MEDIEVAL
TAPESTRIES

MEDIEVAL TAPESTRIES

in The Metropolitan Museum of Art

ADOLFO SALVATORE CAVALLO

The Metropolitan Museum of Art, New York

Distributed by Harry N. Abrams, Inc., New York

This publication was generously supported by The Andrew W. Mellon Foundation, The Mary C. Fosburgh
Endowment Fund, and the National Endowment for the Arts.

Published by The Metropolitan Museum of Art, New York
John P. O'Neill, Editor in Chief
Barbara Burn, Executive Editor
Margaret Aspinwall, Editor, assisted by Katharine A. Ray and Tonia Payne
Bruce Campbell, Designer
Peter Antony, Production

Type set by The Sarabande Press, New York
Printed and bound by Stamperia Valdonega, Verona, Italy

Photography of all Museum holdings is by the Photograph Studio, The Metropolitan Museum of Art;
new photography is by Joseph Coscia, Jr., Bruce Schwarz, and Carmel Wilson, Photograph Studio.
Other photographs were supplied by the owners of works of art listed in the captions,
except as noted on page 674.
Slipcase: Detail of 37, *A Hawking Party*
Frontispiece: Detail of 35, *Shepherd and Shepherdess Making Music*

Library of Congress Cataloging-in-Publication Data
Metropolitan Museum of Art (New York, N.Y.)
Medieval tapestries in the Metropolitan Museum of Art / Adolfo
Salvatore Cavallo.
p.   cm.
Includes bibliographical references and index.
ISBN 0-87099-644-4.—ISBN 0-8109-6420-1 (Abrams)
1. Tapestry, Medieval—Catalogs.   2. Tapestry—New York (N.Y.)—Catalogs.
3. Metropolitan Museum of Art (New York, N.Y.)—Catalogs.
4. Tapestry, Medieval—History.   I. Cavallo, Adolfo S.   II. Title.
NK3005.M48 1993
746.394'09'020747471—dc20   92-15540
CIP

Contents

Foreword

The word "tapestry" brings to most people's minds a vision of great stone walls covered with fantastic scenes in glorious color. For the first centuries of the widespread use of tapestry hangings in Europe, the vision tells the truth, though the word, in its strictest sense, as so ably elucidated in this book, refers to a basic weave discovered and used in many parts of the world. Nowhere, however, has this fairly simple technique produced such spectacular works of art as in the southern Netherlands from the late fourteenth to the early sixteenth century. As church and cathedral walls became more and more glass-filled, huge translucent colored spaces, so the rooms of town houses and castles of great princes became alive with stories of heroes and saints, legends of Troy and histories from the Bible.

The Metropolitan Museum, thanks to generous donors and farsighted curators, has acquired a substantial number of these rare treasures. One introductory section of this catalogue gives a vivid account of how tapestries were used, continually traveling with their possessors, sometimes hung in the street for a festival or procession; later owners cut them up or stored them in attics or barns. Only a tiny fraction of what once existed has come down to us. The tourist must go to Angers to see an impressive range of late fourteenth-century tapestry, or he can come to The Cloisters in New York to enjoy the only slightly later *Five Worthies*. Fifteenth-century tapestries are still rare, but this book bears witness to the fact that the Metropolitan Museum has splendid examples. It is only from the end of the century and from the first few decades of the next that substantial numbers of tapestries have survived and can be found in modern collections, most conspicuously in the Spanish Patrimonio Nacional and in Wawel Castle in Cracow. Among these too, however, the Metropolitan

Museum can offer its jewels, such as the second most famous unicorn tapestries in the world—first place, of course, going to those in the Musée de Cluny in Paris.

The art of the late Middle Ages has an immediate appeal in its richness of detail, its wealth of color and brilliance, and what is sometimes, to modern eyes, its charming naïveté. To study and explain it, on the other hand, requires awesome learning and long experience. The Metropolitan Museum has been fortunate in obtaining Adolfo S. Cavallo to make this catalogue of its medieval tapestries. He is the author of a number of tapestry catalogues, including that of the important collection of the Museum of Fine Arts, Boston. He is also a costume specialist, a field of knowledge particularly valuable in dating early tapestries; many entries here reflect this expertise. He has read every pertinent book and article and consulted specialists in many fields, but, more importantly, he has looked at every square inch of the tapestries represented in the sixty-four catalogue entries. Tapestries deserve to be treated as works of art, as if they were, say, old master drawings, and Mr. Cavallo has so treated them. The book, however, is far more than a conventional item-by-item catalogue. The introductory essays on the character, the stylistic development, and the weaving of tapestries in Europe during the late Middle Ages are, in effect, the most up-to-date history and historiography of tapestry in print and amount to a substantial contribution to the history of art.

We are also indebted to Margaret Aspinwall, who edited this catalogue and the catalogue of Renaissance and later tapestries in the Metropolitan Museum, and to The Andrew W. Mellon Foundation, The Mary C. Fosburgh Endowment Fund, and the National Foundation for the Arts for their generous financial support of this study and its publication.

Philippe de Montebello
Director

Acknowledgments

It would be impractical to print the names of everyone who helped me with the preparation of this book and the tasks associated with my part in its production. The list is too long, and my debts too many and too diverse. In the notes for many catalogue entries I have thanked those who helped with particular research problems. Other people who contributed in less specific but equally important ways know who they are and that I am grateful to them. In most cases their names are associated with the institutions and business firms I have cited as owners of works of art that I had the privilege to consult at first hand, or to study in photographs, or to illustrate. However, some people are so much a part of this book that their contributions demand special mention.

The project originated with Philippe de Montebello, Director of The Metropolitan Museum of Art, and it was he who did me the honor of inviting me to participate in its creation. Both William D. Wixom, Chairman of the Department of Medieval Art and The Cloisters, and John P. O'Neill, Editor in Chief and General Manager of Publications, supported the venture enthusiastically, and throughout the seven years I spent writing and helping to edit the book, they and their respective staffs sustained me in countless ways. I want especially to thank Barbara Burn, Executive Editor, and Margaret Aspinwall, Senior Editor.

In studying the tapestries discussed here, I was lucky enough to work with Nobuko Kajitani, Conservator in Charge of the Department of Textile Conservation, who was my forbearing helpmate throughout the project. In so many ways, from providing access to tapestries that were not on view to making the remarkably clear diagrams and photographs of weaves that appear in the essay on tapestry-weaving procedures, she and her staff supported and encouraged me. To William B. Walker, Arthur K. Watson Chief Librarian, Thomas J. Watson Library, and his staff, especially Patrick F. Coman and his force at the circulation desk, I am deeply indebted for the easy and amiable access to publications and library reference services that I enjoyed throughout the years of writing and editing. I am also grateful for the help and guidance given me by Jeanie M. James, Archivist, and her staff. Edith Appleton Standen, Consultant in the Department of European Sculpture and Decorative Arts, has stood by me as a colleague and friend throughout the project; among other things, she allowed me to borrow her copies of esoteric publications and to use the preliminary notes and drafts of catalogue entries that she had prepared for certain medieval tapestries before concentrating on the post-medieval pieces in this Museum.

Friends and colleagues from outside the Metropolitan Museum also made important contributions to the book. Katharine A. Ray obtained and kept track of the photographs I requested, Alice Blohm and her assistants made conservation reports and technical studies concerning about half the pieces published here, and Nadine Orenstein searched for design sources. Ruth Scheuer kindly read my description of weaving procedures and made some valuable suggestions that improved it. Kathryn Hiesinger in Philadelphia, Deborah Kraak in Boston, Christa Mayer Thurman in Chicago, and Anne Wardwell in Cleveland, all cheerfully sent me material concerning tapestries in their collections. William H. Forsyth, former curator of the Department of Medieval Art in the Metropolitan Museum, was always prepared to answer my questions about any number of tapestries in the collection. At his suggestion, I consulted Elizabeth Beatson in Princeton when I was struggling with my perennial inability to accept the so-called *Glorification of Charles VIII* (27a–c in this catalogue) for what it was said to be; and it was Mrs. Beatson who gave me the insight I needed to solve the puzzle. My graduate school classmate Lilian Randall generously answered my stream of questions about a manuscript in the collection she keeps in the Walters Art Gallery, Baltimore, and also about some medieval bookbindings. In that regard she referred me to Christopher Clarkson of West Dean, Sussex, who, as a practicing bookbinder and historian of his field, gave me the answers I was looking for.

Through correspondence with colleagues abroad or personal visits, I had the privilege of consulting, in Paris, Chantal Coural, Nadine Gasc, Fabienne Joubert, and Nicole Reynaud, all of whom helped me make this text more complete and authoritative than it would have been otherwise. I had other invaluable talks and correspondence with Anna Rapp Buri and Monica Stucky-Schürer of Basel, Leonie von Wilckens of Nuremberg and Munich, and Scot McKendrick of London. Richard Marks, then director of the Burrell Collection in Glasgow, Valerie Blyth, his conservator of textiles, and his administrative staff, let me see every tapestry in that fabulous collection and every written word concerning it. Dr. Marks and William Wells, the former's predecessor as keeper of the Burrell Collection, granted me the privilege of studying Mr. Wells's unpublished catalogue of the Burrell Collection tapestries. Wendy Hefford, Associate Keeper of Textiles in the Victoria and Albert Museum in London, and Guy Delmarcel, former keeper of the tapestry collection in the Musées Royaux d'Art et d'Histoire in Brussels, have given me a great deal of time, either answering my questions on specific tapestries or tapestries in general or preparing material to send to me. On matters of heraldry and related subjects, I was fortunate enough to be able to consult Jean-Bernard de Vaivre of Paris, who on many occasions put his brilliant knowledge of those subjects at my disposal. Whatever errors I have made in this book concerning matters heraldic stem from my not having had time to consult M. de Vaivre on those matters, and the errors are mine alone.

While searching for photographs that show the ways tapestries are woven, I had occasion to consult and correspond with a number of photographers, weavers, and publishers, most of whose names are mentioned in the captions or credit lines for those illustrations. However, I want to single out for special thanks Mme. Julien Coffinet, Yves Debraine, J. P. Levet, James J. More, and Ruth Scheuer.

Numbers of collectors and dealers in this country and abroad generously answered my questions about tapestries in their possession. Their amiable cooperation stirred memories of the benevolent encouragement I never failed to find in the company of the late Milton Samuels of French and Company who, like Adele Coulin Weibel and Gertrude Townsend, my late mentors at the Detroit Institute of Arts and the Museum of Fine Arts in Boston, set me, a raw student of art history, on this path of specialization. That I have walked this far and completed this book may be ascribed to my having been inspired and encouraged by William E. Woolfenden and sustained by Edward Y. Liang.

Preface

The convenient term "medieval" applies only in a limited way to tapestries that have survived from the years before 1525. Except for a handful of pieces dating from the eleventh to the thirteenth centuries, all so-called medieval tapestries represent the art as it was practiced in Europe in the late Middle Ages, from about 1350 to 1525.

It is as difficult to single out the moment when "medieval" becomes "Renaissance" in this art as it is in the other arts. It has been said that the new tapestry style superseded the old in the southern Netherlands about 1520, when the Brussels entrepreneur Pieter van Aelst produced the *Acts of the Apostles* tapestries after Italian Renaissance cartoons by Raphael. However, Netherlandish tapestries that were woven in the two preceding decades already show some of the form and much of the ornament characteristic of Italian Renaissance art. The same pieces also show a painterly but entirely Netherlandish tapestry style that had developed in the late fifteenth and early sixteenth centuries. Neither the *Acts of the Apostles* cartoons nor any other single set of exotic tapestry designs could divert so strong a native current. When a fully pictorial high Renaissance Netherlandish tapestry style did assert itself about 1530 in tapestries woven after designs by Bernaert van Orley or his shop, like the *Hunts of Maximilian*, it slid smoothly into place: certainly novel and Italianate, it was no more

nor less than another development in an indigenous tapestry style that had been evolving for at least two centuries.

Lamenting the passing of what he clearly viewed as a tapestry style that was particularly well suited to the medium, Louis de Farcy wrote in 1897, concerning the introduction of the Renaissance style into the art of tapestry in the early sixteenth century:

La tapisserie n'est plus la *décoration rationelle d'une surface plane,* comme l'étaient jadis les peintures murales et les verrières; elle devient *tableau.* A dater de cette epoque, il n'y a plus d'art particulier à la *tapisserie;* on copie des tableaux, absolument comme on l'a fait dans les vitraux. Est-ce un progrès? Assurément non, au point de vue *décoratif,* qui doit ici primer tout le reste (Louis de Farcy, *Histoire et description des tapisseries de l'église cathédrale d'Angers* [Angers, 1897] p. 72).

(Tapestry is no longer the logical decoration of a flat surface, as wall painting and stained glass used to be; it becomes a picture. From this time forward there is no longer a style peculiar to tapestry; people copy pictures, exactly as they did in stained glass windows. Is this progress? Certainly not from the standpoint of decoration, which in this case should override every other consideration.)

History of the Collection

Although The Metropolitan Museum of Art had been collecting works of art since its foundation in 1870, it was only after 1904, when J. Pierpont Morgan, who collected tapestries as well as other artifacts, was named president of the Museum, that the first medieval tapestry entered the collection. We have to assume that in earlier years no staff member or trustee was motivated to make such an acquisition. However the trustees were examining their ideas about the collections, and change was in the wind. In their annual report for 1905 they stated as their purpose "not merely to assemble beautiful objects and display them harmoniously, still less to amass a collection of unrelated curios, but to group together the masterpieces of different countries and times in such relation and sequence as to illustrate the history of art in the broadest sense, to make plain its teaching and to inspire and direct its national development." This enlightened and liberal policy may have inspired Mr. Morgan to bring into the Museum artifacts that would broaden the scope of the holdings. He inaugurated the medieval tapestry collection with a gift whose brilliance the staff would find hard to emulate in the future. In February 1907, while visiting the New York gallery of the Paris dealer M. Bacri, Mr. Morgan saw five large and handsome fragments of a huge mid-fifteenth-century south Netherlandish tapestry of the *Story of the Seven Sacraments and Their Prefigurations in the Old Testament* (7a–e), bought them, and had them shipped directly to the Museum as his gift. In atypical fashion, this collector of collections bought on this occasion just a few fragments of a single work of art. It is obvious that he had appreciated the quality of what he had seen at Bacri's. The passing years have proved his intuition correct. Only a few other fragments of this tapestry have come to light since 1907, and all of them depend for their context on the five pieces in the Metropolitan Museum. The surviving fragments have stimulated three generations of scholars to ponder over them, trying to date them and associate them with certain historical figures. Only recently have we found that the historical importance of the original tapestry is different, though greater, than what had been supposed: it once belonged to Isabel la Católica, who bequeathed it to the royal chapel that she and Fernando caused to be built in the cathedral of Granada early in the sixteenth century. Curiously enough, Mr. Morgan, who gave Renaissance and baroque tapestries to the Metropolitan Museum later, never repeated his gesture toward the collection of medieval pieces. However the Museum eventually acquired two medieval tapestries that he had owned, the *Apostles' Creed* (53) and the *Crucifixion* (54).

Mr. Morgan's gift of the *Seven Sacraments* fragments encouraged the Museum to acquire more fine medieval tapestries. In 1909 it used the Rogers Fund to buy four more fifteenth-century hangings. Three of them are large fragments from a set of tapestries showing courtly figures in a rose garden (8a–c). The fourth piece shows episodes in the *Story of the Vengeance of Our Lord* (10). In 1916 the Museum bought Mr. Morgan's *Crucifixion* (54) with the Francis L. Leland Fund and a gift from Mitchell Samuels. Woven in southern Germany about 1325–50, it was and still is the earliest European tapestry in the Museum and one of the earliest to have survived anywhere in the world.

Although the collection was not yet a large one, every piece in it was handsome and important; and so generous donors were inspired to help it grow. The *Infant Christ Pressing the Wine of the Eucharist* (22) and the *Scenes from the Life of the Virgin* (18) came to the Museum in 1913 in the bequest of Benjamin Altman. The *Adoration of the Magi* (21) entered the collection in 1915 in the bequest of Lillian Stokes Gillespie. In 1917 the *Fall and Redemption of Man* (15) came as the bequest of Oliver H. Payne.

Naturally a collection containing examples of such importance would continue to attract donors. In 1921 the *Scenes from the Passion of Christ* (44), rich with gilt and silver yarns, came in the bequest of Michael Dreicer; and in 1925 Dr. Ernest G. Stillman gave the *Coronation of the Virgin and Related Subjects* (28), woven about 1500–1515, and the somewhat later *Moses and Aaron before Pharaoh* (47). The next medieval tapestries were acquired in 1931, when the majestic *King Arthur* (2a) from the *Nine Worthies* series was bought through the Munsey Fund, and the *Arcades with Riders in Fantastic Thickets* (50a, b) came to the Museum in the bequest of Michael Friedsam.

After 1934, when James J. Rorimer was appointed

curator of a newly established Department of Medieval Art, the collection grew rapidly. Rorimer had a special gift for appreciating and acquiring tapestries and for inspiring colleagues and donors to support him in his role as champion of this small but choice collection. He made his first purchase in 1935, acquiring the *Shield of Arms and Wreath on an Arabesque of Thistle Branches* (26) through the Rogers Fund. In the same year, Mrs. Daniel Guggenheim gave four handsome sixteenth-century hangings of the *Story of Hercules* (48a–d), in memory of her husband.

As Rorimer worked on plans for The Cloisters with John D. Rockefeller, Jr., he dreamed of having in that magical building in Fort Tryon Park the six exquisite *Hunt of the Unicorn* tapestries (20a–f) that hung in the Rockefeller house in New York. Mr. Rockefeller agreed that the tapestries belonged in The Cloisters and gave not only them but also two related fragments (20g, h) that were still in the hands of the La Rochefoucauld family who had owned the six other tapestries. All eight pieces were hanging in The Cloisters when the building opened in 1938. That same year Rorimer bought for The Cloisters Collection two tapestries representing the great *Story of the Redemption of Man* series (29a, b), pieces which had been for centuries in the cathedral of Burgos. In 1939 he acquired, through the Fletcher Fund, a large fragment of tapestry showing Andromache and Hector urging Priam not to go to war (13c), one of the subjects in the *Story of the Trojan War* series. In later years Rorimer acquired two more pieces representing the same composition in that cycle (13a, b), which has become one of the most celebrated and avidly studied series of tapestries that we have from the last third of the fifteenth century.

During Rorimer's first ten years as curator, another twenty-six tapestries entered the collection, all of them either gifts or bequests from George Blumenthal, Mr. and Mrs. Frederic B. Pratt, George D. Pratt, Harriet Barnes Pratt, Mrs. Van Santvoord Merle-Smith, and Helen Hay Whitney. Among these pieces are some of the most handsome and important ones in the collection, including two showing courtly falconers against pink millefleurs grounds (3b, 4), the earlier *Annunciation* (5) of two in this collection, some hunting and country-life pieces (25a–f, 34, 37, 40, and 49a–d), an altar hanging of the *Lamentation* (17), and two tapestries from a series inspired by Petrarch's *I Trionfi* (33a, b).

So in less than forty years the collection had grown from nothing to a presence to be reckoned with. The international importance of this small but choice group of medieval tapestries, together with the fact that Rorimer was an energetic collector, attracted more gifts to the

Museum and inspired more purchases. In 1946 Frank Jay Gould gave two fifteenth-century pieces, the dramatic *Judith Taking Holofernes' Head* (9) and the *Falcon's Bath* (3a) which, because it shows in reverse the same composition as the piece given earlier by Mr. and Mrs. Frederic B. Pratt (3b), was desirable both for its historical importance and its lyrical charm. About the same time, Rorimer showed a particular interest in tapestry weaving of the second half of the fourteenth century, a period from which only a few tapestries other than the *Apocalypse* of Angers have survived. In 1946 he bought a fragment of mid- to late-fourteenth-century tapestry that had been designed to cover the walls or furniture of a room (1). It shows a decorative arrangement of heraldic elements referring to the Beaufort, Turenne, and Comminges families of France. Just a year later Rorimer embarked on a project that he must have had in mind for some time, one involving the reconstruction of most of a set of *Nine Worthies* tapestries that he believed could be dated in the late fourteenth century. He already had in his care the *King Arthur* fragment (2a) that was bought in 1932 and thought to have come from a lost set of *Nine Worthies* hangings. In 1936 he discovered more *Nine Worthies* fragments in the art market and realized not only that they belonged with the *King Arthur* piece but also that they comprised a good part of the missing *Nine Worthies* set. So he moved quickly. Between 1947 and 1949, Rorimer, with Mr. Rockefeller's encouragement, methodically gathered about a hundred other fragments from this set from three different sources. Mr. Rockefeller gave most of them, and one came as a gift from George A. Douglass. After a short time, during which the fragments were renovated and reassembled, Rorimer could exhibit four large and two small hangings at The Cloisters, thus miraculously reviving more than half of the original set.

In 1949, immediately after unveiling the *Five Worthies with Attendant Figures* (2a–i), the Museum announced a major gift as part of The Jules Bache Collection. It was the *Resurrection* (45), a splendid example of early sixteenth-century Netherlandish tapestry weaving. The next year two large fragments of tapestry representing the same period and place, but totally different in character, came in the bequest of Mary Stillman Harkness. They show episodes from the story of the *Hunt of the Frail Stag* (32a, b). They were to be joined fifteen years later by five tapestry fragments bequeathed by Adele L. Lehman, in memory of Arthur Lehman, that represent the same allegorical tale of man's perilous journey through life (24a–e).

Meanwhile, the collection of German and Swiss tapestries was growing. In 1948 Richard C. Hunt gave an altar hanging with *Scenes from the Life of the Virgin* (62), dated 1538, in memory of his grandfather. Three years later, Mrs. Leo S. Bing gave a later sixteenth-century German antependium showing the *Madonna with Eight Saints* (64). In 1953 Rorimer bought a third German sixteenth-century altar hanging, *Esther Pleading before Ahasuerus* (63), for The Cloisters Collection.

Records for the decade of the 1950s show that Rorimer, who by this time was certainly the most imposing single acquisitor of medieval tapestries in the country if not the world, cast his net far and wide in an attempt to round out the collection. He also tapped his own talent for creative collecting by enhancing the importance of pieces that were already in the Museum, as he had done for the *King Arthur.* In 1939 he had bought with the Fletcher Fund a piece of tapestry showing the right quarter of the sixth composition in the *Story of the Trojan War* series (13c). In 1952, again with the Fletcher Fund, he bought a larger fragment representing slightly less than the left half of the same composition (13a) and in 1955, for The Cloisters Collection, a small fragment from a different tapestry woven after the same cartoon (13b). Meanwhile, Rorimer was thinking about a hanging that George Blumenthal had given in 1941 (27c) and that Rorimer knew was incomplete at the left end. In 1953 he found and acquired for The Cloisters two other incomplete hangings (27a, b) because he believed that they had originally formed, with the Blumenthal piece, one exceptionally long, late fifteenth-century tapestry. Having reconstructed the hanging, Rorimer named it the *Glorification of Charles VIII* and unveiled it in 1954. Many years later we discovered that, while Rorimer was right to rejoin the edges of these three fragmentary tapestries and thereby reconstitute a hanging that had been disassembled (the central section of 27a–c, which we have entitled *Christ the Judge on the Throne of Majesty*), the composite piece he re-created was itself a concoction that had been made up at some time in the past from parts of three separate tapestries.

During the next decade or so Rorimer strove to diversify the holdings by buying for The Cloisters Collection the mid-fifteenth-century *Honor Making a Chaplet of Roses* (6), the *Armorial Bearings and Badges of John, Lord Dynham* (16) which can be dated on internal evidence between 1488 and 1501, and the exquisite *Resurrected Christ Appearing to Mary Magdalen in the Garden* (30), which dates from the first quarter of the sixteenth century. Meanwhile a number of important gifts and bequests came in. Among them was the imposing yet charming *Apostles' Creed* (53) given by The Hearst Foundation, Inc., and a small but choice group of fifteenth- and sixteenth-century tapestries with country-life, Christian, or mythological subjects that were either given by Mrs. Mellon Bruce (38), or bequeathed by Charles F. Iklé (56) or Adele L. Lehman in memory of Arthur Lehman (23, 24a–e, 31, 39, 46). Two mid-sixteenth-century *Thickets with Large Leaves, Flowers, Animals, and Architectural Enframements* (52a, b) were a posthumous gift from Rorimer, made by his widow, Katherine S. Rorimer.

The collection grew less rapidly after Rorimer's death in 1966; but his colleagues and successors in the Department of Medieval Art and The Cloisters—chiefly Florens Deuchler, William Forsyth, Carmen Gómez-Moreno, Thomas Hoving, Timothy Husband, and William Wixom—continued to make important acquisitions. During this period the Museum received two early sixteenth-century country-life millefleurs tapestries: the *Shepherd and Shepherdess Making Music* (35), which came in the bequest of Susan Vanderpoel Clark in 1967, and the *Falconer with Two Ladies, a Page, and a Foot Soldier* (36) in the bequest of Harriet H. Jonas in 1974. The Cloisters Collection fared particularly well in this period. In 1971 the staff bought an *Annunciation* (11) that was woven in the third quarter of the fifteenth century in the southern Netherlands, a piece of the greatest historical interest, and also the *Two Riddles of the Queen of Sheba* (59), a prime example of somewhat later Upper Rhineland weaving. Another piece from the same region and period, part of one of the celebrated weavings inspired by the poem *Der Busant* (58), entered the collection in 1985 as the gift of the Honorable Murtogh D. Guinness. In 1990 the staff bought another important Rhenish piece for The Cloisters Collection. This one, a *Fantastic Beast* (55), represents early fifteenth-century tapestry weaving in the Basel region.

In just eighty-odd years the staff, trustees, and patrons of the Metropolitan Museum have succeeded in building a collection of medieval tapestries which, in terms of variety, quality, and range of geographical and chronological representation, rivals that of any other public institution. It is an impressive record.

The Fabric, Weaving Procedure, and Yarns

In this catalogue the word *tapestry* is used to signify a particular kind of textile produced for a particular purpose. In general usage the word may refer to any material used for covering walls or furniture. In most European languages its equivalent term can refer to paper or leather as well as to any woven, embroidered, printed, or painted textile. It is in effect a synonym for *upholstery*. In Great Britain *tapestry* is used to refer to tent-stitch embroidery. However, among textile historians *tapestry* refers only to a particular fabric woven in a particular way. Although the term may properly be applied to tapestry-woven fabrics used for dress or dress accessories, in this catalogue it is used only in reference to tapestry-woven fabrics meant to cover walls or furniture.

THE FABRIC

Tapestry weave is extremely simple. It requires only one warp system and one weft system. Except for rare variations of tapestry weave, like the twill tapestry used in Indian and Persian shawls and other garment fabrics,

tapestry weave is akin to simple cloth or *tabby* weave (bed sheeting, for example). Like that weave, tapestry uses a single set of fixed yarns (the *warp*) parallel to the length of the fabric. The other system of yarns, which is not fixed (the *weft*), intersects the warp at right angles and interweaves with it. In ordinary tabby weave, each line of weft yarn that traverses the width of the fabric from one edge (the *selvage*) to the other passes alternately in front of, then behind, every successive warp yarn. It then returns, passing behind the warp yarns it had passed in front of on the previous run and in front of the ones it had passed behind (fig. 1).

Tapestry differs from tabby weave in two basic ways. First, in tapestry the weft yarns do not usually pass completely across the warp. Each line of weft is made up of any number of colored yarns that engage the warp only in those places where each weft color is required in the pattern. Second, the weft yarns are usually finer than the warp yarns and they are packed close together. They cover the warp completely. In a finished tapestry, the warp is perceived indirectly, as a series of ribs or ridges lying under the colored wefts (fig. 2).

Fig. 1. Model of the structure of tabby weave. The warp yarns run vertically. The weft yarn intersects the warp at right angles, passing behind one warp yarn, in front of the next, behind the next, and so on in each row.

Fig. 2. Model of the structure of tapestry weave. The warp yarns run vertically, the weft yarn horizontally. The weft has been interwoven with the warp in tabby binding and then packed down tightly.

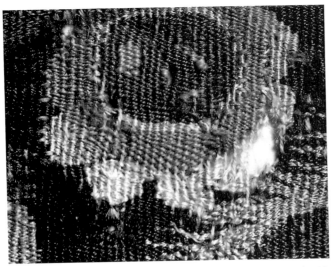

Thus, a tapestry is a weft-faced tabby-weave fabric made up of a series of discontinuous colored weft yarns that form patches of color accommodating each other in shape like the pieces of a jigsaw puzzle and held together by the underlying yarns of the undyed warp (fig. 3). By making his patches of weft color correspond to the colors painted on the full-sized pattern or *cartoon* that guides him, the weaver slowly builds up the pattern and the fabric simultaneously. Since there are no secondary warp or weft systems in this weave, the same pattern appears on both the front and the back of the fabric; on the back it appears in reverse.

Fig. 3. Detail of a medieval tapestry in The Cloisters (13b). The warp runs vertically and holds together the patches of weft yarns.

THE WEAVING PROCEDURE

The following technical notes represent a simple introduction to the subject. For a more detailed account, see François Tabard, "The Weaver's Art," in Great Tapestries *(ed. Joseph Jobé [Lausanne, 1965] pp. 225–61), or Julien Coffinet,* Arachne ou l'art de la tapisserie *([Geneva, 1971] pp. 59–148), which treats high-warp weaving only.*

Now, as in the Middle Ages, tapestry weavers use two basic types of loom. In both types the warp yarns are stretched between two rollers or *beams*. In the *high-warp* or upright loom, the warp is held in a vertical plane. The ends of the yarns are tied to a beam at the top of the structure and a beam at the bottom (fig. 4). The warp is somewhat longer than the finished tapestry will be, longer than the distance between the two beams, and so the excess warp is rolled onto the upper beam. The weaver sits at the back of the loom and works on the lower part of the exposed warp (fig. 5). When he has woven the fabric up to a comfortable level, he rolls the finished web onto the lower beam; this causes a corresponding amount of warp to unroll from the upper beam, and at the same time the unused warp immediately above the finished web moves down to be worked on next.

In the *low-warp* or horizontal loom, the warp is stretched between a beam set at the front of the loom and another set at the back. The weaver sits before the front beam and works on the forward part of the warp (fig. 6). As the finished portion of the web is rolled onto the front beam, a like amount of warp unrolls from the back beam. The weaver then works with the fresh supply of warp that has moved to the front of the loom.

Weavers at the two types of looms use basically the same procedures and produce the same kind of fabric. The looms differ primarily in the way they enable the weaver to control the warp yarns. If these yarns were fixed in one plane like the strings of a harp, the weaver

Fig. 4. A high-warp tapestry loom, shown from the front. The warp is stretched vertically between the upper and lower beams.

Fig. 5. A tapestry weaver working at a high-warp loom. The finished web fills the lower part of the unrolled warp. The cartoon hangs behind the weaver. He faces the back of the growing fabric and can see the front of it reflected in the mirror placed before, and just above, the lower beam.

would have to pass the bobbins carrying the weft yarns laboriously in and out among them, in front of one yarn, behind the next, in front of the one next to that, and so on. However he can create a passage or *shed* between the alternate warp yarns, through which he can pass his bobbins easily in one sweep, by placing each successive yarn in one of two movable planes that have a narrow space between them. These planes can then be made to move forward and back (or up and down), penetrating each other so that the yarns in one plane are first in front of (or above) the others and then behind (or below) the others. Therefore the space between the two planes, the shed, lies first in front of one set of warp yarns and behind the other and then behind the first set and in front of the second. In this way, the weft yarns carried on bobbins that follow the course of the two sheds automatically interweave with the warp in a regularly alternating sequence.

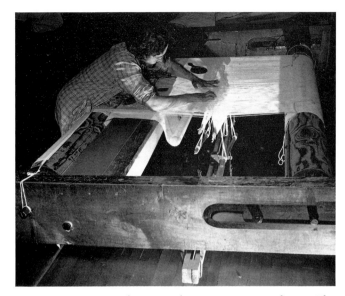

Fig. 6. A weaver working at a low-warp tapestry loom. The warp is stretched horizontally between the front and back beams. The cartoon lies under the warp and is supported on a board that extends across the loom next to the front beam.

The weaver prepares the yarns to form the two sheds by making a *cross* in the warp: he separates the odd-numbered yarns from the even-numbered ones and fixes them in two separate planes with the aid of two rods (fig. 7). When this crossed warp is installed on a high-warp loom, the two sets of yarns are held in separate planes by one or more crossbars that remain in the warp near the top of the loom (see fig. 22). The yarns in one plane lie slightly nearer the weaver's hands than the yarns in the other. The space between the two warp planes at rest will serve as the first of the two sheds that the weaver needs. However since this space is too narrow to pass a

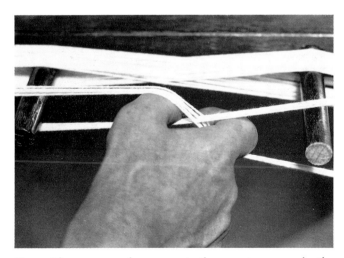

Fig. 7. The weaver makes a cross in the warp to prepare for the two sheds through which the bobbins carrying weft yarns will pass alternately when the warp is mounted on the loom.

Fig. 8. A weaver working at a high-warp loom opens the first shed by pulling some of the warp yarns in the nearer plane forward and then passes the bobbin through the shed from right to left.

Fig. 9. A weaver working at a high-warp loom opens the second shed by pulling on some heddles; this brings the warp yarns in the farther plane to a position in front of the yarns in the nearer plane, and the weaver passes the bobbin through the shed from left to right.

bobbin through easily, the weaver widens it by grasping a group of warp yarns in the nearer plane and pulling them forward. He can then pass a bobbin carrying weft yarn of the required color through this shed which lies behind the yarns in the nearer plane and in front of the ones in the farther plane (fig. 8). As the bobbin passes through this shed, some of the weft yarn it carries is left behind, ultimately to become part of the fabric and the pattern. To open the second shed, the weaver releases those warp yarns and pulls on the adjacent loops of cord or *heddles* hanging from rods near the top of the loom (see fig. 11), loops through which each warp yarn in the farther plane passes. This pulls the yarns forward, past the yarns in the nearer plane and closer to the weaver than the nearer warps are (fig. 9). The space between the two warp planes is now in the alternate position, in front of the warp yarns in the nearer plane and behind the farther yarns which the heddles have pulled forward. The weaver then passes the same bobbin through this shed in the opposite direction, depositing another length of weft yarn in the warp. In this way the weft

yarns, passing with the bobbins to and fro, in front of one set of warp yarns in one pass and behind the same set in the next pass, interweave with the warp and so create the tapestry fabric (fig. 10). The weaver keeps several bobbins working in sequence, using each one as the color of the yarn it carries is required in the pattern. The bobbins hang at the back of the fabric when they are not being used (fig. 11).

The weaver at a horizontal loom works in essentially the same way. However in this loom the sheds are created by a different method. The two sets of yarns lie in a single plane when at rest; but the even-numbered yarns pass through heddles fixed in one of two sets of *harnesses* hung above or below the warp, and the odd-numbered yarns pass through the heddles in the other set of harnesses. The weaver can raise or lower the harnesses (depending on whether they are mounted above or below the warp) by pressing on the pedals attached to them (fig. 12). In this way he can raise or lower one set of warp yarns while leaving the alternate set in the plane of rest (see fig. 6). By depressing the

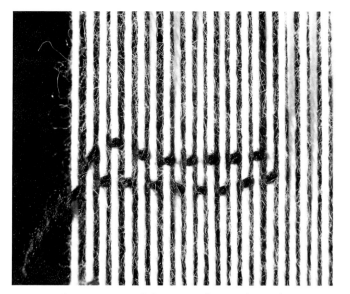

Fig. 10. The tapestry web begins to form. The weft yarn has passed with the bobbin through two sheds, in front of one set of warp yarns and behind the other.

Fig. 11. A weaver working at a high-warp loom. The various bobbins he uses, each of which carries weft yarn of a different color, hang from the edge of the web on the back of the growing tapestry. The heddles through which every other warp yarn passes hang from rods suspended just above the weaver's head.

Fig. 12. A low-warp tapestry loom viewed from below. One set of warp yarns passes through the heddles in one of two sets of harnesses, and the alternate set passes through the heddles in the other set of harnesses. Each harness is controlled by a pedal connected to it by chains and cords.

pedals alternately, the weaver can open one shed and then the other.

Tapestry weave has no secondary weft system that builds up a web separate from the one created when the colored wefts interweave with the warp, and so openings occur in the weave where the pattern requires that two different color areas meet along a line parallel to the warp. The bobbin carrying weft yarn of one color turns back after passing around the warp yarn that borders the line separating the colors on one side, and the bobbin carrying weft of the other color does the same on the other side. A narrow gap or *slit* will form in the fabric at this place (fig. 13). If the slit continues for any distance it will weaken the finished tapestry when it is hung. Weavers have three basic ways of controlling these slits. The simplest way is to close them with needle stitches after the fabric comes off the loom (fig. 14). Or the weaver can avoid forming slits as he weaves, either by dovetailing the opposing wefts on the warp yarn lying between the edges of the two color areas (figs. 15, 16) or

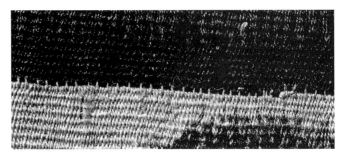

Fig. 13. Model of a tapestry fabric showing the formation of a slit where two contiguous patches of color meet along a line parallel to the warp.

Fig. 14. Detail of a medieval tapestry in The Cloisters (13b) showing a slit closed with needle stitches (front of the fabric).

Fig. 15. Model of a tapestry fabric showing weft yarns from two contiguous patches of color engaging a common warp yarn lying between the patches before turning back in the next row of weaving. Since the opposing weft yarns are now dovetailed on the same warp yarn, no slit can form along the line of color change.

Fig. 16. Detail of a medieval tapestry in the Metropolitan Museum (42b) showing dovetailed weft yarns (face of the fabric).

Fig. 17. Model of a tapestry fabric showing weft yarns of two contiguous patches of color looping through each other before turning back in the next row of weaving. Since the opposing weft yarns are now interlocked, no slit can form along the line of color change.

Fig. 18. Model of a tapestry fabric showing double interlocked wefts, each weft loop of one color engaging two, rather than one, weft loop of the other color.

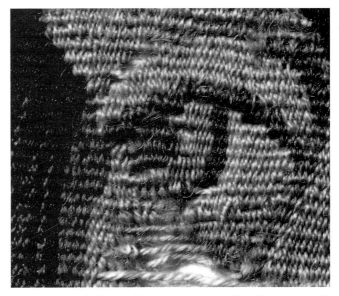

Fig. 19. Detail of a medieval tapestry in The Cloisters (13b) showing the loops of double interlocked wefts on the back of the fabric.

Fig. 20. Detail of a medieval tapestry in The Cloisters (13b) showing a passage of double interlocked wefts on the front of the fabric. The loops are invisible, and the adjacent color patches meet along a smooth line.

Fig. 21. Weavers working side by side at a low-warp loom.

by interlocking opposite wefts in one of two ways before turning each one back to begin the next line of weaving (figs. 17–20).

Weavers at both types of looms face the back of the web as they work. In order to see the right side of his fabric, the high-warp weaver can walk around to the front of the loom or look between the warp yarns into a mirror placed there (see fig. 5). The low-warp weaver can see only small portions of his fabric's face at a time, by sliding a mirror under the warp and looking into it through the spaces between the yarns.

The high-warp weaver hangs his cartoon behind the loom (see fig. 5) and turns his head constantly to consult it. He draws its broad outlines on the warp; then, as he works, he carries the image in his mind from the cartoon to the loom. Since he is working at the back of the fabric, he must execute the image in reverse in order to give it the proper left-right orientation on the face of the hanging. In low-warp weaving the cartoon is placed on the loom, underneath the warp, face-to-face with the tapestry being woven (see fig. 6). The weaver can see the pattern in the spaces between the warp yarns and so copy the cartoon more precisely than the high-warp weaver can. This, along with the fact that his hands are free to manipulate the bobbins because his feet are controlling the sheds, enables him to work faster. Since this fabric lies face-to-face with the cartoon, it will show the pattern in reverse just as a print shows the image on a plate or stone in reverse when the paper is peeled off. Knowing this, painters who prepared cartoons for execution on the low-warp loom reversed the composition so that the image in the tapestry would have the same right-left orientation as the original design.

Since neither high- nor low-warp weavers could work efficiently on a section of web much wider than the distance between their hands extended forward and slightly to the sides, it took several weavers working side by side to build up the full width of the fabric (figs. 21, 22). For a number of reasons—including the artistic and technical advantages the weavers found in executing vertical pattern lines on the horizontal, the greater stability weft yarns have when they cover a warp hanging horizontally rather than vertically, and the impracticality of building and housing wide looms—medieval weavers executed the characteristically long, narrow tapestry patterns from end to end rather than from bottom to top, with the longer dimension of the pattern running parallel to the warp rather than the weft. A tapestry forty-five feet long and eighteen feet high (not an uncommon dimension for the period) woven from bottom to top would require a loom at least forty-five feet wide, whereas the same tapestry could be woven from end to end on a loom just over eighteen feet wide. Almost all late medieval tapestries were woven from end to end, and so their warp yarns run horizontally when they are hung.

Fig. 22. Weavers working side by side at a high-warp loom.

The Yarns

Tapestries woven in the southern Netherlands in the late Middle Ages invariably had warps of woolen yarn. The weft yarns were primarily of wool, but more expensive pieces also had silk wefts, particularly in the light areas and highlights. The richest pieces had silk in all parts of the design. The most sumptuous pieces contained not only quantities of silk, which was prized for its rich glossiness, but also wefts of silver and silver-gilt yarns made by wrapping a core yarn of white or yellow silk spirally with a narrow, flat wire of metal showing one metallic color or the other. During the late Middle Ages colored yarns were dyed with vegetable substances fixed to the fibers with *mordants* of metallic oxides or salts.

Figure 23. Miniature painting in the Book of Hours of Alfonso V of Aragon. Spain (?), about 1450. British Library, London (Add. MS 28962, fol. 14v). The king and bishop kneel in a chamber whose walls are covered with a hunting tapestry hung on hooks. The bed canopy and curtains are made of woven silk; the bedcover appears to be silk embroidered with silver-gilt yarns.

How Tapestries Were Used in the Middle Ages

Most medieval tapestry weavings were designed to be used as wall hangings. But since the fabric happened to be rich, warm, and durable, it was also used to cover beds, seat furniture, cushions, and tables. These were the days before furniture frames were fitted with upholstery fixed in place, and so it was necessary to have loose textile covers unless one were prepared to live among the bare wood or metal frames. Fourteenth- and fifteenth-century household accounts and inventories list quantities of tapestry *chambers,* as these fabric room suites were known. Not every chamber contained the same kind or number of pieces, but normally such a suite included wall hangings, bed furnishings—that is, curtains, cover, ceiling, and valances—and bench and cushion covers. Some of the tapestry furniture covers had patterns related to those on the walls; others showed different patterns. Still other chambers had tapestry wall coverings but bed furnishings made partly of tapestry, partly—or completely—of woven or embroidered silk or other fabrics (fig. 23).

Although affluent burghers could afford to furnish their homes with tapestry, the medieval tapestry industry needed the support of princes and nobles, men and women who maintained numbers of houses in cities and the country and who traveled frequently on state or social occasions from one residence to another. The interiors were minimally furnished unless the owner was in residence, and when he or she proceeded to a different house it had to be made habitable and attractive as quickly and economically as possible. Wall tapestries and tapestry covers could create instant environments, and they were easy to move and to store. They were also colorful, entertaining, warming, and impressive. They answered the need perfectly. Most interiors had metal hooks set into the walls so that the tapestries, fitted with rings or tapes along the top, could be installed easily and relatively quickly. The weavings were hung from floor to ceiling or to the springing of a vault or some other horizontal line on the wall. They were placed edge to edge, completely covering the wall, like wallpaper in a modern room (fig. 24). Since most of these residences had been built as fully or partially fortified structures, there were few openings in the walls for windows and doors. Tapestries were hung along the walls in front of what openings there were. If a door or window had to be opened, the hangings could be pushed aside or, if left in place for some time, cut through and fitted into the thickness of the wall (fig. 25). Where a chimney breast interrupted the course of a wall, the tapestry was turned under or pulled back to accommodate it (fig. 26). The stock of tapestries of a great noble contained pieces of different lengths and heights. Some sets of hangings were made to fit a given space. For example, the large tapestry inventoried in the gallery of the château Beauté-sur-Marne after the death of Charles V of France in 1380 seems to have been woven to size: "Item, one large cloth of Arras work with the deeds and battles of Judas Maccabeus and Antiochus, stretching from one of the turrets of the gallery at Beauté to just beyond the turret at the far end of the same, and being of the same height as the said gallery."[1] Although we are not given the dimensions of the tapestry, we know that it could have measured at least as much as some eighteen feet in height and almost eighty feet in length, the original dimensions that have been estimated for most of the duc d'Anjou's six *Apocalypse* tapestries.

Great princes did not fail to exploit the capacity of rich tapestry environments to impress each other and the public at large. When Philippe le Bon visited Paris in 1461 to attend the coronation of Louis XI at Reims, he brought with him some of the most precious tapestries in his extensive collection. Lodging at his hôtel d'Artois, he opened his doors to the people of Paris who trooped through the house marveling at the *Story of Gideon,* the *Story of Alexander,* and numbers of other hangings equally resplendent with bright silk, silver, and gilt yarns. If Parisians had not known beforehand how rich and powerful this duke of Burgundy and king's protector was, they knew it now. When not in use, these tapestries, along with many others, were probably kept in the vaulted stone storeroom that the duke had built in his residence in Arras, where he also provided guards, handlers, and restorers for these precious hangings. Charles VII of France used tapestries as a symbol of his position when he covered the walls of the courtroom in the château de Saint Georges at Vendôme with hangings

Fig. 24. *Richard II Surrenders His Crown to Henry of Bolingbroke, Earl of Derby*, miniature painting in a copy of Froissart's *Chronicles*. France, about 1470. British Library, London (MS Harl. 4380, fol. 184v). In this view of a meeting room, a battle tapestry shares the back wall with a tapestry showing a formal arrangement of trees and urns of flowers. The pieces are hung edge to edge, and they cover the wall completely from the springing of the barrel vault to the floor.

Fig. 25. Stanza dei Pappagalli, Palazzo Davanzati, Florence. Painted about 1395 (?). The decoration of the lower two-thirds of the walls simulates tapestries, or possibly needle-worked hangings, hung there. The fictive hangings are shown turning back and over at the ends of each wall and the edges of the fireplace and showing a lining resembling fur (vair). At the windows, the painting indicates that the hangings have been cut and fixed to the thickness of the wall.

showing his emblems of roses and winged stags together with his coat of arms, all against a ground striped with his colors of red, green, and white (fig. 27).

Any great occasion for a procession, whether related to church or state, was a call for hanging tapestries and other decorative fabrics along the route. The greatest parades were those produced for Corpus Christi day and for the state entry of a prince into one of his cities. There are records of such occasions dating back at least to 1380 when Charles VI of France made his first entry into Paris where "the streets and thoroughfares of the city were hung with tapestries."[2] For Henry VI's entry into Paris on December 2, 1431, "all the streets along which the said king passed [were] hung and adorned with very rich tapestries in several places."[3] At a meeting of the town authorities of Tournai, held on October 4, 1463, to set up guidelines for the commissioners who would prepare the city for Louis XI's entry on February 6 of the next year, they ordered "that the residents on the streets along which he will pass have their houses adorned with tapestries, cloths, or other rich and showy decorations, and grasses and greens spread out on the streets."[4] When Louis entered Lyon twelve years later, the streets were decorated with a variety of hangings and with tapestries showing "several stories in honor and praise of the King."[5] At least some of the hangings used to decorate streets during processions were bought specifically for the purpose: in 1531 Pierre de la Comté of Arras inherited from his uncle "two large pieces of tapestry of Julius Caesar, because they were bought for the front of the house for Corpus Christi day."[6]

On the battlefield or when two rulers met in the field, tapestries lined their tents to provide warmth and diversion and also to remind visitors that the occupant was a person of consequence (fig. 28). This practice sometimes led to a change of ownership, as when the Swiss forces that defeated Charles le Téméraire at Grandson in 1476 carried off the tapestries that the duke had brought with

Fig. 26. *January* (detail), miniature painting in the *Très Riches Heures* of Jean, duc de Berry. France, 1411–16. Musée Condé, Chantilly (MS 65). The hall is hung with a battle tapestry hooked along the top of the walls. It continues around the corner of the room at rear left and has been turned under where it passes the chimney breast to leave the fireplace open.

Fig. 27. *Trial of Jean, duc d'Alençon* (detail), miniature painting in Laurent Girard's French edition of Boccaccio's *De casibus virorum illustrium*, with additions. Painting attributed to Jean Fouquet, France, 1458. Bayerische Staatsbibliothek, Munich (cod. gall. 369, fol. 2v). Charles VII of France is seated on the throne at center rear.

Fig. 28. *The King of Hungary Holding a Council in His Tent on a Battlefield,* miniature painting in a copy of Froissart's *Chronicles.* France, about 1470. British Library, London (MS Harl. 4380, fol. 84r). The interior of the tent is hung with millefleurs tapestry.

Fig. 29. Interior view of the abbey church of Saint-Robert in La Chaise-Dieu (Haute-Loire) showing the set of tapestries donated in 1518 by the abbot, Jacques de Saint-Nectaire, as they hang in the choir. See a detail of one of the tapestries in fig. 32.

him to the battlefield, including the handsome mille-fleurs hanging with the arms and devices of Philippe le Bon which now hangs in the Bernisches Historisches Museum (see fig. 78).

Great personages traveled with tapestries on display in civilian as well as military contexts. The Este inventory of 1457–69 tells us that Borso d'Este bought tapestries showing his arms and devices from Rainaldo Boteram, a merchant weaver from Brussels, to use as decorations on his large barge. In the mid-fifteenth century René d'Anjou had four large armorial hangings, eight bench covers, and two square covers woven in Paris for the council chamber of the treasury at Angers, but he occasionally used the four hangings on his boat. Other princes used tapestries to decorate their land vehicles. In 1412 Jean sans Peur bought five tapestries from Pierre de Beaumetz of Paris to decorate his chariot.

Princes and civic officials gave tapestries as diplomatic gifts or payments. The history of Europe abounds with such references during the late Middle Ages, from the time that Jean sans Peur of Burgundy offered tapestries as part of his ransom to Sultan Bayezid I after his defeat at Nicopolis in 1396, to more than a century later when a seemingly endless round of tapestries was given by the magistrates of Tournai to their ever-changing rulers in France, England, and the Holy Roman Empire during the first quarter of the sixteenth century.

Not every tapestry showing a religious subject was intended to be hung in a church or private chapel, but there are frequent references in contemporary documents to their use in ecclesiastical interiors. Religious hangings were used either as devotional objects or as an aid in teaching Christian lessons to the illiterate. Tapestries of any size, shape, or subject might be hung more or less at random in a church building to decorate it on festival occasions. It seems that the only kind of tapestries that were habitually woven specifically to fit a particular ecclesiastical space—other than above or in front of the altar—were the choir hangings that have survived in relatively large numbers. These differ from other tapestries in two ways. First, they are in most cases exceptionally long in the aggregate—each set comprised several pieces—for their height. Second, their subjects concern primarily the lives of Christ or the Virgin, stories of the lives of the patron saints of the church for which they were designed and woven, or religious texts like the *Biblia Pauperum* or *Speculum Humanae Salvationis* that were intended to teach theological or ethical lessons. Furthermore, choir tapestries often contained inscriptions giving the name of the donor, the date, and sometimes the name of the weaver and the place of manufacture. Such sets of hangings were meant to go completely around the choir (usually semicircular but sometimes rectangular) of the church, extending from the top of the choir stalls to some clearly defined architectural boundary higher up, like the top of an iron screen set above the stalls or the baseline of the entablatures on columns or piers supporting the vaulting or ceiling above the choir. Numbers of such choir hangings may still be seen in the settings for which they were designed, as for example in the abbey church of Saint-Robert in La Chaise-Dieu (fig. 29). While the congregation could enjoy the spectacle of these hangings on feast days, the rest of the year both they and the clergy had to content themselves with seeing only the painted cloth cartoons from which they had been woven. These are often mentioned in the church inventory along with the tapestries. In at least one instance, documented in the records of the cathedral church at Angers, people occupying the choir were completely surrounded by tapestries on feast days and by the painted cloth cartoons the rest of the time. The *Story of Saint Maurice*, in six pieces, which had been ordered in Paris in 1459, lined the space above the stalls, and the *Story of Saint Maurille*, in three pieces, brought from Paris two years later, lined the inside of the rood screen, so that the two cycles of hangings faced each other and completely surrounded the space. Since late medieval choir tapestries could reach heights of more than sixteen feet (the *Life of Saint Rémi* in Reims) and lengths of over two hundred and thirteen feet (the surviving pieces in the abbey church at La Chaise-Dieu), they made a considerable visual impact in even the largest ecclesiastical interiors they decorated.

NOTES

1. Quoted from Pierre Verlet, "Gothic Tapestry from the 12th to the 16th Century," in *Great Tapestries*, ed. Joseph Jobé, trans. Peggy Rowell Oberson (Lausanne, 1965) p. 11.
2. Quoted from Bernard Guenée and Françoise Lehoux, *Les entrées royales françaises de 1328 à 1515*, Sources d'Histoire Médiévale 5 (Paris, 1968) p. 18. The French text reads, "les rues et les carrefours de la ville étaient tendus de tapisseries...."
3. Quoted from Guenée and Lehoux, *Les entrées royales*, p. 70. The French text reads, "... toutes les rues par ou le dit roy passa [estoient] tendues et parees de moult riches tappisseries en plusieurs lieux...."
4. Quoted from Guenée and Lehoux, *Les entrées royales*, p. 188. The French text reads, "... que les demourans es rues par ou il passera ayent leurs maisons parees de tapisseries, linges ou autres aournemens riches et notables, et sur les rues herbes et verdures espandues...."
5. Quoted from Guenée and Lehoux, *Les entrées royales*, p. 21. The French text reads, "... plusieurs histoires en l'honneur et loüange du Roy."
6. Quoted from Jean Lestocquoy, *L'art de l'Artois* (Arras, 1973) pp. 43–44. The French text reads, "deux grandes pièces de tapisserie de Jules César, à cause qu'elles ont été achetées pour la devanture de la maison le jour du Sacrement."

Fig. 30. *Saint Luke Drawing the Virgin and Child.* Tapestry, southern Netherlands, late fifteenth century. Musée du Louvre, Paris.

The Character of Medieval Tapestry Design

In the Middle Ages and also later, designs for tapestries commissioned by a patron or producer-merchant were made to order. But the majority of tapestries were woven after existing designs that were kept in a producer's or weaver's stock. The custom design might be completely original or it might be adapted from an existing composition or series of compositions. For example, it is thought that the *Trajan and Herkinbald* tapestry (see fig. 60) in the Historisches Museum in Bern was designed after Rogier van der Weyden's murals with the same subjects that were painted on the walls of the city hall in Brussels and destroyed when that city was bombarded in 1695. A tapestry showing Saint Luke drawing the Madonna, now in the Musée du Louvre, was woven after a cartoon based on Rogier's painting of that subject (figs. 30, 31). Prints offered tapestry designers another source of ready-made images. A number of late medieval tapestries, of which the early sixteenth-century choir hangings in the abbey church of Saint-Robert in La Chaise-Dieu (Haute-Loire) are a prime example, were designed after printed illustrations in the *Biblia Pauperum* or the *Speculum Humanae Salvationis*, popular books that dealt with the mystical connections among the Old Testament, Christ, and the Virgin (figs. 32, 33). Certain stock figures, some of them known to have been borrowed verbatim from print sources, were used over and over again in weavers' shops as motifs in millefleurs pieces, whose lack of iconographic and spatial continuity allowed weavers to concoct perfectly acceptable compositions using figures that had been taken out of other contexts, and in tapestries with simple narrative subjects (figs. 34–40). Even when they were producing tapestries of the finest quality, weavers or producer-merchants might use figure compositions that were borrowed from some familiar or particularly admired painting, a kind of borrowing that easel painters also indulged in. The Baptism panel in Rogier van der Weyden's triptych of Saint John the Baptist, now in the Staatliche Museen in Berlin-Dahlem (fig. 41), inspired the central figures that appear in slightly altered forms and contexts in several early sixteenth-century tapestries of the *Baptism of Christ* (figs. 42–45). Designers also borrowed groups of figures whose action was so neutral that it could suit almost any subject. Whether

Fig. 31. *Saint Luke Drawing the Virgin and Child,* by Rogier van der Weyden. Panel painting, about 1435–40. Museum of Fine Arts, Boston; Gift of Mr. and Mrs. Henry Lee Higginson.

he took them from the tapestry design or from a common source in a print or painting, the designer of the *Childhood of Hercules* tapestry in Brussels repeated in the upper right corner of this composition three half-figures of fashionably dressed men that appear in somewhat different and slightly earlier costumes in the right-central section of the *Hunt of the Calydonian Boar* in the Walters Art Gallery in Baltimore, which was woven about ten years earlier (figs. 46, 47).

When tapestry designers did not depend on figures or compositions created by other artists in their own or different media, they could draw on a number of alternate kinds of visual inspiration. The design of certain

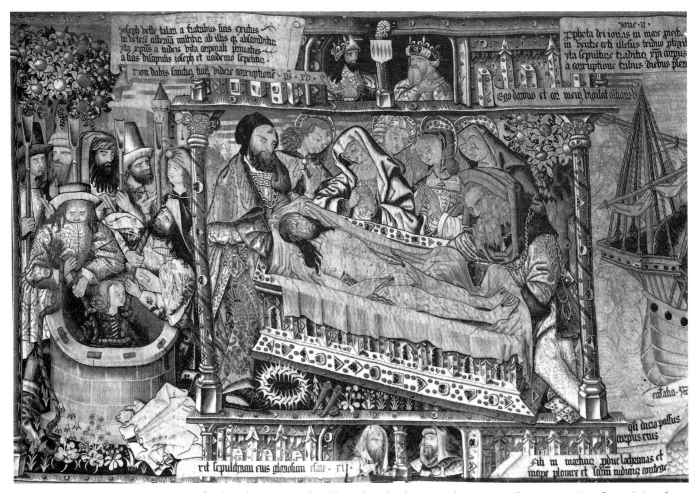

Fig. 32. *The Entombment*, section of a choir hanging in the abbey church of Saint-Robert in La Chaise-Dieu (see fig. 29). Southern Netherlands, woven between 1492 and 1518. The tapestry designer took his inspiration directly from a woodcut like the one illustrated in fig. 33.

ornamental tapestries depended upon pattern systems and motifs borrowed from contemporaneous woven or embroidered silks (see 1). From the performances of miracle and mystery plays a designer could borrow figures and simple settings (see 29a, b). When royal or noble personages made state entries into a city, some of the citizens took part in pageants during which they greeted the honored visitor either as part of a welcoming committee, or in a brief drama, or as living statues in elaborately costumed and decorated tableaux set up on scaffolds along the route of the procession. Contemporary accounts abound with descriptions of such allegorical and laudatory productions, many of which included installations of placards inscribed with verses identifying the figures or explaining their actions. Such placards or scrolls, inscribed in French or Latin or both, frequently appeared in a tapestry designer's scheme to serve the same purpose. Some of these pageants were designed by artists who also designed tapestries. A case in point is that of Jacquemart Pilet, one of the painters

Fig. 33. *The Entombment*, woodcut from an edition of the *Biblia Pauperum*. Germany, late fifteenth century. Albertina, Vienna.

34

Fig. 34. *Five Soldiers and a Turk on Horseback*, by Albrecht Dürer. Engraving, Germany, end of the fifteenth century. MMA, Fletcher Fund, 1919 (19.73.100). The halberdier standing right of center served as the model for figures in the tapestries illustrated in figs. 35 and 36, as well as others.

Fig. 35. *Miracle of Saint Julien* (detail). Tapestry, southern Netherlands, early sixteenth century. Mobilier National, Paris. The head and shoulders of Dürer's halberdier, and perhaps also the figure standing next to him, appear at the right.

Fig. 36. *A Falconer with Two Ladies, a Page, and a Foot Soldier*, tapestry (36 in the present catalogue). The figure of the halberdier, and perhaps also the figure standing next to him, taken from Dürer's print (fig. 34), are used in a new context.

Fig. 37. *The Alfresco Banquet.* Tapestry, southern Netherlands, early sixteenth century. The Burrell Collection, Glasgow Museums and Art Galleries.

trained in the atelier of Bauduin de Bailleul in Arras. In 1468 Pilet and two colleagues were commissioned by the aldermen of Arras to paint fourteen narrative scenes on paper that would then be acted out by members of the city corporations when Charles le Téméraire made an entry into that city on March 16, 1469. The subjects were drawn from Scripture and ancient history. Some years later, in 1496, the parishioners of the church of Saint-Géry in Arras commissioned the same Pilet to design five tapestries of the *Life of Saint Géry* based on a written account that they provided. It has been suggested that Jean Perréal, court painter to Charles VIII, Louis XII, and François I, who is known to have designed scenes for royal entries, also designed tapestries, some of

which show subjects related to those he used in his pageant designs.

Except for the hodgepodge compositions that weavers assembled (rather than designed) in their shops, tapestry designs of the kinds described above passed through two or three stages before they reached the weavers. First, the designer prepared a small sketch of the composition either as a drawing or small painting. It was customary during the Renaissance and later to have the sketch enlarged in full color to the size of an easel painting. Since no paintings of this sort seem to have survived from the Middle Ages and no documents mention their use, it may be that medieval designers eliminated this intermediate step and worked directly from the sketch

Fig. 38. *Falconry and Sheep Tending*. Tapestry, southern Netherlands, early sixteenth century. The Corcoran Gallery of Art, Washington; William A. Clark Collection. The figures of the jester, the young man pouring from a ewer, and the seated lady holding a glass appear in this tapestry (now reversed) and the one in fig. 37.

into the final stage of preparation, or the cartoon. This was a full-size pattern painted in colors on paper or cloth from which the weavers would work. The cartoon painter was an artist with special technical knowledge that enabled him to translate the designer's shapes and details into forms suited to the weaver's medium. His was the most important function in the process of preparing the design for execution in tapestry. He may have been—but was not always—the man who designed the original sketch.

Because tapestry design was subject to particular technical, economic, and functional limitations that were different from those affecting mural, easel, or miniature painting, it developed an aesthetic of its own. In the Middle Ages, important tapestries were required to cover dozens if not hundreds of running feet of wall space, much of it at least sixteen feet high. Therefore the elements in the design had to be bold, the pattern ornamental, the color strong, the spatial composition subject to interpretation from many different viewpoints. Concerning the question of color, Tommaso Portinari, the Medici agent in Bruges, had become so sensitive to the particular character of tapestry art he could tell Giovanni de' Medici in a letter dated February 18, 1463, that he wondered if a particular color should not be changed if certain tapestries were woven again since the color in that part of the cartoon was not effective when woven. When one realizes that a freshly woven tapestry

rich with silk, silver, and gilt yarns must have looked like nothing so much as a gargantuan enameled plaque, one understands that tapestry design was perhaps more akin to the design of precious metalwork—whose value it approximated—than to the design of easel pictures.

In later eras, tapestries were often left hanging in place indefinitely or set into wall panels where they served essentially as fixed and relatively inviolable mural decorations or large easel paintings. In contrast to this, medieval usage required that tapestries be frequently moved,

Fig. 39. *Departure for the Hunt.* Tapestry, southern Netherlands, early sixteenth century. Musée de Cluny, Paris. The mounted falconer and his two mounted attendants at the left end of the tapestry in fig. 40 appear again in this example.

Fig. 40. *Falconry and Pastoral Merrymaking.* Tapestry, southern Netherlands, early sixteenth century. The Corcoran Gallery of Art, Washington; William A. Clark Collection.

sometimes combined with other tapestries of different dimensions and subjects, turned around corners, folded under or draped back around fireplaces, cut through to make openings for doors and windows—in short, be regarded as anything but fixed and inviolable. Consequently the medieval tapestry designer was obliged to forego the satisfaction of creating compositions with a marked center of interest and subtly subordinated secondary passages. He had to keep his whole surface equally strong, mobile, and visually engaging. His job was not an easy one, and not least because he knew that some patron, producer, or weaver was quite apt to alter his design before, or even after, it was executed as a woven fabric. We have many accounts of such changes. To cite one example of a change of design before weaving, we can note that in 1477 the Brussels weaver Gilles Van den Putte contracted to produce for the London merchant Jean Pasmer a tapestry in which the central scene of the Last Supper would be replaced with a scene showing the Four Doctors of the Church. In an example of a change after weaving, between 1399 and 1402 two Arras weavers, Colart d'Auxy and Jean de Nieuport, acting under orders from Philippe le Hardi, removed the figure of Louis de Mâle from an existing tapestry of the *Twelve Peers of France* because the duke thought the figure was not impressive enough. He had it replaced with a figure of the same count richly worked with gilt and silk yarns. Designers also had to plan ahead for the possibility that very large tapestries might be cut into smaller pieces if after several installations the single monumental hanging was found to be too large and heavy to handle. This was the fate of the great *Battle of Roosebeke*, begun in 1387 and woven in one piece to a size of some forty-one and a half meters long by some five and a third meters high. In 1402 it was cut into three pieces by the same Colart d'Auxy. His work was complimented with the observation that the separation was so well done the three pieces seemed to have been woven separately in the first place. If such operations were not successful, weavers would be engaged to add fabric along the sides of the cuts to complete inscriptions, figures, or trees that had been mutilated. Indeed medieval tapestry designs were not deemed to be inviolable. They were regarded first as designs for serviceable wall coverings and only secondarily as pictures.

One need only compare a late medieval tapestry with a contemporaneous painting showing the same or similar composition to demonstrate the profound formal differences that separated the two media. The tapestry version of Rogier van der Weyden's *Saint Luke Drawing the Virgin and Child* in the Musée du Louvre (fig. 30) virtually repeats the composition of the painting in the

Fig. 41. *The Baptism of Christ,* central section of the altarpiece of Saint John the Baptist, by Rogier van der Weyden. Panel painting, about 1450–65. Gemäldegalerie, Staatliche Museen Preussischer Kulturbesitz, Berlin-Dahlem.

Museum of Fine Arts, Boston (fig. 31), of which four versions exist. The tapestry shows the composition in reverse and so was probably woven on a horizontal loom from a cartoon that did not prepare for the reversal. The main figures are proportionately smaller than the figures in the painting, and they are set farther back in the space. The tapestry designer has made them less important in the composition, no more imposing visually than the other forms represented. The garments on both figures have been arranged in more complex and decorative folds. The tapestry designer has shown more of the Virgin's patterned gown and more of the patterned cushion on which the saint kneels. The linear perspective in the painting that helps create a sense of depth through the drawing of the canopy above the Virgin's

Fig. 42. Kunsthistorisches Museum, Vienna.

Fig. 43. Abegg-Stiftung Bern, Riggisberg.

Fig. 44. Museo de la Catedral de La Seo, Saragossa.

Fig. 45. Museo degli Argenti, Palazzo Pitti, Florence.

40

Fig. 46. *Episodes in the Childhood of Hercules* (detail, upper right corner). Tapestry, southern Netherlands, here dated about 1480–85. Musées Royaux d'Art et d'Histoire, Brussels.

Fig. 47. *Hunt of the Calydonian Boar* (detail, upper right corner). Tapestry, southern Netherlands, here dated about 1470–75. Walters Art Gallery, Baltimore.

head and the bases and capitals of the colonnettes at the back has been eliminated in the tapestry. The carved ornaments in the tapestry setting are more detailed, and an urn, a table with a vase of flowers, and an open book have been added. The horizon line in the distant landscape has been raised, and more buildings, trees, and hills fill the space outside. In short, everything has been done to change a picture into a decorative pattern without losing the painter's narrative intent.

When comparing compositions in painting and tapestry that are similar rather than virtually identical, one sees yet more striking contrasts, even when the tapestry is also essentially a picture. Hans Memling's *Adoration of the Magi* in the Museo del Prado (fig. 48) shows a

composition very much like that in the tapestry dossal with the same subject in the cathedral of Sens (fig. 49). In the woven picture the Magus at the right kneels beside, rather than partly in front of, the Virgin and Child, and all the other main figures stand closer to the front of the space than they do in the painting. They are all more or less the same height, which is nearly that of the composition itself. Their heads, the Virgin's throne, and the heads of the two shepherds at the rear left all obscure the open space in the distant landscape and effectively block it out. The Magi in the tapestry wear garments of elaborately patterned silks, which relate these figures to the richly decorated woven frame surrounding the scene and thus tend to bring the eye back to the picture plane.

In the painting, the five main figures—Virgin and Child, Joseph, and the two elder Magi—have been made the center of interest not only because they were placed in the center of the picture's width but also because each of them occupies a point on a great imaginary circle on the ground extending from the Madonna at the front through the semicircular apse at the rear. The youngest Magus and the attendant figures do not participate in this circular arrangement nor are they included in the vast space that surrounds the main figures and flows out into the distance through the arched windows in the rear wall. So it is obvious that the easel painter established a strong center of interest and subordinated other forms to it, and it is equally obvious that the tapestry designer neutralized the power of the Virgin's central position by eliminating the illusion of deep space and by giving all the figures approximately equal importance in his composition.

It seems likely that in the Middle Ages it was the cartoon painter rather than the designer—except of course in those instances when the same man prepared both the initial sketch and the cartoon—whose job it was to turn essentially narrative compositions into essentially decorative ones. Comparing the fragmentary sketch for the *Andromache and Priam Urging Hector*

Not to Go to War in the *Trojan War* series (fig. 50) to an example of the finished tapestry (fig. 51), one sees quite clearly that the cartoon painter caused the tops of the figures and architectural elements in the lower, nearer, space of the tapestry to overlap the figures and elements in the upper, more distant space, in order to unify the two spaces and thus emphasize the composition's surface pattern rather than its depth. In this case the designer was probably a painter of miniatures who was trained to emphasize the separation of contiguous spaces like these in order to clarify the narrative.

Until the late fifteenth century, when painters of easel pictures apparently began to take a more active part in designing tapestries, cartoon painters did not ask weavers to stretch the limitations and conventions of their craft. A weaver could not blend colors or trace diagonal or graceful curving lines as a painter could do. He could produce a rough equivalent of color blending by means of *hatching*, or weaving reciprocal comb-like teeth of color to make contiguous color areas interpenetrate along the boundary and so produce the illusion of a blended middle tone (fig. 52). He could also soften the sharp contours along lines of color change by dovetailing the wefts of adjacent color areas, and he could approximate the appearance of diagonal and curved lines

Fig. 48. *The Adoration of the Magi,* by Hans Memling. Panel painting, about 1475–85. Museo del Prado, Madrid.

Fig. 49. *The Adoration of the Magi.* Tapestry dossal, southern Netherlands, about 1476–88. Cathedral, Sens.

Fig. 50. *Andromache and Priam Urging Hector Not to Go to War.* Fragment of the original design (*petit patron*) for the tapestry illustrated in fig. 51. Drawing, northwest France (?), about 1465–70. Cabinet des Dessins, Musée du Louvre, Paris.

Fig. 51. *Andromache and Priam Urging Hector Not to Go to War* (13c), fragment of a tapestry from the *Story of the Trojan War* series.

43

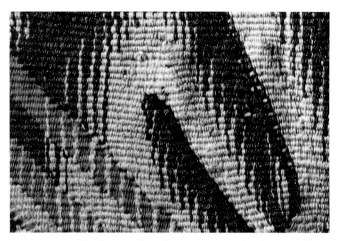

Fig. 52. Detail of a medieval tapestry in the Metropolitan Museum (42b). The effect of shading from light to dark is achieved by hatching, or shaping the edges of the adjacent areas of light and dark yarns like the interpenetrating teeth of two combs.

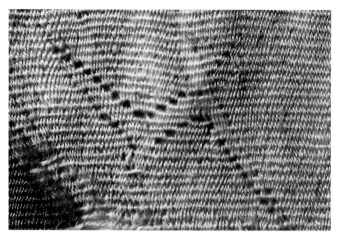

Fig. 54. Detail of a medieval tapestry in the Metropolitan Museum (13b). The delicate contours in the flesh of a hand are rendered by lines of shadows cast by small slits deliberately left in the monochromatic weave rather than by hard lines made with weft yarns of a darker tone.

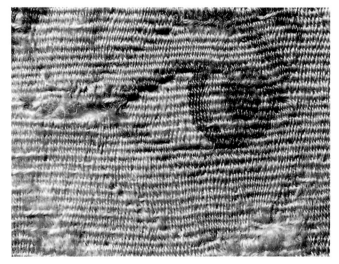

Fig. 53. Detail of a medieval tapestry in the Metropolitan Museum (13b). The dark weft yarns delineating the outer part of the eyelid directly above the iris have been dovetailed with the adjacent lighter wefts in order to soften the contour and also to keep a slit from forming. The effect of a diagonal contour defining the inner edge of the same eyelid was achieved by stepping short, straight lengths of the dark line to the side and down.

by means of *stepping,* or building up the contour with short lines or small blocks of color gently offset one from the next as they traced out the direction of the line (fig. 53). Small slits in the weave parallel to the warp direction were a boon to the weaver since they cast small shadows which he could use to define subtle contours in places where strong lines and color contrasts were not wanted (fig. 54).

Economic considerations determined the relative fineness of a tapestry's texture and that, in turn, affected the amount of detail the tapestry would show. The more warp yarns a piece contained, the finer each yarn could be and consequently the finer the texture and the more complicated the detail. A tapestry with a high warp count cost more than one with fewer warp yarns per measure. Economic factors also determined the number of colors that would be used and whether silk, silver, and gilt yarns would be included in the piece.

Stylistic Development of Tapestry Design in France and the Southern Netherlands, 1375–1525

The art of tapestry design followed its own course during the period 1375–1525, developing compositions based on styles created by contemporary printmakers and painters of easel, mural, and miniature pictures but altered to suit the requirements of tapestry design. The aesthetic, economic, and functional factors that obliged tapestry designers to modify the character of current images did not change the essential style of those images during most of the period. Occasionally tapestry designers deliberately ignored some of the basic precepts of a pictorial style, but in doing so they merely created a derivative, parallel style that served their purpose better. They were making special kinds of pictures, but they were indeed making pictures. Like printmakers and painters, tapestry designers had to consider the problem of how to represent space, how to interpret subject matter, how to deal with the question of using static or dynamic balance, clear or obscure form—these and other problems that any image maker must address. Therefore the same art-historical method one uses to analyze the style of an easel painting may properly be used when attempting to trace stylistic development in tapestry design. However the results of such a study may be valid only where the tapestries being considered show original designs and not simply compositions made up of images borrowed from one or more preexisting sources.

Stylistic analysis can help one perceive the fact that modes of representation in pictorial tapestries did indeed change and develop during the late Middle Ages. The exercise can also help date a tapestry, but no more precisely than to a particular half century or perhaps quarter century. One needs specific internal evidence, like fashionable dress or accessories, or heraldic motifs, to date the design of a tapestry with any degree of precision. Also, unless the tapestry itself is dated in the weave or by virtue of a documentary reference, its date of manufacture cannot be determined precisely, even by the date of the cartoon after which it was woven. Popular cartoons continued to be used for some years after they were made, and they were sometimes, not always, brought up to date through changes in the fashionable details. The tapestries that will be discussed here to

illustrate the styles of successive periods between 1375 and 1525 were chosen because most of them can be dated by document or firm internal evidence.

In the years around 1380, when documents suggest the *Apocalypse* tapestries at Angers were finished, the chief image makers were the painters of monumental murals and the illustrators of fine books. The images in the *Apocalypse* tapestries (fig. 55) reflect primarily the style of contemporaneous book illustration (fig. 56). These artists had developed a style that got the message across quickly, clearly, and with the greatest economy of means. Human figures and the elements of the minimal settings were given fairly simple silhouettes but complex decorative details within those contours. Space was treated as an abstraction, something the mind knew had to exist if these people could move, these objects stand, against these flat plain or decorated backgrounds. People and animals moved almost exclusively in a shallow plane close to and parallel to the picture plane. All forms and spatial relationships were crystal clear. One mass balanced another with equal visual weight. Each shape was complete in itself. The drawing of figures and other forms—nervous, attenuated, and essentially decorative—reflected the sophisticated and exquisitely mannered International Style that dominated late fourteenth-century court painting not only in France but also in the major capitals of western Europe. In these respects, the style of late fourteenth-century book illustration was a perfect style for the tapestry designer whose goal was to decorate walls first and tell stories second.

By 1402, the year specified in a lost document as that in which the *Story of Saints Piat and Eleuthère* tapestries were finished, a marked change had taken place. Four of the nine tapestries in this set, woven in Arras for the cathedral of Tournai, have survived and are preserved in the treasury of that cathedral church (fig. 57). Although some of the figures show the attenuation of the International Style, they have few of its decorative mannerisms. The tapestry designer, like the painter who pointed the way for him, has moved on to a more plastic conception of the body and of the space it inhabits. The designer has attempted to suggest deep space by causing his figures and objects to overlap one

Fig. 55. *Michael and His Angels Defeating Satan and His Angels*, detail from one of the hangings in the *Apocalypse* series. Tapestry, southern Netherlands, about 1373–80. Musée des Tapisseries, Château d'Angers.

Fig. 56. *Michael and His Angels Defeating Satan and His Angels*. Miniature painting, France, first half of the fourteenth century. Bibliothèque Nationale, Paris (MS lat. 14410, p. 34).

another and also by introducing a high horizon line in his exterior settings. These devices tend to emphasize the spatial relationships among elements in the composition, and they also set them in motion, turning the contained balance of the *Apocalypse* compositions into a dynamic rather than static equilibrium.

Even artists in the major fields of painting would not find a convincing way to represent depth and air in real space until some years later. By 1434, Jan van Eyck had achieved a totally illusionistic representation of space and of solid forms moving through it in his astonishing portrait of Giovanni Arnolfini and his wife in their wedding chamber, now in the National Gallery in London (fig. 58). At this point, pictorial styles in painting and tapestry design began to develop separate courses, and the divergence lasted until late in the fifteenth century. Tapestry designers realized that illusionistic effects would not suit their purpose. Furthermore, they knew the current limits of their medium, a medium that had not yet been pushed to the point of being able to suggest transparent or blended color in direct imitation of oil painting. Nevertheless, van Eyck and his peers had made a bold new statement. To the extent that the patrons of tapestry designers demanded it and weavers could provide it, the designers found a way of adapting the new images to their medium. By about 1440 they had developed a believable if nonillusionistic means of representing depth and open space without destroying the reality of the tapestry's own surface. This is evident in the four great hunting tapestries in the Victoria and Albert Museum (see fig. 59), which, though their dates vary slightly among themselves, have been dated in the second quarter of the fifteenth century. The device of overlapping forms, used some forty years earlier in the *Saints Piat and Eleuthère* tapestries, is carried a step further and coordinated with the convention of placing the more distant figures on a distinctly higher level than those in the foreground. The designer also arranged his figures, buildings, and natural forms in diagonal and curving lines that carry the observer's eye into and around the space. It is as though one were observing the action from a moving point somewhat above the stage on which these scenes are being played out. People and things, richly patterned and detailed, describe themselves and their positions clearly and succinctly. The surface of the composition is also decorated with a network of curving, diagonal, and undulating paths for the eye to follow. The surface scintillates with a thousand

Fig. 57. *Saint Piat Begins His Preaching in Tournai,* detail of one of the choir hangings of the *Story of Saints Piat and Eleuthère.* Tapestry, woven in the shop of Pierre Féré, Arras, 1402. Cathedral, Tournai.

Fig. 58. *Portrait of Giovanni Arnolfini and Giovanna Cenami,* by Jan van Eyck. Panel painting, dated 1434. National Gallery, London.

decorative details of costume and setting. It is in fact by virtue of the designer's laying small, complex details of pattern over his clearly defined forms that he achieves the effect of surface integrity while simultaneously convincing the observer that these people, buildings, and greenery are solid and that they occupy deep space.

This style seems to have continued until the sixth decade of the fifteenth century when the designers who had achieved this delicate balance between surface and depth moved into what can only be called a baroque phase. The *Trajan and Herkinbald* tapestry in the Historisches Museum in Bern shows a style in transition (fig. 60). It is generally agreed that the tapestry was woven not long after 1450, but we have no firm justification for that date. The spatial clarity of the earlier style survives in the interior scenes, more cluttered but essentially the same. The exterior scenes show a very different mode of representation. There the figures, now completely plastic and more carefully observed from nature, press forward against the picture plane in a constricted space that is too shallow to contain them. In an effort to find breathing space they push up toward the top of the composition or down toward the bottom. Formal clarity gives way to confusion, and everything is in a state of dynamic motion. The problem of representing depth no longer concerns the designer who seems obsessed with the need to decorate the surface of the fabric and to maintain its integrity. Other tapestries datable to about 1460, like the *Story of Alexander* in

Fig. 59. *Deer Hunt.* Tapestry, southern Netherlands, about 1425–50. Victoria and Albert Museum, London.

Fig. 60. *Story of Trajan and Herkinbald* (detail, left half). Tapestry, southern Netherlands, about 1450–55. Bernisches Historisches Museum.

Rome (fig. 61) and the *Story of the Swan Knight* in Vienna and Cracow (fig. 62), as well as the *Story of the Vengeance of Our Lord* in the Metropolitan Museum (see 10), show the same tendency to press the forms against the picture plane. The fully developed baroque style of this third quarter of the fifteenth century is to be seen in the *Story of the Trojan War* series to which there are references in documents of 1472, 1476, and 1488 (see 13a–c). The tapestries in this series were therefore probably designed late in the 1460s, and the vogue for them lasted almost until the end of the century. In them, the designer achieved the ultimate goal of the decorator of monumental surfaces. He succeeded in telling a story and simultaneously entertaining the eye with an endless succession of visual diversions, never asking the observer to choose between one experience and the other. His work succeeds in the same way that a well-made opera or ballet succeeds, by offering the viewer multiple perceptions simultaneously which, when expertly combined, can offer an agreeably rich experience.

As the fifteenth century moved into its fourth quar-ter, tapestry design turned to the example of easel painting. The reason for this abrupt change is not clear. It may have been brought about by a pronounced change in patrons' taste. It may also have been an immediate and direct result of the Brussels ordinance of 1476 which required that weavers in that city use only cartoons designed by members of the painters' guild for all but their verdure tapestries, a term that might have signified not only landscape pieces but also millefleurs and other pieces featuring greenery and plants. Some designers working during these years frankly set out to imitate easel pictures complete with illusionistic effects and imitations of carved and gilded frames. Among these pieces are the two dossals in Sens (figs. 49, 63), the *Annunciation* and *Adoration of the Magi* in the Mobilier National in Paris (figs. 64, 65), and the *Madonna of the Living Water* in the Musée du Louvre (fig. 66). All of these examples are dated, or may be dated, between 1475 and 1490. Not only has the designer created the illusion in each case that his tapestry is in fact an altarpiece made of painted panels held in a carved and gilded

Fig. 61. *Alexander in a Flying Machine*, detail of a hanging in the *Story of Alexander* series. Tapestry, southern Netherlands, about 1459. Galleria Doria Pamphili, Rome.

Fig. 62. Scenes from the *Story of the Swan Knight*. Tapestry, southern Netherlands, about 1461. Wawel Castle Museum, Cracow.

Fig. 63. *The Coronation of the Virgin and Related Scenes from the Old Testament.* Tapestry dossal, southern Netherlands, about 1476–88. Cathedral, Sens.

50

frame, but also the weaver has succeeded in forcing his technique to suggest the chromatic and textural effects of painting and of gold and silver leaf. In some of the *Hunt of the Unicorn* hangings (20b–e and 20g, h in the present catalogue), the designer and weavers simulated the quality of oil-glazed painting specifically.

Other tapestry designers—and it seems that there were more of them than there were imitators of easel painting—returned to the realm of painting styles but without violating the integrity of their own art. In tapestries like the *Life of the Virgin* in the church of Notre-Dame in Beaune, a set of choir hangings dated 1500 in the weave, the designer presented fully modeled figures arranged in compartmented shallow spaces in the foreground and mildly illusionistic landscapes beyond them (fig. 67). This example may have been somewhat advanced for its time, for by comparison with it the style of the tapestries of the *Life of Saint Anatoile*, woven in Bruges between 1502 and 1506, seems conservative (fig. 68). Here, figures move diagonally through spaces in landscapes or interiors that are drawn with a rudimentary kind of linear perspective. The illusion of depth is

Fig. 64. *Annunciation, with Scenes and Figures from the Old Testament.* Tapestry dossal, southern Netherlands, about 1475–85. Mobilier National, Paris.

Fig. 65. *The Adoration of the Magi, with Scenes from the Old Testament.* Tapestry dossal, southern Netherlands, about 1475–85. Mobilier National, Paris.

Fig. 66. *Madonna of the Living Water.* Tapestry dossal, southern Netherlands, dated 1485. Musée du Louvre, on deposit from the Mobilier National, Paris.

Fig. 67. *The Visitation*, detail of one of the choir hangings of the *Life of the Virgin.* Tapestry, southern Netherlands, about 1500. Church of Notre-Dame, Beaune.

less convincing than it is in the hangings in Beaune. In tapestries like the *Lives of Christ and the Virgin* in the Cathedral of Saint-Sauveur in Aix-en-Provence, which are dated 1511 in the weave (fig. 69), and the *Legend of Herkinbald* of 1513 or the fourth hanging from the *Legend of Notre-Dame du Sablon* set of 1518, both in Brussels (figs. 70, 71), the designer minimized the compartmentalization of spaces and tried instead to create an illusion of coherent, flowing open space occupied by fully credible three-dimensional figures.

As Renaissance forms from Italy influenced the painterly conventions of Flanders in the second and third decades of the sixteenth century, the swing toward illusionism in south Netherlandish tapestry design accelerated. While they are still clearly northern and late medieval in style, the *Sablon* tapestries, believed to have been designed by Bernaert van Orley, look decades later—that is, more illusionistic and Italianate—than the *Herkinbald* piece that was designed by Jan van Roome, a traditionally oriented Brussels designer, only

Fig. 68. *Saint Anatoile's Body Transported in State to the Church of Saint Symphorien at Salins,* eighth piece in the set of the *Life of Saint Anatoile.* Tapestry, woven in the shop of Katherine Wilde, Bruges, 1502–6. Musée du Louvre, Paris.

Fig. 69. *Entry into Jerusalem,* section of a hanging in the series *The Lives of Christ and the Virgin.* Tapestry, southern Netherlands, dated 1511. Cathedral of Saint-Sauveur, Aix-en-Provence.

five years earlier. In the third and fourth decades of the sixteenth century, south Netherlandish weavers used more designs in the Italian mode, or showing Italian influence, presumably in response to a growing demand for them. However the *Life of the Virgin* choir hangings in Reims (fig. 72), finished by 1530, and the similar *Life of Saint Rémi,* woven sometime between 1523 and 1531, also in the cathedral of Reims, prove that the traditional south Netherlandish tapestry style continued for some years after the initial success of tapestries in the Italianate mode.

This brief essay on the succession of styles in late medieval tapestries has been limited to a consideration of the main developments in the major class of tapestries that have survived, that is, tapestries that show pictorial compositions. The other kinds of tapestries, all of which are essentially ornamental, like heraldic or millefleurs pieces, do not follow the same lines of development. The design of such hangings does not involve the formal elements that enable one to analyze the style

of pictorial compositions. For the present we are obliged to rely on other kinds of evidence in order to arrange these pieces in chronological sequence. Matters like the character of ornaments, the design of costume or other fashionable accessories, or the interpretation of heraldic motifs may help determine the date when a particular tapestry was designed. Various attempts have been made to arrange millefleurs tapestries in chronological sequence according to criteria based on the style of the floral motifs represented in each piece. Those deliberations have produced no reliable results. However if, in the future, many more millefleurs tapestries can be securely dated by other means, this kind of investigation might be worth pursuing. It seems possible that when such dates are coordinated with the tapestry designs, certain trends in the way the plants and flowers are drawn, and the way they are scaled and arranged, may become apparent.

Fig. 70. *Legend of Herkinbald.* Tapestry, Brussels, 1513. Musées Royaux d'Art et d'Histoire, Brussels.

Fig. 71. *The Miraculous Statue Is Brought to Brussels,* fourth piece in the set of the *Legend of Notre-Dame du Sablon.* Tapestry, believed to have been produced in Brussels, 1518. Musées Royaux d'Art et d'Histoire, Brussels.

Fig. 72. *The Annunciation, with Figures and Scenes from the Old Testament*, detail of a hanging in the set of the *Life of the Virgin*. Tapestry, southern Netherlands, completed by 1530. Cathedral, Reims.

Fig. 73. Scene from the *Story of Jourdain de Blaye*. Tapestry, southern Netherlands, late fourteenth century. Museo Civico, Padua.

History of Tapestry Weaving in Europe during the Late Middle Ages

THE PRESENT STATE OF OUR KNOWLEDGE

Since Achille Jubinal published the first scientific study of historical tapestries in 1838, the authors of countless books and articles have examined the subject in increasingly greater detail and from different points of view. But what we have today, a century and a half later, is essentially a vast body of data, largely miscellaneous and undigested, concerning primarily the sale of tapestries in the late Middle Ages, details like the names of clients, merchants, patrons, weavers, and a few designers, together with notes on prices, dimensions, subject matter, and materials used to design and execute the tapestries. We also have some information about the regulations controlling the manufacture of tapestries and the methods of marketing them. Historians collected these data from a broad miscellany of sources including inventories, household accounts, receipts, civil and ecclesiastical records of all sorts, ordinances and other forms of public legislation, and private legal documents. A host of dedicated scholars produced most of this information before the close of the nineteenth century. Houdoy followed Jubinal's general work with a special study of the industry in Lille, and Wauters and Soil followed soon afterward with their documentation concerning the industries in Brussels and Tournai, respectively. Guiffrey, Müntz, and Pinchart made the most important single contribution in their cooperative work *Histoire générale de la tapisserie* in which they published original material relating to the history of tapestry in most parts of Europe. In the early years of the twentieth century, W. G. Thomson published two books that brought additional documentary material to light, particularly with reference to British patrons and weavers. A few years later Heinrich Göbel produced his monumental *Wandteppiche*, a general history of the art and industry of tapestry throughout Europe, in which he coordinated most of the material published earlier with valuable new data developed in his own files.

None of these scholars was primarily an art historian. Taken in the aggregate, their work amounted to the beginning—and only the beginning—of a comprehensive history of the tapestry industry. It would remain for the art historians, examining data gathered from these archive-oriented sources and from their own firsthand

study of surviving tapestries, to begin writing a history of the art of tapestry. The early generations of art historians comprised people whose primary training and expertise involved the art of painting. Not understanding the subtle but critical differences that set the two arts apart from each other, these scholars fell into the trap of treating the essentially impersonal, industrial art of tapestry as though it were the personal, conceptual art of painting. Following their natural tendency to construct intellectual and intuitive systems by means of which they thought they could attribute any given tapestry to a particular place, time, designer, and weaver, as they might determine the particulars concerning a painting, these neophyte tapestry historians veered off course. They believed that a weaver was a creative artist whose personal manner affected the appearance of the images he created. They also believed that there were regional schools of tapestry design in the Middle Ages as there were regional schools of painting. Furthermore, these scholars lived in modern times when anyone acquainted with the visual arts would at least have heard of the Gobelins, Beauvais, Aubusson, and other highly organized manufactories of the seventeenth century and later whose products could be recognized through certain visual peculiarities. However a modern self-contained tapestry manufactory is very different from a medieval tapestry-weaving shop. But these early art historians gave undue importance to the factors of region and workshop when studying medieval tapestries because they were used to thinking in terms of these later manufactories whose artistic and technical directors saw to it that their products would have a particular look. These scholars also believed (and many others still believe) that they could identify the hand of a particular painter, usually a seminal painter of distinction, in the design of these early tapestries. They did not acknowledge that during the Middle Ages the entrepreneurs who produced the weavings patronized primarily a class of artists who specialized in decorative design and painting and worked at everything from painting coats of arms and coaches to designing mimes for the state entries of sovereigns, stained glass, and tapestry. A few of these painters were artists of note who created original

Fig. 74. *The Gift of the Heart.* Tapestry, southern Netherlands, early fifteenth century. Musée du Louvre, Paris.

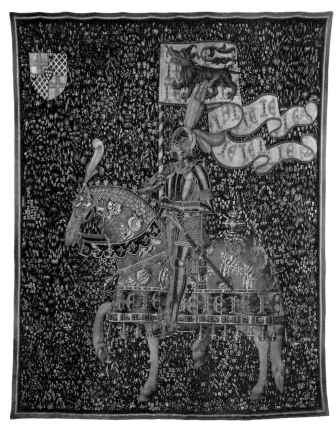

Fig. 75. *Mounted Knight with the Arms of Jean de Daillon.* Tapestry, southern Netherlands, Tournai, about 1483. Montacute House, Yeovil (Somerset); The National Trust.

tapestry designs, but most of them were image makers who based their designs on the work of leading painters of the moment.

So, for better or worse, art historians of the late nineteenth and early twentieth centuries began drawing the broad outlines of the history of tapestry weaving in the late Middle Ages according to their own lights, combining the incomplete miscellanea unearthed by the archivists with their own conclusions based on observation of the few dated or datable and geographically locatable tapestries that have come down to us, and then generalizing from there. In this way, the extant pieces of the great *Apocalypse* tapestries in Angers, which were woven sometime between about 1373 and 1380 and until recently believed to have been woven by Nicolas Bataille in Paris (fig. 55), became the touchstone by which all tapestries showing related images would be attributed to Paris in the late fourteenth century and, more often than not, to Nicolas Bataille. The same historians defined a "style of Arras" based curiously enough less on the analysis of the *Story of Saints Piat and Eleuthère* (dated 1402) in the cathedral of Tournai, the

only documented early Arras hangings we have (fig. 57), than on analyses of pieces like the tapestry from the *Story of Jourdain de Blaye* series in Padua or the *Gift of the Heart* in Paris, for neither of which is there any documentation connecting it with Arras nor giving it any date (figs. 73, 74). To establish regional styles for the second half of the fifteenth century, these historians looked for tapestries that could be more or less securely placed and dated in that period, and they found two pieces of a *Story of Alexander the Great* in the Galleria Doria Pamphili in Rome (fig. 61), some fragments of a *Story of the Swan Knight* in Cracow (fig. 62) and Vienna, and a host of fragments and complete hangings of the *Story of the Trojan War* in various European and American collections (see 13a–c). Most historians believed that the *Alexander* and *Swan Knight* hangings could be identified with tapestries of these subjects that Philippe le Bon of Burgundy bought from the Tournai producer-merchant Pasquier Grenier in 1459 and 1461 respectively. There is no proof to support these contentions. On the other hand, there is no doubt that the surviving pieces of the *Trojan War* tapestries show designs that

Fig. 76. *The Stoning of Saint Stephen,* from the set of the *Life of Saint Ursin.* Tapestry, southern Netherlands, Tournai, about 1500. Musées de Bourges.

correspond to those that Grenier sold to Henry VII of England in 1488. But we cannot be sure that Grenier had the tapestries designed and woven in Tournai. Nevertheless, using these three series of tapestries and a number of other pieces that can reasonably be dated stylistically in the second half of the fifteenth century, tapestry historians isolated the "style of Tournai" and attributed quantities of other surviving tapestries to that city as their place of manufacture. Some historians went so far as to identify certain pieces as the work of Pasquier Grenier, who, they thought, was operating as a weaver. We now know that he made his fortune not as a weaver but as an entrepreneur in the tapestry and wine trades. We also know that only two extant examples of tapestry weaving can be documented as having been woven in Tournai in the second half of the fifteenth century. The earlier piece is a millefleurs tapestry now in Montacute House, Somerset. It shows a mounted knight in armor and, in the upper left corner, the coat of arms of Jean de Daillon, seigneur de Lude, for whom it was woven by Wuillaume Desreumaulx of Tournai. It was delivered in 1483 (fig. 75). The later example com-

prises three fragments from a *Life of Saint Ursin* in the Musées de Bourges which date from about 1500 (fig. 76). These fragments show no stylistic affinities with the millefleurs tapestry, and none of them bears any resemblance to the *Trojan War* tapestries which may or may not have been woven in Tournai.

As for the first quarter of the sixteenth century, there are no extant tapestries that can be documented certainly as Tournai work. The only tapestries that we can date and locate securely for that period are the three pieces of the *Life of Saint Anatoile* in the Musée du Louvre and Mobilier National in Paris (fig. 68), the *Legend of Herkinbald* in the Musées Royaux d'Art et d'Histoire in Brussels (fig. 70), and probably also the several pieces of the *Legend of Notre-Dame du Sablon* to be found in the same museum in Brussels (fig. 71) and the Musée Communal there, the Hermitage Museum in Saint Petersburg, the Burrell Collection in Glasgow, and elsewhere. The *Saint Anatoile* tapestries are documented as having been produced in Bruges between 1502 and 1506, the *Herkinbald* in Brussels in 1513, and the *Sablon* pieces probably in Brussels in 1518. Curiously enough, no historian attempted to establish a "style of Bruges," but the "style of Brussels" based on the *Herkinbald* and *Sablon* tapestries has been current among tapestry historians for as long as the "styles" of Paris, Arras, and Tournai.

No responsible art historian would have had the temerity to define a local style of late medieval painting on the basis of so inadequate a body of data. And yet tapestry specialists insisted on establishing regional tapestry styles. We do not know that the few documented pieces we have show images that are typical of images in tapestries woven in the same time and place. It is quite possible that they are atypical. We simply know that they are securely fixed in time and space, and we have conveniently forced them to be typical so that art-historical theories could be constructed on the evidence they provide. What we have as a result is a mass of literature repeating a host of misleading theories, opinions, and conclusions. It ought to have been clear to us along the way that any stylistic similarities one can find among these tapestries would reflect not the style of a city, weaver, or shop, but the general style of a culture or perhaps the style of a designer with a strong personality. Nevertheless, it became the custom early in this century to view the art of tapestry during the late Middle Ages as a simple linear development from obscure beginnings in Paris during the second half of the fourteenth century to a brilliant flowering in Arras during the next fifty years. Then, according to this theory, Tournai became the tapestry center of Europe during the second half of the fifteenth century, enjoying a monopoly on the art and industry of tapestry until Brussels superseded it around 1500. After that, all fine tapestries were produced in Brussels, while somewhat coarser pieces originated in Tournai.

Thanks to the recent efforts of a group of French and Belgian scholars who have brought more imaginative methods of research and reasoning to bear, we now know that medieval tapestries cannot be assigned to a place of manufacture through the application of these overly simplified criteria, and we also have come to understand how important it is to find correct interpretations for key terms that keep turning up in the documents. As Francis Salet, the chief innovator in this field, has pointed out, these terms seem to mean different things according to when and where they occur, and the signification can vary from one document to another even at any given moment and place. He also called attention to the fact that these terms were written in old French and Netherlandish rather than in Latin and that they obeyed no standard rules of spelling or syntax. Furthermore, many of these terms acquired different meanings in later years. For example the words *haute lisse* apparently did not necessarily describe a high-warp (vertical) loom before the end of the sixteenth century. Salet demonstrated that *haute lisse* was used in reference to luxury fabrics of different kinds, including yardage with repeat patterns and embroideries, as well as figured tapestry hangings, and that at times it seems to have connoted high quality, like the modern term *haute couture.* The word *tapisserie* referred then, as now, both to tapestry fabrics and to other kinds of upholstery materials. In the late Middle Ages, the term *tapissier* referred not only to the professionals who made or installed tapestries and other upholstery fabrics, including embroideries, but also to the restorers, keepers, and merchants who handled such materials. The *tapissier* who functioned as a merchant and producer of fabrics was in fact an entrepreneur capitalist who enjoyed high social standing. He might have a business as a grain or wine merchant as well. If he had begun his career as a weaver or director of a weaving shop, he became an entrepreneur who held stocks of cartoons and tapestries, took commissions from the wealthy and powerful, arranged for custom designs to be made and cartoons painted, advanced capital to buy materials and pay the weavers, and finally delivered the tapestries to the patron (of whom he might be a confidant). When dealing with stock tapestries, the *tapissier* functioned simply as a merchant, dealing in cartoons and finished textiles.

Therefore it is clear that a *tapissier* mentioned in a medieval document was not necessarily a tapestry weaver. Furthermore he was not in business to impose his own design sense on the products he dealt with, although he probably required that the designers and weavers he commissioned must work according to his standards. He had only one goal: to provide furnishing fabrics that would please his clients. The weavers he employed were skilled artisans who followed the patterns they were given. They did not seek to impress whatever personal artistic sensibilities they might have upon the fabrics growing on their looms. The concept of the designer-craftsman is a nineteenth-century one; it did not exist in the industrial art of tapestry during the fourteenth to sixteenth centuries. Tapestry weavers were craftsmen who were motivated to avoid personal idiosyncrasies in their work so as to be in a position to serve any of the great producer-merchants and work from cartoons showing any number of styles. While it is conceivable that a weaver might have developed characteristic quirks of execution that identify any given tapestry as his work, we have not yet isolated any instances of this sort.

The story of the two late fourteenth-century weavings of Hennequin de Bruges's designs for the *Apocalypse* tapestries shows how futile it is to try to assign stylistic characteristics to weaving centers, shops, or individual weavers during this period. The project was initiated at the command of Louis I, duc d'Anjou, sometime after 1373. Payments were made to Nicolas Bataille, the producer, in 1378 and 1379 and to Hennequin de Bruges (also known as Jean Bandol), the designer, in 1378. Current thinking favors the idea that the tapestries were woven in Paris or Arras or possibly in both cities, being subcontracted to shops in one place or the other directed by Robert Poinçon (also Poisson), an Arras shop director then living in Paris. The second recorded weaving of the series—a single hanging having been woven separately for Jean, duc de Berry—was executed for one of Louis's other brothers, Philippe le Hardi, duc de Bourgogne, between 1386 and 1395. The Arras entrepreneur Jean Cosset produced it, putting it out to be executed in weaving shops in Arras directed by the same Robert Poinçon who in 1397, two years after the four pieces then finished were ready to hang, was enrolled as a burgher of Lille. So we have Robert Poinçon, master weaver active in Paris, Arras, and Lille; Nicolas Bataille, a Parisian producer-merchant who is also known to have sold tapestries made in Arras; Jean Cosset, an Arras producer who had close ties with his counterpart Pierre de Beaumetz in Paris; Hennequin de Bruges, a Netherlandish painter in the service of a French king—how is it possible to assign either of the two editions of tapestries woven after the same cartoons to any one of these weaving centers and then to claim that the particular style of the men or towns involved with their manufacture had impressed itself on the tapestries? And yet in all but the most recent literature the *Apocalypse* tapestries at Angers are regarded as showing the "style of Paris" in the late fourteenth century and in some cases also the "style of Nicolas Bataille." In reality the only style they show is that of the designer (and cartoon painter if he was not the same man), possibly shaded by the taste of his client.

In order to establish the style of a weaving center—if a regional style indeed existed there—one would have to know for certain that the tapestries being analyzed for this purpose were both woven and designed in one place. But contemporary documents frequently indicate that late medieval tapestries were designed by artists associated with places other than the place where the tapestries were woven. For example we know that the *Story of Gideon* series woven for Philippe le Bon was designed by Bauduin de Bailleul of Arras but woven in shops directed by Robert Dary and Jean de l'Ortie of Tournai. The fact that these two master weavers were located in Tournai does not necessarily mean that the weaving shops were also there nor that some of the weaving was not subcontracted to other shops. It seems unlikely that so enormous a commission, involving some 550 square meters of tapestry that were woven between 1449 and 1453, could have been executed without subcontracting part of the work. To reverse the example, we know that the Tournai painter Jacques Daret designed tapestries for Arras producers. The Valenciennes painter Simon Marmion registered as a member of the guild of Saint Luke in Tournai so that he could design tapestries for producers there. Giovanni and Piero de' Medici each sent designs from Florence via their agents in Bruges to the producer Pierre de Los of Lille to have them enlarged into cartoons and then woven as tapestries under his direction. The Tournai producer Philippe le Scellier furnished cartoons to weavers in Brussels and Audenarde. Finally, it must be noted that for lesser stock, producers and weavers frequently used cartoons made up from parts of other cartoons or based on compositions or parts of compositions borrowed from preexisting paintings and prints, sources that might represent the styles of any number of distant places.

There are very few extant late medieval tapestries that are firmly fixed in time and space by documentary evidence. Tapestries and documents have survived by chance, and some of the most important weavings and records that we know existed have not survived. The documents that have been studied were chosen erratically, and more often than not the choice of papers reflects the researcher's tendency to use local sources.

Furthermore, we do not know how to interpret some of the most critical terms that occur in these documents. The result of these and related limitations is that the study of the art of tapestry weaving during the late Middle Ages is still in its infancy, and the study of the industry is not much farther along. However the recent work of European scholars is producing new data and broadening our understanding. These scholars have returned to the classic sources published over a hundred years ago and have found new insights in those documents. They have also brought to light quantities of new archival sources not only in the Netherlands and France but also in Spain, Italy, and elsewhere on the Continent. They have emphasized the dangers of attributing any given tapestry to a particular place and date without the help of documents, and they have called attention to the value of internal visual evidence like representations of armorial bearings and fashionable details of dress and furnishing in determining the date of a tapestry or the cartoon after which it was woven. Most important of all, they have made it clear that for the history of the art of tapestry during this period the question of where a tapestry was woven is of relatively minor importance. It is far more significant to determine when the piece was woven, who designed it or what it was designed after, and who the patron and producer were.

Origins and Ancestors

The art of tapestry weaving in the West can be traced through surviving examples back to the fifteenth century B.C. Excavations at the tomb of Tuthmosis IV (ca. 1425–1417 B.C.) in Egypt yielded some fragments of plain linen decorated with hieroglyphs pertaining to Tuthmosis III (ca. 1504–1450 B.C.) worked with colored yarns in tapestry weave into the plain linen. There was another fabric in this find, entirely tapestry-woven, showing the cartouche of Amenhotpe II (ca. 1450–1425 B.C.). The fragments are preserved in the Egyptian Museum in Cairo. These examples do not indicate that tapestry weaving originated in Egypt at that time. Nor can we be sure that the technique was practiced only in that part of the eastern Mediterranean world. Textiles happened to survive in Egypt from this period and later because the mode of burial and the local climate favored their preservation. There is every reason to believe that tapestry-woven ornaments and furnishing fabrics were produced in antiquity throughout the eastern Mediterranean basin and probably also in Asia Minor and Europe. Conditions simply did not favor their survival. The craft is a simple one, and we know that it developed apparently independently in China and the Andes.

Fig. 77. *The Virgin and Child with the Archangels Michael and Gabriel; Christ in Majesty Above.* Tapestry icon, eastern Mediterranean, sixth century A.D. The Cleveland Museum of Art.

A number of tapestry curtains and hangings of the fifth and sixth centuries (A.D.) have survived. One of them, now in the Cleveland Museum of Art (fig. 77), shows the Virgin enthroned holding the Child on her lap and flanked by the archangels Michael and Gabriel. In a smaller compartment above, a pair of angels support an oval cartouche containing a representation of the mature Christ enthroned. Of all the hangings that have survived from the late classical and early Christian periods, this piece, with its developed pictorial form and wide border, must be cited as the earliest known surviving ancestor of European wall tapestries.

We do not know where or when tapestry hangings were first woven in Europe. The traditional view holds that the craft traveled from Egypt and Asia Minor westward across North Africa with the spread of Islam during the seventh century, eventually entered Spain, and from there the rest of Europe. However if we seek an origin outside Europe then we must acknowledge the possibility that Islamic settlers in southern Italy brought the craft with them to the peninsula in the ninth century. And yet what appear to be tapestry-woven ornaments on garments represented in late Roman and Byzantine paintings and mosaics produced on the Italian peninsula suggest that the technique was known there from antiquity. It is likely that tapestry weaving was being practiced in most or all of Europe throughout late antiquity and the early Middle Ages. There is no other way to explain the fact that we have sophisticated, fully developed tapestry weaving exemplified in a few surviving twelfth-century German tapestries (see the section Tapestry Weaving in Germany below), as well as supremely expert work in the late fourteenth-century *Apocalypse* tapestries in Angers.

Theories favoring the notion that tapestry weaving was imported from Islamic countries found support in the German term *Heidnischwerk* (literally, "heathen work") and the French term *tapisserie sarrasinois* (Saracenic tapestry). Proponents of this idea trotted these terms out to demonstrate that in the Middle Ages, when the terms were current, tapestry weaving was regarded as being of Islamic origin. However, beyond knowing that the two terms referred both to tapestry weaving and knotted pile weaving, we do not know why these terms were used.

LATE MEDIEVAL WEAVERS AND THEIR
PRODUCTS: PROBLEMS OF INTERPRETATION

The term *tapissiers sarrasinois* appears in the list of trades whose statutes Etienne Boileau, then provost of Paris, registered there between 1258 and 1270. As noted above, the term *tapissier* did not necessarily designate a weaver of tapestries: it could also refer to a supplier of furnishing fabrics, an embroiderer, a restorer or keeper of furnishing fabrics, or a producer-merchant. In any case this reference indicates that men dealing in luxury furnishing fabrics were operating in Paris during the third quarter of the thirteenth century.

The terms *tapis sarrasinois* and *tapissier sarrasinois* were used so loosely in medieval documents that at present it is not possible to attempt to define them in simple or consistent terms. It has been suggested that the adjective *sarrasinois* indicates that the fabric was constructed with a knotted pile in the fashion of oriental carpets. While that may be true in certain early references, it could not always have been so. For example, in 1386 the Paris merchant Jacques Dourdin sold to Philippe le Hardi some hangings showing the *Story of the Golden Apple* and the *Story of Jourdain de Blaye* that were described as "deux tapis sarrazinois ouvré à or, de la fachon d'Arras." If, as we believe, the term *arras* was already being used as a synonym for the flat-woven, pileless fabric we call tapestry, then this reference and others like it suggest that the term *tapis sarrasinois* was used to designate tapestry as well as knotted pile fabrics. There are many late fourteenth- and fifteenth-century texts that refer to one and the same man as a *tapissier sarrasinois* and an *hautelisseur.* However, in a document of 1303 concerning an altercation that the *hautelisseurs* were having with the *tapissiers sarrasinois* in Paris, the *hautelisseurs* were referred to as "une autre manière de tapicier que l'on appelle ouvrier de haute lice." But as Salet has shown, the term *hautelisseur* was not associated exclusively with a weaver at the vertical loom; it also referred to men who dealt in luxury furnishing fabrics including embroideries, tapestries, and patterned yardage. Therefore we cannot claim that the *tapissiers sarrasinois* differed from the *hautelisseurs* in that the first worked at the horizontal loom and the others at the vertical loom.

Another allied trade whose statutes Etienne Boileau registered in Paris between 1258 and 1270 was that of the "tapissiers de tapis nostrés." Souchal suggested that the fabric these men produced was neither tapestry nor knotted pile fabric but a wool or part wool furnishing fabric woven in standard lengths and, presumably, showing a regularly repeating pattern rather than pictorial subjects. That is possible, but it is conjecture; we do not know for certain what the term means.

Salet pointed out that the word *tapis* could refer to a wall hanging, a floor carpet, or a cover for a packhorse, mattress, or trunk. This term, along with the Latin *pannum* and its Spanish and Italian forms *paño, panno,* appears in contexts that clearly describe hangings of many different kinds including tapestries, appliqué-work wall hangings, and hangings worked with a needle.

Salet also suggested that a *marcheteur* was not a weaver making tapestry at a horizontal loom fitted with treadles (*marches*), as has been thought. In 1442 Jacquemart Largeche of Lille was referred to both as a *marcheteur* and a *hautelisseur*; therefore, unless Largeche used both horizontal and vertical looms, these words were not limited to designating men by the kind of loom at which they plied their craft. The inventory of tapestries (1422) belonging to Charles VI of France contains a number of citations of "tapisserie faicte à la Marche" which, according to Salet's new interpretation of this term, referred not to tapestries woven on the horizontal loom but to furnishing fabrics of lesser quality and price that had been made for stock.

It is hard to interpret the term *patron* in early documents. In some contexts it clearly signifies a preliminary sketch. In others, it refers to the full-size painted cartoon from which the weavers worked. In yet other contexts *patron* could mean one thing or the other. The point is important since certain artists provided only the sketch, others painted only the cartoon, and still others executed both the preliminary sketch and the cartoon.

The terms *fin fil* (or *filé, fille*) *d'Arras* and *gros fil* (*filé, fille*) *de Paris* or *fil délyé de Paris* suggest to some historians that the tapestries containing these yarns were woven in one city or the other. But in certain contexts it becomes clear that these terms are simply descriptions of grades or qualities of yarn. For example, in Charles VI's inventory of 1422, three tapestry valances are described as "tappicerie d'Arras, de fil délyé de Paris" and two hangings of the Old and New Testaments are described as "de fille d'or et fille d'Arraz." Did *tappicerie d'Arras* mean that the fabric in question had been produced in Arras or simply in the manner of Arras, as the frequently encountered term *de la fachon d'Arras* suggests? Do the terms *de l'oeuvre d'Arras* and *de l'ouvrage d'Arras* mean that the fabrics so designated were woven in Arras, as the corresponding term *de l'ouvrage de Paris* suggests that the piece in question was woven in Paris, or simply that they exemplified some kind of work done in one city or the other?

Until these and other contemporary terms are properly defined and understood, all histories of tapestry will continue to express not absolute and objective truths (which we have not yet grasped) but rather, like the brief survey that follows here, simply the opinions of the writer. But we are making progress. We are beginning to understand that diverse activity took place simultaneously in many different weaving centers and tapestry markets and that this activity transcended regional boundaries. It is no longer believed that the *Apocalypse* tapestries in Angers were certainly manufactured in Paris nor that Paris was the chief tapestry market of Europe during the last quarter of the fourteenth century. It appears now that Arras harbored at least as much tapestry production and marketing at that time. Furthermore, it seems clear that tapestry weavers and merchants were plying their trades not only in Paris and Arras in the fourteenth century but also throughout the southern Netherlands, in Bruges, Brussels, Ghent, Lille, Louvain, and Valenciennes, and in other places as well, including London. Now that the traditional hold that Paris and Arras have had on our thinking has been broken, it is a matter of searching for records in these other places and of looking for evidence that tapestries were being woven, and perhaps also designed, rather than just marketed, in them.

The brief historical notes that follow were written solely with the purpose of demonstrating that tapestries were being designed, woven, and marketed in many different places in late medieval Europe simultaneously rather than (as it seemed in the recent past) chiefly only in one place after another. These notes should also demonstrate how rash it is to claim that more than a handful of extant medieval tapestries can be associated with a particular weaving center or producer, and those few only by virtue of documentary evidence.

Tapestry Weaving in France and the Southern Netherlands, 1375–1525

Because we know that Arras enjoyed a position of supremacy in the wool manufacturing and export trade at least as early as the eleventh century, and also because we have documentary references to the tapestry industry there in the fourteenth century, we may ask whether this story should begin in Arras as well as in Paris where it is traditionally thought to have begun.

It has been suggested that when Arras became less important in the wool trade around the middle of the thirteenth century, that city's capitalists realized that they could maintain their strength by converting from the manufacture of cloth to the weaving and trading of luxury furnishing fabrics of various kinds. We may assume that this new industry was well established by 1313, for in that year Mahaut, comtesse d'Artois, bought from Ysabeau Caurrée, a textile merchant in Arras, five hangings and two seat covers for the countess's son's house in Paris. Between 1310 and 1320 she bought other furnishing fabrics, some in Arras, others in Paris. They may have been produced in one city or the other, in both, or in neither one.

The conflict that the *tapissiers sarrasinois* had with the *hautelisseurs* in Paris in 1303 suggests that men who may have been tapestry weavers were working in Paris at that time. At present the earliest reference we have to a tapestry weaver or upholsterer in Arras dates from 1317 when Jean de Créqui is mentioned as a *tapissier*. In 1337 there is a reference to Thomas le Cordonnier, "ouvrier de haute lisse"—perhaps a tapestry weaver. Among the properties listed in the testamentary inventory of 1360 of Isabella, wife of Edward II of England, is a large old dossal "de opere de rivera d'Arras." Similar terms, like *de l'oeuvre d'Arras, de l'ouvrage d'Arras, de opere Atrabatensi, operis de Arras,* crop up frequently in fourteenth- and fifteenth-century inventories and other records. The contexts suggest that the writers using these terms are less concerned with designating the place where the textiles had been woven than with describing the fabric itself in a generic sense; that is, probably as tapestry. From at least the fourteenth century onward that city's name was used in this way, as a synonym for "tapestry," perhaps tapestry of some special kind or quality, not only in French but also in Latin (*opus atrabatensum*), English (*arras*), Italian (*arazzo*), and Spanish (*paño de ras*). This, together with the fact that at present we have more references to what we believe was the tapestry industry in Arras than in Paris during the first three-quarters of the fourteenth century, would, on the face of it, suggest that the industry developed to a position of importance in Arras earlier than it did in any other city in the northwest part of the Continent. This is pure conjecture. It may be that by chance more Arras-related documents were preserved or studied than documents relating to other centers.

There are early references to the industry in other cities. Johannes Crane, "tapijtwever" (tapestry weaver?), was active in Brussels in 1321. The dukes of Brabant bought tapestries in Brussels, their capital, in 1366. In the preceding two years Jeanne, duchess of Brabant, bought some chambers of tapestry from Jean Hont of Valenciennes who was either a weaver or a merchant or both. Jean Castelains, "ouvrier de haute-lice," native of Quévrain, entered the bourgeoisie of Valenciennes in 1368. The corporation of "tapissiers" (weavers or upholsterers?) is first recorded in Ghent in 1336. In 1356 it was said that there were sixty members in that corporation. In 1352 Jean Capars of Arras, "ouvrier de haute lisse," was established at Tournai. We know also that there were tapestry weavers and perhaps also upholsterers in

England at this time: fourteenth-century documents there refer to Arras work and "tapicers."

Few as these references are, they prove that any extant tapestries of the fourteenth or early fifteenth century that have been traditionally ascribed to Paris or Arras might just as well have been woven in Brussels, Ghent, Louvain, Valenciennes, London, or another place whose early activity as a tapestry-producing center has not yet been discovered. Surely it is because we know so much more about Paris and Arras as tapestry centers during these early years, and because we have before us tapestries from the great *Apocalypse* series documented as having been woven sometime between 1373 and 1380 through an agent in Paris and also pieces of the *Story of Saints Piat and Eleuthère* documented as having been woven in Arras in 1402, that these two cities have come in for more than their proper share of attention.

Certainly, both Paris and Arras were bustling with activity in the tapestry trade during this period. Throughout the last quarter of the fourteenth century and the early decades of the fifteenth, the kings and queens of France, the dukes of Anjou, Berry, Burgundy, and Orléans, and princes in other parts of Europe bought quantities of tapestries from the great producer-merchants of each city, some of whom were active in both places. Nicolas Bataille, Jacques Dourdin, and Pierre de Beaumetz appear to have been the busiest suppliers in Paris. But Bataille sold some tapestries that may have come from Arras. Dourdin operated both in Paris and Arras. Pierre de Beaumetz worked in close association with the Arras producer Jean Cosset. The fortunes of the industry in both cities seem to have waxed and waned according to the degree to which the chief producers remained active. Nicolas Bataille's name fades out of notice at the end of the fourteenth century, but Dourdin continued to provide tapestries until his death in 1407. Pierre de Beaumetz sold tapestries, primarily from Paris, until his death in 1418. What has been regarded as the decline of Paris as a tapestry center was probably more the result of his passing than of the English invasion of 1420, which historians have usually given as the reason for the weakening of the industry there. In fact Paris continued as a tapestry market, if not a manufacturing center, well into the early years of the sixteenth century, after which manufacturing developed there again.

Arras continued as a tapestry center and grew more important as the fifteenth century progressed but not, as has been traditionally asserted, to the exclusion of other south Netherlandish cities. During the first half of the century, Tournai developed as a manufacturing center and market. City ordinances dated 1397 and 1408 mention regulations concerning respectively "ouvriers a le marche," "ouvriers de hauteliche," and "draps nommés hauteliche." In 1423 the *hautelisseurs* of Tournai broke away from the mercers' guild and formed their own corporation. In 1449 the rising producer-merchant of Tournai, Pasquier Grenier, who was then described as a *marcheteur*, was selling tapestries through warehouses in Bruges and Antwerp, both of which were fast becoming the tapestry markets of Europe. He also sold pieces directly out of Tournai and through agents in Puy (Auvergne), in Lyon, and in Reims. In 1448 Philippe le Bon ordered one of the most sumptuous series of tapestries ever woven, the *Story of Gideon*, from the merchant-weavers Robert Dary and Jean de l'Ortie of Tournai.

During this first half of the fifteenth century, Lille was also active in the tapestry and upholstery trades. Robert Poinçon, who had directed the weaving of the *Apocalypse* series for both Louis d'Anjou and Philippe le Hardi, entered the bourgeoisie of Lille in 1398. During the next thirteen years, Lille harbored six *hautelisseurs* who were all natives of Arras or its environs. Relatively large numbers of tapestry-woven furnishing fabrics were sold in Lille during the second quarter of the century. Pierre de Los, the leading producer in Lille during the next few decades, was named in 1448 as one of the three agents there of the brothers Truye, who seem to have been the leading upholstery suppliers in Arras at that time. In the same year the Truyes listed five agents in Bruges. By then Bruges had become the chief tapestry marketplace of Europe. It was there that in 1423 Philippe le Bon bought six pieces of the *Life of the Virgin* from the Italian merchant Giovanni Arnolfini as a gift for Pope Martin V. In 1439 the same duke bought a *Story of the Sacrament* from the Bruges merchant Paule Mélian. The tapestry or upholstery industries in Saint Omer, Thérouanne, and Valenciennes had grown enough to support respectively six, four, and three agents of the Truye brothers of Arras.

This brief discussion of the industry during the first half of the fifteenth century makes it clear that, far from having a monopoly on the trade, Arras had to contend with energetic competition from cities in the rest of the southern Netherlands. Like Paris, Arras flourished as long as aggressive producer-merchants functioned within her walls. The three most important ones were Jean Cosset, Jean Walois, and Guillaume au Vaissel. Jean Cosset served as valet de chambre to Philippe le Hardi and sold him a set of tapestries each year from 1385 to 1402. Between 1413 and 1445 Jean Walois enjoyed the patronage of Jean sans Peur, Philippe le Bon, and the duc de Touraine, among other princely clients.

Both Cosset and Walois, like Guillaume au Vaissel, owned stocks of cartoons and occasionally had cartoons made for special commissions. These men also had inventories of tapestries and warehouses in Bruges. They engaged in the wine trade as well. In 1448 the Truye brothers, the merchants in Arras, named ten agents, including another brother, as their representatives at home in Arras. Although Philippe le Bon bought tapestries frequently in Tournai after 1450, at least one of his sources there was Jehan de Gamand, an Arras merchant. The luxury upholstery industry in Arras seems to have diminished during the third quarter of the fifteenth century, but tapestries continued to be sold there until at least the second quarter of the sixteenth century.

Entrepreneurial energy seems to have waxed in Tournai as it waned in Arras. However the two cities never operated entirely independently. Two of Philippe le Bon's purchases demonstrate this quite clearly. In 1445 he ordered from the Arras producer-merchant Guillaume au Vaissel a chamber of verdure tapestries showing children going to school. The court accounts for the next year record not only the duke's payment to Vaissel for the chamber but also a payment to Jehanne Pottequin of Tournai for a tapestry wall hanging of the same design, a piece that the duke had ordered to accompany the chamber. The second instance concerns Philippe's commission of the *Story of Gideon* to be woven in the richest possible manner with silk, silver, and gilt yarns as well as the finest wool. The dimensions were impressive: the eight hangings had a height of approximately 5.60 meters and a total running length of some 98 meters, an area of about 550 square meters. The duke's agents in the enterprise were his chamberlain Philippe de Ternaut and his keeper of tapestries Jean Aubry. Aubry was a native of Arras, and it may have been he who chose Bauduin de Bailleul, an Arras painter, as the designer. The agents also chose Robert Dary and Jean de l'Ortie, two merchant-weavers living in Tournai, to execute the hangings. In the same year the contract was signed, 1448, these two men were named as agents in Tournai for the Truye brothers, the merchants in Arras.

The third Truye agent in Tournai was Pasquier Grenier who sold quantities of important tapestries to Philippe le Bon and then Charles le Téméraire during the second half of the fifteenth century. Most of what we know about the industry in Tournai during this period concerns these purchases. In August 1459, Philippe le Bon bought from Grenier a chamber of tapestries of the *Story of Alexander* comprising bed furnishings and six wall hangings. Earlier in the same year Grenier's son and nephew took a group of tapestries, including a set of the

Story of Alexander, to Milan at the request of the duke, Francesco Sforza. Although we have no record of that duke's having bought the tapestries, it has been suggested that he did indeed buy them and that they eventually found their way into the hands of the Doria family of Genoa. According to this theory, the two *Story of Alexander* tapestries now in the Galleria Doria Pamphili in Rome (see fig. 61) came from that set. Other specialists believe that these two tapestries belonged to Philippe le Bon's chamber of that subject. In either case, it is believed that they were tapestries handled by Pasquier Grenier, whether they were woven in Tournai or not. In 1461 Philippe bought a *Passion* in six pieces from Grenier, and the next year he bought two other important sets from the same merchant. One showed the *Story of Esther and Ahasuerus;* the second was the *Story of the Swan Knight,* in three pieces. Fragments from one or more hangings of a *Swan Knight* set are preserved in Cracow (fig. 62) and Vienna. Again, specialists do not agree whether or not these pieces come from the duke's tapestries. In 1466 he bought two chambers of tapestries from Grenier, one showing people with orange trees, the other showing woodsmen. Until recently it was believed that the fragments of a *Story of the Seven Sacraments* preserved in the Metropolitan Museum (7a–e), the Victoria and Albert Museum, and the Burrell Collection were vestiges of one or more tapestries that Grenier and his wife were said to have given to their parish church of Saint Quentin in Tournai about 1475. It is demonstrated in this catalogue that the fragments came instead from a hanging woven twenty-five to forty years earlier that had belonged to Isabel la Católica of Spain. Sometime before September 1472, Grenier supplied to the magistrate and Franc of Bruges, for presentation to Charles le Téméraire, a *Story of the Trojan War* set. In 1476 Federico da Montefeltro made a partial payment to Jean Grenier for a set of eleven *Trojan War* tapestries, and in 1488 Henry VII of England bought from Pasquier and Jean Grenier another eleven pieces. Five pieces from Henry's set eventually appeared on the walls of the Painted Chamber in Westminster Palace. By good fortune an architect made watercolor drawings of them in 1799 before they were removed from the walls and later lost track of. These sketches, now in the Victoria and Albert Museum, show parts of compositions that appear in a particular group of *Trojan War* tapestries preserved in this country and elsewhere (13a–c). Therefore we can be certain that this *Trojan War* series, unlike the *Alexander, Swan Knight,* and *Seven Sacraments* tapestries, may confidently be associated with Grenier. This extraordinary man died in 1493. He left his stock of tapestry cartoons to his sons and widow along with his other

property. But he left neither looms nor weaving materials. Having begun his career as a *marcheteur* (weaver or merchant?), he died as a substantial patrician of Tournai.

Because we know so much about Pasquier Grenier's activities and also because so many extant tapestries have been associated with him, he and Tournai with him have dominated our view of tapestry weaving in Europe during the second half of the fifteenth century. We have been left with the impression that Tournai had a monopoly on the industry during this period; but that misconception is easily corrected. Men and women of wealth bought tapestries at this time not only in Tournai but also in Paris, Arras, Lille, Bruges, and Brussels. In 1442 René d'Anjou bought six tapestry hangings and eight seat covers, all decorated with his coat of arms, in Paris. When the Truye brothers of Arras named their agents in 1448, they chose eight *hautelisseurs* in Paris, more than they had appointed anywhere else outside their own city. In 1459 the chapter of the cathedral of Angers bought six tapestries of the *Life of Saint Maurice and His Companions* from Jean Despaing in Paris and the next year three pieces of a *Life of Saint Maurille* from an unnamed merchant in the same city. The magistrate of Tournai bought a chamber of tapestries in Paris in 1484 as a gift for one of Charles VIII's courtiers. The king himself bought eight verdure hangings with shepherd folk from the Parisian merchant Michel de Chamans in 1487.

The industry was also active in Arras in and after the second half of the fifteenth century. A client of the first importance, Charles de Bourbon, cousin and brother-in-law of Charles le Téméraire and later a cardinal, bought some tapestries of the *Story of Godefroy de Bouillon* in Arras in 1469 while he was there as abbot of Saint Vaast. In 1496, the Arras painter Jacquemart Pilet, who had worked in Bauduin de Bailleul's shop, designed five choir tapestries of the *Life of Saint Géry* that were woven in Arras by Jean de Saint Hilaire.

Only recently have we begun to understand the importance of the industry in Lille during the second half of the fifteenth century. The trade there can be traced to the beginning of the fourteenth century, but the important activity seems to have been concentrated in the second half of the fifteenth century. In 1454 Philippe le Bon paid Jehan Picart, a weaver in Lille, for six seat covers showing the duke's coat of arms. Four years later Philippe ordered a hanging of the *Baptism of Clovis* from Jehan Lecoq of Lille, a man who may have been a weaver or a producer-merchant. It has been suggested that this piece might have been woven after the cartoons that served for the *Story of Clovis* tapestries represented by two extant pieces in Reims, pieces that have traditionally been attributed to the looms of Tournai. In 1467 the duke paid Camus Dugardin, a leading producer-merchant of Lille, for some tapestries. A year later, his son Charles le Téméraire ordered a tapestry seat cover from the same man. In 1469 Charles de Bourbon, who the same year bought the *Story of Godefroy de Bouillon* in Arras, bought some wall hangings, a portiere, a seat cover, and a carpet from Dugardin.

Meanwhile another producer-merchant of Lille was enjoying the patronage of the Medici and their clients. Pierre de Los is first mentioned in 1448 as one of the Truye brothers' agents in Lille. From that year until 1466 he lent tapestry cartoons executed on cloth to the sheriffs' hall in Lille to decorate it on festival occasions. In 1453 he began to work with the Medici agents in Bruges. Gierozzo de' Pigli, Giovanni de' Medici's agent, bought from de Los a *Story of Samson* tapestry chamber for shipment to Astore II Manfredi of Faenza, a client of the Medici. At the same time Gierozzo commissioned de Los to produce for his master in Florence five hangings and a portiere of the *Triumphs of Petrarch* using designs brought from Italy. The next year Gierozzo conveyed another Medici commission to de Los but this time from Piero rather than Giovanni. Piero sent his own master weaver, Jacquet d'Arras, to Bruges to supervise the production of six hangings, six bench covers, and three portieres. The cartoons were to be sent from Italy. Pierre de Los was to recruit the workers and gather the materials while Jacquet would direct the weaving. By 1459, when a third commission came from Florence, Tommaso Portinari had replaced de' Pigli as the Medici agent in Bruges. In that year Portinari commissioned de Los to produce for Giovanni de' Medici three wall hangings, three seat covers, and twelve cushions, all based on the subject of the largest hanging, which showed six seated figures separated by passages of verdure and pendant coats of arms. The designs were brought from Italy and converted into cartoons in de Los's shops. Among other tapestries that de Los had woven for Italian clients was a suite of ten pieces that he produced for Gaspar, count of Vimercato, in 1459.

While these Italians were ordering tapestries in the southern Netherlands, others were having pieces woven at home. They employed Netherlandish weavers in patron-sponsored shops. Weavers from Arras staffed an atelier at the court of Milan for the Sforza while another group from Arras wove tapestries for the Este at Ferrara. Other weavers worked in Mantua, Siena, Rome, Correggio, Venice, and Perugia. Weavers and producer-merchants went to most of the same cities from Bruges, Brussels, Tournai, and Paris. Presumably all the tapestries produced in these shops were woven after Italian designs.

Bruges is mentioned so often in documents as an international tapestry market during the second half of the fifteenth century that its role as a manufacturing center is scarcely considered. Throughout this period, from 1448 when the Truye brothers of Arras named five agents in Bruges until the late years of the century, great personages like Charles de Bourbon, Isabel of Spain, Maximilian, and Marie de Bourgogne bought tapestries in Bruges. Between 1502 and 1506, the widow of Jean de Wilde wove fifteen pieces of a *Life of Saint Anatoile* for the canons of that saint's church in Salins. Shortly afterward Margaret of Austria ordered from Bruges eight armorial hangings and a set showing thistles. By the end of the sixteenth century Bruges had become an important tapestry-weaving center as well as a marketplace.

Along with Arras, Bruges, Lille, Paris, and Tournai, Brussels harbored an active tapestry industry during the second half of the fifteenth century. There are records indicating that during the second quarter of the century some five hundred *tapissiers* (weavers or upholsterers?) were active there. In 1446 the guild of *tapissiers* withdrew from the corporation of wool workers and formed their own guild. Some of these men were certainly tapestry producers or weavers. We have no idea what their work looked like. The only surviving tapestry that can be associated with a documentary reference to a Brussels commission during the second half of the fifteenth century—and not with absolute certainty—is the wall hanging showing the arms and emblems of Philippe le Bon against a millefleurs ground that is now in the Bernisches Historisches Museum (fig. 78). Many historians believe that this is one of the eight such pieces that the duke bought from Jean de Haze in Brussels in 1466. Others believe that the Bern tapestry is either an earlier or later version of one of the pieces in that order, and yet other specialists have suggested that it may be part of a similar set of hangings delivered to the duke by Perceval van Hersele of Middelburg in 1470. In 1467 Philippe paid de Haze for a chamber of verdures decorated with rinceaux. In the same year he paid the same man or another (the name was transcribed, perhaps erroneously, from the manuscript record as Jean de Rave) for six hangings of the *Story of Hannibal* that had been sent as a gift to Pope Paul II. In 1469 the magistrate of Antwerp bought a chamber of tapestries from Jean de Haze in Brussels as a gift for Charles le Téméraire. The next year Charles bought four armorial tapestries from de Haze, and in 1472 de Haze was mentioned as a "valet de chambre" and "ayde de la tapisserie" to this duke. While there can be no question that de Haze was work-

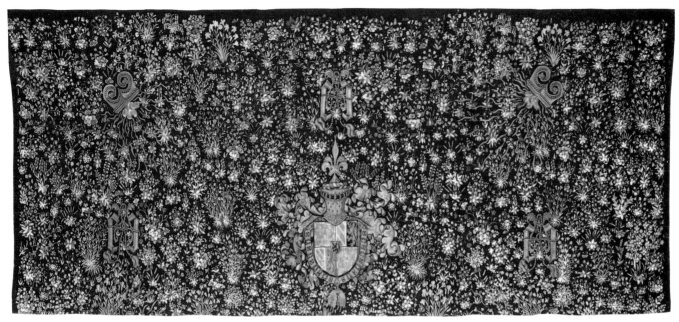

Fig. 78. *Coat of Arms and Emblems of Philippe le Bon* (incomplete at the bottom). Tapestry, southern Netherlands, probably Brussels, about 1466. Bernisches Historisches Museum, Bern.

ing in Brussels during the third quarter of the fifteenth century, we know that he was trained in Lille and entered the bourgeoisie of that city in 1461. He served as a sheriff of Lille throughout the years that he enjoyed the patronage of the dukes of Burgundy in Brussels.

On June 6, 1476, the magistrate of Brussels issued an ordinance to confirm an agreement that the Brussels painters' guild had reached with the tapestry weavers' guild. The painters had complained because some weavers were using cartoons or drawings executed on paper with charcoal or chalk that had been made by persons who were not members of the painters' guild. The painters opposed this practice and ultimately agreed to let the weavers design for each other the accessory details—trees, animals, boats, plants, textile patterns—in their "verdure" tapestries (landscapes, millefleurs, or some other kind of greenery). Most historians have cited this ordinance as grounds for supporting a prejudicial and as yet unproved contention that from that moment onward Brussels produced the most painterly, pictorially sophisticated, and refined tapestries in the southern Netherlands. Arguing from this position and also from the attribution of the design of a number of small, extremely refined altar tapestries to the Brussels painters Vrancke Van Der Stockt and the Master of the View of Saint Gudule, historians have assigned these and related pieces to the looms of Brussels. But in fact there is nothing to indicate that such pieces, like the two tapestry dossals in the cathedral of Sens (figs. 49, 63), or the *Annunciation* and *Ado-*

ration of the Magi in the Mobilier National (figs. 64, 65), or the *Madonna of the Living Water* in the Musée du Louvre (fig. 66)—although perhaps designed by Brussels artists—were not woven instead in Bruges, Lille, Tournai, or any other south Netherlandish weaving center that was active during these years.

It has been suggested that the letters BRVXEL woven into the lower border of the alb worn by the celebrant in the *Mass of Saint Gregory* tapestry of about 1500 in the Patrimonio Nacional in Madrid indicate the piece was woven in Brussels. The composition shows a more conservative style and somewhat less painterly execution than the tapestry dossals mentioned above; but it is otherwise rich and refined, like the dossals and the few hangings of the next quarter century that are documented as having been woven (or probably having been woven) in Brussels. The earliest of these is the *Legend of Herkinbald* in the Musées Royaux d'Art et d'Histoire in Brussels (fig. 70). The Brotherhood of the Holy Sacrament in the Church of Saint Peter in Louvain commissioned the piece. In 1513 they paid Jan van Roome of Brussels for making the original design, a certain Philips for painting the cartoon, and a Brussels weaver named Lyoen for weaving the hanging. The other documented tapestries of this period are the four pieces of the *Legend of Notre-Dame du Sablon* set which were commissioned in Brussels in 1516 or 1517, completed in 1518, and believed to have been designed by the Brussels artist Bernaert van Orley (fig. 71). Two of the pieces are complete; one is in the Musées Royaux d'Art et d'Histoire in

Brussels, the other is in the State Hermitage Museum in Saint Petersburg; fragments of the other two hangings are now in the Hôtel de Ville and the Musée Communal, both in Brussels, the Staatliche Museen in Berlin, the Burrell Collection in Glasgow, and the Musée Ile-de-France in Saint-Jean-Cap-Ferrat.

In 1521 the last of the twelve *Acts of the Apostles* tapestries, designed by Raphael and produced by the Brussels tapestry entrepreneur Pieter van Aelst, came off the loom. A few years later van Aelst was producing for the emperor Charles V the magnificent set of hangings called *Los Honores* which is now in the collection of the Patrimonio Nacional in Madrid. Here are two sets of tapestries that were certainly produced in Brussels, and they are supremely rich and refined. Van Aelst's signature has been identified on two weavings of *Christ Carrying the Cross,* one in Madrid, the other in the Museo Diocesano in Trent where there is also a signed *Resurrection* from the same *Story of the Passion* series. Another signed hanging, a *Bathsheba at Her Bath,* is in the Schloss Sigmaringen, Germany. Many other hangings of the highest quality have been attributed to van Aelst's enterprise among which may be cited the four *Life of the Virgin* tapestries (the so-called *paños de oro*) and the *Mass of Saint Gregory,* all in the Patrimonio Nacional, and the four versions of the so-called *Glorification of Christ,* one of which is in The Cloisters and now called *Christ the Judge on the Throne of Majesty* (see 27a–c).

At present we cannot say whether the consistently high quality of the design and execution in tapestries associated with van Aelst's name is due to the man's own insistence on excellence or to the standards set by the Brussels corporation of tapestry weavers. Certainly van Aelst was in a position to influence much or all of the tapestry production in Brussels during the first quarter of the sixteenth century. Born about 1450 in Enghien and trained in Alost (or Aelst) as a weaver, he settled in Brussels in the late fifteenth century where he became a prominent producer-merchant. Soon he was appointed *tapissier* to the archduke Philippe le Beau and later to the courts of the Empire and the Holy See. So it is not unreasonable to believe that Pieter van Aelst, with the support of his powerful and wealthy patrons, raised the art of tapestry weaving in Brussels in the first quarter of the sixteenth century to a pinnacle of excellence that may never have been reached before.

However we cannot be sure that Brussels produced nothing but superb tapestries during the first quarter of the sixteenth century and that superb tapestries of that period were being produced only in Brussels. There is good reason to believe that tapestries of the first quality

were being manufactured elsewhere as well. In Tournai, for example, where the producer-merchants and presumably also the weavers remained actively engaged in the industry throughout these years, Pasquier Grenier's sons Jean and Antoine continued their father's highly successful trade. In 1497 Antoine sold an altar frontal showing the Adoration of the Shepherds to the archbishop Georges d'Amboise for the episcopal palace in Rouen, and in 1508 he sold other pieces to the same patron for the château de Gaillon. Although Philippe le Beau had bought tapestries from Pieter van Aelst in 1497 and appointed him *tapissier* in 1502, the archduke patronized Tournai producer-merchants as well. In 1501 he bought four tapestries "à personnages à manière de Bancquet" from Colart Boyart, and in 1504 he paid Jean Grenier for a tapestry "à la manière de Portugal et de Indye" which was described as "bien richement faicte." The next year he paid the same Tournai merchant for six "histoire du Bancquet" hangings that were qualified as "riche" and also for two chambers of tapestry, one showing vintners, the other woodsmen. Hangings described as "bien richement faicte" and "riche" at this time would have contained metal as well as silk yarns along with the woolen ones. In 1510 the emperor Maximilian acquired from Arnould Poissonnier, another leading Tournai merchant, eight hangings showing the triumphs of Julius Caesar, a chamber with a falconry theme, and some pieces "a ystoire de gens et de bestes sauvaiges à la manière de calcut."

The records we have concerning the industry in Tournai during the first quarter of the sixteenth century are full of references to commissions that city officials gave to local producer-merchants. These involve tapestries that were sent as state presents to representatives of the various governments which controlled Tournai in succession during these troubled years. The French lost Tournai to the English in the autumn of 1513 when Henry VIII took it during his invasion of northern France. In 1517 Henry sold Tournai to François I, who held it until 1521 when it became one of the possessions of the emperor Charles V. At each turn the magistrates or city council of Tournai gave tapestries to the succeeding governors. These city officials bought tapestries from Jean Grenier, Arnould Poissonnier, Jean Devenin, Clément Sarrazin, and others. Among the subjects mentioned were the "Voyage de Caluce," "douze mois de l'année," "histoire d'Hercule," and "cité des dames." These and other series, whose titles vary slightly in phrasing and spelling from one document to another, are cited repeatedly in Tournai records of the first third of the sixteenth century. Arnould Poissonnier's testamentary inventory of 1522 lists among other tapestries seventeen pieces of the "histoire de Carrabarra dit des Egiptiens." A number of extant tapestries show compositions suggesting this title, and we have others that can be associated with most of the other titles in the documents.

Historians depended upon these and similar tapestries to define a so-called "style of Tournai" for the first third of the sixteenth century which involves not only the character of the figures and landscapes but also the border patterns. It has been thought that those borders are different from the ones used in Brussels. Although these criteria no longer seem reliable, many tapestry specialists still classify as Tournai work certain tapestries of the first third of the sixteenth century that do not rise to the standards of excellence traditionally associated with Brussels pieces. However the tapestries that Philippe le Beau bought from the Tournai producer-merchant Jean Grenier in 1504 and 1505 were described as "bien richement faicte" and "riche." Therefore, unless one believes that Grenier was selling Brussels tapestries, which is certainly possible, it appears that some tapestries of the first rank may have been produced by Tournai entrepreneurs at this time. Conversely, some hangings of lesser quality that show versions of compositions known (or thought) to have been produced in Brussels may in fact be Brussels products made for a lesser market rather than—as has been suggested—Tournai pieces. Some extant pieces of the "douze mois de l'année" and of "los honores" fall into this category.

At present we have little information about the tapestry industry outside of Brussels, Tournai, Arras, and Paris during these years, although documents make it clear that tapestries were being woven in most of the southern Netherlands, particularly in Enghien, Grammont, Ghent, Bruges, Alost, Antwerp, Louvain, and Middelburg. In Arras Jacquemart Pilet and other painters who had trained and worked with Bauduin de Bailleul continued to design tapestries, stained glass, mimes, and other projects at least until the opening years of the sixteenth century. The guild of *tapissiers* of Arras changed their regulations for the last time in 1528. The industry seems to have declined and disappeared soon afterward. Paris fared better. Erard de la Marck, who made an important collection of tapestries during this period, commissioned two series of choir tapestries in Paris in 1514, and it has been suggested that they were probably woven there. De la Marck and Georges d'Amboise bought other tapestries in both Paris and Tournai. In 1514 François d'Angoulême bought some pieces of a *Twelve Months of the Year* set from Michel de Chamans, a Tournai merchant operating in Paris. The future king also bought in Paris a suite of tapestries of Leda and her Nymphs from the *tapissiers* (weavers or merchants?) Miolard and Pasquier de Montaigne. In 1543, Cardinal Givry, bishop of Langres, ordered a set of tapestries of the *Life of Saint Mamas.* The cartoons were designed by Jean Cousin the elder and woven by Pierre II Blassey and Jacques Langlois, the two Parisian weavers who are thought to have established the tapestry workshop at Fontainebleau about 1540.

Soon the days of uncertainty about a tapestry's place of origin would be over, at least in the Netherlands. On May 16, 1528, the magistrate of Brussels issued an ordinance requiring that every tapestry woven in that city that contained more than six square aunes (about $3^{1}/_{3}$ square meters) be marked in a certain way. At one side of the bottom border must appear the mark of the weaver, merchant, or upholsterer who had it woven, and at the other side must appear the city mark, a small red shield flanked by the letters B B (for Brussels and Brabant). The tapestry had to show these marks before it could be sold or delivered to the buyer. This ordinance anticipated by some years a general edict issued from the imperial court in 1544 which required that all weaving centers in the Netherlands mark every tapestry costing at least 24 sous per square aune with the mark of the city where it was woven. Certain irregularities occurred. Since Brussels tapestries were highly regarded, the city name was occasionally woven illegally into pieces woven elsewhere, or legitimate Brussels marks might be removed from one tapestry and fitted into another. In any event, by the time these regulations were observed to the letter, the Middle Ages had passed.

MILLEFLEURS TAPESTRIES

To judge from the quantities of tapestries showing this generic kind of pattern that have survived, they were woven in very large numbers between roughly 1400 and 1550. The element they share, and on the basis of which they have been treated in the literature as a kind of subgroup in the body of late medieval tapestries, is the background rendered as a flat plane of color, usually dark green but occasionally pinkish red, studded with many varieties of blooming plants, floral sprigs, or flowering branches with broken or cut ends. Figures, animals, trees, heraldic motifs, and other kinds of objects are set against this background of "a thousand flowers," a modern term used to designate the group. In their time these tapestries were probably referred to as *verdures*, although that term also was applied to tapestries showing landscapes or other kinds of greenery. The subject matter in a millefleurs piece, when it is not purely ornamental in character, deals with hunting,

Fig. 79. *A Mon Seul Desir*, one of the hangings from the set *The Lady with the Unicorn*. Tapestry, France or the southern Netherlands, late fifteenth century. Musée de Cluny, Paris.

courtly or country life, mythology, allegory, heraldry, and narrative or devotional Christian themes. The most celebrated example of the group is the enchanting *Lady with the Unicorn* series in the Musée de Cluny in Paris (fig. 79).

Recent research has shown that tapestries of this kind were certainly woven in Brussels, Tournai, Ghent, and Bruges. But it is likely that they were woven in all the tapestry-producing centers of the southern Netherlands. Historians had proposed earlier that millefleurs tapestries were woven by itinerant weavers who worked for patrons in the Loire valley where so many examples have been found. Another group of country-life tapes-

tries, related to these in style and general character but without the flowered grounds, was also attributed to France. There is no documentary support for the itinerant workshop theory and no real evidence that tapestries like these were woven in France. We now believe that both groups of tapestries, although perhaps designed by French artists, were woven in the southern Netherlands and exported to France and also to Italy where paintings of the period show millefleurs hangings fairly frequently.

There are two millefleurs tapestries in this collection whose style and fashionable accessories place them in the first quarter of the fifteenth century (3a, b). A few related examples in other collections may date from around the middle of the century. The earliest piece that can be dated by document fairly exactly is the example in Bern showing the coat of arms and emblems of Philippe le Bon (fig. 78). It is considered to be one of eight such pieces that the duke bought from Jean de Haze in Brussels in 1466 or part of a somewhat earlier or later series. The next documented piece dates from about 1480. It is the tapestry showing an armored knight on horseback and the coat of arms of Jean de Daillon, for whom it was woven in Tournai (fig. 75). The latest millefleurs tapestries that can be firmly dated are the three pieces showing angels carrying the instruments of the Passion preserved in the chapel of the château d'Angers. They show the coat of arms of Charles de Rohan and his wife and can be dated by means of these bearings between June 1512 and April 1513.

Figures that appear in one millefleurs tapestry sometimes turn up in another, usually in a different context. Often single figures or groups of figures have no logical relationship to one another and seem to have wandered into a verdant field with no common purpose. The weavers evidently used stock figures taken from any number of sources and simply combined them more or less at random. However in many examples the figures engage in simple narrative activities; and in these instances they may have been designed especially for the pieces or borrowed from pictorial tapestries or from secondary sources showing groups rather than single figures.

TAPESTRY WEAVING IN GERMANY, 1350–1550

Late medieval tapestries woven in the parts of Europe that Germany and Switzerland now occupy have survived in large numbers. They are products of looms located primarily in the Rhineland, from Cologne to the Lake of Constance, including the adjacent parts of northern Switzerland; in central Germany, especially around Nuremberg; and in Lower Saxony. At present we know much less about medieval tapestry weaving in this region than in the southern Netherlands, but our knowledge is expanding rapidly thanks to the research that Cantzler, Heinz, Rapp and Stucky-Schürer, and von Wilckens have published in recent years.

The oldest European tapestries and pictorial knotted pile hangings we have were woven in Germany. The earliest piece, believed to date from about 1150, was discovered after World War II in the cathedral in Halberstadt, Germany, where it is now preserved. It is a fragment of a large knotted pile carpet or hanging, probably made locally, showing a wide ornamental border enclosing parts of two arcades, one above the other, each of which contains a figure. Fragmentary inscriptions identify one of the figures as Temperantia, one of the seven Virtues, and the other figure as Xenocrates, one of the seven philosophers of antiquity. Fragments of another knotted pile hanging, dating from about 1200 and believed to have been woven in a convent in nearby Quedlinburg, are preserved there in the parish church of Saint Servatius. They are part of a hanging made of knotted pile fabric, and they show figures from the story of the marriage of Mercury and Philology in the prose-and-verse allegory *De Nuptiis Philologiae et Mercurii et de septem Artibus liberalibus libri novem*, by the fifth-century writer Martianus Capella (fig. 80). (A fragment of German knotted pile fabric of considerably later date, about 1500, is in the Metropolitan Museum. It comes from a hanging or cover of the Annunciation and shows part of Gabriel's body, some of the words in his greeting, the pot of lilies, and part of a border [fig. 81].)

The earliest tapestry-woven example in this group of medieval German weavings comprises three fragments, one in the Germanisches Nationalmuseum in Nuremberg, another in the Musée Historique des Tissus in Lyon, and the third in the Victoria and Albert Museum in London. The pattern does not show human figures but a purely ornamental design derived from some Byzantine silk weaving, of which likely examples exist, with a typical drawloom-woven repeating pattern (figs. 82, 83). The design unit in the tapestry consists of a roundel enclosing a griffin attacking an ox, and there is an outer rectangular border showing a leafy arabesque punctuated with ox masks. The tapestry is believed to have been woven in Cologne during the second half of the eleventh century.

The oldest German tapestries that show human figures are preserved in the cathedral of Halberstadt. It is believed that they were all woven locally, in Lower Saxony. Of the three pieces in the cathedral, two are long and narrow and may have been woven as choir hangings. The longer of the two, which is just over ten meters long and a bit more than a meter high, shows scenes from the story of Abraham (fig. 84) and, at the extreme right, Saint Michael slaying a dragon. It has been dated about 1150. The second long piece is almost nine meters long and just over a meter high. In the center is a representation of Christ seated in a mandorla which is supported by the archangels Michael and Gabriel and flanked by six apostles at the left and six at the right. This piece has been dated about 1170. The third tapestry in Halberstadt is more or less square. It shows Charlemagne seated in a lozenge-shaped compartment in the center and incomplete figures of four ancient philosophers, in-

Fig. 80. *The Marriage of Mercury and Philology,* fragment of a knotted pile hanging or carpet. Lower Saxony, Quedlinburg, about 1200. Church of Saint Servatius, Quedlinburg.

Fig. 81. *Angel of the Annunciation,* fragment of a knotted pile hanging. Southwest Germany, early sixteenth century. MMA, Rogers Fund, 1928 (28.15).

cluding Cato and Seneca, in the triangular corners of the field. This example has been dated somewhat later than the other two, in the first half of the thirteenth century. By good fortune, a large fragment of an embroidered hanging from Lower Saxony has survived and is now in the Kunstgewerbemuseum in Berlin. It dates from about 1160–70. It shows scenes from the New Testament enclosed within a border of compartments containing palmettes or busts of saints. The figure style and general composition relate this piece intimately to the long, narrow tapestries in Halberstadt.

These large hangings prove that ambitious weaving and embroidery projects were being executed in Germany by highly skilled needleworkers and weavers, during the twelfth and thirteenth centuries; but we have no evidence that these craftsmen and women functioned in the context of a highly capitalized and organized luxury industry like that which existed in the fourteenth to sixteenth centuries in the southern Netherlands. At present, it appears that the industry did not develop along similar lines in Germany until considerably later, some years after a number of professional weavers from the Netherlands settled there in the second half of the sixteenth century.

According to all but the most recent literature, tapestries woven in Germany and northern Switzerland in the fourteenth to mid-sixteenth centuries were domestic or monastic products made either by civilian women at home or by nuns in convents. A number of considerations encouraged historians to reach this conclusion. In all the known depictions of German tapestry weavers of this period, only nuns are shown at the looms (see, for example, fig. 85). Also, as Rapp and Stucky-Schürer noted, the names of tapestry weavers (*Heidnischwerker, Heidnischwerkerin*, in the feminine) that have survived in contemporary household and convent account books, city tax rolls, and court records in the Basel–Strasbourg region are preponderantly women's names. The same two authors reconsidered earlier interpretations of these and other documents that mention tapestries, weavers, patrons, and tapestry-weaving equipment and materials and concluded that other interpretations can be made of the same data. Rapp and Stucky-Schürer argued that, at least for the region of Basel–Strasbourg, the frequent mention of tapestries, materials, and equipment in domestic and monastic accounts and inventories does not necessarily indicate, as earlier historians had thought, that the residents of those houses or convents wove tapestries themselves but, instead, that they were civilian or religious patrons who employed professional weavers to make tapestries. These were modest establishments: most German tapestries that have survived from the fourteenth, fifteenth, and early sixteenth centuries are small and simply executed, obviously not the products of a large workshop having elaborate equipment, expensive stocks of materials, and a large staff of weavers.

This paints quite a different picture of the tapestry industry in Germany at this time, at least in the Basel to Strasbourg area. The image we had cultivated of girls and women weaving tapestries as amateurs at home or in convents now becomes one of women, and some men, trained for this profession, plying their trade as independent employees in a kind of cottage industry system in which a patron provided the workplace, the equipment, and the materials and also had a role in distributing the employee's work. The high quality of most of these tapestries supports this newer concept of the craft structure. On the other hand, a fair number of less well executed tapestries have survived, and so it is reasonable to ask whether weavers with less than professional skill were also producing tapestries. We know that some nuns wove tapestries, for a few late medieval German

tapestries (see an example in fig. 85), and one painting, show them working at small tapestry looms, and we have documentary evidence that nuns in Nuremberg were weaving tapestries. It has been claimed, but not proven, that burghers' daughters wove tapestries.

As for the patterns and looms, references in contemporary documents indicate that artisans were employed in the Basel–Strasbourg region to paint cartoons (*Bildner*) for tapestry weavers, and it is fair to assume that the same activity was carried on also in other parts of Germany and neighboring Switzerland. We know from the reports of men who saw tapestry weavers at work in the late fifteenth and early sixteenth centuries that both horizontal and vertical looms were used. After reviewing literary evidence and the physical evidence in the tapestries themselves, Rapp and Stucky-Schürer

Fig. 82. *Griffins Attacking Oxen,* fragment of a tapestry, from the Church of Saint Gereon, Cologne. Germany, Cologne (?), 1050–1100. Germanisches Nationalmuseum, Nuremberg.

Fig. 83. *Griffins Attacking Quadrupeds,* fragment of drawloom-woven silk. Byzantine, eighth century. Museum of Fine Arts, Boston.

Fig. 84. *The Three Angels at Abraham's Table*, detail of the Abraham and Michael tapestry. Lower Saxony, Quedlinburg (?), about 1150. Cathedral, Halberstadt.

concluded that weavers in the Basel–Strasbourg area used only vertical looms.

The technique of weaving in the late Middle Ages was the same in Germany as it was in the Netherlands, including manipulations like dovetailing, interlocking, and hatching. However certain procedures, and some materials, were different. In places where German weavers did not use hatching, they produced middle tones by juxtaposing tiny blocks of different colors in a checkerboard pattern. Occasionally German weavers did not blend tones but simply placed areas of unmodulated color next to each other. The warps in their tapestries invariably were made up with linen, rather than woolen, yarns. Like the wefts in Netherlandish tapestries of the same period, the wefts in German pieces were made primarily of wool. The richer pieces also contained silk and metallic yarns. However unlike the Netherlandish pieces, German examples occasionally contained wefts spun of cotton, linen, and goat's hair, with bleached linen or white goat's hair serving in some cases as a substitute for white silk. In many instances, these weavers did not give their figures facial features on the loom but embroidered the features into place after the fabric had been woven.

Most of these tapestries were woven from end to end rather than from bottom to top so that, like the warps in most Netherlandish tapestries, these warps lie horizontally when the pieces are hung. Since most of the tapestries are no more than a meter high, they could be woven on very narrow looms. The same is true of a small group of fifteenth- and sixteenth-century German tapestries with tall, narrow formats that were woven from bottom to top, with warps running vertically rather than horizontally (see 57). However some of the tapestry funeral hangings and bier covers that have survived, which are two to three meters high and woven from end to end, required wide looms. Judging from the tapestries that have survived from the late Middle Ages in Germany, we conclude that wide tapestry looms were the exception in that culture. It was not until after Netherlandish weavers began to work for patrons in Germany in the second half of the sixteenth century that the characteristically taller patterns and wider looms of the Netherlands became common in Germany.

During the fourteenth, fifteenth, and early sixteenth centuries, the subject matter of German tapestries was drawn from the Old and New Testaments, the lives of saints, love poems, romances, and allegories. Both contemporary civilian men and women and wild folk appear in the secular pieces, the wild folk constituting a theme category of their own in the fifteenth century. Like many tapestries woven in the southern Netherlands, some of these examples contain inscriptions that explain the action represented. However in the German pieces, the inscriptions convey the characters' speech rather than the author's narrative or descriptive text. The words usually appear on curling scrolls whose sinuous curves are exploited for their decorative value in the total design.

Since dates and coats of arms are represented in certain late medieval German tapestries, it has been possible to arrange some of them in chronological and geographical order. With this information in hand, specialists have attempted to establish stylistic criteria as a means of dating a tapestry and identifying its place of manufacture. Certainly, well-executed tapestries with elaborate compositions have enough artistic individuality to enable one to make valid stylistic judgments that may lead to an informed estimate of the date of manufacture. But, while it seems likely that tapestries showing the same or similar styles were woven in the same place as well as in the same time frame, in most instances there are no documents to confirm that assumption. To make attributions based on that assumption is to imply that we know German tapestries were woven exclusively after designs that originated locally, that the pieces woven in a particular shop or by a particular weaver show characteristics exclusive to that shop or weaver, and, finally, that we are certain that all German tapestries showing coats of arms were woven in the immediate locality where the person or persons represented by those arms lived. All of that may be true; but since we know that none of it is true in regard to tapestries woven in the southern Netherlands, we believe it is prudent to reserve judgment about contemporary German tapestries until we have more documentary evidence concerning the specific production practices that were current in Germany and northern Switzerland in the late Middle Ages.

The characteristic long, narrow tapestries that have survived from this culture were designed as altar frontals, dossals, or choir hangings if the subjects were religious, or, regardless of whether the subjects were secular or religious, as hangings (*Rücklaken*) to be used on walls in domestic settings above long seats or chests. Small squarish pieces were made to cover cushions, and larger squarish ones served as wall hangings or covers for tables and other horizontal surfaces. A few tall, narrow pieces, with formal floral textile patterns and warps running vertically rather than horizontally, were presumably woven to be made into curtains or furnishing fabrics or, perhaps, bier covers (see 57).

Fig. 85. Two Dominican nuns working at a high-warp tapestry loom. Detail from the lower border of a tapestry showing scenes from the Passion. Germany, Franconia, end of the fifteenth century. Cathedral, Bamberg.

Selected Sources and Suggestions for Further Reading

The following list of publications includes works that the present author used in preparing the preceding introductory essays. The list also serves as a guide to the reader who wishes to learn more about the history of the art and industry of tapestry in the Middle Ages. The selections include the classic works dealing with this subject as well as more recent publications (dating after 1960) which express points of view that question the traditional opinions and open fresh avenues of inquiry. Additional sources concerning medieval tapestries are cited in each catalogue entry under the headings Exhibitions, Publications, and Notes.

Ainsworth, Maryan Wynn. "Bernart van Orley as a Designer of Tapestries." Ph.D. diss., Yale University, New Haven, 1982.

——. "Bernart van Orley, Peintre-Inventeur." *Studies in the History of Art*, National Gallery of Art, Washington, 24 (1990) pp. 41–64.

Artes Textiles: Bijdragen tot de Geschiedenis van de Tapijt-, Borduur-, en Textielkunst. Centrum voor de Geschiedenis van de Textiele Kunsten, Ghent. Annual, beginning in 1953. This serial is devoted to presenting serious contributions dealing with the history of textiles, particularly Netherlandish tapestries. Although many other scholars publish here, *Artes Textiles* has served largely as the vehicle for disseminating new ideas generated at the Centrum by specialists associated with that institution, especially Erik, Joseph, and Magda Duverger, Jan-Karel Steppe, J. Versyp, and their disciples.

Asselberghs, Jean-Paul. *La tapisserie tournaisienne au XVe siècle.* Exh. cat. Tournai, 1967.

——. *La tapisserie tournaisienne au XVIe siècle.* Exh. cat. Tournai, 1968.

Azuas, Pierre-Marie, et al. *L'Apocalypse d'Angers: Chef-d'oeuvre de la tapisserie médiévale.* Fribourg, 1985.

Bellmann, Fritz. "Ein Knüpfteppichfragment des 12. Jahrhunderts im Dom zu Halberstadt." In *Denkmäle in Sachsen-Anhalt.* Weimar, 1986, pp. 389–410.

Bernheimer, Richard. *Wild Men in the Middle Ages: A Study in Art, Sentiment, and Demonology.* Cambridge, Mass., 1952.

Brunard, Andrée. "Les deux fragments de la tapisserie de la légende de Notre-Dame du Sablon au Musée communal de Bruxelles." *Bulletin des Musées de Belgique* 4 (1962–63) pp. 153–54.

Cantzler, Christina. *Bildteppiche der Spätgotik am Mittelrhein 1400–1550.* Tübingen, 1990.

Cetto, Anna Maria. *Der berner Traian- und Herkinbald-Teppich.* Bern, 1966.

Coffinet, Julien. *Métamorphoses de la tapisserie.* Paris, 1977.

Crick-Kuntziger, Marthe. *Catalogue des Tapisseries (XIVe au XVIIIe siècle).* Musées Royaux d'Art et d'Histoire, Brussels, 1956.

——. "La tapisserie bruxelloise au XVme siècle." In *Bruxelles au XVme siècle.* Exh. cat., Musée Communal. Brussels, 1953, pp. 85–102.

David, Henri. *Philippe le Hardi.* Dijon, 1947.

Delmarcel, Guy. "La légende d'Herkenbald et la justice de l'empereur Trajan: Notice iconographique." In *Tapisseries bruxelloises de la pré-Renaissance.* Exh. cat., Musées Royaux d'Art et d'Histoire. Brussels, 1976, pp. 243–53.

——. *Tapisseries anciennes d'Enghien.* Exh. cat. Mons, 1980.

Delmarcel, Guy, and Erik Duverger. *Bruges et la tapisserie.* Exh. cat., Musée Gruuthuse and Musée Memling. Bruges and Mouscron, 1987.

Delmarcel, Guy, and Jan-Karel Steppe. "Les tapisseries du Cardinal Erard de la Marck, prince-évêque de Liège." *Revue de l'Art*, no. 25 (1974) pp. 35–54.

Deuchler, Florens. *Der Tausendblumenteppich aus der Burgunderbeute: Ein Abbild des Paradieses.* Zurich, 1984.

Dhanens, Elisabeth. "L'importance du peintre Jean van Roome, dit de Bruxelles." In *Tapisseries bruxelloises de la pré-Renaissance.* Exh. cat., Musées Royaux d'Art et d'Histoire. Brussels, 1976, pp. 231–38.

Digby, George Wingfield, assisted by Wendy Hefford. *The Devonshire Hunting Tapestries.* Victoria and Albert Museum, London, 1971.

——. *The Tapestry Collection: Medieval and Renaissance.* Victoria and Albert Museum, London, 1980.

Dumoulin, Jean, and Jacques Pycke. "La tapisserie de Saint-Piat et de Saint-Eleuthère à la cathédrale de Tournai (1402), son utilisation et son histoire." *Revue des Archéologues et Historiens d'Art de Louvain* 15 (1982) pp. 184–200.

Duverger, Joseph. "Jan de Haze en de Bourgondische Wapentapijten te Bern." *Artes Textiles* 6 (1965) pp. 10–25.

Duverger, Magda. "De Externe Geschiedenis van het Gentse Tapijtweversambacht." *Artes Textiles* 2 (1955) pp. 53–104.

Erlande-Brandenburg, Alain. "A propos d'une exposition: La tapisserie de choeur des anges porteurs des instruments de la Passion dans la chapelle du château d'Angers." *Le Journal des Savants*, 1974, pp. 62–69.

——. *La Dame à la Licorne.* Paris, 1978.

———. "Les tapisseries de François d'Angoulême." *Bulletin de la Société de l'Histoire de l'Art Français*, 1973, pp. 19–31.

———. *La tenture de Saint Rémi*. Reims, 1983.

———. "La tenture de la Vie de la Vierge à Notre-Dame de Beaune." *Bulletin Monumental* 134 (1976) pp. 37–48.

Erlande-Brandenburg, Alain, et al. *La tenture de l'Apocalypse d'Angers*. Nantes, 1987.

Forti Grazzini, Nello. *L'arazzo ferrarese*. Milan, 1982.

Gay, Victor. *Glossaire archéologique du Moyen Age et de la Renaissance*. 2 vols. Paris, 1887–1928.

Gilbert, Pierre. "Les nouveaux panneaux de la tenture de Notre-Dame du Sablon aux Musées royaux d'Art et d'Histoire et au Musée communal de Bruxelles." *Bulletin des Musées de Belgique* 4 (1962–63) pp. 149–50.

Göbel, Heinrich. *Wandteppiche: I. Die Niederlande*. 2 vols. Leipzig, 1923.

———. *Wandteppiche: II. Die Romanischen Länder*. 2 vols. Leipzig, 1928.

———. *Wandteppiche: III. Die Germanischen und Slawischen Länder, Deutschland einschliesslich Schweiz und Elsass (mittelalter), Süddeutschland (16. bis 18. Jahrhundert)*. Berlin, 1933.

———. *Wandteppiche: III. Die Germanischen und Slawischen Länder, West-, Mittel-, Ost-, und Norddeutschland, England, Irland, Schweden, Norwegen, Dänemark, Russland, Polen, Litauen*. Berlin, 1934.

Grönwoldt, Ruth. Catalogue entries for nos. 797, 806, 807a, b. In *Die Zeit der Staufer*, vol. 1. Exh. cat., Württembergisches Landesmuseum. Stuttgart, 1977.

Guenée, Bernard, and Françoise Lehoux. *Les entrées royales françaises de 1328 à 1515*. Sources d'Histoire Médiévale 5. Paris, 1968.

Guiffrey, Jules. *Histoire de la tapisserie en France*. Pt. 1 of *Histoire générale de la tapisserie*. Paris, 1878–85.

———. "Inventaire des tapisseries du roi Charles VI vendues par les anglais en 1422." *Bibliothèque de l'Ecole des Chartes* 48 (1887) pp. 59–110.

Heinz, Dora. *Europäische Wandteppiche I*. Brunswick, 1963.

Houdoy, Jules. *Les tapisseries de haute-lisse: Histoire de la fabrication lilloise du XIVᵉ au XVIIIᵉ siècle, et documents inédits concernant l'histoire des tapisseries de Flandres*. Lille and Paris, 1871.

d'Hulst, Roger-A. *Flemish Tapestries from the Fifteenth to the Eighteenth Century*. New York, 1967.

Hunter, George Leland. *The Practical Book of Tapestries*. Philadelphia and London, 1925.

———. *Tapestries: Their Origin, History and Renaissance*. New York, London, and Toronto, 1912.

Husband, Timothy, with the assistance of Gloria Gilmore-House. *The Wild Man: Medieval Myth and Symbolism*. Exh. cat., MMA. New York, 1980.

Jarry, Madeleine. *World Tapestry: From Its Origins to the Present*. New York, 1969.

Joubert, Fabienne. "L'Apocalypse d'Angers et les débuts de la tapisserie historiée." *Bulletin Monumental* 139 (1981) pp. 125–40.

———. "Jacques Daret et Nicolas Froment cartonniers de tapisseries." *Revue de l'Art*, no. 88 (1990) pp. 39–47.

———. "Remarques sur l'élaboration des tapisseries au Moyen Age." *Annales d'Histoire de l'Art et d'Archéologie*, Université Libre de Bruxelles, 10 (1988) pp. 39–49.

———. *La tapisserie médiévale au musée de Cluny*. Paris, 1987.

———. "La tenture de choeur de Saint-Etienne d'Auxerre et la peinture bruxelloise vers 1500." *Revue de l'Art*, no. 75 (1987) pp. 37–42.

Jubinal, Achille. *Les anciennes tapisseries historiées, ou collection des monumens les plus remarquables, de ce genre, qui nous soient restés du moyen-âge, à partir du XIᵉ siècle au XVIᵉ inclusive . . . d'après les dessins de Victor Sansonetti*. 2 vols. Paris, 1838.

———. *Recherches sur l'usage et l'origine des tapisseries à personnages dites historiées, depuis l'antiquité jusqu'au 16ᵉ siècle inclusivement*. Paris, 1840.

King, Donald. "How Many Apocalypse Tapestries?" In *Studies in Textile History in Memory of Harold B. Burnham*. Ed. Veronika Gervers. Toronto, 1977, pp. 160–67.

Kroos, Renate. *Niedersächsische Bildstickerein des Mittelalters*. Berlin, 1970.

Kurth, Betty. "Die Blütezeit der Bildwirkerkunst zu Tournai und der burgundische Hof." *Jahrbuch der Kunsthistorischen Sammlungen des allerhöchsten Kaiserhauses* 34 (1918) pp. 53–110.

———. *Die deutschen Bildteppiche des Mittelalters*. 3 vols. Vienna, 1926.

———. *Gotische Bildteppiche aus Frankreich und Flandern*. Munich, 1923.

de Laborde, Léon E. S. J. *Les ducs de Bourgogne*. 3 vols. Paris, 1849–52.

Lestocquoy, Jean. *L'art de l'Artois: Etudes sur la tapisserie, la sculpture, l'orfèvrerie, la peinture*. Arras, 1973.

———. "L'atelier de Bauduin de Bailleul et la tapisserie de Gédéon." *Revue Belge d'Archéologie et d'Histoire de l'Art* 8 (1938) pp. 119–37.

———. *Deux siècles de l'histoire de la tapisserie (1300–1500): Paris, Arras, Lille, Tournai, Bruxelles*. Arras, 1978.

Manufacture Nationale des Gobelins. *La tapisserie gothique*. Paris, [1928].

Marquet de Vasselot, J. J., and Roger-Armand Weigert. *Bibliographie de la tapisserie, des tapis et de la broderie en France*. Paris, 1935.

Müntz, Eugène. *Histoire de la tapisserie en Italie, en Allemagne, en Angleterre, en Espagne, en Danemark, en Hongrie, en Pologne, en Russie, et en Turquie*. Pt. 2 of *Histoire générale de la tapisserie*. Paris, 1878–85.

Pinchart, Alexandre. *Histoire de la tapisserie dans les Flandres*. Pt. 3 of *Histoire générale de la tapisserie*. Paris, 1878–85.

Planchenault, René. *L'Apocalypse d'Angers*. Paris, 1966.

Pomarat, Michel, and Pierre Burger. *Les tapisseries de l'abbatiale de Saint-Robert de La Chaise-Dieu*. Brioude, 1975.

Prost, Bernard. *Inventaires mobiliers et extraits des comptes des ducs de Bourgogne de la maison de Valois (1363–1477)*. 2 vols. Paris, 1908–13.

Rapp Buri, Anna, and Monica Stucky-Schürer. *Zahm und Wild: Basler und Strassburger Bildteppiche des 15. Jahrhunderts*. Mainz, 1990. Companion volume to the exhibition of the same name held at the Historisches Museum, Basel, 1990.

Riefstahl, Elizabeth. *Patterned Textiles in Pharaonic Egypt*. Brooklyn, 1945.

Salet, Francis. "Chronique: Broderie, tapisserie," review of

Schneebalg-Perelman, "Les sources de l'histoire de la tapisserie bruxelloise . . ." (see listing below). *Bulletin Monumental* 124 (1966) pp. 433–37.

———. Introduction in *Chefs-d'oeuvre de la tapisserie du XIVe au XVIe siècle*. Exh. cat., Grand Palais. Paris, 1973, pp. 11–25.

———. "Remarques sur le vocabulaire ancien de la tapisserie." *Bulletin Monumental* 146 (1988) pp. 211–29.

———. Summary of his lecture "Le vocabulaire ancien de la tapisserie" delivered at a meeting of the Société Nationale des Antiquaires de France, December 12, 1984. *Bulletin de la Société Nationale des Antiquaires de France*, 1984, pp. 239–43.

Savigny, Sophie. "La tenture de la Vie de la Vierge de la cathédrale de Reims: Etat de la question." *Mémoires de la Société d'Agriculture, Commerce, Sciences et Arts du département de la Marne* 100 (1985) pp. 60–72.

Schmitz, Hermann. *Bildteppiche: Geschichte der Gobelinwirkerei*. Berlin, [1919].

Schneebalg-Perelman, Sophie. "'La Dame à la Licorne' a été tissée à Bruxelles." *Gazette des Beaux-Arts*, 6th ser., 70 (1967) pp. 253–78.

———. "Un grand tapissier bruxellois: Pierre d'Enghien dit Pierre van Aelst." In *De Bloeitijd van de Vlaamse Tapijtkunst (Internationaal Colloquium, 23–25 mei 1961)*. Koninklijke Vlaamse Academie voor Wetenschappen, Letteren en Schone Kunsten van België, Klasse der Schone Kunsten. Brussels, 1969, pp. 279–323.

———. "Un nouveau regard sur les origines et le développement de la tapisserie bruxelloise du XIVe siècle à la pré-Renaissance." In *Tapisseries bruxelloises de la pré-Renaissance*. Exh. cat., Musées Royaux d'Art et d'Histoire. Brussels, 1976, pp. 161–91.

———. "Richesses du garde-meuble parisien de François Ier: Inventaires inédits de 1542 et 1551." *Gazette des Beaux-Arts*, 6th ser., 78 (1971) pp. 253–304.

———. "Le rôle de la banque de Médicis dans la diffusion des tapisseries flamandes." *Revue Belge d'Archéologie et d'Histoire de l'Art* 38 (1969) pp. 19–41.

———. "Les sources de l'histoire de la tapisserie bruxelloise et la tapisserie en tant que source." *Annales de la Société Royale d'Archéologie de Bruxelles* 51 (1962–66) pp. 279–337.

———. "La tenture armoriée de Philippe le Bon à Berne." *Jahrbuch des Bernischen Historischen Museums in Bern* 39–40 (1959–60) pp. 136–63.

Shepherd, Dorothy G. "An Icon of the Virgin: A Sixth-Century Tapestry Panel from Egypt." *Bulletin of the Cleveland Museum of Art* 56 (1969) pp. 90–120.

Soil, Eugène. *Les tapisseries de Tournai: Les tapissiers et les hautelisseurs de cette ville, recherches et documents sur l'histoire, la fabrication, et les produits des ateliers de Tournai*. Tournai and Lille, 1892.

Souchal, Geneviève. Catalogue entries in *Chefs-d'oeuvre de la tapisserie du XIVe au XVIe siècle*. Exh. cat., Grand Palais. Paris, 1973.

———. "Etudes sur la tapisserie parisienne. Règlements et technique des tapissiers sarrazinois, hautelissiers, et nostrez

(vers 1260–vers 1350)." *Bibliothèque de l'Ecole des Chartes* 123 (1965) pp. 35–125.

Steppe, Jan-Karel. "Inscriptions décoratives contenant des signatures et des mentions du lieu d'origine sur les tapisseries bruxelloises de la fin du XVe et du début du XVIe siècle." In *Les tapisseries bruxelloises de la pré-Renaissance*. Exh. cat., Musées Royaux d'Art et d'Histoire. Brussels, 1976, pp. 193–230.

Stucky-Schürer, Monica. *Die Passionsteppiche von San Marco in Venedig*. Bern, 1972.

Les tapisseries de la Vie du Christ et de la Vierge d'Aix-en-Provence. Exh. cat., texts by M. H. Krotoff et al. Musées des Tapisseries. Aix-en-Provence, 1977.

Thomson, W. G. *A History of Tapestry from the Earliest Times until the Present Day*. Rev. ed., London, 1930.

———. *Tapestry Weaving in England from the Earliest Times to the End of the XVIIIth Century*. London, 1914.

de Vaivre, Jean-Bernard. "L'origine tournaisienne de la tapisserie de Jean de Daillon." *Archivum Heraldicum* 88 (1974) pp. 17–20.

———. "La tapisserie de Barthélemy de Clugny." *Gazette des Beaux-Arts*, 6th ser., 105 (1985) pp. 177–90.

———. "La tapisserie de Jean de Daillon." *Archivum Heraldicum* 87 (1973) pp. 18–25.

Conde Viudo de Valencia de Don Juan. *Tapices de la Corona de España*. 2 vols. Madrid, 1903.

Van Ruymbeke, Anne. "La légende de Notre-Dame du Sablon." In *Tapisseries bruxelloises de la pré-Renaissance*. Exh. cat., Musées Royaux d'Art et d'Histoire. Brussels, 1976, nos. 20–23, pp. 85–99.

Versyp, J. *De Geschiedenis van de Tapijtkunst te Brugge*. Brussels, 1954.

Viale, Mercedes and Vittorio. *Arazzi e tappeti antichi*. Turin, 1952. Memorial catalogue of the exhibition held at Palazzo Madama, 1948.

Wauters, Alphonse. *Les tapisseries bruxelloises: Essai historique sur les tapisseries et les tapisseries de haute et de basse-lice de Bruxelles*. Brussels, 1878. Reprinted Brussels, 1973.

Weigert, Roger-Armand. *La tapisserie française*. Paris, 1956.

Wells, William. "Four Loire Tapestries in the Clark Collection." In *The William A. Clark Collection: An Exhibition Marking the 50th Anniversary of the Installation of the Clark Collection at the Corcoran Gallery of Art*. Washington, 1978, pp. 39–50.

von Wilckens, Leonie. Catalogue entry for no. 1019. In *Stadt im Wandel: Kunst und Kultur des Bürgertums in Norddeutschland 1150–1650*, vol. 2. Landesausstellung Niedersachsen 1985, exh. cat. Brunswick, 1985.

———. "Der Michaels- und der Apostelteppich in Halberstadt." In *Kunst des Mittelalters in Sachsen: Festschrift Wolf Schubert*. Weimar, 1967, pp. 279–91.

———. "Nuremberg: Medieval Tapestries." *Hali*, no. 29 (1986) pp. 19–25.

Wyss, Robert L. *Ein brüsseler Bildteppich mit Taufe Christi*. Bern, 1977.

Notes to the Reader and Frequently Cited Sources

BIBLIOGRAPHIC REFERENCES

Each catalogue entry contains two sets of notes, one set given parenthetically in the main body of the text, the other set given as endnotes signaled by superscript numbers. The in-text notes cite the author, date, and page or illustration number for books or periodical articles; and for exhibition catalogues they cite the place, date, and catalogue or page number. The works referred to in these in-text notes are listed under the headings Publications or Exhibitions near the end of each catalogue entry. The endnotes appear under the heading Notes at the end of each entry. Some of the works listed under all three headings are cited in abbreviated form; the complete references appear in the list of Frequently Cited Sources.

BIBLICAL QUOTATIONS

The biblical quotations in Latin that appear in this catalogue are given according to the Vulgate, the version of the Bible that the tapestry designers used. The texts were translated into English according to the Reims-Douay version, whose text is closer to the Vulgate than that of any other modern Bible.

TRANSLATIONS FROM FOREIGN LANGUAGES

Translations into English of texts other than biblical ones were made by the author unless otherwise stated in the main text or notes.

FREQUENTLY CITED SOURCES

Coffinet 1977
Coffinet, Julien. *Métamorphoses de la tapisserie.* Paris, 1977.

Digby 1980
Digby, George Wingfield, assisted by Wendy Hefford. *The Tapestry Collection: Medieval and Renaissance.* Victoria and Albert Museum, London, 1980.

Göbel 1923
Göbel, Heinrich. *Wandteppiche: I. Die Niederlande.* 2 vols. Leipzig, 1923.

Göbel 1928
Göbel, Heinrich. *Wandteppiche: II. Die Romanischen Länder.* 2 vols. Leipzig, 1928.

Göbel 1933
Göbel, Heinrich. *Wandteppiche: III. Die Germanischen und Slawischen Länder, Deutschland einschliesslich Schweiz und Elsass (mittelalter), Süddeutschland (16. bis 18. Jahrhundert).* Berlin, 1933.

Göbel 1934
Göbel, Heinrich. *Wandteppiche: III. Die Germanischen und Slawischen Länder, West-, Mittel-, Ost-, und Norddeutschland, England, Irland, Schweden, Norwegen, Dänemark, Russland, Polen, Litauen.* Berlin, 1934.

Hunter 1912
Hunter, George Leland. *Tapestries: Their Origin, History and Renaissance.* New York, London, and Toronto, 1912.

Hunter 1925
Hunter, George Leland. *The Practical Book of Tapestries.* Philadelphia and London, 1925.

Joubert 1987
Joubert, Fabienne. *La tapisserie médiévale au musée de Cluny.* Paris, 1987.

Kurth 1926
Kurth, Betty. *Die deutschen Bildteppiche des Mittelalters.* 3 vols.: vol. 1, text and plate captions; vol. 2, pls. 1–168; vol. 3, pls. 169–344. Vienna, 1926.

Lestocquoy 1978
Lestocquoy, Jean. *Deux siècles de l'histoire de la tapisserie (1300–1500): Paris, Arras, Lille, Tournai, Bruxelles.* Arras, 1978.

New York 1974
Masterpieces of Tapestry from the Fourteenth to the Sixteenth Century. Translation of *Chefs-d'oeuvre de la tapisserie du XIVe au XVIe siècle,* Paris, 1973, with additional entries by J. L. Schrader. Exh. cat., Metropolitan Museum of Art. New York, 1974.

Paris 1973
Chefs-d'oeuvre de la tapisserie du XIVe au XVIe siècle. Introduction by Francis Salet, catalogue entries by Geneviève Souchal. Exh. cat., Grand Palais. Paris, 1973.

Thomson 1930
Thomson, W. G. *A History of Tapestry from the Earliest Times until the Present Day.* Rev. ed., London, 1930.

Verlet 1965
Verlet, Pierre. "La tapisserie gothique du XIIe au XVIe siècle." In *Le grand livre de la tapisserie,* ed. Joseph Jobé, pp. 9–76. Paris and Lausanne, 1965.

THE TAPESTRIES

I

Heraldic Composition with the Arms of Beaufort, Turenne, and Comminges

Fragment from a suite of room furnishings

Southern Netherlands, 1350–75
Wool warp, wool wefts
7 ft. 7 in. × 3 ft. 9³/₄ in. (2.31 m × 1.16 m)
12 warp yarns per inch, 5 per centimeter
Rogers Fund, 1946 (46.175)

CONDITION

The hanging is composed of a number of irregularly shaped fragments of tapestry weaving joined together. We can distinguish two large and eighteen small pieces in this mosaic, but some of them may comprise even smaller fragments whose contours are not apparent. The edges of the pieces were joined by means of reweaving with new warp and weft yarns. There are also small spot repairs by reweaving throughout the piece but especially in its lowest third part.

DESCRIPTION AND SUBJECT

The pattern shows lozenge-shaped units arranged as a trellis. The motifs are rendered in polychrome tones against a ground of dark blue. A chevron-shaped battlemented wall, with a turret at the center and each end, defines the lower contour of each unit. An angel stands in each outer turret and bends forward at the waist, extending one arm diagonally downward, the other diagonally upward. Their raised hands support an open coronet whose upper edge shows fleurs-de-lis alternating with low points. A double five-petaled rose drawn in frontal view appears above each coronet, and it carries in its own center a round shield charged with armorial bearings. A pair of storks, the legs spread wide apart, stretch out between the roses and the end turrets, pressing their bodies close to the angels' wings. Within each lozenge-shaped compartment formed by the contours of wall, angels, birds, coronet, and rose there appears an animal wearing a mantle charged with armorial bearings. The species of the animals, as well as the arms on their mantles, vary according to the unit's position in the overall design. The blazon in the center of the rose also changes as the rose changes position. The animals

inside the lozenges are arranged so that unicorns, lions, stags, and an elephant appear in diagonal rows and face alternately left and right. Some of the animals wear mantles showing the coat of arms of Beaufort (argent, a bend azure accompanied by six roses gules in orle) quartering Turenne (bendy or and gules), which represents Guillaume III Rogier, comte de Beaufort. Other animals wear mantles showing Beaufort dimidiating Comminges (argent, a cross paty gules [alternately described as gules, four otelles argent in saltire]) with the addition of four small shields of Turenne placed on the arms of the cross (or, the spaces between the otelles) which identify this dimidiated blazon specifically as that of Aliénor de Comminges who, as the wife of Guillaume III Rogier de Beaufort, bore her husband's arms in the dexter half of her shield and, in the sinister half, the arms of Comminges differenced by the four shields of Turenne to represent her claim to the viscountcy of Turenne in her own right.[1] The centers of the roses display either Beaufort or Turenne; the Comminges arms do not appear in the roses. Elie de Comminges (1972, 283) believed that since the tapestry was woven for Guillaume III Rogier de Beaufort there was no reason to include his wife's arms in the roses. If that observation is correct, one wonders why Aliénor's arms appear in the pattern at all.

Using examples in the Burrell and Thyssen collections (see Related Tapestries), de Comminges (1972, 271–72, pls. 2, 3) analyzed the standard pattern system and then commented on the variations found in all the other surviving pieces (1972, 272–78, pls. 4–11; see also Related Tapestries in this catalogue entry). As de Comminges observed, the example in the Metropolitan Museum departs more from the norm than any of the others does. The second diagonal row from the bottom ought to contain only elephants; instead it has two unicorns and one elephant. The row containing stags ought to appear between the rows of unicorns and of lions rather than to the right of the elephants. Some of the animals heading left wear mantles with the arms of Beaufort quartering Turenne and some of those heading right wear Beaufort dimidiating Comminges, which is the reverse of the norm. The sequence of arms inside

Detail of 1

the roses is also irregular. The standard pattern shows rows of one blazon alternating with the other in the vertical direction, but here the arms in the roses do not follow that or any other system. The uppermost center rose is the only one in all the surviving fragments that shows the Beaufort blazon in its correct left-right orientation. In all the other hangings with this pattern the centers of the roses show this coat of arms and the Turenne arms in reverse.

As de Comminges (1972, 272) wrote, the mantles on the animals in the standard pattern are blowing out behind them, and so the arms can be read correctly only if one imagines the mantles as being pivoted around the creatures' necks into the upright position; but he did not specify that in doing so one must read the free end of the mantle as the top or chief of the shield and the end around the animal's neck as the shield's bottom or point. In the Metropolitan Museum's piece, the dimidiated arms on the elephant at the center of the right side may be read properly in this way; but the same arms on the mantles of the lions at the center of the left side and near the top of the right side can be read properly only if one accepts the neck end of the mantle as the chief of the shield and the free end as the point. This is the way that these mantles should be read since, as de Vaivre (1974, 297) pointed out, they are meant to be perceived as coats of arms or herald's tabards; that is, with the end near the head representing the chief of the shield. Thus, as de Vaivre (1974, 301) also noted, the mantles on these two lions are the only ones in 1 that show the arms marshaled correctly on the mantles. In order to read the dimidiated arms on the mantle worn by the stag at the bottom of the center row one must not only accept the neck end of the mantle as the chief of the shield but also reverse the arms since, as de Vaivre (1974, 300) pointed out, these blazons appear in reverse where the creatures wearing them face in the opposite direction from the norm. The mantles worn by the two unicorns in the center row also show the arms in reverse but oriented so that the free end of the mantle must be accepted as the chief of the shield. All the mantles showing Beaufort quartering Turenne may be read with either end of the mantle as the chief of the shield; none of these mantles displays the arms in reverse.

Several explanations have been offered for the variations and apparent errors that the designer or weavers made in the surviving tapestries, that is, the occasional unit containing the wrong animal, an animal facing the wrong way, or a coat of arms reversed and sometimes also turned end for end. Coffinet (1977, 12) observed that there is no consistency in the way these errors occur, and so he reasoned that the weavers could not have been working from a master cartoon showing the whole pattern because any errors in that cartoon would have showed up consistently in the finished product. Therefore he concluded, as some other writers before him had done, that the weavers were working from separate patterns for each part of the design, that is, the wall-angel-crown lozenge, the animals within each lozenge, and the coats of arms for either the roses or the mantles. De Vaivre (1974, 302) suggested that since the weavers were probably working in a place where these coats of arms were unfamiliar, the men may occasionally have reversed the patterns unwittingly.

We believe there may be a different explanation for these inconsistencies. Since the Metropolitan Museum's hanging was made up from at least twenty pieces of the original fabric or set of fabrics, it may be that the restorer who composed this hanging (and perhaps also all or some of the others like it) occasionally inserted a unit in a place it had not originally occupied. He may also have finished off certain pieces neatly on the back so as to be able to turn them over and show a surface in better condition than the true face. If that were done, the viewer would see any turned-over armorial mantles in reverse. The blazons inside the roses may have been reversed in the same way; if not, they may have been caused by an error on the part of a weaver who was not following a cartoon for the rose centers but simply transferring to each one the arms he saw on the mantle below. If he did that, then the centers of the roses would show the Turenne and Beaufort arms in reverse because the blazons on the mantles, which blow out horizontally rather than hang vertically, appear ninety degrees off their normal positions and thus show the bends in both coats of arms reversed, as bends sinister.

This is not the only example of late medieval tapestry weaving to show blazons with bends in reverse. There are some instances of it in the *Dame à la Licorne* tapestries in the Musée de Cluny, Paris. The piece representing the sense of taste, in which both the lion and the unicorn wear armorial mantles, has the lion's mantle showing the crescented bend of the Le Viste arms correctly, whereas the unicorn's mantle shows it in reverse as a bend sinister. In Erlande-Brandenburg's monograph on this set of tapestries, he noted this reversal but located it on the mantle of the lion rather than the unicorn.[2] He also noticed, as we have done, that in the piece representing the sense of smell the shield hung around the lion's neck shows the bend reversed again whereas the charge on the unicorn's shield is correctly oriented. We can add that in the hanging representing the sense of hearing the unicorn's standard shows the bend in the correct direction on the back of the fabric although it appears as a bend sinister when seen from the front. The viewer does not immediately recognize this "error" because the blazon reads correctly as shown. Since heraldic irregularities like this could occur in a set of hangings of such high quality, in which the blazons are so prominent a part of the design, it may be fair to conclude that for some reason or other—perhaps simply because the designs are more balanced this way—the patron (in this case a most important one) approved of these deviant representations of his coat of arms. Therefore, unless the reversed and inverted blazons in Guillaume III Rogier de Beaufort's tapestries represent a restorer's manipulations, we may assume that he might have been willing to accept these variant forms of his coat of arms.

Only a few historians have attempted to interpret the significance of the animals and motifs other than blazons that appear in the pattern of the Metropolitan Museum's hanging and the others related to it. In Wells's study of the Rogier de Beaufort family's connections with the popes at Avignon and with Avignon itself, he has suggested more interpretations than anyone else. According to him (1977, 98–100) the stork refers to Agricola, a seventh-century saint and the first bishop of Avignon, and to this saint's protecting the city walls that Guillaume III Rogier de Beaufort and his son, Raymond, were prepared to defend. Therefore, Wells conjectured, the four animals in the tapestry pattern represent the "vassals they could call on in time of need," apparently meaning the vassals living in the lands of Beaufort, Turenne, and Comminges. Observing that the pattern on an enameled candlestick in Baltimore shows lion heads and complete lions along with the dimidiated arms of Comminges-Turenne and the arms of France ancient, Wells deduced that the lion may have been a badge of the Comminges family. As for the stags in the tapestry pattern, Wells associated them with the Beaufort family and gave a number of examples to support his suggestion (1977, 99–100). At a reception given near Avignon for Pope Clement VI, who was Pierre Rogier de Beaufort, uncle of Guillaume III, there appeared "a sort of castle . . . enclosing a gigantic stag and a number of smaller creatures. . . ." It was Clement who had hunting murals painted in his study in the papal palace at Avignon, the room known as the Chambre du Cerf. Numbers of objects showing deer or stags, including two textiles decorated with deer wearing mantles showing the arms of Guillaume II Rogier de Beaufort, are listed in some late fourteenth- and early fifteenth-century inventories of the Rogier de Beaufort household. Although Wells did not go on to suggest interpretations for the unicorns and elephants in the tapestry pattern, he did

suggest that the battlemented walls are a canting reference to the name Beaufort, referring both to the image of a fortress that the name invokes and also the fortress-palace at Avignon which Clement VI enlarged. Wells (1977, 100) found a possible meaning for the rose, relating it to the rose used as a motif on family wares or the golden roses that the popes distributed at Lent. He (1977, 96) also noted the canting significance of the roses in the Rogier de Beaufort arms which refer to the seigneurs de Rosiers, their ancestors. While these suggestions seem convincing, it is important to remember that lions and stags frequently appear in the decorative arts of the late Middle Ages, and that while the battlemented walls could refer to "Beaufort," as Nickel (1972, 115) also suggested, there is another, purely formal, explanation of that motif (see Source of the Design).

Citing a seal affixed to a document of 1383, de Vaivre (1974, 301 n. 1, fig. 5) demonstrated that Guillaume III Rogier de Beaufort used at that time a unicorn's head for a crest and a pair of mermaids for supporters. Nickel

Fig. 86. Woven fabric (brocaded lampas). Polychrome silk and gilt yarns; Italy, Venice or Lucca, about 1350–1400. From Friedrich Fischbach, *Die wichtigsten Webe-Ornamente bis zum 19. Jahrhundert* (Wiesbaden, 1902–11) pl. 78.

(1972, 114) also commented on the unicorn's head crest. That may explain the presence of unicorns in the tapestry pattern; but then why are there no mermaids? At present we cannot prove that these animals, the storks, and the angels, had any particular symbolic significance. As Wells (1977, 95) has said, Kurth's interpretation of the four mantled beasts as symbols of the virtues courage, prudence, loyalty, and chastity is misleading.[3] We believe that some, if not all, of these animals may simply have been appropriated from, or inspired by, the pattern in one or more silk textiles from which the form of the tapestry design probably was derived.

Source of the Design

Although the specific source of the individual motifs in the pattern has not been ascertained, the structure of the pattern, based on the regular repetition of a design unit displayed against a monochrome ground, is the same kind of organization that one finds in woven textiles, as Heinz also observed in her catalogue entry for the Rijksmuseum piece when it was exhibited in Vienna in 1962 (*Europäische Kunst um 1400*, 454). Certain drawloom-woven furnishing and dress fabrics attributed to fourteenth-century Lucca or Venice—specifically, a class of luxury silks that show bilaterally symmetrical units arranged in lozenge trellis systems (see, for example, fig. 86)—have motifs closely related to the ones in the tapestry. Some examples show the motifs in metallic or polychrome silk yarns, or both, against monochrome grounds; others, woven as velvets, show as many as four colors, sometimes also with metallic yarns, against the plain ground.[4]

In these silks, there are affronted or addorsed animals in pairs, some with heads turned away from the direction in which the bodies are oriented, like the stags in the tapestry pattern; and there are unicorns, elephants, lions, stags, and stork-like birds, as well as dogs and fantastic creatures.[5] Many of the silks also show battlemented, turreted, and moated castles.[6] In the example shown here (fig. 86), a pair of addorsed, winged dogs displayed above castle walls recalls the affronted storks displayed below castle walls in the tapestry pattern. Other silks show figures leaning out of castle towers or over castle parapets or out of trees near castles; they are not the angels leaning out of the turrets in the tapestry pattern, but they are reminiscent of them.[7] One silk shows a chevron-shaped battlemented wall with three turrets rather like the one in the tapestry, but it defines the top, not the bottom, of a pattern unit.[8]

The lozenge trellis, a standard pattern system well suited to the requirements of textile design, appears also in the fictive tapestry-woven or needleworked hangings painted on the walls of some rooms in the Palazzo Davanzati in Florence (fig. 87; see also fig. 25) and the Schloss Runkelstein (Castello di Roncolo) near Bolzano[9] in the late fourteenth century. However the motifs in those hangings lack the variety of form and naturalistic grace that relate the pattern of 1 so intimately to the silk patterns. Everything the tapestry designer needed to produce the pattern for the Metropolitan Museum's tapestry—that is, the choice and character of the motifs and the mode of organizing them—was available to him in the vocabulary of contemporary textile design, particularly the language characteristic of these luxury silks. Except for the heraldic details, which the patron probably submitted to him directly, the designer could have developed his pattern directly from these textiles. The broader color range of his pattern follows from the nature of his medium: it was easier and economically more feasible to multiply colors in tapestry than in drawloom weaving.

Manufacture and Date

The coats of arms had been identified by 1903 when the related fragment in the Rijksmuseum, Amsterdam, was first published.[10] Because the wedding represented by the dimidiated blazon took place in 1349, when Guillaume III Rogier de Beaufort married Aliénor de Comminges, and since both lived almost to the end of the century, scholars have dated these fragments in the second half of the fourteenth century. Because the couple lived in France, the pieces have been most often attributed to Paris or Arras. At the time the fragments then owned by Edouard Jonas were exhibited in Detroit in 1928, in Rochester in 1929, and in Providence in 1930, and again when the Metropolitan Museum's piece was exhibited in Hartford and Baltimore in 1951–52, it was said that the tapestries were woven between 1375, when Guillaume III Rogier de Beaufort became the "duc de Beaufort," and 1396 (correct date is 1394), when he died; and the coronet held aloft by the paired angels was described as a ducal coronet.[11] These arguments carry no weight. Guillaume III Rogier never held the title of duke: the property of Beaufort (Beaufort-en-Vallée, near Angers) was a county, not a dukedom. Furthermore, as de Comminges (1972, 272 n. 18) observed, the coronet is not specifically that of a duke but simply the usual kind of coronet that was represented before the fifteenth century.

Weinberger believed that the drawing of the angels recalls the style of Jean Fouquet and Jean Bourdichon, and so he suggested that the tapestry fragments were

Fig. 87. Wall paintings imitating tapestry or needle-worked hangings in the Camera Nuziale, Palazzo Davanzati, Florence, about 1395 (?).

woven in France but no earlier than 1480.[12] Ackerman compared the two fragments in the Macomber collection to a millefleurs tapestry showing "the lion with the same shield," a tapestry that she believed was woven in the southern Netherlands, perhaps Tournai, in the late sixteenth century.[13] Erkelens[14] and Cavallo (1967, 49) suggested that the tapestries might have been woven either in France or the southern Netherlands. Later, de Comminges (1972, 283) noted that Erkelens had abandoned the idea of an origin in France. Cavallo (1967, 50) observed that although the coats of arms appear to be those of Guillaume III and Aliénor it seemed possible that the tapestries might have been made in reference to them by some descendant like Anne de Beaufort, great-niece of Guillaume, who gained claim as heiress in her own right to the same properties and titles in 1444. Therefore, he considered a date in the middle of the

fifteenth century as well as the second half of the fourteenth century. However both de Comminges (1972, 278, 283) and de Vaivre (1974, 300–302) refuted Cavallo's suggestion, arguing that in view of the conventions of heraldic usage at that time, the coats of arms indicate that these fragments would have been woven exclusively for Guillaume and Aliénor.

Wells (1977, 95–100) made an intensive study of Guillaume III Rogier's life in relation to his uncle Pope Clement VI, his brother Pope Gregory XI, as well as his son, Raymond, and concluded that if the tapestries were woven after 1375, they would have been produced for Guillaume (alone or with his wife) in conjunction with his son. Wells advanced this theory partly because he knew that Guillaume had given the title of vicomte de Turenne to Raymond in 1375 and partly because he believed that Guillaume did not quarter his arms; therefore, he reasoned, the mantles showing Beaufort dimidiating Comminges represent Guillaume, while the others, showing Beaufort quartering Turenne, must represent Raymond. However, de Vaivre (1974, 301, fig. 5) demonstrated that Guillaume III Rogier did indeed quarter Beaufort and Turenne on a seal affixed to a document of 1383. Wells (1977, 97, 98) also suggested that the tapestries could have been woven between 1376 and 1378 for Guillaume and Raymond as leaders of their vassals within the Papal State in Avignon. In a somewhat earlier publication, Wells had suggested that the pieces might have been produced for Guillaume III "as Grand-master of some religious-military order connected with the defence of the city" (that is, Avignon).[15] These opinions reflect Wells's conviction that the stork, the battlemented wall, and the four beasts wearing heraldic mantles have military significance in relation to Avignon. Arguments based on the interpretation of these motifs must be considered with some reservation, since, as we have shown (Source of the Design), most of the motifs could have been derived from standard pattern elements in contemporary textile design.

No other tapestries that might be used as comparative material in dating these fragments have survived. However, there is important evidence in the trompe-l'oeil tapestries or embroideries painted on the walls of three rooms in the Palazzo Davanzati in Florence which have been illustrated by Mariacher (see note 9). In the Stanza dei Pappagalli (see also fig. 25) the fictive wall covering shows a lozenge trellis with a simple quatrefoil motif in each of its compartments. In the bands forming the trelliswork itself there are parrots stretched out diagonally like the storks in 1 and the other pieces related to it. In the Camera da Letto the painted hanging shows lozenges containing lions facing left alternating in diagonal rows with grotesque creatures facing right. The pattern on the walls of the Camera Nuziale is the one most like that in the tapestry fragments (fig. 87). Although the paintings in the other two rooms are not dated, it is thought that this room was decorated in 1395 when Tommaso Davizzi married Caterina degli Alberti. Here, the lozenges contain five different centers: a cluster of four fleurs-de-lis, a pair of crossed keys, a lion, the Davizzi coat of arms, and a crown. They are arranged so that each motif repeats in horizontal, rather than diagonal, rows. There is a change of rhythm at the bottom where a row of keys and a row of lions have been omitted above a row of Davizzi arms. This irregularity suggests that the deviations from the normal pattern system that were noted in the Beaufort-Turenne-Comminges tapestry pattern (see Description and Subject) perhaps should not necessarily be regarded as errors.

The Badezimmer in the Schloss Runkelstein near Bolzano also has walls painted to represent tapestry or embroidered hangings (see note 9). One wall shows eagles with wings displayed that are arranged in a repeating lozenge pattern. Another shows animals within the lozenge-shaped compartments of a trellis, the lozenge points decorated with rosettes. These paintings have been dated to about 1390–1400.

However, we know that textiles with patterns even more closely related to the pattern in the Metropolitan Museum's tapestry were being produced before these two groups of wall paintings of about 1390–1400 were executed, in fact before 1379. An entry in the inventory of the church of the Saint Sépulcre in Paris of about that date reads in part as follows: "Item une autre thapis losengé à lyons et à lycornes, en mantelles [enmantellés?] de manteaux armoiez des armes de Castile et d'Alençon . . ." (Item, another tapestry [or carpet?] lozenged with lions and unicorns, wearing mantles bearing the arms of Castile and Alençon . . .).[16] Therefore we believe that 1 and the pieces related to it could have been woven in the third quarter, rather than the second half, of the fourteenth century. As Coffinet (1977, 10) wrote, it would seem logical for the tapestries to have been produced not long after the Beaufort-Comminges marriage took place in 1349. Furthermore, we know that Guillaume III Rogier de Beaufort's uncle Pope Clement VI helped arrange his marriage to Aliénor de Comminges in order to settle a dispute over the succession to the fiefdoms of Turenne and Comminges and also that, as Elie de Comminges (1972, 269–70) noted, Guillaume was confirmed in his rights over Turenne by letters patent from Jean II de France dated in December 1350 and February 1351 (new style). It seems reasonable to suppose that Guillaume would have had the tapestries woven not much later than this time to celebrate both his recent marriage and his coming into his new estate through that marriage. In reference both to the date and place of production, it may be significant that Clement VI had become bishop of Arras in 1328 and that he might have arranged for his nephew's tapestries to be produced or bought in Arras just before his own death in 1352.

RELATED TAPESTRIES

The hanging in the Metropolitan Museum and the others like it have often been referred to in the literature as parts of a large hanging or as pieces of a set of room furnishings. The fact that the pattern units in 1 are only three-quarters as large as the units in the Burrell Collection pieces indicates that the extant fragments came from more than one hanging.[17] Furthermore, this discrepancy suggests that some of the fabric was woven to cover large surfaces, presumably walls, and some to cover smaller surfaces, presumably bed and seat furniture. Inventories and household accounts of the late fourteenth and fifteenth centuries abound in references to tapestry rooms or "chambers." A typical chamber is cited in an inventory of 1420 among the tapestries that Philippe le Bon inherited from his father. The entry reads as follows: "Une autre riche chambre de tapisserie de haulte-lice, de file d'Arras, faicte à or, appellée la Chambre du Couronnement Nostre-Dame, garnye de ciel, dossier, couverture de lit et six tapiz à tendre" (another rich chamber of high warp [or high quality?] tapestry, of thread of Arras, made with gold, called the Chamber of the Coronation of Our Lady, comprising canopy, back cloth, and cover for the bed, and six wall hangings).[18] Other chambers included valances and curtains for the bed, and bench and cushion covers. Some chambers had certain covers and hangings made of tapestry and the rest of silk or other yardage that was either patterned in the weave or embroidered; others, perhaps less common, contained tapestry fabrics exclusively.

De Comminges (1972, 271–72, 285, Appendix A) made a summary of data concerning the Beaufort-Turenne-Comminges fragments he knew. He listed and illustrated (1972, pls. 2–11) nine pieces whose present locations are known and mentioned five to nine others that seem to have been lost. The pieces in the first group are as follows: the one in the Metropolitan Museum; three pieces in the Burrell Collection, Glasgow; one in the Rijksmuseum, Amsterdam; one in the Museum of Fine Arts, Boston; one in the Museum of Art, Rhode Island School of Design, Providence; one in the Guennol Collection, New York; and one in the Thyssen-Bornemisza Collection in Lugano. We can cite further some fragments in the Hunt Museum in Limerick, Ireland.[19] Among the lost pieces, de Comminges listed one formerly in the Macomber collection, two in the possession of "N. N." in Paris in 1947, and two that were offered for sale to Sir William Burrell, but not acquired, in 1936. Finally, de Comminges (1972, 271) noted that if the four pieces that were exhibited in Detroit in 1928 were not the same as those that are now in the Metropolitan Museum, the Burrell Collection, and the Thyssen-Bornemisza Collection, then they, too, are lost. We believe that these four pieces are indeed the ones de Comminges thought they might be and that the five fragments he designated as being lost are in fact the only ones that are now missing. However it seems possible that the pieces now in the Hunt Museum are the ones that had belonged to "N. N." in Paris.

HISTORY

Possibly inherited by François II de la Tour, vicomte de Turenne, grandson of Anne de Beaufort, great-niece of Guillaume III Rogier de Beaufort, in the first quarter of the sixteenth century.[20]
Property of E. Lowengard, Paris, in 1901.
Property of Hector de Economos, Paris.
Property of Edouard Jonas, New York.
Property of Stephen Vlasto, Buenos Aires and Paris.
Purchased from Vlasto by the MMA through the Rogers Fund, 1946.

EXHIBITIONS

Detroit Institute of Arts, 1928. *The Seventh Loan Exhibition: French Gothic Art of the Thirteenth to Fifteenth Century.* Catalogue of tapestries by Adele C. Weibel. Cat. no. 96b, not illus. Lent by Edouard Jonas.
Hartford, Wadsworth Atheneum, and Baltimore Museum of Art, 1951–52. 2000 *Years of Tapestry Weaving: A Loan Exhibition.* Text by Adele Coulin Weibel. Cat. no. 68, pl. ix.

PUBLICATIONS

Taylor, Francis Henry, Horace H. F. Jayne, and Laurence S. Harrison. "Review of the Year 1946." Annual Report for 1946. In *MMA Bulletin,* n.s. 6 (1947–48) p. 18. Discussed briefly.
Rorimer, James J. *Mediaeval Tapestries: A Picture Book.* MMA, New York, 1947, p. [2]. Discussed; illus.
Europäische Kunst um 1400. Exh. cat., Kunsthistorisches Museum. Textiles catalogued by Dora Heinz. Vienna, 1962, p. 454. Mentioned.
Verlet 1965, p. 25. Mentioned.
Cavallo, Adolph S. *Tapestries of Europe and of Colonial Peru in the Museum of Fine Arts, Boston.* Boston, 1967, p. 51. Mentioned.
de Comminges, comte Elie. "Une tapisserie aux armes Beaufort, Turenne et Comminges." *La Revue de Comminges* 85 (1972) pp. 270–72. Discussed; illus. pl. 7.
Nickel, Helmut. "'a harnes all gilte': A Study of the Armor of Galiot de Genouilhac and the Iconography of Its Decoration." *Metropolitan Museum Journal* 5 (1972) pp. 113–15, 124. Discussed briefly; illus. fig. 67.
de Vaivre, Jean-Bernard. "Mélanges: A propos d'une tapisserie aux armes Beaufort-Comminges." *Bulletin Monumental* 132 (1974) p. 300. Discussed; illus. fig. 1.
Coffinet 1977, p. 13. Mentioned; illus. p. 11 (color detail).
Wells, William. "Tapestry with the Arms of Beaufort, Turenne and Comminges." *Apollo* 105 (1977) p. 94. Mentioned.
Marks, Richard, et al. *The Burrell Collection.* London and Glasgow, 1983, p. 101. Mentioned.

NOTES

1. See Jean-Bernard de Vaivre, "Mélanges: A propos d'une tapisserie aux armes Beaufort-Comminges," *Bulletin Monumental* 132 (1974) pp. 297–302, for a discussion of the coats of arms shown in the tapestry fragments and particularly p. 301 for an explanation of why Aliénor de Comminges's coat of arms was marshaled in this way.
2. Alain Erlande-Brandenburg, *La Dame à la Licorne* (Paris, 1978) n. pag.; all six tapestries in this set are illustrated.
3. William Wells, "Tapestry with the Arms of Beaufort, Turenne and Comminges," *Apollo* 105 (1977) pp. 95, 100 n. 7, referred to this suggestion that Betty Kurth made in her unpublished catalogue of the tapestries in the Burrell Collection, submitted in 1947.
4. The examples listed in notes 5–8 below are typical metallic and

polychrome silks; for an illustration in color, see Otto von Falke, *Kunstgeschichte der Seidenweberei* (Berlin, 1913) vol. 2, fig. 450. For typical polychrome velvets, see W. Mannowsky, *Der Danziger Paramentenschatz: Kirchliche Gewänder und Stickereien aus der Marienkirche* (Berlin, [1931]) vol. 1, pt. 2, pls. 82, 83, caption p. 17, and von Falke, *Kunstgeschichte der Seidenweberei*, vol. 2, fig. 494 (in color).

5. See von Falke, *Kunstgeschichte der Seidenweberei*, vol. 2, figs. 472 (unicorns), 395, 427, 437 (elephants), 396, 404, 406, 488 (lions), 446, 483 (stags), and 396, 398, 399 (stork-like birds).

6. See von Falke, *Kunstgeschichte der Seidenweberei*, vol. 2, figs. 428, 429, 450; also Friedrich Fischbach, *Die wichtigsten Webe-Ornamente bis zum 19. Jahrhundert* (Wiesbaden, 1902–11) pl. 52 (examples in center and at right).

7. See Fischbach, *Die wichtigsten Webe-Ornamente*, pls. 47, 52 (example at left), and 44, respectively.

8. Von Falke, *Kunstgeschichte der Seidenweberei*, vol. 2, fig. 432.

9. For illustrations of the painted walls in the Palazzo Davanzati, see Giovanni Mariacher, *Ambienti Italiani del Trecento e Quattrocento* (Milan, 1963) illus. p. 79 (Stanza dei Pappagalli), p. 80 (upper illus., Camera da Letto), and facing p. 80 (Camera Nuziale, in color); the walls in the Badezimmer in the Schloss Runkelstein are illustrated in *Die Parler und der schöne Stil 1350–1400: Europäische Kunst unter den Luxemburgern*, exh. cat., Schnütgen-Museum (Cologne, 1978) vol. 3, p. 238.

10. *Catalogus van de Textiele Kunst in het Nederlandsch Museum voor Geschiedenis en Kunst te Amsterdam* (Amsterdam, 1903) no. 365.

11. *The Seventh Loan Exhibition: French Gothic Art of the Thirteenth to Fifteenth Century*, Detroit Institute of Arts (Detroit, 1928) no. 96b; *Loan Exhibition of Gothic Art*, Memorial Art Gallery (Rochester, 1929) no. 50; M. A. Banks, "The Tapestry Exhibition," *Bulletin of the Rhode Island School of Design* 18 (1930) p. 14; and *2000 Years of Tapestry Weaving: A Loan Exhibition*, Wadsworth Atheneum, Hartford, and Baltimore Museum of Art (Hartford, 1951) no. 68.

12. Martin Weinberger, "Sammlung Schloss Rohoncz: Plastik und Kunstgewerbe," *Der Cicerone* 22 (1930) p. 378.

13. Phyllis Ackerman, *A Catalog of the Tapestries in the Collection of Frank Gair Macomber* (n.p., [1927]) p. 37.

14. A. M. Louise Erkelens, *Wandtapijten 1: Late gotiek en vroege renaissance*, Facetten der Verzameling, Rijksmuseum, 2d ser., no. 4 (Amsterdam, 1962) p. 6, fig. 1.

15. *Treasures from the Burrell Collection*, exh. cat. by William Wells, Hayward Gallery (London, 1975) no. 80.

16. Achille Jubinal, *Recherches sur l'usage et l'origine des tapisseries à personnages dites historiées depuis l'antiquité jusqu'au 16e siècle inclusivement* (Paris, 1840) p. 28.

17. The maximum width of the units in the three Burrell Collection pieces, from the rear talon of one stork to that of its mate, ranges from $38^1/_2$ inches to $40^1/_2$ inches; the corresponding width of the units in the Metropolitan Museum's hanging is $27^1/_2$ inches average.

18. Alexandre Pinchart, *Histoire générale de la tapisserie*, pt. 3, *Histoire de la tapisserie dans les Flandres* (Paris, 1878–85) p. 32.

19. The author thanks Patrick F. Doran, curator of the Hunt Museum, for his kindness in informing him that the fragments formerly in the collection of Mr. John Hunt are now in the Hunt Museum. No illustration of those pieces, now combined with passages of needlework in order to show the complete pattern unit, is known to have been published.

20. See Helmut Nickel, "'a harnes all gilte': A Study of the Armor of Galiot de Genouilhac and the Iconography of Its Decoration," *Metropolitan Museum Journal* 5 (1972) p. 114. Nickel believed that Guillaume Rogier de Beaufort's tapestries descended with the title, land, and castle to François II de la Tour, vicomte de Turenne (1497–1532), because the etched gilt armor thought to have been made for the latter shows the unicorn, lion, stag, elephant, and crane among the creatures in its decoration. The point is well taken; however it seems equally possible that other family furnishings could have inspired the designs on the armor.

2

Five Worthies with Attendant Figures

Four reconstructed hangings derived from a set
of three tapestries depicting *The Nine* (or *Ten?*)
Worthies

a *King Arthur (as reconstructed at MMA)*

b *Two Attendants: Swordsman and Courtier
(fragment sewn along left edge of 2a when it was
received at MMA, now placed at right end of 2c)*

c *Joshua and David (composed of 2b and fragments
acquired from other sources)*

d *Hector of Troy*

e *Julius Caesar*

f *Three Attendants: Cardinals (fragments now
placed along top of 2a but acquired from a
different source)*

g *Miscellaneous fragments, including three pieces
showing figures of cardinals (not used in the four
reconstructed hangings)*

h *Attendant: Standard-Bearer (fragment now placed
at right of David in 2c but acquired from a
different source)*

i *Attendant: Bishop (not used in the reconstructed
hangings)*

Southern Netherlands, 1400–1410

Wool warp, wool wefts

Dimensions of the four main hangings as reconstructed:

2a and f (King Arthur): 14 ft. × 9 ft. 9 in. (4.27 m × 2.97 m)

2b, c, and h (*Hebrew Worthies*): 14 ft. × 20 ft. 10 in. (4.29 m × 6.35 m)

2d (Hector): 13 ft. 9¹/₂ in. × 8 ft. 8 in. (4.21 m × 2.64 m)

2e (Caesar): 13 ft. 9¹/₂ in. × 7 ft. 7 in. (4.21 m × 2.38 m)

12¹/₂ warp yarns per inch, 5 per centimeter

2a and b: Munsey Fund, 1932 (32.130.3; after reconstruction
changed to 32.130.3a,b)

2c–g: Gift of John D. Rockefeller, Jr., 1947 (47.101.1–10; after
reconstruction changed to 47.101.1–5)

2h: Gift of George A. Douglass, 1947 (47.152)

2i: Gift of John D. Rockefeller, Jr., 1949 (49.123)

CONDITION

Apparently all the fragments were preserved together
until around 1870 when they were dispersed to two or
more different collections (see History). Nevertheless
they seem to have survived in approximately the same
condition. All the fragments are worn, and most of them
show losses and a good deal of repair by reweaving,
much of which has been left intact. The colors have
faded more in some places than others; where they have
survived well, particularly in the row of attendants at
the top of the *Hebrew Worthies,* they are bright and
clear. The fragment showing a standing bishop (2i; he
was seated originally, see Source of the Design) had been
almost completely rewoven below the level of the pallium, and the sections of fabric showing a twisted column at the left and flowers below are part of that
restoration. The restorations have been removed. However the fabric showing the rear right of the room he
occupies, which comes from some other part of the
original tapestry, was left in place when the other corrections were made.

The main consideration in terms of condition is the
reconstruction itself and the degree to which the fragments have or have not been correctly assembled. This
question is so critical that it will be treated as a special
subject in the following discussion.

THE RECONSTRUCTION

When Ackerman (1922–23) first published the King
Arthur piece as one that obviously came from a set of
hangings of the Heroes or Worthies (see Subject) she,
along with Hunter (1925), Göbel (1928), and Marillier
(1932), assumed that such a cycle once existed, but they
could not identify the set of hangings from which this
fragment came. It remained for Rorimer to make the
discovery just a few years later. In 1936 he saw at Joseph
Brummer's gallery in New York five pairs of window
curtains which the dealer had recently acquired.
Rorimer realized that they had been made up of fragments of the lost set of hangings combined with strips of
modern fabric (figs. 88–92). Eleven years later, in 1947,
having succeeded in buying the curtains, he established
a team of restorers at The Cloisters to reconstruct as
much of the original tapestry set as possible (Rorimer
and Freeman 1948–49, 243–44; 1953, frontispiece text).

In planning for the reconstruction Rorimer must have
seen that the figures representing each of the three
groups of Worthies (Pagan, Hebrew, and Christian; see
Subject) were associated with three different kinds of
architectural settings and that the smaller figures of
attendants also occupied three different kinds of settings. Therefore he would have concluded that the original set of hangings comprised three pieces, each one

2a and f

Figs. 88–92. Five pairs of curtains composed of fragments of the *Worthies* tapestries combined with strips of modern fabric. MMA, Gift of John D. Rockefeller, Jr., 1947 (47.101.1–10).

showing one type of setting, each setting occupied by either Pagan, Hebrew, or Christian Worthies and their attendants. Rorimer knew that Charles VI had owned three similar tapestries showing the *Preuses,* the female counterparts of the Worthies or *Preux* (see Related Tapestries), and this was confirmation, he probably concluded, that The Cloisters set was complete in three pieces. However, he did not acknowledge in any of his publications the fact that Charles's tapestries showed ten rather than nine female Worthies and therefore that ten rather than nine male Worthies might have been represented in the pieces he was reconstructing. Furthermore, in writing about Philippe le Hardi's tapestries of the Worthies and their female counterparts, Rorimer and Freeman (1948–49, 253–54) did not specify, as the accounts do, that the duke owned not only one tapestry or set of tapestries of the *neuf preux* and *preuses* but also one or two of the "dix preux et 9 preuses."[1]

We are obliged here to write assumptions rather than reports about Rorimer's planning since no detailed account of the reconstruction project is known to have been recorded. The only surviving pieces of documenta-

tion are small photographic paste-ups that Rorimer prepared. They are in effect jigsaw puzzles whose pieces are mostly simple rectangles that jibe because of their consistent shape or else irregularly shaped pieces whose contours do not correspond at all. Rorimer and Freeman (1948–49, 244) stated that the vertical cuts had been neatly made and that "it was comparatively easy to reweave the fragments once their positions had been determined." What is more to the point is that since these straight cuts all looked alike they could not help Rorimer determine the relative positions of the various fragments. However almost every one of the figures in these fragments was associated with one or another of the three kinds of architectural settings, and he could use that as a clue to help him place each figure (both the Worthies and the smaller figures) in the correct tapestry. This would not tell him where each of the three Worthies appeared on that original tapestry—that is, whether in the center, or left, or right—or with which one of them each of the attendant figures was associated. We assume that Rorimer and his team chose a place for each figure within each hanging according to two basic

Fragment of 2g, obverse of fabric

Fragment of 2g, reverse of fabric

criteria. First, since some of the details of the architectural settings and the Worthies' thrones were drawn according to the principles of linear perspective, these elements could be placed left or right of center if one assumed, as seems correct, that the designer placed his vanishing point roughly in the center of each composition. Second, the small figures in each building might be placed according to whatever iconographic reason there might be to associate them with any particular Worthy. When the fragment showed clues of both kinds these must have helped the staff considerably; but the illusion of linear perspective is not equally convincing in all parts of the hangings, and in many instances there seems to be little iconographic reason to associate any of the attendant figures at the sides with any Worthy in particular (see Subject).

There is another factor to take into account in considering the accuracy of the reconstructions. Our examination of 2g, the unmounted fragments that were not used in the reconstruction, demonstrates that the tapestries

were woven so that the front and back faces are identical except for occasional manipulations (for example, weft carry-overs where adjacent yarns of different colors are passed over one another for short distances) that distinguish the back from the front quite clearly.[2] One could thus easily mistake the back of a fragment for the front. Therefore it seems possible that the restorers may unwittingly have mounted some of the fragments in reverse, but we cannot pursue this question further because the ninety-odd fragments that make up the four hangings were fixed firmly to their mounts and to pieces of plain modern tapestry-woven fabric in 1947–49.

The four hangings that resulted from the reconstruction represent more than half the substance of the three original tapestries including five of the nine or ten Worthies. However, significant parts of them—the passages of fabric showing four or five of the Worthies (Alexander the Great, Judas Maccabeus, Charlemagne, Godefroy de Bouillon, and possibly also one more Pagan or Christian Worthy; see Related Tapestries), most of

98

their attendant figures, and parts of the architectural and landscape settings in which they appeared—are missing. They have either perished or they survive unidentified someplace else. It is also obvious that the top and bottom portions of the original tapestries are missing. Rorimer and Freeman (1948–49, 243) calculated that each of the three tapestries measured more than 21 feet in length and about 16 feet in height. Presumably they based this estimate on the dimensions of the nearly complete *Hebrew Worthies* (2b, c, h), which measures 20 feet 10 inches in length and 14 feet in height. The three original tapestries may have had large inscriptions beneath each figure and coats of arms above them (see Related Tapestries). In any case it is clear that most of the band of sky along the top and all of what must have been the masonry base of the building together with a strip of meadow below it, as appears in the *Apocalypse* tapestries in Angers, are missing from each of the Metropolitan Museum's reconstructed hangings. It seems

fair to estimate that each of the three original tapestries was at least 16 feet, and perhaps as much as 18 feet, high.

DESCRIPTION

One of the reconstructed hangings (2b, c, h) shows two of the three Hebrew Worthies in their settings and nearly all their attendant figures. Another represents King Arthur (2a and f), one of the three or possibly four figures (see Related Tapestries) that appeared in the original tapestry devoted to the Christian Worthies together with some attendant figures. The third and fourth pieces represent respectively Hector of Troy (2d) and Julius Caesar (2e), with attendants, all taken from the third tapestry which depicted the three Pagan Worthies. A number of other fragments (2g and 2i), which show architectural elements, bits of the landscape in which the buildings are set, and incomplete figures of three cardinals and a bishop, all apparently

2b, c, h

Detail of 2b, c, h

unconnected to those parts of the three original hangings that had survived, were not used during the reconstruction of 1947–49 and are preserved separately in the
Metropolitan Museum.

The *Hebrew Worthies* is the largest of the reconstructed hangings and preserves almost the entire substance of the original tapestry. The only missing figures

are those representing Judas Maccabeus and one of the
attendants.

Joshua is seated on his throne in a room occupying the
left end of a masonry building. David appears on his
throne in the center. Each occupies a vaulted octagonal
room whose three front walls are open. The three corresponding vaults are carried on round-headed arches sup-

ported on columns at the sides and ending in pendants in the center. Round-headed windows fitted with delicate mullions and tracery are installed in the three rear walls of each room. Rich fabrics showing regularly repeating patterns cover the seats and fronts of the thrones and the surfaces beneath the Worthies' feet. The textile on Joshua's throne has a pattern of floriated Greek crosses. His footrest is covered with what appears to be a brocaded silk patterned with winged dragons and blossoms or stars. The seat and front of David's throne are covered with a fabric showing an eagle displayed, but the pattern on the surface beneath his feet is not clear. Both men wear ermine-lined surcoats with flat, round collars and wide shoulder capes over their plate body armor which is visible on the forearms, lower legs, and feet. Each carries a sword upright in his right hand. David holds an open book, presumably the Book of Psalms, on his left knee. Both Worthies have moustaches and long beards. Joshua's hair reaches only to his jawline while David's falls in curls behind his shoulders. Joshua wears a crown in the form of a narrow jeweled fillet. David has a jeweled crown fitted with slender points that support large strawberry leaves alternating with small trefoils. A shield emblazoned with each Worthy's arms hangs from a strap passed over a hook in the vaulting above and to the right of his head. Joshua's arms are blazoned or a wyvern (winged dragon) vert passant. David's shield is blazoned azure a harp or. The vault boss above each man is made in the shape of an octafoil with a shield at its center. Both octafoils are red (the one above David having been incorrectly restored as golden orange) with white borders. Both shields are blazoned azure a fleur-de-lis or (the single flower representing a semy of fleurs-de-lis or: see note 5), the royal arms of France as they were marshaled at this time. We believe, as Adam (1949, 75–76) also did, that the red field was intended to represent the border in the arms of Louis, first duc d'Anjou, who marshaled his arms France, a border gules. His arms appear in this form—that is, France against a decorative background of red that reads as the border gules—in the *Apocalypse* tapestries in Angers.[3]

Flanking the Hebrew Worthies' rooms are narrow flat walls pierced by round-headed arches giving on to small vaulted rooms on two levels. A corresponding wall appears at the right end of the hanging where it would have flanked the room containing Judas Maccabeus. Round-headed arches crowning windows fitted with delicate tracery carry the vaults at the back and sides of these smaller rooms. The form of the vaulting indicates that the rooms are rectangular in plan. Each room contains one standing figure. On the lower level, left to right, appear a warrior in full armor with spear and shield; a

spearsman wearing a hip-length houppelande over his armor; a warrior dressed in a similar way, prancing toward the left and carrying a spear from the upper end of which flies a pennon showing three balls inside a crescent; and, at the far right, a warrior wearing a sword belt and a long houppelande with wide sleeves over his armor. On the upper level the figures (visible only from the thigh upward) are, left to right, an archer in jerkin and hose, bending a bow; a crossbowman in a long houppelande about to loose a bolt; and a warrior wearing a sword belt over his long houppelande.

This main section of the facade, which accounts for the lower two-thirds of the depicted building's total height, terminates at the top in a low battlemented parapet that extends the full width of the building and forms a balcony in front of its uppermost story. Behind the parapet rises a wall articulated like the main wall below, with three projecting bays set between four narrow, flat walls pierced by round-headed arches giving on to small, rectangular vaulted rooms closed at the back by tall windows decorated with elaborate tracery. The facade's entablature has a frieze decorated with pierced quatrefoils below the cornice and a battlemented turret at every change of planes. What seems to be an inscription containing four capital letters appears in the center of the cornice. From left to right the motifs resemble an *M* whose second vertical stroke has been combined with the first stroke of a *W*, then a *T* inverted, then an *M*, and finally a *Y*. They are all modern restorations and may be later additions rather than replacements of letters that appeared in the original design. Above this entablature and at the left side of the building appear passages of dark sky set with small stars and clouds. At the right edge of the hanging the left ends of a butterfly's spotted

Detail of right edge of 2b, c, h

2a as received in 1932

(representing heraldic ermine?) wings (see detail) appear against the sky a short distance below the turret at the far right end of the balcony. (See below, discussion of other butterflies along the left side of the Hector tapestry.)

In each of the thirteen rooms on the top level stands a male or female figure, which is visible above the battlemented parapet only from the waist up. From left to right they represent an armored warrior holding a battle-ax, a lady playing a rebec, a crowned lady fondling a cheetah, a lady playing a harp, an armored warrior carrying a mace upright in both hands, a lady holding a crown in her arms, a crowned lady holding a falcon on her left fist and a bird's leg in her right hand, a crowned lady with folded hands looking at the falconess, an armored warrior holding a sheathed sword in both hands, a crowned lady holding a small dog in her lap, a lady playing a psaltery, a lady holding a small round object in her right hand, and a man carrying a pole arm over his right shoulder and a small shield in his left hand. All the women wear fitted houppelandes cut with high waists,

wrist-length sleeves, and either high or low round necklines. Those who do not wear crowns have either caps or floral chaplets and many of them also have veils. Some of them wear their hair coiled at the sides of the face, but most of them have long plaited or loose tresses. The men's hair falls to their shoulders and they all have bifurcated beards of varying lengths. The three men at the left wear surcoats and the one at the far right wears a short houppelande. They all have caps.

Fourteen square banners fly from the roofs of turrets set into the battlemented wall that runs in front of these figures. The first banner at the left is blazoned azure a semy of fleurs-de-lis or, an engrailed border gules, the border extended at the left to form three short projections. These are the arms of Jean, duc de Berry. The projections represent the tails of the duke's pennon that would be cut off when he was granted the privileges of a knight banneret.[4] The second banner shows the same arms without the border; these were the arms of the king of France. Following these, left to right, five banners repeat the arms of the duc de Berry, one the royal

Detail of 2a

arms, two the arms of Berry, and then the royal arms again. The next banner to the right is blazoned bendy of six, or and azure, which may represent the arms of the first ducal house of Burgundy but without the border of gules that usually surrounds the bends; and finally, at the far right end of the line, the duc de Berry's arms appear once again.[5]

In regard to the accuracy of the reconstruction in this hanging, we believe that since the design of the architectural elements in the building's uppermost story allows for no variations in form, and since all of the thirteen figures that occupy that story and the banners flying near them were already associated with bits of their setting before the fragments were assembled, the upper third of the hanging has been correctly reconstructed. As for the lower part, we believe that the two Worthies' thrones and footrests were drawn in linear perspective with reference to a vanishing point in the center of the hanging. Since Joshua's setting was drawn to be viewed from the right and David's from a point directly in front of itself, we conclude that these two figures now occupy

the positions they had in the original tapestry, or at the left end and in the center, respectively. Judas Maccabeus would have appeared in his room at the right end. As for the attendant figures in the two levels of rooms flanking the Worthies, it appears that the lower figure at the far left has been properly placed since the fabric on which he is represented is an integral part of the fabric representing the corner buttress that rises along the left side of the building. That is not true of the bowman directly above him; but what perspective there is in the drawing of the bowman's setting suggests that he too is now where he appeared originally. The perspective effect is so slight in the other four small settings that it is not possible to be sure they are correctly positioned.

In 2a and f, the hanging that represents a bit more than one-third of the original tapestry of the *Christian Worthies*, King Arthur is seated on his throne in a large vaulted room occupying the lower center section of a masonry building. A five-petaled white rose with a blue center decorates the vault boss. The conformation of the vaulting indicates that the room is hexagonal in plan, and the disposition of the three lobed, pointed, and gabled arches that carry the outer ends of the vaults on columns at the sides and pendants in the middle indicates that the three front walls project forward in front of the facade. The back walls are represented as tall windows with elaborate tracery; they rise from the floor to the arches that carry the vaulting. The king wears a mantle thrown back over his left shoulder to reveal the armorial surcoat covering most of his plate armor. Three golden crowns on whose points large strawberry leaves alternate with small oval leaves appear on the front of the blue surcoat, two above, one below. This is King Arthur's coat of arms which is blazoned azure three crowns or, two in chief, one in point. The same three crowns appear again in a single row on the blue pennon that flies from the upper end of the staff or lance which he holds upright in his right hand. On his head the king wears a matching golden crown set with gemstones. The seat of his throne and the dais on which

it rests are covered with a carpet or cloth decorated with a regularly repeating pattern of foliated Greek crosses. The king's lightly waving hair falls to the base of his neck at the sides and back. His beard, short at the sides, descends in a bifurcated point to his chest in front. He holds a dagger in his left hand.

The three arches at the front of this room have spandrels fitted with small stained-glass trefoils. The arches carry low walls that serve as the parapets of a balcony above. The figure of a cardinal, visible only from the waist upward, stands in a hexagonal pavilion that rises above the balcony. Like those in the rooms below, the three front walls of this pavilion are open and its back walls contain windows fitted with elaborate tracery. Flying buttresses that are also decorated with fine tracery flank the pavilion.

Twin towers rise to the left and right of the central bay. Each one contains lozenge-shaped rooms on three levels. The two forward walls are carried on pointed,

2i after restoration in 1949

2i as received in 1949

104

Three fragments of 2g

lobed, and gabled arches. The two rear walls contain corresponding arches crowning tall windows whose tracery is like but does not match that in the windows of the central bay. Each of the two lowest rooms contains a seated bishop. The one at the left wears a cope over an alb, buskins, gloves, and a miter; he holds a crosier in his right hand and an open book in his left. The bishop at the right wears a chasuble and pallium, gloves, buskins, and a miter; he holds a crosier in his left hand and an open book in his right. An archbishop stands in each of the two mid-level rooms; the men are visible only from the waist up. Each wears a cope over an alb, gloves, and a miter, and has a book in his right hand and a procession-al cross in his left. Above them, two cardinals stand in the side bays of the top story, flanking the cardinal directly above King Arthur. The three cardinals are dressed alike: each wears a gown, a hood, and a hat denoting his office, and each of them holds a book. The figure at the left and the one in the center are identical except that the first wears a red gown and the second wears a green one. Bits of dark blue sky punctuated with clouds and stars appear above and between the pavilions that the cardinals occupy.

At least two other Christian Worthies, Charlemagne and Godefroy de Bouillon, were represented in the original tapestry and perhaps a fourth Christian Worthy was also present with his attendants (see Related Tapes-tries). No fragments showing these other main figures

are known to have survived, but we have fragments representing four of their attendants. Three pieces among the fragments in 2g show cardinals in settings like the ones in the King Arthur hanging. Another (2i) shows the figure of a bishop. It had been restored incor-rectly to show a standing figure, but the bust on this fragment matches that of the bishop seated in the lower right corner of the King Arthur piece.

A narrow corner buttress projects forward from the outer end of the uppermost room at the left. Its presence indicates that this bit of setting and the figure of a cardinal that it contains must always have occupied the upper left corner of the building and therefore also the left end of the original tapestry of the *Christian Worthies* before it was mutilated. However there is nothing to prove that this figure and its setting origi-nally belonged with King Arthur rather than one of the other Christian Worthies nor for that matter with the two other cardinals in this piece. No one of these frag-ments is connected to any other: they all survived as separate pieces. The fact that the cardinal in the center repeats (that is, was woven after the same cartoon as) the one at the left suggests that those two figures were not placed side by side originally. The restorers had three other figures of cardinals to choose from, the three among the fragments in 2g. Two of them occupy side rooms and the third is shown in a central room. One of the first of these pieces and the last one could have been

2d

used in the reconstruction of the King Arthur hanging instead of the ones that were used. However the third of these cardinals, who occupies an end room, would not have suited here because there is a corner buttress rising along the right side of the room, indicating that this figure must have occupied the upper right corner of the original tapestry. We can only guess that the restoration team chose to use the first three cardinals rather than the others because of this, because the former all face to the right (as the king also does), and finally because they are much more complete and in better condition than the three cardinals in 2g.

The fabric on which the bishops and archbishops are represented appears to be a continuous part of the fabric on which King Arthur is shown. Since his throne and the platform supporting it are drawn in perspective to be viewed head on rather than from a vantage point slightly to the right, it is fair to ask whether the king and his four attendants were originally in the center of the complete tapestry rather than at its left end as this reconstruction suggests they were.

The *Pagan Worthies* tapestry is represented by the third and fourth reassembled hangings (2d and 2e), which together make up more than two-thirds of the substance of the third tapestry in the original set. The figures of Hector and Julius Caesar in their settings, each surrounded by smaller figures, have been preserved. The representations of Alexander and attendants above him are missing.

In 2d Hector, wearing a cape over his tunic and body armor, sits on a throne in the center of a vaulted room. A fillet set with blossom-shaped jewels encircles the crown of his head. Beneath it his hair sweeps back from the sides of his face. He has a bifurcated beard that falls to his chest. His throne has a high gabled back decorated with crockets and a lily finial. Its four stiles terminate in tall, slender crocketed spires. He holds a sword upright in his right hand; his left hand rests on his thigh. A large shield covers the left half of his upper body. It is blazoned with his coat of arms: gules a lion or armed and langued argent, seated on a chair, holding a sword argent with a handle azure. The two rear walls of this room are hung with a dark fabric that shows a repeating pattern of grotesque dragons from whose mouths sprout swirling leafy tendrils.

The structure of the vaulting in this room and of the two pointed arches that carry the front of it indicate that the room has a lozenge-shaped plan. Like the arches in the King Arthur piece, these are lobed and gabled and carry a low angled wall that is pierced with slender panels of monochrome stained glass. There are only two rather than three arches here and their spandrels are decorated not with stained-glass trefoils but with lion-masks carved in relief, the lion-mask perhaps referring to the main charge on Hector's shield. None of the spandrels of the arches in the room directly above contains these masks, but the spandrels of the arches on the lowest level of the flanking bays contain leaf motifs like those in the Caesar piece (see below). The two low walls rising above the pair of arches in the center carry a balcony that runs in front of a smaller room set on the third floor of this bay. A pair of flying buttresses flank the room. A young woman with flowing coils of blond hair, dressed in a loose girdled gown with long tight sleeves, stands in this upper room. She is visible only from thigh level upward. She gazes toward the right, rests her right hand on the balustrade, and holds a lily stalk upright in her left hand. The back wall of her room is covered with a fabric showing double oval motifs that sprout leafy shoots at their tops. In the center of each oval appears a single lowercase letter, what appear to be either an *a* and an *n* or two of one or the other (both in the upper left section), a *y* (twice, lower left), and a *u* (lower and upper right) and also repetitions of some of these (right edge).

On the first and second levels of the building four smaller rooms constructed like Hector's flank his room. An armored archer occupies the room on the lowest story at the left. The hanging on the back wall is made of a dragon-patterned fabric matching the one in Hector's room. A warrior wearing a girdled, knee-length surcoat over his armor stands in the lowest room on the right. He holds a standard-topped spear upright in his right hand and an oval shield in his left. The back of his room is hung with a fabric decorated with a repeating motif of a bird's head with a three-leafed branch held in its beak. A helmeted warrior wearing a mail gorget, a cape, and a girdled surcoat over his armor stands in the second-story room at the left side. He holds a spear upright in his right hand. The dark fabric covering the rear walls of this room has a repeating pattern of eagles displayed. A warrior wearing a helmet, mail gorget, plate armor for breast and legs, along with a short tunic stands in the corresponding room at the right. He carries a round shield in his right hand and rests his left hand on the hilt of the sword that hangs from his girdle. The fabric covering the wall behind him is like the corresponding fabric at the left, but here the displayed eagles face left rather than right.

On the third and uppermost level of this facade two rooms flank the one in the center. They are constructed like it with flying buttresses at the sides. In the left bay only parts of the head, the pointed cap, and the left hand of a male figure have survived. The hanging behind him

shows a repeating lyre-shaped motif. In the right bay stands a warrior wearing a houppelande, a belt with a large round buckle slung over his right shoulder, and a pointed hat tied with a scarf. The wall behind him is covered with a fabric showing a repeat pattern of floriated Greek crosses.

A wide band of dark fabric runs along the left edge of 2d. The right-hand third of its width is an integral part of the adjacent fabric. The rest was pieced together from at least three fragments. Since parts of the pattern match up along the edges of most of these fragments we conclude that this band was reassembled correctly. It shows small trees and flowers at the bottom and a bird and two butterflies in flight higher up, all against a dark blue sky. The wings of the lower butterfly have a pattern that resembles a blazon but probably is not one.[6] It shows white rings with blue centers on a red ground and what appears to be a fess enhanced paly of six or and azure (see detail). However the pattern on the insect above may have heraldic significance (see detail). The body is blazoned bendy of six or and azure, from chief sinister to base dexter, and the antennae and tail are or. This butterfly has two pairs of wings. The upper ones show what appears to be a field of ermine but the tinctures are unclear because the motif is so faded. The lower wings

show a field paly of eight, gules and azure. As noted above, what may be ermine-patterned butterfly wings also appear along the right edge of the *Hebrew Worthies*; but since in their present condition they seem to have fields not of white but of pale yellow and pink, the patterns may not have been intended to represent heraldic ermine. If the patterns on two or three of these sets of butterfly wings do in fact function as blazons they are blazons we have not yet identified. Should they be identified, they could help significantly in the search for the name of the person or persons who commissioned the tapestries (see Manufacture and Date). If the fabric showing the insect with the body patterned bendy or and azure was unwittingly reversed during reconstruction, so that the back now appears as the face, the blazon on the upper butterfly's body would match that on the banner flying second from the right at the top of the *Hebrew Worthies*. It may represent the blazon of the first ducal house of Burgundy (see note 5).

The facade of 2d resembles the facade of the building in the King Arthur piece in almost every detail except that it is not open to the sky behind and between the rooms on the uppermost story. Instead a solid masonry wall rises behind those rooms, true also in the Caesar piece (2e) whose architectural setting matches that for

Hector except that the spandrels of the arches above Caesar are carved with a radial pattern composed of three leaves or feathers. If they are in fact feathers they may refer to the double-headed displayed eagle blazoned on Caesar's shield.

The emperor, wearing a mantle over his armor and a closed crown, is seated in the large central room. His throne has a gabled back and stiles that terminate at the top in crocketed spires. He holds a falchion upright in his right hand and rests his left hand in a fold of the mantle. His shield, blazoned with his coat of arms (or an eagle with two heads displayed sable), hangs on a belt tied just below the tip of a spear that rests against the back of the throne.

In the room directly above Caesar, which, like the central upper room in the Hector piece, has flying buttresses at either side, stands a woman dressed in a low-necked houppelande trimmed with a wide ermine collar. On her head she wears a windswept veil secured with a jeweled fillet. The features and costume of this woman, as well as the features and garments of most of the men standing in the rooms at the sides on this level and below, all have a decidedly oriental cast. In the lowest of the three rooms at the left a bearded man wearing a short houppelande over hose, boots with long turned-up toes, and a horn at his waist, dances to the sound of the tambourine he is playing. In the room opposite him a man wearing the same kind of clothes and a hood as well dashes toward the left (see detail). He carries a handful of long darts and a round shield. There is a sword on his left hip. The circular object that hangs from the back of his girdle is decorated with three red balls nestling in an upturned red crescent on a yellow ground, all within a green border. The balls and crescent appear again as design elements in the border pattern of this warrior's shield. At first glance this appears to be an armorial motif; but since it is the same one that appears again with different tinctures (blue charges on a white field) on the standard carried by the prancing figure in the lower right-central section of the *Hebrew Worthies,* it cannot be that strictly speaking. It may be an emblem intended to suggest that these figures are orientals, perhaps Turks.

In the right-hand room on the second level of this facade, a man wearing a hooded and girdled robe and a pointed hat with an upturned brim draws a bow across the strings of a fiddle. Opposite him a hatless man with a longer beard and a houppelande buttoned down the front holds a standing shield in his left hand and turns his head to look sharply upward and to the right. Both of these figures are visible only from the waist upward, as are the two above them. The dark-skinned man standing

Detail of 2e

in the room on the third story at the left is younger than most of the others and beardless. He wears a turban and a houppelande buttoned down the front, and he plays a harp. The bearded man on the third story at the right is also dressed in a houppelande with a belt across one shoulder. He has a cap with a drooping point at the top. In his right hand he holds a ball or tidbit which he offers to the small greyhound-like dog cradled in his right arm.

Most of the dark fabrics hanging behind these figures show repeat patterns of small stylized plant forms or stars. The hanging at the back of Caesar's room is decorated with double-headed eagles displayed. The back wall of the room on the middle story at the left is unpatterned. Outside the building, at the far right, is a passage of dark sky against which appears a bit of foliage.

The corner buttress that rises at the left side of the building in the Hector piece seems to be represented on an integral part of the adjacent fabric, and the same is true of the buttress that rises along the right side of the building in the Caesar hanging. Therefore we can assume that these were the left and right ends of the building in the original hanging. However it seems that the figures of Hector and Caesar, neither of which is represented on an integral part of the adjacent fabrics, are not in their original positions. The spandrels of the arches in the lowest side rooms in the Hector piece contain the triple feather or leaf motif that appears above the figure of Caesar and not the lion-mask that accompanies Hector. This suggests that the restorers placed the figure of Hector, and the arches above him that are part of the same fabric, in the place that Caesar and his setting should occupy. The fact that Hector's throne is drawn in perspective to be seen directly from the front and Caesar's to be viewed from the right seems to confirm our suggestion. In other words, and in our opinion, the original tapestry showed Caesar at the left end of the facade, accompanied by the armored warriors, even though this would place him so that he faced away from, rather than toward, the other two Pagan Worthies. Hector appeared in the room at the center, flanked by figures that have not survived. Therefore the oriental figures that now flank Caesar would have accompanied the missing figure of Alexander at the right end of the facade. To give Alexander oriental attendants makes sense iconographically, and it makes equally good sense to give Caesar western attendants. As for the oriental figures who occupy the upper story of the Caesar hanging as it was reconstructed, we believe that they were correctly placed in relation to the four attendants below since they are all figures of the same type. However the left half of the flying buttress at the left of the central room at the top appears to be missing, which might indicate that there is an error in the reconstruction in this part of the hanging. As for the figures in the uppermost story of the Hector piece as reconstructed, we see no way of determining whether they are or are not in their original positions.

Subject

In publishing 2a, Ackerman (1922–23, 48) did not hesitate to identify King Arthur as one of the Worthies, and Hunter (1926, 39–40), Göbel (1928, vol. 1, 15), and Marillier (1932, 14) agreed that 2a probably did belong to a set dealing with these famous men. When Rorimer associated this hanging with fragments from a complete set of tapestries of the *Worthies* that Joseph Brummer brought to New York in 1936, he proved Ackerman right. The pieces were consistently referred to in the literature after that time as a cycle celebrating the *Nine Heroes* or *Worthies.*[7]

The theme of the Worthies as a class of wise, good, and valiant men derives from some unknown thirteenth-century source. In the form of the *Nine Worthies* it appears first in a romance entitled *Les Voeux du Paon* (The Peacock's Vows) written by the poet Jacques de

Longuyon about 1312 at the behest of Thibaut de Bar, the bishop of Liège. Somewhat later Guillaume de Machaut resumed the theme in his poem *La Prise d'Alexandrie.* Later still Eustache Deschamps used it in his ballads, and it is thought that it was he who introduced the idea of establishing a group of female Worthies to complement the men.[8]

The subject involves nine men who were regarded in the Middle Ages as embodiments of wisdom and chivalric heroism. Three represent the Pagan Law (Hector of Troy, Alexander, and Julius Caesar), three the Hebrew Law (Joshua, David, and Judas Maccabeus), and three the Christian Law (Arthur, Charlemagne, and Godefroy de Bouillon). Marillier (1932, 14) noted that Frederick I, Holy Roman Emperor, or Guy de Lusignan, king of Jerusalem and Cyprus, both twelfth-century figures, or Bertrand du Guesclin, champion of France against the English during the late fourteenth century, sometimes appeared among the Christian Worthies, and also that Shakespeare named Pompey and Hercules among the Pagan Worthies. Because the female Worthies must count as examples of courage and devotion also, usually with military achievements to their credit, they were drawn primarily from the ranks of the Amazons. We have a pictorial representation of both the male and female Worthies that is approximately contemporary with the Metropolitan Museum's tapestries. A miniature painting of the nine Worthies appears on the obverse and the nine female Worthies on the reverse of a page in a unique manuscript of the allegorical novel *Le chevalier errant* written by Tommaso di Saluzzo of Piedmont at the end of the fourteenth century.[9] The female Worthies' names (spelled in a variety of ways but listed here according to the inscriptions in the Saluzzo manuscript) are as follows: Deyphille, Synoppe, Yppollitte, Menalyppe, Semiramis, Lampheto, Thamaris, Theuca, and Penthezillee.

All the Worthies, both male and female, were assigned coats of arms. These varied from one representation to another.[10] The coats of arms shown in the tapestries on the shields associated with Joshua, David, and Caesar correspond to those characteristically assigned to each man. In some instances the field of King Arthur's shield is red (gules) rather than blue (azure) as it is here.[11] The major confusion involves the arms of Hector and Alexander. Rorimer and Freeman (1948–49, 246, 251) identified the Worthy in 2d as Alexander, and subsequent writers followed suit until Souchal (in Paris 1973, 39–40, 43) pointed out that de Vaivre had proved these to be Hector's arms. However it should be noted that according to the blazon Souchal quotes from an unpublished lecture by de Vaivre, and also in the blazon shown on

Hector's shield in the Saluzzo manuscript, the seated lion carries a halberd rather than a sword as he does in the tapestry. In the early fifteenth-century murals at the Castello della Manta in Piedmont, Alexander's shield is blazoned with a lion sitting on a chair and holding a halberd; Hector's shield shows a leopard sitting on a stool and holding a sword.[12] Plotzek (1978–80, vol. 3, 120) referred to the figure in the tapestry as either Alexander or Hector. We believe that the figure in the tapestry represents Hector.

The attendant figures at the sides and tops of each of the four hangings have excited the curiosity of only a few writers. Rorimer (1933, 48) suggested that the figures in the Arthur piece—and at that time 2b, which was still attached to its left side, was thought to be part of this hanging—represented the king's ecclesiastical and noble advisers. Later, he and Freeman (1948–49, 251) noted that the figures do not appear in any literary account of the Worthies and suggested that the designer of these tapestries had invented them. In his review of their publication, Adam (1949, 76) said that until someone else resolved the question he was inclined to identify the ladies standing on the upper level of the building in the *Hebrew Worthies* as royal princesses and among them (presumably the one standing next to the banner bearing what may be the arms of the first ducal house of Burgundy) Philippe VI's wife Jeanne de Bourgogne. We cannot agree with this interpretation since it seems unlikely that any designer would have represented ladies of that station in such subordinate parts of the composition and also since figures like these appear as stock attendants in the arts of miniature painting and stained glass during the fourteenth century (see below). Stucky-Schürer (1972, 64) saw many of these figures as reminders of the drolleries that appear in mid-fourteenth-century miniatures. Wyss (1957, 78–79) believed that the male warriors and musicians represent the men who accompanied the Worthies to war. He also thought that while the ladies in the upper level of the *Hebrew Worthies* could not be identified by the musical instruments and animals they hold, nevertheless the five wearing crowns could be related to the five Amazon queens among the female Worthies—that is, Semiramis, Synoppe, Lampheto, Thamaris, and Penthesilea. Plotzek (1978–80, vol. 3, 120) suggested that the nine women in the upper rooms were in fact the nine female Worthies.

Figures like these, both the warriors and the musicians, of both sexes, frequently appear in comparable positions in fourteenth-century manuscripts and stained-glass windows. For example, literally dozens of the illustrations in the *Romance of Alexander* in the Bodleian Library in Oxford, illustrations that were completed in 1344, show similar small figures standing in side rooms or at the top of buildings inside which the main scenes of the story are being enacted.[13] Folio 101v shows a building that has five polygonal rooms carried on corbels along the top. Through the arched windows in each room an armored warrior is visible from the thighs upward; four of the men hold shields and spears while the fifth, in the center, fits an arrow to his bow. Four female musicians, playing on horns or drums, stand on the roof between the rooms; they are visible from the knees upward. Folio 51v shows a similar building with polygonal rooms, turrets, battlemented walls, and conical towers flying square banners. Six female musicians, visible only from the knees up, stand on the roof. They play horns, an organ, a rebec, a psaltery, and a hurdy-gurdy. In a late fourteenth-century manuscript of the *Bible historiale* that had belonged to Jean, duc de Berry, and is now in the Walters Art Gallery, Baltimore, the Judas Maccabeus page shows a tripartite structure whose general format is rather like that in the King Arthur, Hector, or Caesar hangings.[14] Judas stands in the central bay of a building behind a battlemented parapet; at each side there are towers with gabled, round-headed arches giving on to smaller rooms in which stand the figures of armored warriors holding shields and swords or maces. Both here and in the Bodleian's *Romance of Alexander* these subordinate figures appear to be supernumeraries (military guards and warriors, court entertainers, or retainers) whose function seems to be simply to modify the character of the main figures they attend.

The same is true of the comparable figures who appear frequently in fourteenth-century stained-glass windows. Among these may be cited the choir windows of Saints Thomas Becket and Eloi in the abbey church of Saint-Ouen in Rouen where musical angels, an apostle, a magus, a prophet, and an archbishop stand in the rooms above and beside those in which scenes from the stories of these saints are represented. Attendants like these also appear in other choir windows here which, though much restored, still show their original formats of about 1318 to 1339.[15] Panels in the windows of Saint Michel show numbers of figures in niches that occupied several levels of a Gothic facade, figures representing falconers among whom is a young lady playing with a hawk.[16] Perrot thought it exceptional for these secular figures to appear among the others in these windows, all of whom in one way or another have some religious significance. She related them to the figure of a male falconer who appears in a representation of the Ages of Man in one of the Saint Matthieu windows in this church.[17]

The lowercase letters decorating the oval motifs in the background of the central room at the top of the Hector piece (2d) have been the subject of some controversy. Rorimer and Freeman (1948–49, 252) read them as *u* and *y* and suggested that the *u* could be the initial of the mysterious lady associated with Berry's emblem showing a bear and a swan (*ours-cygne*, thus "Ursine" according to one interpretation) or at least with the *V* (or *U?*) in his secret cipher, or the *u* that appears as a repeating motif on the liveries of the duke's attendants in the January and May pages of the *Très Riches Heures* in the Musée Condé, Chantilly (see fig. 26, for January). As for the *y* they suggested that this letter, which also occurs as a decorative motif on hangings represented in the first, fourth, and fifth pieces of the *Apocalypse* tapestries in Angers, may refer to Ysabeau de Bavière, wife of Charles VI, or perhaps instead, taken as an alternate for the letter *j*, the initial of the Christian name of both of Berry's wives (Jeanne d'Armagnac and Jeanne de Boulogne).[18] Rorimer and Freeman did not claim that their interpretations were necessarily correct but concluded that the two letters had some special meaning, perhaps a secret meaning, for the owner of the tapestries. Most later writers who studied both the *Apocalypse* tapestries and the Metropolitan Museum's *Worthies* rejected these interpretations. Some offered other explanations. De Vaivre's study of the heraldry and emblems in the *Apocalypse* summarized Planchenault's interpretations of the *y*.[19] Planchenault did not believe the *y* was a personal device. He considered and rejected the idea that it referred to Yolanda de Aragón, wife of Louis II d'Anjou, who was born in 1381, the year after we believe the tapestries were completed. He then went on to consider other possibilities including the notion that the *y* read as an *i* might stand for Saint Jean or Jean (also Hennequin) de Bruges, court painter to Charles V and designer of the *Apocalypse* tapestries, or that the letter in its original form might represent the Trinity or Pythagoras's image of the bivium, the crossroad of virtue and vice. De Vaivre (1983, 104–13) proposed another explanation of the letter, one derived from a representation of it associated with a harrow. According to his interpretation, to cultivated Frenchmen of the period the *y* was a symbol of Life. Because of that it was associated with Pythagoras's concept of the bivium, the stem of the *Y* representing childhood and the fork representing the age of reason when life seems split into two paths, one of them the way of virtue, the other that of vice. De Vaivre's interpretation seems to be the correct one in reference to the *Apocalypse* pieces, and it may also apply to the *y* in the Metropolitan Museum's tapestry where, as he pointed out (1983, 113 n. 54), it appears in the center of a rooting seed as it does in some of the pieces in Angers. However, since it seems that the letters *a*, *n*, and *u* also appear in these "seeds," we may ask whether the *y* has some other meaning here. Adam (1949, 76) noted that pending an examination of the hanging itself, which apparently he had not seen, he thought one might find the name *Anjou* in these letters. Van Ysselsteyn (1969, 100) accepted the *y* as a symbol of the bivium and because of it suggested that the woman standing in front of the hanging where it appears at the top of 2d is in fact a symbol of Wisdom. What seems at first glance to be a lowercase letter *y* reversed, used again as an ornamental motif on a hanging at the back of a room, appears in one of the two somewhat later *Passion of Christ* tapestries in La Seo in Saragossa. It decorates the fabric hanging in the background of the scene showing Pilate washing his hands.[20] However the letter is most likely a *p* instead and may refer to Pilate.

SOURCE OF THE DESIGN

Ackerman (1922–23, 48) maintained that because the King Arthur piece was so close in style to the Angers *Apocalypse* it was almost certainly designed by the same hand and produced at the same time on the same looms. None of the specialists who wrote after her considered the question of a designer as such until Rorimer (1947–48, 98) observed that no information concerning a designer had yet been found. All earlier writers, believing that a merchant-weaver or local "school" could determine the character of a tapestry design, were content to say that the Metropolitan Museum's tapestries had been woven either in Nicolas Bataille's shop or a shop associated with him. Göbel (1928, vol. 1, 14) went only so far as to say that the piece had come from a shop in Paris.

Rorimer and Freeman (1948–49, 254–59) addressed the question of the designer's identity as directly as Ackerman had done. They called attention to what they regarded as technical and formal considerations relating these tapestries to the *Apocalypse* hangings in Angers; and then because they were convinced that the *Worthies* had been woven for Jean, duc de Berry (see Manufacture and Date), they concentrated on the stylistic similarities that link the *Worthies* to certain works of art that were either made for the duc de Berry or belonged to him. These included the sculptured figures and stained-glass windows commissioned for the duke's palace at Bourges (Rorimer and Freeman 1948–49, 256, illus.) and a number of manuscripts he owned. They called attention particularly to the duke's *Psalter* (Bibliothèque

Nationale, Paris, MS fr. 13091), which contains twenty-four figures of prophets and apostles (Rorimer and Freeman 1948–49, 256, two illus.); his *Petites Heures* (Bibliothèque Nationale, MS lat. 18014; Rorimer and Freeman 1948–49, 255, illus.), which contains an Annunciation page showing the figures in a generically similar architectural setting; and the Albumasar astrological treatises (Pierpont Morgan Library, New York, MS M.785; Rorimer and Freeman 1948–49, 258–59, illus.), which shows some similar figures. Ultimately they rejected the idea that any of the painters who produced these miniatures—among them possibly André Beauneveu and Jacquemart de Hesdins—could have designed the tapestries of the Worthies. They also considered and rejected the possibility that Hennequin de Bruges (also known as Jean Bandol, Jean de Bondolf), who designed the *Apocalypse* for Berry's brother Louis I d'Anjou, designed the *Worthies* because they considered the style of the drawing to be too different. They concluded (1948–49, 259) that the tapestry designer was "a Flemish master, perhaps from Bruges, working in France under the influence of Beauneveu." Presumably they specified Bruges because the Albumasar astrological treatises were illuminated in a shop near Bruges. Later writers followed the lead of Rorimer and Freeman, discussing the tapestry designs in terms of the works of art associated with the duc de Berry that they had identified. Only two of these scholars offered slightly variant opinions. Meiss (1967, 59) suggested that the designs derived from late fourteenth-century French court painting as it was practiced in the borderland of France and the southern Netherlands. Sterling (1987, 202) believed that the tapestries were designed by a Flemish painter.

Freeman (1955–56), in an article about the duc de Berry's *Belles Heures*, gave a reverse twist to the earlier theories concerning the design of the tapestries. She suggested that the now-missing figure of Charlemagne in the tapestries might have served as the model for the representation of Charlemagne in the manuscript. Later, Wieck made a similar suggestion; that is, that the lost section of the *Hebrew Worthies* tapestry in which the figure of Judas Maccabeus appeared flanked by attendant figures might have inspired the miniaturist who painted the Judas page in the first volume of Guiart des Moulins's *Bible historiale* now in the Walters Art Gallery, Baltimore, a manuscript that also belonged to Jean, duc de Berry.[21] In that illustration, which shows figures occupying arched spaces in a facade, Judas stands in the center behind a battlemented parapet. At either side appear two armored warriors standing behind parapets on two levels. As noted above (see Subject) details

like the architectural settings and the small figures in subsidiary spaces are to be found in other miniature paintings and in stained-glass windows. Similar motifs, more simply presented, also appear on seals.[22]

We believe that the style and composition of the Metropolitan Museum's tapestries have less to do with contemporary miniature paintings than with stained-glass windows, which they resemble in many ways, and that this similarity is not fortuitous. Since the main figures have been foreshortened, and since the attendant figures are smaller at the bottoms of the hangings than at the tops, it seems clear that the designer intended the tapestries to be seen from a low vantage point. In other words, it appears that they were meant to be installed, as most stained-glass windows were, high on the walls. (It is largely because they have been foreshortened that the Worthies look rather stubby and squat or, as Souchal [in Paris 1973, 42] described them, "représentés avec une certaine maladresse." It is also because of the shifts of scale, together with the extensive restoration and reconstruction to which the smaller figures have been subjected, that she could say they "ne s'intègrent pas toujours avec aisance dans leurs niches.") Furthermore, the slim red, blue, and green lines that rise above the gables in the *Pagan* and *Christian Worthies* represent panels of stained glass. The patterned grounds that appear behind the figures, some of them representing woven or embroidered silks and others simulating the "damask" patterns in contemporary windows, come directly from the vocabulary of stained-glass design. As already noted by Rorimer and Freeman (1948–49, 255) the yellow decorations on the gables, columns, crockets, and finials also derive from stained-glass design, but not the red contours, as these writers implied. The yellow accents imitate the silver stain passages in contemporary and earlier stained glass. The architectural enframements themselves appear over and over again in European windows dating from the thirteenth to sixteenth centuries. As early as 1878, in the first published notice we have of any one of the Metropolitan Museum's *Worthies* hangings, Giraud noted that the King Arthur piece looked like a stained-glass window and suggested that it was probably woven after a cartoon for one.

Therefore we agree with Rorimer and Freeman (1948–49, 255–58), who compared the tapestry designs to the stained-glass windows from the Sainte-Chapelle in the duc de Berry's palace at Bourges and to the windows in the Trousseau and Aligret chapels of the cathedral there (see Manufacture and Date) as well as to certain stylistically related pieces of sculpture in the palace. However we cannot agree with their claim that these windows are quite different from others designed in the International Style or that the tapestry designer was somehow associated with the windows at Bourges. Furthermore we know that the windows from the Sainte-Chapelle illustrated by Rorimer and Freeman (1948–49, 256, 257) were reconstructed when they were installed in the crypt of the cathedral in the nineteenth century. It was then that the figures were placed in their present architectural settings, settings which indicate that the figures must have appeared originally on two or more levels and not just the one they now occupy.[23] It is true that these window fragments contain facial and figure types related to those in the tapestries, but we regard these as elements in the pictorial style of a particular period and place rather than the style of a particular hand. The faces in the tapestries were certainly not drawn by the artist or artists who created the stained glass and stone faces at Bourges nor those of the prophets in the duke's *Psalter* to which they are often compared.[24]

The overall format used by the tapestry designer for the *Pagan* and *Christian Worthies*, with figures on several levels in small rectangular or polygonal rooms opening out from a Gothic facade whose gables and spires soar upward, may be found not only in the windows at Bourges but also in windows made in other parts of France as well as in England, Germany, and the Netherlands in the fourteenth and fifteenth centuries. At first glance it would appear that the designer did not use the same kind of composition for the *Hebrew Worthies*; but beyond the superficially Norman details of the building and the greater freedom of movement of the fourteen figures occupying the upper story, we see essentially the same composition. There is a precedent for this kind of variation in the choir windows of the abbey church of Saint-Ouen in Rouen (mentioned above under Subject).[25] These windows show structures and figures that in their general form recall those in the Metropolitan Museum's tapestries. However since the windows date between 1318 and 1339 (see note 15), the style of the figures and compositions is naturally quite different. Allowing for these differences, and allowing also for the fact that both the tapestries and the windows have been heavily restored, one is struck by the similarity of concept that relates one set of works to the other. For example, the central lancets of the Saint Nicaise windows show scenes from the saint's life in spaces surmounted by triple-lobed arches on the lowest of three levels of a soaring facade that features gables, buttresses, and spires. Other figures appear in smaller arched niches set on two upper levels. Musical angels stand facing inward in the eight small niches flanking

the spaces on the first and second stories; some of them play instruments, others are singing. In these windows, now restored, only some of these figures are original.[26] The Saints Eloi and Thomas Becket windows are similar. The small flanking figures are present in all but the two central lancets. In some of the windows there are figures on the second and/or third stories as well. Among the figures that flank the scenes in the first story —figures corresponding to the ones in the two first levels of the buildings in the tapestries—are an apostle in the first window, a magus and two angels playing instruments in the second, two bishops and the Gabriel and Mary of an Annunciation in the fifth, and a prophet and an archbishop in the sixth.[27] There are also windows like these devoted to Saint Etienne. The central pair shows towers with two stories rather than three. The rooms in the upper stories are remarkably like those in the King Arthur tapestry (2a). The four end windows show pairs of musical angels standing on balconies under the trilobate arch of the main gable. They recall the figures standing on the balcony in the *Hebrew Worthies*.[28]

Although the windows at Saint-Ouen and the miniatures in the *Romance of Alexander* (see note 13) were made much earlier than the Metropolitan Museum's *Worthies* tapestries, they serve to demonstrate that the tapestry designer was thoroughly familiar with characteristic modes of design in the arts of both manuscript illustration and stained-glass windows but particularly the latter. As Helbig has shown,[29] numbers of Netherlandish painter-glassworkers were active in France at this time in the courts of the king, the duc de Berry, and the duc de Bourgogne. They came from Ghent, Mechelen, and Bruges, undoubtedly bringing pattern books with them. It seems reasonable to suggest that it was one of these men who either designed the *Worthies* or influenced their design. Although the compositions have a powerful decorative impact and the heads of the Worthies have great character, neither the drawing nor the quality of the designs as a whole shows the elegant sophistication one would expect of a French court painter at this time. The tapestries show a more robust style that belongs to some designer working at a distance from Paris, perhaps in the southern Netherlands as Rorimer and Freeman (1948–49, 259), Meiss (1967, 59), and Sterling (1987, 202) have already suggested. The fact that the designer represented costumes whose fashions span a period of almost twenty years (see Manufacture and Date) also suggests that he was working in a relatively provincial context.

The artist or shop that executed the tapestry cartoons —and it could have been the designer himself—repeated certain figures in different parts of the compositions. Joubert has shown that the cartoonists did this in the *Apocalypse* tapestries at Angers.[30] In 2a–i such repetitions appear a number of times. Two of the three cardinals among the fragments in 2g (not used in the reconstruction) were woven after the cartoon that served for the cardinal who now stands at the right end of the uppermost level in the King Arthur piece, but the design appears in reverse. The cardinals standing at the center and left end of the same hanging were woven after one and the same cartoon but not the one that served for the other cardinals. The upper part of the bishop in 2i repeats the corresponding part of the seated bishop in the lower right corner of the Arthur hanging, again in reverse. The man playing a tambourine in the lower left corner of the Caesar piece was woven, with minor changes, after the cartoon that also served for the standard-bearer (2h) to the lower right of David in the *Hebrew Worthies.*

MANUFACTURE AND DATE

There is some confusion in Rorimer's suggestions concerning the date and place of production. At first (1933, 48; 1947–48, 93) he, like every writer before him except Giraud, who attributed the King Arthur piece to Aubusson without giving his reasons, believed that the *Worthies* had been produced in the same shop as the *Apocalypse,* or a shop working under the same supervision by weavers trained in the same way—in other words a shop operated or influenced by Nicolas Bataille. Later, after Rorimer reconstructed the four hangings, he and Freeman became convinced that the tapestries had been woven for the duc de Berry (1948–49, 251–52). At that point they vacillated on the question of origin. They marshaled what they regarded as evidence that Bataille had produced the tapestries, but at the same time they suggested (254–55) that the tapestries might have been woven in the duke's palace in Bourges, perhaps by weavers called from Paris (see below). The two ideas are mutually exclusive. If a leading entrepreneur like Nicolas Bataille were going to produce this relatively modest set of tapestries, he would have no reason to set up a weaving shop in a client's palace. He would certainly have used one of the established shops that he already controlled or patronized in some weaving center we cannot yet identify.

Before examining this question further it is important to ask how likely or unlikely it is that, as Rorimer and Freeman suggested, the duc de Berry commissioned the complete hangings from which 2a–i came or received them as a gift. To support their position, Rorimer and

Freeman cited the presence of the duc de Berry's coat of arms on ten of the fourteen small banners flying near the top of the *Hebrew Worthies* and also (they thought) on the bosses of the vaults above the heads of Joshua and David in that hanging. However these bosses do not show his arms but what appear to be those of his brother Louis I, duc d'Anjou. They also interpreted the letters *u* and *y* that decorate the back wall of the room above Hector's head in 2d as emblems relating to Jean de Berry (concerning these letters, see Subject). They called attention to the three tapestries of the female Worthies in Charles VI's inventory that showed the duc de Berry's coat of arms together with compositions related to the ones in 2a–i (see Related Tapestries). Finally, Rorimer and Freeman (1948–49, 254–55) referred to a document which they thought might indicate, but not prove, that these tapestries were woven at Bourges. The reference concerns a payment made in 1385 to Jehan le Prestre for reroofing the great hall of the duc de Berry's palace in Bourges "ou l'on faisait actuellement sa tapisserie, en même temps que l'on y taillait les pierres pour l'appareil dudit palais" (where they were now making his tapestry at the same time they were cutting stones there for the adorning of the said palace).[31] Rorimer and Freeman understood the word *tapisserie* to mean "tapestry" in one of its modern senses: that is, a tapestry-woven wall hanging. However, as Salet has shown conclusively, in the Middle Ages the word *tapisserie* could refer not only to this kind of tapestry but also to a variety of furnishing fabrics including ensembles of embroidered and woven ones of various kinds and even leather hangings.[32] Furthermore, it is unlikely that tapestry weavers would have been working in a room where stonecutters were raising clouds of dust and making a great deal of noise. On the evidence of this document alone we see no grounds for claiming that any tapestry-woven wall hangings were being produced in the palace, whether these or any others.

Rorimer and Freeman acknowledged (1948–49, 252) that the Metropolitan Museum's tapestries could not be identified with the tapestry ("tappis") of the nine Worthies (which they described as a "set" of tapestries) that appears in the duke's posthumous inventory of 1416 because it contained metallic yarns and 2a–i do not, even though it had dimensions similar to those of the three original hangings from which 2a–i came.[33] While the two authors observed that compilers of inventories sometimes made errors (thereby implying they thought the tapestries of which 2a–i are fragments might have been in the duke's possession when the inventory was taken but overlooked or described incorrectly), they suggested that 2a–i might have been missing from this inventory because the duke had already given them to a relative as a wedding or New Year's Day present. Van Ysselsteyn (1969, 38–39) had a different suggestion: the tapestries were not in the duke's inventory because they were not finished at the time of his death in 1416. It is conceivable that the tapestries were still on the looms at that time, but since we cannot be sure that they were intended for Jean de Berry it is futile to argue the point.

Having stated in his earliest published study of 2a–i that the coats of arms represented in the tapestries were those of the duc de Berry (1933), Rorimer later (with Freeman, 1948–49, 253) acknowledged that the arms of France and of Burgundy (corrected in 1953, 17, to "old" Burgundy) were also represented in the banners that fly at the top of the *Hebrew Worthies*. However he did not attempt to explain their presence. He simply observed that the royal arms may or may not have significance here and that the Burgundian arms had led him to search the accounts of the dukes of Burgundy for possible references to the tapestries. It was at this point that he missed the chance to develop new ideas about the origin of the tapestries and pursue them to some conclusion that would free him from the need to associate their early history exclusively with Berry.

Rorimer and Freeman (1948–49, 244) noted that tapestries of the *Neuf Preux*, and in some cases also the related subject of the female Worthies, belonged not only to Philippe le Hardi and the duc de Berry but also to the kings Charles V and Charles VI, to Louis I, duc d'Anjou, and to the comte de Hainaut.[34]

Philippe le Hardi owned one, two, or three tapestries of the *Preux* and *Preuses* containing metallic yarns (see note 1). Two tapestries of the nine Worthies appear in Charles V's inventory of 1379–80.[35] These may be the two tapestries that appear in his son Charles VI's expense accounts of 1389, when Jean de Jaudoigne was summoned to repair, among other hangings, "deux tapis de salle aux Neuf Preux" (two hall tapestries of the Nine Worthies).[36]

As Rorimer and Freeman (1948–49, 244) noted, Louis I d'Anjou owned a tapestry of the nine Worthies. However neither they nor other writers who have discussed this matter called attention to the fact that among the tapestries listed in this duke's inventory of 1364 there was also a tapestry showing only the three Christian Worthies. The first is described as "un tapis des IX preuz, contenant xviij alnes" (a tapestry of the nine Worthies, containing eighteen aunes), and the other as "un tapis de Charlemaine, du Roy Artus et de Godefroy de Billon, contenant vj alnes" (a tapestry of Charlemagne, King Arthur and Godefroy de Bouillon, containing six

aunes).[37] The latter is the only one among the several *Worthies* tapestries cited in these princely accounts that showed three rather than nine Worthies in one piece. Although it was described as being much smaller—only six square aunes, or about ten square yards—than any of the other pieces, there is nothing in the inventory to indicate that this piece was a fragment of a larger hanging. Furthermore since it showed the three Christian Worthies specifically and not a combination of men representing two different Laws, as it might have done had it been cut out of a larger hanging showing all nine figures, we are inclined to believe that it was one of a set of three hangings which together showed the nine Worthies. If that is so, then this inventory entry serves to indicate that such sets of tapestries, the kind from which 2a–i came, had been produced before 1364.

The documents cited above do not indicate in every instance what materials were used in the hangings; but where such records exist they specify the presence of metallic yarns along with the wool. The only tapestry that was described as containing wool (and therefore presumably no other fibers) was one of the three hangings of the *Preuses* which appeared in Charles VI's inventory of 1422 and again ten years later when the king's tapestries were disposed of (see Related Tapestries). This piece was referred to in 1432 as "ung tappiz de laine," and it was appraised at 16 livres 4 sous. The other two pieces in that set were valued at 8 livres 8 sous (with three figures of female Worthies) and 12 livres 16 sous (four figures).[38] The last two pieces were probably appraised for less than the first because, according to the descriptions, they were old and worn and furthermore, as Souchal (in Paris 1973, 42) and we conjecture (see Related Tapestries), they may have lost some fabric along the top. Even so, it seems certain that they would have been appraised at higher figures than the woolen piece if they had contained gilt and/or silver yarns. It is important to note here that the tapestries owned by great medieval patrons were not exclusively woven with silk and metallic yarns, in combination with wool. Except for the few metallic yarns used in some of the flowers in the fourth hanging of the *Apocalypse* cycle in Angers, those tapestries, produced for Louis I d'Anjou, were woven only of wool. King has pointed out that the *Apocalypse* tapestries (seemingly woven after the same cartoons) owned by Philippe le Hardi and Jean de Berry also contained only wool yarns.[39]

The documents cited here demonstrate that a number of princes owned tapestries of the male and female Worthies during the second half of the fourteenth century and that at least some of these hangings were woven of wool, without gilt and silver yarns. Since the

Hebrew Worthies shows the arms of either Charles V or VI, and also what appear to be the arms of Louis d'Anjou and a form of the arms of the first ducal house of Burgundy as well as the arms of the duc de Berry, it seems possible that any one of those Valois princes or several of them together might have commissioned these tapestries. There were at least two occasions we know of when this might have been done, and there must have been others also. Charles V's brothers assumed the regency after his death in 1380, during the minority of Charles VI. Later, after the new king became ill for the first time in 1392, Jean de Berry and Philippe le Hardi took power again, Louis d'Anjou having died in 1384. Although we believe that the tapestries were woven later than that, it seems possible that the four coats of arms in the *Hebrew Worthies* might have been placed there to celebrate a coalition of Valois power in a France that was in turmoil. Perhaps it was for this reason that what appear to be Anjou's arms were blazoned on the vault bosses below rather than among the banners flying above: the duc d'Anjou was dead when the tapestries were designed. In this connection it seems significant that the arms of Louis, duc d'Orléans, brother of Charles VI, who joined the fight to control the throne but against Burgundy, are not present. However, if this interpretation is valid, it fails to explain why the duc de Berry's arms far outnumber all the others at the top of the tapestry—ten banners for him, three for the king, and one representing what appears to be a form of the arms of Burgundy ancient rather than the arms that Philippe le Hardi used at this time.

Although we have found some grounds for associating the tapestries specifically with Jean de Berry, as Rorimer and Freeman had done at the outset, and also some reason for thinking that he together with one or more of his brothers might have commissioned them, it is important also to consider the possibility that someone outside the royal family who wished to pay homage to the Valois princes commissioned the tapestries from which 2a–i come—someone who wished to celebrate that family or to acknowledge Berry's (or all the princes') suzerainty over himself or the territory in which he lived and perhaps also to acknowledge some instance of patronage. We can cite such an example of homage in the pattern of stained-glass windows in some of the chapels in the cathedral of Bourges, monuments that Rorimer and Freeman (1948–49, 255, 258) referred to in their study of the design influences in 2a–i. In the chapel that Pierre Trousseau founded and had constructed about 1404–6 the lunette at the top of the window contains the arms of the papacy, the arms of the antipopes Clement VII, under whom Trousseau entered the clergy, and Ben-

edict XIII, under whom he became a distinguished ecclesiastic. Below these appear the arms of the duc de Berry, lord of this region, at the left (heraldic dexter) and the royal arms of France at the right (sinister). Donor figures of Pierre Trousseau and his family, with their coats of arms, appear below the lunette in the main part of the window. A similar arrangement appears in the chapel of Simon Aligret (ca. 1405–6). There the arms of Berry occupy the same relative position and the arms of his second wife, Jeanne de Boulogne, comtesse d'Auvergne, appear at the right (sinister). The donor figures, with their coat of arms, appear in the windows below.[40]

If the coats of arms in the *Worthies* tapestries were disposed in the same way for the same or similar reasons, then it is important to consider the possibility that what appear to be heraldic designs on the butterfly wings at the left side of the Hector of Troy and the right side of the *Hebrew Worthies*—and it will require further research to determine whether or not they are heraldic —may be intended to represent the donor. It is also important to consider whether the person who commissioned the tapestries wished to express his regard for the duc de Berry in particular. The answers to these questions could help determine the date of the commission and the range of dates during which the tapestries could have been woven.

Rorimer did not pursue his study of the armorial motifs in the hangings to this point and therefore clung to his belief that the tapestries had been produced for the duc de Berry by Nicolas Bataille or in a shop under his supervision. The notion that the hangings were associated with Bataille and woven in Paris did not originate with Rorimer, who in his earlier studies had proposed that city as the place of origin. He was probably following Hunter who, in his catalogue entry for the exhibition of that piece in Cleveland in 1918, attributed it to Paris in the last quarter of the fourteenth century because of its supposed similarity to the *Apocalypse* in Angers. In his later publications Hunter repeated this opinion, which was shared by every subsequent writer except Coffinet (1971, 1977), Stucky-Schürer (1972), and Sterling (1987), who did not endorse the attribution to Paris.

Rorimer (1947–48, 93, 98) developed arguments involving both stylistic and technical considerations to support his theory that Nicolas Bataille had either woven or produced 2a–i. He observed that both 2a–i and the *Apocalypse* hangings show large figures seated in vaulted golden tan masonry buildings set off against blackish blue grounds and that both used palettes featuring red and blue. He noted that the manner of rendering the figures' hair and beards with slits and shading was the same in both sets of hangings and claimed that this, along with the use of "double" weft yarns (two strands, plied) were "technical peculiarities pointing to the Bataille workshop." Rorimer repeated most of these comparisons in the major study he published with Freeman (1948–49, 254) and added that the *Apocalypse* and the *Worthies* both show butterflies and foliage at the sides and that both were woven with twelve and a half warp yarns to the inch. Had he been writing again some thirty-six years later, when it was discovered that the *Apocalypse* tapestries were woven so that the back was finished as neatly as the front and were therefore effectively reversible, he would have been able to add that information. All of Rorimer's observations (except his remarks concerning the palette which are no longer acceptable now that the variety and brilliance of the colors on the back of the *Apocalypse* pieces have been revealed) are valid as far as they go. However enough new data have come to light since Rorimer's time to enable us to know that the technical "peculiarities" he identified with Bataille's workshop are not limited to the *Apocalypse* and the *Worthies* and furthermore that most of the stylistic similarities belong to the period and place. Although 2a–i share certain artistic and technical features with the *Apocalypse* tapestries, we have no reason to associate those features with any particular weaving center. We know that the duc d'Anjou's *Apocalypse* was produced through the agency of men who were active in Paris and Arras; but since so few records have survived we cannot be sure that entrepreneurs in other parts of France and the southern Netherlands were not producing similar tapestries.

Rorimer and Freeman (1948–49, 258–60) dated 2a–i about 1385 because they found stylistic similarities linking these hangings not only to the Angers *Apocalypse* tapestries (which they believed were still on the looms in 1384) but also to the duc de Berry's *Petites Heures,* his *Psalter,* and the Albumasar treatises (see Source of the Design), all of which they dated in the ninth and tenth decades of the fourteenth century. Most later writers followed Rorimer and Freeman in dating 2a–i about 1385. Others proposed a date generally in the last quarter of the fourteenth century. Among them only Ferrero Viale (1967), Coffinet (1977), and Sterling (1987) specifically wrote that they regarded 2a–i as having been designed later than the *Apocalypse.* Salet (1987) expressed the opinion that the date of 2a–i is uncertain but made no alternate suggestions.

Since the compositions in the *Worthies* are not narrative, the designer had little occasion to deal with the problems of organizing forms on the surface and in depth. All the forms have been placed close to the pic-

ture plane and parallel to it. Therefore, in considering the matter of style, we must depend primarily on the character of the drawing. The forms in the *Apocalypse* tapestries are drawn with sinuous curves and fillips that endow them with an ornamental value totally lacking in 2a–i except for a vague hint of it in the drapery that the main figures wear. The draperies in the Angers tapestries break into a system of small linear folds that have a kind of buoyant energy totally different from the monumental stillness the draperies in 2a–i show. The *Apocalypse* pieces reflect the mellifluous Paris court style of the first half of the fourteenth century. Although the drawing in the *Worthies* shows a residual hint of this style, particularly in the rendering of the main figures, it is modern and vigorous in a way that places the design of 2a–i in a period of transition from the earlier French court style to the direct realism of fifteenth-century Netherlandish painting, as Meiss (1967, 59) and Sterling (1987) have already suggested. Some of the differences we see between the two sets of hangings may fairly be attributed to the personal style of the designers. Beyond that it is clear that we are dealing with a matter of chronological development. In terms of style 2a–i are much closer to the surviving pieces of the *Story of Saints Piat and Eleuthère* in the cathedral in Tournai than they are to the *Apocalypse* hangings, and some of the facial types in the *Worthies* tapestries, particularly the faces of some of the men in the side towers and at the top of the *Hebrew Worthies,* are strikingly similar to some in these tapestries in Tournai.[41] We know that Hennequin de Bruges began to work on the *Apocalypse* designs for Louis d'Anjou before 1378. The *Story of Saints Piat and Eleuthère* tapestries originally contained an inscription, now lost, indicating that they were finished in December 1402. Therefore we suggest that the tapestries from which 2a–i came were designed no earlier than 1400 and, on the grounds of fashion in costume, possibly a bit later.

Three specialists in the art of painting at this period have suggested independently to the author that in terms of style the *Worthies* could not have been designed before 1390–1400.[42] Concerning the matter of fashion in costume, van Buren[43] made a preliminary study of the attendant figures' garments and concluded that the tapestries were probably designed at the beginning of the fifteenth century. She noted that some of the ladies on the balcony of the *Hebrew Worthies* wear the kind of houppelandes that were fashionable in Paris around 1390 and that others have the version of this garment that dates from approximately 1400. The short houppelande on the man at the far right end of the balcony was worn from about 1390 onward. The warrior standing in the lower right corner of the *Hebrew Worthies* has a long houppelande with wide sleeves that is roughly contemporary. Van Buren also called attention to the absence of long points on the shoes (pikes or poulaines) which in itself indicates a date during the first five years of the fifteenth century. Because the garments in 2a–i show a mixture of earlier and later fashions and also because some of the details differ from the corresponding ones that were to be found in Paris at this time, van Buren suggested that the designs were probably created in a provincial center rather than in Paris and between about 1400 and 1405. We endorse these suggestions and are prepared to extend the date to 1410 on the grounds of both van Buren's observations and our own, particularly in reference to the style of the men's hair and beards.[44]

RELATED TAPESTRIES

No other fragments of the set of hangings from which 2a–i came nor of any other set woven after the same cartoons are known to have survived. The tapestry showing King Arthur, Charlemagne, and Godefroy de Bouillon that appears in Louis I d'Anjou's inventory of 1364 (see note 37) and that we believe was one of three hangings which together showed the nine Worthies was much smaller than any of the pieces to which 2a–i belonged. It measured approximately 91 square feet (8.45 square meters) as compared with the minimum area of 336 square feet (31.21 square meters) that we calculate for each of the original *Worthies* tapestries. Unless we assume that the same patterns were scaled down by a factor of three and a half, which seems unlikely, we must conclude that the duke's tapestry was woven after a different set of cartoons.

The three tapestries of the *Preuses* or female Worthies owned by Charles VI are the only hangings of which we have any record that may have formed a companion cycle. Unfortunately the citations in the inventory of 1422 and the slightly different descriptions in the list of the king's tapestries that were distributed in 1432 do not include the dimensions. The largest piece—we assume it was larger than the other two because it contained four rather than three major figures—was described as follows in the documents of 1432, which are more detailed than the earlier inventory: "Item, ung tappiz bien vielz et usé, où il a plusieurs personnaiges de Roynes et autres Dames, nommées: Darphille, Argentine, sa seur, Synoppe et Ypolite, où il y a au-dessoubz desdiz personnaiges escripture et leurs nommes escrips au-dessus; en hault sont les armes de Berry emplusieurs ecussons . . ."

(Item, a very old and worn tapestry in which there are figures of queens and other ladies named Darphille, her sister Argentine, Synoppe and Ypolite, [and] where there is writing under the said figures and their names written above; up top are the arms of Berry on several shields). The compiler of the 1432 list apparently made an error in his notation concerning the placement of the inscription which in the earlier inventory clearly indicates that the names belong with the writing below the figures and not above, as follows: ". . . où il y a au-dessoubz desdits personnages escripture et leurs noms escripz, et au-dessus, en hault, sont les armes de Berry. . . ." The inventory of 1422, in which this tapestry is listed as number 151, suggests that the duke's coats of arms are shown apart from the shields ("au-dessus, en hault sont les armes de Berry—et plusieurs petiz ecussons") rather than, as the later text specifies most importantly, *on* the shields.[45]

The second piece (no. 152 in the inventory of 1422) was listed in 1432 as "Item, ung autre tappiz, vielz et usé, où il y a plusieurs personnaiges de Roynes at autres Dames, c'est assavoir: Thamaris, Theucra et Penthasilée, et au dessoubz d'elles a grans escriptures de leurs noms parescript, et au-dessus par en hault les armes de Berry . . ." (Item, another old and worn tapestry in which there are several figures of queens and other ladies, that is to say: Thamaris, Theucra and Penthasilée, and beneath them [there are] large inscriptions with their names written in them, and above them, up top, the arms of Berry . . .). This piece and the preceding one were among the tapestries listed in a document dated in Paris on October 5, 1432, as having been delivered to the Regent, the duke of Bedford.

The third tapestry (no. 153 in the inventory of 1422), which on February 11, 1432, was given to Pierre le Boursier, the late king's hanger of tapestry chambers, was described as follows: "ung tappiz de laine a iij grans personnaiges de Dames, c'est assavoir: Ménalope, Sem[i]ramis et Lampheto, et au dessus escripture, et leurs noms par escript, avec plusieurs autres personnaiges au dessus d'elles, armoyé en hault des armes de Berry en petis escussons . . ." (a wool tapestry with three large figures of ladies, that is to say: Menalope, Semiramis and Lampheto, and above [them there is] writing and their names written [there] with several other figures above them, [and] blazoned up top with the arms of Berry on small shields . . .). In the 1422 inventory the inscriptions with the names are specified as being below ("au dessoubz") the women rather than above them, and the figures above the female Worthies are qualified as being small ("avecques plusieurs autres petiz personnages au dessus de elles . . ."). However the earlier text does not mention the wool or the fact that the duke's arms are *on* the shields.

Rorimer and Freeman (1948–49, 253) believed that the description of these three tapestries suggests that they were "the exact female counterpart to our Heroes." However the descriptions of the two sets of compositions do not tally as well as that. It can be argued that inscriptions like the ones below, and coats of arms like the ones above, the main figures in the *Preuses* were lost along with the fabric that is obviously missing from the tops and bottoms of the four reconstructed *Worthies* tapestries. But as for the coats of arms "en hault," there are coats of arms in the upper part of the *Hebrew Worthies*, a part of the composition that has also survived in the King Arthur, Caesar, and Hector hangings where there are not now, and never were, any coats of arms. Furthermore, the *Preuses* were described as showing only the arms of Berry and not the arms of France, Burgundy ancient, and probably also Anjou, which appear along with the arms of Berry in the *Hebrew Worthies*. As for the fact that only one of Charles VI's three *Preuses* tapestries (no. 153) showed "several other figures" above the main characters whereas all three of the hangings from which 2a–i came obviously had such figures, Souchal (in Paris 1973, 42) offered a reasonable explanation: that the upper registers of two of the *Preuses* had been lost before they were inventoried in 1422. If that is true, then it is fair to suggest that the three *Preuses* tapestries may have been composed like the three to which 2a–i belonged. However, since no other figures were described as appearing beside the main figures in the *Preuses*, as they clearly did in the three complete *Worthies* hangings, we proceed with caution when attempting to resolve this problem.

The fact that the compositions in these two sets of tapestries were at least very similar if not the same raises a point that has not yet been addressed in the literature: Charles VI's tapestries showed ten, not nine, female Worthies, and Philippe le Hardi owned one or two tapestries that showed ten male and nine female Worthies (see note 1). Therefore it is fair to suggest that the three complete hangings from which 2a–i came may also have shown ten rather than nine Worthies. Because we have enough of the *Hebrew Worthies* to show that it was complete with three main figures, it is clear that the tenth man, if there was one, could not have represented the Hebrew Law. So little of the other two hangings has survived that we cannot say whether the tenth man would have been another Pagan or Christian Worthy, perhaps—to use the list of alternates Marillier (1932, 14) gave—Pompey, Hercules, Frederick I, Guy de Lusignan, or Bertrand du Guesclin, recently deceased (1380).

HISTORY

2a, b property of Joel Joseph Duveen.
In the collection of M. Chabrières-Arlès, Lyon, by 1877.
Property of Duveen Brothers from late 1915.
In the collection of Clarence H. Mackay, New York, from 1924.
Purchased by the MMA with funds from the Frank A. Munsey Bequest, 1932.

2c–g property of Joel Joseph Duveen.
In the possession of Baron Schickler, château Martinvast, Normandy, from about 1872. There made into five pairs of window curtains. It is not clear whether the hangings had been cut up into fragments before this.
In the possession of Count and Countess Hubert de Pourtalès (daughter of Baron Schickler), château Martinvast, in the form of window curtains.
Property of Joseph Brummer, New York, by 1936, in the form of window curtains.
Given to the MMA by John D. Rockefeller, Jr., 1947.

2h in the collection of Clarence H. Mackay, New York.
In the collection of Mr. and Mrs. George A. Douglass, New York.
Given to the MMA by George A. Douglass, 1947.

2i property of John Hunt, Ireland.
Given to the MMA by John D. Rockefeller, Jr., 1949.

EXHIBITIONS

Lyon, 1877. *Exposition rétrospective* [2a (as originally received at MMA)]. See Publications, Giraud 1878.
Cleveland Museum of Art, 1918. *Loan Exhibition of Tapestries.* Catalogue by G. L. Hunter. Cat. no. 2 [2a (as originally received at MMA)]. Lent by Duveen Brothers.
New York, MMA, 1931. *Loan Exhibition of European Arms and Armor.* Cat. no. 534 [2a (as originally received at MMA)]. Lent by Clarence H. Mackay.
Paris 1973. Catalogue entries by Geneviève Souchal. Cat. nos. 3 [2d], 4 [2a (as reconstructed at MMA)], both illus., and color detail of 2a.
New York 1974. Cat. nos. 3 [2d], 4 [2a (as reconstructed at MMA)], both illus., and color detail of 2a.

PUBLICATIONS

Giraud, J.-B. *Recueil descriptif et raisonné des principaux objets d'art ayant figuré à l'Exposition Rétrospective de Lyon 1877.* Lyon, 1878, p. 9. 2a (before reconstruction at MMA) described and discussed briefly.
Ackerman, Phyllis. "Tapestries of Five Centuries: I. The French Gothic Looms." *International Studio* 76 (1922–23) p. 48. 2a (before reconstruction at MMA) described and discussed briefly; illus. in heightened color, p. 41.
Hunter 1925, pp. 17–21, 24–25, 234–35. 2a (before reconstruction at MMA) described and discussed briefly. 2a illus. pls. III,a, b, detail in color and full view.
Hunter, George Leland. *Tapestries of Clarence H. Mackay.* New York, 1925, p. 14. 2a (before reconstruction at MMA) described and discussed briefly; illus. pp. 20, 22, 24–26, full view and details (one in color).
Hunter, George Leland. "Clarence H. Mackay's Gothic Tapestries." *International Studio* 84, no. 351 (August 1926) pp. 39–40. 2a (before reconstruction at MMA) described in detail and discussed briefly; illus. full view p. 40, and color detail p. 43.
Göbel 1928, vol. 1, pp. 14–15. 2a (before reconstruction at MMA) described and discussed briefly; illus. vol. 2, fig. 14.
Marillier, H. C. "The Nine Worthies." *Burlington Magazine* 61 (1932)

p. 14. 2a (before reconstruction at MMA) described and discussed briefly; illus. pl. B.

Ackerman, Phyllis. *Tapestry: The Mirror of Civilization.* New York, London, and Toronto, 1933, pp. 89, 107, 321. 2a (before reconstruction at MMA) described and discussed briefly.

Rorimer, James J. "The King Arthur Tapestry." *MMA Bulletin* 28 (1933) pp. 48–50. 2a (before reconstruction at MMA) described and discussed at length; illus.

Loomis, Roger Sherman. *Arthurian Legends in Medieval Art.* New York, 1938, pp. 38–39. 2a (before reconstruction at MMA) discussed briefly; illus. fig. 12.

Scherer, Margaret R. *About the Round Table.* New York, 1945, pp. 28–29. 2a (before reconstruction at MMA) described and discussed briefly; detail illus.

Rorimer, James J. *Mediaeval Tapestries: A Picture Book.* MMA, New York, 1947, p. [2]. 2a–f and 2h mentioned; 2a illus. fig. 1.

Rorimer, James J. "The Museum's Collection of Mediaeval Tapestries." *MMA Bulletin,* n.s. 6 (1947–48) pp. 92–93, 98. 2a–f and 2h described and discussed at length; detail of 2a illus. p. 93.

Comstock, Helen. "The Connoisseur in America: The Recovery of the Duke of Berry's *Heroes.*" *Connoisseur* 124 (1949) pp. 114–16. 2a–f and 2h discussed at length; 2e and 2b, c, h illus. full view; also a detail of 2b, c, h.

Rorimer, James J., and Margaret B. Freeman. "The Nine Heroes Tapestries at The Cloisters." *MMA Bulletin,* n.s. 7 (1948–49) pp. 243–60. Described and discussed at length; the four reconstructed hangings illus. pp. 245 [2a], 246 [2d], 247 [2e], 248–49 [2b, c, h]; details illus. pp. 243 [2c], 258 [2e]; one of the pairs of curtains from Martinvast illus. p. 250; one pair of curtains hanging in salon at Martinvast illus. p. 251. This article contains the first complete statement by the two authors on which subsequent comments by them and others concerning the iconography, design, and history of the tapestries were based. The same text was reprinted, with minor revisions and ten more illustrations, in the picture books published in 1953 and 1960 (see below).

Adam, P[aul]. "Comptes rendus bibliographiques: La tapisserie aux Preux, Bulletin of the Metropolitan Museum of New-York, vol. VII, no. 9." *Revue Française d'Héraldique et de Sigillographie* 5, no. 12 (1949) pp. 74–76. Review of Rorimer and Freeman 1948–49.

Rorimer, James J. *The Cloisters: The Building and the Collection of Mediaeval Art in Fort Tryon Park.* MMA, New York, 1951, pp. 47–55. Described and discussed in detail (text based on Rorimer and Freeman 1948–49). Detail of 2a illus. fig. 23; detail of 2b, c, h illus. fig. 24; 2d illus. fig. 25; 2e illus. fig. 26. See also 3d ed. rev., 1963, pp. 76–83. Text cut down and reorganized from 1951 edition; detail of 2b, c, h illus. fig. 34; 2e illus. fig. 35; detail of 2a illus. fig. 36.

Art Treasures of the Metropolitan. Marshall B. Davidson, ed. MMA, New York, 1952, p. 222, no. 55. 2a–f and 2h discussed briefly; color detail of 2a illus. fig. 55.

Rorimer, James J. and Margaret B. Freeman. *The Nine Heroes Tapestries at The Cloisters: A Picture Book.* MMA, New York, 1953. 2a–f and 2h described and discussed in detail (see above, Rorimer and Freeman 1948–49). The four reconstructed hangings illustrated along with one of the five pairs of curtains from Martinvast and related works of art. See also rev. ed., 1960, with the same text and illustrations, arranged somewhat differently.

Freeman, Margaret B. "A Book of Hours Made for the Duke of Berry." *MMA Bulletin,* n.s. 15 (1956–57) pp. 101–2. 2a–f and 2h discussed briefly; illus. details of 2d and 2e.

Weigert, Roger-Armand. *La tapisserie française.* Paris, 1956, pp. 37–38. 2a–f and 2h discussed briefly. The same text was reprinted in Weigert, *La tapisserie et le tapis en France.* Paris, 1964, pp. 23–24.

Wyss, Robert L. "Die neun Helden: Eine ikonographische Studie." *Zeitschrift für Schweizerische Archäologie und Kunstgeschichte* 17 (1957) pp. 78–79, 86. 2a–f and 2h described and discussed briefly.

Heinz, Dora. "Gewirkte Monumentalmalerei—Zur Tapisseriekunst in Frankreich und Burgund um 1400." *Alte und Moderne Kunst* 7,

nos. 56/57 (March/April 1962) p. 26. 2a–f and 2h discussed briefly; 2a illus. fig. 4.

Heinz, Dora. *Europäische Wandteppiche I.* Brunswick, 1963, pp. 53–54. 2a–f and 2h discussed briefly; 2a illus. fig. 29.

Verlet 1965, pp. 10, 20–21, 51. 2a–f and 2h described and discussed briefly; color illus. of 2a, pp. 50 (detail) and 51 (full view).

Troescher, Georg. *Burgundische Malerei: Maler und Malwerke um 1400 in Burgund.* Berlin, 1966, vol. 1, pp. 241–42, 289. 2a–f and 2h discussed at length; illus. vol. 2, figs. 412–15.

Ferrero Viale, Mercedes. "Tapestry and Carpets: I. Tapestry." In *Encyclopedia of World Art.* Vol 13. New York, Toronto, and London, 1967, cols. 913–14. 2a–f and 2h discussed briefly; illus. pl. 392 [2b, c, h].

Meiss, Millard. *French Painting in the Time of Jean de Berry: The Late Fourteenth Century and the Patronage of the Duke.* London and New York, 1967, vol. 1, pp. 58, 365 n. 103. Illus. vol. 2, figs. 445, 446 [2e, 2a].

Jarry, Madeleine. *World Tapestry: From Its Origins to the Present.* New York, 1969, pp. 34, 37. Discussed briefly; details illus. pp. 40–42 [2a and 2b, c, h].

van Ysselsteyn, G. T. *Tapestry: The Most Expensive Industry of the XVth and XVIth Centuries.* The Hague and Brussels, 1969, pp. 38–40, 100. Described briefly and discussed at greater length; illus. fig. 16 [2d].

Coffinet, Julien. *Arachne ou l'art de la tapisserie.* Geneva and Paris, 1971, p. 176. Discussed briefly.

Stucky-Schürer, Monica. *Die Passionsteppiche von San Marco in Venedig.* Bern, 1972, pp. 62–64. Described and discussed at length; illus. fig. 43 [2b, c, h].

de Vaivre, Jean-Bernard. "Les trois couronnes des hérauts." *Archivum Heraldicum* 86 (1972) p. 34 n. 25. Mentioned.

de Vaivre, Jean-Bernard. "Artus, les trois couronnes et les hérauts." *Archives héraldiques suisses,* Yearbook, 88 (1974) pp. 4, 11 n. 26. 2a described and discussed briefly; detail illus. fig. 4 [2a].

Coffinet 1977, p. 16. Discussed briefly.

Plotzek, Joachim M. "Alexander der Grosse oder Hektor." In *Die Parler und der schöne Stil 1350–1400: Europäische Kunst unter den Luxemburger.* Exh. cat., Schnütgen-Museum. Cologne, 1978–80, vol. 3, pp. 120–23. Described and discussed at length; illus. p. 121 [2d].

de Vaivre, Jean-Bernard. "L'héraldique et l'histoire de l'art du Moyen Age." *Gazette des Beaux-Arts,* 6th ser., 93 (1979) pp. 102, 104. Mentioned; illus. fig. 1 [2a].

Heslop, T. A. "The Episcopal Seals of Richard of Bury." In *Medieval Art and Architecture at Durham Cathedral.* British Archaeological Association Conference Transactions, 1977. London, 1980, p. 157. Mentioned; illus. pl. XXIV B [2a].

Grand, Paule Marie. *La tapisserie.* Paris and Lausanne, 1981, p. 42. 2a illus. in color.

Pastoureau, Michel. "Héraldique—Sigillographie." In *Les fastes du Gothique: Le siècle de Charles V.* Exh. cat., Grand Palais. Paris, 1981, p. 410. Mentioned.

de Vaivre, Jean-Bernard. "Notes d'héraldique et d'emblématique à propos de la tapisserie de l'Apocalypse d'Angers." *Comptes rendus de l'Académie des Inscriptions et Belles-Lettres,* 1983, pp. 102–3, 113 and n. 54. Mentioned.

Salet, Francis. "Prologue." In Alain Erlande-Brandenburg et al., *La tenture de l'Apocalypse d'Angers.* Nantes, 1987, p. 16. Mentioned.

Sterling, Charles. *La peinture médiévale à Paris 1300–1500.* Vol. 1, Paris, 1987, p. 202. Discussed briefly.

NOTES

1. See Rorimer and Freeman, "The Nine Heroes Tapestries at The Cloisters," *MMA Bulletin,* n.s. 7 (1948–49) pp. 253–54, where the authors discuss "Philip's set of Heroes and Heroines . . ." as though these were the only tapestries of this subject that he had. However, the records of Philippe's payments indicate that he

owned not only one tapestry (or perhaps set of tapestries?—referred to as a "tapis") showing nine male and nine female Worthies but also one or two hangings or sets of hangings showing ten male and nine female figures. See Bernard and Henri Prost, *Inventaires mobiliers et extraits des comptes des ducs de Bourgogne de la maison de Valois*, vol. 2, *Philippe le Hardi (1378–1390)* (Paris, 1908–13) pp. 438 item 2755, 444 item 2777, and 540 item 3345, all of which concern payments made in 1388 and 1389 for work done on a tapestry of the "9 preux et 9 preuvvez" (also spelled "preuses," "preuvves"), and also pp. 429 item 2711 and 642 item 3762, which deal respectively with a payment made in 1388 for a "drap de hautheliche de l'istoire des dix preux et 9 preuses" and another made in 1390 for "un tapiz des dix Preux et des 9 Preuses," both bought from Pierre de Beaumez "tapissier et varlet de chambre de Mgr." It is not clear whether these payments concern one and the same tapestry (or set of tapestries) or two different pieces or sets.

2. The same is true of the reverse face of the *Apocalypse* tapestries in Angers. See Alain Erlande-Brandenburg et al., *La tenture de l'Apocalypse d'Angers* (Nantes, 1987) figs. 48, 55.

3. Two different versions of the duke's coat of arms rendered in this way appear in the cloths of honor hanging behind the figures seated in pavilions at the left ends of the third and fifth pieces of the six *Apocalypse* tapestries in Angers; see Erlande-Brandenburg et al., *La tenture*, figs. 22, 30, 122, 154.

4. The author wishes to thank Jean-Bernard de Vaivre for remarking on the significance of this detail during the course of a conversation.

5. The field of the duc de Berry's arms is represented on the third, possibly the fifth, and the ninth banners from the left end as a small section of a field scattered with fleurs-de-lis, a whole one in the center, and the tips of four others in the corners. However on the fourth, sixth, seventh, tenth, twelfth, and fourteenth banners, there is only a single fleur-de-lis in the field. The duc d'Anjou's arms, with a plain rather than engrailed border of gules, appear in both forms, as well as with a field completely covered with fleurs-de-lis, on banners and shields in the *Apocalypse* tapestries in Angers; see Erlande-Brandenburg et al., *La tenture*, figs. 18–20, 95, 122. The single fleur-de-lis within the engrailed border also appears as the duc de Berry's coat of arms on a French stone medallion of about 1400 in a private collection; see *Les fastes du Gothique: Le siècle de Charles V*, exh. cat., Grand Palais (Paris, 1981) no. 107, illus. Concerning the arms bendy without the border of gules, de Vaivre indicated in conversation that he has occasionally seen examples of the coat of arms of the first ducal house of Burgundy in this form but that he is studying the matter further and will comment on his findings in a forthcoming publication.

6. The wings of the butterflies represented in the Angers *Apocalypse* are patterned with armorial blazons. See Erlande-Brandenburg et al., *La tenture*, figs. 2, 3, 23, 24, 95, 122, 154, which show butterflies having one or two pairs of wings blazoned with either the arms of Louis I, duc d'Anjou, alone or with his arms on the dexter wings and the arms of his wife, Marie de Bretagne (ermine), on the sinister wings.

7. Ackerman and many other writers referred to these nine men as *Heroes*, a term that Rorimer used consistently in his publications. However, since the characters derive from a French literary source and are referred to without exception in French literature as *Preux* (Worthies) and never as *Héros* (Heroes), we prefer to use the former term in this catalogue entry.

8. Concerning the early history of the Worthies theme, see Robert L. Wyss, "Die neun Helden: Eine ikonographische Studie," *Zeitschrift für Schweizerische Archäologie und Kunstgeschichte* 17 (1957) pp. 73–77.

9. Bibliothèque Nationale, Paris, MS fr. 12559, fols. 125, 125v. Pastoureau published the miniatures with the date usually assigned

to them, or about 1394–95, whereas Meiss believed they were painted about 1404. See Michel Pastoureau, "Héraldique—Sigillographie," in *Les fastes du Gothique*, p. 410, the male Worthies illustrated; also Millard Meiss, *French Painting in the Time of Jean de Berry: The Limbourgs and Their Contemporaries* (New York, 1974) vol. 1, pp. 14, 381, and vol. 2, figs. 47, 48, both the male and female Worthies illus.

10. Wyss, "Die neun Helden," pp. 98–102, published charts listing the charges shown on the nine male Worthies' shields in certain French, German, and Swiss works of art dating from the fourteenth to sixteenth centuries, but unfortunately he did not cite the tinctures of the fields and charges. Nevertheless these charts make it clear that the coat of arms assigned to each man frequently varied.

11. The field is gules in a late fifteenth-century tapestry of the *Worthies* in the Historisches Museum, Basel; see Hans Lanz, *Die alten Bildteppiche im Historischen Museum Basel* (Basel, 1985) pp. 52–53, illus. in color. See also Jean-Bernard de Vaivre, "Les trois couronnes des hérauts," *Archivum Heraldicum* 86 (1972) pp. 30–35, for a discussion of Arthur's blazon.

12. See Wyss, "Die neun Helden," chart, p. 98. See also Pastoureau, "Héraldique—Sigillographie," in *Les fastes du Gothique*, p. 410, who notes that Hector's arms were not confused with Alexander's in the Saluzzo manuscript. In Wyss's chart, the Worthy in the Metropolitan Museum's tapestry is identified as Alexander, presumably because Wyss followed the writers who had published the hangings according to the identification of the figures that Rorimer and Freeman had made. For the Manta murals painted between 1411 and 1430, see Paolo d'Ancona, "Gli affreschi del castello di Manta nel Saluzzese," *L'Arte* 8 (1905) pp. 94–106, the walls showing both the male and female Worthies illus.

13. MS Bodley 264; see *The Romance of Alexander* (Oxford, 1933), introductory text by M. R. James. The main section of the book is a facsimile of the manuscript; for the small figures see especially fols. 51v, 67v, 74v, 88v, 101v, 107r, 119r and v, 129r, and intermittently to the end.

14. The author wishes to thank Roger S. Wieck for bringing this miniature to his attention. It appears on fol. 66v of MS w.125; see Lilian M. C. Randall et al., *Medieval and Renaissance Manuscripts in the Walters Art Gallery*, vol. 1, *France, 875–1420* (Baltimore and London, 1989) p. 198, not illus.

15. See Jean Lafond et al., *Les vitraux de l'église de Saint-Ouen de Rouen*, vol. 1 (Paris, 1970) pp. 172–74 and pls. 44–45 (Saints Becket and Eloi), and especially also pp. 141–42 and pls. 30, 32, 33 (Saint Nicaise). See also pp. 39–40, where the windows are dated about 1325, and Françoise Perrot, "Vitraux," in *Les fastes du Gothique*, p. 379, where she dates the construction and glazing of the choir between 1318 and 1339.

16. Perrot, "Vitraux," in *Les fastes du Gothique*, no. 329, illus. See a larger illustration in Lafond et al., *Les vitraux*, pl. 42.

17. Perrot, "Vitraux," in *Les fastes du Gothique*, p. 384, not illus.

18. For illustrations of the *y* motifs in the *Apocalypse* tapestries, see Erlande-Brandenburg et al., *La tenture*, figs. 95, 138, 162.

19. See Jean-Bernard de Vaivre, "Notes d'héraldique et d'emblématique à propos de la tapisserie de l'Apocalypse d'Angers," *Comptes rendus de l'Académie des Inscriptions et Belles-Lettres*, 1983, pp. 97–98, 102–4, for the summary of Planchenault's opinions, and 104–13 and n. 54, and figs. 36–39, for de Vaivre's exposition of his own interpretation which was itself partly anticipated in Rose Graham, "Shorter Notices: The Apocalypse Tapestries from Angers," *Burlington Magazine* 89 (1947) p. 227.

20. This detail of the tapestry is illustrated in color in Eduardo Torra de Arana et al., *Los tapices de La Seo de Zaragoza* (Saragossa, 1985) p. 20.

21. Letter from Roger S. Wieck to the author, February 23, 1989. For details concerning the miniature see note 14 above.

22. Among other miniature paintings may be cited the *Four Evange-*

lists page by the Pseudo-Jacquemart in an early fifteenth-century *Evangeliary* now in the Bibliothèque Municipale in Bourges (MS 48, fol. 1); see Millard Meiss, *French Painting in the Time of Jean de Berry: The Late Fourteenth Century and the Patronage of the Duke* (London and New York, 1967) vol. 1, pp. 320–21, vol. 2, fig. 253. There the figures are arranged in the spaces of an architectural facade somewhat like that shown in the tapestries. Other settings like these that harbor military and musical figures appear frequently in the *Romance of Alexander* in the Bodleian Library whose illustrations were completed by Jehan de Grise in 1344 (see note 13 above). In relation to the category of seals, the author thanks John H. Plummer for calling his attention to it. See for example a seal of 1365 of Marguerite, comtesse de Flandres, showing that lady standing in a niche flanked by smaller niches containing angels holding blazoned shields: Auguste Coulon, *Inventaire des sceaux de la Bourgogne* (Paris, 1912) pl. xx, no. 93, and p. 21 text for no. 92 (the texts for nos. 93 and 92 were confused). See also a number of English seals of the middle and second half of the fourteenth century, in T. A. Heslop, "The Episcopal Seals of Richard of Bury," *Medieval Art and Architecture at Durham Cathedral*, British Archaeological Association Conference Transactions, 1977 (London, 1980) pls. xxiv a, xxv e, xxvi c.

23. See Stephen K. Scher, "Note sur les vitraux de la Sainte-Chapelle de Bourges," *Cahiers d'archéologie et d'histoire du Berry*, no. 73 (December 1973) p. 39, for a brief but carefully considered account of the present condition of the windows.

24. See Scher, "Note sur les vitraux," figs. 5, 9–14, for detail illustrations of examples of all three types of heads. For illustrations of all twenty-four prophets and apostles in the *Psalter*, see Meiss, *French Painting . . . Patronage of the Duke*, vol. 2, figs. 51–74.

25. In the windows that feature six lancets the architectural details of the buildings represented in the four outer windows are virtually the same, but in the two central lancets the facades show different details. See Lafond et al., *Les vitraux de l'église de Saint-Ouen*, pls. 32, 38, 44.

26. The Saint Nicaise windows are illustrated in Lafond et al., *Les vitraux de l'église de Saint-Ouen*, pls. 32–33, with a detail of a lower story on pl. 30. The pertinent commentary appears on pp. 141–42.

27. The Saints Eloi and Becket windows are illustrated in Lafond et al., *Les vitraux de l'église de Saint-Ouen*, pls. 44–45. The pertinent commentary appears on pp. 172–74.

28. The Saint Etienne windows are illustrated in Lafond et al., *Les vitraux de l'église de Saint-Ouen*, pls. 38–39 (commentary on pp. 148–49, 155).

29. Jean Helbig, "Circulation de modèles d'ateliers au XIVe siècle," *Revue Belge d'Archéologie et d'Histoire de l'Art* 8 (1938) pp. 115–17.

30. Fabienne Joubert, "L'Apocalypse d'Angers et les débuts de la tapisserie historiée," *Bulletin Monumental* 139 (1981) pp. 134–35 and figs. 1–12.

31. Quoted from Alfred de Champeaux and P. Gauchery, *Les travaux d'art exécutés pour Jean de France, duc de Berry* (Paris, 1894) p. 64.

32. Francis Salet, "Remarques sur le vocabulaire ancien de la tapisserie," *Bulletin Monumental* 146 (1988) pp. 211–12.

33. For the reference in the duke's inventory, see Jules Guiffrey, *Inventaires de Jean, duc de Berry (1401–1416)* (Paris, 1894–96) vol. 2, p. 209, item 17, ". . . un autre tappis nommé le Tappis des neuf Preux, contenant sèze aulnes de long et quatre aulnes de large ou environ, de l'ouvrage d'Arras, fait d'or, d'argent et de laynne de plusieurs couleurs, qui font a l'aune quarrée LXIIII aulnes . . ." (. . . another tapestry called the tapestry of the Nine Worthies, measuring about sixteen aunes in length and four in width, of Arras work, made of gold, silver and wool of several colors, which comes to sixty-four square aunes . . .). Assuming that the dimensions refer to the Paris aune, which was equivalent to 46³/4 inches, we calculate that the tapestry was about 62¹/3 feet long and 15¹/2

feet high (19 × 4.75 m), or roughly three times as long as Rorimer and Freeman estimated each of the original *Worthies* tapestries to be and roughly just as high.

34. See Alexandre Pinchart, *Histoire générale de la tapisserie*, pt. 3, *Histoire de la tapisserie dans les Flandres* (Paris, 1878–85) p. 21. The comte de Hainaut's tapestry appears in the inventory of 1418 of the Hôtel du Porc-Epic in Paris as "Ung grant tappis des Neufs Preux."

35. For the text of this inventory see Jules Labarte, *Inventaire du mobilier de Charles V, roi de France* (Paris, 1879); the reference to the tapestries, "Item les deux tappis des Neuf Preux," appears as item 3680 on p. 378.

36. Jules Guiffrey, *Histoire générale de la tapisserie*, pt. 1, *Histoire de la tapisserie en France* (Paris, 1878–85) p. 22, where the author recorded rather than quoted the text of this account.

37. See G. Ledos, "Fragment de l'inventaire des joyaux de Louis Ier, duc d'Anjou," *Bibliothèque de l'Ecole des Chartes* 50 (1889) p. 171 no. 184 (5) and p. 173 no. 184 (18) respectively.

38. Transcriptions of the citations for these three tapestries in the inventories of 1422 and 1432 are given in Jules Guiffrey, "Inventaire des tapisseries du roi Charles VI vendues par les Anglais en 1422," *Bibliothèque de l'Ecole des Chartes* 48 (1887) pp. 90–91, 411, 424. The piece specified as being made of wool, which showed Menalippe, Semiramis, and Lampheto, is referred to on p. 424 as having been given to the king's tapestry hanger in 1432.

39. Donald King, "How Many Apocalypse Tapestries?" in Veronika Gervers, ed., *Studies in Textile History, in Memory of Harold B. Burnham* (Toronto, 1977) pp. 161, 164–65.

40. For illustrations of the windows in the Trousseau and Aligret chapels, see A. des Méloizes, *Vitraux peints de la cathédrale de Bourges postérieurs au XIIIe siècle* (Paris, 1891–97) pls. 1 and 3; commentaries appear on pp. 2–4 and 11–12 respectively.

41. For a set of black and white illustrations of the tapestries in Tournai, see Monica Stucky-Schürer, *Die Passionsteppiche von San Marco in Venedig* (Bern, 1972) figs. 44–49; see also a detail in Roger-A. d'Hulst, *Flemish Tapestries from the Fifteenth to the Eighteenth Century* (New York, 1960) pp. 18–19.

42. The author wishes to thank Anne van Buren, Jonathan Alexander, and François Avril for their willingness to consult with him on this question.

43. Professor van Buren was kind enough to make this study at the author's request. Her report, which has not been published and for which he thanks her here, was contained in a letter addressed to the author on April 11, 1989.

44. For illustrations of similar women's houppelandes and coiffures which simply demonstrate that the basic silhouettes and forms van Buren identified primarily in the context of their earliest appearances continued to be represented in other works of art dated at least as late as 1410, see Meiss, *French Painting . . . The Limbourgs*, vol. 2, figs. 12 and 19 (Epître Workshop, 1403–4), 37–42 (Cité des Dames Workshop, ca. 1405–10), 141–42 (Epître Workshop and Cité des Dames Workshop, ca. 1406–10), and 163 (Orosius Workshop, 1407). For some of the male attendants' costumes and hair and beard styles, see figs. 14 and 20 (Epître Workshop, 1403–4), 15 (Cité des Dames Workshop, shortly after 1410), and 49 (Cité des Dames Master, ca. 1404). See also illustrations of men wearing similar garments and hair and beard styles in the tapestries of the *Story of Saints Piat and Eleuthère* in the cathedral in Tournai (dated 1402) in Stucky-Schürer, *Die Passionsteppiche*, figs. 44–49, and a detail in d'Hulst, *Flemish Tapestries*, pp. 18–19.

45. Quoted from Guiffrey, "Inventaire des tapisseries du roi Charles VI" (see note 38 above), pp. 411, 424. The citations in the inventory of 1422 are given on pp. 90–91. It is not clear whether the slightly different descriptions of the tapestries given in the two sources are to be interpreted as different perceptions of different compilers or errors in the descriptions or errors in Guiffrey's transcriptions of the documents.

3
The Falcon's Bath

Two hangings woven after the same or similar cartoons, one tapestry woven in reverse orientation

---

Southern Netherlands, 1400–1415
Wool warp, wool wefts
3a: 10 ft. × 9 ft. 8³/₄ in. (3.05 m × 2.97 m)
12–14 warp yarns per inch, 5–6 per centimeter
Gift of Frank Jay Gould, 1946 (46.58.1)
3b: 8 ft. 4 in. × 7 ft. 7 in. (2.54 m × 2.31 m)
11–13 warp yarns per inch, 4–5 per centimeter
Gift of Mr. and Mrs. Frederic B. Pratt, 1943 (43.70.2)

CONDITION

Cut on all four sides, 3a was probably the major section of a larger hanging. It has been heavily restored by patching and reweaving. Fragments of another red-ground tapestry, together with pieces of later weaving, have been inserted along the left and top sides. Almost the entire lower central portion of the piece has been rewoven with new warp and weft yarns. The passages that fall within this area are as follows: both main figures, except for most of the woman's head, the left part of her standing collar, her right shoulder and right hand, and the man's head, left hand, and most of the fur linings of both of his sleeves; the falcon and most of the basin to the right; almost the entire ground area between the figures and the bottom of the tapestry; all the tree trunks behind the two main figures, some of that foliage, all of the plants and ground area to the right of the man, and parts of all four small figures in the background. There are also smaller repairs on new warp yarns in the upper left and right sections of the background as well as small areas of reweaving with new weft yarns on the original warp in the small figures at left and right, the fur lining of the man's garment, and the base of the plant under the basin. Since the heads and other important parts of each of the main figures have survived, and since these images agree essentially with corresponding images in 3b, it seems likely that the two figures were originally in the places they now occupy and that, despite the extreme nature of the restorations, the composition we now see is, in broad terms, what was there originally. Comparing the details in this piece with corresponding details in 3b, one finds that 3a must have been restored by following the design for the other in reverse. All the tree trunks, for example, were copied from the trunks in 3b. The garments of both main fig-

ures were also copied verbatim from 3b, and the fact that the man's beads are in alternating tones of orange and golden brown, as the restored beads in 3b are rendered, proves that these garments were copied after 3b itself was restored (see below). Through a restorer's mistake in 3a, the seams at the top of the man's set-in sleeves have been eliminated and oak branches take their place. In 3b the construction of the garment at the shoulder line is clearly and logically represented, and these seams have been decorated with needlework representing oak leaves—undoubtedly the prototype for the misunderstood detail that the restorer introduced at that place in 3a.

All four sides of 3b have also been cut, and it was probably also the main section of a larger hanging. It has been very heavily restored by patching and reweaving. The entire bottom of the tapestry, from the hems of the main figures' garments to the lower edge, does not belong to the rest of the fabric. Both upper corners and most of the left and right sides of the field have been rewoven on new warp yarns. These passages include most of the small figure in the background to the left of the man's shoulder and most of the small figure in the tree above and to the right of the woman's head. Parts of the lower garments of both main figures, the woman's chin and collar, and the lappet above her left shoulder have also been restored with new warp and weft yarns. There are small areas of reweaving on the original warp throughout the piece and these have altered the drawing of both main figures' facial features. The large beads strung around the man's body have been changed through this reweaving from what seems to have been their original color, red or reddish brown, to brownish orange alternating with golden brown.

The colors in both pieces have faded appreciably but are still rich, especially in the red passages. The green grass on the island or knoll on which the figures sit has turned to dark greenish blue.

DESCRIPTION AND SUBJECT

In 3a, two fashionably dressed figures, a lady and a gentleman, are seated in the center foreground on a grassy knoll or island where a variety of small blossoming plants grows in profusion. She sits at the left, he at the

3a

3b

right. Orange trees in fruit and blossom and oak trees grow at the rear of the grassy rise. A young man is standing in the upper branches of an oak tree at the far left and another youth, wielding a pruning knife, is perched high in the branches of an oak tree right of center. At the right a young man or a boy runs downhill toward a fashionably dressed man standing below. The space behind the figures and their immediate setting is rendered as a flat plane of pinkish red on which oak branches and flowering branches, all with cut ends, have been scattered, as though tossed there by the pruners.

The lady holds a falcon on her gloved left fist; her tasseled gauntlet and the two tasseled leashes tied to the bird's legs hang below her hand. The gentleman places his right hand on his right knee, and with a rod in his left hand he splashes the water in a small round basin that rests on the ground between him and the lady. Both main figures wear the houppelande, a loose, full outer robe. The lady's garment has a high, round collar standing upright at the back and sides, with the points turned outward at the throat. She wears a jeweled necklace and a jeweled belt cinched very high on the waist. Her funnel-shaped sleeves are long and wide; and they, like the collar and hem, are lined with black and white ermine fur. Her headdress comprises a padded fabric roll, or bourrelet, resting on two "horns" of hair that have been padded and rolled high over the temples. The bourrelet, which is studded with short spikes of yarn or padded fabric, each tipped with a pearl or bead, rises forward and upward from either side of a jeweled pin above the center of the forehead and then turns abruptly backward.[1] An ermine lappet falls from the back of the headdress at the left.

The gentleman's houppelande is cut like the lady's except for the neckline, where the collar remains upright and close to the neck all around, and the sleeves, which are set in at the shoulders rather than made in one piece with the body of the garment as hers are. The details of this construction, which has been altered by the restorer's hand, can be seen clearly in the houppelande worn by the gentleman in 3b. The inner edge of the collar and the turned-back edges of the sleeves and hemline show that this garment is lined with tightly curled brown fur. The gentleman wears a long strand of beads made of coral or some other reddish stone wound once around his neck, then passed over his right shoulder and completely around his body at hip height. At his waist he wears a wide belt from which hang short lengths of chain, a small bell fixed to the end of each one. Similar accessories are represented in numbers of miniature paintings of the early fifteenth century.[2] On his head is a chaperon, a hood twisted into a turban. Its

silhouette is low and wide, and the point of the hood, or a separate tippet, falls forward where it is held to the rest of the fabric with a jeweled pin. The two men pruning the trees and the running man in the background wear hip- or calf-length body garments and hose. The fourth man, at the far right, wears a narrow-sleeved houppelande or robe, a chaperon, and a wide belt trimmed with bells slung over his right shoulder and across his left arm.[3]

The composition of 3b is essentially the same as 3a but in reverse. The figures are somewhat closer together and more elongated in their proportions. The small figure of a man in the far right background of 3a is not present at the left in 3b. The lady sits a bit farther back than the man, and there are other minor differences of design and detail resulting partly from the restorer's work and partly from the fact that the two pieces were probably woven by different artisans, perhaps after cartoons that were not precisely identical. Because the lady in 3a carries the falcon on her left fist, as was usually done, we assume that image shows the left-right orientation that the designer meant the composition to have. In 3b, the red background that so distinguishes 3a appears only in a small portion of the upper left corner and again in the background to the left and right of the man's shoulders. Most or all of these red weft yarns were introduced by the restorer; the rest of the background is dark blue in color. Since a narrow section of this blue ground directly above the man's head appears to be original, and since the areas of background above and to the right of the woman's head were restored with blue rather than red yarns, presumably during a different restoration treatment, one wonders whether the background of this hanging was originally blue or green rather than red.

Destrée (1912), apparently not familiar with the subject matter, thought that the man in 3b was feeding the falcon from the basin with the aid of a rod. He is not in fact feeding the bird but splashing water in the basin to encourage the bird to bathe. This represents only one of many steps in the long process of taming a wild hawk and preparing it for use in the sport of falconry. In his *De arte venandi cum avibus*, written in the second quarter of the thirteenth century, the emperor Frederick II of Hohenstaufen describes this process.[4] The training procedures were described again by Henri de Ferrières in his fourteenth-century manuscript *Le livre du roy Modus et de la royne Ratio*.[5] Frederick's instructions for the bath are fairly simple:[6] he observes first that bathing helps tame the falcon and accustom her to the presence of humans (female hawks were favored over males because they were larger and also performed better as hunters). The tub or basin containing the bath water should be at least two feet wide and deep enough to let the water rise above the bird's legs. The bath, which should contain only cool, clear water, could be located in a protected place out of doors or in a mews. If the bird is not yet tame, the falconer tethers her to an object near the bath and moves away while she bathes. If she is hooded or has closed lids she may be carried on the falconer's wrist to the tub, and the water in the basin is to be splashed to make an inviting sound. When the falcon wants to bathe, she will lower her beak and turn toward the water. The falconer then brings the bird forward so that her feet touch the water, and he splashes it again. After she has stepped into the bath, he splashes the water at intervals to encourage her to bathe completely. She then regains her perch on his wrist. Frederick finishes his brief discussion of the bath by observing that it will not only tame the bird but also keep her well and cool. The bath described by King Modus is essentially the same.[7] He advocates bathing the bird after giving her a meal of live bird flesh. With the hood in position, the falcon may be brought on the hand quite near the basin while the falconer splashes the bath water with a small rod. The hood is then removed, and the fist on which the bird perches is moved to the basin. When the falcon has entered the bath she is left there until she indicates that she wants to emerge. At that point the fist is brought to the basin again so that she may hop up to her perch. Modus also recommends holding a bit of meat in the fist to entice the bird to return to it. According to

him, the bath gives the falcon not only courage and confidence but also an appetite. He then observes that many falcons will not bathe in a basin and that these must be taken to bathe in a river.

Early manuscripts and printed editions of these two major works on falconry include detailed illustrations of the procedures and equipment used to train and fly falcons. Among the many depictions of the bath are those contained in the Vatican copy of Frederick's book (see note 4). Folio 96r shows a drawing of a falcon in the bath inside a mews and a falcon standing on a block of stone near an outdoor tub of water and tethered to a stake driven into the ground next to the block. There is also an incomplete drawing of a falconer holding a bird close to a tub. Folio 108v shows a painting of a falconer holding a hooded bird on his left fist and a bit of meat in his right hand. On the same page another falconer sits next to a tub placed on the ground. He splashes the bath water with a rod held in his right hand while the falcon takes her bath; in his gloved left hand he holds the jesses tied to her legs. In the illustration on folio 79r the falconer crouches beside a bath, splashing the water with a forked stick and holding the jesses of a falcon who perches on the rear edge of the tub.

The painting on folio 60v of the Morgan Library *Roy Modus* manuscript (see note 5) shows a falcon poised similarly on the rim of a low, wide basin on the ground between two falconers, the right one of whom splashes the water with a rod held in his right hand. A woodcut

Fig. 93. *Trainer Inviting a Falcon to Bathe.* Woodcut on the verso of an unnumbered folio in the first edition of *Le livre du roi Modus*, printed by Antoine Neyret in Chambéry, October 20, 1468. Pierpont Morgan Library, New York.

Fig. 94. *Lady with a Dog and a Falcon.* Drawing, French school, about 1400–1410. Musée du Louvre, Paris.

on an unnumbered folio of the first printed edition of *Le livre du roi Modus* (see note 5) shows a crouching falconer splashing the water in a basin with a rod held in his right hand while he holds the falcon on his left fist directly over the bath (fig. 93).

These illustrations prove that the tapestry designer knew his subject well. All the actions represented are correct: the lady holds the falcon—now unhooded—on her left wrist and brings it close to the bath as her companion splashes the water with a rod. The falcon in the tapestries must be a tame one since she seems unafraid of the humans and is not tethered to a stake. The moment represented is that in which the bird is first invited to bathe. A tapestry in the Montreal Museum of Fine Arts shows a similar subject but the moment depicted is the next one, when the bird has hopped up to the edge of the basin and the trainer (the lady in this case) is splashing the water again to encourage her falcon who, like the exemplary bird in Frederick's account of the bath, turns her beak toward the water.[8] Ladies owned their own falcons and flew them at game birds just as men did. One of the appeals of falconry during the Middle Ages was that ladies and gentlemen could enjoy

the sport together, a lady often riding pillion behind her male companion.[9] Since the couple in the Metropolitan Museum's tapestries are bathing the falcon rather than flying it, the designer clearly intended to represent a moment of pleasant dalliance in a noble context rather than an incident in a hunting episode.

SOURCE OF THE DESIGN

The two main figures undoubtedly derive from some lost or unidentified drawings like certain examples at the Louvre (fig. 94) and in Dresden.[10] The figure in the Louvre drawing is not the immediate prototype for the lady in the tapestries but shows that this general image was current during the early years of the fifteenth century. Some drawing very much like this one must have served as the source for the lady falconer in the *Gift of the Heart* tapestry in the Musée du Louvre (fig. 74). Her pose is virtually the same as in the Metropolitan Museum's tapestries; only the details of costume and the falcon's pose have been changed. We can assume that the small figures in the background of 3a and b, and perhaps also the background itself, were derived from another lost or unidentified drawing or from some stock cartoon that could have served as the setting for any number of country-life subjects.

MANUFACTURE AND DATE

In 1912, when 3b was first published, Destrée related it to country-life tapestries listed in a number of late fourteenth- and early fifteenth-century inventories and expressed the opinion that the Metropolitan Museum's tapestry, then owned by Bacri in Paris, was contemporary with the five *Scenes from a Courtly Romance* in the Musée des Arts Décoratifs in Paris and earlier than the *Gift of the Heart* in the Musée du Louvre.[11] Destrée offered no specific dates for the various tapestries but clearly intended to place 3b in the early years of the fifteenth century. He believed that the cartoon was designed by a French artist and that the weave was like that of the *Apocalypse* in Angers. On these grounds, he cautiously and tentatively attributed 3b to Paris. Souchal (in Paris 1973, 88) also felt that the design was French. However, since she dated the tapestry after 1420, she theorized that it would not have been woven in Paris, where the English occupation had damaged the tapestry industry seriously, but probably in Arras. In the absence of evidence supported by documents favoring an attribution of either one of the Metropolitan Museum's tapestries to Paris or elsewhere in France, it is reasonable to suggest that they were woven somewhere in the southern Netherlands where the industry was thriving. After Destrée, most of the specialists who studied 3b, and in certain cases also 3a, believed that one or both were woven in Arras, or probably in Arras. Their reason was simply that they saw in these pieces stylistic elements they identified with Arras work or, for Forsyth (1943–44, 259) and Souchal (in Paris 1973, 88), that by about 1420 the tapestry-weaving industry had been effectively destroyed in Paris. These scholars also dated the pieces between 1420 and 1440 on stylistic grounds (Kurth 1918, 69 n. 1; Margerin 1932, 141; Forsyth 1943–44, 259; Young 1962–63, 346; Souchal in Paris 1973, 88; Lestocquoy 1978, 47, 48, 96, 117). According to Coffinet (1977, 28), both 3a and 3b, along with 4 and a group of hangings in other collections, could be dated from the end of the fourteenth century to around 1440. Weibel, in the catalogue of the Hartford/Baltimore exhibition of 1951–52, dated 3a and by implication also 3b in the third quarter of the fifteenth century without stating her reasons. Souchal (in Paris 1973, 88, 91) correctly refuted this opinion on stylistic grounds and dated 3a about 1420–30 and 3b about 1420 without giving reasons for specifying different dates.

The spatial organization of the scene, with the main and secondary figures ranged in two shallow ranks parallel to the picture plane, suggests a date in the late fourteenth or early fifteenth century. Furthermore, the manner of rendering the draperies in soft, limp, linear folds is characteristic of paintings in the international Gothic style of the same period, particularly those produced by artists constituting the School of Paris. Beyond that, the date can be refined only in terms of fashion in costume. The garments and accessories indicate that the cartoon or cartoons must have been designed between 1400 and 1410. Both gentlemen and ladies wore the houppelande from the last quarter of the fourteenth century through about 1425, men continuing to wear it on ceremonial occasions for some time longer, until about 1450. During this period, women's houppelandes might be cut with the high standing collar with turned-down points, with the falling collar, or with a low, graceful, oval neckline that left the corsage exposed from the base of the neck to the points of the shoulders (see 4).[12] It is not the houppelande itself but some details of fashion that fix the date of the tapestry cartoon within the first two decades of the fifteenth century. We have seen that the strands of large beads and the belts with bells were worn about 1413–16 when the calendar pages of the *Très Riches Heures* of Jean de Berry were painted (see notes 2 and 3). The same pictures show that the headdress of the lady falconer in 3a and b also was being worn at that time. This form of headdress, with the bourrelet rising forward and then backward over horns of hair, and rather low as a whole, was frequently represented in miniature paintings, some of which date from about 1410 (see note 1). By 1425 the bourrelet had become wider, and during the next quarter century the sides sloped backward from the forehead, rather than forward, and then soared upward to form two essentially separate loops at the sides of the head, rising above round, flat panels of jeweled netting that contained the hair.[13] However it is the treatment of the gentleman's hair that narrows the date of the cartoon down from the first two decades of the century to the very first decade. During the last quarter of the fourteenth century civilian males wore their head hair to the shoulder, brushed away to the sides of the head. Some men also wore short pointed beards below moustaches.[14] By 1413–16, as the calendar pages of the *Très Riches Heures* show, the hairstyle for gentlemen had changed completely. Their chins were now clean-shaven and their hair was cropped short all around. The gentleman in the Metropolitan Museum's tapestries wears his blond hair full at the sides and low at the back; he also has a small moustache and a short beard (much obscured by restoration in 3b). Since the subject matter of the composition concerns people of fashion, there can be no doubt that the cartoon was designed by about 1410. For the same reason, it seems unlikely that the tapestry would have been woven much more than five years later, when the gentleman's hair would already have looked old-fashioned.

Princes owned similar tapestries during the early years of the fifteenth century. The inventory of 1416 of carpets, tapestries, and upholstery fabrics belonging to Jean, duc de Berry, shows that he had a "ciel d'une chambre de tappicerie de plusieurs laynes . . . ou milieu duquel a une fontaine et deux personnages de dames alentour, dont l'un tient un esprevier et l'autre un bassin" (ceiling of a tapestry bed made of several wools . . . in the middle of which is a fountain and two ladies next to it, one of whom holds a hawk and the other a basin), and he also had the "dossiel de ladicte chambre, ou milieu duquel est une royne tenant une esprevier et deux dames a l'entour, dont l'une met de l'eaue en un bassin et l'autre bat l'eaue" (the back cloth of the said chamber, in the middle of which is a queen holding a hawk and two ladies in attendance, one who puts water into a basin and the other who beats the water).[15] Many of the tapestries listed in these early inventories had rose-colored grounds. One piece in particular, mentioned among the tapestries inherited by Philippe le Bon and inventoried at Dijon in 1420, must have looked somewhat like 3a and b. It was described as follows:

"Ung tapiz de haulte-lice, sur champ vermeil, de file d'Arras, à plusieurs herbages et fleurettes, ouvré ou mylieu de deux personnages, assavoir: d'un chevalier et d'une dame, et de six personnages d'enfans es quatre cornetz" (A high-warp tapestry, on a rose-colored ground, of Arras yarn, with many plants and little flowers, worked in the middle with two figures, that is: one of a knight and one of a lady, and with six figures of children in the four corners).[16]

RELATED TAPESTRIES

The only tapestry known at present that might have accompanied one or both of these pieces in a series of related hangings is 4. It may be significant that that tapestry was said to have been owned by Bacri in 1912 when the firm also had 3b. Since 3a and 3b show precisely the same subject, although in reverse orientations, and since they show some differences in weaving technique, it is unlikely that they belonged to one and the same set of hangings. Furthermore, if 3b was indeed woven originally with a blue or green background rather than a red one (see above, Description and Subject), it would probably have been made for a different set of tapestries.

HISTORY

3a in the collection of the family of Florence Day Gould (Mrs. Frank Jay Gould).
In the collection of Frank Jay Gould, Paris.
Given to the MMA by Frank Jay Gould, 1946.

3b owned by Bacri Frères, Paris, in 1912.
In the collection of Mr. and Mrs. Frederic B. Pratt, New York, by 1920.
Given to the MMA by Mr. and Mrs. Frederic B. Pratt, 1943.

EXHIBITIONS

New York, MMA, The Cloisters, 1944. *The Noble Sport of Falconry.* 3b exhibited.
Hartford, Wadsworth Atheneum, and Baltimore Museum of Art, 1951–52. *2000 Years of Tapestry Weaving: A Loan Exhibition.* Text by Adele Coulin Weibel. Cat. no. 72 [3a], illus.
Paris 1973. Catalogue entries by Geneviève Souchal. Cat. nos. 25 [3a], 26 [3b], both illus.
New York 1974. Cat. nos. 25 [3a], 26 [3b], both illus.

PUBLICATIONS

Destrée, Joseph. "Deux idylles: Tapisseries de l'époque de Charles VI (1380–1422)." *Annales de la Société Royale d'Archéologie de Bruxelles* 27 (1912) pp. 141–46. 3b discussed; illus. p. 143.
Kurth, Betty. "Die Blütezeit der Bildwirkerkunst zu Tournai und der burgundische Hof." *Jahrbuch der Kunsthistorischen Sammlungen des allerhöchsten Kaiserhauses* 34 (1918) p. 69 n. 1. 3b mentioned.
Mlle. Margerin. "Les tapisseries de verdure, de leur origine au milieu du XVIᵉ siècle, dans les ateliers d'Arras, de Tournai et d'Audenarde." *Bulletin des Musées de France* 4 (1932) p. 141. 3b mentioned.
Forsyth, William H. "The Noblest of Sports: Falconry in the Middle Ages." *MMA Bulletin*, n.s. 2 (1943–44) pp. 256–59. 3b discussed at length; illus. p. 254.
Taylor, Henry Francis, Horace H. F. Jayne, and Laurance S. Harrison. "Review of the Year 1946." *MMA Bulletin*, n.s. 6 (1947–48) p. 18. 3a and b mentioned.
Rorimer, James J. *Mediaeval Tapestries: A Picture Book.* MMA, New York, 1947, fig. 3 [3b].
Young, Bonnie. "Lady Honor and Her Children." *MMA Bulletin*, n.s. 21 (1962–63) p. 346. 3a and b mentioned; 3b illus. fig. 2.
Schneebalg-Perelman, Sophie. "La dame à la licorne a été tissée à Bruxelles." *Gazette des Beaux-Arts*, 6th ser., 70 (1967) p. 266. 3a and b mentioned.
Coffinet, Julien. *Arachne ou l'art de la tapisserie.* Geneva and Paris, 1971. 3a illus. in color, pp. 19 (two details), 183 (full view).
Verdier, Philippe. "The Medieval Collection." *Apollo* 103 (1976) p. 366, no. 16 n. 2. 3a and b mentioned.
Coffinet 1977. 3a and b discussed briefly pp. 28, 30–31; 3a illus. p. 22, color detail p. 23.
Lestocquoy 1978, p. 117. 3a and b mentioned; 3b illus. in color, pls. xxix (detail), xxx (full view).

NOTES

1. Similar headdresses with bourrelets covered with dots or beads, some of them showing studs supporting these points, are to be found in miniature paintings of the early fifteenth century. See two examples of about 1410, both in paintings illustrating a volume of works by Christine de Pisan (MS Harley 4431, fols. 3r, 150r), illustrated in Millard Meiss, *French Painting in the Time of Jean de Berry: The Limbourgs and Their Contemporaries* (New York, 1974) figs. 151, 155. The April page of the *Très Riches Heures* of Jean, duc de Berry, of about 1413–16, shows a lady in the background wearing a similar bourrelet studded with gold dots; see Jean Longnon, Raymond Cazelles, and Millard Meiss, *The* Très Riches Heures *of Jean, Duke of Berry* (New York, 1969) pl. 5. See note 14 below for later examples.
2. See a miniature painted before 1413 showing John Hayton presenting his book to Jean sans Peur (fol. 226r of MS fr. 2810 in the Bibliothèque Nationale, Paris, illustrated in Millard Meiss, *French Painting in the Time of Jean de Berry: The Boucicaut Master* [London, 1968] fig. 98) in which a man in a white houppelande right of center wears a long strand of large beads in precisely this fashion. In the January scene of the *Très Riches Heures* of Jean de Berry, a man standing in the center foreground wears a belt hung with little bells around his waist; see Longnon, Cazelles, and Meiss, *Très Riches Heures*, pl. 2.
3. Two gentlemen and a lady wear belled belts in a similar way in the April and May scenes of the *Très Riches Heures* but in the reverse direction, from left shoulder to right hip. A gentleman standing at the far left in the John Hayton presentation miniature wears a belled belt in the same direction as the small man in the Metropolitan Museum's tapestry.
4. See Casey A. Wood and F. Marjorie Fyfe, trans. and ed., *The Art of Falconry: Being the De arte venandi cum avibus of Frederick II of Hohenstaufen* (Stanford and London, 1943), and also the facsimile reproduction of the illustrated copy of the manuscript that was made for Frederick's son Manfred, king of Sicily, between 1258 and 1266, now in the Biblioteca Apostolica Vaticana (MS Pal. Lat. 1071), published in the series Codices e Vaticanis Selecti, vol. 30/Codices Selecti, vol. 16–16* (Graz, 1969).

5. See an illustrated northern French copy of the Ferrières manuscript dating from about 1465 in the Pierpont Morgan Library, MS 820, and also the first printed edition of the text, published by Antoine Neyret in Chambéry in 1468, illustrated with woodcuts; also two modern critical editions of the text prepared by Gunnar Tilander, both published in Paris, 1931 and 1932, the latter for the Société des Anciens Textes Français.

6. From Wood and Fyfe, *Art of Falconry*, pp. 191–93.

7. From Tilander, *Livre du roy Modus*, 1931 ed., pp. 128–29.

8. The tapestry is illustrated in Philippe Verdier, "The Medieval Collection," *Apollo* 103 (1976) p. 366.

9. See two such scenes, in a stag-hunt tapestry in the Metropolitan Museum (25a) and in a miniature painting in the Morgan Library manuscript of the *Livre du roy Modus*, fol. 70v (see note 5 above).

10. For the pertinent text concerning the drawing illustrated here as fig. 94, see Grete Ring, *A Century of French Painting, 1400–1500* (London, 1949) cat. no. 40. For the drawing in Dresden, which treats a different but equally fashionable subject and is of approximately the same date, see Jacques Dupont, "French School (about 1410)—Fragment of a Larger Composition Representing an Aquatic Tournament," *Old Master Drawings* 9 (1934–35) pp. 51, 52, illus. pl. 51.

11. For illustrations of the *Romance* tapestries, see Monica Stucky-Schürer, *Die Passionsteppiche von San Marco in Venedig* (Bern, 1972) figs. 57–61.

12. Similar garments for both men and women appear in the calendar pages for January, April, May, and August in the *Très Riches Heures* of Jean de Berry (ca. 1413–16); see Longnon, Cazelles, and Meiss, *Très Riches Heures*, pls. 2, 5, 6, and 9.

13. See the intermediate stage in the development of the headdress in a miniature painting of about 1425 by the Valerius Maximus Master (MS 5060, fol. 27r, in the Bibliothèque de l'Arsenal, Paris), the coiffure of the lady in the lower center section, illustrated in Meiss, *The Limbourgs*, fig. 208. For examples of the developed form of the headgear in the second quarter of the century, see the ladies in the Devonshire hunting tapestries in the Victoria and Albert Museum, illus., Digby 1980, esp. figs. 10, 11.

14. For typical examples, see two miniatures in a manuscript of the *Roman de la Rose* dating from the late fourteenth to the early fifteenth century in which men wear the long houppelande and this style of head and face hair, illustrated in François Boucher, *Histoire du costume en occident de l'antiquité à nos jours* (Paris, 1965) p. 196. See also the men in the right foreground of the tapestry of the *Story of Jourdain de Blaye* in Padua, woven about 1390, and the mason in the lower right corner of one of the *Lives of Saints Piat and Eleuthère* tapestries in Tournai, dated 1402, both illustrated in Stucky-Schürer, *Die Passionsteppiche*, figs. 55 and 49 respectively.

15. Jules Guiffrey, *Inventaire de Jean, duc de Berry (1401–1416)* (Paris, 1894–96) vol. 2, p. 216, nos. 78, 79.

16. Alexandre Pinchart, *Histoire générale de la tapisserie*, pt. 3, *Histoire de la tapisserie dans les Flandres* (Paris, 1878–85), p. 24.

4
Lady Holding a Falcon

Southern Netherlands, originally 1400–1415 (altered later)
Wool warp, wool wefts
8 ft. 6 in. × 5 ft. 7 in. (2.59 m × 1.70 m)
12–14 warp yarns per inch, 5–6 per centimeter
Gift of Mr. and Mrs. Frederic B. Pratt, 1943 (43.70.1)

CONDITION

The hanging has been cut on all four sides. It has been heavily restored throughout by patching and reweaving. Most of the figure was cut out of another tapestry, apparently one that was different from the piece or pieces that provided the rest of the field, turned back to front, and then set into place. The fabric in the areas of the corsage and head shows a finer texture than the rest and clearly comes from yet another hanging. The greensward and plants in the foreground do not belong with the background, which is itself composed of many small patches of old and new weaving. The rabbits in the background and the falcon on the lady's hand show both new warp and weft yarns. The crown atop the lady's headdress is a modern invention. Since the figure of the lady (except for the neck and head) and the flower-strewn red ground correspond to details in 3a and b, it is likely that this hanging was made up from a tapestry designed either for that series or a closely related one, in either case with additions from one or more other pieces.

DESCRIPTION AND SUBJECT

In the center of the composition a lady sits on a grassy knoll where flowering plants grow in profusion. She wears a houppelande cut with a low oval neckline and lined with ermine fur. The high waistline is cinched with a jeweled belt. The lady inclines her head to the right and gazes at the falcon perched on her gloved left hand. (As noted above, the fabric representing the body from neckline down was turned back to front during restoration thus reversing its left and right sides.) Her headdress (not original) comprises a relatively high bourrelet that rises up and backward from the center of her forehead, over a pair of jeweled nets that cover the hair brushed back from both temples. A veil hangs from the back and sides of the bourrelet and an open crown (a modern addition) is perched on top. Oak trees and rosebushes rise from the ground at the back of the knoll. The flat red plane behind them is scattered with oak branches and flowering branches, all with cut ends, and with figures of rabbits (not original).

SOURCE OF THE DESIGN

Although the neckline of the houppelande and the pose of the falcon have been changed, the lady is the same figure that appears in 3a and b. It derives from the same drawing that served the designer of those two pieces and possibly also the designer of the *Gift of the Heart* in the Musée du Louvre (fig. 74).[1] The background, where rosebushes have been added to the orange and oak trees of 3a and b and rabbits have also been added, was taken either from the same unidentified source or a related one.

MANUFACTURE AND DATE

When it was shown in the Metropolitan Museum's *Fiftieth Annual Exhibition* in 1920, this tapestry was catalogued as French and dated in the fifteenth century. In 1944, Forsyth (255, 259) suggested a date of about 1420–35 on grounds of pictorial style and costume and indicated that at that late date the tapestry would probably have been woven in Arras rather than in Paris where, he believed, the industry was virtually extinct. Rorimer (1947, caption fig. 4) retained the tentative attribution to Arras and dated the piece in the early fifteenth century. Schneebalg-Perelman (1967, caption fig. 12) gave it the same date and attributed it to Arras. Souchal (in Paris 1973, 88, 91) gave reasons similar to Forsyth's for attributing the tapestry tentatively to the looms of Arras, and she dated it about 1435–40 because of the late form of the headdress. As noted above, this headdress was introduced from a different tapestry, clearly a later one, and thus it cannot be used as evidence in dating the piece. Coffinet (1977, 28) included this tapestry in a group of hangings that he believed could be attributed on the grounds of style to Arras between the end of the fourteenth century and 1430 or 1440. Lestocquoy (1978, 47, 48, 96, 117) dated this piece about 1420 and included it among a list of hangings that he attributed to Arras because he could see no reason to place them elsewhere. He also believed that Arras weavers had a special fondness for the particular kind of stylized rabbit that appears on the red ground of this tapestry, and furthermore that Arras weavers repeated these motifs over a period of many years without altering them. Lestocquoy cited references (1978, 87, 103, 114 n. 12) to certain tapestries used in Ferrara in 1461 as evidence that one piece with rabbits and a few others were bought in Arras since they showed *Rezo* either on the linings or in the border. However, as already noted, the rabbits in 4 are not part of the

original fabric. Furthermore we believe that Lestocquoy misinterpreted these documents. He apparently thought that the word "arezo" in the phrases "quelli d'arezo" or "havuti d'arezo" referred to Arras. But *d'arezo*, spelled with an *e* rather than an *a* after the *r*, refers not to Arras but to the Italian town of Arezzo, presumably the place from which the tapestries were sent to Ferrara or where they were bought. There are at present no reasons for accepting or refuting these attributions to Arras. Like 3a and b, which use the same figure of a lady falconer with a few differences, this piece was probably designed by a French artist but woven in the southern Netherlands. Costume details indicate that the hanging may be dated about 1400–1415. The courtly romance tapestries in the Musée des Arts Décoratifs, which date from the first decade of the fifteenth century, show ladies wearing houppelandes with either high or low necklines.[2] In a miniature of about 1403–4 the female character Richesse appears before the castle of Fortune wearing a white and gold houppelande with funnel sleeves and the same low oval neckline worn by the lady in 4.[3] The April page of the *Très Riches Heures* of the duc de Berry shows ladies wearing funnel-sleeved houppelandes with high round collars, falling collars, and low oval necklines, about 1413–16.[4] By the second quarter of the century, ladies' houppelandes, or gowns resembling them in a general way, were cut with either high round necklines or deep pointed ones that dropped to the belt.[5]

RELATED TAPESTRIES

This hanging may have been woven after a cartoon in the series after which 3a and b were woven. If Rorimer was correct in suggesting that this piece was bought from Bacri in 1911 or 1912 (see History) it might have belonged with 3b, which was certainly with Bacri in 1912. However we now know that that piece might have been woven originally with a blue or green background rather than a red one (see 3b, Description and Subject). At present that is the only other known tapestry that might have accompanied this piece in a series of hangings, unless 3a also belonged to the set.

HISTORY

According to an unpublished note by James Rorimer, perhaps bought for Mr. and Mrs. Frederic B. Pratt from Bacri Frères, Paris, in 1911–12.
In the collection of Mr. and Mrs. Frederic B. Pratt, New York.
Given to the MMA by Mr. and Mrs. Frederic B. Pratt, 1943.

EXHIBITIONS

New York, MMA, 1920. *Fiftieth Anniversary Exhibition.* Cat. p. 13. Lent by Frederic B. Pratt.
New York, MMA, The Cloisters, 1944. *The Noble Sport of Falconry.*
Paris 1973. Catalogue entries by Geneviève Souchal. Cat. no. 27, illus.
New York 1974. Cat. no. 27, illus.

PUBLICATIONS

"List of Loans: Fiftieth Anniversary Exhibition." *MMA Bulletin* 15 (1920) p. 118. Mentioned.
J. B. [Joseph Breck]. "Mediaeval and Renaissance Decorative Arts and Sculpture." *MMA Bulletin* 15 (1920) p. 180. Mentioned; illus. p. 181.
Forsyth, William H. "The Noblest of Sports: Falconry in the Middle Ages." *MMA Bulletin*, n.s. 2 (1943–44) pp. 256–59. Described briefly and discussed; illus. p. 255.
Rorimer, James J. *Mediaeval Tapestries: A Picture Book.* MMA, New York, 1947, fig. 4.
Schneebalg-Perelman, Sophie. "La dame à la licorne a été tissée à Bruxelles." *Gazette des Beaux-Arts*, 6th ser., 70 (1967) p. 266. Mentioned; illus. fig. 12.
Coffinet 1977, p. 28. Mentioned; illus. p. 32.
Lestocquoy 1978, pp. 47, 48, 87, 96, 117. Discussed at length; illus. in color, pls. XXVII (full view), XXVIII (detail). Pl. XXXIV shows a montage of two figures from a Florentine engraving of 1465–70 superimposed on the background of 4, with the lady and falcon deleted.

NOTES

1. The drawing would have been one like that illustrated as fig. 94 in 3. See the text associated with it in Grete Ring, *A Century of French Painting: 1400–1500* (London, 1949) cat. no. 40.
2. See Monica Stucky-Schürer, *Die Passionsteppiche von San Marco in Venedig* (Bern, 1972) figs. 57–61.
3. In a manuscript of Christine de Pisan's *Mutacion de Fortune* in the Musée Condé at Chantilly, MS 494, fol. 13r, illustrated in Millard Meiss, *French Painting in the Time of Jean de Berry: The Limbourgs and Their Contemporaries* (New York, 1974) fig. 1.
4. See Jean Longnon, Raymond Cazelles, and Millard Meiss, *The Très Riches Heures of Jean, Duke of Berry* (New York, 1969) pl. 5.
5. See these later versions of the garment in the Devonshire hunting tapestries of the second quarter of the fifteenth century, illustrated in Digby 1980, figs. 2–11.

5
The Annunciation

Southern Netherlands, 1410–30
Wool warp; wool and a few metallic wefts
11 ft. 6 in. × 9 ft. 9 in. (3.51 m × 2.97 m)
12–14 warp yarns per inch, 5–6 per centimeter
Gift of Harriet Barnes Pratt, in memory of her husband, Harold
Irving Pratt (1877–1939), 1949 (45.76)

CONDITION

The tapestry has been cut along the left, right, and top edges. Although the bottom edge has also lost some of its original fabric, bits of the selvage that remain along three-quarters of its length from the left prove that the design of the tapestry originally ended at the bottom essentially where it does now. The right quarter of this edge, extending from the bottom of the piece upward to the top of the first row of tiles inside the mansion, is a patch of later weaving showing both new warp and new weft yarns. There are other patches of modern fabric scattered throughout the piece, chiefly as follows, from left to right: the left end of the top edge; most of the small tree seeming to float in the sky at the upper left, the clouds and treetops below it and much of the field near the left edge from that point to the bottom; God the Father's torso and right arm and the aura to the right; the heraldic shield held by the two angels and most of the masonry structure beneath them, from the top of the building to a point directly above the Virgin's head; the arched porch except for the upper part of the right-hand column and its entablature; the lower third of that column and virtually the entire base of the porch as well as two sections of the entrance to the pavilion across from Gabriel's torso; all of Gabriel's halo and parts of the wings near it and of his face; his right shoulder and left hand, and the folds of his mantle below that hand; the central section of the mansion's ceiling (restored to look like a barrel vault rather than a pitched roof, which the gabled wall at the right shows it to have been); most of the cloth of honor suspended above the Virgin; and bits of the window frame behind her and of the chamber's front wall rising at the right. There are also patches in the Virgin's face, collar, corsage, both hands, the forward right corner of the dais on which she sits and some of the adjacent floor tiles. There are also many spot repairs made by weaving new weft yarns on the original warp, especially in the figure of the Christ Child carrying the cross, in the two angels, in the greenery beyond the roof line in the upper section of the tapestry, and in Gabriel's

hair. The dark brown passages everywhere in the tapestry, especially in the trees and shrubs at the left and in the floor tiles, are mostly restorations, but the lighter browns in Gabriel's wings are original. Except for the pink initial *A* of *Ave* in the scroll representing Gabriel's greeting, the letters in that inscription have been restored with brown wool of later date. There is a good deal of reddish gilt yarn (yellow metal tinsel wound on white silk core) in Gabriel's wings and the cloth of honor above the Virgin; these too are restorers' yarns. The original metal yarns—whether silver and gilt or only one or the other—have corroded and tarnished. The wool weft yarns have faded a good deal but the reds and blues are still relatively bright. The yellow yarns have lost their hue almost entirely, but where the yellow dye was mixed with blue to produce green, this hue has survived as a distinct (though muted) tone.

DESCRIPTION AND SUBJECT

The interior of a small marble mansion occupying the right half of the composition is open to view through a wide arch. A narrow porch opens into this interior space through the wall at the left. Extensive restoration in the fabric (see Condition) has altered and confused the structural logic of this building. In the original design, the porch probably had a simple pitched roof and an entrance framed by a high, narrow arch carried on colonnettes, perhaps like the porch that leads into the Virgin's house in a late twelfth-century Byzantine icon in Sinai (see note 3). There are traces of a second, taller structure, with a tiled pitched roof over a clerestory, above and to the left of the porch in the tapestry, but it is not clear how the masses related to one another. The so-called Talbot casket published and illustrated by Cherry (1982, 135, pl. XXXIIIa) shows on the inside of its lid an Annunciation set in virtually the same architectural context. It too has a narrow, short porch extending forward from the entrance to the mansion at an angle of about forty-five degrees, and the porch has a simple pitched roof surmounted by a spire. The ceiling inside the Virgin's room is represented as a ribbed and planked barrel vault like most of the ceiling created by the tapestry restorer in the Metropolitan Museum's hanging. The room inside the casket lid also has a tiled floor, but the tiles are set at an angle of forty-five degrees rather than parallel to the walls. In the tapestry, Mary sits on a throne-like chair placed on a low dais in the center of the room. A

5

patterned cloth of honor rises behind her to become a fringed canopy above. Beyond the cloth one sees the back wall which contains a row of tall, narrow arched windows surmounted by a range of small, rectangular clerestory windows. The floor is paved with polychrome tiles patterned with floral and geometric motifs; most of these are the work of a restorer. A lusterware vessel placed on the floor in the left front corner of the room contains a branch of lilies bearing three open blossoms and a fourth about to open. Through the arched opening in the right-hand wall of this room one glimpses an inner room where a number of scrolls rest on a table.

As Frantz (1972, 10–12) noted, the designer has chosen to represent the moment in the story of the Incarnation as it is told in Luke 1:28, 29 and the pseudo-Bonaventure's *Meditationes vitae Christi.* According to these texts, Mary was engaged in reading the Book of Isaias when Gabriel appeared. Here in the tapestry, Mary, wearing a mantle over a simple gown girdled at the waist, her hair falling loose beneath a wreath of flowers and a halo, has been reading a book that rests on the cantilevered and inclined shelf of a reading stand placed on the floor to the right of the dais. She turns toward the left and raises her left hand in surprise as she sees the angel and hears his greeting. Gabriel, wearing a mantle over his gown, stands outside the room, under the arched entrance to the porch, and raises his right hand in salutation. His left arm moves across the front of his body, to the right. His left hand holds the bottom of a scroll which unrolls directly upward. It shows the words *Ave/gratia/ple/na.* His right wing moves outward and back while his left wing rises sharply upward. Above the tip of this wing appears a bust of God the Father surrounded by rays of light. He raises His right hand in blessing and holds a globe in His left hand. A diminutive nude Christ Child carrying a cross flies from the bust toward the building. The Holy Spirit in the form of a dove precedes Him on rays of light, its head touching the Virgin's halo. At the very top of the composition, in the center, two angel busts carry between them a heraldic shield that they seem to be either supporting or lowering to the roof of the Virgin's house. The charges on the shield have been interpreted in a variety of ways (see below). Except at the right, where the composition is incomplete and finishes in an interior space, a verdant landscape surrounds the room and its porch. Small plants and tufts of long grasses are scattered over the greensward at the front. Shrubs and trees with gnarled trunks and a variety of leaves and blossoms grow along the left side of the composition, filling the space between grass and sky, where flat oval clouds of white and light blue float against the dark blue heavens.

The tapestry contains a number of iconographic peculiarities that are of special interest not only in themselves but also in connection with the search for a design source. The fact that Gabriel salutes Mary from an exterior space rather than from within the space she occupies indicates that the designer had been influenced by interpretations of the Annunciation that had developed in Italy from Byzantine prototypes and had in time spread to northern Europe.[1] The tradition can be traced back at least to the sixth century, to monuments like the *Annunciation* mosaic of about 540 in the Basilica of Saint Euphrasius in Poreč. There, the Virgin is seated on a throne attached to the end of a basilica as the angel approaches from the left, outside the building.[2] In a Constantinopolitan icon of the late twelfth century, now in Sinai, the exterior part of the space has developed into a landscape with very specific details, including a stream with water creatures in the foreground, grass and birds in the middle ground, and buildings in the far distance.[3] In this example, Gabriel enters the scene from the left and strides toward Mary, who sits on a throne placed before the entrance to her house which has a steep pitched roof, arched windows above the narrow arched entrance, and a roof garden above a wing whose rectangular doorway or window below is partially covered with a curtain. The facade and roof of this building, set at an angle of forty-five degrees to the picture plane, recall the architecture of the mansion in the Metropolitan Museum's tapestry. Jacopo Torriti's mosaic in Santa Maria Maggiore and the mural painting attributed to Pietro Cavallini in the porch of Santa Maria in Trastevere, both in Rome, demonstrate that the Byzantine formula for the placement of figures in scenes of the Annunciation had been absorbed into Italian art by the end of the thirteenth century.[4] As Souchal (in Paris 1973, 48) observed, some French and Franco-Flemish painters active in the last years of the fourteenth century used the exterior/interior formula when representing the Annunciation, whereas others showed both figures in a single interior space. According to Panofsky (1953, vol. 1, 87), Melchior Broederlam, in his Annunciation on the altarpiece for the Chartreuse de Champmol (fig. 95), was the first northern painter to show Gabriel in an exterior space approaching Mary in her enclosed space. Among other contemporary French or southern Netherlandish paintings showing this disposition of the figures are two panel paintings, one in Baltimore and the other in Cleveland.[5]

Another detail of special iconographic interest is the tiny nude Christ Child that proceeds from God the Father toward the Virgin, following the dove of the Holy Spirit. The dove is a traditional accessory to the scene,

Fig. 95. *The Annunciation,* detail of the exterior of the left altarpiece wing, painted by Melchior Broederlam for the Chartreuse de Champmol. Panel painting, 1394–99. Musée des Beaux-Arts, Dijon.

but the Child—the *puer parvulus formatus*—is not. As Robb indicated, the motif appears to have originated in Italy and then spread outward from there. The earliest known work of art in which it appears, as a detail, is a panel painting of about 1300 of the *Lignum Vitae* by Pacino da Buonaguida in the Accademia in Florence.[6] By the end of the fourteenth century, the *puer parvulus formatus* had appeared fairly frequently in works created not only in Italy but also in Spain, southern Bohemia, and Germany. Among these are two miniatures painted in the Book of Hours of Blanche de Savoie between 1350 and 1378 by Giovanni di Benedetto da Como, the Grabower altar wing painted by Meister Bertram of Hamburg in 1379, and the Netzer altar wing painted about 1400 by a Westphalian master.[7] The motif seems not to have appeared much in France until the second quarter of the fifteenth century. Robb cited a miniature painting of about 1430 in the Morgan Library (MS 157, fol. 57r) as the earliest known French work in

which it appears.[8] The motif had been used in southern Netherlandish painting before that. It is represented in the Merode altarpiece, painted by Robert Campin about 1425, now in The Cloisters.[9] Squilbeck (1966, 12), who believed that the Metropolitan Museum's tapestry was woven in either Arras or Tournai in the first half of the fifteenth century, interpreted it as indicating that the detail of the flying child was known there at that time and that Campin would have become familiar with the motif and then subsequently used it in the Merode altarpiece.

The Christ Child does not always carry the cross, nor does He always follow the dove in the progression moving from God the Father toward the Virgin. The descending Child appears without cross or dove in the early fifteenth-century *Annunciation* panel in the Cleveland Museum of Art (see note 5) and in the *Lignum Vitae* panel (see note 6), but with the cross and without the dove in the Merode altarpiece (see note 9). The *puer parvulus formatus* seems to have been used mostly in popular representations of the Annunciation and only rarely in monumental works. According to Robb, Robert Campin was the only major Flemish painter who used it.[10] Some medieval theologians regarded the motif as heretical and they opposed it. Pope Benedict XIV finally condemned it in the eighteenth century.

The position of Gabriel's wings in the tapestry is also a matter of special interest. They are not displayed at the same angle, either both upright as in the Broederlam panel (fig. 95) or both down as is more usual. In the tapestry Gabriel holds his right wing down and relatively close to his body whereas he lifts his left wing sharply upward. This agitated posture of the wings infuses the scene with a high emotional charge. Gabriel's wings are in similar though less dramatic poses in a number of roughly contemporary paintings including the Grabower and Netzer panels (see note 7) and the Cleveland *Annunciation* (see note 5). It is not only the position of his wings but also the angel's striding posture that invites the observer to read his attitude as one of restrained aggression. Like the tradition of the exterior/interior setting, this one harks back to Byzantine models. The best example to cite in this regard is the icon of the *Annunciation* in Ohrid, which has been attributed to Constantinople at the end of the thirteenth or early fourteenth century.[11] Like the Virgin in the tapestry, Mary in this icon seems to demur, as though more than simply startled, holding one hand up, the other down, and inclining her head. This curious interpretation of the subject probably traveled from East to West through the medium of icons and also illustrated manuscripts. Its appearance in the Metropolitan Museum's tapestry proves that the formula had been adopted in the West by the early fifteenth century.

No study of the tapestry has so far called attention to another unusual iconographic feature. It is the diadem or wreath composed of three concentric rings of pink blossoms and green leaves that encircles the crown of Mary's head. In most contemporary representations of the scene the Virgin's head is bare or partly veiled. In some she wears a crown as she does in certain representations of the Nativity, the Adoration of the Magi, and the Presentation in the Temple. She wears a crown in the Annunciation scene shown on an Upper Rhenish tapestry antependium of around 1400 preserved in the Augustinermuseum in Freiburg im Breisgau.[12] Hall and Uhr have shown that this kind of wreath is in fact a symbolic representation of the *aureola* of virginity.[13] They called attention to its appearance as a metal band covered with white blossoms in Hans Burgkmair's *Allerheiligen Altar* in Augsburg, in which a kneeling angel offers the diadem to Mary as Queen of Heaven, and also to its representation in Dürer's engraving of the Madonna in which a flying angel is about to place on her head a narrow metal circlet covered on the outside with a row of disks or blossoms.[14] Although these early sixteenth-century examples postdate the symbolic representation of the *aureola* in the tapestry, they serve to explain it.

Another important iconographic detail is the object carried by the angels at the top of the tapestry. Everyone but Panofsky (see below) has accepted it as a heraldic shield. Frantz (1972, 26–28) discussed the blazon and the readings that have been offered for it. If the shield is regarded as one showing dimidiated arms, then it may be read as (dexter) "gules, a cross trefoiled and voided or, . . . [sinister] gules (?), on two pallets argent, ladders (?) semé (?) azure." If it is thought to show a single coat of arms then the blazon would read "gules, a saltire enhanced, trefoiled and voided or with, below, on two bends (bendlets?) sinister argent, ladders (?) semé (?) azure." Frantz observed that if one accepts the coat of arms as being dimidiated it follows that the shield is lozenge-shaped. In that case the arms would be those of a lady. He also considered the possibility that the cross and ladders may not have been meant as heraldic motifs but as a reference to the Crucifixion "in heraldic dress."

We believe that the shield is an armorial one. Various attempts have been made to identify the blazon. At first Rorimer (1947, 3) stated that part of the coat of arms (meaning the dexter side of the dimidiated shield) are those of the Villanova family. However when he discussed the matter later (1961–62, 145) he said that only the arms on the sinister side of the shield can be identi-

fied positively and that they represent the Escales family. Other scholars have discussed the shield and acknowledged that because the motif has been damaged and restored it is virtually impossible to interpret the blazon. In a letter to the present author, Sr. J. Ainaud de Lasarte, former director of the Museu d'Art de Catalunya in Barcelona, outlined the results of his own research concerning the coat of arms. He suggested that the arms were those of Francesc de Blanés, bishop of Gerona from 1408 to 1409 and of Barcelona from 1409 to 1410. Sr. Ainaud de Lasarte observed further that Francesc de Blanés's coat of arms contained both a cross and the ladders of the Escales family. He also expressed the opinion, with which we agree, that the unusual position of the shield in the composition suggests that the coat of arms was not part of the original design of the tapestry but was added later, after the bishop had acquired it.

The matter seems to be even more complex than that. A recent cleaning and detailed examination of the tapestry has shown that the shield-like motif was completely rewoven with new warp and weft yarns sometime in the past. Certainly it is a heraldic shield now, but we cannot be sure that such a shield was in the original design. The motif may have originated as a lozenge and then been turned into a shield having a lozenge-shaped top and a long asymmetrical bottom. Panofsky (1935, 450 n. 32; 1953, 134 n. 4) has provided an explanation. Having seen the tapestry or illustrations of it before it was cleaned, he said that this object looked "rather like an embroidered cushion" and suggested that it was a weaver's misunderstood rendering of the capstone (also interpreted as a keystone or cornerstone) image from Psalm 118:22 and other scriptural sources, "The stone which the builders rejected; the same is become the head of the corner." The stone appeared in some illustrations of the Annunciation at this time as a symbol of Christ. Its placement atop the building, as the final stone in the structure, was seen as the promise of His coming.[15] Panofsky (1935, figs. 20, 21) illustrated two examples of the capstone symbol. One is a drawing in a *Speculum Humanae Salvationis* in the Staatsbibliothek in Munich that shows two masons atop a building holding a lozenge-shaped stone above a tower rising between them as they prepare to lay the stone in place. In the second example, the Annunciation panel from the altar painted by the master of Heiligenkreuz, now in the Kunsthistorisches Museum in Vienna, two tiny angels lay a stone on the top of a church wall that rises behind the Virgin's throne. Panofsky (1935, 450 n. 32) described the angels in that painting and in the Metropolitan Museum's tapestry as a seraph and a cherub, in the case of the tapestry presumably because one of the bust figures wears a red robe and the other a blue one. There can be little doubt that the tapestry designer meant these two angels, like those in the drawing and the painting, to be interpreted as figures laying the biblical capstone as a symbol of Christ and of His coming. We may assume that some later owner had that lozenge-shaped passage of weaving (lozenge-shaped because it represents a square stone seen in perspective at an angle of ninety degrees) removed and the heraldic shield woven anew in its place while retaining the silhouette of the upper half of the stone's lozenge shape as the contour of the top of the shield. Further technical and historical investigation must be undertaken to confirm Sr. Ainaud de Lasarte's contention that the owner may have been Francesc de Blanés; but even at this stage of the investigation it seems likely that the coat of arms is a bona fide one.

Frantz (1972, 11) noted and commented upon another curious detail in the composition. It is the little tree bearing round leaves and/or fruits which seems to float in the sky in the upper left corner and differs from all the other trees and shrubs in the hanging. Frantz thought that this tree might represent the Tree of the Knowledge of Good and Evil. One would expect a painter to represent such an important symbol of the Fall of Man in a complete scene preceding the Annunciation, as for example Zanobi Strozzi did in his altarpiece of about 1445 that is now in the Prado.[16] Nevertheless, if we assume that the little tree in the tapestry (heavily restored and partly replaced with later weaving) was in fact originally there, we must also assume that it has a very particular meaning, quite possibly the meaning that Frantz suggested for it.

Finally, the reading stand with its cantilevered arm is also an unusual detail in this composition. Representations of this kind of stand are rare, so rare as perhaps to have exaggerated in the minds of some writers the degree to which the tapestry composition depends on the Broederlam altar wing (fig. 95) in which a very similar reading stand appears. However cantilevered stands like these do occur in other Annunciation scenes of the period, including the one on the Grabower altar of 1379, on a page in Guillaume de Vrelant's *Traité sur la salutation angélique,* on the Heiligenkreuz panel of about 1410, and on a slightly earlier panel in the Walters Art Gallery.[17]

SOURCE OF THE DESIGN

In Ackerman's two earlier studies of this tapestry (exh. cat. San Francisco 1922, no. 1; 1922–23, 50), she attributed its design to some anonymous painter of the Paris school in the circle of Jean Malouel. In her opinion, this anonymous artist also painted the four altar panels showing scenes from the life of Christ that are now divided equally between the Baltimore Museum of Art and the Mayer van den Bergh Museum, Antwerp. Certainly the designer of the Metropolitan Museum's tapestry was working in the international Gothic style of the late fourteenth and early fifteenth century, and his work was indeed close to that of Jean Malouel as it was also to the work of the painter of the presentation pages in the *Belles Heures de Jean de France* (the "Brussels Hours"), where one finds a Madonna with similar hair, face, hands, and smooth, limp drapery.[18] Ackerman (1926–27) then wrote that she had found initials referring to Willem van Roome in the Metropolitan Museum's tapestry. She suggested that this Netherlandish painter, whom she proposed as a designer of tapestries even though he is known only from a reference to his having designed decorations for the wedding of Charles le Téméraire, designed the tapestry. The suggestion does not stand close examination, for what may have appeared to Ackerman to be two capital letters *R* in the pattern decorating the majolica pot holding lilies are more likely pseudo-Arabic letters. The lowercase letter *m* or *w* on the tile directly below the base of the reading stand is a replacement made with new warp and weft yarns that may or may not have followed the pattern that was there originally; if it did, the letter need not have been anything more than a decorative motif.

In 1927, when the tapestry was exhibited at the Jacques Seligmann Galleries in New York, the author of the catalogue entries (text, pl. VII) expressed the opinion that the design and workmanship related this piece closely to the *Apocalypse* tapestries in Angers, an observation that can be discounted out of hand. In 1928, when the tapestry was exhibited in the Metropolitan Museum, the author of the catalogue entry recalled Ackerman's attributions to the follower of Jean Malouel or to Willem van Roome and added that the hanging was reminiscent of the Annunciation on one of the two altar wings that Melchior Broederlam painted for the Chartreuse de Champmol between 1394 and 1399 and is now preserved in the Musée des Beaux-Arts, Dijon. This observation, unlike the earlier ones, has much to recommend it, and it has been repeated with varying degrees of conviction by all writers since that time. Rorimer (1947; with Forsyth, 1953–54, 135) emphasized the tapestry's close relationship to the altar wing Annunciation and later (1961–62, 146) suggested that Broederlam himself might have designed this tapestry and even painted the cartoon for it. Souchal (in Paris 1973, 48) called attention to the ways in which the two compositions differ

Fig. 96. *The Annunciation,* miniature painting in the Book of Hours by the Rohan Master. Paris, about 1418–20. Bibliothèque Nationale, Paris (MS Lat. 9471, fol. 45).

miniature paintings but also the design of the Metropolitan Museum's tapestry. He observed (1953, 134) that the tapestry differed from the picture in two details; that is, that the skein of wool that the Virgin holds in the painting is not in the tapestry and that the flying Christ Child in the tapestry is not in the painting.

Indeed the painting differs from the tapestry in other ways, and these differences are even more critical. In a letter that he addressed to Rorimer on February 13, 1943, Panofsky noted that while the Broederlam panel would have been the chief source of the tapestry design there must have been another source that included the capstone image which is in the tapestry but not in the painting. Also, while the figures in the tapestry and painting occupy roughly the same kinds of spaces and hold approximately the same poses, their psychological content is totally different. The angel in the Broederlam composition approaches Mary humbly, balancing his speech scroll delicately in both hands. Mary turns toward him with mild surprise. But in the tapestry the angel strides toward Mary with some aggression and throws his scroll straight upward. Mary moves her left arm forward and raises that hand in a gesture of defense. Furthermore in the Broederlam painting the room in which Mary reads is shown as a porch projecting forward at an angle of about forty-five degrees and attached at the back to a round building next to two rectangular ones. In the tapestry Mary's room stands alone in the landscape like a pavilion and its front edge is set parallel to the picture plane. Even if the tapestry continued farther to the right to show more buildings constituting a town, as the buildings in the painting do, the effect of the setting in the tapestry would still be static as compared to the dynamic setting in the painting.

It was noted above (Description and Subject) in the discussion of the curious iconographic details in this tapestry that both Gabriel's striding pose and the narrow porch leading into Mary's room from the exterior space can be traced to late Byzantine prototypes.[20] At least one other contemporary European Annunciation shows an equally dynamic and aggressive Gabriel. It is a page in the *Grandes Heures de Rohan* that was painted in Paris about 1418–20 (fig. 96). This angel annunciate shows the same striding stance, the same upward tilt of the head, and a similar crossed position of the arms although it is the other hand that throws the scroll upward. Only the pose of the wings differs greatly. The manuscript page has been attributed by some specialists to an anonymous master who worked in Paris but was, some thought, perhaps a native of Catalonia. Meiss believed that this Book of Hours might have been made originally for either Charles, duc de Berry, later

and suggested that Broederlam and the tapestry designer had access to a common source, an opinion that Coffinet (1977, 30) repeated and endorsed. Panofsky (1953, vol. 1, 86, 88) pointed out that as Philippe le Hardi's court painter from 1391 onward, Broederlam did everything from painting banners and chairs to decorating a pavilion and designing layouts for tile floors. (Other writers also mentioned Broederlam's work with tile design and implied that there was a connection between Broederlam and the tiled floor represented in the tapestry, a matter of no consequence, now that we know the floor is very heavily restored.) While he did not repeat Göbel's reference to a Burgundian court document of September 12, 1390, identifying Broederlam as the designer of some shepherd and shepherdess tapestries[19] (to which Heinz 1963, 59; Souchal in Paris 1973, 48; and Lestocquoy 1978, 48, referred), Panofsky maintained that Broederlam's Annunciation inspired not only many

Charles VII of France, or for Louis III, duc d'Anjou; that the so-called Rohan Master painted only the figure of Gabriel on this page; and that the anonymous artist was not Spanish but someone who began his career in Provence or Champagne, then worked in Troyes and finally in Paris.[21] This anonymous painter and the designer of the tapestry both seem to have been influenced by some image of Gabriel that ultimately drew its inspiration from late Byzantine painting. However the formal sympathies that link the tapestry with the Broederlam Annunciation indicate that the tapestry designer was also influenced by a version of this painting or a common source from which both artists drew inspiration. As Panofsky observed in his letter to Rorimer, since the detail of the capstone does not appear in Broederlam's painting, the tapestry designer's source must have included that detail.

MANUFACTURE AND DATE

Opinions have been fairly consistent in regarding the tapestry as Franco-Flemish work of the end of the fourteenth or beginning of the fifteenth century since Ackerman (in exh. cat. San Francisco 1922) first published that attribution. The author of the Seligmann exhibition catalogue of 1927 (pl. VII and text), Siple (1927), and Panofsky (1935, 450 n. 32; 1953, 134) found the *Annunciation* tapestry reminiscent of the *Apocalypse* of Angers and believed that it was woven in France. The author of the Seligmann exhibition catalogue dated it in the last quarter of the fourteenth century, Siple in the early fifteenth century, and Panofsky about 1450. Rorimer (1947) was the first to suggest that the tapestry might have been woven in Arras; and his attribution to Arras in the early fifteenth century was echoed in publications by Rorimer and Forsyth (1953–54, 136), Heinz (1962, fig. 6; 1963, fig. 31), Wixom (1967), Souchal (in Paris 1973, 48), Stechow (1974), Coffinet (1977, 28), and Lestocquoy (1978, 48). Verlet (1965, 18) dated the tapestry in the first half (rather than the first years or first quarter) of the fifteenth century, and Squilbeck (1966, 12) allowed not only the same range of dates but also an attribution to Tournai as well as to Arras.

Because of certain details that Stucky-Schürer (1972, 99 and fig. 74) believed were common to both the Metropolitan Museum's hanging and the *Resurrection* tapestry in the Louvre, she dated the former about 1435–40. She (1972, 93–99), along with Coffinet (1977) and Lestocquoy (1978), believed that they could isolate and identify in the Metropolitan Museum's tapestry and a group of others dating from the late fourteenth and early fifteenth centuries certain stylistic characteristics they also found in the *Story of Saints Piat and Eleuthère*; and so they attributed the Metropolitan Museum's tapestry along with the others to Arras. In our opinion these "stylistic" comparisons involve not formal considerations but motifs that were almost certainly common property among tapestry designers and weavers at this time in this region and not the exclusive property of weavers in Arras, an opinion shared by Digby (1980, 11). Nevertheless, these similarities do exist, and they help fix the date of the Metropolitan Museum's tapestry in the early years of the fifteenth century.

Erlande-Brandenburg (1970, 172) suggested that the designer might have been a southerner because, he believed, the patches of delicate color in the marble of which the buildings are made give the effect of Cosmati work and also because the twisted columns of the porch, the acanthus decoration on its arch, and the vase all look more Italian than northern. However the dabs of color in the stone look more like natural mottling than mosaic, and the acanthus decoration is not original but restored work. The vase has now been identified as Manises majolica (see below). Lestocquoy (1978, 48) also believed that the ceramic pot containing the lilies was reminiscent of Italy, but that since there was so much influence from Italian art in Arras at this time there is no reason to wonder whether the tapestry might have been woven in Italy. There is a suggestion in unpublished notes in the files of the Metropolitan Museum Department of Medieval Art that the tapestry might have been designed and possibly also woven in Catalonia, a possibility that Souchal (in Paris 1973, 49) considered but did not endorse. In fact there are no grounds to support such a suggestion, which probably represents reverse thinking based on the claim that the tapestry was found in a Catalan church.

Every consideration of style and iconography indicates that the tapestry was designed by an artist in the service of the kings of France or the royal dukes (or by a lesser light deriving images from such an artist) and that it was designed in the early years of the fifteenth century. The only detail that might argue for a slightly later date is the majolica pot containing the lilies. As noted above, it has been referred to as a faience pot of Italian type. But everything about it—its shape, the character of its ornament, the light ocher (meant to represent golden luster) and blue colors of the glazes, and the pseudo-Arabic inscription—points to Spain as the pot's place of design and manufacture. As a number of specialists have said in unpublished notes to the present author, ceramic containers of this shape did not appear in Italy until the late fifteenth century. However this shape and style of decoration are found in majolica vessels from Valencia made at Manises. González Martí published certain pieces as dating from the first half to middle of the fifteenth century.[22] A few of these ceramics are strikingly similar to the pot in the tapestry. Among the pots that González Martí illustrated are a mortar for grinding basil leaves that has a high, wide, splayed foot rather like the foot of the lily pot in the tapestry. He dated it in the first half of the fifteenth century.[23] He dated a very similar vessel decorated with bryony blossoms like the ones on the pot in the tapestry to the middle of the fifteenth century and a surprise jug with the bryony blossoms, the high splayed foot, and four spouts like the two on the pot in the tapestry to the same period.[24] The curious detail of the "pie-crust" edge on the foot of the pot in the tapestry appears around the foot of a flower vase that González Martí published as dating from the end of the fifteenth or beginning of the sixteenth century.[25] It is not clear whether that detail was used only at this relatively late period. Should it be possible in the future to refine the dates of these Manises vessels, the one shown in the tapestry would provide a terminus a quo for the date of the tapestry design. For the present it seems reasonable to follow González Martí and date the lily pot shown in the tapestry sometime in the first half of the fifteenth century and also to acknowledge that in terms of style the tapestry should be dated even more precisely within the first third of the century. Since the weaving is of fine quality and contains some metallic yarns, the hanging was clearly made for a wealthy patron who would not have ordered or bought it after its pattern passed out of fashion.

RELATED TAPESTRIES

As Verlet (1965) has observed, the tapestry could be a hanging in its own right or a fragment of a larger one. If it is indeed but a fragment, the whole piece would have continued for some distance to the right, and possibly also to the left, and would have shown more scenes from the life of the Virgin or of Christ. Since the bottom edge has preserved bits of the original selvage and the top of the field shows passages of sky, it is clear that the mother hanging—if there was one—could not have been a great deal taller than this piece, perhaps some three to four feet at most, bringing the total height to no more than sixteen feet. As it is now the tapestry is too tall to have come from the upper section of a longer and taller tapestry showing scenes on two or more levels, like the two *Passion* tapestries in La Seo in Saragossa (to which this tapestry has often been likened).[26] However it might have been part of a larger hanging showing scenes in

mansions about two-thirds the height of the tapestry alternating with scenes that rose to the full height of the hanging, as one sees in the somewhat later *Good Government* tapestry in the cathedral at Tarragona.[27]

If it has always been a hanging in its own right, the Metropolitan Museum's piece must have belonged to a series of hangings showing scenes from the life of the Virgin or of Christ. Contemporary documents refer to more than one tapestry cycle with these subjects. For example, in 1423 Philippe le Bon paid Giovanni Arnolfini, the Medici agent in Bruges, for such a series in six pieces bought as a gift for Pope Martin V. This set of hangings, described as follows, could have been woven after the series of cartoons from which the Museum's tapestry derives, as Jarry (1969, 63, caption) has suggested: "A *Jehan Arnoulphin*, marchant de Lucques, demourant à Bruges, la somme de trois cens quarante cinq liures du poids de XL gros monnoye de Flandres la liure, pour six pièces de tapisserie faites et ouvrées bien richement de plusieurs histoires de Nostre Dame. C'est assavoir la première de l'Anunciation, la seconde de la Nativité, la tierche de l'Aparicion, la quarte de la Circoncision de NS, la Ve de l'Assumption de Nostre Dame, et la VIe du Couronnement d'Icelle . . . donné a Meleun, le XI jour de septembre M CCCC XXIII."[28]

HISTORY

Said to have been bought by a dealer from the treasury of the cathedral church of Gerona about 1910, then to have passed into the possession of the Spanish Art Gallery, London, before becoming the property of French and Company, New York, sometime before 1922. Rorimer (1961–62, 145) said that a resident of Tarragona had related an alternate tradition—that is, that the tapestry had hung for many years in a chapel in the cathedral church of that city—but Rorimer was not able to substantiate that claim.

Bought by Mrs. Harold Irving Pratt from French and Company in 1924.

In the collection of Mr. and Mrs. Harold Irving Pratt, New York.

Given to the MMA by Harriet Barnes Pratt, 1949, in memory of her husband, Harold Irving Pratt.

EXHIBITIONS

Chicago, Art Institute, 1920. *An Exhibition of Gothic Tapestries of France and Flanders.* Cat. no. 3. Lender's name not listed.

San Francisco Museum of Art, 1922. *Catalogue of the Retrospective Loan Exhibition of European Tapestries.* Catalogue by Phyllis Ackerman. Cat. no. 1. Lent by French and Company.

New York, Jacques Seligmann & Co. Galleries, 1927. *Loan Exhibition of Religious Art for the Benefit of the Basilique of the Sacré Coeur of Paris.* Cat. no. VII. Lent by Mr. and Mrs. Harold I. Pratt.

Cambridge, Massachusetts, William Hayes Fogg Art Museum, 1927. Opening exhibition in the new museum (see Siple 1927 in Publications). Lent by Mrs. Harold I. Pratt.

New York, MMA, 1928. *French Gothic Tapestries: A Loan Exhibition.* Cat. no. 1, illus. Lent by Harold Irving Pratt.

Boston, Museum of Fine Arts, 1940. *Arts of the Middle Ages: A Loan Exhibition.* Cat. no. 110. Lent by Mrs. Harold I. Pratt.

Paris 1973. Catalogue entries by Geneviève Souchal. Cat. no. 6, illus.

New York 1974. Cat. no. 6, illus.

PUBLICATIONS

Ackerman, Phyllis. "Tapestries of Five Centuries: I. The French Gothic Looms." *International Studio* 76 (1922–23) pp. 49–50, 53. Discussed briefly; illus in color p. 43.

Hunter 1925, pp. 26–27, 233. Discussed; illus. pls. III,i, XVII,c (detail). In Limited, Subscription Edition, illus. also pl. S,e (detail).

Ackerman, Phyllis. "Recently Identified Designers of Gothic Tapestries." *Art Bulletin* 9 (1926–27) p. 144. Mentioned.

Ackerman, Phyllis. *A Catalog of the Tapestries in the Collection of Frank Gair Macomber.* N.p., [1927], p. 2. Discussed briefly.

Siple, Walter H. "The New Fogg Art Museum: The Opening Exhibition." *The Arts* 12 (1927) p. 35. Mentioned; illus. p. 4 (hanging on gallery wall).

"Illustrierte Berichte aus Berlin, London, New-York. . . ." *Pantheon* 2 (1928) p. 372. Mentioned.

Breck, Joseph. "The Tapestry Exhibition: Part I." *MMA Bulletin* 23 (1928) p. 147. Mentioned.

Panofsky, Erwin. "The Friedsam Annunciation and the Problem of the Ghent Altarpiece." *Art Bulletin* 17 (1935) p. 450 n. 32. Discussed briefly; illus. fig. 25.

Crick-Kuntziger, Marthe. "De vlaamsche tapijtweverij in de XIVᵉ, XVᵉ, en XVIᵉ eeuwen." In Stan Leurs, ed., *Geschiedenis van de Vlaamsche Kunst.* Vol. 1, The Hague, 1936, p. 483. Mentioned.

Townsend, Gertrude. "Mediaeval Textiles in Boston." *Art News* 38 (February 17, 1940) p. 24. Discussed briefly; illus. p. 16.

Taylor, Francis Henry. "The Middle Ages in Boston." *Parnassus* 12, no. 3 (March 1940) p. 9. Mentioned; illus. facing p. 5.

Ladner, Gerhart B. "The Symbolism of the Biblical Corner Stone in the Mediaeval West." *Mediaeval Studies* 4 (1942) p. 44. Mentioned.

Rorimer, James J. *Mediaeval Tapestries: A Picture Book.* MMA, New York, 1947, p. [2]. Discussed briefly; illus. fig. 2.

Panofsky, Erwin. *Early Netherlandish Painting: Its Origins and Character.* Cambridge, Mass., 1953, vol. 1, pp. 88, 134, 412 n. 4. Discussed briefly; illus. fig. 51.

Rorimer, James J., and William H. Forsyth. "The Medieval Galleries." *MMA Bulletin,* n.s. 12 (1953–54) p. 135. Discussed briefly; illus. p. 136.

Rorimer, James J. "The Annunciation Tapestry." *MMA Bulletin,* n.s. 20 (1961–62) pp. 145–46. Discussed at length; illus. fig. 2 and cover (color detail).

Heinz, Dora. "Gewirkte Monumentalmalerei—Zur Tapisseriekunst in Frankreich und Burgund um 1400." *Alte und Moderne Kunst* 7, nos. 56/57 (March/April 1962) pp. 28–29. Discussed briefly; illus. fig. 6.

King, Donald. "Textielkunst um 1400." In *Europäische Kunst um 1400.* Exh. cat., Kunsthistorisches Museum. Vienna, 1962, p. 438. Discussed briefly.

Heinz, Dora. *Europäische Wandteppiche I.* Brunswick, 1963, p. 59. Mentioned; illus. fig. 31.

Verlet 1965, p. 18. Discussed briefly.

Squilbeck, Jean. "Un aspect peu connu de la personalité du Maître de Flémalle." *Revue Belge d'Archéologie et d'Histoire de l'Art* 35 (1966) p. 12. Discussed briefly; illus. p. 11.

Wixom, William D. *Treasures from Medieval France.* Exh. cat., Cleveland Museum of Art. Cleveland, 1967, p. 242. Discussed briefly.

Jarry, Madeleine. *World Tapestry: From Its Origins to the Present.* New York, 1969, pp. 62, 63. Mentioned; illus. pp. 52 (detail of Virgin's hands), 53 (full view).

van Ysselsteyn, G. T. *Tapestry: The Most Expensive Industry of the XVth and XVIth Centuries.* The Hague and Brussels, 1969, p. 38. Discussed briefly; illus. fig. 14.

Erlande-Brandenburg, Alain. Review of M. Jarry, *La tapisserie des origines a nos jours. Bulletin Monumental* 128 (1970) p. 172. Discussed briefly.

Coffinet, Julien. *Arachne ou l'art de la tapisserie.* Geneva and Paris, 1971, illus. pp. 15 (full view, black and white), 101, 108, 153, 180–82 (color details).

Frantz, James H. "The Annunciation Tapestry in The Metropolitan Museum of Art and the International Gothic Style in Early Franco-Flemish Tapestries." Qualifying paper submitted in partial fulfillment of the requirements for M.A., Institute of Fine Arts, New York University, 1972, pp. 3–28.

Stucky-Schürer, Monica. *Die Passionsteppiche von San Marco in Venedig.* Bern, 1972, pp. 93, 95, 99, 100. Discussed at length; illus. fig. 75.

W. S. [Wolfgang Stechow]. Catalogue entry for no. 8. In *European Paintings before 1500: Catalogue of Paintings.* Cleveland Museum of Art. Cleveland, 1974, p. 23. Mentioned.

Coffinet 1977, pp. 28, 30. Discussed at length; illus. pp. 25 (full view, black and white), 24, 26–28 (color details).

Lestocquoy 1978, p. 48. Discussed at length; color illus. pls. VII (full view), VIII (detail).

Digby 1980, p. 11. Mentioned.

Joubert, Fabienne. *La tapisserie au moyen âge.* Rennes, 1981, p. 15. Discussed briefly; color detail illus. p. 11.

Cherry, J. "The Talbot Casket and Related Late Medieval Leather Caskets." *Archaeologia* (Society of Antiquaries, London) 107 (1982) p. 135. Discussed briefly; illus. pl. XXXIIIb.

NOTES

1. For a brief account of this development, see Erwin Panofsky, "The Friedsam Annunciation and the Problem of the Ghent Altarpiece," *Art Bulletin* 17 (1935) pp. 441–42.

   The present author is indebted to James H. Frantz, who generously allowed him to consult his qualifying paper "The Annunciation Tapestry in The Metropolitan Museum of Art and the International Gothic Style in Early Franco-Flemish Tapestries" (see Publications above), in which Frantz found some new references to published sources used in this catalogue entry and also a number of original observations that stimulated his own thinking about the tapestry.

2. Illustrated in Gertrud Schiller, *Ikonographie der christlichen Kunst* (Gutersloh, 1966–76) vol. 1, fig. 72.

3. Illustrated in Kurt Weitzmann, *The Icon: Holy Images—Sixth to Fourteenth Century* (New York, 1978) pl. 27, with text.

4. Illustrated in Schiller, *Ikonographie,* vol. 1, figs. 96 (Torriti) and 101 (attributed to Cavallini).

5. For the Baltimore panel, see *The International Style: The Arts in Europe around 1400,* exh. cat., Walters Art Gallery (Baltimore, 1962) no. 24, pl. IV. For the painting in Cleveland, see *European Paintings before 1500: Catalogue of Paintings,* Cleveland Museum of Art (Cleveland, 1974) no. 24, fig. 8, and color pl. VI.

6. See David Robb, "The Iconography of the Annunciation of the 14th–15th Century," *Art Bulletin* 18 (1936) pp. 523–26. The detail from the panel is illustrated by Robb as fig. 44, and by Schiller, *Ikonographie,* vol. 1, as fig. 101.

7. See, for the miniatures, Robb, "Iconography," pp. 524–25, fig. 45, and for the panels, Schiller, *Ikonographie,* vol. 1, figs. 103, 104.

8. Robb, "Iconography," p. 525, where he cites also two other French examples of around 1430; illustrated in Panofsky, "Friedsam Annunciation," fig. 15.

9. The central panel containing the Annunciation is illustrated in Schiller, *Ikonographie,* vol. 1, fig. 113. Panofsky illustrates the two wings as well in *Early Netherlandish Painting: Its Origins and Character* (Cambridge, Mass., 1953) vol. 2, fig. 204. See also Katharine Baetjer, *European Paintings in The Metropolitan Museum of Art by Artists Born in or before 1865: A Summary Catalogue* (New York, 1980) vol. 1, p. 23.

10. Robb, "Iconography," p. 526.

11. Weitzmann, *The Icon,* pl. 44; also Robert S. Nelson, "A Byzantine Painter in Trecento Genoa: The *Last Judgment* at S. Lorenzo," *Art Bulletin* 67 (1985) p. 555, fig. 14.

12. Illustrated in *Die Parler und der schöne Stil 1350–1400: Europäische Kunst unter den Luxemburgern*, exh. cat., Schnütgen Museum (Cologne, 1978–80) vol. [5], p. T-104; see also Kurth 1926, pls. 162–63.

13. Edwin Hall and Horst Uhr, "*Aureola super Auream:* Crowns and Related Symbols of Special Distinction for Saints in Late Gothic and Renaissance Iconography," *Art Bulletin* 67 (1985) pp. 566–603, esp. p. 602, where the authors state that "late scholastic writers . . . sometimes refer to the *aureola* of virgins as being made of flowers" as opposed to the *aureola* of martyrs (precious stones) and of doctors (stars).

14. See Hall and Uhr, "*Aureola super Auream,*" pp. 601–2, figs. 33, 34.

15. The image of the stone, in slightly varying forms, appears also in Isaias 28:16, Matthew 21:42, Mark 12:10, Luke 20:17, Acts 4:11, and Ephesians 2:20–21. Panofsky, in *Early Netherlandish Painting*, vol. 1, p. 134, observed that this stone, the *lapis in caput anguli* of the Vulgate, was interpreted as being a keystone as well as a "headstone of the corner." Gerhart B. Ladner, "The Symbolism of the Biblical Corner Stone in the Mediaeval West," *Mediaeval Studies* 4 (1942) pp. 43–60, treated the entire question of the interpretation of the scriptural cornerstone as a foundation stone and as a stone at the top of a building.

16. Illustrated in Schiller, *Ikonographie*, vol. 1, fig. 121.

17. For illustrations of the reading stands, see respectively Schiller, *Ikonographie*, vol. 1, fig. 104; Robb, "Iconography," fig. 35; Panofsky, "Friedsam Annunciation," fig. 21; and *International Style*, exh. cat., Walters Art Gallery, pl. iv.

18. Bibliothèque Royale Albert I, Brussels, MS 11.060–61, fols. 10 and 11. Illustrated in L. M. J. Delaissé, H. Liebaers, and F. Masai, *Medieval Miniatures from the Department of Manuscripts . . . the Royal Library of Belgium* (New York, 1965) nos. 19, 20. The paintings have been attributed to an anonymous French painter and dated about 1390.

19. Göbel 1923, vol. 1, p. 232.

20. Gabriel is shown in the striding pose in the icon at Sinai and the one at Ohrid; the porch appears only in the former. See Weitzmann, *The Icon*, pls. 27, 44, both with text.

21. Millard Meiss and Marcel Thomas, *The Rohan Master: A Book of Hours* (New York, 1973) p. 16.

22. Consultations generously accorded the author in person by Jessie McNab and Carl C. Dauterman at the MMA and through indirect correspondence with John V. G. Mallet, Victoria and Albert Museum, and Anthony Ray, Ashmolean Museum, through the kindness of Tina Levey and John Archer, Victoria and Albert Museum. Messrs. Mallet and Ray called to the author's attention Spanish pottery, especially Manises work, and the publication by Manuel González Martí, *Cerámica del Levante español, siglos medievales* (Barcelona, 1944–52). The author expresses his thanks to all these colleagues.

23. González Martí, *Cerámica*, vol. 1, fig. 300.

24. González Martí, *Cerámica*, vol. 1, figs. 301, 368 respectively.

25. González Martí, *Cerámica*, vol. 1, fig. 382.

26. For text and illustrations in color, see Eduardo Torra de Arana et al., *Los Tapices de La Seo de Zaragoza* (Saragossa, 1985) pp. 61–73.

27. Illustrated in James J. Rorimer, "The Annunciation Tapestry," *MMA Bulletin*, n.s. 20 (1961–62) pp. 146 (fig. 1), 148 (fig. 3).

28. Léon E. S. J. de Laborde, *Les ducs de Bourgogne* (Paris, 1849–52) vol. 1, pp. 196–97.

6

Honor Making a Chaplet of Roses

Southern Netherlands, 1425–50
Wool warp, wool wefts
7 ft. 9 in. × 9 ft. (2.36 m × 2.74 m)
10–12 warp yarns per inch, 4–5 per centimeter
The Cloisters Collection, 1959 (59.85)

CONDITION

The hanging is a mosaic of pieces that have been joined together with new warp yarns. The lines of joining were then covered over with new weft yarns. The constituent pieces are predominantly rectangular in shape, but they vary in size from small bits to a large rectangular fragment in the left-central section, which includes the figures of the seated lady making the chaplet, most of the male figure at the left, almost all of the female figure at the right, and also the hedge, grass, and meadow adjacent to those figures. The next largest fragment, again a horizontal rectangle, has been placed just below the main fragment. It contains the representation of the flowery meadow below the lady's bower as well as parts of the three banderoles inscribed with couplets that flutter in front of this ground. The rather short scroll at the left, the one whose inscription begins *uut a mon bon*, is only the right-hand portion of a longer scroll, its left half or so having been cut off with the rest of the field along that side. What appears to be the fluttering left end of this scroll, curling downward, is in fact a bit of restoration. Furthermore, the letters at the left ends of both lines of the couplet, especially the initial letters *u* and *d*, may be restorations. The scroll running along the bottom of this fragment directly below the figure of the seated lady is in its original state except for its right and lower edges and the fluttering downward-turning end at the left, all of which are restorations. As for the scroll at the right, only a bit more than the left-hand half, whose couplet begins with the word *Pour*, belongs with this large rectangular fragment. The section on which appear *rre a mi* on the first line and *io il* on the second line is woven on a different fragment and therefore must represent part of a totally different scroll. The line separating the two parts of the scroll runs from the upper edge of the scroll directly downward through the first *e* in the word *perre* and the *u* in *capu* to the lower edge. Other pieces of weaving of varying size and shape, though mostly rectangular, have been pieced in below and to the sides of the two fragments bearing the inscriptions.

A tall narrow piece fills the space between the left edge of the hanging and the left sides of the hedge and of the figure of the man standing at the left. Two long narrow fragments and two smaller oddly shaped ones have been pieced to each other and joined to the rest along the top of the hanging. They extend from the left edge of the field almost to the middle of the scroll that flutters above the head of the man standing at the right. All of the meadow above the three figures at the left, the upper half of the girl's hat, and most of the left end of the scroll at the right are represented in this composite section. It was joined to the main section below with a long, wide passage of reweaving which includes the head (from the nose upward) and headdress of the man at the left and also the forehead of the woman standing right of center and the lower half of her hat. This strip of repair also involves wide parts of the flowery meadow lying between and beyond those two heads. The figure of the man standing at the right and the right-hand two-thirds of the scroll above his head belong to one large upright rectangular fragment of weaving that has been joined to the rest. Four other patches fill out the space between the right side of his body and the right edge of the hanging. The fabric representing his ankles and shoes is modern. The fluttering downward-turning left end of the scroll above his head and its entire right end, including the section that curls upward, are all restorations. The first word in the first line of the couplet inscribed on this banderole, *Deduit*, and the upper parts of the first three letters in the second line, *eim* (?), together with the portion of the scroll immediately adjacent, belong to one of the two small patches of weaving that were placed along the top of the field. The lower parts of the letters in the lower line have been restored. The next letters in each line, *ce* above and *ci* below, have also been restored. The words following these, *sui qui ve* (or *de*?) in the upper line and *le ce bien au* in the lower one, are in their original condition. The rest of the word beginning *ve* or *de* and some text that presumably followed *au* have been cut off with the fabric on which the right end of the scroll was represented.

There are a few more patches and spots of reweaving in different parts of the field but they have not affected the composition significantly. The constituent parts of this hanging came either from different parts of one large tapestry or from several tapestries belonging to a particular series of hangings (see Related Tapestries).

Bands of modern fabric have been sewn to the four

6

149

edges of the piece. The colors have for the most part preserved the integrity of their hues throughout; they are fresh and relatively bright. Kurth (1923, 57) claimed that the warp is made of linen yarns; but like all the weft yarns in this hanging the warp yarns were spun of woolen fibers.

DESCRIPTION AND SUBJECT

In the left half of the field a lady wearing an ermine-lined houppelande with a wide falling collar, flaring sleeves turned back at the elbow, and a narrow jeweled girdle sits on a flowered lawn closed in at the sides and back by a green hedge in which more blossoming plants grow. Her floral-patterned undersleeves, ballooning outward from the tight cuffs at the wrists, project beyond the sleeves of the houppelande. Her coiffure is a low, wide bourrelet studded with five-petaled blossoms or jewels. At the ends it rests on twin "horns" of hair gathered over the temples (see similar costumes in 3a and b). In her left hand she holds a half-finished chaplet made of red and pink rosebuds strung on a hoop. The knife used to sever the buds from the stalks has been thrust into the hedge near her left elbow. Her gaze and the gesture of her left hand are directed toward a young lady who stands outside the hedge enclosure at the right. This figure is dressed in a simple fitted gown, or cotte, that laces up the right side of the bodice and has a low round neckline and long sleeves flaring outward at the cuffs. She wears low, round-toed shoes with straps over the insteps. A wide, spotted hat decorated with a jeweled pin perches on the top of her head. Since the lower half of this headdress is represented in an area of restoration and the top half belongs with a patch of weaving that may have come from a different part of this tapestry or from a different tapestry altogether, we cannot be sure that the hat looked like this originally or that it belongs here.[1] This young lady gathers up the folds of her skirt in her right hand and raises the other hand toward her left ear. The fingers appear to be touching her hat; but since the hat may not have been there originally the gesture may have been intended to express some other action, perhaps a greeting to the lady seated in the enclosure. A man wearing a knee-length, ungirdled tunic (a huke) stands close to the outside of the hedge at the left. The ballooning sleeves of his shirt or doublet pass through the side slits in the huke. The laces used to tie his hose to his doublet are visible on his right hip. From the level of his nostrils upward his head and headdress are modern inventions; but since the end of the twisted hood (chaperon) that falls behind his right shoulder is part of

the original weaving it seems likely that his headdress looked more or less like this originally.

As noted above (Condition) the meadowy ground surrounding the large fragment that contains these three figures and the meadow immediately adjacent to them does not belong where it is now. The many fragments on which that ground is represented were joined to the main part of the field in such a way as to have introduced some exceptionally heavy foliage in the meadow above the figures at the left and also to have diminished the extent of the grassy plot on which the lady in the houppelande sits. The banderoles that now appear below the figures may originally have appeared above them. We assume that the only complete scroll of the three, the one whose couplet begins *Ie sui onneur qui fai capiaus*, refers to the seated lady who is making the chaplet and therefore that the fragmentary scroll at the left refers to the man standing outside the hedge at that side and the composite scroll at the right refers to the girl standing at the right. But this is by no means certain.

A young man stands at the far right end of the field and turns his gaze toward the left. He wears a huke over a shirt of mail. He also wears hose, pointed shoes with buckles or straps over the insteps (incorrectly restored), and a chaperon decorated with a jeweled pin. A sword or dagger hangs on his right hip under the huke. As noted above, neither this figure nor the meadow surrounding him belongs in this place. His figure, a bit of meadow immediately behind him, and the right-hand two-thirds of the scroll above his head are all represented on one large fragment which could have come either from the same hanging as the other three figures or from a different hanging in the same series (see Related Tapestries).

Writers publishing their studies before a thorough examination of the tapestry was conducted at the Metropolitan Museum thought that the hanging was all of a piece, although most of them realized that parts of the inscriptions had been incorrectly restored. They found it difficult, therefore, to interpret the subject of the composition as well as the meaning of the couplets written on the banderoles. When Kurth first published the piece (1918, caption fig. 1), she referred to it as "Wandteppich mit Honneur" (Tapestry with Honor). Five years later Göbel (1923, vol. 1, 244–45) described the subject as "Dame Honneur verteilt Ehrenhüte" (Lady Honor distributing honorary hats). When it was sold from the Emil Weinberger collection in 1929 the hanging was entitled "Allegorie auf die Ehre" (Allegory of Honor). Lowry (1929, 3–6) used the English version of that title, which remained with the hanging every time it was exhibited between 1939 and 1954. Kris, who also published the piece at the time of the Weinberger sale, said that it showed Honor represented as a lady who was giving out courtly chaplets to her daughters. Wirth (1958, caption fig. 2) apparently followed Kris when he referred to the subject as "Honneur flicht Kränze für ihre Kinder" (Honor braids crowns for her children), and later writers continued to regard Honor as the mother of the other figures. When the Metropolitan Museum first published the tapestry (Redmond and Rorimer, 1959–60, 47), it was illustrated with a caption reading "Honor and her children in a garden," and subsequently Young (1962–63, 340) called it "The Lady Honor and Her Children." These two titles and some of the ones used earlier derive from the content of the couplet inscribed on the banderole spread out below the figure of the seated lady. It reads as follows:[2]

Ie sui onneur qui fai capiaus
pour mes en fans qui tant sont biaus

(I am Honor who make chaplets
for my children who are so beautiful).[3]

Since the fragment on which Honor appears is not continuous with the fabric in which this and the adjacent banderoles are woven, we have to take it on faith that the couplet just transcribed and translated refers to this lady rather than to some other figure that was shown making chaplets on this or another hanging related to it. For the same reason, we cannot be sure that the other two banderoles in this section of the tapestry refer to the figures that now appear above them. As noted above in the discussion of the hanging's condition, the couplets written on both of these scrolls are incomplete. The scroll at the left contains only the last half or so of both lines of a couplet, and the one at the right combines the first few words of both lines of one couplet with parts of a different one. Aware that something was amiss but not realizing precisely what it was, Kurth (1918, 57–59; 1923), Ernst (in Weinberger sale cat., 1929), Weibel (in exh. cats. Detroit 1945, and Hartford and Baltimore 1951–52), and Young attempted to make some sense out of these two couplets as well as the equally damaged one above the head of the young man standing at the right. Young (1962–63, 343) approached the question more cautiously than the earlier writers, but she used some of the content of their suggestions in her own, so her readings are quite similar to theirs. She suggested that the verses at the left might be read as follows: . . . *a mon bon/dam mon geron* (Homage to my good lady, my protectress).

Young read the verses on the banderole at the right as follows, because she thought the girl represented above it was showing off her hat: *Pour mieus perre a mi/ afulerai ce capu io il* (To please my friend better I will put on this pretty hat). Young also noted that the beginning of the second line of the couplet on the fourth banderole was heavily restored and that both lines were incomplete at the right. She suggested that the couplet might have read more or less as follows: *Deduit ce sui . . . / . . . le ce bien . . .* (Pleasure am I who defend Joy and Mirth [le ce] well loved).

The present author agrees with all the earlier readings of the couplet referring to Honor making the chaplets; but armed with the knowledge of just how incomplete and damaged the rest of the inscriptions are (knowledge that was not available to his predecessors), he suggests that the earlier readings be modified in the following ways. The words on the banderole at the left represent the ends of two lines of a couplet and therefore cannot be interpreted as following directly upon each other, as in ". . . my good lady, my protectress." The initial *uut* of the first line is, apart from being partly restored, the end of a word rather than the beginning, and it cannot be translated as "Homage." The *dam* beginning the second line again represents the end of a word and the *d* appears to have been restored. So for the present the words can neither be transcribed nor translated to make any sense. The same is true of the inscription beneath the girl at the right. The *Pour mieus p* in the first line and *afulerai ce cap* in the second line do indeed represent the initial words in each line. The letter after the *p* in the first line is not an *l* but an *e* correctly or incorrectly restored, and so that word cannot be read as *plerre* (*plaire*) as all writers before Young (who read it correctly) had done. The *u* following *cap* in the second line is also a restoration and may not be correct. Therefore it is chancy to interpret what looks like *capu* as a word that signifies hat. Since the *a mi* at the end of the first line does not rhyme with *io il* below, as it should, we suggest that the right end of this scroll has suffered more damage and restoration that we realize even now. In any case, the lines cannot be interpreted to mean that the girl above is putting on her hat to please a friend. The beginning of what remains of the fourth couplet reads quite clearly *De duit* [c or i?]*e sui qui* [v or d?]*e*, the same kind of identifying phrase that appears in the undamaged inscription referring to Honor. Therefore it seems likely that although the words *duit* and *sui* are rendered on two separate fragments of weaving they do in fact belong together and that the first line of that couplet may fairly be transcribed as *Deduit ie sui qui . . .* (I am Pleasure who . . .). The rest of that line is missing except for the *ve* or *de* that begins the next word. Even given the words *le ce bien* that have survived relatively intact on the second line, we cannot make any sense of that line. The couplet cannot be read as though the two lines were complete, or, according to Young's suggestion, "Pleasure am I who defend Joy and Mirth [*Leece,* see below] well loved." The "loved" here depends on reading what looks like *au* at what is now the end of the second line as the beginning of *aimee,* an interpretation that is open to question.

The allegorical figure of Honor was usually but not always personified as a woman. In a group of early sixteenth-century weavings in the Musée de Cluny whose subject has been identified as the *Triumph and Death of Honor,* Honor is represented as a man.[4] He was also shown as a man in a set of six hangings that were described along with two other tapestry cycles in an anonymous document of the second or third quarter of the fifteenth century.[5] According to that account the hangings, which seem to have been woven partly in pile technique, told the story of how Venus tried unsuccessfully to lure the young man Honor to live and serve in her court. He is surrounded by a family of ugly folk including, among others, the allegorical figures of Toil, Sweat, Hunger, Pain, Illness, and Diligence. It is significant that in this series of tapestries the character *Deduit* (Pleasure, Amusement) is a member of Venus's court rather than of Honor's family. In both of these contexts where Honor is represented as a man, the subject matter has a sober, high-minded, moralizing tone. However the same is true in certain literary works that present Honor as a woman. Young (1962–63, 343) observed that in some fourteenth- and early fifteenth-century sources the words "Dame d'Onneur" refer to a lady of good reputation. She also cited Jean Froissart's *Le trésor amoureux,* in which Honor and six other ladies guard a palace, and furthermore she referred to an anonymous poem that presents Haute Honneur as a queen who passes judgment on brave knights.

The lady Honor in the Metropolitan Museum's tapestry is not shown in a sober or high-minded context. She is to be associated instead with the literature of the period that celebrates courtly love, and she is engaged in an occupation that other gentlewomen of the period engaged in, the making of flowered chaplets. Göbel (1923, vol. 1, 83) related the tapestry to a late fifteenth-century poem written by Jean Molinet, one of the *grands rhétoriqueurs,* entitled *Le chapelet des dames.* The poet tells how Lady Virtue is making a small wreath of flowers in her garden, and by choosing flowers whose names begin with the letters M-A-R-I-E she spells out the name of the Virgin and also that of Marie de Bourgogne. The wreath is a symbol of honor. The painter of the six miniatures in René d'Anjou's manuscript (about 1460) of

Boccaccio's mid-fourteenth-century epic poem *Teseida* shows in one of them the imprisoned Arcita and Palemone watching Emilia making a chaplet of red and white roses as she sits on the hedge of an enclosure rather like the one in the Metropolitan Museum's tapestry.[6] Young (1962–63, 342–44) considered a number of possible literary sources from which the tapestry's subject might have been taken. These included the thirteenth-century poem *Roman de la Rose* in which ladies and gentlemen exchange flowered chaplets. *Deduit* is ruler of the garden of earthly delight and his love is the lady *Leece* (Mirth). Young also cited Eustache Deschamps's late fourteenth-century poem *Le lay amoureux.* In this work Honor is a lady who wears a chaplet or hat of flowers and whom everyone must love. *Deduit, Leece,* and *Joie* (Joy) appear in Deschamps's *Le lay de franchise.* Young also considered other possible sources and concluded that none of them seemed to be the precise source of the scene in the tapestry. We suggest that since each figure in the tapestry stands in its own clearly defined space and seems to have its own speech explaining who he or she is and what he or she does, the designer might have been inspired by the spectacle of some ceremonial entry of an important personage into a town. Those spectacles sometimes featured people dressed to represent characters like these placed in settings constructed on scaffolds, each figure accompanied by a placard identifying the character and explaining his or her meaning.

We have not yet identified the image that inspired the designer. Because of that, and because the tapestry shows a composite image, we cannot name the subject of this piece or of the series of hangings from which it comes. Whatever the subject was, it surely had an erotic rather than moralizing message to convey. The chaplets of flowers were tokens of love, whether given by women to men, men to women, or women to each other.[7] In one of Christine de Pisan's ballads, she urges young girls to wear chaplets of flowers on their blond tresses, to play and dance in the meadows, to laugh and sing and avoid sadness and distress.[8] A number of writers have called attention to tapestries with related subjects that were mentioned in fourteenth- to sixteenth-century documents, but they do not help identify the subject of this piece. Kurth (1918, 59) mentioned three items in Philippe le Bon's inventory of 1420, as follows: "une chambre vermeil de tapicerie de haulte lice, faicte à or, ouvrée d'aournemens de dames faisans personnages d'Onneur, de noblesse, largesse, simplesse et autres . . ." (a red-ground chamber of high-warp tapestry, woven with gold, worked with figures of ladies representing Honor, Nobility, Bounty, Simplicity and others . . .); "trois tapiz de haulte lice et de file d'Arras, faiz richement à or, appellez les tapiz de Fama, ouvrez de plusieurs person-nages qui tendent à Honneur" (three high-warp tapes-tries of Arras thread richly woven with gold, called the tapestries of Fame, worked with several characters who bow to Honor); "un autre grant vielz tapiz bien adom-magié de l'histoire de Jeunnesse et Déduit, appellée la chasse au cerf" (another large, old, badly damaged tapes-try of the story of Youth and Amusement, called the hunt of the stag). The third piece may have been part of a series of hangings representing the *Hunt of the Frail Stag* (see 24a–e) and not related in any way to the subject of the *Honor* tapestry. Kurth also referred to a tapestry that had belonged to Charles VI of France and was sold by the English in 1422, as follows: "une chambre de tapisserie d'Arras sur champ vermeil de l'ystoire de Plai-sance, appellée la chambre d'Onneur, dont les ciel, dos-sier et couverture sont d'or et de soye à plusieurs petitz personnages à pié et à cheval" (a chamber of red-ground Arras tapestry with the story of Pleasure, called the chamber of Honor, whose bed ceiling, head cloth and cover are made of gold and silk with many small figures on foot and on horseback). An entry among the accounts of the dukes of Burgundy in 1391 contains the following citation: "un drap d'or de l'histoire de Déduit et de Plaisance . . ." (a golden hanging of the story of Amuse-ment and Pleasure . . .).[9] Among the tapestries that belonged to Henry VIII of England were listed "2 peces of Pleasaunce" and "1 pece of Tapestrie of honour."[10]

Various attempts, all unsuccessful, have been made to identify the Metropolitan Museum's tapestry with some princess named Margaret or with Isabeau de Ba-vière, wife of Charles VI of France. Kurth (1918, 57) first proposed the idea of "Margaret" on the strength of her identifying the flowers on *onneur*'s headdress as daisies (marguerites) and the fact that the same lady's houppe-lande is lined with ermine. In Weibel's catalogue entries for the tapestry when it was exhibited in 1945 and 1951–52, she repeated this idea, and it was mentioned again in the catalogue for the exhibition in Winnipeg in 1954. But the blossoms—if they are blossoms and not jewels—on *onneur*'s bourrelet are not necessarily daisies, and ermine was not reserved for the use of royalty (see the lady falconers in 3 and 4). The identification of the figure of *onneur* with Isabeau de Bavière appears to have origi-nated with Maurice Brockwell, who prepared a brief essay on the subject.[11] He claimed that the figure in the tapestry was inspired by the portrait figure of the queen in the miniature on the presentation page of a manu-script containing the poems of Christine de Pisan (see Young 1962–63, 346, fig. 5). Young (347–48) examined and correctly rejected the notion that *onneur* represents either Isabeau or Anne, sister of Philippe le Bon.

SOURCE OF THE DESIGN

Like the figures in many other millefleurs tapestries—and this piece does indeed belong to that class of com-positions—these figures have little formal and psycho-logical connection with one another. It seems likely that each figure was taken from a separate source, probably a print, and then combined with the others to make up the compositions that the story required. Since both the figures (especially the hands and necks) and the floral elements show signs of having been drawn by a rather naive hand, it is reasonable to suggest that the motifs may have been both designed and combined in the weaver's shop without the intervention of a professional artist or cartoon painter.

MANUFACTURE AND DATE

Kurth (1918, 60–61) thought that the lack of depth, the arrangement of figures parallel to the picture plane, and the character of the flowering meadow all relate this hanging to tapestries that were woven during the late fourteenth and early fifteenth centuries. She refined the date further by observing that the fashions in clothing fix the date around 1415 when the calendar pages of Jean de Berry's *Très Riches Heures* were painted. As for the place of manufacture, she noted that the verses are writ-ten in Picard dialect and that certain words, specifically *capiau* rather than *chapiau, mieus* instead of *mieux*, and *biaux* for *beaux*, are characteristic of the language of Tournai, but despite these linguistic clues, the tapestry could not be assigned to Tournai because the inscrip-tions could have been copied from any source. Never-theless when she published the piece later, Kurth (1923, fig. 15) attributed it to Tournai and dated it 1415–25. Göbel (1923, vol. 1, 244–45) thought that he could see in the plants, faces, costumes, and hands in this tapestry a drawing style characteristic of Arras work. In his discus-sion of the tapestry in the Weinberger sale catalogue (1929), Ernst attributed the weaving to Arras or Tournai about 1430 and for the first time correctly related the piece to the Devonshire hunting tapestries. When it was exhibited at the New York World's Fair in 1939, the piece was catalogued as French and dated in the fifteenth century. In later exhibitions it was called Arras work and dated at different moments during the second quarter of the fifteenth century. Young (1962–63, 346–47) believed that this tapestry had been woven later than the early fifteenth-century courtly life tapestries in the Musée des Arts Décoratifs in Paris and the two tapestries in the Metropolitan Museum showing a couple next to a fal-con's bath (see 3a, b) but earlier than the Devonshire hunting tapestries. She thought that in its decorative effect the *Honor* tapestry anticipated the millefleurs tapestries of the second half of the fifteenth century and also that it was similar in many ways to the Metropolitan Museum's tapestries showing figures among rose-bushes (8a–d), which she dated about 1435–40. Therefore she dated the *Honor* piece about 1430 and attributed it to looms in Arras or Tournai on the strength of her conviction that at that time one and then the other were the important tapestry-weaving centers of Europe.

Although at first glance it seems that this hanging has nothing to do with the extravagantly designed and executed Devonshire hunting tapestries that Ernst had compared it to, the *Honor* tapestry shows costumes, plants, and grasses that are in many ways like those in the hunting tapestries. The similarity is particularly striking when one compares the Metropolitan Museum's piece to the *Deer Hunt* tapestry in London, allowing all the while for the differences that derive from the more sophisticated drawing and execution of the hunting tapestry (see, in this catalogue, fig. 59). The major difference between the two hangings is that the floral elements count for more in the Metropolitan Museum's piece than they do in the London tapestry both because they are larger in relation to the figures (which are fewer in the Museum's piece) and because in the *Honor* tapestry there seems to be a greater value contrast between the plants and the dark greenish blue ground. The surface pattern in the *Honor* tapestry is simple and its suggestion of movement in depth is minimal, whereas the composition of the *Deer Hunt* is complex on both counts. Nevertheless, both hangings show compositions and fashions in clothing indicating that they were designed during the second quarter of the fifteenth century. As for the place of weaving, we can do no more than observe that the *Honor* tapestry was woven in some provincial shop in the southern Netherlands that was producing tapestries woven after simple rather than sophisticated compositions. A few other pieces that show the same direct clarity of form have survived. Among them may be cited a fragment of millefleurs tapestry in the Victoria and Albert Museum and a fragment with a figure of Hippolyte that was in a private collection when Demotte published it in 1924.[12]

RELATED TAPESTRIES

No other fragments of this hanging or of hangings that might have belonged in the same series are known to have survived. Since Honor has been personified here as a woman rather than a man, we know that the tapestry cycle from which this piece came did not show the story of Venus attempting to win Honor for her court (see

Description and Subject, and note 5). In the early references we have at present, Honor is associated in tapestries of the fourteenth and fifteenth centuries most often with the characters Pleasure or Amusement and in one case with Nobility, Bounty, Simplicity, "and others" (see Description and Subject). In Philippe le Bon's "tapestry of Fame," several figures bow to Honor. Some or all of these characters may have been Honor's "children," and presumably some or all of them appeared in other hangings of the set to which the Metropolitan Museum's composite piece belonged. But since we cannot interpret the meaning of this hanging properly we cannot determine what the subject of the series was or how many tapestries it comprised.

HISTORY

In the collection of Emil Weinberger, Vienna, by 1918. According to Betty Kurth (1918, see Publications) it had been acquired some years earlier by a Paris art dealer.

Sold, *Die Sammlung Emil Weinberger, Wien,* auction houses of Wawra and Glückselig, Vienna, October 22–24, 1929, no. 293. In sale cat., tapestries and textiles catalogued by Richard Ernst. According to Lowry (1929, see Publications) the tapestry was bought for the Louvre by the firm of M. and B. Jonas.

Property of Duveen Brothers Inc., New York, by 1939.

Purchased by the MMA, The Cloisters Collection, 1959.

EXHIBITIONS

New York World's Fair, 1939, Pavillon de la France. *Five Centuries of History Mirrored in Five Centuries of French Art.* Paris, 1939. Cat. no. 16, pl. IV. Lent by Duveen Brothers, New York.

Detroit Institute of Arts, 1945. *Twenty-Seventh Loan Exhibition: Four Hundred Years of Tapestries.* Catalogue by Adele Coulin Weibel. Cat. no. 1. Lent by Duveen Brothers, New York.

Flint Institute of Arts, 1945. *Gothic Tapestries of the 15th & 16th Centuries.* Cat. no. 1. Lent by Duveen Brothers, New York.

Toronto, Royal Ontario Museum, 1945. Lent by Duveen Brothers, New York.

Ann Arbor, Museum of Art, University of Michigan, 1946. *Four Centuries of Tapestry Weaving.* Lent by Duveen Brothers, New York.

Grand Rapids Art Museum, 1946. Lent by Duveen Brothers, New York.

Hartford, Wadsworth Atheneum, and Baltimore Museum of Art, 1951–52. *2000 Years of Tapestry Weaving: A Loan Exhibition.* Text by Adele Coulin Weibel. Cat. no. 71, illus. Lent by Duveen Brothers, New York.

Winnipeg Art Gallery, 1954. *Exhibition of the High Art of Tapestry Weaving.* Cat. no. 1, illus. Lent by Duveen Brothers, New York.

PUBLICATIONS

Kurth, Betty. "Die Blütezeit der Bildwirkerkunst zu Tournai und der Burgundische Hof." *Jahrbuch der Kunsthistorischen Sammlungen des allerhöchsten Kaiserhauses* 34 (1918) pp. 57–61. Described and discussed at length; illus. fig. 1.

Göbel 1923, vol. I, pp. 83, 244–45. Discussed briefly.

Kurth, Betty. *Gotische Bildteppiche aus Frankreich und Flandern.*

Munich, 1923, pp. 3–4. Described and discussed at length; illus. fig. 15.

Kris, Ernst. "Die Sammlung Emil Weinberger in Wien." *Pantheon* 4 (1929) pp. 431–32. Discussed briefly and illus.

Lowry, L. "Weinberger Art Sale in Vienna Totals $205,000." *Art News* 28 (November 16, 1929) pp. 3, 6. Described incorrectly.

Breuning, Margaret. "France Loans Us an Acre of Her Tapestry Treasures: Gothic Tapestries at Duveen." *Art Digest* 22, no. 5 (December 1, 1947) p. 11. Mentioned.

Wirth, Karl-August. "Ehre." In Otto Schmitt et al., eds., *Reallexikon zur Deutschen Kunstgeschichte.* Vol. 4, Stuttgart, 1958, col. 848. Described and discussed briefly; illus. fig. 2.

Redmond, Roland L., and James J. Rorimer. "Review of the Year 1958–1959." *MMA Bulletin*, n.s. 18 (1959–60) p. 39. Mentioned; illus. p. 47.

Young, Bonnie. "The Lady Honor and Her Children." *MMA Bulletin*, n.s. 21 (1962–63) pp. 340–48. Described and discussed at length; illus. fig. 1.

Freeman, Margaret B. *The Unicorn Tapestries.* MMA, New York, 1976, pp. 123–24. Discussed briefly; illus. fig. 154.

Verdier, Philippe. "The Medieval Collection." *Apollo* 103 (1976) p. 366, no. 16, n. 3. Mentioned.

NOTES

1. A lady's hat that is narrower and taller than this, but decorated very much like it, appears in one of the miniatures of a manuscript of *L'Ystoire de Helayne* painted approximately 1460–70 (Bibliothèque Royale, Brussels, MS 9967). See Millia Davenport, *The Book of Costume* (New York, 1948) fig. 834 and p. 314, where the manuscript is dated incorrectly 1448. If the resemblance is not simply coincidental, this may indicate that the hat shown in the *Honor* tapestry, if it is not simply a restorer's garbled idea of a bourrelet, represents an earlier form of this headdress.

2. The transcriptions and translations offered here for all the inscriptions in the tapestry differ in some details from earlier readings. They represent the present author's own interpretation of the texts.

3. Both Adele Coulin Weibel, in her catalogue entries for the exhibition in Detroit in 1945 and the exhibition in Hartford and Baltimore in 1951–52, and Bonnie Young, "The Lady Honor and Her Children," *MMA Bulletin*, n.s. 21 (1962–63) p. 342, correctly translated *capiaus* as chaplets. Aside from the fact that the seated lady is making a chaplet, it should be noted that while *capiau* is a form of the word *chapeau*, both words in French can refer to a chaplet as well as to the more complete head covering we call a hat.

4. See Joubert 1987, pp. 140–49. He is called "decus."

5. Betty Kurth, "Die Blütezeit der Bildwirkerkunst zu Tournai und der Burgundische Hof," *Jahrbuch der Kunsthistorischen Sammlungen des allerhöchsten Kaiserhauses* 34 (1918) pp. 59–60, first mentioned this document, a seventeenth-century manuscript that is believed to convey the contents of a letter written by an agent or courtier to a duke, perhaps Philippe le Bon or Charles le Téméraire, who saw the three tapestry cycles in the palace in Vienna. The first published account of the document was given in Achille Jubinal, *Les anciennes tapisseries historiées* (Paris, 1838) vol. 2, pp. 28–31. He referred to it as MS no. 7406 in the Bibliothèque du Roi.

6. MS cod. 2617 in the Österreichische Nationalbibliothek, Vienna; see H. Leporini, "Das Rätsel der Bilderhandschriften König Renés von Anjou," *Pantheon* 15 (1935) color illus. facing p. 117.

7. See Margaret B. Freeman, *The Unicorn Tapestries*, MMA (New York, 1976) p. 123, for brief notes on the giving of floral chaplets, and G.-J. Demotte, *La tapisserie gothique* (Paris and New York, 1924) pl. 147, or Monica Stucky-Schürer, *Die Passionsteppiche von San Marco in Venedig* (Bern, 1972) fig. 60, for an illustration of one of the five courtly scenes hangings in Paris in which a lady who is already wearing a chaplet of flowers places another on the head of a seated lady who holds a falcon on her left fist.

8. The text of this ballad is given in *Oeuvres poétiques de Christine de Pisan*, vol. 1, Maurice Roy, ed., Société des Anciens Textes Français (Paris, 1886) pp. 218–19.

9. Baron de Sainte-Suzanne, "Les tapisseries d'Arras," *Bulletin Monumental* 45 (1879) p. 94.

10. Thomson 1930, p. 248. In the king's posthumous inventory of 1548 the tapestries were listed as being in the palace at Westminster.

11. Part of an unpublished typescript study of the tapestry, apparently made when it was with Duveen Brothers, now in the files of the MMA Department of Medieval Art.

12. For the fragment in London, see Digby 1980, pl. 17; for the Hippolyte, see Demotte, *La tapisserie*, pl. 160.

7

Seven Scenes from the Story of the Seven Sacraments and Their Prefigurations in the Old Testament

Five fragments of a wall hanging

a   *Matrimony and Extreme Unction*
b   *God the Father Uniting Adam and Eve, and*
    David Being Anointed King at Hebron
c   *Namaan Being Cleansed in the Jordan*
d   *Jacob Blessing Ephraim and Manasseh*
e   *Baptism*

Southern Netherlands, 1435–50
Wool warp; wool and silk wefts
7a: 7 ft. 9¹/₂ in.× 10 ft. 1 in. (2.38 m × 3.07 m)
7b: 6 ft. 8 in.× 10 ft. 2 in. (2.03 m × 3.10 m)
7c: 7 ft. 7 in.× 6 ft. 10 in. (2.31 m × 2.08 m)
7d: 7 ft. 7 in.× 4 ft. 6 in. (2.31 m × 1.37 m)
7e: 5 ft. 3¹/₂ in.× 7 ft. 6 in. (1.61 m × 2.29 m)
(Note: these are the sight dimensions of the fragments as they were mounted between 1937 and 1940; the actual dimensions, which include turned-under edges of varying size, are only slightly greater.)
12 warp yarns per inch, 5 per centimeter
Gift of J. Pierpont Morgan, 1907 (07.57.1–5)

CONDITION

All of the fragments have been cut along the edges, and there are a number of irregularly shaped holes in each one. The two scenes represented in 7a preserve their full height and width but have lost their lower outer corners. These corners, which were cut away with the lowest quarter of the piece sometime in the past, were presumably lost before the main part of that quarter was remounted in its original position. The inscribed scrolls that run along the top are part of the original fabric. 7b has lost a small strip along the left edge where the back of Adam's figure is missing. The inscribed scroll along the bottom of 7c was cut off at some time and its left-hand two-thirds was lost; the rest was later returned to its rightful place. The scroll along the bottom of 7d is an integral part of the weaving. It has lost only a bit of its length, at the right; the missing piece is now mounted between two sections of a scroll along the bottom of the composite fragment from the same tapestry that is now in the Burrell Collection in Glasgow (fig. 97). 7d has lost a bit of fabric along its right edge where the back of the woman is missing; but since its left edge contains parts of the base and collar of the colonnette rising along the right edge of 7c, it is clear that 7d is complete at that side and that the two pieces belong together as they are now

mounted. 7e has suffered minor losses along the top and right sides but a major loss along the bottom where approximately one-quarter of the fabric is missing. The strip of landscape pattern along the left edges of 7c and e suggests that there were corresponding strips along the right edges of 7a and b which have been lost. The pattern at the bottom of 7a indicates that there was a strip of flowering greensward along the bottom of 7e when it was whole, and we may assume that there was originally a strip representing sky or other landscape elements along the tops of 7b, c, and d. The narrow stripes of pink and variegated white weaving along the left edges of 7c and e probably are vestiges of a decorative guard that bordered the whole hanging.

The darkest wool wefts and the lightest silks have deteriorated and fallen out in many places; they have not been replaced. The losses occurred mainly in the letters of the inscribed scrolls, in the dark ground of the damask-patterned backgrounds, and in the darkest shadows and highest lights of the garments. In these places the undyed wool warp yarns are visible; and, since they are lighter than the yarns that once covered them, the value relationships have been reversed in these areas. Because of this it is hard to read some of the planes and contours in the garments; also, in the damask backgrounds, the pattern units now appear darker than the ground whereas they were once considerably lighter.[1] Otherwise the drawing and modeling appear essentially as they did originally.

The yarns that survive have retained their intense colors except in most of the flesh tones and the brickwork at the right sides of 7a and b where the yarns have faded somewhat. Before the fragments were acquired by the Metropolitan Museum, 7a, 7b, and 7e had been hung with their backs outward, presumably because the colors were then brighter on the back than the front. This circumstance may account for the brightness of most of the colors on what is once again presented as the correct face of each fragment.[2]

156

If the compositons shown in 7a–e are to be described and interpreted properly, they must be studied in terms of the design and iconographic plan of the hanging from which these fragments came. Most of the evidence that is needed to reconstruct that tapestry is found not only in these five pieces but also in other fragments of the tapestry that are now in the Burrell Collection, Glasgow, and the Victoria and Albert Museum, London (see figs. 97 and 98, and Related Tapestries). More evidence is provided in an early description of this tapestry and also in descriptions of two others that we believe were woven after the same cartoon or a version of it. The documents containing those descriptions will be discussed more fully below (Manufacture and Date).

The earliest known reference to this hanging appears in the inventory of Isabel la Católica's possessions that were housed in the Alcázar in Segovia in 1503.[3] It was one of nineteen tapestries that the queen bequeathed to the Capilla Real in Granada in 1504. It remained there until 1871 when Mariano Fortuny bought it in much deteriorated condition. The second document concerns a tapestry in one or more pieces that was said to have been given to the church of Saint Quentin in Tournai by the tapestry and wine entrepreneur Pasquier Grenier and his wife (see below and note 10). The third text describes a tapestry that Jean Chevrot, bishop of Tournai from about 1438 to 1461, bequeathed in 1458 to the church of Saint Hippolytus in Poligny in Burgundy (see below, and Fourez 1954, 105). It is clear that all three of these texts could, and we believe do, describe one composition or versions of one composition. The description of it in Isabel's inventory tells us that it showed seven inscribed panels across the middle. The other two descriptions refer to the scenes from the Old Testament that prefigured the Seven Sacraments.

There is sufficient evidence in fragments 7a–e to show how these scenes and inscriptions were arranged in the original hanging. The episodes from the Old Testament were placed side by side in a horizontal row above another row of scenes representing the Seven Sacraments. The inscribed scrolls were spread out end to end entirely across the tapestry, between the upper and lower registers. This agrees with the entry in Isabel's inventory of 1503 that mentions seven inscribed panels with black letters along the center of the tapestry.

The fragments preserved in the Metropolitan Museum, the Victoria and Albert Museum, and the Burrell Collection contain all or major portions of five scenes showing sacramental ceremonies and five others representing the prefigurations of sacraments. These are Baptism (7e) with its prefiguration, Namaan being cleansed in the Jordan (7c); Confirmation (Victoria and Albert Museum; fig. 98) with its antecedent, Jacob blessing Ephraim and Manasseh (7d); Communion prefigured by Melchizedek offering bread and wine to Abraham (both in the Burrell Collection; fig. 97); Matrimony (left part of 7a) and its prefiguration, God the Father uniting Adam and Eve (left part of 7b); and Extreme Unction (right part of 7a) and its prototype in the Old Testament, David being anointed king at Hebron (right part of 7b).

The scenes representing Ordination and Penance and their prefigurations are missing. We have no visual or documentary evidence to indicate what those two scenes looked like, nor what the subjects of the two related scenes from the Old Testament showed. However it is reasonable to suggest that the designer may have chosen the subjects that appear in a series of woodcuts in the edition of *L'art de bien vivre* published by Antoine Vérard in Paris in 1492. The prints illustrate the same iconographic theme and the compositions are arranged like those in the tapestry: one of the Seven Sacraments is represented below in the central bay of a building and its prefiguration appears in the center of a canopy above.[4] Although the scene prefiguring Confirmation in the prints is not the Jacob episode but one showing a king being anointed, the prefigurations for Baptism, Matrimony, Communion, and Extreme Unction are the same in prints and tapestry. Therefore the chances are good that the prefigurations of Ordination and Penance in the book were also the ones that appeared in the tapestry. The scene above the printed illustration of Ordination shows Moses, the two horns prominent on his forehead, consecrating Aaron as high priest (Exodus 29:7, Leviticus 8:12). The scene above Penance shows one man kneeling before another; a crown rests on the ground behind them. It seems likely that this represents David confessing to Nathan that he has murdered Uriah and taken his wife (2 Kings 12:13).

Armed with some or all of this information, three specialists offered three different theoretical reconstructions of the original tapestry. Rorimer (1940, 86), believing that the Confirmation fragment in London represented both that sacrament and also Ordination, included only six sections in his reconstruction (fig. 99). In his scheme only those parts of the original tapestry that showed Penance and its prefiguration were missing. Wells (1959, 97) observed correctly that the piece in London does not represent both Confirmation and Ordination but only the former. To make his reconstruction Wells (1959, fig. 21; also fig. 100 here) used Rorimer's as a starting point and added a seventh section in the center. In Wells's proposal the central scene comprises two fragments of weaving from the right end of

7b

7a

158

Fig. 97. Composite hanging made from pieces of painted cloth and fragments of the *Seven Sacraments* and another tapestry. Southern Netherlands, here dated 1435–50. The Burrell Collection, Glasgow Museums and Art Galleries.

the composite piece in the Burrell Collection and a large fragment from another Burrell Collection tapestry whose subject he identified as the consecration of an altar or of liturgical objects. In adding this seventh section Wells correctly provided a place for the main Sacrament—Communion—in the center of the composition where it was in most depictions of the Seven Sacraments at this time. However the fragments Wells placed there do not show the celebration of the Eucharist, and we believe they were never part of this tapestry.

Retaining most of Rorimer's proposals and strengthening them with Wells's corrections and his argument for adding a seventh section in the middle, the present author developed a third reconstruction (fig. 101). According to this plan, the original tapestry would have shown, left to right, top to bottom, Namaan being cleansed in the river Jordan above Baptism; next, Jacob blessing Ephraim and Manasseh above Confirmation; then Moses anointing Aaron (?) above its corresponding scene of Ordination; next, in the center of the hanging, Abraham and Melchizedek above Communion; then David confessing his sin to Nathan (?) above Penance; next, God the Father uniting Adam and Eve above Matrimony; and finally, at the right end, David anointed king at Hebron above Extreme Unction. Although Ordina-

tion and Penance, with their prefigurations, might have been shown in reverse order, we have reason to believe that Ordination preceded Penance (see Related Tapestries).

The dimensions of the whole tapestry, before it was reduced to a number of fragments, are recorded in Isabel la Católica's inventory of 1503.[5] It was $16^3/_4$ varas long and $5^3/_4$ varas high which, given the value of the Castilian vara as .8359 meter, translates into just over 14 meters (46 ft.) long and 4.81 meters (15 ft., 9 in.) high. The extant fragments as assembled in Rorimer's, Wells's, and Cavallo's reconstructions (figs. 99–101) measure some 14 feet 7 inches in height. The difference between this and 15 feet 9 inches would be accounted for by a missing strip of sky or landscape above and another of ground pattern below. We cannot comment on the width of the reconstruction because we know the widths of only four of the fourteen compartments (the Namaan and David scenes, Matrimony, and Extreme Unction), and they are not equal. It is clear that the width of the compartments varied according to the number of figures they contained.

Because 7a–e all show bits of the setting surrounding the narrative scenes, they provide evidence of how the overall composition of the tapestry looked when it was

160

complete. These fragments indicate that the biblical and sacramental episodes took place within compartments viewed through openings in the facade of a two-storied brick building that was set in a wooded and flowered field. The backgrounds of the seven scenes are represented as flat walls covered with a damask or voided velvet fabric featuring a stylized leaf pattern. The floors in the six scenes of 7a–b and 7d–e are paved with polychrome tiles in various patterns. The ground in 7c, the single exterior scene in this group, is represented as a grassy riverbank where flowering plants and small trees grow.

The scenes were separated from each other in the horizontal direction by slender colonnettes and in the vertical direction by horizontal rows of brickwork. The uppermost of these rows represented the top of the building, the lowest one the bottom, and the intermediate row, against which inscribed scrolls were displayed, represented the floor separating the two stories. Columns of brickwork represented the right and left ends of the building. As Hunter (1912, 312, 314) observed, the

designer drew the jeweled inner edges of the brick columns and courses in perspective as they would appear to a person standing on the ground in front of the building and to the right of its center. Hunter (1912, 312; 1925, 50) thought that the brick elements and the landscape beyond them served as a border for the tapestry. Although the brickwork and greenery do indeed function incidentally as a border for the narrative scenes, these architectural and botanical elements are an integral part of the field design and not part of a border surrounding the field. However the original tapestry apparently did have a border of some kind: the pink and variegated white stripes that run down the left edges of 7c and 7e represent either a section of a narrow guard or the inner parts of a wider band whose outer portions are missing.

Taking the seven scenes in the order they followed in the original hanging, top to bottom, left to right, they may be described as follows.

Namaan being cleansed in the Jordan, 7c, shows the climactic moment in the story of Namaan's miraculous cure (4 Kings 5:1–14). Having heard from his wife's serving girl that a prophet in Samaria could cure his leprosy, Namaan, army commander to the king of Aram, went to seek help from the king of Israel. Elisha learned of Namaan's plight and let him know that he should wash seven times in the river Jordan. Namaan would have ignored what he regarded as useless advice but for the encouragement of his servants. He went to the river, bathed as directed, and was cured. The scene in the tapestry shows Namaan standing nude in the Jordan, at the lower left. Two servants dressed in tunics decorated at the neck, shoulders, sleeve cuffs, and hems with patterned bands, each man wearing a hat, stand on the banks of the river; the man at the left holds Namaan's robe. The man standing in the right foreground and talking to Namaan is probably meant to represent Elisha. He wears a long, patterned velvet houppelande trimmed at the edges with fur, a purse tied to his heavy girdle, and a chaperon on his head. A narrow brick wall borders the scene at the left and a colonnette does the same at the right.

In 7e, Baptism, mounted directly below the Namaan scene, a tonsured priest, wearing an alb and a stole over his high-necked houppelande, holds a nude infant above a font filled with water while the parents or godparents stand at the right with their right hands clasped. The gilt box containing the anointing oil rests on the forward lip of the font. The mother or godmother wears a patterned damask or velvet houppelande and, on her head, a patterned bourrelet; she holds a towel in her left hand. The man is dressed in a girdled, unpatterned, and fur-trimmed houppelande. Another tonsured priest or

Fig. 98. *Confirmation,* fragment of the *Seven Sacraments* tapestry. Southern Netherlands, here dated 1435–50. Victoria and Albert Museum, London.

Fig. 99. Theoretical reconstruction of the *Seven Sacraments and Their Prefigurations in the Old Testament* tapestry according to James J. Rorimer, before 1959.

acolyte and another man stand behind the officiating priest. A man wearing a hood and a long unpatterned jacket pleated down the front, and holding a battle-ax, stands in the foreground at the left. The same narrow brickwork wall rises along the left side of this scene but there is no colonnette at the right.

Jacob blessing Ephraim and Manasseh, 7d, mounted immediately to the right of the Namaan scene, shows the bearded and nearly blind patriarch seated in the center of the space. He wears a patterned mantle over a plain tunic decorated with ornamental bands at the edges and, on his head, a tall domed miter. He is represented in the act of blessing his two grandsons, as recounted in Genesis 48:10–20. In taking his two sons to Jacob to be blessed, Joseph placed the elder boy, Manas-

seh, at Jacob's right and the younger one, Ephraim, at his left. In this representation both boys are bareheaded and they wear sleeveless tunics with ornamental bands at the edges. When the old man blessed them he crossed his arms and placed his right hand on Ephraim's head. When Joseph protested, Jacob explained that he deliberately gave Ephraim precedence over his elder brother because it was he who would become the greater man. Jacob is shown at the moment of blessing, with his hands crossed on the boys' heads. The bearded man at rear left, dressed in a mantle over a tunic and wearing a high-crowned hat with a turned-up ermine brim, is probably meant to represent Joseph. The woman at the rear right may be intended as Joseph's wife although there is no mention of her presence, or that of any other woman, in

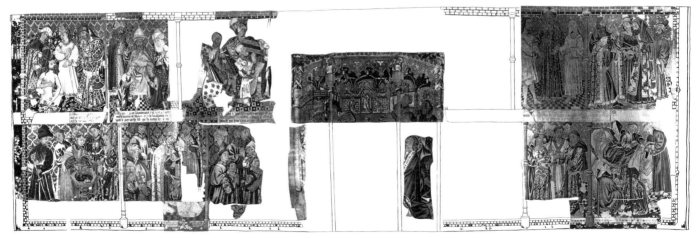

Fig. 100. Theoretical reconstruction of the *Seven Sacraments and Their Prefigurations in the Old Testament* tapestry according to William Wells, 1959.

162

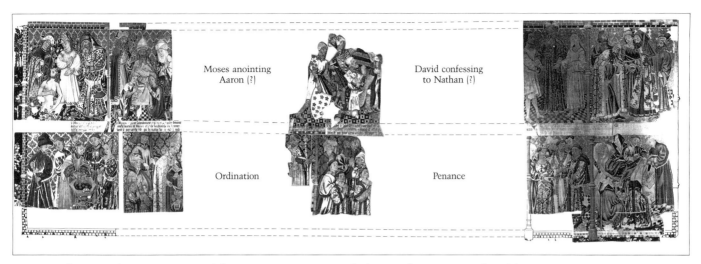

Fig. 101. Theoretical reconstruction of the *Seven Sacraments and Their Prefigurations in the Old Testament* tapestry according to Adolfo S. Cavallo, 1990.

the scriptural account of this episode. She wears an unpatterned houppelande and a turban with a pendant scarf that encircles her face.

These three scenes appeared in the left end of the original hanging. Although the fabric of 7d is not connected to that of 7c, its left edge retains bits of the base and collar of the colonnette that separates the two episodes. Therefore we may be certain that 7d originally occupied the place it now does.

The right end of the original tapestry contained 7a and 7b in the relationship they now bear. The left end of 7b shows God the Father uniting Adam and Eve, the scriptural subject prefiguring the sacrament of Matrimony. It represents the moment when God, having fashioned Eve from one of Adam's ribs, brings her to him as a companion (Genesis 2:22–25). The bearded God the Father, His head surrounded by a cruciferous halo, dressed in a pearl-edged and patterned houppelande, stands in the center of the space. His head and halo appear in front of the two courses of bricks above. Adam stands at the left, Eve at the right. God takes their right hands and brings them together.

The left end of 7a, in which the sacrament of Matrimony is represented, was mounted directly below this in order to place it in the position it occupied in the original hanging. A colonnette rises at each side of the scene. They separate this episode from the one that adjoined it at the left (now missing) and also from Extreme Unction which flanks it at the right. In Matrimony the bride, wearing a crown and a patterned gown with long sleeves and a low round neckline, stands to the left of the priest who wears a girdled alb, an amice, and a stole crossed over his breast. The groom, dressed in a patterned fur-trimmed houppelande, his chaperon

resting on his left shoulder, stands at the right and extends his right hand to clasp that of his bride. The priest places his left hand on the groom's right wrist and with his own right hand shakes holy water from an aspergillum onto the clasped hands. Two women wearing houppelandes and low linen headdresses stand behind the bride. The head of a man standing behind the priest is visible.

David being anointed king at Hebron, the seventh and last of the biblical scenes in the original tapestry, is shown in the right part of 7b. A colonnette separates it from God uniting Adam and Eve at the left. The David scene derives from three stories in the Old Testament, two in 2 Kings (2:4 and 5:3) and one in 1 Paralipomenon (11:3). In these three accounts it is told that the elders of Israel anointed David king after making a covenant with him in the city of Hebron. In the tapestry David, wearing a patterned ermine-trimmed mantle over a plain fur-trimmed houppelande girdled low on the waist, stands in the left foreground and bends forward to receive the crown that a bearded and hooded man wearing a patterned sleeveless tunic over a houppelande places on his head. Two other bearded elders wearing plain robes stand behind them at left and right; the one at the right also wears a high-crowned turban. A young man wearing an unpatterned, long robe stands between them and holds a small bowl of anointing oil.

Extreme Unction, at the right end of 7a, appears in its original place directly below David's anointment. The composition shows a woman lying in a bed that extends into the room from the left, from a wall or space that disappears behind the colonnette separating this episode from Matrimony which occupies the left end of the same fragment. She wears a scarf wrapped around her head but her arms and feet are bare. The priest, tonsured and wearing a fur-trimmed houppelande, stands at the foot of the bed and applies anointing oil to the invalid's ankles, which are exposed, as an acolyte standing behind the bed lifts the bottom of the bedclothes. A hooded woman reading from a book she holds stands next to the acolyte at the left. Two other hooded women, who also wear houppelandes, one patterned, one plain, are seated in the left half of the foreground and are also reading, the one at the left from a book, the other from a scroll. The priest reads from a book held in his left hand.

The original tapestry showed seven inscribed scrolls spread out along the middle, between the two rows of episodes. The triplet verses on each scroll refer to both the sacramental scene below and its prefiguration above. Only the right end of the scroll that ran along the bottom of the Namaan scene and the top of Baptism has survived. What remains of its verses reads as follows:

> . . . (?) · *histores de lescripture*
> . . . (?) *sait baptesme purgies*
> . . . [u]ue (eaue?) *de jourdin lavez*

> (. . . [?] stories from Scripture
> . . . [?] baptism purified
> . . . [?] washed [in the water?] of the Jordan).

Before it was returned to its rightful place this inscribed fragment had been mounted as the right end of the scroll spread out beneath the Jacob scene. The true right end of that scroll had at some time been inserted between the left and right portions of the scroll along the bottom of the composite fragment in the Burrell Collection (see fig. 97, and Related Tapestries). This transposed fragment shows one word on each of three lines: *donnent,* [o]*iture, mist.* These are the terminal words in the lines of the triplet on the scroll spread out under the Jacob scene (7d). Returning these words to their proper place, we read as follows:

> *Adfin qua vigheur sabandonnent · creatures prelas leur donnent*
> *confirmacion et tonsure · et de che samblance en droiture*
> *jacob le patriarche fist · qui ses mains sur · ii · enfants mist*

> (Priests give children confirmation and tonsure so that they will devote themselves to strength. Jacob the patriarch did the same righteous thing when he laid his hands on two children).

The first line of this triplet and the first half of the second line refer to the sacrament of Confirmation which was represented in the scene below. A large part of that section of the original tapestry is preserved in the

Victoria and Albert Museum in London (see fig. 98, and Related Tapestries).

The entire scroll extending between Adam and Eve and Matrimony has survived. Its verses read as follows:

> *Le sacrement de mariage · dont multiplie humain lignage*
> *moustra dieux quand Adam crea · et de sa coste eve fourma*
> *qui fu des femmes la premiere · et a adam amie chere*

> (God demonstrated the sacrament of Matrimony whereby human life continues when he created Adam and with his rib fashioned Eve who was the first woman and Adam's beloved companion).

The inscription on the scroll running between David being anointed and Extreme Unction is also complete. It reads as follows:

> *Mais la darniere unction · qui contre la temptation de sa vertu donne vigheur · moustra lunction dhonneur*
> *faite en ebron a david roi · pour estre de pluffort arroi*

> (The anointing of honor given to David at Hebron to make him a stronger king presaged the last anointing which by its power gives strength against temptation).

SOURCE OF THE DESIGN

Schmitz (1919, 190) believed that the style of the heads and patterned backgrounds in these compositions relates them to the work of Robert Campin. Heinz (1963, 80) and Cetto (1966, 159) suggested that the designer was a painter in the circle of Rogier van der Weyden. Morelowski (1936, 221) thought that the tapestry fragments are close in style to the *Story of the Swan Knight* pieces in Cracow and Vienna and observed furthermore that the dying figure in Extreme Unction bore a striking resemblance to an invalid in a miniature painted by the Master of Antoine de Bourgogne.

None of these suggestions helps identify the tapestry designer who must remain anonymous for the present. The choice of Rogier as the focus of the search depends in part on the fact that stylistic comparisons have been drawn among the tapestry fragments and a number of other mid-fifteenth-century Netherlandish works of art that illustrate the Seven Sacraments: an embroidered orphrey and hood in the Historisches Museum in Bern, some silverpoint drawings in the Ashmolean Museum in Oxford and the collection of baron Edmond de Rothschild in Paris which show the same compositions as the embroideries, and two altarpieces attributed to followers of Rogier, one (formerly called the Cambrai altarpiece) in the Museo del Prado in Madrid, and the other in the Musée Royal des Beaux-Arts in Antwerp.[6] Winkler and Bach, in their studies of the drawings and embroideries, found them superior to the scenes in the niches of the paired towers flanking the arch in the center of the Madrid altarpiece and concluded that the small compositions were probably derived from a lost work by Rogier himself.[7] Châtelet (1989, 15), in his discussion of the Antwerp altarpiece which shows the sacraments being administered in the nave and aisles of a church, saw a close enough resemblance between those scenes and several of the ones in 7a–e to conclude that the painting and the tapestry fragments are related. He added that "les modèles rogeriens sont repris un peu lourdement pour occuper un plus grand espace."

However, the expressive but stolid figures in 7a–e are not even distant cousins of the slim and vibrant characters who act out the sacramental scenes in the drawings, embroideries, and altarpieces. Furthermore, since the fashionable costume worn by the husband in the Matrimony scene in 7a antedates by at least a decade the one worn by the man kneeling in the right foreground of Penance in the drawings and embroideries and also by the husband in the Matrimony scene of the Antwerp altarpiece, the tapestry designer could not have been inspired by any of these works which are attributed to Rogier or his followers. Certainly, the designer of 7a–e was working in the artistic milieu from which Rogier emerged and which he soon dominated; but the tapestry fragments share nothing with these other works of art beyond the iconography and the style of that period and place. Rorimer (1940, 87) came to the same conclusion when he related 7a–e to the embroideries and Antwerp altarpiece in his first publication of the Metropolitan Museum's fragments. The compositions in the tapestry-woven scenes are totally different from all the others. The designer probably found his immediate source of inspiration in some unidentified series of Netherlandish drawings or prints that antedated the drawings and embroideries and the Antwerp altarpiece by a decade or a bit more, as suggested above.

MANUFACTURE AND DATE

When 7a–e were offered for sale in 1875 and again in 1888 they were called "gothic" or "fifteenth century." No place of origin was suggested except for Baptism, which was attributed tentatively to Arras (Goupil sale cat., 1888, 101). Dean (1907, 40–44) called the fragments Burgundian and suggested Arras as a possible place of origin because the verses in 7d were said to contain some words in Picard dialect. He dated the fragments in the first half of the fifteenth century on the grounds of fashion in costume and also because he found them similar to the *Story of Saints Piat and Eleuthère* tapestries that were woven in Arras about 1402.[8] Hunter (1907, 185–86) agreed with Dean on the date of 7a–e, citing the relatively coarse weave and the style of the costumes and accessories, and he repeated the attribution "Burgundian." Later, Hunter (1912, 388) stated that 7a–e came from the *Histoire du Sacrament* tapestry that Philippe le Bon bought in Bruges in 1439 (old style; 1440 new style).[9] Schmitz (1919, 189–90) and Breck and Rogers (1925, 114–15) considered that possible, while Marillier (1936, 46, 50) vacillated and neither accepted nor rejected the idea. Göbel (1923, vol. 1, 271; vol. 2, figs. 208, 209) assigned the fragments to Tournai, about 1445, on stylistic grounds and added that they might have come from some other edition of the tapestry that the duke had bought. Crick-Kuntziger (1936, 215) pointed out that since the fragments contain no metal yarns they could not have come from the duke's tapestry because it was described as "bien riche," that is, containing gilt and silver yarns. Digby (1980, 20) also rejected this identification because he believed that the tapestry from which the fragments came could not have been woven as early as 1440.

The tapestry in question could not be the one that the duke bought in 1440 but not for these reasons. The writers who discussed the matter seem to have missed the fact that Philippe le Bon's tapestry was described as "ung tapis de l'istoire du sacrement" or a tapestry of *the* Sacrament (Communion) and not of the *Seven* Sacraments. It is clear that a distinction was drawn between the two subjects at least by the end of the fifteenth century. Among the twenty-two tapestries that Isabel la Católica gave to Margaret of Austria in September 1499 were "otro paño del sacramento rico en oro" (another tapestry of the Sacrament rich with gold) and "otro paño del sacramento sin oro" (another tapestry of the Sacrament without gold). However the tapestry mentioned in the inventory of Isabel's possessions in the Alcázar in Segovia in 1503, the hanging from which the extant fragments came, was described as "Otro paño grande de lana e seda que es de los siete sacramentos e tiene por medio siete letreros de letras negras tiene de largo diez e seys varas e tres quartas e de cayda çinco varas e tres quartas" (Another large tapestry of wool and silk of the Seven Sacraments and it has seven inscribed panels with black letters across the middle it is sixteen and three-quarters varas long and five and three-quarters varas wide).[10]

Not realizing that this tapestry was the source of 7a–e and the related fragments in London and Glasgow, earlier writers attempted to assign the original tapestry a date and place of origin by identifying it with hangings mentioned in two other fifteenth-century documents. Rolland (1936, 212–14) proposed an attribution to Tournai around 1475 because he believed that the original hanging was one that the Tournai entrepreneur Pasquier Grenier and his wife were said to have had made for their parish church of Saint Quentin in Tournai about that time to decorate its choir. The text that Rolland interpreted in this way appeared in the undated and unpublished "Projet manuscrit d'Histoire de Tournai" by Sanderus.[11] The pertinent part reads as follows: ". . . ut patet ex tapetibus, quos confici curarunt ad ornamentum chori, septem ecclesiae sacramenta, cum suis figuris ex antiguo testamento depromptis, luculenter exprimantibus" (. . . there covered with tapestries which they undertook to have made for the decoration of the choir, of the Seven Sacraments of the Church, with prototypes derived from the Old Testament, beautifully represented). Crick-Kuntziger (1936, 215–18) accepted this assertion with reservations. Morelowski (1936, 218–22) endorsed it after devising some ingenious paths circumventing the logical objections one might raise against Rolland's theory. Rolland (1936, 214) argued that Grenier would not have made the gift before 1474 when the renovations at the east end of the church were completed, and Morelowski (1936, 220) maintained that Grenier and his wife, generous supporters of a parish they loved, would have wanted to have a tapestry woven especially for it, one that also made reference to their children. Marillier (1936, 46–50) discussed Rolland's theory but could not accept it wholeheartedly because he could not reject out of hand the tradition that the fragments had not come from the church of Saint Quentin in Tournai but from the Capilla Real in Granada. Rorimer (1940, 87; 1947, 3) accepted Rolland's theory. Wells (1959, 101) quoted and agreed with Kurth's statement in her unpublished catalogue of the Burrell Collection tapestries: she wrote that the fragments were "known to have been woven in the workshops of Pasquier Grenier at Tournai . . . [and are] dated by documents about 1475." Verlet (1965, 19, 55), Jarry (1969, 79), and Digby (1980, 20) also accepted the tradition that Grenier had a tapestry woven for his church, and so they dated 7a–e and the related fragments in the third quarter of the fifteenth century.

Rolland's theory must be reconsidered for it is based on a number of assumptions that do not bear close scrutiny. He began by observing that Grenier and his wife paid some of the cost of adding an ambulatory around the sanctuary and one of three new chapels opening off the ambulatory. This chapel, which they dedicated to the Seven Sacraments, was intended to be their family burial chapel. Rolland (1936, 209–10) quoted documents that leave no doubt such a gift was made. However, in regard to the gift of the tapestries, Rolland depended on Sanderus's account of them: that it was Grenier and his wife who had the tapestries (in the plural) made for the choir of the church (not for their own chapel). Sanderus did not give any documentary evidence to support this claim which, if his manuscript has been correctly dated about 1650, he would have made almost two hundred years after the fact. Neither did he say when the tapestries were given, whether they were still hanging at the time he was writing, or whether he had even seen them. However, Rolland (1936, 212, 214) accepted Sanderus's account of the gift as fact and went on to make the assumptions, which most later writers accepted without question, that Grenier and his wife had the tapestries woven to fit the new dimensions of the choir and consequently that the hangings were woven after and not before the east end of the building was renovated between 1464 or 1469 and 1474. He also assumed that they were still hanging in the church about 1650 when Sanderus wrote his history of Tournai. Sanderus's and Rolland's assertions concerning the history of the tapestries may be true, but it is important to realize that we have no documents to support them.

Other writers, following Fourez (1954, 82 n. 4) rather than Rolland (1936, 212–14), proposed that 7a–e and the related fragments are to be associated with a different fifteenth-century document. Fourez published the text of a will that Jean Chevrot, bishop of Tournai from about 1438 to 1461, made in 1458. In part, the testament reads as follows (Fourez, 1954, 105): "Nous donnons et leguons a legle colleal de saint ypolite de Poligny pour la decoracon du choer dicelle aux fetes solenniez trois tappis des Sebilles avec ung autre tapis des VII sacremens de sainte egle figurez selon le viel testament et le nouviel lesquelz avons fait faire pardeca" (We give and bequeath to the collegiate church of Saint Hippolytus in Poligny for the decoration of its choir on solemn feast days three tapestries of the Sibyls with another tapestry of the Seven Sacraments of the Holy Church illustrated according to the Old Testament and the New which we had made here). Fourez interpreted "pardeca" as meaning "here" in Tournai. However Chevrot could have been using the term in its broader sense of "on this side," that is, in this part of the Burgundian territories (the southern Netherlands) as opposed to "that side" (Burgundy in France), the region to which he was bequeathing the tapestries. Fourez (1954, 82 n. 4) also suggested that the cartoons for this tapestry might have been the ones that Robert Dary, a tapestry weaver and producer of Tournai, delivered to Chevrot in 1444.[12] It is a tenuous possibility: the cartoons in question could just as well have been the ones for the Sibyls tapestries as for the *Seven Sacraments.*

Cetto (1966, 157–59) accepted Fourez's theory and then observed that we cannot be sure Chevrot's *Seven Sacraments* tapestry got to Poligny, that somehow it might have found its way to Spain, where 7a–e are known to have been found. She also suggested that the kneeling saint that Wells placed in the lower right-center of his reconstruction of the original tapestry (fig. 100 here) represents Chevrot's patron Saint John the Evangelist and furthermore that the main part of Wells's central scene may commemorate Chevrot's ordination as bishop of Tournai. Wells agreed, two years after publishing his reconstruction, that the extant fragments of the *Seven Sacraments* hanging should perhaps be associated with Chevrot's tapestry rather than with the one that Grenier is said to have given to the church of Saint Quentin.[13] Asselberghs (1967, 35), Digby (1980, 20), and Châtelet (1989, 20 n. 45) suggested that Chevrot's tapestry might represent another edition of the piece in Grenier's gift.

None of these arguments need be considered further since recent research has made it clear that 7a–e and the fragments in London and Glasgow came from the tapestry that Isabel la Católica bequeathed to the Capilla Real in Granada in 1504. Sánchez Cantón published the list of tapestries in her bequest for the first time in 1950 but he cited all but one of them according to his own numbering system rather than by subject or title.[14] Apparently no one before us had associated the number in his list with this tapestry and so most earlier writers did not accept Dean's assurance (1911, 140) that 7a–e had come from the Capilla Real. Only Asselberghs (1967, 35) came close to the truth. He found the *Seven Sacraments* tapestry in Isabel's inventory of 1503 (which none of the other writers had done), but he did not realize that it was among the pieces she had left to the royal chapel. Therefore, while he did not deny that the extant fragments came from the chapel, he did not identify them with the tapestry in the inventory.

These writers questioned the history of the tapestry as it involved the Capilla Real primarily because most of them accepted Rolland's theory and could not explain how the tapestry got to Granada from Tournai after 1650. Furthermore Rolland had made a claim they found

too enticing to resist: he suggested that the hanging (or hangings?) in Grenier's gift contained portraits of himself, his wife, and their seven children (the fragment mounted in the left part of the Burrell piece). Rolland (1936, 214) and Morelowski (1936, 220) rejected the Granada history out of hand as a presumption; and Morelowski went so far as to suggest that the persons from whom Fortuny bought the fragments may have invented the provenance in order to hide the true source. However Crick-Kuntziger (1936, 218) observed correctly that if the Granada story were true one would have to conclude that Grenier had woven several hangings after the same cartoon, sometimes in one piece, sometimes in two or more pieces. Verlet (1965, 19), Asselberghs (1967, 35), Digby (1980, 20), and Châtelet (1989, 21 n. 45) all wrote that the composition had been woven more than once.

According to Dean (1911, 140), one of the Metropolitan Museum's curators (an undated letter that Dean wrote to Edward Robinson, the director of the Metropolitan Museum, from Geneva reveals that the curator was Dean himself) paid a visit to Fortuny's brother-in-law Ricardo de Madrazo and saw a photograph which showed some of the tapestries in a corner of Fortuny's studio. Madrazo told the curator that the "tapestries" (what we now know were fragments of a larger tapestry) had hung before the main altar of the Capilla Real in Granada. Dean also said in his article that the chapel authorities had discarded them in 1871 because they were in poor condition and that Fortuny, hearing about this while in Granada, arranged to buy them. Ricardo de Madrazo then wrote to Dean from Madrid on June 26, 1910, and confirmed the story as follows: "En efecto los tapices del siglo XV, que están ahora en el Museo Metropolitano de New York, pertenecieron a mi amado Mariano Fortuny, el cual los compró en Granada en la Capilla de los Reyes Católicos el año 1871. Luego se vendieron en Paris, en 1875, cuando tuvo lugar la venta de todo el estudio. Con mucho gusto he contestado a su pregunta" (Indeed the fifteenth-century tapestries that are now in the Metropolitan Museum of New York belonged to my beloved Mariano Fortuny who bought them in Granada in the Chapel of the Catholic Kings in the year 1871. Later they were sold in Paris, in 1875, when the sale of the whole studio took place. I have been happy to answer your question).[15]

Baron Davillier, who was in close touch with Fortuny during this time, indicated that the painter, his wife, children, and brother-in-law visited Madrid and Seville after leaving Paris in 1870 and then settled in Granada until the end of 1872, when they proceeded to Rome.[16] Fortuny, who was an active collector of works of art, wrote to Davillier from Granada on December 26, 1871, a letter which Davillier (1875, 72) later published, to tell him that he had not found any objects of Christian art but that "Pour les objets laissés par les rois catholiques Ferdinand et Isabelle, nous sommes plus heureux, car si tout n'a pas été conservé, il reste au moins quelque chose, et on garde encore dans la *Capilla Real* les objets que voici. . . . Il y avait aussi des tapisseries dont je possède quelques fragments en très-mauvais état" (As for the objects left by the Catholic monarchs Fernando and Isabel, we are more fortunate, for although not everything has been preserved something at least remains, and in the Royal Chapel they still have these objects. . . . There were also some tapestries of which I own some fragments in very bad condition).

There can be no doubt that 7a–e were among the fragments Fortuny was referring to in this letter. Ciervo (n.d., pls. 2, 3, 8) published some photographs showing Baptism, Namaan, Matrimony, and Extreme Unction hanging on a wall in the painter's studio in Rome before his death in 1875; and the David and Adam and Eve piece appears in a similar context in a photograph taken of the interior of Albert Goupil's house in Paris at the time of the sale of his property in 1888 (Goupil sale cat., illus. facing p. 100). Only 7d was not illustrated in either of these photographs. Neither it nor 7b was listed in the Fortuny sale catalogue in 1875; but all five fragments and the composite Burrell Collection piece, but not the fragment now in London, appeared in the Goupil sale of 1888.[17] Since Goupil was Fortuny's dealer in Paris and must have known him well, we may assume that he had bought 7b, 7d, and the Burrell piece either from Fortuny before the latter died in 1875 or from his heirs or estate before 1888.

Morelowski's suggestion (1936, 220) that Fortuny may have bought the fragments from someone who had dissimulated their true provenance cannot be credited. In addition to the evidence that Madrazo, Davillier, and Fortuny himself provided, it would be hard to believe that some unscrupulous vendor could have found such a tapestry, or fragments of one, somewhere else and then told Fortuny they had come from the Capilla Real in Granada when we know that Isabel had bequeathed such a piece to the chapel in 1504. Other documents indicate that the tapestries in that bequest did indeed go to the chapel. On July 22, 1505, Fernando ordered these nineteen tapestries removed from the others that would be sold to provide money for Isabel's legacies; the nineteen pieces were then sent to the chaplain of the Capilla Real in Granada.[18] According to Sánchez Cantón these tapestries, together with seven others that Fernando had bequeathed, were in the chapel in 1536; in 1737 only

seventeen pieces in poor condition remained; and by 1777 the surviving fragments had been burned in order to recover the gold from the metallic yarns.[19] However the *Seven Sacraments* that Isabel bequeathed to the chapel did not contain any metallic yarns. It was probably because of this that the tapestry survived. During the nineteenth century the Capilla Real fell into poverty, its staff was reduced, and by papal order it became subject to the jurisdiction of the prelate of the diocese. The chapel was not declared a national monument until 1884; and it was not until 1913 that the crown established the Museo Capitular to protect what treasures had survived in the chapel.[20] It is easy to understand how in these circumstances the authorities might sell off what were by then badly deteriorated fragments of tapestry. This was not a unique instance of such a sale: in 1907 the chapter of the cathedral in Saragossa sold the badly damaged left end of a late fifteenth-century hanging showing the sixth subject in the *Story of the Trojan War* (see 13).[21]

All of this supports Madrazo's affirmation that the fragments in the Metropolitan Museum are the ones that Fortuny had bought from the Capilla Real. That a large fragment of another tapestry in the queen's bequest turned up in Fortuny's sale in 1875 further bolsters Madrazo's account. This tapestry showed certain saints of Spain with the Madonna; like the *Seven Sacraments*, it contained no metal yarns. The fragment from this hanging is now in the Fine Arts Museums of San Francisco.[22]

If there is any basis in fact for the story that a physician bought the *Seven Sacraments* fragments from a family in France, a tradition that Rorimer (1947–48, 91) mentioned only once in his published work on 7a–e, that purchase would have occurred later, after the fragments left Fortuny's hands and before Goupil sold them.[23]

This proof of provenance tells us nothing certain about the date and place of manufacture of 7a–e, but it serves to show that these fragments could not have come from the tapestry that Jean Chevrot bequeathed to the church of Saint Hippolytus in Poligny in 1458 nor from the hangings that Pasquier Grenier is said to have given to his church in Tournai about 1475. However as noted above it seems possible, even likely, that all those tapestries were woven after the same cartoon or some version of it. If they were, then there are grounds for suggesting that all of them may have been produced through the Tournai-based enterprise run by Grenier who, it is said, commissioned one of the three editions of the design.

In terms of pictorial style the compositions in 7a–e are much closer to the hunting tapestries in the Victoria and Albert Museum of about 1425–50 (see fig. 59) with their simply silhouetted figures clearly located in uncluttered space than to the tapestries of the third quarter of the century, like the *Trojan War* pieces designed about 1465–70 (see 13) with their cramped spaces and crowded figure groups. The few fashionable garments represented in 7a–e suggest that the designer was working between about 1435 and 1450. The bourrelet that the mother or godmother in Baptism wears has tall points, and the men's boots wherever they appear have relatively pointed toes. The horns of the headdress were lower before about 1435 and taller after about 1450, and the toes of the boots were rounder before and more pointed afterward. By 1450 the men's heavy chaperons and their houppelandes with pleated fronts and low girdles hung with purses would have looked outmoded to anyone rich enough to have owned such an enormous hanging, and the same is true of the bulky, round-shouldered, and full-sleeved houppelande that the lady in Baptism wears. Appreciably different fashions appeared in the early years of the sixth decade of the century. Examples of the new mode may be seen in the garments worn by the ladies and gentlemen in the *Figures in a Rose Garden* pieces (8a–d).

Since the *Seven Sacraments* tapestry must have been designed no later than 1450, the figures who stand or kneel at the left end of the Burrell Collection piece cannot represent Pasquier Grenier and his family, as Rolland (1936, 213) believed, because the people shown there are all too old. According to Rolland (1936, 214), Grenier, who was admitted a burgher of Tournai in 1447 and had an established reputation in 1449, must have been approaching the age of thirty at that time. The bearded man in the Burrell Collection piece is certainly well over thirty, and at least four of the young men near him are about that age or perhaps a bit younger; in any case these youths are certainly too old to be the children of a man in his late twenties or early thirties.

RELATED TAPESTRIES

In addition to 7a–e and the fragments in London and Glasgow, there are a number of uncatalogued fragments of varying size in the Metropolitan Museum which were removed from the large pieces after they were acquired. Neither the *Seven Sacraments* tapestry commissioned by Jean Chevrot nor the one (or several) said to have been made at the order of Pasquier Grenier and his wife (see Manufacture and Date) are known to have survived. These are the only more or less contemporary tapestries we know of which, because they were described in similar terms, could have been woven after

the same or similar cartoons. In addition to this, we know that Louis d'Orléans (died 1407) owned two hangings showing scenes that apparently illustrated the same subjects, and also that François I owned a piece that probably illustrated the episode of Namaan bathing in the Jordan. Since Louis d'Orléans's hangings must have been at least fifty or so years older than the tapestry from which 7a–e came, it is unlikely though not impossible that they showed similar compositions. His tapestries were described as follows: "Deux grans tappis de haulte lisse pour salez ouvres dor de soye et de laine bien richemont et sont de listoire de vieux testament et du nouvel dont le premier se commence a Naaman qui se baigne en fleuve Jourdain et lautre se fruit [se finit?] alistoire Sacrement de mariage" (Two large hall tapestries worked with gold, silk and wool, very richly, of the story of the Old Testament and the New, of which the first starts with Namaan bathing in the river Jordan and the other [ends?] with the Sacrament of Marriage).[24] François I's tapestry, listed in the inventories of the Garde-Meuble in Paris in 1542 and 1551, was not described as being old at that time but it could have been. If so, it might have been woven after the composition that was used for 7c or some version of it. The description of this piece reads as follows: "Troys pièces de riche tappicerie sur or et soye faict de marcheterie, façon de Brucelles. . . . La tierce d'un homme nud qui se lave au fleuve Jourdain" (Three pieces of rich tapestry with gold and silk made of low-warp weaving, [in the] style of Brussels. . . . The third of a nude man who bathes in the river Jordan).[25]

The *Seven Sacraments* fragment in the Victoria and Albert Museum was called "Tonsure" when it was exhibited in London in 1921.[26] Rorimer (1940, 86) called it "Orders and Confirmation (?)"; Rolland (1936, facing p. 212) captioned an illustration of it "L'Ordre (tonsure) (et la Confirmation?)"; and Wells (1959, 98) referred to it as "*Confirmation* and minor orders." However Digby (1980, 19) and other writers have called it simply "Confirmation," which is correct.

There is good reason to question the identification of this scene. It does not show the bishop anointing a child's forehead, as one would expect a representation of Confirmation to do; but it does show the bishop cutting the hair of a boy kneeling in front of him and also a girl whose head has been shaved at the back except for a short fringe just above the neck. Furthermore, the inscription accompanying this episode and its prefiguration in 7d, the scene showing Jacob blessing his grandsons, reads, in part, "Priests give children confirmation and tonsure so that they will devote themselves to strength. . . ."

That the girl's head has been shaved and that a lock of the boy's hair is being cut at the side of the head rather than over the forehead are both confusing facts. The slightly later scenes of Confirmation in the drawing in Oxford and the embroidery in Bern (see note 6) show a bishop using his right hand to cut a boy's forelocks with scissors while he holds a box of chrism in his left hand. In the background, at the left, an assistant clergyman ties a cloth band around the crown of a boy's head. The Confirmation scene in Rogier's *Seven Sacraments* altarpiece in Antwerp (see note 6) shows the bishop simply anointing a boy's forehead, not cutting his hair, while a priest ties a band around another boy's head in the background and two boys and a girl, their heads bound with cloths, walk away from the clergymen. Since this girl is shown only from the front, we do not know whether the back of her head was shaved.

The Reverend Donald W. Hendricks has made the following observations which help explain these mid-fifteenth century representations of Confirmation.[27] First, he noticed that the bishop in the Oxford drawing and the Bern embroidery seems to be cutting the boy's forelocks away in order to clear the child's forehead for the anointing; and, second, he pointed out that the headband was used in confirmations during the Middle Ages as a means of covering the sign of the cross made with the holy oil; three days later, the child was to return and have the priest remove the chrism. Therefore, it seems strange that the head of the boy in the Victoria and Albert Museum tapestry was bound before the bishop cut his hair, presumably to clear his forehead to receive the chrism. The only explanation that seems reasonable (but not necessarily convincing) is that the designer condensed time in this representation and showed the boy at two moments during the ceremony, as his hair was being cut and after his head was bound.

Nevertheless, it is clear that the action of the bishop cutting the boy's hair and the presence of the band around his head both refer to the ceremony at which the sacrament of Confirmation is administered and not to the rite of ceremonial tonsure which is associated with the sacrament of Holy Orders. The "tonsure" of the tapestry inscription must therefore represent a generic use of that word in the sense of any clipping or shaving of hair. In the context of Confirmation, the tonsure probably began as a practical procedure to prepare the forehead to receive the sign of the cross in chrism and later acquired ritual significance as a covenant, as its mention in the inscription suggests. Therefore we believe that the Victoria and Albert Museum fragment comes from a representation of Confirmation specifically and exclusively. Incidentally, it is only in the

acquired-ritual sense of the word "tonsure" that we can understand the shaving of the girl's head in the Victoria and Albert Museum tapestry. It seems to have nothing practical to do with the application of the sign of the cross in chrism on the forehead or with the subsequent binding of the head.

The left end and center of the Burrell Collection piece (fig. 97) contain three large fragments and a number of small ones from the original *Seven Sacraments* tapestry. In its right end are two large fragments of what we believe was a different tapestry. These pieces of tapestry weaving were combined with bits of painted cloth to form one large rectangular hanging. At the left end three men—the head of the one farthest to the right is missing —and a woman stand against the leaf-patterned background. A colonnette rises to the left of them. A boy swinging a censer stands in front of the men and three young men kneel in the foreground. These are the figures that Rolland (1936, 213–14) believed were portraits of Pasquier Grenier, his wife, and their seven children. Most writers accepted his interpretation. For reasons given above (Manufacture and Date) we believe it is unfounded.

Rolland identified this group as part of the scene representing Communion. Wells (1959, 98, 105) believed that Communion was not represented in the tapestry because the Eucharistic theme of Grenier's chapel in the church of Saint Quentin had been planned to complement the subjects in the hanging. Therefore he suggested that this group of figures had been taken from the Ordination scene. We agree instead with Rolland because in at least two contemporary representations of Ordination there are no civilian women present, nor are there civilian men kneeling with their hands in an attitude of prayer as there are in the scene at the left end of the Burrell Collection piece (see note 6). Everyone here appears to be preparing to receive Communion from a priest whose figure, which would have stood at the right, has not survived. The presence of an acolyte swinging a censer further endorses this interpretation.

The figure group in the middle of this fragment shows part of the episode that prefigured Communion: that is, Melchizedek offering bread and wine to the victorious Abraham (Genesis 14:17–19). The armored Abraham and three of the kings who accompanied him in the defeat of Chedorlaomer stand or kneel before Melchizedek whose figure is missing except for the hands holding bread and a veiled chalice. The verses inscribed on the scroll that runs along the bottom of this fragment, toward the right, read as follows (deleting the fragment near the center that contains three words from the scroll in the Jacob scene):

De l'altel le saint sacrement · ou quel est Jhesu
vraiement
Melchisedech representa · quand il offri et
(reserva?) pain et vin pour abraham qui · iiii
(mecreants rois?) vanqui

(Melchizedek anticipated the Holy Sacrament of the altar where Jesus truly is when he gave and [reserved?] bread and wine for Abraham who vanquished four [rebellious kings?]).

The incomplete figure of a priest who appears to be standing between the kneeling figures in Communion and the first soldier in the Abraham scene is represented on a separate fragment of weaving. Rorimer, in his reconstruction of the original tapestry (fig. 99), placed this priest to the right of the tonsuring bishop in Confirmation, and Wells did the same (fig. 100). Rolland (1936, 213–14) and Marillier (1936, 48–49) had suggested this solution some years earlier. However, since the top of the crosier held by the priest overlaps the brickwork of the second-story floor directly beneath the soldier standing at the left end of the Abraham scene (see fig. 97), it is clear that in the original tapestry the priest stood below and just to the left of that soldier. Rorimer and Wells were right to place the priest in that position; but in that position he could not have figured in Confirmation. That sacrament was represented in the second lower compartment from the left end of the whole tapestry, whereas this figure must have been standing at the far right end of the third lower compartment, below the left end of the Abraham scene and immediately to the left of Communion. As we have indicated above (Description and Subject), this third lower compartment must have contained the representation of Penance or Ordination. In the Ordination episode (but not Penance) in the Oxford drawings and the Bern embroideries (see note 6), there is a priest holding the bishop's crosier in a similar way. Therefore it seems reasonable to suggest that Ordination rather than Penance may have appeared immediately to the left of Communion in the original *Seven Sacraments* tapestry.

HISTORY

Perhaps in the collection of Juan II of Spain, then of his son Enrique IV, in the Alcázar in Segovia.[28]
Collection of Isabel la Católica, Alcázar, Segovia, in 1503.
Bequeathed to the Capilla Real in Granada by Isabel la Católica in 1504.
In the Capilla Real in Granada, possibly by 1505, certainly by 1536.[29]
Bought from the Capilla Real in Granada before December 26, 1871, by Mariano Fortuny y Marsal.
Collection of Mariano Fortuny y Marsal, Granada and Rome, 1871–75.

7a, c, and e sold, *Atelier de Fortuny,* Hôtel Drouot, Paris, April 26–30, 1875, p. 143, no. 139 in section "Etoffes Anciennes." The Namaan scene is identified incorrectly as Baptism and the true Baptism scene is not identified at all.
7a–e sold, *Catalogue des objets d'art . . . composant la collection de feu M. Albert Goupil,* Hôtel Drouot, Paris, April 23–28, 1888, pp. 100–101, nos. 613 [7d], 614 [7a–c], 615 [7e]. Baptism is identified correctly, but the other subjects are misunderstood: Manasseh is called a pope; David being anointed king is described as a coronation scene, and either Matrimony or God uniting Adam and Eve is described simply as a "scène de fiançailles." The Namaan scene is not cited by title. 7b is illustrated, in reverse, in the plate facing p. 100.
Property of M. Bacri, Paris and New York.
Bought from M. Bacri, New York, by J. Pierpont Morgan, 1907.
Given to the MMA by J. Pierpont Morgan, 1907.

EXHIBITIONS

None known.

PUBLICATIONS

Ciervo, Joaquín. *El arte y el vivir de Fortuny.* Barcelona, n.d., 7a and 7e mentioned pp. 12–13; 7a, 7c, 7e illus. pls. 2, 3, 8.
Davillier, Baron. *Fortuny, sa vie, son oeuvre, sa correspondance* (Paris, 1875) pp. 71–72. Mentioned indirectly as fragments of tapestries that Fortuny bought from the Capilla Real in Granada.
Dean, Bashford. "A Suite of Early Gothic Tapestries (Burgundian)." *MMA Bulletin* 2 (1907) pp. 40–45. Discussed at length; illus. figs. 1–7.
Hunter, George Leland. "Art in America: The Burgundian Tapestries in the Metropolitan Museum." *Burlington Magazine* 12 (December 1907) pp. 185–86. Discussed; illus. pls. I–III.
"Fifteenth Century Tapestries." *MMA Bulletin* 4 (1909) p. 149. Mentioned.
B. D. [Bashford Dean]. "Recent Accessions and Notes: The Tapestries of the Sacraments." *MMA Bulletin* 6 (1911) p. 140. Discussed.
Candee, Helen Churchill. *The Tapestry Book.* New York, 1912, pp. 38–40. Discussed; 7a, c, d illus. facing pp. 34, 38, 39.
Hunter 1912, pp. 30, 45, 312, 314, 386, 388, 390, 392, 394. Discussed at length; illus. pls. 46, 47.
Hunter, George Leland. "Tapestries at the Metropolitan Museum." *International Studio* 45 (February 1912) pp. LXXXV–VI. Discussed at length; 7a illus. p. LXXXIX.
J. B. [Joseph Breck]. *The Pierpont Morgan Wing: A Brief Guide to the Art of the Renaissance, Medieval and Earlier Periods.* MMA, New York, 1918, p. 10. Mentioned; 7a and e illus. p. 9.
Schmitz, Hermann. *Bildteppiche.* Berlin, [1919], pp. 189–90. Discussed.
Göbel 1923, vol. 1, p. 271. Discussed briefly; 7a and e illus. vol. 2, figs. 208, 209.
Breck, Joseph, and Meyric R. Rogers. *The Pierpont Morgan Wing: A Handbook.* MMA, New York, 1925, pp. xviii, 114–15. Mentioned; 7b illus. fig. 64.
Hunter 1925, pp. 46–50, 53–55, 239. Discussed at length; 7a, d, and e illus. pls. IV,a–c.
Thomson 1930, p. 107. Mentioned.
Samuels, Milton, in collaboration with Avery Strakosch. "Hang'd with Tapestry." *Saturday Evening Post,* April 18, 1931, p. 137. Mentioned; 7e illus. p. 23.
Rolland, Paul. "Le tapissier Pasquier Grenier et l'église Saint-Quentin à Tournai." *Revue Belge d'Archéologie et d'Histoire de l'Art* 6 (1936) pp. 203–14. Mentioned pp. 212–14; illus. on unnumbered pages of pls. facing p. 212.

Crick-Kuntziger, Marthe. In "Le tapissier Pasquier Grenier et l'église Saint-Quentin à Tournai." *Revue Belge d'Archéologie et d'Histoire de l'Art* 6 (1936) pp. 215–18. Mentioned pp. 215–17.

Morelowski, Marjan. In "Le tapissier Pasquier Grenier et l'église Saint-Quentin à Tournai." *Revue Belge d'Archéologie et d'Histoire de l'Art* 6 (1936) pp. 218–21. Mentioned pp. 220–21.

Marillier, H. C. "Sir William Burrell's 'Sacrament' Tapestry." *Archaeological Journal* 93 (1936) pp. 45–50. Discussed at length.

Crick-Kuntziger, Marthe. "Le Moyen Age: Les arts décoratifs." In *L'Art en Belgique du moyen âge à nos jours.* Ed. Paul Fierens. Brussels, 1939, pp. 153–75. Mentioned pp. 167–68.

Rorimer, James J. "A XV Century Tapestry of the Seven Sacraments." *MMA Bulletin* 35 (1940) pp. 84–87. Discussed; illus. figs. 1, 2.

Rorimer, James J. *Mediaeval Tapestries: A Picture Book.* MMA, New York, 1947, p. [3]. Mentioned; illus. figs. 9, 10 (details of 7c and of 7e).

Rorimer, James J. "The Museum's Collection of Mediaeval Tapestries." *MMA Bulletin,* n.s. 6 (1947–48) pp. 91–92. Mentioned.

Bacri, Jacques. "La tapisserie d'Arras au moyen âge." *Travaux et Documents de la Bibliothèque d'Humanisme et Renaissance* 13 (1951) p. 360. Mentioned.

Rorimer, James J., and William H. Forsyth. "The Medieval Galleries." *MMA Bulletin,* n.s. 12 (1953–54) p. 135. Mentioned; 7e illus. p. 137.

Fourez, Lucien. "L'évêque Chevrot de Tournai et sa Cité de Dieu." *Revue Belge d'Archéologie et d'Histoire de l'Art* 23 (1954) pp. 73–110. Mentioned p. 82 n. 4.

Weigert, Roger-Armand. *La tapisserie française.* Paris, 1956, p. 59. Discussed briefly; detail of Extreme Unction illus. pl. 9.

Wells, William. "The Seven Sacraments Tapestry—A New Discovery." *Burlington Magazine* 101 (March 1959) pp. 97–105. Discussed; illus. figs. 15 (only known published illustration of Rorimer's reconstruction) and 21 (Wells's reconstruction).

Heinz, Dora. *Europäische Wandteppiche I.* Brunswick, 1963, p. 80. Mentioned.

Verlet 1965, pp. 19, 55. Mentioned; 7e illus. p. 55.

Cetto, Anna Maria. *Der Berner Traian- und Herkinbald-Teppich.* Bern, 1966, pp. 154–61. Discussed.

Cònsoli, Giuseppe. "'El servo' del 'Trionfo' Sclàfini." *Arte Antica e Moderna* 33 (1966) fig. 18a. 7e illus.

Asselberghs, J. P. *La tapisserie tournaisienne au XVᵉ siècle.* Exh. cat. Tournai, 1967, pp. [14], [35]. Discussed.

Cavallo, Adolph S. *Tapestries of Europe and of Colonial Peru in the Museum of Fine Arts, Boston.* Boston, 1967, p. 46. Mentioned.

Quinn, J. R. "Sacraments, Theology of." *New Catholic Encyclopedia.* New York, etc., 1967, vol. 12, p. 809. 7a and 7b illus. fig. 2.

Jarry, Madeleine. *World Tapestry: From Its Origins to the Present.* New York, 1969, p. 79. Detail of Matrimony illus. pp. 78–79.

Coffinet 1977, pp. 41–42. Mentioned.

Digby 1980, p. 20. Discussed briefly.

Châtelet, Albert. "Roger van der Weyden et le lobby polinois." *Revue de l'Art,* no. 84 (1989) pp. 15, 20–21 n. 45. Mentioned; illus. figs. 13, 14.

NOTES

1. The damask-patterned backgrounds in the related fragments in Glasgow and London (see figs. 97 and 98) have not sustained this kind of loss and consequently show the leaf units as being lighter in value than the ground tone.

2. In *Atelier de Fortuny,* sale cat., Hôtel Drouot, Paris, April 26–30, 1875, no. 139, 7e is described in reverse. Illustrations of 7b in *Catalogue des Objets d'art . . . composant la collection de feu M. Albert Goupil,* sale cat., Hôtel Drouot, Paris, April 23–28, 1888, plate facing p. 100, and of 7a, c, and e in Joaquín Ciervo, *El arte y el vivir de Fortuny* (Barcelona, n.d.) pls. 2, 3, 8, show 7a, b, and e in reverse. Hunter called attention to the reversals and illustrated the five pieces in their correct orientation; see George Leland Hunter, "Art in America: The Burgundian Tapestries in the Metro-

politan Museum," *Burlington Magazine* 12 (December 1907) pp. 185–86, pls. I–III.

3. The inventory of 1503, entitled *Libro de las cosas que están en el tesoro de los alcaçares de la cibdad de Segovia . . . el qual hizo Gaspar de Grizio Secretario . . . Mes de noviembre de mill e quinientos e tres años,* is published in Francisco Javier Sánchez Cantón, *Libros, tapices y cuadros que coleccionó Isabel la Católica* (Madrid, 1950) pp. 109–14; the reference to the *Seven Sacraments* tapestry appears as no. 84 on p. 112.

4. See A. Claudin, *Histoire de l'imprimerie en France au XVᵉ et XVIᵉ siècles* (Paris, 1901) vol. 2, pp. 427–38. The sacraments with their prefigurations are illustrated on pp. 431–37 in the following order: Baptism, Penance, Communion, Confirmation, Ordination, Matrimony, Extreme Unction. In some cases Claudin did not identify the subject correctly and in others he described the action represented but did not name the subject.

5. Sánchez Cantón, *Libros, tapices y cuadros,* no. 84, p. 112.

6. The orphrey and hood in Bern, which Jacques de Savoie, comte de Romont and baron de Vaud (1440–ca. 1486), gave to the cathedral of Lausanne, are discussed and illustrated in Eugene Bach, "Les broderies de la chape donnée par Jacques de Romont à la cathédrale de Lausanne et leurs sources d'inspiration," *Zeitschrift für Schweizerische Archaeologie und Kunstgeschichte* 7 (1945) pp. 39–42 and pls. 14–16. For notes on the drawings and illustrations of them, see Friedrich Winkler, "Some Early Netherland Drawings," *Burlington Magazine* 24 (1913–14) pp. 224–31; and pp. 224, 231, a postscript by Campbell Dodgson calling attention to two more drawings of the set that belonged then to baron Edmond de Rothschild in Paris (not illus.), which, together with the five drawings in the Ashmolean Museum, shows all seven sacraments. The drawings are also discussed in K. T. Parker, *Catalogue of the Collection of Drawings in the Ashmolean Museum,* vol. 1 (Oxford, 1938) pp. 40–41. The altarpiece in Madrid is illustrated in Max J. Friedländer, *Early Netherlandish Painting,* vol. 2, *Rogier van der Weyden and the Master of Flemalle* (New York and Washington, 1967) no. 47, pl. 67. See also an illustration of its central section in Bach, "Les broderies de la chape donnée par Jacques de Romont à la cathédrale de Lausanne," fig. 1. The Antwerp altarpiece is discussed and illustrated in Albert Châtelet, "Roger van der Weyden et le lobby polinois," *Revue de l'Art,* no. 84 (1989) pp. 9–21 and fig. 1.

7. Winkler, "Some Early Netherland Drawings," p. 224; Bach, "Les broderies de la chape donnée par Jacques de Romont à la cathédrale de Lausanne," p. 41.

8. For notes on the *Saints Piat and Eleuthère* tapestries, and illustrations, see Roger-A. d'Hulst, *Flemish Tapestries from the Fifteenth to the Eighteenth Century* (New York, 1967) pp. 17–24.

9. For the text of the account relating to this purchase, dated at Saint Omer, March 17, 1439, see J. Versyp, *De geschiedenis van de tapijtkunst te Brugge* (Brussels, 1954) p. 145. It reads as follows: "A Paule Melian, marchant demourant au dict Bruges . . . 316 lb. 17s. 6d. pour ung tapis de l'istoire du sacrement en tapisserie bien riche que mon dit seigneur a fait prendre. . . ."

10. Concerning the two Sacrament tapestries in Isabel's gift, see Sánchez Cantón, *Libros, tapices y cuadros,* p. 108; the reference to the *Seven Sacraments* in the inventory of 1503 is on p. 112 (no. 84).

11. This section of text from Sanderus, "Projet manuscrit d'Histoire de Tournai," preserved in the Bibliothèque Communale de Tournai, no. 184, fols. 701-2, is published in Paul Rolland, "Le tapissier Pasquier Grenier et l'église Saint-Quentin à Tournai," *Revue Belge d'Archéologie et d'Histoire de l'Art* 6 (1936) p. 209 n. 27.

12. See Eugène Soil, *Les tapisseries de Tournai* (Tournai and Lille, 1892) p. 232, item 47, payment in 1444 to Robert Dary for having furnished Jean Chevrot, bishop of Tournai, with some "patrons" for tapestry. It was Dary, together with Jean de l'Ortie, who produced the *Story of Gideon* tapestries for Philippe le Bon between 1449 and 1453; see Soil, *Les tapisseries,* p. 233, item 52.

13. William Wells, "The Earliest Flemish Tapestries in the Burrell

Collection, Glasgow (1380–1475)," *De Bloeitijd van de Vlaamse Tapijtkunst (Internationaal Colloquium, 23-25 Mei, 1961)* (Brussels, 1969) p. 457.

14. The bequest is discussed, and the tapestries are listed, in Sánchez Cantón, *Libros, tapices y cuadros*, pp. 96–97 and n. 57. The *Seven Sacraments* tapestry is no. 84 in Sánchez Cantón's numbering system.

15. The letter from Dean to Robinson reporting his talk with Madrazo, and Madrazo's letter to Dean are preserved in the Archives of the Metropolitan Museum.

16. Baron Davillier, brief biographical essay in Fortuny sale cat., 1875, p. 6.

17. See Goupil, sale cat., 1888, nos. 613–16. The entries do not identify all the subjects precisely. No. 613 describes the Jacob episode but does not give it a title. No. 614 is a lot described as "trois tapisseries représentant un couronnement, une cérémonie de fiançailles, etc.," with the height given as 2 meters and the (aggregate) length as approximately 7.5 meters. The "coronation" must refer to David being anointed king (right end of 7b) and the "engagement" surely refers to the uniting of Adam and Eve (left end of 7b). That piece now measures 3.10 meters in length. The "etc." must refer to 7a (Matrimony and Extreme Unction) together with 7c (Namaan) since the length of those pieces is now 5.15 meters, and together with 7b these fragments have an aggregate length of 8.15 meters which, allowing for possible errors in the measurements taken in 1888 and the variations of size that tapestries normally sustain over the years, compares well enough with the approximately 7.5 meters given as the aggregate length of no. 614 in the catalogue entry. No. 615 is described in the catalogue as a baptism scene; it certainly refers to 7e. The catalogue description of no. 616 fits the right-hand section of the Burrell Collection piece but the dimensions given for that lot refer to the whole composite fragment as it exists today. Therefore, the only surviving fragment of the original tapestry that was not in the Goupil sale is the Confirmation fragment now in London. Digby 1980, p. 20, conjectured that it too came from the Capilla Real through Fortuny, but its later history remains unknown until 1921 when it appears in the possession of Miss Enid du Cane in London.

18. Sánchez Cantón, *Libros, tapices y cuadros*, p. 97 and n. 57.

19. Sánchez Cantón, *Libros, tapices y cuadros*, p. 100.

20. Antonio Gallego y Burín, *La Capilla Real de Granada* (Madrid, 1952) p. 29.

21. See Manuel Gómez-Moreno, "La gran tapicería de la guerra de Troya," *Arte Español* 4 (1919) pp. 270–71.

22. Sánchez Cantón, *Libros, tapices y cuadros*, p. 111, described in the inventory of 1503 as "Otro paño en que estan los santos de España y nuestra señora en medio con el niño en los braços . . . sin oro . . ."; see also Fortuny sale cat., 1875, p. 143, no. 140. The fragment has been discussed and illustrated in Anna G. Bennett, *Five Centuries of Tapestry from the Fine Arts Museums of San Francisco* (San Francisco, 1976) pp. 34–35. The figure of a bishop saint from the same hanging, now surrounded by a millefleurs ground, was lent to the Philadelphia Museum of Art; see Bennett, *Five Centuries of Tapestry*, p. 34, illus.

23. The story was first published by Milton Samuels in collaboration with Avery Strakosch, "Hang'd with Tapestry," *Saturday Evening Post*, April 18, 1931, p. 137, where the authors state that a doctor making a call in a humble house in France bought the fragments which were covering the kitchen floor, and that sometime later the doctor sold them to a dealer.

24. Text published in Thomson 1930, p. 118.

25. Text published in Sophie Schneebalg-Perelman, "Richesses du garde-meuble parisien de François Iᵉʳ: Inventaires inédits de 1542 et 1551," *Gazette des Beaux-Arts*, 6th ser., 78 (November 1971) p. 277.

26. See *The Franco-British Exhibition of Textiles 1921*, Victoria and Albert Museum (London, 1922) p. 9, pl. xxiv.

27. The present author thanks Father Hendricks, pastor of the Church of Saint Anthony, Yonkers, New York, for his kindness in consulting with him, by means of letters (now in the files of the Department of Medieval Art, MMA) and telephone conversations, on the matter of the hair cutting shown in these representations of Confirmation. In relation to the use of the headband, Reverend Hendricks cited "Confirmation," in *The Catholic Encyclopedia*, C. G. Hebermann et al., eds. (New York, 1907–22) vol. 4, p. 221.

28. Although Isabel bought tapestries and received others as gifts, she inherited a quantity of them that had belonged to her father, Juan II, and then her brother Enrique IV. Their tapestries were stored in the Alcázar in Segovia where her *Seven Sacraments* tapestry was inventoried in 1503. It is therefore possible that Juan II (died 1454) owned the tapestry first and that it passed from him to Enrique (died 1474) and finally to Isabel. See Sánchez Cantón, *Libros, tapices y cuadros*, pp. 92–96, and José Ferrandis, *Inventorios reales (Juan II a Juana la Loca)* (Madrid, 1943) pp. IX–XVII, 19.

29. The present author thanks Ronda J. Kasl, who found the following reference, for bringing it to his attention. Among the warrants issued in 1505 by Juan López, royal clerk and keeper of receipts to the Catholic kings, are three that record payments for services and material in connection with shipping books, tapestries, and other furnishings to Granada for the royal chapel. The texts, recorded on folios 35, 36, and 37, respectively, of the manuscript "Casa y descargos de los Reyes Católicos," Legajo 5, in the Archivo General del Reino in Simancas, read as follows (transcribed here not from the original manuscript but from Amalia Prieto Cantero, *Casa y descargos de los Reyes Católicos: Catálogo XXIV del Archivo General de Simancas* [Valladolid, 1969] p. 145): ". . . a Bernaldino de Loarte, para ir a Granada con los libros y paños de la tapicería de la capilla real . . ." (. . . to Bernaldino de Loarte, to go to Granada with the books and [the] tapestries of the textile furnishing of the royal chapel . . .); ". . . para comprar lienzos de 'vitre' a fin de envolver los paños de la tapicería que se enviaban a la referida capilla real de Granada" (. . . to buy hemp cloths for wrapping up the tapestries of the textile furnishing that were being sent to the said royal chapel of Granada); and ". . . al referido Bernaldino de Loarte, lo que tenía que pagar a Martín Rico, arriero, que llevaría los repetidos paños, tapicería, y libros, a Granada" (. . . to the said Bernaldino de Loarte, who had to pay Martín Rico, muleteer, who would transport the said tapestries, textile furnishing, and books, to Granada). It is possible but not certain that Isabel's *Seven Sacraments* tapestry was among these unnamed hangings. If so, it must have been placed temporarily somewhere other than the present Capilla Real which was not completed until 1519 and did not contain the sepulchers of the king and queen until they were transferred there from the convent church of San Francisco on the Alhambra on November 10, 1521 (see Gallego y Burín, *La Capilla Real de Granada*, pp. 21–24). However we can be sure that the *Seven Sacraments* tapestry, together with the eighteen other hangings in Isabel's bequest and seven more that Fernando had bequeathed to the chapel were in the present Capilla Real in 1536, for they were listed in the chapel inventory of that year; see Sánchez Cantón, *Libros, tapices y cuadros*, p. 100.

8

Figures in a Rose Garden

Four fragments

a   Three Gentlemen and Two Ladies
b   A Lady and Two Gentlemen
c   Four Gentlemen and Four Ladies
d   A Gentleman

Southern Netherlands, 1450–55
Wool warp; wool, silk, and metallic weft yarns
8a: 10 ft. 3 3/4 in. × 8 ft. 1 1/2 in. (3.15 m × 2.48 m)
8b: 9 ft. 5 3/4 in. × 10 ft. 8 in. (2.89 m × 3.25 m)
8c: 12 ft. 5 in. × 8 ft. 8 in. (3.79 m × 2.64 m)
8d: 6 ft. 6 in. × 3 ft. 2 in. (1.98 m × .97 m)
8a–c: 13–15 warp yarns per inch, 5–6 per centimeter
8d: 12 warp yarns per inch, 5 per centimeter
8a–c: Rogers Fund, 1909 (09.137.1–3)
8d: Gift of George Blumenthal, 1941 (41.100.231)

CONDITION

The four sides of all the hangings have been cut and the edges covered with narrow bands of modern fabric. None of the selvages or loom finishes have survived. 8a, b, and c, the three largest hangings, were made up from fragments of three tapestries—8a may also include a small piece from a fourth hanging—joined together with lines of reweaving and insertions of modern fabric, as follows.

In 8a there are three large vertical fragments and two small horizontal ones from a tapestry whose original shape and dimensions cannot be determined. A sixth fragment, much smaller than the others, was taken either from the same tapestry or from a different hanging in the same set. It represents the bottom of the white stripe at the right edge of the field. The three largest fragments are joined together by two vertical lines of reweaving. The first line runs from the top of 8a down through the middle of the headdress worn by the man standing in the upper left corner and continues down through his left side, the right arm of the woman standing below him, the right side of her skirt, and then to the bottom edge of the tapestry. Another join was made from the top edge to the bottom, along the right edge of the white stripe in the center. A third join extends horizontally from this one straight across to the right edge of the fabric at the level of the hips of the man in the lower right corner. There is an insertion of modern fabric at the lower left, from the edge of the hanging through the rosebush and the lower third of the skirt worn by the

woman standing next to it and continuing into the bottom of the white stripe behind her. A long, narrow fragment of original weaving completes the bottom of the field on that side. Most of the brown wool weft yarns in this piece have been replaced, and there are other repairs by reweaving in most of the contours of all the figures, the pleats in their garments, and several small spots in the white headdress of the woman standing in the right half of the field.

In 8b there are seven rectangular fragments of another tapestry in the same series. The five largest ones are vertical in format; the two smallest are horizontal. Four major lines of reweaving join the five tall pieces to one another to form most of the field. The first line follows the left edge of the red stripe against which the lady's right arm appears. The second join extends down a line just to the left of center in the middle white stripe. A third line runs parallel to the second one just to the right of it, grazing the tips of the fingers on the lady's left hand. The fourth join is in the center of the right-most green stripe. A short horizontal join runs from a point near the bottom of this fourth line to the right edge of the field; it connects the bottom of the vertical fragment at the right to the top of one of the horizontal fragments from the original tapestry. Another horizontal join extends from the left edge of the fabric just below the man's right foot to the lowest fold of the lady's train. An insertion of modern fabric extends from that point to the right edge of the field; it represents the bottoms of all the stripes from the center to the right edge of the hanging and the lower parts of the shoes worn by the man standing at the right. There are other small insertions to the right of the monkey in the lower left corner and also along the top of the white and red stripes just to the right of center. Much of the brown wool in the contours of the figures has been replaced, as have many of the silk wefts used in the highlights of their costumes.

Two large and four small fragments from a third related tapestry were joined together with lines of reweaving and insertions of modern fabric to produce 8c. The two major pieces are tall, wide rectangles that were joined down the center of the field; they constitute the

8b

8d

across the figures of the lady and gentleman to the right edge of the fabric, the upper join crossing the figures at the level of their hips, the lower one at mid-thigh level. The lower third of the left half of the hanging consists of an insertion of modern fabric combined with two small rectangular fragments of the original tapestry. The insertion is shaped like the letter L with its longer stroke running horizontally; the fragments of the original tapestry fill the space between that stroke and the bottom edge of the hanging. The skirt of the lady standing there, the lower part of her right arm and hand, and most of the white stripe behind her are represented on the modern fabric. The lower half of the jacket worn by the man standing next to her, his right hand, and a small rectangular section of the green stripe behind him are also represented on this insertion. The dark brown contours of all the figures have been replaced with modern weft yarns, and a great many of the silk and wool wefts in the women's robes as well as the men's jackets have been replaced.

Kajitani (forthcoming) has given a complete account of the condition of 8a–c, together with an exhaustive study of the fibers, yarns, and dyes, the structure of the fabrics, and the technical procedures involved in their manufacture, as well as a history of the restoration and conservation treatments undergone by each of the three hangings before and during the present century.

In 8d there is a wide insertion of modern weaving from the top of the fragment to the middle of the man's headdress and another smaller insertion in the lower right corner from the bottom edge up to the ankle of his left leg. There is also a small insertion on his right breast. Most of the dark brown wefts are modern as are many of the silk yarns in the highlights throughout the piece.

Because all four pieces contain the many repairs by reweaving and the insertions of modern fabric that were noted above, the original drawing and modeling have suffered considerably. Furthermore the bright and varied tones on the backs of the fabrics indicate that all the dyes have faded a good deal, the yellows having suffered the most. Because of that, the tones that were originally green now read as blues with a greenish cast.

Description and Subject

The four hangings show similar compositions. In each of them, male and female figures dressed in garments of elaborately patterned silk velvet or damask, or plain fabrics, many of them trimmed with fur at hem, collar, and cuffs, stand in relatively static poses against grounds showing vertical stripes of unmodulated color.

upper two-thirds of the hanging. A narrow band of modern weaving has been added along the top. It extends completely across the piece and includes the representations of the tops of the cockades on both men's headdresses and the top of the headdress of the woman at the right. The lower third of the right half of the field contains two small, horizontal fragments that are joined to the bottom of the upper fragment and to each other with lines of reweaving that extend from the join in the center

Heavily pruned rosebushes are scattered over the stripes, some behind the figures, some in front of them. The stripes, which are red, white, and green, alternate in a regular sequence from left to right; but the sequence is not the same in all four pieces. In 8a, c, and d (the latter showing only a red and a white stripe), the stripes are arranged in a sequence of white, green, red from left to right, whereas in 8b the sequence runs white, red, green. The designer may have reversed the sequence in 8b so that its stripes would appear as mirror images of the others if it were hung on a wall between and at right angles to them (see Related Tapestries).

In 8a there are all or part of five figures. In the upper left corner stands a man wearing long hose and a velvet or damask fur-trimmed jacket over a doublet made of another patterned silk. The jacket is gathered into deep vertical pleats down the front and has a thigh-length skirt that is slit to the hips at the sides. The shoulders are not heavily padded, but they move upward and outward with the tops of the sleeves as these swell out over the upper arm. The sleeves are slit down the front from a point just below the shoulder to a point just above the wrist; the edges of the slits are lined with fur. This man wears a chaperon (a hood twisted into a turban-like headdress, with the dagged opening for the head piled on top like a cockade), a narrow girdle around his waist with a dagger hanging from it in front, and a pair of ankle-high boots terminating in short points. His body faces left but he turns his head to the right, his right arm bent across his body and his left arm bent, with the knuckles and thumb resting on that hip. In the lower right corner of the field is another man, visible only from the knees upward and facing left, dressed in a simpler version of the same costume. Part of the head and body of a third man dressed like the second one appears at the lower left edge of the hanging. There are two ladies in the composition, one standing in the upper right half, the other in the lower left half of the field. Both wear long, straight gowns (the upper one of plain fabric, the lower one patterned) that are deeply pleated in front from the waist downward; above, the gowns open outward away from the neck and have a flat white collar that tapers to the waist. The top of the kirtle or dress worn under the robe appears at the base of the neckline. The sleeves are straight and tight from shoulder to forearm, and then they taper outward slightly to meet loose, wide cuffs at the wrists. Each lady wears a necklace, a wide girdle, and an elaborate headdress, the one at the top made of fine white linen draped over a high wire frame supported on a cap, the other a bourrelet (a padded roll of fabric) worn high on the forehead and, at the sides, above jeweled net pads that cover the hair over the tem-

ples. This headdress also has a pair of lappets falling to the back on one side and a tippet or liripipe hanging to a point below waist level on the other side. The lower figure has been cut off at ankle level; because the upper one has been preserved full height, one can see that her gown extends below and beyond her feet, turning into a train and forming a decorative flourish of drapery in the lower right corner of the field. The lady and gentleman at the right carry rose sprigs. The lady in the lower left carries a whole small rosebush. The man whose figure is only partly preserved at the lower left is plucking a branch of roses from one of the bushes. In this piece, there is a narrow bit of white stripe along the left edge, then, moving toward the right, the stripes are green, red, white in sequence twice across the field, ending with a white stripe along the right edge.

There are only three figures in 8b. A lady dressed like the one in the lower left section of 8a, but wearing a richer headdress and a gown terminating in a long train, stands just left of center. The upper part of her figure sways to the left and her arms are bent and extended to the sides. In her right hand is a rose sprig that she offers to a man standing at the left end of the field. Dressed like the men in 8a, this gentleman wears a cap and holds his chaperon in both hands with the open crown forward. A rose sprig nestles inside. Below this man's feet appears the upper part of a monkey holding a kitten in the crook of its left arm. A gentleman wearing a knee-length jacket of plain material over a patterned doublet stands in the lower right corner of the hanging. He, like the other man, faces the lady in the center but he is not involved in the action that unites the other two figures. He looks in their direction but seems not to see them as he raises his right arm to grasp a rose branch and slips his left hand under the loosely buckled girdle at his waist. The rosebushes in this hanging are taller and fuller than those in the other three pieces. However, unlike those, which are represented as shrubs growing out of crowns planted in the ground, the ones in 8b are shown as branches growing out of thick stalks that were neatly cut, not broken, from the crown. The stripes in the background begin with a red section at the left, then white, red, green in sequence twice, and ending with a white stripe at the right end of the field.

In all particulars 8c resembles 8a, including the color sequence of the stripes (red, white, green), which begins with a red stripe at the left and ends with another at the right. There are eight figures arranged in couples, with two couples in the upper register and two below. The ladies wear the same basic costume, gowns of damask or velvet, and all have necklaces. The two in the upper register wear the towering white headdress, and the two in the lower row wear the high bourrelet with two short lappets on one side and a liripipe on the other. The men all wear hose, the pleated jacket, and the chaperon with a pendant liripipe. The gentleman in the upper left corner wears a hip-length damask or velvet jacket, the others have longer jackets of plain fabrics, and all four garments have fur trimmings. The two figures at the left end of the field face toward the right; the other six face left. Rosebushes of varying heights and densities are liberally scattered over the stripes, all rising out of firmly planted, heavily pruned crowns. The figures carry rose sprigs, except perhaps the man in the upper left corner whose left hand is hidden and the lady in the upper right corner who crosses her hands in what appears to be a meaningless gesture.

In 8d there is only one figure, a gentleman standing rather unsteadily on slightly bent legs, in the center of the field, which is half red (left) and half white (right). The man's right ankle and foot are hidden behind a rock or low hillock in the lower left corner. Six small rosebushes are scattered over the ground. All but the two at the bottom appear to grow from crowns planted in the earth; those two seem to grow from stalks that were cut off the crown of the shrub. The man wears long hose like the men in 8a–c, but over his hose he wears a tabard-like pleated huke rather than a jacket. It has short caps or wings over the armholes through which pass the swelling damask or velvet sleeves of his doublet. The huke is trimmed with fur along each side and at the collar, shoulders, and hem. The gentleman faces toward the right but his shoulders and torso twist to the left. Both arms are bent and the empty hands hang in the air one above the other in a meaningless gesture.

All of the figures represented in these tapestries, both the men and the women, are dressed in the height of fashion. They wear modish clothes and each of them has shaved the natural hairline away in order to avoid having any head hair show around the edges of the various forms of headdress. These are people of consequence and wealth, the kind of people for whom these costly tapestries were woven. Along with the ordinary wool yarns the tapestries contain not only silk wefts but also metallic wefts made of silver and possibly also gilt tinsel (narrow, flat wire) wrapped spirally around core yarns of silk. Since all the metal elements have blackened, it is not clear whether they were both gilt and silver originally or just one or the other. The silk yarns were used primarily for highlights in the garments and the plants. The metallic yarns appear not only in the jewelry and garments (where they represent the metal yarns woven into the damask and velvet dress fabrics) but also in the rendering of the roses and rosebushes.

The subject of these four hangings has been, and remains, a matter for speculation. When two of the pieces were exhibited in Paris in 1904 (see Exhibitions) and for many years afterward, no writer in Europe referred to the three large pieces—the only ones known until 8d was sold in 1921—as the *Baillée des Roses*, the title that seems to have been invented for the series at the time 8a–c were bought for the Metropolitan Museum in 1909. That title first appears in an article published in the Metropolitan Museum *Bulletin* for that year. The ceremony of the Baillée des Roses was described there briefly according to the account given in Larousse's *Grand dictionnaire universel*. Before 1918, when Rubinstein discredited the idea, some of the writers who discussed the tapestries—specifically, Candee and Hunter, both in 1912, and Rosenthal in 1916—believed that the tapestries did indeed illustrate the Baillée. This was a ceremony during which the peers of France presented roses to members of the parliament and other court officers in Paris and Toulouse during the rose season in late spring and also on other occasions when parliament was to judge a case involving a peer or a peerage.[1] Rubinstein (1918, 167–71) argued that the images in the tapestries had nothing to do with that ceremony and her reasoning was unassailable. Nevertheless a few writers continued to use the title in connection with the tapestries, specifically Migeon (1929), Rorimer (1947), and Weigert (1956 and 1964), with less conviction by Seligman (1961) and Verlet (1965), by Jarry (translated as "The Presentation of the Roses," 1969), and by Joubert (1981).

Other writers have interpreted the subject matter in different ways, but none of these interpretations seems to lead us to a correct understanding of the designer's plan. Guiffrey (1911, 73) said the tapestries were of the sort he called in generic terms "conversations galantes" and that they showed "des seigneurs et des dames . . . vêtues à la dernière mode, se promènent en échangeant des propos galants" (lords and ladies . . . dressed in the latest fashion [who] stroll and flirt). Some years later Rubinstein (1918, 167, 173) converted Guiffrey's generic class of tapestries into a specific series of hangings she dubbed "Conversations Galantes." When 8b was exhibited in Los Angeles and Chicago in 1970, Ostoia restored to that term the general, rather than specific, meaning that Guiffrey meant it to have. She also said that the hangings were now called *Courtiers with Roses* because the figures wear courtly costumes and stand in courtly poses. Furthermore, she noted that the subject of the hangings had been associated with literary texts like the *Roman de la Rose* but that the notion had been abandoned when no one could find anything in the tapestries that would justify such an interpretation. The alleged association with that romance dates back to 1919 when Schmitz first used the word "Rosenroman" in connection with these tapestries. Göbel (1923, vol. 1, 60, 78) took up the banner in earnest when he interpreted the figures as lovers conversing with personified Virtues and Vices and the rosebushes as a proper setting for the romance. Fels (1923) said simply that the hangings showed "Rosen werden gepflückt" (roses being gathered). Hunter (1925, 107) believed the ladies and gentlemen were "having a party in a garden of roses," while Breck and Rogers (1925 and 1929, 130) referred to the subject as "courtiers . . . gathering roses," a description which probably developed in time into *Courtiers with Roses*, the title that the Metropolitan Museum has usually used since then. Bossert (1932) referred to the subject as "Paaren in Rosen" (couples among roses). Yver (1946) called one of the pieces "l'offrande de la rose" and the other simply "jardin de la rose." This brings to mind the theme of the Garden of Love where ladies and gentlemen come to meet for a few hours' dalliance. The tapestries could perhaps reflect that theme: Rosenthal called attention to the fact that the swaying lady in 8b resembles a similar figure shown in the larger print of the *Garden of Love* by the Master of the Love Gardens (Rosenthal, 1916, fig. 11).

It is also possible that these four fragments came from a series of tapestries whose subject was based loosely on the idea of a group of courtiers strolling through a rose garden. Since the lady standing in the lower left half of 8a holds a small rose plant, crown and all, one wonders whether these elegant people are in fact planting, tending, and harvesting the rose garden in which they stroll. The woman in 8b could be gathering a small bouquet by plucking rose sprigs and collecting them with the help of her companion in his inverted chaperon. The other figures wander through the garden plucking roses or simply enjoying the experience of walking among these lovely and fragrant shrubs. There seems to be no literary content here. However there may be some allegorical or heraldic meaning in a related fragment of tapestry that was formerly in the collection of Octave Homberg in Paris (see Related Tapestries). That piece showed similar rosebushes against a striped ground and also the word *vertueuse*—perhaps a personal device?—woven into the fabric (see discussion of striped-ground armorial tapestries below). There are no figures in this fragment; but what appears to be the hemline of a patterned robe at the top of the field suggests that figures were indeed present in the original tapestry. Although it seems unlikely that this fragment came from the series of hangings to which the Metropolitan Museum's pieces belonged, it must have come from a closely related set. Because of that,

and because it contains what may be a heraldic device, it suggests the possibility that 8a–d were designed as armorial hangings and that the missing parts of these fragments, or other hangings in the set, may have shown armorial elements including one or more devices.

A number of other writers, including Migeon (1909), Kurth (1923), Heinz (1963), and Weigert (1964), observed correctly that the figures in the Metropolitan Museum's tapestries have no real psychological or narrative connection with each other and that they are merely decorative motifs in a brilliantly ornamental scheme of wall decoration. Both Lafenestre (both 1904 publications) and van Marle (1931) regarded the designs as wall decorations first and foremost, and van Marle observed further that their ultimate purpose was simply to show the elegance of the nobility. Kurth (1923) and Heinz (1963) called attention to the fact that the figures were treated as elements in an overall textile pattern. Indeed that is what they seem to be, and it is hard to support a claim that they represent couples engaged in conversation. Only two of these "couples," the man and woman in the lower left half of 8c and perhaps also the two figures in the left half of 8b, could be described as figures who are talking to one another. Furthermore, as we shall see below (Source of the Design), what appear to be many different figures in 8a and 8c are in fact just a few figures, some of which have been reversed or slightly modified and then given different costumes. Viewed in this light the four fragments reveal an undeniable kinship with millefleurs tapestries, a kinship that Yver (1947), Heinz (1963), and Young (1962–63) all commented upon. It seems perfectly clear that the figures derive from stock patterns that merchants and weavers used in different compositions, few if any of which had any intrinsic narrative content. Here they have been placed against an abstract, spaceless background of stripes rather than against an abstract, spaceless flowery meadow. Furthermore the monkey holding a kitten in the lower left corner of 8b reminds one of millefleurs tapestries. It is the kind of monkey that mimics human behavior or echoes underlying themes in a number of millefleurs hangings of the fifteenth and sixteenth centuries.[2]

When Rubinstein (1918) argued against the assertion that these tapestries represent the Baillée des Roses, she not only carried her point on that score but also emphasized and developed the most important observation that Bouchot had made when he published the tapestries in 1904. That is, she called attention again to the hangings that appeared on the walls of a room in the château de Saint Georges in Vendôme where the trial of the duc d'Alençon took place in 1458. The scene is shown in a miniature painting by Jean Fouquet which serves as the frontispiece in a copy of Boccaccio's *De casibus virorum illustrium* (translated into French as *Des cas des nobles hommes et femmes*) that is preserved in the Bayerische Staatsbibliothek in Munich (cod. gall. 369; see, in the present catalogue, fig. 27). Those hangings showed a red, white, and green striped ground covered with rose branches on which were superimposed paired winged stags supporting the arms of France. Charles VII of France is shown seated on a canopied dais in the corner of the room. Rubinstein (1918, 171–72), followed by certain later writers, said that red, green, and white were Charles VII's livery colors and the rose tree was a personal emblem of his. Rubinstein (1918, 173) also agreed with Bouchot (1904) in maintaining that the lady in 8b resembles the Madonna in Fouquet's Melun altarpiece, now in Antwerp. The model for that head was supposed to have been the king's mistress Agnès Sorel.[3] On these grounds—the general similarity of design that relates 8a–d to the ones shown in Fouquet's miniature and the supposed resemblance of the swaying lady in 8b to Agnès Sorel—Rubinstein (1918, 171–73) suggested that the tapestries in Vendôme and the ones now in the Metropolitan Museum were made for the king, the latter possibly for Agnès Sorel.

However neither Rubinstein nor any of the later writers (all of them following her in the identification of the colors and rosebush with Charles VII and some of them also repeating the alleged association with Agnès Sorel) noted that the king did not use these colors throughout his lifetime or that he also used other personal emblems and badges including an iris, a sun, a rose, and a winged stag.[4] The rose branches or bushes that appear against the stripes in the Munich miniature and the red or white blossoms they bear are not rendered naturalistically, as the ones in 8a–d are, with a wide variety of hues and tones in the stalks, branches, and blossoms, but hieratically, as though they were heraldic charges. Furthermore the hangings shown on the walls in the Munich miniature are decorated not only with red, white, and green stripes and rosebushes or branches but also with the winged stag, another emblem that Charles used. The narrow border framing the scene shows iris stalks alternating with rose sprigs in a series of rectangular compartments. Every heraldic element on that page refers specifically to Charles VII. Nor did Rubinstein or the writers following her mention the fact that the face of the Melun Madonna was the archetypal fashionable face of the moment, which Reynaud later pointed out quite clearly.[5] But more important than that, the facial features of the lady in 8b simply are not the same as the Melun Madonna's. Any argument based on that claim carries no weight.

As for the red, green, and white colors, the rosebushes and roses in the tapestries, any one of the king's subjects who was in a position to commission works of art could have used these or other visual references to the king, in his honor. Jacques Coeur, Charles VII's High Treasurer, used royal emblems together with his own when he decorated buildings he had commissioned.[6] He also owned tapestries showing the king's colors, arms, and emblems as well as three bench covers, one red, another white, and the third green, showing his own arms and device.[7] A hanging rather like the ones represented in the Munich miniature of 1458 appears in royal context (although the reference is to an event that took place almost a hundred years earlier) in a miniature painting of about 1470 in the British Library's copy of Froissart's *Chronicles*.[8] What appears to be a tapestry with red, white, and green stripes hangs on a wall in the middle distance at the right. On each of these stripes appears a double row of plants, some of which are roses and others possibly irises. To support a claim that that hanging and the four Metropolitan Museum's fragments necessarily were made for Charles VII or for someone to whom he gave them, one would have to prove that no one but this king used red, white, and green as his livery colors at this period. While we do not yet know for certain which colors Charles used at every specific moment in his lifetime, we do know that he used red, white, and blue in the early years of his reign and that he had changed the blue to green by 1437, presumably because the duke of Bedford (and, for a brief time, the duke of Burgundy) also used the first combination of colors. There is also ample evidence to show that Charles used red, white, and green during the period when the Museum's tapestries were woven. Charles V and Charles VI had used red, white, and green earlier, the latter king with the addition of black.[9] We have documents proving that people other than these three kings had tapestries striped red, white, and green, but it is not clear whether or not the colors were used in reference to any one of the kings. An example appears in an inventory of furnishings belonging to the duc de Bourbon dated November 18, 1507: "Une chambre de tapisserie de même verdure, faicte à bandes vertes, blanches et rouges, où il y a dix pièces, et le ciel et pendans de mesmes" (A tapestry chamber of the same verdure, made with green, white and red stripes, of ten pieces, and the [bed] ceiling and valances of the same).[10] Another piece with a striped ground of the same or similar colors is listed in the inventory dated May 12, 1514, of the château de la Motte-Feuilly, the residence of the duchesse de Valentinois: "Une autre pièce de tapicerie de Feulletin à menue verdure sur bandes rouges, blanches et vert brune" (Another piece of

Felletin tapestry with small verdure on red, white and green-brown stripes).[11]

Furthermore, we know that many tapestries with roses and other flowers, human figures, creatures, and armorial elements set against striped grounds were woven at this time and later in reference to other patrons. Bouchot mentioned that toward the end of the fifteenth century Cardinal Charles de Bourbon had similar tapestries with blue, white, and red stripes. One of these may be represented in a drawing that has survived in the Collection Gaignières in the Bibliothèque Nationale, Paris.[12] It shows the Bourbon coat of arms and device together with a lady and a unicorn, all against a ground of red, white, and blue stripes. On the stripes are pairs of branches bearing bell-shaped blossoms arranged in reverse-C arabesques. The Collection Gaignières also contains drawings showing other tapestries with striped grounds, all of them armorial. One piece that must have been commissioned before 1507 (the year of his death) shows the arms, ciphers, and devices of René II, duc de Lorraine, and his wife Philippine de Gueldre, all against a ground of stripes of four different colors.[13] Arabesques of plant tendrils are superimposed on the striped ground (three or four colors) of a heraldic tapestry woven for Jacques III d'Estouteville and his wife Jeanne who were married in 1509.[14] Two other striped-ground pieces, both of which must have been ordered before 1553 when each of the principals died, show in the first instance heraldic motifs referring to Adrien de Croy, comte de Roeux, and his wife, and in the second the armorial bearings of Hugues de Melun, prince d'Espinoy. The first tapestry had a ground of red, yellow, and blue stripes.[15] The second had stripes of two tones, each stripe decorated with a letter *h* and either a flame or two sprigs bearing bell-shaped blossoms placed in reverse-C arabesques.[16] The same kind of arabesques appear again on the striped grounds (two or more tones) of a set of armorial tapestries woven for Antoine de Bourbon, king of Navarre, and his queen, Jeanne d'Albret; they were married in 1548.[17] Henry VIII of England's inventory of 1548 lists various tapestries showing striped grounds, as follows: "7 peces of olde Verdours paned [that is, striped] white and redd. . . . 3 peces of Verdours, paned Murrey [mulberry red] and blew having the *Kings Armes* in them. . . . 2 peces of Verdours paned with yellow and redde. . . ."[18] The second pieces listed sound as though they might have looked very much like a tapestry of the second quarter of the sixteenth century, two fragments of which are now in Winchester College. They show what is said to be the coat of arms of Belinus, king of Britain, against a ground of red (possibly to be described as "murrey") and blue stripes decorated with a damask

pattern of the period. They were exhibited in Tournai in 1970 along with another piece showing heraldic motifs against a ground of red and white stripes (about 1450–1500) and the piece mentioned above that shows the arms of Adrien de Croy and his wife against a ground of red, yellow, and blue damask-patterned stripes (between 1531 and 1553).[19]

As this brief discussion of the matters of livery colors and striped-ground tapestries shows, it seems possible, even likely, that the design of 8a–d may contain some heraldic connotation, but also that it would be extremely risky to claim that they were woven for Charles VII either for his own use or to be used as gifts.

Source of the Design

Although three generations of writers have tried to assign literary content of one sort or another to these compositions, the tapestries seem in fact to be no more nor less than ornamental hangings based on a specific class of heraldic compositions that—as we have demonstrated—present the patron's coat of arms, badges, emblems, and devices in front of a background of stripes whose colors (usually or always?) repeat those of the patron's heraldic tinctures. Kurth (1923, XIII–XIV) and Heinz (1963) both called attention to the architectonic character of these pieces, Kurth implying and Heinz stating that the designs were conceived essentially as textile patterns. Heinz, along with Yver (1947) and Young (1962–63), also noted that the hangings are conceptually related to, and may be forerunners of, the millefleurs tapestries of a somewhat later period. Like those hangings, 8a–d offer the viewer a glimpse of attractive figures, shrubs, and flowers arranged casually against a two-dimensional background of fairly uniform character. The monkey in 8b also fits in with the subject matter found in millefleurs tapestries. Like those pieces, 8a–d show figures that seem to have been arranged to satisfy the requirements of a formal plan rather than a literary one and so the people have little to do with one another in narrative terms. Therefore we are dealing not with compositions that were borrowed whole from some particular preexisting source but with individual design units that were taken from one or more such sources and then assembled with a suitable setting either in the cartoon painter's shop or the weaver's shop, exactly in the way that most or all millefleurs tapestries were designed.

It was noted above (Description and Subject) that some of the figures in 8a–d were repeated in different places. The most striking examples of this are the following ones. The man in the lower right corner of 8a reappears (with a slight change of facial features) in the same position in 8c. The woman in the upper right of 8a is the same as the one in the lower left but wearing a different gown and headdress. She reappears, again with a change of gown and with a rosebud instead of an open blossom, in the upper left half of 8c. The man standing in the lower left half of 8c (his right hand missing, a result of the restoration process) appears again, reversed, wearing a different jacket, and holding the hilt of a dagger in his right hand, in the upper left corner of the same hanging. The man standing in the upper right half of 8c is a close variant of the same figure. The man in 8d, who at first glance looks nothing like the others because his costume is so different and his pose so awkward, is in fact a variant of the man in the upper left corner of 8a. His left hand is in a different position and his legs have been reversed. The figures in 8b do not repeat any of the others, which sets it apart from 8a, c, and d, as do also the facts that the facial features are more elegantly drawn and modeled and the rosebushes are different in a number of ways from the bushes in the other three pieces. It seems reasonable, therefore, to suggest that the artist who painted the cartoons for 8a and c was not the one who painted those for 8b and d, and that the painters used two sets of related designs.

Over the years writers have attributed the compositions to a number of different artists. As early as 1904 Bouchot suggested the name of Jean Fouquet because the hangings represented in the miniature painting of the trial of the duc d'Alençon are related to these; but he qualified the attribution by observing that the hands and legs in the Metropolitan Museum's tapestries look like the work of a lesser artist and so one would have to assume that the weaver had weakened Fouquet's drawing. Candee (1912) believed that the tapestries were designed by some French artist under Fouquet's influence, but Rubinstein (1918, 173) recalled Bouchot's attribution and endorsed it. She also believed that the lady in 8b resembles Agnès Sorel, and that the figures in the tapestries resemble others in the miniature already mentioned as well as miniatures painted by Fouquet in the Book of Hours of Etienne Chevalier, which are opinions that we do not share. Breck and Rogers (1925 and 1929, 131), and Verlet (1965, 28) considered without much conviction the proposition that Fouquet might have designed the Metropolitan Museum's tapestries. Even Bouchot had wavered in his tentative attribution to Fouquet, observing, as he said it, that the compositions represented a transitional style of painting which developed between the time the painters who worked for the duc de Berry were active and Fouquet's time.

Kurth (1923, XIII) included the tapestries among a small group of pieces in whose design she saw the influence of Simon Marmion. We see no grounds for connecting these designs with that painter.

Rosenthal (1916) and Fischel (1947) related the figures represented in the tapestries to certain print sources. Their arguments seem to us more pertinent and potentially fruitful than the ones summarized above. For Rosenthal (1916, 26–27), the tapestry designs were related both to the design of a series of xylographs entitled the *Exercitium super pater noster*, which he believed were made in the southern Netherlands in the decade 1430–40, and also to the larger of the two prints of the *Garden of Love* by the Master of the Love Gardens.[20] He further believed that the Metropolitan Museum's tapestries had been designed by an artist who also designed a hypothetical tapestry to which the print may have been related. Following Rosenthal's idea of a relationship between certain figures in tapestries and in prints made at this time, Fischel (1947, 31) suggested that the figure of the man standing in the lower right corner of 8b and a very similar figure engraved by the Master of the Playing Cards both derive from some common source, perhaps a drawing of Duke Philip of Brabant that was attributed to Jan van Eyck.[21] Fischel believed that the duke's figure could have inspired the figures in the print and the tapestry since the drawing appears to be earlier than both the print and the tapestry, since the figure shown in it uses both hands meaningfully (he holds his hat in his right hand and a falcon in his left hand) whereas the other two figures make arbitrary gestures, and since the duke faces in the opposite direction. Both Rosenthal and Fischel overstated the point. We believe that they were correct in tracing the figures of the swaying lady and of the man at the right in 8b to these prints but that the connections are much more complex and distant than these writers thought. The cartoon painter or weaver used many more figures than just these two, and he may have taken them from some common sources rather than directly from these prints or others that have survived.

Whoever it was who collected the figures he needed for the Metropolitan Museum's tapestries, varying and multiplying them for these settings, also worked on some tapestries of which fragments have survived in Saumur, Baltimore, Paris, and Regensburg. All of those fragments show fashionably dressed men and women riding horses.[22] Most of the riders have stock faces that came from the same hand or hands that drew the faces in the cartoons after which 8a–d were woven. The figures themselves, like the figures in the Metropolitan Museum's pieces, could have been taken from several different prints or pattern books.

MANUFACTURE AND DATE

When the tapestries were first published in 1904, Bouchot attributed some or all of 8a–c to France and dated them around 1450. He believed that the costumes could be dated a bit earlier but that, since tapestry cartoons continued to be used for some years after they were designed, the weavings themselves could belong to a somewhat later period. He also believed that the tapestry designs were related to the style of French court painting of roughly the second quarter of the fifteenth century. Curiously, in the catalogue entry concerning these hangings when they were exhibited in Paris in 1904, Bouchot's attribution to France was retained but the pieces were dated to the end of the fifteenth century. This confusion recurs in the Metropolitan Museum's first publication of the tapestry, in its *Bulletin* for 1909, where in the text the pieces were called French, about 1425–50, but in the captions to the illustrations they were labeled as dating from the end of the century. From 1909 until 1965, when Verlet (28) suggested indirectly that the tapestries might have been woven in the Loire valley, a number of writers (Migeon 1909, Candee 1912, Hunter 1912, Rubinstein 1918 and 1927, Yver 1946, and Weigert 1956 and 1964) considered them French and dated them around 1450 or a bit earlier or later. These dates, like the dates suggested by writers who believed the tapestries were woven elsewhere, were based on the premise that the costumes represented are from the reign of Charles VII (actually about 1445–60). When 8a–c were exhibited at the Metropolitan Museum in 1974, Souchal suggested in the catalogue entry that a detail in the women's headdresses placed the design a bit after 1450. This author also observed that it was more likely that tapestries of this degree of richness would have been bought in France after, rather than before, Charles VII had recovered his kingdom from the English and the country had recovered from the disastrous economic effects of the Hundred Years' War, that is, after the truce of 1444.

Another group of writers, more numerous than those just cited, regarded the tapestries as products of looms located in northern France or the southern Netherlands, and most of them mentioned Arras or Tournai specifically. In 1916 Rosenthal (26–27) started this trend when he associated the tapestry designs with the xylographs he had attributed to the southern Netherlands during the decade 1430–40. Kurth (1917, 1923), Schmitz (1919), Göbel (1923), Hunter (1925), Migeon (1929), and most major specialists writing after that time, and all publications by the Metropolitan Museum (or based on them) continued to attribute the tapestries to Arras or Tournai around the middle of the fifteenth century. When reasons were given for the dates, they were usually based on considerations of fashion. Davenport (1948) and Payne (1965), who published the tapestries from the point of view of costume history, dated them respectively 1438–40 and around 1450. Hunter (1925) and Migeon (1929) believed that the tapestries were probably made for Charles VII (as many other writers, including Souchal in Paris 1973, 69, also did) and believed further that they were woven for the king in Tournai or in France by weavers from Tournai. None of these specialists was able to give any convincing support to his arguments and indeed there appears to be none. Although the designs have a decidedly French flavor, the fabrics themselves could just as well have been produced in any of the southern Netherlands shops that were weaving fine tapestries at this time as in France. We know so little about tapestry weaving in France during this period that it is pointless to pursue the question.

Since the figures represented in these tapestries express little beyond their own being as creatures of fashion, it is reasonable to assume that the tapestries would have been woven not long after the compositions were designed. The clothing indicates a date at or just after the middle of the fifteenth century, slightly later than the *Deer Hunt* tapestry in the Victoria and Albert Museum showing fashions of about 1440–45.[23] One sees in the women's costumes in 8a–c that the bulk of the gowns is less, the sleeves slimmer along the arm and looser at the cuffs, the waistlines lower, the corsages more open, and the bourrelet headdresses slightly higher and narrower than in the hunting tapestry. Also in 8a–c the men's jackets are slimmer and shorter, the sleeves somewhat slimmer, the waistlines higher, and the shoes more pointed than in the *Deer Hunt*. These differences announce the basic change of fashion for both sexes that developed in all its details around 1460 and continued throughout the next two decades (see 12). Men's shoulders became wider and were padded higher, the skirts of their jackets became shorter, and the points of their shoes longer. Women's gowns became even slimmer and the corsage became more open on the shoulders. The two sides of the bourrelet were folded closer together and higher. The men's body garments and headgear already show some of these later fashion details in Fouquet's miniature painting of 1458. The conclusion to be drawn from these comparisons is that 8a–d must have been designed, and probably also woven, no earlier than about 1450 and no later than about 1455.

RELATED TAPESTRIES

The five tapestry fragments in Baltimore, Paris, Regensburg, and Saumur that seem to have been designed by the same hand or in the same shop as 8a–d (see note 22) are not related to the Metropolitan Museum's four pieces in any other ways. None of them shows the striped ground or rosebushes and all five appear to have narrative subjects. None could have belonged to the series of cartoons or hangings to which 8a–d belonged.

There are, however, two pieces, both of which have striped grounds ornamented with plants, that are related to 8a–d in terms of both design and content. The two were sold from the collection of Octave Homberg in Paris in 1931.[24] The smaller piece, number 143 in the sale catalogue, shows parts of five rosebushes like those in 8a–d against a ground of white at the left and blue (according to the catalogue) at the right. This is almost certainly part of a striped ground. The "blue" stripe could have been green originally and (as often happened) have come to appear blue as the yellow component in the green dye faded out over the years. What appears to be the bottom of a damask or velvet robe or gown runs completely across the top of the fragment, and the word *vertueuse* is woven in the fabric just below the center of the field near its right edge. Since the blue (or green?) stripe in this piece is considerably more than half a meter wide, while the stripes in 8a–d are somewhat less than half a meter in width, it is unlikely that this fragment was part of the same set of hangings. However it must have belonged to a closely related series. The other fragment, number 142 in the Homberg sale, shows a lady dressed in a costume similar to those in 8a–c standing against a ground that has a white stripe at the left and a red stripe at the right, each stripe approximately as wide as the stripes in 8a–d. Plants of different varieties (not rosebushes) are arranged in vertical rows on the stripes. An oak tree rises directly behind the lady, who holds a bird in her hands. A dog seated at the left looks up at her. (The tree, the dog, and the woman's pose and activity relate this hanging to certain millefleurs tapestries where details like these are to be found.) The tapestry from which this fragment comes was closely related to 8a–d in terms of design; but the subject and the character of the drawing are essentially different. This piece could not have been woven after the series of cartoons that served the weavers of 8a–d.

Breck and Rogers (1925 and 1929, 130), writing about 8a–c, and Rubinstein-Block (1927), writing about 8d, believed that all of the Metropolitan Museum's fragments came from a single hanging. There are certain inconsistencies of design that repudiate their theory. In fact there is reason to ask whether all four fragments originally came from a single set of hangings. A number of factors set 8b and d apart from the other two pieces. First, there is the curious circumstance that when the tapestries were exhibited in Paris in 1904 only 8a and c were noted in the catalogue (see History), and they were listed as having been lent by M. L. Bardac. All subsequent notices and literature list M. Sigismond Bardac as the owner. Since 8b was not listed in the exhibition catalogue but was first cited in print when Bouchot published it in 1904, we cannot be sure that it was exhibited with 8a and c on that occasion or that it came from the same source as the other two fragments. As we noted above (Source of the Design), 8b differs from 8a, c, and d in terms of design on a number of counts. The figures' faces are more elegantly drawn, more individualized, and more convincingly modeled. The rosebushes are taller and fuller, and they spring not from the crowns of plants growing in the ground but from thick branches with cut ends. The color sequence of the stripes is different from the sequence in the other pieces, the white stripe having a green one to the left and a red one to the right rather than the reverse. The three figures in this piece do not repeat each other or any of the figures in 8a, c, or d.

Nevertheless, we believe that 8b belonged with 8a, c, and d in one and the same set of hangings. The difference one sees in the drawing, modeling, faces, and plants undoubtedly follows from the fact that at least two, and possibly three, painters executed the cartoons for the series.[25] As for the change of color sequence in the stripes of 8b, there is a precedent for it in the miniature of the duc d'Alençon's trial. There, the hanging on the wall at the left shows a sequence of red/green/white/red stripes whereas the sequence in the one on the adjacent wall is red/white/green/red. The designer must have planned them to hang in the room in this way, as mirror images of each other, and the designer of 8a–d may have done the same.

Even though the form of his costume and the drawing of his legs make the man in 8d look different from the others, details that may again be viewed as the work of a different cartoon painter, his facial type agrees with the types in 8a and c. Furthermore, as indicated above (Source of the Design), his figure repeats with a few changes the figure of the man standing in the upper left quarter of 8a.

We know of one other tapestry that is related to 8b in a

different way. In 1919 the Edgewater Tapestry Looms in New Jersey exhibited a tapestry that had been designed after 8b but with the image reversed, with minor changes of detail, and with important differences in the character of the drawing.[26]

HISTORY

8a–c in the collection of Sigismond [and/or L.?] Bardac, Paris, in 1904 (see Exhibitions).

Property of the firm of Jacques Seligmann, Paris.

Purchased by the MMA through the Rogers Fund from Seligmann, 1909. According to Germain Seligman (1961, 21–22) the MMA, under the guidance of trustees William M. Laffan and J. Pierpont Morgan, made an offer to Seligmann for the three tapestries that was higher than the amount that museum officials in France, who also wanted the hangings, would make, and so Seligmann sold the tapestries to the MMA. According to Seligman (1961, 21–22), the press reported that during the succeeding week authorities at the Louvre tried unsuccessfully to buy one of the pieces from the MMA. Reinach (1910, 433) wrote that 8a–c "avaient été acquises, à l'unanimité" (had been acquired, unanimously) by the Consultative Committee of the Musées Nationaux in France, but that since the minister in charge "refusa sa signature" (refused to sign), the tapestries were sold to the MMA the next day, which he lamented. It was probably because of these reports, and also because only 8a and 8c were listed in the catalogue of the Paris exhibition of 1904—Bouchot having published 8b separately—that a number of specialists wrote of the tapestries during the next half-century as though some of them were in the MMA and some elsewhere. Although the earliest publication of the three pieces by the MMA, in the *Bulletin* in 1909, made it perfectly clear that the MMA had bought and kept all three pieces (8a–c), Kurth (1917, 88; 1923, XIII) wrote as though the MMA owned only 8b and 8c. Göbel (1923, vol. 1, 60, 78) thought that two pieces were in New York and the third in the Louvre. Writing in 1931, van Marle seemed unsure whether 8c, which he acknowledged was in the MMA, was also one of the "two" pieces he said had been exhibited in Paris in 1904. As late as 1946 Yver thought that the MMA owned only two of the hangings, and in 1964 Weigert (65) said that the three pieces belonged to the MMA and to Sigismond Bardac. A year later, Verlet (1965, 24) confirmed that the MMA had all three hangings but then observed that they had passed through the Bardac and Morgan collections. In view of the confusion surrounding the acquisition of the tapestries in 1909, this error is not surprising, but while Mr. Morgan was a key figure in the negotiations on behalf of the MMA, he never owned the tapestries in his own right.

8d sold, *Collections de M. Raoul Heilbronner*, pt. 2, Hôtel Drouot, Paris, November 9–12, 1921, no. 520, illus.
In the collection of George and Florence Blumenthal, New York.
Given to the MMA by George Blumenthal, 1941.

EXHIBITIONS

Paris, Palais du Louvre and Bibliothèque Nationale, 1904. *Exposition des primitifs français*. Cat. nos. 260 [8a] and 260 bis [8c], not illus. Lent by M. L. Bardac. It must be noted here that when Bouchot, one of the organizers of this exhibition, published his volume of annotated illustrations of works of art shown on that occasion (see Bouchot 1904 in Publications), he discussed the two pieces mentioned in the catalogue (8a and c) but illustrated only 8b, which was not cited there. He also noted that the tapestries belonged to M. Sigismond (not L.) Bardac. In the two publications issued by Lafenestre in 1904 concerning this exhibition (see Publications),

there was mention of only two of the tapestries, presumably 8a and 8c, the two listed in the exhibition catalogue. We are left to wonder whether 8b was in fact ultimately exhibited with the other two pieces and—if the "L." can be regarded as a typographical error—whether all three belonged to Sigismond Bardac at that time.

Boston, Museum of Fine Arts, 1940. *Arts of the Middle Ages*. Cat. no. 115 [8b], not illus.

Hartford, Wadsworth Atheneum, and Baltimore Museum of Art, 1951–52. *2000 Years of Tapestry Weaving: A Loan Exhibition*. Text by Adele Coulin Weibel. Cat. no. 70 [8b], pl. VI.

New York, MMA, 1967. *In the Presence of Kings: Royal Treasures from the Collections of The Metropolitan Museum of Art*. Text by Helmut Nickel. Cat. no. 12 [8b], illus.

Los Angeles County Museum of Art, and Art Institute of Chicago, 1970. *The Middle Ages: Treasures from The Cloisters and The Metropolitan Museum of Art*. Catalogue entry by Vera K. Ostoia, no. 97 [8b], color illus.

New York 1974. Catalogue entries by Geneviève Souchal. Cat. nos. 28 [8c], 29 [8a], 30 [8b], illus.

PUBLICATIONS

Bouchot, Henri. *L'exposition des primitifs français: La peinture en France sous les Valois*. Paris, [1904], pl. XXXIX. Two pieces exhibited in Paris in 1904 (presumably 8a and c) discussed briefly; illus. 8b only.

Lafenestre, Georges. *L'exposition des primitifs français*. Paris, 1904, p. 24. Two pieces (presumably 8a and c) discussed briefly.

Lafenestre, Georges. "L'exposition des primitifs français," pt. 2. *Gazette des Beaux-Arts*, 3d ser., 31 (1904) pp. 461–62. Two pieces (presumably 8a and c) discussed briefly.

"Fifteenth Century Tapestries." *MMA Bulletin* 4 (1909) pp. 149–52. 8a–c described and discussed at length; illus.

Migeon, Gaston. *Les arts du tissu*. Paris, 1909, p. 274. 8a–c discussed briefly; 8c illus. p. 275.

S. R. [Salomon Reinach]. "Nouvelles archéologiques et correspondance: Au Musée de New-York." *Revue Archéologique*, 4th ser., 16 (1910) p. 433. Observations on purchase of 8a–c by MMA.

Guiffrey, Jules. *Les tapisseries du XIIe à la fin du XVIe siècle*. Paris, [1911], p. 73. Discussed briefly.

Candee, Helen Churchill. *The Tapestry Book*. New York, 1912, pp. 42–44. 8a–c discussed briefly; 8b illus.

Hunter 1912, pp. 51, 374, 376, 378. 8a–c discussed at some length; 8b illus. pl. 53.

Hunter, George Leland. "Tapestries at the Metropolitan Museum." *International Studio* 45 (February 1912) p. LXXXIII. 8a–c discussed in terms of design character and texture; 8b illus. p. LXXXV.

Rosenthal, Erwin. "Die kunstgeschichtliche Stellung des chiroxylographischen Exercitium super pater noster." *Mitteilungen der Gesellschaft für vervielfältigende Kunst. Beilage der "Graphischen Künste"* 39, no. 2 (1916) pp. 26–27. 8a–c discussed briefly; detail of center of 8b illus. fig. 12.

Kurth, Betty. "Die Blütezeit der Bildwirkerkunst zu Tournai und der burgundische Hof." *Jahrbuch der Kunsthistorischen Sammlungen des allerhöchsten Kaiserhauses* 34 (1918) p. 88. 8b and c discussed briefly; illus. figs. 16 [8b], 17 [8c].

MMA, The Pierpont Morgan Wing: A Brief Guide to the Art of the Renaissance, Medieval, and Earlier Periods. New York, 1918, pp. 12–13. 8a–c discussed briefly; 8b illus. facing p. 12.

Rubinstein, Stella. "Three French Gothic Tapestries hitherto Known as the 'Baillée des Roses.'" *American Journal of Archaeology*, 2d ser., 22 (1918) pp. 166–74. 8a–c discussed at length; illus. figs. 1 [8c], 2 [8a], pl. VI [8b].

Schmitz, Hermann. *Bildteppiche*. Berlin, [1919], p. 186. 8a–c discussed briefly; 8b illus. fig. 96.

Göbel 1923, vol. 1, pp. 60, 78, 171, 243. 8a–c discussed at length; 8c illus. vol. 2, fig. 191.

Kurth, Betty. *Gotische Bildteppiche aus Frankreich und Flandern.* Munich, 1923, pp. x, xiii–xiv. 8b and c discussed briefly; illus. figs. 44 [8c], 45 [8b].

Fels, Florent. *Die altfranzösischen Bildteppiche.* Berlin, [1923], pl. 17. 8b illus. with brief caption.

Breck, Joseph, and Meyric R. Rogers. *MMA, The Pierpont Morgan Wing: A Handbook.* New York, 1925; 2d ed., 1929, pp. 130–31. 8a–c discussed at length; 8c illus. fig. 42.

Hunter 1925, pp. 106–8. 8a–c discussed; 8c illus. as tinted black and white photo pl. vi,a; lower half of the same illus. on cover.

Rubinstein-Bloch, Stella. *Catalogue of the Collection of George and Florence Blumenthal, New York.* Vol. 4, *Tapestries and Furniture.* Paris, 1927, pl. 1, illus. and text. 8d discussed briefly; identified as belonging with 8a–c.

Migeon, Gaston. *Les arts du tissu.* Rev. ed. Paris, 1929, p. 318. 8a–c discussed briefly; 8c illus. p. 319.

van Marle, Raimond. *Iconographie de l'art profane au Moyen-Age et à la Renaissance.* Vol. 1. The Hague, 1931, p. 26. Two or three pieces discussed briefly (identifications confused); 8c illus. fig. 21.

Bossert, H. Th. *Geschichte des Kunstgewerbes.* Berlin, 1932, vol. 5, p. 462. Pieces (not specified) mentioned; lower half of 8c illus. fig. 1.

Townsend, Gertrude. "Mediaeval Textiles in Boston." *Art News* 38 (February 17, 1940) p. 25. 8b mentioned; 8b illus. p. 17.

Art News Annual 1945–46, 1945, p. 33. 8a–c discussed briefly; 8c illus.

Yver, Gislaine. "Résumé chronologique du moyen age à 1900." In Germain Bazin et al. *La tapisserie française: Muraille et laine.* Paris, 1946, p. [2 of "Résumé chronologique"]. Two pieces (not specified) discussed briefly.

Fischel, Lilli. "Oberrheinische Malerei im Spiegel des frühen Kupferstichs." *Zeitschrift für Kunstwissenschaft* 1 (1947) p. 31. 8a–c mentioned; figure of man in lower right corner of 8b discussed briefly in terms of pattern source, illus. fig. 29.

Rorimer, James J. *Mediaeval Tapestries: A Picture Book.* MMA, New York, 1947, p. [3]. 8a–c discussed briefly; detail of main central section of 8a illus. on cover, 8b illus. fig. 5.

Yver, Gislaine. "French Tapestry from Its Origins to the Foundation of the Gobelins Factory." In *French Tapestry,* ed. André Lejard. Paris, 1947, p. 37. Piece or pieces (not specified) mentioned; detail of left half of 8c illus. fig. 45.

Davenport, Millia. *The Book of Costume.* New York, 1948, pp. 307–38. 8a–c discussed briefly in terms of costume; illus. figs. 820 [detail of 8a], 821 [8c], 822 [8b].

Rorimer, James J., and William H. Forsyth. "The Medieval Galleries." *MMA Bulletin,* n.s. 12 (1953–54) p. 135. 8a–c mentioned; 8b illus. p. 137.

Weigert, Roger-Armand. *La tapisserie française.* Paris, 1956, pp. 79–80. 8a–c discussed briefly; left-hand two-thirds of 8b illus. pl. xxi.

Seligman, Germain. *Merchants of Art: 1880–1960.* New York, 1961, pp. 13, 21–22. 8a–c discussed briefly in terms of history of their acquisition; 8b illus. fig. 4.

Young, Bonnie. "The Lady Honor and Her Children." *MMA Bulletin,* n.s. 21 (1962–63) p. 347. 8a–c discussed briefly; 8b illus. fig. 4.

Heinz, Dora. *Europäische Wandteppiche I.* Brunswick, 1963, pp. 80–81. 8a–c discussed briefly.

Weigert, Roger-Armand. *La tapisserie et le tapis en France.* Paris, 1964, pp. 65–66. 8a–c discussed briefly.

Payne, Blanche. *History of Costume: From the Ancient Egyptians to the Twentieth Century.* New York, 1965, p. 213. 8a–c discussed briefly in terms of costume; 8a illus. fig. 234.

Verlet 1965, pp. 24, 28, 33, 36. 8a–c discussed at some length; 8b illus. in color p. 56.

Jarry, Madeleine. *World Tapestry: From Its Origins to the Present.* New York, 1969, p. 81. Right half of 8a illus., with caption.

Souchal in Paris 1973, p. 69. 8a–c mentioned.

Hibbard, Howard. *The Metropolitan Museum of Art.* New York and Toronto, 1980, pp. 174, 180. 8a–c mentioned; 8b illus. fig. 334.

Grand, Paule Marie. *La tapisserie.* Paris and Lausanne, 1981, p. 60. 8c illus.

Joubert, Fabienne. *La tapisserie au moyen âge.* Rennes, 1981, p. 18. 8a–c discussed briefly.

Chevalier, Dominique, Pierre Chevalier, and Pascal-François Bertrand. *Les tapisseries d'Aubusson et de Felletin 1457–1791.* Paris, 1988, p. 17. 8a–c discussed briefly; 8b illus.

Kajitani, Nobuko. "Conservation of the *Courtiers in a Rose Garden,* a Fifteenth-Century Tapestry Series." *Proceedings of the Joseph V. Columbus Tapestry Symposium.* National Gallery of Art, Washington, forthcoming. 8a–c described and discussed in detail; illus. figs. 1–17.

NOTES

1. For a brief but detailed account of the ceremony, see *La grande encyclopédie* (Paris, [1895–1900]) s. v. "Baillée des Roses."

2. See Pierre Verlet and Francis Salet, *La Dame à la Licorne* (Paris, 1960) color pls. on pp. 13, 17, 19, 21, 23, where monkeys appear in five of the six tapestries in this series. In the piece representing the sense of Smell the monkey is holding a flower to his nose; in Taste he puts a berry to his mouth; and in Touch there are two monkeys, one chained to a heavy roller, the other unencumbered except for a belt buckled around his middle. See also J.-J. Marquet de Vasselot, *Catalogue raisonné de la collection Martin Le Roy,* fasc. 4, *Tapisseries et broderie* (Paris, 1908) pls. iii and iv, where two tapestries from one series are illustrated. Both show human figures standing on islands against millefleurs grounds; in one piece a monkey is seated at the right combing the hair on its head and looking into a mirror, in the other the monkey scratches its right knee with both paws. The first tapestry is illustrated also in Göbel 1928, vol. 2, fig. 314.

3. For a brief discussion and illustration of the Melun altarpiece, see Nicole Reynaud, entry for cat. no. 5 in *Jean Fouquet,* exh. cat., Musée du Louvre (Paris, 1981) pp. 18–22, illus. p. 19. Reynaud notes that the custom of associating Agnès Sorel's face with the Virgin's in this picture dates from the seventeenth century, but she acknowledges that a resemblance exists even though Mary's face has been idealized to suit contemporary taste.

4. Christian de Mérindol, "L'emblématique des demeures et chapelles de Jacques Coeur. Une nouvelle lecture. La grande loge de Montpellier et les monuments de Bourges," *Etudes languedociennes: Actes du 110e Congrès national des sociétés savantes, Montpellier, 1985, Histoire médiévale,* vol. 2 (Paris, 1985) pp. 156–59 and note 16, which contains a brief bibliography of recent works concerning Charles VII's use of colors and emblems. See also Jean-Bernard de Vaivre, "Les cerfs ailés et la tapisserie de Rouen," *Gazette des Beaux-Arts,* 6th ser., 100 (1982) pp. 93–108, concerning the heraldry of Charles VII, and also de Vaivre's review of de Mérindol's essay in "Comptes Rendus," *Bulletin Monumental* 144 (1986) pp. 378–81. The present author wishes to thank M. de Vaivre for sending him a copy of de Mérindol's article.

5. Reynaud, *Jean Fouquet,* cat. nos. 5 (Melun Madonna), 10 (sixteenth-century copy of a drawing of a lost portrait of Agnès Sorel by Jean Fouquet, pp. 34–35, illus.), and 3e (portrait drawing of Marie d'Anjou, wife of Charles VII, in the Collection Gaignières, illus. p. 16). The two portrait drawings show different features in an absolute sense; but the general effect is the same in both, and both resemble to some degree the Melun Madonna. Reynaud (p. 35) refers to this similarity, using a phrase from an article by Bouchot, "les physiognomies accordées au canon mondain de l'époque."

6. See de Mérindol, "L'emblématique des demeures et chapelles de Jacques Coeur," pp. 154–56, 160–62, 170–71, for discussions of Jacques Coeur's use of the royal emblems and his own in the *grand loge* at Montpellier (since destroyed), his town house in Bourges, and his family chapel in the cathedral of that city.

7. See de Mérindol, "L'emblématique des demeures et chapelles de Jacques Coeur," pp. 160 and 162, for references to these and other tapestries that belonged to Jacques Coeur.

8. British Library, MS Harl. 4380, fol. 40. See G. G. Coulton, *The Chronicler of European Chivalry* (New York and London, 1930) pl. VI, p. 67, captioned "The French King receives the English Envoys."

9. For recent discussions concerning Charles VII's use of livery colors, see de Mérindol, "L'emblématique des demeures et chapelles de Jacques Coeur," pp. 158–59, and the references he gives in his note 16. In addition to those studies, see Jean-Bernard de Vaivre, "Chronique: Héraldique," *Bulletin Monumental* 141 (1983) pp. 92–95, a review of the article by Colette Beaune cited by de Mérindol.

10. "Inventaire des meubles estans en la maison de Monseigneur le duc Bourbonnoys et d'Auvergne, estans en sa ville d'Aiguesperce; ledit inventaire commence le jeudi XVIIIe jour de novembre l'an mil cinq cens et sept," *Mélanges de littérature et d'histoire*, Société des Bibliophiles François (Paris, 1850) Appendix I, p. 113, no. 20.

11. Quoted in Digby 1980, p. 28, with a reference to Göbel 1923, vol. 1, p. 178, where the inventory number is given as 502.

12. See Joseph Guibert, *Les dessins d'archéologie de Roger de Gaignières*, ser. 3, *Tapisseries* (Paris, [1911–14]) no. B. 1733, pl. 23, and the description of the drawing in Henri Bouchot, *Inventaire des dessins exécutés pour Roger de Gaignières* (Paris, 1891) vol. 1, p. 181.

13. Guibert, *Les dessins*, no. B. 3711, pl. 77.

14. Guibert, *Les dessins*, no. B. 3737, pl. 51.

15. See Guibert, *Les dessins*, no. B. 3713, pl. 42, and also J. P. Asselberghs, *Tapisseries héraldiques et de la vie quotidienne*, exh. cat. (Tournai, 1970) no. 10, illus.

16. Guibert, *Les dessins*, no. B. 3714, pl. 88.

17. Guibert, *Les dessins*, no. B. 1735–41, pls. 5–11.

18. W. G. Thomson, *Tapestry Weaving in England from the Earliest Times to the End of the XVIIIth Century* (London, 1914) pp. 38–39.

19. Asselberghs, *Tapisseries héraldiques*, nos. 5, 4, and 10, all illus.

20. For illustrations of both the large and small prints of the *Garden of Love* by the Master of the Love Gardens, see Max Lehrs, *Geschichte und kritischer Katalog des deutschen, niederländischen und französischen Kupferstichs im XV. Jahrhundert* (Vienna, 1908–34; Kraus Reprint, Nendeln, Liechtenstein, 1969) plate vol. 1, fig. 101 on pl. 39 (Lehrs no. 20, the smaller print) and fig. 102 on pl. 40 (Lehrs no. 21, the larger print).

21. For illustrations of the print, a detail of the tapestry, and the drawing, see Lilli Fischel, "Oberrheinische Malerei im Spiegel des frühen Kupferstichs," *Zeitschrift für Kunstwissenschaft* 1 (1947) figs. 28, 29, 26, respectively. For the print, which Lehrs referred to as "Blumen-Unter A" (his no. 46 for this artist), see also Lehrs, *Katalog*, plate vol. 1, fig. 7 on pl. 5. A closely related figure, labeled "Wilden-Ober" (Lehrs no. 55), is illustrated as fig. 12 on pl. 6.

22. The fragment that belongs to the church of Notre-Dame de Nantilly in Saumur shows a falconing party of two ladies and three gentlemen; see George Wingfield Digby assisted by Wendy Hefford, *The Devonshire Hunting Tapestries*, Victoria and Albert Museum (London, 1971) fig. 24. The fragment in Baltimore, at the Walters Art Gallery, showing five horsemen, was published by Souchal in Paris 1973, pp. 68–69, illus., and New York 1974, no. 15, illus. For the fragment in Paris, at the Musée des Arts Décoratifs, less well-known than the others and showing a mounted battle between gentlemen and wild men, see G. T. van Ysselsteyn, *Tapestry: The Most Expensive Industry of the XVth and XVIth Centuries* (The Hague and Brussels, 1969) fig. 60; or *Les nouvelles collections de l'Union Centrale des Arts Décoratifs au Musée du Louvre, Pavillon de Marsan*, 4th ser., *Tissus, Soieries, Tapisseries, Décorations* (Paris, n.d.) pl. 6. The two pieces in the Rathaus in Regensburg show ladies and gentlemen riding out to hunt and wearing costumes that are somewhat later than the ones shown in the other tapestries. Nevertheless it seems possible that they were designed by the same hand or shop; see Leonie von Wilckens, *Museum der Stadt Regensburg: Bildteppiche* (Regensburg, 1980) pp. 47–48, for a brief discussion of those two fragments in relation to the others in Saumur and Baltimore (all of which, she says, have red grounds), the larger Regensburg piece illus. p. 45; for illustrations of both pieces, see Digby with Hefford, *The Devonshire Hunting Tapestries*, figs. 26, 27.

23. Digby with Hefford, *The Devonshire Hunting Tapestries*, p. 25, pl. IV.

24. *Catalogue des tableaux anciens . . . composant la collection de M. Octave Homberg*, Galerie Georges Petit, Paris, June 3–5, 1931, nos. 142, 143, illus. pls. LXII, LXIII.

25. See Joubert 1987, p. 31, and Fabienne Joubert, "Remarques sur l'élaboration des tapisseries au moyen age," *Annales d'Histoire de l'Art et d'Archéologie*, Université Libre de Bruxelles, 10 (1988) pp. 39–49, for a discussion of the effect that cartoon painters had on the final appearance of tapestry images.

26. The following references concerning this tapestry are taken from Alice M. Zrebiec, *The American Tapestry Manufactures: Origins and Development, 1893 to 1933*, Ph.D. diss., New York University, 1980 (Ann Arbor, Mich.: University Microfilms International, 1980) pp. 204, 313, and fig. 113. The tapestry, which was exhibited at the MMA, January 13–February 16, 1919, in the special exhibition *The Museum as a Laboratory: [3d] Exhibition of Work by Manufacturers & Designers*, was also illustrated in *Good Furniture* 15 (September 1920) p. 47 of the advertisements.

9
Judith Taking Holofernes' Head

A hanging from a series of tapestries whose
comprehensive subject has not been identified

Southern Netherlands, 1455–65
Wool warp; wool and silk wefts
13 ft. 6 in. × 10 ft. 8 in. (4.12 m × 3.25 m)
11–13 warp yarns per inch, 4–5 per centimeter
Gift of Frank Jay Gould, 1946 (46.58.2)

CONDITION

The fabric has been cut along all four sides. Most of the
silk yarns, which were used only in the rendering of the
yellow highlights, have deteriorated and been replaced
with modern yarns. The darkest wool yarns, which were
used to render most of the contours throughout the
composition and the shadows in the deep folds of the
fabrics of the tent curtains and the women's gowns, have
also been replaced. The darkest parts of the tent, including its interior walls, the window openings and frieze of
the lantern on its roof, the dark parts of the valance over
the doorway, and the darker motifs in the fabric of the
coverlet on the bed, have also been restored by weaving
modern weft yarns on the original warp. The name *oli fer
ne* inscribed across the bed pillow has been restored as
have also some of the horse trappings, some of the foliage of the trees or shrubs silhouetted against the sky,
and the contours of the hills. Because some of the modern weft yarns have faded to a relatively light brownish
red, the modeling, especially of the tent curtains and of
the two women's gowns, has been weakened. However
the drawing has not been altered significantly. The colors have faded a good deal but the red and blue tones still
show a wide range of hue and value.

DESCRIPTION AND SUBJECT

A rectangular tent rises in the center foreground. It has
a pitched roof with a rectangular lantern set at an angle
in the middle. The lantern has two windows, a fringed
frieze, and a spherical finial from which rays descend
along the sides of the point supporting it. The ridgepole
is decorated with a series of points along its upper edge,
and at each end there is an onion finial from which rises
a small banner decorated with three small spots. The six
panels on the front slope of the roof are decorated with a
pattern of paired leaves with curling stems and tendrils.

The fringed valance hanging over the entrance to the
tent is decorated with a trellis pattern. The curtains,
which have been tied back to the guy lines at left and
right, are made of large-scale patterned velvet or damask
lined with plain fabric. Another patterned fabric covers
the back of a bed that occupies the center of the tent's
interior. A pillow has been propped up against this back
panel. In front of it appears the headless trunk of a man
whose name, *oli fer ne* (Holofernes), is inscribed across
the pillow. Drops of blood spurt from the severed neck.
The upper bedsheet has been turned back over the patterned coverlet.

Two women stand at the foot of the bed. They both
wear gowns of large-scale patterned velvet or damask
cut with fitted bodices whose V-shaped necklines drop
to high, girdled waists; the sleeves are long and narrow,
and the skirts are full and round. The gown that the
woman at the left wears has a collar, cuffs, and hem
flounce of ermine. The skirt flares out at the back to
form a train. This woman wears a gold necklace set with
gemstones and a tall, patterned hennin banded at the
forehead with pearls and covered with a fine linen veil.
In her right hand she holds a scimitar upright, and with
her left hand she grips by the hair the severed head of a
bearded man. Her name, *ju di que* (Judith), is written
across the grass below her feet. The other woman, standing at the right, leans forward to receive the head in an
open bag that she holds in both hands. Her collar and
cuffs are made of a striped white fabric that also appears
as the stuff of a stole or mantle wound around her skirt
below the waist. She too wears a jeweled necklace. Her
headdress is a tall, flattened bourrelet tied around the
middle with a scarf whose ends fall down behind to form
a short liripipe or tippet.

Six mounted warriors appear outside the tent, three at
either side. Although some of them look in the direction

of the tent, it is clear from the settled expressions on their faces that they are not aware of the action that is taking place there. The men all wear hip-length jackets with wide shoulders and slashed sleeves over armor. The two in the foreground wear hats; the other four wear helmets. Three of the warriors—one at the left, two at the right—carry spears fitted at the ends with swallowtail pennants, one of which, at the left, is decorated with the letter O. One of the men next to him carries a sword, the other a baton. The third man at the right carries a glaive, a pole arm with a blade at its upper end. Trees or shrubs with large foliage rise behind each group of men; between them the space opens out into a deep landscape with the walls, gate, and towers of a city rising in the distance. Above these buildings a band of white clouds meanders across the dark blue sky.

The scene shows the critical moment in the story of Judith, Israelite widow of Manasses of Bethulia, the wise and beautiful heroine who saved her people from destruction at the hands of the Assyrians led by Nebuchadnezzar's commander in chief, Holofernes. The story is told in the apocryphal Book of Judith which has been dated variously at the end of the second century B.C. or near the end of the first century A.D.[1] According to the story, King Nebuchadnezzar of Assyria sent Holofernes out with an army to punish all the people living in Persia and to the west who six years earlier had refused to help Nebuchadnezzar in his war against Arphaxad, king of Media. Holofernes and his troops swept across these nations and finally approached Bethulia, an outpost of Judaea. Hearing that he was coming, Eliachim, high priest of Jerusalem, instructed the people of Bethulia and other towns nearby to hold the hill passes leading to Judaea. The citizens of Bethulia did as they were bid and also laid in supplies and prepared for battle. Holofernes asked Achior, leader of the Ammonites, who the Israelites were, and he was told that they worshiped a god who would protect them against all evil as long as they did not sin against him. Holofernes accused Achior of having uttered treason and sent him to be dealt with by the Israelites in Bethulia. He then blockaded the city and took control of the springs that supplied it with water. The residents suffered for thirty-four days and then urged their leaders to surrender. However the magistrate Ozias pleaded with them to hold out for five more days, saying that if God had not sent help by then they would surrender. Judith, a devout widow of the town, chided the magistrates for putting God to the test and reminded them that He would act if He saw fit. She said that God would save them through her, but she would not explain further. She then prayed and asked for divine help. Dressing in her finest clothes, she took her maid and a bag of food and went down to the Assyrian camp. There she arranged to have an audience with Holofernes and convinced him that she had left her people and would tell him how to overcome them. She stayed in the camp for four days, going out into the valley for the first three nights to pray, with Holofernes' permisssion. On the fourth night Holofernes invited her to join a banquet he was giving for his personal staff. She ate and drank moderately while he drank far more wine than he was accustomed to take. When the feast was over and his retainers had departed, Holofernes and Judith were left alone in the tent. As he lay drunk on his bed, Judith took his sword from the bed rail, cut off his head, and put it into the food bag that she had brought with her from Bethulia and that her maid now held open to receive the trophy. The two women then went out of the camp unmolested since the Assyrian warriors thought they were simply going once again to the valley to pray as they had done, with Holofernes' permission, for the previous three nights. When she reached Bethulia, Judith gave the head to the Israelite leaders and told them to hang it on the city walls to discourage the Assyrians. Holofernes' troops lost heart when they saw it and the troops from Bethulia easily overcame them. The Israelites looted the Assyrian camp and then thanked God and celebrated their liberation and their liberator with songs and dances. Judith's fame increased and she lived in comfort and peace for many years more, to die in Bethulia at an advanced age.

The designer followed this account literally except that he, like the designers of some slightly later hangings treating the same subject (see Related Tapestries), showed the headless body of Holofernes in his bed, whereas in the Book of Judith the body is described as lying on the bed before the attack and rolling off the bed after it. The scabbard of the general's sword is shown hanging on the bedpost at the foot of the bed rather than at the head where the apocryphal account places it. In all other respects the composition follows the story as it is told in the Apocrypha. The six mounted warriors surrounding the tent are probably meant to represent Holofernes' bodyguard. Waking soldiers stand behind the tent at the left in a tapestry of about 1510–20 that is now in the Palazzo Venezia, Rome; other soldiers are shown asleep behind the tent on the other side.[2] Knowing that the murder took place late at night, the designer of 9 has represented a dark sky filled with smoldering, meandering clouds that suggest the coming of dawn. However he lit the foreground and middle distance as though it were midday.

While the notion that a clever, virtuous, and patriotic

woman could outsmart a villainous and powerful chieftain is intriguing and romantic enough to make the story of Judith popular at any time, it had special appeal during the Middle Ages because of its connection with the Virgin Mary. Judith was regarded as a type, or prefiguration, of the mother of Christ. In the thirtieth chapter of the *Speculum Humanae Salvationis,* which deals with the Virgin overcoming Satan, three prefigurations are invoked. The text explains that as Christ defeated Satan and death once and for all through His Passion and Mary saves us from the devil through her compassion for mankind, Judith slayed Holofernes, Jael put a nail through Sisera's brain, and Tomyris took Cyrus's head.[3] The *Speculum* also compares Judith's habit of fasting and praying to Mary's chastity and her state of purity when Joseph found that she was with child.[4] Judith's dressing herself in her finest raiment to conquer Holofernes is compared to Mary's donning the *arma Christi* to battle Satan.[5] Holofernes was regarded as the embodiment of evil, as the devil and the personification of Lechery and Pride, while Judith appears, in Prudentius's *Psychomachia,* as the pre-Christian exemplar of Chastity.[6] An early sixteenth-century tapestry in Brussels contains a scene that illustrates in vivid terms the association of Judith with the Virgin at this period. The composition shows Holofernes receiving Judith at his camp in the foreground and, in the upper left corner, Judith and her maid kneeling at prayer outside a tent while a vision of the Virgin and Child appears in the sky above them as though it were the focus of their meditations.[7]

SOURCE OF THE DESIGN

None of the figures has been traced to a pictorial source, but it seems likely that the three main figures and the tent, if not the entire composition, were taken from a woodcut, perhaps an illustration from an edition of the *Speculum Humanae Salvationis.* The hard, heavy contours and the simple masses of the forms arranged in a few clearly defined planes parallel to the surface all give the image a strong graphic quality which suggests that a woodcut rather than a painting was its source. However there is a curious discrepancy of style between the subtly drawn and modeled faces of the two women and the hard, hieratic drawing of the warriors' faces that suggests the two groups of figures may have come from different sources.

MANUFACTURE AND DATE

When Frimmel published the tapestry in connection with its exhibition at Salzburg in 1888, he called it

Burgundian work but did not attempt to date it. Tietze (1911) attributed it to the Netherlands and dated it in the second half of the fifteenth century. Kurth was more specific: she (1923, 6, caption pl. 25) believed that it was woven in Tournai between 1460 and 1470. The catalogue entry that was prepared for the tapestry when it was exhibited in Rouen in 1931 followed Kurth in attributing the hanging to Tournai but broadened the date to include the entire third quarter of the fifteenth century. On the other hand Coffinet (1971) listed the tapestry among a group of pieces he regarded as showing the fully developed style of Arras; later (1977) he illustrated details of it in a section of his text devoted to tapestries showing a survival of the so-called Arras style. None of these writers gave reasons for attributing the tapestry to the regions they suggested, but it is clear that Kurth and Coffinet believed that certain stylistic details could be found consistently in tapestries made in one center or the other. Even if that were true, this hanging shows an exceptionally particular kind of drawing, spatial composition, and palette—so particular that it clearly represents the style of an individual designer rather than the style of some weaving center if indeed such regional, rather than individual, styles existed at this time.

In considering the date of manufacture we are on more solid ground. As both Kurth and Coffinet have correctly indicated, the tapestry belongs to a family of hangings that has been convincingly dated through documentary evidence or stylistic analysis between about 1455 and 1465: the *Story of Alexander* in Rome, the *Story of the Swan Knight* in Cracow and Vienna, the *Story of Trajan and Herkinbald* and the *Story of Caesar* in Bern, the *Story of Jephtha* in Saragossa, and the tapestry in Vienna that shows Pilate sending a messenger to Rome.[8] All of these tapestries, like the Metropolitan Museum's piece, show the figures and other forms arranged so that they read on the surface of the composition and in depth with great clarity and integrity. This style is entirely different from that found in hangings designed about 1465–75 which show the figures pushed together, up, down, and forward, creating an extraordinarily rich but confusing surface pattern and little illusion of depth (see, for example, 13a–c).

The garments and accessories of the figures in 9 were in fashion during the same period—that is, approximately 1455–65—but also somewhat later. The main details of fashion in the costumes of the men and women are to be found in the miniature paintings in a manuscript edition of Jean Wauquelin's *Histoire de Sainte Hélène* that was produced for Philippe le Bon and illustrated in the shop of Loyset Liédet of Bruges about 1470; it is preserved in the Bibliothèque Royale Albert I in

Brussels.[9] For the tapestry, however, the evidence of fashion is less reliable than the style of design because around 1465–75 fashions were not changing as abruptly as tapestry design. The cut of the women's garments and the steeple-shaped hennin worn by Judith were in fashion from about 1450 to 1480; but the maid's tall, flattened bourrelet would have seemed outmoded by the later date. The cut of the men's wide-shouldered, hiplength jackets suggests a date between about 1455 and 1475. A tapestry in the Musée des Arts Décoratifs in Paris depicting a fashionable couple standing before a tent shows the lady wearing a headdress like the one on Judith's maid. The gentleman has on a short jacket cut like the ones worn by the soldiers in 9, which continued in fashion until around 1475, but on his head is a large chaperon with a long, dagged liripipe that would have been out of fashion after about 1460.[10]

While it is true that the subject of Judith taking away Holofernes' head was represented in essentially the same way in one of the roughly contemporary painted cloths in Reims and a number of tapestries of somewhat later date (see Related Tapestries), it may nevertheless be significant that a composition answering this description appeared in two of a set of four hangings bought by Borso d'Este in 1457 and listed in the Este inventory of 1457–69.[11] The two pieces in question were relatively small portieres (antiporti). The representation on one of them is described as follows in the inventory (the other is listed as being the same): "uno pavaione morelo, sotto el quale e in uno leto olifernes nudo cum una dona che li ha talgiato la testa, che ha la spada da una mane e da laltra la testa del dito olifernes per li capili cum la quale porze dita testa a unaltra dona che ha uno carniero in mane, el quale epsa porze per metere dentro dita testa" (a blackish tent under which Holofernes is nude in a bed, with a lady who has cut his head off [and] who holds the sword in one hand and the head of Holofernes, by the hair, in the other, with which [hand] she gives the head to another lady who holds a game bag in her hand which [bag] she carries in order to put the head into [it]). This description is ultimately a generic one that could apply to any number of similar compositions and it would be imprudent to claim that it describes the very image that we see in 9. However, if it does, it is not surprising that the soldiers at the side are not mentioned since each antiporto was only 1.62 meters wide as compared with the 3.25-meter width of 9.[12] Unfortunately the inventory does not enumerate the scenes depicted on the two large wall hangings that accompanied these antiporti; but the listings make it clear that between them the two large pieces showed the complete story of Holofernes. This suggests that the episode of Judith taking away Holofernes' head was represented not only on both antiporti but also on one of these two large hangings. Since the Metropolitan Museum's tapestry is almost precisely as tall as those two pieces were and approximately half as wide as either one of them, it is easy to imagine that it might have been woven after the cartoon that served for half of one of the Este pieces.[13]

Taking into account the evidence of pictorial style, of fashions in clothing, and also the possibility that Borso d'Este bought a tapestry woven after the same cartoon in 1457, we conclude that the Metropolitan Museum's tapestry was designed and woven between approximately 1455 and 1465.

RELATED TAPESTRIES

We do not know any duplicate hangings that have survived nor any tapestries that were woven after the same series of cartoons. In attempting to identify the cycle of hangings to which this piece belonged, one is inclined to assume that it treated the chief episodes in the story of Holofernes' attack on Bethulia and Judith's success in saving her people from destruction at his hands. However it is equally reasonable to suggest that the tapestry belonged to a series of compositions that dealt with the Nine Heroines, the Stories of Virtuous Women, chapter 30 of the Speculum Humanae Salvationis, or perhaps some series celebrating the deeds of selfless Hebrew women. Although the list of women celebrated as Heroines or Female Worthies, counterparts to the nine Heroes or Male Worthies, varied during the late Middle Ages, Judith's name did figure among them.[14] She also appeared as one of the women noted for their chastity in a somewhat later series of ten hangings (the cycle now referred to as the Stories of Virtuous Women) that is represented today by some fragments in the Museum of Fine Arts, Boston, which celebrate Penelope and the Cimbri women.[15] Judith as one of three pre-Christian women regarded in the Speculum as types of the Virgin has been discussed above (Description and Subject). An early sixteenth-century tapestry in the cathedral in Sens made up from parts of two tapestries (see below) shows three scenes from the story of Judith at the left and, at the right end, a scene showing Ruth refusing to leave Naomi on the road to Bethlehem.[16] The two hangings that were combined to make this piece probably came from a cycle celebrating Hebrew women noted for their courage and unselfishness.

If, on the other hand, we regard 9 as a tapestry belonging to a set that told the story of Judith and/or Holofernes, it is difficult, if not impossible, to identify the subjects that were represented in it. We have only one contemporary reference to such a cycle: it is the citation in the Este inventory of 1457–69 already mentioned (Manufacture and Date). The listings do not indicate how many subjects each of the two wall hangings showed or what the subjects were. However since each of those tapestries had approximately the same height as 9 but was approximately twice as wide, it is fair to suggest that whereas 9 shows one subject, each of the others showed two (see note 13). It was noted above that according to the inventory listings those two tapestries alone, not including the two portieres that accompanied them, told the entire story of Holofernes; therefore we conclude that there were only four subjects in the cycle.

The only other early tapestries and references we have concerning a *Story of Judith* series date from some sixty years later, so the evidence they offer may not be apposite. Nevertheless they are worth considering when thinking about the subjects that might have appeared in an earlier cycle. Two tapestries dating from around 1515–20 and having approximately the same dimensions as the Este pieces each show two main subjects in the foreground and others in the background (see list of subjects below). One piece is preserved in the Musées Royaux d'Art et d'Histoire in Brussels; the other is in the Palazzo Venezia in Rome (see notes 2 and 7). We know from documents of that period that Arnould Poissonnier of Tournai produced a chamber of tapestries of the *Story of Judith* which the magistrates of that city gave to the earl of Suffolk in 1516. It contained six pieces and, like the two hangings just mentioned, may have shown more than one subject in each piece.[17] Crick-Kuntziger thought that the tapestries now in Brussels and Rome probably came from Poissonnier's shop; if that is true then we know that the cartoons he used showed the subjects listed below as numbers 1 and 3–8.[18] Two sets of tapestries showing the *Story of Holofernes* (probably the same as the *Story of Judith* just mentioned) were listed as being in Poissonnier's stock at the time of his death in 1522. One set included six pieces and the other seven.[19] In the same year Cardinal Wolsey bought seven pieces of a *Story of Judith and Holofernes* from Richard Gresham for Hampton Court.[20] Soil, Thomson, and Demotte all called attention to the fact that the *Story of Judith and Holofernes* tapestry in Sens, which shows three scenes from that story, a scene from the story of Ruth or Naomi patched in at the right end, and a band along the top where Cardinal Wolsey's arms appear with those of the cathedrals of York and Canterbury, apparently figured in that purchase.[21] This hanging adds subject 2 to the others listed below.

Arranged according to narrative sequence, the sub-jects of the tapestries in Brussels, Rome, and Sens may be listed as follows:

1. Holofernes receives Judith in his tent: main subject in the left half of the piece in the Musées Royaux d'Art et d'Histoire, Brussels (see note 7).
2. Judith invited to Holofernes' banquet and dressing to attend it: double subject in the left quarter of the piece in the cathedral in Sens (see note 16).
3. Judith attends Holofernes' banquet: only subject in the right half of the piece in Brussels; also subject in the second quarter of the piece in Sens (see notes 7 and 16).
4. Judith with the head of Holofernes: main subject in the left half of the piece in Rome; also subject in the third quarter of the piece in Sens (see notes 2 and 16).
5. Holofernes' men find him murdered: main subject in the right half of the piece in Rome (see note 2).

In addition to the main subjects listed above, which appear in their foreground spaces, the tapestries in Brussels and Rome show the following scenes:

6. Judith and her maid pray at night outside the Assyrian camp: in the background of the scene in the left half of the piece in Brussels (see note 7).
7. Judith brings Holofernes' head to Bethulia and shows it to Achior: in the background of the scene in the left half of the piece in Rome (see note 2).
8. The Israelites leave the gates of Bethulia to attack the Assyrian army: in the background of the scene in the right half of the piece in Rome (see note 2).

Any or all of these subjects might have appeared in the set of hangings represented by the Metropolitan Museum's tapestry. None of these eight subjects deals with the early or late incidents in the story of Judith; that is, none of them shows Nebuchadnezzar sending Holofernes on his mission of vengeance; Holofernes approaching Bethulia and interviewing Achior; Judith hearing of the plan to destroy her city and people; Judith telling Ozias that God would save them through her hand; or Judith leaving Bethulia. Nor are there any scenes dealing with events that took place at the end of the story; that is, the people celebrating their victory and their heroine and distributing the booty taken from the Assyrian camp; or Judith dedicating her share of Holofernes' furnishings to God. However a tapestry designed in the so-called Brussels style and woven in the latter part of the first quarter of the sixteenth century does show Judith dressing to go into Holofernes' camp, receiving the homage of Ozias and the people of Bethulia, and bidding farewell to Ozias.[22] While such speculation may be valid with reference to these later hangings, we cannot claim that it applies also to the cycle from which 9 came if, indeed, it came from a set of the *Story of Judith and Holofernes* at all.

HISTORY

In the Benedictine convent of Nonnberg in Salzburg at least by 1738, when it was listed in the convent inventory.
Said to have been sold in Spain about 1916.
On the art market when Kurth published it in 1923.
In the collection of Frank Jay Gould, Paris.
Given to the MMA by Frank Jay Gould, 1946.

EXHIBITIONS

Salzburg, Künstlerhaus, 1888. Exhibition of notable works of art owned in the region. Lent by the convent of Nonnberg. (See Frimmel 1888 in Publications.)
Musée de Peinture de Rouen, 1931. *Exposition d'art religieux ancien.* Cat. no. 265. Lent by Frank Jay Gould. (See Vitry, Guey, Lafond 1932 in Publications.)

PUBLICATIONS

Frimmel, Th. "Les tapisseries à l'Exposition de Salzbourg." *La chronique des arts et de la curiosité,* 1888, p. 238. Described briefly.
Tietze, Hans, with Regintrudis von Reichlin-Meldegg. *Die Denkmale des Stiftes Nonnberg in Salzburg Österreichische Kunsttopographie,* Kunsthistorische Institut der K.K. Zentral-Kommission für Denkmalpflege, vol. 7. Vienna, 1911, p. 174. Described and discussed briefly; illus. pl. xxxii.
Kurth, Betty. *Gotische Bildteppiche aus Frankreich und Flandern.* Munich, 1923, pp. xi, 6. Discussed briefly; illus. pl. 25.
Vitry, Paul, Fernand Guey, and Jean Lafond. *Exposition d'art religieux ancien.* Rouen, 1932, p. 94. Described and discussed briefly; illus. pl. lxxv.
Coffinet, Julien. *Arachne ou l'art de la tapisserie.* Geneva and Paris, 1971, pp. 185–86. Mentioned; illus. (two details).
Coffinet 1977, pp. 68–69. Illus. (three details).

NOTES

1. Louis Réau, *Iconographie de l'art chrétien,* vol. 2, pt. 1. (Paris, 1956) p. 329.
2. For details concerning the tapestry in Rome and illustrations of it, see Marthe Crick-Kuntziger, "La tenture tournaisienne de l'histoire de Judith et d'Holoferne," *Bulletin des Musées Royaux d'Art et d'Histoire,* 3d ser., 12 (1940) pp. 26–34, fig. 3 (the tapestry was then in a private collection outside Belgium); also J. P. Asselberghs, *La tapisserie tournaisienne au XVIe siècle,* exh. cat. (Tournai, 1968) no. 28, illus.; and M. V. B[rugnoli], "Acquisti dei musei e gallerie dello stato: Manifattura di Tournai circa 1515: 'Giuditta e Oloferne,'" *Bollettino d'Arte,* 5th ser., 50 (1965) pp. 232–33, illus. fig. 64. In a tapestry of the same period that is now at Sens there are both sleeping and wakeful soldiers behind the tent containing Holofernes' body; see note 16 below.
3. It is believed that the text of the *Speculum* was written in the early fourteenth century; the author and place of origin are not identified. For the text from an early fifteenth-century manuscript combined with late fifteenth-century woodcuts, see Avril Henry, *The Mirour of Mans Saluacioun, a Middle English Translation of* Speculum Humanae Salvationis: *A Critical Edition of the Fifteenth-Century Manuscript Illustrated from* Der Spiegel der menschen Behältnis, *Speyer: Drach, c. 1475* (Philadelphia, 1987). For these references to Mary, Judith, Jael, and Tomyris, see p. 159, ll. 3219–24, and p. 161, ll. 3275–98; also, in the Prohemium [Proem], p. 39, ll. 211–19.
4. Henry, *Mirour,* p. 67, ll. 910–19.
5. Henry, *Mirour,* p. 159, ll. 3219–30. Woodcuts showing the Virgin with the *arma Christi* and Judith about to cut off Holofernes' head are illustrated on p. 158. The latter composition is totally different from the one in the Metropolitan Museum's tapestry.
6. Réau, *Iconographie de l'art chrétien,* vol. 2, pt. 1, p. 330.
7. The tapestry is preserved in the Musées Royaux d'Art et d'Histoire, Brussels; see Crick-Kuntziger, "La tenture . . . de l'histoire de Judith," pp. 26–34, fig. 2, and her *Catalogue des tapisseries (XIVe au XVIIIe siècle),* Musées Royaux d'Art et d'Histoire (Brussels, 1956) pp. 29–31, pl. 18; also Asselberghs, *La tapisserie tournaisienne au XVIe siècle,* no. 27, illus.
8. For illustrations of the *Alexander, Swan Knight,* and *Trajan and Herkinbald* pieces, see figs. 61, 62, 60 in the present catalogue. For the *Caesar* pieces, see Robert L. Wyss, *Die Caesarteppiche* (Bern, 1957) pls. 1–4; for the *Jephtha* tapestry, see Eduardo Torra de Arana et al., *Los tapices de La Seo de Zaragoza* (Saragossa, 1985) pp. 122–29, with color pls.; for the piece in Vienna, see Göbel 1923, vol. 2, fig. 215.
9. Bibliothèque Royale Albert I, Brussels, MS 9967. See especially Millia Davenport, *The Book of Costume* (New York, 1948) fig. 833. For documentation on the manuscript, see *Le siècle d'or de la miniature flamande: Le mécénat de Philippe le Bon,* exh. cat., Palais des Beaux-Arts, Brussels, and Rijksmuseum, Amsterdam (Brussels, 1959) no. 151.
10. See *Cent chefs-d'oeuvre du Musée des Arts Décoratifs,* exh. cat. compiled by Yvonne Brunhammer, Palais du Louvre, Pavillon de Marsan (Paris, 1964) pp. 24–25, illus. See also illus. in Göbel 1923, vol. 2, fig. 207.
11. For the painted hanging at Reims, see M. Sartor, *Les tapisseries, toiles peintes & broderies de Reims* (Reims, 1912) pp. 174, 178, fig. 81. The cloth is in the Musée de Reims (Hôtel de Ville). In the foreground it shows a scene very much like the one in the foreground of the Metropolitan Museum's tapestry, though drawn in quite a different style, and in the background the siege of Bethulia by the Assyrian army; Holofernes' head appears at the end of a pike on the castle walls. For the Este tapestries, see Nello Forti Grazzini, *L'arazzo ferrarese* (Milan, 1982) pp. 37, 216, 225.
12. The dimensions of the *antiporti* are given in Forti Grazzini, *L'arazzo ferrarese,* p. 225, as $3^1/_2$ *bracci* tall and $2^1/_2$ *bracci* wide. The measure of the *braccio* in Modena at that period corresponded to 64.8 centimeters, and the conversion of dimensions from *bracci* to meters given in the text here and farther on are based on the calculation of one *braccio* equaling 64.8 centimeters.
13. See Forti Grazzini, *L'arazzo ferrarese,* p. 216, where *coltrina* no. 27 is described as "Una coltrina de razzo noua da salla afigurada cum parte de la Jstoria de olifernes . . . ," and no. 28 is cited as "Una coltrina de razzo noua da salla figurada cum el resto de la Jstoria de olifernes la quale va compagna cum la soprascritta coltrina sig(nata) n° 27." The same inventory entries give the dimensions of *coltrina* no. 27 as $6^1/_4$ *bracci* wide (that is, tall as it hung) and $11^1/_4$ *bracci* long (that is, wide as it hung), which converts to 4.05 meters by 7.29 meters. *Coltrina* no. 28 was measured at $6^3/_8$ *bracci* tall by $9^1/_4$ *bracci* wide, or 4.13 meters by 5.99 meters. The Metropolitan Museum's tapestry measures 4.12 meters tall by 3.25 meters wide.
14. Réau, *Iconographie de l'art chrétien,* vol. 2, pt. 1, p. 330; also Karl Künstle, *Ikonographie der christlichen Kunst,* vol. 1 (Freiburg im Breisgau, 1928) p. 181.

15. See Adolph S. Cavallo, *Tapestries of Europe and of Colonial Peru in the Museum of Fine Arts, Boston* (Boston, 1967) pp. 56–61, pls. 4–11. The list of ten subjects in this cycle, which included the *Story of Judith*, is given on p. 60.

16. Concerning the tapestry in Sens, see G.-J. Demotte, *La tapisserie gothique* (Paris and New York, 1924) pls. 105–6 and accompanying text on p. 6; also Thomson 1930, p. 187, illus. facing p. 248, and additional notes and references in note 21 below. The scene with Naomi, Ruth, and Orpah clearly is not part of the Judith piece; but the section of floral border that seems to belong with the former shows an inscribed red banderole bearing Ruth's name which matches precisely the banderoles set against the flowers on the border of the Judith piece. Therefore we conclude that the composite hanging in Sens was made up from parts of two hangings belonging to one and the same series, one having Judith as its subject, the other Ruth or Naomi.

17. See Eugène Soil, *Les tapisseries de Tournai* (Tournai and Lille, 1892) p. 257.

18. Crick-Kuntziger, "La tenture . . . de l'histoire de Judith," p. 33.

19. Soil, *Les tapisseries de Tournai*, pp. 47, 412.

20. Thomson, 1930, p. 240. See also note 21.

21. See E.-J. Soil, "La Tapisserie de Judith et Holoferne à la cathédrale de Sens," *Bulletin Monumental* 64 (1899) p. 318, quoted from E. Chartraire, *Inventaire du trésor de l'église primatiale et métropolitaine de Sens* (Sens, 1897); also Thomson 1930, p. 187; and Demotte, *La tapisserie gothique*, text for pls. 105–6 on p. 6. In Henry VIII's inventory, there were listed at Hampton Court one piece "of Oliphernes" and three "of Olyfernes," all with "bordres of the late Cardinall's arms," and Thomson (pp. 187, 249) suggested that the tapestry in Sens may have been one of these. Soil and Demotte were more certain that this tapestry had belonged to Cardinal Wolsey. At Hampton Court there was also a "post pece" of Holofernes and at The More a "windowe pece" of Judith and Holofernes; see Thomson 1930, pp. 251, 254.

22. The tapestry is in the Musées Royaux d'Art et d'Histoire in Brussels; see Crick-Kuntziger, *Catalogue des tapisseries*, p. 34, illus. pl. 22.

Episodes in *The Story of the Vengeance of Our Lord*

Southern Netherlands, 1460–70
Wool warp; wool wefts with a few silk wefts
13 ft. 9 in. × 28 ft. (4.19 m × 8.54 m)
13–15 warp yarns per inch, 5–6 per centimeter
Rogers Fund, 1909 (09.172)

CONDITION

The tapestry has preserved none of its original edges. A recent intensive examination of the fabric has shown that it is not a single, integral piece but a composite hanging made up from parts of three separate tapestries. The central three-fifths of the piece came from a hanging that dealt with the sack of the Temple of Jerusalem and the enslavement and murder of the Jews in the town. The left-hand fifth came from a tapestry that illustrated some early incidents in the story, including Veronica's visit to the emperor Vespasian to cure him of his illness. The right-hand section of the tapestry, which accounts for somewhat more than a fifth of the full width, shows incidents that took place during Titus's assault on Jerusalem.

The two roughly vertical lines along which the three fragments were joined together may be traced as follows. The boundary between the right side of the scene of Veronica's visit and the left side of the sack and enslavement scene begins as a horizontal line extending from the left edge of the tapestry halfway between the tops of the hills and the upper edge of the hanging and then turns downward through the curious leaf-shaped clouds above the man standing atop a tower near the upper left corner, continuing downward and to the left of his right hand, cutting across the carved figure next to the man's face, then downward along the left edge of the tower and through the left side of the man standing in front of the tower, and around the right side of the girl seated below him to the level of her hip. It then turns to the left, moves diagonally downward across her skirt to the top of the stone ledge in front of her, and then downward and to the left until it reaches the bottom of the hanging. Therefore the man standing in front of the tower belongs with the sack of the Temple scene whereas the seated girl is part of the scene of Vespasian's cure. The lower parts of her skirt and most of the tiled floor to the right of this figure have been replaced with new warp and weft yarns.

10

At the right end of the tapestry the line of demarcation begins at the top of the fabric directly above the second tent from the right, the one with the trapezoidal roof, then moves down along the left edge of that tent and then along the right edge of the group of three prisoners standing to the left of the tent, and then down along the left edge of the swiveled slab and the right side of the civilian man standing next to the machine. The line then moves around the head of the fallen man below, under his left arm, and to the bottom of the fabric at a point under his elbow. Thus the scene showing armored warriors in a military camp at the right end of the tapestry does not belong with the scene of enslave-

Detail of 10, lower left corner

Detail of 10

ment and murder shown at the left. There are other insertions of fabric from other parts of this or related tapestries in the sky and the ground row, particularly in the right half of the tapestry as a whole. The right shoulder of the man standing in front of the tower at the left and the entire right part of his body below the waist have also been inserted. The leafy branches of the tree above the line of prisoners at right-center and the head of the horse that appears above and to the right of this are both restorations that were made with modern warp and weft yarns. There are a few other restorations of this kind in the regions of the sky and ground and a great deal of reweaving with modern weft yarns on the original warp yarns throughout the piece. It is this kind of restoration that has thickened most of the contours and also given the hanging an overall orange-brown tonality it did not originally have.

The three tapestries that contributed parts of their fabrics to this hanging were almost certainly taller than the composite piece is now. Since most surviving tapestries of this type and period show inscribed banderoles across the top and in some cases also along the bottom, it seems likely that the three donor tapestries also displayed such texts to identify the figures and explain the action, especially since none of the human figures here is labeled with its name. Both Destrée (1903, 17) and Breck (1910, 117) suggested that 10 once had explanatory inscriptions. The *Story of Caesar* tapestries in Bern, the *Story of Clovis* pieces in Reims, and the *Story of Jephtha* tapestries in the cathedral church in Saragossa, all of which resemble 10 in style and detail, have quatrain verses inscribed along the top of the field. In their original condition the *Jephtha* tapestries were probably about 16 feet (4.88 m) tall. The *Clovis* tapestries are approximately that tall now (4.75 m). If, as we believe, each of the three tapestries that were used to make up the Metropolitan Museum's hanging also had inscriptions running along the top, then it seems likely that in their original state they, too, were approximately 4.75 to 5 meters tall.

The letters SEMIRAM in the lower left corner of the piece are not part of the original weaving (see below).

DESCRIPTION AND SUBJECT

From the time of its acquisition, the tapestry had been known at the Metropolitan Museum as the *Siege and Capture* (or, alternatively, the *Sack*) *of Jerusalem.* In 1941 Rorimer discovered the letters SEMIRAM in the corner of the tapestry and renamed it the *Story of Queen Semiramis.* Later, he published it (1947, caption, fig. 7) with that title. Between 1947 and 1971, when Zrebiec

(p. 1) noted that the inscription seemed not to be part of the original fabric, the tapestry was known under both titles. In 1973 Zrebiec and Nobuko Kajitani, conservator of textiles at the Metropolitan Museum, examined the fabric on which the inscription appears and confirmed that it is not original. Lapaire, who did not know this when he mentioned the piece in print (1975, 145 n. 14), referred to 10 as a tapestry illustrating an incident in the story of Semiramis. In subsequent literature only the correct title and subject matter have been acknowledged.

Writers who studied the tapestry before we discovered that it is a composite piece were hard put to explain the action it represents. Zrebiec (1971), who made the only concerted effort to identify the subject of each and every scene, was naturally misled into thinking that the narrative was fairly complete in this one piece because it shows scenes from the early part of the story, with Veronica approaching the invalid Vespasian, to the late part, in which soldiers are encamped in Jerusalem and the prisoners who had managed to survive the sack of that city are being sent off in ships.

It is essential that one understand the subject matter of the *Story of the Vengeance of Our Lord,* a blend of fact and legend, before attempting to describe the scenes in the tapestry. The story has four major subjects. The first is the episode in which Veronica miraculously cures Vespasian's (or, in other versions, Tiberius's) leprosy (or cancer, or a plague of hornets in the nose) by means of her Holy Veil. The second theme concerns the cured man's vow to avenge Jesus' death by punishing Pilate, the man who had condemned Him. The third element is the siege and sack of Jerusalem. The fourth is the execution of Pilate.

The accounts of the war in Jerusalem were based loosely on Flavius Josephus's *The Jewish Wars,* written between A.D. 69 and 79. Josephus was a Jewish historian and commander who tried to bring about a reconciliation between the Jews and Rome at the time of the rebellion of A.D 66. When he and his troops were defeated during Vespasian and Titus's attack on Palestine the next year, Josephus surrendered to the Romans. He was released two years later, when his prediction that Vespasian would be named emperor came true. He then adopted the family name of Flavius and became a Roman citizen. It was then that he wrote *The Jewish Wars,* the only historical text on which the anonymous compilers of the *Story of the Vengeance of Our Lord* drew. The other three elements in the story—Veronica's working of the cure, the emperor's vow to avenge Jesus' death, and the execution of Pilate for his part in the crucifixion —are apocryphal. Scholars have made exhaustive

Fig. 102. *The Romans Enter Jerusalem and Find the Inhabitants Starving.* Tapestry, southern Netherlands, 1460–70. Musée d'Histoire et d'Archéologie, Tournai.

searches for the origins of these legends which date back to early Christian times. For our purposes in studying the late medieval tapestries based on the tale, it is needless to seek farther than *La Venjance de Nostre Seigneur,* a French chanson de geste of the twelfth century.[1] This literary work drew its narrative elements primarily from the life of Saint James the Less in Jacobus de Voragine's *Golden Legend* but also from other apocryphal works like the *Acti Pilati,* the *Cura sanitatis Tiberii,* the *Victoria Salvatoris,* and the *Mors Pilati.* Over a period of centuries, these disparate sources were blended into a narrative legend that enjoyed enormous popularity during the Middle Ages. From poetic form the story developed into both narrative and dramatic form. Mystery plays of the *Vengeance de Nostre Seigneur* (variously spelled in contemporary sources) were performed at least as early as 1396 when, as usual, a performance of the *Vengeance* followed immediately upon a production of the mystery of the *Passion.* Other performances are documented in 1437, 1446, 1458, and 1463, in Metz,

Amiens, and Abbeville respectively.[2] A complete précis and part of the text of a play of the *Vengeance de Nostre Seigneur,* attributed to a certain Jehan Michel, has been published.[3] Antoine Vérard published the earliest known printed edition of the *Vengeance* in Paris on May 28, 1491. He issued a second edition in 1493. Other texts were printed early in the next century, but all of them appeared after the tapestries were designed. Nevertheless the great number of printed versions of the play proves that the story was extremely popular during the late Middle Ages. It is not surprising to find that at least three different sets of tapestry designs illustrating the *Vengeance de Nostre Seigneur* (or, as the tapestries were most often called, the *Destruction de Jherusalem*) have survived from the third quarter of the fifteenth century.

No single literary source contains all the elements of the story as it was represented in the tapestries. It seems likely that the author of the scheme composed an original narrative for the purpose, one that he based on the then-standard sources. In the most general terms, the basic outline of the story is as follows. In searching for someone to cure his illness, a ruler—in some cases the emperor Tiberius, in others the Spanish duke Vespasian, in yet others a king of Aquitaine named Titus or Tyrus—ultimately hears of the existence of a prophet and physician in Jerusalem called Jesus. In some versions of the story the ruler asks that Jesus be brought to him; in other versions it is acknowledged that Jesus has been crucified but that some piece of his clothing will effect a cure. Emissaries are sent to Pilate, either to bid him produce Jesus or a relic or, in some cases, to advise Pilate that he has been condemned to death for his part in the execution of Jesus. In most accounts Pilate is taken to Europe and ultimately tortured and murdered or left to commit suicide; in one version he is taken to Rome later, after the destruction of Jerusalem. In all the stories, the ruler who sought Jesus is cured either by adoring the veil brought to him by Veronica or simply by swearing vengeance on the Jews for having killed Jesus. The authorities in Rome order an attack on the rebels in Jerusalem. Their motives vary from one tale to another. In most of them, it is Vespasian who decides either on his own or under orders from a higher authority to lay siege to Jerusalem for the purpose of punishing Pilate and the people of Jerusalem for having crucified Jesus. In other versions of the story it is Nero, determined to force the Jews to display statues of Roman emperors in the Temple in Jerusalem, who orders the siege. In either case, Vespasian and his son Titus are sent to Palestine and for seven years they ravage the land and ultimately approach Jerusalem. But before they begin the attack Vespasian succeeds Nero as emperor and returns to Rome, leaving Titus to invade the city. Having made the Jews inside the city suffer hunger and thirst, the Romans enter Jerusalem, burn most of the buildings, torture and mutilate the inhabitants, sell some as slaves, take the handsomest and tallest back to Rome for their triumphal entry, and finally send the others out by boat, some to be shipped to Rome to die in the arenas, others to be sent to other ports in Europe, the rest to fare as they might. Many of those who were sold thirty for a denarius (in retribution for Jesus' having been sold for thirty denarii) had swallowed their gold in the hope of preserving their wealth if they were fortunate enough to escape with their lives. Discovering the ruse, the Roman soldiers and Turkish and Syrian merchants who bought these captured citizens disembowel them to recover the coins. Titus, having sacked the Temple, collects the booty and sails back to Rome in the year A.D. 70.

The narrative is presented in the Metropolitan Museum's tapestry as a series of scenes set in a rocky landscape whose dark greenish blue ground is covered with flowering plants and small trees or shrubs. A strip of sky filled with small, flat oval clouds runs along the top. The horizon line is punctuated by hilltops and small buildings rising in the far distance. The figures move in the foreground and middle ground amid buildings, towers, and campaign tents. In the upper left-hand corner of the tapestry a soberly dressed woman rides out of the distance toward the foreground in a cart or chariot drawn by a horse and its rider. Three other riders (apparently mounted on a single horse) follow along behind. Below this company appears a building whose interior is open to view. Inside, a man wearing a nightcap lies in a canopied bed. Two men in long robes are standing at the left and a young woman stirring soup or food in a bowl is seated in the foreground. The two men are probably courtiers; the girl is a maid or nurse. The woman in the chariot, holding a box on her lap, is Veronica, shown on her way to cure the invalid Vespasian. As noted above (Condition), neither the man standing against the tower that rises to the right of the bedroom nor the man atop the tower belongs with this scene. They are part of the main section of the tapestry, the large fragment from a different hanging that occupies the central three-fifths of the piece. The soldier in the tower is gesticulating at

Fig. 103. *Nero Sends Vespasian and Titus to Wage War on Jerusalem.* Tapestry, southern Netherlands, 1460–70. Musée d'Histoire et d'Archéologie, Tournai.

some action that was represented at the left end of this large fragment, which is now lost. The woman standing on the balcony next to and below him is either calling to or expressing distress at seeing the soldiers passing below. The man standing beneath her balcony seems to be handing a basket of precious objects to a soldier. This may be part of a scene showing the Romans looting the Temple.

In the upper left of the central section of the hanging a warrior seated before his campaign tent receives a young armored soldier who kneels before him and presents a cart full of treasure. The Ark of the Covenant rests across the top. Three more warriors approach the two main figures from the left, bringing with them a horse laden with two large chests. Behind them a fourth warrior sits in his tent, resting his arms on a poleax. Other warriors stand behind the chief, who is crowned and sceptered like an emperor and who is probably meant to represent Titus as he accepts booty taken from the Temple. To the right, in the distance, a civilian leads three bound prisoners toward a sailing vessel. They are some of the survivors of the siege of Jerusalem who are being shipped away. In the central section of the tapestry below these two scenes some Jewish prisoners are being sold for a denarius, probably to a Turkish or Syrian merchant. A civilian presses a coin into the hand of a soldier who leads five bound prisoners by a rope while a second warrior points to the captives. To the right of this group another soldier sells some elegantly dressed prisoners to a civilian. The woman and two men in the front line of prisoners watch in horror as two soldiers cut open the stomachs of three men to recover the coins they had swallowed. At the right end of this scene, above and behind the figure of a soldier eviscerating one of the victims, a man wearing a luxurious long robe and carrying a purse drops a handful of coins into the hat that a soldier holds before him. Two other soldiers and three civilians stand behind these two men.

The right-hand section of the tapestry comes from a different hanging, as noted above (Condition). At the top a warrior sits before his campaign tent and seems to be addressing the three Jewish prisoners who stand at the left. But the two tapestry fragments were joined along a line that separates the officer from the prisoners. The scene as we view it today is an illusion created by the restorer; no such scene existed in the original design. The chieftain in the tent is probably Titus, rather than Vespasian, who in the dramatic legend had returned to Rome before this moment. Five soldiers appear behind and to the right of the chieftain. Directly below this group, four soldiers are working in an artillery installation. Two of the men pull on ropes attached to the top

end of a slab that swivels on its stand to uncover the mouth of the cannon that a third man is about to fire. (Two very similar installations, where both the equipment and the action of the men are easier to see, appear in the lower left and central sections of one of the two *Story of Alexander* tapestries in Rome.[4]) A fourth warrior, standing at the right and wearing an elegant fur-trimmed gown over his armor, directs the operation. Behind and above him three other soldiers are setting up two campaign tents.

SOURCE OF THE DESIGN

Ever since 1903, when Destrée (p. 17) first noted the stylistic similarities that closely relate the Metropolitan Museum's tapestry to the four *Story of Julius Caesar* hangings in the Historisches Museum in Bern, most writers have emphasized that relationship and either stated or implied that they believed those five pieces, together with two other related tapestries formerly in the Heilbronner collection and now in Tournai (figs. 102, 103), were designed in the same shop.[5] Zrebiec (see note 1) observed that in 1911 Weese had associated the style of 10 with the work of Loyset Liédet and Guillaume de Vrelant, both of whom had provided miniature paintings for a manuscript of *L'histoire des nobles princes de Haynaut* and, in Liédet's case, also miniatures in *L'histoire de Charles Martel*.[6] Wyss (1957, 98–101) thought that the four *Caesar* tapestries and the two pieces in Tournai were designed by one and the same artist, but that the Metropolitan Museum's tapestry, more confused in its spatial organization, was designed by someone else. He suggested that the designer of the *Caesar* pieces depended for the drawing of his figures on the work of Loyset Liédet and that this anonymous artist must have seen the miniature paintings in a manuscript of the *Vengeance de Nostre Seigneur* that Philippe le Bon paid Liédet for in 1468.[7] However Lestocquoy (1938, 132, 135), like Crick-Kuntziger (1931, 160), regarded the Metropolitan Museum's piece as one of a group of Tournai tapestries of approximately the mid-fifteenth century that had been designed at one time by a particular group of artists in a single center. He believed that these pieces—which include, among others, the *Passion* and *Trajan and Herkinbald* tapestries in Brussels, the *Swan Knight* fragments in Vienna and Cracow, the *Jephtha* pieces in Saragossa, and the *Messenger before Pilate* in Vienna—all had been designed in Arras by a circle of painters that included Bauduin de Bailleul, Jacques Daret, Jacquemart Pilet, Robert de Monchaux, and Collart Boutevillain.

In the present author's opinion, any stylistic relationships that exist between these tapestries and the work of a particular artist or school of artists are bonds reflecting the common style of a particular time and place. There are no historical, documentary, or artistic grounds for attributing the design of any of the pieces cited above, or of the Metropolitan Museum's tapestry, to any of these artists or indeed any other. On the other hand, Reynaud's attribution (1973, 16) of a later series of *Vengeance de Nostre Seigneur* tapestries to the designers she identified at that time as Henri and Conrard de Vulcop is convincing (see Related Tapestries). Dudant (1985, 30), apparently believing that the two tapestries in Tournai and the one in the Metropolitan Museum belonged to other editions of that series, stated that all of them had been designed by the de Vulcops rather than, as Reynaud had indicated, only the pieces in the later series represented by the fragments in Lyon, Saumur, and Florence.

While it is reasonable to suggest that the compositions used in the Metropolitan Museum's tapestry might have been based on a series of miniature paintings illustrating a manuscript of the *Vengeance de Nostre Seigneur*, it is also reasonable to suppose that the designer or author created entirely new compositions for this assignment, drawing his inspiration directly from some literary source or from the performances of a mystery play or perhaps from the stage designs that might have been created for such a production. Although no stage designs for this play are known to have survived, a series of seven large painted cloths illustrating scenes in a mystery of the *Vengeance de Nostre Seigneur* have been preserved in Reims.[8] These late fifteenth- or early sixteenth-century cloths, which range in height from 2.90 to 3.20 meters, were made as wall hangings to be used in their own right or, as has been suggested, as cartoons to guide tapestry weavers.

Manufacture and Date

Tapestries with subjects that correspond to episodes in the *Vengeance de Nostre Seigneur* are mentioned in inventories from the years both before and after the date of 10. The earliest known reference occurs in an inventory of Louis I d'Anjou (1364). Such subjects appear in connection with tapestries inventoried in the next century for Philippe le Bon (1420) and Charles VIII of France (1494), and the subjects also appear in the mid-sixteenth-century inventories of Henry VIII, the duke of Calabria, and François I.[9] We do not know when these pieces were woven, but the earlier inventories prove that tapestries with these subjects had been woven at least by the middle of the fourteenth century, and the fact that

Charles VIII bought his six pieces of "L'istoire de la destruction de Jherusalem" in the winter of 1490–91 suggests that they were still being produced around that time.

Breck (1910, 117, 118), who first discussed its date and place of manufacture, believed that 10 had been woven in Burgundy, and he dated it in the middle of the fifteenth century. He, like Destrée (1903, 17), noted the stylistic similarities that link this piece with the four *Caesar* tapestries in Bern which Breck believed had been woven in Arras in the first half of the fifteenth century. Kurth (1918, 78) assigned the Metropolitan Museum's tapestry on stylistic and technical grounds to the group of weavings of which the *Story of Alexander* in Rome and the *Story of the Swan Knight* in Cracow and Vienna are the chief examples. In doing so she implied that 10 was woven in Tournai around 1460 and added that it, like the others, might have been produced by Pasquier Grenier, an opinion shared by Schmitz (1919, 190–92). Göbel (1923, vol. 2, figs. 212–15) captioned illustrations of this piece and the two hangings from the Heilbronner collection (now in Tournai) as having been woven in Tournai around 1460. Wyss (1957, 133) published the Metropolitan Museum's tapestry as Tournai work and dated it between 1460 and 1470, whereas Zrebiec (1971; see note 1), who also compared 10 to the *Caesar* tapestries, dated it in the late 1460s or early 1470s by comparison with Loyset Liédet's illustrations in the manuscript *Les faits et gestes d'Alexandre* (1470). Dudant (1985, 30) dated the design of both the Lyon/Saumur/Florence and Tournai/New York series about 1465–75 but thought that they were woven somewhat later, perhaps as productions of Pasquier Grenier and his sons.

Among the surviving pieces representing the theme of the *Vengeance de Nostre Seigneur*, 10 and the pieces in Tournai are similar in terms of drawing and also in their particular use of compact masses sharply contrasted with sudden, uninterrupted views into the far distance that relieve the sense of clutter. Figures huddle together in tight columnar or cubic groups. Crowds are viewed from the front rather than from above so that the figures in the first row block out all but the tops of the heads of people behind. In these ways the compositions are more closely related to those found in hangings like the *Story of Alexander* in Rome, the *Story of Clovis* in Reims, and the *Story of Jephtha* in Saragossa than they are to the *Story of the Trojan War* tapestries of the 1470s.[10] The hangings mentioned first have been dated in the years around 1460, partly on the grounds of style, but also, in the case of the *Alexander* and *Clovis* tapestries, by reference to documents of the period mentioning tapestries that could be identified with these. Furthermore, the design of the fashionable civilian clothing in 10 suggests that the series to which it belonged was designed during the sixth, or possibly early seventh, decade of the century. The three tapestries that gave part of their fabrics to the Metropolitan Museum's composite hanging might have been woven as early as 1460 or as much as ten years later. There are no grounds for attributing the weaving to Tournai, Arras, or any other particular weaving center or shop in the southern Netherlands.

RELATED TAPESTRIES

It is now clear that 10 was made up from parts of three related tapestries, but we have no way of knowing how many pieces there were in the set to which it belonged. In early inventories one finds mention of one to eight *Destruction of Jerusalem* tapestries, but none of the groups of hangings was described as a complete set. While Charles VIII was in Moulins in the winter of 1490–91, he bought six pieces of "l'histoire de la destruction de Jherusalem."[11] In the middle of the next century, Henry VIII of England owned seven pieces of "the siege of Jerusalem" and the duke of Calabria owned four pieces of tapestry illustrating "la destruccion de Hierusalem" and a single hanging of the same subject.[12] The description of the last tapestry indicates that it showed the whole story of the destruction of Jerusalem in one piece that was almost 38 feet (11.49 m) long. Another mid-sixteenth-century inventory, that of François I, mentions eight pieces of "l'histoire de la destruction de Hierusalem" (see note 9). The documents do not specify that the four, six, seven, or eight pieces were complete tapestries rather than sections of hangings that had been cut into smaller pieces. Nor can we be sure that they showed scenes from the story of the *Vengeance de Nostre Seigneur* as well as scenes from the more general theme of the *Destruction of Jerusalem.*

By studying the subjects illustrated in the existing pieces one can attempt to determine the minimum number of subjects, if not hangings, that the entire series comprised. First it is necessary to isolate the group of hangings to which 10 belongs. We believe, as Göbel (1923, vol. 1, 272–73), Wyss (1957, 133), Souchal (in Paris 1973, 61), and Reynaud (1973, 21 n. 34) also did, that the two tapestries now in Tournai (figs. 102, 103), and the Veronica fragment formerly attached to one of them, all belong to the same series of cartoons if not to the same set of hangings. Unlike the other existing tapestries that deal with these or closely related subjects (see below), none of these three pieces shows labels identifying the characters in the various scenes. Also, in addition to the similarities of style, figure and facial types, and accesso-

ries, these tapestries share some specific details. For example, the curious undecorated tiles set diagonally on the floor of the scene at the far left in the Metropolitan Museum's piece reappear on the floor of the courtyard shown right of center in one of the tapestries in Tournai (fig. 102). The figure representing Veronica in the New York hanging is also the one shown in the fragment that was attached to the other Tournai piece when it was in the Heilbronner collection.[13] Finally, while the Metropolitan Museum's tapestry is some two feet taller than either of the Tournai pieces, it shows more of the sky at the top and a bit more of the ground at the bottom. Thus the three pieces might originally have been woven to the same height. Kurth (1918, 78) is the only writer to suggest that the Metropolitan Museum's tapestry belonged with the *Messenger before Pilate* in the Museum für Angewandte Kunst in Vienna.[14] However that piece shows a somewhat earlier style and undoubtedly was woven after a different series of cartoons that antedate the ones after which 10 and the two related pieces in Tournai were woven. The other tapestries that sometimes have been associated with 10—the examples in Lyon, Saumur, Florence, Geneva, and the two formerly in the collection of William R. Coe on Long Island (see below)—belong in terms of style to yet another, and later, series of cartoons.

When it was in the Heilbronner collection one of the two tapestries now in Tournai had, attached to its left end, a fragment showing Veronica kneeling before Vespasian's bed and curing him with her holy veil while some attendants watch (see note 13). That section is now in a private collection. The part in Tournai shows Nero sending Vespasian and Titus to wage war on Jerusalem (fig. 103). The second hanging in Tournai shows scenes of battle and famine in Jerusalem (fig. 102). The Metropolitan Museum's tapestry comprises a fragment of a scene in which Veronica approaches the home of an invalid (presumably Vespasian) at the left end, a scene of enslavement and mutilation in the center, and episodes in the setting up of a camp and artillery installations at the right end. We conclude from this brief survey of the three pieces that the series of cartoons after which they were woven included at least the following main subjects:

1. Veronica visits Vespasian and cures him of his illness: probably only part of the subject of a complete hanging.

2. Nero sends Vespasian and Titus to Jerusalem: probably only part of the subject of a complete hanging.

3. The Romans set up camp and lay siege to Jerusalem: probably only part of the subject of a complete hanging.

4. The Romans enter Jerusalem and find the inhabitants suffering from starvation: probably only part of the subject of a complete hanging.

5. Titus receives booty from the Temple, and the Jews are enslaved and mutilated: probably the entire subject of a complete hanging.

There are no scenes in 10 or the two pieces in Tournai that show an emperor dealing with Pilate and nothing to represent Titus's triumphal entry into Rome after the conquest of Jerusalem. Only one surviving tapestry associated with this subject illustrates a scene taken specifically from the *Vengeance de Nostre Seigneur*—the hanging in Vienna (see note 14). Although this tapestry is usually described vaguely, with the imprecise title of the *Imperial Messenger before Pilate*, it does in fact show a subject taken directly from the life of Saint James the Less in the *Golden Legend*. There it is said that Pilate sent his emissary Albanus to Rome, instructing him to appear before Tiberius and request that the emperor pardon Pilate for having condemned Jesus to death. Albanus was driven ashore off Galicia and brought to Vespasian, who suffered from a wasp nest in his nose. He was cured of his malady when he heard of Jesus and professed faith in Him. After his cure, he swore vengeance on Jerusalem and applied to Tiberius for aid and support. The scenes are laid out as usual in tapestries of this period, in serpentine form, moving left to right and up and down. Albanus kneels before Pilate in the lower left corner, receiving his instructions, then embarks, sails away, and is shipwrecked (upper right corner). The series of hangings to which the Metropolitan Museum's piece belonged may have begun with such a scene or series of scenes. Perhaps it closed with a scene of Titus's triumphal entry into Rome, with a display of the booty and prisoners from Jerusalem.

Variant interpretations of the subjects that appear in 10 and the two related pieces in Tournai, together with some new subjects, are to be found among the seven tapestry fragments from at least four different sets of weavings that were produced after the latest of the three sets of *Vengeance de Nostre Seigneur* cartoons. Five of the seven fragments are now in museums in Lyon, Saumur, Florence, and Geneva; two were formerly in the collection at Coe Hall in Oyster Bay, Long Island. The fragment in the Musée Lyonnais des Arts Décoratifs shows a scene of Nero sending Vespasian and Titus to Jerusalem and also their preparations for departure.[15] One of the two pieces in the château de Saumur represents the siege of Jerusalem which is also the subject of a nearly duplicate fragment in the Bargello in Florence. The other piece in Saumur shows the coronation of Vespasian.[16] The fragment in the Musée d'Art et d'Histoire in Geneva shows a bloody scene in which Roman soldiers slaughter or mutilate defenders of the city.[17] Of the two fragments formerly in Oyster Bay, one showed the upper part of the same scene in its lower half and, in the upper half, scenes of people inside the city walls eating children or swallowing coins. The other piece showed Vespasian receiving the keys of a city from a group of men who kneel before his horse.[18] Reynaud (1973, 16) suggested that a tapestry fragment showing the martyrdom of Saint James the Less might have belonged in this series of hangings as a kind of prologue scene. Her suggestion was based on the fact that the character Jesus son of Ananias, the unheeded prophet who foretold the destruction of Jerusalem, is shown in this fragment and that his story is told in the *Golden Legend* in connection with the day devoted to Saint James the Less.

Joubert (1987, 27) was led by information written on a photograph in the files of the Musée de Cluny to state that there is an exact duplicate of 10 in the church of Notre-Dame de Nantilly in Saumur. On further investigation, it developed that the photograph is one of 10 itself.[19]

HISTORY

In the collection of M. Velghe in 1900 (see Exhibition).
Purchased by the MMA in 1909, from Seligmann, through the Rogers Fund.

EXHIBITION

Paris, Exposition universelle de 1900. *L'exposition rétrospective de l'art français des origines à 1800*. Cat. p. 304, no. 3174, called *Scène de massacre*. Lent by M. Velghe.

PUBLICATIONS

Destrée, Joseph. "Etude sur les tapisseries exposées à Paris en 1900 au Petit Palais et au Pavillon d'Espagne." *Annales de la Société d'Archéologie de Bruxelles* 17 (1903) pp. 16-17. Discussed; illus. pls. v (center section) and vi (right-hand section).

J. B. [Joseph Breck]. "A Tapestry of the Fifteenth Century." *MMA Bulletin* 5 (1910) pp. 117-19. Discussed; details illus.

Candee, Helen Churchill. *The Tapestry Book*. New York, 1912, pp. 45-46. Discussed briefly; detail illus. facing p. 46.

Hunter 1912, p. 414. Discussed briefly; illus. pls. 410 top (full view), 411 (detail).

Kurth, Betty. "Die Blütezeit der Bildwirkerkunst zu Tournai und der burgundische Hof." *Jahrbuch der Kunsthistorischen Sammlungen des Allerhöchsten Kaiserhauses* 34 (1918) p. 78. Discussed briefly; illus. fig. 9 (center section).

Schmitz, Hermann. *Bildteppiche*. Berlin, [1919], p. 192. Mentioned.

Göbel 1923, vol. 1, pp. 76, 272-73, 408. Discussed briefly; illus. vol. 2, fig. 212.

Hunter 1925, pp. 51-53. Discussed; color detail illus. as frontispiece.

Migeon, Gaston. *Les arts du tissu*. Paris, 1929, p. 234. Mentioned.

Crick-Kuntziger, Marthe. "Les 'Compléments' de nos tapisseries gothiques" (continued). *Bulletin des Musées Royaux d'Art et d'Histoire*, 3d ser., 3 (1931) p. 160. Mentioned.

"Rare Early Gothic Tapestries in Important Loan Exhibition at the Albright Gallery in Buffalo." *Art News* 31 (December 17, 1932) p. 3. Mentioned.

Siple, Ella S. "Une Tapisserie inédite, à Boston." *Gazette des Beaux-Arts*, 6th ser., 12 (1934) p. 66. Mentioned.

The Gallery of Medieval Art. Exh. cat., Brooklyn Museum. Brooklyn, [1935], p. 84. Mentioned.

Lestocquoy, J[ean]. "L'atelier de Bauduin de Bailleul et la tapisserie de Gédéon." *Revue Belge d'Archéologie et d'Histoire de l'Art* 8 (1938) p. 132. Mentioned.

Rorimer, James J. *Mediaeval Tapestries: A Picture Book*. MMA, New York, 1947, p. [3]. Mentioned; illus. fig. 7 (detail).

Weigert, Roger-Armand. *La tapisserie française*. Paris, 1956, p. 51. Mentioned. The same text was reprinted in Roger-Armand Weigert. *La tapisserie et le tapis en France*. Paris, 1964, p. 38.

Wyss, Robert L. *Die Caesarteppiche*. Bern, 1957, pp. 98, 101, 133. Discussed briefly.

d'Hulst, Roger-A. *Flemish Tapestries from the Fifteenth to the Eighteenth Century*. 1960; English translation, New York, 1967, p. 72. Mentioned.

Asselberghs, J. P. *La tapisserie tournaisienne au XVe siècle*. Exh. cat. Tournai, 1967, p. [16]. Mentioned.

van Ysselsteyn, G. T. *Tapestry: The Most Expensive Industry of the XVth and XVIth Centuries*. The Hague and Brussels, 1969, p. 51. Mentioned; illus. fig. 26.

Zrebiec, Alice. "A Reinterpretation of the Tapestry Entitled The Story of Queen Semiramis." Qualifying paper submitted in partial fulfillment of requirements for M.A., Institute of Fine Arts, New York University, 1971, 35 pp.; copy in the files of the MMA Department of Medieval Art. Discussed at length.

Souchal in Paris 1973, p. 61 (see also New York 1974, p. 58). Mentioned.

Reynaud, Nicole. "Un peintre français cartonnier de tapisseries au XVe siècle: Henri de Vulcop." *Revue de l'Art*, no. 22 (1973) p. 21 n. 34. Mentioned.

Holben, Margaret J. "Subject Matter versus Title of 'The Story of Queen Semiramis'—A Gothic Tapestry." Paper submitted, Barnard College, Columbia University, New York, 1974, 41 pp.; copy in the files of the MMA Department of Medieval Art. Discussed at length.

Lapaire, Claude. "Une tapisserie gothique à Genève." *Genava*, n.s. 23 (1975) p. 145 n. 14. Mentioned.

Dudant, Anne. *Les tapisseries tournaisiennes de la seconde moitié du XVème siècle au Musée d'Histoire et d'Archéologie de la ville de Tournai*. Mons, 1985, p. 30. Mentioned; illus. pp. 20 (left-hand section) and 37 (full view).

Joubert 1987, pp. 10, 27, 28, 31. Mentioned; illus. fig. 23.

NOTES

1. Alice Zrebiec made an intensive study of the iconographic sources of the theme and recorded her findings in her qualifying paper "A Reinterpretation of the Tapestry Entitled The Story of Queen Semiramis," 1971 (copy in the files of the MMA Department of Medieval Art; see Publications), and the reader is referred to that work for further details. The present author is indebted to her study for general orientation and guidance, for references to the sources in this catalogue entry and notes concerning the subject matter and history of the legend, and for the discussion in this catalogue entry and notes concerning Liédet and Vrelant as possible authors of the tapestry designs. Concerning the chanson de geste, see Loyal A. T. Gryting, ed., *The Oldest Version of the Twelfth-Century Poem "La Venjance de Nostre Seigneur"* (Ann Arbor, 1952) pp. 1–22; and Paul Meyer, "Notice du manuscrit de la Bibliothèque Nationale fonds fr. 25415, contenant divers ouvrages en Provençal," *Bulletin de la Société des Anciens Textes Français* 1 (1875) pp. 50–53.

2. These and other performances of the play, including some that were produced too late to have inspired the tapestry designer, are listed in L. Petit de Julleville, *Les mystères* (Paris, 1880) vol. 2, pp. 185, 644.

3. For the text of the play and comments on it, see Louis Paris, *Toiles peintes et tapisseries de la ville de Reims ou la mise en scène du théâtre des confrères de la Passion* (Paris, 1880) vol. 2, pp. 605–918. He (pp. 608–10) believed that the play had been written by Jehan Michel, bishop of Angers, and noted that the text he was using had been printed by Jehan Petit (active ca. 1478) and dated, for reasons unknown, to 1491. However, as noted by Zrebiec ("Reinterpretation of the Tapestry," p. 7), Petit de Julleville (*Les mystères*, vol. 1, pp. 326–28) believed that the Jehan Michel in question may not have been the bishop of Angers but a physician who died in 1501.

4. See the large illustration of the Alexander tapestry in Roger-A. d'Hulst, *Flemish Tapestries from the Fifteenth to the Eighteenth Century* (New York, 1967) pp. 50–51.

5. For text and illustrations of the four *Story of Caesar* tapestries in Bern, see Robert L. Wyss, *Die Caesarteppiche* (Bern, 1957). For the two tapestries now in Tournai, see Anne Dudant, *Les tapisseries tournaisiennes de la seconde moitié du XVème siècle au Musée d'Histoire et d'Archéologie de la ville de Tournai* (Mons, 1985) pp. 30–38, illus.; see also Göbel 1923, vol. 2, figs. 213, 214. Fig. 213 shows the Veronica subject still attached to the left end of the piece with Vespasian and Titus leaving for Jerusalem (see note 13 below).

6. See Artur Weese, *Die Cäsar-Teppiche im Historischen Museum zu Bern* (Bern, 1911) p. 10, and also Wyss, *Caesarteppiche*, pp. 103–8.

7. Paul Durrieu, in "Découverte de deux importants manuscrits de la 'librarie' des ducs de Bourgogne," *Bibliothèque de l'Ecole des Chartes* 71 (1910) p. 58, cites an entry in Léon de Laborde, *Les ducs de Bourgogne*, vol. 1 (1849) p. 502, concerning a payment to Liédet in July 1468 for "encoires xx ystoires de plusieurs couleurs ou livre intitulé: *la Vengance de Nostre Seigneur Jhesu-Crist*."

8. See note 3 above for the major study by Paris concerning these painted cloths. The publication also includes a folio volume containing reproductions of line drawings made by Casimir Leberthais of each of the seven hangings. See also detailed catalogue entries for each piece in M[arguerite] Sartor, *Catalogue historique et descriptif du Musée de Reims* (Paris, 1909) pp. 202, 211–13, and a reproduction of a photograph of the cloth showing the capture of Jerusalem by Titus, facing p. 208.

9. Göbel 1923, vol. 1, p. 70, cites the pertinent entries in Louis d'Anjou's inventory as follows: "Item, un tapis de la Véronique et de Vespasian qui fu gueri de sa meselerie. Item, un tapis de Vespasien qui fait metre Pilate en la tour de Vienne"; and on p. 72 he quotes from Philippe le Bon's inventory, "Ung tapiz de haulte lice fait à or de petites ymaiges de la Passion de N.S. et y a au dessoubz une Véronique et les personnages de Vespasian, Titus et autres et est de Brabant." Nicole Reynaud, "Un peintre français cartonnier de tapisseries au XVe siècle: Henri de Vulcop," *Revue de l'Art*, no. 22 (1973) p. 15, quotes from Charles VIII's inventory as follows: "L'istoire de la destruction de Jherusalem contenant six pièces de tappicerie toute garnie, achaptée par led. Sr à Moulins." Thomson 1930, p. 253, lists, among the tapestries inventoried at Windsor in 1548 after the death of Henry VIII, "7 peces of the Siege of Jerusalem." The duke of Calabria's tapestries are listed in the inventory of 1550 published by F. Vignau, "Variedades: inventario del duque de Calabria," *Revista de Archivos, Bibliotecas y Museos* 1 (1871) pp. 252, 284, as follows: "11. Quatro pannos de la destruccion de Hierusalem de lana y seda de diuersas colores . . ." and "20. Vn panno rico de oro, plata, seda y lana, en que está toda la historia de

la destruccion de Hierusalen y una muger assando su hijo y co-miendo el vn bracillo...." Sophie Schneebalg-Perelman, "Ri-chesses du garde-meuble parisien de François Iᵉʳ: Inventaires inédits de 1542 et 1551," *Gazette des Beaux-Arts,* 6th ser., 78 (1971) pp. 299–300, cites among the tapestries in the king's inven-tory of 1551 "... huict pièces de tappicerie de haulte lisse de l'histoire de la destruction de Hierusalem ... [of which] deux pièces, qui sont le département de Vespasien et Titus et le tri-umphe de Vespasien ..." [were apparently without holes and in usable condition].

10. See G. T. van Ysselsteyn, *Tapestry: The Most Expensive Industry of the XVth and XVIth Centuries* (The Hague and Brussels, 1969), for illustrations of the two *Alexander* tapestries (figs. 27, 28) and both of the *Clovis* pieces (figs. 44, 45). For the *Jephtha* pieces, see Eduardo Torra de Arana et al., *Los tapices de La Seo de Zaragoza* (Saragossa, 1985) pp. 122–28. For the *Trojan War* pieces, see 13a–c in this catalogue.

11. Reynaud, "Un peintre français ... Henri de Vulcop," p. 15. See also note 9 above for the reference to these tapestries in the inventory of 1494.

12. See the inventory entries for the king's and the duke's tapestries in note 9 above.

13. See *Catalogue des objets d'art ... composant les collections de M. Raoul Heilbronner,* sale cat., Galerie Georges Petit, Paris, June 22–23, 1921, no. 241, illus. The catalogue entry stated that only the right-hand part of this composite piece belonged to this series of tapestries. However we believe that the Veronica scene was taken from another hanging woven after one of the cartoons in this series. The composite hanging was illustrated in the same condition by Göbel in 1923 (vol. 2, fig. 213), and in 1925 Hunter (p. 52) described it as showing both scenes. Sometime after 1925 and before 1932, French and Company acquired the composite hang-ing and presumably separated the two sections. The firm lent both pieces to an exhibition in Buffalo; see *Exhibition of Gothic Tapes-tries,* Albright Art Gallery (Buffalo, 1932) nos. 7, 11. In 1954 French and Company lent the right-hand section to an exhibition in Winnipeg; see *Exhibition of the High Art of Tapestry Weaving,* Winnipeg Art Gallery (Winnipeg, 1954) no. 4. The left-hand sec-tion appeared later on the London art market and is now in a private collection. Claude Lapaire, "Une tapisserie gothique à Genève," *Genava,* n.s. 23 (1975) pp. 139, 142, using Göbel as his source, mentioned and illustrated the *Departure of Vespasian and Titus* piece at Tournai in its former state, with the Veronica scene still attached to its left end. A small fragment from another tapes-try woven after the cartoon for the Veronica episode was sold from

the Galerie Moderne, Brussels, November 20–21, 1979, no. 1544, illus.

14. Illustrated in Göbel 1923, vol. 2, fig. 215. See also a colorplate in d'Hulst, *Flemish Tapestries,* p. 73.

15. The piece in Lyon is discussed and illustrated by Souchal in Paris 1973, pp. 62, 64, 65. See also Reynaud, "Un peintre français ... Henri de Vulcop," p. 15 and fig. 31; Lapaire, "Une tapisserie go-thique," pp. 139 (illus.), 142; and J. P. Asselberghs, *La tapisserie tournaisienne au XVᵉ siècle,* exh. cat. (Tournai, 1967) no. 30, illus. For an illustration in color, see Dario Boccara, *Les belles heures de la tapisserie* (Zug, 1971) p. 19; and Robert Wernick, "Medieval Tapestry Masterpieces Cast New Spell in a Spectacular Show," *Smithsonian Magazine* 4 (1974) pp. 52–53; also detail in color in New York 1974, p. 59.

16. For the two pieces in the château de Saumur (on deposit from the church of Notre-Dame de Nantilly), see Souchal in Paris 1973, pp. 64, 65, both illus.; also J. P. Asselberghs, *La tapisserie tournai-sienne au XVᵉ siècle,* nos. 31, 32, illus. See also Madeleine Jarry, *World Tapestry: From Its Origins to the Present* (New York, 1969) pp. 66—67, for color illus. of the *Capture of Jerusalem* only. See also Lapaire, "Une tapisserie gothique," pp. 140–42 for both pieces, mentioned and illus. For the piece in the Bargello, see Reynaud, "Un peintre français ... Henri de Vulcop," p. 15 and fig. 33, and also Lapaire, "Une tapisserie gothique," pp. 141, 142, mentioned and illus.

17. The piece now in Geneva is the one that Hunter (1925, p. 52) cited as being the property of the firm of Arnold Seligmann, Rey and Company. It shows part of a scene that also appears in one of the Coe Hall pieces (see note 18). Reynaud, "Un peintre français ... Henri de Vulcop," fig. 40, illustrated it with a note that its location was unknown at the time (1973). It was sold from the estate of the Honorable Lady Baillie, Leeds Castle, at Sotheby's, London, on December 13, 1974, no. 219, illus., and bought for the Musée d'Art et d'Histoire in Geneva. See Lapaire, "Une tapisserie gothique," pp. 135–45, illus.

18. The two hangings formerly in the collection of William R. Coe at Coe Hall, Oyster Bay, were bought from Charles of London, New York, after they were offered for sale at auction in 1920. They were said to have come from the collection of comte Vital, château de Vigny; see *De Luxe Illustrated Catalogue of the ... Property belonging to ... Charles of London,* American Art Galleries, New York, November 15–20, 1920, nos. 726, 727 illus.

19. Discussed in correspondence between the present author and Mme. Joubert in the summer of 1990; letters in the files of the MMA Department of Medieval Art.

The Annunciation

Part of an antependium, dossal, or choir hanging

Southern Netherlands, 1460–80
Wool warp; wool and silk wefts
3 ft. 3 $^1/_3$ in. × 6 ft. 11 in. (1.00 m × 2.11 m)
15–17 warp yarns per inch, 6–7 per centimeter
The Cloisters Collection, 1971 (1971.135)

CONDITION

There are selvages along the top and bottom edges of the fabric. Both ends have been cut. When the tapestry was sold in February 1924 (see History), its length was reported as 2.70 meters and its height as one meter. Those dimensions were repeated in two published accounts of the sale that appeared in April of that year (see Publications). Since the tapestry now measures only 2.11 meters in length it is clear that unless that dimension was reported incorrectly in 1924 the piece lost some 59 centimeters of fabric from its length sometime after that date.[1] We believe that the piece may originally have had an ornamental border whose upper and lower sections were removed before the sale in 1924 and whose end

sections were removed afterward (see Description and Subject).

In a few places the silk yarns used to represent the highlights in the Virgin's mantle have deteriorated and fallen out, leaving some of the warp yarns exposed. A thin, tapering piece of new fabric has been applied along the lower half of the left side. Most of the darkest contours have been replaced, and there are passages of repair by reweaving throughout the field. The most important repairs occur in and around the holly and orange trees at the sides, in the foliage of the flowering plants, and in the upper sections of Gabriel's wings. There are also repairs at intervals along both selvages. None of these losses and repairs has affected the design appreciably.

Although the colors are bright it is clear from an examination of the reverse of the fabric that many of the dyes have faded dramatically. The most notable variations appear in the patterned velvets that both figures wear: they show tones of beige, mauve, and black on the front whereas the same yarns appear as pale yellow, brick red, and blackish red on the reverse. It is important to note here that some of the darkest tones that now read as black or blackish brown may have looked different as late as about 1926 when Ackerman (ca. 1926, 1–2) described the hanging behind the Virgin as "orange and

11

Detail of 11

Detail of 11, reverse of fabric

dark blue damask." It now appears to be orange and dark brown. The grass in which the plants grow now appears on both the face and the reverse as a dark blue tone; however since the dye contains substances that produce both blue and yellow, the grass probably was green originally.[2] Yellows and greens, although pale, have survived in other parts of the composition, particularly in the foliage of the plants and the floor tiles of the anteroom of the Virgin's chamber. An unpublished note that Marillier wrote in or soon after 1938 indicates that the coloring in this piece was the same on the face and the reverse at that time.[3]

DESCRIPTION AND SUBJECT

In the center foreground Gabriel, bending on one knee on the grass outside the portico of a house, greets Mary, who kneels at her prayers inside. He wears an alb with an amice at the neck and a velvet apparel on the cuff of the right sleeve; over this is a patterned velvet cope trimmed with a wide orphrey decorated with pearls and large cabochons. A larger cabochon is set in the center of the oval gold morse. A large cross rises from behind another cabochon set into the front of the fillet around Gabriel's head. Mary wears a loose tunic made of the same patterned velvet as Gabriel's cope under an unpatterned mantle trimmed along the front edges with rows of pearls set in clusters of three. Both figures have halos that match the jeweled plush of Gabriel's orphrey.

Three columns support the roof above the porch; only the two in the foreground are visible from top to bottom. Their gold-collared shafts of glossy stone rise from sculptured gold bases set on hexagonal stone plinths and they support gold capitals decorated with double rows of acanthus leaves which in turn support hexagonal turrets with slate-covered roofs. Small ceramic tiles arranged in a pattern of light and dark lozenges cover the roof sections above the porch. Inside, a book lies open on the stool that serves as the Virgin's prie-dieu. The book covers are encased in a chemise that extends well beyond the boards at the head and sides; two long straps fitted with gilt clasps drop down over the near edge of the stool. The angel looks directly at Mary as he raises his right hand from which issues a scroll on which are inscribed the words *Ave grā plena dūs/tecum*. He holds in his lowered left hand the end of a scepter whose top is decorated with a jeweled gold lily. Mary bows her head and lowers her eyes as she crosses her hands over her breast. The white dove of the Holy Spirit, its head encircled with a cruciferous halo, is poised above her head, flying on three rays of light that enter the space through the edge of a window set in a wall outside the portico. A

patterned curtain is stretched across the open space directly behind Mary and separates the portico she occupies from what appears to be an oratory in her house. Diagonally behind her at the right a doorway opens into her chamber where the end of a curtained bed appears at the far side of the tiled floor. On the opposite side of the portico the space opens out beyond the oratory interior to show an exterior wall flanking the right end of a flagstone terrace on which two beds of flowering plants are set. Three stone walls decorated with the same arched filigree pattern that appears on the hexagonal elements in the portico columns close in the garden at the back, left side, and front. Two matching towers, each capped with a ribbed and rayed onion-shaped dome, rise at the intersections of these walls.

The house and its garden are set in a flowery meadow that opens at the sides and back into a broad landscape. A number of plants including a violet, a forget-me-not, a daisy and a plantain grow in the foreground at the left. On the other side are two more violets, another forget-me-not, and a strawberry plant. These and the garden, the *hortus conclusus*, are associated with Mary.[4] A clump of holly trees bearing berries rises beyond a rocky outcropping at the left while at the right three orange trees in flower and fruit rise from beyond a low hill. City walls and small conical trees appear as a fringe along the horizon. Narrow clouds with tapered ends float low in the sky above.

Like the one in 5, this composition shows Mary interrupted at her reading inside the portico of her house by Gabriel who approaches from outside; and in both images there is a glimpse into an adjoining room at the right. However the designer of 11 added the oratory interior behind Mary and the view into the walled garden in the middle distance. The garden (or at least a comparable walled space with a turreted tower in the near corner) had become part of certain settings for the Annunciation by the early fifteenth century. It appears for example in a miniature in the duke of Bedford's breviary of 1424-35 which is now in the Bibliothèque Nationale in Paris.[5] That *Annunciation* also shows a multiple setting that includes the portico in which the Virgin kneels, the oratory interior beyond a patterned hanging, and, at the right, a view into a third room containing either a cushioned bench or a bed. A related interior setting, without the garden outside, appears in a woodcut published by Joubert in connection with an *Annunciation* represented at the left end of a fragment of tapestry in the Musée de Cluny which comes from a set of choir hangings that was given to the cathedral of Bayeux in 1499.[6] The print, from a Book of Hours published by Pigouchet in Paris in 1496, shows the angel in a similar pose (though reversed) and greeting the Virgin in a space that represents her oratory at the back of which is a doorway leading into her chamber. Therefore it is clear that the composition of the Metropolitan Museum's tapestry, with the two figures placed in a multiple setting that includes a view into Mary's chamber and sometimes also a walled garden, had become a commonplace by the end of the fifteenth century.

This tapestry has been referred to in the literature as an antependium, a dossal, and a choir hanging. We believe that it could have served any of these functions. As a long, horizontal rectangle measuring 1 by 2.11 meters in its present state but 59 centimeters longer at one time (see Condition), it has the format and dimensions of many late medieval pieces that are believed to have been woven to hang either in front of, or behind and above, an altar (for example, see tapestries 14, 17, 54, 61–64 in this catalogue). However it is also possible that this was not made as a self-contained hanging but rather as part of a longer choir tapestry, probably one of several pieces illustrating episodes in the life of the Virgin or of Christ. The height of one meter is considerably less than the height of most surviving late medieval choir tapestries; but if we assume, as we believe we have reason to do, that the Metropolitan Museum's tapestry originally had border sections not only at the ends (see below) but also along the top and bottom edges, it might have measured some 1.25 to 1.35 meters in height, which is still a small dimension for a choir hanging but not an impossible one.[7] We postulate upper and lower borders because the composition is slightly truncated along the top and bottom edges: the first conical tower at the left is incomplete at the top, and the bases of the two columns in the foreground rise directly from the present edge of the weaving. The unfinished upper and lower edges of the pattern are less disturbing if we imagine borders along those edges, borders that were stitched to the selvages at the top and bottom of the field. The fields of tapestry choir hangings, antependia, and dossals with pronounced pattern elisions along the edges look disturbingly incomplete without borders. The pattern of the tapestry dossal of the *Adoration of the Magi* in the cathedral in Sens (see fig. 49) is truncated in this way, but the observer's eye accepts the incomplete image because it is surrounded by a strong border which implies the presence of an opening through which one has a limited view of the scene beyond.

The Sens tapestry, which has narrow sections of border along the top and bottom edges and wider ones at each side, measures 1.38 meters in height and 3.31 meters in length. The Metropolitan Museum's *Annunciation* might also have had a vertical border at each end if

it had been woven as an altar hanging; and, as a section cut out of a choir hanging, it might well have retained at one or both ends all or part of some architectural or botanical motif that separated this scene from its neighbors or from the end of the hanging. In its present state 11 has neither border sections nor buffer motifs at the sides. However when this piece was sold in Paris in 1924, it was 59 centimeters longer than it is now. It seems likely that the missing fabric, removed for reasons unknown at some time unknown, was taken partly from one end of the piece and partly from the other and also that the lost portions represented either upright border sections or buffer motifs. The pertinent entry in the Paris sale catalogue (see History) is not accompanied by an illustration, but it does mention "bandeaux de verdure rapportés à droite et à gauche." We do not know whether the word "bandeaux" referred to the landscape greenery that appears at both sides of the hanging in its present state or to border or buffer motifs that are missing.

SOURCE OF THE DESIGN

Ackerman (ca. 1926, 2–4) attributed the design to Pieter Roen whom she identified with an artist who was listed several times between 1422 and 1438 as an officer of the painters' guild in Bruges. She believed that his name is inscribed on two tapestries that she attributed to him, the *Passion* tapestry in the Musées Royaux d'Art et d'Histoire in Brussels and a hanging showing the Annunciation combined with the Nativity and Annunciation to the Shepherds that is now in the Burrell Collection in Glasgow (fig. 104).

We cannot agree with Ackerman's interpretation of these inscriptions, nor can we see the same designer's hand at work in the Metropolitan Museum's *Annunciation* despite the fact that the Burrell Collection tapestry contains a number of closely related details. For reasons that will be discussed below (Manufacture and Date), it seems certain that this designer was not a bona fide guild painter but a concocter of cartoons who was either primarily a weaver or an artisan who prepared cartoons for one or more weaving shops.[8] Although his work in this instance seems to be a pastiche of borrowed parts, it shows a consistent personal style characterized by a dry and metallic style of drawing. This is apparent principally in the two faces, in the architectural details (especially the portico columns and their acanthus-leaf capitals), and in the rocky outcroppings at the left. The character of the setting, the costumes, the architectural details, the flora, the buildings on the horizon—all the motifs in the Metropolitan Museum's *Annunciation*

Fig. 104. *The Annunciation, the Nativity, and the Annunciation to the Shepherds.* Tapestry, southern Netherlands, 1460–70. The Burrell Collection, Glasgow Museums and Art Galleries.

seem to have been common property among the designers of a particular group of Netherlandish tapestries produced around 1455 to 1470 (see Manufacture and Date). This designer seems to have depended particularly on one set of hangings in this group, the *Life of Saint Peter* tapestries (see an example in fig. 105) that were commissioned by Guillaume de Hellande in 1460.[9] He could have derived his Gabriel and Mary from some prototype in a miniature painting, a woodcut, or a tapestry cartoon. As noted above, Gabriel's pose is similar to that of the angel annunciate in a woodcut of 1496 (see note 6) which shows the figure in reverse. However a more comparable figure, facing in the same direction and having essentially the same head, costume, and wings, appears in the Burrell Collection tapestry (fig. 104) which is contemporary with the Metropolitan

Museum's piece. That composition also includes a closely related setting comprising portico, chamber, and oratory.

Our study of the tapestry's design source involves the question of its date of design and manufacture so intimately that we have elaborated upon it in the following section rather than here.

MANUFACTURE AND DATE

When the Metropolitan Museum's hanging was sold in Paris in 1924, it was described as dating from the reign of Louis XII (1498–1515) but not assigned to a place of manufacture. In 1971, when it was catalogued for sale at auction, it was listed as French, probably Touraine, and dated late in the fifteenth century. Other writers have

Fig. 105. *Saint Peter Released from Prison,* fragment from *The Life of Saint Peter* set. Tapestry, southern Netherlands, ordered in 1460, finished by 1461. Musée de Cluny, Paris.

dated the tapestry within the third quarter of that century or toward its end, and they have considered the possibility of an origin in France or the southern Netherlands, possibly in Tournai or Arras.

Our own interpretation of the tapestry's pictorial style, figure types, and ornamental details suggests that it was designed and woven in the southern Netherlands either concurrently with certain closely related tapestries dating from around 1455–65 or, because its style seems to have been derived from them rather than developed with them, no earlier than 1460 and perhaps as late as 1480. To name a few typical tapestries in this group: the *Legend of Trajan and Herkinbald* and the four pieces of the *Story of Julius Caesar,* all in Bern; several pieces of the *Life of Saint Peter* that were all originally in the cathedral of Beauvais and are now

partly there and partly divided among a number of collections in this country and abroad (see fig. 105 for a piece now in Paris); the fragments of the *Story of the Swan Knight* in Cracow and Vienna; and the two surviving pieces of the *Story of Alexander* in Rome.[10]

The design of 11 differs from the design of the other tapestries in this group in a number of subtle but important ways. The organization of forms is much looser and the colors are harsher and more limited in range. Certain details in the pattern are rendered correctly while others are completely misunderstood. The definition of space is not dense and confused, as it is in most tapestries of this period, but strangely lucid and yet, at the same time, ambiguous in some places and illogical in others. Therefore it seems fair to ask whether 11 was designed and woven not in the third quarter of the fifteenth century but at a much later date. Marillier, in the notes he made after he saw the piece in or soon after 1938, seems to have had a similar question in mind.[11]

Laboratory analyses of the dyes in five weft yarn samples taken from different parts of the fabric show that the dyes contain natural materials that are commonly found in late medieval tapestries (see note 2). However these dyestuffs were used later as well. The fabric undeniably shows signs of age and wear and certainly has been repaired and rewoven in places. That in itself does not prove that this piece is antique. On one hand the wear and aging could have been produced artificially to dupe the viewer; and, on the other, a tapestry woven as late as the eighteenth or early nineteenth century, especially an abused one, could show as much wear and repair as this piece does.

A carbon 14 test of the original warp yarns shows that their calibrated radiocarbon age can be determined with 95.4 percent confidence as ranging between A.D. 1410 and 1650.[12] The analysis demonstrates that the tapestry is not modern, but it does not prove that these yarns were manufactured in the fifteenth, or even sixteenth, century rather than the first half of the seventeenth century.

Since these physical examinations cannot be used to support our contention that the tapestry was produced in the third quarter of the fifteenth century or only slightly later, this dating must be defended on stylistic grounds alone, specifically on our interpretation of the anomalies in the design and our explanation of their presence. The arguments on which we based this date are set out in detail below.

The errors that the designer made in his representation of space stem less from an ignorance of the devices used to depict space than from a tendency to borrow parts of the composition from different sources and then combine them in contexts they were not designed for. For example, he has not explained how the two main spaces that adjoin the portico in which the Virgin kneels relate to that space and to each other. A bedchamber with an anteroom gives on to the portico at the right; but the space the chamber should occupy at the left is taken up by the right end of the oratory interior behind Mary. The bedchamber simply ceases to exist at that point. The colonnette supporting the left end of the patterned textile that hangs behind Mary seems somehow to mark an incomprehensible transformation of interior into exterior space: behind it, the interior wall (brown masonry) of the oratory suddenly turns backward at right angles and magically becomes an exterior wall (blue masonry), presumably the same oratory. To the left of this exterior wall a garden patio opens out. Two tall walls decorated with arched filigree work enclose the garden at the back and left sides; the front wall, behind Gabriel, is only half as high as the other two and less wide. The right end of the back wall seems to butt up against the church wall; its left end terminates at a domed tower. A matching tower rises forward of this one and engages both the nearer end of the garden's side wall and the left end of the lower front wall. The artist offers no explanation for the disparate height of that wall, nor —more important still—does he show how and where the right end of the low forward wall ends, somewhere behind Gabriel. The same may be said of the shaft of the column whose capital rises behind Gabriel's head. The roof poised precariously on that capital and extending from there to the capital atop the forward column seems to be shorter than the distance between the bases of these two columns, a distance great enough to accommodate the bulk of Gabriel's body and the space between his left knee and the forward column. That bit of roofing does not join the ridge of the tiled roof in the foreground and it seems to have no structural relation to it. It is literally impossible to understand how these upper structures relate to the spaces they are supposed to shelter. Furthermore, while the paving blocks surrounding the garden beds in the patio are drawn accurately in linear perspective, none of the tiled floors in the portico or the bedchamber is rendered in that way. By contrast, the various parts of the building in the closely related Annunciation scene in the Burrell Collection tapestry (fig. 104) are clearly related to each other in space, and the effect of linear perspective is consistent throughout. Here, the roof convincingly covers the space that the two main figures occupy.

The holly and orange trees in the middle distance at the sides rise out of mysterious spaces that fall out of sight behind the crag at the left and the hill at the right. That is exceptional. In other tapestries of this period trees like these are rooted in a meadow or on the crests of such rises. Furthermore such trees do not usually appear as incidental accessories decorating an otherwise empty landscape. They are gathered into thickets that function as coulisses at the sides of major scenes to enframe the action.[13]

The errors or misinterpretations that seem to have plagued the designer of 11 appear not only in the form of the composition but also in its details. For example, in the Burrell Collection tapestry the rays of light on which the dove flies come in through the central roundel of a trefoil window and splay out radially whereas in 11 the source of the rays is unclear and they are parallel rather than radial. The first representation is more usual for the period. While no figure of God the Father as the source of the light is apparent in the Burrell Collection piece, it may have been shown in the adjacent section of weaving which is now missing. In any case it is clear that the rays descend from above as they do almost invariably in representations of this kind, whereas in the Metropolitan Museum's tapestry the rays run almost horizontally and on the level of the Virgin's head.[14] Here, this may be regarded either as a designer's error or as a condition imposed on him by the long, narrow format of the composition.

The pearls in the clusters of three that border the Virgin's mantle in the Burrell Collection tapestry (fig. 104) seem to be in scale with the figure whereas in 11 they seem much too large.

The halos surrounding both Gabriel's head and the Virgin's in 11 are rendered as though they were made of the same curly pile fabric as the orphrey of the angel's cope. A comparable but very different juxtaposition of halo and orphrey may be found in one of the Saint Peter tapestries. There, the ground of the jeweled halo is represented with vertical hatchings suggesting the presence of light whereas the ground of the orphrey is covered with the small crescent shapes that presumably represent a fabric covered with long curling pile.[15]

In the Metropolitan Museum's tapestry Gabriel and the Virgin wear garments made of the same patterned velvet. In itself this is an unusual detail; but beyond that the pattern has been rendered incorrectly. It includes what appear to be dark stripes decorated with a simple trellis motif as well as carnations and leaves. It was certainly meant to depict one of the patterns that tapestry designers and painters of the middle and second half of the fifteenth century represented often, but the light and dark tones in the trellis motif have been reversed and the overall disposition of the pattern has not been represented. A similar pattern, shown correctly and in its entirety, appears for example in a number of tapestries illustrating the Story of Esther and also in a painting by Rogier van der Weyden.[16]

The pattern on the fabric that hangs behind the Virgin in 11 has also been misunderstood. The designer obviously intended to represent a well-known type of damask or velvet pattern based on the repetition of a lozenge-centered leaf or pomegranate surrounded by floral arabesques. Such a textile is represented as a cloth of honor hanging behind the Virgin in the Saint Luke Drawing the Virgin and Child by Rogier van der Weyden, now in the Museum of Fine Arts, Boston (see fig. 31). Many fabrics showing this type of pattern have survived from the second half of the fifteenth century.[17]

The book that Mary has been reading also seems to have been represented with less than a complete under-

standing of its construction. It is shown as a volume whose cover boards have been slipped into the pockets of a chemise of cloth or soft leather whose wide head flap hangs in regular folds over the back of the stool or prie-dieu. The end flap on the near side has been pushed back over the pages and the two straps that secure the covers hang loose outside the chemise. Normally there are no straps visible in illustrations of bindings with such ample chemise flaps. In cases where long straps do show, there is no chemise. Where there are straps along with end flaps not as wide as these, the straps are represented as attached to the inside of the fore edge of the board and therefore inside the chemise flaps; they clasp the book shut before the flaps wrap over the ends and head of the boards. Straps that lie outside the chemise flaps, as they do in this Annunciation, normally are attached to one of the two end flaps and their clasps engage a pin set into the side of the opposite board. In these cases the straps are much shorter than the ones shown in the tapestry. In another type of binding a long strap, which has no metal clasp at its end, wraps entirely around the outside of the book.[18] Clarkson has indicated that while the long straps lying outside the ample chemise flap are unusual, nevertheless the binding shown in the Metropolitan Museum's Annunciation could have existed.[19] A related arrangement, using a metal clasp that is shorter than the cloth straps in the tapestry but still lying free outside the flap, was used on some girdlebooks.[20]

Finally, it should be noted that the sky in the Metropolitan Museum's Annunciation is treated differently from those represented in other tapestries of this group. The skies in them are filled with long, low, oval clouds rendered in several tones of blue; here the clouds are wedge shaped and less varied in their tonality.

Nevertheless, although the cartoon painter could not always interpret details in current paintings and tapestries correctly, the following observations will demonstrate that he was familiar with the most subtle ones.

The peacock feathers growing along the edges of Gabriel's wings in the Burrell Collection tapestry (fig. 104) continue from one tip to the other as they do in most representations of this kind. The wings of an angel in one of the Saint Peter tapestries are feathered like this as are also Saint Michael's wings in Rogier van der Weyden's Last Judgment altarpiece in the Hôtel-Dieu in Beaune.[21] However in the Metropolitan Museum's tapestry peacock feathers grow only on the lower two-thirds of Gabriel's wings, and although the upper thirds show areas of restoration it is clear that there never were any peacock feathers there. The cartoon painter did not invent this subtle variation. The first angel kneeling at the right in the Adoration of the Shepherds panel in

Hugo van der Goes's Portinari Altarpiece in the Galleria degli Uffizi in Florence has wings like Gabriel's.[22]

The Virgin's patterned tunic falls free from the neckline in pleats that are not girdled at the waist. This kind of garment for Mary, which is less usual than a girdled gown at this time, may be found in Rogier van der Weyden's *Annunciation* panel now in the Musée du Louvre.[23]

Mary's small oval head, with its high forehead, sharply arched brows, and flowing hair, reflects a type known in Netherlandish painting in the works of artists like Petrus Christus.[24] The head does not appear in the *Saint Peter* tapestries or in any others of this group, but the figure of Venus in a tapestry of the same period that is in the Musée des Arts Décoratifs in Paris has a similar head though with somewhat softer features.[25]

The particular features of Gabriel's head, with its long narrow nose, small chin, broad cheekbones with the eyes placed close together, and short, loosely curled locks of hair, appear again, more softly drawn, not only in the Burrell Collection tapestry (fig. 104) but also in a number of others of the period including two of the *Saint Peter* tapestries (see one of them in fig. 105), the *Swan Knight* piece in Cracow, and a fragment from an *Old Testament* series in the Musée Municipal in Saint Omer.[26] The tightly bent toes of Gabriel's bare left foot appear again on Saint Peter's right foot in one of the tapestries in that set.[27] The long, slender fingers of Gabriel's and Mary's hands are found frequently in fifteenth-century tapestries: they appear, for example, in the Metropolitan Museum's somewhat earlier *Annunciation* (5) and especially in several of the *Saint Peter* hangings.[28]

The cluster of three acanthus leaves on the three main capitals in 11 and on the corbels supporting the end towers of the roof in the Burrell Collection piece appears among many other places in several of the *Saint Peter* tapestries, although in a single row of three rather than a double row.[29] Columns like the ones in the foreground of 11, which have slightly tapering cylindrical shafts rising from high plinths and supporting turret-like capitals, also appear in other tapestries of the period, for example in the center of the *Legend of Trajan and Herkinbald* in Bern, where the shaft also passes through a molded collar in the middle, and in another fragment from the *Old Testament* series in the Musée Municipal in Saint Omer.[30]

The cinquefoil rosettes that decorate the plinth supporting the nearest garden tower in the Metropolitan Museum's tapestry appear frequently in the *Saint Peter* set, sometimes projecting beyond the surface of the stone, as they appear to do here, sometimes recessed in

it.[31] The arched filigree pattern on the garden walls and towers in the Museum's *Annunciation* is a common architectural ornament in hangings of the period. It appears in several of the *Saint Peter* pieces, in two fragments from a *Story of David* now in Winchester College, England, and also in the *Prince des Malices* tapestry in the Walters Art Gallery in Baltimore.[32]

Bulbous domes like the two that cap the pair of garden towers in 11 also appear in other contemporaneous tapestries, usually in oriental settings and particularly in scenes set in Jerusalem. In number 10 of this catalogue, in which most of the setting represents Jerusalem, somewhat more squat ribbed domes cap a tower near the upper left corner of the scene. In the first *Story of Julius Caesar* tapestry in Bern, there is a cluster of towers capped with ribbed domes just left of center in a setting that represents Turkey. Hemispherical domes decorated with sunrays rather than expressed ribs appear atop twin towers in the foreground of a tapestry in Vienna that shows Pilate dispatching a messenger from Judaea to Rome, whereas in the *Life of Saint Peter* tapestries there are hemispherical domes with both the rays and the ribs.[33] These domes all have the same kind of boss-like finial that appears in the Metropolitan Museum's tapestry; in some cases the finial supports a slender spire or flagpole.

Domes having ribs, rays, ribs together with rays, or other patterns appear in a late fifteenth-century fragment from a *Capture of Jerusalem* tapestry in the château of Saumur. That piece shows the domed towers associated with a long pitched roof paved with tiles in a lozenge pattern like the two blue roofs in the Metropolitan Museum's tapestry. The roof in the Saumur tapestry is colored red and white. Lozenge-patterned roofs of this kind appear in tapestries throughout the fifteenth century. Two roofs with light and dark blue tiles appear in one of the *Story of Saints Piat and Eleuthère* tapestries, which date from 1402, in the cathedral of Tournai. Tiled roofs in two shades of blue or orange and brown are shown in one of the *Story of the Passion* hangings in the cathedral of Saragossa that dates from the first third of the same century.[34] The turret roofs covered with slates in the upper foreground of the Metropolitan Museum's piece are often represented in tapestries of this period, for example in the *Saint Peter Released from Prison* in the Musée de Cluny (fig. 105), where the roof takes the shape of a round cone rather than a hexagonal one.

The landscapes in contemporary tapestries show many details like those in the Metropolitan Museum's *Annunciation.* The most noteworthy instances and related examples are these. The curiously hard representation of layers of rock exposed in an eroded outcropping appear in much the same form, and with similar blue and brown tones, in the center of the third *Caesar* tapestry in Bern and, in less striking form, near the horizon right of center in the Metropolitan Museum's piece from the series the *Story of the Vengeance of Our Lord* (10).[35] Conical trees like the ones in the upper left corner of the Museum's *Annunciation* appear in one of the *Saint Peter* tapestries and again, less stylized, in the *Swan Knight* fragment in Cracow. A building whose walls seem illogically to follow the downward slope of the hill in front of it, like the buildings in the upper left and right corners of 11, appears on the horizon in one of the two *Old Testament* fragments in Saint Omer.[36]

The flowering plants in the foreground of the *Annunciation* resemble any number of comparable motifs in the tapestries under discussion here, but the armorial verdure woven for Philippe le Bon and now in the Historisches Museum in Bern shows plants drawn most like these.[37] The holly trees at the left and the orange trees at the right of 11 have been drawn differently from the trees that appear in most other hangings of the group. However part of an orange tree whose blossoms, fruit, and leaves are drawn in exactly the same way projects beyond a column at the right end of one of the *Saint Peter* tapestries.[38]

All of these observations indicate that the *Annunciation* was woven after a cartoon whose designer knew the motifs in current tapestry design intimately, so intimately that it is impossible to believe he could have lived at any other time. He was inept at interpreting the spatial implications of the motifs he borrowed and he could not reproduce all the details accurately and with finesse; but his familiarity with them and with their subtlest variations lies beyond the understanding of a modern interpreter or forger. If we assume (as we must do, since 11 is clearly not a modern piece) that this hanging was woven after a cartoon concocted by a fifteenth-century painter or weaver who was not a professionally trained designer, then we can account for the misunderstood details, the spatial ambiguities, the metallic hardness of the drawing, and the harshness of the color scheme. We know that cartoons were made up at that time by men who were not legitimate artists, for their activities were outlawed (but probably not terminated) in Brussels by an ordinance that the magistrate of that city promulgated in June 1476. The ordinance confirmed an agreement that the tapestry weavers and members of the painters' guild in Brussels had reached. By its terms the weavers would cease drawing their own cartoons or using cartoons or drawings executed in charcoal or chalk on paper by men who were not members of the painters' guild and would limit their own design

efforts to creating subordinate details in landscape tapestries or to completing or correcting cartoons in charcoal, chalk, or pen.[39]

Therefore we conclude that 11 was both designed and woven in the seventh or eighth decade of the fifteenth century concurrently with, or slightly later than, every tapestry on which its design depends.

RELATED TAPESTRIES

No other weavings produced after the same cartoon are known to have survived. As noted above (Description and Subject) it seems possible that this was woven not as an antependium or retable but as part of one or more choir hangings. No other weaving that appears to have come from such a tapestry or set of tapestries has been identified.

HISTORY

Sold, *Objets d'Art et d'Ameublement . . . Tapisseries Anciennes . . . ,* Hôtel Drouot, Paris, February 29, 1924, no. 156.
Bought by M. Cornillon, rue du Cherche-Midi, Paris.
Bought from M. Cornillon by Duveen Brothers.
Property of Duveen Brothers, about 1926–65.
Bought by the Norton Simon Foundation, 1965.
Sold, *Chinese Porcelain . . . Gothic & 18th Century Tapestries . . . Property of the Norton Simon Foundation . . . ,* Parke-Bernet, New York, May 7–8, 1971, no. 224A, illus.
Purchased by the MMA, The Cloisters Collection, 1971.

EXHIBITIONS

Winnipeg Art Gallery, 1952. *Artists of the Middle Ages.* Cat. no. 9. Lent by Duveen Brothers.
MMA, The Cloisters, New York, 1965–71. Lent by the Norton Simon Foundation.
MMA, The Cloisters, New York, 1968–69. *Medieval Art from Private Collections: A Special Exhibition at The Cloisters.* Catalogue by Carmen Gómez-Moreno. Cat. no. 210, illus. Lent by the Norton Simon Foundation.
MMA, New York, 1975–76. *Patterns of Collecting: Selected Acquisitions 1965–1975.*

PUBLICATIONS

"Le carnet d'un curieux: Un panneau de tapisserie gothique." *La Renaissance de l'Art Français et des Industries de Luxe* 7 (April 1924) p. 220. Discussed briefly.
"Les ventes: A Paris." *Le Bulletin de l'Art Ancien et Moderne.* Supplement to *La Revue de l'Art Ancien et Moderne* 45 (April 1924) p. 101. Discussed briefly.
Ackerman, Phyllis. Unpublished essay written for Duveen Brothers; undated but presumably written soon after the firm acquired the tapestry in or before 1926. Copy in the files of the MMA Department of Medieval Art. Discussed at length.

Breuning, Margaret. "France Loans Us an Acre of Her Tapestry Treasures: Gothic Tapestries at Duveen." *Art Digest* 22, no. 5 (December 1, 1947) p. 11. Mentioned.

"Medieval Tapestry." *Winnipeg Tribune*, Thursday, January 24, 1952. Discussed briefly; illus.

MacMillan, Susan L. "An Annunciation Tapestry in the Cloisters." Qualifying paper no. 2, Institute of Fine Arts, New York University, September 1, 1971. Discussed at length.

J. L. S. [Joseph L. Schrader]. "Tapestry: The Annunciation." In *MMA Notable Acquisitions 1965-1975*. New York, 1975, p. 165. Discussed briefly; illus.

Coffinet 1977, p. 74. Color illus.

Kutnick, Sheldon L. "Notes on a Fifteenth Century Franco-Flemish Tapestry in The Cloisters." Class paper, Hunter College, New York, January 29, 1979. Discussed at length.

NOTES

1. Since the dimensions were listed in exclusively French language contexts, it seems certain that they were recorded accurately. It could be argued that an English-speaking person taking them down from a verbal report might have heard "two meters eleven" or "two meters seventeen" as "two meters seventy." However a French-speaking person hearing "onze" could not mistake it for "soixante-dix."

2. A laboratory report on the dye analysis by Jan Wouters, Institut Royal du Patrimoine Artistique, Brussels, July 12, 1989, is in the files of the MMA Department of Medieval Art. The dye used for the yarns in the grass area contains the substances indigotin, luteolin, and apigenin, the first used in dyeing fibers blue, the other two used in producing yellow tones. Since Wouters noted that the combination indigotin and luteolin (weld) has been found in both blue and green tapestry yarns, it is the presence of the apigenin in the dye from the grass area of 11 that encourages us to believe that those yarns were green rather than blue. Wouters also reported that one of the several red yarns in 11 contains madder and another contains redwood. One of the black yarns contains ellagitannins.

3. H. C. Marillier's note is in his manuscript "Subject Catalogue of Tapestries," vol. T.37F-1946, "Christ and the Virgin: Sales, etc.," p. 61, in the Department of Textiles and Dress, Victoria and Albert Museum, London. See also note 11 below.

4. See notes on the symbolic meaning of these plants in Margaret B. Freeman, *The Unicorn Tapestries*, MMA (New York, 1976) pp. 115-18, 132, 135. The strawberry is the fruit of the blessed, the plantain a healing herb, the daisy a symbol of innocence, the violet of humility, the forget-me-not of fidelity.

5. Bibliothèque Nationale, MS lat. 17294; the manuscript is discussed in Charles Sterling, *La peinture médiévale à Paris 1300-1500*, vol. I (Paris, 1987) pp. 435-49; fol. 440, the *Annunciation* page, illus. in Abbé V[ictor] Leroquais, *Les bréviaires manuscrits des bibliothèques publiques de France* (Paris, 1934) plate vol., pl. LXIII.

6. For a discussion of the tapestry and the print, with illustrations, see Joubert 1987, pp. 60-65, figs. 55, 59, 60.

7. We calculate that the choir hanging from which the five *Hunt of the Frail Stag* fragments in the Metropolitan Museum came (see 24a-e in this catalogue) was probably about 1.58 meters high. See Joubert 1987, pp. 60-65, for an account of the choir hangings of the *Life of the Virgin* that were given to the cathedral of Bayeux in 1499 and survive today only in the form of six fragments, three in the United States and three in France. The taller of the two fragments in the Musée de Cluny, Paris, is 1.38 meters high in its present state; and with upper and lower borders, which we believe it may have had, it may perhaps have been as much as 1.50-1.60 meters high.

8. See Fabienne Joubert, "Remarques sur l'élaboration des tapisseries au Moyen Age," *Annales d'Histoire de l'Art et d'Archéologie* (Université Libre de Bruxelles) 10 (1988) pp. 39-49, for an innovative study, with bibliography, of how medieval cartoon painters worked, with emphasis on those whose personal style altered the character of a painter's original image and those who, not trained painters themselves, concocted cartoons for tapestry producers by using stock-figure patterns and existing cartoons, varying these preexisting images in different contexts as needed. See also note 39 below.

9. For details concerning the *Saint Peter* tapestries ordered by Guillaume de Hellande, bishop of Beauvais from 1444 to 1462, and illustrations of the surviving pieces, see Philippe Bonnet-Laborderie, "Les tapisseries de la cathédrale de Beauvais," *Bulletin du G.E.M.O.B.* 14-15 (1982) pp. 2-32; and also Joubert 1987, pp. 17-35.

10. For illustrations of these tapestries, see the following sources. For the *Caesar* and *Trajan and Herkinbald* tapestries in the Bernisches Historisches Museum, see Michael Stettler and Paul Nizon, *Bildteppiche und Antependien im Historischen Museum Bern* (Bern, 1966) pp. 9-15 and 28-29 respectively, and for a large illustration of the *Trajan and Herkinbald*, see Roger-A. d'Hulst, *Flemish Tapestries from the Fifteenth to the Eighteenth Century* (New York, 1967) pp. 62-63. For the *Saint Peter* pieces, see note 9 above; for the *Swan Knight* fragment in the Museum für Angewandte Kunst, Vienna, see Dora Heinz, *Europäische Wandteppiche I* (Brunswick, 1963) fig. 46, and for the one in the Wawel Castle Museum in Cracow, see, in this catalogue, fig. 62; for the two *Alexander* tapestries in the Palazzo Doria, Rome, see d'Hulst, *Flemish Tapestries*, pp. 50-51, and Heinz, *Europäische Wandteppiche*, fig. 39.

11. Marillier wrote next to an illustration of this piece in his "Subject Catalogue of Tapestries" (see note 3) that it was "difficult to account for its perfect condition and identical colouring back and front. According to [Tancred?] Borenius several details and combinations of details are not like [or late?] 15th century, though the whole is undoubtedly based on Van der Weyden."

12. From the report of an analysis of original warp yarn samples, made by Dr. A.J.T. Jull, NSF-Arizona AMS Facility, University of Arizona, dated August 15, 1990, copy in the files of the MMA Department of Medieval Art. The raw radiocarbon age was quoted as 1521-1661 and the calibrated, or absolute, age as 1431-1624 for 1-sigma (68 percent confidence) and 1410-1650 for 2-sigma (95.4 percent confidence).

13. For examples of this kind of coulisse made from a thicket of trees arranged vertically along the sides of a main scene, see a somewhat earlier *Annunciation* tapestry in the Metropolitan Museum (5). In a *Last Supper* in the Vatican and one of the two *Story of Alexander* pieces in the Palazzo Doria in Rome, both roughly contemporary with 11, the coulisses are defined by trees combined with outcroppings of rock; for an illustration of the former, see Sophie Schneebalg-Perelman, "Un nouveau regard sur les origines et le developpement de la tapisserie bruxelloise du XIVe siècle à la pré-Renaissance," in *Tapisseries bruxelloises de la pré-Renaissance*, exh. cat., Musées Royaux d'Art et d'Histoire (Brussels, 1976) p. 176, fig. 4; and for the latter, see Göbel 1923, vol. 2, fig. 201.

14. In a few other contemporary Annunciation scenes, the rays also approach the Virgin's head almost horizontally. See for example the diptych scene on two leaves from the Book of Hours of Charles of France that are now in The Cloisters; illustrated in John Plummer assisted by Gregory Clark, *The Last Flowering: French Painting in Manuscripts, 1420-1530, from American Collections*, exh. cat., Pierpont Morgan Library (New York and London, 1982) nos. 64b and c.

15. See Bonnet-Laborderie, "Les tapisseries de la cathédrale de Beauvais," fig. 14.

16. Among the *Esther* tapestries are one in the Minneapolis Institute of Arts and another in the Musée du Louvre that show the pattern very clearly; see Göbel 1923, vol. 2, figs. 222, 223. For the painting, which shows Mary Magdalen wearing sleeves made of a similar fabric, see Erwin Panofsky, *Early Netherlandish Painting: Its Origins and Character* (Cambridge, Mass., 1953) vol. 2, fig. 334.

17. See for example a piece of patterned velvet of the second half or last quarter of the fifteenth century in the Kunstgewerbemuseum der Stadt Köln, illustrated in Barbara Markowsky, *Europäische Seidengewebe des 13.–18. Jahrhunderts* (Cologne, 1976) no. 50.

18. The author wishes to thank Lilian M. C. Randall, Walters Art Gallery; William Voelkle, Pierpont Morgan Library; and especially Christopher Clarkson, West Dean College near Chichester, West Sussex, for their invaluable help as he attempted to understand the complexities of this subject. For illustrations of bindings of the kinds cited above, see Harry B. Wehle and Margaretta Salinger, *MMA: A Catalogue of Early Flemish, Dutch and German Paintings* (New York, 1947) p. 39, a painting of the Annunciation now attributed to a follower of Rogier van der Weyden in the Metropolitan Museum showing the Virgin reading a book that has a wide chemise but no straps; also Giulia Bologna, *Illuminated Manuscripts: The Book before Gutenberg* (New York, 1988) p. 135, an illustration of a page from the Hours of Mary of Burgundy (ca. 1467) showing a woman reading a book with a similar chemise. For illustrations of bindings with long straps fitted with clasps, see the page in the *Chroniques de Hainaut* (Bibliothèque Royale Albert I, Brussels, MS 9242, fol. 1r) showing the book being presented to Philippe le Bon, illustrated in Florens Deuchler, *Der Tausendblumenteppich aus der Burgunderbeute: Ein Abbild des Paradieses* (Zurich, 1984) p. 63; also the Annunciation page painted by Jean Fouquet in a Book of Hours of about 1460 in the Pierpont Morgan Library (M. 834, fol. 29), illustrated in Plummer with Clark, *The Last Flowering*, pl. 42a. A different kind of binding with short straps attached to the inside fore edge of the boards and lying inside the end flaps of the chemise may be seen in two northern French paintings of about 1451 in the Friedsam Collection in the MMA (32.100.110, 111); see Charles Sterling, *MMA: A Catalogue of French Paintings XV–XVIII Centuries* (New York, 1955) pp. 2, 3. For illustrations of the type of binding in which short straps are attached outside the chemise and engage side pins, see Heinz Petersen, *Bucheinbände* (Graz, 1988) pp. 102–3, 104–5, and for the type with a single strap that wraps entirely around the book, pp. 100–101.

19. Christopher Clarkson, in conversation with the author, 1989.

20. A facsimile of such a girdlebook dating from 1484 is illustrated and discussed in Petersen, *Bucheinbände*, pp. 196–97.

21. See Bonnet-Laborderie, "Les tapisseries de la cathédrale de Beauvais," fig. 19, and Panofsky, *Early Netherlandish Painting*, vol. 2, fig. 327.

22. The author thanks Carl N. Schmalz, Amherst College, for bringing this example to his attention. For a clear illustration of this painting in color, see Gigetta Dalli Regoli et al., *Uffizi, Florence*, Newsweek, Great Museums of the World (New York, 1968) pp. 138–39.

23. Illustrated in Panofsky, *Early Netherlandish Painting*, vol. 2, fig. 309b.

24. Especially the head of the Madonna in a panel painting by Petrus Christus now in the Nelson-Atkins Museum of Art in Kansas City; see Robert A. Koch, "A Rediscovered Painting by Petrus Christus," *Connoisseur* 140 (1957–58) pp. 271–76, illus. pp. 271–72.

25. Illustrated in G.-J. Demotte, *La tapisserie gothique* (Paris and New York, 1924) pl. 155.

26. For an illustration of the other angel's head in the *Saint Peter* set, see Bonnet-Laborderie, "Les tapisseries de la cathédrale de Beauvais," fig. 19, and for the heads in the *Swan Knight* and *Old Testament* pieces, see J. P. Asselberghs, *La tapisserie tournaisienne au XVe siècle*, exh. cat. (Tournai, 1967) nos. 14 and 16 respectively.

27. See Bonnet-Laborderie, "Les tapisseries de la cathédrale de Beauvais," fig. 9, and another example, less similar, in fig. 105 in this catalogue entry.

28. See especially fig. 105 here, and Bonnet-Laborderie, "Les tapisseries de la cathédrale de Beauvais," figs. 15, 16.

29. See Bonnet-Laborderie, "Les tapisseries de la cathédrale de Beauvais," figs. 11, 13, 15.

30. For the *Trajan and Herkinbald* tapestry, see d'Hulst, *Flemish Tapestries*, pp. 62–63, and for the piece in Saint Omer, see Asselberghs, *La tapisserie tournaisienne au XVe siècle*, no. 15, illus.

31. The motif is represented in a variety of ways; see fig. 105 here, and also Bonnet-Laborderie, "Les tapisseries de la cathédrale de Beauvais," figs. 11, 13, 15.

32. For examples in the *Saint Peter* set, see fig. 105 here, and also Bonnet-Laborderie, "Les tapisseries de la cathédrale de Beauvais," figs. 9, 25; for the *David* pieces, Asselberghs, *La tapisserie tournaisienne au XVe siècle*, nos. 17, 18, illus.; and for the tapestry in Baltimore, Schneebalg-Perelman, in *Tapisseries bruxelloises de la pré-Renaissance*, p. 179, fig. 6.

33. The *Caesar* tapestry is illustrated in Stettler and Nizon, *Bildteppiche*, p. 11. For the tapestry in Vienna, see Göbel 1923, vol. 2, fig. 215, and for the *Saint Peter* tapestries, see fig. 105 in this catalogue entry, and also Bonnet-Laborderie, "Les tapisseries de la cathédrale de Beauvais," fig. 15.

34. The fragment in Saumur is illustrated in color in Madeleine Jarry, *World Tapestry: From Its Origins to the Present* (New York, 1969) pp. 66–67. For a color illustration of the tapestry in Tournai, see Paule Marie Grand, *La tapisserie* (Paris and Lausanne, 1981) pp. 74–75. For the hanging in Saragossa, see Eduardo Torra de Arana et al., *Los tapices de La Seo de Zaragoza* (Saragossa, 1985) colorplates facing p. 64 and on p. 65.

35. The *Caesar* tapestry is illustrated in Stettler and Nizon, *Bildteppiche*, p. 13, with a color detail that includes the rocks on p. 15.

36. The conical tree in one of the *Saint Peter* tapestries is illustrated in Bonnet-Laborderie, "Les tapisseries de la cathédrale de Beauvais," fig. 11. See Asselberghs, *La tapisserie tournaisienne au XVe siècle*, no. 14, for conical trees in the *Swan Knight* fragment, and no. 16 for the buildings on the horizon in one of the *Old Testament* fragments.

37. A large color illustration of this armorial millefleurs tapestry, followed by details in color, may be seen in Deuchler, *Der Tausendblumenteppich*, figs. 1, 3–13.

38. Illustrated in Bonnet-Laborderie, "Les tapisseries de la cathédrale de Beauvais," fig. 10.

39. For a brief account of the ordinance, see Alphonse Wauters, *Les tapisseries bruxelloises* (Brussels, 1878) pp. 47–48. In 1988 Fabienne Joubert (see note 8 above) discussed a number of tapestries in relation to the practices that were cited in the ordinance as disallowed and as permissible. The timeliness of her publication and the force of her arguments inspired the present author to search for an explanation of the disturbing elements in 11 in terms of these outlawed practices. Thanks to this lead and an exchange of letters with Mme. Joubert, he found what he believes is the correct answer. He wishes to thank Mme. Joubert for her invaluable guidance.

12

Six Courtiers

Fragment of a tapestry with an unidentified allegorical subject

Southern Netherlands, 1465–80
Wool warp; wool wefts with a few silk wefts
3 ft. 7 3/4 in. × 5 ft. (1.11 m × 1.52 m)
15 warp yarns per inch, 6 per centimeter
Bequest of George Blumenthal, 1941 (41.190.229)

CONDITION

The fragment shows cut edges on all four sides. It is composed of three pieces taken from one or more hangings showing the same subject or closely related subjects. The largest of the three component pieces contains the figures of the four gentlemen and the lady in the left-hand two-thirds of the field. It has been joined with new warp and weft yarns to a somewhat smaller fragment containing the figure of the man standing at the right and the lower parts of the robes of one or more figures standing behind him. The line connecting the two pieces runs vertically straight from the top of the fragment to the bottom, beginning at a point just to the right of the head of the man standing in the center and runs down through his left shoulder, hip, and thigh, then through the left shoulder of the man standing below him, and so to the bottom edge of the hanging. The third component piece is only a narrow strip of weaving along the left edge of the fragment; it contains a bit of the ground pattern and the right edges of a sleeve and skirt of a garment. It has been joined to the piece it abuts with new warp and weft yarns. The line of demarcation begins at the top just to the left of the basal leaves of the large plant in the upper left corner of the field and then continues down through the flowery ground to a point just to the left of the lower edge of the gown worn by the man at the far left.

The fragment shows a fair amount of reweaving with new weft yarns on the original warp and—especially in the areas showing brown wefts—occasionally also on new warp yarns. These repairs occur primarily in the region of the lady's right arm and breast and also in the darker patterns and shadows of the gentlemen's gowns. The high conical hat worn by the man at bottom center is almost entirely rewoven. A horizontal line of reweaving runs straight across the largest of the three component fragments at the level of the lady's shoulders. There is a small curved patch of old fabric on the left breast of

the man standing in the upper center and a rectangular insertion made with new warp and weft yarns next to the left elbow of the young man standing at the right. None of these repairs has changed the original drawing to any significant degree.

Assuming that we are correct in associating this hanging with a larger and apparently complete one that shows a related subject (see Description and Subject), we conclude that the largest of the three component pieces in this fragment, with figures facing to the right, comes from the left half of the original tapestry and that the second largest piece, with the figure of the gentleman facing left, comes from the right half of that tapestry or a related one. The third piece, which has been sewn along the left side here, may have come from the right edge of one of these hangings.

DESCRIPTION AND SUBJECT

The fragment shows five gentlemen and a lady standing in three horizontal registers against a dark blue (originally green) ground covered with small flowering plants of many varieties. The six figures are dressed in rich and elaborate garments and accessories, all in the highest fashion. The two men standing at the sides in the uppermost register wear loose, ungirdled gowns cut with full sleeves that are gathered and puffed at the shoulders and slit along the outside from upper arm to cuff to reveal slashed doublet sleeves beneath and full linen sleeves under the doublets. The necklines of the gowns have high mounting collars above which appear the yet taller collars of the doublets worn beneath. Both of these men have wide scarves gathered and draped across their breasts. The man at the left wears a patterned scarf over his plain robe, and the man at the right has a plain scarf over a robe of patterned velvet or damask. The young man in the center of the upper register wears a plain

12

gown with vertical pleats over the shoulders and down the sides that create a fullness at the waist which is controlled by a narrow girdle. The man standing at the left of the lowest register wears an outer garment whose fabric and cut are like those of the man at the right of the upper register. The man in the center of the lowest register wears an unpatterned garment that is cut with fullness at the shoulders and center front; it seems to be closed along the top of the right shoulder with a row of large buttons. All five men have hats with conical crowns of different shapes and heights; all of them are brimless except for the one belonging to the man in the upper left corner. The gentleman in the center of the uppermost register has softly waving hair that falls to his shoulders. The other four men wear their hair to the same length but dressed in tight, serpentine curls.

The lady is in the middle register just left of center. She has a patterned gown cut with a fitted bodice and long sleeves. At her waist is a girdle of velvet or damask, whose pattern is related to that on the fabric of her tall conical hat or hennin. A veil of transparent linen falls from the point of the hennin to the level of her eyes in front and below her shoulders at the sides and back. Her neckline is open in a low oval from the points of the shoulders to the top of the breasts, and there are two bands of linen along its inner edge and a narrow falling collar studded with large gemstones along its outside edge. The lady also wears a wide jeweled necklace high on her breast. The two men standing above her in the center and at the right wear narrower necklaces, and the man in the upper left corner has a twisted torque or double strand of beads around his neck. The wide sleeve cuffs of the gown on the gentleman at the right are trimmed with pearls and large square-cut gemstones.

As noted above (Condition) the three pieces that make up this fragment appear to have come from different parts of one or more tapestries. In 1909, when the piece was first published, Migeon suggested that the subject must have been a historical one. Rubinstein-Bloch (1927) observed that the fragmentary condition of the piece made it difficult to identify its subject matter, but nevertheless she suggested that it belonged with a series she referred to as "Conversations Galantes." Rorimer (1947) most sensibly called this piece simply "Lady and gentlemen." Davenport (1948), Coffinet (1977), and Ostoia (exh. cat. Los Angeles and Chicago 1970) used the Metropolitan Museum's working title of "A Noble Company," but Ostoia deduced correctly that the subject of the original tapestry must have dealt with a "courtly gathering."

A tapestry representing such a gathering was sold in New York in 1987.[1] It shows a company of male and female courtiers wearing the same kind of costumes and hairstyles and, like the figures in 12, they are represented against a millefleurs ground. These ladies and gentlemen stand toward the back of the space, flanking a queen who is seated before a cloth of honor in the center of the composition. A shield emblazoned azure, three fleurs-de-lis or, a baston or cotise gules overall (if a cotise, the blazon of the dukes of Bourbon) appears against the cloth at the top, right of center. The word *Cupido* is inscribed on the cloth to the right of the shield. The queen and her courtiers are watching a ceremony that takes place in the foreground. It seems to involve an allegory of the months and seasons. An imposing male figure wearing a mantle trimmed with ermine over a jewel-trimmed gown stands in the center foreground and points with his left hand to an armored knight who kneels at the right. That figure is labeled *Este* (*été*, or Summer) on the ground below his left thigh. The standing figure directs his gaze in the opposite direction and looks at another armored warrior who kneels at the left. This man is labeled *pritāps* (*printemps*, or Spring) on the ground beneath his right knee. An armored squire stands behind each of the kneeling figures, and two more squires or attendants stand in front of a tent in the upper left corner of the field. These figures seem to be participating in the judgment of a joust. The man standing in the center is probably the judge, as the long arrow held in the crook of his right arm suggests. *Printemps* and *Eté* have jousted already, once on horseback with lances and again on foot with swords, as the broken lances and cut feathers that lie about on the ground at their feet indicate.[2] At this moment each knight holds an ax. It is not clear whether they have already completed a round of jousting on foot with these weapons or whether they are about to do so. In any case, the judge is giving the victory for whatever round it might be to *Eté* whose lady May (*mai*, labeled over her left hip) stands complacently behind him. Opposite May, on the other side of the judge, April (*avril*, labeled over her left hip) expresses distress, presumably because her champion *Printemps* was not the victor.

Given all the features in common between this tapestry and the Metropolitan Museum's fragment, there can be little doubt that the fragment is from one or more tapestries woven after one or more cartoons in this series of compositions. The subject probably derives from a poem, a play, or the scenario for a pageant, a triumphal entry, or a grand banquet, and it probably deals with the allegory of the succession of seasons throughout the year, with Summer overcoming Spring, Autumn overcoming Summer, Winter succeeding Autumn, and Spring winning out over Winter. Because a somewhat earlier fragment of tapestry now in Paris shows a closely related subject that includes a seated and crowned female figure labeled *venus* and a woman in the right foreground labeled *mai* (see Related Tapestries), it is reasonable to ask whether the queen figure in the tapestry sold in 1987 (see note 1) might also have been meant to represent Venus and whether the subject of that tapestry and of the related one or ones from which the Metropolitan Museum's fragment came might have involved not only the succession of the seasons but also a love theme. The presence of the word *Cupido* on the piece sold in 1987 suggests the same possibility.

SOURCE OF THE DESIGN

The design was probably based on the painted or printed illustrations that would have been made for a publication or a pageant dealing with the theme of the succession of the seasons of the year and possibly also secondary themes combined with it.

MANUFACTURE AND DATE

Both Migeon (1909) and Rubinstein-Bloch (1927) believed that the fragment was woven in France. Migeon saw an elegance and charm in the design that he characterized as being French, whereas Rubinstein-Bloch believed that the figure types and the style of the costumes were French. As comparative material she cited a miniature by Jean Fouquet (see below) and two contemporaneous tapestries, the so-called *Three Coronations* dossal in the cathedral in Sens and the *Bal des Sauvages* in the church of Notre-Dame de Nantilly in Saumur.[3] Migeon dated the Metropolitan Museum's fragment in the second half of the fifteenth century, but Rubinstein-Bloch narrowed the span of years down to the third quarter of the century although she believed that the costumes represented in the fragment could be dated in the reigns of both Louis XI and Charles VIII (1461–98). Ostoia (exh. cat. Los Angeles and Chicago 1970) published the piece as French or Flemish and dated it in the second half of the century on the evidence of fashion in costume, whereas Rorimer (1947) called it Franco-Flemish and narrowed the date down to 1460–70.

Certain characteristics of costume relate the figures in the fragment to works of art dated in the last third of the fifteenth century. Both the men's and the women's costumes appear in these forms in Loyset Liédet's illustrations for *L'Ystoire de Helayne* painted in or about 1470 and now in the Bibliothèque Royale Albert I in Brussels (MS 9967), and the basic features of the men's costumes are to be found in a miniature by Jean Fouquet that shows Louis XI instituting the Order of Saint Michael in 1469, the frontispiece of a copy of *Les statuts de l'Ordre de Saint-Michel* in the Bibliothèque Nationale in Paris (MS fr. 19819).[4] The lady's costume, including a version of the hennin and a similar bodice and necklace, is found in Hans Memling's portrait of Maria Maddalena Baroncelli, wife of Tommaso Portinari, now in the Metropolitan Museum and dating from about 1470–71.[5] At the other end of this span of some thirty years may be cited the evidence in Israhel van Meckenem's engraving of the *Dance of Herodias*, which dates from the end of the fifteenth century.[6] It shows similar costumes for ladies, complete with the tall hennin and its veil and, in the near foreground left of center, a knee-length man's gown, girdled at the waist, that is cut with the same pleats at the sides that appear in the gown of the young man in the center of the Metropolitan Museum's fragment. However certain telling points of fashion are missing here: the men's shoulders are narrower and less sloping; their high conical hats have disappeared; and while two men wear shoes with long points (early second half of the century), one man wears shoes with rounded toes (late second half). The costumes in the tapestry fragment belong to an earlier period. The curious serpentine curls in the men's hair ought to help date the piece but they do not. They appear again in the coiffure of the gentleman standing to the left of the vintner trampling grapes in the *Vendanges* tapestry at the Musée de Cluny, a hanging that may be dated on points of fashion to the late fifteenth or early sixteenth century.[7] This particular hairstyle appears in an Italian painting of 1443–44, and it may perhaps have been represented even earlier.[8] All details of fashion in costume that appear in the Metropolitan Museum's fragment are to be found again in the so-called *Bal des Sauvages* tapestry preserved in the church of Notre-Dame de Nantilly in Saumur (see note 3). While many of the people shown in that piece are garbed in fanciful confections, the man in the lower left corner wears the loose gown with long sloping shoulders and neck-scarf that appears in the upper corners of the Metropolitan Museum's fragment; two ladies in the upper central section wear the hennin veiled to eye level; and almost all the men wear some form of the high conical hat. The men's shoes are long and pointed, and their shoulders are broad, sloping, and padded at the points. On the basis of fashion in costume, the Saumur tapestry may be dated about 1465–75. The Metropolitan Museum's fragment must have been designed at approximately the same time, probably in France, and woven in the southern

Netherlands around that time or possibly as late as 1480, when the costumes would not yet have seemed dated.

RELATED TAPESTRIES

Other than the tapestry showing Summer overcoming Spring that was sold in 1987 (see note 1), no other hangings or fragments of hangings belonging to this series of compositions are known to have survived. If our assumptions concerning the subject of the series (see Description and Subject) are correct, it would seem proper to postulate the existence of four separate hangings, each showing a jousting judge declaring the approaching season to be the victor over the expiring season. If, on the other hand, the subject dealt only with Summer succeeding Spring, then the series would probably have included hangings showing the cause of the succession, the preparations for the contest between the antagonists, the rounds of the joust itself, the declaration of the winner, and the details of the triumphant new season's rewards and installation. A fragmentary hanging showing a subject that has been described as *La Cour de Vénus*, now in the Musée des Arts Décoratifs in Paris, shows a rather similar arrangement of figures (including *mai*) in the context of a gathering at court and also rather similar costumes.[9] However the style of that piece is somewhat earlier, about 1450–60. It may be related to the Metropolitan Museum's fragment insofar as subject matter is concerned, but it could not have been woven after the same series of cartoons.

HISTORY

Sold, collection Dupont-Auberville, 4ᵉ vente, Paris (Charles Mannheim, expert), April 3–4, 1891, no. 160.
In the collection of Charles Mège, Paris.
In the collection of George and Florence Blumenthal, New York.
Bequeathed to the MMA by George Blumenthal, 1941.

EXHIBITIONS

New York, MMA, 1920. *Fiftieth Anniversary Exhibition.* Cat. p. 13. Lent by George and Florence Blumenthal.
New York, MMA, 1943. *Masterpieces in the Collection of George Blumenthal: A Special Exhibition.*
Los Angeles County Museum of Art, and Art Institute of Chicago, 1970. *The Middle Ages: Treasures from The Cloisters and The Metropolitan Museum of Art.* Catalogue entry by Vera K. Ostoia, no. 116, illus.

PUBLICATIONS

Migeon, Gaston. "Collection de M. Ch. Mège." *Les Arts,* no. 86 (February 1909) pp. 16–17. Discussed and described; illus. p. 11.
"Supplementary List of Loans: Fiftieth Anniversary Exhibition." *MMA Bulletin* 15 (1920) p. 145. Mentioned.
J. B. [Joseph Breck]. "Mediaeval and Renaissance Decorative Arts and Sculpture." *MMA Bulletin* 15 (1920) p. 181. Mentioned.
Rubinstein-Bloch, Stella. *Catalogue of the Collection of George and Florence Blumenthal, New-York.* Vol. 4, *Tapestries and Furniture.* Paris, 1927, pl. II. Discussed at length; illus.
Rorimer, James J. *Mediaeval Tapestries: A Picture Book.* MMA, New York, 1947, fig. 6.
Davenport, Millia. *The Book of Costume.* New York, 1948, p. 337. Discussed from the point of view of costume; illus. fig. 879.
Coffinet 1977, p. 71, illus.

NOTES

1. *European Works of Art, Arms and Armour, Furniture and Tapestries,* sale cat., Sotheby's, New York, November 23, 1987, no. 478, illus. in color.
2. The author thanks Dr. Helmut Nickel for calling his attention to the probable significance of the long arrow held by the central figure and also of the cut feathers at his feet in the foreground.
3. For an illustration of the miniature by Fouquet, see note 4 below. For the tapestry dossal in Sens, see in the present catalogue, fig. 63. For the *Bal des Sauvages* in Saumur, see Coffinet 1977, p. 70, where it is illustrated directly opposite the Metropolitan Museum's fragment.
4. Two illustrations from *L'Ystoire de Helayne* appear in Millia Davenport, *The Book of Costume* (New York, 1948) figs. 832, 833; the manuscript is documented, under the title *Histoire de Sainte Hélène,* in *Le siècle d'or de la miniature flamande: Le mécénat de Philippe le Bon,* exh. cat., Palais des Beaux-Arts, Brussels, and Rijksmuseum, Amsterdam (Brussels, 1959) no. 151. For the frontispiece in *Les statuts de l'Ordre de Saint-Michel* and related documentation, see Nicole Reynaud, *Jean Fouquet,* exh. cat., Musée du Louvre (Paris, 1981) no. 22, illus. This copy of the manuscript is dated about 1470.
5. MMA acc. no. 14.40.627, Bequest of Benjamin Altman, 1913; see Katharine Baetjer, *European Paintings in The Metropolitan Museum of Art by Artists Born in or before 1865: A Summary Catalogue* (New York, 1980) vol. 1, p. 123; illus. vol. 3, p. 336. For a large illustration in color, see Guy Bauman, "Early Flemish Portraits: 1425–1525," *MMA Bulletin,* n.s. 43, no. 4 (Spring 1986) p. 55, captioned on p. 53, no. 89.
6. Illustrated in Blanche Payne, *History of Costume: From the Ancient Egyptians to the Twentieth Century* (New York, 1965) fig. 268.
7. Illustrated in Francis Salet, *La tapisserie française du moyen-âge à nos jours* (Paris, 1946) pl. 42, captioned as dating from the beginning of the sixteenth century.
8. Domenico di Bartolo's fresco in the Pellegrinaggio of the Ospedale di Santa Maria della Scala in Siena showing the rector of the hospital with Pope Celestine III. A young man standing in the foreground, seen from the back, wears his hair in this fashion; see Payne, *History of Costume,* fig. 223.
9. Illustrated in G.-J. Demotte, *La tapisserie gothique* (Paris and New York, 1924) pl. 155.

13

Scenes from *The Story of the Trojan War*

a *The Battle with the Sagittary and the Conference at Achilles' Tent*

b *Busts of Achilles, Agamemnon, and Hector in Conference*

c *Andromache and Priam Urging Hector Not to Go to War*

Southern Netherlands, probably produced through Pasquier Grenier of Tournai, 1470–90

Wool warp; wool wefts with a few silk wefts

13a: 14 ft. 6^{1}/$_{2}$ in.×13 ft. 1 in. (4.43 m×3.99 m)

15–17 warp yarns per inch, 6–7 per centimeter

Fletcher Fund, 1952 (52.69)

13b: 2 ft. 7 in.×5 ft. 6 in. (.79 m×1.68 m)

15–16 warp yarns per inch, 6 per centimeter

The Cloisters Collection, 1955 (55.39)

13c: 15 ft. 10 in.×8 ft. 8 in. (4.83 m×2.64 m)

13–16 warp yarns per inch, 5–6 per centimeter

Fletcher Fund, 1939 (39.74)

CONDITION

These three pieces are fragments of two or more tapestries that were woven after the cartoon illustrating the sixth of the eleven compositions in the *Trojan War* series. This composition showed four major episodes: the fifth battle, in which the centaur or Sagittary fought on the side of the Trojans; the conference held in Achilles' tent to arrange single combat between Hector and Menelaus; the eighth battle; and Hector arming for war. The largest of the Metropolitan Museum's fragments, 13a, shows slightly less than the left-hand half of the complete sixth composition, that is, the fifth battle and the conference. The smallest fragment, 13b, repeats a small section of the conference. The third fragment, 13c, shows the right-hand quarter of the complete composition—Hector arming for war.

Fragments 13a and c have been restored by reweaving modern weft yarns on the original warp and by inserting patches of fabric made with modern warp and weft yarns. When 13b was received at the Metropolitan Museum the small rectangle of original fabric representing Achilles' right shoulder was stitched directly above his head, and immediately to its right was mounted a tall, narrow piece of original fabric showing a floral pattern. That piece is now correctly placed next to the similar passage of fabric adjacent to Hector's left shoulder, and Achilles' right shoulder is restored to its proper position. In its present state 13c shows a good deal of wear and a number of holes and bare warp yarns but very little

reweaving, and most of that is in the region of Hector's chest.

Of the three pieces 13a has suffered the most. Approximately half of the fabric has been restored with modern warp and weft yarns, and within these completely rewoven areas there are lines along which adjacent sections of modern fabric have been joined to each other as well as to sections of the original fabric. The hanging is in fact a mosaic of pieces of original weaving and modern weaving, and it is not possible to find any warp yarns that extend unbroken across the width of the hanging. The largest single modern insertion is the trapezoid of weaving that can be traced from a point near the lower right edge of the hanging just above the *r* in Hector's name (written across his left thigh) straight across to the left side of the tent and then diagonally down through the right half of the Latin inscription below that, to the lower edge of the tapestry. There is also a small rectangle of modern weaving on which Hector's head and chest are represented. Other insertions of modern fabric appear left of the tent: the three adjacent horses' heads, the falling warrior, almost all of the centaur's body, and irregular passages to the right and left of his head both at its own level and above—these are all restorations. The torso and head of the mounted warrior (Hector) above and to the right of the centaur's head are original but the rest of his figure and his horse's neck are modern. Most of the left third of the piece, including the upper left corner and most of the figures and tents, is original. The upper two-thirds of the rocky cliff in the foreground is modern, while the lowest third, with its flora and the bit of ground at the bottom, is made up of patches of old weaving that seemingly do not belong to this hanging. The rumps of the first and third horses to the right of this are original together with most of the figures of their riders. However most of the rump of the middle horse and much of the figure of his rider, together with the left arm of the rider to the right (Ajax Telamon) are modern insertions. There are small repairs by reweaving everywhere throughout the rest of the hanging. Since it appears that both the passages of reweaving and the modern insertions in the right-hand third of this piece

13b

were patterned after the analogous sections of the corresponding tapestry in Zamora, the drawing (except for that of Hector's head and torso) is relatively true to the original. The banderole inscribed with the French verses along the top shows a number of insertions. It has also been cut down to half its original height and moved from its original position. The banderole at the bottom showing verses in Latin has also been moved (see Description and Subject). At certain points along the top and bottom edges of the field, just inside the inner edges of both ranges of banderoles, there are bits of original selvage. This suggests that the strips of tapestry showing the banderoles were either woven separately on a different loom and then stitched to the field or woven simultaneously with the field on the same loom bordering slits that were then closed with stitches.

In making his mosaic of old and new pieces of weaving, the restorer shifted the positions of a number of men, horses, and accessories out of the locations they occupy in the corresponding tapestries in Zamora and Worcester (see figs. 106, 108). Because the piece presents these problems, Scot McKendrick suggested that the left and right sections of 13a might have come from different hangings.[1] He believed that the right portion, comprising essentially the tent and the figures in front of and above it, might once have been part of a tapestry in the château de Sully, a fragment of which is now in Worces-

ter (see Related Tapestries). McKendrick observed that the left edge of the tent section of 13a would fit neatly against the right edge of the Worcester fragment. He also suggested that the left-hand section of 13a might have come from the tapestry in Zamora whose left-hand quarter section, including the composition of the battle with the Sagittary, from the left end of the piece to the left edge of the tent, was said to have been partly burned in the early years of this century, removed from the rest, and then sold by the authorities of the cathedral church in 1907 (see Related Tapestries). It is certainly possible that 13a was made up in this way, but to come to any valid conclusion on the point one would have to make detailed technical analyses of the tapestries in Worcester and Zamora to ascertain whether their materials, warp counts, and textures agree with corresponding elements in the left and right sections of 13a. There does in fact seem to be a slight difference between the colors and textures of the section around the tent and its figures and the rest of the piece; but that could be a result of the restorer's work. If not, and if this is indeed a composite piece, it may be that the left part with the Sagittary comes not from the damaged piece in Zamora but from one of the tapestries formerly in the château d'Aulhac. The illustration that Jubinal published of that piece (fig. 107) shows a centaur with a very particular look about the head that appears to resemble the corresponding

231

head in 13a. However since the latter is a modern insertion this would mean either that the piece was heavily restored before 1838 when Jubinal published the illustration or that the restorer created the head any time after that, working from that illustration. Much the same question arises in relation to the inscription PONIPENAR on the bridle of Polixenar's horse which appears just to the left of Achilles' right elbow in the conference scene (see note 9 below).

The tallest fragment, 13c, shows cut edges along all four sides. The lower edge of the banderole at the top, showing verses in French, has been sewn to the upper edge of the field. The narrow U-shaped border surrounding the banderole on the top and sides is part of the original fabric; but since it has been sewn to the inscribed panel it is probably not in its original position. The banderole with the Latin inscription at the bottom appears to have been treated like both ranges of inscriptions in 13a; that is, it was woven either separately and then stitched to the field or simultaneously with the field but bordering a slit that was then closed with stitches. Comparing the upper and lower banderoles to those that appear in the relatively complete hanging in the cathedral church of Zamora that shows this subject (fig. 106), one sees that the inscribed scrolls in 13c are approximately where they ought to be. This comparison also shows that the first one or two letters at the left ends of each of the verses in the upper banderole of 13c have been altered through restoration. There is relatively little restoration in the field itself. There are small repairs by reweaving with modern weft yarns scattered throughout the area, but none of them affects the drawing. There are insertions of modern weaving in the regions of the hair of the steward helping Hector to dress, the masonry wall and horse's head and neck directly below him, the thighs of the steward standing next to Hector's horse in the lower register, and the upper part of the plinth behind him, as well as a few small spots in the tower at the right. These modern insertions, like those in 13a, appear to have been designed after the original passages in the tapestry in Zamora and therefore have not altered the drawing of the original design. The small section of weaving that shows the end of a banderole and some flowers in the lower left corner has been inserted but it is original, whereas the flowers in the lower right corner appear on a modern insertion. Of the three fragments this is the only one that seems to have lost none of its original height. The height of the corresponding hanging in Zamora is given variously as 4.55 meters and 4.67 meters which is slightly less than the 4.83 meters recently recorded for 13c. Comparing illustrations of the two pieces one sees that the upper banderole in 13c is

placed higher up in the scene than the corresponding scroll in the Zamora piece and the lower banderole is placed lower down. That difference could explain the greater height of 13c.

DESCRIPTION AND SUBJECT

Asselberghs (1970, 157–61) gave a clear and concise account of the sources from which the author or designer of the tapestries could have taken the story of the Trojan War.[2] Although Homer's *Iliad* was known in the Middle Ages, it was regarded as faulty and not to be trusted as the most authoritative source for information about the war. Rather, writers and painters depended on two other authors who worked in the first or second century A.D. Telling the story of the Trojan War with a prejudice in favor of the Greeks, Dictys of Crete pretended that he had been an eyewitness of the battles as did his Trojan-oriented counterpart, Dares of Phrygia. Their accounts served most purposes until the end of the twelfth century when, about 1184, a Norman cleric, Benoît de Sainte-Maure, composed an epic poem in contemporary taste at the command of Eleanor of Aquitaine. Entitled *Roman de Troie*, Benoît's poem comprised thirty thousand octasyllabic verses written in French. He followed the accounts of Dictys and Dares, ignoring Homer and any reference to the intervention of the gods of Olympus. Benoît's poem was soon translated into virtually every modern language of Europe. In 1287 a Sicilian judge named Guido delle Colonne composed a simplified adaptation of the poem in Latin prose. Because Benoît's poem was written in French and Guido's prose version of it was in Latin, and because Guido did not acknowledge his monumental debt to Benoît but cited Dares as his source, readers considered Guido's account of the wars more authoritative than Benoît's. By the middle of the fifteenth century other literary works based on Guido's text had been written including a number of dramatic works of which Jacques Millet's mystery play *La Destruction de Troie la Grande*, written about 1450, is the best-known example. A few years later Philippe le Bon commissioned his chaplain Raoul Lefèvre to write a new version of the story of the Trojan War. As Forsyth (1955–56, 77) noted, the dukes of Burgundy claimed Priam as an ancestor; and so the legend would have held a special appeal for Philippe le Bon. In 1464 Lefèvre wrote the first two books of his work entitled *Recueil des Histoires de Troie*. These dealt only with the first two destructions of Troy, by Hercules. By 1468 the *Recueil* included a third book that treated the final war. This was in fact simply a translation of Guido delle Colonne's Latin text covering that subject but presented without giving credit to the author. In 1474 an English translation of the *Recueil* commissioned from William Caxton by Margaret of York was printed in Bruges. Entitled *The Recuyell of the Historyes of Troye*, it was the first book printed in English.

Asselberghs suggested that although it would seem correct to regard Lefèvre's *Recueil* as the literary source of the tapestry series, the designs were probably based not on Lefèvre's book but on Guido's first translation into Latin of Benoît's poem (1287).

In Scherer's opinion the tapestry series was conceived by some author who did not draw on any one particular source.[3] None of the other writers who considered this question was able to make any more specific a suggestion. Too many possible sources and too many variables are involved. There is every reason to believe that some poet whose name we do not know wrote not only the French and Latin stanzas that appear along the upper and lower edges of the hangings but also a verse or prose scenario for the designer. Asselberghs (1970, 160) cited two abbreviated poems of the period, the *Ystoire de Troie abrégée* in one quatrain and thirty-three hexastichs, and the *Estoire abrégée de Troie, selon Darès et Ditis* with forty-six quatrains and three hexastichs. De Ricci (1924) made a special study of the French (but not the Latin) verses in the tapestries with the help of transcriptions from the four hangings in the cathedral church of Zamora and also the French verses written out on paper that are kept in the Musée du Louvre along with the preliminary drawings for the series.[4] He was able to reconstruct thirty-one stanzas of the forty-five that Asselberghs later deduced must once have existed. De Ricci concluded that the poem was a literary work in its own right.

Ackerman suggested that the final scene in the eleventh and last tapestry in this series perhaps was meant to show the cartoon painter (the bearded man) and two assistants discussing the design "in a kind of workshop."[5] Asselberghs (1970, 124) and Souchal (in Paris 1973, 59) both believed, as the present author does, that the bearded man represents the scenario writer or poet, and not the designer. As Asselberghs (1970, 124–26) pointed out, figures like these are found in illustrated manuscripts as well as in other late fifteenth- and early sixteenth-century Netherlandish tapestries. When they appear in tapestries they are accompanied by inscriptions whose content is less narrative than it is moralizing. The figure of a man leaning out of a window at the left end of the *Story of Jephtha* tapestry (woven about 1460–70) in Saragossa appears above an inscription praising prudence and patience.[6] The left and right ends respectively of the first and tenth

hangings of the *Story of David and Bathsheba* (about 1510–15) in the Musée de Cluny in Paris show men conversing over book stands in scenes that virtually duplicate the one at the right end of the last tapestry in the *Story of the Trojan War* series.[7] The texts inscribed on plaques below each of these scenes summarize the action shown in the main fields of the tapestries but in highly moralizing terms. At the right end of the ninth and last hanging in the tapestry series called *Los Honores* (designed by about 1520) that belongs to the Patrimonio Nacional in Spain is another scholarly figure seated in his studio. In this instance the man is labeled AUTHOR, and the text inscribed on the panel above his room summarizes the moral themes illustrated in the tapestry series. Delmarcel, in his study of these hangings, expressed the opinion, which the present author shares, that this is not a portrait of Jean Lemaire de Belges or any other specific literary figure but a generic symbol telling the viewer that what he is seeing is a morality.[8] This interpretation could pertain equally well to the *Jephtha*, *David*, and *Trojan War* tapestries. On the other hand the symbol has indeed been personified; and perhaps in some instances at least the figure might have been intended also as a reference to a specific author. In the case of the *Trojan War* series, the bearded man could be meant to represent Benoît de Sainte-Maure, Guido delle Colonne, Raoul Lefèvre, or the anonymous writer who created the scenario and poem for the tapestry designer. Asselberghs (1970, 126 and n. 3) cited Crick-Kuntziger as having suggested that these narrator figures might have been derived from the theater. However that may be, there is a strong moralizing content here. The verses that appear both above and below the "narrator" and his guests in the eleventh and last tapestry of the *Trojan War* series (see Asselberghs 1970, 128; or Souchal in Paris 1973, 59) lament the ignominious fate of the once glorious and powerful city of Troy.

By analyzing information gathered from visual and documentary sources, Asselberghs was able to reconstruct the content of the tapestry cycle to which these pieces belonged. Thanks to him, we know that the Metropolitan Museum's three pieces represent the first, second, and fourth scenes in what is the sixth hanging of the series, the one known, for the sake of brevity, as *The Tent of Achilles*. A tapestry showing the second, third, and fourth scenes is preserved in the cathedral church of Zamora (fig. 106).

The composition for *The Tent of Achilles* shows four major episodes placed next to each other and bordered along the top by red banderoles bearing white inscriptions, specifically, quatrains in French. Along the bot-

Fig. 106. *The Tent of Achilles* (left quarter missing). Tapestry, southern Netherlands, last quarter of the fifteenth century. Cathedral, Zamora.

tom there are narrower scrolls of the same kind showing distichs in Latin.

The first episode, which shows the fifth battle in the Trojan War, occupies the left two-thirds of 13a. In the lower left corner some mounted Greek warriors are being driven back to their tents by the terrifying figure of the Sagittary, a centaur bowman whose powerful figure dominates the center of the scene. The monster has just shot an arrow deep into the chest of the Greek warrior Polixenar, who is seen falling from his steed in the foreground, his name (misspelled PONIPENAR) inscribed on the horse's bridle.[9] Hector (labeled *hector* across his left forearm), who appears on his mount immediately beyond the centaur, plunges his sword into the neck of the warrior who falls behind the beast. In this part of the hanging the restorers have shifted the relative positions of the figures to such an extent that this passage has been diminished and the warrior's name eliminated. The detail is to be seen in its complete form in the drawings published by Jubinal (see note 10), in the frag-

ment in Worcester, and to a lesser extent at the left edge of the large hanging in Zamora (figs. 106–8). Hector's victim is labeled clearly in the first two examples; he is the Greek king Scedius (*roy cedius*). The figure of Diomedes (labeled *dyomedes* across the breast) rises to the left of the centaur's bow and is about to strike the monster with his sword. Directly above Diomedes, Achilles (labeled *achilles* across his breastplate) gathers all his strength behind the spear thrust he directs deep into the chest of the giant Hupon le Grand (labeled *hupon le grand* on his right arm), who topples over backward in the upper right corner of this scene. The head and shoulders of Aeneas (labeled *eneas* across the helmet) appears just below Hupon's sagging head. Directly below Aeneas appears the top of another warrior's helmet. The rest of his head and his face are missing but the letters *op* remain on the helmet. The corresponding helmet in the tapestry in Zamora is clearly labeled *epistropus*, thus identifying the figure as Epistrotus, brother to Scedius, as Asselberghs (1964, 36) pointed out. Ajax Telamon,

235

labeled *thelamōala* (the last three letters restored) across the lower back, sits astride his horse at center bottom and aims a double-barbed spear at the Sagittary. The Trojan Antenor (labeled *athenor* along his right forearm) locks swords with another soldier labeled ᴀᴇꜱᴏ on the edge of his sleeve or shoulder plate at the very top of the scene, in the center. A warrior who resembles the Agamemnon standing in front of the tent in both the Zamora piece and in 13b moves in from the left for an attack on the Sagittary with a sword whose blade shows a much restored (and now illegible) inscription. There is no inscription on this sword in the Worcester Museum fragment or the illustration that Jubinal published (see figs. 108 and 107).

The action represented in the scene is described on banderoles, quatrains in French along the top and distichs in Latin along the bottom of the field. As Asselberghs (1970, 111) noted, this French quatrain was mutilated and its elements were rearranged. In their present form, arranged on two rather than four lines, the verses make sense only in part:

> *Achilles vint impetueusemēt · En bataillant avec le sagitaire orrible & espatant · Polixenar tua en cest effort/Qui cōbatoit mlt vertueusemet · Fort terrible nōme Diomedes vertueux & puissant · Le sagitaire occit et mist a mort.*

Asselberghs reconstructed the quatrain by combining parts of this inscription with parts of one taken from another edition of the same tapestry and then sewn to the bottom of a hanging showing the *Anniversary of Hector's Death* that is now in the Burrell Collection in Glasgow (see Asselberghs 1970, fig. 17). As reconstructed, it reads as follows:

> *Achilles vint impetueusement · En bataille ou tua ung joyant*
> *Qui cōbatoit mlt vertueusement · Fort terrible nōme hupō le grant*
> *Le sagitaire orrible et espatant · Polixenar tua en cest effort*
> *Diomedes vertueux et puissant · Le sagitaire occit et mist a mort*

(Achilles came impetuously into battle where he killed a most terrifying giant named Hupon the Great who fought very bravely. The horrible and terrifying Sagittary killed Polixenar in this battle. Brave and powerful Diomedes killed the Sagittary).

The Latin distich at the bottom, most of whose right half has been restored with both new warp and weft yarns, reads as follows (not in complete agreement with transcriptions by Asselberghs 1970, 111–12, or Souchal in Paris 1973, 54):

Fig. 107. Illustration of a seemingly incomplete tapestry of *The Tent of Achilles* formerly in the château d'Aulhac near Issoire in central France. From Achille Jubinal, *Les anciennes tapisseries historiées . . . d'après les dessins de Victor Sansonetti* (Paris, 1838) vol. 2, pls. 2–4.

> *Intervint huiomem [huponem] achilles · Sagittarius fortiter certavit*
> *Tradit morti diomedes miles · Et la[r?]tus hostes prostravit*

(Achilles defeated Hupon. The Sagittary fought bravely [but] surrendered to death [at the hand of] the warrior Diomedes and overcame the enemy's flank).

236

Scherer (1963, 79–80) pointed out that the giant and the centaur archer were brought into the story in the Middle Ages and that the next scene, showing Achilles and Hector in conference, was also a medieval embellishment on the classical sources. She noted that Hupon was based on the character of the king Hipparchus or Hippothoos who, in the *Iliad*, was a Trojan partisan whom Ajax killed after Patroclus's death. Scherer also indicated that it was Benoît de Sainte-Maure who gave the Trojans a warrior centaur for an ally and that he was called the Sagittary in the tapestry verses because the Latin term *sagittarius* referred both to a mounted archer in general and also to the constellation of that name.

It was also the medieval accounts of the Trojan War that introduced the idea of a truce after the fifth battle, during which Hector visited Achilles in his camp, the

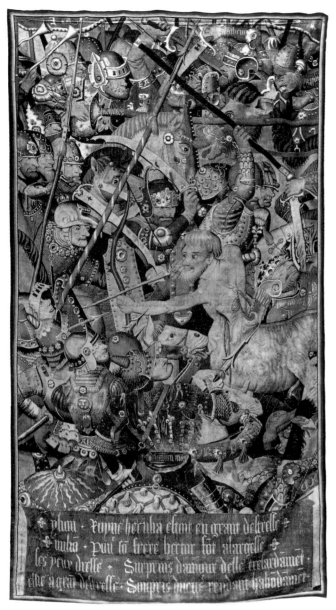

Fig. 108. *The Battle with the Sagittary.* Fragment of a tapestry, southern Netherlands, last quarter of the fifteenth century. Worcester Art Museum; Gift from the Estate of Mrs. Aldus Chapin Higgins.

subject of the second scene in the sixth tapestry. It appears in the lower right-hand third of 13a. During his visit to the Greek camp Hector entered Achilles' tent at the latter's behest. During their conversation Achilles boasted of how he would take pleasure in dispatching Hector both because of the wounds he himself had received by Hector's hand and because Hector had slain his beloved friend Patroclus. Hector responded by proposing that they engage in single combat to decide the outcome of the war. If Achilles were to win, the Trojans would depart and leave their land to the Greeks; but if Hector won, then the Greeks would depart and leave the Trojans in peace and Helen with them. When Agamem-

non heard of this discussion he went to the tent to object. In 13a the left two-thirds of the complete scene has been preserved. Comparing this to the larger hanging in Zamora (fig. 106) one sees that three other men, a horse, and a page are missing at the right side along with the right half of the tent itself. Present in 13a, however, are the figures of Achilles (labeled *achilles*, a restoration, on the bottom of his right sleeve) standing at the left in front of the embroidered watered-silk tent; Hector (labeled *hector*, a restoration, on his left thigh) standing opposite him at the right; and Agamemnon (labeled *agamenō*, not restored, on the front of his robe at hip level) standing behind and between the two main characters. One of the three men missing from the scene in this hanging but present in the piece in Zamora, a man standing directly beside and behind Hector, is Menelaus (labeled *menelas* on the collar of his robe). The letters represented as embroidered in pearls and alternating with rosettes along the valance bordering the bottom of the tent's roof—E, S, G, P—may have some significance or may simply be meaningless ornaments, as the letters on one of the Greek tents at the left edge of the tapestry seem to be.

This scene has lost both of its inscribed banderoles but the banderoles have been preserved in the corresponding hanging in Zamora. The verses in French that appear along the top of that hanging read as follows:

Treves pendant cōme est acoustume · Hector vint veoir achilles en satente
Que veu navoit ōcque synō arme · Dēprēdre champ chascūdeux secōtente
Hector vaincu rend helayē la gente · Ou achilles vaincu fait de partir
Tout lost des grecz par p[ro]messe patente · Mais les princes ny voldrēt consētir

(During the customary truce Hector came to visit Achilles whom he had never seen out of his armor. They both agreed to go to the battlefield. If Hector were beaten he would give Helen back to the people. Or if Achilles lost he would have all the Greeks leave for good. But the princes did not want to agree to this).

The verses in Latin at the bottom read as follows:

Achilles it hector tentoria · Paciscuntur se solos bellare
Hector stat pax pro victoria · Huic helena duces nolūt dare

(Hector went to Achilles' tent and they made a pact to fight in single combat. If Hector won there would be peace; but the chiefs did not want to give Helen to him).

Fragment 13b shows at the left the face, chest, right shoulder, and left arm of Achilles. Hector's torso and a bit of Menelaus's face, beard, and robe appear at the right end. Agamemnon's torso and head (labeled *agame/no* [*nō?*] on the upturned brim of his hat), together with a bit of the figure standing behind him, appear between the figures of Achilles and Hector.

The third episode in *The Tent of Achilles* does not appear in any of the Metropolitan Museum's fragments. It has been preserved complete in the middle third of the tapestry in Zamora (fig. 106) and in fragmentary form in a piece now or formerly in a private collection in Paris (see Related Tapestries). It represents the main events that took place during the eighth battle in the Trojan war. Briseide, Troilus, Andromache, Helen, and Polyxena watch from the walls of Troy as the battle rages around them. There are warriors attacking one another everywhere; but in the lower center section the designer has singled out for special notice the scene of Hector killing the king Menon as Achilles moves in from the left to deliver a blow at Hector and Troilus approaches from behind to help his brother. Asselberghs (1970, 112) and Souchal (in Paris 1973, 54) give transcriptions of both the French and Latin verses that accompany and explain this episode.

The fourth and last scene in *The Tent of Achilles*, which appears in the right third of the hanging in Zamora (fig. 106), has been preserved in its entirety in 13c. It deals with the subject of Hector's arming for battle and the efforts of his wife and parents to dissuade him from taking part in the conflict that day. In the upper section of the composition, Hector's wife, Andromache, who had had a dream in which she saw Hector killed in battle the next day, kneels at the left and pleads with Hector as his steward outfits him for the battle. Both of the main figures are labeled with their names, hers (rendered as *andromata*) is written across the lower part of her gown; his (as *hector*) runs across his left thigh (where it appears also in the tent scene). Andromache holds one of their two sons, Astromatas (also called Astyanax, here labeled *astromata*), in her arms while their other son Laomedon (not labeled) stands between his parents. Five richly dressed ladies shown in attitudes of distress and supplication surround Andromache. Three of them are identified by their labels as Helen (*heline*), the letters partly restored, far left; Polyxena (*polixene*), to the right of Helen; and Hecuba (*heccuba*), directly above Andromache. The figure of Hector, mounted and fully armed for battle, occupies the center of the lower half of the composition. His name (*hector de troye*) is inscribed on his scabbard. Two warriors and a second horse emerging from behind the tower at the

right follow along behind Hector. A steward stands at the far left in front of Hector's horse, and the mounted figure of King Priam (labeled *roy priam* on his right shoulder) appears immediately behind the steward, raising his hand and entreating his son on Andromache's behalf and his own, not to go to battle that day. Hunter (*Tapestries of Clarence H. Mackay,* 1925, 36) thought that the letters inscribed on the edge of the arch at the very top of this scene could be read in part, at the center, as *Ilion Regis.* Since most of these letters have been restored, it would be pointless to pursue this suggestion. Letters like these in other tapestries of the series indeed do spell out the name of a building; see for example the inscription on the central arch of the Temple of Apollo in one of the tapestries in Zamora (Asselberghs 1970, fig. 19).

The verses in French inscribed in the banderole along the top of 13c have been mutilated in part through restoration. The transcription that follows was taken from the verses that have been preserved seemingly intact at the top of the hanging in Zamora:

> *Andromata la mort hector doubtans · Quavoit sōgie vīnt agēou plourer*
> *Lui pōta en grans pleurs les enfans · En lui priant en ce jour non allerr*
> *En bataille hector se fist armeer · Ce non ostāt et acheval monta*
> *roy priāt le constrait retourneer · Par la pitie quil prīnt dādromata*

(Having dreamed of his death, Andromache brought the children to him tearfully and kneeling before him begged him not to go to battle that day. In spite of this Hector had himself armed and mounted his horse. King Priam coerced him to return out of pity for Andromache).

The Latin verses along the bottom are inscribed on a banderole that has been placed somewhat lower down in the field than the corresponding scroll in the Zamora tapestry, but the words are identical. They read as follows:

> *Andromatha de flens excidium · Hectoris qd vidit dormiendo*
> *Offert prolem huic in remedium · Priamus hunc vocat retinendo*

(Andromache grieves over Hector's death which she saw in her sleep. She brings her children to him to prevent it. Priam calls to him and detains him).

SOURCE OF THE DESIGN

The *Story of the Trojan War* tapestries are exceptional in a number of ways. There are some fifteenth-century documents mentioning the name of the producer and the delivery dates of two sets of weavings that have survived. Furthermore, this is the only extant late medieval tapestry series whose original designs (or most of them) have also survived. Ten whole or fragmentary pen and ink drawings on paper, heightened with watercolor, have been preserved. Nine of them were discovered in Dresden in the collection of Adolf Gutbier and published by Schumann in 1898.[10] They are now in the Cabinet des Dessins in the Musée du Louvre (nos. R.F. 2140–47). The nine drawings are mounted on eight sheets, each measuring a bit less than $12^{1}/_{4}$ inches in height by $22^{1}/_{2}$ inches in width (.31 m × .57 m). The complete drawings (nos. R.F. 2140–42 and 2144–47), some of which display lacunae due to loss of the paper support, show the compositions for the first, fourth, fifth, eighth, ninth, tenth, and eleventh subjects. Mounted on the fourth sheet in the series (no. R.F. 2143) are two narrow fragments. One shows the left end of the seventh subject and the other shows part of the arming of Hector (fig. 50) at the right end of the sixth composition, *The Tent of Achilles.* A tenth drawing was found more than seventy years later in the collection of the Cabinet des Estampes in the Bibliothèque Nationale, Paris, and it was published in 1976.[11] Its subject is the celebration of the anniversary of Hector's death, which has survived in tapestry in one of the two fragments in the Burrell Collection (see Related Tapestries).

In spite of overwhelming evidence that these are the preliminary drawings from which cartoons would be painted on the correct scale for the weavers, Hunter, in two publications in 1925 and one in 1926, held fast to the opinion that the nine drawings in the Louvre were merely crude copies of the tapestries made by an inferior artist. Every other writer on the subject has accepted the drawings for what they clearly are except for Weigert (1964, 39–40), who entertained doubts about their priority in relation to the tapestries. Asselberghs (1970, 101–2, 127) advanced a number of arguments supporting the priority of the drawings. One of his most convincing observations concerned details in the last composition where the draftsman mistakenly placed a votive figure of Minerva on the altar in the temple of Apollo and the cartoon painter corrected the error for the weavers. With Asselberghs, the present writer believes that no copyist would have deviated so strikingly from the models, that is, the tapestries themselves. A copyist would have included much more of the decorative detail in the textiles and accessories than the drawings show, and, particularly, no one working from the finished weavings would have concentrated the rendering of details toward the bottoms of the compositions (as the draftsman has done)

instead of showing details in similar density at top and bottom, as they are in the tapestries. Furthermore, the cartoon painter consistently reinterpreted the organization of the compositions in the drawings in such a way as to diminish the illusion of depth and emphasize the reality of the surface of the tapestry. Comparing the drawing for 13c (fig. 50) with the tapestry, one sees that the cartoon painter enlarged the lower figure of Hector and gave his helmet a tall panache. He also lowered the wall that runs behind Hector and Priam and caused the tops of the figures in the lower register to overlap the lower parts of the composition in the upper register. These changes have the effect of uniting the scenes in the two registers and giving the surface of the composition more power than it has in the drawing. Finally, some words in one of the penned French stanzas that have been preserved with the drawings show the letter *n,* but in the tapestry these are elided and represented only by horizontal lines in superscript. That is, *constraint* in the ink inscription becomes *constraīt* in the tapestry and *dandromata* becomes *dādromata.* It seems unlikely that a copyist would make such changes if he were literally copying existing images, whereas it makes sense to assert that the cartoon painter or the weavers themselves would introduce the elisions in order to save time and labor, especially since elisions like these were the rule in tapestry inscriptions at this time rather than the exception. On the other hand, in a few instances words in the tapestries contain one more letter than the same word does in the penned inscription.[12]

Ever since they were first published, the nine drawings in the Louvre have been attributed to a number of different artists. In 1898 Müntz expressed the opinion that they were the work of some anonymous artist who was active in Paris.[13] The next year Guiffrey, prophetically and with great insight, attributed the drawings to the anonymous designer who created the composition of the *Destruction of Jerusalem* fragments in Saumur.[14] Reynaud (1973, 15) called attention to the same relationship almost seventy-five years later. She also observed that Henri Bouchot had attributed the Louvre drawings to the same French artist who had designed the woodcuts in the *Heures de Simon Vostre;* that Jean Lafond likened the style of the drawings to the style of Parisian stained glass; and that, like Jean Porcher, Lafond thought that the tapestry designer should be sought among the artists who worked for the great Parisian printers of the end of the fifteenth century, Porcher singling out the printer Antoine Vérard.[15] Schmitz,[16] Rorimer (1939, 227), and Forsyth (1955–56, 80) proposed Jean le Tavernier of Audenarde as the author of the Louvre drawings because they felt that these drawings resemble the miniatures that le Tavernier executed in the *Cronicques et Conquestes de Charlemagne* in Brussels and also because it is known that Philippe le Bon paid le Tavernier in 1454 for "trois histoires de Troie" which were apparently drawings on paper.[17] The present author agrees with Asselberghs (1970, 180) and Reynaud (1973, 7), who believe that le Tavernier's style—although found in similar kinds of compositions—is entirely different from that of the author of the Louvre drawings. The present author also maintains that le Tavernier's style of painting, as well as his representation of fashion in costume mark him as an artist working too early and too conventionally to have created the Louvre drawings. Göbel (1923, vol. 1, 407, 599 n. 174), following A. Thiéry, looked for and believed he had found a partly hidden form of the name of the Brussels designer Jan van Roome in 13a, in the letters on the bridle of Ajax Telamon's horse (some of which had in fact been restored) and which Göbel misread as I. N.; RON IPENAR. Dhanens corrected this misapprehension and the erroneous deduction Göbel had drawn from it.[18] Lugt[19] and Asselberghs (1970, 181) each suggested that the artist who created the Louvre drawings was not a miniature painter but one of the painter-decorators who worked among other things for tapestry producers. They agreed that this anonymous artist was to be found in the circle of men like Bauduin de Bailleul and Jacques Daret. Hunter's suggestion (1926, 45) that the unidentified artist was associated with the school of Rogier van der Weyden and was possibly a member of the shop staff of that master may be discounted out of hand.

Reynaud has produced the most convincing attribution to date. She has identified the author of the Louvre drawings with the miniature painter whom Paul Durrieu had earlier named the "Maître de Coëtivy" and to whom Reynaud attributed certain other miniature and altar paintings and some stained glass.[20] Durrieu had already suggested that this man might be identical with Henri de Vulcop. Through an ingenious if not entirely convincing series of assumptions and deductions, Reynaud came to the conclusion that the Coëtivy Master could be identified as a brother team of Henri and Conrard de Vulcop and that one or both of them created the Louvre drawings. The few extant documents that concern these brothers of Netherlandish origin indicate that Conrard was court painter to Charles VII between 1446 and 1459 and that Henri worked as court painter to Marie d'Anjou, Charles's queen, in 1454–55, and then to Charles's eldest son, Charles de France, duc de Berry, brother of the future Louis XI.

Whether or not one or both of the Vulcop brothers was the Coëtivy Master, the present writer is convinced that

Reynaud is correct in stating that the Louvre drawings were made by the man who also painted the miniatures in the manuscript of Orosius's *Histoire Universelle* in the Bibliothèque Nationale in Paris (MS fr. 64). Although the Trojan War drawings in the Louvre have been worked over with various instruments and pigments more than once, some more than others, whether by the cartoon painter or by some later enthusiast, their character suggests that they were made by an artist who was accustomed to painting miniatures and who was working here on a larger scale.

In the present writer's opinion, the descriptions of these drawings that have been published to date are sadly inadequate. Other writers have referred to them as pen drawings in brown ink touched with watercolor, chiefly in red and blue. That is quite untrue. Although the pigments are for the most part applied thinly, they are definitely handled as pigments, not just as washes. Some are quite opaque. The colors include pale but vibrant yellows, mauves, and lavenders, various greens and whites, as well as the reds and blues. The convention of shading a form by means of hue changes rather than value gradations of the same hue, the touch, the handling of line for purposes of modeling—everything about these drawings indicates that they are the work of a man who was a master at painting miniatures, whatever else he may have done. His pictorial handwriting, his handling of color, and his figure and facial types also identify him either as the illustrator of the Orosius manuscript in the Bibliothèque Nationale or a member of his shop, an associate whose hand was for all intents and purposes indistinguishable from the master's.

From 1898 when Schumann first published the drawings, scholars have used the two watermarks in the paper support as a means of dating them and determining their place of origin.[21] Some scholars, more intent on collecting data to prove a preconceived point than on investigating the validity of this test without prejudice, have accepted what others reported without fully understanding the limitations and dangers implicit in using watermarks of this early period as a means of determining the date and place of manufacture of a paper and of the words and images it supports. The introductory text in the latest edition of C. M. Briquet's *Les filigranes* gives fair warning.[22] Reynaud (1973, 7), who depended perhaps mostly heavily on the watermarks for evidence, declared that *the* watermark (taking into account only one of the two watermarks that Schumann published), showing the arms of France accompanied by a Gothic *t*, indicates that this is a large-size French paper manufactured in the region of Troyes and distributed toward the north of France and in Paris between 1460 and 1470. She then observed that this dating agrees with the style of the drawing and certain aspects of the costumes. Erlande-Brandenburg, in his review of Reynaud's brilliant article, stated that the watermark allows us to date the paper between 1460 and 1470 in the region of Troyes and that the artist was therefore French or at least working in France.[23] Even Asselberghs, attempting to verify the claims that Schumann and later writers had made for the paper's date and place of manufacture, did not take all the possibilities into account.

To begin with, Schumann in 1898 did not publish photographs of the watermarks but only drawings of them; and he compared these drawings to drawings that Midoux and Matton had published in 1868.[24] These kinds of archaeological drawings are only as accurate as the draftsman was capable of making them. Having made his comparisons, Schumann stated that the paper was probably manufactured in northern France and used in the region of Laon and Soissons between 1463 and 1481.[25] Over the years his followers have chosen to narrow the range of dates down to 1460–70. Some scholars have checked other authorities on watermarks, possibly because they realized that Midoux and Matton's search for dated documents using paper showing these watermarks was limited to archival sources in northern France and naturally would report that the paper had been used there. Asselberghs also studied Briquet's work on watermarks; and while he indicated consequently that the paper had been distributed far more widely than had hitherto been admitted, he did not acknowledge Briquet's much broader range of dates. Instead, Asselberghs (1970, 101–2) concluded that the watermark showing an inverted anchor (the second one that Schumann published) was similar to one used in Champagne, perhaps most in the region of Troyes, whereas Briquet, in the reference Asselberghs used, said that the mark appeared on papers used not only in Troyes and Champagne but also in Lorraine and other places. Following Briquet, Asselberghs indicated that the watermark with the arms of France and the Gothic t showed that the paper was probably made at Troyes. The same mark used on smaller size paper appears, according to Asselberghs, in manuscripts in Troyes, Mézières, Chalons-sur-Marne, and Holland, whereas Briquet indicated that similar variants of the mark were found in papers preserved not only in those places but also in Cologne, Bar-le-Duc, Gaillon, Beauvais, Colmar, Carden, Leiden, Eppelsheim, Amsterdam, Strasbourg, Burgundy, Paris, and Middelburg, and that the dates found in these manuscripts range from 1468 to 1482. Furthermore, in Briquet one can find other variants of these watermarks in paper of manuscripts dating as late as 1521.[26] Neither Matton and Midoux nor Briquet could or did derive their information from paper manufacturers' records but were obliged to deduce all the information they offered from the evidence in the documents in which they found the watermarks. Furthermore the line drawings reproduced in all these books of reference vary slightly among themselves. It is clear that the identification and interpretation of these watermarks is at best a subjective exercise on the parts of both the archivist and the art historian. It is also clear that no one studying this question has yet examined the problem of paper supply and trade in the second half of the fifteenth century. The present author believes it is prudent to treat with a healthy degree of reserve any attribution made of the drawings and tapestries on the grounds of the watermarks found in these papers.

MANUFACTURE AND DATE

Thanks to the extraordinary documentation we have concerning this series of hangings, there is no need to rely on the test of stylistic analysis in order to arrive at the probable date of their manufacture, although the result would be the same. The fully developed style used for narrative subjects in tapestries during the last third of the fifteenth century appears in these pieces as well as in such contemporaneous tapestries as the *Battle of Roncevaux,* of which there are fragments among other places in the Musées Royaux d'Art et d'Histoire in Brussels and the Victoria and Albert Museum in London (Digby 1980, no. 7, pl. 15). In reference to the *Story of the Trojan War* tapestries, we have documents indicating that Charles le Téméraire, duc de Bourgogne, received a set of *Trojan War* tapestries as a gift by September 1472, which most writers believe was the first set woven after this series of cartoons, and that Henry VII of England bought another set in 1488. In both instances the hangings were provided by Pasquier Grenier of Tournai (see Asselberghs 1970, 162–68). An inventory made in 1494 at the château d'Amboise shows that Charles VIII owned a set of eleven pieces (Asselberghs 1970, 168). Souchal produced convincing evidence that Matthias Corvinus, king of Hungary (died 1490), owned a set of these *Trojan War* tapestries.[27] Gómez-Moreno (1919, 268) suggested that the four pieces now in the cathedral church in Zamora may have belonged originally to Fernando I, king of Naples, before 1487. Asselberghs (1970, 172) tended to accept this theory but regarded it only as a hypothesis. This group of early references has been examined by most writers on the subject of the *Trojan War*

242

tapestries. It would be redundant to refer again here to all the sources. The present author refers his readers instead to Asselberghs (1970, 162–72) and Digby (1980, 14–18) as the most complete summaries of the pertinent facts, while wishing to acknowledge at the same time the important critical contributions that Souchal (in Paris 1973) and Reynaud (1973) have made. Recently it was discovered that in 1476 Federico da Montefeltro paid Jean Grenier one-third of the price of a set of eleven *Trojan War* tapestries, clearly a set woven after this series of cartoons.[28]

Every writer who has studied the subject has assumed that the tapestries cited above in connection with specific names and dates were woven after one and the same series of cartoons. That assumption cannot be justified. Most writers, tempted to exploit what appears at first sight to be a set of incontrovertible historical facts, have chosen to ignore certain evidence we have indicating that there may have been different *Trojan War* tapestries being woven about the same time. For example, we know from the inventory of Henry VIII's tapestries (1549) that there were a total of twenty-four *Trojan War* tapestries in the king's collection (Thomson 1930, 252, 253, 258). It is possible but unlikely that all of them were woven after the cartoons for the present series and produced by Pasquier Grenier or his sons.

It is only because an English architect named John Carter made watercolor drawings in 1799 of five *Trojan War* tapestries that were hanging in the Painted Chamber in Westminster Palace at that time that we can associate any surviving *Trojan War* tapestries with Pasquier Grenier. The five hangings Carter illustrated represent the second, third (see fig. 109), fourth, fifth, and tenth compositions in the series under discussion here. Carter made the drawings in connection with his campaign to save these five tapestries, which were damaged and out of fashion, from destruction (see Marillier 1925, and Asselberghs 1970, 99–100). His efforts were successful to the extent that the tapestries were removed from the palace and later sold in London, privately in 1820 and then at auction in 1825. Within a few years they were lost track of. Asselberghs (1970, 166–68) gathered evidence that argues in favor of identifying these five pieces with the set of eleven *Trojan War* tapestries that Henry VII bought from Jean Grenier, one of Pasquier's sons, in 1488. It appears that those hangings can be traced through royal inventories and other documents to 1713 when six of them were prepared for hanging in the House of Commons. Therefore we can be relatively sure that the series of hangings represented by 13a–c and the pieces related to them were being produced by the

Grenier family around 1488. Since it is not impossible but unlikely that Pasquier Grenier and his sons were producing more than one series of *Trojan War* tapestries of such formidable size during those years, we believe that the set of hangings supplied by Pasquier Grenier and given to Charles le Téméraire in 1472 was woven after the same series of cartoons. Reynaud (1973, 14–15) developed an ingenious theory holding that Charles's set was not the editio princeps. However that may be, we know that the cartoons must have been designed at least by 1468 or 1469 because, as other writers have already observed, it would have taken the weavers three or four years to complete so large a set of hangings. We also know that sets of tapestries woven after these cartoons were still being sold in 1488 when Henry VII bought his tapestries, and that they were still in fashion in 1494 or 1495 when, as Souchal has shown, Charles VIII had his emblem woven into the eleven pieces he owned.[29]

As for the place of manufacture, Reynaud (1973, 7) believed that the *Trojan War* tapestries were woven in Tournai. However, as Erlande-Brandenburg observed in his review of Reynaud's article (see note 23), Pasquier Grenier did not necessarily have the hangings woven in Tournai even though his seat of operations was there. Göbel (1923, vol. 1, 407–9) thought he had found the words BRVS. BRABAN. in the Victoria and Albert Museum's tapestry, and he offered that as proof that the *Trojan War* tapestries were woven in Brussels. In fact there is no such inscription in that hanging. We have no reason to attribute these *Trojan War* tapestries to any particular Netherlandish center.

RELATED TAPESTRIES

We know of five fragments of two or more other hangings woven after the same cartoon as 13. The largest fragment, which shows the conference in front of Achilles' tent, the eighth battle, and Hector being armed for war, is preserved in the cathedral church in Zamora (fig. 106). According to Gómez-Moreno (1919, 275) and Asselberghs (1970, 98), its left quarter, showing the battle with the Sagittary, had been partly burned early in this century. That end was then cut off and sold by the cathedral chapter in 1907. The tapestry in its present state has been published by Gómez-Moreno (1919, 275, 277), Asselberghs (1970, 109–11), Souchal (in Paris 1973, 49–55), and, in greatest detail, by Gómez Martínez and Chillón Sampedro.[30] It is one of the four *Trojan War* tapestries that the sixth conde de Alba de Aliste gave to the cathedral in 1619. Tapestry-woven shields bearing his coat of arms appeared at intervals along the top of each hanging. It was discovered early in this century that those shields had been sewn over others in the same places, and the superimposed ones were removed in or before 1925. This revealed the earlier set of shields, bearing the arms of Don Inigo López de Mendoza, second conde de Tendilla and first marqués de Mondéjar (died 1515), as they appear today. However because Don Inigo's coats of arms were woven with weft yarns that differ slightly from the adjacent ones, albeit on the original warp, they must have been added after the tapestries were woven for the original owner. Gómez-Moreno (1919, 268) suggested that this person was probably Fernando I, king of Naples, and that he may have given them to Don Inigo together with some other furnishings in 1487. Other writers have accepted this suggestion with varying degrees of conviction. It seems tenuous at best.

Another fragment, much smaller than the one in Zamora, shows only the figure of the Sagittary and the tangle of bodies that surrounds him. It is now in the Worcester Art Museum (fig. 108). It came from the château de Sully, Maine-et-Loire, and then passed into the collection of Otto Kahn. Later it became the property of Mrs. Aldus Chapin Higgins from whose estate it went as a gift to the Worcester Art Museum. Sewn across the bottom of this fragment is an inscribed banderole that does not belong to it but to some edition of the seventh tapestry in the series, the one illustrating the commemoration of the anniversary of Hector's death (see below). The fragment in Worcester has been published by Asselberghs (1970, 97, 110) and Schrader (in New York 1974, 52).

The third extant fragment from a tapestry representing the sixth subject comprises parts of two banderoles bearing French inscriptions. It is a composite piece that was sewn along the bottom of one of the two *Trojan War* fragments now in the Burrell Collection, the one that shows the ceremony observed on the anniversary of Hector's death (Asselberghs 1970, fig. 17). The left third of the inscription shows part of the verses that appear above the conference episode in the example in Zamora. The right two-thirds portion shows part of the verses that belong on the banderole at the top of the battle with the Sagittary. The Burrell piece, like the fragment in Worcester, came from the château de Sully. It then passed through the Otto Kahn collection and the firm of Arnold Seligmann, Rey, from which Sir William Burrell acquired it.

The fourth fragment is another inscription showing verses in French that refer to the third scene in *The Tent of Achilles*, the eighth battle in the war.[31] It was taken from the top of a complete hanging and sewn across the top of a fragment of tapestry showing a battle; but the composition does not belong to this series of cartoons.

The fifth fragment is one that is not referred to in Asselberghs's work but was discovered later by Reynaud (1973, 10, fig. 28) in a private collection in Paris. It is a composite piece showing primarily the upper left section of the scene of the eighth battle but also including the head of Hupon le Grand from the fifth battle scene and the wounded head of King Menon which appears in a different section of the scene showing the eighth battle. Reynaud (1973, 20 n. 8) suggested that the component parts of this piece may have come from the tapestries that were formerly in the château d'Aulhac.

It has not been mentioned in the literature before this that when 13c was sold from the F. G. Roybet collection in 1877 (see History), two, not one, Gothic tapestries depicting subjects taken from "l'histoire d'Hector" were listed under lot 21. The one whose dimensions were recorded as 4.70 by 2.65 meters must be 13c; it now measures 4.83 by 2.64 meters. It seems possible that the other piece, measuring 3.95 by 1.80 meters, might have come from the same tapestry. If it did, it is now either lost or not yet recognized for what it is.

As early as 1919 Gómez-Moreno had worked out the general outline of the series. He used the evidence of existing pieces, the drawings illustrated by Jubinal (see note 10), and the drawings and fragments of inscriptions in the Louvre. It was he who first established the fact that there were eleven hangings in the series. In only two instances does his identification of specific subjects with specific hangings differ from what we believe is correct today. It was not until 1964 when Asselberghs produced his brilliant and exhaustive study of the tapestries in the cathedral church in Zamora that we had a complete (and apparently accurate) idea of which subjects belong with which pieces. Coming to his subject much later than Gómez-Moreno, Asselberghs could work with the John Carter watercolor drawings, which no student of the subject knew about until 1924 when the Victoria and Albert Museum acquired them. Asselberghs also knew the few more pieces of tapestry that came to light after Gómez-Moreno published his work in 1919.

Asselberghs (1964 and 1970) has shown that the full complement of eleven pieces telling the *Story of the Trojan War* may be described as follows:

1. The mission of Antenor: Priam orders Antenor to travel to Greece and negotiate the return to Troy of the king's sister Hesione. The Greeks refuse the request. Mercury shows the sleeping Paris a vision of the three goddesses and the apple of discord (Asselberghs 1970, 102).

Fig. 109. *The Greeks Capture the City of Tenedon, and Other Subjects,* by John Carter. Drawing, England, 1799. Victoria and Albert Museum, London.

No tapestry showing this subject is known to have survived. The whole composition, except for a bit of the left end where some other figures relating to the eleventh subject have been added, has been preserved in a drawing in the Louvre (no. R.F. 2140; Asselberghs 1970, fig. 1). The left third of the composition is shown in one of the drawings published by Jubinal (Asselberghs 1970, fig. 2).

2. The rape of Helen: Priam sends Paris on the mission that Antenor had failed to bring to the desired end. Instead of following his father's orders, Paris finds Helen in the Temple of Venus on the island of Cythera and takes her to Troy, where she is received in Priam's court (Asselberghs 1970, 103).

There is a complete tapestry of the subject in Zamora (Asselberghs 1970, fig. 3; Souchal in Paris 1973, no. 7, illus.). A small fragment of another edition of the subject, showing heads of soldiers, is in the Museum of Fine Arts, Boston, original source unknown (Asselberghs 1970, fig. 4 bis; Schrader in New York 1974, no. 7, illus.). There is a drawing for the composition in the Victoria and Albert Museum (no. E.2225-1924; Asselberghs 1970, fig. 4).

3. The Greeks prepare to retrieve Helen: Menelaus grieves over the loss of his wife. Achilles and Chalcas each consult the oracle at Delphi. The Greeks attack and capture the city of Tenedon. Ulysses and Diomedes visit Priam's court to discuss Helen's return to Greece, and Telephus prevents Achilles from slaying King Teutras (Asselberghs 1970, 105-7).

A fragment of tapestry in the Burrell Collection, Glasgow, shows the scene at Priam's court (Asselberghs 1970, fig. 5b). Its provenance is not known, but the piece passed through the collections of Lord Howard de Walden and Edson Bradley before Sir William Burrell acquired it. One of the John Carter drawings in the Victoria and Albert Museum (no. E.2235-1924) shows part of the composition (fig. 109 here; Asselberghs 1970, fig. 5a).

4. The Greeks land at Troy: the Greeks, having sailed to Troy, leave their ships and encounter the Trojans in the first great battle of the war (Asselberghs 1970, 107-8).

No tapestry showing this subject is known to have survived. A record of its composition is preserved in two incomplete drawings, one in the Louvre (no. R.F. 2141;

245

Asselberghs 1970, fig. 6) and one in the Victoria and Albert Museum (no. E.2251–1924; Asselberghs 1970, fig. 7).

5. The fourth battle: Helen and Hecuba watch the armies fighting before the walls of Troy. The Trojans capture King Thaos and imprison him in a tower. The Trojan women congratulate their warriors (Asselberghs 1970, 108).

No tapestry showing this subject is known to have survived. The details of the composition as recorded in one of the John Carter drawings (Victoria and Albert Museum, no. E.2245–1924; Asselberghs 1970, fig. 9) differ significantly from those shown in the corresponding drawing in the Louvre (no. R.F. 2142; Asselberghs 1970, fig. 8).

6. The tent of Achilles: see details in the present catalogue entry; also Asselberghs 1970, 109–12.

7. The tenth and twelfth battles: Hector is killed in the tenth battle; later the anniversary of his death is commemorated. Achilles falls in love with Polyxena and consequently tries to convince the Greek chieftains to abandon the siege of Troy. The twelfth battle ensues (Asselberghs 1970, 112–15).

Two fragments from a tapestry woven after this composition have been preserved. One, showing the Trojans commemorating Hector's death, is in the Burrell Collection (Asselberghs 1970, fig. 17). Sewn along the bottom of the field are parts of two banderoles inscribed with verses in French; they were taken from the top of a hanging showing the subject of *The Tent of Achilles* (see details in the present catalogue entry). The other fragment, now in the Worcester Art Museum, shows a scene from the twelfth battle and a conference during which the Greeks agree to continue fighting. Both of these fragments came from the château de Sully, Maine-et-Loire, and passed through the collection of Otto Kahn in New York before going in one case to the Burrell Collection and in the other to the museum in Worcester through the estate of Mrs. Aldus Chapin Higgins (Asselberghs 1970, fig. 18a). A narrow fragment of the drawing for the twelfth battle and the conference is preserved in the Louvre (no. R.F. 2143; Asselberghs 1970, fig. 18b). It is mounted on a sheet next to the narrow drawing for the scene of the arming of Hector (fig. 50 here). A drawing for the scene showing the commemoration of the anniversary of Hector's death is in the Cabinet des Estampes, Bibliothèque Nationale in Paris.[32]

8. Death of Achilles: the eighteenth, nineteenth, and twentieth battles, in which Achilles kills Troilus and Ajax kills Paris, rage on either side of the Temple of Apollo where Achilles falls victim to Paris's arrow (Asselberghs 1970, 115–18).

One of the four tapestries in Zamora shows the entire composition (Asselberghs 1970, fig. 19; Souchal in Paris 1973, no. 9, illus.). One of the drawings in the Louvre (no. R.F. 2144; Asselberghs 1970, fig. 20) also shows this composition.

9. The Amazons come to the aid of the Trojans: the Amazon queen Penthesilea arrives with a thousand of her women to join the Trojans in the twenty-first battle. Ajax Telamon gives Achilles' armor to Pyrrhus to wear, and Penthesilea unseats this young warrior during the twenty-second battle (Asselberghs 1970, 118–20).

A tapestry showing the left three-quarters of the composition is preserved in the Victoria and Albert Museum (Digby 1980, no. 6, pls. 12, 14; Asselberghs 1970, fig. 22). In the early nineteenth century it passed from the château de Bayard (near Grenoble) into the hands of a painter named Richard and then to Achille Jubinal. Jubinal gave it to the Bibliothèque Nationale in Paris, whence it went to his heirs and eventually was acquired by the Victoria and Albert Museum. One of the drawings in the Louvre shows this subject (no. R.F. 2145; Digby 1980, pl. 13; Asselberghs 1970, fig. 21).

10. The death of Penthesilea and the treachery of Antenor and Aeneas: in the twenty-third battle Pyrrhus kills Penthesilea. Antenor and Aeneas steal the Palladium, the statue of Minerva that protects Troy from conquerors. Ulysses and Diomedes pretend to make peace with Priam, and evil omens foretell the fall of Troy (Asselberghs 1970, 120–23).

A fragment of tapestry now in the Montreal Museum of Fine Arts shows the right-central quarter of the composition (Asselberghs 1970, fig. 25b; Schrader in New York 1974, no. 11, illus.).[33] The piece came from the château d'Aulhac and passed through the collections of Count Schouvaloff, Countess Benckendorff, and Duveen Brothers before the museum acquired it. Jubinal's illustrations of the tapestries in the château d'Aulhac show the hanging in its complete state, continuing to both the left and right of the space occupied by this piece (Asselberghs 1970, fig. 25a). A complete hanging woven after the same cartoon but showing a somewhat softer rendering of forms is preserved in the collection of the duque de Alba at the Palacio de Liria in Madrid (Asselberghs 1970, fig. 26). Drawings of the composition are in both the Louvre (no. R.F. 2146; Asselberghs 1970, fig. 23) and the Victoria and Albert Museum (no. E.2238–1924; Asselberghs 1970, fig. 24).

11. The capture and destruction of Troy: the Greeks pretend to leave Troy but stop at Tenedon. Greek war-

riors reenter the city at night and are joined by others who were hidden in the great horse that the Trojans had taken inside the gates. The Greeks ravage Troy. Pyrrhus kills Priam and Polyxena. The narrator in his study laments the fate of the once-great city (Asselberghs 1970, 123–28).

There is a complete hanging illustrating this subject in Zamora (Asselberghs 1970, fig. 27; Souchal in Paris 1973, no. 10, illus.). One of the drawings in the Louvre (no. R.F. 2147; Asselberghs 1970, fig. 28) shows this composition but without the narrator at the right end. A narrow drawing that relates to that scene has been fixed to the left end of the drawing (no. R.F. 2140) that shows the first subject in the series (see paragraph 1 above).

Asselberghs (1970, 172–79) tried to associate the surviving *Trojan War* tapestries with one or another of the sets of hangings that are mentioned in early documents. His work is more convincing than that of his predecessors who made the same attempt; but even Asselberghs, whose command of every detail of this subject was prodigious, landed in a mire of probabilities, possibilities, and questions from which he could draw little that was new concerning the provenance of these pieces. Furthermore this line of inquiry has led writers to regard the few documented sets of hangings as being the only ones that were ever woven and, in some instances, to claim on the slimmest evidence that certain pieces came from sets of hangings owned by important historical figures. In the present writer's opinion, such efforts—except in those few cases where a document or a piece of internal evidence precludes guesswork—are pointless.

PROVENANCE

Various attempts have been made to trace the early history of 13a–c, but none of them has produced convincing results. It was noted above (Condition) that there is reason to ask whether 13a is not all of a piece but rather a composite hanging consisting of a right-hand section taken from the tapestry that was formerly in the château de Sully and a left-hand section taken either from the left end of the tapestry in Zamora or the left end of one formerly in the château d'Aulhac. That question requires further study and must remain unanswered for the present.

As for 13b, Forsyth (1955–56, 82) maintained that it is a fragment of one of the château d'Aulhac tapestries. He pointed to the fact that the colors, the representation of hair and jewels, and particularly the way Agamemnon's name is inscribed on his hat in 13b agree precisely with the corresponding details in Jubinal's illustration of the château d'Aulhac piece[34] and, furthermore, that these details are slightly different in other surviving tapestries that show the same subject. Asselberghs (1964, 37; 1970, 109–10), Reynaud (1973, 10), and Salet (1973, 175–76) all thought it possible or likely that 13b came from the château d'Aulhac tapestry. We agree that there is reason to consider associating 13b with that piece, but neither Forsyth's arguments nor those of his followers prove the point. On one hand, some other details in the Jubinal illustration do not correspond exactly to those in 13b and, on the other, the motifs that Forsyth and Asselberghs cited could have appeared also in one or more other weavings of the sixth composition that have not survived.

Gómez-Moreno (1919, 271), followed by Rorimer (1939, 224), thought that 13c was once part of the corresponding tapestry formerly in the château d'Aulhac. Forsyth (1955–56, 82) and Asselberghs (1964, 37–38) stated that 13c could be the missing right end of that tapestry, specifically because the pattern at the left edge of 13c seems to continue the pattern along the right end of the tapestry that Jubinal illustrated (see Asselberghs 1970, figs. 11a, b). Forsyth observed furthermore that the textile on Hector's horse shows the same pattern as the tabard worn by the figure of Diomedes standing at the left in a *Trojan War* fragment in Montreal (Asselberghs 1970, fig. 25b) and therefore that the two fragments must have come from the same set of hangings. The Montreal piece is believed to have come from one of the château d'Aulhac tapestries. However neither of these arguments offers sufficient proof that 13c came from that hanging. It could have come instead from some undocumented tapestry that has not survived. The textile pattern in question was undoubtedly present in the cartoon and therefore would have appeared in any hanging that was woven from it.

Forsyth (1955–56, 77, 82), believing as Rorimer (1939, 224; 1947, 3) had done that the château d'Aulhac hangings were among the *Trojan War* tapestries that had been given to Charles le Téméraire in 1472, concluded that 13b and c had once belonged to that duke. However Asselberghs (1964, 59–60) found that the château d'Aulhac tapestries had been associated with the duke only on the strength of a vague local tradition. Asselberghs (1970, 164–66) also showed that Charles le Téméraire's tapestries, which were inherited by the emperor Charles V and then by Philip II of Spain and inventoried for the last time in 1598 (when they were described as being in poor condition, some lacking their inscriptions), may have been destroyed in a fire that broke out in 1731 in the royal palace in Brussels. In any event, Asselberghs (1964, 124) made it clear that 13c could not have come from Charles le Téméraire's tapestry of *The Tent of Achilles* because the inventory of 1598 indicates that that piece had lost its inscriptions, and 13c still has inscriptions at the top and bottom.

HISTORY

13a sold, *Collections de M. Raoul Heilbronner*, Galerie Georges Petit, Paris, June 22–23, 1921, no. 240, illus.
Property of Demotte, Paris.
Property of French and Company, New York.
Property of Raimondo Ruíz, Spain.
Purchased for the MMA through the Fletcher Fund, in 1952, from Raimondo Ruíz.

13b purchased in Paris for the MMA, The Cloisters Collection, 1955.

13c sold, [Collection of] M. Roybet [et al.], Hôtel Drouot, Paris, March 24, 1877, no. 21.
Sold, *Collections de M. Jean Dollfus*, pt. 3, Galerie Georges Petit, Paris, April 1 and 2, 1912, no. 189, illus.
Property of Gimpel and Wildenstein in 1915.
Property of French and Company, New York.
Collection of Clarence H. Mackay, New York, from 1916.
Purchased by the MMA through the Fletcher Fund, in 1939, from the estate of Clarence H. Mackay.

EXHIBITIONS

Philadelphia, Pennsylvania Museum, 1915. *Loan Exhibition of Tapestries.* Catalogue by George Leland Hunter. Cat. no. 3 [13c], illus. Lent by Gimpel and Wildenstein.
Amsterdam, Rijksmuseum. 13a said to have been exhibited sometime before 1928 (see Detroit 1928 and Brooklyn 1935 exhibition catalogues below).
Detroit Institute of Arts, 1928. *The Seventh Loan Exhibition: French Gothic Art of the Thirteenth to Fifteenth Century.* Catalogue of tapestries by Adele Coulin Weibel. Cat. no. 98 [13a], illus. Lent by French and Company.
Providence, Rhode Island School of Design, 1930. [Tapestry exhibition], no. 7 [13a]. Lent by French and Company. (See Publications, Banks 1930.)
Philadelphia, Pennsylvania Museum, 1931. *The Art of the Middle Ages.* 13a lent by French and Company. (See Publications, "French & Company Loan Tapestries," 1931; Marceau 1931; and Taylor 1931.)
Brooklyn Museum, 1935. *The Gallery of Medieval Art.* Cat. no. 223 [13a]. Lent by French and Company.
New York, MMA, 1931. *Loan Exhibition of Arms and Armor.* Cat. no. 535 [13c]. Lent by Clarence H. Mackay.
Tournai, 1967. *La tapisserie tournaisienne au XVᵉ siècle.* Catalogue by J. P. Asselberghs. Cat. no. 1 [13c], illus.
New York 1974. Catalogue entry by J. L. S[chrader], no. 8 [13a, b, c]; illus.
Athens, National Pinakothiki Alexander Soutzos Museum, 1979. *Treasures from The Metropolitan Museum of Art, New York: Memories and Revivals of the Classical Spirit.* Cat. no. 5 [13a], illus.

PUBLICATIONS

Gómez-Moreno, Manuel. "La gran tapicería de la guerra de Troya." *Arte Español* 4 (1919) pp. 270–71. 13c mentioned as still in Dollfus collection; illus.

Göbel 1923, vol. 1, p. 407. 13a mentioned; illus. vol. 2, fig. 221.
de Ricci, Seymour. "Résumé d'une note sur les tapisseries gothiques du Siège de Troie." *Comptes rendus de l'Académie des Inscriptions et Belles-Lettres*, 1924, p. 252. 13c mentioned.
Hunter 1925, pp. 73–74, 77, 78. 13a and c discussed briefly; illus. pls. v,a (color detail of 13c), v,b (full view of 13c). In the Limited, Subscription Edition, also pls. s,j–l (details of 13c).
Hunter, George Leland. *Tapestries of Clarence H. Mackay.* New York, 1925, pp. 13, 28–31, 43. 13c discussed; 13c illus. pp. 32, 36–37 (full views), and 28–29, 34, 39–42 (details). Fragment of the MS poem in the Louvre used for the French verse on 13c illus. p. 29.
Marillier, H. C. "The Tapestries of the Painted Chamber." *Burlington Magazine* 46 (1925) pp. 36–37. 13a mentioned.
Hunter, George Leland. "Clarence H. Mackay's Gothic Tapestries." *International Studio* 84, no. 351 (August 1926) pp. 39, 40, 45. 13c discussed; 13c illus. pp. 42 (color detail), 45 (full view).
Frankfurter, Alfred M. "Gothic Trojan War Tapestries." *International Studio* 92, no. 383 (April 1929) pp. 36, 40. 13a and c discussed briefly; 13c illus. p. 36.
Migeon, Gaston. *Les arts du tissu.* Rev. ed. Paris, 1929, pp. 235–36, 238. 13c described, 13a mentioned; 13c illus.
Banks, M. A. "The Tapestry Exhibition." *Bulletin of the Rhode Island School of Design* 18 (1930) pp. 14–15. 13a mentioned.
Thomson 1930, p. 120. 13a mentioned.
"French & Company Loan Tapestries to Pennsylvania." *Art News* 29 (March 21, 1931) p. 17. 13a discussed briefly.
Marceau, Henri G. "The Art of the Middle Ages at Philadelphia." *American Magazine of Art* 22 (1931) pl. facing p. 251. 13a illus. in color, shown on wall of exhibition gallery.
Taylor, Francis Henry. "The Art of the Middle Ages." *The Arts* 17 (1931) p. 483. 13a illus.
Rorimer, James J. "A Fifteenth-Century Tapestry with Scenes of the Trojan War." *MMA Bulletin* 34 (1939) pp. 224–27. 13c discussed in detail; illus. fig. 2 (full view) and cover (detail).
Rorimer, James J. *Mediaeval Tapestries: A Picture Book.* MMA, New York, 1947, p. [3]. 13c discussed briefly; illus. fig. 8.
Forsyth, William H. *A Brief Guide to the Mediaeval Collection.* MMA, New York, 1947, p. 13. 13c mentioned.
Forsyth, William H. "The Trojan War in Medieval Tapestries." *MMA Bulletin*, n.s. 14 (1955–56) pp. 76–84. All three pieces discussed; illus. pp. 77 [13b], 78 [13a], 83 [13c].
Seligman, Germain. *Merchants of Art: 1880–1960.* New York, 1961, pp. 216–17. 13c mentioned.
Scherer, Margaret R. *The Legends of Troy in Art and Literature.* New York, 1963, p. 241. All three pieces mentioned; illus. pls. 64 [13a], 66 [13c].
Asselberghs, J. P. *Les tapisseries flamandes de la cathédrale de Zamora.* Ph.D. diss., Université Catholique de Louvain, 1964, pp. 58–60, 64, 75–76, 124. All three pieces discussed briefly. See also Asselberghs 1970.
Weigert, Roger-Armand. *La tapisserie et le tapis en France.* Paris, 1964, p. 39. 13a and c mentioned; 13c illus. facing p. 27.
Verlet 1965, p. 19. 13c mentioned.
Asselberghs, J. P. "Les tapisseries tournaisiennes de la guerre de Troie." *Revue Belge d'Archéologie et d'Histoire de l'Art* 39 (1970) pp. 94–98, 109–11, 173–75. All three pieces discussed; illus. figs. 11b [13c], 12 [13b], 13 [13a].
Reynaud, Nicole. "Un peintre français cartonnier de tapisseries au XVᵉ siècle: Henri de Vulcop." *Revue de l'Art*, no. 22 (1973) p. 20 n. 8. 13b mentioned.
Salet, Francis. "Chronique." *Bulletin Monumental* 131 (1973) pp. 175–76. All three pieces mentioned.
Souchal in Paris 1973, pp. 52–54. All three pieces mentioned.
Freeman, Margaret B. *The Unicorn Tapestries.* MMA, New York, 1976, fig. 243. 13c illus. next to the Louvre drawing for it.
Coffinet 1977, p. 59. 13a illus.
Digby 1980, p. 17. 13a and c mentioned.

NOTES

1. Letter to the present author from Scot McKendrick, London, July 24, 1985, now in the files of the MMA Department of Medieval Art.

2. Jean-Paul Asselberghs began his monumental study of the *Trojan War* tapestries in connection with the doctoral dissertation he submitted in 1964, and he continued and refined his study in several later publications (see Publications). The mass of information he gathered from primary and secondary sources has become the foundation on which all subsequent studies are based. The present author acknowledges his own debt in this regard. Asselberghs, in reference to his study of the literary sources that the author or designer of the tapestries might have used, acknowledged that he based his own work on A. Joly, *Benoît de Sainte-More et le Roman de Troie* (Paris, 1871); see Asselberghs, "Les tapisseries tournaisiennes de la guerre de Troie," *Revue Belge d'Archéologie et d'Histoire de l'Art* 39 (1970) p. 157.

3. Unpublished note by Margaret R. Scherer in the files of the MMA Department of Medieval Art, submitted in connection with her intensive study of the Trojan War story as represented in the arts, *The Legends of Troy in Art and Literature* (New York, 1963).

4. Four of the handwritten octaves in French that have been preserved with the drawings in the Louvre were illustrated by Schumann, *Der trojanische Krieg*, text volume (see note 10 below); Asselberghs, "Les tapisseries tournaisiennes de la guerre de Troie," p. 101, stated that eighteen stanzas mounted on a single sheet had survived with the drawings and that a prose comment on the war deaths had been inserted between two of them by a different hand. We found that seventeen bits of paper inscribed with French verses are mounted on one sheet. Sixteen of them have one stanza each. The seventeenth bit has one octave at each end and, between them, the addition that Asselberghs mentioned.

5. Phyllis Ackerman, *Tapestry: The Mirror of Civilization* (New York, London, and Toronto, 1933) pp. 214–15.

6. See Eduardo Torra de Arana et al., *Los tapices de La Seo de Zaragoza* (Saragossa, 1985) pp. 122–29, text and illus.

7. See *David and Bathsheba: Ten Early Sixteenth-Century Tapestries from the Cluny Museum in Paris*, exh. cat., MMA (New York, 1974) nos. 1 and 10, text and illus.

8. Guy Delmarcel, "Colecciones del Patrimonio Nacional: Tapices I. Los Honores," *Reales Sitios* 16, no. 62 (1979) pp. 46, 48, text and illus.

9. See Asselberghs, "Les tapisseries tournaisiennes de la guerre de Troie," fig. 11a, which reproduces Jubinal's illustration of the corresponding tapestry formerly in the château d'Aulhac in which the name is spelled PONIPENA.R. It is spelled correctly, as POLIXENAR, in the tapestry in Zamora. The misspelling might have appeared in the cartoon after which 13 and the château d'Aulhac tapestry were woven; on the other hand, Jubinal's illustration may depict 13a itself in a former state; or, if 13a is not part of that hanging, it may have been restored using the illustration as a pattern.

10. Paul Schumann, *Der trojanische Krieg* (Dresden, 1898), was published in two volumes. The smaller one contains text treating the drawings and their two watermarks, drawings of the watermarks, illustrations of four French octaves, and reproductions of the prints after drawings by Victor Sansonetti that accompany the texts for the *Trojan War* tapestries in Achille Jubinal, *Les anciennes tapisseries historiées* (Paris, 1838) vol. 1, pp. 39–40, vol. 2, pp. 9–10. The folio volume of Schumann contains photographic reproductions of the drawings now in the Louvre.

11. Michèle Hébert, "Un 'petit patron' de tapisserie du XVᵉ siècle au Cabinet des Estampes, la 'Commémoration de la Mort d'Hector,'" *Gazette des Beaux-Arts*, 6th ser., 87 (1976) pp. 109–10.

12. These variations became apparent as we compared words in the French verses in 13c with words in the corresponding inscription on one of the paper fragments in the Louvre which is illustrated in

George Leland Hunter, *Tapestries of Clarence H. Mackay* (New York, 1925) p. 29. Two words are longer in the tapestry inscription than in the penned one: *aler* and *pleur* become *aller* and *pleurs* in the tapestry, which are spelling changes, not elisions.

13. Eugène Müntz, "Bibliographie" (review of Schumann, *Der trojanische Krieg*), *La Chronique des Arts*, August 20, 1898, p. 263.

14. Jean Guiffrey, "La guerre de Troie: A propos de dessins récemment acquis par le Louvre," pt. 2, *La Revue de l'Art Ancien et Moderne* 5 (1899) pp. 515–16.

15. Nicole Reynaud, "Un peintre français cartonnier de tapisseries au XVᵉ siècle: Henri de Vulcop," *Revue de l'Art*, no. 22 (1973) pp. 19, 21nn. 55–57. Mme. Reynaud's brilliant article on the Louvre drawings represents the most authoritative and provocative study we have concerning the search for the tapestry designer. The present author acknowledges his debt to her leadership.

16. Hermann Schmitz, *Bildteppiche* (Berlin, [1919]) pp. 196, 200.

17. Asselberghs, "Les tapisseries tournaisiennes de la guerre de Troie," p. 180. The note of payment in complete form reads as follows: "Item en trois parques de pappier, trois histoires de Troie, pour ce un écu" (from comte De Laborde, *Les ducs de Bourgogne*, pt. 2 [Paris, 1849–52] vol. 2, pp. 217–18).

18. Reference from J. P. Asselberghs, *La tapisserie tournaisienne au XVᵉ siècle*, exh. cat. (Tournai, 1967) n. 36: E. Dhanens, "Jan Van Roome alias Van Brussel, Schilder," *Gentse Bijdragen tot de Kunstgeschiedenis* 11 (1945–48) p. 106.

19. Frits Lugt, *Inventaire général des dessins des écoles du Nord: Maîtres des anciens Pays-Bas nés avant 1550*, Musée du Louvre (Paris, 1968) p. 17.

20. Nicole Reynaud, "La résurrection de Lazare et le Maître de Coëtivy, *La Revue du Louvre* 15 (1965) pp. 171–82; see pp. 173 n. 4 and 181 n. 15 for citations of Durrieu's studies.

21. Schumann, *Der trojanische Krieg*, gave drawings of the two watermarks on p. 7 of the text volume.

22. C. M. Briquet, *Les filigranes* (1907; reprint, Amsterdam, 1968) vol. 1, pp. 31–34.

23. A. Erlande-Brandenburg, "Chronique" (review of Reynaud, "Un peintre français cartonnier de tapisseries"), *Bulletin Monumental* 133 (1975) p. 88.

24. Etienne Midoux and Auguste Matton, *Etude sur les filigranes des papiers employés en France au XIVᵉ et XVᵉ siècles* (Paris, 1868) drawings of watermarks following p. 20.

25. Schumann, *Der trojanische Krieg*, text vol., pp. 6–8.

26. Briquet, *Les filigranes*, vol. 3 (plates), variants of watermarks numbered 1739, 1740, 1741, 1748, ranging in date of use from 1458 to 1521 and in place of use from northern France through the Netherlands to Germany.

27. Geneviève Souchal, "Charles VIII et la tenture de la Guerre de Troie," *Revue Belge d'Archéologie et d'Histoire de l'Art* 39 (1970) p. 187 n. 4.

28. See C. H. Clough, "Economic Documents Relating to the Decoration, 1472–1482, of Federico da Montefeltro's Palaces at Urbino and Gubbio," *Notizie da Palazzo Albani* 15, no. 1 (1986) pp. 26–29.

29. Souchal, "Charles VIII et la tenture de la Guerre de Troie," p. 186.

30. Amando Gómez Martínez and Bartolomé Chillón Sampedro, *Los tapices de la Catedral de Zamora* (Zamora, 1925) pp. 70–74.

31. Present location unknown. See *Catalogue des sculptures . . . composant la Collection de M. F. Roybet*, sale cat., Galerie Georges Petit, Paris, November 19, 1920, no. 109, illus. The catalogue describes the verse as rendered in white letters on a red ground.

32. Hébert, "Un 'petit patron,'" p. 109, fig. 2.

33. See also Philippe Verdier, "The Medieval Collection," *Apollo* 103 (1976) pp. 366–67, and pl. 1. Verdier accepted the tradition that the tapestries in the château d'Aulhac had belonged to Charles le Téméraire but, following Reynaud, he believed that they were not the first set of weavings made from the cartoons.

34. Jubinal, *Les anciennes tapisseries historiées*, vol. 2, pl. 3 of "Tapisseries d'Aulhac" following text p. 10.

Antependium or dossal for an altar

Southern Netherlands, 1475–1550
Wool warp; wool, silk, silver, and gilt wefts
3 ft. 8 1/4 in. × 6 ft. 11 in. (1.12 m × 2.11 m)
17–20 warp yarns per inch, 7–8 per centimeter
The Cloisters Collection, 1952 (52.34)

CONDITION

The fabric has been cut on all four sides and bands of modern weaving have been sewn to the edges. A narrow strip of tapestry taken from another part of this piece or from a closely related hanging has been sewn along the left side. Since there is a virtually uninterrupted line of plants with complete bases across the bottom, that edge seems to have lost little of its original fabric. The pattern is also fairly complete along the top. However the plants along the right side have been cut into and that edge has been completely rewoven. Therefore it appears that the tapestry has preserved all or most of its original height but lost some of its field at each end.

There are other repairs by reweaving along the left and right ends of the bottom edge, in a few of the floral motifs near the upper left and lower right corners of the field, and in both heraldic shields. The representations of the instruments of the Passion have also been rewoven in part, most notably the shaft of the trumpet at the left, the ground of Veronica's veil, the hexagonal pot near the base of the cross at the right, and parts of the face and aura of the moon in the upper right section. The effect that these changes have had on the original drawing is negligible. Although the metal yarns have darkened, the wool and silk yarns still show fairly bright colors. The ground behind the flowers, which was probably dark green originally, is now dark blue.

DESCRIPTION AND SUBJECT

The hanging shows a field densely covered with flowering plants of many kinds.[1] Each plant occupies what is essentially a rectangular compartment of space, and these compartments have been arranged in vertical rows. The instruments of the Passion, which are also the charges in the *Arma Christi*, or coat of arms of the Savior, are displayed against this ground. In the center the cross rises from the hill of Golgotha; Adam's skull appears at its foot. The three nails are still in place on

the cross, and two scourges hang from the crossbar, next to the crown of thorns which has been hung over the top of the cross. The sign INRI (*Iesus Nazarenus Rex Iudaeorum*) is fixed to the top of the shaft. The ladder rests with its upper end against the left end of the crossbar, and Veronica's veil hangs between the ladder and the shaft of the cross. What appears to be the fine robe in which Herod sent Christ back to Pilate, rather than the plain seamless coat that is usually represented in this context, has been hung over one of the ladder's lower rungs. Two torches made of bound reeds or faggots stand upright in the middle distance, one to the left of the ladder, the other to the right of the cross. The thieves' crosses, each with its base set in a hillock, flank these elements. From the right end of the crossbar at the left hangs Judas's purse. The ewer and basin of water in which Pilate washed his hands, together with the hammer used to nail Christ to the cross, rest on the hillock below. Above them appear the head of a man spitting, a hand clenched into a fist, and another hand with the palm flat, all referring to the taunting and beating of Christ during His interrogation. There is another symbol connected with these, a hand pulling locks of Christ's hair, to the left of the shaft of the other thief's cross. To the left of the first thief's cross rises the pillar where Christ was flogged, together with the rope that bound Him to it. The cock that crowed after Peter had denied Jesus three times stands atop the pillar. A tall trumpet with a banner hanging from its shaft stands upright next to the pillar. This probably refers to the trumpet in Matthew 24:30–31, the trumpet that sounds when Christ's angels bring His elect together.

Between the main cross and the thief's cross at the right stands the reed carrying the sponge dipped in vinegar that was held up to the crucified Christ. From the left end of the crossbar of this thief's cross hangs a knife that refers to Peter's cutting off Malchus's ear when Christ was apprehended. Below it appear the three dice

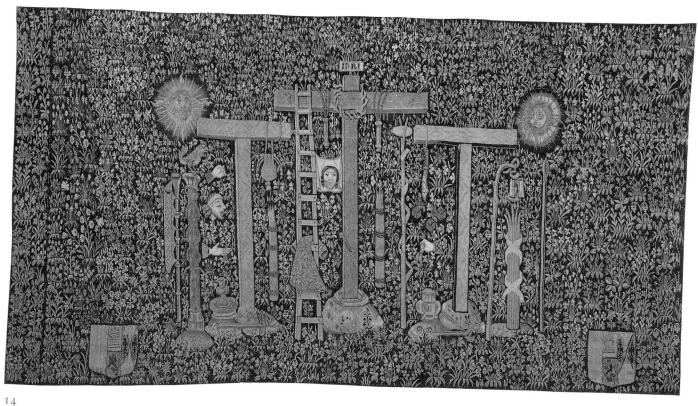

that the soldiers used to gamble over Christ's garments. The pot of vinegar stands on a rock next to the base of the cross, and the pincers used to remove the nails rest on the ground. To the right of this cross, and hanging from the curved end of a gnarled staff, is the lantern with which Judas's men sought out Christ after the betrayal. Beneath the lantern stands a bundle of reeds bound together with a girdle or stole. It may refer to the reeds that Christ's mockers struck Him with. To the right of this stands the lance with which the centurion pierced Christ's side. At the upper corners of the field appear the veiled sun (above the crowing cock next to the left-hand thief's cross) and the veiled moon (above the lance at the right). The plain dark ground that surrounds each heavenly body may be interpreted either as a reference to the darkness that engulfed the earth between the sixth and ninth hours on that day or, more likely, simply as a formal device to set the rays of light off from the rather similar plant forms that surround them.

A shield blazoned with the arms of the dukes of Segorbe appears in each lower corner of the field. The arms are as follows: tierced in pale; 1, or, four pales gules (Aragón); 2, party per fess, gules, a castle with three towers or, voided azure (Castile), and argent, a lion gules, langued and crowned or (León); 3, or, four pales gules, flanked saltirewise argent, two eagles sable, crowned or (Sicily). When the tapestry was exhibited in Paris in 1928, and again when it was sold in 1938 (see Exhibitions and History), the coat of arms was described as that of Isabel and Fernando of Spain. In 1953 Rorimer published the arms correctly as referring to a member of the house of Aragón-Segorbe, specifically to Don Enrique II, cousin of Fernando el Católico, Infante de Aragón, who held among other titles those of duque de Segorbe and conde de Ampurias. In connection with a study van de Put made of this coat of arms as it appeared on a Valencian earthenware bottle of the first half of the sixteenth century, he noted that in this form the arms could have been borne by any one of the three successive dukes of Segorbe, that is, by Enrique II (died 1522), Alfonso (died 1562), or Francisco de Aragón Folch de Cardona (died 1575).[2] Although Rorimer did not specify his reason for associating the coat of arms with the first duke, he probably did so because he believed that the tapestry was woven during the last quarter of the fifteenth century. However it is possible that the piece dates from a later period and that it was ordered by Enrique's son Alfonso, second duque de Segorbe (see Manufacture and Date).

Silk weft yarns were used in the passages of weaving showing the flowers, the instruments of the Passion, and the coats of arms. The metal yarns, made of flat, narrow silver or gilt metal wires wrapped spirally around silk core yarns, appear in the representations of the heads, the instruments, and the shields.

As noted above (Condition) the tapestry appears to have retained almost all of its original height, but it has lost some of the field at both sides. While its height, which originally must have been at least 45 inches (1.14 m), is still within the range of dimensions for an antependium, it is also a suitable height for a dossal. The present width, almost 7 feet (2.11 m), seems suitable for a dossal but narrow for an antependium. However the width has been reduced and there is no way of determining what the original dimension was.

SOURCE OF THE DESIGN

The composition of the instruments of the Passion probably derives from a drawing, painting, or print showing the *Arma Christi* as represented by a special cult or order (the choice of symbols is very particular). A note written on the back of an early photograph of the tapestry that was taken before it left Spain states that it came originally from a Carthusian monastery, that of Val de Cristo near Segorbe in the province of Valencia.[3]

MANUFACTURE AND DATE

The tapestry was exhibited in Paris in 1928 as a Franco-Flemish piece dating from the end of the fifteenth century. When Crick-Kuntziger (1928, 215–16) discussed it in the context of that exhibition, she accepted the date but for a number of reasons concluded that the tapestry had been woven in Spain. Her arguments included the fact that it displays a Spanish coat of arms and an unusual kind of millefleurs ground. Furthermore, she knew no other pieces in which there is such a discrepancy between the character of the drawing, which she regarded as crude, and the delicacy of the execution. Finally, she cited studies indicating that tapestry weavers were active in Barcelona in the late fourteenth century and the fifteenth century and that tapestries "à décors d'armoiries et à fond de fleurettes" were being woven there. On the strength of this, Crick-Kuntziger suggested that the tapestry might be one of the pieces

that had been woven in Barcelona. When it was sold at auction in 1938 it was described as a Franco-Flemish piece of the end of the fifteenth century. Rorimer (1952–53, 276) repeated the date but changed the attribution to Brussels without explanation. Berliner (1955, 90), following Crick-Kuntziger, thought the tapestry was probably Spanish.

Crick-Kuntziger's tentative attribution to Barcelona is ingenious but untenable. We do not know what late fourteenth- or fifteenth-century tapestries woven in Barcelona looked like. Furthermore we know that during the fifteenth century and later, affluent clients in other parts of Europe sent designs to the southern Netherlands to be executed in tapestry. Others imported Netherlandish weavers to produce tapestries for them on home ground. It seems more than likely that one of the dukes of Segorbe arranged with a tapestry producer to have the piece woven in the Netherlands.

Since we cannot date millefleurs grounds with any degree of precision, and since there is nothing else in the pattern to enable us to date the piece stylistically, we are bound to conclude that it could have been woven anytime from the late fifteenth century to the middle of the sixteenth. The history of the dukes of Segorbe bears out this conclusion. Enrique II de Aragón, who was made duke in 1472 and died in 1522, could have ordered the tapestry, as his son Alfonso (died 1562) also could have done. The third duke was not born until 1539, so it is unlikely that it would have been he who ordered it. According to an entry in the catalogue of the Valencian exhibition of 1910 (see Exhibitions) this piece is listed in the inventory of Don Berenguer Torres y Aguilar which is dated April 30, 1507. If the tapestry was correctly identified as the piece mentioned in the inventory then certainly it was woven before 1507. Further research will be required to confirm this identification. As for the place of manufacture, it could have been anywhere in the southern Netherlands.

RELATED TAPESTRIES

The tapestry appears to have survived as a unique piece. No duplicate hangings, no pieces that might have been associated with it in a series of ecclesiastical decorations, are known to have survived. The narrow strip of millefleurs tapestry that was added along the left edge agrees in pattern precisely with the rest of the field, so it probably came from another part of this hanging. However the strip might have come from a corresponding antependium if this was a dossal, or the reverse. It could also have come from another dossal or antependium belonging with this example in a set of altar hangings with matching fields but different motifs pertaining to certain days or seasons in the liturgical year.

In terms of subject matter only the Metropolitan Museum's hanging is related generically to three millefleurs tapestries in the chapel of the château des ducs d'Anjou in Angers that show angels carrying instruments of the Passion. Erlande-Brandenburg discovered that these pieces would have been ordered between June 2, 1512, and April 22, 1513.[4]

HISTORY

Said to have come from the charterhouse of Val de Cristo near Segorbe in Valencia.
Said to have belonged to Don Berenguer Torres y Aguilar, Spain, in 1507.
In the collection of the marqués de Dos Aguas, Valencia, by 1910.
Bought by Maurice Harris, Spanish Art Gallery, London, in 1928.
Sold, *Italian Majolica . . . Tapestry . . . by order of George Durlacher,* Christie's, London, April 6–7, 1938, no. 234, illus.
Property of F. A. Drey, London.
Purchased by the MMA, The Cloisters Collection, 1952.

EXHIBITIONS

Valencia, 1910. *Exposición Nacional de Valencia, Sección de arte retrospectivo.* Cat. no. 1073, pp. 40, 42 note. Lent by the marqués de Dos Aguas.
Paris, Musée de la Manufacture Nationale des Gobelins, 1928. *La tapisserie gothique.* Cat. no. 36. Lent from a private collection.
New York, MMA, The Cloisters, 1953. *New Acquisitions for The Cloisters.*
Ithaca, New York, Andrew Dickson White Museum, Cornell University, 1968. *A Medieval Treasury.*
Utica, New York, Munson-Williams-Proctor Institute, 1968. *A Medieval Treasury.*

PUBLICATIONS

Manufacture Nationale des Gobelins. *La tapisserie gothique.* Paris, [1928], no. 58. Described briefly; illus. pl. 58.
Crick-Kuntziger, Marthe. "L'exposition de tapisseries gothiques au Musée des Gobelins." *La Revue d'Art* 29 (1928) pp. 215–16. Discussed at length; illus. fig. 3.
Die Weltkunst 12, no. 18/19 (1938) p. 2. Illus., with caption.
Rorimer, James J. "Acquisitions for The Cloisters." *MMA Bulletin,* n.s. 11 (1952–53) p. 276. Discussed briefly; illus. p. 281.
Berliner, Rudolf. "Arma Christi." *Münchner Jahrbuch der Bildenden Kunst,* 3d ser., 6 (1955) p. 90. Mentioned.
Verlet 1965, p. 19. Mentioned.
Crockett, Lawrence J. "The Identification of a Plant in the Unicorn Tapestries." *Metropolitan Museum Journal* 17 (1982) pp. 16–17 and n. 7. Discussed briefly; illus. figs. 6, 8 (detail).

NOTES

1. Lawrence J. Crockett, "The Identification of a Plant in the Unicorn Tapestries," *Metropolitan Museum Journal* 17 (1982) pp. 16–17, observed that there are four representations of the rarely depicted sawfruit among the plants in this tapestry.
2. Albert van de Put, *Hispano-Moresque Ware of the Fifteenth Century: Supplementary Studies and Some Later Examples* (London, 1911) pp. 54–57, figs. 20, 23, 24.
3. The photograph was sent to Rorimer with a letter from Juan Ainaud de Lasarte dated in Barcelona, February 23, 1955. Both the letter and the photograph are now in the files of the MMA Department of Medieval Art.
4. See Souchal in Paris 1973, nos. 40–42, for illustrations and discussion of the tapestries in Angers. For details on dating these pieces by means of the coats of arms represented on them, see Alain Erlande-Brandenburg, "A propos d'une exposition: La tapisserie de choeur des anges porteurs des instruments de la Passion dans la chapelle du château d'Angers," *Le Journal des Savants,* January–March 1974, pp. 62–69. See also Jean-Bernard de Vaivre's comments on the dating by heraldry in "Chronique," *Bulletin Monumental* 133 (1975) p. 87, and also in de Vaivre, "L'héraldique et l'histoire de l'art du moyen âge," *Gazette des Beaux-Arts,* 6th ser., 93 (1979) p. 105.

15
The Fall and Redemption of Man

Southern Netherlands, 1480–90
Wool warp; wool, silk, silver, and gilt wefts
10 ft. 2 ¹/₄ in. × 12 ft. 9 in. (3.11 m × 3.89 m)
17–18 warp yarns per inch, 7 per centimeter
Bequest of Oliver H. Payne, 1917 (17.189)

CONDITION

Except for some losses and restorations that the hanging has suffered along the left edge, the bottom, and the left end of the top edge, the extent of the original fabric remains relatively intact. The wide striped guards bordering the four sides are modern. A narrow wedge-shaped piece of modern weaving has been inserted along the top of the field from its left end to a point about midway along the top of the compartment that occupies that corner. The slender column that rises along the left side of the field is a modern restoration duplicating the original column at the right. The scalloped band along the bottom of the field and the jeweled band below it are also restorations. A few more insertions of modern weaving appear in the field. The most important ones occur next to the right hand of the thief at Christ's right side, in the regions of the right hand and left ankle of the woman standing in the lower left compartment, and also in the head of the ox or horse in the background of the same scene.

The fabric has been repaired extensively by reweaving new weft yarns on the original warp. These restorations appear in all parts of the field but especially in the highlights where the silk yarns had deteriorated and fallen out and also in the places where the darkest wool yarns were missing. Many of these wefts were replaced either with a bright yellow-green wool yarn or wool yarns that are now brown but were originally dark blue and possibly also other dark hues. Most of the costumes and some of the letters in the inscriptions have been repaired in this way. The restorations have affected the color balance of the design more than the quality of its drawing, which seems for the most part to have been changed relatively little. However the repairs have made the letters inscribed on the scrolls and on some of the garment borders virtually illegible. There was a wide range of both pale and intense tones in the original palette and most of these have survived, some having faded more than others. Both the gilt yarns (narrow, flat gilded wires wound spirally on a core of pale orange silk) and the finer silver ones (narrow, flat silver wires wound spirally on a white-silk core) have tarnished and now read either as black or dark bluish gray yarns.

DESCRIPTION AND SUBJECT

The field is divided into five roughly circular compartments, each of which contains a narrative scene, and seven interval spaces of irregular shape and size. The ground in these spaces looks like a plain surface of polychrome marble. The two smallest spaces, which are the spandrels of arches that border the top of the field in the center, are filled with filigree work. The three largest spaces, in the upper left and right corners of the field and in the center at the bottom, contain human figures holding inscribed scrolls. The two remaining interval spaces, in the lower corners of the field, contain a pelican and its young (left) and a lion and its cubs (right). Grapevines bearing fruit and leaves appear alongside these figures. The five pictorial compartments have borders made of wide gold moldings decorated with cabochons of various colors, pearls, and short vine branches bearing leaves and bunches of grapes. The molding at the top of the central medallion is elevated and becomes an arch carried on a pair of short faceted marble shafts that also support the inner ends of the moldings belonging to the two compartments at the sides. A pair of slender columns with segmented shafts rise along the left and right sides of the field. As noted above, the column at the left, while not original, is an exact copy of the one on the right. The lowest segment of the shaft, a bit more than a third of the column's total height, is encrusted with small rectangles of polychrome marble wrapped diagonally in two directions with narrow bands of gold. A molded gold collar tops this segment and becomes the base of the next section which is encrusted with gold set with ovoid gemstones. Another gold collar separates this segment from the uppermost one, which is made of a slender marble cylinder wrapped spirally with a gold

254

15

Detail of 15

band whose sides are serrated like the edges of a holly leaf. What may have been a small statue representing a human figure—the poor condition of the fabric in this place makes it difficult to interpret the form precisely—surmounts the column at the right. Since such a figure stands atop the restored left-hand column, it seems likely that the restorer placed it there to balance one that was present on the other side at the time the repair was done.

A representation of the Crucifixion fills most of the space inside the central and largest compartment. An abbreviated version of the Nativity occupies the lower left curve of the same compartment. The cross has an elaborately carved shaft and cross beam and a short top represented as a shallow tabernacle inside which the letters INRI are inscribed. The figure of Christ, nude except for a loincloth, hangs on the cross with closed eyes, His head crowned with thorns and dropping to the left. Behind Him appear the two thieves on their crosses, the beardless one to the left of Christ hanging with drooping arms and head in an attitude of submission. The other one, with a small beard standing erect, arches his body violently backward in his struggle to be free. Above the three figures a cloudy sky appears with the sun at the left and the crescent moon at the right. Below this a rolling landscape stretches not only into the far distance but also to the left and right where it also serves as the landscape setting for the scenes enclosed in the compartments that flank this one in the upper corners of the field. At the base of the cross the skull and one bone of Adam's skeleton lie on the ground, having been thrown up from his tomb as the earth trembled and shook at the moment Christ died. To the right of this, in the scene that fills the right half of the foreground, John looks up at the tortured figure while he and a woman standing next to him support the arms and shoulders of the swooning Mary. John wears a patterned cope-like mantle over a patterned gown. The Virgin, dressed in a patterned mantle over a loose, patterned gown, wears a white headcloth with a veil under her chin. The cuffs of her narrow sleeves are embroidered with pearls and gemstones, and the border of her mantle is inscribed with Latin letters that seem to be purely decorative and without meaning. The woman holding her from behind wears a gown with a fitted bodice and a girdle, and she has a striped scarf around her head. The two elder men among the four who stand behind this group of figures raise their hands in gestures of distress. Another man stands opposite them on the other side of the cross, and in front of him appear the mounted figure of Longinus plunging his lance into Christ's side and also the figure of a turbaned man who from his position behind the

blind soldier guides the lance with his own left hand. The garments that both of these men wear, and the horse's panoply, are elaborately patterned.

The Nativity scene is set in the stable; but since there is no clear line of demarcation separating its actors from those in the Crucifixion, and since both groups of figures are drawn to the same scale and lighted from the upper left, the two events seem to be occurring in the same place and simultaneously. Mary, wearing a patterned mantle over a patterned loose gown, her long fair hair falling to the sides in soft waves, kneels in prayer before the nude Child who lies on a fold of her mantle on the ground before her. Rays of light emanate from the tiny figure who looks up at His mother and raises His right hand in benediction. Joseph, wearing a patterned hood, mantle, and gown, sits in the background at the entrance to the stable, his head bowed slightly forward, his hands clasped over the top of a cane on which he leans. His gaze is directed to the right, toward the Crucifixion, his face sad, his forehead set in a frown.

In the upper left compartment Adam and Eve are shown in the verdant landscape of Paradise. They walk toward the right in the company of two angels who guide them forward. The man and woman are nude. Each holds one hand down to cover the groin and one hand up in a gesture that indicates they are speaking. The angels wear elaborately patterned copes bordered with pearls and gemstones over patterned robes. The lower right hem of the cope worn by the angel at the left is inscribed with letters that are partly hidden but seem to read (left to right) R or B, OEL, and then A or T. These have been interpreted in a number of different ways (see Source of the Design). The scene continues in the compartment at the upper right corner of the field. There God the Father stands in the company of three angels. All four figures are richly dressed in patterned garments trimmed with pearls and gemstones. God, wearing the tiara on His head, raises His left hand in a gesture that indicates that He is talking to Adam and Eve.

Directly below this another scene appears in a larger compartment whose upper left quarter disappears behind the adjacent part of the central compartment. An elderly bearded man wearing a rich mantle over a girdled tunic and a longer robe beneath that, all elaborately patterned, stands in the center of the space. The tables of the Law which he holds in his right hand and points to with his left hand identify him as Moses. The letters inscribed on the stones are nearly illegible now, but in 1918 Porter studied them and believed they represent words paraphrased from the Decalogue combined with meaningless letters.[1] He thought he could read the words *nec jura vana* (referring to Exodus 20:7: "Non assumes nomen Domini Dei tui in vanum" ["Thou shalt not take the name of the Lord thy God in vain"]) and also *mm̃ sabba scīfices* (Exodus 20:8: "Memento, ut diem sabbati sanctifices" ["Remember that thou keep holy the sabbath day"]). Five richly dressed people are seated around Moses, two men at the left, two men and a woman at the right. A broad landscape opens out behind the figures. In the middle distance at the left Moses is shown kneeling before a figure of God the Father in the clouds. The Deity hands him the two inscribed tables. This scene must represent the second occasion on which God gave the Law to Moses, the first set of tables having been broken when Moses returned from Mount Sinai the first time and dashed them to the ground in his anger at finding the Israelites worshiping the golden calf. He is shown here explaining the Commandments to his repentant people.

The scene in the compartment in the lower left corner of the field shows in the foreground an elderly bearded man wearing a plain hood and a patterned mantle standing between two women. He raises his right hand straight upward and points toward it with his left hand. The gesture suggests that he is engaged in conversation with the woman standing at the left; but he may also be pointing to one or both of the men who stand behind her. One of these men, the one standing at the right, seems to be shouting in anger. Two younger men and another figure, perhaps a woman, stand in the middle distance at the left, outside the vaulted structure in which the first five figures stand. The young man at the left wears a mantle decorated at the hem with a band of letters which do not seem to spell words. Both women inside the structure wear richly patterned fitted gowns; the dress on the one standing at the left is also embroidered with pearls. This woman has a turban and two veils and in her left hand carries by its handle a covered wicker or reed basket. The other woman, seated, wears a hood over a veil; in her lap she holds a small basket that has a cover but no handle. A bit of landscape appears in the distance in the upper left corner of the scene while in the lower right corner there is a partial view into a space occupied by two quadrupeds. One of them has the antlers of a stag, the other the head of a horse.

In the upper left corner of the field, between the compartment containing the Paradise scene and the column that rises along that side of the tapestry, sits an elderly man dressed in a plain hood and a richly patterned velvet or damask gown. In his left hand he holds the bottom of an inscribed scroll that curls upward to fill the space above his head, a space that also shows a section of a grapevine complete with its leaves and fruit. The inscription, like the others that will be recorded here presently, was first read by Porter in 1918 when the letters and figures were more legible than they are now.[2] All subsequent transcriptions derive from his. Our own readings are based on a fresh study made in 1988, but they necessarily incorporate Porter's transcriptions in the places where the letters are now illegible because they have faded, deteriorated, or been restored incorrectly. We offer the following transcription of the text on this scroll:

Vinea · dabit · fructū/suum · zacha[rie?] vii

(The vine shall yield her fruit. Zacharias 7 [from Zacharias 8:12: "But there shall be the seed of peace: the vine shall yield her fruit, and the earth shall give her increase"]).

It is clear therefore that the figure in the upper left corner of the field is the prophet Zacharias. There is what appears to be another inscription in the border that runs along the bottom of his gown. It has been read in several different ways. Our own reading is as follows:

DIT · DEET · DOEN [the N reversed] MA K [or V?]. . . .

Steppe (1976, 205–6) read these letters as DIT(s) · (?) IEETS · DOEN · MAK . . . and interpreted them variously as "Dit ieets doen mak . . ." or "Dit heeft doen maken" or "Dit dede maken" which he identified as expressions that have been found on south Netherlandish paintings and picture frames of this period meaning "this was had made [by]." The letter s after the DIT in Steppe's transcription must have derived from one of the ornamental stops between the words which indeed are shaped like that letter.

In the upper right corner of the field sits the figure of a young man wearing a crown and a richly patterned velvet or damask girdled robe. His name, *salomō*, is clearly inscribed on a portion of the original fabric that has survived virtually intact and represents the lower end of the inscribed scroll that flutters above the man's head in a space that also contains some grapevines. This is King Solomon, who looks toward the compartment containing the figure of God the Father and says (on his scroll):

De fractu [for fructu] · manuū · suarū · plātavi[t]/vinea[m] · pu XXX°

(With the fruit of her hands she hath planted a vineyard. Proverbs 30 [from Proverbs 31:16: "She hath considered a field, and bought it: with the fruit of her hands she hath planted a vineyard"]).

A third man holding a scroll sits at the bottom of the field in the center. He is middle-aged, bearded, and barefoot, and he wears a patterned gown and mantle embroi-

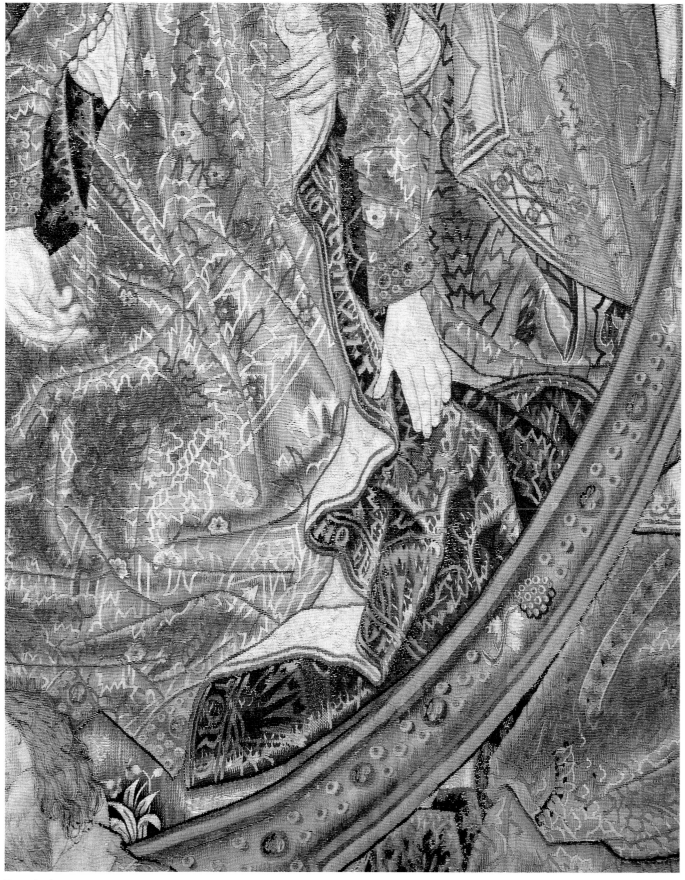

Detail of 15

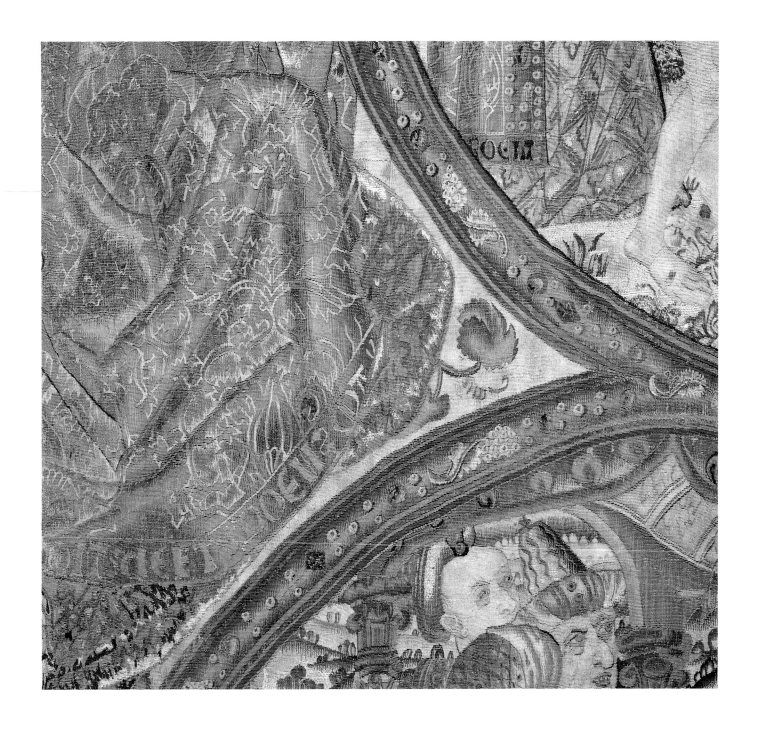

Details of 15

Detail of 15

dered with pearls at the hemline. His head overlaps the bottom of the central compartment just to the right of the recumbent figure of the Christ Child. More fruiting grapevines appear against the flat marble field behind him. His scroll reads as follows:

Misit · deus · filium · suum · ut ens [for *eos*] · *qui/Sub · lege · erant · redi[m]eret · gal 4°*

(God sent his Son to redeem them who were under the law [from Galatians 4:4–5: "But when the fulness of the time was come, God sent his Son, made of a woman, made under the law: That he might redeem them who were under the law: that we might receive the adoption of sons"]).

This quotation from the Epistle to the Galatians identifies the figure as that of the apostle Paul.

The two remaining open spaces in the field, the spandrel-shaped areas in the two lower corners, are occupied by figures other than human ones. In the left corner a pelican with upraised wings bends its head down, pecking at its own breast. In the opposite corner a lion directs its open mouth at two cubs lying on the ground in front of it. The pelican, in medieval bestiaries a profoundly charitable creature who revives with its own blood the young it had killed in annoyance, is a familiar symbol of Christ. In these bestiaries the lion, also a symbol of Christ, was a creature that breathed life into its young three days after they were born dead.

Gilt yarns were used to brighten the highlights of objects represented in warm tones—red, orange, yellow, brown—and the silver yarns, more sparsely used, appear as highlights in areas of blue, green, or gray. Both metallic yarns were also used to represent the metallic parts of the patterns in the various rich textiles represented throughout the piece. Silk yarns were used to render the light tints that appear in the highlights of the figures and objects. The weavers left many small slits in the weave in places where bare flesh is represented; the shadows they cast trace out the contours of the forms more delicately than color changes could have done.

The subject of the tapestry is a complex one involving the Law given to mankind by God, how man's disobedience led to his fall, and how he was in time redeemed through the obedience of the Virgin and Christ's mission on earth. The story is told in both narrative and symbolic terms: scenes from Scripture and later texts are combined with a number of allegorical and allusive images. The vines, grapes, and revivifying blood of the pelican all allude to Christ as the "true vine," to His blood, and to the Eucharist. The lion who gives life to its cubs three days after they had been born dead is a symbol of the resurrected Christ and of the new life He gives

to mankind. Standen observed that Saint Paul's words in his letter to the Galatians confirm that Christ's mission was to redeem mankind, and the prophecies of Zacharias and Solomon reveal that He would accomplish this through His own blood.[3] Standen was the first writer to express the theme of the composition as a whole succinctly and, we believe, correctly. She observed that "as well as the general idea of the Old Law and the New, the quality stressed is obedience, or submission to the will of God" and also that through representations of the Nativity, the Crucifixion, Adam after the fall, Moses as receiver of the Commandments, and Mary living under the Law before the Incarnation—through these images "the whole history of the world until the Crucifixion is summed up." In preparing her study, which unfortunately was never published, Standen consulted Lady (formerly Mrs. Trenchard) Cox in London and, through Lady Cox, Professor Francis Wormald, also in England, as well as Professor Kenneth M. Cameron in this country, all specialists in Christian iconography or early church drama. These correspondents agreed with Standen's exposition of the tapestry's theme, as we do also, but their interpretations of the scene in the lower left compartment (see below) differed slightly from hers.

There has been little disagreement concerning the scenes in the other four compartments. Souchal (in Paris 1973, 171) emphasized the fact that the scenes in the upper left and right corners of the composition represent two aspects of the same event and not separate or successive episodes. Standen had already perceived this and noted that in the compartment at the left Adam and Eve are shown neither breaking God's command nor being punished for it but approaching Him to hear His judgment.[4] Certainly both figures are nude and hiding their nudity, and they are being moved along into the Lord's presence (in the compartment at the upper right) by a pair of angels. Standen's interpretation is convincing.

As in most late medieval art the Nativity is shown here, in the lower part of the central compartment, as an adoration of the Child by the Virgin with Joseph present (a Holy Family). Also as usual, He is shown lying on a fold of His mother's gown (when not on a bed of hay) with rays of light emanating from His body. In this representation Joseph's gaze is not directed at the Child but toward the representation of the Crucifixion. In that scene the artist chose to represent the moment when, seeing that Christ was dead, the soldiers did not break his legs as they had done to the two thieves; but one of them pierced His side with a lance and from the wound poured water and blood. John (19:32–34), the only Evangelist who mentions this incident, does not name the soldier but in the Acts of Pilate he is called "Longinus,"

263

from the Greek word for "lance" (*longke*).[5] He is shown here as a blind man whose arm must be guided by the sighted man who stands or rides behind him. His blindness, which was cured when some of Christ's blood dropped into his eyes, is mentioned in the *Golden Legend.*

The significance of the scene showing Moses presenting the second set of the tables of the Law to the Israelites is clear enough; but the meaning of its pendant scene at the left is less obvious. From the time the tapestry was first published, by Destrée in 1912, various attempts have been made to identify these characters and their actions. Destrée did not mention this scene at all in his description of the hanging. Breck (1918, 48–52) believed that it represented the Visitation. He reasoned that Elizabeth, who was the first to recognize what Mary's pregnancy meant, served as a link between the past and the future, that the Visitation is the connection that joins the old covenant and the new, but he did not name the figures. Nor did he attempt to explain the other figures who must have some role in the story, particularly the angry man standing behind the older woman, or to explain why both women are carrying baskets. His interpretation is not satisfactory. Souchal (in Paris 1973, 171) suggested that since the scenes in the two upper compartments describe a single incident it is reasonable to assume that the two lower scenes are connected in a similar way and therefore the one at the left also illustrates some episode in the story of Moses. She could not find such an incident but thought that this scene might have something to do with the women who brought brightly colored yarns and fine linen when Moses told the Israelites what was needed to build the Tabernacle (Exodus 35:25–27). She then rejected that idea because it did not explain the presence of the two men standing in the background at the left. Souchal also believed that Carmen Gómez-Moreno (reference not cited, but apparently based on Standen 1968–69 preliminary draft; see note 3) might be correct in identifying the scene as one showing Mary's family visiting her in the temple before her marriage, and that the closed box she holds is a symbol of her virginity.

However, in view of the fact that the scenes in both upper compartments represent episodes in the story of Adam and Eve, Souchal's suggestion (in Paris 1973, 171) that the scene in the lower left compartment may have been taken from the story of Moses cannot be dismissed lightly. There are a number of such episodes to consider, but none of them seems to suit the composition precisely. The elderly man could perhaps represent Aaron who, like the other Israelites tired of waiting for Moses to return from his first trip up Mount Sinai, told the women to bring their gold earrings to him to be melted down and cast into an idol of the golden calf (Exodus 32:2–4). The angry man in the background may represent a dissenter who objected to the women's bringing their jewelry in the wicker baskets if indeed that is what these baskets contain. On the other hand this could represent an earlier incident in the story when God told Moses to bring unleavened loaves and cakes in a basket, together with a bullock and two rams, to the consecration of Aaron and his sons as His priests (Exodus 29:1–31). This interpretation could explain the presence of the baskets and the animals in the background. But these are not the right creatures: the one that looks like a horse could perhaps have been meant for a bullock, but the other is certainly a stag, not a ram. The elderly man may represent Moses, the angry or shouting (but for what reason?) man Aaron, and the young men his sons. It does not help to consult traditional typologies. While representations of the Nativity and the Crucifixion in the *Biblia Pauperum* involve Moses and Aaron—the Burning Bush, Aaron's flowering rod, the sacrifice of Isaac, and Moses raising the bronze serpent—none of them explains this scene.[6]

Taking a totally different tack, Steppe (1975, 357, 359) believed that the scene is related iconographically to the figure of Paul seated outside the compartment at the right and to the allegorical content of his letter to the Galatians. Seeing in the scene a reference to the Lutheran allegory of Man freed from the Mosaic law through the mercy of Christ, he believed that it showed Abraham sending Hagar and Ishmael (the slave woman and her child born of the flesh) out of his house while Sarah and her son Isaac (the free woman and the child born of promise) were kept at home. However Steppe made no attempt to identify the figures in the tapestry by name or to explain where the two boys were or what the baskets signified (in Scripture, Abraham sends Hagar and Ishmael away with a bottle of water and some bread). This interpretation leaves too many figures unexplained and too many details unaccounted for. Furthermore, while much of the content of Paul's letter to the Galatians (esp. 4:7–31) indeed has the allegorical content that Steppe refers to, we believe that Paul and the message on his scroll relate specifically either to the scene in the center or, as Wormald implied (see below), to the entire field rather than just to the episode illustrated in the lower left compartment.

Standen's interpretation of the scene in the lower left compartment, and the variant suggestions made by her three correspondents seem to us more reasonable and correct than any of the others outlined above.[7] She believed that the composition shows Mary living in the

Fig. 110. *The First Four Articles of the Creed.* Tapestry, southern Netherlands, last quarter of the fifteenth century. Museum of Fine Arts, Boston.

temple during her childhood (from her third to twelfth year, as recounted in the Protevangelium of James) and that the man standing behind her is the high priest even though he does not wear the usual tall, miter-like head-dress. Standen accepted the birds perched on the pole behind this man as doves and thus as references to Mary who in James's writing was compared to a dove living in the temple; and she suggested that the closed box (a covered basket) in Mary's lap is a symbol of her virginity. She also suggested that the woman standing to the left of the man might be Saint Anne and that the other figures could be suitors except for the fact that two of them look like women. She observed that the stag and horse might represent sinful desires overcome by Mary's virtue or perhaps instead the quality of obedience to God. Such a scene would have taken place at a time not long before the Incarnation and thus, Standen reasoned, it would complete her interpretation of the tapestry's overall theme; that is, that it treats the entire history of the world under the Law, from the time of Adam to the moment of the Crucifixion.

Lady Cox and Professors Wormald and Cameron agreed that the scene in the lower left compartment does indeed show the Virgin in the temple but at a later moment, at the time when Mary, having reached the age of thirteen, must be espoused according to the bishop's law.[8] In this interpretation, which we believe is the correct one, the young lady seated at the right is Mary, the man behind her is Joachim, and the woman at the left is Anne. Joachim is explaining to his wife that according to the Law Mary must be espoused. The figures in the background are the suitors (only the figure stand-ing behind the two at the left could perhaps be a woman). One of these men, who stands behind Anne, is aggressively angry or impatient. Cameron suggested that this man, and another in the background who also wears a tall hat might represent clergymen who insist that the bishop's law must be observed. He also sug-gested that the baskets might be read as symbols of sacrifice, since sacrificial doves were taken to the tem-ple in such containers, and furthermore that the animals behind Mary (are they the requisite sheep and rams, he wondered?) might also be sacrificial beasts. In Lady Cox's opinion, these quadrupeds could represent the ox and ass from the neighboring Nativity scene, the de-signer having given antlers to one of them by mistake. Wormald did not comment on these animals but con-centrated his attention on the logic of the composition as a whole. He perceived it as an expression of the idea of the Law, of the lawgivers God and Moses in the two compartments at the right compared to the original lawbreakers Adam and Eve and the perfect law keepers Mary and her parents, all in the two compartments at the left.

Source of the Design

The surface composition is unusual for tapestries that have survived from this period. The format itself, one in which figures or scenes are enclosed within circular compartments arranged symmetrically on a rectangular field, dates back to late antiquity in the art of tapestry weaving.[9] It also appears in antique floor mosaics and in medieval decorative arts and manuscript illustrations. One such painting, which serves as the title page of a missal that has been dated about 1481, the approximate date of the Metropolitan Museum's tapestry, shows a pair of curling rose branches that form five compartments disposed rather like those in the tapestry.[10] In the central compartment Adam, Eve, the Virgin, the crucified Christ, and Death appear with the Tree of the Knowledge of Good and Evil. An allegorical figure appears in each of the upper compartments and allegorical scenes fill the lower ones and the space between them. Pages showing this basic format also appear in fourteenth-century illustrations for the *Biblia Pauperum.*[11] Therefore it is clear that the tapestry format, while unusual in the context of its peers, reflects a design tradition that was relatively common in the other decorative and representational arts.

Destrée (1912, 7) recorded that he did not agree with G. Vermeersch who had said to him in conversation that he regarded Quentin Massys as the designer of this tapestry. Destrée believed that it was not a Brabant artist but some other south Netherlandish painter who had designed it, perhaps Justus van Ghent whom he (1912, 3) and Bernath[12] believed had designed the stylistically similar *Creed* tapestry (fig. 110) in the Museum of Fine Arts, Boston. That tapestry is indeed related to this one in a number of ways. Apart from the details Destrée noted—the similarity of the figures of the thief with the convex chest and chin beard and the resemblance of the David in the Boston piece to the God the Father in 15—we can add the fact that the pose of Peter in the Boston tapestry (lower right corner of the Creation of Eve scene) is virtually identical to that of Paul in 15, and the observation that the figures of the crucified Christ and of the swooning Virgin are similar in both tapestries. Another, nearly identical, representation of the crucified Christ appears in a tapestry that was sold from the James A. Garland collection in 1909.[13] Destrée and some later writers also noted that the figure and facial types in the Boston and New York tapestries are closely related. These points of resemblance do not necessarily indicate that the Boston, New York, and Garland tapestries were designed by a single artist—although that may be true—but only that parts of their compositions were taken from the same design sources.

Those sources were either paintings, some of which have been identified, or unknown sources that had been consulted by both the tapestry designer and the painters. Standen noted that the figure of John supporting the fainting Virgin appears in reverse in a painting of the *Deposition* in Munich (fig. 111) that has been attributed to a follower of Rogier van der Weyden.[14] She observed also that some of the figures standing on the other side of the cross in this painting resemble corresponding figures in the tapestry and furthermore that the skull and bone at the foot of the cross appear in both the tapestry and the painting. Standen found a similar bearded, convex-chested thief in the left wing of a painted triptych of the *Deposition* in the Walker Art Gallery in Liverpool (fig. 112) that is regarded as a fifteenth-century copy after an altarpiece by Robert Campin.[15] Earlier, Destrée (1912, 8) had noticed that the figure of Joseph leaning on a stick in the Nativity in 15 is similar to the corresponding figure in Rogier's composition for the *Holy Family* panels in Berlin and Granada (fig. 113). In the painting he is shown asleep, but in the tapestry he is very much awake and looking with distress at the Crucifixion. We can add that the figures of Adam and Eve in 15 were derived from the van Eyck altarpiece in Ghent, the figure of Adam virtually identical except for the reversed positions of the arms, the Eve precisely the same but entirely reversed.[16]

Breck (1918, 46) claimed that the tapestry was signed by Jan van Roome (the artist who designed the *Legend of Herkinbald* in Brussels), but he offered no evidence to support this claim. It appears not only at the head of his article but also in the text below, immediately preceding the sentence "The inscriptions will be discussed in a later article." This suggests that Breck thought he had found such a signature in one of the inscriptions on the tapestry. He transcribed and translated (1918, 46, 48) the texts associated with the figures of Zacharias, Solomon, and Paul, none of which contains a combination of letters that could be interpreted as Jan van Roome's signature. Therefore, since Breck never addressed the subject again in print, we have to assume that he found what looked like the word ROEM somewhere else in the composition, probably in the two places that Porter thought he had seen it (see notes 1 and 2): that is, once on the cope worn by the angel standing next to Eve and again among the words on Zacharias's robe. We do not know

Fig. 111. *The Deposition*, by a follower of Rogier van der Weyden. Panel painting, southern Netherlands, middle or second half of the fifteenth century. Pinakothek, Bayerische Staatsgemäldesammlungen, Munich.

Fig. 112. *The Deposition*, believed to be a copy after an altarpiece by Robert Campin. Panel painting from a triptych, southern Netherlands, fifteenth century. Walker Art Gallery, Liverpool.

Fig. 113. *The Holy Family*, by Rogier van der Weyden. Panel painting from a triptych, southern Netherlands, second quarter or middle of the fifteenth century. Capilla Real, cathedral of Granada.

whether Göbel and Hunter found what was thought to be the word ROEM through correspondence with Breck or on the tapestry itself; but Göbel (1923, vol. 1, 410–11) claimed that an abbreviated version of Jan van Roome's name appeared in more than one place on the tapestry and suggested that it had been designed by van Roome working in collaboration with Philip van Orley. Hunter (1925, caption pl. XVIII,e) was more cautious and referred to the word on the angel's cope as the "so-called" signature of this painter. Ackerman (1926–27, 152) transcribed as HOENS what Porter had read as ROEM on the border of Zacharias's robe and she believed that it represented the name of a Brussels weaver (see Manufacture and Date). However Ackerman also thought that the designer's signature was here also. With some difficulty she read the name of I (for Joris) Waelkin on the border of the mantle worn by one of the young men in the lower left compartment, and she identified Waelkin as a pupil of Jean Fabiaen, a designer of Bruges tapestries. However her reading of the inscription seems to be incorrect. Rorimer (1953–54, 295–96) accepted the word on the border of the angel's cope as ROEM and claimed that it was Jan van Roome's signature. Souchal (in Paris 1973, 173–74) discussed the so-called signature and the attribution to Jan van Roome, but she hesitated to accept the critical word as ROEM and preferred to attribute the design to some unnamed south Netherlandish follower of Rogier van der Weyden. Soon afterward Steppe (1976, 203–6) made it quite clear that the word on the angel's cope cannot be read as ROEM but possibly as BOELA, ROELA, BOELT, or ROELT, and furthermore that what was thought to be ROEM on the border of Zacharias's gown is in fact DOEN. He did not believe that the letters referred to the weaver or cartoon painter but suggested that it could be the name of the producer or commissioner of the tapestry because he thought it continued the inscription that appears on the border of Zacharias's robe which he read as DIT(s) · (?) IEETS · DOEN · MAK . . . or, in Flemish, "this was had made [by]." As noted above, our reading of the inscription on Zacharias's robe differs from Steppe's. (We read the letters as DIT · DEET · DOEN [the N reversed] MA K [or v?].) Coffinet (1977, 90) followed Steppe in his interpretation of the inscription. Although he did not suggest a name for the designer of the Metropolitan Museum's tapestry Coffinet believed that it could have been produced by Pieter van Aelst.

We see no grounds for associating the style of this tapestry with that of the *Herkinbald* piece in Brussels which in any case may look as much like the work of Philips, the man who painted the cartoon, as that of Jan van Roome who provided the original design. We cannot name the designer of 15 but believe that he was a south Netherlandish painter who drew inspiration from the work of Robert Campin and Rogier van der Weyden and their followers.

MANUFACTURE AND DATE

Destrée (1912, caption, fig. 15) published the tapestry as a Flemish piece dating from the second half of the fifteenth century. Breck (1918, 46) retained the general attribution to Flanders and dated it about 1500. Göbel (1928, vol. 1, 410; vol. 2, caption fig. 368a) published it as a Brussels piece dating from the beginning of the sixteenth century or about 1500. Souchal (in Paris 1973) thought it was probably woven in Brussels and dated it about ten to fifteen years before 1498 (the year some writers believe it was given to Isabel la Católica; see History) or around 1483–88. Steppe (1975, 357; 1976, 203) believed that the hanging was woven in Brussels about 1480. None of these writers specified their reasons for assigning the hanging to Brussels. Breck, Göbel, and Rorimer (1953–54, 295–97) thought that a Brussels painter had designed it. Probably they and the other writers regarded the painterly style and fine quality of the weaving to be reason enough to make the attribution. Ackerman (1926–27, 152), who read the letters inscribed on the border of Zacharias's robe as FET JEENS HOENS MA . . . , believed that it was woven by a Brussels weaver she identified as "Jean Hoens, Maître." Coffinet (1977, 90) thought the tapestry showed the same qualities of design and execution as the superb *Story of the Virgin* tapestries in Madrid that Juana of Spain bought from Pieter van Aelst in 1502, and therefore he considered it a Brussels product.

The tapestry is another in the series of relatively small, exquisitely designed and executed (always with lavish use of metal yarns) late fifteenth-century tapestries with religious subjects that have traditionally been ascribed to Brussels, chief among which are the two altarpieces in the cathedral in Sens and the *Annunciation, Adoration of the Magi,* and *Madonna of the Living Water* in Paris (see in this catalogue, figs. 49, 63–66). There is no proof that any of these pieces was woven in Brussels. Concerning the date of 15, it is significant that the stylistically similar *Madonna of the Living Water* (fig. 66) shows the date 1485. That falls within the span of ten years or so (about 1480–90) during which we believe 15 was designed and woven, judging from the tapestry's pictorial style and, to a lesser but material degree, the fashion of the garments worn by the two women in the scene at the lower left.[17] In any case, since we know that in 1498 Isabel la Católica received as a gift what must have been one or two hangings woven after the same or a similar cartoon (see History), we can be sure that the design antedates that year and that at least one hanging had been woven from it before that date.

RELATED TAPESTRIES

No tapestries that could have belonged with this piece in a series of hangings are known to have survived. While it is possible that other tapestries showing typological relationships between Old and New Testaments once accompanied this example, the fact that it summarizes entirely within itself what is central to the Christian faith suggests that it was designed to hang alone, perhaps as a dossal above an altar, and to be contemplated as an object of devotion.

PROVENANCE

In a letter to Rorimer in 1956, Steppe proposed with some hesitation that this tapestry was identical with one that had been given to Isabel la Católica at Alcalá de Henares on April 2, 1498.[18] In that letter he acknowledged that several tapestries could have been woven after the same composition and implied that 15 might not in fact be the one in question. However by the time he published the piece in 1975 (357) he decided that it had indeed belonged to the queen. He published it again (1976, 205) with references to two citations of tapestries that were given to the queen at Alcalá de Henares on April 2, 1498, citations that referred either to one tapestry listed twice or to two tapestries woven after the same or similar cartoons.[19] According to information provided in Steppe's letter to Rorimer in 1956, the bishop of Palencia who was mentioned as donor of one of the tapestries (no. 147 in Sánchez Cantón's list; see note 19) was probably Don Alonso de Burgos (bishop 1486–99), confessor to both the king and the queen. Steppe identified the hanging given by the bishop of Palencia with the one cited among those that were sold at Toro in January 1505.[20] The buyer was listed as the bishop of Málaga whom Steppe suggested in his letter of 1956 might be identified as Don Diego Ramírez de Fuenreal (or, de Villaescusa), the queen's chief chaplain who was bishop of Málaga in 1502. Steppe was not able to produce any evidence that would connect that tapestry with 15.

Sánchez Cantón lists a tapestry with the subject of 15 in a group of seven that were recorded as having been given to the queen and delivered to her at Alcalá de Henares on April 2, 1498.[21] The last piece in that list (Sánchez Cantón's no. 147) was described as follows: "Vn paño Ryco de Ras de devoçion grande con oro e plata en questa nuestro Señor en la Cruz e al un costado esta dios padre con vnos angeles al derredor e al otro Adan y Eba e al pie de la cruz el nasçimiento de Nuestro Señor con otras muchas figuras que tiene de largo quatro baras e tres quartas e de cayda tres varas e une terçia es traydo e mucho amarillo el qual dio el Obispo de palençia" (A rich large devotional tapestry with gold and silver in which our Lord is [shown] on the cross and on one side is God the Father with some angels around Him and on the other side Adam and Eve and at the foot of the cross the birth of our Lord with many other figures[;] it is four and three-quarters varas wide and three and one-third varas high[;] it is worn and much yellowed [and it is] the one that the bishop of Palencia gave). What was either the same tapestry showing the Nativity and Crucifixion together or a version of it was among another group of seven tapestries that were also given to the queen at Alcalá de Henares on April 2, 1498.[22] The other six pieces in this second gift were different from the six pieces that accompanied the Nativity and Crucifixion tapestry in the first group of seven. There were thus two separate gifts of seven pieces. Therefore it seems quite possible that two similar tapestries existed and that this is not a matter of one piece having been listed twice by mistake.

The second citation of a Nativity and Crucifixion tapestry given to the queen on April 2, 1498 (Sánchez Cantón's no. 172; see note 22 here), describes it as follows: "Un paño de Ras grande Rico con oro en que esta nuestro Señor en la cruz entre dos ladrones e en lo alto del en la vna parte Adan y eva y de la otra dios padre con dos Angeles y en lo baxo el nascimiento de nuestro Señor e de la otra moysen con las tablas de la ley que tiene de largo çinco varas e de cayda tres varas e media" (A large tapestry rich with gold in which our Lord is on the cross between two thieves and at the top on one side Adam and Eve and on the other God the Father with two angels and at the bottom the birth of our Lord and on the other [side] Moses with the tables of the Law which is five varas wide and three and a half varas high).

Only one tapestry (Sánchez Cantón's no. 309) that could have answered the description of one or both of those hangings was recorded among the pieces that were sold at Toro in January of 1505, soon after the queen's death.[23] It was described as follows: "que se vendió al obispo de Málaga un paño de Ras rico con oro en que está Nuestro Señor en la crux entre dos ladrones y en lo alto Dios Padre y Adán y Eva y en lo baxo del Nascimiento de Nuestro Señor, en cient ducados de oro" (there was sold to the bishop of Málaga a tapestry rich with gold in which our Lord is on the cross between two thieves and at the top God the Father and Adam and Eve and at the bottom the birth of our Lord, for a hundred gold ducats).

Presumably this was one of what we believe were two similar tapestries in the queen's collection. One of them was said to contain both gold and silver yarns, the other, only gold. Presumably the latter was the one sold at Toro which was also said to contain only gold yarns. Among the documents that Sánchez Cantón published there is no reference to the disposition by sale or other means of any second tapestry with this subject. Steppe (1975, 357; 1976, 205 and n. 58) believed that Isabel owned only one such tapestry, but Souchal (in Paris 1973, 173) thought there might have been two of them and noted that the two descriptions differ. That fact indicates either that two different pieces were involved or that one of the inventory takers made some errors or perceived the same compositions and materials differently. Sánchez Cantón's number 147 was described as containing both gold and silver, with the figure of God the Father surrounded by "some" angels, measuring the equivalent of 156$^1/_3$ inches in width and 109$^7/_8$ inches in height (3.97 × 2.79 m), as being worn and much yellowed, and as given to the queen by the bishop of Palencia. The other citation (Sánchez Cantón's no. 172) describes a piece that was said to have been "rich with gold," with figures of God the Father and "two" angels, measuring 8 inches (20.3 cm) wider and 6$^1/_2$ inches (16.5 cm) taller than the other, and with no mention of either damage or a donor's name.

The Metropolitan Museum's tapestry is more like the one that Sánchez Cantón numbered 147 than his number 172. It shows signs of wear now (was it "worn" in 1498?); it contains both gold and silver yarns; and there are "some" (three, not two) angels standing with God the Father. But it is not "much yellowed" (presumably the yarns had discolored through oxidation by 1498), and it now measures 153 inches in width and 122$^1/_4$ inches in height (3.89 × 3.11 m). Comparing these dimensions to the ones given in 1498 for Sánchez Cantón's number 147, one can ascribe the 3-inch discrepancy in width either to error or to shrinking (as Souchal had already noted) and the 12 or so additional inches in height partly to the widths of the modern guard bands at the top and bottom of 15 and partly to the height of the restoration at the bottom (see Condition). On the other hand these discrepancies might indicate that this tapestry is not the one mentioned in either citation in Isabel's inventory. In the case of the *Story of the Seven Sacraments* fragments in the Metropolitan Museum (7a–e), we can identify them with the tapestry that Isabel had bequeathed to the Capilla Real in the cathedral of Granada because Fortuny bought the fragments from that source. However in the case of 15 we know nothing about the history of the tapestry before the late nineteenth century and

therefore cannot connect it with a source that could be traced back to the queen's collections.

HISTORY

According to Destrée (1912, 7, caption fig. 15) the tapestry had been in the Gavet collection, presumably the collection of Emile Gavet, which was sold at the Galerie Georges Petit, Paris, May 31–June 9, 1897. If Destrée was correct, Gavet (who had died before the date of the sale) must have disposed of the tapestry beforehand; it is not listed in the catalogue of that sale nor in the catalogue of the sale of pictures from the Emile Gavet collection that was held at the Hôtel Drouot, Paris, May 8, 1906.

Bequeathed to the MMA by Oliver H. Payne, 1917.

EXHIBITIONS

Tournai, Halle aux Draps, 1958. *Tapisseries d'occident.* Cat. no. 11, pl. VIII.

Paris 1973. Catalogue entries by Geneviève Souchal. Cat. no. 73, illus.

New York 1974. Cat. no. 78, illus.

PUBLICATIONS

Destrée, Joseph. "Juste de Gand (Josse van Wassenhove)," pt. 2. *L'Art Flamand & Hollandais* 18 (1912) pp. 7–8. Described briefly and discussed; illus. fig. 15.

Wood, D. T. B. "'Credo' Tapestries," pt. 1. *Burlington Magazine* 24 (1913–14) p. 254. Discussed briefly.

J. B. [Joseph Breck]. "A Tapestry Bequeathed by Colonel Oliver H. Payne." *MMA Bulletin* 13 (1918) pp. 46–52. Described and discussed in detail; illus. full view plus details of each section.

Göbel 1923, vol. 1, pp. 410–11. Described and discussed briefly; illus. vol. 2, fig. 368a.

Hunter 1925, p. 253. Mentioned; illus. pl. XVIII,e, detail of inscription on border of angel's cope in upper left scene.

Ackerman, Phyllis. "Recently Identified Designers of Gothic Tapestries." *Art Bulletin* 9 (1926–27) p. 152. Discussed; illus. fig. 4, detail of inscribed border on Zacharias's robe.

Rorimer, James J. "The Glorification of Charles VIII." *MMA Bulletin*, n.s. 12 (1953–54) pp. 295–97. Discussed briefly; illus. full view plus detail of inscription on border of angel's cope.

Steppe, Jan-Karel. "'De Overgang van het Mensdom van het Oude Verbond naar het Nieuwe,' een Brussels wandtapijt uit de 16e eeuw ontstaan onder invloed van de Lutherse ikonografie en prentkunst." *De Gulden Passer*, Bulletin van de Vereeniging der Antwerpsche Bibliophielen 53 (1975) pp. 357, 359. Described; iconography discussed.

Steppe, Jan-Karel. "Inscriptions décoratives contenant des signatures et des mentions du lieu d'origine sur des tapisseries bruxelloises de la fin du XVe et du début du XVIe siècle." In *Tapisseries bruxelloises de la pré-Renaissance.* Exh. cat., Musées Royaux d'Art et d'Histoire. Brussels, 1976, pp. 203–6. Discussed briefly; illus. figs. 1, 2, detail of upper left quarter and of inscription on border of angel's cope.

Coffinet 1977, pp. 88, 90–91. Described and discussed; illus. full view black and white plus color detail of bottom of Moses scene.

NOTES

1. Letter from A. Kingsley Porter to Joseph Breck dated March 24, 1918. In a letter of March 22, 1917 (error for 1918), also to Breck, Porter referred in less detail to the same inscription. Both letters are in the files of the MMA Department of Medieval Art.

2. In his letters of March 22 and 24, 1918, Porter transcribed his

version of the inscriptions on all three scrolls and in the borders of the angel's cope and Zacharias's robe as well as the words on Moses' tables.

3. Edith Appleton Standen, notes, correspondence, and preliminary draft for a catalogue entry concerning this tapestry, 1968–69, in the files of the MMA Department of Medieval Art.

4. Standen, preliminary draft, 1968–69.

5. Louis Réau, *Iconographie de l'art chrétien* (Paris, 1955–59) vol. 2, pt. 2, p. 496.

6. See a number of fourteenth-century examples in Henrik Cornell, *Biblia Pauperum* (Stockholm, 1925) pls. 1, 10, 21b, 22, 28, and 39, where the typologies for the Nativity are the episodes of Moses and the burning bush and the flowering of Aaron's rod, and for the Crucifixion the episodes of the sacrifice of Isaac and of Moses raising the bronze serpent.

7. Standen, preliminary draft, 1968–69.

8. Correspondence between Standen (see note 3) and Lady Cox, Professor Francis Wormald, and Professor Kenneth Cameron.

9. See a typical example in Jules Guiffrey, *Les tapisseries du XIIᵉ à la fin du XVIᵉ siècle* (Paris, [1911]) fig. 1.

10. For an illustration of the title page and further details concerning the missal, see Ernst Guldan, *Eva und Maria: Eine Antithese als Bildmotiv* (Graz and Cologne, 1966) frontispiece in color and pp. 142, 161.

11. See Cornell, *Biblia Pauperum*, pls. 21b, 22, 54.

12. Morton H. Bernath, "Notes on Justus van Ghent," *American Journal of Archaeology*, 2d ser., 14, no. 3 (1910) p. 335. For a discussion and detail illustrations of the Boston *Creed*, see Adolph S. Cavallo, *Tapestries of Europe and of Colonial Peru in the Museum of Fine Arts, Boston* (Boston, 1967) pp. 83–87, pls. 21–21d.

13. *The James A. Garland Collection*, sale cat., American Art Association, New York, March 19–20, 1909, no. 131, illus.

14. Standen, preliminary draft, 1968–69. Concerning the painting, see also Max J. Friedländer, *Early Netherlandish Painting*, vol. 2, *Rogier van der Weyden and the Master of Flémalle* (New York and Washington, 1967) no. 95, pl. 111.

15. See also Walker Art Gallery, Liverpool, *Foreign Catalogue* (Liverpool, 1977) vol. 1, pp. 37–38.

16. For a large illustration of the two figures in their settings, see Lotte Brand Philip, *The Ghent Altarpiece and the Art of Jan van Eyck* (Princeton, 1971) fig. 1.

17. Both women wear high-waisted gowns with fitted bodices, long narrow sleeves, and rather high straight necklines softened at the top of the arm by the cap of the sleeve. The silhouette corresponds to that which was fashionable during the eighth and ninth decades of the fifteenth century. For example a miniature illustration of about 1480 shows Marie de Bourgogne wearing a gown cut in the same way (see Margaret B. Freeman, *The Unicorn Tapestries*, MMA [New York, 1976] fig. 180); and in Hans Memling's version in the Metropolitan Museum of the central panel of his altarpiece of the *Mystic Marriage of Saint Catherine* in Bruges, which dates from about 1475–79, Saints Catherine and Barbara are shown wearing gowns cut along similar lines (see Guy Bauman, "Early Flemish Portraits 1425–1525," *MMA Bulletin*, n.s. 43 [1985–86] fig. 18, illus. of MMA acc. no. 14.40.634, Bequest of Benjamin Altman, and fig. 19, illus. of the example in Bruges). In that painting, the silhouette of Barbara's headdress, coming to its highest point over the forehead, corresponds to the silhouette of the headdress worn by the seated woman in the tapestry even though the component parts of the headdresses are quite different. Later in the century women apparently preferred to see the highest point at the back of the head (see 17 in this catalogue). The tight sleeves with turned-back white cuffs on Saint Catherine's gown also appear on the gown worn by the same woman in the tapestry.

18. Letter from Jan-Karel Steppe to James J. Rorimer, May 23, 1956, in the files of the MMA Department of Medieval Art. Steppe noted that the listing for Isabel's tapestry appeared twice in the texts, but he did not give his source in the letter. It was presumably the book by Sánchez Cantón cited in note 19.

19. Francisco Javier Sánchez Cantón, *Libros, tapices y cuadros que coleccionó Isabel la Católica* (Madrid, 1950). The documents concerning tapestries are discussed on pp. 89–150; the references to the tapestry or tapestries under discussion here appear on pp. 122–23 (no. 147), and 128–29 (no. 172).

20. Sánchez Cantón, *Libros, tapices y cuadros*, p. 148 (no. 309).

21. Sánchez Cantón, *Libros, tapices y cuadros*, pp. 122–23.

22. Sánchez Cantón, *Libros, tapices y cuadros*, pp. 128–29 (no. 172).

23. Sánchez Cantón, *Libros, tapices y cuadros*, p. 148 (no. 309).

16

16
The Armorial Bearings and Badges of John, Lord Dynham

Southern Netherlands, 1488–1501
Wool warp; wool wefts with a few silk wefts
12 ft. 8 in. × 12 ft. 1 in. (3.86 m × 3.68 m)
12–14 warp yarns per inch, 5–6 per centimeter
The Cloisters Collection, 1960 (60.127.1)

CONDITION

All four sides show cut edges, but there is a bit of the original selvage along the top. Before it entered the Metropolitan Museum's collection the tapestry appeared to be less complete than it is. A portion of the upper field, extending along a straight line running from the left edge to the right edge, on a level with the inner curve of the Garters encircling the two armorial shields at the top, had been turned over and stitched to the back. The hanging was illustrated in this condition in 1929 in the *Bulletin of the Needle and Bobbin Club* (pl. III) and in the Myron Taylor sale catalogue in 1960. When the hidden portion was released at the Metropolitan Museum, 26 inches more fabric became visible. The presence of some of the selvage along the top edge proves that the pattern is complete at the highest point of that line. However a significant amount of the original fabric is missing from the left side and the bottom, including the following parts of the field which have been replaced: starting at a point just below and to the left of the broken mast in the upper left corner and following along the left edge of the mast below that, dropping to the flourish of the mantle's leaf directly below, around the next flourish and the stag's right rear leg, then moving irregularly right across the piece, from the level of both stags' rear hooves downward. The replacements for these lost portions were fragments taken from one or more related hangings. There are other patches in the upper left corner of the field, near the bottom of the Garter at upper left, and also in the space in the central armorial motif between the Garter and the upper left curve of the shield. Basing our calculations on the organization of the units here and also on the pattern of a similar tapestry in Haddon Hall (fig. 114), we conclude that the tapestry has lost little of its original width but about 48 inches of fabric below the stags' lower hooves. Therefore in its original state the hanging would have measured some 16½ feet in height, which is approximately the same height that Young (1961–62, 315) had suggested (17 ft.).

The yarns have faded appreciably and the light neutral tones have darkened. The white and yellow silk yarns and the brown wool yarns that appear in many parts of the piece are not original. There are small repairs by reweaving throughout the piece.

Fig. 114. *Royal Arms of England.* Tapestry, southern Netherlands, third or fourth quarter of the fifteenth century. Haddon Hall, Bakewell, Derbyshire.

Flowering plants of many kinds are scattered over the dark blue (originally dark green) field that appears intermittently between the floral units. A complete achievement of arms, that of Sir John, first Lord Dynham, Knight of the Garter, occupies the lower two-thirds of the field. Two more coats of arms, each encircled by the emblem of the Order of the Garter, appear in the upper corners of the field. Lord Dynham's personal badge, a topcastle and broken mast, appears eleven times in the spaces between the main heraldic elements. The eleven units are arranged in three horizontal rows of five, two, and four. There is also a nearly complete unit in the lower right corner of the field and the top of a streamer from another one below the hind hooves of the stag at the right. The placement of these two incomplete badges suggests that in its original state the hanging may have shown another eleven badges below the stags, arranged in reverse order, in lines of four, two, and five, and surrounding the two missing shields as the badges in the upper third of the field do.

The following description of the heraldic elements is taken from Nickel's (1984/85) exhaustive treatment of the subject. The full achievement of arms centers around a shield shaped like a tournament targe that shows the arms of the Dynhams of Devonshire, which are blazoned as gules, a fess of four lozenges ermine. The emblem of the Order of the Garter, a blue garter inscribed with the device *hony soit qui male y pense,* surrounds the shield. A pair of stags proper serve as supporters; but rather than holding the shield as supporters normally do, they hold the edges of the Garter between their forehoofs. A helmet with a barred visor, shown in three-quarter view, surmounts the Garter and is embellished with elaborate mantling tinctured gules, lined ermine (but ermine, lined gules, on the dexter side, according to Nickel). The crest is as follows: on a chapeau gules, upturned ermine, an ermine statant between two lighted candles proper. The badge consists of the topcastle of a warship, broken at the mast, with five javelins resting inside the structure against the railing, and flying a swallow-tailed pennant with red and white streamers and a cross of Saint George next to the staff. The coat of arms encircled by the Garter in the upper left corner of the field repeats the charges on the main shield. The other shield shows the same (Dynham) arms in the dexter half impaling the arms of Arches, which are gules, three arches argent, the two in chief conjoined, in the sinister half. The similar tapestry in Haddon Hall (fig. 114) shows four Garter-encircled coats of arms in the corners of the field. In that case all four shields show the royal arms of England, as the main shield in the

center also does. Young (1961–62, 315), Souchal (in Paris 1973, 124), and Nickel (1984/85, 25) agreed that in its original state the Dynham piece also showed a shield in each of its four corners. Young thought it likely that the two missing shields at the bottom bore the same arms as those at the top. Nickel (1984/85, 28) observed that the missing shields would also have been surrounded by the Garter and suggested that they might have shown the same arms as the shields above, or other family arms, or Dynham's arms impaling those of his two wives. While it is possible that at times Dynham marshaled his arms with those of his wives, we have no example of it. Since the arms that are present in the tapestry refer only to his parents and himself, we believe it is likely that one of the two absent shields bore the Dynham arms alone and that the other showed Dynham either impaling or quartering Arches. We know that Lord Dynham did quarter his arms with his mother's since that marshaling appears on his stall plate in Saint George's Chapel at Windsor Castle (Young 1961–62, fig. 6).

The heraldic motifs in the pattern relate to persons and events connected with the life of John, Lord Dynham. The accounts of his life vary somewhat according to the source one uses. The following brief biography combines details taken from the accounts offered by Longstaffe (1876), Young (1961–62), Nickel (1984/85), and Chope.[1] John Dynham of Dynham (fifth of that name), Knight, Lord Dynham, was born in 1433, the eldest son of Sir John Dynham of Devonshire and his wife, Jane (or Joan) Arches, daughter of Sir Richard Arches of Eythorpe, Buckinghamshire. According to Chope, the Dynhams appear first in the records of Devon in 1122 when Geoffrey, lord of Dinan (later Dynham), granted the manors of Nutwell and Harpford in Devon to the abbey of Marmoutier-les-Tours.[2] In 1457 or 1458 the fifth John Dynham's father died, and this eldest son received in his inheritance the manors of Nutwell (or Bocland-Dynham, according to Longstaffe) and Hartland in Devonshire. Soon afterward, in 1459, (now Sir John) Dynham embarked on a military career that spanned the reigns of five English kings and the crucial years of the War of the Roses. He was at first loyal to Henry VI, as his father also was, but soon switched allegiance to the house of York. In 1459 he played a key role in Prince Edward's escape from the battle of Ludlow. Dynham continued to serve the Yorkist cause, and for his military action at sea and on land King Edward rewarded him, sometime between 1461 and 1467 (when he was first called to Parliament as Lord Dynham), with a peerage. Dynham served the king chiefly as naval commander in the English Channel; and when Edward died in 1483 Lord Dynham held the title of Deputy Captain of Calais. He became Captain of Calais under Richard III and then continued in that post until after Henry VII's accession to the throne in 1485. Dynham appears to have been a favorite of the Tudor king, who appointed him Privy Councillor and Treasurer of England in 1485 or 1486. He continued in the office of Treasurer until his death in 1501. In 1487 or 1488, after four unsuccessful bids to election under Edward, Dynham was at last elected to the Order of the Garter and served as a remarkably active member of that distinguished group of knights until the end of the century. He died in London in January 1501 and was buried at Grey Friar's as he had directed. His mother had died in 1496 or 1497. His first wife, Elizabeth, Lady Fitzwalter, daughter of Sir Walter Fitzwalter, whom he had married in 1467, predeceased him, as did their two children. In 1488 he married Elizabeth, daughter of Robert Willoughby, Lord Brook. They had no children. Therefore Lord Dynham died childless and his four sisters' children ultimately became his heirs.

The heraldic motifs in the pattern reflect most of this history. As Young (1961–62, 309) pointed out, the ermine in the Dynham arms (the fur and also the animal standing in the crest) was associated with Brittany and especially with Dinan, the family's original home. Ermine appeared not only in the arms of other branches of the family of the lords of Dinan but also in the arms of that municipality. Nickel (1984/85, 28; 1985, 173) suggested that the stag supporters in the full achievement of arms in the center, interpreted as harts, refer to the manor of Hartland in Devonshire, whereas Longstaffe (1876, 206) interpreted them as bucks, referring to the other manor of Bocland-Dynham. Longstaffe (1876, 205) correctly identified the sharply tapered cones flanking the ermine on the crest as lighted candles. Nickel (1984/85, 28; 1985, 173) explained the candles by observing that an alternate heraldic term for "lozenge," the charge on the Dynham shield, is "fusil," a steel flint striker, which with the flint was the means of lighting a candle in the Middle Ages. All writers on the subject agree that the topcastle badge refers to Dynham's naval career, and Nickel (1984/85, 29) developed that idea with specific suggestions for the interpretation of the javelins inside the structure and the pennant flying above it. He wondered whether the choice of five (rather than more or fewer) javelins—if it were not simply the normal number shown in this context—might not refer to five chief naval commands. He also stated that the Saint George's cross in the foreward section of the pennant, next to the staff, and the pennant's red and white tails were common to all English military standards.

Furthermore Nickel (1984/85, 29 and fig. 3) also called attention to the standard of Sir John Carew, a descendant of one of Sir John Dynham's sisters, which shows virtually the same topcastle badge but with the black lion taken from the Carew crest rising from among four javelins.

SOURCE OF THE DESIGN

Enough millefleurs tapestries with heraldic patterns have survived from the second half of the fifteenth century to prove that John Dynham's hanging represents a mode of composition that was in fashion during those years as well as the first years of the next century. The piece in Bern with the arms and devices of Philippe le Bon, believed to have been woven in Brussels by Jean de Haze in 1466, shows the duke's shield of arms, with crest and collar of the Golden Fleece, in the center of the field, his sparking flint strikers in each of the upper corners, and the cryptic pairs of affronted letters *e* beside and above the shield (see fig. 78 in this catalogue).[3] In its complete form (the piece has lost approximately the lower third of its field) two more flint strikers and one more pair of letters *e* would have appeared in corresponding positions along the bottom. A tapestry in the château de Langeais with the arms and device of Jacqueline de Luxembourg shows her own arms dimidiating those of her husband, Philippe de Croÿ, in the center, encircled by a wreath of intertwined branches bearing leaves and blossoms. Similar wreaths surround pairs of addorsed letters *e* placed one in each of the four corners of the field.[4] The hanging must have been commissioned between 1455, the year Jacqueline de Luxembourg married, and 1513, when she died.

Even more closely related to the pattern of the Dynham tapestry is the pattern of the hanging at Haddon Hall, which shows the royal arms of England, marshaled as they were from 1405 to 1603, surrounded by the Garter in the center and again in each corner of the field (fig. 114). Except for the absence of supporters, the central achievement, with mantled and crested helmet, is arranged like the corresponding achievement in the Dynham tapestry. The character of the plants and their drawing and arrangement are also similar, and from every point of view the two tapestries appear to be more or less contemporary.

It seems clear that during the late fifteenth century tapestry producers could offer their clients formats for armorial hangings showing the clients' arms, devices, and badges on a millefleurs ground, and we may assume that John Dynham patronized one of these suppliers. The client probably commissioned the heraldic pattern

275

from an artist specializing in armorial compositions, and the producer's designers adapted it for use in tapestry. This particular five-spot compositional formula continued to be used, with a change from millefleurs grounds to grounds filled with great scrolling leaves, well into the next century, as two hangings with the arms, heraldic beasts, and device of Margaret of Austria demonstrate. These tapestries, now in the Iparmü-vészeti Múzeum, Budapest, were woven in Enghien in 1528 by Henri van Lacke.[5]

MANUFACTURE AND DATE

Longstaffe, who published the tapestry for the first time in 1876, deduced from the absence of heraldic elements referring to Elizabeth Fitzwilliam, John Dynham's first wife, who died sometime between 1483 and 1485, that the tapestry was woven after she died and before Lord Dynham married Elizabeth Willoughby in 1488, or in other words early in the reign of Henry VII (1485–1509). Later writers dated the tapestry between 1487 or 1488, when John Dynham was elected to the Order of the Garter, and 1501 when he died. Thomson (1930, 160), Young (1961–62, 316), and Souchal (in Paris 1973, 125) believed that he might have ordered the tapestry to commemorate his election. Young (1961–62, 316) and Nickel (1984/85, 27) called attention to the fact that (as Thomson 1930, 151–52, had shown) in 1486 Henry VII commanded safe conduct and protection in England for Pasquier and Jean Grenier of Tournai and also permission for them and their servants to bring tapestries and other textiles into England, and furthermore that in 1488 the king ordered his Keeper of the Privy Seal, customs officers, Treasurer, and barons of the Exchequer to allow Jean Grenier to bring some altar cloths and tapestries of the Trojan War into the country duty free. Therefore, they suggested, Dynham, who held the office of Treasurer, might have thought of ordering some tapestries for himself at that time (which coincidentally was also the first time he could use the Garter with his coat of arms). Certainly the presence of the Garter in this piece proves that it could not have been ordered before 1487 or 1488. It seems equally certain that Dynham himself ordered the hanging. Therefore the commission could not have been let after January 1501, when he died.

Even though John Dynham may have ordered the hanging from the Tournai merchant-entrepreneurs Pasquier and Jean Grenier, it could have been woven in any of the tapestry-producing centers of the southern Netherlands.

RELATED TAPESTRIES

The hanging almost surely belonged with others in a series of furnishings for a room. However no other pieces of the set are known to have survived.

HISTORY

In Appleby Castle, Westmoreland, in 1876, when Longstaffe described it as hanging in a bedroom there. Described again as being in Appleby Castle by Thomson (1914, 25).[6]

Property of the Spanish Art Gallery, London, before 1929.

In the collection of Mr. and Mrs. Myron C. Taylor, New York, from at least 1929 to 1960.

Sold, *Gothic and Renaissance Furniture . . . Gothic Tapestries . . . Collected by the Late Myron C. Taylor*, pt. 2, Parke-Bernet, New York, November 11 and 12, 1960, no. 1019, illus.

Purchased by the MMA, The Cloisters Collection, 1960.

EXHIBITIONS

Tournai, 1970. *Les tapisseries héraldiques et de la vie quotidienne.* Catalogue by J. P. Asselberghs. Cat. no. 6, illus.

Paris 1973. Catalogue entries by Geneviève Souchal. Cat. no. 45, illus.

New York 1974. Cat. no. 48, illus.

PUBLICATIONS

Longstaffe, W. Hylton Dyer. "Tapestry in Appleby Castle." *Archaeologia Aeliana*, n.s. 7 (1876) pp. 205–9. Discussed at length, with notes on John Dynham and his family.

Thomson, W. G. *Tapestry Weaving in England from the Earliest Times to the End of the XVIIIth Century.* London, 1914, p. 25. Discussed briefly.

"Club Notes." *Bulletin of the Needle and Bobbin Club* 13 (1929) pp. 50–52. Discussed briefly; illus. pl. III.

Thomson 1930, p. 160. Described briefly.

Advertisement of Parke-Bernet Galleries. *Art News* 59 (December 1960) p. 24. Mentioned; illus. hanging on the wall of one of the firm's galleries before the sale of the Myron C. Taylor collection.

Young, Bonnie. "John Dynham and His Tapestry." *MMA Bulletin*, n.s. 20 (1961–62) pp. 309–16. Discussed at length, with bibliography; illus. figs. 1 (full view) and 2, 3, 5, 7 (details).

"Chronache: New York." *Emporium* 136 (1962) p. 122. Mentioned; illus. p. 124.

Rorimer, James J. *The Cloisters: The Building and the Collection of Medieval Art in Fort Tryon Park.* MMA. 3d ed., rev., New York, 1963, p. 183. Discussed briefly.

Coffinet 1977, p. 65. Illus.

Nickel, Helmut. "Heraldry." In Joseph R. Strayer, ed., *Dictionary of the Middle Ages.* Vol. 6, New York, 1985, p. 173. Discussed briefly; illus. with line drawing of the main achievement of arms and two of the badges.

Nickel, Helmut. "Some Remarks on the Armorial Tapestry of John Dynham at The Cloisters." *Metropolitan Museum Journal* 19/20 (1984/85) pp. 25–29. Discussed at length with reference to matters of heraldry; illus. figs. 1 (full view) and 2 (detail).

NOTES

1. R. Pearse Chope, "The Last of the Dynhams," *Report and Transactions of the Devonshire Association for the Advancement of Science, Literature and Art* 50 [3d ser., 10] (1918) pp. 431–92.

2. Chope, "The Last of the Dynhams," p. 432.

3. Concerning the tapestry in Bern, see Florens Deuchler, *Der Tausendblumenteppich aus der Burgunderbeute: Ein Abbild des Paradieses* (Zurich, 1984).

4. See Souchal in Paris 1973, pp. 126–28, illus. p. 127.

5. See Guy Delmarcel, *Tapisseries anciennes d'Enghien*, exh. cat. (Mons, 1980) nos. 1, 2, illus.; also Göbel 1923, vol. 1, pp. 520–21; vol. 2, fig. 475.

6. Since W. G. Thomson, *Tapestry Weaving in England from the Earliest Times to the End of the XVIIIth Century* (London, 1914) p. 25, wrote of the tapestry as being in Appleby Castle at that time but of its not being there when the revised edition of his *History of Tapestry from the Earliest Times until the Present Day* was published in 1930 (p. 160), we assume he knew that the piece was indeed still in Appleby Castle in 1914. Bonnie Young, "John Dynham and His Tapestry," *MMA Bulletin*, n.s. 20 (1961–62) p. 314, believed that this tapestry could have been one of the "hangyngs aboute the halle parlour chambre" that were among the things in Lord Dynham's residence at Lambeth that he bequeathed to his second wife, and Souchal (in Paris 1973, p. 125) agreed. However the evidence is too slim to credit. The "hangyngs" were not described and they may not have been tapestries.

17

The Lamentation

A dossal or antependium

Southern Netherlands, 1490–1505
Wool warp; wool, silk, and gilt wefts
3 ft. 8 in. × 6 ft. 9¹/₄ in. (1.12 m × 2.06 m)
16¹/₂–22 warp yarns per inch, 6¹/₂–9 per centimeter
Gift of George Blumenthal, 1941 (41.100.215)

CONDITION

Neither the field nor the border has been cut or diminished in size. The outer edges of the upper and lower sections of the border retain their original selvages. There are small spots of reweaving on the original warp in the upper and side borders and in a few contours of the figures in the field. The only area whose drawing could have been affected to any appreciable degree is that which represents the Magdalen's inner garment, from the waist downward; however that passage reads convincingly as restored. The colors throughout the piece are still rich and bright; they show a wide range of pastel tones and some more intense ones. The gilt yarns have tarnished in some places but most of them have retained their original color and luster.

DESCRIPTION AND SUBJECT

The scene is set in a landscape, with the figures clustered together in the foreground. Behind them the blue sky fades down to white at the horizon, and at both sides there are vistas with trees, rocks, hills, and buildings. In the middle of the landscape at the left, in the first fold of the hills, there is a small human figure standing or running with his right hand placed on the back of a large quadruped. Part of the shaft of the cross of the Crucifixion appears above Christ's head, immediately below the upper border. In the foreground there are small stones, bits of bone, and a whole bone scattered on the grass. A primrose plant bearing pink blossoms grows in the grass next to John's left foot.

The semirecumbent body of the dead Christ appears just right of center. Mary supports most of His weight on her lap and left knee; she holds His head with her left hand and wraps her right hand around the front of His rib cage. She wears a plain mantle over a patterned velvet or damask gown and a white kerchief wrapped around her head and under her chin. John the Evangelist,

also dressed in a patterned gown and a plain mantle, supports Him on the other side, placing his left hand under the armpit. He presses his right hand against the Virgin's forehead. A young woman fashionably dressed in a long patterned tabard over a patterned tunic and wearing a high-crowned bonnet with a pendant scarf stands to the left of the main group. She bends her right knee and wrings her hands. We can identify her as Mary Magdalen because she occupies the place at Christ's feet that is traditionally reserved for her in representations of this subject. Standing opposite her, partly hidden behind John's figure, is Joseph of Arimathea shown as an old man wearing a wide-sleeved robe over a tunic and, on his head, a chaperon. In his left hand he holds the three nails that he took from the cross as he removed the body of Christ. In the far right foreground of the scene, in front of Joseph, stands a woman holding a cylindrical box which probably contains the spices to be used in preparing the body for burial. She wears a moiré gown with a deep V neckline and hanging sleeves over a plain long-sleeved kirtle. On her head she has a turban with a rosette and plume at the center and, at the back, a long scarf puffed into a crown before it falls behind her shoulders. This may be Mary Salome who, according to Mark (15:40, 16:1), was with the Virgin and Mary Magdalen at the Crucifixion and who, with them, brought the spices for the burial (although John 19:39 says it was Nicodemus who brought the myrrh and aloes). Or it is Mary Clopas who, according to John (19:25), was the third Mary to be present on these occasions. Opposite this woman, on the other side of the composition, appears an old man wearing a short-sleeved patterned gown over a plain tunic and a hood on his head. Standen suggested that this figure, who is shown kneeling and holding his hands in an attitude of prayer, may represent a donor.[1] It is a reasonable interpretation. On the other hand he may represent Nicodemus, who would meet with Jesus only clandestinely during the Savior's lifetime but who came forward after the Crucifixion and helped Joseph of Arimathea prepare the body (John 19:39–40) and lay it in his own unused tomb. A bearded man with almost the same face stands behind the Virgin and raises his right hand as though about to touch her head to comfort her. If this is Nicodemus then the man at the left may indeed represent the donor of the tapestry. However the donor —if there is one in this hanging—could just as well be

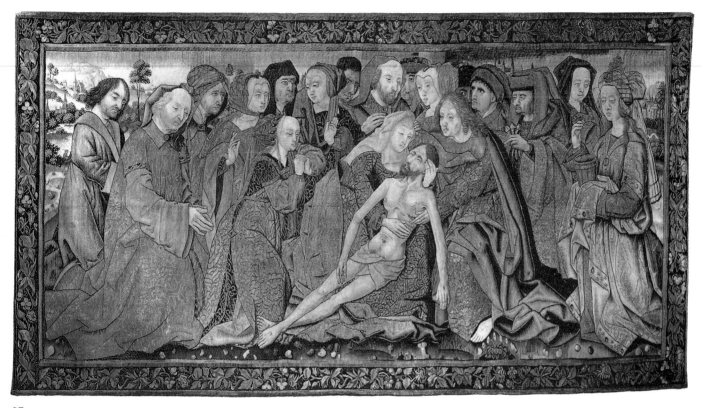

17

the figure directly behind the old man in question, a younger man kneeling in precisely the same pose.

With the exception of Joseph of Arimathea and the bearded man standing behind the Virgin, the characters mentioned thus far all occupy a clearly defined plane that runs parallel to the picture plane in the immediate foreground. The other figures, seven men and four women, stand in a plane set immediately behind the first one. Their poses and gestures show that they are all deeply involved in the principal drama that takes place in the foreground.

The border shows a band of floral motifs that is flanked by narrow guards of plain silk picked out here and there with gilt highlights. The main band shows a course of rose branches bearing red buds and open blossoms alternating with violet plants, all against a dark blue ground.

The weaving is extremely fine throughout the piece. Tiny slits are used in the flesh parts to render delicate shadings and contours; this is particularly noteworthy

in the rendering of the folds of skin that occur on the outside of the knuckles. In the representation of Christ's body the modeling is achieved by means of a combination of slits and subtle tonal variations in the wool weft yarns. Gilt yarns are used primarily to render the highlights on the garments and on the border guards.

The subject, which is not mentioned in the Gospels but does appear in later writings like the *Meditations* formerly attributed to Saint Bonaventure and the *Revelations* of Saint Bridget, represents the moment following the removal of Christ's body from the cross (the Deposition) and preceding the moment when it is placed in the tomb (the Entombment). In the literature of art this subject is called either the Lamentation or, in Italian, the Pietà. From the twelfth century onward it was represented as a subject in its own right, first in Byzantine art, then in Italian, and soon afterward in art north of the Alps. It was also occasionally combined with the Deposition. The composition for the Lamentation always involves the figures of the Virgin and Christ but

Detail of 17

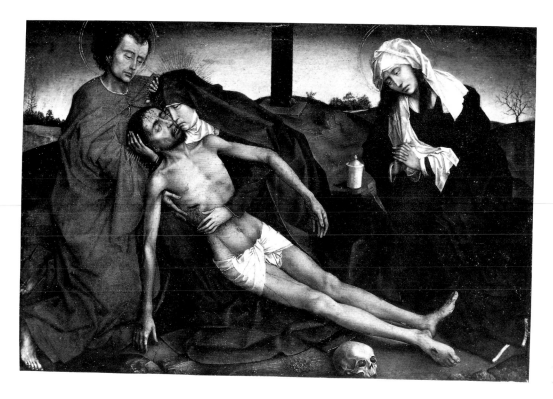

Fig. 115. *The Lamentation,* after Rogier van der Weyden. Panel painting, probably Brussels, second half of the fifteenth century. Musées Royaux des Beaux-Arts de Belgique, Brussels.

sometimes none of the others that are shown here (see Source of the Design for some variations). As Standen pointed out, there is an unusually large company in 17, and she suggested it may represent Christians in general rather than specifically the contemporary followers of Christ.[2] Usually the setting includes a more complete view of the cross whether or not the figures involved in the Deposition are present. In this instance the observer has been given only a glimpse of the shaft of the instrument because the shape of this tapestry, which was determined by its intended function as an altar hanging, precluded the possibility of representing a large vertical form. The proximity of the cross and the presence of bones among the pebbles in the foreground indicate that the drama is taking place on the hill of Golgotha. In most of the similar tapestries we know of, the scene is also set at Golgotha rather than at some distance from it. Among those that depict the Lamentation at Golgotha are tapestries in the Saint Louis Art Museum (fig. 116), the Philadelphia Museum of Art, and two pieces whose present locations are unknown, one formerly in a private collection in New York and the other formerly in the collection of Sir Herbert Cook in England. Among the other tapestries, which show the Lamentation taking place at a distance from the hill, we may list a tapestry in the cathedral in Palencia and another in the Kunsthistorisches Museum in Vienna.[3]

The primrose plant that grows in the grass so promi-

nently next to John's foot was placed there either as a symbol—it was used among other things as a sign of the keys to heaven—or because it blooms early in the spring and so may be an allusion to renewal (Resurrection) or, more simply, to the time of year when the Crucifixion took place.[4] Therefore there is reason to ask whether the violets and roses that decorate the border in this hanging were placed there as symbols. Roses and violets (in some cases the "violets" may be pansies) also appear along with other flora in the borders of the Lamentation tapestries that were cited above as formerly in the Cook collection and as in Palencia, Philadelphia, and Vienna, but not in the pieces now in Saint Louis or formerly in New York. However roses and violets appear together with other flora in the borders of countless tapestries of the period whose subjects are essentially Christian but do not concern the Lamentation (see, for example, one of the two *Prodigal Son* tapestries in the Metropolitan Museum, 41a). Roses, grapes, daisies, violets, pomegranates, and oranges—the flora most often found in borders of this type—all had symbolic significance. Each flower or fruit conveyed several meanings; but most commonly red roses were used to signify martyrdom; grapes, the Eucharistic wine; daisies, purity and innocence; violets, humility; pomegranates, the church, Christ, the Virgin, fertility; and oranges, love or the fruit of the tree of the knowledge of good and evil.[5] However border designers may have chosen these flora simply because all of them have lovely forms and are pleasantly scented. On the other hand the thorny branches that dominate the border design of the *Lamentation* in Saint Louis (fig. 116) make direct reference to the Crucifixion (the crown of thorns), as do also the enframed motifs at the corners and sides—the pelican feeding her young with her own blood, the monogram IHS, and a motif that may include the crown of thorns.

If this tapestry had been hung in front of the altar, the priest's body and vestments would have obscured most of the field during the celebration of Mass. Since the subject is critically involved with that Sacrament, it seems likely that the tapestry was not made to hang there, as an antependium, but above the altar as a dossal where it would be seen more clearly throughout the service.

SOURCE OF THE DESIGN

As Standen has indicated, a panel painting in the Musées Royaux des Beaux-Arts de Belgique in Brussels (fig. 115) appears to be the ultimate source of the design for the figures of the dead Christ, the Virgin, Saint John, and the Magdalen.[6] The picture is one of several that repeat with slight variations a composition by Rogier van der Weyden that appears in a panel painting in the Capilla Real in Granada and also in a virtually identical panel in the Altar of the Virgin in the Gemäldegalerie der Staatlichen Museen, Berlin-Dahlem. Other versions of the composition also appear in paintings now in London, Berlin, and Madrid. In those the figures of John and/or the Magdalen have been replaced by figures of saints or donors or both.[7] In the Brussels and Madrid pictures and the second Berlin picture, the poses of the Virgin, John, and the body of Christ are almost identical to those in the tapestry but in reverse. The major difference is to be found in the position of Christ's legs and feet which in the tapestry are crossed at the ankles. This detail does not appear in the paintings associated with Rogier or his shop, but it is present in works by other artists who used this composition. The feet are crossed more or less in the same way in some pictures painted after a lost original by Dieric Bouts.[8] A *Lamentation* painted by Gerard David and now in the John G. Johnson Collection at the Philadelphia Museum of Art virtually repeats the design of the four main figures as they appear in the Brussels picture but with variations that make it clear the David was not the source of the tapestry's composition.[9]

There can be little doubt that 17 was designed by someone who used for the central section of his picture a composition after Rogier van der Weyden as it was modified by one or more of that master's followers. We cannot tell whether the facial types that are so distinctive in the tapestry, with their rather small features pinched together in the center of the face and in some cases their long hooked noses, were designed by the artist who drew the original sketch or *patron* or by the cartoon painter, assuming they were not one and the same man. But one hand or the other may have created the designs of at least four other surviving pieces; that is, the closely related *Lamentation* in the Saint Louis Art Museum (fig. 116), the *Mass of Saint Gregory* in Nuremberg, the *Esther before Ahasuerus* formerly with a dealer in New York, and the *Christ and the Adulteress* formerly in the collection of Baron Hirsch in London, then in the Joseph Widener collection in Elkins Park, and now in the National Gallery of Art in Washington.[10] In the last the head of the man standing behind and between Christ and the adulteress is almost identical to that of the man kneeling in the left foreground of the Metropolitan Museum's tapestry.

Standen noted that the design of a *Lamentation* tapestry in Vienna had been associated with the name of Quentin Massys and also that some of the facial types in 17 are similar to faces in Massys's paintings.[11] While the observation is valid, neither Standen nor the present writer accepts Quentin Massys as the designer of 17. The fact that almost all the figures seem to have been created for the places they occupy indicates that they are not standard models taken from some cartoon painter's or weaver's stock but figures that were designed expressly for this composition.

The same design source, or perhaps another version of the same cartoon, was used for the *Lamentation* in the Saint Louis Art Museum (fig. 116). Not only are the figures of the Virgin, Christ, John, and the Magdalen the same, but also the two men and the woman who stand behind the Magdalen, the bearded man standing behind the Virgin, and the man behind Saint John all find their counterparts in the Metropolitan Museum's tapestry in more or less the same locations. Although the costumes and postures are somewhat different in the Saint Louis tapestry and the cross and ladder are prominently displayed in its background, it is clear that the two tapestries were woven after versions of the same design. Similar though not identical figures of the Virgin and the dead Christ appear in a *Lamentation* that was in an unidentified private collection in New York in 1923.[12]

MANUFACTURE AND DATE

Rubinstein-Bloch (1927), Patterson (1930), the catalogue for the Blumenthal collection exhibition at the Metropolitan Museum (1943), Rorimer (1947), and Standen

Fig. 116. *The Lamentation.* Tapestry, southern Netherlands, late fifteenth or early sixteenth century. The Saint Louis Art Museum.

(see note 1) attributed this tapestry to Brussels without stating their reasons. Tapestries like this usually were assigned to Brussels because of their painterly compositions and fine quality even though there is nothing to prove that such pieces were produced only there. We suggest no place of origin other than the southern Netherlands in general.

Except for Patterson who dated it in the fifteenth century and the Brooklyn Museum exhibition catalogue of 1936 which placed it in the second half of the fifteenth century, the tapestry has been published as dating from sometime in the first quarter of the sixteenth century. Standen called attention to its similarity to the *Mass of Saint Gregory* in the Germanisches Nationalmuseum in Nuremberg which is dated 1495 in the weave, and she suggested that the *Lamentation* was designed and woven between 1495 and 1510.[13] The facial types in the two pieces are strikingly similar. However it is more important, as Standen indicated, that the tapestries are similar in terms of pictorial style. The figures in both are arranged in rows parallel to the picture plane and all the figures are pressed close to it. This was characteristic of tapestry design in the last third of the fifteenth century. We may cite as typical examples of that style, as seen in so-called

Brussels tapestries, the dossal of the *Adoration of the Magi* in the cathedral in Sens and the dossal of the *Madonna of the Living Water* in the Louvre, both of which may be dated about 1480–85 (see figs. 49, 66). It may be seen in quite a different form in tapestries that have been associated with Tournai, like the *Trojan War* tapestries in the Metropolitan Museum and elsewhere (see 13a–c), that were designed a decade or two earlier than the "Brussels" pieces.

What little information the conventionally dressed figures in 17 can give us about fashions in civilian costume at the time the tapestry was designed points to a date in the last decade of the fifteenth century. The fashion for the deep V neckline on the gown worn by the woman in the foreground at the right waned after about 1490 but the high-crowned silhouette of her headdress and the one worn by the Magdalen continued to be in favor during the last decade of the century.[14] This, together with the fact that the stylistically similar *Mass of Saint Gregory* in Nuremberg was either designed or woven in 1495, suggests that 17 was designed about 1490–95 and that, because it was an expensive piece to produce and therefore presumably meant for a fashionable client, it would not have been woven much later.

RELATED TAPESTRIES

No tapestries that could have accompanied this one in a set of altar furnishings are known to have survived. As noted above (Source of the Design) the figures in the central group as well as most of the others appear again in the *Lamentation* in Saint Louis (fig. 116). There is no other connection between the two pieces.

HISTORY

Sold, *The James A. Garland Collection,* American Art Association, New York, March 19–20, 1909, no. 127, illus.
In the collection of George and Florence Blumenthal, New York, in 1909.
Given to the MMA by George Blumenthal, 1941.

EXHIBITIONS

New York, MMA, 1909. Lent by George and Florence Blumenthal.
New York, Jacques Seligmann & Co. Galleries, 1927. *Loan Exhibition of Religious Art for the Benefit of the Basilique of the Sacré Coeur of Paris.* Cat. no. XII. Lent by George and Florence Blumenthal.
Brooklyn Museum, 1936. *An Exhibition of European Art 1450–1500.* Cat. no. 154, illus. Lent by Mr. and Mrs. George Blumenthal.
New York, MMA, 1943. *Masterpieces in the Collection of George Blumenthal: A Special Exhibition.* Cat. no. 27, illus.

PUBLICATIONS

Hunter 1925, p. 124. Mentioned.

International Studio 87 (June 1927) p. 4. Illus., with caption.

Rubinstein-Bloch, Stella. *Catalogue of the Collection of George and Florence Blumenthal, New-York.* Vol. 4, *Tapestries and Furniture.* Paris, 1927, pl. XII. Described and discussed briefly; illus.

Patterson, Augusta Owen. "Furniture in the Blumenthal Collection." *International Studio* 97 (November 1930) p. 45. Illus. hanging on the wall of a room in the Blumenthal house in New York.

"European Art, 1450–1500: Painting, Tapestries, Sculpture and Objects of Art Lent to Brooklyn." *Art News* 34 (May 16, 1936) p. 6. Illus.

Rorimer, James J. *Mediaeval Tapestries: A Picture Book.* New York, 1947. Illus. fig. 20.

NOTES

1. Edith Appleton Standen, unpublished draft manuscript of a catalogue entry for this tapestry, ca. 1968–1969, in the files of the MMA Department of Medieval Art.

2. Standen, draft MS. Standen calls attention to a somewhat later tapestry of the Lamentation (combined with figures from the Deposition) in Brussels that also shows a large number of figures; see Marthe Crick-Kuntziger, *Catalogue des tapisseries (XIVe au XVIIIe siècle)*, Musées Royaux d'Art et d'Histoire de Bruxelles (Brussels, 1956) no. 20, pl. 26.

3. See, respectively, for the first group of four, Saint Louis Art Museum, *Handbook of the Collections* (Saint Louis, 1975) p. 83, illus. (see also fig. 116 in text above); Joseph Downs, "Gothic Tapestries," *Pennsylvania Museum Bulletin* 21 (1925–26) pp. 175–81, illus. p. 174; Göbel 1923, vol. 2, fig. 370; and *Porcelain and Objects of Art . . .* [various properties including some] *. . . Sold by Order of the Trustees of the Cook Collection . . . .*, sale cat., Christie's, London, July 24, 1947, no. 174, not illus., but see Wolfgang Schöne, *Dieric Bouts und seine Schule* (Berlin and Leipzig, 1938) pp. 145–47, illus. pl. 40. For the other two pieces, see, respectively, J. K. Steppe, "Vlaamse Wandtapijten in Spanje. Recente Gebeurtnissen en Publicaties," *Artes Textiles* 3 (1956) p. 52, illus. fig. 16; and Dora Heinz, *Europäische Wandteppiche I* (Brunswick, 1963) illus. pl. 79.

4. Margaret B. Freeman, *The Unicorn Tapestries*, MMA (New York, 1976) pp. 132–33, referred to the primrose as a symbol of the keys to heaven, and also to the fact that it is one of the first plants to bloom in spring.

5. These and other interpretations for the flora listed above, except the grapes, are given in Freeman, *Unicorn Tapestries*, pp. 115–16, 121–25, 131–32.

6. Standen, draft MS. Concerning the painting in Brussels, see Max J. Friedländer, *Early Netherlandish Painting*, vol. 2, *Rogier van der Weyden and the Master of Flémalle* (New York and Washington, 1967) p. 64, no. 20a, pl. 41; the author describes it as a workshop version of the similar painting in the National Gallery, London (see below, note 7).

7. For the Altar of the Virgin panels in Granada and Berlin, see Friedländer, *Early Netherlandish Painting*, vol. 2, p. 60, nos. 1 and 1a, pl. 1; and Lorne Campbell, *Van der Weyden* (London, 1980) pp. 6, 37, 38, illus. For the *Lamentation* paintings in London, Berlin, and Madrid, see Friedländer, *Early Netherlandish Painting*, vol. 2, p. 64, nos. 20, 20b, 20d, pls. 40, 41. The London version is also illustrated in Campbell, *Van der Weyden*, p. 94.

8. For the pictures after Bouts, see Schöne, *Dieric Bouts*, pp. 120–23, 182, and pls. 43–44 where four of the versions of this composition are illustrated, including the one in the Städelsches Kunstinstitut in Frankfurt which Schöne regards as the one closest to the original.

9. See *John G. Johnson Collection: Catalogue of Flemish and Dutch Paintings* (Philadelphia, 1972) p. 28, no. 328, illus. p. 134.

10. For the last three tapestries see, respectively, Göbel 1923, vol. 2, figs. 120, 371, 372. Standen, draft MS, called attention to the stylistic similarities between 17 and the *Mass of Saint Gregory*.

11. Standen, draft MS. For the tapestry, see Heinz, *Europäische Wandteppiche*, pl. 79. For the Massys paintings that Standen cited, see Friedländer, *Early Netherlandish Painting*, vol. 7, *Quentin Massys* (New York and Washington, 1971) pl. 1, John's face in the *Lamentation* panel in Antwerp, and pl. 7, left, the young man holding a document in the panel of the *Holy Kindred* in Brussels.

12. See Göbel 1923, vol. 2, fig. 370.

13. Standen, draft MS. For the Saint Gregory tapestry, see Göbel 1923, vol. 2, fig. 120.

14. The V neckline had come into fashion about 1460; see C. Willett and Phillis Cunnington, *Handbook of English Mediaeval Costume* (London, 1952) p. 156. For headdresses like those worn by the Magdalen and the woman in the right foreground of the tapestry, see Freeman, *Unicorn Tapestries*, figs. 250 and 255 (woodcuts dating from the last decade of the fifteenth century) and fig. 202 (painting of about 1492 showing Mary Magdalen wearing a headdress reminiscent of the one she wears in the Metropolitan Museum's tapestry).

18

Scenes from the Life of the Virgin

Southern Netherlands, 1490–1510
Wool warp; wool, silk, and metallic wefts
7 ft. 2³/₄ in. × 6 ft. 10 in. (2.20 m × 2.08 m)
16–19 warp yarns per inch, 6–7¹/₂ per centimeter
Bequest of Benjamin Altman, 1913 (14.40.707)

CONDITION

The field and border have not been cut or diminished. In many areas the weft yarns, particularly the silks, have deteriorated and fallen out. They were replaced with new weft yarns woven on the original warp. These repairs are scattered over the whole surface of the piece, but they are particularly prevalent in the inner and outer guards of the top and bottom segments of the border and, to a lesser extent, in the side guards. There are also repairs in the floral part of the border. Almost all the areas of highlight in the garments throughout the field have been rewoven. These restorations occur mainly in places where the pattern shows relatively flat, unmodulated tones rather than contours; and so the drawing has been affected very little. The colors have survived moderately well. The metallic yarns, made of narrow flat silver and/or silver-gilt wires wrapped around silk core yarns, have tarnished. They were used to render highlights in some of the garments and also some of the architectural details.

DESCRIPTION AND SUBJECT

A symmetrical system of stone and metal structural elements divides the field into five compartments of irregular shape and unequal size, a conformation that invites comparison with some painted altarpieces of the period. The column that rises in the center of the lower portion of the field carries on its capital the left and right ends of two adjacent cusped, curved arches which do not continue their normal courses but terminate at their centers where each one meets the base of a column that rises upward to the top of the field. Just above their points of joining the cusped arches, the two upper columns support the inner ends of a pair of flat arches with curved ends. These columns and arches are all decorated with dentated leaves that either form a cresting on the cusped arches or wind around the shafts of the columns and the middle parts of the flat arches.

The system creates two small rectangular compartments in the upper corners of the field. The one at the left contains a scene showing the presentation of the young Mary in the temple. She is greeted at the entrance to the building by the rabbi, a man wearing a yoked plain velvet tunic over an unpatterned gown. The girl wears a loose trailing gown cut with a high round neck. She kneels on a platform at the top of the flight of steps that leads to the temple. A bearded man and a woman, the Virgin's parents, Joachim and Anne, both wearing hoods and plain gowns, stand in the background beyond the steps. A landscape opens into the distance behind them. The Visitation is represented in the rectangular compartment at the upper right. Elizabeth and Mary greet each other in a landscape setting. Mary, wearing a mantle over a patterned velvet or damask gown and a scarf wound around her head, stands at the left and extends her left hand to touch her cousin's shoulder; her right hand is raised in salutation. Elizabeth wears a long hood and a simple unpatterned gown, and she bends her knee to the Virgin and raises both hands toward her.

These two scenes flank a pentagonal compartment that contains a representation of the Assumption. Six angels in flowing robes and mantles bear Mary upward, above a landscape in which a turreted building and numbers of trees are visible. The Virgin wears a simple round-necked sleeved tunic made of patterned velvet or damask over a plain velvet kirtle. Her blond hair is parted in the middle and falls in waving tresses to a point below her shoulders. She faces directly forward, her eyelids downcast and her hands pressed together before her breast in an attitude of prayer. In a number of related paintings and tapestries (see Source of the Design) a similar figure of Mary, again assisted by angels, stands on a crescent moon and in some cases is about to be crowned as queen of heaven, either by other angels or by the persons of the Trinity. A very similar image that appeared in a tapestry fragment formerly in Berlin showed the Trinity at the top of the composition, about to place a crown on the Virgin's head.[1] Since that composition is otherwise nearly a duplicate of the one in 18, it seems fair to ask whether the latter represents an abbreviated version of what was in fact a Coronation of the Virgin combined with an Assumption. Eisler noted that in northern European painting the Assumption was rarely depicted as a separate subject until the end of the fifteenth century; that before that it was combined with

18

the Death and Coronation of the Virgin; and that in the painted versions of the scene (see Source of the Design) there are allusions to the Woman of the Apocalypse from which developed the image of the Immaculate Conception.[2]

The arched compartment at the lower left corner of the field contains the scene of the Annunciation. It is set in a room with a patterned tile floor. Mary is dressed in the same way as in the Assumption scene above but with the addition of a white veil over her head and shoulders. She is shown in the right foreground kneeling before a low stand on which an open book rests, her hands crossed over her breast. Gabriel, wearing a cope over a long-sleeved gown, the whole bordered with floral arabesques, rushes in from the left with his wings raised and his right hand lifted in salutation. He holds a scepter in his lowered left hand. A length of damask or velvet decorated with a large conventional floral pattern hangs behind him. A ewer containing two stalks bearing lily buds and blossoms rests on the floor in the left foreground.

The compartment in the lower right corner of the field shows Mary, dressed as in the Annunciation but with a larger and heavier head covering, sitting in the right foreground and holding the infant Jesus on her lap. The scene, which represents the Adoration of the Kings, is set in a room with a carpeted floor. There is a glimpse of a broad landscape through the open doorway in the wall at the left. A bareheaded and beardless man holding a chaperon stands behind Mary at the right; he probably represents Joseph. On the other side of the Virgin appear the three kings. In the foreground the eldest one, whose wide-brimmed hat is set on the floor to the right of the Virgin's feet, kneels before the Christ Child and raises both hands toward Him, taking the infant's right hand in his own left hand. This king, the most richly dressed of the three, wears an ermine-lined patterned tunic over a plain funnel-sleeved gown and a jeweled necklace with pendants. An ovoid metal box rests on the floor next to his right foot. The king behind him, bareheaded and wearing what appears to be a cloak over a striped garment, raises his hands in prayer and gazes at the Child. The third king stands behind these two. His unpatterned garment is cut with a high round neck and full sleeves gathered in at the wrists. He removes his turban with his left hand and holds a covered cup in his right.

The border comprises narrow guards flanking a wide band of dark blue against which are scattered branches with rose blossoms and leaves alternating with daisy stalks and grapevines.

If this tapestry had been designed as part of a series of narrative hangings it would almost certainly have shown incidents representing only one or two periods in Mary's life, and the other pieces would have shown the rest. But the five episodes depicted in 18 represent events that took place both early and late in her life. This, together with the relatively small size of the hanging, suggests that it may have been made as a dossal to be hung above an altar and contemplated by itself. It also suggests that the choice of subjects may represent the stated preference of some lay patron or religious order or establishment.

SOURCE OF THE DESIGN

Schmitz (1919, 214, 216) listed this hanging and the similar *Assumption* fragment formerly in Berlin (see note 1) among a group of tapestries that he believed had been designed by Philips, the man whose name is recorded as the painter of the cartoon for the *Legend of Herkinbald* in Brussels. Göbel (1923, vol. 1, 411) suggested that 18 was designed by Jan van Roome, who painted the model for the *Herkinbald* tapestry, when he

Fig. 117. *The Annunciation,* by Gerard David. Panel painting, Bruges, late fifteenth century. Städelsches Kunstinstitut, Frankfurt.

287

was working with Bernaert van Orley late in his career. Heinz listed the Berlin *Assumption* fragment among a group of hangings that she thought might have been designed by Quentin Massys.[3] Until and unless documentary evidence turns up to support these attributions they cannot be considered further.

Although we have no prints or paintings to designate as the source of the compositions in 18, Standen traced some of the figures to what may be their primary or, more likely, their secondary sources.[4] The figure of Gabriel in the Annunciation is almost identical to the corresponding figure in a late fifteenth-century panel painting by Gerard David that is now in the Städelsches Kunstinstitut in Frankfurt (fig. 117).[5] Since a very similar figure appears considerably earlier, in the *Annunciation* miniature which serves as the frontispiece of a manuscript of the *Traité sur la salutation angélique* in Brussels, we cannot be sure that David invented it.[6] That manuscript page, painted in 1461 in Bruges in the shop of Guillaume Vrelant, also shows the Virgin kneeling in a similar pose but with her body turned more to the left.

The figure of the Virgin in the Assumption scene in 18 resembles the corresponding figure in the panel painting of *Mary Queen of Heaven* that was executed in Bruges between 1480 and 1490 by the Master of the Saint Lucy Legend. It is now in the National Gallery of Art in Washington (fig. 118).[7] In that painting there are eight angels lifting Mary to heaven and a host of others, singing or playing musical instruments, surrounding her. However there are only six angels supporting Mary, as there are in the tapestry, in another *Assumption* panel in the National Gallery. The picture was painted by Michiel Sittow who may have been apprenticed to the Master of the Saint Lucy Legend in Bruges when the latter was painting his Assumption. Sittow executed this small panel in Spain for Isabel la Católica about 1500–1502.[8] In Sittow's version of what appears to be the Master of the Saint Lucy Legend's interpretation of the subject, there is a detail that shows his painting to be more closely related to 18 than the other painting is. Sittow depicted one of the angels at the left placing his right arm under the Virgin's cloak at the side as he helps her upward. Both paintings show Mary rising above an open landscape with buildings in it, just as the tapestry does. However there are two major differences between the painted and woven images. Both panel paintings show the Virgin standing above a crescent moon (inverted in the Sittow example), and in both she is about to receive her crown as queen of heaven—from the Trinity in the Master of the Saint Lucy Legend's painting, from three angels in the Sittow panel. The similar *Assumption* tapestry fragment that was formerly in Berlin included both the crescent moon and the Coronation by the Trinity (see note 1). Another similar tapestry *Assumption*, with the crescent moon, appears in the center of a hanging in Saint Mary's Hall in Coventry. In this hanging, which shows male and female saints, a king, a queen, gentlemen, and ladies reverently watching the Assumption from the sides as angels with instruments of the Passion move above, the central group must have been taken from the same or a closely related composition.[9]

Some of the figures in the Adoration of the Kings in the Metropolitan Museum's tapestry—the Virgin and Child and particularly the figure of the king in the foreground—seem to have been derived from the same source as the models for the corresponding figures in a tapestry in the Bayerisches Nationalmuseum in Munich.[10] The figure of the Virgin in the Annunciation scene in 18 is closely related to the figure of Mary in the Nativity scene in a tapestry of the same period in Trent.[11]

MANUFACTURE AND DATE

Von Bode (1906) believed that this tapestry was produced in the Netherlands at the end of the fifteenth century, whereas it was attributed specifically to Brussels in the *Handbook of the Benjamin Altman Collection* (1914, 1915, 1928), and by Hunter (1915), Göbel (1923), and Monod (1923), with dates ranging from about 1500 (MMA *Handbook* and Hunter) to about 1520 (Göbel). Monod placed it in the transitional period between the Gothic and Renaissance styles but offered no specific date. Presumably these writers chose Brussels as the place of manufacture because the tapestry shows the painterly style that has become associated with Brussels and because its border resembles the borders of tapestries that are associated with Brussels (see discussion in 41a, b). Göbel must further have designated Brussels because he attributed the design of the tapestry to Jan van Roome. The fact that some of the figures in these scenes may derive from paintings executed in Bruges or by artists associated with Bruges does not indicate necessarily that the tapestry was designed there and certainly not that it was woven there. It might have been commissioned from a producer in Bruges, but the hanging itself could have been made anywhere in the southern Netherlands.

The paintings by Gerard David, the Master of the Saint Lucy Legend, and Michiel Sittow cited above (Source of the Design) that might have provided models for some of the figures in the Metropolitan Museum's tapestry may all be dated between 1480–90 and 1502.

The fact that the tapestry field was designed to resemble an altarpiece with small, irregularly shaped panel paintings set into an elaborate framework relates this hanging intimately to others that are dated convincingly in the last quarter of the fifteenth century (see figs. 64–66). Finally, among the scenes represented in the choir hangings of the *Lives of Christ and the Virgin* in Aix-en-Provence, tapestries that are dated 1511, there are similar compositions for the Annunciation, Visitation, and Assumption.[12] Those tapestries show columns separating the scenes and, as Standen pointed out, some of the columns are carved with classical ornaments.[13] However the upper part of the column in one piece is wrapped spirally with leaves and it resembles the shafts of the columns in the Metropolitan Museum's tapestry.[14]

Taking into account the dates of the paintings that may have inspired some of the figures in the tapestry together with the late fifteenth-century form of the composition and the date of the Aix tapestries, we conclude that the Metropolitan Museum's hanging was probably designed after about 1490 and woven no later than about 1510.

RELATED TAPESTRIES

As noted above (Description and Subject) we believe that this tapestry may have been designed to hang alone as a dossal above an altar because it is relatively small and also because the events it represents took place both early and late in the Virgin's life rather than at just one stage. However it is possible that it is part of a series of hangings that illustrated the episodes without regard for chronological sequence. No tapestries that might have belonged in such a cycle are known to have survived. The other subjects would have depicted the usual key events—the birth of the Virgin, her marriage, the Nativity, the Christ Child presented in the temple, the Crucifixion and Lamentation, Pentecost, the Dormition, and the Coronation. Since there are no devotional or laudatory representations in this piece, the other hangings would probably have contained only narrative scenes also; but it is difficult to imagine how they would have been grouped. The most closely related Lady cycle known to have survived is contained in, and intimately connected with, the series of scenes from the life of Christ that appear in the set of choir hangings in the Cathedral of Saint-Sauveur in Aix-en-Provence.[15] There, the designer showed the birth of the Virgin, her presentation in the temple, the Annunciation, the Visitation, the Nativity combined with the Adoration of the Shepherds, the Crucifixion and Lamentation, Pentecost, the Virgin greeting the apostles, the Dormition, the funeral of the Virgin, and her Assumption. The Coronation is not present, but the figure of Mary appears on Christ's right hand in the Last Judgment. Any or all of these episodes might have been represented among the hangings to which this piece belonged if it did indeed belong to such a set.

HISTORY

According to Müntz (1882, 139, caption), this or a duplicate hanging was in the Spitzer collection in or around 1882 (see Publications). If this piece indeed did belong to Frédéric Spitzer, he disposed of it before his collection was offered for sale at auction in Paris in 1893; it is listed neither in the sale catalogue nor in the catalogue of the Spitzer collection that was published in Mâcon in 1890–91.[16] Monod (1923) and the author of the MMA *Handbook of the Altman Collection* (1914, 1915, 1928; see Publications) believed that the tapestry had belonged to Spitzer.

In the collection of Oscar Hainauer, Berlin, before 1894, when he died and it passed into his widow's possession. Presumably sold with the rest of the Hainauer collection by Frau Julie Hainauer to Joseph Duveen in 1906.[17]

In the collection of Benjamin Altman, New York.

Bequeathed to the MMA by Benjamin Altman, 1913.

EXHIBITION

Berlin, 1898. *Ausstellung von Kunstwerken des Mittelalters und der Renaissance aus Berliner Privatbesitz veranstaltet von der Kunstgeschichtlichen Gesellschaft.* Illus. pl. LVII, hanging on a wall of one of the exhibition galleries. Lent by Frau Julie Hainauer.

PUBLICATIONS

Müntz, Eugène. *La tapisserie.* Paris, [1882], p. 139. This or a duplicate piece is illustrated in a small-scale engraving; not mentioned in the text.

von Bode, Wilhelm. *Die Sammlung Oscar Hainauer.* Berlin, 1897; English imprint, London, 1906, no. 449. Described briefly; illus. pl. following p. 48.

Handbook of the Benjamin Altman Collection. MMA, New York, 1914; rev. ed., 1915, pp. 144–45. Described and discussed briefly.

Hunter, George Leland. "The Tapestries of the Altman Collection." *Arts and Decoration* 5 (1914–15) pp. 92–94. Discussed briefly; illus. p. 92.

Schmitz, Hermann. *Bildteppiche.* Berlin, [1919], pp. 214, 216. Mentioned.

Göbel 1923, vol. 1, pp. 76, 411. Discussed briefly; illus. vol. 2, fig. 58.

Monod, François. "La galerie Altman au Metropolitan Museum de New-York," pt. 3. *Gazette des Beaux-Arts,* 5th ser., 8 (1923) p. 373. Described and discussed briefly.

Hunter 1925, pp. 124, 240. Mentioned.

Handbook of the Benjamin Altman Collection. MMA. 2d ed. (rev. from 1914 and 1915 eds.), New York, 1928, p. 145. Described and discussed briefly.

Catalogue of . . . [various properties including] . . . *the property of Captain Denzil Cope,* sale cat., Sotheby's, London, March 13, 1931, nos. 121[a, b]. Mentioned.

NOTES

1. Illustrated in Göbel 1923, vol. 2, fig. 57. Formerly in the Kunstgewerbemuseum in Berlin. Another hanging woven after a similar cartoon was owned by Major Darley, England, earlier in this century; photo in H. C. Marillier's manuscript "Subject Catalogue of Tapestries," Victoria and Albert Museum, London.

2. Colin T. Eisler, "The Sittow Assumption," *Art News* 64 (September 1965) pp. 35–37.

3. Dora Heinz, *Europäische Wandteppiche I* (Brunswick, 1963) pp. 122–23.

4. Edith Appleton Standen, unpublished draft of a catalogue entry on this tapestry, ca. 1968–69, now in the files of the MMA Department of Medieval Art.

5. See also Max J. Friedländer, *Early Netherlandish Painting,* vol. 6, pt. 2, *Hans Memlinc and Gerard David* (New York and Washington, 1971) no. 176, pl. 189.

6. Bibliothèque Royale Albert I, Brussels, MS 9270, fol. 2v. See *Le siècle d'or de la miniature flamande: Le mécénat de Philippe le Bon,* exh. cat., Palais des Beaux-Arts, Brussels, and Rijksmuseum, Amsterdam (Brussels, 1959) no. 141, pl. 48.

7. See also Friedländer, *Early Netherlandish Painting,* vol. 6, pt. 2, no. Add. 277, pl. 257.

8. The picture was one in a series painted by Michiel Sittow and Juan de Flandes, both painters to the court, for the oratory in the queen's private chapel. After her death it was sold with some of the other panels in that group to Margaret of Austria's treasurer, and it became her property. See Eisler, "The Sittow Assumption," pp. 34, 52–53; and Jazeps Trizna, *Michel Sittow, peintre revalais de l'école brugeoise (1468–1525/1526)* (Brussels, 1976) pp. 25–26, 59, 73, 91. Eisler (pp. 37, 52) suggested that Sittow may have been trained in Bruges under the Master of the Saint Lucy Legend rather than under Memling.

9. See Thomson 1930, pp. 150–51, for an illustration and brief discussion of this tapestry; for an exhaustive discussion of it, see George Scharf, Jr., "The Old Tapestry in St. Mary's Hall at Coventry," *Archaeologia* 36 (1856) pp. 438–53. Both authors believed that the tapestry was woven to fit the north wall of Saint Mary's Hall

which was used as the guildhall in Coventry. They also indicated that the figure of Justitia that now occupies the center of the upper register in the composition, directly above the representation of the Assumption, replaced a representation of either the Trinity (Thomson) or symbols of the four Evangelists (Scharf). Scharf (p. 446) noted that depictions of angels and part of a throne and mantle remain from the original subject. This might indicate that the missing figures indeed represented the Trinity and that this is another instance of an Assumption combined with a Coronation of the Virgin.

10. Göbel 1923, vol. 2, fig. 369a.

11. The tapestry, one of a series, is preserved in the Museo Diocesano in Trent; see Enrico Castelnuovo et al., *Gli arazzi del cardinale: Bernardo Cles e il Ciclo della Passione di Pieter van Aelst* (Trent, 1990) illus. pp. 120-21.

12. See *Les tapisseries de la Vie du Christ et de la Vierge d'Aix-en-Provence*, exh. cat., Musée des Tapisseries (Aix-en-Provence, 1977) pp. 30, 41, illus. This catalogue contains a number of essays that discuss the tapestries from several specialized points of view.

13. Unpublished note by Edith A. Standen; see note 4 above.

14. Illustrated in *Les tapisseries . . . d'Aix-en-Provence*, p. 29. This column separates the episode of the birth of the Virgin from that of her presentation in the temple.

15. The subjects represented in this series of hangings are listed in *Les tapisseries . . . d'Aix-en-Provence*, pp. 85-92.

16. *La collection Spitzer: Antiquité, moyen-âge, renaissance*, 2 vols. (Mâcon, 1890-91); and *Catalogue des objets d'art . . . composant l'importante et précieuse collection Spitzer*, 2 vols., sale cat., 33 rue de Villejust, Paris, April 17-June 16, 1893.

17. The story of Duveen's purchase of the collection is given in James Henry Duveen, *The Rise of the House of Duveen* (New York, 1957) pp. 251-54.

19
Wreath on a Ground of Flowers, Birds, and Rabbits

Fragment of a wall hanging

Southern Netherlands, 1490–1550
Wool warp, wool wefts
6 ft. 7 in. × 4 ft. 1 in. (2.01 m × 1.25 m)
14 warp yarns per inch, 5 1/2 per centimeter
Bequest of George D. Pratt, 1935 (42.152.6)

CONDITION

The hanging, which has been cut along all four sides, is a fragment of a larger tapestry. Bands of modern weaving showing a narrow light stripe next to a wide dark stripe have been sewn to the four edges. There are a few small spot repairs by reweaving throughout the piece but none of them has affected the original drawing. Two small rectangular patches taken from another part of the original tapestry or from a closely related piece have been inserted in the lower corners. The colors are fresh and vibrant.

DESCRIPTION AND SUBJECT

A wreath tied with lengths of ribbon at the centers of the top, bottom, and two sides appears against a dark greenish blue ground richly strewn with a variety of blossoming plants. One rabbit nibbles at a bit of food at center bottom while a second rabbit sitting slightly above and to the left turns to watch the first. A cock and a hen pheasant stand in the space enclosed by the wreath. Two short-tailed game birds, perhaps quail, appear against the ground near the upper left and right corners of the field.

The wreath is composed of four quadrant-shaped swags of leaves, flowers, and fruits that are similar to each other but not identical. The ends of the swags issue from large stylized acanthus leaves, the stem ends of which are tied to each other with lengths of ribbon whose centers form flat loops inside the wreath at each knot. The two ends of each ribbon flutter past the outside edge of the wreath to loop loosely once before coming to rest at or near that edge. Since the exterior loops at the bottom form a more elaborate and dominant horizontal mass than the others, and also since all the birds and rabbits stand in the same orientation on the ground,

it would seem that this weaving was meant to be viewed in a vertical plane, as hung on a wall, rather than in a horizontal plane, as lying on a bed, table, or bench.

Wreaths of leaves (with or without fruits, flowers, and ribbons) have been used as decorative motifs since classical antiquity. They appear to have been especially popular during the fifteenth and sixteenth centuries in all the decorative arts and in architecture. During that period wreaths appear frequently in the textile arts, not only in tapestry but also in weaving and needlework. As Callmann (exh. cat. Allentown 1980, 81) pointed out, a sumptuous Italian gilt-ground voided velvet featuring a wreath of oak leaves and fruits enclosing a shield with the arms of Matthias Corvinus, king of Bohemia and Hungary (1458–90), has survived from the second half of the fifteenth century.[1] This wreath is tied at the sides by fluttering, tasseled ribbons and at the top and bottom by narrow bands apparently made of grooved metal. Other silks of the same sort and period have also survived, including two voided velvet antependia, one with a wreath enclosing the arms of a Cardinal Mendoza of Toledo and the other with a wreath surrounding an oak tree and scroll referring to Pope Sixtus IV (1471–84).[2] In the second example the wreath, which is made of oak leaves, is tied at the sides, top, and bottom by lengths of fluttering ribbon that also wrap around some adjacent oak branches. To contemporary eyes, a wreath surrounding a coat of arms or a personal device undoubtedly carried with it implications of honor, valor, and victory, memories of the honorific crowns of antiquity.

In most surviving tapestries showing wreaths used in this way, the circular form reads as a frame for a secondary field that is different from that against which the wreath itself appears. Often the wreath encircles a landscape setting featuring an armorial shield (see Manufacture and Date). A tapestry in the Cleveland Museum of Art shows emblazoned shields hanging on ribbons inside the wreaths and directly against the flowered ground.[3] A tapestry with leaf, fruit, and flower swags that are virtually identical to the ones in 19, and tied together with the same looping ribbons in the same way, shows the wreaths enframing scenes representing proverbs, the whole against a flowered ground inhabited by birds.[4] The Metropolitan Museum's tapestry differs from these other hangings in that it shows a wreath used not as an enframement for another motif but as an ornament in its own right that has simply been superimposed on the flowered ground. Wreaths of this kind also appear in certain Spanish knotted carpets of the sixteenth century; some of them enclose secondary motifs, others do not.[5]

Callmann (exh. cat. Allentown 1980, 80–81) believed that the tapestry from which 19 came had the same format as two millefleurs tapestries with armorial wreaths, the one in the Cleveland Museum of Art and another in the Victoria and Albert Museum.[6] Each of them shows the wreaths arranged in a row along the center of the long, narrow ground which, in the latter piece, is inhabited by animals and birds. A small hanging that shows three wreaths that are virtually identical to the one in 19, placed close together in a horizontal row against a similar ground inhabited by similar birds and rabbits (fig. 119), came to light some years after Callmann made her observation. It is not part of the same tapestry but may represent one woven after the same, or a closely related, set of cartoons (see Related Tapestries).

SOURCE OF THE DESIGN

Callmann (exh. cat. Allentown 1980, 81) suggested that the wreath may have been based on an Italian silk or an Italian drawing that was interpreted in a northern weaving shop. While the motif might well originally have come from Italy, it seems likely that by the time this piece was woven such motifs would be found in the stocks of Netherlandish tapestry designers and weavers.

MANUFACTURE AND DATE

In the only published opinion we have concerning the date and place of manufacture of the fragment, Callmann (exh. cat. Allentown 1980, 80–81) observed that the wreath in this context points to a date in the sixteenth century but that late fifteenth-century Italian silks showing decorative wreaths were known in northern Europe as well. She concluded that the fragment was Franco-Flemish and could be dated in the late fifteenth century. Other closely related millefleurs hangings decorated with wreaths associated with heraldic motifs may be dated in the first half of the sixteenth century. Two such hangings show wreaths enclosing landscapes in front of which hang the arms of the Province of Salzburg and of Matthäus Lang von Wellenburg, the whole surmounted by an ecclesiastical hat. Palm trees hung with military trophies flank the wreaths. Von

Wellenburg served as archbishop of Salzburg from 1519 until his death in 1540. One of these pieces, complete with border, is in the Museum Carolino Augusteum in Salzburg; the other, without its border, is in the Fogg Art Museum, Cambridge, Massachusetts. Erik Duverger dated these hangings between 1520 and 1530.[7] There is a tapestry in the Victoria and Albert Museum that shows three wreaths on a millefleurs ground, each of which encloses a landscape opening out behind a shield blazoned with the coat of arms of the Giovio family of Como. As Digby (see note 6) noted, the Giovio arms are marshaled there as borne by Paolo Giovio (1483–1552) after Pope Leo X (1513–21) honored him with the Medici charges that appear in the first and fourth quarters of the shield. A scroll inscribed with Paolo's device FATO PRU-DENTIA MINOR wraps around the wreath. The internal evidence points firmly to a date in the second quarter of the sixteenth century, as Digby concluded. Later Delmarcel suggested that this tapestry and its mate in the collection of the prince of Liechtenstein might have been produced for the palace that Giovio bought in Como in 1543 and therefore that the pieces may have been woven between that year and 1552, when Giovio died.[8]

A different but closely related group of millefleurs tapestries showing wreaths and armorial elements may be dated in the same period because their borders resemble a particularly sumptuous kind of enframement that is frequently found on tapestries attributed to Brussels in the second quarter or middle of the sixteenth century. This kind of border shows tightly packed bands of fruits, leaves, and flowers; in the side sections are iris plants with tall lanceolate leaves. Among the many tapestries of this type that have survived may be listed an example that was formerly with L. Bernheimer in Munich and one in the collection of Arthur Curtiss James. These, together with three similar tapestries that Erik Duverger identified as Bruges weavings, have floral grounds of much finer scale than 19 or the other examples discussed here.[9]

If the Metropolitan Museum's tapestry were more directly related to the pieces cited above it would seem reasonable to date it in the first half of the sixteenth century. However it does show marked differences of composition and style, and there is nothing to indicate that this piece may not have been woven during the last years of the preceding century. The millefleurs tapestry featuring virtually identical beribboned wreaths enframing scenes representing proverbs (see note 4) contains a clue to its date of design. The scene showing a man carrying a lady on his shoulders and the one below it, in which a man approaches a dog, contain figures

Fig. 119. *Wreaths on a Ground of Flowers, Birds, and Rabbits.* Tapestry, southern Netherlands, here dated 1490–1550. Collection De Wit/Blondeel-Belgium.

wearing costumes for men and women that came into fashion in the last decade of the fifteenth century. Since this piece and 19 effectively have the same wreaths it is clear that the two hangings are closely related. However we cannot say whether they share only a design source or also a time frame and a shop context.

As for the place of manufacture, there is no evidence that the Metropolitan Museum's tapestry was woven in any particular south Netherlandish center. Its subject matter is similar to that of the tapestries attributed to Brussels and the von Wellenburg, Giovio, and other hangings that have been attributed to Bruges; but that does not indicate that it was produced in one place or the other.[10]

RELATED TAPESTRIES

The Metropolitan Museum's piece may be a fragment of a long, narrow hanging like the ones in the Victoria and Albert Museum and the Cleveland Museum of Art (see Description and Subject, Manufacture and Date). If it is such a fragment, the hanging from which it was cut would probably have been accompanied by one or more matching pieces to make up a set of long, narrow dossals meant to hang around a room above the seat furniture.

The virtually identical wreaths that appear in a similar millefleurs hanging (fig. 119) contain hen pheasants whose silhouettes correspond to that of the cock pheasant inside the wreath in 19.[11] However the ground of 19 is more densely covered with larger, more luxuriantly blossoming plants than the other ground. The two pieces may, nevertheless, have come from the same set

of hangings or from two closely related sets. The discrepancy in the ground patterns could be due to their having been produced by different weavers, or in different shops, using the same or closely related sets of cartoons.

HISTORY

In the collection of George D. Pratt, New York.
Bequeathed to the MMA by George D. Pratt, 1935.

EXHIBITION

Allentown (Pennsylvania) Art Museum, 1980–81. *Beyond Nobility: Art for the Private Citizen in the Early Renaissance.* Catalogue by Ellen Callmann. Cat. no. 79, illus.

PUBLICATIONS

None known.

NOTES

1. Illustrated in Otto von Falke, *Kunstgeschichte der Seidenweberei* (Berlin, 1913) vol. 2, fig. 546.
2. See von Falke, *Kunstgeschichte,* vol. 2, figs. 545, 544.
3. The shield in this tapestry, which is displayed twice in the width of the field, bears the coat of arms of a member of the Medici family; see J. P. Asselberghs, *Les tapisseries flamandes aux Etats-Unis d'Amérique* (Brussels, 1974) p. 21, fig. 8.
4. Discussed and illustrated in Phyllis Ackerman, *Catalogue of a Loan Exhibition of Gothic Tapestries,* Arts Club of Chicago (Chicago, 1926) no. 14.

5. Two examples in the Textile Museum, Washington, illustrate the type well; see Ernst Kühnel and Louisa Bellinger, *Catalogue of Spanish Rugs, 12th to 19th Century* (Washington, 1953) pls. xxvii (Alcaraz, early sixteenth century), and especially xxxv (Cuenca?, second half of the sixteenth century).

6. For the tapestry in Cleveland, see note 3 above. The tapestry in the Victoria and Albert Museum is discussed and illustrated in Digby 1980, pp. 47–48, pls. 58A (full view) and 58B (detail of upper left section). More recently the London tapestry and its mate in the prince of Liechtenstein's collection were discussed and illustrated by Guy Delmarcel in *Bruges et la tapisserie*, exh. cat. by Delmarcel and Erik Duverger, Musée Gruuthuse and Musée Memling (Bruges, 1987) nos. 5 and 6, illus. in color and black and white.

7. The complete tapestry in Salzburg is illustrated in J. Duverger, "Mededelingen en Kanttekeningen: Tentoonstellingen van Doornikse tapijten," *Artes Textiles* 7 (1971) fig. 1; it is mentioned on p. 203. The hanging in Cambridge from the same series, without its border, is mentioned in Asselberghs, *Les tapisseries flamandes aux Etats-Unis d'Amérique*, p. 15, and discussed briefly and illustrated in J. P. Asselberghs, *Tapisseries héraldiques et de la vie quotidienne*, exh. cat. (Tournai, 1970) no. 8. For notes on these and some other closely related pieces, together with illustrations of both of the above examples, a detail of the wreath in the Salzburg piece, and a full view of a piece in Buenos Aires, see Candace Adelson, "Florentine and Flemish Tapestries in Giovio's Collection," *Atti del Convegno Paolo Giovio: Il Rinascimento e la Memoria (Como, 3–5 guigno 1983)*, Raccolta Storica, vol. 17 (Como,

1985) p. 253 nn. 40–42, figs. 7–10. Erik Duverger discussed and illustrated the von Wellenburg and Buenos Aires pieces in *Bruges et la tapisserie*, no. 4.

8. Delmarcel, *Bruges et la tapisserie*, p. 201.

9. For the Bernheimer piece, see Göbel 1923, vol. 1, p. 287; vol. 2, fig. 253. For the other, see *The Arthur Curtiss James Art Collection*, sale cat., Parke-Bernet, New York, November 13–15, 1941, no. 392, illus. For the similar pieces woven in Bruges, see Erik Duverger, *Bruges et la tapisserie*, p. 188, figs. 3/8–3/10.

10. The von Wellenberg, Giovio, and related tapestries (see note 7 above) have been attributed to Bruges because their borders resemble the borders of some tapestry fragments that are now in the Gruuthusemuseum in Bruges. In its original state, the tapestry showed a wreath on a millefleurs ground and the arms of the Franc de Bruges. See Erik Duverger, *Bruges et la tapisserie*, no. 3, figs. 3/1, 3/2, 3/4. Duverger stated that the tapestry from which the fragments came was woven in the shop of Antoon Segon of Bruges about 1530 or possibly 1545. These fragments were also published by J. Versyp, *De Geschiedenis van de Tapijtkunst te Brugge* (Brussels, 1954) fig. vi, and by V. Veermersch, in *Zilver & Wandtapijten*, exh. cat., Gruuthusemuseum (Bruges, 1980) pp. 224–27.

11. See *Bloemen en Wandtapijten, Fleurs et Tapisseries*, exh. cat., Refugie Abdij van Tangerlo (Mechelen, 1990) p. 14 and color illus. pp. 16–17. The author thanks Guy Delmarcel for bringing this piece to his attention.

20

The Hunt of the Unicorn

Six hangings and two fragments from two or
more sets of tapestries

a *The Start of the Hunt*
b *The Unicorn Is Found*
c *The Unicorn Leaps across a Stream*
d *The Unicorn at Bay*
e *The Unicorn Is Killed and Brought to the Lord
and Lady of the Castle*
f *The Unicorn in Captivity*
g *A Hunter Sounds the Capture of the Unicorn by
the Maiden*
h *The Maiden's Companion Signals to the Hunters*

Southern Netherlands, 1495–1505
Wool warp; wool, silk, silver, and gilt wefts
20a: 12 ft. 1 in. × 10 ft. 4 in. (3.68 m × 3.15 m)
20b: 12 ft. 1 in. × 12 ft. 5 in. (3.68 m × 3.79 m)
20c: 12 ft. 1 in. × 14 ft. (3.68 m × 4.27 m)
20d: 12 ft. 1 in. × 13 ft. 2 in. (3.68 m × 4.01 m)
20e: 12 ft. 1 in. × 12 ft. 9 in. (3.68 m × 3.89 m)
20f: 12 ft. 1 in. × 8 ft. 3 in. (3.68 m × 2.52 m)
20g: 6 ft. 6 in. × 2 ft. 1 1/2 in. (1.98 m × .65 m)
20h: 5 ft. 6 1/2 in. × 2 ft. 1 1/2 in. (1.69 m × .65 m)
16–19 warp yarns per inch, 6–7 1/2 per centimeter
20a–f: Gift of John D. Rockefeller, Jr., 1937 (37.80.1–6)
20g, h: Gift of John D. Rockefeller, Jr., 1938 (38.51.1,2)

CONDITION

All eight pieces contain small patches of old or modern
fabric and passages of reweaving. In an inventory of 1728
of the château de Verteuil, published by de Fleury (1884–
85, 126, 163), it was noted that the group of five tapestries hanging in the large bedroom of the new building
was "presque mi-usée" (almost half worn out) and that
two others in a furniture storeroom were "trouées en
divers endroits" (having holes in several places). Some of
the restorations, most of which are readily visible in the
illustrations, were probably made in the mid-nineteenth
century after the tapestries were returned to the château
de Verteuil from which they had been taken in 1793 (see
History, and Freeman 1976, 227), some were possibly
made later, and others were made at the Metropolitan
Museum in 1937–38, when many of the earlier repairs
were allowed to remain. The restorations have not altered the original drawing and modeling to any significant degree. The most disturbing repair is in 20d; it
involves the head, shoulders, and breast of the woodsman with an ax who stands in the left background and
points toward the hunters at the right. Two other major
restorations appear in the lower sections of 20a and 20e.
In 20a, both the warp and weft yarns have been replaced
below a line that runs irregularly from the left edge at a
point near the bottom of the cipher AE (the E reversed)
up to the soles of the shoes worn by the hunter at the far
left, down across the legs of the forward-most greyhound (the foreparts of three of them are missing), and
then more or less straight across to the right edge, just
skirting the bottom loops of the cords that tie the A to
the E in the lower right corner of the field. The passage of
restoration in the lower right corner of 20e is smaller but
equally obtrusive. The bottom hem of the chatelaine's
gown, the feet of her lord, and the lower legs of the page
standing behind them, as well as the lower half of the
hound he fondles, have been lost along with the adjacent
part of the flowering meadow. The entire area has been
filled in with patches taken from later verdure tapestries. The lower left corner of 20f was lost (and with it
the cipher AE) and has been replaced with strips of
tapestry that seem to have been taken from the missing
left and right sides.

Six of the pieces (20a–f) are nearly complete. Each of
these has been cut along its four sides and has lost part of
its field. The probable extent of the losses will be discussed below (Description). A short passage of the original striped guard or narrow border has survived along
the lower left side of 20c, and strips of modern fabric
imitating its pattern have been sewn to the edges of
20a–f. There is a narrow stripe of solid color along the
left edge of 20g which represents its guard or narrow
border. This stripe is red, whereas the guard or border in
20c shows a white inner stripe, then a red one, and along
the outside edge a wider blue stripe. 20g and 20h are
small fragments from the upper left section of a seventh

hanging, the rest of which seems to have been missing since about 1888 when Barbier de Montault (114, n. 2) reported that this hanging showed a loss and that one of the seven hangings, apparently this one, had been converted to serve as a portiere (see a suggested reconstruction of 20g, h in Nickel 1982, fig. 10). In 1974, 20g and 20h were treated further at the Metropolitan Museum. The uppermost 11 1/2 inches of 20g, which consisted of modern weaving imitating that immediately below it, was removed; and the lower section of 20h, which had been turned under earlier to make that piece the same length as 20g in its restored form, was released. In that operation the unicorn's back and the forelegs of the forward hound and the muzzle of the farther one were made visible once more.

It has been said in most of the literature that the tops of the tapestries were cut away along lines following the treetops but that is not strictly true. There are bits of the original sky adjacent to the buildings and foliage in the distance. The upper parts of the skies, which were replaced with plain canvas in the nineteenth century, are now represented by insertions of modern ribbed weaving dyed various blue tones. These were applied at the Metropolitan Museum in 1937–38. Speculations concerning the missing passages of sky and when they were removed will be discussed below (Description).

The colors of the wool and silk yarns have survived in exceptionally good condition. The range of tones, which is rarely seen in tapestries that have come down to us from this period, includes intense yellows, oranges, pinks, and greens, and a rich variety of reds and blues. The silver and gilt yarns (narrow, flat wires wound spirally on silk core yarns) have oxydized in some places, but for the most part they have retained both their color and luster.

DESCRIPTION

In 20a five hunters with their hounds face or walk toward the right in the foreground of a flowering meadow.[1] A scout perched in the branches of one of the trees that border the meadow at the right raises his right hand to signal to the others. A cipher consisting of an A tied with a looped and knotted cord to a reversed E is shown in the field five times: it appears in each of the four corners and again among the upper branches of the cherry tree that grows just to the left of center. The cord is made of several strands of yarn plied together so that the twist is apparent, and there is a tassel at each end. The three men standing at the left are gentlemen hunters; they wear sleeveless jerkins with thigh-length skirts over their

doublets and hose. Their garments are made of plain and patterned fabrics which have been used either whole or, to decorate them further, paned and slashed. The two men at the left wear fur or thrum hats fitted with one or two ostrich feathers while the third man has an elaborate panache on his small round cap.[2] They all wear low-cut, round-toed shoes that taper outward from the heel to become wide at the front. From the left, the first and third men carry spears in their right hands and have swords on their left hips. The first man also holds a collared greyhound on a lead. The second man has a hunting horn hanging over his right hip and a sword over his left. The two men to the right of these three are keepers of the hounds. They both wear unpatterned jerkins with loose sleeves and thigh-length skirts over plain hose. Each has a hunting horn hanging from a strap over his shoulder; the farther one carries a spear in his left hand. The man in the foreground holds a pair of collared greyhounds on a double lead, the other a pair of uncollared scent hounds. The greyhound in the foreground has a collar decorated with the cipher AE shown twice (neither reversed, and not tied together with the cord). The other hound has a collar showing two capital letters A alternating with three shields blazoned with quartered arms (see Subject, and The Ciphers, the Coat of Arms, and the Original Owner).

In 20b a stone fountain decorated with carved leaves, a gilt pomegranate finial, and gilt lion-masks rises in the center of a wood. The water spills from the basin through a lion-mask at the front into a stream that spreads toward the left and right in the foreground of a flowering meadow. A cock and a hen pheasant and two goldfinches are perched on the rim of the basin; the cock pheasant dips its beak to the water. The cipher showing the knotted A and E (reversed), but drawn and colored differently from the motif in 20a, appears at the center of the fountain and in each of the four corners of the field. A unicorn kneels in front of the fountain with its head down and the tip of its horn in the stream. A lion and its mate, a panther, a genet, and a hyena rest on the forward bank while a stag lies on the far bank near two rabbits. A thicket of shrubs and small trees rises beyond the fountain; it partially hides a company of hunters behind whom rise the tall trees of the forest. A castle appears in the middle distance beyond a clearing at the left, and there is a passage of sky (modern, unpatterned weaving) across the entire top of the field. There are four gentlemen and eight working huntsmen in the party. The keepers of the hounds have with them a number of scent hounds and greyhounds on leads. Seven of the men hold spears and two have hunting horns hanging from straps over their shoulders. The working hunters wear sleeve-

20a

299

20b

Detail of 20b

less jackets over their doublets and hose and either small round hats with upturned brims or hats made of fur or thrum fabric. The gentlemen wear open sleeveless coats or jackets over doublets and hose, the upper garments made of plain or patterned velvet or watered silk. Two of them wear fur or thrum hats decorated with a single feather; the other two have small round caps.

The same kind of forest setting, with plain sky along the tops of the trees and a view to distant buildings through a clearing in the trees at the back (this time at the right), appears in 20c. The cipher showing the A tied to the reversed E is displayed against the flora in each corner of the field and again tied to a branch of the oak tree that rises in the center of the composition. Directly above this tree, sewn to the modern fabric that now replaces the sky portion of the original weaving, appears another cipher comprising an F tied with the same kind of tasseled cord to an R. It is not certain that this cipher appeared here originally or indeed that it belongs with these hangings at all. Freeman (1976, 173) noted that it shows more warp yarns per inch than the main weavings do and also that the alloy in its silver yarns is slightly different from that used for the yarns woven into the field of 20c. Further discussion of this issue involves the search for the original owners of the tapestries (see below, The Ciphers . . .).

The oak tree to which one of the AE ciphers is tied rises from the near bank of the stream which, as in 20b, flows parallel to the picture plane. A wide tributary running in from the background joins the stream in the center of 20c. The unicorn bounds across the tributary, its rear legs still in the water, its forelegs raised to leap onto the bank at the right, where two hunters with raised spears prepare to attack it. Three scent hounds and a pair of greyhounds have been slipped, and they pursue the unicorn from behind. Two hunters with spears follow them, one about to thrust his spear into the quarry's haunch. At the left two gentlemen hunters discuss the attack while one working hunter blows his horn and another stoops to slip his pair of greyhounds. His forward dog and one of the pair bounding ahead on the near side of the stream wear collars decorated with the AE cipher. A third gentleman, dressed in an open, long-sleeved coat over doublet and hose, appears in the middle distance just right of center. He gestures toward the huntsman at the right who blows on his horn. Of the men whose lower legs are visible, two wear round-toed shoes, one wears thigh-length boots, one knee-length boots, and one (left foreground) wears shoes over his thigh-length boots. Most of the hunters wear small round hats with upturned brims; two wear fur or thrum hats; and the gentleman standing in the middle distance

right of center wears a headband of striped cloth trimmed with a feather fastened by a brooch.

The setting of 20d has the same kind of elements as appear in 20b and c, but the clearing at the back is broader and affords a wider view of the hills, buildings, and passages of sky in the distance. The stream continues across the foreground, and an orange tree bearing both blossoms and fruit rises in the center of the composition. The letters A and E (reversed), tied together with a tasseled cord, are placed at the springing of the tree's branches and in the four corners of the field. The unicorn appears prominently in the right-central foreground on the far bank of the stream. It kicks out at the hunter behind it to ward off the impending thrust of the spear, and with its horn it gores a greyhound in the chest. Two other hunters standing at the right trap the quarry with their spears. The hounds have all been slipped, and most of them bound around or toward the unicorn. The greyhound in the center foreground has a collar decorated with the AE cipher, and the one to the left of it wears a collar decorated with the letters OFANCRE. There is also an inscription on the scabbard of the horn blower who stands in the left foreground; it reads AVE · REGINA · C (see Subject). All the hunters in this episode are dressed as gentlemen, with hip-length coats whose wide sleeves have been slashed to allow the tighter sleeves of the doublet to pass through. They all wear plain hose except for the man in the right foreground, whose hose are striped, and they wear either shoes alone or shoes over knee- or thigh-length boots. Their upper garments are made of watered silk or plain or patterned velvet. Their heads are covered with either the fur or thrum hat or the small round hat with an upturned brim that appears in the other hangings. Two of these men stand in the middle distance right of center, one of them holding his greyhound by the collar. Across from them, on the other side of the orange tree, two woodsmen observe the hunting scene. They are simply dressed in plain jackets over hose (one with leggings over the lower leg). One of these men carries a pole and a flask, the other an ax.

In 20e the scene is set at the edge of the forest, in the castle precinct. The buildings rise in the middle distance and occupy the entire upper right quarter of the composition. In this hanging the cipher A and E (reversed) does not appear in the center of the composition but only in the corners. In the upper right corner the E was cut away from the A when some of the original sky was removed, and the cipher is entirely missing from the lower right corner, where the fabric has been replaced with fragments of later weaving. The stream in the foreground—which the human and animal figures in

302

20C

Detail of 20c

20d

the left and central foreground almost completely hide from view—empties into the castle moat. On the high embankment that rises on the far side of the stream two hunters spear the unicorn in the neck and chest from the front while the lord of the hunt moves in from the rear with his sword unsheathed to render the coup de grace. Four hounds attack the quarry from the left while a huntsman in front of them sounds the kill on his horn. In the left foreground, on the near bank of the stream, three hunters with hounds escort the horse bearing the dead unicorn. The unicorn's head and forelegs hang over the near side of the horse, and its horn is tied to its neck by a thorny branch bearing oak leaves. The lord and lady of the castle, accompanied by a party of ladies and gentlemen and a page who fondles his dog, stand in the right foreground and receive the returning hunters. Two men watch the scene from the tower that rises behind this party and a man and woman watch through a tower window. The hunters are dressed as before, some with jackets or coats of watered silk or velvet, others with garments of plain fabric over their hose. They wear either just shoes, shoes over high boots, or low boots alone. The lady of the castle wears a fitted, figured velvet gown with long funnel sleeves over a linen shirt. On her head is a black hood, at her waist a long scarf knotted as a girdle with rosary beads hanging from it, and around her neck a necklace with a pendant gold cross. Her lord is dressed in a knee-length, pleated, plain velvet surcoat with long funnel sleeves, striped hose, and a bowl-shaped fur or thrum hat. A heavy gold chain hangs around his shoulders. The ladies in their retinue wear gowns cut like the chatelaine's but made of less sumptuous fabrics; three of them have similar hoods while a fourth has a patterned veil pinned with a brooch to her plaited hair.

In 20f the field is completely covered with flowering plants of many varieties. The cipher AE, drawn and colored as it is in 20a but not 20b–f, appears tied to the branches of a pomegranate tree (a fanciful rendering, not botanically correct) and again in the upper left and right corners of the field and in the lower right corner.[3] It is not present in the lower left corner where patches of fabric from the missing left and right sides of 20f have been inserted. The main motif in this tapestry, the unicorn lying at rest in the center of a circular fenced enclosure, fills the center of the composition. The fence is made of posts and rails, with a small gate at the front. The unicorn faces left. It wears a broad collar of jeweled cloth or leather with gold fittings. A gold chain with rectangular links runs from a loop in the collar to the pomegranate tree where it fastens to the trunk below

the cipher. Drops of red, which some writers interpret as blood and others as pomegranate juice (see Subject), appear at the base of the unicorn's neck, on its left shoulder directly below the tongue of the collar, at the center of the back, and on the rump.

20g and 20h are fragments that were taken from the upper left quarter of a hanging (see a suggested reconstruction in Nickel 1982, fig. 10). The cipher AE, which is drawn and colored as it is in 20b–e but not 20a and 20f, appears in the upper left corner of 20g against the foliage of a holly tree which rises from the ground inside a post-and-rail fence made of small branches or dowels; rose-bushes bearing white or red blossoms grow against the fence. The upper half of a hunter's figure is visible beyond the fence at the left in the midst of an oak thicket. He is simply dressed in an unpatterned doublet and a small round hat with an upturned brim. He carries a pole over his right shoulder and with his left hand holds a horn to his mouth. A scent hound and a greyhound accompany him, the greyhound wearing a collar inscribed with three letters that have been read variously as IHS and CHS (see Subject). The back of the head and neck of another greyhound, and part of the hindquarters of another scent hound, appear in the lower right corner of this piece. They correspond to the parts of hounds that appear in the lower left corner of 20h. Both these dogs wear decorated collars. What appear to be a reversed E and a forward-facing E appear in the pattern of the scent hound's collar, while the left half of an A appears on the other. These two hounds have their forepaws on the back of a unicorn. The scent hound's muzzle appears immediately above a bleeding wound on the unicorn's back; there is a second wound behind this one. The unicorn faces toward the right; it raises its head and gazes upward, as though into the face of the woman whose right hand rests on its neck. Her velvet-sleeved arm appears beyond its neck, but the rest of her figure is missing. Another woman appears behind the unicorn at the left. She is standing in front of a section of the rose-covered fence which, with the portion of fence in 20g, forms the back and side of a rectangular enclosure. This woman is dressed in a fitted gown of fur-trimmed plain velvet. She wears a dark hood over a light cap, a heavy gold chain around her neck, and a gold girdle set with pearls or jewels. She grasps the lower part of her skirt with her right hand and raises her left hand in a signaling gesture. She lowers her eyes as she turns her head to communicate slyly with either the horn blower or a figure who is out of range. To the right of her left hand appears the left third of an A that is presumably part of another of the ciphers. From its position in the

20e

Detail of 20e

fragment, one concludes that it was tied to the branches of an apple tree, some of whose branches are visible; the trunk apparently rose behind the woman whose right hand rests on the unicorn's neck.

It is clear that 20g, h represent only the upper left part of the field of a hanging and also that each of the other six pieces has been cut on all four sides. Freeman (1976, 220–21) published for the first time the extremely important information that an inventory taken in 1680 in Paris listed the dimensions of these seven pieces as approximately 22 aunes in length (width, as they hang) in the aggregate and 4 aunes in height.[4] Since both this document and an inventory taken at the château de Verteuil in 1728 refer to seven pieces of unicorn tapestry and to none that are fragments, we may assume that the piece from which 20g, h came was still whole in those years. Freeman calculated that on the basis of the Paris aune this meant that the seven hangings together were a little over 84 feet (25.60 m) long and a bit more than 15 feet (4.57 m) tall. She then noted that today the six large pieces measure about 70 feet (21.34 m) in length and 12 feet 1 inch (3.68 m) in height. She concluded that each of those six pieces has lost about 3 feet (.914 m) from its height and estimated that all six together have lost about a foot or perhaps a bit more in width. That would leave 12 to 13 feet (3.66 to 3.96 m) to account for the width of the seventh piece, from which 20g, h came. In making these calculations, Freeman assumed that in 1680 the hangings had their original dimensions. Since 20a–f are still nearly complete in width, we agree.

Our own calculations have given a different result. Using $47^{1}/_{4}$ inches (1.20 m) as the value of the Paris aune, rather than the 46 inches (1.17 m) that Freeman used, we arrived at an aggregate length of 86 feet $7^{1}/_{2}$ inches (26.40 m) for the seven pieces and a height of 15 feet 9 inches (4.80 m) for each. We figure the present width of the six large hangings as 70 feet 11 inches (21.62 m) in the aggregate, which leaves 15 feet $8^{1}/_{2}$ inches (4.79 m) to account for the amounts missing from the sides of 20a–f plus the original width of 20g, h. Our calculations also indicate that 20a–f are each about 3 feet 8 inches (1.12 m) shorter than they were in 1680, remembering always that those measurements were noted in the inventory citation as approximate ones.

A fair indicator of the amounts of fabric that may have been lost at the sides of 20a–f exists in the cipher that appears in the upper left corner of 20g. Its position relative to the left edge of the field is firmly fixed by the remains of a guard along that side. In the corners of 20a, 20d, and 20e the ciphers seem to be placed in the same relationship to the sides as in 20g, but in the corners of 20b, 20c, and 20f the ciphers are a bit too close to the

sides of the field. However not much fabric can have been lost from these fields. As Freeman noted (1976, 221), the present width of 20g, h (including the gap between them as mounted) is 4 feet 6 inches (1.32 m). The fixed left edge of 20g and the position of the fragment of cipher at the right edge of 20h, which would have been just left of center, indicate that the two pieces together represent somewhat less than half the width of the field, which therefore may have measured approximately $10^{1}/_{2}$ feet (3.20 m) across. Subtracting that amount from the 15 feet $8^{1}/_{2}$ inches (4.79 m) we estimated above as the figure representing the fabric that has been lost from the aggregate width of the seven pieces, we arrive at a figure of 5 feet $2^{1}/_{2}$ inches (1.59 m) which we suggest represents the approximate amount of fabric that is missing from the sides of 20a–f in the aggregate.

As for the height, Freeman (1976, 221–22) noted that the compositions show losses at both the bottoms and the tops, and she believed that the tops had suffered more. Ever since Rorimer suggested in 1938 (*The Cloisters*, 95) that there may have been "identifying insignia" in the lost portions of the sky, every writer has believed that major portions of the tops of the tapestries were cut away deliberately. After Rorimer developed his theory that the tapestries had been woven for Anne de Bretagne, he suggested (1942–43, 20 and fig. 26) that the fabric representing the skies was cut away in order to remove royal insignia that appeared there, like the coats of arms represented against the sky along the tops of some of the tapestry fragments from the *Stories of Virtuous Women* in the Museum of Fine Arts, Boston. In that publication as well as his studies of 1945 (2d ed., *The Unicorn Tapestries*, 1938) and 1963 (174), Rorimer wrote that the skies were probably removed in order to save the tapestries from the revolutionaries at Verteuil who in 1793 were ordered by the Société Populaire of Ruffec to destroy all tapestries having royal insignia. Freeman (1976, 163) corrected this by quoting from the directive in question, a letter of December 2, 1793, sent from the Comité de Surveillance at Ruffec to the Société Populaire of Verteuil, directing the latter to "examine these old tapestries. Respect them because they show no signs of royalty; they contain stories."[5] In Freeman's opinion (1976, 222) the skies did not contain coats of arms because there were none mentioned in the inventory of 1680. She suggested instead that they may have contained inscribed bands which had become worn and were therefore cut off. In any case, Freeman (1976, 163) noted, there were no members of the La Rochefoucauld family at the château de Verteuil in 1793 to remove fabric from the tapestries. Salet (1978, 105) believed that the missing fabric at the tops of the hangings contained

312

either coats of arms (which the 1680 inventory did not mention) or, more likely, inscriptions. On the other hand, Souchal (1973, 86; 1980, 315–16) believed that the sky portions of the tapestries had been removed specifically because they contained coats of arms and added that someone at Verteuil other than a family member could have cut these portions off in 1793. She argued furthermore (1980, 316) that only this kind of removal would explain the fact that the sky portions were "cut away along the tortuous line of the tree tops."

All of these hypotheses carry some weight. However we agree with Freeman and Salet in believing that the missing parts of the sky may have shown inscriptions rather than armorial bearings. We also believe that the character of the compositions suggests that each tapestry has lost about the same amount of fabric at the bottom as at the top and consequently that there would have been less sky at the top than Freeman and Salet thought there was, or approximately sixteen inches rather than two or three feet. We suggest this because the ciphers in the corners of 20a–f are now approximately the same distance away from the present baseline of each field and from the highest point of each clump of tree foliage. Also, since the compositions in 20a–f are tightly controlled within a long oval mass in the center of the field and the ciphers are tucked neatly into the spandrels of these ovals, it may be fair to assume that the ciphers were originally more or less equidistant from the top and bottom of the field. It follows that there probably never was much more sky above the trees than there is now and that there may never have been supplementary motifs—whether coats of arms or inscriptions—there at all. As for the observation that the tops of the tapestries were cut around the contours of the foliage, we believe that this would be the natural way for those who restored the tapestries the first time to prepare hangings with ragged edges for joining to lengths of new fabric representing the sky. Freeman (1976, 223) indicated that the tapestries were restored at Verteuil after they were returned to the family and installed again in the castle in 1856. According to tradition they had been used for the preceding sixty-odd years as coverings for potatoes in barns or for espaliered trees. We can imagine that the tops and bottoms of the tapestries might thus have been damaged after the Revolution rather than during it. In any case it is normal for the tops and bottoms of tapestries to wear out first: the tops from handling as the tapestries are hung and taken down and as they are fitted with hanging devices that must be replaced from time to time, and the bottoms as the hanging tapestries are abraded by contact with furniture and passing legs and feet.

SUBJECT

Although the hangings show a unicorn rather than a stag as the quarry, the ones that illustrate the stages of the hunt as such (20a–e) represent episodes characteristic of the progress of a late medieval stag hunt (see 25a–f, and Forsyth 1951–52). However historians have thought they contain some symbolic and allegorical significance beyond the immediate narrative of the hunt.[6] This can be traced at least as far back as 1888, when Barbier de Montault offered a particularly romantic interpretation of the episodes, an interpretation that does not bear scrutiny. For him, the apparent subject, the unicorn hunt, masked a moral tale involving the guilt that the lady of the castle feels as she recalls that she, as a young virgin, helped capture this innocent creature who is now brought before her, dead. The anonymous author of the Notice sur Verteuil (before 1905, 13–14) believed that the episodes shown in the hunt take place on the grounds at Verteuil and that the tapestries present an allegory of the battle between Good and Evil. Biais (1905, 677) and Serbat (1913, 133–34), referring to Biais, both mentioned this interpretation.

Ackerman (1922–23, 292) also treated the unicorn hunt as an allegory but specifically as a Christian one. It appears that she was the first tapestry specialist to associate this hunt with a related allegory that interprets the Incarnation as a hunt by the angel Gabriel of the unicorn (Christ) in the bosom of the Virgin. The hunter is aided in his quest by his four hounds, Peace, Truth, Justice, and Mercy. These represent the Four Daughters of God, through whose pleading the Incarnation was realized (see 29a, b). Ackerman thought that the initials AE (E reversed) were in fact AM (the M turned on its side), a familiar reference to the Virgin Mary (Ave Maria). She also interpreted the inscription (AVE · REGINA · C[OELORUM]; see detail illustration) on the scabbard of the horn-blowing huntsman in the left foreground of 20d as another salute to the Virgin, who she believed was represented as the chatelaine in 20e. She observed furthermore that the unicorn is not usually killed but only "wounded unto death" and that in this instance an older version of the legend must have been used. Breck (1928, 150) accepted the interpretation of the unicorn hunt as an allegory of the Incarnation in the same terms but added that the designer seemed to be less interested in the symbolism than in the action of the hunt itself. He also maintained that 20f, which shows a living though apparently wounded unicorn in captivity, represents the ultimate purpose of the Incarnation—that is, the Resurrection of Christ—and that the fenced enclosure is the hortus conclusus, another symbol of Mary.

Shepard (1930, 71) was alone in not embracing the

Detail of 20d

Christian allegorical interpretation that would prevail in all subsequent literature on the subject when he wrote that, in spite of the presence of the cipher which he accepted as AM, the "theme is tending toward a purely secular treatment." Rorimer (*The Cloisters*, 1938, 85) endorsed the idea that the hangings represent the allegory of the Incarnation even as he acknowledged that the designer had emphasized the secular appeal of the hunting party over the religious content. Further-more he believed (1938, 88, 90) that 20f represents not only the realization of the Incarnation, with the fenced enclosure as the *hortus conclusus* symbolizing the Virgin, but also the consummation of marriage because he interpreted the golden chain by which the unicorn is tethered to the tree as a symbol of marriage and the pomegranate fruit as a well-known symbol of fertility. This interpretation led him and also later writers to theorize that the tapestries were made to celebrate a wedding, although he (1938, 90–91) and others did not think the tapestries were woven about 1450 to com-memorate the marriage of Jean II de La Rochefoucauld and Marguerite de Barbezieux, as a family tradition claimed (see below, The Ciphers . . .). Soon Rorimer (1942–43, 8) found other names and dates to associate with his theory: except for 20a and 20f (which he thought were added later, perhaps for François I) the

314

tapestries were woven to celebrate the marriage on January 8, 1499, of Anne de Bretagne and her second husband, Louis XII of France. (Curiously, this removes 20f, which Rorimer had specified as the piece representing the consummation of marriage, from consideration in this context. Later [1945 ed., *The Unicorn Tapestries*, 1938] he associated 20f by implication with the marriage of François I and Anne's daughter Claude in 1514 when, he speculated, 20a and 20f may have been added to the earlier set of hangings.) In this new interpretation Rorimer (1942–43, 12) retained the story of the Incarnation. The maiden in 20g, h, of whom only the right hand and forearm remain, should be associated with the Virgin and the unicorn with Christ, since what Rorimer interpreted as IHS (and we read as CHS), the monogram of Christ, appears on the collar of one of the dogs in the background of 20g at the left (Rorimer 1942–43, fig. 11). According to Rorimer's study, this maiden also represents Anne de Bretagne, as does the lady of the castle in 20e; and the salutation AVE REGINA C on the hunter's scabbard in 20d refers to her while the inscription OFANCRE on the collar of the hound standing to the right of this hunter (see detail illustration), which he expanded to read O F[R]ANC[ORUM] RE[X], refers to Louis XII. Rorimer (1942–43, 12) concluded that the main group of hangings—that is, 20b–e, g, h—"tell of the hunt of the unicorn, the courting and wedding of Louis, and at the same time the Incarnation of Christ."

Most writers succeeding Rorimer accepted this interpretation, until, in 1976, Freeman (156–62) reconsidered every one of Rorimer's arguments concerning the identification of the lady and lord of the castle with Anne and Louis and concluded that there is no proof that the identifications are correct. Souchal (in Paris 1973, 84) had already pointed out the weak points in Rorimer's theory that the tapestries were made to celebrate the wedding of Anne and Louis; but both she and Freeman continued to believe that the hangings contained symbolism concerning the Incarnation. The reasons to argue against this notion were first advanced by Erlande-Brandenburg (1975) and then Salet (1978), who pointed out that if, as the legend claimed, a unicorn could be subdued by a maiden and taken back to the palace alive, there would be no reason for the hunters to continue to pursue and kill it as they do in 20d and 20e. The two writers concluded that, on these grounds and considering the slight stylistic differences that distinguish 20g, h from 20b–e, 20g, h belong neither with 20b–e nor with 20a and 20f, which were acknowledged by every writer from the beginning as having come from a different set of tapestries. Erlande-Brandenburg and Salet suggested that 20g, h probably come from yet a third set of hang-

ings, one whose narrative ended not in the death of the unicorn but in its capture alive. Salet observed furthermore that 20b–e, which represent some of the stages in a standard medieval stag hunt, could have come from a set of hangings that showed such a hunt with a unicorn substituted for the stag. In refuting Freeman's theory that 20f shows the resurrected unicorn (Christ) in captivity, Salet (1978, 106) pointed out that the unicorn had never before been treated in art or literature as a resurrected being (however, see below, Thomas of Cantimpré's allegory) and also that Freeman's suggestion that this piece may have served as the canopy or cover of a bed (and thus explain its presence and that of 20a among the otherwise quite different 20b–e) was unacceptable.

By separating this group of hangings into three parts rather than two, Erlande-Brandenburg and Salet paved the way for others to study the tapestries without the encumbrance of earlier prejudices. We agree that 20a and 20f come from a different set of tapestries than that represented by 20b–e, and possibly also 20g, h (see below), and that all the sets were made for one client whose cipher AE appears on all of them. As Salet (1978, 106) pointed out, the Le Viste family, for whom the *Dame à la licorne* in the Musée de Cluny was woven, owned several sets of hangings with unicorns on pink grounds, not just the one. It is essential that we reconsider the relationships among 20a–h before attempting to disentangle the mutually exclusive strands of what has been treated as an impossibly complex subject—the hunt of a unicorn plus the Incarnation plus the marriage of Anne de Bretagne and Louis XII and the consummation of their marriage.

Freeman (1976, 176–79) attempted to explain away the notable stylistic difference between 20a, f and 20b–e, g, h not by assuming that 20a and 20f were woven somewhat later than the others, as Rorimer thought, but by suggesting that they may have been designed by different men, produced by less skillful weavers, or designed for a different use. She suggested that 20a and 20f, which she regarded as the two more "static" compositions, were designed to serve as canopy, cover, or back cloth of a bed set up in a chamber whose walls were decorated with 20b–e. No subsequent writer has endorsed this suggestion. It seems clear to us that 20a and 20f, with their millefleurs grounds and their differently drawn and colored ciphers, were not originally part of the set of hangings from which 20b–e, and possibly also 20g, h, came. Indeed we ask whether 20a and 20f come from one and the same set of hangings. The style of drawing is hard and rather coarse in 20a, soft and fine in 20f. One may argue that they were designed by different artists. However there are iconographic as well as stylistic reasons to question their kinship. As a number of writers, most recently Salet (1978, 106) and Nickel (1982, 10 n. 5), have observed, there is nothing in 20a to suggest that it represents the start of a unicorn hunt rather than a hunt for any other kind of game. Furthermore, the captured beast in 20f clearly does not represent the unicorn revived after its death as shown in 20e nor the unicorn as a symbol for the resurrected Christ. This beast is not once again free and active: it is collared and chained, decidedly a captive in its fenced enclosure. It is the unicorn that serves in the pictorial arts as a symbol of the lover vanquished by the god of love and held captive by his lady. This iconography appeared fairly frequently in the later Middle Ages, as Freeman (1976, 45–46, 52, figs. 43, 44, 55) has shown. But the imagery associated with this allegory does not include a representation of all the preceding stages of the hunt, as 20b–e do. Therefore it is fair to assert that 20f probably did not belong with 20a but that it either came from a different set of millefleurs tapestries featuring the unicorn as a lady's beloved or, as Nickel (1982, 10 n. 5) suggested, that it may not have been part of a set at all but meant to hang alone.

It was not until the tapestries were exhibited in 1973 at the Grand Palais, Paris, where 20g, h were hung separately from 20b–e, that anyone questioned the kinship of 20g, h and 20b–e. Until then, from the time Rorimer (*The Unicorn Tapestries*, 1938) first summarized the narrative as it is represented in the hangings, it was considered that the tapestry from which these two fragments came showed the unicorn being tamed in the lap of a virgin so that the hunters, who had failed to capture it by ordinary means, could subdue it. Souchal (1973, 47 n. 11) disagreed with those who separated 20g, h from 20b–e, saying that the episode of 20g, h occurs logically in the sequence of events: the hunters, unable to take the beast in the usual way, use a maiden to subdue it and "ils peuvent alors en venir a bout" (they could then succeed). By using this elliptical language and not saying that the hunters then killed the tamed unicorn, Souchal avoided the inevitable problem of explaining how and why the hunters had to pursue and kill the beast (as they do in 20e) if it had already been subdued by the maiden in this supposedly peaceful enclosure. Erlande-Brandenburg (1975, 89–90) addressed the problem and observed that since the enclosure (and the hounds and girls inside it) were protecting the unicorn from the hunters, this hanging must have come from a different set showing a unicorn hunt in which the beast is not killed but taken prisoner alive. The fact that 20g shows a red stripe along its left edge, presumably one of the inner stripes of a narrow border or guard, rather than a white one as the bit of original border on 20c does, may or may not be significant; it suggests, but does not prove, that the tapestries belong to different sets of hangings.

It is curious that although Freeman (1976, 176, fig. 226) mentioned and illustrated the six unicorn hunt scenes in the series of engravings that Jean Duvet produced between the late 1540s and about 1560, neither she nor any other writer has yet investigated the prints as a guide to understanding the subject or subjects of 20a–h.[7] Eisler, in his study of the engravings, made it clear that they were issued at different times and that at least two of them, one showing the king and Diana receiving the fewterer and the other the unicorn dipping its horn in a stream, might have been issued as separate prints.[8] Therefore it is important to realize that this "series" of engravings (as we now regard it) may not have been conceived as an integral unit. Nevertheless, the prints in the order in which they can be and usually are arranged (Freeman 1976, fig. 226) seem to illustrate a story in which the unicorn is hunted first by force, then with the aid of the maiden, and so taken alive; later it is carried on a triumphal car and finally appears in triumph in heaven before God the Father. As Eisler has indicated, the iconography seems to correspond to a late medieval text by Thomas of Cantimpré in which the unicorn is clearly a metaphor for Christ who, like the unicorn, was ferocious—before being made incarnate He punished angels and men—and could not be tamed by any man; He was led by an angel to the Virgin Mary where he was made incarnate; He then allowed Himself to be captured by the Jews, rose up, and ascended to heaven.[9] While the Thomas of Cantimpré text, which treats the Incarnation, Passion, and Resurrection, corresponds more to the interpretation Rorimer (first in *The Unicorn Tapestries*, 1938) and his followers endorsed for 20a–h (that the maiden tames the unicorn, which is then killed by men), the prints themselves, which show the unicorn alive after being tamed by the maiden, illustrate a narrative like the one Erlande-Brandenburg (1975, 89) postulates for 20g, h, one in which the tamed unicorn is not killed, as 20e shows it to have been.

Erlande-Brandenburg (1975, 89–90) also called attention to a number of stylistic inconsistencies that he said obliged the staff at the Grand Palais to hang 20g, h away from 20b–e because they looked so out of place among them. Salet (1978, 106) wrote that he had doubted for some time that 20g, h belonged with the others both because of the iconographic non sequitur and the stylistic difference which he did not think could be explained away by postulating different designers, but he preferred to leave that question open. However he made an observation that may be the clue to solving this puzzle of interpretation: when the unicorn is shown massacred on the maiden's knees, the beast is then the symbol of Christ made incarnate in the Virgin's womb and sacrificed by His enemies. This iconography, which concerns the Incarnation (and, when Adam pierces the unicorn's breast with a spear and Eve collects the spilling blood, also the Crucifixion), was often represented in late medieval prints, paintings, and tapestries. It is very different from the one that deals with a unicorn hunt conducted like a stag hunt and that, like it, ends in the death of the quarry. Ackerman (1922–23) introduced the idea of associating 20a–f with the Incarnation version of the unicorn hunt, and writers between her time and Salet's (1978) have perpetuated that association much to the confusion of the issue at hand. Those compositions show Mary seated in her enclosed garden and receiving the unicorn in her lap (with or without the Adam and Eve figures) while the hunter, Gabriel, with his hounds representing the Four Daughters of God or other Virtues, approaches from the left (see for example Freeman 1976, figs. 51–53). A contemporary tapestry woven in the Middle Rhine region makes the meaning of the subject as the Incarnation quite clear: it appears at the beginning of a series of scenes from the life of Christ, just before the Nativity.[10]

If we remove 20g, h from the place they have been given in the sequence of the tapestries, as we believe it is necessary to do, then we can rethink an interpretation of the subject of 20b–e. Salet (1978, 106) has suggested that 20b–e may simply be a narrative that tells the story of a typical late medieval game hunt but with a unicorn substituted for the stag, wild boar, bear, or other quarry. The unicorn's horn was prized as a panacea, a protection from poison and an indicator of the presence of poison, so it was a quarry worth hunting in imagination even though, as a mythical being, it could never be hunted in fact.

We would accept this interpretation if 20b–e did not contain three iconographic details that Salet did not comment upon and that make it incumbent upon us to consider the possibility that the subject of 20b–e is specifically an allegory of the Incarnation and Crucifixion of Christ and nothing else. The details are these. First, as it was pointed out frequently before, the hunter blowing the horn in the left foreground of 20d is wearing a sword whose scabbard is inscribed AVE · REGINA · C[OELORUM] (see detail illustration), a salutation to the Virgin Mary. Second, there are two oak branches unaccountably bearing thorns that tie the dead unicorn's horn to its neck in 20e. Third, also in 20e, the chatelaine, who looks so sadly at her lord, points to the dead beast with her right

hand and touches her rosary with her left. Although the hunter in 20d has no wings, he may represent Gabriel announcing the Incarnation; the wreath of oak branches with the inexplicable thorns suggests nothing so much as the crown of thorns; and the woman to whom the dead unicorn is brought in her sorrow may be Mary. If this interpretation is correct, the scene in front of the castle is a Deposition, perhaps with John, whose expression is equally tragic, standing next to the Virgin, the three Marys behind them, and the other people the followers of Jesus who were present at that moment. 20b then would represent Christ's ministry; 20c the beginning of His persecution; 20d His betrayal and Passion; and 20e the Crucifixion and Deposition. The Resurrection is missing.

It is conceivable that the Fall of Man and the Incarnation are partly present in 20g, h. Instead of representing a stage in the unicorn hunt as has been proposed, this piece may represent Christ as the unicorn coming to the Virgin's womb, as in the Gelnhausen tapestry (Freeman 1976, fig. 51), but with the added feature of Eve as the evil woman at the left probably balancing the treacherous Adam now missing from the right who, in a similar scene in a Swiss tapestry of 1480 now in the Landesmuseum, Zurich (Freeman 1976, 51 and fig. 53), says as he thrusts a spear into the unicorn's chest, *ipse · aut · vulneratus · ē · prop/ter · iniquitates · nostras* (But He is wounded through our sins). Finally, the tree that is thought to have been in the center of this tapestry, represented by the branches in the top right corner of 20h, is an apple tree, the symbol of the Tree of the Knowledge of Good and Evil, the tree from which Eve fed Adam and because of which mankind was expelled from Paradise. As we calculated above, the tapestry from which 20g, h come may originally have measured only some 10^1/$_2$ feet (3.20 m) wide, which would provide room for relatively few figures. They may have included not only the Virgin and Eve but also Gabriel with his hounds at the left and Adam at the right. If such a tapestry did not occupy a place at the beginning of the cycle, then it may have constituted a separate devotional piece to be contemplated in association with the other four or, finally, if it followed a text based on (or derived from a common source with) the Thomas of Cantimpré text that Eisler quoted (see note 8), it could have appeared in the hunt sequence exactly where Rorimer and his followers placed it. In any case, it need not have been designed by the artist who produced the compositions for 20b–e.

Williamson (1986), who studied the tapestries in terms of their plant symbolism and the blending of pre-Christian and Christian iconographies, believed that the hangings dealt with the Passion, Crucifixion, and Resurrection as well as with numerous pagan references to the seasons of the year and to death and renewal. He (1986, 142) believed that the unicorn is depicted without ears deliberately in 20d because the designer wished to emphasize the idea of silence as an introduction to the betrayal of the unicorn by the maiden in 20g, h. Our examination of the fabric in the part of 20d showing the unicorn's head suggests not that the ear is missing but that it was rendered very lightly, primarily by means of slits; the color modulations that are present are extremely subtle. Therefore we believe that the ear is there but almost invisible owing to some fading and puckering in the fabric at that place. Nevertheless, Williamson's observations are fascinating and helpful, whether one considers that symbols are used here consciously or as an intuitive expression of a cultural heritage. For example, he suggests (1986, 192) that the botanically incorrect oak-thorn wreath on the dead unicorn in 20e was inspired both by the pre-Christian belief in the annual winter rebirth of the Oak King (with the subsequent regeneration of plant life) and by the crown of thorns.

Detail of 20a

THE CIPHERS, THE COAT OF ARMS, AND THE ORIGINAL OWNER

The paired and knotted letters A and E (reversed) that appear in the center and fields of all seven tapestries, the knotted F and R that appear against the modern weaving representing the sky in 20c, and the two shields blazoned with a quartered coat of arms on the collar of one of the greyhounds in 20a (see detail illustration) have excited a great deal of interest because of their potential usefulness in identifying the person or persons for whom the tapestries were woven. Unfortunately none of the investigations that have been undertaken thus far —and there has been a great deal of discussion in the literature—has netted any positive result. We still do not know whom the ciphers and the coat of arms represent.

Biais (1905, 675–76) believed that the AE referred to the lords for whom the tapestries were woven, not to members of the La Rochefoucauld family but probably to two families related to them. The only La Rochefoucauld he could find who had a given name beginning with A around this time was Antoine who lived in the first half of the sixteenth century and was the second son of François I de La Rochefoucauld, and since the name of Antoine's wife, Antoinette, also began with an A rather than an E he did not propose that the cipher referred to them. Hunter (1925, 96) also thought that the

A and the E represented the initials of the lord and lady for whom the tapestries were woven and suggested that they in turn were represented as the couple receiving the dead unicorn in 20e. Except for Ackerman (1922–23, 292) and Shepard (1930, 71) who, as noted above, believed that the letters were to be read as AM (for *Ave Maria*) rather than AE, most writers thought that the A and the E were either the initials of the given names of a couple or the secret cipher of an individual but in any case a reference to the unidentified person or persons for whom the tapestries were woven. Guiffrey (1911, 99), Rodière (1916, 310), Breck (1928, 150), and the author of the entry for the catalogue of the exhibition at the Metropolitan Museum in 1928 (20) all wrote that the initials were those of the couple for whom the hangings were woven. Rorimer (*The Cloisters*, 1938, 92) agreed and added that the cipher could also refer to some device like *Amour et Eternité* or perhaps *Animae* (for "two souls," the married couple). However a few years later Rorimer (1942–43, 7) proposed that the A and E are the first and last letters of Anne de Bretagne's given name and also of her device, *A ma vie.* As evidence supporting the first suggestion he pointed to two pages in a prayer book made for Anne about 1496 in the region of Tours, now in the Pierpont Morgan Library, New York (Rorimer 1942–43, figs. 1, 2). The borders of both pages show the letters A, N, and E repeated within the ogival or lozenge-shaped compartments of a network of knotted cords. Rorimer interpreted these cords, and also the cords tying the A to the E in the tapestries, as the cordelière of the Franciscan order of the Cordeliers, a motif closely associated with Anne both by virtue of her own use of it and the fact that in 1498 she established the chivalric order of the Dames de la Cordelière. The cords in the tapestries are not the true cordelière (a plied cord knotted tightly at measured intervals along its length) but simply twisted and tasseled cords. This interpretation of Rorimer's was repeated in subsequent literature including the catalogue entry for the exhibition of 20b at the Metropolitan Museum in 1970. Souchal (in Paris 1973, 83–84) advanced cogent arguments against Rorimer's theory that the tapestries had been woven to celebrate the marriage of Anne de Bretagne and Louis XII and his suggestion that 20a contained a portrait of François I, and she did not accept his interpretation of the AE cipher, observing that the letters in such motifs never refer to the first and last letters of a given name but rather to the initials of the given names of a couple, the initials of a person's given and family names, or to a secret, personal cipher. Furthermore, as she observed, we can cite no work of art that belonged to Anne and showed this cipher.

Freeman (1976, 156–70) argued against Rorimer's association of the tapestries with Anne and Louis, made it clear that the tasseled cords tying the A to the E in the tapestry fields are not the Franciscan cordelière, and proceeded to discuss and evaluate previous interpretations of the cipher itself. She cited instances in which similarly knotted letters were the initials of an individual's given and family names, as they are in the ciphers of the Paris printers Antoine Denidel and Robert Gourmont (the surnames spelled with lowercase rather than capital *d* and *g*), of a French gentleman or noble named Estienne Petit, of Netherlander Jean Floreins who commissioned Hans Memling's altarpiece of the *Adoration of the Magi* in Bruges, and of the Englishmen Sir John Dygby and Lord Thomas Dacre (Freeman 1976, figs. 212–14, and p. 168). She also reviewed the secret ciphers that earlier writers had mentioned and added a number of new examples. She concluded, as others had done before her, that the AE remains a mystery.

Salet (1978, 105) agreed that the cipher does not refer to Anne de Bretagne and that it could be a personal device. He pointed out that it is by no means certain that the initials are those of the given names of a husband and wife or of any member of the La Rochefoucauld family.

We can add only two observations that seem significant: first, the greyhound's collar in 20a that shows the three armorial shields also shows the letter A alone, and second, on another greyhound's collar the letters A and E, but not tied with the cord, appear twice side by side (see detail illustration). These letters, used singly in this way, may indicate that each one is the initial of the given name of two people or the initials of one person's first and last names. In any event, they suggest that the AE is not a cipher representing a secret device since if that were so the A would not appear alone. There is a somewhat later tapestry in the Metropolitan Museum (31) that has in the two lower corners of its field (and had in the upper two before it was cut down) a cipher comprising the letters n and G tied together with a plied, tasseled cord. The letters represent the given names of the couple for whom the tapestry was woven, Nicolas and Guillemette Bouesseau; his device, *Selon le temps*, appears inscribed on a scroll set among the branches of a tree that rises in the center of the field.[11]

The other cipher, the F and R tied together with a similar tasseled cord that had been sewn to the modern fabric in 20c before Mr. Rockefeller acquired the tapestries, has been the subject of equally frustrated but less extensive discussion in the literature. Biais did not mention it in his study of 1905. In 1911 Guiffrey discussed it on an equal footing with the AE and regarded both as a reference to the affianced or married couple for whom the tapestries were woven. Ackerman (1922–23, 292–93) thought it was the monogram of François I de La Rochefoucauld for whom, she believed, 20b–e had been woven about 1480. Hunter (1925, 97) wrote that these could be the initials of the same man and observed further that it would have been natural for La Rochefoucauld to add his initials to the fabric if he had received the tapestries as an inheritance or a gift. Rorimer (*The Cloisters*, 1938, 92) said that these initials may have inspired the tradition that the tapestries were made for François de La Rochefoucauld but that they could have been added to 20c at any time, thereby implying that he did not endorse the tradition. However a few years later (1942–43, 19–20) he considered the possibility that the letters do indeed refer to this member of the La Rochefoucauld family to whom his godson, François I, may have given the tapestries. He favored this idea since it would provide the "missing link" between Anne de Bretagne, for whom Rorimer now thought the tapestries had been woven, and the La Rochefoucauld family in whose possession they had been for so long.

Souchal (in Paris 1973, 78, 84), the first specialist to question this thesis of Rorimer's, observed that the FR shows a higher warp count than the tapestries themselves (8–9 per cm as against 6–7½) and so could not have been part of the original fabric. Freeman (1976, 173) wrote that the FR showed not only a finer weave but also a slightly different alloy in the metal yarns from those used in the rest of 20c. She proposed the idea that fabric with the FR cipher could still have been part of the original suite of tapestries if the whole set was a chamber and the FR had appeared on the bed valances which were narrower than the other pieces and possibly woven on a narrow loom using a finer warp. The theory is not convincing. Salet (1978, 105) did not accept it either and went on to argue that the letters do not refer to François de La Rochefoucauld: great nobles did not usually use monograms composed of the initials of their given and family names, and if these were regarded as the initials of two given names, they could not refer to François because his first wife was named Louise and his second, Barbe. Freeman (1976, 170) noted that the FR "seems to offer better evidence [than the AE] for association with the La Rochefoucauld family." She reviewed (1976, 170–74) earlier interpretations of the FR and explored some new ones, none convincing. Like most writers before her, she rejected (1976, 163–65) the family tradition that the tapestries were produced for Jean II de La Rochefoucauld and his wife Marguerite de Barbezieux, mainly on the grounds that he died in 1471 and the style of the tapestries is later, adding that while there is no proof of it the tapestries could conceivably have been woven for Marguerite and her second husband, Hardouin IX de Maillé (died ca. 1492). She concluded her discussion (1976, 174) with the observation that there is no proof that the cipher belonged with these tapestries originally or that it can be identified with François I de La Rochefoucauld.

Freeman (1976, 172) published for the first time the information that another FR like this one, also cut out from its original fabric, is applied to the modern border of a late sixteenth-century tapestry still in the château de Verteuil. Salet (1978, 105) believed that the existence of the second FR, sewn as it was to the modern border of a totally different tapestry, suggested that both ciphers were applied in the nineteenth century. It seems likely that this is the case. Furthermore, we may observe that there is no place in 20b–e and 20g, h for the FR to have appeared except in the sky portion, and it seems unlikely that it would have been placed there when five AE ciphers would have held prominent positions in the fields of each of those five hangings. There would have been no place for it at all in 20a and 20f. It seems unlikely, therefore, that the FR ever appeared in any of these hangings.

The quartered coat of arms blazoned on the three shields decorating the collar of one of the greyhounds in the right foreground of 20a (see detail illustration) has inspired as much discussion, with as little positive outcome, as the two ciphers. It appears that Rodière (1916, 310) was the first writer to notice and comment upon this detail. Convinced that the AE did not refer to any

member of the La Rochefoucauld family, he was free to study the armorial motif without the prejudices that encumbered later investigations. He read the blazon as follows: "écartelé: 1 et 4, fascé d'or et d'azur, à trois annelets de gueules brochant sur les deux premières fasces; 2 et 3, d'or à trois maillets de gueules" (quartered: 1 and 4 barry or and azure, three ringlets gules over the upper two bars; 2 and 3, or, three mallets gules). Rodière believed that these arms, which he said could not be confused with any others, were in the first and fourth quarters the arms of La Viefville of Picardy and the Artois, and that quarters 2 and 3 were blazoned with the arms of Mailly-Lorsignol. He then discussed (1916, 310–11) the members of that family to whom the arms could refer and traced the alliance back to Jean I, sire and baron de La Viefville, seigneur de Blessy, vicomte d'Aire, serving as governor and captain-general of the Artois in 1328, who married Marie de Mailly, dame de Nédon. Marie inherited from her father, Jean, knight, and so her descendants quartered their arms. Rodière could find no married couples in this family whose given names began with A and E but he had another idea. Marie, the last descendant of the senior branch of the La Viefville, married in 1453 Antoine, illegitimate son of Philippe le Bon, duc de Bourgogne, who died in 1504. Rodière, implying that the A and E could refer to Antoine, suggested that the absence of Antoine's arms could be explained by their removal from the tapestries either during a restoration or when some member of the La Rochefoucauld family acquired them. While this conclusion is not entirely convincing—especially since we are asked to believe that Marie's arms are represented on the hound's collar together with her husband's first initial but none of her own anywhere in the tapestries—nevertheless it is significant that Rodière identified the arms as La Viefville quartering Mailly-Lorsignol, a reading that de Vaivre (1979, 105, 108 n. 11) provisionally endorsed.[12]

It appears that this interpretation of the coat of arms did not come to the Metropolitan Museum's notice until considerably later than its publication in 1916. In 1928 when the tapestries were exhibited at the Metropolitan Museum, R. T. Nichol (exh. cat., p. 21) interpreted the arms as follows: "sable, 2 bars gold, in chief 3 roses of same, quartering . . . gold, 3 escutcheons gules." He read these as Chavagnac d'Amandine of Auvergne quartering Du Bost la Blanche of Forez. Some years later, after the tapestries had been cleaned and restored, Forsyth read the blazon again: "1 and 4 argent, a bouquet of three flowers gules with stems and leaves or; 2 and 3 or, three escutcheons gules." More than a dozen other readings have been offered.[13]

Freeman (1976, 171–72) pointed out that since the

shields on the greyhound's collar are only about one inch tall and badly worn it is difficult to decipher the arms. She also observed that the arms are not necessarily those of the original owner of the tapestries but may have belonged to another family member or a friend. In support of this she illustrated (1976, fig. 205) the coats of arms placed along the tops of some of the fragments of the *Stories of Virtuous Women* tapestries in the Museum of Fine Arts, Boston, which have been thought to represent relatives or friends of Ferry de Clugny who is said to have commissioned the tapestries. Freeman (1976, 95) further cited the fact that in 1405 Marguerite of Flanders owned greyhound collars showing the devices of the duc de Bretagne and the duc de Berry and ones decorated with the letters P and M or Y. However Freeman also referred to dog collars listed in Philippe le Bon's inventory of 1420 that were decorated with that duke's own coat of arms and device. We can add a reference to the coat of arms of Nicolas Rolin, chancellor of Burgundy (1422–61), that appears on a shield decorating the collar of a hound standing in the foreground of a tapestry of woodcutters in the Musée des Arts Décoratifs in Paris (Jarry 1969, 82). The tapestry also shows the same coat of arms in the field itself. Freeman (1976, 224–25) finally rejected Rodière's reading of the blazon on the grounds that the weavers could have represented the charges more accurately if they had meant to, and that the alliance between the La Viefville and Mailly families that Rodière referred to had taken place in 1328, at least one hundred and fifty years before 20a–h were woven. She accepted (1976, 172) the following reading of the blazon on the dog's collar in 20a as follows: 1 and 4, "barred gold and blue with three red roses passing over the first two bars," and 2 and 3, "gold or silver with three red shields." She then suggested that the arms might be those of Guillaume de La Rochefoucauld, cousin to François de La Rochefoucauld, and Guillaume's wife, Françoise de la Haye, because the la Haye family (Normandy) bore "three red shields on silver" and because in 1506 Guillaume used as a seal a device having "in the left corner, as a quartering, three roses or cinquefoils." However, a device—its form not explained—used on a seal does not necessarily serve as a coat of arms. All of Freeman's reasons for rejecting Rodière's reading of the blazons are untenable. The charges on the greyhound's collar are so small that the wefts rendering the ringlets or roses and the mallets or shields pass over only three or four fine warp yarns, and in those circumstances it would have been extremely difficult if not impossible to make rings that did not also look like cinquefoils (roses?) and mallets that did not also look like shields. Furthermore, Rodière wrote not that the marital al-

liance between Jean I de La Viefville and Marie de Mailly took place in 1328 but that Jean de La Viefville was serving as governor and captain-general of the Artois in that year. Freeman did not take into account Rodière's suggestion that the arms might be those of Marie de La Viefville, who married Antoine, grand bâtard de Bourgogne, in 1453.

It is clear that further investigation is needed to interpret correctly the AE, the FR, and the arms on the greyhound's collar. In the meanwhile we do not know whom these motifs represent and therefore who commissioned the Metropolitan Museum's tapestries.

SOURCE OF THE DESIGN

Few early writers concerned themselves with the question of the design of 20a–h, becoming absorbed instead with matters of iconography and the question of who commissioned the tapestries. Serious investigation of the design source did not begin until Reynaud and Souchal published articles of critical importance in 1973. Ackerman (1922–23, 292) was the first to express an opinion concerning the designer but only in general terms; she suggested that the drawing of the first four pieces shows the style of the stained-glass painters of the late fifteenth century in the Ile de France. Later (1926–27, 148) she claimed to have found the signature of the Tournai designer Jean III le Quien on two of the hangings but without identifying them or the motifs that contain the alleged signatures. We assume that she was referring to the two sets of letters that appear inscribed on hunting horns in 20b and 20c and which Freeman (1976, 194) later discussed. The first inscription appears on the side of the hunting horn worn by the fair-haired hunter standing to the left of the fountain in 20b (see detail illustration). Freeman thought she could read the letters (right to left) JONES "(Johannes?)," then AN followed by some unintelligible letters, then ON followed by several other letters of which one near the end might be the E of FECIT. Therefore she suggested tentatively that the name of one of the designers might have been Jean or Johannes. Freeman did not offer an interpretation of the second inscription, which appears on the horn hanging on the hip of the hunter standing in the right foreground of 20c who points a spear at the unicorn's breast (Freeman 1976, fig. 122). We cannot agree with Freeman's reading of the first inscription and find (as she apparently did also) the second one illegible. Both sets of letters, like the majority of such "inscriptions" in tapestries of this period, are most likely just decorative motifs that convey no message at all.

Detail of 20b

When the tapestries were exhibited at the Metropolitan Museum in 1928, the author of the catalogue entry attributed the design of 20a and 20f to Touraine and of 20b–e to Tournai based on what were then commonly applied, if unfounded, stylistic criteria. The tendency to set 20a and 20f apart from the others in every sense continued throughout the history of these studies until Freeman (1976, 178) courageously ran counter to the current and expressed the opinion that these two pieces, while admittedly different from the other five on a number of stylistic counts, were indeed part of the same set of hangings. She depended heavily on the presence of the AE cipher in all seven pieces to carry her point. However, many earlier writers and every later one interpreted this to mean simply that all seven hangings had been commissioned by the same person or persons even though they belong to two, three, or four different sets of hangings (see Subject). Freeman suggested (1976, 178) that 20a and 20f were probably not produced later than the others, as Rorimer had suggested, but at the same time, either after the designs of a different artist or after the same designer's work by different and less skillful weavers. However, she concluded that the cartoons

for 20a–h were probably supplied by more than one designer.

Souchal (exh. cat. Paris 1973, 86) identified the designer of 20b–e and 20g, h as a man she dubbed the "Maître de la Chasse à la Licorne." She discussed his oeuvre at length in her article of the same year in *Revue de l'Art*. Her thesis derived from discoveries and suggestions that Reynaud had made and published in her own article in the same issue of *Revue de l'Art*. Reynaud discussed primarily the work of the Coëtivy Master, whom at that time she identified with the brothers Henri and Conrard Vulcop, to whom she attributed the design of the *Story of the Trojan War* (see 13a–c), and she called attention to a number of motifs and mannerisms in their work that reappear in some of the *Hunt of the Unicorn* hangings. She cited primarily the men's facial types, with prominent chins and sunken upper lips, the poses and modes of movement that characterize many of their figures, and particularly (Reynaud 1973, 19, figs. 49, 50) the fact that the figures of the page and his dog in the right foreground of 20e virtually repeat the same motif in the first of the series of Trojan War drawings in the Louvre.

Souchal (1973) developed this idea, collecting masses of visual material to illustrate the work of what she believed was one man, a disciple of the Vulcop brothers who inherited their shop drawings and traditions, a man who had a host of followers and imitators. This was her "Maître de la Chasse à la Licorne," an artist whom she thought (1973, 44) must have been born no later than 1450, among whose earliest works were the printed illustrations for the *Missel de Verdun* of 1481, and who continued to work in Paris for the following thirty years painting easel pictures and miniatures in manuscripts and also designing woodcuts for Paris publishers and stained-glass windows in Paris and Rouen. She compared the compositions, details, and motifs in 20b–e and 20g, h to works she identified with this master, particularly to the prints he had designed for the Paris publishers Simon Vostre and Antoine Vérard. Souchal (1973, 45–46) noted also that this master, for all he depended on the forms and motifs inherited from the Vulcop brothers, had been subtly influenced by contemporary Italian art, either directly or through Italian influence on Netherlandish art. She, along with Reynaud (1973, 18), believed furthermore that he had also designed other sets of tapestries that have survived, notably the *Dame à la licorne* in the Musée de Cluny, a *Life of the Virgin* of which pieces survive in that museum and also the Bob Jones University Museum (Souchal 1973, figs. 66, 67), a tapestry of the *Story of Perseus* in a private collection in France (Souchal 1973, fig. 76), and the *Stories of Vir-*

tuous Women of which fragments survive in the Museum of Fine Arts, Boston (Souchal 1973, fig. 79). Souchal pointed out both in this article and in her exhibition catalogue entry (Paris 1973, 86) that the composition of 20h, particularly the pose of the unicorn and of the arm and hand by its neck, repeats in reverse the composition of the *Sight* tapestry in the Musée de Cluny, and that the sly girl standing at the left of 20h looks like the women in the *Hearing* and *A Mon Seul Désir* hangings. She noted other details that she thought were similar in both sets of hangings and cited them as further support for her claim that the two unicorn series were designed by the same man. According to Souchal the visual differences that distinguish one series from the other result from the fact that 20b–e and 20g, h were woven on low-warp looms, whereas the tapestries in Paris were produced on high-warp looms.

In giving a logical and convincing summation of Souchal's thesis, Joubert (1987, 84) observed that since we have no archival documents to illuminate the artistic world of Paris at the end of the fifteenth century, we must imagine numbers of design shops producing compositions in the current style, the style in fashion, whose vocabulary of forms was accessible to all through the medium of the illustrations in contemporary printed books.

Erlande-Brandenburg (1975) considered Souchal's thesis concerning the "Maître de la Chasse à la Licorne" and, while acknowledging its usefulness, he disagreed with the idea that all these works of art could represent the activity of a single man. He did not believe that Souchal had succeeded in finding the designer of the Metropolitan Museum's tapestries. He observed (1975, 89) that the prints she cited could be compared convincingly among themselves but they did not relate as well to the tapestry designs. He also noted (1975, 90) that the material Souchal had gathered as illustrating her master's production represented most of the artistic activity of Paris at the end of the fifteenth century and that one day it would be seen as the work of more than one artist, and furthermore, that the undeniable similarities that relate some of these works of art to each other could be explained either as the influence of one man who may have affected a whole generation of artists or through the fact that stock patterns were then very much in fashion. He also believed that the designers of the *Dame à la licorne* and of the *Hunt of the Unicorn* had nothing in common except that they happened to live in the same place at the same time.

We regard Souchal's study as a contribution of major importance; and while it does not convince us that the works of art she studied are in fact the work of one man

or even of one man and his school, it serves to prove beyond any possible doubt that the design source of 20b–e and 20g, h is to be sought in the work of a Parisian painter or design atelier active during the end of the fifteenth century. His figures, settings, and details seem for the most part to be original inventions, but it is clear that he—or the design shop in which he worked—also had recourse to stock patterns, as the figure of the page with his dog in 20e and the composition of the unicorn with an arm about its neck in 20h indicate. In addition, this artist had access to a pattern very much like the one used for the figures of the lord and lady of the castle in 20e, which recall in general form the corresponding couple at the castle gate in the *Visit of the Gypsies* in the Currier Gallery of Art in Manchester, New Hampshire.[14] While 20a and 20f clearly were woven after cartoons designed by someone else, we see no reason to seek him outside this context. Not every tapestry designed in the current Parisian style need have looked like every other.

It seems to us significant that the tapestries woven after the designs for 20b–e and 20g, h show, particularly in the passages representing red velvet and in many of the foliage passages, a particular painterly effect reminiscent of easel paintings executed with oil glazes. The images in 20a and 20f, like those in most tapestries that have survived from this period, have the look of paintings executed with unglazed opaque tempera pigments. At present we do not know how to interpret this difference, but its existence may perhaps be significant in connection with future searches for the identities of the designers of the *Hunt of the Unicorn* tapestries.

Freeman (1976, 193–205) considered the question of the design source, taking into account the theories that Reynaud and Souchal advanced in 1973, and concluded that the designer of 20b–e and 20g, h was an artist working in Paris at the end of the fifteenth century who was influenced, particularly in his choice of colors, by Netherlandish painting, and that while he had also designed the *Perseus* tapestry, he was not the same man who produced the compositions for the *Dame à la licorne*. We agree with Freeman except for her inclusion of the *Perseus* among the artist's works and the matter of color choice which, we believe, is a false criterion since the extraordinarily varied and intense tones in 20a–h seem to us to follow naturally from the excellent state of their preservation. Such colors simply have not been seen, or have not been reported, in any other hangings that have survived from this period. In the future, when more tapestries are examined from the back, as the *Apocalypse* tapestries in Angers were in 1985,[15] it may become apparent that the palette which appears so striking and unusual in the *Hunt of the Unicorn* was not so unique as has been thought.

MANUFACTURE AND DATE

Like most late medieval tapestries that show elegant figures wearing fashionable costumes in verdure settings, particularly if they have (or are associated with pieces that have) millefleurs grounds, 20a–h were until recently thought to have been designed in France and also manufactured there. Biais (1905, 673–76) published them as French and noted that other writers had suggested Aubusson or the Loire valley as the place of manufacture but that he himself had reservations about both opinions. He noted (1905, 675 n. 1) an item in the inventory of the château de Verteuil of 1728 (de Fleury 1884–85, 75) which mentions a room in the castle where "travaillait le tapissier" (where the *tapissier* was working), and he concluded, we believe correctly, that this did not refer to a tapestry weaver but to a restorer of tapestries (or, we believe, perhaps an upholsterer). Biais dated the *Hunt of the Unicorn* tapestries at the end of the fifteenth or first quarter of the sixteenth century on the basis of fashion in costume, the same criterion that Guiffrey (1911, 100 and caption fig. 56), who also called the tapestries French, used to suggest a date at the end of the fifteenth century.

Ackerman (1922–23, 292) also attributed the tapestries to France, but she was the first specialist to separate 20a–f (20g, h had by now disappeared temporarily from the literature; see Publications) into two groups of different date. She believed that 20b–e were woven about 1480 and that 20a and 20f, which she said show different kinds of figures and drawing, were added in the sixteenth century. The catalogue entry for their exhibition at the Metropolitan Museum in 1928 (p. 18) and the related article by Breck (1928, 150) called 20a–f French and dated all of them about 1500, but except for these publications the division of the six pieces into two groups, one slightly later than the other, was repeated from time to time in the literature. Hunter (1925, 95) observed the distinction and added that the first four pieces (20b–e) were produced "by weavers with Tournai training," the later two (20a, f) in France. Migeon (1929, 325–26) and Marillier (1935, 293) also regarded 20a and 20f as being later than 20b–e, and Marillier expressed the opinion that all of them were probably woven in Touraine. Siple (1938, 89) considered 20a and 20f to be "less spirited," but she dated all the hangings, which now included 20g, h, to the end of the fifteenth century and labeled them as Franco-Flemish work.

Rorimer, from the time of his earliest publication of the tapestries (*The Cloisters*, 1938, 86, 90), acknowledged that there was insufficient evidence for a claim of France or the Netherlands as the place of manufacture and that 20a and 20f looked later than the others. A few years later he published his hypothesis (1942–43, 8) that 20b–e and 20g, h were produced to celebrate the marriage of Anne de Bretagne and Louis XII in 1499. Soon afterward, he suggested (1945 ed. of *The Unicorn Tapestries*, 1938) that 20a and 20f may have been added to the set later, when François I married Claude, Anne's daughter and heir, in 1514. He dated the two groups of hangings accordingly. Rorimer held to these attributions in all his later writings. When 20b was exhibited at the Metropolitan Museum in 1970–71, it was catalogued as Franco-Flemish work of about 1500.

Following Rorimer, Shepherd (1961, 175) dated the design of 20b–e and 20g, h to the period 1498–99, during the time that Anne became Charles VIII's widow and then Louis XII's bride; and she expressed the opinion that they had not been woven in the Loire valley. Schneebalg-Perelman (1962–66, 308–9) also followed Rorimer in associating the earlier pieces with Anne de Bretagne and the two laters ones with François I and, further, included them in her discussion of tapestries she believed were of Brussels manufacture that were listed in Anne's inventories of 1494 and 1501. Salet (1966, 435–36), in his review of this article, observed that it is difficult to distinguish Brussels millefleurs tapestries from those woven in other parts of the southern Netherlands and that there is no proof that 20a–h were woven in Brussels. However some writers continued to entertain the idea that 20a–h had been woven there. In Coffinet's opinion (1971, 202–3) all but 20a show the workmanship of Brussels and 20f could have been woven only in Brussels. He also acknowledged that 20a and 20f could have been produced later than the others and after designs by a different artist. Souchal (exh. cat. Paris 1973, 86) dated the entire series at the end of the fifteenth century and, after acknowledging that there were other weaving centers in the southern Netherlands using low-warp looms (and in her opinion 20a–h were certainly woven by this method), she tended to favor Brussels as the place of manufacture because it seems that the most luxurious low-warp tapestries were being woven there at this time.

Freeman (1976, 206–7) dated the designs of 20a–h about 1500, allowing a range of dates from 1490 to 1505. She based her opinion on the overwhelming evidence that they correspond in style to the many woodcut book illustrations that were produced in Paris at the turn of the century. As she observed, the details of the fashionable costumes also appear in the prints. After considering earlier opinions about the place of manufacture (1976, 212–18), she settled in favor of Brussels where she believed tapestries of the best quality were being woven at the time.

It seems correct, given the limited data we have to serve as criteria for dating fashionable costumes of this period, to date the designs for 20a–h in the years 1495–1505 and to assume that because these are hangings of the highest quality they would not have been woven any later. As for the place of weaving, we agree with Salet (1978, 106) who noted in his review of Freeman's book that he was prepared to accept 20a–h as Brussels work even though the place of manufacture is not a prime consideration. We also agree with Souchal (exh. cat. Paris 1973, 86) and Freeman (1976, 217) who viewed Brussels as the place where luxurious tapestries were being woven at this time; but as we have said elsewhere in this catalogue, we have no reason to believe that equally fine and rich hangings were not being woven in other parts of the southern Netherlands as well. It seems to us more important, for the sake of future investigations, to note here that we believe 20a–h were produced under the auspices of the finest entrepreneurs of the period of whom Pieter van Aelst of Brussels is the best known today. Whether the producer was van Aelst or some other, in this instance it is important to note that he used a method of manufacture that somehow enabled 20b–e and 20g, h to look like oil-glazed easel paintings (see Source of the Design), which the original sketches or the *petits patrons* may indeed have been. In our experience this effect is unique among surviving late Gothic tapestries. Certainly neither 20a nor 20f, which we see no reason to date later than the others, do not give this impression. In itself that may indicate, as Freeman suggested, that they were not produced under the same auspices as the other hangings in this series.

RELATED TAPESTRIES

No duplicate weavings, and none that seem to belong with this group, appear to have survived. As noted above (see Subject), we believe that among 20a–h there are remnants of at least two, probably three, and possibly four sets of hangings, all dealing with some aspect of the theme of the unicorn, all woven for the same patron.

In the literature, 20b–e have been treated as comprising a series that is complete in itself, a cycle illustrating the hunt of a unicorn according to the stages of a typical stag hunt of the period. However in those terms a number of pieces could be missing. For example there is no episode showing fewterers bringing the animal's droppings for inspection and no scene showing the hunters leaving the castle, only 20e which shows their return (see 25a–f for a list of typical scenes in a stag hunt and an example of a set of tapestries showing both the departure of the hunters from the castle and their return to it). Also as noted above, 20a shows hunters who seem to be posting the hounds as a limerer or fewterer calls to them. There is nothing to indicate that their quarry is a unicorn. Therefore this piece could belong to a set of hangings illustrating a hunt for a stag, a wild boar, a bear, or any other game animal, a set of which the other pieces have either not survived or not been identified. If, as it has been suggested, 20g, h do not belong with 20b–e, then they must have been produced either as a single hanging showing Gabriel hunting the unicorn in the *hortus conclusus* or as part of a set showing several scenes from a version of the unicorn hunt in which the quarry is tamed by a maiden but not killed (see Subject above, and Freeman 1976, 49–51). As for 20f, we agree with Nickel (1982, 10 n. 5) who suggested that it may have been produced as a single hanging rather than as part of a series. If that is not so then we are left to conclude that it formed the last piece in a cycle illustrating the story of the unicorn hunted as the lover (Freeman 1976, 45–48).

HISTORY

In the collection of the comtes de La Rochefoucauld, France.

In 1680 seven pieces listed in the inventory of François VI de La Rochefoucauld as hanging in the great chamber of his residence on the rue de Seine, Paris.

In 1728 seven pieces listed in the inventory of François VIII de La Rochefoucauld at the château de Verteuil (Charente), five in the large bedroom in the new building, two in a large low hall near the chapel where furniture was being stored.

Said to have been looted from the château de Verteuil in 1793 and to have been used in the neighborhood to protect potatoes from freezing and to cover espaliered trees; acquired again by members of the La Rochefoucauld family and installed in a salon in the château de Verteuil in 1856.

20a–f acquired by John D. Rockefeller, Jr., from comte Aimery de La Rochefoucauld through Edouard Larcade in 1923.

In the collection of John D. Rockefeller, Jr., New York.

Given to the MMA by John D. Rockefeller, Jr., 1937.

20g, h acquired from the comte Gabriel de La Rochefoucauld and given to the MMA by John D. Rockefeller, Jr., 1938.

EXHIBITIONS

New York, Anderson Galleries, 1922. 20a–f exhibited by Edouard Larcade.

New York, MMA, 1928. *French Gothic Tapestries: A Loan Exhibition.* Cat. nos. 4–9 [20a–f]. 20f illus. Lent "by friends."

New York, MMA, 1970. *Masterpieces of Fifty Centuries.* Cat. no. 176 [20b], illus.

Paris 1973. Catalogue entries by Geneviève Souchal. Cat. nos. 18–24 [20a–h], illus.

New York 1974. Cat. nos. 18–24 [20a–h], illus.

PUBLICATIONS

de Fleury, P. "Inventaire des objets mobiliers existant dans les châteaux de La Rochefoucauld, Verteuil et La Terne à la mort de François VIII de La Rochefoucauld (1728)." *Bulletin de la Société Archéologique et Historique de la Charente*, 5th ser., 7 (1884–85) pp. 126, 163. Seven unicorn tapestries mentioned.

X. B. de M. [X. Barbier de Montault]. Review of G. Callier, *Note sur les tapisseries de Boussac (Creuse)* (Guéret, 1887). *Revue de l'Art Chrétien* 38 (1888) p. 114. 20a–h described and discussed briefly.

Notice sur Verteuil. Ruffec, n.d. [before 1905: cited in Biais 1905, p. 669 n. 1], pp. 13–14. 20a–f discussed briefly.

Biais, Emile. "Les tapisseries de 'la Licorne' du château de Verteuil." *Réunion des Sociétés des Beaux-arts des Départements* 29 (1905) pp. 669–77. 20a–f described and discussed at length; 20b, c illus.

Guiffrey, Jules. *Les tapisseries du XIIᵉ à la fin du XVIᵉ siècle*. Paris, [1911], pp. 98–100. 20a–f described and discussed; 20c illus. fig. 56.

Hunter 1912, p. 52. 20a–f described briefly.

Serbat, Louis. "Troisième excursion: Château de Verteuil." In *Congrès archéologique de France: LXXIXᵉ session tenue à Angoulême en 1912*. Vol. 1, *Guide du Congrès*. Société française d'archéologie. Paris and Caen, 1913, pp. 133–34. 20a–f discussed briefly.

Rodière, R. Communication, read by C. Enlart at the meeting of November 8, 1916. *Bulletin de la Société nationale des antiquaires de France*, 1916, pp. 308–11. 20a–f mentioned; 20a discussed.

Ackerman, Phyllis. "The Hunt of the Unicorn." *International Studio* 76 (1922–23), pp. 292–96. 20a–f described and discussed; illus.

Göbel 1923, vol. 1, pp. 169–70. 20a–f described and discussed.

Hunter 1925, 95–98. 20a–f described and discussed at length; illus. pls. vi,b–d (20b, full view and details), vi,e (20b, full view). In the Limited, Subscription Edition, also pls. S,a,b (20f, full view, and 20d, detail).

Ackerman, Phyllis. "Recently Identified Designers of Gothic Tapestries," *Art Bulletin* 9 (1926–27) p. 148. Two pieces, not identified, mentioned.

Breck, Joseph. "The Tapestry Exhibition: Part I." *MMA Bulletin* 23 (1928) pp. 147, 150. 20a–f described and discussed; 20b, d, f illus. figs. 3–5.

Migeon, Gaston. *Les arts du tissu*. Rev. ed., Paris, 1929, pp. 325–26. 20a–f discussed briefly; 20b illus.

Shepard, Odell. *The Lore of the Unicorn*. Boston and New York, 1930, p. 71. 20a–f discussed briefly; 20f, b, d illus. pls. iv–vi.

Marillier, Henry C. "Shorter Notices: The *Hunt of the Unicorn* Tapestries." *Burlington Magazine* 66 (1935) p. 293. 20a–f discussed briefly.

Marquand, Eleanor C. "Plant Symbolism in the Unicorn Tapestries." *Parnassus* 10, no. 5 (October 1938) pp. 2–8, 33, 40. Discussed at length; includes a list of plants represented in the tapestries; 20a, c, f illus. full view, and details of 20d, h.

Rorimer, James J. "New Acquisitions for The Cloisters." *MMA Bulletin* 33, no. 5, section 2 (May 1938) pp. 14, 16, 19. 20a–f discussed; illus. cover [20e] and figs. 12 [20c], 13 [20e detail], 14 [20e].

Rorimer, James J. *The Cloisters: The Building and the Collection of Mediaeval Art in Fort Tryon Park*. MMA, New York, 1938, pp. 85–95. Described and discussed at length; 20b–e illus.

[Rorimer, James J.]. *The Unicorn Tapestries: A Picture Book*. MMA, New York, 1938. Described and discussed; illus. figs. 1–20, full views and details. Revised as *The Unicorn Tapestries at The Cloisters: A Picture Book*, published in 1945 (2d ed.), 1946 (3d ed.), and 1962 (4th ed.).

Siple, Ella S. "Art in America—Medieval Art at the New Cloisters and Elsewhere." *Burlington Magazine* 73 (1938) p. 89. Discussed briefly.

Alexander, E. J., and Carol H. Woodward. *The Flora of the Unicorn Tapestries*. Reprinted from the *Journal of the New York Botanical Garden*, May–June 1941. New York, 1941, 1947, 1965. Discussed; 20a illus. full view, details of others.

Rorimer, James J. "The Unicorn Tapestries Were Made for Anne of Brittany." *MMA Bulletin*, n.s. 1 (1942–43) pp. 7–20. Discussed at great length; 20a, e illus. full view and in detail, also details of several others.

Schneider, Hildegard. "On the Pomegranate." *MMA Bulletin*, n.s. 4 (1945–46) p. 120. 20f discussed briefly; illus. p. 119, detail of 20c.

Rorimer, James J. "The Museum's Collection of Mediaeval Tapestries." *MMA Bulletin*, n.s. 6 (1947–48) pp. 92, 98. Discussed briefly; illus. p. 94, full view of 20a–f, and pp. 96, 97, details of 20d and 20e.

Freeman, Margaret B. "A New Room for the Unicorn Tapestries." *MMA Bulletin*, n.s. 7 (1948–49) pp. 237–42. Discussed at length in terms of the various settings in which the tapestries are known to have been hung; illus. installations in château de Verteuil and residence of Mr. and Mrs. John D. Rockefeller, Jr., New York.

Forsyth, William H. "The Medieval Stag Hunt." *MMA Bulletin*, n.s. 10 (1951–52) pp. 207–9. Discussed; illus. details of 20b, c, e.

Weigert, Roger-Armand. *La tapisserie française*. Paris, 1956, pp. 85–86. Discussed briefly; 20b illus. pl. 29.

Verlet, Pierre, and Francis Salet. *La dame à la licorne*. Paris, 1960, pp. 33–34. Discussed briefly.

Shepherd, Dorothy G. "Three Tapestries from Chaumont." *Bulletin of the Cleveland Museum of Art* 48 (1961) pp. 174–76. Discussed at length; 20d illus. fig. 15.

Schneebalg-Perelman, Sophie. "Les sources de l'histoire de la tapisserie bruxelloise et la tapisserie en tant que source." *Annales de la Société Royale d'Archéologie de Bruxelles* 51 (1962–66) pp. 308–9, 321. Discussed briefly; 20b illus. fig. 13.

Rorimer, James J. *The Cloisters: The Building and the Collection of Medieval Art in Fort Tryon Park*. MMA. 3d ed., rev., New York, 1963, pp. 162–75. Described and discussed at length; illus. 20b, f, g, h full view, and details of 20c, d, e.

Weigert, Roger-Armand. *La tapisserie et le tapis en France*. Paris, 1964, p. 72. Discussed briefly (same text as this author's *La tapisserie française*, 1956).

Verlet 1965, pp. 23–24, 68–69. Discussed, illus.

Salet, Francis. "Chronique: Broderie, tapisserie," review of Schneebalg-Perelman, "Les sources de l'histoire de la tapisserie bruxelloise . . . ," 1962–66. *Bulletin Monumental* 124 (1966) p. 436. Mentioned.

Holm, Edith. *Die Einhornjagd auf den Teppichen der Anne de Bretagne*. Die Jagd in der Kunst. Hamburg and Berlin, 1967. Described and discussed according to Rorimer; 17 illus. including color of 20d.

Jarry, Madeleine. *World Tapestry from Its Origins to the Present*. New York, 1969, pp. 121, 123. Discussed; 20f illus. p. 120.

Coffinet, Julien. *Arachne ou l'art de la tapisserie*. Geneva and Paris, 1971, pp. 202–3, 205. Discussed; illus. pp. 201, 203, color details of 20b and 20c.

Beer, Rüdiger Robert. *Einhorn: Fabelwelt und Wirklichkeit*. Munich, 1972, pp. 153–58. Described and discussed at length primarily according to Rorimer; 20a–f illus. pp. 163–65.

Reynaud, Nicole. "Un peintre français cartonnier de tapisseries au XVᵉ siècle: Henri de Vulcop." *Revue de l'Art*, no. 22 (1973) pp. 18, 19. Discussed briefly.

Souchal, Geneviève. "Un grand peintre français de la fin du XVᵉ siècle: Le maître de la Chasse à la Licorne." *Revue de l'Art*, no. 22 (1973) pp. 22–49. Discussed at great length in terms of the source of the design; illus.

Sipress, Linda. "The Unicorn Tapestries." *MMA Bulletin*, n.s. 32 (1973–74) pp. 177–224. Described and discussed in detail, adapted from a then-unpublished study by Margaret B. Freeman (see below, Freeman 1976); illus. full views and details, many in color.

Erlande-Brandenburg, Alain. In "Chronique: Tapisseries," review of Souchal, "Un grand peintre français . . . ," 1973. *Bulletin Monumental* 133 (1975) pp. 88–90. Discussed at length.

Einhorn, Jürgen W. *Spiritalis Unicornis: Das Einhorn als Bedeutungsträger in Literatur und Kunst des Mittelalters*. Münstersche Mittelalter-Schriften, vol. 13. Munich, 1976, pp. 243, 259, 302, 355–56. Discussed briefly, primarily according to Rorimer.

Freeman, Margaret B. *The Unicorn Tapestries.* MMA, New York, 1976, 244 pp., 306 illus. (51 in color), index. Described and discussed in detail from every pertinent point of view; completely illustrated with full views and details; most related materials discussed in the text are also illustrated.

Schneebalg-Perelman, Sophie. "Un nouveau regard sur les origines et le développement de la tapisserie bruxelloise du XIVᵉ siècle à la pré-Renaissance." In *Tapisseries bruxelloises de la pré-Renaissance.* Exh. cat., Musées Royaux d'Art et d'Histoire. Brussels, 1976, p. 174. Discussed briefly.

Coffinet 1977, pp. 104–6. Discussed at length; illus. pp. 108, 109, color details of 20b and 20c.

Schneebalg-Perelman, Sophie. In "Comptes rendus," review of Freeman, *The Unicorn Tapestries,* 1976. *Revue Belge d'Archéologie et d'Histoire de l'Art* 46 (1977) pp. 58–59. Discussed at length.

Erlande-Brandenburg, Alain. *La Dame à la Licorne.* Paris, 1978, n. pag.; section near end entitled "Le maquettiste." Discussed briefly; illus. details of 20a, b.

Lestocquoy 1978, p. 115. Arms on dog collar in 20a discussed briefly.

Salet, Francis. In "Bibliographie," review of Freeman, *The Unicorn Tapestries,* 1976. *Bulletin Monumental* 136 (1978) pp. 104–6. Discussed at length.

de Vaivre, Jean-Bernard. "L'héraldique et l'histoire de l'art du Moyen Age." *Gazette des Beaux-Arts,* 6th ser., 93 (1979) pp. 105 and 108 n. 11. Arms on dog collar in 20a discussed briefly.

Souchal, Geneviève. In "Book Reviews," review of Freeman, *The Unicorn Tapestries,* 1976. *Art Bulletin* 62 (1980) pp. 313–16. Discussed at length.

Crockett, Lawrence J. "The Identification of a Plant in the Unicorn Tapestries." *Metropolitan Museum Journal* 17 (1982) pp. 15–22. 20a, f discussed; illus. full view and details figs. 1–4.

Nickel, Helmut. "About the Sequence of the Tapestries in *The Hunt of the Unicorn* and *The Lady with the Unicorn.*" *Metropolitan Museum Journal* 17 (1982) pp. 9–14. Discussed; illus., including suggested reconstruction of 20g, h in fig. 10.

Reynaud, Nicole. "La Galerie des Cerfs au Palais ducal de Nancy." *Revue de l'Art,* no. 61 (1983) pp. 21, 24. Discussed briefly; 20d illus. fig. 24.

Williamson, John. *The Oak King, the Holly King, and the Unicorn: The Myths and Symbolism of the Unicorn Tapestries.* New York, 1986. Described and discussed at great length primarily in terms of the plant and animal symbolism and correspondence of pre-Christian and Christian myths and symbols; illus., some in color.

Joubert 1987, pp. 83–84. Discussed briefly.

NOTES

1. For detailed descriptions of the various flora and fauna in these tapestries, and notes on the symbolism with which they were associated in the Middle Ages, see studies by Marquand (1938), Alexander and Woodward (1941), Freeman (1976), and Williamson (1986) listed in Publications above.

2. Some of the hunters in 20b–e also wear shaggy fur-like hats. Most of these hats are simply resting on the top of the head; some are worn over a cap. However in 20c and 20d some men wear the hats tied to their heads with a scarf that passes over the crown and brim, or through the brim, and then under the chin. Hunters depicted in 25a, c, and f also wear this kind of hat tied to the head. A hanging in the Musée de Cluny shows a hunter wearing the same kind of shaggy hat tied on in this way with a scarf passing around the chin and brim and tied in a bow on top of the crown; see Joubert 1987, illus. p. 122; see also fig. 40 in the present catalogue. A tapestry formerly in the collection of Genevieve Garvan Brady showed the same detail; see Marvin Chauncey Ross, "Four Tournai Tapestries," *Corcoran Gallery of Art Bulletin* 9, no. 2 (November 1957) fig. 6. A hanging formerly in the collection of Rita Lydig showed a hunter with a hat tied on with a scarf that passes through the brim; see *The Rita Lydig Collection of Notable Art Treasures of the Gothic and Renaissance Periods,* sale cat., American Art Galleries, New York, April 4, 1913, no. 137, illus. A somewhat different version of the same hat appears in another tapestry in the Metropolitan Museum (see 36 in the present catalogue). If these shaggy hats were not made of dyed fur or of some fur-like textile, they were probably made of a fabric covered with short lengths of yarn or "thrums," like the "Hattes thrommyd with silke of diuerse collours" mentioned in a manuscript of ca. 1525 (*Oxford English Dictionary,* 2d ed., s.v. "thrum" [vb. 2]).

3. See a brief description of the pomegranate tree or bush as it grows in nature in Hildegard Schneider, "On the Pomegranate," *MMA Bulletin,* n.s. 4 (1945–46) p. 118, and on p. 119 an illustration of a correctly rendered example in the lower left corner of 20c; see also Margaret B. Freeman, *The Unicorn Tapestries,* MMA (New York, 1976) fig. 164 (in color). While the representation of the fruit on the tree in 20f is accurate, the extraordinarily long radial leaves seem to be the designer's invention.

4. When Freeman discovered the inventory in 1967, she recorded the entry concerning the tapestries in a letter (in the files at The Cloisters) to then-director Thomas Hoving. The 1680 inventory entry reads: "Item, une tenture de tapisserie de haute lisse représentant une chasse de licorne en sept pièces contenant vingt-deux aulnes de cour sur quatre aulnes de haut ou environ, prisé la somme de quinze cens livres. . . ."

5. Reference in Freeman, *Unicorn Tapestries,* p. 238 n. 9, to Abbé J. F. Chevalier, *Verteuil sous la Révolution* (Ruffec, 1930) pp. 117–18; present author's translation of the French text, which is recorded as follows in the files of the Department of Medieval Art: "Examinez ces vieilles tapisseries. Respectez-les pour ce qu'elles ne représentent aucuns signes de royauté; elles contiennent des histoires."

6. Freeman, *Unicorn Tapestries,* pp. 11–65, discussed the history of the unicorn image and the symbolism and allegory that have been traditionally associated with it. For further information, see in Publications above works by Shepard (1961), Beer (1972), and Einhorn (1976).

7. Colin Eisler, *The Master of the Unicorn: The Life and Work of Jean Duvet* (New York, 1979) pp. 114–15, dated the prints in this period.

8. Eisler, *Master of the Unicorn,* pp. 112–13.

9. Eisler, *Master of the Unicorn,* pp. 118–19, 124.

10. Kurth 1926, pl. 216.

11. For more information concerning the emblems and device in this tapestry and works of art made for Nicolas Bouesseau, see Jean-Bernard de Vaivre, "Deux tapisseries inédites de la fin du Moyen Age commandées par des Bourguignons," *Comptes rendus de l'Académie des Inscriptions et Belles-Lettres,* 1988, pp. 133–40.

12. M. de Vaivre intends to investigate the coat of arms further and will give an account of his findings in a forthcoming publication.

13. Forsyth's reading of the blazon, together with other interpretations, are recorded in the files of the MMA Department of Medieval Art.

14. For the tapestry in Manchester, see Souchal in Paris 1973, no. 53, illus.

15. The backs of the *Apocalypse* tapestries were exposed when the linings were removed in connection with a conservation project undertaken by the Service des Monuments Historiques. See Alain Erlande-Brandenburg et al., *La tenture de l'Apocalypse d'Angers* (Nantes, 1987), for color illustrations made of the tapestries at that time.

21

The Adoration of the Magi

An antependium, a dossal, or part of a choir hanging

Southern Netherlands, about 1500
Wool warp; wool, silk, and linen wefts
3 ft. 5 1/4 in. × 6 ft. 4 1/2 in. (1.05 m × 1.94 m) as mounted
15 warp yarns per inch, 6 per centimeter
The Lillian Stokes Gillespie Collection, Bequest of Lillian Stokes Gillespie, 1915 (15.121.1)

CONDITION

The fabric has been cut along all four sides. The left and right edges have been rewoven with modern warp and weft yarns. They show a pattern resembling what appear to be bits of the original narrow yellow and brown tessellated bands running along the top and bottom of the field and which are most clearly visible directly below the figure of the Virgin. There are important areas of reweaving along the edges of the field, especially in its upper and lower left corners. These restorations have faded and now read as irregularly shaped smoke-like intrusions on the dark spotted background or the light tiled floor. A section of the background that runs vertically between the figures of the two Magi standing at the right has been rewoven as have also parts of their costumes and the accessories they hold. The most important restorations in this area appear along the back edge of the black Magus's right leg and in most of his left shoe. In these two places the drawing has been altered significantly. There are other passages of reweaving in Joseph's hood, cloak, and sleeves; in the Virgin's patterned velvet garment and the locks of her hair; and in the jeweled bands bordering the right-hand parts of the sleeve opening and the hem of the kneeling Magus's robe. There is a large passage of reweaving that involves the back of his robe just below shoulder height and the light flame-like mass that moves from there outward across a bit of the dark background.

Most of the weft yarns used in the rewoven passages are made of wool. Pale yellow silk yarns were used to repair certain areas that read in the photograph illustrated here as a tone slightly darker than the lightest light; it appears for example on the right shoulder of the Virgin's mantle and at several points below that on the same garment. However the yellow, green, and blue silks that render highlights in areas of those hues are original. The lightest lights, most of which have survived vir-

tually intact, were woven with linen yarns dyed a pale warm yellow tone. This and the other colors have faded somewhat, but for the most part they are still strong and varied. The two shades of dark blue in the background and the greens and oranges in the garments of the two Magi at the right are particularly intense.

DESCRIPTION AND SUBJECT

Six figures are arranged in two rows that are parallel to each other and to the picture plane. Both rows occupy the foreground of an interior space defined only by a tiled floor at the bottom and a velvet curtain at the back. The rectangular tiles of the floor are decorated with squares or rosettes. The background has been described as a starry sky, but it was certainly intended to represent a hanging of plain cut velvet decorated with small loops of gilt yarn (see below).

An elderly, balding, and bearded man, who wears a doublet of patterned velvet with fur cuffs under a long plain velvet robe trimmed at the collar, armholes, and hem with bands of pearls and gemstones, kneels in the center of the composition in the forward plane. His golden crown rests on the floor beyond his left knee. He offers an uncovered casket of gold coins to the nude Christ Child, who is seated on His mother's lap and leans forward, holding His hands out toward the gift. A halo of pale gold overlaid with a red cross paty and border surrounds His head. Mary is seated in the forward plane, left of center. She wears an unpatterned tunic under a cope-like mantle of sumptuous patterned voided velvet whose sides are held together over her breast with two jeweled brooches and a band running between them. Her fair hair falls loose to her waist and a halo of pale gold darkened at the edges surrounds her head. Joseph, represented as an elderly bearded man, sits behind Mary and apparently in a farther plane. Although the designer has not clarified the relationship of the two figures in space, the fact that Joseph's right hand passes in front of Mary's hair at the point of her right shoulder suggests that he is sitting on the rear part of the bench that she occupies. Joseph wears a long hood and cloak over his doublet and breeches; all his garments are of unpatterned fabric. A purse hangs from the girdle that encircles his waist. He rests his crossed arms on the

21

head of a walking stick wedged between his knees and raises his right hand in salutation as he directs his gaze toward the visitors.

Two men approach this main group from the right. Each of them wears a golden crown with strawberry-leaf points like the one that rests on the floor near the elderly man kneeling before the Child. The man walking in the forward plane at the far right wears a calf-length tunic of patterned voided velvet with short sleeves over hose and a patterned doublet, a long scarf tied in a knot behind his head, ankle-high shoes with turned-back tops, and pendant gold earrings. His skin is swarthy and his facial features are negroid. In his left hand he carries what appears to be a golden incense burner in the shape of a chapel supported on a round flaring foot. His companion, who stands in the farther plane a bit to the left, wears an unpatterned velvet mantle draped around his figure. He has a loose, wide-sleeved doublet, hose, and

calf-length boots. He raises his right hand to remove his crown. With his left hand he proffers a covered gold cup shaped like the hull of a sailing vessel supported on a round flaring foot.

In 1915 Friedley (248) wrote that the background suggests "bands of cloud starred with small crescents in white, the effect approximating that found in the earliest examples of European tapestry known to exist." The last comment is probably a reference to the early or mid-fourteenth-century German tapestry of the Crucifixion with the Virgin and saints that was on exhibition in the Metropolitan Museum from 1914 until 1916 with works of art lent from the J. Pierpont Morgan collection.[1] Friedley undoubtedly knew it before the Museum acquired it in 1916 (54 in this catalogue). That hanging has a background of dark blue sky scattered with six-pointed yellow stars. Migeon (1929, 207) described the *Adoration* as having a "blue starred ground" and discussed it specifically in the context of the earlier *Crucifixion.* However what both writers read as an expanse of sky was not meant to represent the sky nor are the light spots scattered over it meant to be seen as stars. What Friedley interpreted as bands of cloud in the *Adoration,* the small cloud-like patches of lighter blue scattered irregularly over the dark blue ground, represent highlights on velvet pile. The same effect may be seen on the top and front fall of the dark, plain velvet cover on Saint Anne's bed in the scene showing the Birth of the Virgin in one of the five *Life of the Virgin* choir hangings in the collegiate church of Notre-Dame in Beaune.[2] The crescent-shaped pale yellow "stars" scattered over the dark blue ground in the Metropolitan Museum's *Adoration* were meant to represent loops of gilt yarn woven at regular intervals into the ground of the velvet. The same small crescents, woven with the same pale yellow yarn (linen), appear again in the pile parts of the patterned velvet of which the Virgin's mantle is made; they appear most clearly to the right of the Infant's legs. (The "cloud" effect appears in the highlights of the same velvet in the same place.) If these observations are not enough to demonstrate that the background was not meant to represent the sky, there are the two narrow parallel bands of red that run along the bottom of the dark ground where it meets the tiled floor. These lines are meaningless if one reads the background as sky, especially since parts of the "clouds" are visible between them; but they make perfect sense as two decorative tapes or cords that border the base of a textile wall cover. The same kind of double banding runs along the bottom edges of the velvet hangings that cover the backs of the Circumcision and Coronation of the Virgin scenes in the tapestries in Beaune; and in the scene showing the Virgin reading alone in her room, next to the one showing the flowering of Joseph's rod, the bands border not only the lower edge of the velvet hanging but also its left side and upper edge (see note 2). Therefore we can be sure that the dark background in the Metropolitan Museum's *Adoration of the Magi* represents not a starry sky but a hanging of dark blue, plain velvet decorated with loops of gilt yarn and trimmed at the lower edge, and perhaps also the side and upper edges, with two bands of tape or cord.

In the New Testament the story of the Magi's visit appears only in the Gospel according to Matthew (2:1–12). Other accounts appear in the apocryphal books including the Protevangelium of James. Matthew's account contains few details of the visit. He tells that "wise men" came from the "east" to Jerusalem to seek the child born to be king of the Jews; that after conferring with Herod, who had heard of their mission, they proceeded to Bethlehem, continuing to follow a star that had appeared to them and that stopped over the place where the Child lay; and that after entering the house and finding Him with His mother, they fell down and adored Him and offered Him gifts of gold and frankincense and myrrh. The Evangelist does not say how many men there were nor where they came from, nor when, nor what their names were. These details developed later, and they were not stated consistently. Early Christian artists portrayed two, three, or four men in the company; in Syrian art there might be as many as twelve.[3] At first they all were given the same appearance; they wore Persian costume, with trousers and the Phrygian cap; and they were all of the same age. Eventually they were called by the Persian name *magi,* the plural of *magus,* a term interpreted as "magician" in the sense of a priest or an astrologer. It was thought that they had been watching for the star that Balaam had foretold would "rise out of Jacob" (Numbers 24:17), a star that became associated in Christian times with the star of Bethlehem.[4] Because the idea of a "magician" suggested the Antichrist to early Christians, and also because the Magi were eventually regarded as symbolic representatives of the three parts of the world as it was then known —that is, Europe, Asia, and Africa—these men came to be described as kings, specifically as three kings, one for each part of the earth. Other factors favored the number three. It is the number of the Trinity. Matthew spoke of three gifts and so the notion of one man per gift developed. What was said to have been the relics of these men, taken from Constantinople to Milan and then eventually to Cologne in the middle of the twelfth century, corresponded to the remains of three bodies. The number three was also associated with three ages of man, and so one of the Magi came to be represented as a beardless youth, another as a mature man, and the third as a bald and bearded elderly man. The one representing Europe was shown as a Caucasian and curiously enough the Asian was too; the third, representing Africa, was given negroid features and coloring. The names Gaspar, Melchior, and Balthasar do not appear before the ninth or tenth century, and it was not until later that the youth was associated with Gaspar, the mature black man with Balthasar, and the elderly man with Melchior.

The Metropolitan Museum's tapestry shows the iconography in its fully developed late medieval form. Melchior, Gaspar, and Balthasar approach the Child with their gifts in attitudes of homage. Melchior, his crown removed and placed on the ground, kneels before Him. Gaspar raises one hand to remove his crown in deference to the Child and with the other he offers his gift; his legs bend as he prepares to kneel. Balthasar walks forward, leaning back from the waist upward either to counterbalance the weight of the vessel he carries or to throw the weight of his torso over his trailing left leg in preparation for a graceful kneeling. He extends his arms to offer his gift, his hands covered with a scarf in a gesture of respect. Here are the three kings who rule the earth, come to pay homage to the King of Kings. Their gifts are symbolic. Gold represents the royal station of Christ; frankincense refers to His divinity; and myrrh, used in embalming, symbolizes His death. The Child, shown here as a chubby baby whose eyes are wide with wonder, reaches forward to touch the bright, shining coins that Melchior offers Him. Mary holds the nude Infant tenderly and watches His action with dignified amusement. Joseph sits quietly in the background gesturing a welcome to the visitors but remaining essentially an observer. The velvet curtain or hanging behind them shuts out the exterior world, so that it is impossible to tell at what time of day or year the scene takes place. Matthew does not specify either one. According to one tradition, which eventually became the most commonly accepted one, the Magi came to the Child soon after His birth. Another held that they did not arrive until sometime later since Herod (Matthew 2:7, 16), having asked the Magi when the star appeared to them, ordered all male children in Bethlehem and environs who were under the age of two to be killed. Here the designer seems to have accepted the first tradition since he shows the Child as a nude infant.

In its present state, the tapestry has the shape and approximate dimensions of a typical altar frontal or dossal of the late fifteenth century (see 17). The fact that the left and right edges have been cut indicates that some fabric has been lost from both ends, but we cannot determine the extent of the losses nor whether the piece was woven as an independent rectangle with these general proportions or as a section of a much longer hanging. Therefore, it is possible that 21 was not an altar hanging but part of a choir tapestry that showed several scenes from the life of the Virgin or of Christ arranged in a row as they are, for example, in some choir hangings that have survived from two contemporary cycles of the *Life of the Virgin.* One of those cycles, comprising five pieces showing seventeen scenes, was woven in or about 1500 for the collegiate church of Notre-Dame in Beaune and is still in that church.[5] The other cycle was presented to the cathedral of Bayeux in 1499 and has survived only as a series of fragments, one in a private collection in France, two in the Musée de Cluny in Paris, two in the J. B. Speed Museum, Louisville, and one in the Bob Jones University Collection of Religious Art in Greenville, South Carolina.[6] Both cycles show interior and exterior settings in which the narrative scenes unfold.

Although the figure and facial types in the Metropolitan Museum's tapestry resemble those in both the Beaune and Bayeux hangings, the simple pictorial style of 21 relates it more closely to the Beaune pieces. Many of the episodes in that cycle are enacted in outdoor settings; but the scenes showing the Wedding of Mary and Joseph, the Circumcision, the Presentation of the Child in the Temple, the Slaughter of the Innocents, and the Coronation of the Virgin are set in interiors whose back walls are covered with hangings of dark blue velvet. A pattern of rectangular lines representing fold marks relieves their plain surfaces. The setting for the Circumcision and a number of the other episodes shows the top of the velvet meeting the base of a pitched ceiling or vault along a simple horizontal line that runs parallel to the front edge of the floor; and it is tempting to think that the tessellated band across the top of 21, which is also parallel to the front of the floor, is the springing line of a similar ceiling or vault that is now missing. However this band has a distinct pattern that matches the pattern on the band running along the bottom of the field, and so it is clear that both bands represent the inner edge of a decorative border. Therefore, the setting could not have continued above the band, and the field could never have been any wider than it is now, or 1.05 meters. If 21 was once part of a choir hanging, it must have had wide borders along the top and bottom to raise the height to some figure more like the 1.50–1.60 meters which we have postulated for the hypothetical choir hanging from which 24a–e may have come (see 24, Description and Subject) and for the taller Bayeux fragment in the Musée de Cluny (see note 6), which is 1.38 meters high without the upper and lower borders we believe it may once have had. The choir hangings in Beaune are 1.80–1.90 meters tall and have no borders (see note 5).

SOURCE OF THE DESIGN

It was noted above that 21, in terms of pictorial style, is particularly close to the tapestries in Beaune, and that the figure and facial types in 21 are similar to the ones in both the Beaune choir hangings and the fragments from Bayeux. The heads in the *Marriage of Cana* piece from Bayeux, which is now in the J. B. Speed Museum (see note 6), are particularly like the ones in 21. Ackerman suggested that the Bayeux tapestries were designed by some pupil of the painter Gilles van Everen who worked in Brussels and then Antwerp; but her arguments are not convincing.[7] We agree instead with Souchal's and Joubert's contention that that designer was an anonymous artist who borrowed figures and motifs from existing painted or printed book illustrations and reworked them to suit his current needs.[8] Souchal and Joubert have each demonstrated that the figure of Mary in the Annunciation scene in the Bayeux fragment in the Musée de Cluny resembles that in a woodcut of the same subject in a Book of Hours, dated September 27, 1501, printed by Philippe Pigouchet for the publisher Simon Vostre in Paris. Another of Souchal's comparisons shows that the figure of Gabriel in that tapestry is close to the one on the Annunciation page of the *Très petites Heures d'Anne de Bretagne*.[9] Joubert credits Ackerman for having noted that the scene in the Bayeux fragment showing Mary and Joseph at home was inspired by "one of the Vérard Books of Hours" which Souchal later identified as another one printed by Pigouchet for Vostre, this dated September 17, 1496.[10]

Despite the similarities that link the Metropolitan Museum's *Adoration of the Magi* with the Beaune and Bayeux tapestries—they are essentially commonalities of period and place—we cannot claim that 21 was designed by the artist who created the cartoons for one or the other of those choir cycles. However, it seems likely that the designer of 21 also took some or all of his figures from preexisting sources in woodcuts or miniature paintings. None of his sources has been found. He had a markedly personal style—note especially the Virgin's head, Balthasar's head, and the Child's body—that must be taken into account in any future search for his identity.

Manufacture and Date

When the Metropolitan Museum acquired the tapestry in 1915, Friedley published it as an example of German, specifically Rhenish, tapestry weaving of about 1500. He gave no reasons for this attribution, but it is clear from the context of his discussion that he was comparing the piece to the German *Crucifixion* fragment (54) that was then on exhibition in the Metropolitan Museum. The *Adoration of the Magi* was still thought to be German eight years later, when Ackerman (1923, 297), with no discussion, captioned an illustration of it as "probably Nuremberg, the sixteenth century." Shortly afterward Breck and Rogers (1925, 153) referred to 21 not as German but "presumably made in Touraine about 1470–80." Their second edition of the same publication (1929) changed the attribution without giving their rea-

sons: the tapestry was referred to as Franco-Flemish work, probably made in Tournai about 1475–1500. Also in 1929 Migeon compared it to the earlier *Crucifixion* because of what he thought was its background of a starry sky, and because he thought the figures suggested the work of German painters of the first third of the fifteenth century, implying rather than stating that he regarded the *Adoration* as an example of German weaving. He dated it in the mid-fifteenth century. Rorimer (1947) called the tapestry Franco-Flemish work, and he dated it correctly in the late fifteenth or early sixteenth century. It was attributed simply to the fifteenth or sixteenth century when it was published in 1952 (*Art Treasures of the Metropolitan*).

In terms of style the *Adoration of the Magi* is so much like the choir hangings of the *Life of the Virgin* in Beaune that it seems correct to date it, too, about 1500. What few details of fashion in clothing are visible—really only the shape of the Magi's boots and shoes—do not argue against such a date. Erlande-Brandenburg, who published a study of the date and design of the Beaune tapestries, suggested that their designer was an artist who had been trained in the Netherlandish school of painting and sculpture and that the hangings had been woven somewhere in the southern Netherlands.[11] We agree with his suggestions and believe that the *Adoration of the Magi* was also produced in that region despite the fact that the presence of so much linen weft yarn in the fabric—the halos, the middle tones of the Virgin's hair and of the three crowns, and many of the light tones in her garments and those of the three Magi—suggests some connection with Germany. Except for that, the materials and the weaving technique bear no relation to German work of the period; they are entirely characteristic of tapestries produced in the southern Netherlands. We have no simple explanation for what appears at present to be a contradiction. The tapestry may have been woven somewhere in the eastern reaches of the Netherlands (see 51 in this catalogue), or it may have been woven in some German territory by emigrant Netherlandish workers. On the other hand future research may show that linen wefts were used outside of Germany more commonly than we have reason at present to believe they were.

Related Tapestries

No duplicate tapestries are known to have survived, nor do we know of any that belonged with this piece in a series of hangings.

As noted above (Description and Subject), 21 was woven either as an antependium or dossal for an altar or, possibly, as a section in one of a set of choir hangings. Since the length of such hangings was a function of the length and width of the choir they were designed to decorate (or the length of the arc, if the stalls were curved), we cannot calculate the length of the hanging to which this piece may have belonged or how many episodes it might have shown. Nor can we know whether the cycle concerned the life of the Virgin, the life of Christ, a combination of the two, or some theme related to one or the other.

HISTORY

Said to have belonged to Mme. Lelong, Paris.[12]
In the collection of Henry W. Poor, New York; said to have been acquired on the advice of Stanford White.[13]
Sold, *Valuable Artistic Furnishings . . . of Henry W. Poor, Esq.*, American Art Association, New York, April 21–24, 1909, no. 203, illus.
Property of Duveen Brothers from April 1909.
In the collection of Mrs. Robert McM. Gillespie, New York and Stamford.
Bequeathed to the MMA by Lillian Stokes Gillespie, 1915.

EXHIBITION

New York, MMA, in the Morgan Wing, 1925–29, and possibly longer (see Publications, Breck and Rogers).

PUBLICATIONS

D. F. [Durr Friedley]. "An Important Bequest of Tapestries." *MMA Bulletin* 10 (1915) pp. 247–48. Described briefly and discussed; illus.
Ackerman, Phyllis. "Tapestries of Five Centuries: IV. The Weavers of Germany." *International Studio* 76 (January 1923) p. 297. Illus. with caption.
Breck, Joseph, and Meyric R. Rogers. *MMA, The Pierpont Morgan Wing: A Handbook.* New York, 1925; 2d ed., 1929; p. 153. Discussed briefly.
Migeon, Gaston. *Les arts du tissu.* Rev. ed., Paris, 1929, pp. 206–7. Described and discussed; illus.
Rorimer, James J. *Mediaeval Tapestries: A Picture Book.* MMA, New York, 1947. Illus. fig. 19.
Art Treasures of the Metropolitan. New York, 1952, p. 221, no. 46. Discussed briefly; illus. fig. 46 on p. 56.

NOTES

1. See Robert T. Nichol, "Gallery Twelve, Gothic Period," in *MMA, Guide to the Loan Exhibition of the J. Pierpont Morgan Collection* (New York, 1914) p. 27, illus. facing p. 30.

2. See an illustration of the Birth of the Virgin scene in Francis Salet, *La tapisserie française du moyen-âge à nos jours* (Paris, 1946) pl. 16, upper left. This kind of amorphous highlight also appears on large, unbroken expanses of other plain, glossy silk weaves, especially satin. It is as characteristic of the way these fabrics reflect light as are the passages of reflected light that appear along lines where such silks have been tightly draped or folded. Reflected lights of this kind as they appear on plain velvet may be seen along the fold lines on the same bedcover and on the velvet wall hangings that appear at the backs of a number of scenes in the Beaune tapestries: the Circumcision; a scene of Mary reading in her chamber next to the room in which Joseph's rod flowers; the Wedding of Mary and Joseph; the Presentation of the Christ Child in the Temple; the Slaughter of the Innocents; and the Coronation of the Virgin. For illustrations of these episodes, see respectively Salet, *La tapisserie française*, pl. 16, lower right and upper right; and Göbel 1928, vol. 2, figs. 324, upper left, and 325, upper left and right and lower right.

3. The notes on the development of the iconography of the Adoration of the Magi as discussed here and in the following text were derived from Louis Réau, *Iconographie de l'art chrétien* (Paris, 1955–59) vol. 2, pt. 2, pp. 236–49.

4. See a representation in the upper right corner of the Metropolitan Museum's tapestry *Christ Is Born as Man's Redeemer* (29b) of three astrologers keeping watch for Balaam's star and next to them a scene showing the three Magi (represented as kings) washing their feet in a pond and looking upward at the star which has the form of a nude child carrying a cross in the midst of rays of light.

5. For illustrations of the five hangings at Beaune, see Salet, *La tapisserie française*, frontis. (Adoration of the Magi, in color) and pl. 16, two of the hangings, with notes on their dimensions in the captions; also Göbel 1928, vol. 2, figs. 324, 325, one of the same hangings plus the three others. For a discussion of the design source, donor, and date of weaving, see Alain Erlande-Brandenburg, "La tenture de la Vie de la Vierge à Notre-Dame de Beaune," *Bulletin Monumental* 134 (1976) pp. 37–48.

6. For illustrations and notes on the history and design of the tapestries formerly in the cathedral of Bayeux and the surviving fragments, with dimensions of the pieces now in Paris, see Joubert 1987, pp. 60–65; also Phyllis Ackerman, "The Reappearance of a Lost Bayeux Tapestry," *International Studio* 96 (July 1930) pp. 17–20.

7. Ackerman, "Reappearance," pp. 19–20.

8. See Geneviève Souchal, "Un grand peintre français de la fin du XVᵉ siècle: Le maître de la Chasse à la Licorne," *Revue de l'Art*, no. 22 (1973) p. 38; also Joubert 1987, p. 65.

9. See Souchal, "Un grand peintre français," p. 38 and figs. 13 (the woodcut), 15 (the miniature painting), and 18 (the tapestry); also Joubert 1987, figs. 59 (tapestry) and 60 (woodcut).

10. Joubert 1987, pp. 62, 65.

11. Erlande-Brandenburg, "La tenture de la Vie de la Vierge," p. 46.

12. D.F. [Durr Friedley], "An Important Bequest of Tapestries," *MMA Bulletin* 10 (1915) p. 248. Friedley did not give any documentation to support this statement. Presumably he was referring to Mme. Camille Lelong.

13. See Friedley, "An Important Bequest of Tapestries," p. 248, for the report, given as hearsay, that Henry W. Poor bought the tapestry on Stanford White's advice.

22

The Infant Christ Pressing the Wine of the Eucharist

Southern Netherlands, about 1500
Linen warp; wool, silk, and gilt weft yarns
19⁷/₈ in. × 18¹/₄ in. (.505 m × .46 m)
33 warp yarns per inch, 13 per centimeter
Bequest of Benjamin Altman, 1913 (14.40.709)

CONDITION

Since the warp runs parallel to the vertical axis of the pattern, the selvages, which are present except for a few small losses, appear along the left and right sides of the weaving rather than at the top and bottom. Therefore we know that the tapestry has retained its original width. The top and bottom edges of the fabric have been cut, but very little of it could have been lost at these ends because the border is complete along the top and bottom of the field and there are narrow gold and silk ornamental bands outside the border but inside the cuts. There are a few breaks in the central part of the fabric and some small spots of reweaving in the passages representing the Child's hands and the grapes as well as in the oval surround. A short slit that developed between a pair of adjacent warp yarns along the right side of the cross on the orb has been closed with needle stitches. None of these repairs has altered the drawing or modeling of the original design. All the colors have faded somewhat. The flesh tones have suffered most; the subtle color modulations they once showed are now gone and they read as rather flat areas of beige. The gilt yarns (narrow, flat, gilded metal wires wrapped spirally around a silk core) still have their original color and brilliance.

When it came to the Metropolitan Museum, the tapestry was mounted in a rectangular frame of linen decorated with a pattern of roses, grapes, other fruits, and stalks of iris executed in *or nué* needlework, fine colored silks stitched sparsely over parallel rows of heavier gilt yarns (see fig. 120). The pattern was based on some prototype like the pattern in the border of the closely related piece that is now in the Art Institute of Chicago (fig. 121). The top and bottom edges of the embroidered frame have secondary borders, and a narrow strip of oval motifs surrounds the whole. The subsidiary borders at top and bottom show a repeating pattern of stylized lilies inside lyre-shaped units rendered in couched cord work. The cross of the Spanish chivalric Order of Calatrava, set in the center of a shield-shaped compartment,

all worked in split stitches and couched cords, appears in the center of each of these two borders. The tapestry was illustrated with the frame in place, but with the secondary borders at top and bottom turned under, by Hunter (1915–16) and Göbel (1923, 1924) and in the two editions of the Metropolitan Museum handbook of the Altman collection (1914, 1928). In 1961 the needlework frame was removed when the tapestry was cleaned. The frame itself was then cleaned and replaced but inadvertently upside down so that the iris plants appeared inverted (fig. 120). The illustration published by Janson (1985) shows the tapestry and frame in that condition. The frame has since been removed.

DESCRIPTION AND SUBJECT

The upper half of the infant Christ's body appears in the lower half of an oval compartment in the center. He wears a simple tunic cut with a high round neckline and full sleeves. The end of a marble table or low wall appears in front of Him at the left; in the center a crystal orb intervenes between the figure and the oval frame that surrounds the pictorial part of the field. Two gold straps encircle the orb and a gold cross set with a pearl at the center rises from its top. The Child's left hand, holding a branch bearing two small clusters of grapes, is reflected in the crystal. As Standen noted, the reflected index finger appears to be pointing to the cross.[1] A parapet hung with a patterned silk velvet or damask rises behind the figure to the height of His shoulders, and a different patterned silk hangs on a rope as a small cloth of honor behind His head. A landscape with buildings and tall trees is visible above and to the sides of this cloth. At the left end of the parapet stands a closed book, and at the right end, a lozenge-patterned glass beaker containing some water with light shining through it rests on a sheet of paper. There is an apple in the mouth of the beaker. The Child's head, covered with blond curls

22

Fig. 120. The tapestry, 22, in its embroidered frame as mounted in 1961.

Fig. 121. *The Holy Family.* Tapestry, southern Netherlands, here dated about 1500. The Art Institute of Chicago; Bequest of Mr. and Mrs. Martin A. Ryerson.

and elongated at the back, is turned toward the left, but the eyes look straight out at the observer. His right hand is raised above the mouth of a low cup or chalice that has a flat lobed foot and a pair of embossed rings around its center. He holds a bunch of grapes in this hand and squeezes their juice into the cup. Except for the elements in the landscape background, all these forms are rendered with gilt as well as wool and silk yarns. The ground of the oval surround is woven only with gilt yarns, and the floral motifs that appear in the spandrels are woven entirely with silk yarns. In the upper left corner there is a rose sprig with an open blossom. Opposite this appears a strawberry with its stalk and leaves and a pansy blossom with its stem. Another pansy, with stem and leaves, fills the lower left corner and a rose sprig with a closed bud, the lower right.

The rectangular border shows a narrow band of gold set in the center of a wider band of simulated velvet or plush. There are unpatterned silk and gold bands along the upper and lower edges of this border. An inscription in the side sections of the border reads as follows: PORREXIT · MANVM · SVAM · INLIBATIONEM, along the left side, and along the right, ET · LIBAVIT · DESANGVINE · VVE · ECCL · CI · C · LO.[2] The text is taken from one of the apocryphal books of the Old Testament, Ecclesiasticus or the Wisdom of Jesus the son of Sirach (50:16): "He stretched forth his hand to make a libation, and offered of the blood of the grape." "He" in this context refers to Simon, the high priest, son of Onias. In the next verse (50:17) Simon pours out the wine at the foot of the altar. Sacrificial wine, interpreted in Christian terms, is the ultimate subject of the Metropolitan Museum's tapestry. The infant Christ squeezes the juice of the grapes into a chalice. The ends of the rope on which the small cloth of honor hangs—they are not visible in this composition— are probably tied to the screws of a winepress, just like the ends of corresponding ropes in the related tapestry in Chicago (fig. 121) and another tapestry formerly with French and Company that shows the adult Christ in a related context (fig. 122). As Wardwell (1975, 21) and Janson (1985, 63) indicated, this is the "mystical winepress" in which grapes yield their juice, an allegorical reference to the cross on which Christ's blood flowed.

Wardwell (1975, 17–23) made an exhaustive study of the theme of the mystical grapes and its allusions to the blood of Christ and His role as Redeemer of mankind. She called attention not only to the parallels that were drawn between the Child squeezing the grapes and the mystical winepress but also to the symbolic meanings of the seemingly commonplace objects that are shown in this tapestry and others related to it. The orb with a cross on top refers to the catholicity of the redemption

Fig. 122. *Christ of the Mystic Winepress.* Tapestry, southern Netherlands, here dated about 1500. Formerly property of French and Company, New York; present location unknown.

Fig. 123. *The Mystical Grapes.* Tapestry, southern Netherlands, about 1500. The Cleveland Museum of Art.

that Christ won for mankind through His own sacrifice and also to His sovereignty in the world. The apple resting on the beaker is the apple that Adam and Eve ate, the apple of original sin, symbol of sin and death. The glass beaker, through which light passes without breaking it, signifies the Virgin; and the water in it is the Water of Life, or Christ.[3] Wardwell pointed out that the shape of this beaker and the presence of the apple on top of it refer to a related image often found in late medieval paintings, that of an apothecary jar with an apple resting on it, like the one in the painting of *Saint Jerome in His Study* in the Detroit Institute of Arts (Wardwell 1975, fig. 4). There, the label on the jar reads *tyriaca,* an antidote for poisonous bites and mortal diseases. Therefore, as Wardwell indicated, the image of the apple on top of the beaker symbolizes the Incarnation of Christ who saved mankind from death, the "illness" to which humanity had become subject when Adam and Eve ate the forbidden fruit. The book resting on the parapet represents the Bible. The flora in the spandrels of the oval frame also have symbolic significance. The open rose in the upper left corner and the rosebud in the lower right corner are red and signify martyrdom, in this case Christ's own death on the cross. The pansies in the other two corners connote remembrance and therefore may have been included as a reference to the celebration of the Eucharist and the command that Christ left with

His disciples at the Last Supper, an exhortation to remember Him when taking wine and bread. Pansies also stood for reflection and meditation; and the late medieval observer probably saw in them an invitation to meditate upon the image inside the oval surround. The strawberry in the upper right corner was one of the fruits of Paradise; but, as Wardwell (1975, 20) noted, it could also signify a hidden danger to the spirit.

The image of the infant Christ and the collection of symbolic objects surrounding Him refer to His sacrifice and to the wine of the Eucharist as His blood. Wardwell (1975, 20–21) observed that the table on which the symbolic objects are placed in the closely related tapestry in the Cleveland Museum of Art (fig. 123)—specifically the cup or chalice receiving the "blood" of the grape— represents the altar or table on which the sacrifice of the Eucharist is performed. The same may be said for the marble parapet or table on which the chalice rests in the Metropolitan Museum's tapestry. Wardwell (1975, 21– 22) noted further that by the time these tapestries were woven the cult of the Holy Blood had developed and had inspired representations of this subject and other closely related ones. The theme, central to the Christian faith, became the subject matter of many Netherlandish paintings and tapestries of the late fifteenth and early sixteenth centuries, examples of which both Wardwell and Standen have identified. They are listed below.

A painting by Joos van Cleve in the Metropolitan Museum shows the Virgin nursing the Child beyond a parapet in the foreground. He holds an apple in His left hand, and on the parapet there are a beaker of wine and a plate of fruit, including a bunch of grapes.[4] Another picture by the same artist may be cited. Now or formerly in a private collection in Paris, it shows the Child lying on a cushion and eating grapes from the bunch He holds in His left hand.[5] A painting of 1509 by Gerard David, in the Musée des Beaux-Arts, Rouen, shows the Virgin seated in the center of the space surrounded by saints and angels and holding the Child on her lap. He holds a bunch of grapes in both hands.[6]

A tapestry that virtually duplicates the Metropolitan Museum's piece has survived (see fig. 124, and Related Tapestries). Two others, already mentioned, resemble these both in terms of subject matter and style, one in the Art Institute of Chicago and the other in the Cleveland Museum of Art (figs. 121 and 123).[7] Standen called attention to a number of other closely related tapestries.[8] Two pieces with the same subject were listed in the inventory of Juana la Loca of Spain, one or both of which may have survived (see Related Tapestries). A miniature tapestry showing Christ as a somewhat older child pressing the grapes into a cup resting on a parapet and accompanied by much the same group of symbolic objects was sold from the collection of Heinrich Wencke in Cologne in 1898.[9] Another miniature tapestry that shows the Virgin seated in the center foreground holding the Child in her lap and a branch bearing an open rose and a bud, both red, was formerly in the collection of Martin Le Roy in Paris.[10] In that example the books, scrolls, and beaker of water topped by an apple appear at the sides, and the same cup, with the grapes nestling in it rather than held above it, rests on the right end of a parapet that separates the figures and their setting from the landscape beyond. Out there, at the left, is a wine-press in the form of a cross with an inscribed tablet hung on it. In the Museo Arqueológico in Madrid there is a tapestry showing the Virgin enthroned in the center holding the Child on her lap.[11] He reaches out to take an apple that His mother holds in her right hand. A bunch of grapes rests on the arm of the throne just below the apple. An angel kneels at the right and holds an illustrated manuscript open for the Virgin to read. Standen also found a slightly later example that was formerly in the collection of Henry G. Marquand. In the center it shows the Virgin holding the Child, who is about to press a bunch of grapes into a chalice held by a woman kneeling at the left, whom Standen identified as Charity, while Justice, standing at the right, sheathes her sword.[12] A number of tapestries of the Holy Family in

Fig. 124. *The Infant Christ Pressing the Wine of the Eucharist.* Tapestry, southern Netherlands, here dated about 1500. Dutch Renaissance Art Collection, Amsterdam.

which the Virgin, Saint Joseph, or Saint Anne offers the Child grapes, an apple, a pear, or a red rose also have survived (see 23).

The compositions in two other contemporary tapestries from the southern Netherlands reveal the subject's significance even more directly. One of them has already been mentioned. It shows the adult Christ standing or kneeling behind a bench or prie-dieu in the immediate foreground (fig. 122). Only the bust of the figure is visible; He rests His left hand on the orb and raises His right hand in a sign of benediction. The rope supporting the small cloth of honor behind His head is tied at each end to the screw of a winepress. A marble column, probably the column to which He was tied when flagellated, rises directly behind His head. A book and scroll appear at the left on the parapet that runs behind Him, and the apple and beaker rest on a sheet of paper on an oval box at the right.[13] A rectangular plaque fixed to the center of the lintel that runs across the top of the field shows, at left, a rose sprig and, at right, the same ringed and footed chalice that appears in the other tapestries of this group.

In the second tapestry singled out for discussion here, the sacrificial significance of the Child's action is literally spelled out for the observer. It is a small hanging preserved in the Appartamento Pontificio in the Vatican.[14] There the Child, sitting on His mother's lap, turns toward the left and squeezes the bunch of grapes into a chalice held by a kneeling woman who, like the corresponding figure in the Marquand tapestry (see note 12), may represent Charity. A scroll that flutters above the head of the man standing at the left is inscribed with the same verse from Ecclesiasticus (50:16) that appears in the side borders of the Metropolitan Museum's tapestry. It refers to the sacrificial wine that the high priest Simon poured at the foot of the altar. Another inscribed scroll flutters across the center of the top border. It reads: BIBITE · VINVM · / Q[UO]D · MISCVI · VOBIS · / PROVB 9°. The quotation is from the Book of Proverbs, chapter 9, and is the last half of Wisdom's speech in verse 5. The text of the complete verse in translation reads: "Come, eat my bread, and drink the wine which I have mingled for you." The reference to bread as well as wine relates the verse to the idea of the Eucharist. A third inscribed scroll, falling from the left hand of the man standing at the far right, reads: AMMRM · / ERIT · POTIOBIBĒTIBUS · ILLAM / VSA · 24°. The words are taken from the Prophecy of Isaias, chapter 24, the second half of verse 9, whose complete text in translation is as follows: "They shall not drink wine with a song; the drink shall be bitter to them that drink it." The context is that in which God has laid waste to sinful Tyre where people have broken faith with the eternal covenant. So all three quotations in this tapestry—the first referring to the sacrificial use of wine at an altar, the second to Wisdom's offering her guests bread and wine, and the third to wine as being antipathetic to evil folk—make it abundantly clear that this designer and the designer or designers of the tapestries cited above intended the observer to understand that Christ's pressing the grapes, and the "blood" of the grape, refer specifically to the saving grace of Christ's blood in the sacrament of the Eucharist.

SOURCE OF THE DESIGN

Hunter (1914–15, 93) believed that this tapestry was woven after an existing painting rather than a design created especially for it. Although we do not know of any panel paintings with this subject that have survived, it seems reasonable to assume that such paintings existed in the late Middle Ages. They would have been produced in quantity to serve as devotional pictures to aid worshipers in their religious meditations. However since we have at least two tapestries showing the same design, 22 and the example from Amberley Castle (fig. 124), and since two additional pieces may have been listed in the inventory of Juana la Loca (see Related Tapestries), it seems likely that, contrary to what

Hunter thought, a cartoon was indeed prepared and used several times. We cannot agree with Monod (1923, 374), who saw the style of Gerard David in the composition; we do not believe that it was designed by a painter whose name is celebrated today. The workmanlike artist or artists who created the cartoons for this piece and the several others related to it (see below) used traditional forms and stock motifs. Some or all of these elements may have been taken originally from one or more prints or miniature paintings or perhaps from panel paintings. While we cannot identify a likely source of this kind, it is significant that a manuscript illustration of about 1510 that Standen referred to shows an image of the adult Christ which in a general way resembles the figure represented in the tapestry mentioned above that was once with French and Company (fig. 122).[15]

Hunter (1915–16, 500) noted that 22 is remarkably like the related pieces, one now in Chicago and one formerly in the Martin Le Roy collection, as well as the *Holy Family* in the Metropolitan Museum (23), and he concluded that all four pieces were designed by the same hand. He did not publish the closely related piece that is now in Cleveland. It, like the ones in the Metropolitan Museum and the Art Institute of Chicago, shows the same Child with elongated head covered with curls seen in three-quarter view. These three pieces, together with the one formerly in the Martin Le Roy collection, have the chalice, the book standing upright, and all or the lower part of the oval surround. Three of them also have the beaker with the apple on top, and three show the same orb. To Hunter's list we can add not only the Cleveland example but also the tapestry with the adult Christ which has the beaker and apple, the book, the orb, the chalice, the open rose, a winepress like the one in the Chicago piece, and the lower part of the oval surround (fig. 122). The Christ Child's hands are very similar in the Chicago piece and 22, although they are placed in different positions. The cloth of honor in 22 is the same one that appears in the example in Chicago, and the Cleveland piece and the one formerly with French and Company have similar hangings behind Christ's head. The scale-patterned silk that hangs in front of the parapet rising behind Christ in the last piece appears again in the corresponding position in 22. These similarities suggest, as Hunter thought, that the tapestries were designed by the same hand. However they could indicate instead that several different designers (or design shops) were working with the same sources. The orb, beaker, apple, chalice, roses, book, and surround are obviously stock motifs. The head of the Christ Child appears again, in slightly different form, in the tapestries in the Museo Arqueológico, Madrid, and the

Vatican (see notes 11 and 14), which are otherwise very different in style. Wardwell (1975, 22) commented on the fact that this elongated head with curly locks was not uncommonly represented in Netherlandish painting at this time and gave examples to illustrate her point.

MANUFACTURE AND DATE

Hunter (1915–16, 500) included this tapestry in his discussion of a group of miniature pieces that he judged to be Flemish work of the end of the fifteenth century. Göbel (1923, 1924) attributed it to Brussels and dated it in the first third of the sixteenth century. Standen believed that it was woven in Brussels between 1490 and 1510.[16] None of the three gave their reasons for making these attributions, but it seems likely that the last two regarded the painterly quality of the design and the fineness of the weave as characteristic of Brussels pieces and the pictorial style as corresponding to that found in other Netherlandish tapestries woven about 1500.

Certainly we know that tapestries with painterly compositions showing this degree of fineness and richness were being produced in Brussels about 1500, which is the date that the style of this composition suggests; but we cannot be sure that such tapestries were not also being produced elsewhere in the southern Netherlands at the same time. Neither this piece nor any of the closely related ones contain any visual clues that could lead to a more precise dating of the design and weaving. 22 shows no armorial bearings and no fashionable costumes. The only documentary evidence we have concerning tapestries that apparently showed the same subject dates from 1555 when two such pieces were listed in the inventory of tapestries belonging to Juana of Spain (see below).

RELATED TAPESTRIES

Only one near-duplicate tapestry is known to have survived (fig. 124). It belonged to J. A. Garland in 1895 when it was exhibited in the Art Loan Exhibition at the Ortgies Galleries in New York. Later it passed to his grandson Thomas Emmet and then to Emmet's widow, baroness Emmet of Amberley. It was sold with the contents of Amberley Castle in 1981 and became the property of the Victor Franses Gallery in London, whence it passed into the Dutch Renaissance Art Collection, Amsterdam.[17]

Two other tapestries that showed the same or a similar subject are mentioned in two mid-sixteenth-century inventories. Standen found the reference in the inventory of 1555 of the personal property of Juana la Loca, queen of Spain. Two of her tapestries are described as follows: "dos niños ihus de oro y sedas y lanas de colores que son de la çinta arriba y tenia el vno en la mano vn mundo y en la otra vn rrazimo de hubas apretandole en vn bajo y el otro de la misma manera y hechura" (two infants Jesus of gold and colored silk and wool which are from the waist up and one of them was holding a world in one hand and in the other a bunch of grapes squeezing it into a cup and the other [was] of the same kind and make).[18] As Standen noted, the Child in the Metropolitan Museum's tapestry does not actually hold the orb in His hand. If the compiler of the inventory described the queen's tapestries accurately, then neither this piece nor the one from Amberley Castle can be identified with them.

HISTORY

Perhaps in the collection of Juana, queen of Spain, before 1555 (see Related Tapestries).
At one time owned by a member of the Order of Calatrava (see Condition), which was established as a military and religious order by Sancho III of Toledo in the mid-twelfth century.[19]
In the collection of Benjamin Altman, New York.
Bequeathed to the MMA by Benjamin Altman in 1913.

EXHIBITIONS

None known.

PUBLICATIONS

MMA, Handbook of the Benjamin Altman Collection. New York, 1914, pp. 145–46. Described and discussed briefly; illus. facing p. 145. 2d ed., 1928, pp. 146–47; illus. facing p. 146.
Hunter, George Leland. "The Tapestries of the Altman Collection." *Arts and Decoration* 5 (1914–15) p. 93. Described and discussed briefly.
Hunter, George Leland. "Miniature Tapestries of the Infant Christ." *Arts and Decoration* 6 (1915–16) p. 500. Described and discussed briefly; illus.
Göbel 1923, vol. 2, fig. 135. Illus. with caption.
Monod, François. "La galerie Altman au Metropolitan Museum de New-York (pt. 3): II, Les sculptures et les objets d'art." *Gazette des Beaux-Arts*, 5th ser., 8 (1923) p. 374. Discussed briefly.
Göbel, Heinrich. *Tapestries of the Lowlands.* Trans. by Robert West. New York, 1924, fig. 135. Illus. with caption.
Virch, Claus. *The Adele and Arthur Lehman Collection.* MMA, New York, 1965, p. 96. Mentioned.
Wardwell, Anne E. "The Mystical Grapes, a Devotional Tapestry." *Bulletin of the Cleveland Museum of Art* 62 (1975) pp. 17, 21. Discussed briefly; illus. fig. 2.
Freeman, Margaret B. *The Unicorn Tapestries.* MMA, New York, 1976, p. 127. Mentioned; illus. fig. 157.
Victor Franses Gallery, London, advertisement. *Apollo* 114 (December 1981) advertising p. 63. Mentioned.

Janson, Dora Jane. "Visions of the Vine: A Symbolic History." In Hugh Johnson, Dora Jane Janson, David Revere McFadden. *Wine: Celebration and Ceremony.* New York, 1985 (published to accompany the exhibition of the same name, Cooper-Hewitt Museum, New York, 1985) p. 63. Described briefly; illus. in color p. 65.

NOTES

1. Edith Appleton Standen, notes and preliminary draft for a catalogue entry concerning this tapestry, ca. 1968, in the files of the MMA Department of Medieval Art.
2. The letter N is reversed wherever it appears in this inscription.
3. Erwin Panofsky, in his *Early Netherlandish Painting: Its Origins and Character* (Cambridge, Mass., 1953) vol. 1, p. 144, quotes lines of a hymn that explain the meaning of the transparent glass (in his example, a carafe): "As the sunbeam through the glass / Passeth but not breaketh, / So the Virgin, as she was, / Virgin still remaineth."
4. MMA acc. no. 32.100.57, The Friedsam Collection, Bequest of Michael Friedsam, 1931. For an illustration of this painting, which shows Joseph in the background, see Anne E. Wardwell, "The Mystical Grapes, a Devotional Tapestry," *Bulletin of the Cleveland Museum of Art* 62 (1975) fig. 7, or Panofsky, *Early Netherlandish Painting*, vol. 2, pl. 333, fig. 494.
5. See Georges Marlier, "Joos van Cleve—Fontainebleau and Italy," *Connoisseur* 165 (1967) p. 27 and fig. 1.
6. Illustrated in Marcel Nicolle, *Le Musée de Rouen: Peintures* (Paris, 1920) p. 30, with caption.
7. See Christa Charlotte Mayer, *Masterpieces of Western Textiles from the Art Institute of Chicago* (Chicago, 1969) pp. 25, 29, pl. 12; and Wardwell, "The Mystical Grapes," pp. 17–23, fig. 1. In both tapestries the warp runs parallel to the vertical axis of the pattern.
8. Standen, notes and preliminary draft, ca. 1968.
9. *Ausgewählter, hervorragender Kunstsachen und Antiquitäten aus der Sammlung des Herrn Heinrich Wencke, Hamburg,* sale cat., J. M. Heberle (H. Lempertz' Sohne), Cologne, October 27–28, 1898, no. 228, illus. facing p. 58. In this example the warp runs parallel to the horizontal axis of the pattern.
10. J. J. Marquet de Vasselot, *Catalogue raisonné de la collection Martin Le Roy,* fasc. 4, *Tapisseries et broderie* (Paris, 1908) pp. 33–36, pl. VI. The warp runs parallel to the vertical axis of the pattern.
11. J. K. Steppe, "Vlaamse Wandtapijten in Spanje. Recente Gebeurtenissen en Publicaties," *Artes Textiles* 3 (1956) pp. 58–59, fig. 17.
12. Standen, notes and preliminary draft, ca. 1968. *Illustrated Catalogue of the Art and Literary Property Collected by the Late Henry G. Marquand,* subscriber's edition of sale cat., American Art Association, New York, January 23–31, 1903, no. 1331, illus. facing nos. 1316-19. The warp runs parallel to the horizontal axis of the pattern.
13. Wardwell, "The Mystical Grapes," p. 20, wrote that a similar box shown in the tapestry in Cleveland represents a container for the Host and thus is a symbol of the Virgin.
14. See *The Vatican Collections: The Papacy and Art,* exh. cat., MMA, Art Institute of Chicago, and Fine Arts Museums of San Francisco (New York, 1983) no. 15, illus. in color. The warp runs parallel to the horizontal axis of the pattern.
15. Standen, notes and preliminary draft, ca. 1968. Fol. 153v of S. C. 21604 (MSS Douce 30), Bodleian Library, Oxford, a Netherlandish Book of Hours in Latin with a calendar of the diocese of Utrecht; see A. W. Byvanck and G. J. Hoogewerff, *La miniature hollandaise dans les manuscrits des 14e, 15e et 16e siècles* (The Hague, 1922–26) pl. vol. 1, pl. 60F, and text vol. p. 70, no. 174.
16. Standen, notes and preliminary draft, ca. 1968.
17. See *Art Loan Exhibition for the Benefit of the New York Cancer Hospital: Catalogue,* Ortgies Galleries (New York, 1895) no. 1052; illus. in J. Getz, *A Short Historical Sketch on Tapestry and Embroidery,* Art Loan Monographs published for the benefit of the Art Loan Exhibition (New York, 1895) facing p. 12. See also *The Contents of Amberley Castle, Amberley, West Sussex,* sale cat., Sotheby's, London, September 30–October 1, 1981, no. 80 (illus. in color), and text on frontispiece page; also advertisement of Victor Franses Gallery, London, *Apollo* 114 (December 1981) advertising p. 63, illus. in color.
18. Standen, notes and preliminary draft, ca. 1968. The inventory entry is given in José Ferrandis, *Inventarios reales (Juan II a Juana la Loca),* vol. 3 of *Datos documentales para la historia del arte español* (Madrid, 1943) p. 345.
19. For a brief discussion of the Order of Calatrava, see Harrold E. Gillingham, *Spanish Orders of Chivalry and Decorations of Honour,* Numismatic Notes and Monographs, no. 31 (New York, 1926) pp. 9–12. The badge of the order is illustrated as pl. I on p. 11; it shows the complete design, which includes not only the red cross fleury that appears within a shield-shaped compartment on the secondary borders of the tapestry frame but also a plumed helmet and a trophy of flags.

23
The Holy Family with Saint Anne

Southern Netherlands, about 1500
Linen warp; wool, silk, silver, and gilt wefts; the fabric
embroidered in a few places with gilt and silver yarns
3 ft. 5 3/4 in. × 4 ft. 7 in. (1.06 m × 1.40 m)
20 warp yarns per inch, 8 per centimeter
Bequest of Adele L. Lehman, in memory of Arthur Lehman, 1965
(65.181.15)

CONDITION

The tapestry has suffered little damage or alteration and
retains its original dimensions. The selvages are present
along the top and bottom edges. The left and right ends
have been cut, but the pattern is complete along those
sides. There are a few small areas of wear throughout the
piece and some linear repairs by reweaving on the original warp in the outer edges of the border and immediately below the letters VI (of VITA) in the inscription
along the bottom of the field. The colors, particularly
the flesh tones, have faded somewhat. The silver yarns
have tarnished, but the gilt yarns have for the most part
retained their original color and brilliance. A few small
slits that were left by the weaver in the areas representing flesh have been closed with needle stitches, and as a
result the original modeling has been weakened slightly
in those places.

DESCRIPTION AND SUBJECT

The field shows the Virgin and Christ Child, Saint
Joseph, and Saint Anne seated in the immediate foreground of a shallow space enclosed at the back by a
parapet that is half as tall as the picture space itself. A
patterned silk damask or velvet hanging covers the front
of the parapet; above and beyond it appears a deep landscape filled with hills, buildings, trees, and birds.

The three adult figures, all in sitting positions, are
shown only to their knees. The Virgin is in the center,
with a cloth of honor behind her and a fringed canopy
above her. The back cloth and the valances of the canopy
are made of silk damasks or velvets showing two different patterns. Mary holds the Child in both arms,
clasping His left hand in her right, and she looks down at
Him pensively. She wears a plain mantle over a narrow-
sleeved tunic and an undergarment whose tight sleeves
project beyond the fur cuffs of the tunic. A large scarf
trimmed at the edges with pointed oval drops is draped

around her head. The Child, wearing a plain narrow-
sleeved tunic, places His right hand on His mother's
breast. He turns His head toward the left and looks at
Saint Anne, who is seated at Mary's right hand, the
position of honor. Anne wears a hood and a mantle over a
tunic and underdress cut like the Virgin's, and she places
her left hand on an open book on a marble surface in
front of her and raises her right hand to offer the Child a
red rose, gazing at Him as she does so with a soft smile
and great tenderness. Joseph, wearing a loose robe over a
tunic, an undergarment with tight sleeves, and a hood
that covers the top and back of his head, sits at the right
side of the composition, facing the other figures. He
extends both hands toward them, holding a bunch of
grapes in his right hand and an apple in his left. He gazes
at the apple with furrowed brow and a face full of sorrow.
A closed book fitted with a clasp and covered by an
inscribed scroll lies on the parapet above and beyond his
right hand.

The border consists of a wide, light-colored central
band decorated with plants and flanked by narrow bands
along its inner and outer edges. The flora in the central
section include branches bearing rosebuds and blossoms, violet plants, and lengths of grapevine, all arranged in a single undulating row. (We read the plant
blossoms as violets rather than pansies, which they also
resemble, because they appear now in tones of brown
and gray rather than yellow and blue.) The band along
the outer edge of this central section shows a series of
narrow polychrome stripes inside a wider stripe that
simulates plush or deep velvet. The band along the inner
edge takes the form of a quarter-round molding decorated at the top and sides with slender vines rendered in
gilt and silver satin stitches and couched work. At the
bottom this molding becomes wider and shows an inscription whose words were embroidered with silver
satin stitches. Gilt satin stitches were used for the orna-

342

23

343

mental stops between the words and next to the saints' names. The inscription reads as follows:

S · ANNA—OBEATA · INFANTIA · PER · QVAM · NOSTRI · GENERIS · EST · VITA · REPARATA—IOSEP · S

(St. Anne—O, blessed Infancy through whom life has been restored to our kind—St. Joseph).[1]

Gilt yarns were used to weave the highlights in the garments and some of the clothing details. The gilt and silver yarns are composed of flat, narrow metal wires wrapped spirally on cores of silk yarn. The wool weft in several places consists of two different colors (blue and brown) woven in together as a single yarn. In other places silk yarns of three different colors (blue, beige, and tan) were used in the same way.

In terms of subject matter this tapestry is closely related to the tapestry-woven pictures showing the infant Christ squeezing the mystical grapes into a cup or chalice, with or without Mary and Joseph in attendance (see 22). In all of these examples there are symbolic objects (and in this piece and 22, also inscriptions) that refer to the fall of man and his redemption through the shedding of Christ's own blood, the blood of the Eucharist. Here, Joseph offers the Child the apple of original sin and the grapes of salvation while Anne offers Him the red rose of martyrdom. As she does, she holds her hand on a book (one of her attributes) that probably represents the New Testament in which His story is told. The closed book on the parapet behind Joseph probably represents the Old Testament and the scroll may represent one of the prophecies.[2] The red roses and blue grapes in the border may refer respectively to the martyrdom and blood of Christ, just as the violets may denote His humility; however since these flora also appear in the borders of tapestries with non-Christian subjects they may have been used here without symbolic intent.

Standen noted that about 1500 Saint Anne appeared more frequently than before in Netherlandish art and that her popularity increased as people accepted the doctrine of the Immaculate Conception.[3] She cited as an example of this new interest in the mother of Mary a painting by Joos van Cleve in the Musées Royaux des Beaux-Arts de Belgique in Brussels which shows a tender family scene with Anne seated in the center on a throne with a cloth of honor falling behind her. She holds the sleeping Child on her lap. Mary and Joseph, seated at the sides, are smiling and Mary reaches out toward the Infant. In this picture it is Anne who holds the apple and whose face expresses her knowledge of the impending sacrifice.[4] In another painting by the same artist, in the Museo Estense in Modena, the infant Jesus stands on His mother's lap and is about to take the apple from her as Anne, seated at the right, offers Him a bunch of grapes.[5] Standen also called attention to a tapestry-woven picture in the Musées Royaux d'Art et d'Histoire in Brussels that shows a scene rather like this. There, Anne and Mary sit next to each other on a throne, and the Child, seated on His mother's lap, squeezes a bunch of grapes into a chalice that Anne holds.[6]

Foster has shown how a new interest in Joseph, indeed a cult of the saint, developed during the fourteenth and fifteenth centuries, to culminate in the mid-sixteenth century at the Council of Trent when the liturgy of the saint's feast was made standard. Meanwhile, Pope Sixtus IV established a feast of Saint Joseph in the Roman church about 1479.[7] In discussing the iconography of the Holy Family with Saint Anne, Foster referred to a painting by Cornelis Buys that shows Mary seated on the ground in the center with the Child on her lap; He leans forward and reaches out to Anne, who sits on a canopied throne at the left. A knight of the Order of the Holy Sepulcher kneels at the right, and Joseph appears as his patron saint.[8] Foster also observed that Joseph's offering fruit to the Child in these contexts is the same action he displays in the theme of the Rest on the Flight into Egypt.[9] She illustrated her point with a reference to a painting by Quentin Massys now in the Worcester Art Museum, a panel from an altarpiece of the *Seven Sorrows of the Virgin* dating from 1509–13, that shows the three figures resting in a landscape, Mary seated on the ground at the left with the Child in her arms, and Joseph standing at the right and offering Him an apple.[10] A different composition for the Rest on the Flight into Egypt, in tapestry rather than painting, shows Joseph offering Him a bunch of grapes instead. Two versions of that composition may be cited: one is a small tapestry picture in the Philadelphia Museum of Art; the other is a large hanging that was formerly in the Spitzer Collection.[11] Another tapestry-woven picture, formerly owned by French and Company, shows a composition similar to both of those; it has Joseph offering the Child a pear, a fruit that was occasionally used instead of the apple as a symbol of the fall of mankind.[12] A figure that we believe represents Joseph in a tapestry in the Musée Lyonnais des Arts Décoratifs shows him offering the infant Jesus a fruit that is either a pear or an apple.[13]

SOURCE OF THE DESIGN

Hunter (1915–16, 500) believed that whoever designed this piece also designed the Metropolitan Museum's tapestry-woven picture of the infant Christ with the

344

mystical grapes (22), the Holy Family with the grapes and winepress in the Art Institute of Chicago, and the picture showing the Virgin and Child with the grapes, press, and other related symbols that was formerly in the collection of Martin Le Roy in Paris.[14] Furthermore he observed that the pose and expression of the Child's head is the same in all four pieces, that Saint Joseph's head is the same in 23 and the Chicago tapestry, and that the same model served for the representation of Mary in those two tapestries as well as the one in the Le Roy collection. We cannot agree with all of Hunter's opinions. The head of the Christ Child in 23 is very much like that in the Le Roy piece but not like the other two except for the pose. Joseph has much the same head, in the same pose, in the Chicago tapestry and 23, but the expression and details are not quite the same. The Virgin's face in 23 is full and round like the face in the Chicago example, but both of these differ considerably from the face in the Le Roy tapestry. The variations in details and expressions that we perceive in these three heads—of the Child, Mary, and Joseph—are the variations one expects to find in work done by artists with different skills and sensibilities who have used the same design source. It seems clear that several artists produced the cartoons for the *Infant Christ Pressing the Wine of the Eucharist* (22) and the miniature tapestries that are closely related to it as well as for the present example but that they depended on the same or closely related sources. These sources were either prints or manuscript illustrations or possibly panel paintings of a particularly conventional kind.

Standen noted that symbolic still-life objects like the ones that appear in these tapestry pictures are to be found in Flemish paintings about 1500 and particularly in the works of Joos van Cleve. However she did not believe that he could have designed the weavings because their pictorial style belonged to an earlier time. Standen also pointed out certain formal and iconographic characteristics that the tapestry shares with some paintings by Colijn de Coter and the Master of the Embroidered Foliage, but she did not believe that either of those men designed the Metropolitan Museum's tapestry.[15] We endorse her conclusions.

Although 23 is more narrative in form and content than 22, this tapestry, like that one, was designed to serve as an aid to religious meditation. We believe that both pieces reflect some rigidly formalized tradition rather than the personal style of any painter we can identify today. These two hangings, along with all or most of the other tapestry-woven pictures that have been compared to them in the present text and the text for 22, were undoubtedly designed in some shop or group of shops that specialized in producing cartoons for small devotional tapestries.

MANUFACTURE AND DATE

Hunter (1915–16, 497) included this piece in a group of tapestries he regarded as Flemish work of the end of the fifteenth century. Breck (1920, 181) attributed it to the Netherlands about 1500. Virch (1965, 96) as well as Gómez-Moreno (1975, 163) agreed with that date but thought the tapestry was woven in Brussels. Standen thought that Brussels was its probable place of origin.[16] Wardwell (1975, 23) dated it about 1500 and attributed it to Flanders.

Like 22, to which it is intimately related in terms of subject and style, this tapestry shows all the qualities we associate with southern Netherlandish tapestry weaving of the period about 1500 but nothing that justifies an attribution specifically to Brussels nor a date any more refined than that. No fashionable costumes or armorial elements are present, and we have no documents that might help date the design or weaving.

RELATED TAPESTRIES

We do not know of any surviving tapestries that belong with this example in a group of seminarrative pictures dealing with the theme of the Holy Family or the lives of Christ or the Virgin.

HISTORY

Said to have been acquired from the cathedral in Burgos.
Said to have belonged to Lionel Harris, London.
Property of French and Company, New York.
In the collection of Arthur Lehman, New York, from 1916.
Bequeathed to the MMA by Adele L. Lehman, in memory of Arthur Lehman, 1965.

EXHIBITIONS

New York, MMA, 1920. *Fiftieth Anniversary Exhibition.* Cat. p. 13. Lent by Arthur Lehman.
Said to have been shown in the *Masterpieces of Art* exhibition at the New York World's Fair of 1939, lent by Mrs. Arthur Lehman. Information from a label fixed to the back of the frame in which the tapestry had been kept; not so far confirmed by documents or publications.
Billings, Montana, Yellowstone Art Center, 1978. *A Christmas Exhibition from the Collections of The Metropolitan Museum of Art and The Cloisters.*
New York, Cooper-Hewitt Museum, 1985. *Wine: Celebration and Ceremony.*

PUBLICATIONS

Hunter, George Leland. "Miniature Tapestries of the Infant Christ." *Arts and Decoration* 6 (1915–16) pp. 497–500. Described and discussed at length; illus.

"List of Loans: Fiftieth Anniversary Exhibition." *MMA Bulletin* 15 (1920) p. 118. Mentioned.

J. B. [Joseph Breck]. "Mediaeval and Renaissance Decorative Arts and Sculpture." *MMA Bulletin* 15 (1920) pp. 181–82. Mentioned; illus. p. 183 in view of gallery installation during *Fiftieth Anniversary Exhibition.*

Hunter 1925, p. 124. Mentioned.

Virch, Claus. *The Adele and Arthur Lehman Collection.* MMA, New York, 1965, p. 96. Described and discussed in detail; illus. p. 97.

Forsyth, William H. "Reports of the Departments: Medieval Art and The Cloisters, the Main Building." Annual Report for 1965–1966. In *MMA Bulletin*, n.s. 25 (1966–67) p. 87. Mentioned.

C. G.-M. [Carmen Gómez-Moreno]. "Tapestry: Madonna and Child with Saint Anne and Saint Joseph." *MMA Notable Acquisitions 1965–1975.* New York, 1975, p. 163. Discussed briefly; illus.

Wardwell, Anne E. "The Mystical Grapes, A Devotional Tapestry." *Bulletin of the Cleveland Museum of Art* 62 (1975) pp. 22, 23. Discussed briefly; illus.

NOTES

1. Earlier writers offered slightly different translations for this inscription. George Leland Hunter, "Miniature Tapestries of the Infant Christ," *Arts and Decoration* 6 (1915–16) p. 498, translated it as "Saint Anne. Oh, blessed Infant through whom the life of our race has been restored. Joseph Saint." Claus Virch, *The Adele and Arthur Lehman Collection*, MMA (New York, 1965) p. 96, read it as "St. Anne [.] O blessed Infant through whom the life of mankind has been restored [.] St. Joseph." Edith Appleton Standen, in her notes and preliminary draft for a catalogue entry concerning this tapestry, ca. 1968, on file in the MMA Department of Medieval Art, offered "St. Ann. Oh blessed childhood by which the life of our race is restored. St. Joseph." Standen correctly translated "infantia" as "childhood" (or, more properly, "infancy" since the word connotes the preverbal stage of childhood). The Reverend Donald W. Hendricks, Saint Anthony's Parish, Yonkers, observed that the word may have been used here as a vocative, "Your Infancy." We believe that his interpretation is correct and that Standen's interpretation of the inscription, modifed by changing "childhood" to "infancy," is the right one. The present author thanks Father Hendricks, Sister Janet Baxendale, S.C., Liturgy Office, Archdiocese of New York, and the Reverend Monsignor William B. Smith, Saint Joseph's Seminary, Yonkers, for generously consulting with him on the meaning of this inscription.

2. Standen, notes and preliminary draft, ca. 1968, suggested that the book behind Saint Joseph presumably represents the Old Testament and the scroll on the book, one of the prophecies; she also observed that one of Saint Anne's attributes is a book, presumably the Old Testament.

3. Standen, notes and preliminary draft, ca. 1968.

4. For an illustration of this painting, see Ludwig Baldass, *Joos van Cleve, der Meister des Todes Mariä* (Vienna, 1925) fig. 40.

5. See Baldass, *Joos van Cleve*, fig. 13.

6. Standen, notes and preliminary draft, ca. 1968. See Marthe Crick-Kuntziger, *Catalogue des Tapisseries (XIVᵉ au XVIIIᵉ siècle)*, Musées Royaux d'Art et d'Histoire (Brussels, 1956) no. 18, pl. 24.

7. Marjory Bolger Foster, *Iconography of St. Joseph in Netherlandish Art 1400–1500*, Ph.D. diss., University of Kansas, 1978 (University Microfilms International, Ann Arbor, 1979) pp. 187–89.

8. Cited by Foster, *Iconography of St. Joseph*, p. 210. For an illustration of the painting, see G. J. Hoogewerff, *De Noord-Nederlandsche Schilderkunst*, vol. 2 (The Hague, 1937) fig. 170. When Hoogewerff published the picture, it was in the collection of the marquess of Bute.

9. Foster, *Iconography of St. Joseph*, pp. 159–60.

10. Discussed and illustrated in E. Haverkamp-Begemann, "Flemish School," *European Paintings in the Collection of the Worcester Art Museum* (Worcester, 1974) vol. 1, pp. 190–93, vol. 2., illus. p. 574.

11. The picture in the Philadelphia Museum of Art (reg. no. 1980–118-1, gift of Elizabeth Donner Norment) is illustrated in *Italian Primitive and Renaissance Paintings . . . Gothic Tapestries . . . Collected by the Late Leon Schinasi . . . .*, sale cat., Parke-Bernet, New York, November 3–4, 1944, no. 405. For the tapestry from the Frédéric Spitzer collection, see Eugène Müntz, "Les tapisseries," in *La collection Spitzer* (Paris, 1890–92) vol. 1, p. 164 and pl. III.

12. Photograph in the Photo Archives, J. Paul Getty Center for the History of Art and the Humanities, Santa Monica, French and Company photo collection, no. 4189-21816.

13. For discussions and illustrations of this tapestry, see Souchal in Paris 1973, no. 80, illus., and in New York 1974, no. 85, illus.; see also *Le XVIᵉ siècle européen: Tapisseries*, exh. cat. by Germain Viatte, Mobilier National (Paris, 1965) no. 17. Souchal thought it might show a scene from the life of "un pieux personnage," that is, the male figure kneeling on one leg in the right foreground who we believe represents Joseph. Viatte suggested that the same composition, as it appears in a variant version in a tapestry in the Vatican, might represent the Holy Family; we believe that is the subject of the piece in Lyon. He did not refer to the man in the foreground as Joseph but mentioned a tradition holding that this figure represents Ambrose of Ravenna. Souchal noted that a tapestry in the Saint Louis Art Museum shows another variant version of the same composition.

14. For an illustration of the tapestry-woven picture in Chicago, see 22 in the present catalogue, fig. 121, and for that piece and the one formerly in the Le Roy collection, see Hunter, "Miniature Tapestries of the Infant Christ," figs. II and IV, respectively.

15. Standen, notes and preliminary draft, ca. 1968.

16. Standen, notes and preliminary draft, ca. 1968.

24

The Hunt of the Frail Stag

Five fragments of a hanging, perhaps a choir hanging

a   *Nature Sets Her Hound Youth after the Stag*
b   *Vanity Sounds the Horn and Ignorance Unleashes the Hounds Overconfidence, Rashness, and Desire*
c   *Old Age Drives the Stag out of a Lake and the Hounds Cold, Heat, Anxiety, Vexation, Heaviness, Fear, Age, and Grief Attack Him*
d   *Sickness Spears the Stag and Death Sounds His Horn*
e   *The Poet with His Epilogue*

Southern Netherlands, 1495–1510
Wool warp; wool and silk wefts
Sight dimensions of each piece as mounted: 3 ft. ³/₈ in. × 2 ft. 11 in. (.924 m × .89 m)
14–15 warp yarns per inch, 5–6 per centimeter
Bequest of Adele L. Lehman, in memory of Arthur Lehman, 1965 (65.181.18–22)

CONDITION

Each piece is mounted and is somewhat wider than noted above. The excess fabric, irregularly shaped, has been turned over the edges of the mount at the sides. Each fragment also retains a narrow strip of weaving seven-eighths of an inch wide along the bottom; this grayish white fabric has also been turned over and sewn to the bottom edge of the mount.

Photographs published in 1913 show that these five pieces had suffered significant losses by that date.[1] Since then each fragment was restored as described below. All five fragments also show many small spot repairs by reweaving scattered over the surface and especially in the inscriptions where some of the original black yarns (now blackish brown) deteriorated and fell out of the fabric. They were replaced with yarns that have turned a slightly different shade of dark brown. The ground weaves surrounding the inscriptions are for the most part intact, but some of them show considerable repair.

There are insertions of modern weaving, with new warp and weft yarns, along both sides of 24a (see Picot 1913, pl. LI). At the left the restorations involve the foliage and fruit in the upper corner and the narrow strip of ground and flowers that lies between that area and the left end of the inscribed banderole at the bottom of the field, including the first letters in the last three lines of the stanza. In the photograph published in 1913 the

words *Et le* were still present at the left of what is now the first word in the second line, or *cerf*. In place of the capital letter *O* that now introduces the third line the remnants of a word, possibly *Qui*, were still visible. The fourth line began with a word containing two *f*'s followed by an *i* or an *n* and several other indefinite letters. The entire right side of the piece, a narrow strip of fabric filling the space bounded by the left edge of the tree and the present right edge of the fabric, from top to bottom, is a modern insertion. The photograph published in 1913 also shows a narrow band of light-colored fabric along the bottom of the field and, below that, a wider band of dark-colored fabric. It is likely, though not certain, that these horizontal strips of weaving, which also appeared in the early photographs on some of the other fragments, are segments of the original border or guard that ran along the bottom of the whole hanging from which the fragments were cut (see Description and Subject). As already noted, the light-colored band has survived on all five of the fragments.

Very narrow strips of modern weaving were added along the left and top edges of 24b (see Picot 1913, pl. LII). The right edge was cut partway through the representation of a balustered column and what appears to be the springing of an arch above. An irregularly shaped piece of modern weaving runs across the piece just below center from the left edge to the upper right corner of the inscribed banderole; it passes through the lower part of *Ignorance*'s skirt, the thighs, lower body, and forelegs of the first hound, and the lower body and forelegs of the second one. The name inscribed on the body of the first dog, [*ou*]*ltrecuidáce*, has been altered significantly in this restoration whereas the next dog's name, *haste*, was scarcely affected by it.

The modern insertions in 24c include a narrow strip of sky along the top and a wider strip of landscape

24a

behind the figure of *vielles*[se]. The upper corner of the right end of the scroll and all of the ground and tree trunk to the right of it, as well as the right-hand clump of holly foliage above, have been restored (see Picot 1913, pl. LIII). There are also small insertions in the lower part of the body of the hound *doubtāce* and in the lower jaw of *ēnuy*. The word left of center in the second line of verse below was almost entirely lost and has been replaced by letters that make no sense. The name of the hound in the upper right corner, which now reads as *froi*, was originally written as *froit*.

Like 24a, b, and c, 24d shows bands of modern fabric inserted along the top and both sides (see Picot 1913, pl. LIV). On the left side the restoration extends from the patch of grass to the left of the banderole upward through the right foot of the character *maladie*, past her right hand, and to the top of the dark leaves above her right arm. The strip of modern weaving that was added

at the top begins at that point and passes just above *maladie*'s head, through the top of Death's skull, and then straight across to the right edge of the fragment. The insertion at the right side extends from the lower right-hand corner of the banderole upward through its turned-back end and the hind quarters of the hounds *soucy* and *aage* to a point just above the tip of the stag's right-most antler. There it meets the restoration running along the top edge.

There are insertions of modern weaving along both sides of 24e (see Picot 1913, pl. LV). The one at the left runs the full height of the piece and involves all the fabric to the left of the inscribed tablet. The restoration at the right begins at a point just to the right of the strawberry plants below the poet's left foot and continues in a straight line upward through the poet's left hand (of which only the thumb and adjacent part of the palm are original). Just above that point the insertion expands

348

24b

to the left to include the clump of lighter colored leaves in the upper right corner of the piece. There is some repair by reweaving in the right side of the man's face, in the ground of the inscribed tablet, and in the bottom of his gown where the yarns representing the dark blue shadows have been replaced and are now dark brown. Except for the red initial letter in the first line of the stanza, the letters show either the original black weft yarns (now dark brown) or modern yarns in tones of gray brown, red brown, and beige brown. The coat of arms that appears in the upper central section of the fragment is surrounded by dark brown modern weft yarns, but the warp appears to be original and continuous with the rest of the fabric. The staff of what we may assume was an abbot's crosier passes behind the shield; only its lower tip and a small bit of its upper shaft are visible. Such a crosier, together with a miter that either surmounts it or is pierced by it, appears in two other tapestries showing the same coat of arms.[2] The top of the crosier and the miter are both missing from 24e. In one of the other tapestries the two motifs together are approximately one and a quarter times as tall as the shield, and in the other piece they measure approximately four-fifths the height of the shield. Assuming that the designer of 24e used one or the other of those proportions in his depiction of the crosier and the miter, and noting further that the shield in 24e is $8^{5}/_{8}$ inches tall, we can estimate that the missing part of the crosier and the miter together would have occupied a strip of fabric somewhere between $6^{7}/_{8}$ and $10^{3}/_{4}$ inches (.174 and .27 m) tall which, together with more of the field that must have been shown above and around these motifs, has been lost.

DESCRIPTION AND SUBJECT

The first four fragments show episodes in the story of an allegorical stag hunt, the hunt of the "frail stag," a creature treated as a metaphor for Mankind which, in pursuing its journey through life, is assailed by the moral and physical weaknesses of its own flesh. The progress of the hunt is illustrated in 24a–d as though it were an actual stag hunt in the late Middle Ages, but with allegorical characters substituted for the hunters and hounds (see 25a–f for a description of a typical medieval stag hunt). In 24e is shown a venerable male figure who represents the author of the poem on which the compositions are based. He stands beside a tablet inscribed with the verses expressing the moral in the allegory of *le cerf fragile.* In 24a–e the verses appear on white grounds and the letters are dark brown or black (originally all black) except for the initial letter in each of the five stanzas, which is red. When the five fragments were exhibited in Paris in 1904 and again when des Forts published them in 1906, 24e was treated as the first, rather than the last, panel in the series. Later writers invariably placed it last in the series and referred to it as an epilogue piece. The stanza could be interpreted equally well as a prologue or an epilogue. We elect to regard it as an epilogue partly because a closely related miniature painting is bound into its manuscript at the end of a similar series of allegorical hunting scenes (see below) and also because representations of authors with their moralizing verses usually appear at the end, rather than the beginning, of a number of tapestry series of this period (see pertinent discussion in 13a–c).

In 24a the stag hunt begins when the lady *nature* (Human Nature) who stands left of center, having used her limer (a carefully trained scent hound) to find a stag suitable for hunting, flushes him out of his covert. He had been harbored in a forest of trees, rosebushes, pansies, columbines, strawberries, pinks, and other flowering plants that fill the field almost to the top (where a bit of sky appears) in the manner of a millefleurs tapestry. *Nature* wears a patterned velvet gown over a plain velvet kirtle or underdress, a hood, and two necklaces, one made of pearls or round beads, the other a chain with a cross suspended from it. The hound *jeunesse* (Youth) appears just to the right of *nature* and springs forward to pursue the stag. The octave inscribed on the scroll spread out across the bottom of the field reads as follows:[3]

Cy voiez le buissō denfance · Ou nature sō chemin dresse
[Et le] cerf fragille h[o]rs lance · Avec sō beau limyer jeunesse
Q[ui] le met sus & pas ne cesse · Davoir de laproucher ēvie
[Affin qu'?] en rep[os?] ne le laisse · Es bois de transitoire vie

(Here you see the forest of childhood to which Nature makes her way
And flushes out the frail stag with her handsome hound Youth
Who sets upon him and never relents in his attack
So that he will have no rest in the woods of [this] transitory life).

In 24b the hunt continues in another part of the same forest. Two other allegories personified as fashionably dressed ladies stand at the left side of the field. They are two of the relays who have been posted along the stag's projected path of flight, and they have with them scent hounds and greyhounds who are unleashed as the quarry passes. Lady *Ignorance*, wearing a plain silk gown over a patterned velvet kirtle, a gold chain with a locket around her neck, and a turban headdress with flowing lappets, stands at the far left. Next to her is the lady *vanite* in a costume that comprises a short patterned tunic with long open sleeves under which show the linen sleeves of her kirtle, and a patterned petticoat. She also wears a string of beads with a pendant cross, various ornaments hanging from her girdle, and a cap with a brim turned down in front. She has lifted a hunting horn to her lips and blown the three notes that order the release of the hounds. *Ignorance* has unleashed the greyhound [*ou*]*ltrecuidāce* (Overconfidence) and the scent hounds *haste* (Rashness) and *vouloir* (Desire) who go bounding after the stag. The poem continues in the inscription below, as follows:

Les chiens que tenoit acouplez · Dedās le bois dame Ignorance
Apres le cerf a descouplez · Cest vouloir haste oultrecuidance
Qui plāis de mōdaine plaisāce · Luy fōt maīt sault de travers faire
Et lors vanite si savance · De corner cōme elle scet faire

(The dogs that she held leashed in the woods Dame Ignorance
has let loose after the stag; they are Desire, Rashness, Overconfidence
Who, filled with worldly pleasure, make him take many an erratic leap
And then Vanity comes forward to sound the horn as she knows how to do).

The scene changes in 24c from the depths of the forest to a clearing at the edge of a lake. The stag has dashed into the water to refresh himself and to try to shake off his pursuers. The near shore of the lake is covered with flowering plants. Grass and trees grow on the far shore. The lady *vielles[se]* (Old Age) hobbles into the scene from the left with a walking stick in each hand. She

Puis lassault viellesse a oultrāce · Qui le fait hors du lac saillir
Et luy lasche peine et deage · EChault et froit et fait venir
Soucy ēnuy pour le tenir · Et aage a la chere ridee
Et pesanteur le fōt fouyr · Deuers maladie la doubtee

24c

wears a dark hood and a gown of plain fabric tied with a girdle of tasseled cords; a rosary hangs from the girdle. In the middle distance eight hounds have caught up with the stag; four of them bite into his flesh as he struggles to jump out of the water. The hounds are labeled (clockwise, starting at the upper right) *froi[t]* (Cold), *chault* (Heat), *soucy* (Anxiety), *enuy* (Vexation), *pesanteur* (Heaviness), *doubtāce* (Fear), *aage* (Age), and *peine* (Grief). The verses inscribed on the banderole running across the bottom of the field read as follows:

> *Puis lassault viellesse a oultrāce · Qui le fait hors*
> *du lac saillir*
> *Et luy lasche peine et deage* [doubtance, incorrectly restored] · *E[t] Chault et froit et fait venir*
> *Soucy ēnuy pour le tenir · Et aage a la chere ridee*
> *Et pesanteur le fōt fouyr · Devers maladie la doubtee*

(Then Old Age, who makes him leap up out of the lake, attacks him with a vengeance

And unleashes Grief and Fear and Heat and Cold after him and then brings in
Anxiety [and] Vexation to hold him fast; and Age with its wrinkled skin
And Heaviness make him flee toward Illness, the dreaded one).

The hunt reaches its climax in 24d, where the trials of Old Age move in and make their kill. The scene shifts to another part of the forest, where there is a field of flowering plants in the foreground and a screen of trees reaching to the sky in the distance. Lady *maladie* (Illness) stands at the left. She wears a long plain hood and a plain gown bordered with gemstones and lined with ermine over a patterned velvet kirtle. She lunges forward and thrusts the point of her spear into the stag's side as he falls under the assault of the eight hounds that found him in the stream. Four of the hounds (*enuy*, *pesant[eur]*, *chault*, and *soucy*) stand or pace about in the foreground while *peine* sinks its teeth into the stag's

24d

rump, *doubtace* leaps up behind him ready to follow suit, and *froit* and *aage* bite deep into his neck. The head and shoulders of Death, not labeled but represented as an emaciated body topped by a skull, rise above the shrubs in the middle distance. He lifts his horn and blows the notes to signal that the stag has been taken. The action is described in the octave written on the banderole that runs across the bottom of the field, as follows:

Voy le veneur espouventable · Qui la mort du cerf a emprise
Cest maladie la doubtable · De qui la charōgne est sourprise
Elle luy fait forte ētreprise · Car de lespieu le coup luy dōne
Apres la mort viēt cornez · prise · Aīsi que tēps si lordōne.

(See the frightening hunter who has set out to kill the stag;

It is fearful Illness by whom the flesh is overtaken.
She does him great violence, for she strikes him with her spear.
Then Death comes to sound the capture as the occasion demands).

The last of the five fragments, 24e, shows the poet with a rectangular tablet inscribed with the epilogue to the story he has told in the verses along the bottom of 24a–d. The tablet is near the left edge of the piece, and the poet stands at the right. He wears a hat with a tall crown and a turned-up brim and a plain, long-sleeved tunic over a velvet gown. He gathers the folds of the tunic in his right hand and lifts his left hand as though in greeting or bidding attention. The setting shows a narrow strip of flowering plants and grass in the foreground and a view into a grassy meadow above and behind the tablet and figure. Oak trees close the scene in at the left, and orange trees do the same at the right. A coat of arms appears in the center of the fragment, above the tablet. The bottom of the shaft of a crosier projects from beneath the point of the shield and overlaps the upper molding of the frame surrounding the tablet. The shield is blazoned as follows: quarterly, 1 and 4 bendy of four, azure and argent, with three hearts gules two and one on the argent, crowned or on the azure (for Baudreuil); 2 and 3 ermine a fess azure semée-de-lis (for the abbey of Saint-Martin-aux-Bois). The coat of arms is that of Guy de Baudreuil, abbot of Saint-Martin-aux-Bois, near Beauvais, from 1491 or 1492 to 1530.[4] In two of the other three tapestries we know on which his armorial shield is illustrated (see Manufacture and Date), a crosier rises behind the shield and is accompanied by a miter which the crosier either pierces or supports on its curved upper end. The fringed ends of the miter's lappets fall to the sides of the shield at the top. In the third tapestry the crosier and miter are missing, and the shield is tied to the branch of a tree with a ribbon whose lower ends float at the sides of the shield. There are no lappets near the shield in 24e, and there is no other indication that a miter accompanied this crosier.

The stanza on the tablet reads as follows:

Gens de briefve duree mōdaīē
qua chasse mortelle & soubdaīē
etes comme cerf asservis
cōsiderez la vie humaine
et la fin ou elle vous maine
et les metz dont serez servis
alors que serez desservis
de Jeunesse et aurez adviz
advisez atel propoz prendre
que qāt serez de mort Ravis
et les vers serōt au corps vifz
que puissiōs adieu lame Rendre

(You people whose life on earth is brief,
Who, to a short and deadly hunt,
Like the stag, are subject:
Think of human life and the end it leads you to
And the things that will be dished up to you
When you have lost
Your youth and realize what has happened:
Think of how you are going to manage
So that when death overtakes you
And the worms are eagerly at your flesh
We can commit our souls to God).

These tapestries illustrate some of the key episodes of a typical stag hunt in Europe during the Middle Ages, as do 25a–f, which show stag hunters and their attendants engaging in many of the activities involved in the chase from the moment the party leaves their castle until they return. However in 24a–e the hunters and hounds are allegorical creatures rather than real beings. The hunters are represented as women personifying Human Nature and certain weaknesses and ills of the human body and spirit while the hounds represent some of the chief enemies of man's physical and moral well-being. The stag they are chasing is not labeled, but it is clear that he represents unfortunate Man, the pilgrim in medieval and later literature who fritters his life away during the carefree years of his youth and then falls under the crushing burden of his fleshly weaknesses and his sins. Ultimately he seeks salvation through the practice of virtue in the hope of claiming the right to the eternal life he was promised at his baptism. But he must make his peace with God before his death; and this is the message that the poet expresses in the verses written on the tablet he stands next to in 24e.

In this context the stag is the hart that Saint Augustine (of Hippo) likened to mortal man "still bearing about the frailty of flesh" in his *Enarratio in Psalmum XLI*, the *cerf fragile* who appears in manuscript illustrations and tapestry hangings produced in the sixteenth century (see Source of the Design and Related Tapestries), the stag that would have been seen in the hanging entitled *Le cerf fragille de S. Augustin* that figured in Florimond Robertet's testamentary inventory of August 4, 1532.[5] It was this reference that led the present writer, with the help of a student of this field, to find the source of the allegory in the writings of Saint Augustine.[6] The saint's commentary takes as its point of departure the second verse of Psalm 41: "As the hart panteth after the fountains of water; so my soul panteth after thee, O God." Saint Augustine compares sinful man to the thirsty stag, the stag (hart in the text) who becomes more thirsty as he destroys serpents and then seeks water. The serpents are compared to man's vices, and Saint Augustine calls upon man to destroy them and thus thirst for "the Fountain of Truth," for God who is the fountain of life. In paragraph 9 of the commentary, Saint Augustine not only speaks of man's "frailty of flesh" but also says that he is "in peril in the midst of the 'offences' of the world."[7] Whether by direct means or indirect, this commentary seems to have become the inspiration for the allegory of the frail stag and for the poems that treat the subject. In discussing references to the stag in medieval bestiaries, Freeman noted that in the bestiary of Bishop Theobald "the stag . . . devours [serpents]" and then drinks cool water whereby "the poison is quenched," and also that "men, when they gather poisons from the serpent, such as 'luxury, hatred, anger . . . [or] lusts of the heart . . . should run with all haste to Christ who is our living water, who when he cleanses our souls, drives all poison away.'"[8]

The stag as a symbol of Mankind threatened, hunted,

24e

and tormented by human weaknesses and the forces of evil also appears in other contexts in medieval art. He is also the "White Stag" of Antonio Fileremo Fregoso's morality *La cerva bianca*, published in Italy in the early sixteenth century. Van Marle (1932, fig. 125) illustrated a woodcut bound in an edition of this work that was published in Venice in 1525; it shows a hunter with the hounds *Desio* (Desire) and *Pensier* (Worry) hotly pursuing a hapless stag. The stag is also depicted as *le cerf humain*, pausing to refresh himself in the waters of a stream while the hunters and hounds run bounding past him in the distance, as shown in a tapestry that belonged formerly to the marquess of Breadalbane and then to Henry Symons.[9] There the stag is once again the hart of Psalm 41 and of Saint Augustine, the soul who yearns after God as the hart thirsts after water. In a related but different context the stag is the human soul who after a life of sin is brought to his salvation by Divine Mercy through Reason, as illustrated in a tapestry that was formerly at Ockwells Manor in Windsor Forest and is now in the Musée d'Histoire et d'Archéologie in Tournai.[10] The hanging shows a garden setting in which a woman standing at the left holds a leash tied to the collar of a stag which *Raison*, seconded by an unlabeled woman kneeling before the dais, presents to the enthroned *Misericordia Dei*. According to Oursel, this subject derives from some sixteenth-century moral treatise, presumably the *Miroir de l'âme pécheresse*.[11] An iconography closely related to this one, again with a happy ending, concerns the so-called *cerf privé* whose story is told in a poem contained in an illustrated manuscript in the Bibliothèque Nationale in Paris entitled *La chasse d'ung cerf privé* and dating from about 1543.[12] In these eight illustrated episodes the stag is at first free and happy but is soon pursued by *Envie* (Jealousy), *Mauvais Conseil* (Bad Advice), and *Faux Rapport* (False

354

Witness). *Vérité* (Truth), *Honneur, Bon Renom* (Good Character), and *Joyeux Espoir* (Happy Hope) come to his aid along with his parents and friends and strengthen him against the further assaults of *Soucy* (Worry), *Regret*, and *Desplaisir* (Unhappiness). Finally the stag finds a safe harbor in a lovely park where *Liberté* (Freedom), *Discretion, Prudence, Bon Renom*, and *Honneur* are his companions.

In other contexts the stag served as a symbol for Christ, as for example it did in a cycle of mural paintings commissioned by Antoine, duc de Lorraine, for the Galerie des Cerfs in his palace in Nancy. Reynaud (1983, 7–28), who discovered the surviving preparatory drawings, discussed the project in detail. The paintings were executed between 1524 and 1529 by Hugues de la Faye, court painter to the duke, and Georges Gresset. The paintings themselves were destroyed when the palace burned in 1871, but the drawings indicate that there were twenty-two compositions in the cycle, compositions inspired by the concept of a comparison between the life of Christ and the life of a stag, from birth (the birth of a fawn and the Nativity) to death (the death of the stag at the hands of hunters and the Crucifixion). The image of the stag hunt comes into play only when the story reaches the betrayal of Judas, which is compared to the preparations for the stag hunt. The paintings were accompanied by verses that Reynaud (1983, 25) believed might be the work of Pierre Gringore, who was court poet and herald of arms at the court of Nancy during the time the murals were painted. Among his other works was a pamphlet entitled *La chasse du cerf des cerfz* that he wrote against Pope Julius II in 1510. Although Gringore used the image of the stag in the pamphlet, there is no reason to think that he wrote the verses that the designer of 24a–e used, for it is clear that the allegory of the stag hunt was a commonly accepted convention by then, as the stag as a symbol of Christ also was. Freeman quoted from a passage in a twelfth-century bestiary by Philippe de Thaun: "The stag has that nature . . . that he goes seeking a hole where there is a serpent lying. When he has found a serpent, he takes water in his mouth and throws it in and then blows. He blows there . . . so long that he draws [the serpent] out with great labor. The stag is angry and kills it with his feet. . . . By this stag we rightly understand Jesus Christ. The water is wisdom which is in his mouth; . . . holy inspiration is understood by his blowing, and by the serpent, the Devil."[13]

The Metropolitan Museum's fragments have always been referred to in the literature as five separate tapestries. Only Virch (1965, 105) suggested that they may once have been cut out of a single, longer hanging which

Fig. 125. *Nature Sets Her Hound Youth after the Fragile Stag.* Drawing in an illustrated manuscript of the *Chasse du cerf fragile.* France, late sixteenth century. Bibliothèque Nationale, Paris (MS fr. 25429, fol. 2r).

he referred to as a "frieze." He came to this conclusion, which we believe is correct, because as he observed there is a "border" (a guard band) along the bottom of each piece. Another clue to the original arrangement of the fragments is the incomplete representation of a balustered column carrying a portion of an arch at the right side of 24b. The presence of this architectural element in this place suggests that each scene originally appeared within one of the open spaces of an arcade, like the scenes from the life of the Virgin in the choir tapestry in the church of Notre-Dame in Beaune.[14] In that hanging some of the scenes are set in interior spaces, but others appear in landscapes with bits of flowered meadow in the foreground like those that one sees in 24a–e. Within limits we can estimate the dimensions of the hanging from which the fragments came. Taking the present height of each piece, or approximately 37 inches, as a point of departure, and adding to it some 8 inches for the guard band at the bottom and another along the top, plus about 15 inches to account for the parts of the field that are now missing at the top, including the thickness of each arch and some space above each one, we reach a total height of some 60 inches (1.52 m). As for the length of the original hanging, we can estimate that each of the seven scenes—we have reason to believe there were seven (see Related Tapestries)—measured some 3 feet in width, giving a total of 21 feet; and adding to that about 32 inches for the combined widths of the eight columns that carried the seven arches in the arcade, we reach a total length of some 23 feet 6 inches (7.16 m). If the hanging included an inscription, a figure of the donor, and possibly also a patron saint, it might have reached a total length of some 26 feet 6 inches (8.08 m) or perhaps even a bit more. Given these dimensions, that is, approximately 1.50 by 8 or more meters, we conclude that the tapestry may have been produced as a choir hanging.

Source of the Design

It was Picot (1913, 60–63, pls. LVI–LVIII) who first called attention to the close relationship that exists between the Metropolitan Museum's tapestries and an illustrated manuscript in the Bibliothèque Nationale in Paris (MS fr. 25429). That book, which Picot dated toward the end of the sixteenth century, contains nine gouache drawings and nine related sets of verses (seven octaves and two quatrains), plus a quatrain inscribed on the easel near the author. They are remarkably like the designs and verses in 24a–e in terms of composition and content (fig. 125). Reynaud (1983, 28 n. 50) believed that the miniatures in the Paris manuscript illustrate the text that 24a–e also illustrate, and in general terms her observation is correct. However the verses in the manuscript and in the tapestry fragments show notable if minor differences in the choice and arrangement of the words. There are also differences in the way the pictures were composed. However the similarities suggest that the tapestry fragments and the miniature paintings derive from some common source. That source was probably an illustrated book, either a printed volume or a manuscript.

Manufacture and Date

A hanging or set of hangings listed in the inventory of Philippe le Bon's tapestries taken in 1420 was called "l'Histoire de la Jeunesse et déduit, appelée la Chasse du cerf" (The Story of Youth and Pleasure, called the Hunt of the Stag).[15] Although we cannot be sure that the subject matter was the same as in 24a–e, this listing could indicate that tapestries with this or a similar subject were being made in the late fourteenth or early fifteenth century. However 24a–e obviously were woven much later than that. Until 1932, when van Marle (105–6) referred to the tapestries as having been woven in Tournai or somewhere in northern France, writers had called 24a–e French and dated them anywhere from

the fifteenth century to the third decade of the sixteenth century. It was Guiffrey (1911, 197) who proposed the later date, which both Göbel (1923, vol. 1, 131) and Virch (1965, 100) also used. Forsyth (1966–67, 87) believed that the five fragments were Franco-Flemish, and he dated them in the early sixteenth century. All subsequent publications have followed his suggestion.

Picot (1913, 60) thought that 24a–e, together with the other two tapestries then known to show Guy de Baudreuil's coat of arms (see below), could have been woven in Beauvais, presumably because it was close to the abbey of Saint-Martin-aux-Bois. Since we have no reason at present to think that fine tapestries like this were being woven at Beauvais at that time, it seems more reasonable to locate the place of weaving in the general region of the southern Netherlands. We are not justified in attributing them to any specific weaving center.

Because Guy de Baudreuil's coat of arms, which includes those of Saint-Martin-aux-Bois, together with what appears to be the bottom of the shaft of a crosier, is present in 24e, we conclude that the hanging from which these fragments come must have been commissioned between 1491 or 1492, when Guy succeeded his brother Guillaume as head of the abbey of Saint-Martin-aux-Bois, and 1530, when Guy moved to Corbigny (see note 4). A drawing in the Collection Gaignières in Paris illustrates a tapestry showing the same quartered coat of arms, with the miter and crosier, along with the shield of each quarter in its own right, and an inscription that reads "messire Guy de Vaudreuil ma fait faire lan 1520."[16] So we know that he was commissioning tapestries in that year. The coat of arms appears again, but without the miter and crosier, in one of two tapestries representing the allegory of Sacred and Profane Love, both in the Musée des Arts Décoratifs, Paris.[17] The pictorial style, border pattern, and fashions represented in those hangings suggest a date around the same time. The same quartered shield of arms, with the miter and crosier, appears in a tapestry that des Forts published in 1906 (557, illus. facing 556) as belonging to the comte de Baudreuil at the château de Favelles (Loir-et-Cher).[18] That hanging, which shows Minerva standing in the center of an ornamental composition featuring a variety of heraldic and symbolic elements, must have been woven earlier than the three tapestries just mentioned. The drawing of Minerva's figure is sophisticated and fashionable, only slightly removed from its prototypes in late fifteenth-century Florentine painting. This suggests that the tapestry was both designed and woven not much later than 1500–1510. Compared to these four hangings, 24a–e look retrospective and outmoded. Furthermore, while most of the women in 24a–e wear fancy dress, the costume of *Jeunesse* reflects the fashion of civilian women's garments in the last decade of the fifteenth century or the first decade of the sixteenth.[19] It seems correct, therefore, to date the five fragments no later than about 1510 and no earlier than 1495, a few years after Guy de Baudreuil could have begun to marshal his coat of arms as it appears in these tapestries.

RELATED TAPESTRIES

No other fragments of the original hanging are known to have survived. However we have reason to believe that at least two other fragments may once have existed. As noted above, the sixteenth-century manuscript in Paris that illustrates the same subject (see Picot 1913, 60–63) contains nine scenes and stanzas. Virch (1965, 105) noted that the first, fifth, and ninth subjects and stanzas in the manuscript correspond to the first, third, and fifth subjects and stanzas in the tapestry fragments. The second tapestry subject, shown in 24b, combines in one scene the subjects of the second and third scenes and verses (quatrains rather than octaves) in the manuscript, while the fourth tapestry subject, in 24e, shows in a single composition both the sixth and seventh subjects of the manuscript but only the seventh stanza (an octave). Therefore, only two subjects that are present in the manuscript are missing from the tapestry series; that is, the fourth subject which deals with *Necessite* driving the stag into the *lac de Cognoissance* (the Lake of Knowledge), and the eighth subject which shows *Mort* (Death) allowing the worms to have their reward of the hunt.[20] It may be fair to assume that these two subjects once appeared along with 24a–e in the hanging from which they were taken. A fragment of a much larger tapestry, showing the female figure of *necessité* accompanied by the hound *simplesse* at the edge of a lake (all mentioned in the stanza accompanying the fourth subject in the manuscript), was formerly in the Larcade collection in Paris.[21]

Two large hangings from another set of tapestries whose design was based on the same verses and woven after similar cartoons are now in the Metropolitan Museum (32a, b).

A fragmentary tapestry woven after a cartoon that was based on a similar but different text was sold in London in 1968.[22] It shows the female figure of *Jonesse* watching four hounds (the name of only one, *gloutanie*, is legible) barking at the stag, labeled *le cerf fragille*, which is just about to leap into a lake filled with fish. The female huntress *ennuee* (Vexation) stands at the far left while the male hunter *faulxraport* (False Witness), who stands to the right of her, blows his horn.

HISTORY

Commissioned by Guy de Baudreuil, abbé commendataire of the abbey of Saint-Martin-aux-Bois in the diocese of Beauvais.
Collection of M. and Mme. de Kermaingant, Paris, by 1886.
Property of French and Company, New York, by 1923.
Collection of Mr. and Mrs. Arthur Lehman, New York, 1923.
Bequeathed to the MMA by Adele L. Lehman, in memory of Arthur Lehman, 1965.

EXHIBITIONS

Paris, Palais du Louvre and Bibliothèque Nationale, 1904. *Exposition des Primitifs Français.* Cat. no. 409 [24a–e]. Lent by M. de Kermaingant.
Paris, Jacques Seligmann (former hôtel de Sagan), 1913. *Exposition d'objets d'art du Moyen Age et de la Renaissance . . . organisée par la Marquise de Ganay.* Catalogue by Seymour de Ricci. Cat. nos. 333–37 [24a–e]. Lent by M. de Kermaingant.
New York, MMA, The Cloisters, 1952. 24a–e lent by Mrs. Arthur Lehman.
Providence, Museum of the Rhode Island School of Design, 1974. *Europe in Torment: 1450–1550.* Cat. no. 45 [24a–e]; all illus.
South Hadley, Massachusetts, Mount Holyoke College Art Museum, 1977. *Monsters, Gargoyles, and Dragons: Animals in the Middle Ages.* Cat. no. 32 [24a–e]; 24d illus.
Katonah, New York, Katonah Gallery, 1978. *Medieval Images: A Glimpse into the Symbolism and Reality of the Middle Ages.* Cat. no. 50 [24a–e]; all illus.
Binghamton, New York, Roberson Center for the Arts and Sciences, 1978. *Medieval Images: A Glimpse into the Symbolism and Reality of the Middle Ages.* 24a–e exhibited.
Aspen Center for the Visual Arts (now the Aspen Art Museum), 1979–80. *Medieval Images.* 24a–e included in brochure; 24b illus.
New York, Center for African Art, and Houston, Museum of Fine Arts, 1988–89. *Africa and the Renaissance: Art in Ivory.* 24b exhibited.

PUBLICATIONS

Müntz, Eugène. "La tapisserie à l'époque de Louis XII." *Les lettres et les arts* 3 (1886) p. 215. 24a–e discussed briefly as in the de Kermaingant mansion on the Champs-Elysées; 24a, b illus. facing pp. 212, 214.
Müntz, Eugène. "Tapisseries allégoriques inédites ou peu connues." *Fondation Eugène Piot: Monuments et Mémoires,* Académie des Inscriptions et Belles-Lettres, Paris, 9 (1902) pp. 114–16. 24a–e discussed, with transcriptions of the verses.
des Forts, Philippe. "Les tapisseries de Gui de Baudreuil, abbé de Saint-Martin-aux-Bois." In *Congrès Archéologique de France: LXXIIᵉ session tenue à Beauvais en 1905.* Société française d'archéologie. Paris and Caen, 1906, pp. 558–59. 24a–e discussed briefly.
Guiffrey, Jules. *Les tapisseries du XIIᵉ à la fin du XVIᵉ siècle.* Paris, [1911], p. 197. 24a–e mentioned.
Picot, Emile. "Le cerf allégorique dans les tapisseries et les miniatures." *Bulletin de la Société française de reproductions de manuscrits à peintures* 3 (1913) pp. 58–60. 24a–e described, with transcriptions of the verses; 24a–e illus. pls. LI–LV.
de Ricci, Seymour. "L'art du Moyen Age et de la Renaissance à l'hôtel de Sagan." *Gazette des Beaux-Arts,* 4th ser., 10 (1913) p. 75. 24a–e mentioned.
de Ricci, Seymour. *Exposition d'objets d'art . . . organisée par la Marquise de Ganay à l'ancien hôtel de Sagan (mai–juin 1913).* Paris, 1914, pls. 23, 24. 24a–e discussed briefly; 24a–d illus.
Fels, Florent. *Die altfranzösischen Bildteppiche.* Berlin, [1923], p. 16. 24b mentioned; 24b illus. pl. 46.
Göbel 1923, vol. 1, p. 131. 24a–d described briefly, transcription of verses in 24e given; brief bibliography for 24a–e, p. 580 n. 138.
Hunter 1925, pp. 71–72. 24a–e discussed briefly.
de Mély, F. "Pierrefonds et son architecte Jean Lenoir." *Gazette des Beaux-Arts,* 5th ser., 13 (1926) p. 205. 24a mentioned.
van Marle, Raimond. *Iconographie de l'art profane au Moyen-Age et à*

la Renaissance. Vol. 2. The Hague, 1932, pp. 105–6. 24a–e mentioned as formerly in the de Kermaingant collection, and again, with a different attribution, as in the collection of Arthur Lehman.

Forsyth, William H. "The Medieval Stag Hunt." *MMA Bulletin*, n.s. 10 (1951–52) p. 209. 24a–d described and interpreted briefly.

Virch, Claus. *The Adele and Arthur Lehman Collection*. MMA, New York, 1965, pp. 100–106. 24a–e discussed at length, with transcriptions and translations of the verses, and bibliography; illus.

Forsyth, William H. "Reports of the Departments: Medieval Art and The Cloisters, the Main Building." Annual Report for 1965–1966. In *MMA Bulletin*, n.s. 25 (1966–67) p. 87. 24a–e mentioned.

C. G.-M. [Carmen Gómez-Moreno]. "Tapestries: Le Cerf Fragile." *MMA Notable Acquisitions 1965–1975*. New York, 1975, p. 164. 24a–e discussed briefly; 24b illus.

Reynaud, Nicole. "La Galerie des Cerfs au Palais ducal de Nancy." *Revue de l'Art*, no. 61 (1983) pp. 25, 28 n. 50. 24a–e mentioned; 24b illus. fig. 27.

NOTES

1. Emile Picot published photographs of all five pieces in 1913; see Picot, "Le cerf allégorique dans les tapisseries et les miniatures," *Bulletin de la Société française de reproductions de manuscrits à peintures* 3 (1913) pls. LI–LV. The photographs of 24a and 24b published in Eugène Müntz, "La tapisserie à l'époque de Louis XII," *Les lettres et les arts* 3 (1886) pp. 212, 214, showed them to be in virtually the same condition. In 1914, Seymour de Ricci (*Exposition d'objets d'art du Moyen Age et de la Renaissance . . . organisée par la Marquise de Ganay à l'ancien hôtel de Sagan [mai–juin 1913]* [Paris, 1914] pls. LXXIII, LXXIV) published the photographs that Picot had used, or similar ones; only 24a–d illus.

2. The miter appears above the top of the crosier in the central section of an armorial tapestry inscribed "messire Guy de Vaudreuil ma fait faire lan 1520" which is known only from a drawing of it that is preserved in the Collection Roger de Gaignières in the Bibliothèque Nationale, Paris; see Henri Bouchot in note 16 below and Philippe des Forts, "Les tapisseries de Gui de Baudreuil, abbé de Saint-Martin-aux-Bois," *Congrès Archéologique de France, LXXIIe session tenue à Beauvais en 1905*, Société française d'archéologie (Paris and Caen, 1906) p. 559, illus. facing p. 558. The shaft of the crosier passes through the miter in an allegorical tapestry featuring the figure of Minerva which was in the possession of the comte de Baudreuil in the château de Favelles (Loir-et-Cher) when des Forts published it in 1906; see des Forts, "Les tapisseries," p. 557, illus. facing p. 556.

3. The transcriptions and translations of the verses given here differ in several details from the readings offered in earlier publications. The present author has used the Picot photographs (see note 1 above) and also the virtually identical verses shown in two closely related hangings in the Metropolitan Museum (see 32a, b) to arrive at the transcriptions offered in the text here.

4. According to Picot, "Le cerf allégorique," p. 58, Guillaume resigned his office at the abbey in favor of his brother Guy in 1492, whereas according to des Forts, "Les tapisseries," p. 555 n. 2, Guy was already abbot in July 1491. Des Forts, p. 560, wrote that Guy left the abbey in 1530 and went to Corbigny in his native department of Nièvre.

5. Göbel 1923, vol. 1, p. 131.

6. The author expresses his thanks to Martin Fleischer for the latter's generous sharing of his knowledge of pertinent sources and for providing texts for the author to study.

7. See Philip Schaff, ed., *A Select Library of the Nicene and Post-Nicene Fathers of the Christian Church*, vol. 8, *Saint Augustine, Expositions on the Book of Psalms* (reprint, Grand Rapids, 1979). The *Enarratio in Psalmum XLI* appears on pp. 132–38; paragraph 9 is found on p. 135.

8. Margaret Freeman, *The Unicorn Tapestries*, MMA (New York, 1976) pp. 73, 233 n. 18 (her source was *Physiologus, a Metrical*

Bestiary of Twelve Chapters by Bishop Theobald, trans. Alan Wood Rendell [London, 1928] p. 27).

9. The tapestry was sold from the collection of the marquess of Breadalbane, Taymouth Castle, by Dowell's Ltd., Edinburgh, April 22–28, 1922, no. 29, illus. It appeared next in the sale of the Henry Symons collection at the Anderson Galleries, New York, January 27–February 3, 1923, no. 1175, illus. It then became the property of French and Company, New York.

10. The tapestry was hanging in the Great Hall at Bray, Ockwells Manor, the seat of Sir Edward Barry, Bt., when it was published in 1924; see Christopher Hussey, "Ockwells Manor—II. Bray," *Country Life* 55 (January 19, 1924) illus. pp. 92, 96 (the author thanks Wendy Hefford for this reference). Later it entered the collections of the Musée d'Histoire et d'Archéologie in Tournai. It was exhibited in Arras in 1966 and in Tournai in 1968; see *Tapisseries françaises et flamandes du XVIe siècle*, exh. cat., entries by H. Oursel, Musée d'Arras (Arras, 1966) no. 11, pl. 3, and also *La tapisserie tournaisienne au XVIe siècle*, exh. cat. by J. P. Asselberghs (Tournai, 1968) no. 12, illus. According to Asselberghs there is a replica of this tapestry, cut into two pieces, in the château de Chenonceaux.

11. H. Oursel, in *Tapisseries françaises et flamandes du XVIe siècle*, cat. no. 11, observed that the *Miroir de l'âme pécheresse* is the best known of these moralizing treatises and also that in terms of Psalm 41 the stag does in fact symbolize the sinful soul.

12. MS fr. 379; see Picot, "Le cerf allégorique," pp. 63–67, scenes 1 and 6 illustrated on pls. LX, LXI. Picot (p. 67) expressed the opinion that these miniatures were made as designs for tapestries, whereas Nicole Reynaud ("La Galerie des Cerfs au Palais ducal de Nancy," *Revue de l'Art*, no. 61 [1983] p. 28 n. 52) believed that the paintings were intended only as illustrations for the manuscript text.

13. Freeman, *Unicorn Tapestries*, pp. 73, 233 n. 17. Her source was Thomas Wright, *Popular Treatises on Science Written during the Middle Ages* (London, 1841) p. 86.

14. See Alain Erlande-Brandenburg, "La tenture de la Vie de la Vierge à Notre-Dame de Beaune," *Bulletin Monumental* 134 (1976) particularly pp. 41–46, illus. pp. 42, 44. See also illustrations in Göbel 1928, vol. 2, figs. 324, 325.

15. A. Wauters, *Les tapisseries bruxelloises* (Brussels, 1878) p. 13.

16. See note 2 above for des Forts's discussion and illustration of the tapestry. See also the description in Henri Bouchot, *Inventaire des dessins exécutés pour Roger de Gaignières* (Paris, 1891) vol. 1, p. 495, no. 3736. The illustration, made from a tracing of the drawing in the Collection Gaignières, shows the surname spelled as Vaudreuil, which may be an artist's error, and a date that looks like 1420 but is clearly a slight misrendering of 1520 using the medieval form of the numeral 5.

17. Both tapestries are illustrated and discussed briefly in Erwin Panofsky, *Studies in Iconology: Humanistic Themes in the Art of the Renaissance*, 2d ed. (New York, 1962) pp. ix, 51, figs. 116, 117.

18. For a color lithograph illustrating this tapestry, see Eugène Müntz, *Histoire de l'art pendant la renaissance*, vol. 1 (Paris, 1889) frontispiece.

19. Gowns and hoods of essentially the same fashion appear in two miniatures showing Anne de Bretagne in various companies; one is dated to 1492–98, the other about 1507. See Freeman, *Unicorn Tapestries*, figs. 195, 200.

20. For transcriptions of the verses accompanying the fourth and eighth miniatures and also for illustrations of the paintings, see Picot, "Le cerf allégorique," pp. 61 and 62, pls. LVII and LVIII.

21. Known only from a photocopy of what appears to be a page in a sale catalogue, in MMA Department of Medieval Art files accompanied by a note stating that the tapestry was sold at the Galerie Charpentier, Paris, "Sambon-Warneck et à divers amateurs." At the time of writing it was not possible to trace this sale.

22. The tapestry, formerly belonging to M. Georges de Vergie, château de Touffou, was sold from the collection of David Ogilvy, Esq., at Sotheby's, London, April 18–19, 1968, no. 220, illus.

25
Incidents in a Stag Hunt

Six fragments from a set of hangings

a A Hunting Party Leaving a Castle
b Following the Stag's Trail
c The Stag at Bay
d Preparing to Undo the Stag in the Field
e Rewarding the Hounds
f A Hunter Returning to a Castle

Southern Netherlands, 1495–1515
Wool warp, wool wefts
25a: 7 ft. 10 in. × 6 ft. 6 in. (2.39 m × 1.98 m)
25b: 7 ft. 10 in. × 4 ft. 9 in. (2.39 m × 1.45 m)
25c: 7 ft. 7 in. × 12 ft. (2.31 m × 3.66 m)
25d: 7 ft. 11 in. × 4 ft. 4 in. (2.41 m × 1.32 m)
25e: 8 ft. 2 in. × 6 ft. 6 in. (2.49 m × 1.98 m)
25f: 7 ft. 10 in. × 5 ft. (2.39 m × 1.52 m)
11–13 warp yarns per inch, 4–5 per centimeter
Bequest of Helen Hay Whitney, 1944 (45.128.19–24)

CONDITION

Before coming to the Metropolitan Museum the six fragments had been joined to each other and to some strips of modern weaving. The modern sections were removed at the Museum, and these six fragments were finished at the edges so that they could be hung individually. Each piece shows an appreciable amount of repair and patching as follows.

Fragment 25a is made up of two main pieces that are joined vertically along a line passing between the two figures on horseback, through the body of the hound below them, and then through the drawbridge and stream to the bottom edge of the hanging. Another join appears along the left side; it runs from the top of the window in the turret straight down to the bottom of the foliage. At that point another patch, which includes the representation of a hound's forelegs, joins the strip above and continues to the bottom of the hanging. There are a great many small patches and passages of reweaving in the head of the mounted gentleman, his headdress and the adjacent parts of the turret that rises beyond it, his right leg and foot, the horse's stomach and forelegs, and the body of the hound below. The rider's watered-silk collar and sleeve linings and what appears to be a pleated tunic beneath his patterned velvet coat are all insertions of modern weaving. There are traces of the body of a falcon next to his left hand; only its tail remains relatively intact. (See the illustration of 25f to

form an idea of how this figure, which was woven after the same pattern, originally looked.) The shoes of the page or valet standing with his back to the viewer are modern insertions. There are also insertions and passages of reweaving that have distorted the shoulders, face, chest, and left arm of the falconer standing behind the page.

At some time 25b was cut into two pieces that were later rejoined. A bit of fabric was turned under or lost along both sides of the seam, which runs along a straight line passing through the center of the horse's neck and bridle, the upper part of its right foreleg, the rider's right toe, and the hindquarters of the hound below; it then continues to the bottom edge of the tapestry. There are some small spots of repair scattered throughout the piece, particularly in the right part of the rider's skirt, the leg and foot directly below, and the hind legs of the hound below the horse's forelegs.

The pattern is incomplete at the top and both ends of 25c, which is the central section of a larger hanging. Narrow strips of old weaving have been joined to it at both sides, and a small rectangular piece of tapestry with the same kind of ground pattern has been patched in at the lower left corner. A shield-shaped patch of similar fabric appears near the top of the tree trunk that rises to the right of the stag's antlers. It replaces the representation of a shield, certainly an armorial shield, that once hung there. The belt that held the shield to a branch is still visible (Jarry [1972, 47] published illustrations of two very similar tapestries showing armorial shields hanging on or in front of the branches of trees). Another patch of old fabric showing the pattern of the ground and shaped like the blade of a sword—which is probably what was represented there originally, accompanying the coat of arms—appears below the right side of the shield. The tree trunk itself, apparently taken from another part of this or a related hanging, was also patched in. There is more patching with old fabric, and a good deal of reweaving, throughout the piece. In the

359

25a

lower right corner a rectangular section, bounded at the top by a straight line passing through the rider's lower left thigh and the horse's chest and at the left by a line passing through the steed's forehoofs, was cut out at some time and later rejoined to the hanging.

In the upper and lower left corners of 25d there are patches of old tapestry whose patterns match that of the ground, and there are more such patches in and near the tree trunk below the landscape at the right. The entire landscape is represented on a number of patches taken from some other tapestry. The center back of the valet's patterned velvet doublet is a modern insertion. There are areas of reweaving throughout the piece particularly in the ground pattern and along a straight line from the top of the piece to the bottom through the valet's right hand and long arrow.

A strip of modern fabric a bit less than a sixth of the width of the whole piece occupies the left side of 25e; it extends from the top of the hanging to a point near the bottom, where it meets a rectangular patch of old weaving that shows the same pattern. There are other rectangular patches of the same kind above and to the left of the huntsman's head. A patch of flowered fabric, shaped like the shield it replaced, appears halfway up the trunk of the tree in the upper right corner of the field. The buckled belt from which the shield hung is still in place, passing over a broken branch that grows from the trunk just above the patch. There are patches along the lower edge of the piece at the right, in the lower right corner, and in the region of the neck of the upper hound at the right. A pair of parallel lines of wear, now repaired, extend from the top of the hanging to the bottom through the huntsman's right shoulder and side and the right hind leg of his hound. Spots of reweaving show in many parts of the piece, and large areas of this kind of repair appear in the region of the hindquarters of the two upper hounds at the right and the neck of the hound below them. The right side of the man's face and throat also contains passages of reweaving.

A shield-shaped patch of old tapestry with a flowered pattern appears in 25f near the top of the tree trunk at the left. A small, irregularly shaped piece of the same kind of fabric has been patched in above the back of the upper hound. There is also a small patch in the lower right corner. The rider's right leg and foot have been repaired with reweaving and insertions of modern fabric. There are other small spots of reweaving throughout the piece.

All six of the fragments have retained much of their original brilliant coloring. The reds and blues are especially well preserved; the green tones are still distinctly green but less intense than the other hues.

A gentleman on horseback, accompanied by a lady seated behind him, rides out of a castle whose walls rise along the left side of 25a. It has been assumed that this man is the lord of the castle, and he may be; but there is nothing in the scene to identify him in that role rather than the role of a guest at the lord's hunt. His horse has proceeded halfway across a drawbridge spanning the width of a moat. The outer end of the bridge rests on the far bank of a flowered meadow extending toward the right. The near bank of this meadow appears in the immediate foreground. Water from the moat flows off to the right to become or to join a stream running along the bottom of 25b, 25c, and 25f; in 25f it once again joins or becomes a moat passing under a castle drawbridge. At the back of 25a, an open, rolling landscape with a screen of tall trees fills the middle distance. The gentleman wears a short, patterned velvet coat lined with watered silk that shows at the collar (incorrectly restored) and inside the sleeves. The pleated knee-length jacket he wears under the coat is a restoration. A much damaged representation of a falcon appears next to his left hand. A shaggy hat with a wide, upturned brim is tied to his head by a scarf that passes over the brim and crown and under his chin. A number of hunters shown in other tapestries of the period wear similar hats secured to the head in this and other ways. It is not clear whether these hats, which often show bright colors, were made of dyed fur, of cloths with a fur-like finish, or of fabrics covered with short pieces of yarn called "thrums" in English.[1] The lady wears an unpatterned gown girdled at the waist and, on her head, a long hood over a cap. Below the mounted couple a hound sniffs at the drawbridge. To the right a page standing with his back to the observer turns to speak to the rider and points toward the right. He wears hose, a doublet whose full upper sleeves are slashed down the back, shoes with slightly rounded toes, and a small round cap with an upturned brim and a short straight feather rising from the front of the shallow crown. Behind him and slightly to the right stands a falconer wearing an unpatterned knee-length coat lined with watered silk (all much restored) over his hose and doublet. He wears a large hat like the rider's but with the addition of a pair of ostrich plumes that rise from its top in front. A sword hangs at his left side. He holds a falcon on his left wrist and a rod in his right hand.

In the upper right-hand quarter of 25b another mounted gentleman wearing a short patterned velvet coat with hanging sleeves and lined with watered silk rides toward the right. He holds a long rod upright in his right hand and the horse's reins in his left hand; a hunting horn hangs from his girdle. Two greyhounds and a scent hound run free on the flowery meadow in front of him at the edge of the stream that flows across the bottom of the field. A second scent hound, held on a leash by a kennelman walking behind the rider, sniffs the ground just beyond the horse. His master wears an unpatterned, thigh-length jacket through the armholes of which pass the sleeves of his doublet; these, like the doublet sleeves of the page in 25a and many of the men in the other fragments, are wide and loose over the upper arm and gathered in at the elbows, where they meet the tight part of the sleeves that cover the forearms. He wears shoes with rounded toes, a low round cap, a length of cord as a girdle, and a wide-mouthed game or equipment bag on his right hip. He carries a spear over his left shoulder. A wide, rolling landscape opens out beyond the edge of the meadow in the distance.

The scene shown in 25c is set in the midst of a forest. A flowery field occupies most of the space on the far side of the stream that runs across the immediate foreground. At the back of the field rises a thicket of oak and fruit trees in which, at the left and center, appear a rider, three hounds, and a hunter blowing a horn. The rider's head is missing, and the hunter's head is partly missing, along with the top of the field (see Condition). Two other hunters appear in the left foreground. The one standing farther to the left blows his horn while the other holds tightly to the leashes of a pair of agitated hounds. A stag is held at bay in the center of the field. Three large hounds jump up against its body while two others rush in to attack it from the right. At the far right end of the field a gentleman rider, wearing a plain knee-length coat lined with watered silk over a doublet patterned with motifs resembling fleurs-de-lis, rushes in toward the stag. Like the two falconers in 25a, he wears a large shaggy hat tied under the chin with a scarf. His legs are sheathed in tight leather leggings. Just in front of him rises a tree trunk on which once hung a shield and a sword (see Condition). The man blowing the horn in the distance at center left wears hose, and a jacket with slit hanging sleeves over a doublet whose sleeves are cut full over the upper arm and tight over the forearm. The two huntsmen at the left wear doublets with similar sleeves under their thigh-length jackets, hose, and round-toed shoes. The hunter standing farther to the left also has slashed leather leggings.

The action continues in 25d in the midst of the forest. Two hunters and the body of a stag lying on its back occupy the space in the foreground. The man at the left, who wears hose, a plain thigh-length jacket, a low round cap, and a large bag on his right hip, grasps the lower parts of the stag's hind legs. The other man, in hose and a short patterned velvet jerkin over a plain doublet with

sleeves that are slit behind from elbow to shoulder, stands to the right and holds a long arrow in his upraised right hand. This figure, seen from the back, was woven after a version of the cartoon that was used for the figure of the page or valet in 25a, differing only in certain details of costume and the positions of the head and right forearm. The figure holding the stag's legs is essentially the same as the one restraining the two hounds at the left end of 25c and the one walking behind the rider in 25b; details of costume and the positions of the heads and forearms distinguish one figure from the other. As noted above (Condition) the landscape scene that fills the top of the field has been patched in here; it was not part of the original design.

In 25e a hunter wearing a plain knee-length coat lined with watered silk over a slashed doublet, round-toed shoes, and a large shaggy hat over a cap stands in the center of a flower-strewn forest. He holds a spear in his left hand and a dog's leash in his right. In the right foreground a greyhound begins to feed at the neck of a stag's severed head while another hound approaches from the right. Behind them two other hounds stand with necks bent downward. Although the representation of their heads has been cut away with the rest of the fabric along the right edge of the piece, it is clear that they are bending to a meal.

A gentleman hunter on horseback in the center of 25f rides toward the gates of a castle whose walls rise at the right, presumably, but not certainly, the same castle that the rider and his lady left in 25a. The figure in 25f and his mount were woven after the same pattern that served for the hunter and horse in 25a but with some changes in detail. The rider wears the same patterned velvet coat lined with watered silk and the same shaggy hat tied under the chin in both 25a and 25f, and he carries the falcon on his left fist. But the colors of the garments and horse are different, and in 25f the figure of the lady riding behind the man has been eliminated. The horse in 25f is about to place its right front hoof on the end of a drawbridge that spans a moat whose waters—or the waters of the stream that appear along the bottoms of 25a, 25b, and 25c—flow in from the left. A tree trunk rises in the middle distance between the rider and his valet, who brings up the rear. This man has a patterned velvet doublet under a plain thigh-length jacket, a large shaggy hat, a sword, and a hunting horn. He carries a long pole (probably the shaft of a spear) over his right shoulder. The foreparts of two greyhounds on leashes appear in the foreground at the left edge of the hanging.

Forsyth (1951–52, 207) wrote of these tapestries, in the context of stag hunting, that "a medieval hunt is portrayed from the time the lord rides out over the

drawbridge of his château until his return." This implies that the six fragments all belonged to a single set of tapestries dealing with a stag hunt, which we agree they did (see below). However the fact that a lady rides out to the hunt with her male companion in 25a, where they are attended only by a falconer but no one equipped to hunt for stags, and that what appears to be the same man riding back into the castle in 25f wearing a different costume, riding a different horse, without his lady but in the company of a valet fitted out to hunt for stags are apparent discrepancies that must be accounted for. Forsyth also implied that all or most of the key episodes that took place in a late medieval stag hunt are represented in these six hangings. However a number of important incidents are not depicted here.

25a and 25f cannot show the same gentleman at the beginning and end of one and the same hunt even though the figures of the two men were woven after the same pattern. The man in 25a wears a blue coat and rides a brown horse, whereas the man in 25f wears a red and tan coat and rides a spotted white horse. Furthermore, there is a lady mounted behind the hunter in 25a, and the man in 25f rides alone. Unless we accept the unlikely possibility that the designer arbitrarily changed the costume and mount of one of his chief characters in the midst of his story, we must conclude either that these figures represent two different members of one hunting party, who for reasons of industrial economy became twins in the weaver's shop, or that these two riders represent the same man leaving a castle with his lady and falconer in 25a to engage in a hunt on one occasion (the subject of one set of hangings) and on a different occasion (the subject of a separate set of tapestries) entering a castle upon his return from a hunt without a lady but with a valet equipped for stag hunting in 25f. The gentleman leaving the castle in 25a carries a falcon on his fist and takes as his attendants (at least the two who appear in this fragment) only a falconer on foot and a page. There is nothing here to indicate that he is going out to hunt for stags. The presence of the lady suggests that the couple is leaving the castle solely to hunt with falcons, a relatively gentle sport in which ladies often took part.[2] It is therefore tempting to suggest that this piece comes from a different but closely related series of hangings showing a falcon hunt, a series whose other pieces have disappeared. However we have evidence that ladies did accompany gentlemen on hunts for stags and other wild beasts. For example, while most of the fashionable ladies represented in the *Deer Hunt* tapestry in the Victoria and Albert Museum are hunting with falcons, one of them stands immediately next to a dead stag, from whose open belly the hounds are being given their reward. In the three related tapestries whose subjects deal with hunts for boars, bears, otters, swans, as well as hunts with falcons, ladies are shown among the male hunters.[3] Also, we are told that ladies were present at stag drives or hunts that were held within limited boundaries rather than in open spaces and that Margaret of Austria could undo a stag.[4] Therefore it seems that 25a, with its lady hunter and two male falconers, probably did belong to the same set of hangings as 25b–f, which depict only episodes in a stag hunt. It also seems likely that a number of pieces from this series of hangings have not survived (see Related Tapestries). Perhaps one or more of them showed some falconing episodes as adjuncts to the stag hunt for, like the company shown in the London *Deer Hunt* (see note 3), some of the members of the hunting party in 25a–f were equipped to hunt with falcons as well as for a stag. A number of tapestries of the same period seem to show parties prepared to hunt for both beasts and winged quarry.[5]

Some of the incidents that typically occurred in a late medieval stag hunt are depicted in 25a–f. Among contemporary treatises dealing with the subject of the hunt, the most important for purposes of interpreting the tapestries is the *Livre de la chasse,* which Gaston III, comte de Foix, wrote toward the end of the fourteenth century. The count was dubbed "Gaston Phébus" because of his remarkable beauty and noble bearing. His book reflects not only his own extensive firsthand knowledge of the noble sport of hunting wild game of many kinds but also his acquaintance with earlier books on hunting, primarily Henri de Ferrières's *Livre du roy Modus et de la royne Ratio* and Gace de la Buigne's *Roman des déduits et des oiseaux,* both of which were written between ten and thirty years earlier. Gaston's book, which is known today in a number of manuscript examples, comprises eighty-five chapters arranged in four sections or "books." The first section, numbering fourteen chapters, concerns the natures of various tame and wild animals. The thirteen chapters of the second book deal with the characteristics of several breeds of dogs and their training for the hunt. In the third book Gaston devotes twenty-two chapters to the question of training hunters and to the method of hunting by force of hounds, that is, hunting for a variety of wild game with the aid of highly trained dogs of at least five different breeds—the scent hound, the greyhound, the alaunt (related to the wolfhound), the mastiff, and the spaniel. The fourth and last book, numbering thirty-six chapters, deals with methods of hunting by other means including the use of traps, subterfuge, and the crossbow. All the details are there: how to shout the various commands and messages, how to blow signals on the horn, how to train and care for the hounds, how to teach a valet to hunt under a variety of conditions, how to dress for the hunt, how to post the relays along the course the hunters expected the stag to run, how to find a lost trail, how long to keep a stag at bay, how to undo a stag, how to conduct the ritual of rewarding the hounds (the *curée*, or "quarry") and the distribution of meat to the various members of the hunting party—these and a host of other subjects with which the sportsman-hunter must be acquainted.

The sections of Gaston's book that concern stag hunting are lengthy and complex, and his description of a typical hunt includes so many incidents that one cannot begin to guess (and it would be a guess) how many episodes a designer might think necessary to include in his scheme for a series of tapestries, prints, miniatures, or mural paintings based on the theme. W. A. Baillie-Grohman, Forsyth, Freeman, and Digby and Hefford have all written excellent summaries of Gaston's discussion of stag hunting, and the present author refers the reader to them for further details and some illustrations.[6] The most frequently cited and richly illustrated surviving manuscript of *Le livre de la chasse* is an early fifteenth-century example in the Bibliothèque Nationale in Paris (MS fr. 616) which has been published, with illustrations, several times.[7]

Among the numbers of incidents that might be used to illustrate the progress of a typical stag hunt, the Metropolitan Museum's tapestries show six. As already noted, the subject of 25a, a gentleman and his lady leaving a castle in the company of a page and a falconer, indicates that the company would enjoy some falconing during the course of the stag hunt. In 25b a gentleman hunter is shown riding next to a kennelman who has a limer, a specially trained scent hound, on a leash. This may represent one of several moments between the start of the hunt and the goal of bringing the stag to bay. Possibly the limer which found the stag chosen as the day's quarry has been brought forward to trail the beast. Since two greyhounds and a limer appear unleashed in 25b, it seems likely that this hanging illustrates a moment when the hounds have lost the trail, for at the start of the hunt the hounds would still be held in pairs or groups of three by the men stationed as relays along the stag's anticipated path of flight. The long rod the lord carries in his right hand would have served a number of purposes. As Gaston Phébus explained it, a rider would hold the stick in front of him in the woods to keep branches from hitting his face. When changing trails the rider could strike his boot with it to get the hounds' attention and spur them on. If a mount or hound or valet failed to perform as the lord wished, he would be given a light blow with the rod. Finally, Gaston observed, the hand is more adroit if it is holding something.[8]

In 25c the hounds have the stag at bay. The scent hounds and smaller greyhounds have done their work in tracking it down and the larger, heavier greyhounds have been released to attack and hold it until the lord or master of the hunt can ride in and dispatch it with a bow and arrow or a sword. A valet or kennelman who had been posted as a relay restrains another pair of greyhounds in the foreground at the left. Two other hunters, one at the far left and another standing behind him just left of center, lift their horns to blow the notes of the *prise*, the signal that the stag is now held. Other hunters and hounds rush in from the distance at the left to be present at the kill. The rider at the right is probably meant to represent the lord of the manor or the master of the hunt. It is he who will make the final and dangerous approach with his sword, moving in from a direction as much as possible out of the stag's line of sight. The alternative was to shoot the stag from a distance with bow and arrow, a weapon that this hunter appears not to have with him. Gaston described the maneuvers at this stage of the hunt in considerable detail.[9]

After the hapless stag was dispatched the body was usually undone on the spot, and in 25d the men are preparing for that ceremony. Gaston observed that the body could instead be transported to the lord's castle or house, but he thought it was better to undo the stag at the site of the kill. Otherwise the hounds could easily become lazy if they learned that their reward was to be had at home rather than in the field as part of the chase.[10] However a number of works of art of this period show that hunters did not undo the stag where it fell. For example the fifth hanging (20e) in the series of the *Hunt of the Unicorn*, which treats that hunt in terms of a stag hunt, depicts the dead unicorn brought to the castle slung over the back of a horse. Freeman illustrated a woodcut in a book of hours published by Thielman Kerver in Paris in 1504 that shows a dead stag being transported in the same way.[11] Freeman also noted a fifteenth-century description of a hunt by Jacques de Brézé in which the deer was transported whole to the castle, then undone and the *curée* held.[12] However in 25d the huntsman at the left, watched or aided by the page holding a long arrow, is turning the dead stag onto its back prior to undoing it, just as Gaston directed in chapter 40 of *Le livre de la chasse* and as depicted in two other fifteenth-century tapestries.[13]

25e

In 25e only the left-hand part of what must have been a complete representation of the *curée*, or rewarding of the hounds, has survived. The hunter standing in the center of the space holds the leash of a greyhound that chews the neck of the stag's head. What appears to be a scent hound approaches the head from the other side. According to Gaston the head of the slain beast, a highly prized part, was given (along with words of praise) to the limer that had found the stag in its covert.[14] So if this greyhound is indeed being allowed to eat from the head, and not just nibble at it, this representation is unusual. The two hounds in the background (their heads are missing along with the right-hand section of the original hanging) are eating their share of the body parts that were mixed with blood and bread and spread out on the ground on top of the stag's skin as a reward for all the hounds.

The hunter riding into the castle in 25f may be the lord of the manor or one of his guests in the hunting party. As already noted, he could not be the same man who rode out of the castle in 25a. The presence of an attendant equipped for stag hunting suggests that they have just returned from such a hunt even though the rider has his falcon with him. The greyhounds would have been taken along whether the men were hunting for stags or birds or both.

SOURCE OF THE DESIGN

The designer probably based his compositions on the illustrations in a manuscript or printed book dealing with hunts of various kinds, perhaps an edition of Gaston Phébus's treatise. The richly illustrated manuscript in the Bibliothèque Nationale (MS fr. 616; see note 7) contains miniatures that illustrate the subjects of 25d and 25e but the compositions are not the same.[15] Nickel (1968, 83 n. 1, and fig. 40) observed that the figure of the page or valet holding a long arrow in 25d seems to have been based (in reverse) on a similar figure in a woodcut by Urs Graf that was published in Strasbourg in 1508. The two figures are indeed similar, the main difference being that the man in the print bends his torso toward the arrow while the other bends it away.

As noted above (Description and Subject) the figures of the riders in 25a and 25f are the same, and the figures of the pages or valets in 25a and 25d are virtually duplicates of one another, as are the men at the left ends of 25b, 25c, and 25d. This suggests that those figures at least were not derived from a primary source but from stock patterns that belonged to the cartoon painter or the weaver.

MANUFACTURE AND DATE

Forsyth (1951–52, 205) published the tapestries as Franco-Flemish work of the early sixteenth century. Like other millefleurs tapestries of this kind, these were probably woven in the southern Netherlands after designs made in France or for the French market. The fashions in clothing suggest that the pieces could have been designed as early as 1495. Freeman dated the design of the *Hunt of the Unicorn* tapestries (20a–g) about 1500 or a few years before or after that date, perhaps about 1490–1505, based on their relation to a particular group of prints and on the style of the costumes and weapons.[16] Even though the men's garments in 25a–f are much less rich than those in the *Unicorn* tapestries, they are cut in precisely the same way. Freeman's dating is convincing and may be applied to these six fragments as well as to the *Unicorn* tapestries, but allowance should be made for a time lag since the relatively modest execution of 25a–e suggests that they were made for a less wealthy and therefore perhaps less fashionable client. The armorial shields whose traces appear in 25c, 25e, and 25f (see Condition) and which might have helped date the tapestries and even place them geographically were removed at some time in the past, perhaps during or shortly after the French Revolution.

RELATED TAPESTRIES

No other fragments of the set of hangings from which 25a–f come are known to have survived. We have no way of estimating the number of pieces the series would have contained originally, but the missing hangings might well have shown events like the limerer finding the stag in its covert, the hunters' assembly, various incidents in the chase itself, the kill, and probably also some incidental hawking scenes.

A number of tapestries showing episodes in stag hunts against millefleurs grounds and dating from approximately the same period may be cited. The most similar in terms of style are three large fragments in the château de Langeais (Institut de France, Indre-et-Loire) that Jarry published (1972, 47–48). One shows essentially the same scene as 25d, again with the dead beast having been laid on its back in preparation for the undoing; but Jarry referred to it as "la mort du cerf" (the death of the stag). When that tapestry was exhibited in Tournai in 1970, Asselberghs used the same title but noted that two valets have already started to undo the body.[17] A second piece in that group shows the rewarding of the hounds (the *curée*, or "quarry"), and the third shows the presentation of one of the stag's hooves to a hunter. Two hangings showing hunters and hounds in hot pursuit of a stag against a millefleurs ground with a screen of trees across the upper half of the field are known. One was sold in Paris in 1924, and the other is in San Simeon, California.[18] The style of drawing in these two pieces is quite different from that of 25a–f.

HISTORY

Thought to have been bought by Stanford White early in the twentieth century for use in the residence he designed for Mr. and Mrs. Payne Whitney at 972 Fifth Avenue, New York.
In the collection of Mr. and Mrs. Payne Whitney, New York.
Bequeathed to the MMA by Helen Hay Whitney (Mrs. Payne Whitney), 1944.

EXHIBITIONS

None known.

PUBLICATIONS

Forsyth, William H. "The Medieval Stag Hunt." *MMA Bulletin*, n.s. 10 (1951–52) p. 207. 25a–f discussed briefly; 25c–e illus. p. 205.
Nickel, Helmut. "Ceremonial Arrowheads from Bohemia." *Metropolitan Museum Journal* 1 (1968) p. 83 n. 51. 25d mentioned.
Jarry, Madeleine. "La collection de tapisseries du château de Langeais." *Bulletin de la Société de l'Histoire de l'Art Français*, 1972, p. 48. 25a–e mentioned.

NOTES

1. See 20, note 2, in the present catalogue for a discussion of hats like these and a reference to "thrums."
2. See five tapestries in the Metropolitan Museum's collection (in this catalogue, 3a and b, 4, 37, 38) that show ladies training falcons or hunting with them. A tapestry in the William A. Clark Collection in the Corcoran Gallery of Art, Washington, shows two couples on horseback hunting with falcons; see Marvin Chauncey Ross, "Four Tournai Tapestries," *Corcoran Gallery of Art Bulletin* 9, no. 2 (November 1957) fig. 3.
3. The four hunting tapestries are discussed in Digby 1980, cat. nos. 2–5. The *Deer Hunt* is illustrated in pl. 3B, the other three pieces in pls. 2A, 2B, 3A, with details of all four in pls. 4–11.
4. George Wingfield Digby assisted by Wendy Hefford, *The Devonshire Hunting Tapestries*, Victoria and Albert Museum (London, 1971) pp. 44, 48.
5. Among these may be cited a tapestry in the Fogg Museum, Cambridge, that shows two gentlemen and their attendants leaving a castle equipped to hunt for both birds and beasts and a fragmentary piece in the Museum of Art, Rhode Island School of Design, Providence, which shows a man apparently engaged in a stag hunt but turning his head to look at a falcon in flight; for both pieces, see J. P. Asselberghs, *Tapisseries héraldiques et de la vie quotidienne*, exh. cat. (Tournai, 1970) nos. 20, 21, both illus. Another

piece, formerly the property of French and Company, showed among other figures a gentleman riding out of a castle with a falcon on his fist, another mounted hunter blowing a horn, two valets standing nearby with spears and hounds, and a third man setting up a net; see a French and Company photograph, neg. no. 16036, in the J. Paul Getty Center for the History of Art and the Humanities, Santa Monica.
6. W. A. Baillie-Grohman, "The Finest Hunting Manuscript Extant," *Burlington Magazine* 2 (1903) pp. 15–21; William H. Forsyth, "The Medieval Stag Hunt," *MMA Bulletin*, n.s. 10 (1951–52) pp. 203–8; Digby with Hefford, *The Devonshire Hunting Tapestries*, pp. 43–49; and Margaret B. Freeman, *The Unicorn Tapestries*, MMA (New York, 1976) pp. 91–107. All four publications include illustrations from the manuscript in Paris referred to in note 7 below. Early in the fifteenth century, Edward, second duke of York, Master of Game at the court of his cousin Henry IV, translated those parts of Gaston Phébus's book that dealt with the kinds of game and hounds to be found in England at that time, added five chapters of his own, and published his book under the title *The Master of Game*; see W. A. and F. Baillie-Grohman, eds., *The Master of Game* (London, 1904).
7. Concerning MS fr. 616, see especially Gaston Phébus, *Le livre de la chasse*, translated into modern French by Robert and André Bossuat, introduction and commentary by Marcel Thomas ([Paris], 1986), which contains the entire text in modern French and a number of illustrations in color. See also *Livre de la chasse par Gaston Phébus, comte de Foix*, Bibliothèque Nationale (Paris, [1909]), for reduced reproductions in black and white of the eighty-seven miniature paintings. The manuscript has also been published in a facsimile edition as vol. 53 in the Codices Selecti series (Graz, Austria, 1976).
8. *Livre de la chasse*, Bossuat and Thomas eds., p. 117.
9. *Livre de la chasse*, Bossuat and Thomas eds., p. 129.
10. *Livre de la chasse*, Bossuat and Thomas eds., p. 112.
11. Freeman, *Unicorn Tapestries*, p. 107 and fig. 136.
12. Freeman, *Unicorn Tapestries*, p. 107.
13. *Livre de la chasse*, Bossuat and Thomas eds., p. 108. See Digby 1980, pls. 3B and 11, for illustrations of the *Deer Hunt* tapestry in the Victoria and Albert Museum, which shows a dead stag being undone as it lies on its back, a hunter gripping its forelegs. See Asselberghs, *Tapisseries héraldiques*, no. 23, for a similar scene in a tapestry in the château de Langeais.
14. *Livre de la chasse*, Bossuat and Thomas eds., p. 111; see also pl. facing p. 128 (MS fr. 616, fol. 72) showing the *curée* and the stag's head being given to a limer.
15. For the subjects of 25d and 25e, see MS fr. 616, fols. 70 and 72, *Livre de la chasse*, Bossuat and Thomas eds., color illus. facing pp. 121 (showing the master of the hunt and the valets beginning to undo the dead stag, which has been laid on its back) and 128 (showing the hounds eating from the stag's skin at the *curée* and, in the lower right corner, a man placing the stag's head before a limer).
16. Freeman, *Unicorn Tapestries*, pp. 206–7.
17. Asselberghs, *Tapisseries héraldiques*, no. 23, illus.
18. The present author is indebted to Maurice Hudkins, who brought these two tapestries to the Metropolitan Museum's attention and who, with additions from Polly Sartori, contributed notes concerning them to the files (Department of Medieval Art). The first tapestry was sold from the collection of M. L . . . , Hôtel Drouot, Paris, April 11, 1924, no. 100, illus. The other hanging was published by Carleton M. Winslow, Jr., and Nickola L. Frye, *The Enchanted Hill: The Story of Hearst Castle, San Simeon* (Millbrae, Calif., 1980) pp. 99, 109–11, illus. in color.

26

Shield of Arms and Wreath on an Arabesque of Thistle Branches

Cover for a bed or table

The Netherlands (?), 1495–1550
Wool warp, wool wefts
9 ft. 2 in. × 7 ft. (2.79 m × 2.13 m)
12–15 warp yarns per inch, 5–6 per centimeter
Rogers Fund, 1935 (35.67)

CONDITION

The fabric has been cut on all four sides. The edges of both shorter sides have been rewoven along most of their lengths with modern warp and weft yarns. The upper edge (upper in relation to the orientation of the coat of arms) was finished to resemble a selvage. Some two dozen rectangular or irregularly shaped patches of modern weaving have been inserted throughout the piece. There are also small areas of reweaving scattered throughout. Since these seem to follow the original contours of the design, and since the rectangular insertions occur almost entirely in areas of unpatterned ground, the original drawing of the pattern has been affected very little. The colors are fairly bright and fresh throughout.

At some time in the past a lining fabric was sewn against the face of the tapestry and its reverse side was presented to view, presumably because the front had faded and the colors were brighter on the back. That reversal was possible only because the back of the fabric was finished off almost as neatly as the front when the piece was woven, something not encountered often in surviving Netherlandish tapestries of this period. Two small technical details distinguish the back from the front of the fabric. On the back, small loops of yarn appear along lines where double interlocking was used to prevent slits from occurring during the weaving process, and in some areas where hatching was used to blend adjacent color areas, the points where yarns were interchanged are visible. The restorations noted above were executed with the back of the fabric outward, so the raw surface of each repair is visible on the true face of the tapestry. For this reason the piece has been left with its reverse side outward. To show the pattern in its correct left-right orientation in this catalogue, the photographic negative was reversed when it was printed.

DESCRIPTION AND SUBJECT

A number of stalks from a thistle plant, in their natural colors and with cut ends visible in places, have been tied together with ribbons to form an arabesque pattern on the light, unpatterned neutral ground. In some places the outer ends of the stalks sprout fanciful, brightly colored blossoms, most of which have long, twisting pistils. A wreath of laurel leaves, small flowers, and fruits bound with knots of ribbon at the top, bottom, and sides is at the center of the arabesque. Inside the wreath is a rectangular shield of arms. It is blazoned with this coat of arms: parted per pale; dexter, a dimidiation of barry of six, azure and argent; sinister, a dimidiation of azure, a chevron argent accompanied by three garbs or. The owner of this coat of arms has not yet been identified. Because the tapestry was thought to be French when it was acquired, the search was originally limited to families in France. Within that context, the arms in the dexter side have been identified with only one family, the Pequigny.[1] The arms on the sinister side were borne by members of two families, the Cueillette of Burgundy and the Francon of Dauphiné.[2]

The tapestry, which belongs generically to a class of hangings and furnishing fabrics showing armorial bearings in association with fields of verdure (see 19), seems to have been designed to be viewed in a horizontal plane. Although the shield of arms is naturally oriented only in one direction, the arabesque and wreath may be viewed equally well from any direction. Rorimer believed that the patched holes indicate that the piece had been used as a furniture cover, perhaps for a bed. The dimensions of the piece and the character and orientation of the pattern are indeed suitable for a bedcover, but they also answer the requirements of a table cover.

SOURCE OF THE DESIGN

The thistle arabesque probably derives from an ornamental print of the kind produced in Germany during the late fifteenth and early sixteenth centuries by Israhel van Meckenem, the Master b g, the Master h w, and Daniel Hopfer among others.[3] The closest parallel we have found is the pattern in a late fifteenth-century

373

26

Fig. 126. *Ornamental Page with Morris Dancers,* by Israhel van Meckenem. Engraving, Germany, about 1490–1500. MMA, Gift of Henry Walters by exchange, 1931 (31.31.28).

print by Israhel van Meckenem showing a lady surrounded by morris dancers in the midst of an arabesque of spiky thistle or holly branches that grow out of the two main limbs of the tree in which the lady stands (fig. 126).

The stylized and fanciful flowers that grow on some of the stalks in the tapestry also may derive from a German source. They often appear in German and Swiss embroideries and tapestries dating from the second half of the fifteenth century through the first quarter of the seventeenth century. They are sometimes found in association with wreaths enclosing shields of arms against arabesque grounds.[4] These curious flowers appear in an early sixteenth-century south Netherlandish verdure arabesque tapestry then in the Kaiser Friedrich Museum in Berlin which Schottmüller published as being woven after an Italian design influenced by ancient Roman ornaments of the imperial period.[5] The present author believes that although the ultimate source of the arabesque may be found in Roman ornament, the design of the tapestry in Berlin is typically Netherlandish and simply reflects the strong Italian influence that was felt in the north in the early sixteenth century.

MANUFACTURE AND DATE

When the tapestry was sold from the Allenby collection in 1935 (see History), it was attributed to France and dated about 1500. Göbel, in a letter to Harris, expressed the opinion that the piece was woven about 1525, proba-

bly in Tournai or Brussels but possibly in Enghien or Grammont.[6] When Harris published the tapestry in 1936, he used Göbel's suggestion as a tentative attribution. Some months later Marillier observed that the piece might be Dutch, Flemish, or German, the last because the pattern seemed "abnormal"—that is, for Netherlandish tapestries.[7] Rorimer summarized these opinions soon afterward by observing that the tapestry was thought to be German or Flemish work of the sixteenth century.

The fact that the pattern of 26 is closely related to German design sources and the fact that the fabric was finished almost as neatly on the back as on the front—a technical peculiarity one often finds in late medieval German tapestries—argue for an attribution to some tapestry-producing region in Germany. However the warp is made of woolen yarns and not of the linen or other bast fiber yarns that were invariably used for warp yarns in the German regions. Furthermore, we know that tapestry designers and weavers in the southern Netherlands sometimes borrowed figures and figure compositions from German prints (see 36, 48a–d). The pattern of 26 is certainly unusual. Its strong affinity with German sources may indicate simply that it was woven somewhere in the Netherlands away from those centers where French taste held sway, that is, in the northern or eastern Netherlands. The same problem of attribution obtains in another tapestry in the Metropolitan Museum's collection (51). Its pattern shows strong German influence but its structure is characteristically

Netherlandish. Two possible solutions suggest themselves: that tapestries like 26 were woven in the Netherlands for German patrons, or that they were woven in Germany, for German patrons, by emigrant or itinerant Netherlandish weavers.

The related prints, embroideries, and tapestries mentioned above (Source of the Design) indicate that the main pattern elements in the Metropolitan Museum's bed or table cover—the branch arabesque, the wreathed shield, and the fanciful terminal blossoms—were well established in Germany by the end of the fifteenth century and continued to be used there in the textile arts through the early years of the seventeenth century. In the case of 26 it is not the choice of motifs but the strong Gothic flavor of the pattern that argues for a date in the late fifteenth or first half of the sixteenth century. It has been suggested that the series of thistle tapestries that are now in Glasgow, Copenhagen, and Bourges may be associated with two documented purchases of thistle hangings, one in 1503, the other in 1518.[8] Those tapestries show rows of somewhat stylized thistle plants growing upright in the earth. The plants are treated as ornamental motifs in their own right rather than as elements in an artificial confection as they are in 26. Nevertheless, these pieces indicate that tapestries using thistles as motifs were fashionable during the first quarter of the sixteenth century, and there is no reason to think the motif would have passed out of favor suddenly. If the owner of the coat of arms in the center of 26 can be identified, it may be possible to assess the date of manufacture with some degree of precision.

RELATED TAPESTRIES

No other tapestries showing the same pattern are known to have survived. Since this probably served originally as a bed or table cover, it may have belonged to a suite of matching covers for the furniture and walls of a room; that is, a tapestry chamber.

HISTORY

Property of Demotte, Inc., New York.
In the collection of F. S. Allenby, New York.
Sold, *English & French Furniture . . . Property of F. S. Allenby . . . and of Other Owners,* American Art Association, Anderson Galleries, New York, March 29–30, 1935, no. 397, illus. (inverted and with the back of the fabric outward).
Purchased by the MMA, through the Rogers Fund, 1935.

EXHIBITIONS

None known.

PUBLICATIONS

P. S. H. [Paul S. Harris]. "Notes: A Verdure Tapestry." *MMA Bulletin* 31 (1936) pp. 242–44. Discussed in detail; illus. p. 243, with the back of the fabric outward.
Rorimer, James J. *The Cloisters: The Building and the Collection of Mediaeval Art in Fort Tryon Park.* MMA, New York, 1938, p. 104. Discussed briefly; illus. fig. 54 (shown hanging on the wall of the Spanish Room, with the back of the fabric outward).

NOTES

1. J. B. Rietstap, *Armorial Général* (Gouda, 1884–87; reprint, Baltimore, 1972) vol. 2, p. 410. See also Victor Rolland, *Planches de l'Armorial Général de J.-B. Rietstap,* vol. 5 (The Hague, 1921) pl. XXXII (Pequigny).
2. Comte Théodore de Renesse, *Dictionnaire des figures héraldiques* (Brussels, 1894–1903) vol. 3, p. 693. See also Rietstap, *Armorial Général,* vol. 1, pp. 494 (Cueillette), 703 (Francon); and Rolland, *Planches,* vol. 2 (Paris, n.d.), pls. CLX (Cueillette), CCCLVI (Francon).
3. See Peter Jessen, *Der Ornamentstich* (Berlin, 1920) fig. 7, a print by Israhel van Meckenem showing a pair of lovers seated in the midst of scrolling fine-leaved acanthus branches, two of which terminate in fanciful flowers like those in the Metropolitan Museum's tapestry; fig. 3, a wild man climbing scrolling thistle branches, by Master b g; and fig. 5, a lion confronting a buck goat in the midst of an arabesque of thistle or holly branches with cut ends, by Master h w. See also Rudolf Berliner and Gerhart Egger, *Ornamentale Vorlageblätter des 15. bis 19. Jahrhunderts* (Munich, 1981) vols. 1 and 2, nos. 44 and 46, by Daniel Hopfer, ca. 1510 and ca. 1515, illus., showing arabesques of thistle or holly branches.
4. For the embroideries, see Verena Trudel, *Schweizerische Leinenstickereien des Mittelalters und der Renaissance* (Bern, 1954) pls. V, IX, X, XXII, and XXIV, ranging in date from the second half of the fifteenth century to the end of the sixteenth century; and also Jenny Schneider, *Schweizerische Bildstickereien des 16. und 17. Jahrhunderts* (Bern, 1978) nos. 2, 10, and 13, illus., ranging in date from the early sixteenth to early seventeenth century. For examples in tapestry, see Göbel 1934, figs. 51, 69, 75, and 85, ranging in date from the beginning of the sixteenth century to the early seventeenth century.
5. [Frida] Schottmüller, "Kaiser-Friedrich-Museum: Italienische Verdurateppiche," *Amtliche Berichte aus den königlichen Kunstsammlungen* 37 (1915–16) cols. 25–28, fig. 11.
6. Unpublished letter from Heinrich Göbel to Paul S. Harris, dated November 8, 1935, in the files of the MMA Department of Medieval Art.
7. Unpublished letter from H. C. Marillier to Paul S. Harris, dated April 30, 1936, in the files of the MMA Department of Medieval Art.
8. The first reference concerns a series of thistle tapestries ordered by Pierre II, duc de Bourbon, sometime before his death in 1503; see Betty Kurth, "En ukendt fransk Gruppe af Verdurer fra Overgangen til det 16. Aarhundrede," *Kunstmuseets Aarsskrift* (Copenhagen) 27 (1940) pp. 54–60, figs. 6–8, three thistle tapestries illustrated; one in Det Danske Kunstindustrimuseum in Copenhagen, one now in the Burrell Collection, Glasgow, and the third from the Maison Jacques in Bourges, later in the Louvre, Paris. The second reference concerns a series of tapestries that Charles V bought from Pieter van Aelst of Brussels in 1518; see Sophie Schneebalg-Perelman, "Un grand tapissier bruxellois: Pierre d'Enghien dit Pierre van Aelst," *De Bloeitijd van de Vlaamse Tapijtkunst (Internationaal Colloquium, 23–25 mei 1961)* (Brussels, 1969) p. 304 and fig. 11, the piece in the Burrell Collection illustrated.

27
Christ the Judge on the Throne of Majesty and Other Subjects

A composite hanging made up from parts of three or four tapestries

a Scenes from the Story of Esther and Ahasuerus, *left end of an otherwise lost tapestry, joined at its right edge to the leftmost section of a tapestry showing* Christ the Judge on the Throne of Majesty *in its center section*

b Christ the Judge on the Throne of Majesty, *center section whose left and right sections were removed and joined to the right and left edges of 27a and 27c, respectively*

c Scenes from the Story of Charlemagne (?), *right end of an otherwise lost tapestry (perhaps incorporating another part of that tapestry or part of a second lost tapestry with a different subject), joined at its left edge to the rightmost section of a tapestry showing* Christ the Judge on the Throne of Majesty *in its center section*

Southern Netherlands, 1500–1510
Wool warp; wool, silk, and metallic wefts
Entire piece: 11 ft. 8 in. × 30 ft. 3 in. (3.56 m × 9.22 m)
27a: 15–16 warp yarns per inch, 5–6 per centimeter
27b: 15–17 warp yarns per inch, 5–6 per centimeter
27c: 13–18 warp yarns per inch, 4–7 per centimeter
27a: The Cloisters Collection, 1953 (53.80)
27b: The Cloisters Collection, purchase and by exchange, 1953 (53.81)
27c: Gift of George Blumenthal, 1941 (41.100.214)

CONDITION

Parts of three or four different hangings have been joined to make up 27, and except for the fact that the lowest quarter of 27b is missing, each of the pieces is remarkably well preserved in terms of structure and color. The wefts have worn away in some places and left small areas of bare warp yarn. There are small passages of reweaving throughout the three pieces, particularly in the contours, but these repairs have had virtually no effect on the original drawing and modeling. The fabric representing the right shoe of the man digging with a shovel in the upper right-hand compartment of 27a is a modern replacement. The upper and lower borders across the entire hanging have also been replaced, but the main bands in these borders are contemporary with the three fields except for the section directly below 27b,

which is modern. Each band comprises several pieces of varying lengths. Both side borders are original and are an integral part of the fabric adjoining them. In the four corners, they meet the replaced top and bottom borders along the inner edges of the latter. The lower end of the right-hand border was once cut across its width about a foot from the bottom, raised slightly, and then sewn back into place.

The condition of the metallic yarns varies. Some of the gilt yarns (narrow flat gilt-silver wires wrapped spirally on silk core yarns) are still bright, but others have oxidized significantly. Other metallic yarns that now have a dull, grayish blue surface may have been silver originally; it is also possible that they were gilt-silver yarns which lost their surface coating.

The most significant factor in the condition of the piece is the matter of continuity. In 1953 the component parts of the hanging were assembled, and it was presented as a single tapestry. However, our recent examination proves that it was made up from one complete hanging and parts of two or three totally different tapestries. For this reason, it has been impossible for anyone to interpret the iconography of the whole tapestry. In order to understand what is represented, one must consider first how the piece was assembled.

ASSEMBLY OF THE COMPONENT TAPESTRIES

In his first publication on the subject Rorimer (1953–54, 281–84) explained how he put the hanging together. He had recognized that the composition was continuous from the right end of 27a to the left end of 27b, and from the right end of 27b to the left end of 27c. After acquiring 27a and 27b, Rorimer rejoined the edges of the three pieces, and he noted that the fabrics corresponded "perfectly, thread by thread." He also noted that there were earlier joins along the sides of the third and sixth (from the left) columns and interpreted this as evidence that the hanging had been woven in three pieces, on at least three different looms, in order to complete the task as fast as possible. To explain the discrepancy in the warp counts that he measured along these two seam lines, Rorimer wrote that "the number of warp threads had to be increased or decreased as the work progressed so that the component parts would have the same height" and

377

that "medieval warp threads varied in thickness and in tightness of weave." He also referred to descriptions by Göbel of the practice of weaving borders and parts of the field separately on different looms.

While it would have been possible for the hanging to be produced in sections, as Rorimer thought it was, all the technical, iconographic, historical, and stylistic evidence we have argues against his conclusion. A weaver could not add or delete warp yarns in a tapestry of this kind once the warp had been tied to the two beams of the loom and the weaving had begun, and furthermore he would have had no reason to do so: it is neither the absolute number nor the relative diameters of the constituent yarns in a warp that determines the width of the web (and thus the height of the finished hanging) but the width of the warp in the aggregate as it has been installed on the loom. Any variations in the diameters of the individual yarns would have been taken into ac-

count as the width of the web was being established. As for manufacturing a tapestry in parts that would later be joined together, it is true that borders were sometimes woven separately from fields, both in medieval tapestries and in later ones. However those joins were made parallel to the warp and thus could be connected to the field fabric quite easily with needle stitches. The kind of joins that Rorimer envisaged, which we have never encountered in any late medieval tapestry, are quite different: they would require delicate and time-consuming insertions of extra warp and weft yarns to allow the ends of three separate weavings to be connected along lines that run at right angles to the warp rather than parallel to it. Such joins are also different from the kind of insertions (figures let into landscapes woven separately) that Rorimer also cited to support his argument. Finally, there would have been no need to weave 27a–c, which is 30 feet 3 inches (9.22 m) long, in three sections. The

27a–c

tapestry from which the fragments described in 7 came was a bit more than 46 feet (14 m) long, and there is no evidence that it was woven in sections. Any shop equipped to produce a hanging as fine as 27a–c would have had looms capable of accommodating a warp long enough to allow it to be woven in one piece.

The field that has been created by joining the three component parts of 27a–c is cohesive stylistically and iconographically only in the center, between the third and sixth columns, where the joining has reconstituted a triptych-like tapestry we have dubbed *Christ the Judge on the Throne of Majesty.* (We shall refer to it in this entry as the reconstituted tapestry in the center of 27a–c.) The rest of 27a–c is asymmetrical in a way we have not seen in any other tapestry of this kind (see typical examples in figs. 130, 131).[1] Also, while the composite hanging 27a–c shows episodes in relationships that cannot be explained logically, the reconsti-

tuted tapestry in the center shows a meaningful composition within itself, one that has survived also in three other versions. One of them is the so-called Mazarin tapestry in the National Gallery of Art in Washington (fig. 127); the other two versions are in the cathedral of La Seo in Saragossa (fig. 128) and the Musées Royaux d'Art et d'Histoire in Brussels (fig. 129). Earlier writers, specifically Hunter (1912, pl. 371; 1925, 115–16), Rubinstein-Bloch (1927, pl. XI), McCall (1932, 21), and Crick-Kuntziger (exh. cat., Brussels 1935, no. 610), had noticed that the right side of 27a and the left side of 27c repeated the compositions in the outer ends (or "wings" if one understands the field as representing a triptych) of these other three tapestries. What neither they nor Rorimer realized was that 27a and 27c were themselves composite pieces put together from the outer "wings" of the reconstituted tapestry in the center of 27a–c and the left and right ends, respectively, of two

379

27a as received in 1953

completely different tapestries and possibly part of a
third (see Description and Subject).

Apart from considerations of iconography, there are a
number of other observations to indicate that 27a–c was
made up from parts of several different tapestries. The
composition in the reconstituted central tapestry is
more crowded and dense than those in the major portions of 27a and 27c. The heads in the reconstituted
tapestry are slightly smaller than the others, and the
facial types are quite different. The brick-red shadows
on the masonry plate that carries the columns at the
bottom of 27a–c are more faded in the two "wings" of the

reconstituted central tapestry—the bottom of 27b, its
own central section, is missing—than they are in the
main portions of 27a and 27c. Finally, and most important in terms of style, the disposition of compartments
in 27a does not match that in 27c, so that the overall
composition of 27a–c is a jumble of disparate shapes.
Normally, and in every other tapestry of the type that
we know, this kind of composition shows a symmetrical
disposition of compartments (see note 1). Two closely
related tapestries may be cited as examples. One is a
Queen of Sheba Presenting Gifts to Solomon in the
Musée du Louvre (fig. 130); the other, also in the Louvre,

380

27b as received in 1953

shows an unidentified classical subject (fig. 131). There are also versions of these two pieces in the cathedral of La Seo in Saragossa (see Related Tapestries). In those four hangings there is a central compartment that rises the full height of the piece. Narrow flanking compartments rise to two-thirds of the height at left and right. The lintels that separate the tops of these side spaces from the bottoms of the paired spaces above them arch upward in the center (as they do also at the sides of 27a–c), and the inner ends of the lintels are cantilevered out into the central space where they arch again, turn upward, and become colonnettes (as the one at the left

side of 27a–c also does). In all these examples the central compartment is characteristically wider than the others, and it rises the full height of the composition. The compartments flanking it may take a number of forms, but they are invariably mirror images of each other in terms of mass if not detail (see note 1). Therefore we believe that the left-hand two-thirds of 27a originally was the left end and most of the center of some tapestry showing scenes from the story of Esther and Ahasuerus. As for 27c, its right half, which shows an emperor and queen seated beneath an arched lintel that supports two compartments above, came from the right end of some

27c as received in 1941

tapestry where, we believe, it flanked a tall compartment which is now missing. The subject of the complete tapestry is thought to have been the *Story of Charlemagne.* Although there is no visible seam following the column that separates these three compartments from the two bordering them at the left (the upper one showing a boy kneeling and the lower one a group of men standing), it seems possible that the two left-hand compartments come either from a different hanging or a different part of the same hanging, for we have never seen two compartments of less than the full height next to each other, rather than at the sides of a tall compartment, in a tapestry of this kind.

It seems clear that at some time before any of the three pieces, 27a, 27b, or 27c, was published, someone made up for the first time the composite hanging that Rorimer

subsequently reassembled. Although the outer components of 27a and 27c did not come from the cycle of hangings to which the reconstituted tapestry in the center of 27a–c belonged, it would not have been difficult for the first person who assembled these pieces to find three or four contemporary tapestries showing different subjects but having quite similar architectural elements. A number of such pieces have survived, among them the two tapestries in Paris (figs. 130 and 131), in which the stone plate that carries the columns is a duplicate of the one that runs across the bottom of the field in 27a–c. The component parts of 27a, 27b, and 27c shared not only details of this kind but also the palette and the quality of the weaving. Obviously they all came from the same industrial context—that is, the same producer or the same design or weaving shops—and it is

The reconstructed tapestry in the center of 27a–c

not surprising that Rorimer thought the three pieces were parts of a single hanging, especially since they have survived in approximately the same condition. Having been assembled once, this composite hanging was at some later time cut into three pieces but not, as Rorimer observed, along the seams where the three sections (or, as we now know, the three hangings) had been joined to each other. Those seams had been made along both sides of the third column from the left end, the right side of the sixth column, and, we believe, possibly also along one side of the seventh column. The cuts that turned the long pastiche into three separate pieces (that is, 27a, 27b, and 27c as they came to the Metropolitan Museum) were made down the centers of the two columns in the middle of the composition. Those were the two cuts that mutilated the original (now reconstituted) triptych-like

tapestry in the center of 27a–c and gave its left "wing" to 27a and its right "wing" to 27c.

Believing with good reason that he was right to join the edges of the three hangings he had brought together, Rorimer (1953–54, 292) observed (ironically, as it developed) that only after the pieces had been reassembled could one identify certain scenes that had previously frustrated attempts to interpret them and also that only then could one revise earlier interpretations of some of the episodes. However it was precisely because he himself, Freeman, and later writers were struggling to interpret what was in fact three separate tapestries with three or four different subjects rather than, as they believed, a single hanging with one subject, that they found it difficult and in some cases impossible to identify many of the scenes. They expected to find some

Fig. 127. So-called *Triumph of Christ* ("The Mazarin Tapestry"). Tapestry, here attributed to the southern Netherlands, late fifteenth century. National Gallery of Art, Washington; Widener Collection.

common theme that united the episodes. Rorimer and Freeman had trouble trying to explain the scenes dealing with the story of Esther and Ahasuerus in the third (and, Freeman thought, also the second) main bay from the right end since this story had already appeared in the two bays at the far left end of the composite piece. A second problem interfered with their attempts to interpret the hanging. Rorimer had developed an elaborate hypothesis holding that some of the main figures, especially those representing kings and emperors, were portraits of historical characters. For example, Rorimer (1953–54, 287) identified the figure of Ahasuerus in the right-hand section of the tapestry as "Charles VIII, perhaps representing King Ahasuerus."

THE QUESTION OF PORTRAITS

To clarify matters we must eliminate from further consideration the incorrect and distracting notion that the hanging contains portraits of historical figures. Rorimer did not invent the idea. It had appeared in the literature several times before. These earlier studies undoubtedly influenced him even though he cited none of them in the brief bibliography he gave (1953–54, 299) at the end of his article. Ganz, writing in 1925 about 27b in connection with the related hanging in Brussels (fig. 129), noted that some of the faces were similar and that they might be portraits. A few years later McCall (1932, 15–16) noted that Lenoir had written of the Mazarin tapestry (in 1824, a later edition of a work he published in 1819; see

Fig. 128. So-called *Royalty of Christ.* Tapestry, here attributed to the southern Netherlands, early sixteenth century. Museo de la Catedral de La Seo, Saragossa.

note 2) that the marriage of Esther and Ahasuerus in the tapestry symbolized that of Charles VIII and Anne de Bretagne; however McCall believed that if the Ahasuerus and Esther in the tapestry represented any sovereigns at all they would be Philippe le Beau and Juana of Spain rather than Charles and Anne. Rorimer was convinced that the royal figures involved were indeed Charles VIII and Anne de Bretagne, and he proceeded to develop (1953–54, 284–92) an even more complex theory: Charles VIII was depicted as "the principal figure . . . at least five times" in 27a–c and possibly again as King Arthur. Rorimer noted that the king's features changed slightly according to each context, just as they varied somewhat in the three contemporary

painted portraits that Rorimer chose to illustrate (1953–54, 283–85). According to Rorimer, Charles's head with its "large nose and flowing hair" was "somewhat idealized" in the tapestry but could always be recognized by virtue of the crown he wore, which Rorimer described as the royal crown of France, worn over a blue cap. He also characterized blue as the royal color of France and the red and yellow (gold) that appear in Ahasuerus's mantle as well as throughout the tapestry as Charles's own colors. These arguments do not bear scrutiny. The form of Ahasuerus's crown in the tapestry, with its points bearing alternately fleurs-de-lis and fleurons, is simply the standard form used at this time to represent a royal crown, not specifically the crown of the king of France.

385

The red, yellow, blue, and white that, as Rorimer observed, appear throughout the tapestry are the chief colors that were normally used in any Netherlandish tapestry at this time.

Rorimer also claimed that the inscription *karlus,* which is written across Charlemagne's mail skirt in the narrow upper compartment third from the left end, is the key to the identity of Charles VIII in the tapestry. Since neither of the other two Christian Worthies, King Arthur and Godefroy de Bouillon, depicted in the upper compartment fourth from the right end was labeled, Rorimer interpreted this to mean that the designer had singled out Charlemagne as the king's ancestor and namesake. He also called attention to the fact that French kings of the period delighted in identifying themselves with distinguished forebears and with characters from ancient history and the Old Testament. This, he believed, explained the presence in the tapestry of Ahasuerus and Augustus.

Building on the hypothesis that the tapestries contained portraits of contemporary figures, Rorimer wrote (1953–54, 289, 292) that, among the nobles gathered below and to the right of the enthroned Christ in 27b, Margaret of Austria, Charles's first betrothed, was represented (as the young woman standing to the right of the emperor), together with her father, Maximilian (as the king), and her grandfather Frederick III (as the emperor). He supported his identification of Margaret by pointing out that the girl in the tapestry wears a pendant featuring a double-headed eagle and by comparing her head with a contemporary painted portrait of Margaret. In the tall compartment of 27a, Rorimer saw Anne de Beaujeu, Charles's elder sister and regent, as the woman who approaches "her brother's" throne, an identification he supported by illustrating (1953–54, 289) a painted portrait of Anne.

None of these identifications is convincing, either on the basis of contemporary portraiture or, especially, of contemporary history. Rorimer (1953–54, 292) noted that by 1491, when Charles, having renounced his betrothal to Maximilian's daughter Margaret in 1489, married Anne de Bretagne, who had been betrothed to Maximilian, relations between France and the Hapsburgs were strained. To accommodate this problem he theorized that the tapestry must have been in production, if not delivered, before 1491. Shepherd (1961, 171) endorsed Rorimer's identification of Charlemagne in the tapestry as Charles VIII because the king's betrothal to Margaret of Austria united the arms of France with those of the Holy Roman Empire, a union that is expressed in the blazon of Charlemagne's shield. Van Ysselsteyn (1969, 102) believed, as had McCall

(1932, 15–16), that because of the tension the betrothals created between France and the Empire the figures of Esther and Ahasuerus in the Mazarin and Metropolitan Museum tapestries could not represent Charles VIII and Anne de Bretagne. Van Ysselsteyn (1969, 102 and pl. 83) denied Charles VIII any role in 27a–c, substituted Maximilian in his place, introduced Marie de Bourgogne among the historical characters, and wrote further that Philippe le Beau gave the tapestry to his father, Maximilian, "in loving memory of the marriage of the late Mary of Burgundy and Maximilian of Austria."

We agree with Souchal (in Paris 1973, 178) who, in discussing the Mazarin tapestry, referred briefly to these theories and rejected them as "conjectures." Destrée had already discredited Lenoir's hypothesis that there are portraits of Charles, Anne, and Frederick III in the Mazarin tapestry while pointing out that Lenoir had completely missed the point of the central scene showing Christ in majesty.[2] That is another argument we can cite against the notion that 27a–c contains portraits. Furthermore, since the main central section—the reconstituted central part of 27a–c—was woven, albeit with slight variations, at least three other times (see Related Tapestries), it was clearly an industrial product, a stock pattern that any patron could order, and therefore it would not include portraits. The tapestry from the *Legend of Notre-Dame du Sablon* series that is now in the Musées Royaux d'Art et d'Histoire in Brussels (see, in this catalogue, fig. 71), which contains a number of portraits of the imperial family, including Margaret of Austria, as well as of the donor François de Tassis, imperial postmaster, and members of his family, serves as a rare example of the kind of bespoke tapestry that does contain portraits. The features given to portrait figures in such circumstances do not recur on other figures in other parts of the composition. In 27a–c, the face that serves for Ahasuerus in the second bay from the left also serves for the man standing at the far left in the scene in the upper right corner of 27a. King Arthur's face, which Rorimer thought might be a portrait of Charles VIII, recurs as the face of the shopkeeper in the compartment immediately to the left of the one containing Arthur and Godefroy de Bouillon, in the upper left section of 27c.

DESCRIPTION AND SUBJECT

The field is divided into seven major vertical sections, some of which show scenes on two levels. An elaborate system of jeweled columns, lintels, and arches separates the space into eighteen compartments of varying shapes and sizes. A narrow band of ornament flanked by light and dark guards borders the entire field. Stalks and

Fig. 129. So-called *Glorification of Christ*. Tapestry, here attributed to the southern Netherlands, early sixteenth century. Musées Royaux d'Art et d'Histoire, Brussels.

branches of rose, thistle, and grape appear against the dark blue ground of the band. They are tied about with ribbons at intervals and harbor a variety of birds.

In the tall compartment second from the left end a king is seated on his throne and gestures toward a queen who approaches him in an attitude of supplication. She places her left hand on his knee and raises her right hand to her breast. Two helmeted men and a number of other men and women stand in the background watching this encounter. An imposing figure of a man wearing an unpatterned, girdled gown and a hood stands in the left foreground. He places his left hand on his hip and gestures toward the king and queen with his right hand. A page wearing a striped doublet and upper stocks stands in the foreground and removes the top of a covered cup as he looks up at the gesturing man. A collared grey-

hound stands between the page and the steps of the king's dais.

Rorimer (1953–54, 285, 289) referred to the king simply as Charles VIII, not as Ahasuerus, and to the queen as Anne de Beaujeu. Later (1963, 181) he wrote that the scene "may represent Esther and Ahasuerus with Haman standing in the foreground." In this he agreed with Freeman, who wrote (1953–54, 300) that the scene may represent Esther and Ahasuerus with Haman but that "it could be intended as well for Solomon and the Queen of Sheba or King David with Bathsheba, or another famous royal pair." Freeman also observed (1953–54, 301) that in the *Speculum Humanae Salvationis* Solomon's "glory" is "a prefiguration for the 'eternal glory' of the blessed," and that Solomon was a "prototype for the . . . Christ Child." Hunter (1925, 115) and Crick-Kuntziger

387

Fig. 130. *The Queen of Sheba Presenting Gifts to King Solomon.* Tapestry, southern Netherlands, early sixteenth century. Musée du Louvre, Paris.

(exh. cat. Brussels 1935, 60) had both characterized this scene as a representation of Esther pleading with Ahasuerus to rescind the decree he had issued against the Jews. (At the urging of Haman, Ahasuerus's chief official, the king had ordered that all Jews in his kingdom of Persia were to be killed and their possessions taken.) However Esther made her plea during the banquet at which she entertained Ahasuerus and Haman (Esther 7:3–4). It seems more likely that this episode, which is set not in a banqueting hall but at the king's throne, represents instead the moment when Esther invited Ahasuerus, and Haman (the man standing in the left foreground) with him, to her banquet (Esther 5:2–5).

In the upper left corner of the field a king wearing an ermine-lined patterned mantle over a patterned gown is seated on his throne. He holds a scepter in his right hand and gestures with his left hand toward the man kneeling before him at the left. Five men stand in the background. In the compartment to the right the same king is seated at a carpet-covered table before a scribe who is writing

388

Fig. 131. Unidentified classical subject, formerly called *Esther and Ahasuerus* or, in another version, *Jephtha's Daughter*. Tapestry, southern Netherlands, early sixteenth century. Musée du Louvre, Paris.

in a book. A man wearing a hood stands behind the king at the left, and the heads of two ladies wearing caps and hoods appear behind him. A queen wearing a crown over her hood is next to the king at the right, and a bare-headed young man stands next to her. Rorimer did not interpret these episodes in his earlier publication, but in 1963 (180–81) he followed Freeman (1953–54, 300) in saying that the first scene shows Esther's cousin and foster father Mordecai asking Ahasuerus to revoke his order against the Jews and that the second scene shows

the king and queen watching the order of revocation being written. However in the Book of Esther it is not Mordecai but Esther who pleads for the revocation. Hunter (1925, 115) and Crick-Kuntziger (exh. cat. Brussels 1935, 60) described the first scene simply as one showing Mordecai kneeling before Ahasuerus. It probably shows Mordecai coming before the king at Ahasuerus's command when Ahasuerus learned how Mordecai was related to Esther (Esther 8:1). Hunter thought the second scene showed Esther dictating the

Detail of 27a–c

order to revoke the first edict; Crick-Kuntziger suggested that it was Ahasuerus who was dictating. In either case the significance of the scene is clear.

In the main compartment below these two, at the left end of 27a, finished at the top by a jeweled lintel that arches upward in the center, the same king and queen stand on a stepped dais at the left behind a balustrade covered with a length of patterned velvet or damask and in front of another hanging of a similar kind. A page dressed in hose and a patterned velvet doublet stands in the lower left corner. The left thigh of his hose has a pattern that includes in the center the letters REOON, the R, E, and N reversed, the two O's interlocked (see Source of the Design). The boy faces the royal pair but turns his head to gaze at the man genuflecting before them at the right. This man, who wears a patterned coat over his unpatterned gown, holds a hat in his left hand and gestures toward the king with his right hand. A young man wearing a helmet and a short coat grasps the suppliant's left arm. Another helmeted man behind him places his hands on the shoulders of a bearded man who gazes at the king and wrings his hands. Four more men stand in the background at the right and a woman stands behind the king at the left. Hunter (1925, 115), Crick-Kuntziger (exh. cat. Brussels 1935, 60), and Freeman (1953–54, 300) wrote, and we concur, that this scene shows the arrest before Esther and Ahasuerus of the two men in the king's service who had plotted against his life and later were exposed by Mordecai. In the account given in both the Old Testament (Esther 2:21–23) and the Apocrypha (Esther 12), Esther was not mentioned as being present at the interrogation.

The scenes in the three large (below) and six small (above) compartments that follow to the right of this belong to a different tapestry which, thanks to Rorimer's having assembled the component parts, is now complete except for the lower quarter of the central section (27b). This is the reconstituted central part of 27a–c, whose form invites us to regard it as a triptych, with a wide central panel (27b) flanked by a pair of narrow panels or wings.

In the left wing appears an episode in which a young woman kneels before an emperor standing at the left. He wears the imperial crown, a plain ermine-lined mantle over a patterned gown, and a large jeweled brooch on his wide ermine collar. He holds a sword upright in both hands and looks down at the woman. He is labeled *Octavian* by a gilt inscription across his knees. The woman is labeled *sebilla* across the left hip. She wears a plain mantle over a patterned gown which is girdled by a wide sash and, on her head, a kerchief over a cap. She looks up at the emperor and holds her hands in a gesture

signifying that she is talking to him. A group of six men is in the immediate background behind the emperor and four women stand behind the kneeling woman. In the distant background at the right the emperor and kneeling woman appear again, but this time their postures are reversed. The emperor kneels and gazes upward, his hands raised in wonder as he contemplates a vision of the Virgin and Child in the heavens. Almost every writer has accepted this as a representation of the story in the *Legenda Aurea* which tells how the emperor Augustus consulted the Tiburtine Sibyl to find out whether there would ever be a ruler greater than he (see 28 for a discussion of this subject). After a time she showed him a vision of the Virgin and Child in the sky and told him that here was the altar of Heaven and that this Child would be greater than he. Only Destrée, writing about the Mazarin tapestry (fig. 127) in which the figure of Octavian is not labeled but mentioned in the accompanying inscribed plaque, hesitated to affirm that the figures in the foreground were meant to represent the emperor and the Sibyl even while accepting the obvious interpretation of the small scene in the background. He did not believe that the young woman was meant to represent a Sibyl and so suggested that the scene might show David receiving Abigail or Solomon crowning Bathsheba because in the Mazarin piece the man standing behind the kneeling woman holds a crown in his hands.[3] Since the same emperor is labeled *Octavian* in 27a–c, there can be no question that the scene in the foreground refers to Octavian's consultation with the Sibyl. When the related tapestry in Brussels (fig. 129) was catalogued a few years later, Destrée and Van den Ven still did not accept this interpretation. They suggested that the scene in the foreground showed Octavian surrounded by his court and receiving Cleopatra.[4] In his discussion of this scene in the Mazarin tapestry, McCall (1932, 44–45) suggested that the crown held by the man standing behind the emperor and the Sibyl was the crown that Octavian's successor would wear. Souchal (in Paris 1973, 177) accepted the female figure kneeling in the foreground as the Tiburtine Sibyl and agreed with McCall's interpretation of the crown.

In the compartment above this stands the figure of the emperor Charlemagne in front of a patterned velvet hanging. It is not only his shield that identifies him—it shows the arms of the Holy Roman Empire (or, an eagle with two heads displayed sable) dimidiating the arms of France (azure, a semy of fleurs-de-lis or)—but also the name *karlus* inscribed across his thighs. He wears an ermine-lined mantle over full armor and a jeweled hat surmounted by the imperial crown. He holds a sword

Detail of 27a–c

In writing about the Mazarin piece Destrée and, later, Destrée and Van den Ven interpreted the scene as an illustration of the parable likening the kingdom of Heaven to the man who found a treasure buried in a field, buried it again, and then bought the field (Matthew 13:44).[5] At first Crick-Kuntziger (exh. cat. Brussels 1935, 60) accepted this interpretation when writing about 27a, but she later (1956, 25) qualified it as being a possibility, as Freeman (1953–54, 300) also did. Writing about this scene in the Mazarin tapestry, Hunter (1925, 114) and McCall (1932, 45) claimed that it showed workers preparing for the construction of the Ara Coeli on the Capitoline Hill in Rome where Augustus had seen his vision and ordered the structure to be built. Wieck (1975–76, 14), also writing about the Mazarin piece, offered what seems to us a more reasonable interpretation: that is, that the scene illustrates a passage relating to the Second Coming of Christ (Matthew 24:39–42). There it is said that only one of two men in a field would be taken. As Wieck observed, this could explain the surprised expression on the digger's face and the presence of a second man in the woods (the men to be taken and left, respectively). Later Wieck offered another interpretation based on his associating the digger with personifications of labor in a sixteenth-century stained-glass roundel and a woodcut of about 1499.[6] Souchal (in

upright in his right hand. The head and shoulders of a turbaned and moustached man appears next to his left leg.

In the compartment to the right of this, three cloaked men approach a hooded man who is digging in the ground with his shovel. One visitor raises his right hand toward the man and places his left hand on his own breast. The laborer turns to gaze at him and raises his right hand to his head as though in distress or astonishment. There have been a number of attempts to interpret this scene, but to date no explanation that has been offered is wholly convincing. Before examining the matter further, it is important that one take into account the fact that this scene is represented quite differently in the Mazarin tapestry (fig. 127), which we believe shows the cartoon in its original form (see Source of the Design). In the reconstituted central part of 27a–c only one man is shown digging in the woods and just three visitors approach the laborer. In the Mazarin hanging there is another man working in the woods beyond and to the right of the first one, and they have seven visitors.

Detail of 27a–c

Detail of 27a–c

Paris 1973, 177) considered all the opinions that had been expressed before Wieck's and rejected them, concluding instead that the scene must illustrate some unidentified text.

We believe that the scene illustrates not a text but a common late medieval concept of the road to salvation, a concept that is closely associated with the idea of labor. Developing Wieck's association of the figure with the idea of labor, we suggest that the man approaching the digger in the Mazarin piece, 27a–c, and the two other woven versions of this cartoon (figs. 128, 129) represents

the Tempter (or a Vice accompanied in the Mazarin piece by six other Vices, significantly a total of seven figures) who diverts sinful man from the labors he has undertaken as a first step on his way to redemption. The digger's gesture of deference—in the Mazarin tapestry he is clearly lifting his hood, not holding his brow as he does in 27a–c—makes sense in this context. The concept of tempting mankind away from his resolve to be saved in the context of Vices diverting him from his labor is illustrated more than once in contemporary tapestries. In the upper left-central section of the *Vices*

Detail of 27a–c

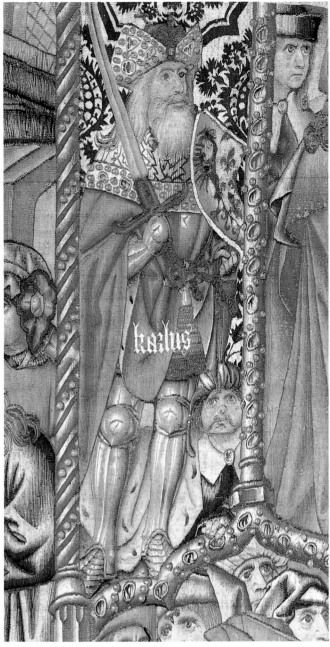

Detail of 27a–c

comparable episode in the upper left corner of a tapestry in the cathedral in Saragossa that shows scenes from the stories of Judas Iscariot and Joseph.[8] If we are right in identifying the digging episode as an allegory of temptation, then this juxtaposition suggests that it may refer here to Judas's being drawn toward the evil that led him to betray Jesus for the thirty pieces of silver (Matthew 26:14–16). However since it is a woman rather than a second male laborer who stands behind the digger here, the episode may refer specifically to Adam and Eve in their fallen state, doomed to labor because of their sin. We believe that the scene balancing this one on the right side of the central section of 27a–c (see below), which shows a young woman leading a young man to a shop dealing in luxury goods, is also an allegorical representation of Temptation.

The next compartment to the right, which rises the full height of the piece, serves as the central panel of the triptych-like tapestry that was reconstituted in the center of 27a–c. The lowest quarter of this section (27b) is missing, but the top and sides of the field are complete. The figure of the youthful Christ enthroned before a cloth of honor appears in the middle at the top. He wears an unpatterned cope with jeweled orphrey and morse over His robe and the imperial crown on His head. He raises His right hand in benediction and places His left hand on a gold-girdled crystal orb that rests on that knee. A host of angels, their hands held in attitudes of prayer, surround Him. Two female figures wearing bonnets and plain mantles over patterned gowns stand before Him at either side. The woman at the left holds a stalk of lilies which identifies her as the personification of Mercy. The woman opposite, holding a sword, is a personification of Justice. A host of people representing churchly and civil society is gathered in the foreground, and all gaze upward at the Savior. To the left of center are the ecclesiastics. A pope wearing a cope over his alb, gloves, and the tiara, and two cardinals in their proper vestments kneel in the foreground. The pope and the cardinal next to him at the left each hold a jeweled processional cross upright. Behind them are a bishop in cope and miter carrying a ceremonial mace and a group of nuns and tonsured monks. Secular society, led by a kneeling emperor and a standing king, appears opposite this group. A queen and a young woman wearing a bonnet stand next to these two men, and behind the women appear a lord wearing an ermine hat, three burghers (one of whom, standing behind and between the king and lord, looks directly out at the observer; see detail illustration and Source of the Design), and, in the rear at the right, a peasant man and woman. The nude figure of Adam, holding a leaf over his genitals, stands in the narrow

Attack Man tapestry in the Fine Arts Museums of San Francisco, *labor* hands *homo,* sitting in the midst of the Vices, a shovel. In the lower right corner of the same composition *homo,* surrounded again by the Vices, leans on his shovel as *labor* walks away from him. The reference also involves Adam who, when expelled from Paradise, was doomed to work the earth in order to live. Adam holds a shovel in the *Prodigal Son* tapestry in the Walters Art Gallery which the Metropolitan Museum exchanged for 27b.[7]

None of the writers who discussed the meaning of this scene in the Mazarin tapestry seems to have found the

Detail of 27a–c

compartment that a branching colonnette forms to the left of Christ, while a nude Eve, holding a leaf in her left hand and the apple in her right hand, stands in the corresponding compartment at the right.

This scene has been interpreted in a variety of ways. It also provides the grounds for naming the tapestries in which it appears. Destrée called the Mazarin piece "The Kingdom of Heaven," while Hunter (1925, 58) and Souchal (in Paris 1973, 174) preferred "The Triumph of Christ," and Thomson (1930, 174) called it "The Adoration of the Eternal Father." Destrée and Van den Ven referred to the tapestry in Brussels as "The Triumph of Christ," but later Crick-Kuntziger (1956, 24) used the title "The Glorification of Christ." The corresponding piece in Saragossa has been called "The Royalty of Christ."[9] Ganz (1925, 304) used that same title in reference to 27b, but it was called "The Triumph of Christ"

by Demotte (1924, 3) and in the Walters Gallery *Handbook* (1936, 84).

The title that Rorimer gave 27a–c, "The Glorification of Charles VIII," does not take this scene into account. He wrote (1953–54, 284) that "we have decided to entitle this tapestry The Glorification of Charles VIII, . . . as we believe the principal figure, . . . appearing at least five times in the tapestry, represents this monarch in his youth," an explanation he later repeated (1963, 178).

Most writers following Rorimer continued to use that title and to ignore the critical importance of the central scene. Wieck, who used Rorimer's title for 27a–c, was the only one among them to study 27a–c in relation to its main subject and, correctly, with reference to that subject as it appears in the Mazarin tapestry and in terms of its relation to the van Eyck altarpiece of the *Adoration of the Holy Lamb* in Ghent. His discussion (1975–76, 9–14) centers on an interpretation of the Mazarin tapestry as not only a Triumph of Christ but also as a reference to the Second Coming as described in Revelation and to the concept of the Millennium which derives from it. Wieck (1975–76, 12) explained that the Last Judgment itself is not shown because this is a representation of only the first Resurrection, the act by which Christ raised the virtuous who would inhabit heaven; later he would raise the damned. Wieck believed that the iconographic details which enable the Mazarin composition to express these secondary meanings are absent in 27a–c. He pointed out that in the Mazarin tapestry Christ holds the Book of the Gospels (a reference to the Book of the Seven Seals) rather than an orb; that there are only four angels (the number in Revelation) surrounding Him rather than a host of angels; that above and around the figure of Christ there is open space showing a sky with clouds in it and a wide landscape below; and also (he believed) that in the lower central section there are a host of people in contemporary costume who were living at the time the tapestry was woven and some of whom could be identified. Wieck (1975–76, 10) also identified the Christ in the Mazarin piece as the Christ of the Second Coming by virtue of his "radiant robes, throne, and cloth of honor, his crown and gesture, and the symbolic sword and lily carried by the angels." Wieck (1975–76, 11) suggested therefore that the Mazarin tapestry shows the Second Coming on earth, whereas 27a–c represents "the celestial court of heaven."

It is true that the angels surrounding the enthroned Christ in 27b block out the distant views of the cloud-filled sky mentioned in Revelation and of the pleasant landscape below which, as Wieck observed, represents the abode on earth of Christ and the blessed. However as

Detail of 27a–c

Detail of 27a–c

398

we shall demonstrate below (Source of the Design) this crowding results not from a deliberate wish on the part of the designer to change the iconography of the tripartite composition of the Mazarin tapestry but to alter the form itself here and there for aesthetic reasons which incidentally altered the logic of the subjects in those places, particularly in this and in the digging and shop scenes. It is true that in 27b Christ holds an orb rather than a book. However this Christ and the Christ in the Saragossa and Brussels tapestries, like the figure in the Mazarin piece, also wears radiant robes, sits on a throne before a cloth of honor, wears the crown and gestures His blessing. The sword and lily are also depicted, albeit held by personifications of Justice and Mercy rather than by angels. The people below wear contemporary costumes because such figures in tapestry designs at this period were normally dressed in this way rather than in archaeologically correct ancient costume. They are to be read no more or less as contemporary figures than those in the Mazarin hanging, and none of them, in any of the four versions, can be identified with any person living at the time the tapestries were woven or designed. They are all meant to represent the blessed who share the glory of heaven with the resurrected Christ. This is clear from the close iconographical relationship that, as Wieck also noted, this composition—whether in the Mazarin piece, 27b, or the pieces in Saragossa and Brussels—shares with the van Eyck altarpiece in Ghent. As Philip has pointed out, the figures of the apostles, prophets, knights, judges, martyrs, pilgrims—representatives of the ecclesiastical and secular worlds—that appear in the lower level of that altarpiece represent the blessed in one of two heavens (the lower of two strata of the "celestial hierarchy") and not people on earth.[10] Philip also discussed the relationship of this image to the concept of the Second Coming (but without a representation of the Last Judgment as such) and furthermore explained how the figures of Church and Synagogue (which appear in the Mazarin hanging but not in the reconstituted central part of 27a–c and the Brussels and Saragossa hangings) also belong to this theme.[11]

As Wieck (1975–76, 9) indicated, the iconography of the Christ in Triumph derives from early Christian representations of the *Majestas Domini* in which the Savior is shown seated on a throne or a globe, blessing with his right hand, and holding the Gospel in his left hand, all sometimes within a glory. This observation is particularly important in relation to 27b and the title that seems to have been given this composition in the early sixteenth century. The comparable piece in Saragossa was listed in the cathedral inventory of 1521 as follows: "Item otro paño grande rico con seda y mucho oro con la historia 'de sede majestatis' en medio a la man drecha la misericordia con un ramo de lirio blanco en la mano y de la otra parte la justicia con una espada en la mano con otras historias" (Item another large tapestry, rich with silk and much gold, with the story "from the seat of majesty" in the center [and] at the right side Mercy with a white lily branch in her hand and on the other side Justice with a sword in her hand [and] with other episodes).[12] Therefore it seems likely that the phrase "de sede majestatis" was used in reference to 27b in the early sixteenth century.

The right-hand wing of the reconstituted central part of 27a–c shows a queen wearing an ermine-lined mantle over a patterned robe genuflecting before a richly dressed, enthroned king. The monarch holds a scepter upright in his right hand, and with his left he hands a ring to the bareheaded elderly man standing next to the throne at the left. A dark bearded man wearing a hat and a simple gown stands behind the throne at the right and watches the action intently. Two other gentlemen and three ladies stand behind the throne in the center and at the left. In the distance at the left two men have met at a table; the hooded man places coins on the table while the other writes on a sheet of paper. In the right foreground of the scene stand three small boys dressed as pages in doublets, hose, cloaks, and hats. In the Mazarin tapestry this episode is represented differently: the king hands the ring to the queen who is seated beside him on a throne and feeds a squirrel perched on her left arm. The same three pages, dressed differently, are also present but they are on the left side of the foreground. A comparable group of lookers-on appears near the throne. The small scene at the back shows not the two men at the table but the queen kneeling before the enthroned king, her hands held in an attitude of prayer.

Writing about the version of the scene in the Mazarin tapestry, Destrée described it as one showing Ahasuerus giving Esther a ring as a symbol of their marriage and, in the background, Esther pleading with Ahasuerus.[13] McCall (1932, 45–46) agreed that the scene refers to the marriage, but Souchal (in Paris 1973, 177–78) preferred to interpret it as one showing Ahasuerus giving his signet ring to Esther and Mordecai so that they could use it to seal a letter revoking the edict against the Jews. The versions of this scene in the tapestries in Brussels and Saragossa match not that in the Mazarin piece but the one in the reconstituted central part of 27a–c. In their description of the Brussels tapestry, Destrée and Van den Ven wrote that the scene in the foreground shows Ahasuerus listening to Esther while in the background two figures seal a letter, perhaps the edict against the

Detail of 27a–c

originally had had no connection with the central or right-hand sections of the composite hanging. Freeman (1953–54, 300) wrote of the scene that it may show Esther interceding with the king while in the background Haman pays a bribe into the royal treasury. Rorimer (1953–54, 287) illustrated a detail of the king's head in that episode and captioned it as "Charles VIII, perhaps representing King Ahasuerus." Later (1963, 181) he wrote that the story of Esther and Ahasuerus continues in this part of the tapestry. We believe that the episode must be interpreted in terms of the interplay that is taking place between Ahasuerus and Mordecai, the elderly man standing next to the throne at the left. None of the writers who have discussed 27a–c noted that the king is in fact handing a ring to Esther's relative. It is undoubtedly Ahasuerus's signet ring which, as Souchal has already noted, he is giving to Esther in the Mazarin tapestry. However in the version of the scene in 27a–c and in the Brussels and Saragossa pieces, Ahasuerus gives the ring to Mordecai (Esther 8:2). Finally, we believe that Freeman (1953–54, 300) had identified the scene in the distance at the left correctly. It surely refers to Haman's offer to pay ten thousand talents of silver into the royal treasury at the time he urged Ahasuerus to order the destruction of the Jews (Esther 3:9–10).

Above this compartment appear two smaller ones separated by a colonnette rising from the arched lintel below. In the left compartment, a lady dressed in a watered silk gown and a bonnet with a veil at the back stands before the counter of a draper's or upholsterer's shop and touches a partially unrolled bolt of cloth with her right hand. Another lady standing behind her gestures toward the shopkeeper behind the counter and seems to be engaged in conversation with him. Bolts of cloth fill the shelves at the back of the shop. A young man with long curling hair, wearing a wide-sleeved coat over his robe and a fur or thrum hat on his head, stands in the background at the left.

This scene, like the corresponding one at the left, which shows the laborer digging in the earth, deviates significantly from the representation in the Mazarin tapestry (fig. 127) from which both scenes were derived. In the Mazarin tapestry, it is a young woman who tends the counter while a young man behind her reaches up to the shelves for a bolt of cloth. The lady customer rests her left hand on the counter but turns away from it and places her right hand on the arm of a richly dressed young gentleman who gazes intently at her as he lifts his hat. Six other figures (a lady and five gentlemen) stand immediately behind this pair. Here also is the explanation of the colonnette that seems so illogically placed near the right side of the scene in 27a–c: in the Mazarin

Jews.[14] Crick-Kuntziger (1956, 25) simply noted that the episode shows Ahasuerus receiving the kneeling Esther in the presence of Mordecai.

Rorimer and Freeman hesitated at first to recognize this as a scene from the story of Esther and Ahasuerus because five scenes from that story were already shown at the left end of 27a–c. They did not realize that those scenes had been taken from a different tapestry which

Detail of 27a–c

Detail of 27a–c

tapestry it is the post that supports the end of the counter and, presumably, continues upward to meet the shop's roof or ceiling.

This shop scene, like the digging scene, has been interpreted in several different ways. Destrée, writing about the Mazarin piece and also the related one in Brussels, identified the shop scene as one illustrating the parable that likens the kingdom of Heaven to a merchant who searches for fine pearls and who, finding a particularly valuable one, sells all he owns and buys it (Matthew 13:45–46).[15] Later Hunter (1925, 112) and McCall (1932, 46) interpreted the scene in the Mazarin tapestry as one showing Esther making preparations for the banquet to which she invited Ahasuerus and Haman, while Thomson (1930, 174–77) in his discussion of the same piece thought it showed the treasure closet containing the fine hangings and vessels that Ahasuerus used for the banquet he gave for the people in his capital of Susa (Esther 1:6–7). Freeman (1953–54, 300) considered these suggestions but preferred to interpret the scene as an illustration of the parable likening a man who has learned about the kingdom of Heaven to a householder who can bring forth from his store both the new and the old (Matthew 13:52). Crick-Kuntziger (1956, 25) made

the same suggestion in reference to the related tapestry in Brussels. Souchal (in Paris 1973, 178) rejected all of these theories and suggested that this, like the digging scene, illustrates some text we have not yet identified. Wieck (1975–76, 14) suggested that the scene in the Mazarin tapestry may illustrate the parable concerning a master who, before going abroad, puts his capital into the hands of his servants and then returns to settle accounts with them (Matthew 25:14–28). Wieck proposed that the young woman in front of the counter might be one of the servants who had invested profitably in the textile trade and that the young man tipping his hat to her might be the master's messenger. Later he suggested that the image might have been included as an iconographic pendant to the digging scene at the left —that one representing the laborers in society, this one the merchants.[16]

We believe that the shop scene in the Mazarin piece is indeed a pendant to the digging scene but not in the sense Wieck suggested. Rather, it seems to repeat the idea that temptations lead Man away from his salvation. Here, the Tempter of the digging scene becomes the Temptress, the young lady who leads the richly dressed and entranced (lifting his hat and bowing) young man—

a type of the Prodigal Son—to indulge in extravagance, to separate him from his money. There are six people who accompany her, making a total of seven. Like the seven figures who approach the laborer in the woods, these may be the seven Vices. Wieck (1975–76, 15 n. 35) suggested that the right side of the Mazarin tapestry, with the figures of Eve, Esther, and what he interpreted as the female servant who had done well with her investments, was the "female" side of the composition as opposed to the left side, the "male" side, where Adam, Augustus, and the male laborers appear. The suggestion seems reasonable. If our interpretation of the shop scene is correct, it reinforces his argument.

To the right of the shop scene in 27a–c is a narrow compartment containing the figures of two men. The one standing in the foreground wears a plain mantle over jerkin and hose and a crown on his head. He holds a scepter in his right hand, and there is a shield buckled around his neck and hanging over his left shoulder. The blazon (azure three crowns or, two in chief one in point) identify him as King Arthur. The other man, whose head and shoulders are visible, wears a hat and holds a shield in his right hand. De Vaivre (1974, 13 n. 66) believed that the object was not a shield but a book (see Source of the Design); however he agreed that it bore a blazon. He described the arms (which are half hidden in this image) as "parted gules with a fess argent and argent with a cross potency or accompanied by small crosses of the same." This is the blazon associated with Godefroy de Bouillon. Here then are the other two Christian Worthies to balance Charlemagne, who appears in the compartment at the left end of the reconstituted central part of 27a–c, next to the digging scene.

The compartment to the right of the one with the two Christian Worthies and the compartment immediately below it do not belong with the reconstituted central tapestry but either to the tapestry of which the right end of 27c was the right-hand section or to yet another tapestry that contributed part of its fabric to serve as the central section of 27c. (In other words we believe that 27c could have been made up from parts of three, rather than two, tapestries.) We have not found any evidence of seaming along the right side of this section but the matter is still under investigation.

The upper compartment contains a scene centered around the figure of a bareheaded boy who kneels before a hooded man wearing a patterned gown and holding an open book in his hands. The boy, who wears a plain mantle over a patterned tunic, raises his right hand toward the book while a man kneeling behind him places his right hand on the boy's shoulder. Four other men, all wearing mantles and hats or hoods, stand in the background and watch the action. The rightmost one holds a sword upright. Rubinstein-Bloch (1927, pl. XI) interpreted this as an episode showing a young man being baptized, but she offered no specific identifications of the figures. Freeman (1953–54, 300–301) thought that it showed the king of Moab sacrificing his eldest son as a means of saving his people who were dying in a siege (4 Kings 3:26–27) and added that in chapter 23 of the *Speculum Humanae Salvationis* this sacrifice was cited as a prefiguration of the Crucifixion. It seems unlikely that either one of these suggestions is correct. There is no font or container of chrysm to suggest a baptism, and while the sword suggests a slaying rather than a baptism, the passage in the Old Testament that refers to Moab's sacrifice specifically states that it was offered on the city wall. We do not know what this episode depicted in 27c represents. The possibility that it shows the boy Samuel being presented for service in the Temple comes to mind, but there is no clear context in the tapestry to help us evaluate the likelihood of that identification.

The episode below with the kneeling boy also may or may not belong with the three episodes that appear at the right. It shows a man wearing a plain mantle lined with watered silk over a knee-length patterned velvet tunic, boots, and a turban on his head, standing at the right. In his right hand he carries a heavy gilt scepter in the form of a column with an eagle standing on its capital. A small dog lies curled on the floor at his feet. Behind the dog stands a man wearing a simple girded robe and a hood; he gazes at the turbaned man and raises his right hand as though addressing him. Two other men stand at either side in the immediate background and behind them appear two more men and a woman. Freeman (1953–54, 300), believing that this compartment belonged with the compartment at the left, suggested that this scene may represent another episode in the story of Esther and Ahasuerus, Haman plotting against the Jews in Persia. We know now that the two fabrics do not belong together, and therefore that there is no connection between their subjects.

The last section of 27a–c at the right end is composed like the section at the left end. There are a tall, wide compartment below and two smaller compartments above. A lintel that rises in the center to form an arch separates the two levels. The scene in the lower compartment shows an elderly bearded man seated on a throne in the left foreground. He wears the imperial crown and a plain mantle with a jeweled border and an ermine cape collar over a patterned gown. Beneath his feet a patterned carpet covers the tiled floor. Around his neck is a ceremonial collar from which hang oval and

Detail of 27a–c

lily-shaped jewels at the sides and a double-headed eagle at the center in front. A woman wearing an elaborate crown and an ermine-caped, jewel-bordered and patterned mantle over her plain fitted gown is seated on the throne next to the emperor. They appear to be engaged in a conversation that concerns the richly dressed young girl who stands before them and gazes up at the emperor. Two young women kneel behind the girl and gaze upward at the eagle flying above the queen and holding a dove in its claws. The dove has an olive branch in its beak. In the background, outside the building in which the action takes place, is a group of men and women. Some of them watch the figures inside, but others look at the birds.

Until Rorimer assembled the three fragmentary tapestries to form 27a–c, he (1947, caption fig. 13) and every other writer identified this scene as one dealing with the story of Charlemagne. Neither Hunter (1912, 371) nor Rubinstein-Bloch (1927, pl. xi) had any question of it. However since Rorimer and Freeman believed that Rorimer had reassembled what was originally a single tapestry, they were obliged to find a different interpretation for this scene. Freeman (1953–54, 300) suggested that the emperor here is more likely Augustus than Charlemagne, that the woman seated beside him may be his sister Octavia, and that it is the imperial eagle with the dove of peace flying above. Rorimer (1963, 181) repeated this identification of the emperor and eagle but did not mention Octavia. Since the emperor's collar has what may be fleurs-de-lis along with the double-headed eagle—the two charges that represent France and the Holy Roman Empire on Charlemagne's shield—

Detail of 27a–c

Detail of 27a–c

the man may be Charlemagne. The other figures are not so easy to name. Rubinstein-Bloch (1927, pl. XI) suggested that the woman seated next to the emperor is Irene, empress of Constantinople, and that the girl standing before them represents Rothrude, the daughter of Charlemagne to whom Irene's son Constantine IV was betrothed in an effort to avoid a confrontation in Italy between the eastern and western factions. If that was true, then the eagle with the dove of peace would symbolize the peaceful alliance between the two parts of the empire. Rubinstein-Bloch acknowledged that this suggestion was not offered as a final interpretation.

In the left-hand compartment above this one four young women, all wearing hoods and plain fitted gowns, surround a younger girl who sits at the right and takes clumps of loose fiber out of a basket and gathers it in her lap. She wears a hooded bonnet with a deep crown, and her gown is of watered silk. The woman in the immediate foreground at the left is talking to the girl, and the woman behind her is manipulating a clump of fiber. Another basket of fiber stands in the center foreground. Hunter did not offer an interpretation for this scene, but Rubinstein-Bloch (1927, pl. XI) suggested that it shows young ladies combing wool in honor of the month of May, the month associated with the Virgin Mary. Freeman (1953–54, 300) and Rorimer (1963, 181) suggested that this scene may represent Tubalcain's sister Noema and her ladies, the Naamah of the Old Testament (Genesis 4:22), who in the *Legenda Aurea* was said to have founded the craft of making textiles. It seems more likely to us that the scene, if this end of 27a–c concerns Charlemagne, shows young ladies being instructed in the art of working wool or some other textile fiber in one of the schools that Charlemagne, in the legends that grew up around him, was said to have established.[17]

In the compartment occupying the upper right corner of the hanging, the same emperor as the one in the large compartment below stands at the right and gestures as though directing the work of a young man dressed in doublet, hose, and an apron who is about to strike the base of a golden figure with what appears to be a chisel and a mallet. The figure, which represents a warrior standing with a shield in his left hand and a standard pole in his right, is set atop the arm of a throne. Three other men watch the action of the young man from the background. Rubinstein-Bloch (1927, pl. XI) thought that the young man was destroying an idol at Charlemagne's command. Freeman (1953–54, 300), who believed that the emperor represents Augustus, suggested that this scene shows him directing work on the Ara Coeli, which he had ordered built in Rome on the site where he had had his vision. She wrote that it might

also refer to Tubalcain, who, in the Old Testament (Genesis 4:22), was the master metalsmith, and in the *Legenda Aurea*, the first man to make metal sculptures. Rorimer (1963, 182) added the observation that the skills of Tubalcain and Noema represent some of the joys of the blessed in Paradise. However since this part of 27a–c was not originally associated with the view of the redeemed in Heaven that 27b offers, and since the emperor may not represent Augustus, neither Rorimer's suggestion nor Freeman's seems correct. Rubinstein-Bloch's interpretation may be the right one because the Charlemagne of the legends is credited with having destroyed the cult of idols. However none of the scenes at this end of 27a–c offers evidence that the emperor represented here is undoubtedly Charlemagne rather than Augustus, Caesar, Trajan, or any of the other emperors who appear in tapestries of this period.

SOURCE OF THE DESIGN

In this catalogue entry we have brought to light the fact that 27a–c was not woven as a single hanging. As the eye moves from one component weaving to the next, one perceives, among other variations, slight differences in the facial types, the scale of the figures, the density of their arrangement, and the details of the architectural elements. However there is nothing to indicate that the component parts were necessarily designed by different artists or design shops. They simply represent three or perhaps four different tapestries.

Hunter (1925, pl. XVIII,ea) interpreted the letters RE-OON (the R, E, and N reversed) decorating the thigh of the page's hose in the lower left corner of 27a as the signature of Jan van Roome, the artist who is documented as having designed the *Legend of Herkinbald* tapestry in Brussels (see fig. 70 in this catalogue). Soon afterward Rubinstein-Bloch (1927, pl. XI) wrote that no one knew who the designer of 27c was and that Jan van Roome was the name most often associated with that hanging. Crick-Kuntziger did not address the question of the designer's name when 27a was exhibited in Brussels in 1935 (exh. cat., no. 610), nor did she suggest a name for the designer of the tapestry in Brussels that is a near-duplicate of the reconstituted central part of 27a–c when she catalogued it (1956, no. 8) some twenty years later. Rorimer (1953–54, 295–99), following Hunter, was convinced that van Roome had designed 27a–c. He called attention to the "signature" REOON (the R, E, N reversed) on the page's hose and also compared the style of the Mazarin tapestry and of 27a–c to that of the Metropolitan Museum's *Fall and Redemption of Man* (15), which, Rorimer thought, bears van Roome's signature in the form of an inscription that had been read as ROEM. However, as Steppe (1976, 202–6, 210) has clearly shown, neither one of those inscriptions can be read as a name or accepted as the signature of Jan van Roome. Verdier (1955, 48 n. 27) placed the Mazarin tapestry in a group of hangings he attributed to Jan van Roome, but he listed 27a–c in a different group which he considered to be less certainly the work of this designer and perhaps instead the work of the Master of the Combat of the Virtues and Vices. Souchal (in Paris 1973, 180), in her discussion of the Mazarin tapestry, noted that the names of Hans Memling, Gerard David, and Quentin Massys had all been suggested as the designer but she did not accept any of them. She believed that the man who had designed the *Story of the Virgin* tapestries (the so-called *paños de oro*) in the Patrimonio Nacional in Madrid had also designed the Mazarin tapestry and thought that he might perhaps be identified as Jan van Roome. She wrote that the faces in the Mazarin piece have the dreamy and absent air of the faces of Jan van Roome's characters but also that there were notable differences between this tapestry and the *Herkinbald* piece, differences that perhaps could be attributed to the artist's development during the years between about 1490 and 1513.

We believe that the stylistic character of a single tapestry, the *Herkinbald* piece in Brussels, is not enough on which to develop a set of criteria that one may use in judging the same artist's work in other tapestries, especially tapestries woven at an earlier time. Apart from the usual problems one encounters when attempting to make such judgments in reference to panel paintings, there is in the art of tapestry the additional problem of accounting for the possibility that the cartoon painter (who, in the case of the *Herkinbald* tapestry, we know was not van Roome) may have contributed something of his own which would affect the appearance of the finished product. Hundreds of surviving tapestries show a generic style to which 27a–c is more closely related than it is to the *Herkinbald* piece. It seems obvious that many designers were involved in the creation and dissemination of this style. Given the imperfect state of our knowledge at present, we do not see how an individual name can be singled out as the designer of 27a–c. Rorimer (1953–54, 297) believed that the man who gazes directly out at the observer from his position below the enthroned Christ and the figure of Justice in the center of 27a–c may be a self-portrait of the artist. Verdier (1955, 48 n. 32) said the same of a man wearing what he called a "painter's cap" in the lower left corner of the *Prodigal Son* tapestry in Baltimore, adding that the man bears a striking resemblance to the man in 27a–c. We

believe that what may create this impression is not any real similarity in the features but rather the fact that the heads in the two tapestries happen to be placed in similar poses and have the same type of face. Rorimer's suggestion may be worth considering further; however we must note here that the man who appears in the same pose in the Mazarin tapestry has a totally different face.

Although we cannot name the designer of 27a–c and the pieces in Saragossa and Brussels (figs. 128, 129) that nearly duplicate its reconstituted central section, it is clear that those two pieces and the central part of 27a–c were woven after variant cartoons of the one that served for the Mazarin tapestry (fig. 127). A number of observations make this dependence clear. The figures needed to understand the digging and shop scenes are present in the Mazarin piece but not in the other three. The post that holds up the forward corner of the counter in the shop scene is logically represented in the Mazarin tapestry but misrepresented as another colonnette in the system of compartments in the reconstituted central part of 27a–c and the version in Brussels and only ambivalently understood in the piece in Saragossa. The man who stands behind the kneeling woman in the Augustus and Sibyl scene in the Mazarin tapestry holds a crown (presumably for the emperor's successor), which is a significant detail in the narrative, whereas in the other three hangings he holds a hat. Most important of all, the designer of these three pieces vitiated the power and significance of the space around the enthroned Christ by compressing it through the addition of the abutting compartments containing Adam and Eve, just as he had forced elisions in the digging and shop scenes by introducing the abutting compartments containing the figures of the three Christian Worthies. Furthermore this compression in the center forced the two groups of the blessed closer together below, and as a result their gaze seems no longer to rest on the figure of Christ. There is a clarity of form in the master design—the cartoon after which the Mazarin tapestry was woven—that expresses its content clearly. The clarity of both the form and the content has been diminished in the derivative designs.

The central part of the composition, showing the enthroned Christ in majesty, angels, Adam, Eve, and the ecclesiastical and civilian blessed, depends ultimately on two formal prototypes. The first, from which the figures of Christ and Adam and Eve come, and also the general concept of the elect arranged below them, is found in the van Eyck altarpiece of the *Adoration of the Holy Lamb* in Ghent. The other, from which derives the composition uniting the Savior, the angels, and the two groups of the blessed, is found in the class of paintings that Panofsky called the "new style" All Saints composi-

Detail of 27a–c

tion. In the form of the Adoration of the Trinity, these showed groups of the elect representing various ranks of ecclesiastical and secular society gathered below another heavenly space in which the Trinity, Mary, John the Baptist, angels, and other exalted figures appear. The example most germane to the reconstituted central part of 27a–c and its related pieces, though later than the tapestry designs, is Albrecht Dürer's *Adoration of the Trinity* (the Landauer Altarpiece) in the Gemäldegalerie in Vienna. Related compositions appeared concurrently with the tapestries in the art of book illustration.[18]

Souchal (in Paris 1973, 177) thought that the figure of the Sibyl in the scene at the left was woven after a cartoon that had been designed for some other purpose, but she did not develop her point. De Vaivre (1974, 9, 13 n. 66) suggested that the figures of Godefroy de Bouillon and King Arthur may have been designed originally to represent a herald of arms and a king of arms rather than

Worthies. Verdier (1955, 57 n. 117) believed that four of the figures in the *Prodigal Son* tapestry in Baltimore appear again, slightly changed, among the blessed in the center of 27a–c. It is certainly possible, even likely, that certain figures in 27a–c were based on stock images.

MANUFACTURE AND DATE

Demotte (1924, 3) attributed 27b to Brussels at the end of the fifteenth century. Ganz (1925, 304–5) also ascribed it to Brussels and dated it "15th–16th century," and he called 27c Flemish work of the end of the fifteenth century. Rubinstein-Bloch (1927, pl. XI) published 27c as Brussels work of the early sixteenth century, which is the same attribution Crick-Kuntizger offered for 27a when it was exhibited in Brussels in 1935. 27c was given the same attribution when it was exhibited at the Metropolitan Museum in 1943, and Rorimer (1947, fig. 13) published it as Brussels work of about 1500.

After 27a–c had been assembled and Rorimer developed his theory that it contained a number of portrait figures, he (1953–54, 292) indicated that it must have been nearly completed, if not delivered, by 1491. At that time, after Charles VIII's betrothal to the young Margaret of Austria had been repudiated, he married Anne de Bretagne, and, Rorimer argued, the relations between France and the imperial family would have been too strained to permit portraits of Margaret, Maximilian, and Frederick III to be included in the design. Believing that it took about two years for the weavers to produce the hanging, Rorimer concluded that the design must have been completed by 1489. Furthermore he believed (1953–54, 293–95) that 27a–c antedated the pieces now in Saragossa and Brussels because in the former the figure he identified as Margaret was no longer wearing the double-headed eagle pendant (she having married Juan de Aragón in 1496) and because he believed the design had been changed in order to make the characters and the crowns look specifically Spanish. He regarded the piece in Brussels as a "crude follower" of 27a–c. Rorimer did not state flatly that he believed 27a–c antedated the Mazarin tapestry too, but he implied it when he captioned (1953–54, 291) illustrations of the Brussels and Mazarin tapestries as "following our tapestry." Also, he stated (1953–54, 294–95) that the design of the central scene and the Augustus and digging scenes in the Mazarin piece depended on the cartoons that had served for 27a–c but that the design of the scene at the right showing the presentation of the ring had to be changed in the Mazarin tapestry because in that scene (he believed) Esther and Ahasuerus represent Charles

Detail of 27a–c

VIII and Anne de Bretagne, and therefore the figure of Margaret (of Austria) had to be replaced with the figure of a kneeling courtier. Souchal (in Paris 1973, 175–80) attributed the Mazarin tapestry to Brussels on the grounds that its extremely refined workmanship is analogous to that of the *Mass of Saint Gregory* tapestry in Madrid, which is believed to be Brussels work because the letters BRVXEL appear inscribed among others on the border of the celebrant's alb.[19] She believed that the Mazarin piece must have been designed no later than about 1490 because the particular kind of head-dresses the women wear were hardly ever represented at the very end of the century.

While the execution of each of the component parts of 27a–c is of the type and quality that has traditionally been ascribed to Brussels, we cannot be sure that tapestries of this class were not also being woven in other centers in the southern Netherlands at this time. As for the date of the design and weaving, the women's high-crowned bonnets worn well back on the head show a fashion of the last decade of the fifteenth century and the early years of the next, while their gowns, which have fitted waists, with no suggestion of a small hump just below the waist at the back, and loose overgar-ments, show a fashion that began in the first decade of the sixteenth century.[20] Since all the parts of 27a–c are richly woven and qualify as luxury products, they were surely owned by fashionable patrons. Therefore it seems reasonable to suggest that they could have been de-signed as early as 1500 and woven within the following decade.

RELATED TAPESTRIES

We have not found any other hangings that show the compositions in the left-hand two-thirds of 27a or the right-hand two-thirds of 27c. As noted above, two other versions of the reconstituted central part of 27a–c have survived, one in the cathedral of La Seo in Saragossa (fig. 128), the other in the Musées Royaux d'Art et d'Histoire in Brussels (fig. 129).[21] We discussed above (Source of the Design) most of the ways in which the images in these three hangings differ from those in the Mazarin tapestry (fig. 127), which represents the primary design of which the other three are versions. One of the most important differences concerns the treatment of the figures of Adam and Eve which appear not only in these three tapestries but also in at least three others from the same period.[22] In 27a–c and the tapestries in Brussels and Saragossa, the two figures are represented as real human beings in landscape settings, each prominently placed in its own compartment on a level with the Savior. In the Mazarin design they appear as two small polychrome sculptures set in niches on the columns that rise at the far left and right ends of the field. Two other figures of this kind, Church and Synagogue, occupy niches on the two inner columns. These two figures do not appear at all in 27a–c and the Saragossa and Brussels versions. It is also important to note that the inscribed plaques suspended from the arches above the side scenes in the Mazarin tapestry do not appear in the other three pieces.

The Brussels and Saragossa tapestries differ from each other and from 27a–c in a number of ways. While the figure of Eve is the same in all three pieces, the Adam in the Saragossa tapestry is walking forward and his right hand is raised at the wrist, whereas in the other two pieces both feet are planted squarely on the ground in a static posture and his hand drops slightly from the wrist. In the three main scenes of the Saragossa piece the ground below the figures is represented as a flowery meadow. The Brussels hanging shows the figures standing or kneeling on interior patterned floors as 27a–c also does. The borders are different in all three pieces. The border of the Brussels tapestry is thinner and simpler than the border of 27a–c, and it contains neither ribbons nor birds. The Saragossa border is much more dense and bushy than the one enframing 27a–c but, like it, contains birds.

The reconstituted central part of 27a–c and the three tapestries in Washington, Brussels, and Saragossa could be regarded as woven retables, each complete in its own right, without reference to any companion pieces. However, while the Mazarin tapestry may have been intended to hang alone, the presence of the three Christian Worthies in the other pieces suggests that they may have belonged to a cycle of three related hangings celebrating subjects from the Pagan, Hebrew, and Christian laws. Tapestries that may have belonged to

such a series have survived. Two are in the cathedral of La Seo in Saragossa, and two other pieces, woven after the same cartoons as the two in Saragossa but with somewhat different details, are in the Musée du Louvre (figs. 130, 131). The two in Saragossa have the same border as the tapestry in that collection (fig. 128) that nearly duplicates the reconstituted central part of 27a–c.[23] One of these compositions (see fig. 130) shows Solomon receiving the Queen of Sheba with her gifts in all three lower compartments, Gabriel addressing Gideon in the threshing room in the larger upper left compartment and again over the fleece in the larger upper right compartment. Figures of the three Hebrew Worthies occupy the smaller upper compartments. David with his harp stands at the left, and Judas Maccabeus and Joshua with his shield of arms stand in the compartment at the right. The subject of the other composition (see fig. 131) has been described as Esther and Ahasuerus or Jephtha greeting his daughter. However since the woman kneeling in the center is exposing one breast as she addresses the armored man standing before her, and since the three Worthies standing in the upper corners of this composition are Pagan rather than Hebrew Worthies, it is clear that this does not represent the Esther or Jephtha subject but rather some episode in classical history. The Worthy standing in the upper left corner wears a crown and carries a shield charged with a lion rampant holding a halberd. He is Alexander. Opposite him, in the compartment that fills the upper right corner of the piece, stands a younger man wearing a turban whose shield is charged with what appears to be a pair of affronted lions. This is Hector. Behind him stands Julius Caesar represented as an older man wearing the imperial crown and holding a sword upright.

It may be that the reconstituted central part of 27a–c once belonged to a set of three hangings that showed these two other compositions. Since the border patterns of the examples in Paris and Saragossa differ from each other and from the one that now enframes 27a–c, it is clear that these hangings represent three different sets of weavings. The Solomon and Sheba subject, with its references to both Christ and the Virgin (see 28) and its inclusion of scenes from the story of Gideon whose fleece was a symbol of Mary, could easily relate to the subject of the reconstituted central part of 27a–c. Until the third subject, the one from classical history, has been identified, we cannot understand how it relates to the Christian theme. Nor can we say what the title of the cycle of three compositions might have been if, indeed, such a cycle ever existed.

As for 27a, it obviously comes from a tapestry cycle dealing with either the story of Esther and Ahasuerus or a series of subjects drawn from the Old Testament. 27c probably belonged in a series dealing with the legends of Charlemagne or of some emperor of ancient Rome.

HISTORY

27a in the collection of baron Arthur Schickler, château Martinvast near Cherbourg, from about 1872.
Property of Duveen Brothers, New York, by 1947.
Purchased by the MMA, The Cloisters Collection, 1953.

27b in the collection of marquis Henri de Vibraye, château de Bazoches du Morvan, Nièvre, until about 1903.
In the collection of Frédéric Engel-Gros, château de Ripaille, Lake Geneva.
Sold, *Collection Engel-Gros . . . importantes tapisseries gothiques*, Galerie Georges Petit, Paris, May 30–June 1, 1921, no. 288.
Acquired by Henry Walters for the Walters Art Gallery, Baltimore, 1921.
In the collection of the Walters Art Gallery.
Acquired by exchanging a tapestry purchased by the MMA, The Cloisters Collection, with 27b at the Walters Art Gallery, 1953.

27c in the collection of marquis Henri de Vibraye, château de Bazoches du Morvan, Nièvre, until about 1903.
In the collection of George and Florence Blumenthal, New York, by 1912.
Given to the MMA by George Blumenthal, 1941.

EXHIBITIONS

27a said to have been exhibited at the Sesquicentennial Exhibition in Philadelphia, 1926.
Brussels, Exposition Universelle et Internationale, 1935. *Cinq Siècles d'Art.* Vol. 2, *Dessins et Tapisseries.* Catalogue entry by Marthe Crick-Kuntziger, p. 60, no. 610 [27a]. Lent by Duveen Brothers, New York.
27a said to have been hung in Westminster Abbey on the occasion of the coronation of George VI in 1937.
New York, MMA, 1943. *Masterpieces in the Collection of George Blumenthal: A Special Exhibition.* Cat. no. 28 [27c], illus.
New York, Duveen Brothers galleries, 1947. 27a exhibited.

PUBLICATIONS

Hunter 1912, pp. 63, 284, 300, and text for pl. 371. 27c discussed briefly; illus. pl. 371.
Bouyer, Raymond. "Une grande vente—Les collections de M. Engel-Gros au château de Ripaille." *Chronique des Arts et de la Curiosité,* May 15, 1921, supplement facing p. 68. 27b mentioned.
"Mouvement des arts: Collection Engel-Gros." *Chronique des Arts et de la Curiosité,* June 15, 1921, p. 88. 27b mentioned.
Demotte, G.-J. *La tapisserie gothique.* Paris and New York, 1924, text for pl. 37 on p. 3. 27b described and discussed briefly; illus. color pl. 37.
Ganz, Paul, et al. *L'oeuvre d'un amateur d'art: La collection de Monsieur F. Engel-Gros, Catalogue Raisonné.* Geneva, [1925], vol. 1, pp. 304–5. 27b described at length and 27b and c discussed briefly; 27b illus. vol. 2, pl. 107.
Hunter 1925. 27a described and discussed briefly, pp. 58, 115; illus. pls.

VII,c (full view) and XVIII,ea (detail of pattern with letters REOON [R, E, and N reversed] on page's hose). 27c mentioned pp. 20, 116.
Rubinstein-Bloch, Stella. *Catalogue of the Collection of George and Florence Blumenthal, New-York.* Vol. 4, *Tapestries and Furniture.* Paris, 1927, pl. XI. 27c described and discussed at length; illus.
McCall, George Henry. *The Joseph Widener Collection: Tapestries at Lynnewood Hall.* Philadelphia, 1932, p. 21. 27c mentioned.
Crick-Kuntziger, Marthe. "Tapisserie." In *Cinq Siècles d'Art: Mémorial de l'Exposition, 1935.* Brussels, 1936, vol. 2. 27a mentioned.
Handbook of the Collection. Walters Art Gallery, Baltimore, 1936, p. 84. 27b discussed briefly; illus.
Breuning, Margaret. "France Loans Us an Acre of Her Tapestry Treasures: Gothic Tapestries at Duveen." *Art Digest* 22, no. 5 (December 1, 1947) p. 11. 27a mentioned.
Rorimer, James J. *Mediaeval Tapestries: A Picture Book.* MMA, New York, 1947, p. [4]. 27c discussed briefly; illus. fig. 13.
Rorimer, James J. "The Glorification of Charles VIII." *MMA Bulletin,* n.s. 12 (1953–54) pp. 281–99. 27a–c described and discussed at length; illus.
Freeman, Margaret B. "Notes on the Religious Iconography." *MMA Bulletin,* n.s. 12 (1953–54) pp. 300–301. The iconography of 27a–c discussed in detail; illus. with a diagrammatic sketch.
Comstock, Helen. "The Glorification of Charles VIII." *Connoisseur* 84 (1954) p. 113. 27b mentioned; 27a–c discussed according to Rorimer 1953–54 and illus. in color detail, p. 112.
Neugass, Fritz. "Kunsthistoriker als Detektive." *Die Weltkunst* 24, no. 15 (August 1, 1954) p. 7. 27a–c discussed at length, following Rorimer 1953–54.
Verdier, Philippe. "The Tapestry of the Prodigal Son." *Journal of the Walters Art Gallery* 18 (1955) pp. 9, 15; 46 nn. 1, 2; 48 nn. 23, 27, 32; 59 n. 117. 27a–c discussed at length; also details of history of 27b and exchange between Walters Art Gallery and MMA.
Crick-Kuntziger, Marthe. *Catalogue des tapisseries (XIVᵉ au XVIIIᵉ siècle).* Musées Royaux d'Art et d'Histoire de Bruxelles, Brussels, 1956, p. 25. 27a–c mentioned.
Mayor, A. Hyatt. "Children Are What We Make Them." *MMA Bulletin,* n.s. 15, no. 7 (March 1957) p. 182. Illus. detail of pattern on page's hose, with brief comment.
Shepherd, Dorothy. "Three Tapestries from Chaumont." *Bulletin of the Cleveland Museum of Art* 48 (1961) pp. 171, 175. 27a–c discussed briefly.
Heinz, Dora. *Europäische Wandteppiche I.* Brunswick, 1963, pp. 106–7. 27a–c mentioned.
Rorimer, James J. *The Cloisters: The Building and the Collection of Medieval Art in Fort Tryon Park.* 3d ed., rev. MMA, New York, 1963, pp. 178–82. 27a–c described and discussed at length; detail illus. fig. 90.
van Ysselstcyn, G. T. *Tapestry: The Most Expensive Industry of the XVth and XVIth Centuries.* The Hague and Brussels, 1969, pp. 101–2. Discussed at length; illus. figs. 83 [27a–c] and 83a [27a].
Souchal in Paris 1973, pp. 178, 180. 27a–c discussed briefly. See also New York 1974, pp. 179–80.
de Vaivre, Jean-Bernard. "Artus, les trois couronnes et les hérauts." *Archives heraldiques suisses,* Yearbook, 88 (1974) pp. 9, 13 n. 66. The figures of King Arthur and Godefroy de Bouillon discussed in detail; detail of those two illus. fig. 17.
Wieck, Roger S. "The Mazarin Tapestry: An Iconographic Analysis." *Marsyas* 18 (1975–76) pp. 11, 14, 15. 27a–c discussed at length; detail of central section illus. fig. 2.
Freeman, Margaret B. *The Unicorn Tapestries.* MMA, New York, 1976, pp. 193, 214. 27a–c discussed briefly; detail of pattern on page's hose illus. fig. 244.
Steppe, Jan-Karel. "Inscriptions décoratives contenant des signatures et des mentions du lieu d'origine sur des tapisseries bruxelloises de la fin du XVᵉ et du début du XVIᵉ siècle." In *Tapisseries bruxelloises de la pré-Renaissance.* Exh. cat., Musées Royaux d'Art et d'Histoire. Brussels, 1976, pp. 200, 210–11. 27a–c discussed briefly.

1. Tapestries of this type occasionally show minor variations in the details of certain parts of the architectural design, but the variations are not so pronounced as the irregularities we see in 27a–c. See, for example, two such tapestries of the Virtues and Vices formerly in baron d'Hunolstein's collection, illustrated in Eugène Müntz, "Tapisseries allégoriques inédites ou peu connues," *Fondation Eugène Piot: Monuments et Mémoires,* Académie des Inscriptions et Belles Lettres, Paris, 9 (1902) pls. VII and VIII, which have seven compartments each: the one in the center rises the full height of the piece while the two flanking it are two-thirds as tall and the four above them make up the other third of the height. Both tapestries show a symmetrical arrangement of columns and arches except for the right-hand third of the tapestry in pl. VIII whose ogee arch develops into an inverted heart-shaped compartment. The corresponding arch in the left third of pl. VIII, as well as the two arches in the tapestry in pl. VII, are normal ogee arches.

2. Joseph Destrée, *Tapisseries et sculptures bruxelloises à l'Exposition d'art ancien bruxellois . . . 1905* (Brussels, 1906) p. 20. See Alexandre Lenoir, *Description d'une tapisserie, rare et curieuse, faite à Bruges, représentant, sous des formes allégoriques, le Mariage du Roi de France Charles VIII, avec la Princesse Anne de Bretagne* (Paris, 1819).

3. Destrée, *Tapisseries et sculptures bruxelloises,* p. 19.

4. J. Destrée and P. Van den Ven, *Les tapisseries,* Musées Royaux du Cinquentenaire (Brussels, 1910) p. 23.

5. Destrée, *Tapisseries et sculptures bruxelloises,* p. 19, and Destrée and Van den Ven, *Les Tapisseries,* p. 23.

6. Letter from Roger S. Wieck to Timothy Husband at The Cloisters, October 26, 1988. The roundel was sold at Sotheby's, New York, November 22–23, 1988, no. 63, illus. in sale cat. The print appears in the incunabulum *Prognasticatio* of J. Lichtenberger (Modena, before 1500), in the Walters Art Gallery, Baltimore, shelf no. L–186. The author thanks Roger Wieck for his kindness in consulting on this matter subsequently.

7. For the tapestry in San Francisco, see Anna G. Bennett, *Five Centuries of Tapestry from the Fine Arts Museums of San Francisco* (San Francisco, 1976) p. 62, illus. pp. 64–65, who pointed out the relationship between labor and redemption. For Adam holding a shovel in the tapestry in Baltimore, see Philippe Verdier, "The Tapestry of the Prodigal Son," *Journal of the Walters Art Gallery* 18 (1955) p. 35 and fig. 14.

8. See Eduardo Torra de Arana et al., *Los tapices de La Seo de Zaragoza* (Saragossa, 1985) series VIII, no. 1, illus. facing p. 164. We cannot agree with the authors who identify this scene as one showing Joseph, as viceroy of Egypt, touring Pharaoh's lands and talking to his subjects.

9. For titles of the Mazarin piece, see Destrée, *Tapisseries et sculptures,* p. 18. For the Brussels tapestry, see Destrée and Van den Ven, *Les tapisseries,* p. 23. For the hanging in Saragossa, see Torra de Arana et al., *Los tapices de La Seo,* p. 132.

10. See Lotte Brand Philip, *The Ghent Altarpiece and the Art of Jan van Eyck* (Princeton, 1971) pp. 53, 58, and fig. 41.

11. Philip, *Ghent Altarpiece,* pp. 102–3. Philip states that "the Lord's rejection of Synagoga and His acceptance of Ecclesia is the basis for the appearance of the two figures in the context of the Last Judgment." In other words, He has judged them. In the Mazarin tapestry Ecclesia appears on Christ's right hand, denoting His acceptance, and Synagoga on His left, denoting His rejection.

12. Quoted in Torre de Arana et al., *Los tapices de La Seo,* p. 47.

13. Destrée, *Tapisseries et sculptures,* p. 19.

14. Destrée and Van den Ven, *Les tapisseries,* p. 23.

15. Destrée, *Tapisseries et sculptures,* p. 19; see also Destrée and Van den Ven, *Les tapisseries,* p. 23.

16. Wieck, letter to Husband, October 26, 1988 (see note 6).

17. The legends appeared at least as early as the tenth century. Some of them treated subjects like this which were illustrated in manuscripts. See, for example, Donald Bullough, *The Age of Charlemagne* (New York, 1966) pl. 84 (center image at left), which shows an emperor labeled as Charlemagne watching girls spinning and reeling yarn, weaving, and doing needlework. The illustration was taken from a manuscript of the *Miroir Historial* in the Musée Condé, Chantilly.

18. For an illustration of Philip's suggested reconstruction of the van Eyck altarpiece, whose form also explains the placement of the Adam and Eve on the same level as the Savior as here, see Philip, *Ghent Altarpiece,* fig. 41, and the text concerning Adam and Eve, pp. 17–18, 54, 59–60. For the All Saints pictures, see Erwin Panofsky, *Early Netherlandish Painting: Its Origins and Character* (Cambridge, Mass., 1953) vol. 1, pp. 212–13, and fig. 66, a typical example in a manuscript in the Bibliothèque Sainte-Geneviève, Paris. For an illustration of the Dürer altarpiece, see Erwin Panofsky, *Albrecht Dürer* (Princeton, 1943) vol. 2, fig. 172; in fig. 173, Panofsky illustrates a page of the *Adoration of the Trinity* from the *Heures à l'Usaige de Rome* printed in Paris in 1498.

19. See Jan-Karel Steppe, "Inscriptions décoratives contenant des signatures et des mentions du lieu d'origine sur des tapisseries bruxelloises de la fin du XVᵉ et du début du XVIᵉ siècle," in *Tapisseries bruxelloises de la pré-Renaissance,* exh. cat., Musées Royaux d'Art et d'Histoire (Brussels, 1976) p. 207, illus. p. 208.

20. For the high-crowned bonnet worn at the back of the head, see one that Mary Magdalen wears in a painting of 1492 in the Musée du Louvre and several others of rather exotic form in two woodcuts in the Metropolitan Museum: Margaret B. Freeman, *The Unicorn Tapestries,* MMA (New York, 1976) figs. 202, 250, 255, respectively. Concerning the cut of the gowns which are covered by loose overgarments, see an early instance in the tapestries of the *Story of Saint Anatoile de Salins* which are dated by document between 1502 and 1506; for a piece from this cycle that is now on deposit at the Musée du Louvre, see *Bruges et la tapisserie,* exh. cat. by Guy Delmarcel and Erik Duverger, Musée Gruuthuse and Musée Memling (Bruges, 1987) fig. 2/1 on pp. 170–71 (color). Compare the cut of those gowns with the typical cut of a decade earlier as seen in the *Hunt of the Unicorn* (20e, 20g in this catalogue).

21. Concerning the tapestry in Saragossa, see Torra de Arana et al., *Los tapices de La Seo,* pp. 132–38, illus. in color. For the tapestry in Brussels, see Destrée and Van den Ven, *Les tapisseries,* p. 23, pls. 11–13; and Marthe Crick-Kuntziger, *Catalogue des tapisseries (XIVᵉ au XVIIIᵉ siècle),* Musées Royaux d'Art et d'Histoire (Brussels, 1956) no. 8, illus.

22. Similar figures of Adam and Eve appear in compartments flanking a tall central scene in a *Deposition* tapestry in the Cappella Palatina, Palazzo Reale, Naples, that has been attributed to Brussels, first quarter of the sixteenth century, and in two versions of a *Nativity* tapestry attributed to the same time and place. One of the Nativities is in the cathedral of La Seo in Saragossa, the other in the Patrimonio Nacional in Madrid. For the piece in Naples, see Mercedes and Vittorio Viale, *Arazzi e tapetti antichi* (Turin, 1952) pp. 40–41, illus. pl. 19 and in color facing p. 64. For the two tapestries in Spain, see respectively Torra de Arana et al., *Los tapices de La Seo,* pp. 155–60, illus. in color; and Paulina Junquera de Vega and Concha Herrero Carretero, *Catálogo de tapices del Patrimonio Nacional,* vol. 1, *Siglo XVI* (Madrid, 1986) p. 7, illus. in color.

23. For details concerning these two companion pieces and illustrations of them, see Torra de Arana et al., *Los Tapices de La Seo,* pp. 139–42 (the Solomon and Queen of Sheba piece, here identified incorrectly as the *Presentation of Esther*), and pp. 143–47 (the unidentified classical subject, here incorrectly identified as *Jephtha's Daughter*). See also pp. 131, 150, where the authors list four pieces under this series they call "La Glorificación de Jesucristo" but acknowledge that one of them, representing the raising of Lazarus, may not belong to the series (no. VI) that the other three pieces represent.

28

Coronation of the Virgin and Related Subjects

Southern Netherlands, 1500–1515
Wool warp, wool and silk wefts
13 ft. 6 in. × 20 ft. 5 ¹/₄ in. (4.12 m × 6.23 m)
16 warp yarns per inch, 6 per centimeter
From the Collection of James Stillman, Gift of Dr. Ernest G.
Stillman, 1925 (25.177.3)

CONDITION

The tapestry has lost some of its original width and part of its upper border. At some time in the past the right-hand border was cut away from the field along the inner guard from the bottom of the lower border to the inside of the upper border. At right angles to this cut, a second cut was made along the top of the field from the edge of the inner guard to a point about two feet to the left and then straight up through the upper border. The right end of the field was cut away, and the inverted L-shaped piece of border that was removed from the right side was then rejoined to the tapestry along the new right end of the field. Assuming that the Coronation episode originally occupied the center of the composition, we can estimate that about a quarter of the field's width was removed at the right.

The upper border is a patchwork of contemporary weavings, some of which belonged originally to this hanging. A section about a foot and a half long at the left end, terminating with two bunches of grapes, is part of the original border but it was not in this position. The section to the right of that, including the first two square compartments containing small blossoming plants and the floral bands between and to the left of them, was taken from the upper or lower border of a different hanging and inserted here. The section in the center of the border, which shows an inscribed scroll on a floral band, is part of yet another tapestry. The next section to the right, including the third and fourth square compartments together with the floral band between them and half of the band at the right, came from the tapestry that yielded the corresponding section at the left, but from one of its side borders (the warp runs vertically here). The right end of the upper border, from a point halfway between the square compartment and the corner, is original as are the right (though moved), left, and lower borders.

There is a great deal of repair in the tapestry, most of it done by weaving modern weft yarns on the original warp in places where the light-colored silks in the highlights and the dark-colored wools in the shadows and contours had deteriorated and fallen out. These repairs affect almost every figure and inscription in the field but especially the angel in the upper left corner and the figures in the adjacent scene, in the Coronation, and in the lower right corner of the field. The repairs have altered the original modeling and drawing throughout the field to a significant degree. There are also a number of important restorations made by inserting into voids in the original fabric patches of weaving that have both modern warp and weft yarns. One of these restorations involves the back of the robe worn by the angel in the upper left corner as well as the wall behind him. The right side of the gown worn by the half-kneeling man in the lower left corner and the portion passing over his right knee have been restored in this way. The back of the cope worn by the cleric kneeling in the foreground left of center and the feet and lower left leg of the man immediately to the right of him are also restorations. Other repairs of this kind are found in the lower half of the garment worn by the woman seated in the center of the group in the upper right corner, the collar of the man standing to the right of the female figure labeled TĒPERĀCIA (Temperance) in the Coronation scene, the entire gown of the woman standing to the right of the king near the right border, the front of the gown worn by the woman standing behind her to the left, and, finally, the lower right part of the gown worn by the woman standing immediately to the left of the greyhound in the lower right corner of the field.

These restorations apparently were made between the time the photograph illustrated in the de Somzée sale catalogue (1904) was taken and the time the piece was illustrated in the Chappey sale catalogue (1907). The earlier photograph shows that by 1904 at least two patches from this or another tapestry had been inserted in the field along the inner edge of the right-hand border below the shoulders of the woman standing to the right of the king and above the head of the greyhound lying on the ground in front of her. The patches seem to have represented parts of the garments of two different figures, one of them showing the name ISAIAS, the other with a name that is illegible in the photograph. The

28

same photograph shows what might have been a name inscribed across the figure of the king, which is part of the original tapestry, at waist level. Although the name itself, if it is a name, is illegible, the letters could have spelled out DAVID. Unfortunately all trace of those letters was obliterated in the restoration process.

DESCRIPTION AND SUBJECT

The composition shows groups of figures arranged on two or three levels across the width of the field. At the left end the figures occupy only two levels. An interior scene appears in the upper left corner. An angel with upraised wings and a scepter in his left hand addresses a man who is labeled SALOMŌ (Solomon) across the fabric of his gown at ankle level. Behind the throne where Solomon sits sleeping there stand two men. A vision of a woman carrying a radiant heart in her hands appears among clouds in the upper left corner, above the angel's

head. Below this group sits an impressive male figure wearing a patterned velvet or damask gown under a plain fur-lined gown. He also wears a large round hat with brim upturned and crown encircled by an open coronet. He looks at the figures assembled at the right and gestures away from them with his left hand. His right hand rests on his thigh, the fingers holding one end of an inscribed scroll that flies upward and flutters around his head. The inscription, much restored, mostly reads as nonsense; but the letters LABIA (on the first deep curl of the scroll, above and to the left of the man's head), SIT (just to the right of that), and SALOM (at the right end of the scroll) appear to have survived virtually intact.

The figures involved in the scene to the right of this are arranged on three levels. At the top is a vision of the Virgin and Child surrounded by rays of light; Mary's half-figure rises from a crescent moon. Below, a company of seven women and four men surround a regal figure whose name, OCTAVIAN, is written on his shoulder cape. He wears a plain ermine-lined mantle over a patterned gown. On his head is an imperial crown. The women have plain or patterned fitted gowns and high-crowned headdresses, some with veils or lappets. The men wear unpatterned gowns and most of them have no head covering. Two of the women standing at the far left on the second level have labels inscribed across their gowns just below the waist. One, wearing a plain mantle and gown and veils around her bonnet and face, is PRVDĒCIA (Prudence). The other, wearing an elaborately patterned velvet or damask gown and a bonnet with a pendant scarf, is TIBVRTINA (the Tiburtine Sibyl). The woman standing in the lower right corner of this scene carries in her left hand a smoking censer suspended on a chain. A page wearing doublet and hose and a small round hat holds the base of the censer with his right hand; he is either filling or lighting it with the curved vessel in his left hand.

On the uppermost level, above and slightly to the right of the scene with Octavian, is a scene depicting four women, in plain or patterned gowns and mantles and wearing hoods or bonnets, who are making columns and hoisting them upright. The three raising a column are labeled on their garments; left to right they are MODESTIA (Modesty), CARITAS (Charity), and TĒPERĀCIA (Temperance). The woman standing in front of them, using a chisel and mallet to carve the capital of a column lying on the platform, is PRVDĒCIA (Prudence). Opposite her sits an elderly bearded man with a jewel-collared mantle over a patterned velvet or damask gown and a small high-crowned hat on his head. He watches the women at their work. The scroll held in his left hand is inscribed SAPĪĒ EDIFICAVIT (probably *Sapientia aedificavit*, Wisdom will build [it]).

Most of what is now the right half of the field, the three-level composition that once occupied the center, shows the Coronation of the Virgin. On the upper level the Trinity, represented as three identical Persons, crowned and sceptered, each use one hand to hold the crown that they are about to place on the head of the Virgin, who is seated directly below. She wears a plain mantle over an unpatterned loose gown. Her head is bare, her long hair parted in the center and falling loosely to the sides. Supporting her at the left is an unidentified female figure in a plain mantle over a patterned velvet or damask fitted gown. TĒPERĀCIA (Temperance), wearing an unpatterned fitted gown, holds Mary's left elbow. A company of angels stands in a bank of clouds behind the Trinity's throne. A number of men are gathered at each side of the throne. Labels identify some of them. DAVID, holding a harp, stands in front of the group at the left. JACOB is behind him, and farther

back the head of NOE (Noah) appears. On the right side of the throne stand MOISES (Moses) holding the Tablets of the Law and, behind him, ARON (Aaron). Below the figure of the Virgin, on the composition's lowest level, nine men are gathered. Four magnificently dressed high clergymen kneel to the left of her feet, and to the right kneels a monarch with crown and sword. Behind him at the right stand four men who are dressed as gentlemen.

To the right of the Trinity, in the upper right corner of the field, a company of two men and four women, all fashionably dressed, is seated on the grass in the foreground of an open landscape. They are taking roses from a bowl that a boy passes among them. Below this group stands a king wearing a plain mantle over a patterned loose gown and on his head an open crown. Six women and one man stand around him. A greyhound lies on the grass in the foreground and a smaller dog stands in front of it.

The settings in the foreground change from scene to scene. The seated man carrying a scroll and the figures involved with Octavian in the lower left corner of the field occupy a meadow filled with blooming plants. The clergymen and civilians worshiping the Virgin in the center of the field are kneeling or standing on an elaborately patterned tile floor. The flowering meadow appears again in the lower right corner of the field. In the upper level a small oak tree separates the Trinity from the scene adjacent to it at the left, and a small orange tree performs the same function at the right.

The border that is original to this tapestry—that is, the lower border, both side borders, and the outer ends of the upper border—shows a course of branches bearing roses in bud or full bloom alternating with thistle stalks and lengths of grapevine on a dark blue ground. Here and there, knotted ribbons and birds of various kinds, including owls, punctuate the parade of flora. In the center of the top border is a scroll inscribed with the word TĒPERENCIA (Temperance). This part of the upper border, together with the four square compartments and the adjacent floral bands, was taken from a different tapestry and inserted here (see Condition). The floral band in that section shows a course of rose branches alternating with violet plants on a dark blue ground; it does not have the grapes, the ribbons, or the birds. All parts of the border have wide striped guards flanking the floral bands.

The subject is a complicated one that involves the Virgin and Christ, prefigurations of the Annunciation and the Coronation, and the typological relationships that medieval theologians found to connect Solomon (and here possibly also Ahasuerus) with Christ and the Virgin.

The scene in the upper left corner illustrates the story of the dream of Solomon (3 Kings 3:5–15), in which God offers to give Solomon whatever he should ask. The young king requests a discerning heart so that he can govern his people justly and distinguish right from wrong. God does not appear in the tapestry. Rather, a vision of a woman holding a heart surrounded by rays of light appears in the upper left corner of the scene. Below her an angel with upraised wings and a scepter seems to be addressing the sleeping Solomon. The figure in the vision probably represents the Virgin, and the angel is probably Gabriel. The presence of these two figures (if we have identified them correctly) would not have seemed so strange to the medieval viewer as it does to us because, as Breck (1922, 59) stated, the juxtaposition of the radiant heart in this scene and the Christ Child in the scene at the right implies that "Christ is the Wisdom (the Logos) of God." Therefore the heart becomes a symbol of Christ in this context, and the figures of the Virgin and Gabriel in the dream scene may be taken as references to the Annunciation or Incarnation.

According to medieval thought there were many ways in which Solomon was connected with the Virgin and Christ. In the Canticle of Canticles (3:7–11), the lover, identified then as Solomon, rides in a litter made of cedar of Lebanon guarded by sixty select warriors. Theologians interpreted the litter as a symbol of Mary's womb, where Christ's human and divine natures were combined, or of the Church; and the guards were compared to the twelve apostles, who stood by Mary's death bed.[1] Also in the Canticle of Canticles (2, 4) the lover praises qualities in the Shulamite bride that later become attributes of the Virgin: the lily of the valley, the lily among thorns, the tower of David covered with shields, the enclosed garden, the sealed fountain, the well of living water. Medieval theologians interpreted the bridegroom or Solomon as a prefiguration of Christ and the Shulamite bride as the Church; furthermore Solomon and Christ were regarded as the great princes of peace.[2] In medieval art the ancient theme of the Virgin in Majesty (the *Sedes Sapientiae*) sometimes showed Mary seated on Solomon's lion throne and surrounded by crowned women symbolizing Solitude, Modesty, Prudence, Virginity, Humility, and Obedience—the virtues she exemplified at the time of the Incarnation.[3]

The instances can be multiplied; but these will suffice to indicate the kinds of typological relationships that linked Solomon to the Virgin and Christ in the medieval mind. The designer of the Metropolitan Museum's tapestry associated Solomon with the Virgin again by juxtaposing the Coronation with the Dream of Solomon and the building of the House of Wisdom.

Concerning the Coronation, we call attention to one of the tapestry dossals in the cathedral in Sens (see fig. 63). There, the coronation of Bathsheba by her son Solomon and of Esther by Ahasuerus (the latter represented by the king's recognizing his queen with his scepter rather than by a coronation as such) were associated with the Coronation of the Virgin as prefigurations. Therefore the references to Solomon in the left end of the Metropolitan Museum's tapestry and possibly also to Ahasuerus in the right end (see below) are directly related to the Coronation in the center.

The scene involving the emperor Augustus Octavian and the Tiburtine Sibyl, drawn from a number of medieval sources, including the *Mirabilia Urbis Romae* and Jacobus de Voragine's *Legenda Aurea*, also had typological overtones even though the story is apocryphal. According to the legend the emperor, whom the senate wished to deify, went to consult the Tiburtine Sibyl to find out whether the world would ever see a man greater than he. When they met on the Capitoline Hill it was the day of the Nativity; and the Sibyl saw in the sky a vision of the Virgin and Child as a voice said, "This woman is the altar of heaven." When the Sibyl showed the vision to Augustus and told him that the Child would be greater than he, the emperor refused to be deified and knelt in worship before the Child. According to Réau, the legend was invented to lend the distinction of antiquity to the Capitoline church of the Ara Coeli.[4] In some representations the emperor is shown kneeling and swinging a censer, a detail that Réau traces to mystery play productions dealing with the legend. In the tapestry it is not Octavian but a woman standing in front of him who holds the censer. Woodcut illustrations in the *Speculum Humanae Salvationis* show the scene involving Octavian and the Tiburtine Sibyl balanced by another showing the Annunciation or the Adoration of the Magi.[5] Thus the vision was associated with one or the other of these events.

As Breck (1922, 59) had noted, the women working with the columns in the scene above and to the right of this are building the House of Wisdom (Proverbs 9:1, "Wisdom hath built herself a house, she hath hewn her out seven pillars"). Their labels identify the women in the tapestry as Modesty, Prudence, Charity, and Temperance, four of the Virgin's virtues. The inscription on the scroll that the bearded man at the right holds confirms this interpretation of the scene. It reads SAPĪĒ EDIFICAVIT (probably *Sapientia aedificavit*, Wisdom will build [it]), and Standen has shown that in a similar text of the fourth century Solomon is associated with the temple of Wisdom.[6] Breck (1922, 59) interpreted the subject (we think correctly) to mean that Christ repre-

416

sents the wisdom of God and the "house" that Wisdom (Christ) built is a symbol of His mother. The twisted columns the builders are handling may refer to the twisted shaft of the fourth-century A.D. so-called column of Solomon that was said to have come from his temple in Jerusalem and been given by the emperor Constantine to the basilica of Saint Peter in Rome.[7]

The Coronation of the Virgin, which now occupies the right-central part of the field but originally appeared at its center, illustrates a theme which does not derive from Scripture but from early apocryphal sources. It appears later in the writings of Gregory of Tours and Jacobus de Voragine.[8] The composition took many forms. In some cases the crown is bestowed by an angel, in others by God the Father or by Christ or, as here, by the Persons of the Trinity; in other representations the Virgin appears already crowned, seated next to Christ, and receiving His blessing. The Virgin is crowned by the Trinity, as she is here, in the tapestry dossal in Sens (see fig. 63) and in a hanging in Madrid.[9] The five labeled figures who surround the Trinity in 28—Noah, David, Moses, Jacob, and Aaron—are patriarchs from the Old Testament. Medieval theologians regarded the first three as types of Christ. Aaron and Jacob could have been depicted here for any number of reasons, but it seems possible that they refer to two of the Virgin's perfections as celebrated in medieval litany; that is, the Star of Jacob and the Virgin of Aaron. Personifications of two of the Virgin's virtues, Temperance at the right and Prudence at the left (not labeled, but recognizable by comparison with her other appearance in the house-building scene), attend her as she receives the crown. Below her the four clergymen at the left, two wearing copes and one holding the papal tiara, kneel in adoration. Opposite them a monarch who seems to have placed an imperial crown at the Virgin's feet also kneels in worship while the other civilians behind him stand and look on in wonder. Similar groups of men who represent various orders of society, arranged in this way, appear in a number of other tapestries of the period that glorify either Christ or the Virgin; see for example the central scene in the *Christ the Judge on the Throne of Majesty* (27a–c) and the hangings in Washington, Brussels, and Saragossa that show similar scenes (see 27) and a tapestry of the *Glorification* (or *Triumph*) *of the Virgin* in the Burrell Collection in Glasgow.[10]

The scene in the upper right corner of the field, where youths and young ladies sit conversing or taking roses from a bowl held by a page, does not explain itself immediately. However, when it is compared to a similar scene in the lower left corner of a tapestry showing mankind surprised by the Seven Capital Sins, which is now in the Musées Royaux d'Art et d'Histoire in Brussels, its meaning becomes clear. In that hanging, a youth touches a bunch of flowers that a young lady holds in her skirt while a lady seated in front of them takes rose blossoms from a basket to continue making the chaplet she holds in her lap. It has been suggested that the scene indicates that seemingly innocent pleasures can lead to mortal sin.[11] It is likely that the scene in the Metropolitan Museum's tapestry was also meant to symbolize man's inclination to sin. An episode like this, which the late medieval mind would readily have understood as a demonstration of man's weakness and his need for redemption, logically belongs in a tapestry celebrating the Virgin, specifically the Virgin as intercessor for mankind in heaven.

The meaning of the composition below this, where one man and six elaborately dressed women surround a king, is obscure because there are no labels to identify the figures. The women resemble the Virtues who appear in the scenes at the left, but they may represent the Vices instead; and, as noted above (Condition), the king may represent David.

The pose of the crowned figure seated in the lower left corner of the field is identical to that of the figure in the lower left corner of a Metropolitan Museum tapestry that shows the Nativity and related scenes (29b). There, the man carries a scroll inscribed with words from Isaias 26:21 and, presumably, he is meant to represent that prophet. Pairs of seated prophets appear in nine of the ten tapestries comprising the *Redemption of Man* series from which that piece comes; and figures like them, whether Old Testament prophets or kings, or Christian apostles or saints, also appear in other tapestries of this period.[12] In the Coronation tapestry this figure almost surely represents Solomon, whose name in the incomplete form SALOM is inscribed at the outer end of the scroll in the place where the textual source of the seated figure's speech appears in those other tapestries. Two unlabeled figures who probably represent Solomon appear on the Coronation of the Virgin page in a fifteenth-century printed *Biblia Pauperum* published by Avril Henry.[13] The words on their scrolls come from the Canticle of Canticles and Wisdom. In the Metropolitan Museum's tapestry, since only the letters LABIA and SIT on the forward part of the scroll seem to have survived from the original weaving, but in bends of the scroll where words may not have been shown in their complete form, it would be hazardous to try to reconstruct the whole inscription and so, presumably, to identify its source in one of the Old Testament writings that were ascribed to Solomon in the Middle Ages.

In its original state, before the right-hand quarter of

417

the field was removed, the tapestry probably showed another figure group in the upper right corner and another seated figure below that group. We are left to guess the subject of this last episode and the identity of the figure in the corner below it. If the king standing near the present right edge of the field is indeed Solomon's father, David (see Condition), then the missing scene may have illustrated an episode associated with him, an episode balancing the dream of Solomon in the upper left corner of the field; and the seated figure may have represented David. On the other hand, if the bits of weaving that were patched into the right edge of the field belonged to this piece, then the name "Isaias" that appeared on one of them before the hanging was restored (see Condition) may indicate that the figure missing from the lower right corner represented Isaias. These two possibilities are confirmed, and a third possibility is suggested, on the Coronation of the Virgin page of the fifteenth-century *Biblia Pauperum* published by Henry (see note 13). The woodcut shows David and a figure speaking words from the Canticle of Canticles (Solomon?) above the illustration of the Coronation in the center of the page, and, below it, Isaias and a figure quoting the Book of Wisdom (Solomon again?). Scenes of Solomon sharing his throne with Bathsheba, and of Ahasuerus motioning Esther to his throne, flank the Coronation scene at left and right, respectively. This suggests that a scene involving Ahasuerus may have appeared in the lost upper right corner of the field balancing the Dream of Solomon, and that the seated figure in the lower right corner, if it did not represent David or Isaias, might have represented Ahasuerus.

The typological associations that are presented on the Coronation page of the *Biblia Pauperum* (see note 13) help clarify the meaning of the rather involved combination of images in this tapestry. Above the woodcut scene that shows Solomon seated on his throne next to his mother are the words (transcribed and translated from the Latin by Henry), "According to 3 Kings ii 19–20, when Bethsabee the mother of Solomon had come to him in his palace, King Solomon himself had his mother's throne placed next to his throne. Bethsabee signifies the glorious Virgin whose throne was placed next to the throne of the true Solomon, that is, of Jesus Christ." Below the same scene is written "His mother has come in and Solomon places her next to him." Above the Esther and Ahasuerus scene is written "According to Esther ii 15–23, when Queen Esther had come to King Assuerus in his palace, King Assuerus himself placed her next to him to honor her. Esther the Queen signifies the Virgin Mary, whom Assuerus (that is, Christ) placed next to himself in celestial glory on the day of her

assumption." Below this scene is written "When Esther goes in and entreats Assuerus." In the center of the page at the bottom is written "By lifting her up you have honored the loving Mary, O Christ."

Henry's interpretation of the iconography on this page applies equally well to the Metropolitan Museum's tapestry. She observed that Bathsheba's petition to Solomon on behalf of his brother, and Esther's to Ahasuerus on behalf of her people, may both be compared to Mary's intercession with Christ on behalf of man.[14]

SOURCE OF THE DESIGN

None of the figures or groups has been traced to a design source. It seems likely that the composition of the Coronation itself derives from some painting (compare the Assumption group in 18 in the present catalogue). The adoring clerical, regal, and civilian figures below almost certainly were designed after the same source that inspired the comparable groups in the *Christ the Judge on the Throne of Majesty* in the Metropolitan Museum and the three tapestries in Washington, Brussels, and Saragossa that show the same motif (see 27a–c). The man seated in the lower left corner of the *Coronation of the Virgin* tapestry, who appears again in a different costume in the corresponding place in one of the two *Redemption of Man* tapestries in the Metropolitan Museum (29b), belongs to the category of stock figures that tapestry producers and weavers used in different contexts.

MANUFACTURE AND DATE

When the tapestry was sold from the de Somzée collection in 1904, it was published as a Brussels work of the beginning of the sixteenth century. Three years later, when it was offered for sale from the collection of Edouard Chappey, it was catalogued as Flemish work of the end of the fifteenth century. In both his publications of the hanging (1922, 1926) Breck attributed it to Brussels and dated it in the first third of the sixteenth century. Göbel (1923, vol. 2, fig. 118) also gave it to Brussels and dated it about 1520. Asselberghs (1974, 41) dated the tapestry about 1500 and implied that it was woven in Brussels when he discussed it in context with the Richmond fragment (see fig. 132, and Related Tapestries), which he regarded as Brussels weaving.

Although none of these writers gave reasons for his attribution to Brussels, it seems clear that they were all influenced by the fact that the painterly style of the field and the design of the border had both become associated with tapestries produced in that city. Those criteria no

Fig. 132. *Courtly Pleasures*. Tapestry fragment, southern Netherlands, first quarter of the sixteenth century. Virginia Museum of Fine Arts, Richmond.

longer seem reliable. The tapestry was certainly produced in the southern Netherlands, but for the present we have no grounds for giving it a more precise geographic attribution. The stylistic devices of arranging the figures on two or three levels without any architectural framework to isolate each group in a space of its own and of using a smaller scale for figures in the upper levels to create an illusion of depth point to a date no earlier than about 1500. The shapes of the women's headdresses, some of which retain the silhouette of the high-crowned bonnets fashionable in the late fifteenth century, and of the men's shoes (some of which are restored but seem to have contours following the original ones), with their relatively narrow rounded toes that were fashionable at the same time, suggest that the cartoon was painted before these fashion details changed significantly about 1510. For the same reason it

seems unlikely that the tapestry would have been woven after about 1515.

RELATED TAPESTRIES

No tapestries that might have accompanied 28 in a series of hangings are known to have survived. It is possible that this was woven as an individual piece, but it seems more likely that it belonged in a series of hangings whose subject celebrated the Virgin's life and perfections.

A fragmentary tapestry in the Virginia Museum of Fine Arts in Richmond (fig. 132) contains a near-duplicate representation of the scene in the upper right corner of the Metropolitan Museum's hanging. The boy holding the bowl and the man and two women seated at the right reappear in the Richmond piece in slightly

419

different garments and a slightly different setting. According to Asselberghs (1974, 41), the Richmond example is made up of parts of two tapestries; only the right-hand section concerns us here. It is possible that this fragment came from another weaving after the cartoon that served for the Metropolitan Museum's tapestry.

HISTORY

Sold, *Collections de Somzée*, pt. 3, *Objets d'art anciens*, J. Fievez expert, Brussels, May 24 and following days, 1904, no. 705, illus. (before restoration).

Sold, *Objets d'art . . . Collections de M. Edouard Chappey*, pt. 4, Galerie Georges Petit, Paris, June 5–7, 1907, no. 1898, illus. (as currently restored).

Collection of James Stillman.

Given to the MMA by Dr. Ernest G. Stillman, from the collection of James Stillman, 1925.

EXHIBITIONS

Bruges, 1902. *Exposition des Primitifs flamands.*
New York, MMA, 1922–25. Lent anonymously.

PUBLICATIONS

J. B. [Joseph Breck]. "A Loan of Tapestries." *MMA Bulletin* 17 (1922) pp. 58–59. Described and discussed at length.

Göbel 1923, vol. 2, fig. 118. Illus. with brief caption.

J. B. [Joseph Breck]. "Accessions and Notes: A Gift of Tapestries." *MMA Bulletin* 21 (1926) p. 21. Discussed briefly.

Verdier, Philippe. "The Tapestry of the Prodigal Son." *Journal of the Walters Art Gallery* 18 (1955) p. 48 n. 27. Mentioned.

European Art in the Virginia Museum of Fine Arts: A Catalogue. Richmond, 1966, p. 123. Mentioned.

Asselberghs, Jean-Paul. *Les tapisseries flamandes aux Etats-Unis d'Amérique.* Brussels, 1974, p. 41. Mentioned.

NOTES

1. Louis Réau, *Iconographie de l'art chrétien* (Paris, 1955–59) vol. 2, pt. 1, p. 299.
2. Réau, *Iconographie de l'art chrétien*, vol. 2, pt. 1, p. 287.
3. Réau, *Iconographie de l'art chrétien*, vol. 2, pt. 2, p. 94.
4. Réau, *Iconographie de l'art chrétien*, vol. 2, pt. 1, pp. 421–24. The outline of the legend as given in this catalogue entry was taken from Réau's account of it.

5. Réau, *Iconographie de l'art chrétien*, vol. 2, pt. 1, p. 423.
6. In notes that Edith Appleton Standen prepared concerning this tapestry (about 1968, now in the files of the MMA Department of Medieval Art), she quoted a text from Aurelius Clemens Prudentius's late fourth century (A.D.) *Tituli Historiarum* which reads "Aedificat templum Sapientia per Solomonis obsequium," and she translated it as "Wisdom builds a temple by Solomon's obedient hands." Like the verse from Proverbs, this text relates Solomon directly to the image of the House of Wisdom.
7. Réau, *Iconographie de l'art chrétien*, vol. 2, pt. 1, p. 292.
8. The present author's brief outline of the origin of the Coronation of the Virgin theme and the variety of visual forms it took was based on Réau's much more complete account in his *Iconographie de l'art chrétien*, vol. 2, pt. 2, pp. 621–25.
9. This tapestry, in the Patrimonio Nacional, Madrid, is one in the set of four known as the "paños de oro." They are said to have been produced by the Brussels entrepreneur Pieter van Aelst and bought by Juana la Loca in 1502. For pertinent text and illustration, see Paulina Junquera de Vega and Concha Herrero Carretero, *Catálogo de tapices del Patrimonio Nacional*, vol. 1, *Siglo XVI* (Madrid, 1986) p. 5.
10. The Burrell Collection, reg. no. 46/117; see *The Burrell Collection: Gothic Tapestries, a Selection*, exh. cat., McClellan Galleries, Glasgow Art Gallery (Glasgow, 1969) no. 92.
11. For a discussion and illustration of this tapestry, one of a group of four in a set dealing with the theme of the triumph of the Virtues, see *Tapisseries bruxelloises de la pré-Renaissance*, exh. cat., Musées Royaux d'Art et d'Histoire (Brussels, 1976) pp. 104–6. A tapestry showing another version of the same composition is in the cathedral of Saragossa; see Eduardo Torra de Arana et al., *Los Tapices de La Seo de Zaragoza* (Saragossa, 1985) pp. 224–27, illus. on foldout color pl. facing p. 224.
12. See in this catalogue two tapestries from the *Redemption of Man* series (29a, b), both with seated prophets in the lower corners; for notes on all ten subjects in that series, with illustrations, see Anna G. Bennett, *Five Centuries of Tapestry from the Fine Arts Museums of San Francisco* (San Francisco, 1976) pp. 54–73. For other tapestries with seated prophets and apostles in the corners, see D. T. B. Wood, "'Credo' Tapestries," *Burlington Magazine* 24 (1913–14) pp. 247–54 (pt. 1) and 309–17 (pt. 2), for a number of pieces from an *Apostles' Creed* series, and Adolph S. Cavallo, *Tapestries of Europe and of Colonial Peru in the Museum of Fine Arts, Boston* (Boston, 1967) pp. 83–87, for a Creed tapestry from a different series; see also Conde Viudo de Valencia de Don Juan, *Tapices de la Corona de España* (Madrid, 1903) vol. 2, pl. 2, for the *Mass of Saint Gregory* in the Patrimonio Nacional, Madrid, where the figures represent Saint Augustine and David. For two other tapestries in the Patrimonio Nacional that have seated figures of Old Testament prophets or kings in their lower corners, see Junquera de Vega and Herrero Carretero, *Catálogo de tapices del Patrimonio Nacional*, vol. 1, pp. 8, 31, both illus.
13. Avril Henry, *Biblia Pauperum: A Facsimile and Edition* (Ithaca, N.Y., 1987). See facsimile of the "q" page, the transcription of the Latin inscriptions, p. 158, and the translations of them by Henry, p. 119.
14. Henry, *Biblia Pauperum*, p. 119.

29

Two Episodes from *The Story of the Redemption of Man*

*a Peace and Mercy Win the Promise of Redemption
    for Man*
b Christ Is Born as Man's Redeemer

Southern Netherlands, 1500–1520
Wool warp; wool and silk wefts
29a: 13 ft. 11 in. × 26 ft. ¹/₂ in. (4.24 m × 7.94 m)
14–15 warp yarns per inch, 5–6 per centimeter
Fletcher Fund, 1938 (38.29)
29b: 13 ft. 7 in. × 25 ft. 9 in. (4.14 m × 7.85 m)
15–18 warp yarns per inch, 6–7 per centimeter
The Cloisters Collection, 1938 (38.28)

CONDITION

Since both hangings retain their original edges and the fabric of the borders is continuous with that of the fields, it is clear that none of the original fabric is missing. The silk wefts that represent the highlights in the fields and borders have been almost entirely replaced with modern yarns. Many of the wool wefts, particularly those that appear now as dark brown, have deteriorated and fallen out of the fabric, but most of these losses have been restored. In a few places the original warp and weft yarns have both been lost. At the time of writing these holes were being repaired with modern yarns.

At some time in the past 29b was cut into four pieces of irregular shape and unequal size. They have since been rejoined with new warp and weft yarns. The upper left corner of the composition and almost all of its lower half are represented on the largest of the four fragments which, like the others, also contains the adjacent parts of the border. The next fragment, in the upper left-central and central parts of the tapestry, contains the scene showing Virtues and angels surrounding the enthroned God the Father, an exterior scene in the distance to the right of that, and, in the foreground, the top of the pavilion in the scene below. The third fragment, to the right of the second, shows two Persons of the Trinity with three other figures in a pavilion and a bit of landscape in front of it. On the fourth fragment, which is joined to the right side of this piece, are represented the third Person standing in the rear right corner of the pavilion, the landscape with six figures in the upper right corner of the field, the upper half of the Nativity scene below, and the head and shoulders of the figure seated in the extreme right foreground.

While these losses, restorations, and repairs have changed the original appearance of both hangings to some extent, they have not significantly altered the character of the original drawing and modeling. The most important restoration involves the image of the double-headed eagle blazoned on the shield above the arch of the tax-collector's building in 29b. The weft yarns used to represent the eagle and the ground of the shield had been entirely replaced at some time in the past, and it is not possible to determine whether or not the eagle in this form was originally shown there, although it seems likely that it was (see Manufacture and Date). A photograph of this hanging published in 1888 (exh. cat. Barcelona, pl. 2 of tapestries) shows that the restored motif was in place at that time, and another published in 1926 (exh. cat. Burgos 1921, pl. XXIV) shows that it was still there shortly before the tapestry left the cathedral of Burgos. The weft yarns that had been used to restore the figure of the eagle and the ground of the shield have since been removed, and the warp yarns that were laid bare in this operation show traces of the figure of a double-headed eagle which could have been made either by the original wefts or by the restorer's yarns.

The colors in both pieces have faded, but each of the hues retains its identity and most of them are still relatively intense.

DESCRIPTION AND SUBJECT

The composition of 29a is built around a large group of figures that occupies the upper two-thirds of the central space. The Persons of the Trinity are represented as three identical mature bearded men who wear unpatterned gowns under their plain copes and closed crowns on their heads. They are seated on a paneled throne in the center. Beside and behind Them masses of angels emerge from the clouds; the two standing at the extreme left and right appear to be pushing the clouds away, toward the sides. The Son, seated at the left, points His scepter toward the earth and rests His left foot on an orb. The Father, in the center, holds His scepter upright and places His left hand on an orb that rests in His lap; His right hand is raised in benediction. The Holy Ghost,

29a

29b

seated at the right, also holds a scepter upright in His left hand and places His right hand on an orb. Directly below the Trinity one woman kneels behind another at the left and two others stand in a similar relationship at the right. They all wear unpatterned gowns and cloaks. The two in the farther plane wear hoods; the nearer two wear open crowns. The farther woman at left, rear, labeled *Pax* (Peace) on her cloak at thigh level, holds an olive branch in her right hand. The nearer figure to the right of her, labeled at hip level *Misericordia* (Mercy), holds a stalk of lilies in her right hand. Across from her in the nearer plane stands *Justicia* (Justice), labeled at hip level; she raises a sword in her right hand. Behind her stands a woman holding an open book; she is *Veritas* (Truth), labeled at ankle level.

Thistles, bulrushes, daisies, primroses, and other plants grow in or along the banks of a stream that runs across the front of this celestial ground. A small plank bridges the stream at the point where it turns and flows forward, bisecting the foreground of the tapestry into two separate meadows. At the left end of the meadow at the left, Justice swings back her sword to attack a man who crouches on the ground next to a seated woman labeled on her skirt as *luxria* (*Luxuria*, or Lechery), but Mercy restrains her. The man, who wears plain hose, a watered silk doublet, a loose funnel-sleeved coat, and wide round-toed shoes, turns to face his attacker and raises his right arm to protect his head. Written across the bottom of his coat is his name, *homo* (Man, or Mankind). His hat and a chaplet covered with flower petals lie on the ground before him. Lechery throws her arms up in horror. Behind her stand three other women who are dressed in gowns and mantles, as is Lechery, but they have hoods on their heads rather than the open crown that Lechery wears. The leftmost woman holds a lute in her right hand. There are no labels to identify any of these figures but it is clear from the context that they represent other Vices.

Across the stream, toward the right end of the meadow at the right, Man appears again, bending his knee in supplication before the kneeling figure of Mercy. Between and behind them stands a female figure whose name, *gra dei* (*Gratia Dei*, Grace of God), appears written on the bottom of her gown. Over the gown she wears a richly patterned velvet or damask cloak caught at the breast with a sunburst brooch. She holds a breastplate before her, offering it to Man. Peace, modestly dressed in a fitted gown and plain cloak, with a kerchief wound around her head, stands at the right. In the crook of her left arm she holds a helmet. Another group, represented on a smaller scale, appears directly above this one. These figures stand in an open field. In the center, Man throws his hands up in terror as three female figures attack him. The one at the far left wears body armor over her gown and a helmet on her head. Her label, written across the bottom of her gown, identifies her as Lechery. In her right hand she holds a spear which she is about to thrust into Man's chest. Between her and Man stands a woman in an unpatterned gown who has been outfitted with a helmet, shoulder armor, and a shield. Labeled *avaricia* (Avarice) on the bottom of her gown, she reaches out and grasps Man around the throat. Behind these two women stands a man wearing a hood and blowing into a large S-shaped horn. His label, written at waist level, is now illegible, but we know from his appearance in other scenes in this series of tapestries that he represents *Temptator* (the Tempter or Temptation). There are other female figures standing behind and to the right of Man. The first one at the right wears a helmet and gauntlets; she places her right hand behind his head and clutches his stomach with her left hand. She has a large curved sword hanging from her waist. On her gown at knee level she is labeled *Gula* (Gluttony). Behind her stands a woman wearing a mantle over her gown and a bonnet. She holds a club wrapped with a scroll that is inscribed with her name, *spes* (Hope). The two women standing directly behind Man are not labeled. The breastplate and helmet that Grace of God and Peace gave Man in the episode below lie on the ground.

To the right of this scene, in the middle distance,

Detail of 29b

Detail of 29a

Christ, dressed as He is in the central scene but with an aureole around His head, is shown seated on a bench. He holds a scepter in His left hand and an orb in His lap; His right hand is raised in benediction. Seven female figures stand or kneel in an arc before Him and look at Him intently. Some of them are wearing mantles or robes over their unpatterned gowns. On their heads these women wear hoods, veils, and, in two instances, crowns. To the left of Him sits the crowned *Caritas* (Charity) who holds a scepter in her right hand; her name is written near her right hip. At the right sits *humilitas* (Humility) who carries a scepter in her right hand and has a white dove perched on her left wrist. Her name is written on her mantle at knee level. Peace, labeled above

her head, stands to the left of Charity. In front of her stands Grace of God whose name appears above her head. Slightly below and to the right of her crouches *Miseria* (Misery) who leans on a stick and holds up a document for Christ to read. *Natura* (Nature, the nature that God had given Man when he was created, see below), labeled near the hem of her robe, kneels in the center and tears at her gown. To the right of her kneels the crowned figure of Mercy whose label appears on the lower part of her mantle; she seems to be calling Pity and Nature to Christ's attention.

An open landscape appears in the distance at the opposite end of the composition. Two women are leaning on the rim of a fountain in the middle distance, and

Detail of 29a

there are other figures in the background. In the fore-ground of this landscape, a man wearing hose, doublet, a robe, and a small round hat with an upturned brim sits on a low brick wall and embraces a young woman standing before him. She wears an unpatterned gown and a high, open crown on her head. To the right of this, and directly behind the episode in which Justice attacks Man with her sword, rises an octagonal pavilion whose front is open. Slender columns decorated with spiral garlands of narrow, thick-veined leaves support the arches that carry the vaulting above. The floor is carpeted with a patterned fabric. Inside the building stand nine women who are discussing the scene represented on a cloth that the two in the center hold up to view. It

shows a fully clothed young man lying on a bed and pulling a nude young woman to him. The women surrounding the cloth all wear gowns and mantles, crowns or hoods. Labels identify only three of them. Justice (holding a sword up in her left hand) stands at the far left and Charity is opposite her at the right. To the left of Charity is *fides* (Faith) whose name appears on the ground beneath her feet.

In the foreground of the composition, the two meadows are covered with blossoming plants and fruit trees of many kinds. Two mature male figures appear at the outer ends of the verdant meadows; one is seated in the lower left corner of the field, the other in the lower right corner. The man at the left wears a plain sleeveless ermine-lined tunic open at the sides over a patterned doublet cut with full crushed sleeves gathered in at the wrists, an ermine tippet, and an unpatterned hood. His name, *ierimie* (Jeremias), is written across the bottom of his tunic. He raises his left arm across his chest. His right arm drops, the hand resting on the right thigh. This hand holds the end of a scroll that falls to the ground in graceful curves and is inscribed:

Ascēdit mors p fenestras

("Ascendit mors per fenestras"; "For death is come up through our windows" [from Jeremias 9:21]).

His counterpart in the lower right corner of the field sits in a heavy armchair. A loose, unpatterned robe with a deep cape collar completely enshrouds his body. He wears a hat that has a high round crown and a wide, jewel-lined brim that is cut away in front and turns sharply upward at the sides, over the ears. He rests his right arm on the chair and raises his left hand in a gesture directed toward the scene in which Man pleads before Mercy. From this hand falls a scroll inscribed:

reddā ulcōnē hostibus deut XXXII

("reddam ultionem hostibus Deuteronomii XXXII"; "I will render vengeance to my enemies Deuteronomy 32" [from Deuteronomy 32:41]).

The fact that this man's quotation comes from the Book of Deuteronomy probably indicates that he represents Moses. As Standen noted, perhaps the horn-like ends of his divided hat brim were meant to allude to his identity.[1]

The scene in the upper left corner of 29b includes most of the figures that took part in the episode shown in the upper right corner of 29a. The narrative continues smoothly from that scene to this one. Here, Christ stands in a field and is accompanied by six female figures. The label across the breast of the woman standing next to Him identifies her as Humility. To the right of them sits the crowned Charity holding the sealed document that Pity had held up for Christ to read in the previous scene. To the right of this the crowned figure of Justice embraces and kisses Peace. The sword that Justice had been brandishing in 29a lies on the ground under her feet. The two women behind this pair lack labels, but they probably represent Mercy and Truth.

In the next scene to the right, which is set closer to the foreground, God the Father sits enthroned under a canopy of patterned damask or velvet supported by four slender columns. A length of patterned fabric hangs behind Him. He holds a scepter in His left hand and raises His right hand in benediction. Two angels stand at the back of the scene at the left and three others appear opposite them at the right. Four women are gathered next to the throne at the left. They all wear unpatterned gowns and mantles and have kerchiefs or veils on their heads. The two nearest the Father also wear crowns. The woman standing farthest to the left is identified as Truth at the bottom of her mantle. She bends forward to show to the crowned Humility a framed oval picture of the Virgin kneeling before the Child in the stable. Inscribed on the frame are letters that are now virtually illegible but which Standen suggested may have formed the words *incarn dmn dei*.[2] Behind Humility is a woman whose crown and sword identify her as Justice. A fourth woman stands behind Truth; there is no label to identify her. On the other side of the throne are an angel and a female figure who wears an ermine-lined gown and a crown. There is no label to identify her, but she probably represents Mercy. She hands the angel a scepter wrapped with a scroll inscribed with the words AVE/GR/PLENA/TECVM. He wears a patterned damask or velvet mantle over a plain tunic. His crown and the words on the scroll identify him as the archangel Gabriel.

To the right of this group the space opens out into the middle distance where a number of figures stand beyond a low battlemented and turreted wall. The stone buildings of a city rise behind them. Three men appear in an arched opening at the right. The leftmost one holds an open book; the one in the center is seated with an inscribed scroll in his hands at a table covered with a patterned cloth. Directly above him, at the center of the arch, an armorial shield charged with a double-headed eagle and surmounted by a coronet in the shape of an imperial crown is fixed on the wall. (The eagle has been removed; see Condition.) Joseph, accompanied by Mary at his left, places a coin on the table next to the others already there. Another man and woman stand behind Mary and Joseph.

To the right of this episode rises a small rectangular pavilion with an open front. A shallow jeweled arch carried on a pair of slender twisted columns enframes the opening. The side and rear walls are closed but fitted with windows. A patterned damask or velvet hanging covers most of the rear wall. God the Father and the Holy Spirit, represented as They were in 29a, stand in front of the hanging. Mary stands with hands crossed on her breast in front of Them and behind the seated figure of the pensive Christ. Gabriel, dressed in a tunic and a plain velvet cope decorated with a jeweled orphrey, stands in the left foreground holding the scepter that conveys his message. Here the inscription on the scroll (much restored) reads *Ave/maria/plne*(?). The crowned and labeled figure of Humility leans toward him with her arms outstretched. A narrow stream bordered by plants with long, slender leaves flows in front of the pavilion.

In the foreground, slightly to the left of this pavilion, is the octagonal temple where Mary and Joseph are being married. The hexagonal dais on which the figures stand is covered with a patterned fabric. The building's vaulted roof, surmounted by a cupola, is carried on arches supported by slender columns wrapped with long, narrow, thick-veined leaves. Mary, wearing a mantle over a loose gown and a crown on her head, is in the foreground at the left. Joseph, wearing a hood and mantle over a long tunic, stands opposite her. He carries a walking stick in his left hand and holds Mary's right hand in his own. A priest, between and behind them, covers their hands with his left one and raises his right hand in benediction. He wears a cope over a chasuble and alb; on his head is an elaborate bonnet with ermine-lined lappets. The heads of four men appear behind the priest; a fifth man, holding a short rod, stands next to Joseph. There are three women next to Mary and the heads of two more are visible beyond them. None of these figures is labeled.

The Nativity appears to the right of this episode. The scene is set in a flowery meadow that spreads out before a thatch-roofed stable. Mary, wearing a veil and an unpatterned mantle over her plain loose gown, kneels in the center, her head inclined slightly forward, her hands clasped in prayer. The nude Child, emanating rays of light, lies on the ground cradled in the cloth of her mantle. Joseph, dressed as he is in the wedding scene, appears in the left foreground, his knee bent, his arms slightly raised, a candle held in his left hand. Three small angels behind him gaze at the Child. A crowned female figure labeled as Humility stands behind Mary and points to the main figures as she addresses the woman beside her who kneels in adoration. This woman, who wears a wreath of roses on her head, is labeled *Castitas* (Chastity). A third woman appears behind these two. Two shepherds, inside the stable behind a low masonry wall, watch what is happening outside.

Two episodes related to the Nativity appear directly above. In the middle distance at the left three men occupy a rise of ground on which two trees grow. The man sitting at the left holds an open book in his lap and gazes into the sky. He wears a loose gown, a short mantle, and a round hat with an upturned brim. The man seated next to him, who wears an ermine-lined velvet robe and a plain chaperon, raises his left hand and addresses the first. The third man, standing behind the man reading, raises his left hand to shield his eyes as he gazes into the sky. In the landscape that opens out at the right beyond these figures, three kings, wearing tunics, mantles, and crowns, are sitting at the edge of a pool and bathing their feet in it. The kings at left and right look up into the sky where they see a vision of the nude Child carrying a cross and surrounded by rays of light.

At the opposite side of the composition, in the left foreground, a scene involving a mass of figures is set in front of a mound of earth. Man, identified by an inscription above his head, sits right of center. His ankles are bound in metal cuffs that are locked and chained to the ground. He gazes at the figures who enter from the left and raises his hands in wonder. Nature, labeled at the bottom of her skirt, sits next to him and clasps her fingers together as she also watches the figures. At the far left, beyond the mouth of a cave from which these figures emerge, stands the hooded Tempter whose name is written near his lips. He holds the shaft of a banner in his right hand and a large key in his left. The man leading the procession out of the cave wears a robe open at the sides over a long velvet gown; he carries a round hat with upturned brim in his left hand. His name, *abrahā* (Abraham), is written on the right shoulder of his cape. The name of the man walking behind him at the left, *Isa* (Isaac), appears written across his collar; and the man next to him is identified in the same way as *jacob*. The men walking next to and behind Jacob are not identified, but the crowned figure probably represents David. The woman who greets Abraham at the head of the procession is identified as Hope on the shoulder of her gown. Behind her stands Misery, identified by a label above her head.

At the left and right ends of the foreground sit two men holding inscribed scrolls. The one at the left wears over his tunic a yoked, ermine-lined sleeveless gown that is open at the sides and bordered with jewels; on his head is a plain tight cap. He raises his left hand to his breast and rests his right hand on his thigh. In this hand he holds the end of a scroll which is inscribed as follows:

Dn̄s · egrediet · de · loco ·/Isaie · xxvi/scō · suo

("Dominus egredietur de loco suo Isaiae 26"; "the Lord will come out of his place Isaias 26" [similar texts in both Isaias 26:21 and Micheas 1:2–3]).[3]

The other man, who sits at the opposite end of the foreground, wears a loose fur-lined robe and a crown encircling an elaborate hat whose upturned brim is studded with pearls. His right hand is raised; his left rests on his knee and holds the end of a scroll inscribed as follows:

Parvulus · nats · est · nobis ysaie ix

("Parvulus enim natus est nobis Isaiae 9"; "For a child is born to us Isaias 9" [from Isaias 9:6]).

Because these two men are not dressed alike, and also because in the other tapestries of this series the two figures in the corners never represent the same man, it seems likely that in this hanging the man at the left represents Micheas and the other man, Isaias (see note 3). Except for differences in the costume and scroll, the figure of the man at the left is exactly like that of the man who occupies the same position in the Metropolitan Museum's tapestry of the *Coronation of the Virgin* (28). However, that man almost certainly represents Solomon.

Like 29a, 29b shows a ground densely covered with flowering plants; and again the designer has used trees, plants, and waterways to separate the various narrative spaces from one another.

Both hangings have the same border design. Narrow stripes of solid color flank a wide band on whose dark blue ground there are stalks bearing roses, daisies, pansies, and round or oval fruits placed end to end, tied to one another with short lengths of ribbon. There are roots at the ends of some of the stalks; the ends of the others have been cut.

The fields of 29a and 29b represent two compositions in a series that we believe may have been complete in ten (see Related Tapestries). These two tapestries show the third and fourth installments of a complex visual narrative whose content derives both from Scripture and from related allegories that were developed in medieval poetry and drama. Writers who have studied these compositions believed that they had been based ultimately on some mystery or morality play. The use of pavilions with open fronts (and often sides as well) or "mansions" to serve as the settings for interior scenes and also the convention of labeling figures with their names derive from the production techniques of medieval theater and related entertainments like the mime shows and pageants that were presented on the occasion of ceremonial entries into cities or ecclesiastical processions.[4] Although some of the characters and incidents that appear in the tapestry compositions are also to be found in certain morality plays or poems whose texts have survived, no single known source contains all of them. It is possible that such a morality play or poem did exist at one time; but it is equally possible, indeed more likely, that the tapestries were designed to illustrate a scenario that had been written especially for the purpose.[5]

The first writer to isolate a group of tapestries illustrating this theme was D. T. B. Wood (1911–12). He identified eight compositions, exemplified by hangings in several different collections, as constituting a series he called the *Seven Deadly Sins*. The title was based on his belief that some tapestries that Cardinal Wolsey bought for Hampton Court Palace in 1521, referred to then as the "Story of the 7 Deadly Synnes," showed this series of compositions.[6] However, as Cavallo (1958, 168 n. 5) noted, we cannot be sure that the two tapestries of this series that are now at Hampton Court Palace, which led Wood to associate the title the *Seven Deadly Sins* with these compositions, were two of the "7 Deadly Synnes" pieces that Wolsey bought. In more recent literature, the series has also been entitled the *Fall and Salvation of Man*, the *Redemption of Man*, the *Struggle* (or *Conflict*) *of Virtues and Vices*, or variations of these. The only reasonably contemporary citation we have that surely refers to four pieces from the series appears in the inventory of tapestries belonging to the chapter of the cathedral of Burgos in 1560 (repeated in abbreviated form in the inventory of 1572) which lists "quatro tapices de las virtudes que dió el obispo don Rodríguez de Fonseca" (four tapestries of the Virtues that Bishop Rodríguez de Fonseca gave: from Steppe 1956, 46). In the inventories of 1777 and 1797 what were presumably the same four pieces were called "4 tapices iguales . . . en 1 paño está el nacimiento, en los demás los siete vicios capitales" (four similar tapestries . . . in one hanging is the Nativity, in the others the seven capital vices).[7] Since the Vices and Virtues represent only one aspect of the subject matter as a whole—that is, Christ's mission to reconcile mankind to God, mankind who had fallen from grace and was unable to resist the temptations of the Vices however much the Virtues attempted to strengthen him—it seems correct to assign the series a title that allows a broader interpretation of the subject. For that reason we prefer the *Redemption of Man* or some variation of it.

Bennett (1976, 55) observed that "three story lines cross, recross, and finally converge" and identified the three themes as follows: "the divine conflict," "the human conflict," and "the story of the Redeemer." Some of the characters who act out these stories represent the Deity and figures from Judeo-Christian Scripture; others are personifications of Virtues and Vices derived ultimately and mainly from Prudentius's fourth-century poem *Psychomachia*, and others are allegorical figures representing mankind and his nature. For all its convolutions, the subject is simply a variation of the story of Everyman and a generalized version of the parable of the Prodigal Son. These themes are so similar that tapestry designers were able to take certain figure groups from the compositions in one series and use them again in related contexts in designs for tapestries illustrating the other themes (see Source of the Design). The theological and moral content of all these narra-

Fig. 133. *The World Is Created and Man Falls from Grace.* Tapestry, southern Netherlands, first quarter of the sixteenth century. The Fine Arts Museums of San Francisco; Gift of The William Randolph Hearst Foundation.

Fig. 134. *The Vices Lead Man in a Life of Sin.* Tapestry, southern Netherlands, first quarter of the sixteenth century. The Fine Arts Museums of San Francisco; Gift of The William Randolph Hearst Foundation.

Detail of 29b

tives had been developed over a period of more than a thousand years; and by the time the *Redemption* tapestries were designed they were inextricably interwoven.

A great deal of confusion surrounds the definition of the two categories of evil to which Man became subject after his fall from grace. Neither early nor modern literature gives a consistent account of these powers, listing the same evils in one context as Sins (whether Capital or Deadly) and in another as Vices. However it is generally agreed that sin refers to an evil act whereas vice refers to an evil habit. The figures in these tapestries represent evil habits. Because of this, and also because most of the evils represented here are referred to in the *Psychomachia* as Vices and because the eighteenth-century inventories at Burgos that mention these tapestries use the phrase "the seven capital vices," we shall refer to these characters as Vices rather than Sins in the following interpretation of the tapestry narrative.

The first of the ten compositions shows the Trinity creating the world, the temptation and fall of Adam and Eve, and their expulsion from Eden (fig. 133). In the second tapestry Man (Adam), having fallen from his state of grace, sinks into a life of evil, seduced by the Vices, prodded on to greater error by the temptations of the flesh (fig. 134). He appears here dressed in worldly finery, "a pure exemplar of the Prodigal Son," as Bennett (1976, 62) observed. Temptation appears in human form as a boorish man labeled as the Tempter who attacks Man with a spear. Lechery appears as a queen receiving homage from Man who approaches her humbly in the company of the female characters Flesh, Gluttony, and Guilt. A number of Virtues personified as women discuss Man's sinful conduct among themselves and then bring their case before the Trinity. Justice raises her sword to express her aggressive disapproval, but before this part of the story ends Man is given a shovel as Labor offers to lead him on his first steps toward redemption. Bennett (1976, 60–63) has described and interpreted the first and second compositions in detail.

The story continues in 29a. In the Garden of Love which is represented in the upper left corner of the field Man continues his lustful pursuits. We see him fervently embracing a young woman in the garden, and on the cloth that is being exhibited to the Virtues in the adjacent building we see him pulling a nude girl to his bed. These revelations strengthen Justice's resolve to punish Man. She discovers him consorting with a group of Vices and raises her sword to strike him. At that moment Mercy intercedes and saves Man from Justice's sword. To settle Man's fate the four Virtues—referred to as the Four Daughters of God, that is, Peace, Mercy, Truth, and Justice—plead their cases before the Trinity during the trial known in contemporary literature as the Trial, or Parliament, of Heaven. This is an allegorical representation of the deliberation that takes place within the mind of God as He considers whether Man should be punished for his sins or returned to his original state of grace. Peace and Mercy argue in Man's favor; Truth and Justice plead against him. The Persons of the Trinity reach Their decision. The Son points His scepter toward earth which lies on the other side of the stream below. He has given Mercy, Peace, and Grace of God leave to defend Man against temptation by giving him armor and inspiration. But the effort fails. The Tempter attacks Man again: with his horn he summons the three armed Vices, Lechery, Greed, and Gluttony. The breastplate and helmet that Grace of God and Peace had given

Man—probably the breastplate of justice and the helmet of salvation mentioned in Isaias 59:17—have not helped him resist these evils; the armor lies useless on the ground at his feet. However the figure of Hope approaches with a club to help Man ward off the attack. To the right of this scene, in the middle distance, Mercy, Peace, and Grace of God return to heaven to plead once again that Man should be redeemed. Misery accompanies them and holds up for Christ to see the document representing the promise He had made to save Man. Nature tears at the bodice of her gown. The words of the two figures in the corners of the field, Jeremiah at the left ("For death is come up through [our] windows") and Moses at the right ("I will render vengeance to my enemies"), endorse these pleas. Seated between Charity and Humility, Christ raises His right hand to indicate that He will become incarnate and die to redeem Man.

The figure of *Natura* (Nature) in this and other scenes in 29a and 29b has been interpreted in a number of different ways. Wood (1911–12, 215) believed that she represented the Law of Nature, while Verdier (1955, 47 n. 15) identified her with the character *Mundus* in the Prodigal Son tapestry in Baltimore who leads the Vices to Man. Cavallo (1958, 154) called her Human Nature. Standen, in support of her interpretation of *Natura* as

Details of 29b

431

Fig. 135. *Christ the Savior as a Child.* Tapestry, southern Netherlands, first quarter of the sixteenth century. Cathedral, Palencia.

the created world which was damaged when Adam fell but restored when Man was reconciled to God, cited Romans 8:22 ("every creature groaneth and travaileth in pain, even till now").[8] In theological terms "Nature" may signify that part of man which can suffer through his sinning. In the tapestry, Nature is certainly in great distress. She pleads with Christ to save Man and restore her well-being.[9]

The next episode in the story appears in the distance at the left end of 29b which represents the fourth composition in the *Redemption of Man* series. Here Christ, still accompanied by Humility and Charity, watches as the Four Daughters of God are reconciled to each other as soon as the decision has been made to redeem Man. Justice has dropped her sword on the ground and is kissing Peace, and Mercy greets Truth in amity. Standen[10] noted that this image of reconciliation, as well as the idea of the Four Daughters of God itself, were derived from the text of Psalm 84:11 where it is said "Mercy and truth have met each other: justice and peace have kissed." The decision has been made, and Christ will sacrifice Himself to save Man.[11] This is the climax of the drama. The rest of the action represents the denouement which begins in the scene to the right of the Four Daughters where, seated under a canopy, the Father

gives Gabriel his commission and Mercy hands the archangel the scepter that carries the scroll bearing the words of the Annunciation. As this is taking place Truth shows Humility the picture representing Mary kneeling before the Child in front of the manger. Now events on earth move rapidly. Mary is married to Joseph in the closer of the two scenes that occupy the center of the hanging. The Annunciation in a form that incorporates the Incarnation appears in the building to the right of this and slightly above it. Humility receives Gabriel who makes his announcement to Mary in the presence of the Persons of the Trinity; and the figure of the adult Christ sits in front of Mary, His head directly in front of her womb. Freeman (1957–58, 131) interpreted the scene as one showing Gabriel making his announcement to Humility rather than to Mary herself; but he is in fact looking past the figure of Humility and at Mary or Christ. Freeman (1957–58, 130) also noted that in his *Meditationes* the Pseudo-Bonaventure wrote that the Trinity was in the room when Gabriel made his annunciation. That text may have inspired the scene in the tapestry.

To the left of this, as Joseph pays his tax in Jerusalem, the way is prepared for the Nativity which appears in the right foreground of the composition. Humility and

Fig. 136. *The Virtues Challenge the Vices as Christ Begins His Ministry.* Tapestry, southern Netherlands, first quarter of the sixteenth century. Museum of Fine Arts, Boston; Gift of the Hearst Foundation in memory of William Randolph Hearst.

Charity, together with a third female figure that Standen correctly suggested may represent Devotion, stand like handmaidens behind the kneeling Mary. The shepherds in the background look on in adoration. Directly above this is the scene showing three men at the left and three kings at the right. The men at the left are astrologers following the text of the ancient pagan seer Balaam's prophecy "I shall see him, but not now: I shall behold him, but not near. A star shall rise out of Jacob and a scepter shall spring up from Israel . . ." (Numbers 24:17). The three kings at the right (shown washing themselves, here just their feet, an unusual but not unknown detail in contemporary painting, as Rousseau [1950–51, 274–75] first noted) are the ones who saw and followed the star of Bethlehem, the star that was already associated in early Christian thought with the star that Balaam foresaw. The *Legenda Aurea* tells that the kings, who knew Balaam's prophecy and had been watching the sky, did see it at last in the form of a child with a cross beneath his head.

The events that take place in the curious grotto-like scene in the left foreground of the composition reveal the allegorical significance of the Nativity. Man and Nature are still shackled to earth (the dust to which they are doomed to return) but will soon be freed. Misery and

Hope are greeting David, Abraham, Isaac, Jacob, and the other patriarchs who will be released and redeemed when Christ descends into Hell after His crucifixion.

The narrative continues in the center of the fifth tapestry of the series where the Adoration of the Kings is represented (fig. 135). To the left of this a number of smaller compositions represent the Circumcision, the Tiburtine Sibyl showing Augustus a vision of the Virgin and Child, and the three kings discussing the star with Herod. In the right-hand section of the tapestry there are three scenes from Christ's infancy and boyhood. In the first, the infant Christ is being presented in the temple. In the second He is shown disputing with the doctors. In the third He greets the young John the Baptist in the presence of Mary and Joseph, Elizabeth and Zacharias. Cavallo (1957, 25–35) described and discussed this composition in detail.

The sixth subject deals with events that took place during Christ's manhood (fig. 136). John baptizes Him and later is beheaded. Christ raises Lazarus and receives the woman taken in adultery. Judas is given the thirty pieces of silver. A number of allegorical scenes appear along with these narrative ones. In the background left of center John preaches to a group of figures that includes Man, Nature, and Abraham while the Tempter

Fig. 137. *The Virtues Battle the Vices as Christ Is Crucified.* Tapestry, southern Netherlands, first quarter of the sixteenth century. The Fine Arts Museums of San Francisco; Gift of The William Randolph Hearst Foundation.

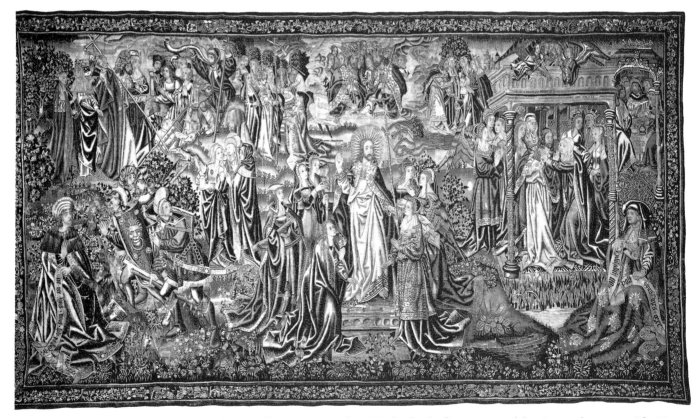

Fig. 138. *Christ Rises and Rescues Man from Hell.* Tapestry, southern Netherlands, first quarter of the sixteenth century. The Fine Arts Museums of San Francisco; Gift of The William Randolph Hearst Foundation.

434

Fig. 139. *Christ Ascends to Heaven and Man is Reconciled to God.* Tapestry, southern Netherlands, first quarter of the sixteenth century. Cathedral, Palencia.

Fig. 140. *Christ Makes His Last Judgment and the Vices Are Vanquished.* Tapestry, southern Netherlands, first quarter of the sixteenth century. Musée du Louvre, Paris.

435

leers in the background; the same characters appear again in a similar scene in the background right of center. In the foreground at the right Charity and Envy are shown as the challengers in an invitation for the Virtues and Vices to do battle. Behind and to the right of this the seven Virtues arm Christ or the Christian Knight as He leads them into battle. Cavallo (1958, 147–68; 1967, 91–94) described this composition and discussed the interpretation of its subject in detail.

The battle between the Virtues and Vices rages in the main section of the seventh tapestry (fig. 137). The Crucifixion is shown in the center background. A figure representing the Old Testament sounds her horn at the left, and opposite her the New Testament answers in kind. The forces of the Christian Knight and the Virtues, all mounted on symbolic steeds of various kinds, charge in from the left to meet the Vices, similarly mounted, entering from the right. Bennett (1976, 66–69) described and interpreted this subject in detail.

The eighth composition (fig. 138) shows the Resurrection of Christ in the center. God the Father and the Holy Spirit look down from above. The soldiers who had been guarding the tomb flee in terror toward the left, and the three Marys who had come to anoint the body appear behind them. At the right there are three scenes showing the risen Christ appearing to Mary Magdalen, to His mother, and to His disciples at Emmaus. In the upper left corner of the field Christ, having descended into Hell, breaks open the doors and releases the souls of Man, Nature, Abraham, and others as the Tempter blows his horn. To the right of this Christ leads the procession of the redeemed to Heaven, past the Fountain of Life. Bennett (1976, 70–73) has given a detailed account of the subject.

In the ninth composition Christ is shown ascending to Heaven to be received by God the Father and the Holy Spirit (fig. 139). In other scenes He is shown appearing to Saints Peter and James and to the Virgin. In the upper right section of the field Grace of God presents redeemed Man to the Trinity while the Vices and the Tempter are sent to their defeat among the demons below.

The tenth and last composition in the series shows a magnificent arrangement of figures that sweeps across the entire width of the field (fig. 140). In the center Christ is seated on a rainbow before His cross, the orb of the world beneath His feet. In the foreground Mercy leads Man, Nature, and the others who have been redeemed forward to receive His blessing while angels above blow their horns or fly toward the throne bearing bundles of saved souls. At the right Justice drives the damned, the Vices, and the Tempter away from Christ as

a host of angels flying above sound their horns or goad them with spears. Taylor (1935–36, 1–15) described and discussed the composition in detail.

In all but the first composition, the *Creation,* there are venerable figures seated in the lower left and right corners of the field. Some of them are labeled with their names. We can deduce the identity of the others from the texts inscribed on the scrolls in their hands. With two possible exceptions these nine pairs of men were clearly intended to represent prophets or other figures from the Old Testament. Among the exceptions may be listed the figure in the lower left corner of the fifth composition who holds a blank scroll. Cavallo (1957, 26, 30) suggested that he may have been meant to represent Jacobus de Voragine since he seems to be pointing directly at the scene showing the Tiburtine Sibyl and Octavian which was derived from Jacobus's *Legenda Aurea.* However since this man's headdress incorporates what could be an open crown he may represent some king instead. In an attempt to identify the figure seated in the lower left corner of the sixth composition whose inscription comes from no known biblical source except perhaps from John 4:1, Cavallo (1958, 157) noted but rejected as improbable the possibility that this man represents John the Evangelist.

Figures of prophets, patriarchs, apostles, or saints flanking scenes from the Bible in these and similar tapestries derive ultimately from the prophetic figures that appear in the *Biblia Pauperum* where they function as interpreters in compositions that bring types from the Old Testament into association with scenes from Christian iconography (see the discussion under 28 concerning the relation of such a tapestry to the *Biblia Pauperum*). Prophets or prophet-like figures of this kind appear in paintings of the period but less frequently than they do in prints and tapestries. Standen found an early sixteenth-century Netherlandish painting of the *Coronation of the Virgin* by Albert Cornelis in which half-figures holding inscribed scrolls appear in the lower left and right corners.[12] Among other tapestries that show figures like these at the sides may be cited the *Coronation of the Virgin* in the Metropolitan Museum (28) in which only one of the figures has been preserved; a *Presentation of the Child in the Temple* and a tapestry dossal of the *Nativity,* both in the Patrimonio Nacional in Madrid; and a somewhat later *Deposition* in the Palazzo Reale in Naples where the two figures are standing at the sides rather than sitting in the corners of the field.[13] These figures represent prophets and kings from the Old Testament. However in the *Creed* tapestry in Boston (see Cavallo 1967, 83–87) one figure in each pair represents an apostle, the other a prophet. The prophet-like figure in the lower right corner of the *Mass of Saint Gregory* in the Patrimonio Nacional in Madrid represents Saint Augustine; the figure in the lower left corner represents David.[14]

SOURCE OF THE DESIGN

A number of the figures and figure groups that appear in these ten compositions are similar to some that have been identified in certain Netherlandish paintings of the second half of the fifteenth century (see below). However each of the compositions as a whole shows formal conventions that differ from those found in contemporary easel paintings. The designer obviously knew Netherlandish painting intimately, and he may have been a painter of easel pictures himself. But he was also able to combine disparate spaces and subjects in ways that satisfied the particular requirements of tapestry design. Cavallo (1958, 167) suggested that this anonymous Netherlandish or Netherlands-trained artist was someone who probably also designed the *Story of the Prodigal Son* tapestries in Baltimore and Louisville (Verdier 1955, figs. 1, 3). Souchal (in Paris 1973, 212–13) considered the question of the designer's identity and concluded, as Cavallo (1958, 167) and Standen[15] had done, that he remains anonymous for the present. Like them, she disagreed with Taylor (1935–36, 10–14) and other earlier writers who had attributed the compositions to a number of artists including Hugo van der Goes and Jan Gossart; and she believed furthermore that the *Redemption* tapestries could have been designed in a workshop rather than by a single artist. She also considered the possibility that Jan van Roome or his followers had designed them, a suggestion that a number of other writers had made; but she concluded, as we have done, that these compositions and many others like them reflect a common style of the time rather than the personal style of any one man. Bennett (1976, 56–57) suggested that the tapestry designer might have been associated with the workshop of Pieter van Aelst because she believed that he may have had access to cartoons for hangings that were produced in that shop.

Certain figures and groups in the ten compositions have been traced to paintings that represent either the direct source of these motifs or, more likely, that share with the tapestries a dependence on some common source. Taylor (1935–36, 11 and fig. 13) believed that there was a close connection between the temptation scene in the *Creation* tapestry and a detail of the same subject in Hugo van der Goes's painting of the *Fall of Man* in Vienna, an opinion with which we cannot agree. On the other hand Standen called attention to two paint-

Fig. 141. *The Wedding of Joseph and Mary,* by the Master of the View of Saint Gudule. Panel painting, Brussels, second half of the fifteenth century. Musées Royaux des Beaux-Arts de Belgique, Brussels.

ings that illustrate the wedding of Mary and Joseph in forms very much like the wedding scene in 29b. One of these, now in the Musées Royaux des Beaux-Arts in Brussels, was painted by the Master of the View of Saint Gudule (fig. 141). The other appears on the left inner wing of an altarpiece of the story of Mary and Joseph in Brussels.[16] Standen also found that the Nativity scene in 29b is similar in form to the Adoration of the Child on the central panel of Rogier van der Weyden's triptych of the Nativity in the Gemäldegalerie der Staatlichen Museen in Berlin.[17] Souchal (in Paris 1973, 212) pointed out the striking resemblance that exists between the figures of Christ, Mary, and John the Baptist in the *Last Judgment* tapestry and those figures in Rogier's altarpiece of the same subject in the Hôtel-Dieu in Beaune, a relation-

437

ship that Taylor (1935–36, 5) had already mentioned.[18] Cavallo (1958, 167–68, fig. 10) pointed out a similarity of form that relates the scene of the beheading of John the Baptist in the sixth composition to a painting of the same subject by the Master of Saint Severin in the Museum of Fine Arts, Boston.

Several writers have called attention to the fact that certain motifs in the *Redemption of Man* compositions appear again in tapestries that belong to other series. These are stock motifs that either were used over again in the same shop or shared among a number of different shops. Verdier (1955, 27 and fig. 3) noted that the scene in the *Prodigal Son* tapestry in Louisville that shows a group of Vices and the Tempter attacking Man virtually duplicates the corresponding scene in 29a. Standen pointed out that the scene in the left foreground of 29a, where Justice prepares to attack Man with her sword, is repeated with slight changes in the central foreground of one of the four *Triumph of the Virtues and Vices* tapestries in Brussels and its near-duplicates in Saragossa, Lisbon, and Hampton Court.[19] A different but closely related figure group occupies the lower central section of a somewhat later tapestry in the Bayerisches Nationalmuseum in Munich.[20] Standen noticed that the figure of the seated Christ in the Incarnation scene in 29b is virtually the same, reversed, as the corresponding figure in the Annunciation tapestry of the *Triumph of the Virgin* set in the Patrimonio Nacional in Madrid and that the figure of Joseph and some of the female figures in the Nativity scene of 29b are similar to corresponding figures in the Presentation of the Christ Child tapestry that belongs in the same set of hangings in Madrid.[21] She called attention to similar figures of Mary, Joseph, and the Child in a tapestry of the Adoration of the Shepherds now in the Museo di Palazzo Venezia in Rome.[22] Bennett (1976, 56) credited Delmarcel with observing that the group of three angels hovering above the Adoration of the Magi scene in the fifth composition of the *Redemption of Man* series reappears in the Presentation of the Christ Child tapestry in Madrid (see note 21). We can add to these observations the fact that the figures of Mary, Joseph, and the Child in the Nativity scene of 29b are virtually repeated, in reverse, in a Nativity tapestry now in the Musée Mayer van den Bergh in Antwerp (Souchal in Paris 1973, 192–94, illus.).

MANUFACTURE AND DATE

Most writers have dated these two tapestries and the others in the series within the first quarter of the sixteenth century on considerations of style. Digby (1980, 34) endorsed this dating with the observation that Don Juan Rodríguez de Fonseca (died 1524) had bequeathed tapestries from the series to the cathedral of Burgos and that Cardinal Wolsey had bought what were thought to be others woven after the same cartoons in 1522 (see note 6). Souchal (in Paris 1973, 213) dated the series in the early sixteenth century or, because the architecture is still Gothic in style, at the end of the fifteenth century. De Ricci (1913, 27) believed that the women's bonnets in 29a indicated that the hanging could not be dated much later than 1510. Steppe (1976, 102) dated the series at the end of the fifteenth century or beginning of the sixteenth but without giving arguments to support his opinion. Cavallo (1957, 34) suggested that the design could be slightly earlier than 1500 but did not spell out his reasons. Standen believed that the Metropolitan Museum's two hangings were designed about 1500 but probably woven a bit later, perhaps as late as 1510.[23] Taylor (1935–36, 10–13) developed an elaborate theory associating the cartoons for the *Redemption of Man* tapestries with the painted hangings that Hugo van der Goes produced to decorate the streets of Ghent for the ceremonial entry of Charles le Téméraire and his bride Margaret of York in 1468; and he proposed furthermore that the "one piece of Arras of the Judgment" that Edward IV, brother of Margaret of York, bought in the same year must have been either the tapestry now in Worcester or one woven after the same cartoon. However the style of these compositions indicates that they could not possibly have been designed as early as 1468–70, the period to which Taylor (1935–36, 1, 14 n. 3) assigned the Worcester hanging. Taylor also believed that the cartoons, altered as necessary to account for changing fashions, continued in use until about 1490–1510, the date to which he assigned the *Last Judgment* tapestry in the Louvre.

Don Juan Rodríguez de Fonseca, who before his death in 1524 had bequeathed 29a and 29b along with two other pieces from the same series (see Related Tapestries) to the cathedral chapter in Burgos as well as another four pieces to the chapter in Palencia, visited the Netherlands in the opening years of the sixteenth century, and it has been suggested that he might have bought the tapestries there at that time or perhaps instead at some other time in Spain, possibly at the annual fair held at Medina del Campo where Netherlandish tapestries were offered for sale.[24] It has also been said that he bought the tapestries in the Netherlands in 1519.[25] In either case, these suggestions do not help us assign the hangings a date any earlier than one which can be deduced on considerations of style alone. In regard to fashions in clothing, what little evidence the tapestries contain—the figures represent historical or allegorical characters rather than contemporary civilian people—points to a date just before or after 1500. The few fashionable elements we can discern in these garments and accessories correspond in basic cut and form (although not in the details which varied from one fashion center to another) to those found in the Metropolitan Museum's *Hunt of the Unicorn* tapestries (20a–h), which we believe were designed and woven between 1495 and 1505. The most notable similarities appear in the shape of the men's wide round-toed shoes; the cut of the women's gowns, especially those with sleeves that are tight and narrow from shoulder to elbow and then flare out like funnels; the loosely tied scarflike girdles that fall to a knotted point below the waist in front; the hoods with lappets and the bonnets worn low and well back on the head; and the men's small, round hats with upturned brims.

The tapestries have the kind of drawing, modeling, figure types, and weaving quality that have traditionally been associated with hangings attributed to Brussels producers. Because Taylor, Rorimer, and some later writers labored under the misapprehension that the double-headed eagle blazoned on the shield in the tax-collecting episode in 29b represented the coat of arms of the emperor Maximilian, they associated these hangings with that emperor and his son Philippe le Beau and Philippe's wife, Juana of Spain. As a result they believed that the tapestries could have been produced by Pieter van Aelst who served as court upholsterer to the Hapsburgs early in the sixteenth century. Even though the double-headed eagle these writers saw in the tapestry was not original (see Condition), we believe there was an eagle, probably a double-headed one, on this shield. In any case, since both double-headed and single-headed eagles were used in the late Middle Ages to represent the ancient Roman empire as well as the Holy Roman Empire, and since the taxation scene is set in the time of the ancient empire, there can be little doubt that the designer intended the eagle, whichever form he gave it, to allude to that empire and not to the Hapsburgs.[26] Standen saw some support for the idea of attributing the production to van Aelst because she believed that the figure of one of the soldiers in the *Resurrection* tapestry in Trent that is thought to have been produced by van Aelst (see discussion under 45) was based on the figure of Man being attacked by Justice in 29a.[27] The figures do indeed resemble one another, but they may represent a common source rather than a stock figure belonging only to this producer. Taylor (1935–36, 9) attributed the manufacture of the Worcester tapestry to Philippe de Mol, whom he identified incorrectly as a weaver rather

than as the man who, some writers thought, had painted the cartoon for the *Legend of Herkinbald* tapestry in Brussels.

If one could prove that Pieter van Aelst had produced the *Redemption of Man* tapestries, it would be reason enough to support the attribution to Brussels. However we cannot be certain that there were no other producers supplying tapestries of this style and quality at the same time and operating someplace other than Brussels. The cathedral of Saragossa owns a tapestry that shows the second composition in the *Redemption* series (see Related Tapestries) and has the Brussels mark (B-shield-B) near the right end of its lower outer guard. However this band of weaving was sewn to the main fabric at some later time and therefore cannot be cited as proof that that tapestry was produced in Brussels.[28]

RELATED TAPESTRIES

Wood's list of eight compositions (1911–12, 215, 216, 221) included the ones cited below under numbers 1, 3, 4, and 6–10. Later, Cavallo (1957, 31) demonstrated that numbers 2 and 5 belong with the others. Therefore we know that there were at least ten compositions in the *Redemption of Man* series. No tapestries showing additional ones are known to have survived. The fact that there were ten pieces in the set of hangings that François Fouquet, archbishop of Narbonne, gave to the chapter of the cathedral of Saint-Just in Narbonne in 1673 tends to confirm our belief that the series contained only ten compositions.[29] However it is possible that other pieces once existed since a number of subjects that would seem pertinent, like some of the episodes in the story of the Passion that preceded the Crucifixion, are not represented in the series as we know it.

No other tapestry showing the composition of 29b is known to have survived, and we know of only one other complete example of 29a. It is preserved in Hampton Court Palace and has been published by Marillier (1962, 14–15 and pl. 11; see fig. 142 here), among others. There are also a number of smaller hangings or fragments that represent the same composition. Two of them show important sections of the design. One of these pieces, which shows a bit more than the left half of the complete composition (fig. 143), is now in the Burrell Collection in Glasgow.[30] A smaller piece with only the eight figures in the left foreground of the complete composition (fig. 144) is in the Victoria and Albert Museum.[31] Since both of these hangings show the scene of Justice attacking Man that appears in the left foreground of the complete pieces in the Metropolitan Museum and Hampton Court Palace, we may conclude that at least

Fig. 142. *Peace and Mercy Win the Promise of Redemption for Man.* Tapestry, southern Netherlands, first quarter of the sixteenth century. Hampton Court Palace, Middlesex.

four different tapestries were woven after the cartoon that served the weavers of 29a or some version of it. A fragment of tapestry showing the four figures in the lower right-central section of the complete composition, where Grace of God and Peace bring a breastplate and helmet to Man, has also survived. It was formerly in the collection of Fernand Schutz in Paris.[32] A smaller fragment representing part of the upper portion of the Parliament of Heaven scene was sold in New York in 1941.[33] Yet another fragment, one with the scene in which the Tempter and Vices attack Man just to the right of the Parliament of Heaven, belonged at one time to French and Company and may be the piece that Hunter (1925, 33) referred to as being in the Kelekian collection.[34] Finally, a fragment showing almost all of the scene in the far right middle ground of 29a, where Christ raises His right hand to signal His promise to redeem Man, is to be made a gift to the Fine Arts Museums of San Francisco.[35]

Bennett (1976, 55–71), Cavallo (1967, 94–95), and Standen[36] compiled comprehensive lists of the known surviving tapestries (both whole and fragmentary) together with notes on their present or most recently known locations. The list that follows incorporates data from these three sources. The titles given below differ

from the ones that Cavallo (1967, 94–95) coined and that Bennett and Standen used later with some variations. In concocting the following titles for each of the ten compositions—we do not know what they were called in the early sixteenth century—we have attempted to suggest both their scriptural and allegorical content.

The various examples of each composition that are cited in this discussion show slight differences in the details and colors: they are not exact duplicates of one another. The pieces that we know may be listed as follows according to their present location and their provenance (when known).

1. The World Is Created and Man Falls from Grace: four complete hangings—Fine Arts Museums of San Francisco (fig. 133), from the cathedral of Toledo (Bennett 1976, 60–61); Kasteel De Haar, Haarzuilens, the Netherlands, from the collection of the duke of Berwick and Alba;[37] cathedral of Saint-Just, Narbonne, sole survivor of the set of ten hangings given to the chapter of the cathedral of Saint-Just by François Fouquet, archbishop of Narbonne, in 1673 (see note 29); in the Vatican in 1855 and by 1878 in the collection of a M. Richard, described as lacking its border.[38] According to Wood (1911–12, 215), a fragment of a tapestry with this subject

440

Fig. 143. *Peace and Mercy Win the Promise of Redemption for Man* (showing somewhat more than the left half of the complete composition). Tapestry, southern Netherlands, first quarter of the sixteenth century. The Burrell Collection, Glasgow Museums and Art Galleries.

was exhibited in Brussels in 1905; however we have no other indication that such a fragment existed, and we believe that Wood probably was referring to a fragment of a tapestry with a related composition that was exhibited on that occasion (see 7 in the list here).

2. The Vices Lead Man in a Life of Sin: four complete hangings—Fine Arts Museums of San Francisco (fig. 134), from the cathedral of Toledo (Bennett 1976, 61–65);

Palencia, cathedral, bequeathed by Juan Rodríguez de Fonseca;[39] Saragossa, cathedral;[40] and in the Vatican in 1855 and by 1878 in the collection of a M. Richard.[41]

3. Peace and Mercy Win the Promise of Redemption for Man: a complete hanging in the Metropolitan Museum (29a) from the cathedral of Burgos; and, as noted above, another complete hanging, two abridged ones, and three fragments.

441

Fig. 144. *Pity Restraining Justice* (lower left section of the complete composition for *Peace and Mercy Win the Promise of Redemption for Man*). Tapestry, southern Netherlands, first quarter of the sixteenth century. Victoria and Albert Museum, London.

4. Christ Is Born as Man's Redeemer: a complete hanging in the Metropolitan Museum (29b) from the cathedral of Burgos; no other extant examples known.

5. Christ the Savior as a Child: one complete hanging in the cathedral of Palencia (fig. 135), bequeathed by Juan Rodríguez de Fonseca;[42] and another, cut into two pieces and lacking a narrow section left of center, in the Fogg Art Museum, Harvard University, Cambridge, said to have come from the Castello Ventoso, Portugal (Cavallo 1957, 25–35, figs. A–C).

6. The Virtues Challenge the Vices as Christ Begins His Ministry: two complete hangings—Museum of Fine Arts, Boston (fig. 136), from the collection of the duke of Berwick and Alba (Cavallo 1958, 147–68); Palencia, cathedral, bequeathed by Juan Rodríguez de Fonseca.[43] There is also a piece in Hampton Court Palace that

shows the right half of this composition (Marillier 1962, 13, 15–16, pl. 12).

7. The Virtues Battle the Vices as Christ Is Crucified: four complete hangings—Fine Arts Museums of San Francisco (fig. 137), from the cathedral of Toledo (Bennett 1976, 66–69); Burgos, cathedral, bequeathed by Juan Rodríguez de Fonseca (Steppe 1956, 46, fig. 14); Kasteel De Haar, Haarzuilens, the Netherlands, from the collection of the duke of Berwick and Alba;[44] in the Vatican in 1855 and by 1878 in the collection of a M. Richard.[45] A fragment showing the figure of the New Testament and angels belonged to Ch. L. Cardon in 1905 when it was exhibited in Brussels, and a fragment with the figure of the Old Testament and angels was sold in New York in 1921.[46]

8. Christ Rises and Rescues Man from Hell: two

complete hangings—Fine Arts Museums of San Francisco (fig. 138), from the cathedral of Toledo (Bennett 1976, 70–73); Burgos, cathedral, bequeathed by Juan Rodríguez de Fonseca (Steppe 1956, 46); and two abridged examples, one in the Art Institute of Chicago, from the collection of the duke of Berwick and Alba,[47] and another in the Vatican in 1855.[48]

9. Christ Ascends to Heaven and Man Is Reconciled to God: two complete hangings—Kasteel De Haar, Haarzuilens, the Netherlands, from the collection of the duke of Berwick and Alba;[49] and Palencia, cathedral, bequeathed by Juan Rodríguez de Fonseca (fig. 139).[50]

10. Christ Makes His Last Judgment and the Vices Are Vanquished: three complete hangings—Worcester Art Museum, said to have come from the Castello Ventoso, Portugal (Taylor 1935–36, 1–15); Musée du Louvre (fig. 140), from the collection of the duke of Berwick and Alba (Souchal in Paris 1973, 208–9); and Palazzo Venezia, Rome (Brugnoli 1965, 232 and fig. 63).

The set of hangings from which 29a and 29b came consisted of eight pieces. Bishop Juan Rodríguez de Fonseca bequeathed four of them to the cathedral chapter of Palencia (cited under titles 2, 5, 6, and 9 in the list above) and the other four to the chapter of Burgos (under titles 3 and 4, the two pieces now in the Metropolitan Museum, and 7 and 8, still in Burgos).

HISTORY

29a and b in the collection of Juan Rodríguez de Fonseca, bishop of Burgos from 1514 to 1524, together with six other hangings from the same set. It has been suggested that he bought the eight tapestries in the Netherlands either in or before 1519 or perhaps instead in Spain sometime before his death in 1524 (see notes 24 and 25).

Bequeathed with two other hangings from this set to the chapter of the cathedral of Burgos by Juan Rodríguez de Fonseca; delivered by his brother and heir Antonio de Fonseca in October 1526.[51]

In the cathedral of Burgos from 1526 to 1926. Mentioned in cathedral inventories of 1560, 1572, 1777, and 1797.[52]

Sold by the chapter of the cathedral of Burgos in 1926.[53]

Property of French and Company, New York, 1931–38.

Purchased by the MMA, 1938: 29a, through the Fletcher Fund, and 29b, The Cloisters Collection.

EXHIBITIONS

Barcelona, 1888. Exposición Universal de Barcelona: Album de la sección arqueológica, pp. 57, 113, pl. 2 [29b] in section illustrating the tapestries. 29b lent by the cathedral of Burgos.

Madrid, 1892–93. Exposición Histórico-Europea de Madrid 1892: Las Joyas de la Exposición. Madrid, 1893, nos. 91, 92, pls. CCIX, CCX (illus. of 29a only). 29a and b lent by the cathedral of Burgos.

Burgos, 1921. VII Centenario de la catedral de Burgos: Catálogo general de la Exposición de Arte Retrospectivo. Burgos, 1926, no. 283 [29b], pl. XXIV. 29b lent by the cathedral of Burgos.

PUBLICATIONS

Müntz, Eugène. "Tapisseries allégoriques inédites ou peu connues." Fondation Eugène Piot: Monuments et Mémoires, Académie des Inscriptions et Belles Lettres, Paris, 9 (1902) pp. 99–100. 29a described and discussed briefly.

Wood, D. T. B. "Tapestries of The Seven Deadly Sins," pts. I (pp. 210–22) and II (pp. 277–89). Burlington Magazine 20 (1911–12) p. 215. 29a and 29b discussed briefly; illus. p. 214, pl. I, nos. 2 [29a] and 3 [29b]; details illus. p. 279, pl. I, b and c [29a], d [29b], and p. 282, pl. II, f–h [29a], j [29b].

Hunter 1912, p. 280. Mentions these two tapestries in Burgos cathedral but not by name.

de Ricci, Seymour. Catalogue of Twenty Renaissance Tapestries from the J. Pierpont Morgan Collection. Paris, 1913. 29a and 29b mentioned p. 25; 29a briefly described and discussed, p. 27.

Kendrick, A. F. Catalogue of Tapestries. Victoria and Albert Museum, London. 1st ed., 1914, p. 38; 2d ed., 1924, p. 35. 29a mentioned.

Göbel 1923, vol. 1, pp. 124–25, 156. 29a and 29b briefly described and discussed.

Hunter 1925, pp. 32, 35, 38. 29a and 29b briefly described.

Thomson 1930, p. 171. 29a and 29b mentioned.

Taylor, Francis Henry. "'A Piece of Arras of the Judgment.'" Worcester Art Museum Annual 1 (1935–36) pp. 9, 12, 14 n. 3. 29a and 29b mentioned as from Burgos cathedral, then as in W. R. Hearst collection; illus. figs. 3 [29a] and 4 [29b].

Rorimer, James J. "New Acquisitions for The Cloisters." MMA Bulletin 33, no. 5, section 2 (May 1938) p. 19. 29a and 29b discussed briefly; 29b illus. fig. 15.

Forsyth, William H. "A Tapestry from Burgos Cathedral." MMA Bulletin 33, no. 6 (June 1938) pp. 148–52. 29a and 29b discussed at length, 29a described in detail; 29a illus. figs. 1 (full view), 2 and 3 (details).

Rorimer, James J. The Cloisters: The Building and the Collection of Mediaeval Art in Fort Tryon Park. MMA, New York, 1938, pp. 99–101. 29a mentioned, 29b described and discussed at length; detail of Nativity scene in 29b illus. fig. 53. References are the same in the 1941, 1944, and 1951 editions of this publication; see below for the 1963 edition.

Kurth, Betty. "Masterpieces of Gothic Tapestry in the Burrell Collection." Connoisseur 117 (1946) p. 8. 29a mentioned.

de Mendonça, Maria José. "Uma tapeçaria dos vícios e das virtudes: 'A Música.'" Boletim do Museu Nacional de Arte Antiga 1 (1946) pp. 32–33. 29a described and discussed, illus. fig. 2; location given erroneously as cathedral of Burgos.

Rorimer, James J. Mediaeval Tapestries: A Picture Book. MMA, New York, 1947, p. [3]. 29a and 29b discussed briefly; 29b illus. figs. 11 (full view) and 12 (detail).

Rousseau, Theodore, Jr. "A Flemish Altarpiece from Spain." MMA Bulletin, n.s. 9 (1950–51) p. 275. 29b mentioned.

Verdier, Philippe. "The Tapestry of the Prodigal Son." The Journal of the Walters Art Gallery 18 (1955) pp. 11, 15, 26, 27, 32, 38, 39, 41, 46 n. 3, 47 n. 15, 48 n. 30, 56 n. 112, 57 n. 125. 29a and 29b discussed briefly and in different specialized contexts; 29a illus. figs. 4 (full view), 17, 21 (details); 29b illus. figs. 2 (full view), 5, 16, 18 (details).

Steppe, J. K. "Vlaamse Wandtapijten in Spanje: Recente Gebeurtenissen en Publicaties." Artes Textiles 3 (1956) pp. 45–47. 29a and 29b discussed briefly; 29a illus. fig. 13.

Cavallo, Adolph S. "Scenes from the Childhood of Christ: A Late Gothic Tapestry." Annual Report of the Fogg Art Museum: 1956–1957. Cambridge, Mass., 1957, p. 32 n. 7. 29b mentioned.

Faure, Lily. "Vlaamse Wandtapijten in Spanje: De Verzameling te Burgos." Handelingen van het XXIIe Vlaams Filologencongres. Ghent, 1957, p. 344. 29a and 29b mentioned.

Freeman, Margaret B. "The Iconography of the Merode Altarpiece." MMA Bulletin, n.s. 16 (1957–58) p. 131. 29b discussed briefly; detail of Incarnation scene illus.

Cavallo, Adolph S. "The Redemption of Man: A Christian Allegory in

Tapestry." *Bulletin of the Museum of Fine Arts, Boston* 56 (1958) pp. 148, 158, 164, 168. 29a and 29b briefly described and discussed.

Marillier, H. C. *The Tapestries at Hampton Court Palace.* London, 1962, pp. 14, 15. 29a and 29b mentioned.

Rorimer, James J. *The Cloisters: The Building and the Collection of Medieval Art in Fort Tryon Park.* MMA. 3d ed., rev., New York, 1963, pp. 176–78. 29a and 29b mentioned, 29b described and discussed at length; detail of Nativity scene in 29b illus. fig. 89.

M. V. B. [M. V. Brugnoli]. "Acquisti dei musei e gallerie dello stato: Manifattura di Bruxelles, 1500 circa; 'Giudizio Universale.'" *Bollettino d'Arte*, ser. 5, 50 (1965) p. 232. 29b mentioned.

Cavallo, Adolph S. *Tapestries of Europe and of Colonial Peru in the Museum of Fine Arts, Boston.* Boston, 1967, pp. 92, 94. 29a and 29b mentioned.

d'Hulst, Roger-A. *Flemish Tapestries from the Fifteenth to the Eighteenth Century.* New York, 1967, p. 122. 29a and 29b mentioned.

Souchal in Paris 1973, p. 210. 29a and 29b mentioned.

Bennett, Anna G. *Five Centuries of Tapestry from the Fine Arts Museums of San Francisco.* San Francisco, 1976, pp. 55, 57, 62–63. 29a and 29b mentioned; illus. figs. 33 [29a] and 34 [29b].

Schneebalg-Perelman, Sophie. "Un nouveau regard sur les origines et le développement de la tapisserie bruxelloise du XIVᵉ siècle à la pré-Renaissance." In *Tapisseries bruxelloises de la pré-Renaissance.* Exh. cat., Musées Royaux d'Art et d'Histoire. Brussels, 1976, p. 185. 29b mentioned; 29a illus. fig. 8.

J. K. S. [Jan-Karel Steppe]. "Le triomphe des Vertus sur les Vices." In *Tapisseries bruxelloises de la pré-Renaissance.* Exh. cat., Musées Royaux d'Art et d'Histoire (Brussels, 1976) pp. 107, 108. 29b mentioned.

Coffinet 1977, p. 100. 29a mentioned, illus.

Digby 1980, p. 34. 29a mentioned.

NOTES

1. Edith Appleton Standen, notes and preliminary draft of a catalogue entry concerning 29a and 29b, ca. 1968, in the files of the MMA Department of Medieval Art.

2. Standen, notes and preliminary draft, ca. 1968.

3. Minor differences occur in the texts of the two books, but neither version agrees totally with the text in the tapestry. The word *sancto* does not appear in Isaias 26:21, but it does occur in Michaeas 1:2 with the difference that the noun it modifies is *templo* rather than *loco* ("... Dominus de templo sancto suo."). On the other hand Michaeas 1:3 gives the verb form as *egreditur* instead of the *egredietur* that appears both in the tapestry and in Isaias 26:21. Therefore we cannot determine which text (or which prophet) the author of the scenario or the designer had in mind when he prepared the inscription on this scroll.

4. For notes on medieval theatrical production techniques and an illustration of a stage design for the setting of a Passion play produced at Valenciennes in 1547, see Henry Francis Taylor, "'A Piece of Arras of the Judgment,'" *Worcester Art Museum Annual* 1 (1935–36) pp. 6–8 and fig. 12. In the foreground ("downstage") of the setting for the Valenciennes production appears a row of mansions very like the ones shown in the tapestry and behind them ("upstage") a high masonry wall fitted with towers and gates, a setting rather like the one in the tax-collecting scene in 29b. According to Gustave Cohen (*Histoire de la mise en scène dans le théâtre religieux français du moyen age* [Paris, 1926] p. 125), the names of characters in morality plays were written on their mantles. We also know that characters in tableaux and pageants presented during ceremonial entries into cities were identified either on placards set up near them or verbally in their speeches.

5. Many of the writers who published tapestries in this and some related series have examined the literature that could have inspired the scenario writer or designer, but none of them could

identify the exact source of the narratives as they develop in the tapestries. See Adolph S. Cavallo, "The Redemption of Man: A Christian Allegory in Tapestry," *Bulletin of the Museum of Fine Arts, Boston* 56 (1958) pp. 164–65, for notes on some of the possible sources. Among the poems mentioned there are Guillaume de Deguileville's *Pèlerinage de la vie humaine*, written in the early fourteenth century, and John Gower's *Mirour de l'omme*, which dates from the late fourteenth or early fifteenth century; among the morality plays listed are *Mundus, Caro, Demonia; L'Homme Pécheur; L'Homme Juste et L'Homme Mondain*; and a Passion play produced at Mons in 1501 which contains most of the elements in the tapestry scenario but was not its direct source.

6. D. T. B. Wood, "Tapestries of *The Seven Deadly Sins*—I," *Burlington Magazine* 20 (1911–12) p. 210, gives the date of Wolsey's purchase as December 22, 1521.

7. From Jan-Karel Steppe, letter to an unidentified staff member at the Metropolitan Museum, dated July 11, 1956, in the files of the Department of Medieval Art.

8. Standen, notes and preliminary draft, ca. 1968.

9. Hope Traver in a letter to W. H. Forsyth, June 8, 1938, in the files of the Department of Medieval Art, mentions a Provençal mystery play in which the Virtues join Dame Nature in pleading that Christ not delay his promise to die for mankind. This is certainly the meaning of the scene in the tapestry.

10. Standen, notes and preliminary draft, ca. 1968.

11. For studies of the theme of the Four Daughters of God and the Parliament of Heaven ("le procès de Paradis"), see Hope Traver, *The Four Daughters of God* (Bryn Mawr, 1909), and Samuel C. Chew, *The Virtues Reconciled: An Iconographic Study* (Toronto, 1947). The theme appears in the twelfth-century writings of Hugues de Saint-Victor and Bernard de Clairvaux as well as in the Pseudo-Bonaventure's thirteenth-century *Meditationes vitae Christi* and then later in a great deal of literature, including poems, moralities, and mysteries. The Trial usually appears as a prologue to the Annunciation, but in some sources the Virtues are not reconciled until after the Ascension; see Chew, *Virtues*, pp. 39–41, 43, 47.

12. Standen, notes and preliminary draft, ca. 1968. The painting, which has been dated 1517–22, is in the church of Saint-Jacques in Bruges; see Max J. Friedländer, *Meisterwerke der niederländischen Malerei des XV. und XVI. Jahrhunderts auf der Ausstellung zu Brügge 1902* (Munich, 1903) pp. 20–21 and pl. 56. The figures are not identified in the text.

13. See respectively Paulina Junquera de Vega and Concha Herrero Carretero, *Catálogo de tapices del Patrimonio Nacional*, vol. 1, *Siglo XVI* (Madrid, 1986) pp. 8, 31; and Mercedes and Vittorio Viale, *Arazzi e tapetti antichi* (Turin, 1952) pp. 40–41, pl. 19.

14. Illustrated and discussed in Junquera de Vega and Herrero Carretero, *Catálogo*, p. 32.

15. Standen, notes and preliminary draft, ca. 1968.

16. Standen, notes and preliminary draft, ca. 1968. The altarpiece wing is illustrated in Joseph Destrée, *Tapisseries et sculptures bruxelloises à l'Exposition d'art ancien bruxellois ... 1905* (Brussels, 1906) pl. XLII; see also text, p. 67.

17. Illustrated in Lorne Campbell, *Van der Weyden* (New York, 1980) pl. 25.

18. The Beaune altarpiece is illustrated in Campbell, *Van der Weyden*, pl. 36.

19. Standen, notes and preliminary draft, ca. 1968. For notes on these tapestries in the Musées Royaux d'Art et d'Histoire in Brussels, the cathedral of La Seo in Saragossa, the Museu Nacional de Arte Antiga in Lisbon, and Hampton Court Palace, together with illustrations of them, see respectively *Tapisseries bruxelloises de la pré-Renaissance*, exh. cat., Musées Royaux d'Art et d'Histoire (Brussels, 1976) pp. 107–9; Eduardo Torra de Arana et al., *Los tapices de La Seo de Zaragoza* (Saragossa, 1985) pp. 228–32 and pl. following; Maria José de Mendonça, "Uma tapeçaria dos vícios e

das virtudes: 'A Música,'" *Boletim do Museu Nacional de Arte Antiga* 1 (1946) pp. 30–36; and H. C. Marillier, *The Tapestries at Hampton Court Palace* (London, 1962) p. 18 and pl. 13.

20. The tapestry is part of the Bayerische Hypotheken- und Wechsel-Bank collection in the Bayerisches Nationalmuseum. See Lorenz Seelig, "Gothic and Early Renaissance Tapestries from the Collection of the Bayerische Hypotheken- und Wechsel-Bank," *Connoisseur* 193 (1976) p. 26 illus.

21. Standen, notes and preliminary draft, ca. 1968. Both tapestries in Madrid are discussed and illustrated in Junquera de Vega and Herrero Carretero, *Catálogo*, pp. 3 and 8 respectively.

22. Standen, notes and preliminary draft, ca. 1968. Discussed and illustrated in Viale, *Arazzi*, p. 45 and pl. 28.

23. Standen, notes and preliminary draft, ca. 1968.

24. Eloísa García, "Los tapices de Fonseca en la catedral de Palencia: Tapices de la Historia Sagrada," *Boletín del Seminario de Estudios de Arte y Arqueología*, Universidad de Valladolid, 13 (1946–47) pp. 173–75.

25. Ramón Revilla Vielva, *Manifestaciones artísticas en la Catedral de Palencia* (Palencia, 1945) p. 63.

26. A single-headed eagle representing the ancient Roman empire appears blazoned on the tabard worn by a man in the tax-collector's office, and again on a banner above this man's head, in the tax-collecting scene painted on the inside of the right-hand wing of the altarpiece of the story of Mary and Joseph in Brussels; see Destrée, *Tapisseries et sculptures bruxelloises*, pl. XLII. Standen (notes and preliminary draft, ca. 1968) found a somewhat later instance of the double-headed eagle used in the same context. It appears, as in 29b surmounted by an imperial crown, on a rectangular plaque fixed to the exterior wall of a house from inside which men are collecting taxes from people lined up outside. The picture, painted by Pieter Bruegel the Elder in 1566, and called the *Numbering* (or *Taxation*) *at Bethlehem*, is in the Musées Royaux des Beaux-Arts in Brussels; see F. Grossmann, *Bruegel: The Paintings, Complete Edition* (London, [1955]) pls. 115, 116.

27. See Enrico Castelnuovo et al., *Gli arazzi del cardinale: Bernardo Cles e il Ciclo della Passione di Pieter van Aelst* (Trent, 1990) pp. 250–51, illus.

28. See Torra de Arana et al., *Los Tapices de La Seo*, pp. 234–36 and pls. following.

29. For notes on the set of ten tapestries given to the cathedral of Saint-Just and the one surviving piece, the *Creation*, see *Le seizième siècle européen: Tapisseries*, exh. cat., Mobilier National (Paris, 1965) no. 19, illus. For the *Creation* tapestry, see also Souchal in Paris 1973, pp. 208–9, illus.

30. The tapestry had belonged earlier to J. P. Morgan; see Seymour de Ricci, *Catalogue of Twenty Renaissance Tapestries from the J. Pierpont Morgan Collection* (Paris, 1913) pp. 24–27, illus. It is mentioned as in the Burrell Collection in Betty Kurth, "Masterpieces of Gothic Tapestry in the Burrell Collection," *Connoisseur* 117 (1946) p. 8.

31. See Digby 1980, pp. 34–35 and pls. 34, 35.

32. Mentioned in Eugène Müntz, "Tapisseries allégoriques inédites ou peu connues," *Fondation Eugène Piot: Monuments et Mémoires* 9 (1902) pp. 99–100, as belonging to M. Schutz and having been exhibited at the Petit Palais in Paris in 1900. Illustrated in Jules Guiffrey, *Les tapisseries du XIIᵉ à la fin du XVIᵉ siècle* (Paris, [1911]) p. 61, fig. 29; no border is shown.

33. See *English & French Furniture . . . Property from the Collection Formed by the Late Mrs. Charles B. Alexander . . .* , sale cat., Parke-Bernet, New York, April 17–19, 1941, no. 579, illus. Erroneously said to be the same as a similar detail in the upper central section of the *Creation* composition.

34. See French and Company photograph, neg. no. 12071, in the Photo Archives, J. Paul Getty Center for the History of Art and the Humanities, Santa Monica.

35. See Anna G. Bennett, *Five Centuries of Tapestry from the Fine Arts Museums of San Francisco*, rev. ed. (San Francisco, forthcoming in 1992).

36. Standen, notes and preliminary draft, ca. 1968.

37. Discussed briefly and illustrated in *Collection de S. A. le duc de Berwick et d'Albe . . .* , sale cat., Hôtel Drouot, Paris, April 7–20, 1877, no. 11.

38. See X. Barbier de Montault, "Rome chrétienne: Les tapisseries de la Fête-Dieu, au Vatican," *Annales Archéologiques* 15 (1855) pp. 235–37; also Barbier de Montault, "Inventaire descriptif des tapisseries de haute-lisse conservées à Rome," *Mémoires de l'Académie des Sciences, Lettres et Arts d'Arras*, 2d ser., 10 (1878) pp. 186–90. Exhibited in Paris in 1878; see Alfred Darcel, "Les tapisseries," in Louis Gonse, ed., *L'art ancien à l'exposition de 1878* (Paris, 1879) pp. 332, 334.

39. See García, "Los tapices de Fonseca en la catedral de Palencia," p. 189, pls. XI–XV.

40. See Torra de Arana et al., *Los Tapices de La Seo*, pp. 234–36 and pls.

41. See Barbier de Montault, "Rome chrétienne: Les tapisseries," pp. 296–98, and "Inventaire," pp. 208–11. Exhibited in Paris in 1878; see Darcel, "Les tapisseries," pp. 332, 334.

42. See García, "Los tapices de Fonseca en la catedral de Palencia," p. 176, pls. I–IV.

43. See García, "Los tapices de Fonseca en la catedral de Palencia," p. 181, pls. V–VII.

44. See *Collection de S. A. le duc de Berwick et d'Albe*, no. 14, illus.

45. See Barbier de Montault, "Rome chrétienne: Les tapisseries," pp. 241–44, and "Inventaire," pp. 201–5. Exhibited in Paris in 1878; see Darcel, "Les tapisseries," pp. 332, 334.

46. The Cardon piece was mentioned in Destrée, *Tapisseries et sculptures bruxelloises*, p. 9. The other fragment was sold, *Gothic and Other Ancient Art Collected by the Late Mr. Henry C. Lawrence of New York*, American Art Association, New York, January 27–29, 1921, no. 578, illus.

47. Described and discussed in Christa Charlotte Mayer, *Masterpieces of Western Textiles from the Art Institute of Chicago* (Chicago, 1969) p. 25, illus. pl. 10.

48. See Barbier de Montault, "Rome chrétienne: Les tapisseries," pp. 239–40. See also Barbier de Montault, "Inventaire," pp. 193–94, 194 n. 1, where he states incorrectly that the Vatican example was owned then by M. d'Erlanger.

49. See *Collection de S. A. le duc de Berwick et d'Albe*, no. 15, illus.

50. See García, "Los tapices de Fonseca en la catedral de Palencia," p. 185, pls. VIII–X.

51. According to J. K. Steppe, "Vlaamse Wandtapijten in Spanje: Recente Gebeurtenissen en Publicaties," *Artes Textiles* 3 (1956) pp. 45–46, Don Antonio held 29a and 29b and the other two tapestries, claiming that the bishop's coat of arms was to be added to them, until the chapter of the cathedral of Burgos took action for possession. The bishop had bequeathed the other four pieces of the set of eight to the cathedral of Palencia, but they were not delivered until 1527 (see García, "Los tapices de Fonseca en la catedral de Palencia," p. 174); and the fact that each of them has three woven coats of arms sewn to the original fabric (for an illustration of one piece, see fig. 135 above) would seem to corroborate Don Antonio's claim concerning the delay in the delivery to Burgos.

52. For the texts of the four inventory listings, see Description and Subject above, and Steppe, "Vlaamse Wandtapijten in Spanje," p. 46, for the citations of 1560 and 1572, and his letter of July 1956 (see note 7 above) for the citations of 1777 and 1797.

53. Roger-A. d'Hulst (*Flemish Tapestries from the Fifteenth to the Eighteenth Century* [New York, 1967] p. 122) thought that 29a and 29b were still in Burgos in 1935–36 and that the Metropolitan Museum bought them at that time. Lily Faure ("Vlaamse Wandtapijten in Spanje: De Verzameling te Burgos," *Handelingen van het XXIIᵉ Vlaams Filologencongres* [Ghent, 1957] p. 344) said that the two hangings were sold during the Spanish civil war but did not name the source of this erroneous information.

30

446

30
The Resurrected Christ Appearing
to Mary Magdalen in the Garden

Southern Netherlands, 1500–1520
Wool warp; wool, silk, and gilt wefts
7 ft. 10 in. × 6 ft. 8 in. (2.39 m × 2.03 m)
15–17 warp yarns per inch, 6–7 per centimeter
The Cloisters Collection, 1956 (56.47)

CONDITION

Bits of yarn from the original loom heading remain woven into the cut ends of the warp at both sides; their presence indicates that the tapestry has lost none of its original width. Since the border is intact on all four sides but missing its dark blue and white striped outer guard along the top and bottom of the tapestry, we know that the piece has lost only about three inches of its original height. There are no patches of old or modern weaving inserted anywhere in the field or border and only a few areas of reweaving. The most important ones occur along the inside of the inner guard at the left of the field and down the right side of the orange tree in the center of the field. There are small spots of reweaving throughout the border, in parts of the landscape background, in the Magdalen's light-colored veil and her sleeves, along the inner contours of Christ's feet, and in His spade. None of these repairs has affected the original drawing or modeling to a significant degree. The colors have faded moderately, but each hue retains its identity and most of them are still intense. The gilt yarns (narrow, flat wires wrapped spirally around core yarns of silk) have darkened in some places but for the most part still read as shining gold.

DESCRIPTION AND SUBJECT

The scene is set in a garden enclosed at the back by a wattled fence and a gate and at the sides by rocky hillocks covered with turf and trees. A narrow path winds through the grass; a variety of flowering plants grow along its edges and in the immediate foreground. In the middle distance at the right there is a lily of the valley; in the foreground there are plantains, pinks, violets, a large winter cherry or Chinese lantern, dandelions, strawberries, and a few other kinds of plants. A tall poppy grows next to a blackberry bush (some of the fruit is red, some black) at the far left next to the Magdalen. Strawberry and other plants grow around the base of the neatly pruned orange tree that rises in the center of the space. Fields open out beyond the garden and in the far distance at the right appear the walls, gabled roofs, and towers of Jerusalem.

The resurrected Christ, with a dark beard and long dark hair that falls in coils over His shoulders, stands in the right foreground. Around His head shines a cruciform halo composed of rays of light woven with gilt yarn. He appears to be wearing only the red ("purple") mantle of the Resurrection, which in this instance is cut like a cope and has a jeweled clasp resembling a morse at the neck. The wounds in His hands, feet, and side are clearly visible. He turns slightly toward the left and bends forward from the waist. In His left hand He holds the handle of a spade; the tip of its metal blade is sunk into the earth. He raises His right arm, the hand open, toward the figure of Mary Magdalen, who is kneeling before Him in the left foreground. She wears a patterned velvet or damask mantle lined with plain fabric over a gown cut with long tight sleeves. The mantle passes over the veil covering her head and shoulders and then falls to the ground in deep folds. She looks up at the Savior and holds her palms together in an attitude of prayer. The pottery jar on the ground behind and between the two figures may represent both the ointment box that is Mary's traditional attribute and the jar in which she and the other Holy Women brought aromatic substances to the tomb to use in anointing the body.

The border comprises a wide, dark blue band flanked by striped inner and outer guards. The central band is decorated with branches with cut ends, some bearing roses alternating with some bearing pansies. Small birds of various kinds fly or perch among these branches. The flora and fauna are densely packed in the section of the border on the right side and the right-hand third of the top and bottom border sections. In the left two-thirds of these border sections and throughout the left section there are fewer motifs set farther apart.

447

Silk yarns were used lavishly throughout the field and border, particularly in the passages of highest light. The gilt yarns appear primarily in the highlights and patterns of the garments but also in the trunk, leaves, and fruit of the orange tree, in the rocks at the right, and in the plants in the extreme foreground.

The incident as it is represented here corresponds specifically to the account given in John (20:11–17). Mary, having looked into the tomb and found it empty but for the two angels who asked her why she was weeping, turned and saw Jesus but did not recognize Him. He asked her why she wept and whom she sought; she, thinking He was the gardener, asked whether He had removed the body and if so where He had laid it. Christ then addressed her by name, and she immediately recognized Him and called Him "Master." Then Jesus said to her, "Do not touch me, for I am not yet ascended to my Father," and He charged her to tell the disciples that he would ascend. It is this moment (John 20:17), when Christ is enjoining Mary not to touch Him and to go tell the disciples He will ascend to God, that the designer has chosen to represent. The garden setting also derives from the account given in John (19:41), which specifies that the sepulcher, which had not yet been used, was in a garden near the place of the Crucifixion. In most late medieval representations of the subject Christ is shown with a spade, and sometimes also in gardener's clothing, because Mary mistook Him for the gardener.

The subject is often referred to by its Latin name, *Noli me tangere,* or "Do not touch me." Réau believed that the use of the verb "touch" reflects a linguistic error in the translation of the Gospels from Greek into Latin and that the sense of Christ's enjoinder was not "do not touch me" but rather "do not hold me" or "do not attach yourself to me" because He knew He would soon ascend.[1] Réau also observed that in some representations of the subject Christ simply extends His arm toward the Magdalen (as He does here) and in others He touches her forehead (see Related Tapestries). Two other tapestries of the subject, one earlier in date than the Metropolitan Museum's piece and now in the parish church in Livré-sur-Changeon (Ille-et-Vilaine) and the other somewhat later, in the Art Institute of Chicago, show the words *Noli me tangere* written across the field near Christ's head.[2]

Standen suggested that although the plants represented in the field portion of the tapestry might normally be found in a garden, the ones that have been featured could have some symbolic significance. She singled out the poppy, the winter cherry, and the blackberry bush for comment and noted that the first two could refer to sleep or death and that the blackberry plant might have sinister connotations because of the thorns on its branches and the color of its fruit.[3] In the context of the Metropolitan Museum's *Hunt of the Unicorn* tapestries (20a–h), Freeman observed that the blackberry was thought to be the bush that Moses saw burning on Mount Horeb and that this plant as well as the winter cherry and the plantain were regarded as antidotes for poisons of various kinds.[4] The lily of the valley that grows so prominently by the path in the middle distance at the right is a familiar visual metaphor for the Virgin. The large tree in the center, an orange, is a tree that tapestry designers often represented in their compositions at this time since it was both decorative and novel. However in this context it may well have a symbolic meaning for, as Freeman noted, in Flanders the orange was called "pomme de Chine" and thus the tree could have been substituted for the apple tree, which designers usually used to represent the tree of the knowledge of good and evil.[5] The tree that grows in the corresponding place in the choir tapestry of the *Noli me tangere* at La Chaise-Dieu is just as clearly a pomegranate and in that context symbolizes immortality.[6] The roses in the border of 30 are all red and could therefore refer to Christ's martyrdom. The pansies might stand for remembrance, inviting the observer to think of His sacrifice. However since these flowers also appear in the borders of contemporary tapestries that have non-Christian subjects in their fields, the roses and pansies may have no symbolic meaning here.

SOURCE OF THE DESIGN

Valentiner wrote, in his introduction to the privately circulated catalogue of the Lydig collection (1913, 98) and in the sale catalogue itself (no. 136), that the design showed Italian influence. He referred to the "southern" quality of the trees and foliage and pointed out that the Magdalen's ointment box is an example of Hispano-Moresque faience. We do not agree that the design shows southern European influence, nor do we agree with the opinion of Breuning (1947, 39) that the tapestry was woven after a cartoon by Bernaert van Orley, citing the "Italianate" quality of the design and the elaborate border as typical of this artist's late work.

Standen observed that the general composition is one that was used frequently in prints, paintings, and tapestries during the fifteenth and early sixteenth centuries in the Netherlands. Among these, she cited a woodcut in a Dutch *Biblia Pauperum* dating from about 1430–40.[7] There, the figure of Christ is similar, in reverse, to the one in the Metropolitan Museum's tapestry, and the

Magdalen, though dressed differently and holding her arms in a slightly different pose, is also similar. The covered cylindrical jar rests on the ground between the two figures, and in the middle distance there is a wattled fence. A walled town appears on a hill in the far distance at the right. Standen cited a painting of the *Noli me tangere* by Jacob Cornelisz van Oostsanen in Kassel as one that is generically similar to, and approximately contemporary with (it is dated 1507), the Metropolitan Museum's tapestry.[8] Although the figures of Christ and the Magdalen in that painting are different from the ones in the tapestry, they hold essentially the same poses (however in the painting Christ touches Mary's forehead), and the general character of the setting is also similar although there is no orange tree in the center and the fence at the back is made of boards rather than wattle.

Regardless of whether the *Noli me tangere* was represented at this period as the principal subject of a composition, as it is in 30, or in the background of paintings and tapestries of the Resurrection, as Standen noted it often was (see, for example, 45), the figures are shown in essentially the same relationship and the settings are basically the same. Only the poses and certain details vary. A prominent tree—although not an orange tree in every instance—rises between or behind the two figures in a number of roughly contemporary tapestries including the ones in the parish church in Livré-sur-Changeon and the Art Institute of Chicago, one belonging to the province of Brabant, others in the Musée du Louvre and the abbey church of Saint-Robert in La Chaise-Dieu, one formerly in the Tollin collection, and one that was offered for sale in Antwerp in 1986.[9] The piece offered in Antwerp and the ones in Paris, Chicago, and Livré-sur-Changeon show a wattled fence with the post and rail gate at the back of the garden rather like the one in 30. The other pieces just mentioned have picket rather than wattled fences at the back. In all but the piece belonging to the province of Brabant, Christ wears the cope-like mantle clasped or tied at the throat.

In view of these basic similarities and slight variations, we conclude that the compositions in these tapestries were derived from different but closely related prints or paintings that have not yet been identified. The figures of Christ and Mary Magdalen in 30 are more like those in the early fifteenth-century *Biblia Pauperum* woodcut mentioned above (see note 7) than like any figures we have found in paintings; but the similarity is not great enough to warrant a claim that the print served as the tapestry designer's source. As a matter of interest, we may note here that the figure of Christ in the tapestry offered for sale in Antwerp in 1986, which is vir-

tually the same figure that appears in the *Noli me tangere* in the Art Institute of Chicago, was probably derived, whether directly or not, from the Christ who emerges from the sarcophagus in pictures of the Resurrection painted by Rogier van der Weyden or Dieric Bouts.[10]

MANUFACTURE AND DATE

When 30 was sold from the Gaillard collection in 1904, it was catalogued as Flemish work of the end of the fifteenth century. In 1913 in the sale catalogue of the Lydig collection (no. 136) and in the privately circulated catalogue (p. 98), Valentiner described it as a Brussels piece of about 1510, an attribution also given by Townsend (1913, 6) in his article on the collection. Göbel (1923, vol. 2, fig. 393) attributed the piece to Brussels and dated it about 1525. When it was exhibited at the Seligmann Galleries in 1927, the tapestry was catalogued simply as Flemish and dated in the early sixteenth century. In the Metropolitan Museum's Annual Report for 1955–56, it was dated in the early sixteenth century and once again attributed to Brussels. Standen assigned the tapestry to Brussels and dated it between 1500 and 1520.[11] None of the writers gave their reasons for making these suggestions.

The attribution to Brussels undoubtedly follows from the various writers' appreciation of the high caliber of the weaving and the accomplished painterly quality of the design. We believe now that these considerations do not in themselves constitute grounds for making this attribution. We know that such tapestries were being woven in Brussels or through the agency of Brussels entrepreneurs at this time, but we cannot be sure that they were not also being produced elsewhere. In theory the tapestry could have been produced by any south Netherlandish entrepreneur who was turning out luxury products and patronizing the best designers. As for the date of production, the general style suggests a time in the first years of the sixteenth century. There are no fashionable details of costume and no accessories represented in the piece that could help refine the date. The Magdalen's majolica ointment box reflects the shape and ornamentation of comparable containers that were represented in Netherlandish paintings during the first half of the fifteenth century; therefore it is of no help in dating the tapestry since an artist working then or at any later time could have represented it.[12]

The Metropolitan Museum's tapestry looks later than the *Noli me tangere* in Livré-sur-Changeon. Macé de Lépinay (1986, 37) reported that Steppe, Souchal, and Delmarcel had dated that tapestry about 1485–90, about

1480, and about 1470–75, respectively. The figures and the tree in the center of that hanging have been placed far forward in the field and the horizon line is high. These devices, together with the row of flowering plants that establish a firm plane in the immediate foreground, represent a developed form of the dominant tapestry-designing style of the seventh and eighth decades of the fifteenth century; see for example in this catalogue numbers 10 and 13a–c. The row of plants in the foreground of 30 and the placement of the two figures in the immediate foreground derive from that style, but the composition as a whole is much more advanced. These considerations suggest that 30 was designed toward the end of the fifteenth century or perhaps at the beginning of the next. It could have been woven some years later than that but probably not later than 1520, when its design would have appeared outmoded.

A tapestry that must have shown a rather similar composition was among those that Juana la Loca of Spain gave to her mother, Isabel la Católica, sometime before Isabel's death in 1504 and that King Fernando returned to Juana shortly afterward.[13] It was described as follows: "Otro paño de devoción de oro y seda y lana que es cómo aparecióó Nuestro Señor a la Madalena después de resucitado, que tiene en medio del un arbol que paresce naranjo e otras verduras; que tiene de largo dos varas e nueve dozavos largos" (Another devotional tapestry of gold and silk and wool which shows how Our Lord appeared to the Magdalen after He had come back to life, which has in the center a tree that looks like an orange [tree] and other greenery; it is two varas and a broad nine-twelfths [of a vara] wide).[14] Translated into modern terms, that tapestry's width was equal to approximately 2.30 meters. It was therefore just a bit wider than the Metropolitan Museum's hanging, whose width today is 2.03 meters.

Related Tapestries

No duplicate tapestries are known to have survived. This tapestry could have been part of a set of hangings illustrating scenes from the life of Christ or perhaps the life of Mary Magdalen, although no tapestries that might have accompanied it in such a series are known to have survived. It is equally possible, especially in view of the small size of the piece, its marked pictorial quality, and the large scale of the figures, that it was designed and produced to be used by itself as a devotional tapestry, to be contemplated on the wall of a chamber or chapel as an aid to religious meditation. The devotional piece owned by Isabel la Católica must have looked very much like it (see above and notes 13 and 14).

HISTORY

Sold, *Objets d'art . . . composant la Collection Emile Gaillard*, Hôtel Emile Gaillard, Paris, June 8–11 and 13–16, 1904, no. 762, illus.

Sold, *The Rita Lydig Collection of Notable Art Treasures of the Gothic and Renaissance Periods*, American Art Galleries, New York, April 4, 1913, no. 136, illus. Catalogue by Wilhelm R. Valentiner with the assistance of Durr Friedley. Said erroneously to have been in the Spitzer collection; the tapestry with the same subject that was in the Spitzer collection is now in the Art Institute of Chicago.[15]

In the collection of Mr. and Mrs. Otto H. Kahn, New York.

Purchased by the MMA, The Cloisters Collection, 1956.

EXHIBITIONS

New York, Jacques Seligmann & Co. Galleries, 1927. *Loan Exhibition of Religious Art for the Benefit of the Basilique of the Sacré Coeur of Paris.* Cat. no. IX. Lent by Mr. and Mrs. Otto H. Kahn.

New York, Duveen Brothers galleries, 1947.

PUBLICATIONS

J. B. T. [James B. Townsend]. "The Lydig Collections." *American Art News* 11 (March 29, 1913) p. 6. Mentioned; illus. p. 9.

Valentiner, Wilhelm R., assisted by Durr Friedley. *The Rita Lydig Collection.* Privately printed, New York, 1913, pp. xxxvii–xxxviii, 98. Described and discussed at length; illus. facing p. 98.

Göbel 1923, vol. 2, fig. 393. Illus.

Hunter 1925, p. 124. Mentioned.

F [Frank E. Washburn Freund]. "Sammler und Markt: Vom New Yorker Markt." *Der Cicerone* 19 (1927) p. 429. Mentioned by name of lender as one of the Gothic tapestries shown in the exhibition of religious art at Jacques Seligmann & Co.

Breuning, Margaret. "France Loans Us an Acre of Her Tapestry Treasures: Gothic Tapestries at Duveen." *Art Digest* 22, no. 5 (December 1, 1947) p. 39. Discussed briefly.

"Additions to the Collection: The Cloisters, Purchases." Annual Report for 1955–1956. In *MMA Bulletin*, n.s. 15 (1956–57) p. 44. Mentioned.

Macé de Lépinay, François. "'Noli me tangere': Une tapisserie bruxelloise du XVe siècle inédite." *Bulletin Monumental* 144 (1986) p. 38. Discussed briefly; illus. fig. 6, p. 37.

NOTES

1. Louis Réau, *Iconographie de l'art chrétien* (Paris, 1955–59) vol. 2, pt. 2, pp. 556–57.
2. See, respectively, François Macé de Lépinay, "'Noli me tangere': Une tapisserie bruxelloise du XVe siècle inédite," *Bulletin Monumental* 144 (1986) pp. 33–39 and figs. 1–4; and Christa Charlotte Mayer, *Masterpieces of Western Textiles from the Art Institute of Chicago* (Chicago, 1969) pl. 13, color illus.
3. Edith Appleton Standen, notes and preliminary draft of a catalogue entry, ca. 1968, in the files of the MMA Department of Medieval Art.
4. Margaret B. Freeman, *The Unicorn Tapestries*, MMA (New York, 1976) pp. 140–41, 143, 135, and figs. 170, 169, and 111, respectively.
5. Freeman, *Unicorn Tapestries*, pp. 124–25, 136–38; orange trees illus. figs. 96 and 156.
6. Michel Pomarat and Pierre Burger, *Les tapisseries de L'Abbatiale de Saint-Robert de La Chaise-Dieu* (Brioude, 1975) pp. 102–3, illus.; see also Freeman, *Unicorn Tapestries*, pp. 131–32 and fig. 164.

7. Standen, notes and preliminary draft, ca. 1968. See Heinrich The-odor Musper, *Die Urausgaben der holländischen Apokalypse und Biblia pauperum* (Munich, 1961) vol. 1, p. 21; vol. 3, illus. p. 31.

8. Standen, notes and preliminary draft, ca. 1968. For an illustration of this painting, see Erich Herzog, *Die Gemäldegalerie der Staatlichen Kunstsammlungen Kassel* (Hanau, 1969) fig. 13.

9. See, respectively, Macé de Lépinay, "Noli me tangere," pp. 33–39, figs. 1–4; Mayer, *Masterpieces of Western Textiles from the Art Institute of Chicago*, pl. 13; *Chefs-d'oeuvre de la tapisserie fla-mande: Onzième exposition du château de Culan* (Bourges, 1971) no. 6, illus.; Louis Guimbaud, *La tapisserie de haute et basse lisse* (Paris, 1928) p. 21, pl. 1; Pomarat and Burger, *Les tapisseries,* pp. 102–3, a *Noli me tangere,* and 142–44, a *Resurrection* with another *Noli me tangere* in the right background, both illus.; *Catalogue des objets d'art . . . composant la collection de M. A. Tollin,* Salle Georges Petit, Paris, May 20–21, 1897, no. 216, illus.; and an advertisement for the forthcoming sale in Antwerp of the *Noli me tangere* tapestry in *Tableau* 9, no. 1 (September 1986) p. 63, illus. The same tapestry had been offered for sale at Palais Galliera, Paris, on March 14, 1970, no. 131, illus.

10. See the scene of the Resurrection in the background of Rogier's *Christ Appearing to His Mother* in the MMA, in Katharine Baet-jer, *European Paintings in The Metropolitan Museum of Art by Artists Born in or before 1865: A Summary Catalogue* (New York, 1980) vol. 1, p. 157; vol. 3, illus. p. 329; and a larger illustration in Hermann Beenken, *Rogier van der Weyden* (Munich, 1951) pl. 33.

For the paintings by Dieric Bouts, see his *Resurrection* panel in the Bayerische Staatsgemäldesammlungen in Munich, discussed and illustrated in *Dieric Bouts,* exh. cat., Palais des Beaux-Arts, Brussels, and Stedelijk Museum Het Prinsenhof, Delft (Brussels, 1957) no. 4, illus., and also the right wing of his triptych of the *Deposition* in the Capilla Real in Granada and the copy of it in the Colegio del Patriarca in Valencia, discussed and illustrated in Wolfgang Schöne, *Dieric Bouts und seine Schule* (Berlin and Leipzig, 1938) cat. nos. 3 and 3a, pls. 9 and 10.

11. Standen, notes and preliminary draft, ca. 1968.

12. See, for example, a rather similar medicine jar with approximately the same straight-sided, tall body shape but quite a different kind of ornamentation, which appears on the shelf behind and above the main figure in the Jan van Eyck and Petrus Christus *Saint Jerome in His Study* in the Detroit Institute of Arts; see Erwin Panofsky, *Early Netherlandish Painting: Its Origins and Charac-ter* (Cambridge, Mass., 1953) fig. 258 on pl. 129.

13. Francisco Javier Sánchez Cantón, *Libros, tapices y cuadros que coleccionó Isabel la Católica* (Madrid, 1950) pp. 92, 97, 149.

14. Sánchez Cantón, *Libros, tapices y cuadros,* p. 150.

15. See note 2 above, and Eugène Müntz, "Les tapisseries," in *La collection Spitzer* (Paris, 1890–92) vol. 1, pp. 163–64, not illus.; also *Catalogue des objets d'art . . . composant l'importante et pré-cieuse collection Spitzer,* sale cat., 33 rue de Villejust, Paris, April 17–June 16, 1893, no. 396, illus. (in plate vol.).

31

31

Five Youths Playing
Blindman's Buff

Southern Netherlands, 1500–1525
Wool warp; wool and silk wefts
8 ft. 9 1/2 in. × 9 ft. 10 in. (2.68 m × 3.00 m)
12–14 warp yarns per inch, 5–6 per centimeter
Bequest of Adele L. Lehman, in memory of Arthur Lehman, 1965
(65.181.17)

CONDITION

The tapestry was cut unevenly along the top, bottom, and right side. These three edges were rewoven with modern warp and weft yarns to make them straight again. The left side, which was not cut, contains bits of the original loom finish. A narrow band of modern fabric has been sewn to all four sides. Judging from the present positions of the ciphers in the lower corners of the field and the traces of two other ciphers in the upper corners, we calculate that the fabric has lost about three feet of its original height (perhaps a foot at the bottom and two feet at the top) but only a few inches of its width, entirely at the right side.

In several parts of the field there are lines of reweaving that are parallel to the warp. The longest one extends more than halfway across the piece about a quarter of the way down from the top, from a point near the left edge to the word *le* on the inscribed scroll. There are a number of spot repairs in the lower left and upper right quarters of the field and also in the face, hat plume, and hands of the youth at the extreme left. The left hand, right arm, and hat of the boy at the right, and the left hand, sleeve, and skirt of the youth crouching right of center have also been rewoven. These repairs have affected the original drawing to some degree, although they have not changed it appreciably. The background color in the left third of the piece is somewhat different from the rest, but the weft yarns in that area are nevertheless original. While the dyes have faded somewhat throughout the field, the hues retain their integrity and most of them are still relatively bright.

DESCRIPTION AND SUBJECT

Against a dark greenish blue ground thickly covered with various blossoming plants, five boys or young men are playing a version of the game of blindman's buff around a tree. A scroll inscribed with the words *Selon/le*

temps is wrapped loosely around the tree at the point where the branches spring from the trunk. The youth whose turn it is to be the blindman stands in the center with his back against the tree trunk. A snake slithers out of a hole in the base of the tree; a lizard and a snail move among the plants near the snake's head. The boy's round hat has been pulled down over his eyes and tied in place with a ribbon passing under his chin. With both hands he swings a rod that has a shoe tied to its upper end by a cord. He is trying to make the shoe strike one of the other youths who surround him, twisting and turning and flailing their arms and hands as they tease the blindman and try to avoid the shoe.

The five youths wear essentially the same costume but the details vary. They all wear hose, wide square-toed shoes tied over the instep, doublets, knee-length skirted jerkins, and round hats with low crowns and turned-up brims. The variations appear mainly in the treatment of necklines and sleeves. The youth at the far left has a square-necked jerkin with open, falling sleeves through which his doublet sleeves pass; they are tight over the forearm and loose above. The four other youths have jerkins with high round necklines and collars; the one crouching to the right of the blindman has wide, loose sleeves whereas the other three have leg-of-mutton sleeves. They all have purses fastened to their girdles; the youth at the far left has a sheathed knife tucked under his purse. Two playthings shaped like golf clubs, two balls, and a quoit lie among the plants at the right. In the lower left and right corners of the field appear the letters nG, each pair of letters tied together with a looped and knotted tasseled cord. The lower ends of two other cords appear along the top of the hanging at left and right, indicating that there were once also ciphers those corners.

There has been some disagreement about how the letters in the cipher and the inscription on the scroll

Detail of 31

should be read. When the tapestry was sold with the A. Tollin collection, the author of the entry in the sale catalogue (1897, no. 219) interpreted the letters in the cipher as P, I, G; but the authors of the catalogue entries for the exhibitions in New York (1928, no. 10) and Indianapolis (1970–71, no. 94) read the same letters as D and G. The first writer to identify the letters as N and G was Virch (1965, 92). He was also right in claiming that these initials refer to the patron for whom the tapestry was woven. By 1985 we knew that the inscription was associated with the Bouesseau family of Burgundy, but it was not until Jean-Bernard de Vaivre studied the piece in 1987 that we could identify the N and G as the initials of the Christian names of Nicolas Bouesseau and his wife, Guillemette Jacqueron.[1]

Although the words on the scroll were read as *Selon le temps* when the tapestry was sold from the A. Tollin collection in 1897, they were interpreted as *le temps scion* by the author of the New York exhibition catalogue (1928, no. 10), as well as by Breck (1928, 184), Virch (1965, 92), and Forsyth (1966–67, 87). Those writers translated the words as "Time whips" or "Time [also] whips" even though *scion* does not correspond to any French verb form and nothing in the phrase justifies the "also." Virch mentioned the earlier reading, *Selon le temps,* but rejected it. In support of his own reading, *le temps scion,* he cited a sixteenth-century Venetian print that shows a figure of Time holding a whip and quoted from Shakespeare's *Hamlet* "the whips and scorns of Time." However the implement that the boy in the tapestry holds is not a whip, and the words are indisputably *Selon le temps*. Both the author of the catalogue entry for the Indianapolis exhibition (1970–71, no. 94) and Gómez-Moreno (1975, 163) accepted this reading.

The words can be interpreted as meaning "according to the weather (or, the season)," as well as "according to the time." Curiously enough, no writer before the present author considered the possibility that these words represent a personal or family device. By chance we found these words inscribed on four scrolls in the painted decoration surrounding an arch in the wall of the fourth bay of the south aisle in the church of Notre-Dame in Dijon. The arch once served as the entrance to a chapel, no longer extant, dedicated by the Bouesseau family of Burgundy to Saint Barbara in the fifteenth century.[2] A carved and painted shield bearing the charges in that family's coat of arms, three crowned lions rising from three barrels, appears under the point of the ogee-arched molding enframing the chapel entrance.[3] A complete device, comprising both motto and emblem, appears in each of the spandrels of this arched molding. It shows the inscribed scroll passing behind a hand issuing from a cloud and holding a watering pot over a mound of flowers. This emblematic image is also found in association with other mottoes and verses.[4] In this instance, since it appears with the motto *Selon le temps*, the meaning seems to be that things prosper as the times (that is, the weather, the season, or perhaps political or economic conditions) favor their growth.

Selon le temps may not be related symbolically to the image on the tapestry: the inscribed scroll, together with the cipher, may have been introduced into the design simply as a means of identifying the person who commissioned the tapestry. On the other hand, as Boehm (1988, 21) observed in her discussion of a contemporary carved ivory sundial leaf from Nuremberg that shows four boys playing the same game, the idea and image of children playing games were associated at that period with time, the seasons, the weather, and also with the allegory of the Ages of Man. Therefore a late medieval artist would have found the device *Selon le temps* an appropriate one to associate with the boys playing fair-weather games in the tapestry. The designer would also have found it appropriate if he were depicting these youths playing games as part of a series of compositions illustrating the age of childhood or youth in a series of compositions dealing with the Ages of Man and their allegorical associations with the months or seasons of the year.[5] However it is pointless to speculate further on this question until we know how to interpret the Bouesseau device, both the motto and the emblem, completely and accurately.

Source of the Design

It seems likely that the figures were taken from a print or painting or from a source common to both. Boehm (1988, 21) suggested that the composition of a similar scene carved on an ivory sundial leaf may have been derived from an early German print. The tapestry composition may also have been taken from such a print; if so, the style of the drawing indicates that some French or Netherlandish tapestry designer or cartoon painter reinterpreted it completely before combining it with stock millefleurs motifs.

Lower left corner of 31

Lower right corner of 31

455

When the tapestry was sold from the A. Tollin collection in 1897, it was said to be French work of the beginning of the sixteenth century. In 1928 it was exhibited in New York with an attribution to Touraine and a date of about 1500. Virch (1965, 92) and Gómez-Moreno (1975, 163) accepted this attribution. Forsyth (1966–67, 87) and the author of the catalogue entry for the exhibition in Indianapolis (1970–71, no. 94) also accepted an attribution to Touraine, although they changed the date to the early sixteenth century.

Like other millefleurs tapestries of its type, this one was probably woven in the southern Netherlands and not in France (see the discussion of millefleurs tapestries in the introductory essay "History of Tapestry Weaving in Europe during the Late Middle Ages"). As for determining the date of its manufacture, the biographies of Nicolas and Guillemette Bouesseau help only to a limited degree. De Vaivre has given a useful summary of the published details of their lives along with some unpublished ones.[6] Nicolas Bouesseau, seigneur de Barjon, the man who commissioned this tapestry, was born sometime before 1450 and died in 1521. In 1472 he was associated with the accounts office of the duc de Bourgogne in Dijon, and in 1477 he was named chief master of accounts to the king. He continued to preside over that office until he died. In 1475 he was mentioned as an alderman juror for the painting and stained-glass trades in Dijon. He built the chapel in the church of Notre-Dame in Dijon (date unknown), and in 1490 commissioned a painted retable for the high altar of the same church. Therefore we know that anytime during the last quarter of the fifteenth century and the first two decades of the sixteenth century he was in a position both financially and as a connoisseur and patron of the arts to order—and perhaps to commission the design and execution of?—the set of hangings to which 31 belonged. We do not know the date of his marriage to Guillemette Jacqueron but deduce that it must have taken place by 1485 at least: Bénigne, one of his three sons, was presumably at least twenty-one years of age in 1506, when he married and held the titles of esquire, seigneur de Barjon, and master of accounts at Dijon. Therefore it seems clear that the tapestries were ordered sometime between about 1485 and 1521, the period during which Nicolas and Guillemette were presumably married and both living. The cut of the boys' costumes suggests a date at the end of the fifteenth century and the beginning of the sixteenth (compare the men's clothes in 20 and 25). However the shape of the shoes in 31, with their wide, square toes, suggests a date no earlier than the first decade of the sixteenth century.

Among the many millefleurs tapestries that are known to have survived from this period, only one resembles this piece in terms of both style and iconography. That tapestry, which is now in the collection of the Bayerisches Hypotheken- und Wechsel-Bank in the Bayerisches Nationalmuseum in Munich, shows a lady and gentleman playing checkers at the base of a tree in the center. Four fashionably dressed youths accompany this couple, one in each of the four corners of the field. The two in the upper corners are hunting birds with bow and arrow. The one at lower left pauses in his game of hoop rolling, and the one in the lower right corner simply holds a standard.[7] As similar as this piece is to 31, the two tapestries could not have come from the same set of hangings because the Munich piece does not have the scroll bearing the Bouesseau device nor does it have the ciphers.

It was noted above (Description and Subject) that 31 might have been part of a set of hangings which, through the depiction of characteristic activities or occupations, alluded to the seasons, the months of the year, the ages of man, or some combination of these time-based measures. It would have required at least four, and as many as twelve, compositions to express the allegorical content of these themes (see note 4).

HISTORY

Sold, *Objets d'art . . . composant la Collection de M. A. Tollin*, Salle Georges Petit, Paris, May 20–21, 1897, no. 219.
Property of Edouard Jonas, Paris.
Property of French and Company, New York.
In the collection of Adele and Arthur Lehman, New York, acquired from French and Company in 1926.
Bequeathed to the MMA by Adele L. Lehman in memory of Arthur Lehman, 1965.

EXHIBITIONS

New York, MMA, 1928. *French Gothic Tapestries: A Loan Exhibition.* Cat. no. 10, not illus. Lent by Mr. and Mrs. Arthur Lehman.
Indianapolis Museum of Art, 1970–71. *Treasures from the Metropolitan.* Cat. no. 94, illus.

PUBLICATIONS

Breck, Joseph. "The Tapestry Exhibition: Part II." *MMA Bulletin* 23 (1928) p. 184. Described briefly; illus. fig. 1.
Virch, Claus. *The Adele and Arthur Lehman Collection.* MMA, New York, 1965, p. 92. Discussed; illus. p. 93.
Forsyth, William H. "Report of the Departments: Medieval Art and The Cloisters, the Main Building." Annual Report for 1965–1966. In *MMA Bulletin*, n.s. 25 (1966–67) p. 87. Discussed briefly; illus.
C. G.-M. [Carmen Gómez-Moreno]. "Tapestry: Five Boys Playing

'Hoodman Blind.'" *MMA Notable Acquisitions 1965–1975*. New York, 1975, p. 163. Mentioned; illus.

de Vaivre, Jean-Bernard. "Deux tapisseries inédites de la fin du moyen âge commandées par des Bourguignons." *Comptes rendus de l'Académie des Inscriptions et Belles-Lettres*, 1988, pp. 133–40. Described and discussed in detail; illus. figs. 9 (detail) and 10 (full view).

B. D. B. [Barbara Drake Boehm]. "Upper Leaf of a Diptych Sundial." *Recent Acquisitions: A Selection 1987–1988*. MMA, New York, 1988, p. 21. Mentioned.

NOTES

1. The present author was able to associate the inscription with the Bouesseau family of Burgundy because he had found the same words painted on a scroll in the church of Notre-Dame de Dijon (see note 2) and then discovered the name of the family in Charles Oursel, *L'église Notre-Dame de Dijon* (Paris, [1938]) pp. 44, 45. In 1987 he brought the tapestry, inscription, and cipher to the attention of M. de Vaivre who, with his own previous knowledge of Nicolas Bouesseau's life and armorial bearings, was able to identify the cipher as that of Nicolas and his wife, Guillemette. The author gratefully acknowledges M. de Vaivre's generosity in sharing his specialized knowledge. For more details on this subject, see Jean-Bernard de Vaivre, "Deux tapisseries inédites de la fin du moyen âge commandées par des Bourguignons," *Comptes rendus de l'Académie des Inscriptions et Belles-Lettres*, 1988, pp. 133–40. See also Jean-Bernard de Vaivre, "Un manuscrit ayant appartenu à Nicolas Bouesseau, maître des comptes du duc de Bourgogne," *Archivum Heraldicum*, 1985, no. 3–4, pp. 39–42.

2. For information concerning the chapel and the painted decorations, with illustrations, see Oursel, *L'église Notre-Dame de Dijon*, pp. 44–45, including a distant view of the wall on p. 43; also de Vaivre, "Deux tapisseries inédites," pp. 137, 140, and figs. 12 (full view of the wall), 13 (detail of the carved shield with the Bouesseau coat of arms), and 14 and 15 (details of two of the four inscribed scrolls and of one of the emblems). Figs. 14 and 15 show that *selon* is spelled with an initial *c* in at least two of the scrolls. Since de Vaivre, "Deux tapisseries inédites," p. 137, noted that the painting on the shield had been restored, we cannot be sure that this variant spelling is original. A longer scroll painted on the wall near the Bouesseau devices, and inscribed with a later dedication to the Five Wounds ("la chappelle des cinq plaies"), is clearly restoration work.

3. De Vaivre has recorded several slightly different blazons for the coat of arms of this Bouesseau family and indicated that the tinctures varied. See de Vaivre, "Un manuscrit ayant appartenu à Nicolas Bouesseau," p. 39, for an illustration of a coat of arms that was added to a page in an early fifteenth-century manuscript in the Walters Art Gallery, Baltimore (MS W 219). De Vaivre gives this blazon as "d'or à trois lions de sable issant de trois paniers du même." He quotes (p. 39 n. 10) a blazon with different tinctures, "dor à trois lions de gueules naissans de trois Bouesseaux d'azur," from Pierre Palliot, *La vraie et parfaite science des armoiries* (1660), facsimile reprint with introduction by Jean-Bernard de Vaivre (Paris, 1979) p. 65, and notes that Palliot also gave that blazon in his *Le parlement de Bourgogne, son origine, son établissement et son progrès . . .* (Dijon, 1649), an example illustrated by de Vaivre, "Un manuscrit ayant appartenu à Nicolas Bouesseau," as fig. 4. De Vaivre (pp. 41–42) also discusses the coat of arms of Thomas Bouesseau, father of Nicolas, that appears in a version of the "armorial de la cour amoureuse" in the state archives in Vienna and illustrates it as fig. 5; he gives the blazon as "de sable à trois demi-lions d'argent issants de trois boisseaux d'or" and observes that these tinctures are the reverse of those in Nicolas Bouesseau's shield in the Baltimore manuscript.

4. See, for example, a tapestry of 1523 showing essentially the same emblem with the motto MVSAS NATVRA LACHRIMAS FORTVNA, illustrated in Joseph Guibert, *Les dessins d'archéologie de Roger de Gaignières*, ser. 3, *Tapisseries* (Paris, [1911–14]) no. B. 1783.

5. For an early sixteenth-century set of tapestries dealing with the allegory of the Ages of Man interpreted in terms of the twelve months and the four seasons of the year, with references to the weather, symbols, and occupations and mythical characters associated with each time frame, see Edith Appleton Standen, *European Post-Medieval Tapestries and Related Hangings in The Metropolitan Museum of Art* (New York, 1985) no. 2.

6. For biographical details concerning Nicolas Bouesseau and his family, see de Vaivre, "Un manuscrit ayant appartenu à Nicolas Bouesseau," pp. 39–42, and also de Vaivre, "Deux tapisseries inédites," pp. 136, 137, 140, and n. 30, in which he credits the detail concerning Bouesseau as a juror to Nicole Reynaud, "Un peintre français de la fin du quinzième siècle: Le maître des prélats bourguignons," in *Etudes d'art français offertes à Charles Sterling*, ed. Albert Châtelet and Nicole Reynaud (Paris, 1975) p. 162 n. 18.

7. See Georg Himmelheber, "Ein Tausendblumenteppich," *Pantheon* 30 (1972) pp. 393–95, illus. in color on cover and p. 393, details in black and white on pp. 392, 395. The tapestry was first published when it was sold from the collection of Mme. C. Lelong in Paris, Galerie Georges Petit, December 8–10, 1902, no. 304, illus. It then belonged successively to Duveen Brothers, Edson Bradley, French and Company, Grace Rainey Rogers, and the Cranbrook Academy of Art, from which it was sold in New York at Sotheby, Parke-Bernet, March 25, 1972, no. 200, illus. in color. See also Göbel 1923, vol. 2, fig. 196.

32a

458

32
The Hunt of the Frail Stag

a   *Vanity Sounds the Horn and Ignorance Unleashes
   the Hounds Overconfidence, Rashness, and Desire*
b   *Old Age Drives the Stag out of a Lake and the
   Hounds Heat, Grief, Cold, Anxiety, Age, and
   Heaviness Pursue Him*

Southern Netherlands, 1500–1525
Wool warp; wool and silk wefts; the fabric embroidered in one
place with wool yarn
32a: 9 ft. 10 in. × 12 ft. 6 in. (3 m × 3.81 m)
11–13 warp yarns per inch, 4–5 per centimeter
32b: 8 ft. 6 in. × 11 ft. 5 in. (2.59 m × 3.48 m)
12–14 warp yarns per inch, 5–6 per centimeter
Bequest of Mary Stillman Harkness, 1950 (50.145.4,5)

Condition

Both tapestries are fragments, each the main section of a
somewhat larger hanging that was cut down at the top
and bottom. The upper left corner of 32a, from the bird's
wings outward, is a modern restoration executed with
new warp and weft yarns. The entire bottom of the piece,
the fabric below an irregular line running through the
lowest hound's legs, is a restoration of the same kind.
There are a few more modern insertions scattered
throughout the piece. The only one that affects the original drawing occurs in the label of the lowest hound,
voloir, whose name has been replaced. There are also
repairs by reweaving new weft yarns on the original
warp in many parts of the fabric. The inscription identifying *vanite*, one of the two women represented, and the
first and last parts of the stag's name have been rewoven
in this way. The yellow tones have faded considerably,
but the other colors are reasonably bright.

The bottom of 32b shows a cut edge, but the left and
right edges retain their original loom headings, indicating that no fabric was lost at the sides. The lower right
corner, an area bounded by a line running from the
shoulder of the hound directly below the stag to the
break in the ground at the right, has been replaced with
modern warp and weft yarns. It is the only insertion in
the piece. There are repairs by reweaving on the original
warp scattered over the surface but particularly in the
areas representing the foliage of the shrub in the center
and the trees in the middle distance at the right. The
colors, including the yellows and greens, have survived
remarkably well.

Description and Subject

In 32a there are two female figures, a stag, and six
hounds in a wooded setting whose foreground is covered
with flowering plants. An orange tree borders the scene
at the right and a cherry or berry-bearing tree does the
same at the left. The top of a pomegranate tree appears
in the upper right corner of the field. A body of water
crosses the scene in the middle distance; on its far shore
a shepherd and shepherdess tend their flock. Two castles
or manor houses appear in the distance at the center. An
inscribed banderole showing yellow letters on a red
ground, with a blue initial letter in the first line of verse,
is spread across the field just above the level of the water.

The stag who is leaping out of the scene at the upper
left is labeled *le [ce]rf fragille*. The hounds chasing him
are, left to right, *haste* (Rashness), *outrecuidanche*
(Overconfidence), and *voloir* (Desire). The same three
hounds appear next to the woman who is unleashing
them directly below. She is labeled *dame ignorance*. The
woman standing above and to the right of her is *vanite*;
she lifts a hunting horn to her lips. *Ignorance* wears a
damask gown with fringed hem and short sleeves
through which the long loose sleeves of her undergarment pass. On her head is a hood surmounted by a hat
with an upturned brim and a high crown tied about with
a flowing scarf. *Vanite* wears a patterned velvet gown cut
like the one worn by *ignorance*. There is a golden chain
with a locket around *vanite*'s neck, and on her head she
wears a hat over a hood. The verses inscribed on the
banderole above read as follows:[1]

*Les chiens qui tenoit acouples dedens leb ois [le
bois] dame / ignoranche apres le cerf a decouplez
ce[s]t voloir haste outrecuidance
qui plains de mondaine plaisanche lui font maint /
sauls et traverssaire [travers faire?] et lors vanite si
savanche de corner come elle scet faire*

(The dogs that she held leashed in the woods Dame
Ignorance has let loose after the stag; they are
Desire, Rashness, Overconfidence
Who, filled with wordly pleasure, make him take
many a leap and crossing; and then Vanity comes
forward to sound the horn as she knows how to do).

459

32b

Light-colored silk yarns were used as highlights throughout. An unusual technical detail appears in the face of the shepherdess seated in the far distance just left of center. Her eyes and mouth have been represented with flat, straight needle stitches; small couched stitches were used to delineate her eyebrows. The embroidery was done with woolen yarns.

Pale-toned silks also appear in the highlights in 32b. That piece contains no needlework. The scene is set in a low, rolling landscape that opens at the back to show a town, a castle on a hill, and a forest in the far distance at the right. An irregularly shaped lake occupies most of the middle ground and some of the left foreground. Next to this part of the lake an old woman hobbles toward the

right, leaning on a walking stick. Her figure is missing from mid-calf down as is the rest of the field. No label appears on or near the visible part of her body, but the verses inscribed on the banderole in the upper right-hand corner of the field indicate that this woman represents *viellesse* (Old Age). In her left hand she holds a leash connected to the collars of three hounds that walk in front of her. The lower parts of their bodies have disappeared along with the bottom of the field, and the names of only two of them are visible. One is *soussi* (Anxiety) and the other is *aige* (Age). Two other hounds have already been unleashed, and they run in front of these three; the name of one, *froit* (Cold), has been preserved. Two other hounds, closer to the stag, who

460

leaps up in the water, are labeled *chault* (Heat) and *peine* (Grief). The verses inscribed on the wide banderole above read as follows:

Puis lassault viellesse aoultrance · Qui le fait hors du lac saillier
Et lui lasche peine et doubtāce · Froet et chault et si fait venir
Soussy laboir pour le tenir · Et eage a la chere ridee
Et pesanteur le font sauie [error for *fouir*?] *· Vers maladie la doubter* [*doubtee*]

(Then Old Age, who makes him leap up out of the lake, attacks him with a vengeance
And unleashes Grief and Fear, Cold and Heat after him and then brings in
Anxiety and Toil to hold him fast; and Age with its wrinkled skin
And Heaviness make him flee toward Illness, the dreaded one).

In the middle of the scene, near the far shore of the lake, a figure sitting in a boat seems to be putting out an anchor line or hauling it in. This is not simply a picturesque detail; it probably refers to the practice of having a boat at the ready in case a stag tried to shake off his pursuers by entering a body of water. The boat could be used if the stag remained in the water for some time or to haul the beast out of the water if he drowned. A boat also provided a means of crossing water too deep to ford. Gaston III, comte de Foix (called Gaston Phébus), made these practical observations in chapter 45 of his late fourteenth-century treatise on hunting, *Le livre de la chasse*.[2]

Both tapestries illustrate incidents in the allegorical story of the Hunt of the Frail Stag. The stages of this hunt follow the course of an actual stag hunt of the period, but the quarry is the Frail Stag, the symbol of Mankind struggling through life at the mercy of his own mortal weaknesses and the trials of old age. The moral of the story, which is the same one told in five tapestry fragments (24a–e) in this catalogue, is that Man must seek and come to terms with God during his time on earth in order to find his salvation. Among the series of compositions to which 32a, b belong, there would have been one showing the poet or author presenting this moral in verse form (see 24a–e and the background information given there concerning the story of this hunt, its moral, and its sources).

The two tapestries show marked differences in the character of the drawing, color, and weaving, but since 32b is much better preserved than 32a, it is difficult to say whether these differences would have been noticed as readily when the two pieces were woven. We cannot say for certain whether or not they come from the same set of hangings. Neither the slight difference in the warp counts nor the different forms of the inscribed banderoles prove that they are from different sets.

SOURCE OF THE DESIGN

Like 24a–e, these two pieces were almost certainly designed after the illustrations in a manuscript or printed book dealing with the allegory of the *cerf fragile* (see Source of the Design in 24a–e). The verses in the two sets of fragments are virtually the same, and the compositions, while different, show some points of similarity. For example the figure of *vanite* in 32a is almost the same as the corresponding figure in 24b but shown in reverse. While the figures of the old woman (*viellesse*) and the hounds in 32b do not correspond to those in 24c, the arrangement of the figures is similar. Therefore it seems possible that 32a, b and 24a–e were woven after cartoons derived ultimately from the same or closely related sources.

MANUFACTURE AND DATE

When 32a was sold in 1914, it was catalogued as French and dated at the end of the fifteenth century. Some years later Göbel (1923, vol. 2, fig. 94) ascribed it tentatively to Tournai and dated it in the first third of the sixteenth century. Hunter (1925, 72 and pl. VI,n) wrote that 32a showed "Tournai-style foliage," but he called it simply "late Gothic." He spoke of it as having been "developed and enlarged" from one of the five Lehman pieces (see 24b), which implies that he believed it had been woven later. Van Marle (1932, 105–6) referred to 32a as being contemporary with those five fragments. Some years later Forsyth (1951–52, 209) called 32a, b Franco-Flemish and dated them in the second quarter of the sixteenth century, an attribution that was used when the two hangings were exhibited in 1961 in Chapel Hill. Later still Virch (1965, 105) repeated the Franco-Flemish attribution but dated the two pieces about 1520–30. None of these writers gave reasons for their attributions except Hunter who, although mentioning the "Tournai-style foliage" in 32a, did not assert that it had been woven in Tournai. The author of the "Note additionelle" (1914–20) wrote that the inscription in 32a shows Picard language forms used by tapestry weavers in Flanders and the Artois. Assuming that his observation is correct, it may perhaps be significant in relation to the place the poem was written but not necessarily where the tapestry was woven. For the present it seems most reasonable to suggest that 32a and b were produced in some unspecified region of the southern Netherlands and to date them tentatively, on the slim evidence provided by the overall style and the costumes (which are fancy dress rather than civilian garb), in the first quarter of the sixteenth century.

RELATED TAPESTRIES

Since the two stanzas shown in 32a, b virtually duplicate two of the five that appear in 24a–e, it is clear that those pieces and the set or sets of hangings represented by 32a, b were designed to illustrate the same poem. Nine miniature paintings illustrate this poem in a late sixteenth-century manuscript preserved in the Bibliothèque Nationale in Paris.3 We estimate that the five fragments in 24a–e originally belonged to a series of seven scenes based on the poem. In both the manuscript and 24a–e the illustrations include one showing the poet or author delivering the moral of the story. Therefore it seems likely that the set or sets of tapestries to which 32a and 32b once belonged included one showing the poet and others illustrating additional incidents in the allegorical stag hunt. None of these pieces is known to have survived. However a fragmentary tapestry that was formerly in the Larcade collection in Paris and whose present location is unknown could have been woven after the same series of cartoons and could perhaps be part of one of these missing hangings.4 Judging from the illustration we have seen, it is more closely related to 32a, b in terms of concept and design than 24a–e are. It shows an incident mentioned in the fourth stanza of the poem, the moment when *necessite*, a female figure, aided by her hound *simplesse*, drives the hapless stag into the Lake of Knowledge.

See Description and Subject and Related Tapestries in 24a–e for details concerning other tapestries and paintings dealing with the *cerf fragile* and other allegorical stags.

HISTORY

32a sold, *Collection de feu M. Charles André*, Hôtel Drouot, Paris, May 18–19, 1914, no. 180, illus.
Property of Wildenstein and Company, by 1925.
In the collection of Mary Stillman Harkness.
Bequeathed to the MMA by Mary Stillman Harkness, 1950.

32b in the collection of Mary Stillman Harkness.
Bequeathed to the MMA by Mary Stillman Harkness, 1950.

EXHIBITIONS

Chapel Hill, William Hayes Ackland Memorial Art Center, University of North Carolina, 1961. *An Exhibition of Medieval Art.* Cat. no. 35 [32b], illus.
Yokohama Museum of Art, 1989. *Treasures from The Metropolitan Museum of Art: French Art from the Middle Ages to the Twentieth Century.* Cat. no. 31 [32a], color illus.

PUBLICATIONS

"Note additionelle sur 'Le cerf allégorique dans les tapisseries et les miniatures.'" *Bulletin de la Société française de reproductions de manuscrits à peintures* 4 (1914–20) p. 8. 32a discussed briefly.
Göbel 1923, vol. 1, p. 131. 32a mentioned and the beginning of the stanza quoted; illus. vol. 2, fig. 94.
Hunter 1925, p. 72. 32a mentioned; illus. pl. VI,n.
van Marle, Raimond. *Iconographie de l'art profane au Moyen-Age et à la Renaissance.* Vol. 2. The Hague, 1932, pp. 105–6. 32a described briefly.
Forsyth, William H. "The Medieval Stag Hunt." *MMA Bulletin*, n.s. 10 (1951–52) p. 209. 32a and 32b mentioned; illus. pp. 206 [32a], 207 [32b].
Virch, Claus. *The Adele and Arthur Lehman Collection.* MMA, New York, 1965, p. 105. 32a and 32b mentioned.
van Ysselsteyn, G. T. *Tapestry: The Most Expensive Industry of the XVth and XVIth Centuries.* The Hague and Brussels, 1969, pp. 185–86. Both pieces described briefly, including the inscriptions; illus. figs. 208, 209.

NOTES

1. The transcriptions and translations of the verses given here differ in some details from readings published earlier.
2. See Gaston Phébus, *Le livre de la chasse,* translated into modern French by Robert and André Bossuat, introduction and commentary by Marcel Thomas ([Paris], 1986) p. 128.
3. MS fr. 25429; see a discussion of the manuscript, together with transcriptions of the verses and illustrations of the miniatures, in Emile Picot, "Le cerf allégorique dans les tapisseries et les miniatures," *Bulletin de la Société française de reproductions de manuscrits à peintures* 3 (1913) pp. 60–63, pls. LVI–LVIII.
4. The fragment is known only from a photocopy of what appears to be a page in a sale catalogue, in the files of the MMA Department of Medieval Art, accompanied by a note stating that the tapestry was sold at the Galerie Charpentier, Paris, "Sambon-Warneck et à divers amateurs." At the time of writing it was not possible to trace this sale.

33

The Triumph of Fame and the Triumph of Time

Two hangings from a set based on Petrarch's
I Trionfi

a *The Triumph of Fame over Death*
b *The Triumph of Time over Fame*

Southern Netherlands, 1500–1530
Wool warp; wool and silk wefts
33a: 12 ft. × 10 ft. 8 in. (3.66 m × 3.25 m)
33b: 12 ft. 6 1/4 in. × 12 ft. 4 1/4 in. (3.82 m × 3.77 m)
11–13 warp yarns per inch, 4–5 per centimeter
Bequest of George D. Pratt, 1935 (41.167.1 [33b], 41.167.2 [33a])

CONDITION

Both hangings were cut along the four sides, and the raw edges were covered with strips of modern weaving. Since 33a shows a bit more than the right half of the complete composition of the *Triumph of Fame* as it is represented in a tapestry in Vienna (see Related Tapestries and fig. 145), 33a is evidently the surviving right-hand section of a hanging that was woven after a version of the same cartoon. The left half of the tapestry is missing along with other sections that extended along the right side, the bottom, and the top. There, the upper of the two lines of verse on the banderole in the sky is missing. On the other hand, 33b shows almost all of the composition in the Vienna tapestry that corresponds to it (see fig. 146). The major losses occur along the left edge and the bottom; very little of the scene is missing along the top and right side.

Both pieces show a good deal of reweaving with new weft yarns, for the most part on the original warp. In 33a the repairs occur spotted about the sky and the inscribed banderole, in details of the landscape and the costumes of the four figures standing at the left, in the nearer elephant's harness, and in the flora along the right side. The hand of justice at the tip of the rod that *Alexandre* holds in his left hand has been rewoven. A line of repair runs irregularly entirely across the piece near the bottom. It begins at the left end of the field at a point level with the emperor's ankles and continues across the chests of the two prostrate female figures in the center. It then goes through the top of the stump at the right and ends at the right end of the field. 33b also has spots of reweaving in the sky and the landscape, but most of the repair appears in the main part of the composition. The

lower half of the seated figure's robe and its left sleeve have been entirely rewoven, and there are spots of repair also in the right side of the robe and in the figure's hat. There are small repairs in the right half of the zodiac ring above his head and in the back of his throne just under the ring. The dark areas beneath the chariot and the stags' bodies—specifically the areas representing *Renommee*'s skirt and the ground behind this figure—have been completely rewoven. There are small repairs in the stags' harnesses and in the rump of the farther animal as well as in the neck of the nearer one. Parts of the birds that fly in front of the stags, and bits of the flora along the right side of the field, also show passages of reweaving. The repairs throughout the tapestry have affected the drawing very little.

In 33b only the major areas of repair—that is, most of the chief figure's robe and the area under his chariot—have altered the original drawing to any appreciable extent. While the colors have faded considerably in both pieces, all the tones are clear and distinct. The greens, blues, whites, pinks, and oranges are especially well preserved.

DESCRIPTION AND SUBJECT

The scene in 33a shows a landscape that has a flowery field in the foreground, a rolling meadow in the middle distance, and a number of turreted buildings nestled among the hills in the far distance. Two trees rising in the foreground at the right close the scene in at that side. In the left foreground the figure of Fame, labeled [Ren]ommee across her skirt at ankle level, stands on the floor of a cart drawn by a pair of white elephants. Flying ahead of the elephants are a cock and a bat, each one tied to the beasts' harnesses by a cord. The procession is moving from left to right. Fame is represented as a winged woman magnificently dressed in a patterned velvet bodice with sleeves that have been decorated with slashings through which puffs of the fabric of her white shirt have been drawn. Her unpatterned velvet skirt has a peplum made of ostrich feathers, each of

which has been represented as a mask with a pair of eyes and a long tongue hanging from the mouth below. Fame wears a cap at the back of her head and a ruffle of clouds over her forehead. She holds a trumpet with four bells up to her lips. Two women lie on the ground next to the cart and the elephants. Only one of them, *atropos,* is identified by the inscription that appears near her right breast. A bearded figure representing the emperor Charlemagne stands in the foreground, in front of the women. There is no label to identify him. He wears an ermine-lined cloak cut like a late medieval chasuble. It is decorated on the right side with the imperial eagle and on the left side with a scattering of fleurs-de-lis. The imperial crown is on his head. He holds a sword upright in his right hand and the imperial orb in his left hand. On the far side of Fame's cart stand three men, all walking toward the right with the rest of the procession. Plato, labeled *platon* across the front of his garment at thigh level, leads the other two. He wears an unpatterned robe with a wide yoke and funnel-shaped sleeves. On his head is a low round cap with an upturned brim. Alexander the Great, labeled *Alexandre* to the right of his left shoulder, wears an unpatterned, ermine-lined cloak cut like Charlemagne's over a patterned velvet robe. On his head is a round cap with an upturned ermine brim and, at its summit, a small open crown. He holds a scepter in his right hand and the staff of the hand of justice in his left hand. He turns his head toward the left to speak to the bearded Aristotle, labeled *aristote* across the back of his cloak. This man wears a headdress that is a cross between a round cap and a chaperon with a pendant tippet. Part of a banderole inscribed with white letters on a pink (originally red) ground is spread out against the sky at the top of the field. This is the lower half of one of two such scrolls on which are inscribed the four lines of verse that refer to the action represented in the complete composition. This line, the last verse of a quatrain poem, reads: *Par son pou[v]oir comme dame estimee* (Through her power as a lady of consequence).[1]

The same kind of open landscape setting appears in 33b. The chariot of Time, whose badly restored label *le temps* is written on his robe near his right knee, is in the left half of the field. A pair of harnessed white stags draws the chariot toward the right. Both creatures move forward, but only one of them looks ahead; the other looks back. Flying before them, and tied to their harnesses, are a hen and a raven. The dead Fame, labeled *Renomee,* lies crushed under the chariot's wheels, the four bells and broken shaft of her trumpet strewn on the ground next to her. Methuselah, labeled *mathusale* across his coat at thigh level, walks next to the rear right wheel of the chariot. He is represented as an old man

wearing a knee-length coat, boots, and a wide-brimmed, high-crowned shaggy hat over a cap. He steps on one of Fame's wings as he hobbles along toward the right. On the far side of the chariot two bearded old men, also carrying walking sticks, are deep in conversation. The one at the left is Noah, labeled *noe* just to the right of his head. In the corresponding tapestry in Vienna (fig. 146), the man at the right is labeled *nestor;* and the third old man walking ahead of him and Noah is labeled *Adam.* In the Metropolitan Museum's tapestry neither Nestor nor Adam is labeled, but the name *nestor* appears inscribed against the landscape some distance to the right of Adam's head.

Time is represented as an old man with a long white beard seated on a throne set in his chariot. He wears an unpatterned velvet robe with a jeweled hem and hanging sleeves through which the sleeves of his doublet pass. He also wears a wide flat collar and a low round hat with an upturned brim. He is seated facing backward, but he turns his torso and head to look forward. In his upraised right hand he holds a clock. A walking stick dangles from his limp left hand. The dark frame of a small circular mirror placed directly above his head is decorated with the signs of the zodiac. At the same level the sun appears in the sky at the left and the moon at the right. Above all of this two banderoles flutter side by side against the sky. The first two lines of a quatrain poem are written in white letters on a pink (originally red) ground on the scroll at the left. The third and fourth lines are inscribed in the same way on the right-hand scroll. The verses (left, then right) read as follows:

Le [t]emps esmeu apres noises debas
V[i]el et casse sans craindre aucun port darmes

A renommee a faict plusieurs a larmes
Et du plus hault il la remise au bas

(Time, roused by quarrels from below,
Old and worn out, fearing no battle,
Has attacked Fame again and again
And knocked her down from her pinnacle).

The weaving was executed primarily with woolen weft yarns. Silk yarns were used to render some of the paler tones in the pattern, especially the highlights.

The meaning of the compositions in these two tapestries is fairly self-evident. In the *Triumph of Fame* we see the chief figure announcing her messages to the four corners of the earth. By virtue of the feather masks hanging around her waist she sees the famous (the eyes) and spreads word of their deeds (the tongues). As Forsyth (exh. cat. Los Angeles and Chicago 1970) noted, the image of the feathers derives from Virgil's description of

33b

Fame in the *Aeneid,* and it survived long after Petrarch's time in sources like Cesare Ripa's *Iconologia.* The two elephants drawing Fame's chariot symbolize great power, having acquired this connotation from their physical strength and from their association with the elephants that drew the chariots of Roman victors. The cock flying ahead of the beasts guides the chariot during the day, the bat during the night. They indicate that the progress of Fame never stops.

Plato leads the procession of famous men as he does in Petrarch's poem. There, Aristotle follows immediately behind him; but in the tapestry he has been moved to the third position, behind Alexander. Forsyth suggested that the Alexander in the tapestry may have been intended to represent Louis XII because he carries the regalia of the king of France and also because his features may refer to those of his ancestor Saint Louis. Scheicher (1971, 45) believed that this figure was meant

466

to represent Louis XII; but Salet (1973, 60) argued that the references to the French monarchy that are associated with this regal figure—the scepters and crown in the Vienna hanging (fig. 145) and 33a; and a crown, the collar of the order of Saint Michael, and a mantle decorated with fleurs-de-lis in the near-duplicate piece in Brussels (fig. 147)—are a normal conceit of the period. It is important to note that this figure is labeled *S. Loys* in the tapestry in Brussels; it is also important that, as Crick-Kuntziger observed, he is identified as Alexander in a late sixteenth-century print published by Charles le Vigoureux (fig. 148) that shows essentially the same composition.[2] The puzzle this figure presents remains unsolved. In any event, he is one of three historical figures who demonstrate Fame's power. A fourth, Charlemagne, is also present. Three other great men of

antiquity, Homer, Cicero, and Virgil, who appear in the left ends of the similar *Triumph of Fame* tapestries in Vienna and Brussels (figs. 145, 147), are not present in 33a because it lacks its left end. Part of that missing section is now in the Seattle Art Museum (fig. 149). It shows almost all of Virgil's figure and part of Cicero's right arm.

As Fame's chariot proceeds, it crushes Death under its wheels. Here Death, unlike the image in Petrarch's *I Trionfi* but like the image in Jehan Robertet's adaptation of it (see below), is represented not by a single figure but by the three Fates. Clotho, who spins the thread of life; Lachesis, who draws it out; and Atropos, who cuts it off, all fall under the wheels of Fame's chariot. Only the bodies of Atropos and Lachesis (not labeled, but lying behind Charlemagne's legs) are visible in the Metropoli-

Fig. 145. *The Triumph of Fame*. Tapestry, here attributed to the southern Netherlands, early sixteenth century. Kunsthistorisches Museum, Vienna.

tan Museum's tapestry. Clotho's body is missing along with the left end of the piece. A bit of her headdress is visible in the lower right corner of the fragment in Seattle.

The tapestry design indicates that Fame, by speaking to the four corners of the earth day and night, triumphs over Death. However the verses inscribed above do not celebrate that action itself but the meaning of Fame's triumph in the succession of triumphs as Petrarch envisaged them. The verses celebrate not only Fame's triumph over Death itself but also over Death as the destroyer of Chastity, the subject of the preceding tapestry in the series, the third in the set of six. The verses of the quatrain inscribed on the two banderoles that flutter across the sky in the complete *Triumph of Fame* in Vienna (fig. 145) read as follows (left, then right):

Fig. 146. *The Triumph of Time*. Tapestry, here attributed to the southern Netherlands, early sixteenth century. Kunsthistorisches Museum, Vienna.

468

Fig. 147. *The Triumph of Fame.* Tapestry, here attributed to the southern Netherlands, early sixteenth century. Musées Royaux d'Art et d'Histoire, Brussels.

de terre vient la haulte renommee
Pour atropos et les deux seurs renger

Car chastete elle a voulu venger
Par son pou[v]oir comme dame estimee

(Loud Fame rises up
To subdue Atropos and her two sisters
Because she has wanted to avenge Chastity
Through her power as a lady of consequence).

In the *Triumph of Time* the main figure holds one symbol of time, a clock, in his hand while another, the ring of the zodiac signs, symbol of the passing year, appears above his head. As Forsyth observed in some unpublished notes, the circular shape of the mirror of which the ring serves as a frame may refer to Petrarch's likening the circular course of the sun to infinity; and the mirror itself may derive from the same unidentified literary source as Cesare Ripa's observation that Time carries a mirror in his hand because one sees time only in the present which is so brief and uncertain that it is

no better than the false image in a mirror.[3] The sun and moon set in the sky at the sides are reminders that day follows night endlessly through time. The old man representing Time sits with his body facing the rear of the wagon, but he turns his head to look forward. Forsyth (exh. cat. Los Angeles and Chicago 1970, 246) noted that this detail indicates "that time 'turns back on itself and never sees the end,'" an idea that he found expressed in Vincenzo Cartari's *Le imagini de i Dei* (Venice, 1580). The stags pulling the chariot are symbols of longevity, and the hen and raven flying ahead signify that time moves forward relentlessly, day and night. The stags, like Time himself, look both forward and back. In *I Trionfi* Petrarch identified Time with the sun, but the artist who designed this composition applied the notion of time to human beings instead and consequently associated Time with old age. Thus, Time himself is shown as an old man, and the three men who walk along behind the chariot, Noah, Nestor, and Methuselah, are all men famed for their longevity. Adam, who walks just ahead of the chariot on its far side, may represent not only lon-

469

Fig. 148. *The Triumph of Fame*, from *Le vray miroir de la vie humaine*, published by Charles le Vigoureux, Paris. Woodcut, France, late sixteenth century. Cabinet des Estampes, Bibliothèque Nationale, Paris.

gevity but also perhaps the first man, the beginning of time for human beings. Time has triumphed over Fame, who is being crushed under the chariot's wheels. The quatrain inscribed on the pair of banderoles in the sky tells the viewer that Time is fearless, and though old and broken he has finally defeated Fame.

In the sequence of six Triumphs that Petrarch (Francesco Petrarca, 1304–1374) described in *I Trionfi*, written between 1352 and 1374, Love made the first conquest and the only one that Petrarch described in terms of a triumphal procession with the key figure riding in a chariot. In the five other Triumphs that he described—Chastity over Love, Death over Chastity, Fame over Death, Time over Fame, and finally Divinity (in later usage, "Eternity") over Time—the scenes are not described as triumphal processions. Rather, Petrarch

speaks of watching in a dream different allegorical figures interacting with various historical figures. They encounter one another in succession, as individuals or in groups. In the three chapters that Petrarch devotes to the Triumph of Fame, he sees Fame arriving across the grass with a host of famous Roman, Greek, Trojan, and Persian emperors, heroes, philosophers, and poets along with the nine male and female Worthies; but there is no triumphal paraphernalia and no procession, no crushing of Death under the wheels of a chariot. Fame simply follows Death in the sequence of events the poet tells of seeing in his dream. In the single chapter he devotes to the Triumph of Time, Petrarch speaks of seeing Time blowing a horn and he identifies Time with the sun, but he does not mention the historical figures who appear in the tapestries and there is no triumphal procession. The

470

other major difference between the tapestry designs and Petrarch's text is that the poet refers many times to his beloved Laura, who had died some years before he began writing the verses. He speaks of her in the Triumph of Love; she is identified with Chastity in that Triumph; Death meets her in his Triumph, and in the Triumph of Divinity Petrarch speaks confidently of seeing her once again in heaven. Laura appears as Chastity in the *Triumph of Chastity* in the Victoria and Albert Museum, a thematically related tapestry of quite different style (see Digby 1980, no. 22), but the figure of Chastity is not so labeled in the corresponding Triumph tapestry in Vienna that belongs to the series of compositions to which 33a and b and their related pieces also belong. A third series of early sixteenth-century *Triumphs of Petrarch* tapestry compositions, represented by a *Triumph of Death* in the Victoria and Albert Museum (see Digby 1980, no. 26), is more faithful to the text of *I Trionfi*. Like the drawings in Paris that show closely related compositions,[4] that *Triumph of Death* and the related pieces cited by Digby do not show triumphal cars or processions; the victorious figures simply stand on the prostrate bodies of the vanquished ones.

Most historians believe that it was the designers of illustrated early editions of *I Trionfi* who invented the theme of six triumphal processions with the chief figures riding in chariots.[5] Others have suggested that the change was brought about through the influence on artists of the work of earlier or later poets who described images like Petrarch's in terms of triumphal processions. In her study of the iconography of the triumph of Fame, Shorr noted that Dante (*Purgatorio*, XXIX) described a scene in which Beatrice appears in a car like the ones that victorious Roman generals and emperors used in their triumphal processions. She was surrounded by a group of elders, virtues, apostles, nymphs, and the Apocalyptic beasts.[6] Shorr also indicated that the theme of allegorical triumphs in the guise of ancient Roman triumphs appears in Boccaccio's *Amorosa visione* (1342), in which the poet described some mural paintings showing the triumphs of Fame (called *Gloria*), Love, and Fortune. Shorr published some late fourteenth-century illustrations of Petrarch's *De viris illustribus* that show Fame as *Gloria* riding forward toward the observer in her triumphal car drawn by two horses.[7] She believed that this image then developed a more secular form—the form it takes in the tapestries and most of the other kinds of pictorial representations of the Triumphs that we know—through the influence on one hand of street processions and on the other hand through the work of the artists who illustrated the various editions of *I Trionfi* in the fifteenth century. Further-

Fig. 149. *The Triumph of Fame*. Part of a tapestry, here attributed to south Netherlands, early sixteenth century. Seattle Art Museum; Gift of Mrs. Donald E. Frederick.

more she noted that elephants rather than horses were shown drawing Fame's chariot as early as the third decade of the fifteenth century, a change that she traced again to the influence of street pageants where, Shorr believed, the designers would have thought it uninteresting to repeat Love's team of horses in connection with Fame's chariot. She quoted part of a letter that the Venetian artist Matteo dei Pasti wrote to Cosimo de' Medici in 1441 asking whether that patron would like to see the Triumph of Fame represented (presumably in a miniature he was painting for a manuscript edition of *I Trionfi*) with "soldiers and maidens to follow or merely famous men of old." In that case the car was being drawn by four white elephants. Shorr also illustrated the Triumph of Fame page in a fifteenth-century Italian manuscript of *I Trionfi* that shows Fame (labeled GROLIA [for GLORIA] MUNDI) riding on a chariot drawn by horses and flanked by famous men of antiquity: Aristotle, Hercules, and Caesar at the left, Samson, Virgil, and Octavian at the right.[8] The letter and the manuscript illustration indicate that by the middle of the fifteenth century the kind of image we see in the Metropolitan Museum's tapestry had been fully developed. In the *Triumph of Fame* miniature the chariot is moving toward the observer rather than sideways across the picture space, but in the same manuscript the illustrations for the triumphs of Chastity and Time show the processions moving toward the right, as they do in the tapestries.[9] Like those two illustrations, the woodcuts in Bernardino da Novara's edition of *I Trionfi* (Venice, 1488) prove that this lateral direction of the processions had developed before the end of the century.[10]

The problem is a complex one. It is not clear whether Petrarch's images, which included only one triumphal procession, that of Love, were changed into a series of six processions solely by the illustrators of *I Trionfi* who had been influenced by Boccaccio's descriptions of the triumphs of Fame, Love, and Fortune and perhaps also by the spectacle of pageants of *I Trionfi* and other triumphal street processions, or whether later versions and adaptations of Petrarch's poem also were influential in bringing this transformation about. Neither the verses in 33a,b and the Vienna hangings, nor those in the set of prints published by Charles le Vigoureux in the late sixteenth century that show essentially the same compositions as those tapestries[11] (except for the French octave that appears in the engraving of the Triumph of Love), nor the verses in Jehan Robertet's heavily moralizing poem of about 1476, the first of several French adaptations of *I Trionfi*, describe the Triumphs as processions. However, one French octave together with one Latin quatrain from Robertet's *Les six Triumphes de Pétrarque* appear in the border of each of the *Triumphs of Petrarch* tapestries at Hampton Court and the Victoria and Albert Museum, all of which show processions.[12] Robertet's poem contains six octaves and title lines in French as well as six quatrains, couplets, and title lines in Latin.[13] All of these French and Latin verses, together with more Latin verse, also appear in the two sets of *Triumphs of Petrarch* drawings in Paris (see note 4). Those drawings, and the *Triumph of Death* tapestry published by Digby (1980, no. 26) that was based on one of them, show the figures arranged in static compositions rather than in processions. It is evident that Robertet's adaptation did not inspire designers to show all the Triumphs as processions. However, his work did influence the iconography of all the *Triumphs of Petrarch* tapestries discussed in this entry in another way. As Joubert noted, it was Robertet who used the three Fates to personify Death.[14] In all the tapestries discussed in this entry, and in all the prints and drawings that relate directly to them, Death is represented by the three Fates rather than by Petrarch's pale, cruel lady dressed in black.

The evidence available at present suggests that the iconography of a succession of triumphal processions, which occurs neither in Petrarch's own text nor in any of the texts discussed above that appear in connection with the images based on that iconography, was probably derived not from some unidentified literary work but from one or more sources in the visual arts and the world of pageants and street processions. However that may be, it is important to acknowledge, when studying so-called *Triumphs of Petrarch* tapestries, that compositions showing all six of Petrarch's Triumphs as processions are not based directly on his text.

SOURCE OF THE DESIGN

Among the many illustrations of Petrarch's *I Trionfi* that Prince d'Essling and Müntz collected and published, only the set of six woodcuts issued by Charles le Vigoureux in Paris about 1590 under the title *Le vray miroir de la vie humaine* show essentially the same six compositions that appear in the tapestries in Vienna.[15] The compositions in the Metropolitan Museum's *Triumph of Fame* and *Triumph of Time* agree in most details with the images in le Vigoureux's corresponding prints (figs. 148, 150). However the verses accompanying those prints were written as double rather than single quatrains and, except for a few words, the texts do not agree with the verses that appear in these tapestries. Göbel,[16] Crick-Kuntziger,[17] Scheicher (1971, 18, 46), and Salet (1973, 60) all noted the close relationship that exists

Fig. 150. *The Triumph of Time*, from *Le vray miroir de la vie humaine*, published by Charles le Vigoureux, Paris. Woodcut, France, late sixteenth century. Cabinet des Estampes, Bibliothèque Nationale, Paris.

between the tapestries and the prints, and Göbel, Crick-Kuntziger, and Salet emphasized that the two sets of images do not derive from each other but from some unknown common source, which was probably a series of prints antedating the tapestry designs. Ackerman believed she saw the name of an early sixteenth-century Tournai designer, Bonaventure Thieffries, inscribed on Charlemagne's robe in the *Triumph of Fame* in Vienna, an observation we cannot agree with.[18] In Reynaud's opinion the design of the Vienna tapestries, or at least the design of the central groups, could be attributed to Georges Trubert, an illuminator from Troyes who worked for René, duc d'Anjou, from 1467 to 1480, and for René II, duc de Lorraine, at least from 1491 to 1499. She did not spell out her reasons for making this attribution

other than mentioning the similarity she saw in the poses, the wide faces, and the narrow eyes, but her suggestion depended in part on her belief that the Vienna tapestries came originally from the ducal collections of Lorraine, a provenance that both Scheicher (1971, 10–11) and Salet (1973, 59 n. 1) regarded as uncertain.[19] Searching for an artist in the circle of the French court who would have had the experience and talent to design this series of hangings, Scheicher (1971, 45) suggested tentatively that Jean Perréal, or someone with his broad vision, would have been equal to the task. Salet (1973, 61) did not agree with that hypothesis, and we see no grounds for supporting it. Joubert did not suggest the name of a designer but thought, as we do, that the Vienna tapestries, like other good allegorical tapestries

473

of its class and unlike the run-of-the-mill pieces, were expressly designed by a painter and not simply concocted by the cartoon makers.[20]

The compositions in the le Vigoureux prints and the Triumph tapestries in Vienna obviously depend on an earlier common source. It seems most likely that the source was a printed book with illustrations or a series of loose prints.

MANUFACTURE AND DATE

Most writers who ventured to make attributions for the Metropolitan Museum's two tapestries based their suggestions on the attributions that had been offered for the corresponding set of hangings in Vienna. When Baldass published those six tapestries in 1920, he called them French and dated them at the beginning of the sixteenth century.[21] In 1928, when 33b was exhibited at the Metropolitan Museum, it was catalogued as French, specifically Touraine, and dated at the same time. Göbel (1928, vol. 1, 317) thought the trees and plants in the Vienna tapestries were designed in the style of Tournai, but he attributed them nevertheless tentatively to Touraine. Weigert (1956, 93; 1964, 80) and Verlet (1965, 74) repeated the attribution to Touraine. Steppe and Delmarcel thought the tapestries in Vienna were products of looms in France or Tournai.[22] Scheicher (1971, 7–9, 40–44) considered both the Loire valley and Brussels as places where the Vienna series might have been woven. Salet (1973, 61) correctly pointed out that there is no evidence to support an attribution of these or the related class of millefleurs tapestries to workshops along the Loire (whose existence has never been proved), and he also implied that the tendency in recent years to attribute all millefleurs tapestries to Brussels is not acceptable. Rorimer (1940, 1947) suggested attributions to either France or Flanders when he published the Metropolitan Museum's two hangings, and he dated them in the early sixteenth century. Forsyth retained these attributions of time and place in his catalogue entry when the two pieces were exhibited in 1970 (exh. cat. Los Angeles and Chicago, nos. 117A, B), and Digby (1980, 38) offered the same ones for the closely related fragment of the *Triumph of Eternity* in London.

Crick-Kuntziger noted that the near-duplicate *Triumph of Fame* in Brussels had been attributed to Audenarde, Tournai, and Touraine.[23] She believed that it could not have been woven in the same shop nor probably in the same locality as the hangings in Vienna. She called attention especially to the differences in the chromatic character of the pieces, the Vienna tapestries showing a wide range of strong hues, the hanging in

Brussels having a limited palette of fairly neutral tones. She suggested that the Vienna pieces might have been woven in Bruges, where weavers used vibrant colors and often worked after French prints. Although she attributed the hanging in Brussels tentatively to some provincial workshop in France, Crick-Kuntziger did not believe that the presence of Saint Louis in the Brussels tapestry indicated that it had been commissioned from a French workshop since that figure appears in tapestries woven in the Netherlands. Since we have no reason to believe that tapestries of this kind were being woven in France at this period, it seems reasonable to attribute the Metropolitan Museum's two hangings to the southern Netherlands, where we are sure there were numbers of shops capable of producing such hangings.

The question of the date of manufacture is more complex. Almost every writer on the subject has dated the Vienna hangings and the others woven after versions of the same cartoons (see Related Tapestries) in the early sixteenth century, presumably on grounds of style. Scheicher (1971, 23–45) narrowed down to 1508–10 the span of years during which she thought the Vienna tapestries could have been woven. She came to this conclusion after developing an elaborate iconographic interpretation of certain figures and details in the various compositions. She related most of them to personalities and emblems associated with the court of France. According to Scheicher, the figure of Claudia, who walks on the far side of the chariot in the *Triumph of Chastity* in Vienna, represents Claude de France, daughter of Louis XII and Anne de Bretagne. She observed also that the figures of Chastity and Abstinence in this tapestry are wearing the habit of the Franciscan tertiaries, with the knotted cord at their waists. This cordeliere was also an emblem of Claude, Anne, and Louise de Savoie, Claude's mother-in-law. Scheicher identified the squirrel sitting on the grass beneath the feet of the forward unicorn as the squirrel that Claude and Anne used as an emblem. Because Pandora, who leads the team of oxen pulling the Fates' chariot in the *Triumph of Death,* carries a cylindrical box rather than a jar, Scheicher (1971, 29–30) believed that the composition could not have been designed before 1508 when the first edition of Erasmus of Rotterdam's *Adagiorum Chiliades tres* appeared. In it he introduced the image of Pandora holding a small box, a pyxis, rather than a dolium, the large storage jar that had been identified with her earlier. Finally, in the *Triumph of Fame* tapestry in Vienna, the figure labeled Alexander is, according to Scheicher, a representation of Louis XII; and here the writer reminded her readers that the corresponding figure is labeled *S. Loys* in the version of this hanging that is now in

Brussels. After making these observations Scheicher (1971, 45) concluded that the cartoons for this series of tapestries must have been designed between 1508 and 1515, the year in which Louis XII died. Finally Scheicher narrowed the likely date of the designs down to 1508–10 because she claimed that the women's costumes could not postdate 1510. Salet (1973, 59–60) correctly challenged these interpretations although he accepted the date of about 1510 as reasonable on stylistic grounds alone. We agree with Salet who doubted that the designer intended to represent Claude de France and Louis XII in this tapestry. We also maintain that the women's costumes, which for the most part represent fancy dress rather than everyday wear, distantly reflect civilian fashions that appear in pictorial sources dating throughout most of the first third of the sixteenth century. Furthermore, tapestries showing a *retardataire* style, not unlike the style of these *Triumph* tapestries, were being woven as late as about 1523–31, the dates associated with the *Life of Saint Remi* tapestries in Reims.[24]

Scheicher (1971, 46) argued that the Vienna tapestries antedate all the others that show the same compositions. She also observed correctly that they may not constitute the first set of hangings woven after these cartoons. In her opinion the Metropolitan Museum's two tapestries were woven next, and the pieces in Brussels and London after those. The criteria on which Scheicher made these judgments—the success or lack of success in suggesting depth in the compositions, the degree of fineness or coarseness of the weave, and the relative sense of volume and life in the figures—seem to us in this case to be criteria relating to questions of quality rather than date of weaving. We believe that it is not possible to arrange these tapestries in order of their date of manufacture on the strength of the evidence that is available at present.

RELATED TAPESTRIES

The compositions in the Metropolitan Museum's two hangings belong to a series of designs that is represented apparently in its entirety in the set of six whole hangings preserved in the Kunsthistorisches Museum in Vienna (see note 15). The six subjects represented in these tapestries deal with the successive triumphs of Love, Chastity, Death, Fame, Time, and Eternity. (The last title does not agree with Petrarch's text, where the final victor is *Divinità* and not *Eternità*.) At present we know of a number of fragmentary hangings in addition to those in the Metropolitan Museum that represent this series of compositions. They may be listed, with their current locations, as follows:

Fig. 151. *The Triumph of Love*. Part of a tapestry, here attributed to the southern Netherlands, early sixteenth century. The Hyde Collection, Glens Falls, New York.

Fig. 152. *The Triumph of Death*. Part of a tapestry, here attributed to the southern Netherlands, early sixteenth century. The Fine Arts Museums of San Francisco; Gift of Mr. and Mrs. Robert Gill to Patrons of Art and Music.

Fig. 153. *The Triumph of Eternity*. Part of a tapestry, here attributed to the southern Netherlands, early sixteenth century. The Hyde Collection, Glens Falls, New York.

1. Triumph of Love: Hyde Collection, Glens Falls, New York (Kettlewell 1981, no. 27, illus.; also fig. 151 here).

[2. Triumph of Chastity: no fragmentary example known; only the complete hanging in Vienna.]

3. Triumph of Death: Fine Arts Museums of San Francisco (Bennett 1976, no. 17, illus.; also fig. 152 here). In the same museum there is a fragment showing most of the last two lines of the quatrain that relates to this subject; it has been sewn across the top of an unrelated hanging showing a scene from the Trojan War. It is not clear whether or not this fragment came from the field of the piece just cited (Bennett 1976, no. 7B, illus.).

4. Triumph of Fame: part of the left end of the Metropolitan Museum's hanging (33a), now in the Seattle Art Museum (fig. 149 here).[25] Another example is in the Musées Royaux d'Art et d'Histoire, Brussels; it lacks the inscribed banderoles along the top (fig. 147 here).[26]

[5. Triumph of Time: only the Metropolitan Museum's piece (33b) and the complete example in Vienna known.]

6. Triumph of Eternity: Victoria and Albert Museum, London (Digby 1980, no. 25, illus.). Another example is in the Hyde Collection (Kettlewell 1981, no. 28, illus.; fig. 153 here).

Of these pieces, at least three—the *Triumph of Love* and the *Triumph of Eternity* in the Hyde Collection and the *Triumph of Fame* in Seattle—originally belonged with the Metropolitan Museum's two pieces in the set of hangings that were said to have come from the collection of the baron d'Ezpleta in the château de Septmonts. According to unpublished notes contributed by Milton Samuels to the Metropolitan Museum's files in 1940, French and Company owned five pieces from the baron d'Ezpleta's set of hangings about 1918; two had gone to

George D. Pratt, two to the Hyde Collection, and one to a "Western collector."[27] It seems likely that the last was the former owner of the fragment now in Seattle.

The surviving hangings and fragments represent at least three sets of tapestries and possibly more. The set in Vienna represents one edition, possibly not the first, as Scheicher (1971, 46) has suggested. The baron d'Ezpleta's hangings (Metropolitan Museum, Hyde Collection, Seattle Art Museum) represent a second set. The piece in Brussels comes from a third edition, and the example in the Victoria and Albert Museum represents a fourth unless it is part of the set from which the Brussels piece comes. The two fragments in San Francisco (see 3 in the list above) would represent a fifth and possibly also a sixth edition if they do not belong to any one or two of the sets just cited.

Bennett (1976, 88) believed that the fragment of the *Triumph of Death* in San Francisco and the *Triumph of Fame* in Brussels, both of which lack inscribed banderoles along the top, were woven without them. However, when one compares their present heights (3.23 m and 3.18 m respectively) to the heights of the complete pieces in Vienna (4.14 m and 4.30 m respectively) and furthermore notes that both pieces have lost more of the composition at the top than at the bottom, it seems likely that a good deal of fabric, including the banderoles, was removed from the top. The same may be said for the pieces in London and the Hyde Collection, which have no inscriptions along the top and measure 3.29, 3.16, and 3.32 meters in height respectively. The *Triumph of Time* in the Metropolitan Museum, which has retained the complete double quatrain along its top but has lost some fabric there and along the bottom, measures 3.82 meters in height as against 4.12 meters, the height of the corresponding complete piece in Vienna. While there is nothing to prove that all tapestries showing these compositions were made the same height, these comparative figures suggest that they were.

Scheicher (1971, 46) noted certain differences of form and detail among these various tapestries, and her observations seem valid. The pieces in Vienna do, as she noted, suggest more depth in the representation of space than the others, and the figures represented in them are more solid and vital. The Metropolitan Museum's *Triumph of Fame* was clearly not woven after the cartoon that served the weavers of either the Vienna or the Brussels tapestries of the same subject. Therefore we conclude that at least three different versions of the cartoons existed; that is, a first (possibly not original) version which is represented by the Vienna hangings, a second version represented by the Metropolitan Museum's two pieces and its mates from the baron

d'Ezpleta series, and the third version after which the tapestry in Brussels was woven.

Other tapestries based on *I Trionfi* and showing them as processions were woven during the first quarter of the sixteenth century, but they represent a different interpretation of the iconography. Most of the surviving examples have been attributed to Brussels as the place of manufacture. These pieces, which have been preserved in the Victoria and Albert Museum, Hampton Court, and a number of other collections, feature double compositions in which the waning force is shown in the act of being vanquished on a chariot in the left half of the field and the victorious force is shown riding triumphantly ahead in another chariot in the right half of the field.[28]

HISTORY

Said to have been in the collection of the baron d'Ezpleta in the château de Septmonts, Aisne, France.
Property of French and Company, New York, by 1918.
In the collection of George D. Pratt, New York, before 1928.
Bequeathed to the MMA by George D. Pratt, 1935.

EXHIBITIONS

Chicago, Art Institute, 1920. *An Exhibition of Gothic Tapestries of France and Flanders.* Cat. nos. 9, 10. Lender's name not listed.
New York, MMA, 1928. *French Gothic Tapestries: A Loan Exhibition.* Cat. no. 16 [33b]. Lent by George D. Pratt.
Hartford, Wadsworth Atheneum, and Baltimore Museum of Art, 1951–52. *2000 Years of Tapestry Weaving: A Loan Exhibition.* Text by Adele Coulin Weibel. Cat. no. 88 [33b].
Los Angeles County Museum of Art, and Art Institute of Chicago, 1970. *The Middle Ages: Treasures from The Cloisters and The Metropolitan Museum of Art.* Catalogue entry by William H. Forsyth, nos. 117A, B, both illus.

PUBLICATIONS

Hunter 1925, p. 70. Both pieces mentioned.
Breck, Joseph. "The Tapestry Exhibition: Part II." *MMA Bulletin* 23 (1928) p. 184. Both pieces discussed at length; 33b illus. on cover.
Göbel 1928, vol. 1, p. 317. Both pieces mentioned.
van Marle, Raimond. *Iconographie de l'art profane au Moyen-Age et à la Renaissance.* Vol. 2. The Hague, 1932, p. 120 n. 1. 33a mentioned.
"Art Throughout America." *Art News* 39 (December 21, 1940) p. 14. Both pieces mentioned; 33b illus.
Rorimer, James J. "The Triumphs of Fame and Time." *MMA Bulletin* 35 (1940) pp. 242–44. Both pieces described and discussed at length; illus.
Rorimer, James J. *Mediaeval Tapestries: A Picture Book.* MMA, New York, 1947, fig. 17. 33b illus.
Weigert, Roger-Armand. *La tapisserie française.* Paris, 1956, p. 93. Both pieces mentioned.

Weigert, Roger-Armand. *La tapisserie et le tapis en France.* Paris, 1964, p. 80. Both pieces mentioned in text reprinted from Weigert 1956.

Verlet 1965, p. 22. Both pieces mentioned.

Jarry, Madeleine. *World Tapestry: From Its Origins to the Present.* New York, 1969, p. 127. Both pieces mentioned.

Scheicher, Elisabeth. "Die 'Trionfi': Eine Tapisserienfolge des Kunsthistorischen Museums in Wien." *Jahrbuch der kunsthistorischen Sammlungen in Wien* 67 (1971) p. 46. Both pieces discussed briefly; illus. figs. 36 [33a], 37 [33b].

Salet, Francis. "Chronique: Tapisserie, La tenture des Triomphes du Musée de Vienne" (review of Scheicher 1971). *Bulletin Monumental* 131 (1973) pp. 60-61. Both pieces mentioned.

Bennett, Anna G. *Five Centuries of Tapestry from the Fine Arts Museums of San Francisco.* San Francisco, 1976, p. 88. Both pieces mentioned.

Digby 1980, pp. 38-39. Both pieces mentioned.

Kettlewell, James K. *The Hyde Collection Catalogue.* Glens Falls, N.Y., 1981, p. 57. Both pieces mentioned.

Aegerter, Mary Jo. "The Triumph Tapestry Panel at the Seattle Art Museum." Graduate paper, Department of Art, Western Washington University, Seattle, 1985. Copies at that university, at the Seattle Art Museum, and in the Department of Medieval Art, MMA. Both pieces mentioned.

NOTES

1. The transcriptions and translations offered for these verses in this catalogue entry vary somewhat from the readings that other writers have given.

2. Marthe Crick-Kuntziger, *Catalogue des tapisseries (XIVe au XVIIIe siècle),* Musées Royaux d'Art et d'Histoire (Brussels, 1956) pp. 40-41.

3. Miscellaneous undated manuscript notes in the files of the MMA Department of Medieval Art.

4. Pen and wash drawings showing Petrarch's six Triumphs in this form appear in MS 5066 in the Bibliothèque de l'Arsenal. These drawings are usually cited in the literature on this subject rather than the somewhat variant drawings in MS fr. 24461 in the Bibliothèque Nationale in Paris which, as Francis Salet, in "Chronique: Tapisserie, La tenture des Triomphes du Musée de Vienne," *Bulletin Monumental* 131 (1973) p. 60 n. 1, pointed out, is the original of the Arsenal manuscript. All six Arsenal drawings are illustrated in Prince d'Essling and Eugène Müntz, *Pétrarque* (Paris, 1902) pp. 234 and 235. The Arsenal drawings of the Triumphs of Love, Chastity, Death, and Time are also illustrated in Elisabeth Scheicher, "Die 'Trionfi': Eine Tapisserienfolge des Kunsthistorischen Museums in Wien," *Jahrbuch der kunsthistorischen Sammlungen in Wien* 67 (1971) figs. 14, 18, 23, 31, respectively.

5. For studies concerning early illustrations of Petrarch's *I Trionfi,* see Prince d'Essling and Müntz, *Pétrarque,* pp. 101-276 (pp. 269-76 are a catalogue of the illustrations, including representations in tapestries), and also Raimond van Marle, *Iconographie de l'art profane au Moyen-Age et à la Renaissance,* vol. 2 (The Hague, 1932) pp. 111-35.

6. Dorothy C. Shorr, "Notes and Reviews: Some Notes on the Iconography of Petrarch's Triumph of Fame," *Art Bulletin* 20 (1938) p. 103.

7. Shorr, "Some Notes," p. 103 and figs. 1-3.

8. Shorr, "Some Notes," pp. 104, 107, and fig. 5. The miniature painting appears on fol. 33r of MS 1129 in the Biblioteca Riccardiana in Florence. See also a catalogue entry for this manuscript in Maria Luisa Scuricini Greco, *Miniature Riccardiane* (Florence, 1958) pp. 205-8.

9. See illustrations of the miniatures of the Triumph of Chastity and of Time on fols. 17r and 42v, respectively, of Biblioteca Riccardiana MS 1129 in Scuricini Greco, *Miniature Riccardiane,* pp. 206-7.

10. See illustrations of Bernardino's woodcuts of the Triumphs of Chastity (mislabeled Fame), Time, and Divinty in Prince d'Essling and Müntz, *Pétrarque,* pp. 174-75.

11. See illustrations of le Vigoureux's prints of the Triumphs of Love, Death, and Fame in Prince d'Essling and Müntz, *Pétrarque,* pp. 213, 249, 251. In this book the prints are incorrectly labeled as copperplate engravings entitled "Figures de la Bible." For correct details concerning the prints, see Jean Adhémar, *Inventaire du fonds français: Graveurs du seizième siècle,* Bibliothèque Nationale, Département des Estampes (1938; reprint, Paris, 1971) vol. 2, pp. 153-54, where they are described as woodcuts under the title "Le vray miroir de la vie humaine"; they are inventoried under the number Ed. 5. g. Rés.

12. None of the literature consulted in the preparation of this entry revealed that the verses in the borders of these tapestries were taken from Robertet's adaptation of *I Trionfi.* The present author thanks Robert A. Baron who, during an exchange of letters in 1988, pointed out to him that Robertet's verses appear in the two sets of drawings in Paris (see note 4 above). It was then clear that the French octaves and Latin quatrains in the tapestries in England also came from Robertet's version of Petrarch's text (see note 13). For comprehensive studies of the three tapestries in the Victoria and Albert Museum and the four at Hampton Court, see Digby 1980, pp. 35-38, pls. 36-43B; and H. C. Marillier, *The Tapestries at Hampton Court Palace* (London, 1962) pp. 19-23, pls. 15-17. Digby (p. 38) gives a list of tapestries in other collections that are closely related to the ones in the Victoria and Albert Museum.

13. For Robertet's poem, which is a much condensed version of Petrarch's text, see Margaret Zsuppán, *Jean Robertet: Oeuvres* (Geneva, 1970) pp. 178-85.

14. Joubert 1987, p. 144.

15. See note 11 for details concerning le Vigoureux's woodcuts and illustrations of some of them. For data concerning the six tapestries in Vienna, and color illustrations of them, see Ludwig Baldass, *Die Wiener Gobelinssammlung* (Vienna, 1920) pls. 1-6; see also Scheicher, "Die 'Trionfi,'" pp. 15-37, figs. 1-6, and details of various pieces in figs. 8, 10, 12, 15, 17, 19, 20, 22, 24-29, and 38, all in black and white.

16. Göbel 1923, vol. 1, p. 105.

17. Crick-Kuntziger, *Catalogue des tapisseries,* p. 41, with reference specifically to the print and tapestry of the *Triumph of Fame.*

18. Phyllis Ackerman, "Recently Identified Designers of Gothic Tapestries," *Art Bulletin* 9 (1926-27) p. 152.

19. Nicole Reynaud, "Georges Trubert, enlumineur du Roi René et de René II de Lorraine," *Revue de l'Art,* no. 35 (1977) pp. 59-60, 63 n. 72.

20. Joubert 1987, p. 149.

21. Baldass, *Die Wiener Gobelinssammlung,* pls. 1-6.

22. Jan-Karel Steppe and Guy Delmarcel, "Les tapisseries du Cardinal Erard de la Marck, prince-évêque de Liège," *Revue de l'Art,* no. 25 (1974) p. 52 n. 78.

23. Crick-Kuntziger, *Catalogue des tapisseries,* p. 40.

24. See Alain Erlande-Brandenburg, *La tenture de la vie de Saint Remi* (Reims, 1983) p. 18. Using the evidence of the donor's blazon as represented in the Saint Remi tapestries, Erlande-Brandenburg demonstrated that the hangings must have been commissioned after 1523. They were finished in 1531, the date cited in an inscription on the tenth and last piece of the set.

25. See *Annual Report of the Seattle Art Museum: Fifty-first Year, 1956,* p. 25 and fig. 18, where the fragment is called incorrectly "Triumph of Eternity over Time."

26. For a discussion of the piece in Brussels, see Crick-Kuntziger, *Catalogue des tapisseries,* no. 22.

27. Notes in the files of the MMA Department of Medieval Art.

28. For studies of these tapestries and others related to them, see Digby 1980, pp. 35-38, pls. 36-43B; and Marillier, *Tapestries at Hampton Court,* pp. 19-23, pls. 15-17.

34
Shepherd and Shepherdesses

Southern Netherlands, 1500–1530
Wool warp, wool wefts
9 ft. 7 in. × 9 ft. 10 in. (2.92 m × 3.00 m)
11–14 warp yarns per inch, 4–6 per centimeter
Gift of George Blumenthal, 1941 (41.100.196)

CONDITION

The top and bottom edges of the tapestry have been completely restored. Parts of the left edge are original, parts are restored. The entire right edge has been pieced. In many places the field shows meandering joins that were made with new warp and weft yarns. It is not clear whether the fabrics next to these joins were originally where they are now or were taken from other parts of this or another tapestry and fitted into place. The figure of the young shepherdess at the right together with the sheep next to her and a rectangular section of the field surrounding them occupy an area that seems to have been patched in. The two other figures and the two sheep near them occupy another large section of relatively unbroken fabric. The shepherd's right shoe, both gaiters, upper stocks, right hand, and lower cape have been partly restored with new warp and weft yarns, as have parts of the elder woman's right hand, purse, petticoat, skirt, and hood. The shepherd's cape and jerkin skirt and the elder shepherdess's petticoat have been rewoven on the original warp with modern weft yarns. The stomacher in the younger shepherdess's bodice has also been rewoven. There are other small repairs by reweaving throughout, but none of them affects the arrangement or drawing of the composition as radically as these major restorations do. The colors have faded appreciably, but the hues are still clearly defined.

DESCRIPTION AND SUBJECT

A shepherd, two shepherdesses, and three sheep are shown standing against a dark greenish blue ground studded with flowering plants of many varieties. The shepherd, at the left, wears a loose, skirted jerkin over doublet and hose; a short cape with dagged edges (badly restored; see a similar cape in 35); a wide-brimmed hat tied over a tightly fitting hood; gaiters of linen cloth wound around the lower leg and gathered and tied at ankle and knee; low, wide, round-toed shoes; and a utensil bag hung on his right hip. His staff with two hooks at

the upper end and a scoop at the lower end, an *houlette*, is propped inside his bent left arm. The elder shepherdess, in the middle of the composition, wears a plain, long-sleeved, fitted gown pulled up at her left to show a plain petticoat. A small drawstring purse hangs from her girdle at her left side, and she wears a folded cloth or loose hood that completely covers her hair. The other shepherdess, at the right, wears essentially the same costume except that her bodice closes with a laced stomacher instead of a simple crossing of the two sides as the other shepherdess's bodice does. As noted above (Condition) the stomacher is not original. Since this kind of bodice belongs to the seventeenth century, the detail is clearly a restorer's mistake. In the original design, this shepherdess's bodice probably matched the other. Her purse is also similar to that of the other, but she wears a low, wide-brimmed hat like the shepherd's and her shoes are daintier versions of his. She holds an *houlette* in her left hand. A sheep grazes to the right behind her and two others appear in the center foreground. A rabbit crouches in the lower left foreground, and a cock pheasant is in a corresponding place at the right.

The actions of the shepherd folk are difficult to interpret. The man at the left bends back at the knees, averts his face, and holds both arms up at the elbow, apparently in an attempt to ward off the elder shepherdess in the center, who leans toward him and grasps his collar with her right hand. The younger shepherdess seems to step backward, away from the other two, and holds her right arm up as though to protect herself from them. Rubinstein-Bloch (1927, pl. IV), the author of the 1928 exhibition catalogue (no. 13), and Forsyth (exh. cat. Los Angeles and Chicago 1970, 240) all believed that the man had made advances to the younger shepherdess and was now being pushed away by the elder woman, who might, Forsyth suggested, be his wife. Cavallo (1979, 33) believed that the characters might be playing a kind of blindman's buff without the blindfold or some sort of

479

34

480

touching game. He further called attention to the fact that the poses of the two main figures in this tapestry were similar to those of two figures in a contemporary tapestry in the Victoria and Albert Museum, a comparison that Göbel (1928, vol. 1, 281) also made. Further study has shown that the figures are not only similar but indeed the same, reversed, with minor changes of costume, and otherwise slightly altered through restoration. The shepherd and shepherdess in the London tapestry are shown in the lower right section of a hanging whose main subject is a game of *la main chaude* (hot cockles) being played by two shepherds and two shepherdesses in the center foreground, while woodcutters, a shepherd, two gentlemen, and a lady go about their business in the background landscape. Another shepherd and shepherdess, in the lower left section of the tapestry, form a small group balancing the pair at the right. The shepherd at the left is reclining; he turns to the right and looks up at the shepherdess standing above him. She raises her right hand in a gesture of greeting or invitation, and he seems to be dismissing her with a gesture of his right hand. The action helps explain the little drama in the right corner, where the shepherdess seems to be pulling a reluctant shepherd by his cape and the skirt of his jerkin toward the game players in the center. If this interpretation of the figures' actions is correct, then it is clear that the two main figures in the Metropolitan Museum's tapestry have suffered the fate of many such figures in millefleurs tapestries. Taken out of their original context, their actions become obscure or open to misinterpretation.

As noted above (Condition) the figure of the younger shepherdess belongs to a section of weaving that might have been let into this hanging from another part of this piece or from a different one. Therefore any interpretation of the subject that includes this figure or her actions must be considered with caution. Since all the figures in 34 have presumably been taken out of some other, original context—whether or not the three belong together— we cannot prove that this elder shepherdess is not chiding the shepherd for making advances to the girl. But it is more likely that the woman is making advances to the man. A tapestry related in style to the piece in London shows shepherdesses making advances to shepherds.[1] One of the women grasps a shepherd by the collar and skirt just as the shepherdess in 34 does (or did, before his skirt was narrowed by restoration). However the fact that the two elder figures in 34 also appear in the London tapestry of *La main chaude* suggests that they were originally designed as bystanders in the context of that game.

SOURCE OF THE DESIGN

The figures of the shepherd and the elder shepherdess were designed after the source, most likely a print, that served for the corresponding figures in the London *La main chaude.* The figure of the younger shepherdess may have been derived from the same source or a related one. All three figures, along with the sheep and smaller animals, evidently served one or more weavers as stock motifs (concerning sheep like these, see 35, Related Tapestries).

MANUFACTURE AND DATE

From 1911, when Guiffrey first published the tapestry, until 1970, when Forsyth (exh. cat. Los Angeles and Chicago, no. 114) pointed out that recent studies by Schneebalg-Perelman and Salet indicated that millefleurs tapestries were woven in Brussels and other parts of the southern Netherlands, writers attributed the tapestry to France on the grounds of style. The author of the 1928 exhibition catalogue (no. 13), Breck (1928, 178), and Rorimer (1947, fig. 15) suggested that it was woven in Touraine, even though Rubinstein (1916–17, 34) had already rejected that regional attribution for lack of proof that tapestries were being woven there in the late Middle Ages. Until further evidence comes to light, it seems correct to attribute the weaving to some unidentified center in the southern Netherlands and to date it on the basis of style as well as costume to the first third of the sixteenth century.

RELATED TAPESTRIES

A number of millefleurs tapestries showing shepherds and shepherdesses have survived.[2] None of them resembles this example closely in terms of drawing, subject, and composition, and so it is evident that none of them was woven after the same series of cartoons. Tapestries with lusty shepherd subjects set in real space rather than the abstract space of the millefleurs setting have come down to us. Among them may be listed the London tapestry with the subject of *La main chaude* and three pieces formerly belonging to dealers in New York.[3]

HISTORY

In the Schutz collection, Paris, in 1911.
In the collection of George and Florence Blumenthal, New York, before 1916.
Given to the MMA by George Blumenthal, 1941.

EXHIBITIONS

New York, MMA, 1928. *French Gothic Tapestries: A Loan Exhibition.* Cat. no. 13, not illus. Lent by George and Florence Blumenthal.

New York, MMA, 1943. *Masterpieces in the Collection of George Blumenthal: A Special Exhibition.*

New York, MMA, 1957–58. *Collector's Choice: Fifty Years of Collecting for the Museum, 1890–1940.*

Los Angeles County Museum of Art, and Art Institute of Chicago, 1970. *The Middle Ages: Treasures from The Cloisters and The Metropolitan Museum of Art.* Catalogue entry by William H. Forsyth, no. 114, illus.

PUBLICATIONS

Guiffrey, Jules. *Les tapisseries du XIIᵉ à la fin du XVIᵉ siècle.* Paris, [1911], p. 57. Illus. fig. 28.

Hunter 1912, p. 51. Mentioned.

Rubinstein, Stella. "Two Late French Gothic Tapestries." *Art in America* 5 (1916–17) pp. 33–34. Described and discussed briefly; illus. fig. 2, p. 31.

Rubinstein-Bloch, Stella. *Catalogue of the Collection of George and Florence Blumenthal, New-York.* Vol. 4, *Tapestries and Furniture.* Paris, 1927, pl. IV. Described briefly; illus.

Breck, Joseph. "The Tapestry Exhibition: Part II." *MMA Bulletin* 23 (1928) p. 184. Mentioned; illus. fig. 4.

Göbel 1928, vol. 1, p. 281. Discussed briefly; illus. vol. 2, fig. 316.

Rorimer, James J. *Mediaeval Tapestries: A Picture Book.* New York, 1947, p. [4]. Mentioned; illus. fig. 15.

Weigert, Roger-Armand. *La tapisserie française.* Paris, 1956, p. 82. Mentioned.

Cavallo, Adolph S. "The Garden of Vanity: A *Millefleurs* Tapestry." *Bulletin of the Detroit Institute of Arts* 57 (1979) p. 33. Mentioned; illus. fig. 5.

NOTES

1. See Göbel 1923, vol. 2, fig. 240.
2. Among them, 35 in the present catalogue and two others, one in Detroit, the other in Paris, from the same series of cartoons or hangings; see Adolph S. Cavallo, "The Garden of Vanity: A *Millefleurs* Tapestry," *Bulletin of the Detroit Institute of Arts* 57 (1979) pp. 31–39, figs. 1, 4. See also a fragmentary piece formerly in the Bossy collection, Paris, now in the Louvre, more like the Metropolitan Museum's piece than these others in that it does not show their coat of arms or inscriptions: Paul Leprieur, "La collection Albert Bossy," *Les Arts*, no. 35 (1904) p. 18, illus.
3. For the piece in London, see Digby 1980, no. 19, figs. 30, 31; and for the other three, see Göbel 1928, vol. 2, figs. 240–42.

35
Shepherd and Shepherdess Making Music

Southern Netherlands, 1500–1530
Wool warp; wool and silk wefts
7 ft. 8 1/2 in. × 9 ft. 7 in. (2.35 m × 2.92 m)
11–12 warp yarns per inch, 4–5 per centimeter
Bequest of Susan Vanderpoel Clark, 1967 (67.155.8)

CONDITION

The tapestry has been cut on all four sides. Strips of modern weaving imitating the tapestry's texture have been sewn to the edges. The hanging must be about as wide now as it was originally since the composition finishes neatly at the sides. However along the top and bottom edges the plants are not complete; therefore, a few inches of field must have been cut off along both margins, more at the top than the bottom. There are some minor repairs by reweaving, especially along the top of the field near the upper left and right corners and in the regions of the shepherdess's hair, bodice, and right arm. There are other repairs spotted throughout the field, but none of them affects the drawing. The major change occurred in the heraldic shield buckled to the tree at the center. Both the warp and weft yarns defining this motif have been replaced except along the bottom of the shield where the blue and yellow repair yarns engage the original warp yarns. Therefore it is clear that the original shield was removed at some time in the past, perhaps during the French Revolution. A small oval spot near the center of the shield was rewoven sometime after the wefts rendering the motif were inserted. The colors throughout the piece are still clear though somewhat faded.

DESCRIPTION AND SUBJECT

The dark greenish blue ground is covered with a variety of grasses and flowering plants. An orange tree rises in the center of the field, and from the space between its two main branches hangs an armorial shield on a buckled strap. The arms blazoned on it, quartered 1 and 4 or, 2 and 3 azure, have not been identifed. Since this motif is not part of the original fabric, the arms may be those of a later owner, the restored arms of the first owner, or merely a fanciful shield of arms invented by the restorer. Cavallo (1979, 39 n. 8) believed that the similar shield of arms in two related tapestries (see below) may be origi-

nal and that the shield in this example might have been copied from them.

A bareheaded shepherdess wearing a long, closed gown with a flat collar is seated on the ground to the left of the tree. A utensil bag hangs over her right hip and a shepherd's *houlette* rests in the crook of her right arm. She reads from a sheet of music that she holds up with both hands. On the other side of the tree a seated shepherd plays a bagpipe while a dog sleeps on the grass behind him. He wears a full-skirted jacket, a short cape with dagged edges over it, hose and gaiters, a hat with a high round crown and turned-up brim, and round-toed shoes. Two sheep stand at the left behind the shepherdess, and another grazes in the distance at the right, behind the shepherd. Two birds fly overhead. Three lines of rhyming verse, representing the characters' speech, are inscribed over each of the figures. Above the shepherdess they read as follows:

> *Chantons sur lerbette*
> *avec ta musette*
> *quelque note double.*

The shepherd responds:

> *Cuant est de georgette*
> *elle a lavoix nette*
> *mes ie faiz le trouble.*

Cavallo (1979, 33) translated the inscriptions as follows:

> Let's sing, on the grass,
> with your bagpipe,
> a tune for two.
>
> When she sings
> her voice is fair;
> but I do the work.

In light of the subject matter and verses in two related tapestries (figs. 154, 155), Cavallo (1979, 35–36) interpreted these lines as having secondary, mostly erotic, meaning. For example, the French term for bagpipe, *musette,* can also refer to a horse's nose bag, an image that in the past has also alluded to the scrotum. The word given in the tapestry as *georgette* is in fact a misspelled rendering of the diminutive form of the French word for throat, or *gorge* (*gorgette*), and *gorge* can refer not only to the throat but to any narrow passage. Furthermore the words *net* (feminine *nette*) and *trouble* are terms used in the wine industry, *net* referring to the

35

clarity of wine and *trouble* to wine sediment. These ideas are developed below in Related Tapestries.

SOURCE OF THE DESIGN

Since 35 and two other surviving pieces woven after the same series of cartoons (figs. 154, 155) reflect some specific and cohesive iconographic theme, it seems likely that the designs and inscriptions were borrowed from an illustrated book or series of loose prints dealing with some popular song, poem, or play with allegorical overtones, all gently satirical. As Cavallo (1979, 35–38) indicated, all the verses in these three tapestries are convoluted, punning, and rife with double entendres. He

noted further (1979, 39 n. 19) that Richard Katz had pointed out some similarities relating these verses— particularly the ones in the Paris piece—to the poetry of a group of contemporary writers known as the *grands rhétoriqueurs* who were active in Burgundy and also that Katz suggested that the verses might have come from a popular song, perhaps a *pastourelle*.

MANUFACTURE AND DATE

The tapestry was first published by Forsyth (1967–68, 83) as Franco-Flemish, late fifteenth century. Cavallo (1979, 30, 31, 34) published this and the two related pieces in Detroit and Paris as Flemish or French and dated them in the early sixteenth century. When it was exhibited at the château de Culan in 1968, the Paris tapestry was attributed to workshops in the region of the Loire and dated about 1500.[1] We now believe that most if not all of the surviving tapestries of this type were designed by French artists (or after their work) but were probably woven in the southern Netherlands. On the basis of pictorial style and fashion in costume, 35 belongs with a group of hangings that have been dated for the same reasons in the first third of the sixteenth century (see especially 37 and 38).

RELATED TAPESTRIES

Among the many millefleurs tapestries with shepherds that are known to have survived from this period, only two pieces, one in the Detroit Institute of Arts (fig. 154) and the other in the Mobilier National in Paris (fig. 155), can be grouped with 35 in a single series of cartoons or perhaps the same set of hangings, as Cavallo (1979, 32–

36) first pointed out.[2] The tapestry in Detroit, which he dubbed "The Garden of Vanity," shows a shepherd and a shepherdess standing in the same kind of setting, she at the left of the tree in the center, he at the right. That tapestry, which is approximately ten inches shorter and fifty-two inches wider than the Metropolitan Museum's piece, also shows a dog, more sheep, and more birds. Aside from the presence in each piece of the coat of arms and the tree, there are other details that relate these three tapestries to one another. The sheep grazing with bent head, left foreleg forward, and left rear leg bent and slightly raised that appears above the shepherd's head in the Metropolitan Museum's tapestry reappears four times (three times in reverse) in the Detroit piece and twice (once in reverse) in the example in Paris. The sheep drawn in foreshortened frontal view near the shepherdess in the Metropolitan Museum's tapestry reappears in virtually the same position in the Paris hanging.

The inscription above the woman's figure in the Detroit tapestry reads as follows (after Cavallo 1979, 32):

Detail of 35

485

Fig. 154. *Shepherd and Shepherdess.* Tapestry, southern Netherlands, early sixteenth century. The Detroit Institute of Arts; Bequest of Eleanor Clay Ford.

Fig. 155. *Shepherd and Shepherdess.* Tapestry, southern Netherlands, early sixteenth century. Mobilier National, Paris.

Mout me plaist ce getil bouchage
ie layme tant que ie nen hobbe
et bref pour fair bon mesnage
ie ne veuil que ma garderobe

(I do like this pretty grove!
I like it so much that I shan't leave it;
and, in a word, in order to live here happily
all I need is my wardrobe).

The shepherd's words are inscribed as follows (Cavallo 1979, 32):

Bergerette plaisant et saige
metryez vous point sous vostre robe
ce que vous baillerai en gaige
afin que on ne le vous desrobe

(Pretty, wise little shepherdess,
won't you put under your dress
what I will give you as my token of love
so that no one can steal it from you?).[3]

The second related tapestry, preserved in the Mobilier National in Paris, shows a shepherd walking from a position to the right of the tree toward a shepherdess seated at the left. This too shows more sheep than the Metropolitan Museum's piece does. It measures about ten inches less in height and nine inches more in width. The shepherdess says (Cavallo 1979, 33):

. . . nt grintotez sur ung point [?]
pensez que ie me lasse
allez la . . . mtre se [?] *basse* [?]
ny [?] *scet faire . . . tre . . .*

(Don't harp on the same point.
Do you think I will weaken?
Go . . . [?]
nor [?] know how to [?] . . .).

The shepherd comments:

Le peschier men pesche
car tant plus y pesche
et mains y proufite

(Sin gets in my way;
for the more I fish around
the less I get).[4]

Cavallo (1979, 33–36) developed a theory whereby the three tapestries belong in a series of hangings whose subject matter deals with a kind of satirical allegory in which women are victims of virtues (grace in the Metropolitan Museum's piece, modesty in the Paris tapestry) or vices (vanity in the Detroit example), and men are bound to the passions of the flesh, all this expressed in terms of the simple, natural rustic or shepherd. He also pointed out the various puns and double entendres with which the poet or author loaded the verses in all three tapestries. The erotic element relates these tapestries in a peripheral way to another series of shepherd and shepherdess tapestries known as the *Story of Gombaut and Macée* that was first woven late in the sixteenth century and contained eight hangings.[5] However that tale does not involve the theme with which 35 and the two related hangings are concerned. There is no continuing narrative in these three tapestries nor any other grounds on which to calculate the number of pieces that may have constituted the series of hangings they represent.

HISTORY

Bequeathed to the MMA by Susan Vanderpoel Clark, 1967.

EXHIBITION

New York, Cooper-Hewitt Museum, 1981. *Gardens of Delight.*

PUBLICATIONS

Forsyth, William H. "Report of the Departments: Medieval Art and The Cloisters, the Main Building." Annual Report for 1966–1967. In *MMA Bulletin*, n.s. 26 (1967–68) pp. 82–83. Mentioned; illus. p. 84.

Cavallo, Adolph S. "The Garden of Vanity: A *Millefleurs* Tapestry." *Bulletin of the Detroit Institute of Arts* 57 (1979) pp. 32–36. Discussed; illus. fig. 3.

NOTES

1. *Chefs d'oeuvre de la tapisserie française au XVIe siècle: Huitième exposition du château de Culan* ([Paris?], 1968) no. 1. For an earlier publication of the Paris piece, see Manufacture Nationale des Gobelins, *La tapisserie gothique* (Paris, [1928]) no. 38, illus.; in this publication, the tinctures of the coat of arms are given as silver and blue rather than gold and blue, probably because the yellow yarns in the first and third quarters of the shield have faded.

2. The piece in Paris is a fragment from the upper section of a larger hanging. It shows parts of the bodies of a shepherd and a shepherdess (who are seemingly hunting with ferrets) against a millefleurs ground; see Paul Leprieur, "La collection Albert Bossy," *Les Arts*, no. 35 (1904) p. 18, illus.

3. Adolph S. Cavallo, "The Garden of Vanity: A *Millefleurs* Tapestry," *Bulletin of the Detroit Institute of Arts* 57 (1979) p. 38 n. 7, noted that he had based his interpretation of the Detroit transcriptions and translations on interpretations made by Geneviève Souchal in 1971.

4. Cavallo, "The Garden of Vanity," p. 38 n. 10, indicated that alternate readings of the Paris inscriptions did not differ substantially from each other or from his own. For one of those readings, see *La tapisserie gothique*, no. 38.

5. For a comprehensive account of the *Story of Gombaut and Macée* tapestries, see Edith Appleton Standen, *European Post-Medieval Tapestries and Related Hangings in The Metropolitan Museum of Art* (New York, 1985) pp. 171–76.

36

488

36

A Falconer with Two Ladies, a Page, and a Foot Soldier

Southern Netherlands, 1500–1530
Wool warp; wool and silk wefts
8 ft. 2^{1}/$_{2}$ in. × 11 ft. 6 in. (2.50 m × 3.51 m)
10–13 warp yarns per inch, 4–5 per centimeter
Bequest of Harriet H. Jonas, 1974 (1974.228.2)

CONDITION

The hanging has been cut along all four sides. The raw edges were covered with strips of modern fabric; the ones at the sides are ribbed tapes and those at the top and bottom are of tapestry weaving. The field fabric was either cut and rejoined or badly worn and restored with new warp and weft yarns along a line from the bottom of the piece up through the foot soldier's halberd to a point about three inches below the top of the fabric. There is another linear repair of this kind in the field pattern just behind the soldier's midsection and yet another that extends upward for a short distance from a point just above the page's right shoulder; from there it joins a seam that borders the left edges of two large rectangular patches of old tapestry that fill in the upper right corner of the piece. Throughout the hanging there are also other patches of old fabric whose pattern matches that of the ground. There are small insertions of new fabric with the same pattern along the lower left edge of the field and below the front of the second lady's petticoat. The fabric representing the left-hand two-thirds of her petticoat is also modern.

There is a great deal of reweaving with modern wefts on the original warp yarns throughout the ground area but especially in the petticoat, sleeves, and bodice of the lady at the far left, the gown and hood of the second lady, the sleeves and borders of the falconer's coat, and the sleeves of the page's coat. The soldier's figure shows virtually no reweaving. Most of the repaired passages occur in places where the light-colored silk used for the highlights has deteriorated and fallen out. In spite of these restorations the figures appear now much as they were originally drawn. Their placement suggests that some of the original field is missing at both sides and the bottom and possibly also at the top, but there is nothing to indicate the extent of those losses.

DESCRIPTION AND SUBJECT

Five figures stand in the foreground against a field of dark blue (probably dark green originally) that is studded with flowering plants of many varieties. The plants, which have been drawn in a particularly naturalistic style, are set close together on the ground. The lady standing at the far left wears a plain gown with a patterned hem over a plain velvet petticoat and a patterned velvet underbodice whose sleeves, slashed underneath from elbow to wrist, pass through the armholes of the gown. She wears a small cap at the back of her head and a gold chain around her neck. Her hair falls down her back in a long, thick mane wrapped with a ribbon. Her left hand is slipped under the right elbow of the lady next to her, who is looking down at the small lion-clipped dog resting its forepaws on her knee. She wears a plain velvet gown over a plain velvet petticoat of a different color (now two colors because of the restoration). Both garments have patterned bands along the bottom. On her head she wears a hood with long lappets over a cap.

The falconer standing in the center of the scene wears a knee-length, fur-lined coat over hose and doublet; round-toed shoes with straps over the insteps; and a round hat with a wide, low crown and an upturned brim. He holds the jesses of a falcon in his gloved left hand. The bird is either rising from his fist or just about to alight on it. A spotted dog resembling a greyhound sits on the flowered ground between this man and the foot soldier who stands next to him at the right and leans forward, holding the pole of his halberd. Over his doublet and hose the foot soldier wears a short jerkin with slashings at the shoulders and pleats at the back. The colors of the left and right halves of the jerkin are counterchanged with those of the left and right legs of his hose. On his head is a shaggy hat decorated with two ostrich plumes and a ribbon or scarf that ties under his

Fig. 156. *Falconer with Ladies, a Page, and a Soldier.* Tapestry, here attributed to the southern Netherlands, 1500–1530. The Art Institute of Chicago; Gift of Kate S. Buckingham.

chin (see 20a–h, note 2, for references to similar hats). A page stands next to the soldier in the lower right corner of the composition. He wears a plain knee-length coat over his shirt, doublet, and hose; round-toed shoes with straps over the insteps; and a low, round hat like the falconer's. A hawk is perched on his gloved right hand; he feeds it a piece of meat that he has probably taken from the tasseled bag hanging on his right hip.

When the tapestry was sold at auction in Paris in 1904, the catalogue entry referred to it as showing "cinq personnages: chasseurs au faucon sur fond de verdure" (five characters: falcon hunters on a ground of greenery). The catalogue of the exhibition in Bordeaux in 1981 described the piece as showing "une scène de fauconnerie" and spoke of a dog jumping up to attract his

mistress's attention, a gentleman about to leave on a hunt, his page, another "servant" holding a staff with a blade that was probably connected with the hunt, and a dog next to him that seems to await the start of the hunt. Gómez-Moreno (1975, 165) referred to the subject matter simply—and we believe correctly—as "five figures on a millefleurs background." A tapestry showing all these figures except the page but including the two dogs, in a somewhat different millefleurs setting, is preserved in the Art Institute of Chicago (see fig. 156 and Related Tapestries). Göbel published the Chicago tapestry with the title *Feudalleben* (Feudal Life), a title that Mayer retained when she published it some years later and referred to the group of figures as "a royal hunting party."[1] Earlier, Rogers and Goetz had said that this tapestry showed a "returning hunter . . . welcomed by his lady. . . . It may well have been one of a series illustrating various phases of courtly life in the country."[2] A tapestry that was woven after a version of the same cartoon is in the Musée de Cluny in Paris (fig. 157). It is a fragment of a larger hanging and shows only the figures of the falconer and the soldier as well as the dog at the right and the rear half of the other dog. Demotte believed that it (and presumably also the Metropolitan Museum's hanging, which he referred to in the same context) showed a "seigneur partant pour la chasse" (a lord going on a hunt).[3] Salet, Verlet, and Joubert each published the Cluny piece with the title *Le départ pour la chasse*.[4] Demotte and the other specialists observed that the hanging in Paris is one of six millefleurs tapestries in the Musée de Cluny that have been dubbed *La vie seigneuriale* (Manorial Life). Like other writers, Verlet regarded these six pieces as a cohesive set of hangings and cited them as an example of a "chambre de tapisseries." He also observed that they show "les loisirs et les occupations favorites des seigneurs et des dames au temps de Louis XII" (the leisurely pursuits and favorite activities of the lords and ladies of the period of Louis XII).[5] A closely related group of three pieces, called *La pastorale* or *La noble pastorale*, formerly in the Larcade collection, is now in the Musée du Louvre.[6]

Like these tapestries in Paris and many other millefleurs pieces elsewhere, including at least one in the Metropolitan Museum (see 34), 36 shows a scene that uses figures taken from other contexts and combines them in a spaceless setting without much narrative purpose. In the case of 36 we know that the figure of the soldier, and possibly also the figure of the falconer, was taken from a print by Albrecht Dürer showing five soldiers standing by the roadside as a Turk rides past (see fig. 34 in the present catalogue and Source of the Design in this entry). The figure of the page may not be that of a boy but of a fully grown man drawn on a smaller scale; and the fact that he holds the falcon on his right fist and feeds it with his left hand suggests that he may be shown here in reverse orientation. A recent search has shown that he appears as an adult and in the correct orientation, with the falcon on his left fist, in a millefleurs tapestry with a different subject in the Mobilier National, Paris. That hanging also contains the figure of a seated lady organist which is a variant of the figure of the lady standing at the far left in the Metropolitan Museum's tapestry (see Source of the Design). This lady may perhaps be looking at her companion, but none of the other figures looks at, or is interpersonally involved with, any of the others. No story is being told here. We are simply shown five human figures and two

dogs in a woodland setting; and only two of the five figures (the gentleman falconer and the page) have any apparent connection with falcon hunting. The two women may be bidding the hunters farewell, as the title *Departure for the Hunt* suggests; but there is nothing in the form of the composition to suggest it, and there are no horses in sight to carry the men to the hunt. The foot soldier leaning on his halberd seems particularly out of context, and indeed he is when one recalls his origin in the Dürer print and also notes his presence in a tapestry showing a miraculous resuscitation that has no connection whatever with soldiering or falcon hunting (see Source of the Design). However it may be significant that a halberdier appears in a similar millefleurs tapestry, walking behind a fashionably dressed gentleman falconer and his lady.[7] If such foot soldiers occasionally accompanied aristocratic hunters as guards in the woods or fields, then Dürer's halberdier has some contextual validity in the Metropolitan Museum's tapestry.

SOURCE OF THE DESIGN

It has been known for some time that the figure of the foot soldier was taken verbatim from the figure of the halberdier who stands at the far right side of an engraving by Albrecht Dürer that has been called among other things *Five Soldiers and a Turk on Horseback* (see fig. 34).[8] We now suggest that the figure of the falconer in the tapestry may also have been derived from the same print, from the figure standing just to the left of the halberdier. His torso, right arm, and right leg are in approximately the same positions in both images; only the tilt of his head and the poses of his left arm and leg are somewhat different. The halberdier and the falconer in the tapestry (the latter with his left arm bent down rather than up and the hand holding a stick rather than the falcon's jesses) appear again in the lower right corner of a tapestry that is thought to show a miracle of resuscitation performed by Saint Julian of Le Mans (see fig. 35).[9] This is another instance in which these two figures have lost all connection with their logical context and have become stock accessories in the hands of tapestry weavers. As noted above, the figure of the page at the far right appears again as an adult, and in reverse, in a millefleurs tapestry in the Mobilier National, Paris. In that piece, which has been given the title *Le concert* (or some variation of it), there is also a lady seated at an organ.[10] The upper part of her body, with the erect torso, the long neck, the head flattened at the back, and the particular pose of the right arm, virtually duplicates the upper body of the lady standing at the far left in the Metropolitan Museum's tapestry. The source of

Fig. 157. *Falconer and Soldier.* Tapestry, here attributed to the southern Netherlands, 1500–1530. Musée de Cluny, Paris.

this figure and of the figures of the page, the other lady, and the dogs have not yet been identified, but there can be little doubt that they too were derived from figures in prints.

MANUFACTURE AND DATE

The hanging was dated at the beginning of the sixteenth century and called Flemish when it was sold in 1904. Gómez-Moreno (1976, 165) published it as French, probably a product of Tournai, early sixteenth century. When it was exhibited in Bordeaux in 1981, the tapestry was catalogued as French and dated at the beginning of the sixteenth century. Discussing the piece in the Musée de Cluny that was woven after a version of the same cartoon (fig. 157), Demotte, Salet, and Verlet attributed it to France and dated it about 1500.[11] Göbel attributed the near-duplicate hanging in Chicago (fig. 156) to Touraine and dated it about 1500.[12] Rogers and Goetz, and later Mayer, attributed the Chicago piece to France and assigned it a date early in the sixteenth century or about 1500.[13] The stylistically similar *Pastorale* tapestries in Paris have been published as French and dated early in the sixteenth century, an attribution that has also been offered for the *Concert* in the Mobilier National.[14]

We have no scientific grounds for asserting that any of these hangings was woven in France. Since we have evidence that millefleurs tapestries were produced in Brussels and Bruges and probably also other centers in the southern Netherlands, it seems reasonable to attribute this example to that region. The design after which the cartoon was painted could not antedate the years around 1495, which is the date usually assigned to Dürer's print of the soldiers and Turk.[15] The design for the tapestry could not have been made much later than 1520, when the civilian clothing shown in it would have been going out of fashion. The tapestry itself could have been executed a few years later. In Joubert's study of the tapestries in the group called *La vie seigneuriale*, including the piece woven after the same design, she (1987, 119–21) considered the question of their origin in the southern Netherlands or France and the problem of their date in detail and correctly advised caution in attributing them to one region or the other. She concluded that the costumes, which she was tempted to consider Flemish, indicated a date around the first quarter of the sixteenth century.

RELATED TAPESTRIES

No other tapestries that can be associated with this piece in a particular series of hangings have been identi-fied. It was noted above (Description and Subject, and Source of the Design) that 36 has been compared with the group of tapestries in the Musée de Cluny called *La vie seigneuriale* and that 36 also shows stylistic and iconographic affinities with the group of three pieces in the Musée du Louvre called *La pastorale* as well as with the piece in the Mobilier National known as *Le concert*.[16] Therefore we assume that the Metropolitan Museum's tapestry once figured in some group of hangings showing aristocratic subjects in country settings. We have no reason to believe that what may appear today to be specific sets of hangings were in fact originally designed and marketed as distinct series with specific titles.

The three versions of this composition that we know at present—that is, 36 and the pieces in the Art Institute of Chicago and the Musée de Cluny (figs. 156, 157)—differ from each other in a number of ways. The Chicago piece has a pink background covered with flowering stalks with cut ends. The four main figures and the two dogs were not placed directly against this background but rather on an island meadow that seems to float against the flowered pink ground. The other two hangings have no island; the figures and dogs have been superimposed directly on the dark blue flowered ground. There is no tree in the Metropolitan Museum's hanging, but there is a tree in each of the other pieces rising from the ground behind or next to the falconer. There are also differences in the details of the costumes and the shape of the blade on the halberd. However there can be no doubt that all three tapestries were woven after cartoons that were copied either from each other or from a common source. Joubert (1987, 119) suggested that in a case like this tapestry merchants may have had copies made of cartoons that belonged to them and then allotted those to the various weaving shops working for them, a hypothesis we endorse.

HISTORY

Sold, *Collection* [Paul] *Mame de Tours*, Galerie Georges Petit, Paris, April 26–29, 1904, no. 437, illus.
Bequeathed to the MMA by Harriet H. Jonas, 1974.

EXHIBITIONS

Bordeaux, Galeries des Beaux-Arts, 1981. *Profil du Metropolitan Museum of Art de New York: De Ramesès à Picasso.* Cat. no. 69, color illus.
San Diego Museum of Art, and Champaign, Krannert Art Museum, University of Illinois, 1981–82. *5000 Years of Art from the Collection of The Metropolitan Museum of Art.* Checklist no. 30a.
Yokohama Museum of Art, 1989. *Treasures from The Metropolitan Museum of Art: French Art from the Middle Ages to the Twentieth Century.* Cat. no. 30, color illus.

PUBLICATIONS

Demotte, G.-J. *La tapisserie gothique.* Paris and New York, 1924, p. 10, text for pl. 178. Mentioned as formerly in Mame collection.

C. G.-M. [Carmen Gómez-Moreno]. "Tapestry: Five Figures on a Millefleurs Background." *MMA Notable Acquisitions 1965–1975.* New York, 1975, p. 165. Discussed briefly; illus.

Joubert 1987, pp. 117, 119. Discussed briefly; illus.

NOTES

1. Göbel 1928, vol. 2, caption for fig. 311. Christa Charlotte Mayer, *Masterpieces of Western Textiles from The Art Institute of Chicago* (Chicago, 1969) caption for pl. 9 and text on p. 25.

2. Meyric R. Rogers and Oswald Goetz, *Handbook to the Lucy Maud Buckingham Medieval Collection,* Art Institute of Chicago (Chicago, 1945) p. 73.

3. G.-J. Demotte, *La tapisserie gothique* (Paris and New York, 1924) p. 10, text for pl. 178.

4. Francis Salet, *La tapisserie française du moyen-age à nos jours* (Paris, 1946) caption for pl. 31; Verlet 1965, caption for illus. on p. 71; Joubert 1987, p. 104.

5. Verlet 1965, p. 70. For a complete study of this group of six pieces, with illustrations in color and bibliography, see Joubert 1987, pp. 104–21.

6. See Salet, *La tapisserie française,* pls. 27–29 and captions on p. xv. Souchal in Paris 1973, no. 31, illustrates the piece showing people playing a board game called *marelle* and gathering fruit, and she discusses it with reference also to the two other hangings in the group.

7. Illustrated in color in Demotte, *La tapisserie gothique,* pl. 163. Now in the Robert Lehman Collection, MMA, acc. no. 1975.1.1912.

8. See F. W. H. Hollstein, *German Engravings, Etchings and Woodcuts, ca. 1400–1700* (Amsterdam, 1954–78) vol. 7, p. 76, where the engraving (B.88, M.81) is illustrated and captioned *Five Soldiers and a Turk on Horseback.* S. R. Koehler, *A Chronological Catalogue of the Engravings, Dry-Points and Etchings of Albert Dürer, as Exhibited at the Grolier Club* (New York, 1897) no. 3, called it *Five Footsoldiers and a Mounted Turk* and noted that it is also called "The Six Warriors." In Walter L. Strauss, ed., *The Intaglio Prints of Albrecht Dürer: Engravings, Etchings & Drypoints* (New York, 1976) no. 6, the print is called *Five Lansquenets and an Oriental on Horseback.*

9. The tapestry, which has been on deposit at the Musée du Louvre from the Mobilier National, was sold from the collection of Mme. de Genevraye at Hôtel Drouot, Paris, December 3–4, 1908, no. 196, illus. The auction catalogue entry calls it *La légende de saint Julien* and notes that it shows Saint Julian stopping a funeral procession and reviving the lady of a manor. Göbel 1928, vol. 1, p. 316, offered a similar interpretation of the subject. Roger-Armand Weigert, *La tapisserie et le tapis en France* (Paris, 1964) p. 67, refers to the subject as "le présumé *Miracle de saint Julien,*" which suggests that he questions the identification of the incident or of the saint. Joubert 1987, p. 117, who also discussed the reappearance of the two figures in this tapestry, accepted it as a piece whose subject deals with the life of Saint Julian.

10. Souchal in Paris 1973, no. 32, published the tapestry with the title *Concert à la fontaine,* illustrated it, and discussed it in some detail. Salet, *La tapisserie française,* pl. 35, illustrated the piece in color.

11. Demotte, *La tapisserie gothique,* pl. 178 and text, p. 10 (see also text for pl. 174); Salet, *La tapisserie française,* p. xvi; Verlet 1965, p. 70. Verlet did not specify France as the place of manufacture but implied a French origin when he wrote of the subject matter as concerning the activities of people in the time of Louis XII.

12. Göbel 1928, vol. 2, caption for fig. 311.

13. Rogers and Goetz, *Handbook to the Lucy Maud Buckingham Medieval Collection,* p. 73; Mayer, *Masterpieces of Western Textiles,* caption for pl. 9.

14. For *La pastorale,* see Salet, *La tapisserie française,* p. xv, captions for pls. 27–29. Souchal in Paris 1973, no. 31, offered no geographical attribution but dated the *Jeu de Marelle* piece about 1510. For *Le concert,* see Salet, *La tapisserie française,* p. xvi, caption for pl. 35. Souchal in Paris 1973, no. 32, gave no geographical attribution for the tapestry but seemed to favor the tradition that it was commissioned by Pierre de Rohan, who died in 1513, thus implying that the tapestry was commissioned by that date.

15. Authorities have dated the print at different times between 1486 and 1500, most of them favoring the years 1495–96. See Koehler, *Chronological Catalogue,* no. 3, and Strauss, *Intaglio Prints of Albrecht Dürer,* no. 6.

16. For references concerning these tapestries, see notes 5, 6, 10, and 14 above.

37
A Hawking Party

Southern Netherlands, 1500–1530
Wool warp, wool wefts
8 ft. 9 in. × 12 ft. 4$^1/_2$ in. (2.67 m × 3.77 m)
13 warp yarns per inch, 5 per centimeter
Gift of George Blumenthal, 1941 (41.100.195)

CONDITION

The tapestry has been cut along all four sides. There is a slightly curved line of restoration from top to bottom just right of center; it suggests that the hanging was once either cut into two pieces or badly worn along that line. There are other important restorations by reweaving and patching along the top of the piece and in both lower corners as well as at the bottom of the second lady's skirt. The drawing of the standing huntsman's hat, left hand, and right foot and of the faces of the three mounted figures has been altered through restoration. There are other repairs by reweaving throughout, especially in the areas of the lead horse's rump and the second horse's neck. The colors have faded appreciably but the hues are still clearly defined.

DESCRIPTION AND SUBJECT

Before a backdrop of flowering plants that almost completely cover the dark bluish green ground, two men and two women are represented at a specific moment in the progress of a hawking party. In the lower left corner a huntsman wearing a doublet with wide, slashed sleeves, hose and breeches, and shoes with rounded toes removes his hat with his left hand and with his right hand holds up a dead or disabled bird for the mounted lady before him to inspect. This young lady rides a white horse whose trappings show a gilt knotted cord and gilt bosses set on a blue ground. She wears an elaborately patterned velvet or damask gown over a plain petticoat. Her sleeves, which match the petticoat in color, are tight over the forearm but wide and slashed over the upper arm, with a white chemise showing through the slashings. She also wears a knotted-cord girdle, an arching cap, and, around her neck, a short string of beads and a long gold chain.[1] A falcon is perched on her gloved left hand.

Following the lady falconer, a young gentleman and lady ride together on a horse. The man, who rides in front and holds the horse's reins in his right hand and the leash of a greyhound in his left, wears a calf-length coat with sleeves that are cut loose and full over the upper arm but tight from elbow to wrist. His shoes have rounded toes, and he wears a low, round hat like that of the huntsman. The lady riding behind him wears a plain gown over a patterned velvet or damask petticoat and a plain cape that partly obscures her sleeves, which are like the other lady's sleeves, complete with their ribbon ties. This lady wears a pendant or locket on a gold neck chain and carries a riding crop in her left hand. Two birds fly above the party.

Before Hunter (1925, 101) noted that the man at the left was holding up "for her inspection the bird that has just met its fate," writers had described the subject as a departure for the hunt or as a hunt with falcons. In the catalogue entry for its exhibition at the Metropolitan Museum in 1928, the tapestry was called "The Departure for the Hunt," but the text notes that "a huntsman, standing in front of her, displays a bird that has been brought down." The hunt has in fact already begun; and the moment represented here, like that shown in the Metropolitan Museum's other millefleurs falconing tapestry with a very similar subject (38), is the moment when a huntsman presents to a lady in a hunting party the game that her falcon has brought down. Weigert (1956, 82) referred to the piece as "le Départ pour la chasse au faucon ou la Chevauchée" (the departure for the falcon hunt or the riding party). The couple at the right have a greyhound with them but no other indication that they are hunting. A similar tapestry in a French private collection shows a lady holding a crop but no falcon, and attended by a page, riding across the field.[2]

SOURCE OF THE DESIGN

The figures may have been designed expressly to be used in tapestries with millefleurs grounds whose compositions dispensed with the formal relationships one expects to find in conventional paintings. Here, as in many millefleurs tapestries, the groups of figures are completely self-contained. Perhaps derived from one or more prints, they were probably stock patterns in a weavers' shop.

MANUFACTURE AND DATE

From 1913 when Bertaux (caption, 7) first published it until 1943 when it was exhibited at the Metropolitan

37

Museum with other works of art from the Blumenthal collection, most writers attributed the tapestry to France, specifically to Touraine or the region of the Loire, and dated it between 1500 and 1515. Bertaux (1913, 12) and Rubinstein (1916–17, 33) gave fashion in costume as the grounds for their dating, both specifically placing the design within the reign of Louis XII (1498–1515). Later writers did not offer alternative datings, but Forsyth (1943–44, 256, caption) agreed with the exhibition catalogue of the Blumenthal collection (1943) in calling the tapestry Flemish rather than French. Rorimer (1947, 4, caption fig. 16) preferred to retain the attribution to Touraine and dated the tapestry at the end of the period favored by earlier writers, specifically about 1515.

The tapestry corresponds in all details to other mille-fleurs pieces that are now believed to have been woven in the southern Netherlands. There are at present no grounds for dating the costumes much before 1500 or much after 1520. However, since fashions in clothing did not change radically in France and the Netherlands until late in the first third of the sixteenth century, the tapestry could have been woven as late as 1530 and still not have looked old-fashioned.

RELATED TAPESTRIES

No other pieces from the same set of hangings are known to have survived. This tapestry probably belonged to a suite of millefleurs hangings treating the subject of hunting or rural pastimes (for example, see 25, 36, 38). Tapestries showing hunts with falcons in pictorial space rather than against millefleurs grounds have also survived from this period in fairly large numbers.[3]

HISTORY

In the collection of Charles Mège, Paris.
In the collection of Charles T. Barney, New York.
In the collection of George and Florence Blumenthal, New York, before 1912.
Given to the MMA by George Blumenthal, 1941.

EXHIBITIONS

Paris, Jacques Seligmann (former hôtel de Sagan), 1913. *Exposition d'objets d'art du Moyen Age et de la Renaissance . . . organisée par la Marquise de Ganay.* Cat. no. 332. Lent by George Blumenthal.
New York, MMA, 1928. *French Gothic Tapestries: A Loan Exhibition.* Cat. no. 12, not illus. Lent by George and Florence Blumenthal.
New York, MMA, 1943. *Masterpieces in the Collection of George Blumenthal: A Special Exhibition.* Cat. no. 29, illus.

PUBLICATIONS

Hunter 1912, p. 52. Mentioned as "a Knight leading a Lady's Horse, in the George Blumenthal Collection."
Bertaux, Emile. "Une exposition d'art du Moyen Age et de la Renaissance." *La Revue de l'Art Ancien et Moderne* 34 (1913) pp. 12, 14. Discussed briefly; illus. p. 7.
Vitry, Paul. "Exposition d'objets d'art du Moyen Age et de la Renaissance, organisée par Madame la Marquise de Ganay." *Les Arts*, no. 141 (September 1913) p. 26. Mentioned; illus. p. 29.
de Ricci, Seymour. *Exposition d'objets d'art du Moyen Age et de la Renaissance . . . organisée par la Marquise de Ganay à l'ancien hôtel de Sagan (mars–juin 1913).* Paris, 1914, pl. LXXV. Mentioned; illus.
Rubinstein, Stella. "Two Late French Gothic Tapestries." *Art in America* 5 (1916–17) pp. 27–28, 33, 34. Discussed at length; illus. fig. 1, p. 29.
Hunter 1925, p. 101. Mentioned; illus. pl. VI,na.
Rubinstein-Bloch, Stella. *Catalogue of the Collection of George and Florence Blumenthal, New-York.* Vol. 4, *Tapestries and Furniture.* Paris, 1927, pl. III. Described; illus.
Breck, Joseph. "The Tapestry Exhibition: Part II." *MMA Bulletin* 23 (1928) p. 184. Mentioned; illus. fig. 3, p. 181.

"Illustrierte Berichte aus Berlin, London, New-York. . . ." *Pantheon* 2 (1928) p. 373. Mentioned; illus.
Forsyth, William H. "The Noblest of Sports: Falconry in the Middle Ages." *MMA Bulletin*, n.s. 2 (1943–44) p. 258. Mentioned; illus. p. 256.
Rorimer, James J. *Mediaeval Tapestries: A Picture Book.* MMA, New York, 1947, p. [4]. Mentioned; illus. fig. 16.
Weigert, Roger-Armand. *La tapisserie française.* Paris, 1956, p. 82. Mentioned.

NOTES

1. The knotted cord that serves as this lady's girdle, and the similar ones that decorate her horse's trappings, may derive from the knotted-cord motif that had topical significance at this time as an emblem of Anne de Bretagne, who established the order of the Dames de la Cordelière in 1498. Anne's cord consisted of twisted strands tied with tight bunched knots at regular intervals. This cord is the one associated with Saint Francis of Assisi, patron saint of Anne's grandfather François, duc de Bretagne, who had also adopted it as an emblem. For further details and examples of Anne's use of the cordelière in works of art made for her, see Margaret B. Freeman, *The Unicorn Tapestries*, MMA (New York, 1976) pp. 156–57 and figs. 193, 195. About the time this tapestry was designed, another, somewhat different, knotted cord was associated with François, comte d'Angoulême, later François I of France. His emblem showed a silver cord tied with loose, looped knots. Alain Erlande-Brandenburg, "Les tapisseries de François d'Angoulême," *Bulletin de la Société de l'Histoire de l'Art Français*, 1973, pp. 23–24, fig. 1, noted that Louise de Savoie, François's mother, had adopted this cordelière for her son in gratitude for his birth and station in life, which Saint Francis de Paola had foretold. This cordelière represents the girdle worn by the monks of the Franciscan order of the Minims, which that saint had founded.
2. See Dario Boccara, *Les belles heures de la tapisserie* (Zug, 1971) p. 35, illus.
3. For example there are four hangings in the Musée de Cluny, Paris, that have rather similar figures; see Joubert 1987, cat. no. 17, especially the two pieces illustrated on pp. 172–73 and 174–75, the latter one showing one female and three male hunters, all mounted, each holding a hawk on the gloved left hand. See also figs. 39 and 40 in the present catalogue.

38

498

38

Huntsman Presenting a Captured Heron to a Lady Falconer

Southern Netherlands, 1500–1530
Wool warp; wool and silk wefts
7 ft. 9$^{1}/_{2}$ in. × 11 ft. 8 in. (2.37 m × 3.56 m)
11$^{1}/_{2}$–13 warp yarns per inch, 4$^{1}/_{2}$–5 per centimeter
Gift of Mrs. Mellon Bruce, 1964 (64.277)

CONDITION

All four sides have been cut. A modern band with multicolored stripes has been sewn to all four sides of the piece. A long, narrow patch of modern weaving has been inserted along the left side beginning about ten inches from the top edge. The huntsman's right shoe, the top of that buskin, and most of his hat have been restored. The heron's wings and tail have been partly restored, and there is restoration also in the areas of the falcon's neck and tail and the partridge's wings and tail. A triangular passage under the lady's right elbow and minor passages in the rest of the hanging have also been restored by reweaving, but the drawing has not been affected appreciably.

DESCRIPTION AND SUBJECT

A grassy island with narrow earth or rock edges occupies the center of the field. A cluster of blossoming and fruiting orange trees rises at the back of the island in the center and three rosebushes grow at center front. To the right of the roses sits a fashionably dressed lady holding in her gloved left hand the jesses of a peregrine falcon which is either alighting on her fist or struggling to get free from it (see below). The blond huntress wears a plain velvet gown over a patterned silk petticoat which shows through the inverted V opening at the front of the gown. A falcon's lure is attached to the sash around her waist. Her tied-on sleeves of figured silk are lavishly beribboned and slashed, exposing the white lawn or muslin shirt beneath. A round hat trimmed with a brooch and two feathers is perched jauntily above a cap or net set on the back of her head. She also wears a strand of gold and gem beads and a gold chain.

Her companion, half-kneeling to the left of the roses, wears a quilted knee-length coat over his hose and breeches, square-toed shoes over slashed leather buskins, and gloves. His chest and back are protected by an open-sided vest set with small metal plates and studs.

On his head is a round hat worn over a cap. He has a sword on his left hip and a pointed staff propped against his right shoulder. His hunting horn and nooses hang from a harness that passes over his left shoulder and rests against his right hip. With his left hand he grasps a heron by the neck and holds it up to the huntress's gaze. Behind the figures and their island the ground is coral pink and strewn with flowering stalks of many varieties, each with a cut end. Most of these are in an upright position, but a few are shown inverted. By contrast, the flowering plants on the green island are represented as growing there. A partridge, a pheasant, and various smaller birds appear on the pink ground in front of the island, at the sides, and above.

When 38 was first exhibited at the Metropolitan Museum in 1928, it was referred to simply as a "hunting scene." It continued to be cited that way until Rorimer (1939, 102) described it as a tapestry showing a huntsman presenting a heron to a lady holding a falcon. Souchal (in Paris 1973, 102) believed that the lady is keeping the falcon away from the heron, and that may be true. The huntress has taken hold of the jesses tied to the bird's legs; but its claws, which have either just let go of the fist or are about to grasp it, are moving free in the air. Therefore it looks as though the falcon could be either struggling to get free and attack the heron or returning to its master's fist after having brought the game down. Since the heron is not flying or running free but being held by the huntsman, it is clear that the bird has already been caught. Therefore it seems most likely that the falcon is shown here returning to its master's hand. The unfortunate heron, with its wings and legs upraised, is clearly still alive, as is the heron held by the neck and presented by a girl to a lady in a tapestry in the Victoria and Albert Museum, London.[1] In 38 any wounds the hawk may have made on the heron's body are not visible. The designer may have chosen not to represent them or perhaps the restorer removed that detail, which can be seen easily in another representation of the sort.[2] Forsyth (1943–44, 258) and later writers made a point of the presentation aspect of the scene.

Souchal (in Paris 1973, 102) referred to the kneeling man as a *seigneur*, or lord, whereas his costume, part armor and part conveyance for his hunting equipment, labels him instead as a huntsman in the employ of this lady or her host. It would have been he who retrieved the stricken heron while the lady or another attendant brought in her falcon with the aid of a lure, perhaps the one now attached to her belt.

Flying falcons at herons was a favorite sport during the Middle Ages. As Digby and Hefford said of it, "This was considered the greatest sport (along with cranes), as the heron with its very light bones was able to rise more steeply than the falcon. It was thought a wonderful sight to see the heron rising steeply, the falcon making great circles as it rose till finally it gained the greater height when it 'stooped' on the heron, which then had no escape but to make for the ground (water if possible) with all speed."[3] Such attacks on herons in midair were shown relatively frequently in late medieval tapestries. Among them are the *Deer Hunt* tapestry from the Devonshire hunts pieces in London; a hunting tapestry in Minneapolis; some falconing tapestries in the Musée de Cluny; a tapestry showing an episode in a heron hunt, in the Burrell Collection, Glasgow; and a fragment of a hawking tapestry in Saumur.[4]

As for the setting, one wonders whether the island on which this lady and her attendant appear is meant to suggest that they are near water. Falconers knew that waterfowl, like the heron, would be found in largest numbers near their own element. The *Falconry* tapestry in London shows a hunt for ducks taking place by a brook, one bank of which rises from a narrow earthen or rocky edge to become a treed and flowered hillock very much like the one shown in this tapestry and others of the type with falconry subjects in this collection (3a, b and 4).[5] Although the subject matter here seems perfectly straightforward, it has been suggested that the crossed rose branches on the pink ground (upper right and possibly also lower left center) provide an erotic theme.[6] However in 38 there is nothing to indicate that the designer intended to endow the scene with that content.

SOURCE OF THE DESIGN

The figures may have been based on prototypes in prints or book illustrations. Like others of their kind, they probably served in one or more weaving establishments as stock motifs to be used in different compositions.

MANUFACTURE AND DATE

The tapestry was attributed to the Loire region of France and dated about 1500 until Forsyth (1943–44, 257) called it Franco-Flemish and extended the date from the late fifteenth to the early sixteenth century. Souchal (in Paris 1973, 103) observed that the style is French although the designer adopted certain characteristics of Flemish painting, like the broad, broken folds of the drapery. Using costume as a criterion, she dated the piece in the early sixteenth century. The design certainly seems to be the work of a French artist, but the weaving was done somewhere in the southern Netherlands. Since red-ground tapestries like this were produced in the early years of the fifteenth century (3a, b) as well as the late years (the *Unicorn* tapestries in the Musée de Cluny), a study of fashion in clothing may help date this tapestry. The man's costume, essentially utilitarian, shows few points of fashion and can help only in a general way by indicating a date in the late fifteenth or first decade or two of the sixteenth century. The lady's gown, with its low, square neckline, tightly fitted bodice, and full open skirt worn over a petticoat, would, as a general form, have been in fashion anywhere from the late fifteenth century to the middle of the sixteenth century. However the exuberantly slashed and beribboned sleeves correspond to sleeve forms represented on such gowns during most of the first half of the sixteenth century. Considering the late medieval quality of the design as a whole, it seems unlikely that the tapestry would have been designed, or woven, after about 1530.

RELATED TAPESTRIES

A tapestry with a similar subject—the presentation of captured game to a lady falconer—is also in the Metropolitan Museum (37). The two pieces could not have belonged to the same series of hangings since 37 shows the figures against the more common bluish green ground and the drawing is entirely different.

Among the few red-ground millefleurs tapestries known to have survived from this period, there is only one whose figures are drawn very much like those in 38. It shows two ladies (one of whom is using a lure to retrieve a falcon), a boy, and a monkey, all standing on an island. The scene clearly has an allegorical meaning, so while it might have been designed by the same artist or shop as 38, it cannot have belonged to the same series of cartoons or hangings. That tapestry was formerly in the collection of Martin Le Roy.[7]

HISTORY

In the collection of Stanford White, New York.
In the collection of Charles T. Barney, then James Barney, New York.
Owned by French and Company, New York, before 1928.
In the collection of the Honorable Andrew W. Mellon, by 1928.
In the collection of Mrs. David K. E. Bruce, by 1938.
Given to the MMA by Mrs. Mellon Bruce, 1964.

EXHIBITIONS

New York, MMA, 1928. *French Gothic Tapestries: A Loan Exhibition*
Cat. no. 11. Lent by the Honorable Andrew W. Mellon.
Detroit Institute of Arts, 1928. *The Seventh Loan Exhibition: French Gothic Art of the Thirteenth to Fifteenth Century*. Catalogue of tapestries by Adele C. Weibel. Cat. no. 105. Lent by the Honorable Andrew W. Mellon.
New York, MMA, 1938–64. Lent by Mrs. Mellon Bruce.
New York, MMA, The Cloisters, 1944. *The Noble Sport of Falconry*. No exh. cat.
Paris 1973. Catalogue entries by Geneviève Souchal. Cat. no. 33, illus.
New York 1974. Cat. no. 36, illus.

PUBLICATIONS

Breck, Joseph. "The Tapestry Exhibition: Part II." *MMA Bulletin* 23 (1928) p. 184. Discussed briefly; illus. fig. 2.
"Illustrierte Berichte aus Berlin, London, New-York. . . ." *Pantheon* 2 (1928) p. 372. Mentioned; illus.
J. J. R. [James J. Rorimer]. "An Important Loan of a Mediaeval Tapestry." *MMA Bulletin* 34 (1939) p. 102. Discussed briefly.
Forsyth, William H. "The Noblest of Sports: Falconry in the Middle Ages." *MMA Bulletin*, n.s. 2 (1943–44) p. 258. Discussed briefly; illus. p. 257.
"Renaissance Splendor on Gramercy Park." *Gramercy Graphic* 15 (1956) pp. 3, 8, 9, 15. Mentioned; shown hanging on wall of reception room in Stanford White's residence at 121 East 21st Street, New York.

Hoving, Thomas P. F. "Reports of the Departments: Medieval Art and The Cloisters." Annual Report for 1964–1965. In *MMA Bulletin*, n.s. 24 (1965–66) p. 69. Mentioned; illus.
Erlande-Brandenburg, Alain. *La Dame à la Licorne*. Paris, 1978, n. pag., in "Etude," facing "III. Les problèmes stylistiques." Mentioned; illus.
Garmey, Stephen. *Gramercy Park: An Illustrated History of a New York Neighborhood*. New York, 1984, pp. 122–23. Discussed briefly; illus. (as above) hanging in the reception room of Stanford White's residence at 121 East 21st Street, New York.

NOTES

1. See the upper central section of the *Otter and Swan Hunt* tapestry, illustrated in George Wingfield Digby assisted by Wendy Hefford, *The Devonshire Hunting Tapestries*, Victoria and Albert Museum (London, 1971) pl. 21. However the brace of herons that a huntsman presents to a lady attending a crossbow and falcon hunt in a tapestry in the Musée de Cluny is clearly dead; see Joubert 1987, illus. pp. 172–73.
2. See Digby 1980, figs. 2B and 7B, the lower right corner of the *Falconry* tapestry in the Victoria and Albert Museum, in which a falconer presents to a lady a duck that has just been killed by a falcon.
3. Quoted from Digby with Hefford, *The Devonshire Hunting Tapestries*, p. 52.
4. See, respectively, Digby with Hefford, *The Devonshire Hunting Tapestries*, pl. IV and fig. 23; Joubert 1987, illus. pp. 168–75; William Wells, "Two Burrell Hunting Tapestries," *Scottish Art Review* 14, no. 1 (1973) fig. 5; Digby with Hefford, *The Devonshire Hunting Tapestries*, fig. 24.
5. For a detail of the hillock rising from the bank of the brook in the *Falconry* tapestry, see Digby 1980, pl. 6.
6. *The Seventh Loan Exhibition: French Gothic Art of the Thirteenth to Fifteenth Century*, exh. cat., Detroit Institute of Arts (Detroit, 1928) no. 105.
7. See J.-J. Marquet de Vasselot, *Catalogue raisonné de la collection Martin Le Roy*, fasc. 4, *Tapisseries et broderie* (Paris, 1908) pp. 21–22, pl. III. See also Göbel 1928, vol. 1, p. 279, vol. 2, fig. 314.

39

39
Flowering Plants and Rosebushes

Southern Netherlands, 1500–1530
Wool warp, wool wefts
8 ft. 7 1/2 in. × 9 ft. 4 1/2 in. (2.63 m × 2.86 m)
11–13 warp yarns per inch, 4–5 per centimeter
Bequest of Adele L. Lehman, in memory of Arthur Lehman, 1965
(65.181.14)

CONDITION

The hanging is made up of six rectangular fragments of tapestry weaving that have been joined together with new warp and weft yarns. Three wide, shallow pieces were set end to end along the top; these account for about one-seventh of the tapestry's height. Three tall fragments, each of which corresponds to the width of the shallow band above it, were placed side by side below them. These three composite columns of weaving increase in width from left to right, the left column accounting for a bit less than a third of the tapestry's width and the right column for a bit more than a third of it. All four sides of the hanging show cut edges, but there are the remains of selvages along the tops of the middle and right upper sections. A few linear repairs made with new warp and weft yarns, and small spots of reweaving on the original warp, appear throughout the field. The colors have faded somewhat, but most of the hues retain a good deal of their original intensity.

DESCRIPTION AND SUBJECT

A multitude of flowering plants almost entirely covers the dark greenish blue ground. A cluster of three rose-bushes grows in the center of the field, and two more clusters of three appear near the lower left corner. A fourth cluster, comprising four bushes, grows at the edge of the field toward the lower right corner.

Although few millefleurs tapestries showing fields of flowers and trees but neither creatures nor man-made objects have survived, there is enough visual evidence in contemporary paintings to show that such tapestries existed in the late fifteenth and early sixteenth centuries.[1] Therefore, it is possible that 39 was designed to look as it does now, with no subject matter other than the plants and rosebushes, but we think that unlikely. Its field is not an unbroken rectangle of weaving: it is a patchwork of six relatively small pieces of tapestry that could have been cut out of one or more millefleurs tapestries displaying birds, beasts, human figures, or

heraldic or religious motifs against the verdure ground (for example, see 14, 16, 31, 34–38). Supposing that this assumption is correct, we can point to a tapestry whose pattern might resemble that of the tapestry or tapestries from which the constituent pieces of 39 could have been cut. It is a tapestry in the Minneapolis Institute of Arts (fig. 158) which, like 39, shows rosebushes with the flowering plants but none of the oak, orange, and holly trees that appear in most surviving millefleurs hangings of the period.[2] In the Minneapolis tapestry a stag, a panther, a unicorn, a lamb, other beasts, and a variety of birds are scattered over the surface against the mille-fleurs ground. These creatures are all drawn to the same scale and they are arranged at regular intervals, with a good deal of space between them, almost like polka dots. It is conceivable that someone could have cut pieces out of one or more tapestries with patterns like this and then fit them together in such a way as to create 39, a hanging that shows plants and rosebushes but neither birds nor beasts.

SOURCE OF THE DESIGN

Verdure patterns of this kind were the stock in trade of tapestry producers. At present we have no way of tracing the designs to a particular source; but it is clear that they were designed by artists who specialized in verdure patterns meant to be painted on walls or wall-covering materials like cloth or leather, to be embroidered, or to be woven as tapestry hangings.

MANUFACTURE AND DATE

Both Virch (1965, 94) and Forsyth (1966–67, 87) attributed the tapestry to France, Virch suggesting Touraine, and Forsyth the region of the Loire. More recent studies have shown that while the designs for some tapestries of this kind may have been created in France, the hangings themselves were produced in the southern Netherlands. It may be significant that the border design of the similar tapestry in Minneapolis (fig. 158) is a simplified version of the border pattern found in a number of tapestries that are either known to have been woven in Bruges or have been attributed to Bruges with good reason.[3] However it is purely an act of faith to consider attributing the Minneapolis piece to Bruges on these grounds since we cannot be certain that such borders were used exclusively for tapestries produced in Bruges. Therefore,

Fig. 158. *Birds, Beasts, and Rosebushes on a Millefleurs Ground.* Tapestry, here attributed to the southern Netherlands and dated in the first third of the sixteenth century. The Minneapolis Institute of Arts; Gift of Mrs. Charles J. Martin in memory of Charles Jairus Martin.

while there is some reason to consider the possibility that 39 may have been woven in Bruges, our knowledge of these matters is still so imperfect that it would be extremely hazardous to do more than submit the question for future study.

We agree with both Virch (1965, 94) and Forsyth (1966–67, 87), who dated 39 in the early sixteenth century, presumably on the basis of the form of the composition and the style of the drawing. However in theory one might date this hanging anytime between about 1480 and 1540, the years during which millefleurs tapestries of this type were in fashion. However one may be justified in suggesting a rough and tentative chronology for tapestries in this class by studying the scale and arrangement of the flora. In 39 the plants have the particular form and arrangement of plants in millefleurs tapestries that can be dated in the second decade of the sixteenth century, tapestries like the ones in Angers that have angels carrying instruments of the Passion, or perhaps as late as the second quarter of the century, like the tapestry with the Giovio arms in the Victoria and Albert Museum.[4] These examples, like the pieces in the so-called *Noble pastorale* and *Vie seigneuriale* series in Paris or certain hangings in the Metropolitan Museum (especially 34–38), which have been dated in the early years of the sixteenth century on the basis of general style and/or fashion in costume, show clearly drawn and defined plants of many different sizes, scales, and types placed close to each other but with an integrity of form that is remarkable considering how jumbled their arrangement appears at first.

This effect is very different from that created in millefleurs tapestries dating from the last quarter of the fifteenth century, like the piece with the arms and badges of Sir John Dynham at The Cloisters (16), which can be dated between 1488 and 1501, or the piece with the arms of Jean de Daillon in Montacute House, Somerset (see fig. 75), which we know from documentary evidence was finished by 1483.[5] In these two hangings the plants —though of myriad varieties, each cleanly and clearly defined—are all drawn in essentially the same scale. This gives the tapestry's ground an even texture which creates the effect of a single plane. In contrast, the design of the later tapestries does not create so unified a surface, and it allows the observer's eye to read the larger plants as existing in a space somewhat closer to him than the smaller plants.

If future research proves this observation to be valid in the context of a larger and therefore more reliable body of data, and if it should prove that the difference noted here is indeed a function of the moment when a tapestry was designed rather than of the place it was woven or of the style of the artist or school of artists who designed it, then it may be fair to date 39 in the first half, or more likely the first third, of the sixteenth century. By the fifth decade of that century, millefleurs tapestries— for example, the pieces woven in Brussels with the arms of the emperor Charles V—had begun to take on the heavily foliate look of large-leaf verdure hangings that were coming into fashion (see 52a, b).

RELATED TAPESTRIES

It is not possible to say whether the six fragments that were used to make up this piece came from different parts of a single hanging or from parts of several hangings in the same set. We do not know any surviving tapestries that could have accompanied 39 in such a set. However, as suggested above (Description and Subject), it seems possible that 39 was made up from pieces of one or more tapestries like the one in Minneapolis (see note 2 and fig. 158) that has birds and beasts amid the similar plants and rosebushes.

HISTORY

EXHIBITIONS

None known.

PUBLICATIONS

Virch, Claus. *The Adele and Arthur Lehman Collection.* MMA, New York, 1965, p. 94. Discussed briefly; illus. p. 95.
Forsyth, William H. "Reports of the Departments: Medieval Art and The Cloisters, The Main Building." Annual Report for 1965–1966. In *MMA Bulletin*, n.s. 25 (1966–67) p. 87.

NOTES

1. For example, see Guy Delmarcel and Erik Duverger, *Bruges et la tapisserie*, exh. cat., Musée Gruuthuse and Musée Memling (Bruges, 1987) fig. 62 on p. 109, for a detail illustration of a painting of the *Marriage at Cana* by Gerard David in the Musée du Louvre which shows a small millefleurs tapestry hanging behind the figures.

2. See "Rare Mille-fleurs Tapestry added to Martin Collection," *Bulletin of the Minneapolis Institute of Arts* 23 (1934) pp. 42–46, details illus. on cover and on pp. 43, 44, 48.

3. For illustrations of the border pattern associated with Bruges tapestries of this period, see Delmarcel and Duverger, *Bruges et la tapisserie*, figs. 3/2 on p. 182, 4/1 on pp. 192–93, and 5/1 on pp. 200–201. However the ground of the Minneapolis border is blue, whereas the borders on most of the surviving tapestries believed to have been woven in Bruges at this period have red grounds; see *Bruges et la tapisserie*, color figs. 6/1 on p. 203, 7/1 on p. 206, and 8/1 on p. 210.

4. Alain Erlande-Brandenburg has demonstrated, on the basis of the heraldic bearings shown in them, that the Angers tapestries were ordered by Pierre de Rohan between June 1512 and April 1513; see Erlande-Brandenburg, "A propos d'une exposition: La tapisserie de choeur des anges porteurs des instruments de la Passion dans la chapelle du château d'Angers," *Le Journal des Savants*, January–March 1974, pp. 62–69; and Jean-Bernard de Vaivre's review of this article in *Bulletin Monumental* 133 (1975) p. 87. Digby 1980, p. 47, dated the tapestry with the Giovio arms in the second quarter of the sixteenth century on the basis of heraldry and genealogy.

5. Jean de Daillon, seigneur de Lude, ordered the tapestry from Wuillaume Desreumaulx of Tournai. He died in 1481 and the tapestry was delivered to his widow in 1483. It belonged with other pieces in a series of hangings but is the only piece known to have survived. See Jean-Bernard de Vaivre (who identified the coat of arms), "La tapisserie de Jean de Daillon," *Archivum Heraldicum* 87 (1973) pp. 18–25, and also his "L'origine tournaisienne de la tapisserie de Jean de Daillon," *Archivum Heraldicum* 88 (1974) pp. 17–20. De Vaivre's identification of the coat of arms enabled Souchal (in Paris 1973, pp. 123–24) to connect the tapestry with the document mentioning the patron's commission to Desreumaulx.

40

40
The Garden of Love

Southern Netherlands, 1510–20
Wool warp; wool, silk, and metallic wefts
10 ft. × 12 ft. 11 in. (3.05 m × 3.94 m)
15–17 warp yarns per inch, 6–7 per centimeter
Gift of Mrs. Van Santvoord Merle-Smith, 1942 (42.202)

CONDITION

The hanging preserves its original width, but the height may have been increased or decreased when the upper parts of the border and the upper third of the field were restored with modern warp and weft yarns sometime in the past. The restoration involves the landscape behind the figures and most of the fountain, the entire top border, and the upper fifth of both side borders. The lower two-thirds of the field, including the figures and the flowery meadow they occupy, is original. The lower four-fifths of the side borders and the entire bottom border, except for its outer guard, also belong to the original fabric. The modern section was joined to the original fabric along a line that starts at the outer edge of the left-hand border at a point level with the hat worn by the man standing there. The line then follows the upper curve of his hat and continues along the tops of the heads of the four women and one man standing to the right of him and then to the left shoulder of the woman nearest the fountain. It crosses the base of the fountain's left wall to the neck of the man standing at center left, over his head to the inner edge of the stone basin behind him and across that edge to its mitered right end, then down along the right wall of the fountain and across to a point slightly above the hat of the man standing behind the chess players. It passes just above his head and the head of his lady, across the trunk of the tree, to the right elbow of the woman standing behind the male chess player. From there it follows the upper contours of that woman's head and the heads of her two companions. The line of joining ends on that level at a point along the outer edge of the right-hand border.

Most of the silk wefts used to render the highlights throughout the hanging, particularly the yellow silks, have deteriorated and fallen out of the fabric. They have been replaced with modern yarns in many places. Most of the wool yarns used to render the dark outlines in the pattern, which now read as brown, have also been replaced. The colors have faded but the hues are easily distinguishable. The metallic yarns that were used to render details in the garments and the women's headdresses appear to have been both silver and gilt. They have tarnished and corroded and now read as black.

DESCRIPTION AND SUBJECT

The scene is set in a garden. The ground is covered with a variety of flowering plants including among others strawberries, poppies, violets, pansies, and daisies. A party of six ladies and three gentlemen is playing cards in the left foreground. The three ladies and one gentleman who seem most directly involved in the game are seated. A gentleman at the right kneels beside the lady closest to him and passes a card across to the one sitting opposite her. Two of the ladies standing behind the seated man also hold cards, but they seem not to be involved in the moves at the moment. All three men wear unpatterned, calf-length sleeveless coats over long jackets and hose. The seated man's coat has a fur-trimmed collar. All the men wear low, round hats fitted with brims at the sides and back that have been turned up and tied across the forehead with ornamental cords or ribbons. Their hair falls loose and full over their shoulders. The men's shoes are not visible except for the ones worn by the man kneeling next to the lady seated at the right of the group; they are cut high at the heel and dagged around the edges at the ankle. The six ladies all wear unpatterned, fitted gowns cut with deep, funnel-shaped sleeves. Some of the gowns have bodices cut with V necklines; others are cut straight across above the breasts. All the ladies wear necklaces of various designs and elaborately decorated and jeweled hoods that are either fitted with lappets at the sides and falls at the back or covered on top with a small bonnet or a kerchief. Another couple, dressed like these gentlefolk, stands in the background at the left; they appear to be deeply absorbed in conversation. The gentleman's coat has an embroidered border at the hemline and a watered silk collar that becomes a short cape at the back.

On the right, in the foreground of the composition, three ladies and two gentlemen stand around a table. It has a pedestal base decorated with slender, twisted columns and a polychrome figure of a saint carrying a bell which Standen noted may represent Saint Anthony Abbot.[1] A chessboard with a raised border rests on the tabletop. The gentleman standing at the right leans forward and moves a piece on the board. The player's lady opponent stands opposite him and watches his move with deep concentration. The lady standing behind the male player leans over the board, as much absorbed in the game as the players. A lady and gentleman stand behind the table and seem to be discussing the progress of the game. Three more ladies stand in the middle distance at the right. They are engrossed in their own conversation, apparently paying no attention to the rest of the figures. The ladies and gentlemen on the right side of the tapestry are dressed essentially like the ones in the left foreground, but the ladies' gowns and headdresses are even more elaborately patterned and bejeweled and the men's coats have wide, funnel-shaped sleeves and embroidered borders along all the edges. The male chess player is standing in such a way that his shoes are visible. They are cut very low at the sides, the back, and over the toes, and there is a narrow strap over the instep.

Two young pages or footmen stand in the center of the composition behind the two gaming groups. They both wear unpatterned, thigh-length jackets with watered silk collars and full sleeves over patterned doublets and plain hose. Their low, strapped shoes resemble the ones that the chess player wears. The boy at the right has a sheathed sword hanging at his waist. He holds the foot of a shallow bowl in his left hand and pours water into it from a ewer held in his right hand. His companion has his right hand on the bowl. Behind them is the great octagonal stone basin of a fountain. From the center of its base a trough projects forward and spills water on the ground through a runnel that may be seen beyond the right leg of the page pouring water. The fountain's basin is filled with rippling water. In the center rises an ornamental waterspout representing a nude boy riding a dolphin. Water spurts from both the boy's mouth and the dolphin's mouth. Beyond the fountain the landscape opens out into grassy meadows in which trees, shrubs, and plants grow. An orange tree rises in the middle distance at the left, and opposite it stands another tree with similar foliage but no fruit.

The border shows a pair of narrow, gold-colored bands decorated with chevrons and grooved collars flanking a wide central band of red on which are spread-out branches bearing white roses and green leaves.

Standen made a study of the subject and concluded that it is not a Garden of Love because in the examples she cited only mixed couples play cards or chess,

whereas here there are single players and onlookers as well.[2] As examples of the typical northern European Garden of Love, Standen cited two tapestries woven in Basel in the second half of the fifteenth century that are now in the Historisches Museum in Basel.[3] One of them shows five couples in a garden closed in at the back by a trellis covered with grapevines. One couple plays chess; another plays cards. Next to the chess players a gentleman hands a lady a basket of fruit. The couple in the center is seated at a table with food and drink, and a male attendant is cutting a bunch of grapes from the vine. Beyond the card players, at the far right end of the piece, a seated lady is making a chaplet of flowers for her lover, who stands at the right. The other tapestry, which has been cut into three pieces, shows in the center section a couple playing cards at a table inside a tent that has been set up in a garden. A page brings them food and drink, which he places on the table. At each side two other couples (only the man appears in the left-hand section, the figure of his companion having been lost) stand and talk. Standen also cited another Rhenish tapestry, attributed to Alsace and dated about 1500, that shows a couple playing chess in a garden setting.[4] In these three tapestries the fountain, one of the most important elements in a Garden of Love, is not present. On the other hand the fountain is featured in a fifteenth-century tapestry in Nuremberg that shows a Garden of Love in which two couples have seated themselves at a table to enjoy a meal to the sound of music.[5] Behind the musicians, who stand at the center of the composition, a young gentleman and his lady are deep in conversation. To the right of them two young men stand at the fountain. The one at the left drinks directly from one of the two spouts while his companion collects water from the other spout in a ewer.

Like the large and small engravings of the Garden of Love made by the Master of the Love Gardens in the first half of the fifteenth century, these tapestries show couples eating, drinking, making chaplets, caressing, or playing games.[6] However the action depicted in the prints is more frankly erotic. A somewhat later engraving by the Master E.S. shows a couple playing chess at a pedestal table in the center of the composition. At the left a lady is making a chaplet of flowers for her lover; at the right another lady reads a letter while a man dressed as a jester watches her in obvious delight.[7]

It is because the dalliance and games in the Metropolitan Museum's tapestry are not limited to couples that Standen did not regard it as a Garden of Love but instead as a kind of outdoor party in which aristocratic folk engage in various pastimes like those shown in the six millefleurs tapestries called *La vie seigneuriale* in the

Musée de Cluny.[8] She also called attention to a similar tapestry that shows gentlefolk making music and eating while pairs of men wrestle or pitch rocks. However we suggest that this may not depict a simple party but athletes and spectators at the Olympic Games.[9] Standen also noted a millefleurs hanging of the early sixteenth century in which a lady and gentleman play chess or checkers in a garden; it has neither a fountain nor any of the other accessories or occupants of the conventional Garden of Love.[10] Ladies and gentlemen were also shown playing chess in interior contexts as well as exterior ones. A late fifteenth-century tapestry, now in the Abegg-Stiftung Bern, shows such a scene with musicians and other folk in attendance.[11] Far from involving simple dalliance, whether in a Garden of Love or not, chess games between women and men, at least in literature, occasionally involved the man's winning the lady's favors if he won the game.[12]

While we agree that 40 does not represent a standard north European fifteenth-century Garden of Love, it does nevertheless contain many elements of that subject and may perhaps be understood as a late version of it that was influenced by the way the subject was treated in fourteenth- and fifteenth-century Tuscan art. As Watson has demonstrated in connection with Tuscan painting of the fourteenth and fifteenth centuries, it is the fountain that identifies the Garden of Love in most representations of the subject. This fountain is the one in which Narcissus saw his own reflection and fell in love with it. In the *Roman de la Rose* it is the fountain in which the narrator saw the rose and was stirred by love. This is Cupid's fountain which inspires love in those who look into its waters or drink them, the fountain which in Boccaccio's fourteenth-century poem *Comedia delle ninfe fiorentine* transformed the insensitive hunter Ameto into a man who can feel love.[13] In a millefleurs tapestry called *Le concert* in Paris, as de Mirimonde pointed out, the fountain's erotic power inspires the lady standing next to it to seize the coat of a youth running away from her with what de Mirimonde referred to as a grasp like Potiphar's wife's while she draws a basin of water for him to drink.[14] Watson also noted that these fountains usually occupy the center of the composition, and they often take the form of a hexagonal basin or well with a smaller structure from which water pours forth, rising from the center.[15] The original part of the fountain in 40—that is, the front wall and bits of the first two side walls—could prepare for either a hexagonal basin or, as it is now in the restored portions, an octagonal one.[16] In the original design its polygonal base may have carried an elaborate superstructure of columns and vaults like the one that ap-

pears above the basin in one of two tapestries of the same type, style, and period that were in 1928 in the collection of Gaston Meunier.[17]

Watson also noted that the theme of the Garden of Love survived north of the Alps well into the seventeenth century, much longer than it did in Italy. Therefore it is not surprising that the northern artist who created this composition early in the sixteenth century probably meant it to be understood as a Garden of Love. Watson emphasized the fact that in the Italian examples there are often unequal numbers of people of each sex in the Garden because "in the pursuit of love somebody is doomed to lose. Not all suitors gain what they desire, nor can all ladies find suitors."[18] The two tapestries referred to above that were in the collection of Gaston Meunier in 1928 show groups of men and women, rather than only couples, engaging in leisurely pursuits around a fountain (see note 17). These ladies and gentlemen make music, converse, eat, or hunt. In one of the two pieces Cupid is shown flying in the upper left corner of the field; he has shot an arrow into the breast of a young man who lounges in a lady's lap in front of the fountain. Another lady approaches from the left and is about to place a chaplet of flowers on his head. There can be no doubt that the subject here is the Garden of Love. The activity and setting in the Metropolitan Museum's tapestry are so much like this that it seems reasonable to refer to it too as a Garden of Love.

SOURCE OF THE DESIGN

None of the figure groups or individual figures has been traced to a source in paintings or prints of the period. However it seems likely that such sources may exist or have existed at one time. The figures and the form of the composition belong to the school of design that dominated one category of southern Netherlandish tapestry production in the early years of the sixteenth century, that class of hangings that traditionally has been regarded as Brussels production. It is not feasible to attempt to attribute the design of this piece to any one of the few artists we can associate with those tapestries, but it may be useful in connection with future investigations to note that the details of costume and the facial types in this composition are particularly like those in the tapestry of the *Destruction of the Egyptians in the Red Sea* preserved in the Museum of Fine Arts, Boston.[19] In discussing that hanging, Cavallo noted that Ackerman had attributed its design to a painter named Philips, who is documented as having made the cartoon for the tapestry of the *Legend of Herkinbald* in Brussels, and that Göbel thought the Boston tapestry had been designed by Philip van Orley working in collaboration with Jan van Roome. We do not know enough about the painter Philips to endorse or reject those suggestions in connection with the search for the designer of the Metropolitan Museum's tapestry.

MANUFACTURE AND DATE

When it was published in the *MMA Bulletin* in 1918 (p. 188), the tapestry was called French and dated in the early sixteenth century. In the *MMA Annual Report* for 1942 (p. 31) the national attribution was changed to Flemish and the date was given vaguely in the sixteenth century. Rorimer (1947, fig. 14) assigned it to Brussels and dated it in the first third of the same century. Standen agreed with the Brussels attribution but dated it specifically between 1505 and 1515 without spelling out the reasons.[20]

Since we have no idea what the upper third of the composition looked like originally it would be imprudent to date the design on the grounds of style alone any more precisely than in the first or second decade of the sixteenth century. The details of costume, particularly the men's hats and shoes and the women's gowns and headdresses, correspond in general terms to those that appear in the *Legend of Herkinbald* in Brussels (dated 1513 by document) and to a lesser degree in the hangings of the *Legend of Notre-Dame du Sablon* that are preserved in Brussels and elsewhere (dated 1516–18 by document).[21] Therefore it seems most reasonable to suggest that 40 was designed during the second decade of the sixteenth century and woven not later than about 1520, when the lines of fashionable clothing were beginning to change significantly.

RELATED TAPESTRIES

No duplicate tapestries are known to have survived. Standen suggested that the tapestry showing a garden party with wrestlers and stone-pitchers (see note 9) may show another subject in the same series of compositions.[22] The subject matter is similar (although, as noted above, we believe this other piece may represent the Olympic Games) but the design is not. The Metropolitan Museum's hanging presents figure groups arranged in much more sophisticated space patterns than the other piece shows. There, the figures have been placed in two horizontal rows, both of which are essentially parallel to the picture plane; and the foreground figures do not define the neat, compact circular parcels of space that contain the corresponding figures in the Metropolitan Museum's hanging. However we agree with Standen

in believing that the other tapestries in the series to which this piece belongs probably showed ladies and gentlemen enjoying pastimes in gardens. The two hangings that belonged in 1928 to Gaston Meunier (see Description and Subject, and note 17) came from a set of tapestries of that kind; as mentioned above they show scenes in the Garden of Love. While 40 clearly does not belong with these two pieces, it probably came from a set of tapestries that showed the same kinds of compositions.

HISTORY

Said to have belonged to the vicomte de la Sayette, château des Bouches d'Azur near Craon, Mayenne.[23]
Property of French and Company, New York.
In the collection of Mrs. Van Santvoord Merle-Smith, New York, from 1918.
Lent to the MMA by Mrs. Van Santvoord Merle-Smith from 1918 except for a few months during 1932.
Given to the MMA by Mrs. Van Santvoord Merle-Smith, 1942.

EXHIBITION

Brooklyn Museum, 1968. *Chess: East and West, Past and Present, a Selection from the Gustavus A. Pfeiffer Collection*. Not listed in the catalogue.

PUBLICATIONS

"List of Accessions and Loans." *MMA Bulletin* 13 (1918) p. 188. Mentioned as an anonymous loan.
"List of Accessions and Loans." *MMA Bulletin* 27 (1932) p. 245. Mentioned as a textile lent by Mrs. Van S. Merle-Smith.
"Review of the Year 1942: Accessions, Department of Mediaeval Art." *MMA Seventy-third Annual Report of the Trustees 1942*. New York, 1943, p. 31. Mentioned.
"Review of the Year 1943: Accessions, Department of Mediaeval Art." *MMA Seventy-fourth Annual Report of the Trustees 1943*. New York, 1944, p. 32. Mentioned; illus. p. 33.
Rorimer, James J. *Mediaeval Tapestries: A Picture Book*. MMA, New York, 1947. Illus. fig. 14.
Nickel, Helmut. "Hunting, Gaming, and Sports." In Thomas Hoving, Timothy B. Husband, and Jane Hayward. *The Secular Spirit: Life and Art at the End of the Middle Ages*. Exh. cat., The Cloisters, MMA. New York, 1975, p. 207. Illus.

NOTES

1. Edith Appleton Standen, preliminary notes and draft of a catalogue entry concerning this tapestry, ca. 1968, in the files of the MMA Department of Medieval Art.
2. Standen, preliminary notes and draft, ca. 1968.
3. Discussed and illustrated in Hans Lanz, *Die alten Bildteppiche im Historischen Museum Basel* (Basel, 1985) pp. 34, 36–37, 54, 56–57. Also illustrated in Göbel 1933, figs. 16a, 17, 29.

4. Illustrated in Göbel 1933, fig. 75.

5. Discussed by Leonie von Wilckens and illustrated in *Gothic and Renaissance Art in Nuremberg 1300–1550*, exh. cat., MMA and Germanisches Nationalmuseum, Nuremberg (New York, Nuremberg, Munich, 1986) no. 67.

6. For illustrations of the two engravings, see Max Lehrs, *Geschichte und kritischer Katalog des deutschen, niederländischen und französischen Kupferstichs im XV. Jahrhundert* (Vienna, 1908–34; Kraus Reprint, Nendeln, Liechtenstein, 1969) plate vol. 1, pl. 39, fig. 101 (Lehrs no. 20, smaller garden), and pl. 40, fig. 102 (Lehrs no. 21, larger garden).

7. Lehrs no. 214; discussed briefly and illustrated in Douglas Percy Bliss, "Love-Gardens in the Early German Engravings and Woodcuts," *Print Collector's Quarterly* 15 (1928) pp. 95, 98.

8. Standen, preliminary notes and draft, ca. 1968. For the millefleurs tapestries, see Joubert 1987, pp. 104–21.

9. See *Catalogue of Fine Works of Art . . .* , Sotheby's, London, July 7, 1961, no. 63, illus. detail and color frontispiece, for the piece Standen referred to. See also a tapestry showing Hercules wrestling with Theseus in the midst of spectators on Mount Olympus: *Artistic Furnishings . . . of Henry W. Poor, Esq.*, American Art Association, New York, April 21–24, 1909, no. 198, illus.

10. Standen, preliminary notes and draft, ca. 1968. The tapestry is now in the collection of the Bayerisches Hypotheken- und Wechsel-Bank, Bayerisches Nationalmuseum, Munich; see Georg Himmelheber, "Ein Tausendblumenteppich," *Pantheon* 30 (1972) p. 395, illus. pp. 393, 395; also Göbel 1923, vol. 2, fig. 196.

11. Discussed briefly and illustrated in "Notable Works of Art Now on the Market: Textiles," *Burlington Magazine* 51 (1927) advertising supplement following p. 332, text and pl. 29.

12. See Charles K. Wilkinson, "Introduction," *Chess: East and West, Past and Present, a Selection from the Gustavus A. Pfeiffer Collection*, exh. cat., Brooklyn Museum (MMA, New York, 1968) pp. XVIII–XX.

13. Paul F. Watson, *The Garden of Love in Tuscan Art of the Early Renaissance* (Philadelphia and London, 1979) pp. 28–33.

14. A. P. de Mirimonde, "La musique dans les allégories de l'amour," *Gazette des Beaux-Arts*, 6th ser., 69 (1967) pp. 337–38, illus. fig. 40. The tapestry, which belongs to the Mobilier National in Paris, shows various figures, including three musicians, near the fountain. It is discussed and illustrated by Souchal in Paris 1973, no. 32. See also Francis Salet, *La tapisserie française du moyen-âge à nos jours* (Paris, 1946) pl. 35, for a larger illustration in color.

15. For paintings showing hexagonal fountains in the Garden of Love, see Watson, *Garden of Love in Tuscan Art*, pls. 51, 53, 56.

16. For an example of an octagonal fountain in the Garden of Love, see Watson, *Garden of Love in Tuscan Art*, pl. 55.

17. Illustrated in Manufacture Nationale des Gobelins, *La tapisserie gothique* (Paris, [1928]) nos. 45, 46.

18. Watson, *Garden of Love in Tuscan Art*, p. 70.

19. See Adolph S. Cavallo, *Tapestries of Europe and of Colonial Peru in the Museum of Fine Arts, Boston* (Boston, 1967), discussion and references on p. 87; illus. pls. 22–22b.

20. Standen, preliminary notes and draft, ca. 1968.

21. See illustrations of some of these tapestries in the present catalogue, figs. 70, 71. They are all discussed and illustrated in *Tapisseries bruxelloises de la pré-Renaissance*, exh. cat., Musées Royaux d'Art et d'Histoire (Brussels, 1976) nos. 19–23.

22. Standen, preliminary notes and draft, ca. 1968.

23. Standen attempted to confirm this history which the donor had from French and Company, but she was unable to find a "château des Bouches d'Azur near Craon." However she found that in 1873 Ludovic Armand Pierre de la Sayette resided at the château des Landes at Loiron, Mayenne, and that Alfred Marie de la Sayette, then head of the family, resided at the château de la Sayette at Vautelis, Deux-Sèvres. See A. Bachelin-Deflorenne, ed., *Etat présent de la noblesse française . . .* , 5th ed., rev. (Paris, 1887) col. 1672.

41a

512

41

Two Episodes from the Parable of the Prodigal Son

a   The Prodigal Offering Jewels to Luxuria
b   The Prodigal among the Harlots

Southern Netherlands, 1510–25
Wool warp; wool and silk wefts
41a: 7 ft. 9 in. × 5 ft. 4¹/₄ in. (2.36 m × 1.63 m)
14–17 warp yarns per inch, 5¹/₂–6¹/₂ per centimeter
41b: 8 ft. 7 in. × 6 ft. 2¹/₂ in. (2.62 m × 1.89 m)
13 warp yarns per inch, 5 per centimeter
The Lillian Stokes Gillespie Collection, Bequest of Lillian Stokes Gillespie, 1915 (15.121.2,3)

CONDITION

Both hangings have survived with their fields and borders uncut and undiminished. Narrow modern tapes have been sewn to the edges of both hangings. Parts of the inner guards have been rewoven, and there are spots of reweaving in both borders and throughout both fields. Many of the silk yarns in the highlights have been replaced, but neither the drawing nor the modeling of the forms has been altered appreciably. The colors are well preserved and comparatively bright.

DESCRIPTION AND SUBJECT

Both scenes take place in outdoor settings. Three figures occupy the entire foreground of the field in 41a. A youth wearing a cloak cut with falling sleeves over an embroidered shirt and a long doublet made of plain fabric decorated at the edges and down the center front with needleworked arabesques is seated on a bench just right of center. A heavy gold chain hangs around his neck. From under his small, round, plumed hat his curling hair falls to the shoulders. His wide-toed shoes are tied over the insteps. A lady wearing a long gown with funnel-shaped sleeves and decorated like the man's doublet sits next to him, at the right. She wears an ermine-lined mantle which, like her gown, has borders of needlework and jewels. Her hair is parted in the middle and swept back over the ears; it then falls in a plaited tail down her back. On her head is an open crown. A young lady whose hair is dressed in the same fashion and who wears a fitted gown with tight sleeves slit at the back and elbows over an embroidered shirt kneels before the young man. He reaches over to the casket that she holds up to him and takes from it a gold bracelet that he is

about to present to the lady seated beside him. This lady tilts her head forward and lifts her hands to her breast in a gesture of deference as he places his left hand on her lap. Flowering plants of various kinds cover the ground in front of these three figures. Three gentlemen and three ladies stand behind the trio. Two of the couples engage in animated conversation while the third pair, at the far left, simply watch the others with apparent indifference. Trees and buildings appear behind them in the far distance. The border comprises striped guards flanking a wide band containing violet plants alternating with branches bearing roses in bud or in full bloom and with stalks of daisies, all against a plain dark ground.

The foreground and distant background in 41b are like those shown in 41a. However in 41b a canopied dais rises in the center of the foreground. The figures are gathered around this structure. A patterned damask or velvet cloth that covers the back of it turns forward at the top to form the interior lining of the canopy, which has a tasseled valance hanging along its front edge, the edge that a pair of metal-collared marble columns support. A small round mirror hangs from a nail set into the top of the back cloth. The young man who lounges at the front of the dais in the center of the composition is dressed like (but not exactly like) the youth in the center of 41a. He probably represents the same character. Four women dressed like the ones in 41a surround this youth and cater to him. The one kneeling in the left foreground offers him a dish of fruit. A woman standing at the left walks toward him; she carries a flagon that presumably contains wine. The woman standing behind his right shoulder bends forward and with her right hand takes his chin and turns his head in her direction. The fourth woman, seated behind him on the other side, places her right hand on his left shoulder. She turns her head to talk to a youth who stands beside her; he holds an unidentifiable rectangular object that he seems to be offering to her. Another man stands in the extreme right foreground and watches intently as the four women make up to the youth. He wears a pleated calf-length coat cut with full sleeves tapered down at the cuffs and a large hat tied under his chin with a ribbon. A tasseled purse hangs on his left hip and the neck of a drawstring purse is visible in his right hand. Two couples standing behind the canopied dais seem to be deep in conversation. The border enframing this composition is like the border of 41a except that orange branches and bunches of grapes have taken the place of the violet plants. Because the two borders differ from one another, and also because 41b is 10 inches (.26 m) taller than 41a, it is fair to ask whether the two tapestries came from the same set of hangings.

It seems likely that both compositions illustrate incidents in the parable of the Prodigal Son. Late medieval artists occasionally blended that tale with more general stories of man the sinner who spends his life hanging in the balance as the Virtues and the Vices support or defeat him. When treated in this way, the Prodigal Son becomes not only the man he is meant to represent in the parable—the misguided son who spends his substance in a life of riotous living and ultimately returns to his loving and forgiving father—but also (as the parable itself implies) the symbol of sinful Man, who is forgiven through the mercy and love of God, redeemed through the mission of Christ on earth. Medieval exegesis added a number of allegorical personifications to the list of characters enumerated by Luke (15:12–32) in his telling of the parable. Verdier published a detailed study of Prodigal Son tapestries dating from this period, and he treated them in terms of these broader concepts.[1] Thus, while 41a and b show a youth bent on gratifying his desire for fleshly pleasures through indulgence in drink, food, and fornication, he could equally well be called the Prodigal Son, the Pilgrim, *Homo* (Mankind, the sons of Adam), Everyman—any name that expresses the idea of the sinful man who ultimately seeks his salvation.

Two examples of this conjunction of themes may be cited here. In the upper right corner of a tapestry of the *Parable of the Prodigal Son* in the Satterthwaite Collection of the J. B. Speed Art Museum in Louisville there is a scene showing the harlots robbing the Prodigal as the Vices drive him away; this as Verdier observed, virtually repeats the scene of evil forces attacking *Homo* in the upper right-central section of the tapestry in the Metropolitan Museum that belongs to a series of hangings dealing with the story of the fall and redemption of man (see 29b).[2] Another tapestry in this series shows the Vices attacking Man; there is one example of it in the Fine Arts Museums of San Francisco and there are others in Spain. A scene in that composition shows *Homo*, having yielded to the temptation to indulge in pleasures of the body, being led to a scantily dressed woman labeled *Luxuria* (Lechery) by female figures representing Flesh and Gluttony. *Culpa* (Guilt) stands directly behind him, and in the background an unnamed Vice dismisses Reason or Contrition from the company.[3] *Luxuria* is

represented as a queen: seated on a throne under a canopy, she wears a crown and holds a scepter. In the tapestry in Louisville the Prodigal Son goes about his debaucheries in the company of clearly identified sinful powers and Vices like *Mundus* (Worldliness), *Cecitas Mentis* (Intellectual Blindness), *Affectio Seculi* (Worldly Wise), *Inconstancia* (Fickleness), *Temptator* (Tempter), and *Dissipatio* (Dissipation). In the Metropolitan Museum's two tapestries, and also in a Prodigal Son tapestry in Minneapolis and another in Brussels, the actors are not identified by labels.[4] Nevertheless in all four pieces some of the characters are meant to represent certain vices and sinful powers who led the unfortunate Prodigal into his debauchery and downfall.

The crowned woman seated beside the Prodigal on the bench in 41a probably represents *Luxuria* although she is more decently clothed than the corresponding figure in the tapestry referred to above (see note 3). In payment of her favors, the youth is offering her jewels from a casket that contains some or all of his share of his father's property. (In the Louisville tapestry it is the woman *Dissipatio* who hands him one of two caskets as he prepares to leave his father's house.) The two women standing directly behind the Prodigal may be Vices, Virtues, or simply incidental figures whose chief function is to fill space.

The allegorical content of 41b is somewhat easier to interpret. The two women who offer the Prodigal Son food and drink are probably meant to represent not only two of the harlots in the house he is visiting but also Gluttony, a vice that is usually represented by one figure alone. A similar scene appears in the lower right-central section of the tapestry in Minneapolis.[5] There, the dandified youth is seated at a table with a female companion while another girl brings a tray of food to them. The older woman in 41b who takes the youth's chin in her hand represents the mistress of the house and possibly also Pleasure. The woman at the other side, the one holding the rose branch, may not have any allegorical significance. The young man talking to her may have a role in the anticipated undoing of the Prodigal, but the four figures in the background appear to be supernumeraries. The man standing in the right foreground probably represents Avarice as well as the pimp or operator of the house. The rectangular object made of watered silk that lies on the ground to the left of his feet may represent the Prodigal's purse, which has slipped away from him. The mirror that hangs on the back cloth above the youth's head is associated with the sin of Pride in the Prodigal Son tapestry in Louisville but with Vanity or Lechery in three other allegorical hangings of the same period.[6] Here it could refer to any one of those three sins.

41b

SOURCE OF THE DESIGN

The three figures in the foreground of 41a appear again, but with slightly changed poses and costumes, in a tapestry that was sold from the collection of Sir John Ramsden, Bart., in 1932, and they reappear, altered slightly, in the lower right corner of a tapestry with a more complex court scene that Boccara published in 1971. The same three figures, although changed more significantly, occupy the center foreground of a court-scene tapestry in the Fine Arts Museums of San Fran-

cisco.[7] Therefore we may safely conclude that both 41a and b show in part, if not entirely, stock designs that more than one tapestry producer had access to. The original design source has not been identified.

MANUFACTURE AND DATE

Friedley believed that the two hangings were woven about 1510, probably in Brussels. The compositions show the painterly style that we associate with the artists who worked for Brussels tapestry producers in the second and third decades of the sixteenth century. The border pattern is almost identical to the border of the so-called *Finding of the True Cross*, which is believed to have been woven after a cartoon by Leonard Knoest, a Brussels artist who specialized in designing tapestries; and it is closely related to the border design of the *Legend of Herkinbald*, which is documented as having been designed and woven by Brussels artisans. Both of these hangings, which are now in Brussels, date from the second decade of the sixteenth century.[8] Nevertheless we cannot be sure that the Metropolitan Museum's two hangings were not produced elsewhere in the southern Netherlands. The fashions of the garments indicate that these tapestries were designed in the second or early third decade of the sixteenth century.

RELATED TAPESTRIES

Although it is not certain that 41a and b belonged to one and the same set of hangings, it seems likely that they were woven after the same series of cartoons. We do not know of any other hangings that might have accompanied these two pieces in the set or sets they represent, nor do we know of any other tapestries that were woven after these cartoons. If the cartoons illustrated the *Parable of the Prodigal Son* specifically and not some exegetical version of it, then we may assume that the other hangings in the series would have shown both earlier and later incidents in the Prodigal's story, from the moment he asks his father for his portion to the moment he returns home and is forgiven. We cannot say how many pieces there would have been in the complete set of hangings. Seven tapestries of the same period but very different style, now in Beaune, show the main events in the story except the son's request for his inheritance.[9]

HISTORY

Bequeathed to the MMA by Lillian Stokes Gillespie, 1915.

EXHIBITION

Austin, Archer M. Huntington Art Gallery, University of Texas, 1982–87. Extended loan of 41a.

PUBLICATION

D. F. [Durr Friedley]. "An Important Bequest of Tapestries." *MMA Bulletin* 10 (1915) p. 248. 41a and b discussed briefly; 41b illus. p. 249.

NOTES

1. Philippe Verdier, "The Tapestry of the Prodigal Son," *Journal of the Walters Art Gallery* 18 (1955) pp. 9–58. Verdier also discussed a number of tapestries of the same period whose iconography is related to that of the story of the Prodigal Son.
2. Verdier, "The Tapestry of the Prodigal Son," p. 15 and fig. 3.
3. Anna G. Bennett, *Five Centuries of Tapestry from the Fine Arts Museums of San Francisco* (San Francisco, 1976) no. 11, illus. pp. 64–65.
4. For the piece in the Minneapolis Institute of Arts, see "Late Gothic Tapestry Acquired for Institute," *Bulletin of the Minneapolis Institute of Arts* 27 (1938) pp. 26–30 and cover, details illus.; for an illustration of the complete hanging, see *Collection of Genevieve Garvan Brady [Mrs. William J. Babington Macaulay]*, sale cat., American Art Association, Anderson Galleries, New York, May 10–15, 1937, no. 2032. There is another version of this tapestry in the cathedral at Vigevano; see Mercedes Viale, "Arazzi fiamminghi nel Duomo di Vigevano," *Bollettino della Società Piemontese di Archeologia e di Belle Arti*, n.s. 4–5 (1950–51) p. 138, fig. 1. The tapestry in the Musées Royaux d'Art et d'Histoire in Brussels is discussed and illustrated, among other places, in *Tapisseries bruxelloises de la pré-Renaissance*, exh. cat., Musées Royaux d'Art et d'Histoire (Brussels, 1976) no. 26; bibliography referring to this piece and three others in the series to which it belongs is on p. 117.
5. See (references in note 4) the full view of the tapestry in the Genevieve Garvan Brady sale catalogue (right-center foreground) and details of this section of the piece on the cover of the Minneapolis Institute of Arts *Bulletin*, as well as an additional detail in Viale, "Arazzi," p. 145, fig. 5.
6. In the lower left corner of the Louisville hanging, in the scene showing the Prodigal asking for his portion, Pride holds a mirror in which the youth's face is reflected; see Verdier, "The Tapestry of the Prodigal Son," p. 12 and fig. 3. In one of the *Redemption of Man* tapestries showing the Vices attacking Man, Vanity sits at the left of the chief figure in the trial scene at upper center and holds a mirror in which the judge, who may be Pride, is reflected; see Bennett, *Five Centuries of Tapestry from the Fine Arts Museums of San Francisco*, no. 11, illus. pp. 64–65. In another tapestry from that series, also preserved in the Fine Arts Museums of San Francisco, which shows the battle between the Virtues and Vices, *Luxuria* appears riding a hog in the lower right section and holding a mirror in which her head is reflected; see Bennett, *Five Centuries of Tapestry from the Fine Arts Museums of San Francisco*, no. 12, illus. pp. 68–69. A tapestry showing the seven capital sins about to attack mankind, preserved in the Musées Royaux d'Art et d'Histoire in Brussels, shows in the lower right corner *Luxuria*, again on a hog, holding a mirror up to her face and looking at her own reflection in it; see *Tapisseries bruxelloises de la pré-Renaissance*, no. 24, illus. p. 105.
7. See *Catalogue of the Important Collection of ... Sir John Ramsden, Bart.*, sale cat., Christie's, London, May 23–26, 1932, no. 117, illus., called "a Betrothal Scene"; Dario Boccara, *Les belles heures de la tapisserie* (Zug, 1971) pp. 46–47, illus., a tapestry then in a private collection in Paris that Boccara called "Scène galante à la cour d'un Seigneur." Both of those pieces could conceivably be connected with the parable of the Prodigal Son, whereas the hanging in San Francisco, which Bennett called "Scenes of Court Life," does not seem to relate to that theme; see Bennett, *Five Centuries of Tapestry from the Fine Arts Museums of San Francisco*, no. 18, illus. p. 91.
8. See *Tapisseries bruxelloises de la pré-Renaissance*, nos. 18 and 19 respectively, both illus.
9. For the tapestries in the Hôtel-Dieu in Beaune, which have been attributed to Tournai and dated about 1520, see J. P. Asselberghs, *La tapisserie tournaisienne au XVIe siècle*, exh. cat. (Tournai, 1968) nos. 18–24, illus.

42
Court Scenes

Two fragments

a A Lady Making a Presentation to a Queen
b A Monarch and a Lady Exchanging a Covered Cup or Box

Southern Netherlands, 1510–25
Wool warp; wool and silk wefts
42a: 22$^{1}/_{2}$ in. × 26$^{1}/_{2}$ in. (.57 m × .67 m)
15–18 warp yarns per inch, 6–7 per centimeter
Bequest of George Blumenthal, 1941 (41.190.89)
42b: 21$^{7}/_{8}$ in. × 25$^{5}/_{8}$ in. (.56 m × .65 m)
12$^{1}/_{2}$–16$^{1}/_{2}$ warp yarns per inch, 5–6$^{1}/_{2}$ per centimeter
Bequest of George Blumenthal, 1941 (41.190.92)

CONDITION

There are traces of a guard along the top of 42a. The other three sides show cut edges. The original selvage has been preserved along the top of 42b and the loom finish appears along its right side. Its left and bottom edges have been cut. Therefore we conclude that 42a once occupied a position along the upper edge of a hanging and that 42b comes from the upper right corner of a tapestry. Since the figures in 42a correspond in scale and arrangement to those in 42b, and since all the figures resemble one another, it seems possible that they were taken either from different parts of one and the same tapestry or, because their warp counts are slightly different, from two different tapestries that were woven after the same series of cartoons.

There are places in both fragments where the surfaces have worn and the wefts have deteriorated, particularly in the dark contours of the figures. In these places the warp yarns are bare. 42b has suffered more seriously in this regard than 42a. Some of the losses were replaced with modern weft yarns, but these restorations were removed later. Therefore neither the drawing nor the colors, which are still bright, have been altered to any appreciable extent.

DESCRIPTION AND SUBJECT

In 42a a gentleman and a queen are shown seated in the right half of the field. The man wears hose, an unpatterned, knee-length jacket or tunic, a cloak with a wide falling collar, and a low, round hat with an upturned brim. The queen wears an unpatterned gown cut with a high waist and a low, square corsage, a shirt with a high round neckline, an unpatterned cloak caught with a pair of brooches at the sides of the bodice, and an open coronet on the back of her head. She holds a scepter in her right hand. Her sleeves, like those of the young lady addressing her, are slit underneath and at the elbows to allow some of the linen shirt to pass through and form decorative puffs. A second man, who looks like either a courtier or an attendant, stands between and behind the queen and her male companion. All three of these figures are watching the young lady who stands in the foreground just to the left of center. This girl wears a costume resembling the queen's but without the cloak. She looks directly at the queen and holds up to view what appears to be a girdle decorated with a row of circles. Her hair, like the queen's, is parted in the center and swept back over the ears. It then falls in a long, plaited tail at the back to a point below her waist. Two other ladies, also dressed in unpatterned gowns and high-necked shirts, wear hoods on their heads. They too are watching the girl in the left foreground. A cloth of patterned velvet or damask hangs behind the two seated figures. A landscape view opens out beyond the two ladies standing at the left.

There are six figures arranged much in the same way in 42b. Two richly dressed men stand at the left before a hanging made of patterned velvet or damask. The gentleman at the far left, who wears a cloak with a wide, fur-lined collar over a jacket and shirt and a low, round hat with an upturned brim over a cap, places his right hand under his cloak and extends his left hand forward. The object held in that hand seems to be a scroll. The man standing behind and to the right of him wears a cloak with a patterned falling collar and over that a neck ornament resembling the collar of some order. He also wears an open coronet around the crown of his wide-brimmed hat. He looks directly at the young woman kneeling before him, and he bends forward either to hand her a gadrooned covered cup or box or to take it from her. His right hand seems to clasp her left hand; the base of the cup or box seems to rest on the fingers of her left hand. This girl, like the lady standing behind her,

42a

wears a fitted gown cut with wide, funnel-shaped sleeves and a low, square corsage, embroidered shirt, and a patterned hood. A third woman, standing behind this one, wears a gown whose sides cross over the breast, an embroidered shirt, and a hood. Both ladies watch the presentation scene in the center of the field. Another gentleman, dressed like the one in the left foreground, stands directly behind the kneeling girl and looks off into the distance toward the right. A bit of landscape is visible behind the four figures in the right half of the composition.

When Rubinstein-Bloch published these two fragments in 1927, she prudently made no attempt to identify the subjects. In discussing the two near-duplicate

pieces that are now in the Burrell Collection (see figs. 159 and 160 and Related Tapestries), the author of the entries in the Seligmann sale catalogue (1935) suggested that 42a apparently represented the marriage of Louis XII of France and Jeanne de France, daughter of Louis XI, and that 42b represented the marriage of Louis XII and Anne de Bretagne. We believe that there are no grounds for supporting these suggestions. None of the figures is shown wearing royal garments of the last quarter of the fifteenth century, when Louis made these two marriages (the first at age fourteen), and nothing in these compositions suggests that they were meant to represent wedding ceremonies. Furthermore, while one of the crowned figures is a man (in 42b), the other is a woman

42b

(in 42a). Wells made the much more reasonable suggestion that the two fragments in Glasgow probably show
scenes from the Old Testament, whose subjects may
have been regarded as prefigurations of scenes in the life
of the Virgin.[1] Kurth suggested that one of the fragments
represents Solomon welcoming the Queen of Sheba
while the other illustrates some episode in the story of
David and Bathsheba.[2] Again the fact that only one of
the two crowned figures is a man argues against this
interpretation of the subject matter.

Apparently these writers did not realize that the two
pieces are not complete tapestries executed on a miniature scale (see 22) but small fragments cut out of one or
two large tapestries. There can be no doubt about this

because, as noted above, the condition of the edges of
42a and b proves that they were taken from the top of one
or two tapestries. Furthermore, the patterns in the costumes and textile hangings, and also the hatchings that
were used to blend the colors, are unusually bold, indicating that the figures were meant to be viewed from some
distance away. Countless hangings of normal size that
have survived from this period show groups of small-
scale figures like these in their upper sections, figures
that act out episodes pertaining to the main event represented in the center of the composition but secondary to
it.[3] Thus 42a and b show either secondary episodes in
the main story or episodes that took place at a time
different from that of the chief event, which may have

Fig. 159. *A Lady Making a Presentation to a Queen.* Fragment of a tapestry, southern Netherlands, first quarter of the sixteenth century. The Burrell Collection, Glasgow Museums and Art Galleries.

Fig. 160. *A Monarch and a Lady Exchanging a Cup or Box.* Fragment of a tapestry, southern Netherlands, first quarter of the sixteenth century. The Burrell Collection, Glasgow Museums and Art Galleries.

been derived from the Old Testament, classical mythology, or, because the three main figures in 42a resemble the three in 41b, perhaps the story of the Prodigal Son.

SOURCE OF THE DESIGN

The main figures in each composition may have been borrowed from one or more prints or paintings, but none of them has been traced to a pictorial source. That the facial features in 42b look softer and rounder than those in 42a may be due to the fact that 42b is in less good condition. It is also possible that the pieces were executed by different weavers. However it seems likely that one and the same hand designed the cartoons after which the fragments were woven. While this anonymous designer belonged to the school of artists who produced designs for countless so-called Brussels tapestries that have survived, his facial types have a distinctive quality that sets them apart from the others.

MANUFACTURE AND DATE

Rubinstein-Bloch (1927) published the two fragments as French work of the early sixteenth century. The near-duplicate pieces that were sold from the Seligmann collection in 1935 were catalogued as Flemish and dated about 1500. When the same two pieces were exhibited in Glasgow more than thirty years later, they were published as Brussels work of about 1500.[4] Both the style of the compositions and the fashion of the garments and

accessories point to a date in the first quarter of the sixteenth century, more precisely in the second decade, the years during which the *Lives of Christ and the Virgin* (1511) in Aix-en-Provence, the *Legend of Herkinbald* (1513) in Brussels, and the *Legend of Notre-Dame du Sablon* (1516–18), now dispersed among museums in Brussels and elsewhere, were woven.[5] The Metropolitan Museum's two fragments show a fully developed painterly style like that which we believe reached its ultimate perfection in the finest tapestries produced in the years around 1500 in Brussels or through the agency of Brussels producers. However we cannot be certain that hangings of comparable style and quality were not being woven at the same time in other parts of the southern Netherlands. While the execution of both 42a and 42b displays considerable refinement, there is a quality in the drawing and spatial composition that is rather awkward but nevertheless positive. At present we have no way of knowing where, or through whose agency, tapestries having this particular quality were produced.

RELATED TAPESTRIES

The two fragments in the Burrell Collection in Glasgow (figs. 159, 160) virtually duplicate 42a and b. The faces differ somewhat and the figures are placed slightly higher or lower in the field. The existence of two almost identical pairs of fragments of this kind is an extraordinary circumstance. It is difficult to understand how and why on two presumably separate occasions these partic-

520

ular fragments either survived by chance the rest of the hangings of which they were part or were chosen as parts to remove from the mother tapestries. The fact that the details are not identical in the two pairs of fragments suggests that one pair is not a copy of the other.

It was noted above (Condition) that both 42a and 42b must have occupied positions along the top edge of the hanging or hangings from which they were taken and furthermore that 42b must have come from the upper right corner of a tapestry. We have not identified any complete hangings that include these particular groups of figures in their compositions.

HISTORY

In the collection of George and Florence Blumenthal, New York. Bequeathed to the MMA by George Blumenthal, 1941.

EXHIBITIONS

None known.

PUBLICATIONS

Rubinstein-Bloch, Stella. *Catalogue of the Collection of George and Florence Blumenthal, New-York.* Vol. 4, *Tapestries and Furniture.* Paris, 1927, pl. v. Both pieces described in detail; illus.

Collection de Madame et Monsieur Arnold Seligmann, sale cat., Galerie Jean Charpentier, Paris, June 4–5, 1935, p. 233. Both pieces mentioned.

NOTES

1. William Wells, manuscript catalogue of tapestries in the Burrell Collection, Glasgow, nos. 166 and 167; consulted through the courtesy of Richard Marks, then director of the Burrell Collection.
2. Comment by Betty Kurth, recorded among other notes on the two Burrell pieces in the files at the Burrell Collection, Glasgow; consulted through the courtesy of Richard Marks.
3. A group of figures remarkably like those represented in both 42a and 42b appears in the upper left corner of a tapestry that was formerly in the de Somzée collection and that Göbel published as having a mythological subject and as Brussels work of about 1530; see Göbel 1923, vol. 2, fig. 373. Among those figures is a young lady kneeling before an enthroned king who extends his right hand to her. A second group of figures, drawn on the same scale, about one-third the height of the pictorial field, appears in the upper right corner of the piece. Another hanging with an unidentified court subject shows a group of figures reminiscent of 42a in the upper central section of the field; see Dario Boccara, *Les belles heures de la tapisserie* (Zug, 1971) p. 42, illus. A group of figures that includes a seated queen holding a scepter and surrounded by attendants, all against a ground of patterned silk and a landscape, appears in the upper left corner of a tapestry in the Victoria and Albert Museum, London, that may illustrate scenes from the story of Aeneas. This group of figures is similar to 42a. See Digby 1980, no. 34, pl. 54. A number of scenes containing small figures of this kind appear along the top of the *Christ the Judge on the Throne of Majesty* tapestry at The Cloisters, MMA (see 27).
4. See *The Burrell Collection: Gothic Tapestries, a Selection*, exh. cat., McClellan Galleries, Glasgow Art Gallery (Glasgow, 1969) p. 30, both illus. Dimensions given as 22 inches high by 26½ inches wide (.56 m × .67 m) for both pieces.
5. For illustrations of these tapestries, see figs. 69–71 in the present catalogue. For pertinent texts, additional illustrations, and bibliographies, see respectively *Les tapisseries de la Vie du Christ et de la Vierge d'Aix-en-Provence*, exh. cat., Musée des Tapisseries (Aix-en-Provence, 1977), and *Tapisseries bruxelloises de la pré-Renaissance*, exh. cat., Musées Royaux d'Art et d'Histoire (Brussels, 1976) nos. 19–23.

43

43
Lady and Gentleman in Front of Two Curtains

A fragment

Southern Netherlands, 1510–25
Wool warp; wool and silk wefts
27 in. × 26¹/₄ in. (.69 m × .67 m)
16–18 warp yarns per inch, 6–7 per centimeter
Bequest of George Blumenthal, 1941 (41.190.94)

CONDITION

The entire lower left corner of the fragment, including the fabric representing the jeweled form at the far left and the puff of drapery in front of the man's right shoulder, is a restoration using modern warp and weft yarns. The fabric representing the mantle that passes over the woman's left shoulder is also an insertion of modern weaving. The rest of the fabric has been heavily rewoven with modern weft yarns on the original warp. These repairs affect more than half of the fragment's surface. The restorations have distorted the original drawing most seriously in the regions of the faces and the headdresses. Where the original colors have survived, especially in the background drapery, they are clear and bright.

DESCRIPTION AND SUBJECT

In the center of the space the bust of a gentleman, wearing a coat of plain fabric lined with patterned damask or velvet over his doublet and embroidered shirt, appears in front of two curtains, one flat and one draped, and below a row of tassels. His thick, curling hair tumbles down from under his round, wide-brimmed hat and falls on both shoulders. He glances toward the right at a lady who stands or sits facing him. Only her head, seen in profile, and her left shoulder are visible. She wears an embroidered shirt under a low, square-necked bodice and, on her head, a patterned cap that features a padded roll of fabric set near the front.

As noted above, the passages representing the lady's left shoulder and the unexplained forms in front of the man's right shoulder were not in the original composition. However the curtain in the background, the draped curtain in the upper left corner of the field, and the tassels hanging from an unseen valance or canopy extending above both figures are part of the original de-

sign. These textile furnishings belong to a tent, a dais with a canopy, or a bed. Although Rubinstein-Bloch (1927) made no attempt to identify the subject when she published this piece, she noted that the man's hair resembles Solomon's hair in a tapestry preserved in the Museo Poldi Pezzoli in Milan.[1] In that tapestry Solomon, who wears a round, plumed, wide-brimmed hat, is seated under a canopy and looks down at the Queen of Sheba kneeling before him. Since we can imagine that the composition from which the Metropolitan Museum's fragment comes could have resembled this one in a general way, it seems possible that the figures in 43 may have been meant to represent Solomon and Sheba. However the young man in 43 also resembles the dandified youths who appear as the Prodigal Son in other tapestries of this period.[2] The man is also related to certain figures found in contemporary tapestries that may represent the story of Ahasuerus.[3] His presence next to what might be a bed suggests that he may represent the young Joseph. The fragment could have been taken from a tapestry that illustrated any one of a number of stories drawn from the Old Testament, classical mythology, ancient history, or the literature of allegory. None of the details in the Metropolitan Museum's fragment is particular enough to serve as a clue that would lead us to an identification of its subject.

SOURCE OF THE DESIGN

The figures and setting belong to a generic group of images that appear frequently in tapestries of this style and period. Like most of those pieces, this one was woven after cartoons designed by some anonymous painter who worked for one or more tapestry producers. He may have borrowed the two figures from an existing composition, but no prototype has been identified.

523

Manufacture and Date

Rubinstein-Bloch (1927) published the fragment as Flemish work of the first half of the sixteenth century. We believe that it could have been woven anywhere in the southern Netherlands. There is nothing beyond its painterly style to associate it with tapestries produced in or through Brussels. The garments, restored though they are, reflect the fashions of the second and third decades of the sixteenth century.

Related Tapestries

No duplicate pieces nor any hangings that can be associated with this fragment in a particular set of tapestries are known to have survived.

HISTORY

In the collection of George and Florence Blumenthal, New York. Bequeathed to the MMA by George Blumenthal, 1941.

EXHIBITIONS

None known.

PUBLICATION

Rubinstein-Bloch, Stella. *Catalogue of the Collection of George and Florence Blumenthal, New-York.* Vol. 4, *Tapestries and Furniture.* Paris, 1927, page between pls. xvii and xviii. Described in detail; not illus.

NOTES

1. See Hunter 1912, pl. 29, the reference Rubinstein-Bloch used.
2. For a discussion of Prodigal Son tapestries of this type, see 41a, b, especially 41b in which there is a rather similar male figure seated under a canopy that has a back cloth of patterned silk and a tasseled valance hung along its front edge. He is surrounded by women catering to him. Other dandified Prodigal Sons appear, among many other places, in a tapestry in the J. B. Speed Art Museum in Louisville and in another in the Minneapolis Institute of Arts. See respectively Philippe Verdier, "The Tapestry of the Prodigal Son," *Journal of the Walters Art Gallery* 18 (1955) fig. 3, and "Late Gothic Tapestry Acquired for Institute," *Bulletin of the Minneapolis Institute of Arts* 27 (1938) pp. 26–30 and cover, details illus.; for a full view of the latter, see *Collection of Genevieve Garvan Brady [Mrs. William J. Babington Macaulay]*, sale cat., American Art Association, Anderson Galleries, New York, May 10–15, 1937, no. 2032.
3. See for example two tapestries in the cathedral in Vigevano that are believed to show scenes from the story of Esther and Ahasuerus, with Ahasuerus (?) standing or seated under a canopy with a tasseled valance in front, illustrated in Mercedes Viale, "Arazzi fiamminghi nel Duomo di Vigevano," *Bollettino della Società Piemontese di Archeologia e di Belle Arti*, n.s. 4–5 (1950–51) pp. 152, 153, figs. 8, 9.

44
Scenes from the Passion of Christ

Probably from a series illustrating this subject

Southern Netherlands, 1510–30
Wool warp; wool, silk, and metallic wefts
6 ft. 9 in. × 9 ft. 1 in. (2.06 m × 2.77 m)
18–20 warp yarns per inch, 7–8 per centimeter
The Bequest of Michael Dreicer, 1921 (22.60.34)

CONDITION

The hanging has been cut along both sides and the bottom. There is a selvage along the upper edge which represents either the top of the hanging as it was originally woven or only the outer edge of the second in a series of guards. A recent examination has revealed that there is a narrow strip of black wefting along the outer edges of the half-columns that finish the field at right and left. This strip could be either the loom finish that marks the beginning and end of the weaving or part of a guard or border. Its presence indicates that the field was never any wider than it is now and that it did not form the central section of a wider hanging, as Forsyth suggested (exh. cat. Los Angeles and Chicago 1970, no. 115). The cut along the bottom of the field has removed a strip of fabric that showed the bases of the plinths supporting the columns at the sides and part of the flowering meadow in the extreme foreground. However, to judge from the appearance of what remains, it seems likely that relatively little of the field is missing at the bottom.

There is a good deal of repair by reweaving new weft yarns on the original warp throughout the piece. Most of it occurs along the contours of the figures, but there are more significant restorations of this kind in the right third of the field. The back of the man riding the dappled horse in the right foreground has been partly rewoven, as have also the back of the man riding the white horse next to him, the entrance to the cave behind the group representing the Entombment, and the grass on the lower part of the hill where the Lamentation is represented in the far distance at the right. None of this restoration has affected the original drawing to any significant degree. However the changes and restorations that were made in two other places are important because they have destroyed the historical clues these passages originally provided. The two tablets hanging on the upper parts of the columns at the sides originally bore inscriptions. A photograph published in von Bode's catalogue of the Hainauer collection (1897) shows that the tablet at the right originally was inscribed with a series of capital letters that may have been AVRC. The tablet at the left also showed an inscription which was already so indistinct that it cannot be transcribed. Since the yarns in the fields of both tablets were replaced at some time after 1897 with pale yellow silk wefts, both sets of letters are now completely missing. If the two armorial shields in the upper corners of the field were original, they could help date the tapestry, but they appear to be later additions, which furthermore have been much restored. The design of the cartouches surrounding them suggests a date in the middle or third quarter of the sixteenth century, so we conclude that, although the wefts representing them are woven on the original warp, both shields were added to the fabric about thirty to sixty years after the tapestry was woven. Significant parts of both shields were rewoven at least once, and we cannot be sure that the restorer's work reproduces the original blazons accurately.

DESCRIPTION AND SUBJECT

The scene appears beyond a proscenium formed by the two half-columns at the sides and the flattened arch they carry. The columns comprise rectangular plinths of stone that rise from gold bases and support polychrome marble balusters. The component parts are trimmed with gold scrolls and leaves. The front surface of the arch is made of polychrome marble. Its lower edge is trimmed with paired gold leaves at the sides and in the center. Stone pistils wrapped with narrow gold bands grow from the ends of both sets of leaves toward each other; their tips, terminating in gold collars and leaves, abut the ends of motifs that resemble tightly packed bunches of grapes.

A hill rises in the middle distance at the center of the space. The Crucifixion appears in front of it. Christ, nude but for a loincloth and the crown of thorns on His head, is stretched out on a tau cross in the center, eyes closed, head dropping toward His right shoulder. Blood pours from the wounds in His hands, feet, and right side.

44

Directly below His right arm the blind centurion astride a white horse, having pierced Jesus' right side, lowers his lance. Above this, an angel flying beneath Christ's right arm collects in two chalices the blood from the hand and chest wounds. Another angel, flying under the left arm, raises a chalice to collect the blood flowing from that hand, and a third angel holds a chalice beneath the feet. A small plaque labeled INRI appears on the cross above His head. The moon appears in the sky to the right of it and a six-pointed black star covers the sun opposite. Under Christ's right arm the repentant thief, his arms tied back over the bar of the cross and his ankles bound to its shaft, his arms and legs cut and bleeding, smiles up at the Savior as an angel above his head carries his soul, represented as a nude child, upward. Opposite him the unrepentant thief, tied to his cross and maimed in the same way, drops his head, eyes closed, as a demon above his head casts his soul downward. This upper portion of the sky is filled with turbulent, boiling cloud banks, light colored on the left, dark and threatening on the right.

In the middle distance at the left there rises a rocky promontory whose summit juts precipitously out over open space. Steps have been cut into it, leading up to a castle or small town at the top. Tall trees surround the structure and smaller ones or shrubs grow at both sides lower down. A city with spires, towers, and walls rests in the hollow between this rise and the one in the center of the field. A lower promontory, also fitted with steps and buildings at its summit, appears in the distance on the other side of the central hill. In front of it, at the right end of the field, another hill rises to the height of the first promontory. The three crosses appear at its summit, a ladder propped against the central one. At the foot of the ladder stands a bearded man wearing a tunic over a long gown; his hands are raised in an attitude of prayer. He probably represents Joseph of Arimathea, who asked Pilate to let him have Christ's body. At the foot of the cross the body of the dead Jesus is laid out on His mother's lap. John supports His head, another man His left hand. A third man, wearing a hood pushed back on his shoulders and a long gown over a doublet, kneels at His feet.

The rest of the figures form a mass of characters that stretches unbroken from the left column to the right across the foreground of the tapestry. There are three scenes of great importance among this crowded display, but most of the figures are essentially supernumeraries—horsemen, soldiers, priests, scribes, and miscellaneous citizens who came to watch the execution and to revile and blaspheme Christ. They wear brightly colored, richly decorated, fashionable garments. The men's clothes are elaborately patterned and slashed, the women's more simply cut but also richly patterned. The scene in the lower left corner of the field shows Christ wearing a simple tunic and the crown of thorns, walking toward the right carrying His cross. A train of dignitaries and soldiers follows. One of His tormentors kicks Him. Just to the right of this, in the foreground, the Virgin swoons in the arms of three women and John. Next to this group, in front of the foot of the cross, two bearded men, using a dagger and a bone as weapons, fight over Christ's tunic while two other men try to restrain them. Farther on toward the right, in the lower right corner of the field, Joseph of Arimathea and Nicodemus lower the Savior's body on its shroud into a sarcophagus while the Virgin and John pray and the other women, who had come with them from Galilee, watch from behind. In the immediate foreground there is a grassy meadow filled with flowering plants of many varieties, some or all of which may have been depicted because of their symbolic connotations. For example the tall iris that grows in the right foreground could represent Christ or the Virgin, and it is also one of the plants that bloom in the Garden of Paradise. The carnation plant that rises in the lower left corner may have been shown here because its fragrance is reminiscent of cloves, the nail-shaped spice that was associated with the nails used at the Crucifixion.[1]

Silk yarns were used to render highlights throughout the field. Metallic yarns, both gilt and silver, appear not only in the highlights but also in the patterns of certain garments and a few special motifs like Christ's gold cruciform halo and the horse's trappings. The gold-colored yarns are made of narrow, flat gilt wire wrapped spirally around a core of yellowish orange silk; the silver yarns are made in the same way but with silver wire and core yarns of pale yellow silk. The metallic yarns have retained a good deal of their original brilliance, and the colors of the wool and silk yarns are clear and intense.

The tapestry has no border but probably had one originally. The tapestry of the *Siege of Dijon* (fig. 161), which shows virtually the same kind of proscenium enframement and closely related figure and facial types, has a border.

A fairly conventional account of the climactic events of Christ's Passion, as they were described in the Gospels and represented in the late Middle Ages, is shown in 44. The carrying of the cross to Golgotha, the crucifixion between two thieves one of whom asks Jesus to remember him when He comes into His kingdom, the people coming to revile Him, the sky darkening between the sixth and ninth hours, the soldier piercing His side with a lance, the entombment in a stone sepulcher in the rock in a garden nearby may all be found in the writings of the four Evangelists and in other representations of the subject at this period (see Source of the Design). The subject of the Lamentation comes not from the Gospels but from later writings like the *Meditations* formerly attributed to Saint Bonaventure and the *Revelations* of Saint Bridget (see 17 in the present catalogue). As for the men fighting at the foot of the cross, they represent the soldiers who shared Christ's clothes after they had crucified Him. According to Matthew (27:35), Mark (15:24), and Luke (23:24), the soldiers cast lots for the garments. However John (19:23–24) specified that four soldiers shared the clothes and then cast lots for the seamless tunic because they did not want to tear it apart. Here the four men are fighting over the tunic, presumably after having gambled for it. Two of them try to separate the two others who are locked in combat directly below Christ's cross; one wields a dagger, the other an arm or leg bone. These two men, together with the one restraining them at the left, appear again, only slightly changed, in a late fifteenth-century *Crucifixion* tapestry in Angers; and in another *Crucifixion* of yet a generation earlier, now in Brussels, only two men are fighting over the tunic and they both wield daggers.[2] Since it was believed that Adam had been buried on Golgotha and that his bones were thrown up at the foot of the cross when tombs opened at the moment Christ died, it seems possible that this contest may have been intended to represent not only the soldiers' dispute but also the deadly fight between Cain and Abel.

Some other details are enigmatic. While the city in the saddle of the hills at the left clearly represents Jerusalem, we are at a loss to explain the rocky promontories with their stepped approaches and castled summits. They may be just decorative fantasies. The man who kneels at Christ's feet in the Lamentation on a promontory at the upper right cannot be a monk, as Forsyth suggested (exh. cat. Los Angeles and Chicago 1970), since he is wearing a red hood, brown gown, and blue doublet. He may perhaps represent Nicodemus, who came to help Joseph of Arimathea entomb the dead Christ (John 19:38–42). The dead tree that appears in the distance between Christ's cross and the unrepentant thief's cross may be intended as a comparison between that thief and the barren fig tree that Christ had cursed (Mark 11:13–14), as Forsyth suggested (exh. cat. Los Angeles and Chicago 1970), but since this tree, unlike the fig tree, has no leaves, it may be simply a symbol of death.

The blazons on the two shields were identified in the 1970 exhibition catalogue as the arms of the Brunavillani of Treviso quartering those of the Alvarotti of Rovigo below a chief charged with a cross. This interpretation was based on a blazon written by an unidentified heraldist around the time the tapestry came to the Metropolitan Museum. His notes also claimed that the chief showed the arms of the Knights of the Order of the Hospital of Saint John of Jerusalem, later known as the Knights of the Order of Malta.[3] As noted above (Condition), the two shields, which were added later to the original tapestry, were subsequently partly restored at least once. Therefore we cannot be sure that the blazons appear now as they did when they were first woven. As we see them, the shields display the following blazons: quarterly 1 and 4 azure a fleur-de-lis gules (pink), 2 and 3 per fess gules (pink) and or, three spurs, rowel down (brown, originally possibly sable), two on or one on gules (pink), a chief gules (pink) a cross or. These do not correspond to the blazons that Rietstap gives for the families cited above. For Brunavillani of Treviso he gives "d'azur à une fleur-de-lis d'arg[ent]" (a silver, rather than red, lily on a blue field in quarters 1 and 4), and for Alvarotti of Rovigo, "coupé d'or sur gules, à la fasce d'argent, brochant sur le coupé, accompagnée de trois éperons de sable, liés du même, la molette en bas, 2 sur l'or et 1 sur gules; au chef d'argent, charge d'une croix de gules" (the same as in quarters 2 and 3 in the tapestry, except that the tapestry shows no silver fess on the gold and red ones and its chief shows a gold cross on a red field rather than this red cross on a silver field).[4] The shield of the Order of the Knights of Malta is blazoned gules a cross argent, whereas the chief in the tapestry is gules a cross or. Since some or all of the original tinctures may have been changed in the restoration, it is fruitless to argue the

matter further. The shields may originally have shown the arms of Brunavillani of Treviso quartering those of Alvarotti of Rovigo but it is by no means certain, and the chief as it appears now corresponds neither to the shield of the Knights of the Order of Malta nor to the chief of the Alvarotti shield.

SOURCE OF THE DESIGN

Ackerman (1924–25, 193) attributed the design of 44 to Jean, son of the Tournai tapestry designer Pierre Ferret. Her argument, based on a circuitous round of associations with a number of other tapestries including an *Annunciation* formerly in the collection of Martin A. Ryerson and now in the Art Institute of Chicago and another formerly in the von Dirksen collection in Berlin, derives from her conviction that Pierre designed the latter. We do not see any stylistic connections among these tapestries nor do we agree that there are grounds for attributing the design of 44 to any member of the Ferret family. However we believe that a number of stylistic analogies relate 44 to certain other tapestries of the early sixteenth century. Chief among these is the single hanging of the *Siege of Dijon* in the Musée des Beaux-Arts in Dijon (fig. 161), in which one finds the same kind of proscenium enframement, similar costumes and figure and facial types, and virtually the same mannerisms in the drawing of clouds. Presumably the tapestry in Dijon was designed shortly after the event in 1513 (we have no documentation whatever concerning the commissioning or making of this piece), and presumably the Metropolitan Museum's hanging was designed about the same time (see Manufacture and Date). These two tapestries also show stylistic similarities to the three pieces surviving from the set of fourteen hangings of the *Life of Saint Anatoile*, which are documented as having been woven in Bruges between 1502 and 1506, and particularly to the piece showing the *Siege of Dole in 1477* (fig. 162).[5] Those tapestries show a similar kind of enframement and related figure and facial types. The *Siege of Dole* also contains a similar rocky promontory with a castle or town perched precariously on the overhanging summit. Therefore it is reasonable to ask whether all these tapestries could have been designed by the same artist or in the same shop. It seems not to have been the same artist, for the drawing in 44 shows some mannerisms—the humorous faces and contorted postures of the repentant thief and some of the figures around the base of the cross—that do not appear in the *Dijon* and *Saint Anatoile* tapestries.

The Metropolitan Museum's tapestry also recalls two hangings in the Musée de Cluny, the *Departure of the*

Fig. 161. *The Siege of Dijon in 1513.* Tapestry, southern Netherlands, here dated probably about 1515–20. Musée des Beaux-Arts, Dijon.

Fig. 162. *The Siege of Dole in 1477,* from the set of the *Life of Saint Anatoile.* Tapestry, Bruges, 1502–6. Musée du Louvre, Paris, on deposit from the Mobilier National.

Fig. 163. *The Departure of the Prodigal Son.* Tapestry, attributed to Tournai (?), about 1520. Musée de Cluny, Paris.

Prodigal Son (fig. 163) and the *Arithmetic* (fig. 164), the latter from the series of the *Seven Liberal Arts.*[6] Both show similar architectural enframements and some similar figure and facial types. In considering these two hangings, Joubert concluded that they, like a number of similar ones, were confected in some shop that specialized in rapidly and cheaply produced tapestries.[7] Since the column at the right side of the *Arithmetic* is virtually a duplicate of the two in the *Scenes from the Passion,* and since similar grape motifs appear in the garland that undulates across the top of the field, it is clear that the designer of the Metropolitan Museum's tapestry had access to the pattern for these motifs, if not direct access then access to a common source. Furthermore one of the figures in the *Arithmetic,* the man standing behind the figure seated next to the lady, has the curious pinched face with a long, scooped, and pointed nose that appears several times in the *Scenes from the Passion.*

The Metropolitan Museum's piece is not, however, a pastiche of disparate parts. While the designer undoubtedly used some stock or otherwise preexisting details, he created a complex and sophisticated arrangement of figures interacting meaningfully with each other. The design was probably made to order, as we know the *Life of Saint Anatoile* was and we may assume the *Siege of Dijon* also was. In creating his pattern the designer of 44 did not hesitate to call on what had by then become a traditional composition in the art of tapestry for the Crucifixion and related scenes. We can trace it back at least to the sixth or seventh decade of the fifteenth century, when the *Scenes from the Passion* in Brussels was woven, and then through the later years of that century and the beginning of the next.[8]

We cannot identify the artist. Duverger suggested that the designers of both the *Saint Anatoile* and *Dijon* tapestries were French, and we believe that the same may be said for the designer of this piece.[9] It is tempting to try to find his name in the letters AVRC that were originally inscribed on the tablet hanging on the right-hand column. Such a signature, that of a cartoon painter surnamed Knoest, does in fact appear on an architectural element, the riser of a step, in a roughly contemporary tapestry now in Brussels.[10] Specialists have attempted to see a designer's name in the letters *d*AVI·F· inscribed on the corresponding tablet hanging on the column in the *Arithmetic* in Paris. Joubert did not indicate whether or not the inscription is original, but she noted that Wauters had interpreted the letters as the signature of the Bruges painter Gerard David; that Souchal was ambivalent about this identification; that Pinchart saw it as the signature of the weaver rather than the designer; and that Steppe rejected the David idea entirely and suggested instead that the designer would have been French.[11]

MANUFACTURE AND DATE

Von Bode (1897) attributed the tapestry to the Netherlands and dated it in the first half of the fifteenth century. When it was exhibited at the Metropolitan Museum in 1920, it was called Franco-Flemish and dated late in the same century. Two years later, when it was acquired, Breck (1922, 106) assigned it to Flanders, probably Brussels, about 1500. Because Ackerman (1924–25, 191–92) thought it came from the shop that wove the Ryerson *Annunciation,* she published it as an Audenarde weaving from the looms of a weaver she identified as Joas Huet. Van Ysselsteyn (1969, 185) was convinced the design was German and included it among a number of tapestries she attributed to the workshop in Rötteln in the Rhineland. Forsyth (exh. cat.

Fig. 164. *Arithmetic.* Tapestry, Tournai (?), about 1520. Musée de Cluny, Paris.

Los Angeles and Chicago 1970) attributed it to Brussels and dated it about 1510–30 because of its similarity to the *Siege of Dijon,* which we assume was produced not long after 1513.

As noted above, we find the design closely related to a number of contemporary pieces that have been attributed in recent literature either to Tournai or Bruges. Joubert suggested that both the *Prodigal Son* and the *Arithmetic* in Paris were woven in Tournai.[12] The *Life of Saint Anatoile* is documented as having been woven in Bruges. Duverger believed that the *Siege of Dijon* might have been woven in Bruges both because it shows certain similarities to the *Siege of Dole* in the *Saint Anatoile* series and because its border shows a pattern related to those associated with tapestries known to have been woven in Bruges or attributed to that city.[13] Soil listed the *Siege of Dijon* among the tapestries he regarded as Tournai work but also thought it possible that it had been woven in Bruges. His tentative attribution to Tournai seems to have been based on Wauters's idea that the letter G in the motif displayed on the shields arranged along the top and bottom of the tapestry indicates that it had been woven in a shop run by some member of the Grenier family although, as Soil then noted, Pinchart did not think that so prominently placed a shield would contain the mark of either a weaver or a shop.[14] A similar motif, also prominently placed, appears twice on a tapestry in the Museum O.L.V. ter Potterie in Bruges that shows the Virgin and Child seated between the two Saints John. Duverger noted that this motif has been interpreted variously as the mark of some Bruges tapestry merchant, of a donor who did not have a coat of arms, or of the hospital of the church of the Potterie, but he did not carry the inquiry further.[15] Delmarcel discussed and illustrated a number of such motifs that appear in certain seventeenth-century tapestries and proved that they are in fact weaving-shop marks masquerading as merchants' monograms.[16] It may be significant that the two hangings we know of that show these motifs so prominently, the *Siege of Dijon* and the *Virgin with Saints John,* have been attributed to Bruges with good reason. The visual elements that the tapestry in Dijon and 44 share—the proscenium, the figure and facial types, the cloud formations, and the tightly controlled organization of masses of figures—are only indications that the two tapestries may have been designed in the same shop or that their designers depended on the same sources. The similarities do not indicate that all three tapestries were woven in the same place, whether in Bruges or any other tapestry-weaving center that was active in the southern Netherlands in the first part of the sixteenth century.

In considering the date of production we have not only the evidence of the costumes, which show the fashions of the second and third decades of the sixteenth century, but also the visual similarities that relate this piece to the *Siege of Dijon* and to the *Departure of the Prodigal Son* and the *Arithmetic* in Paris. Presumably the *Dijon* tapestry was produced not long after the siege took place in 1513. The *Arithmetic* has been dated in the early years of the sixteenth century because the date 1520 is written twice on the right-hand page of the book being consulted on the table, and a corresponding date has been assigned to the *Prodigal Son* piece because of its similarity to that tapestry and to a *Story of Judith* in Brussels.[17] In the light of these considerations it seems correct to suggest that the *Scenes from the Passion of Christ* could have been designed as early as 1510 and woven no later than 1530, when the costumes would have looked outmoded. As noted above, Forsyth had suggested the same range of dates in 1970 (exh. cat. Los Angeles and Chicago).

RELATED TAPESTRIES

There are no duplicate hangings that we know of nor any that can be associated with this piece in a tapestry cycle. Since the Crucifixion is not shown alone but accompanied by the Way to Calvary, the Lamentation, and the Entombment, it is likely that this was not woven to stand on its own as a devotional hanging but that it was part of a *Passion* series. Four pieces from such a cycle are preserved in the Musée des Tapisseries in Angers. They date from about the end of the fifteenth century.[18] The four hangings show Christ before Pilate and Herod, the Way to Calvary, the Crucifixion, the Harrowing of Hell, the Entombment, the Resurrection, and Christ Appearing to the Virgin, Mary Magdalen, and Saint Peter. Originally there were more tapestries, and consequently more subjects, in this set. Five of the additional subjects are shown in a series of embroidered hangings that were based on the Angers tapestries or their cartoons and are now in the church of Saint-Barnard in Romans, Drôme.[19] Those are the Agony in the Garden, the Kiss of Judas, Christ before Caiaphas, Christ and Barabbas, and Pilate Washing His Hands. Most or all of these subjects might have been represented in the set of hangings to which the Metropolitan Museum's tapestry belonged.

HISTORY

In the collection of Oscar Hainauer, Berlin, until 1906.
Property of Duveen Brothers.
In the collection of Michael Dreicer by 1920.
Bequeathed to the MMA by Michael Dreicer, 1921.

EXHIBITIONS

New York, MMA, 1920. *Fiftieth Anniversary Exhibition.* Cat. p. 13. Lent by Michael Dreicer.
Los Angeles County Museum of Art, and the Art Institute of Chicago, 1970. *The Middle Ages: Treasures from The Cloisters and The Metropolitan Museum of Art.* Catalogue entry by William H. Forsyth, no. 115, illus.
Moscow, Pushkin State Museum of Fine Arts, and Leningrad, The Hermitage, 1990. *Decorative Arts from Late Antiquity to Late Gothic* (from The Metropolitan Museum of Art and The Art Institute of Chicago) (in Russian). Cat. no. 80; illus. in color.

PUBLICATIONS

von Bode, Wilhelm. *Die Sammlung Oscar Hainauer.* Berlin, 1897; English imprint, London, 1906, no. 450. Described briefly; illus.
"List of Loans: Fiftieth Anniversary Exhibition." *MMA Bulletin* 15 (1920) p. 118. Mentioned.
J. B. [Joseph Breck]. "The Michael Dreicer Collection, Part II: Decorative Arts and Sculpture." *MMA Bulletin* 17 (1922) p. 106. Described briefly; illus. p. 107.
Ackerman, Phyllis. "Joas . . . of Audenarde." *Art in America* 13 (1924–25) pp. 188, 191–93. Discussed briefly; illus. p. 189.
van Ysselsteyn, G. T. *Tapestry: The Most Expensive Industry of the XVth and XVIth Centuries.* The Hague and Brussels, 1969, p. 185. Discussed briefly; illus. pl. 207. Confused with a different *Passion* series in Paris that is said to bear the arms of Pietro Soderini.

NOTES

1. See Margaret Freeman, *The Unicorn Tapestries*, MMA (New York, 1976) pp. 141, 148.
2. For the hanging in the Musée des Tapisseries in Angers and a fragment in the Rijksmuseum, Amsterdam, that shows part of the same scene, see J. P. Asselberghs, *La tapisserie tournaisienne au XVe siècle*, exh. cat. (Tournai, 1967) nos. 25, 27, illus. For the tapestry in Brussels, see Marthe Crick-Kuntziger, *Catalogue des tapisseries (XIVe au XVIIIe siècle)*, Musées Royaux d'Art et d'Histoire (Brussels, 1956) no. 4, pl. 6.
3. Two sheets of pencil notes preserved in the files of the Department of Medieval Art, MMA.
4. See J. B. Rietstap, *Armorial Général* (Gouda, 1884–87; reprint, Baltimore, 1972) vol. 1, pp. 318 and 39.
5. See Erik Duverger's discussion of the *Saint Anatoile* tapestries and their history together with the piece in Dijon, in *Bruges et la tapisserie*, exh. cat. by Guy Delmarcel and Erik Duverger, Musée Gruuthuse and Musée Memling (Bruges, 1987) pp. 170–79, all illus.
6. See Joubert 1987, pp. 155–61 and 162–67, both illus.
7. Joubert 1987, p. 167.
8. See Crick-Kuntziger, *Catalogue des tapisseries*, no. 4. The procession at the left, the group with the swooning Mary, the men fighting over the garment, the figures gathered under the crosses, and the three crucified figures are all essentially the same in both tapestries. In the Brussels tapestry, the Resurrection occupies the place where the Entombment appears in 44. At the end of the fifteenth century the formula appears again in one of the tapestries of the *Scenes from the Passion* series in the Musée des Tapisseries in Angers; see Asselberghs, *La tapisserie tournaisienne au XVe siècle*, no. 25, illus. A bit later, sometime between the time the Angers tapestries and 44 were woven, it appears again in a tapestry altar hanging preserved in the Kulturhistorisches Museum in Prenzlau; see Göbel 1928, vol. 2, fig. 328.

9. Duverger, *Bruges et la tapisserie*, p. 177.
10. See Crick-Kuntziger, *Catalogue des tapisseries*, no. 13, pl. 17.
11. Joubert 1987, p. 167, and references given there.
12. Joubert 1987, p. 167. This author also noted that an inverted letter B in the garland along the top of the *Arithmetic* had led a number of writers to consider Bruges or Brussels as the place of manufacture.
13. Duverger, *Bruges et la tapisserie*, pp. 177, 179.
14. Eugène Soil, *Les tapisseries de Tournai* (Tournai and Lille, 1892) p. 260. The author reported Wauters's and Pinchart's opinions without indicating his sources.
15. Duverger, *Bruges et la tapisserie*, pp. 220–21.
16. Guy Delmarcel, "Marques et techniques utilisées dans les tapisseries brugeoises," in *Bruges et la tapisserie*, pp. 144–47.
17. Joubert 1987, pp. 167, 161.
18. For illustrations of the hangings in Angers, see Asselberghs, *La tapisserie tournaisienne au XVᵉ siècle*, nos. 23–26, with bibliography. Asselberghs also refers to related pieces in the Rijksmuseum, Amsterdam, the Musée des Arts Décoratifs, Paris (nos. 27, 28, both illus.), and the Museum of Fine Arts, Boston. Another piece is in the Fine Arts Museums of San Francisco; it, like the Boston hanging, shows the subject of Christ before Pilate; see Adolph S. Cavallo, *Tapestries of Europe and of Colonial Peru in the Museum of Fine Arts, Boston* (Boston, 1967) no. 20, illus.; also Anna G. Bennett, *Five Centuries of Tapestry from the Fine Arts Museums of San Francisco* (San Francisco, 1976) no. 6, illus.
19. Concerning the embroidered hangings in Romans, see Ch. Urseau, "La tapisserie de la *Passion* d'Angers et la tenture brodée de Saint-Barnard de Romans," *Bulletin Archéologique du Comité des Travaux Historiques et Scientifiques*, 1917, pp. 54–61, illus.

45
The Resurrection

Southern Netherlands, 1515–25
Wool warp; wool, silk, silver, and gilt wefts
7 ft. 3³/₄ in. × 7 ft. 9¹/₄ in. (2.23 m × 2.37 m)
18–20 warp yarns per inch, 8 per centimeter
The Jules Bache Collection, 1949 (49.7.118)

CONDITION

The fact that the original striped outer guard is present on all four sides of the hanging proves that the piece has lost little if any of its original fabric. The band of striped fabric outside this guard is a modern addition. There are no patches of modern or old fabric anywhere in the field or border, but there are many small restorations by re-weaving on the original warp throughout the tapestry. These occur particularly in areas where the silk yarns had deteriorated and fallen out. However these repairs have altered the original drawing and modeling very little. The colors have faded a good deal, but the red and blue tones are still reasonably intense and varied. The silver and gilt yarns have tarnished and in most places read now as dark gray or black, although glints of gold are still visible here and there throughout the hanging.

DESCRIPTION AND SUBJECT

The scene is set in a landscape that has an outcropping of rock along the center from the foreground to the horizon; there, the rock soars upward to form towering peaks. The rock nearest the observer is the one that was hewn out to make the tomb in which Christ's body was laid. The door to the tomb, a rectangular slab of darker rock set at an angle into the mass, has metal rings fixed to its corners; it seems still to be closed. It has an inscribed border around the left and top edges (the other two edges are not visible in this view). We can identify only two of the letters clearly, an R (reversed) above Christ's right heel and an M to the right of the shaft of His cross. There are traces of unidentifiable letters above the R and to the left and right of the M. The latter may be an I.¹ The resurrected Christ, wearing a loincloth and a cope-like mantle, appears in front of the tomb. His left leg crosses the other as he strides toward the left but turns His torso and head to the front and gazes squarely at the observer. His right arm is bent at the elbow, the hand raised in benediction. His left hand holds the shaft of a processional cross, from the top of

which flutters a pennon showing a white field charged with a red cross. The wounds on His feet, chest, and right hand are clearly visible. A cruciform halo with foliated arms resembling fleurs-de-lis surrounds His head.

The figures of eight soldiers fill the meadow in the foreground. Flowering plants grow here at left and right, and a bird of prey grasps a small creature in its claws. The soldiers wear pieces of plate armor along with their hose and jerkins. Some of them also have tunics or cloaks. Each man wears a helmet or a hat. They are equipped with a variety of weapons—a halberd, a sword, a pike, a war hammer, a bow. (None of the armor or other costume parts resemble body coverings that men wore in battle during the time of the Roman empire. Instead, these costumes were based on military body coverings that had been worn a few generations before the tapestry was designed, changed enough by the designer to make the contemporary observer perceive them as vaguely antique and exotic.) Two of the soldiers are fast asleep: one sits in front and just to the left of Christ's right toe; the other one sits crouched at the far right end of the field, his head resting on his arms. Another soldier, sitting a bit forward and to the left of this one, seems to be on the point of wakening. The other five men open their eyes wide, drop their jaws, and gesticulate in amazement and terror as they behold the resurrected figure.

Two other men are walking into the scene from the left, behind and beyond the group of soldiers. They are dressed like laborers or hunters, and each one carries a pole or baton over his shoulder. They seem to be casual passersby who happen to witness the event that startles the soldiers. Their role in the narrative is not clear. They may be simply supernumeraries brought in to fill up space.

A landscape full of incident opens out beyond Christ's figure. The sky is the sky of earliest dawn, when the rising sun—shown here at the far left edge of the field as a disk reflected in the water and sending dagger-like rays of light upward—begins to illuminate the horizon and the bottoms of the dark clouds above. To the right of the sunburst appear tall buildings perched on a hilltop. In front of this, in the middle distance, there is a garden bounded by a picket fence and a gable-roofed picket gate. A single tree rises at the center of the garden. Next to it stands Christ, dressed in the garments of the Resurrection and with the same halo around His head, holding a spade in His left hand. He bends to address a young woman kneeling before Him. She wears a gown cut with a low, square neckline and wide sleeves, and a bonnet on the back of her head. The cylindrical box, whose cover she is lifting, identifies her as Mary Magdalen. It is her attribute as a saint and, in this context, perhaps a container of the aromatic substances the Holy Women brought to the tomb for the purpose of anointing Christ's body. Opposite this scene, at the right side of the field and farther back in the middle distance, appear the three Holy Women, dressed in gowns, cloaks, and bonnets or turbans. They are walking away from a turreted city—Jerusalem—and toward the tomb.

The border comprises a wide floral band flanked by narrow striped guards. The wide band shows a succession of short floral garlands separated from each other by two different arabesque motifs, all on a dark blue ground. The floral garlands include a variety of plants and blossoms. In some there are rose branches bearing buds and open blossoms; others have grapevines with their leaves and fruit; and some are made up entirely of iris plants. Others of the garlands have pansy plants at one end and a combination of strawberry and violet plants at the other. Small birds perch on the garlands at various points.

The arabesque motifs are essentially architectural ornaments derived from Renaissance versions of classical decorations. One resembles a gadrooned vase with short strings of pearls hanging from its lip, and the other, which resembles an anthemion, consists of curling tendrils and leaves. These two motifs do not alternate at regular intervals or in regular sequence, and in the top and bottom sections of the border they are shown on their sides rather than upright. Such disorder is not commonly found in border designs of this period and type but it is not unknown.[2] In this case, the irregularities were probably caused by what we believe was the method of production. In the side borders short slits appear in the fabric just above and below each vase or anthemion motif. This indicates that the weaving was interrupted every time one of the arabesque motifs was executed, probably to allow the weavers to introduce into the main pattern of garlands these small accent patterns that could be moved about at will. The use of such subsidiary patterns also explains why the vases and anthemions appear on their sides in the top and bottom sections of the border. Since these two motifs are taller than the border is wide, the weavers would have had to repaint the arabesque patterns on a smaller scale in order to weave them upright in the top and bottom border sections where their height was critical (as it was not in the side sections). One can easily imagine that, rather than assuming such trouble and expense, the weavers, who in any case were not fully familiar with these new-style ornaments, did not hesitate to turn the patterns on their sides.

The silver and gilt weft yarns were used primarily to render the highlights on the garments and weapons, but they also appear in the border flowers. The silk yarns were used lavishly throughout all parts of the field and the border.

The form given in this hanging to the main subject, the Resurrection of Christ, corresponds to one used frequently in Western art from about the eleventh century onward. Before then it was customary to allude indirectly to the event by representing an empty cross, by showing the risen Christ about to ascend into heaven, or by showing the Holy Women at the tomb, usually in the presence of one or two angels. By the eleventh century the Resurrection itself was illustrated: Christ was shown emerging from His tomb. The sepulcher was often represented as a rectangular stone sarcophagus, the cover slid aside in some images, still in place in others. In most of these compositions one or two Holy Women and two or more soldiers are present. The image in the Metropolitan Museum's tapestry reflects a later concept involving a representation of the risen Christ at a distance from the tomb, often seeming to float above it, as though this were the moment immediately preceding the Ascension.[3] Because the designer of 45 did not represent cast shadows, it is not clear whether he intended the Savior to appear to be standing on the rock from which the tomb had been cut or hovering somewhat above it. As usual in compositions of this kind, Christ is shown wearing a red—strictly, "purple"—cloak, which identifies Him as the risen Christ, and carrying the cross with its standard showing the red cross on a field of white, the symbol of His triumph over death.

Although the details vary, Matthew (27:60, 28:1–9), Mark (15:46, 16:1–8), Luke (23:53, 24:1–9), and John (19:42, 20:1–13) describe the entombment and allude to the Resurrection in essentially the same terms. Matthew, Mark, and Luke specify that the tomb was cut from the rock, and the first two say that a large stone was rolled across the entrance. Mark, Luke, and John say that the stone had been rolled or moved away from the tomb

Fig. 165. *The Resurrection.* Tapestry, southern Netherlands, about 1520–25. Victoria and Albert Museum, London.

before the Marys arrived, but according to Matthew, the women were at the grave when they saw an angel roll it away. The scene in both 45 and the near-duplicate tapestry in the Victoria and Albert Museum (fig. 165) corresponds most closely to Matthew's account even though the stone is a slab rather than one that can be rolled: Christ has risen, the stone is still in place, and the Marys are on their way but have not yet arrived.

Only Matthew (27:65–66, 28:11–15) mentions the soldiers who appear so prominently in 45. He says that Pilate permitted the chief priests and Pharisees to post guards at the tomb, guards whom the priests later bribed to say that Christ's disciples had removed His body from the tomb at night while the guards slept. The tapestry designer has shown the moment when two of the men are still asleep, one is wakening, and five are not only awake but either cowering or fleeing in terror.

Mark (16:1) specifies that it was Mary Magdalen, Mary the mother of James, and Salome who came at sunrise to anoint the body. Luke (24:10) refers to them as Mary Magdalen, Joanna, and Mary the mother of James. Matthew (28:1) says that only two women came, the Magdalen and "the other Mary." According to John (20:1), it was only Mary Magdalen who came to the tomb and while it was still dark. The tapestry designer seems to have heeded Matthew and Mark in choosing the hour to represent; that is, at or about dawn.

Although Mark (16:9) mentions that the risen Christ appeared to Mary Magdalen first, it is John (20:14–17) who tells how she mistook Him for a gardener until He identified Himself and admonished her not to touch Him. It is also John (19:41–42) who says that the tomb was located in a garden near the site of the Crucifixion (see 30 for further details on this iconography). In a number of tapestries that have survived from the early years of the sixteenth century, the garden is shown as a cultivated enclosure like this one, surrounded by a fence (usually a picket fence) with a gate, often a similar gabled gate, set into it.

When plants like the ones that are represented in the border of 45 are featured in a tapestry composition, as they are for example in 11 and 42, it is clear that the designer intended them to convey symbolic meaning: red roses signify Christ's martyrdom, and grapes, His blood; pansies symbolize remembrance; purple iris refers to Christ or the Virgin; strawberries are food of the spirit and of the blessed; and violets stand for humility. However the flora in the border of 45 do not count as major elements in the composition, and furthermore some of the same flora commonly appear in the borders of countless other tapestries of this type and date. Some of those tapestries, like 29 and 41 for example, have Christian subjects that are basically allegorical. Therefore it does not necessarily follow that the flora in the border of 45 were intended to have symbolic meaning simply because the field shows a particularly sacred Christian subject.

SOURCE OF THE DESIGN

It is not unusual to find several incidents combined in fifteenth-century representations of the Resurrection as they are in 45. A number of paintings that may have inspired the tapestry designer have been found, and they all show the subordinate scenes along with the main subject, although none shows so many soldiers in attendance.

The general composition was based either on a lost painting by Dieric Bouts, of which a number of replicas exist, or on an unidentified common source for both Bouts and the tapestry designer. Standen noted that the version now in the Staatsgalerie in Stuttgart (fig. 166), painted by a German artist dubbed the Master of the Ehningen Altar, resembles the composition in the tapestry most closely, which indeed it does, more than the other version of it that is in the Mauritshuis, The Hague.[4] In the Stuttgart painting the setting, with the massive rock outcropping in the center flanked by deep vistas to the horizon, the scene of Christ appearing to the Magdalen at the left, and the three Holy Women approaching the tomb at the right, is very much like the setting in the tapestry. In both representations there is a soldier who raises one arm to shade his eyes as he gazes at the risen Christ, and in both there is another soldier who wears a broad, flat helmet trimmed with twisted scarves or ribbons and a plume of feathers. The main

difference is that the figure of Christ is shown standing firmly on the ground in the painting but possibly hovering above it in the tapestry. The near-duplicate tapestry in the Victoria and Albert Museum (fig. 165) also shows a risen Christ who may be standing on the rock or hovering above it. Digby (1980, 41), with credit to Johanna M. Diehl, also called attention to the formal similarities that relate the London tapestry to the Stuttgart and Mauritshuis pictures. In the London tapestry Christ's body faces directly forward, as it does in both versions of the Bouts picture. In the Metropolitan Museum's hanging the pose is more complex: the torso and head face the viewer but the hips and legs swing to the left. The pose lends the figure a vivid sense of action. Standen noted the related contrapposto pose of Christ that is shown in a panel painting of the Resurrection by Dieric Bouts preserved in the Capilla Real in Granada and also in another of his paintings of the same subject now in the Bayerische Staatsgemäldesammlungen in Munich.[5] Standen also observed that a similar figure of the risen Christ appears in the background of Rogier van der Weyden's *Christ Appearing to His Mother* in the Metropolitan Museum.[6] In these paintings Christ's right hand is raised in benediction and His left hand holds the cross with its pennon; also, the left leg is crossed in front of the right. However the figure appears to be walking forward, toward the viewer, rather than striding toward the left, as it does in the tapestry. Also in the paintings the figure stands beside an uncovered sarcophagus, another detail that sets these compositions apart from the one in the tapestry. We have now identified an early fifteenth-century painting in Utrecht that shows yet another similar figure in association with an open sarcophagus (the cover has been thrown back at the left).[7] However in this instance the relation of the figure to the sarcophagus explains Christ's curious striding pose in the tapestry: He is in fact stepping out of the sarcophagus, an action that looks perfectly normal in the painting but, because the tapestry designer has removed the sarcophagus, seems extreme and unmotivated in the hanging.

As Standen observed in her notes, the representation of the sun's disk and rays is unusual in these compositions and may derive from the similar sunrise in the left background of the *Resurrection* in Dürer's woodcut series of the *Small Passion* of about 1510.[8]

Since there appear to be a large number of quite disparate design sources for the general composition and the details in this hanging, it seems reasonable to assume that the designer did not invent the composition himself but developed it from some unidentified print or panel painting that combined elements that were in part tra-

Fig. 166. *The Resurrection*, central section of the triptych altarpiece from Ehningen, by an unidentified artist (Master of the Ehningen Altar) after a lost original by Dieric Bouts. Panel painting, Germany, about 1475. Staatsgalerie, Stuttgart.

ditional (like the figure in the Utrecht panel) and in part invented or used by Rogier van der Weyden and/or Dieric Bouts.

MANUFACTURE AND DATE

When the tapestry was sold from the de Somzée collection in 1901, it was attributed to Brussels and dated broadly in the first half of the sixteenth century. In 1920 Breck called it Netherlandish ("the Low Countries") and

gave it a date of about 1500. Soon afterward Göbel (1923, vol. 1, 441; vol. 2, fig. 141) returned to the Brussels attribution and dated the piece about 1525, presumably on stylistic grounds. Roberts (1938, 16) used the same attribution when she published the tapestry some years later. Standen attributed the tapestry to Brussels because of the fine workmanship in it and its general high quality.[9] She dated it about 1515–25 on the basis of the style of the soldiers' armor, the presence of the rising sun in the background (which she traced to Dürer's woodcut of about 1510), and finally because of the Renaissance character of the ornaments in the border. Digby (1980, 41–42) suggested that the related piece in London was probably produced in Brussels because he saw in it certain similarities to the *Passion* tapestries associated with the shop of Pieter van Aelst that are now in Trent, and he dated it 1520–25.

The designer of the Metropolitan Museum's tapestry successfully represented a deep space that stretches unbroken from the immediate foreground to the horizon. Unlike designers working at the turn of the century, he did not use the late Gothic conventions of placing the horizon high in the field and of arranging groups of figures on one or two levels above those in the foreground to suggest that the former occupied a more distant space than the others. He was using ideas about space that later fifteenth-century Netherlandish painters had developed, ideas that began to appear in the world of tapestry design about 1511, the date woven into one of the *Lives of Christ and the Virgin* tapestries in Aix-en-Provence.[10] In discussing a *Christ before Pilate* tapestry in Brussels that belongs to a series of compositions closely related to 45, Steppe argued for a date about 1520 or a bit later, basing his opinion on stylistic considerations.[11] Of the pieces Steppe considered in this study, the seven hangings in the Museo Diocesano in Trent seem to the present writer to be the ones whose style, though perhaps somewhat earlier in terms of the handling of spatial relationships, is most like the style of 45 (see Related Tapestries). Steppe noted that the *Christ Carrying the Cross* in Trent showed the date 1507; he accepted this as the date of the cartoon but not of the weaving, which he believed was about 1515–25.

If, as we believe, the cartoons for the seven hangings in Trent were executed in 1507, then we must accept the fact that the Renaissance ornaments in the border of 45 do not in themselves imply a date any later than that, for at both sides of the fields in the Trent pieces there are columns decorated with late antique ornaments as they were interpreted in Italy from the late fifteenth century onward.[12] The same kind of decoration appears on the face of the narrow columns that separate one scene from another in the *Lives of Christ and the Virgin* tapestries in Aix-en-Provence (1511), and fully developed grotesque ornaments fill the borders of the four *Legend of Notre-Dame du Sablon* tapestries that were produced between 1516 and 1518.[13] It is not just the fact that Renaissance ornaments appear in the border of 45 that helps date the hanging but rather the fact that these ornaments have been combined there with late Gothic floral garlands. The same kind of combination appears in the borders of a number of tapestries of the second and third decades of the sixteenth century, notably in the great *Los Honores* hangings in the Patrimonio Nacional of Spain which were completed in 1523.[14] The combination appears again, in a form very much like that in the Metropolitan Museum's *Resurrection,* in the border of the *Noli me tangere* that belongs to the province of Brabant and which is thought to be Brussels work of about 1520.[15]

Neither the garments that the women in the background of the Metropolitan Museum's tapestry wear nor the soldiers' armor show many details that would help date 45 on the basis of fashion in clothing. The soldiers' costumes were designed to suggest garments worn in an exotic past. However it is significant to note that the bulbous breastplates and narrow waists of the two soldiers who occupy the center foreground in the tapestry agree in general terms of silhouette and mass with the corresponding details of the armor represented in certain German paintings of the first and second decades of the sixteenth century.[16] Furthermore, the shallow helmet decorated with plumes and ribbons worn by the soldier sitting directly below Christ's left foot in 45 reflects the same fashion that inspired the decoration of some military hats during the early years of the sixteenth century.[17] However such details do not help refine the date of the tapestry design; they simply suggest that it was designed and probably also woven during the first quarter of the sixteenth century.

The Metropolitan Museum's tapestry is in a general way reminiscent of the corresponding *Resurrection* tapestry in Trent which is believed to have been produced by the Brussels weaver and entrepreneur Pieter van Aelst.[18] However the resemblance cannot be used to support a claim that 45 was woven in Brussels or through the agency of a Brussels producer.

RELATED TAPESTRIES

A near-duplicate hanging is preserved in the Victoria and Albert Museum in London (see Digby 1980, 41–42; also fig. 165 in the present catalogue entry). It was woven after a version of the cartoon that was used for 45. The composition is somewhat narrower and appreciably taller in the London tapestry, and a number of details in the distant landscape and the immediate foreground have been changed. In the London piece there are trees at either side of the foreground, and their trunks, branches, and foliage form a proscenium before and beyond which the action occurs. However the two versions differ most in the way Christ's figure is represented. In the London tapestry He stands facing the observer more or less squarely, and His right arm is extended straight to the side rather than forward and bent at the elbow. Also, His gaze is directed downward and to the left rather than directly into the observer's eyes. The central band of the London border is more detailed than the border of 45, and the anthemion motifs alternate in a regular sequence with the vases. Both motifs are oriented upright rather than sideways in the top and bottom border sections as well as the side sections.

The *Resurrection* tapestry that belongs in the set of *Passion* hangings in the Museo Diocesano in Trent shows a closely related but decidedly distinct composition.[19] The Savior's pose differs from that shown in both 45 and the London piece: it is more static and placid. The scene of Christ appearing to the Magdalen appears in the background at the right rather than the left, and the other subordinate scene in the background is not the coming of the Holy Women but Christ appearing to Peter. The figures in both subordinate scenes are larger than they are in the New York and London tapestries, and they are all closer to the observer. Like the London tapestry, the one in Trent has vertical forms at the sides to establish the foreground plane. Here they are not trees but a pair of columns with carved decorations.

Since the *Resurrection* in Trent belongs to a set of *Story of the Passion* tapestries, it is fair to assume that 45 and the London tapestry also belonged to sets of hangings illustrating either the Passion or the life of Christ. No hangings that belonged with the Metropolitan Museum's tapestry are known to have survived. However the series of compositions to which it belonged probably contained some or all of the subjects that appear in the Trent tapestries. Each of those hangings shows the principal subject in the center foreground and a number of subordinate incidents that took place at earlier or later times in the background, as follows:

1. The Nativity, with the Adoration of the Magi and the Annunciation in the background, at left and right respectively.

2. Christ washing the disciples' feet, with the agony in the garden (left), Judas leading the soldiers (center), and the kiss of Judas (right).

3. Christ before Caiaphas, with Christ before Annas (left) and the mocking of Christ (right).

4. Christ before Pilate, with the Flagellation (left), the crowning with thorns (left center), and Christ shown to the people (right).

5. Christ carrying the cross, with the Crucifixion (center).

6. The Deposition, with the Harrowing of Hell (left) and the Entombment (right).

7. The Resurrection, with Christ appearing to Peter (left) and Christ appearing to the Magdalen (right).

It is thought, but not certain, that Cardinal Bernard Cles, bishop-prince of Trent, bought these seven hangings from the Antwerp tapestry dealer Joris van Lickaw in 1531.[20] We do not know whether the set was complete in seven pieces.

Some of the compositions in the Trent pieces also appear in somewhat different form in certain extant tapestries that were woven after versions of the same cartoons. Four such hangings are now dispersed among the Patrimonio Nacional in Spain (*Christ Carrying the Cross* and *Deposition*), the Rijksmuseum in Amsterdam (*Christ Washing the Disciples' Feet*), and the Musées Royaux d'Art et d'Histoire in Brussels (*Christ before Pilate*).[21] Another *Deposition* from a set of hangings that Steppe thought was earlier both than those four tapestries and the Trent pieces is also in the Patrimonio Nacional.[22] A *Nativity* from some set of hangings other than the one at Trent (which itself contains a *Nativity*) is now in the Iparművészeti Múzeum (Decorative Arts Museum) in Budapest.[23]

HISTORY

Sold from the collection of Léon de Somzée, Salle des Fêtes du Parc du Cinquantenaire, Brussels, May 20–25, 1901, no. 534, pl. XXVIII. In that catalogue the tapestry is said to have come from the Lafaulotte collection. Unless there were two such hangings in that collection this statement is incorrect. Only one tapestry of the *Resurrection* was sold with the Lafaulotte collection when it was auctioned in 1886; it is the near-duplicate piece that is now in the Victoria and Albert Museum.[24]

In the collection of Jules S. Bache, New York, by 1920.

Received by the MMA with The Jules Bache Collection, 1949.

EXHIBITIONS

New York, MMA, 1920. *Fiftieth Anniversary Exhibition*. Cat. p. 12. Lent by Jules S. Bache.

New York, MMA, 1943. *The Bache Collection*.

Austin, Archer M. Huntington Art Gallery, University of Texas, 1982–87.

PUBLICATIONS

"List of Loans: Fiftieth Anniversary Exhibition." *MMA Bulletin* 15 (1920) p. 118. Mentioned.

J. B. [Joseph Breck]. "Mediaeval and Renaissance Decorative Arts and Sculpture." *MMA Bulletin* 15 (1920) p. 181. Mentioned; illus. p. 183 in a view of the gallery installation during the *Fiftieth Anniversary Exhibition*.

Göbel 1923, vol. 1, pp. 162, 441. Referred to indirectly in discussions of subject and border design treatments; illus. vol. 2, fig. 141.

Roberts, Mary Fanton. "The 'Bache Collection'—A Great Gift to New York City." *Arts and Decoration* 48, no. 3 (May 1938) p. 16. Mentioned; illus. p. 17, hanging in entrance hall of Jules S. Bache house in New York.

Digby 1980. Cat. no. 28, pp. 41–42. Discussed briefly.

1. Digby 1980, p. 42, observed that the letters OBAM, together with some incomplete letters, are inscribed on the front of the tomb in the near-duplicate *Resurrection* tapestry in the Victoria and Albert Museum, London (reg. no. T.139–1921; fig. 165 in the present catalogue entry). The illustration of that piece (Digby 1980, pl. 48) shows that these letters, like the ones in the Metropolitan Museum's tapestry, appear along the left and top edges of the slab covering the tomb and also that the same cryptic, twisted character at the top of the left edge of the New York piece, together with the M to the right of it, also appear in the London tapestry. However in the latter there seems to be an O rather than an I to the right of the M. In Digby's opinion, the O-B-A-M are "presumably random letters suggesting an inscription." We agree with him and believe that the same may be said of the few letters that are visible in the New York tapestry.

2. The sideways orientation of the arabesque motifs in the top and bottom border sections of 45 could easily be explained if it were found that those two portions had been woven as side borders for some other tapestry, then removed, and inserted into this piece. However the warp yarns in the top and bottom sections do not run vertically, as they would if that had happened, but horizontally as they should, and it is clear that these top and bottom sections are integral parts of the original fabric.

   Normally, early sixteenth-century tapestry borders containing arabesque motifs, whether alone or combined with late Gothic floral garlands as they are here, show the units arranged in regular sequence, and oriented upright, in all four border sections; see for example the all-arabesque border of a tapestry of *Christ in the Garden of Olives* in the Musée des Beaux-Arts, Besançon, in *Le XVIe siècle européen: Tapisseries*, exh. cat., Mobilier National (Paris, 1965) no. 22, illus., and the arabesque and garland border of the near-duplicate *Resurrection* tapestry in the Victoria and Albert Museum, in Digby 1980, pl. 48. However other tapestries of this period, like a *Noli me tangere* hanging that is stylistically related to 45 and belongs to the province of Brabant, have borders with arabesque motifs that are arranged irregularly and also oriented sideways in the top and bottom border sections rather than upright as they are at the sides; see *Chefs-d'oeuvre de la tapisserie flamande: Onzième exposition du château de Culan*, exh. cat. by J. P. Asselberghs (Bourges, 1971) no. 6, illus. Another *Noli me tangere*, a hanging in the Musée du Louvre, has a border containing sophisticated Renaissance arabesque motifs which, although arranged in a regular sequence on all four sides, are oriented upright in the side border sections and sideways in the top and bottom ones; see Louis Guimbaud, *La tapisserie de haute et basse lisse* (Paris, 1928) pl. 1.

3. See, for example, the *Resurrection* among the frescoes painted about 1355 by Andrea di Bonajuto and his shop in the Cappella degli Spagnuoli in Santa Maria Novella in Florence which also shows the three Holy Women in the background on one side and Christ appearing to the Magdalen on the other; illustrated in Hubert Schrade, *Ikonographie der christlichen Kunst*, vol. 1, *Die Auferstehung Christi* (Berlin and Leipzig, 1932) pl. 13, fig. 67.

4. Edith Appleton Standen, notes and preliminary draft for a catalogue entry concerning 45, ca. 1968, in the files of the MMA Department of Medieval Art. For further information concerning the Stuttgart picture and notes on, and an illustration of, the Mauritshuis version which has been ascribed to Albert Bouts, see Wolfgang Schöne, *Dieric Bouts und seine Schule* (Berlin and Leipzig, 1938) cat. no. 62a, pl. 73b, and cat. nos. 62b and 104, pl. 73a. See also *Dieric Bouts*, exh. cat., Palais des Beaux-Arts, Brussels, and Stedelijk Museum Het Prinsenhof, Delft (Brussels, 1957) nos. 84 and 61, both illus.

5. Standen, notes and preliminary draft, ca. 1968. The painting in Granada serves as the right wing of a triptych of the *Deposition* whose left wing shows the Crucifixion. See Schöne, *Dieric Bouts*,

cat. no. 3, pl. 9. A copy of the triptych is preserved in the Colegio del Patriarca in Valencia; see Schöne, *Dieric Bouts*, cat. no. 3a, pl. 10. The Munich picture is discussed and illustrated in the Brussels/Delft *Dieric Bouts* exh. cat., no. 4.

6. Standen, notes and preliminary draft, ca. 1968. Concerning Rogier's painting, see Katharine Baetjer, *European Paintings in The Metropolitan Museum of Art by Artists Born in or before 1865: A Summary Catalogue* (New York, 1980) vol. 1, p. 157; vol. 3, illus. p. 329. See also a larger illustration in Hermann Beenken, *Rogier van der Weyden* (Munich, 1951) fig. 33.

7. The painting, which is preserved in the Centraalmuseum's Aartsbisschoppelijkmuseum in Utrecht, is thought to have been painted in the Middle Rhine region about 1400–1410. For notes and an illustration, see Schrade, *Ikonographie*, pp. 185–86, pl. 21, fig. 86.

8. Standen, notes and preliminary draft, ca. 1968. For notes on the Dürer woodcut (B.45) and an illustration, see *The Illustrated Bartsch*, vol. 10, *Sixteenth Century German Artists: Albrecht Dürer*, Walter L. Strauss, ed. (New York, 1980–81) commentary vol., p. 307, illus. vol., p. 140.

9. Standen, notes and preliminary draft, ca. 1968.

10. Concerning the date of the tapestries in the Cathédrale Saint-Sauveur in Aix, see *Les tapisseries de la Vie du Christ et de la Vierge d'Aix-en-Provence*, exh. cat., Musée des Tapisseries (Aix-en-Provence, 1977) p. 4 and illus. on p. 5. As early examples of a tapestry designer's success in representing deep, continuous space, see especially the Visitation, Baptism of Christ, and Resurrection scenes in the color pls. following p. 28.

11. J.K.S. [Jan-Karel Steppe], cat. entry for no. 16, p. 70, in *Tapisseries bruxelloises de la pré-Renaissance*, exh. cat., Musées Royaux d'Art et d'Histoire (Brussels, 1976).

12. For color illustrations of the seven pieces in Trent, see Enrico Castelnuovo et al., *Gli arazzi del cardinale: Bernardo Cles e il Ciclo della Passione di Pieter van Aelst* (Trent, 1990) pp. 88–94. For an intensive study of the tapestries, see Michelangelo Lupo, "Il cardinale Bernardo Cles e gli arazzi fiamminghi," pp. 85–117, and the catalogue, also by Lupo, pp. 118–277, in the same publication, with large color illustrations of each of the seven pieces, including details, interleaved.

13. See *Les tapisseries . . . d'Aix-en-Provence*, color pls. following p. 28, and also *Tapisseries bruxelloises de la pré-Renaissance*, no. 21, illus. pp. 87, 91, 93, 95.

14. For illustrations of these tapestries, with notes and bibliography, see Paulina Junquera de Vega and Concha Herrero Carretero, *Catálogo de tapices del Patrimonio Nacional*, vol. 1, *Siglo XVI* (Madrid, 1986) pp. 35–44.

15. See *Chefs-d'oeuvre de la tapisserie flamande*, no. 6, illus.

16. For example the armor worn by Saints George and Maurice in paintings by Hans Baldung Grien on the inner left and right wings of the *Epiphany* triptych, about 1506, in the Gemäldegalerie in Berlin-Dahlem; see Gert von der Osten, *Hans Baldung Grien: Gemälde und Dokumente* (Berlin, 1983) pp. 42–47 and pl. 8. Note also armor detailed more like that in the Metropolitan Museum's *Resurrection* tapestry in paintings by Lucas Cranach of the *Crucifixion*, about 1515–20, in the Städelsches Kunstinstitut in Frankfurt, and of the *Crucifixion* and the *Resurrection*, panels of a triptych of about 1520 now or formerly in a collection in Berlin; see Max J. Friedländer and Jakob Rosenberg, *The Paintings of Lucas Cranach*, rev. ed. (Ithaca, 1978) nos. 92 and 95, both illus.

17. For example Saint George's plumed hat in the *Epiphany* triptych in Berlin-Dahlem; see von der Osten, *Hans Baldung Grien*, pl. 8.

18. Only the tapestries of *Christ Carrying the Cross* in Trent and Madrid show Pieter van Aelst's signature, but it is thought that he produced all seven pieces. See Jan-Karel Steppe, "Inscriptions décoratives contenant des signatures et des mentions du lieu d'origine sur des tapisseries bruxelloises de la fin du XVe et du début du XVIe siècle," in *Tapisseries bruxelloises de la pré-Renaissance*, pp. 215–16, and fig. 11, p. 216; see also cat. no. 16, p. 70.

19. For color illustrations of the Trent *Resurrection*, including details, see Castelnuovo et al., *Gli arazzi del cardinale*, pp. 94, 250–53, 255–58, 260–61. The tapestry is discussed in detail by Lupo, in that publication, pp. 248–49, 254, 256, 259, 262–67.

20. See Steppe, in *Tapisseries bruxelloises de la pré-Renaissance*, pp. 217–18; and especially Lupo, "Il cardinale Bernardo Cles," in *Gli arazzi del cardinale*, pp. 85–89.

21. For the two pieces in the Patrimonio Nacional, see Junquera de Vega and Herrero Carretero, *Catálogo*, pp. 28 and 29, illus.; for the Amsterdam hanging, see A. M. Louise Erkelens, *Wandtapijten 1: Late gotiek en vroege Renaissance*, Facetten der Verzameling,

Rijksmuseum, 2d ser., no. 4 (Amsterdam, 1962) illus. pp. 36–39; and for the tapestry in Brussels, see *Tapisseries bruxelloises de la pré-Renaissance*, cat. no. 16, illus.

22. See Steppe, in *Tapisseries bruxelloises de la pré-Renaissance*, p. 71; for notes concerning this *Deposition*, and illustrations, see Junquera de Vega and Herrero Carretero, *Catálogo*, p. 34.

23. See Steppe, in *Tapisseries bruxelloises de la pré-Renaissance*, pp. 71–73, with references to illustrations of the piece in Budapest.

24. *Catalogue des objets d'art . . . composant l'importante collection de Lafaulotte*, Hôtel Drouot, Paris, April 5–10, 12, 13, 1886, no. 1032, illus.; called "l'Ascension." See also Digby 1980, p. 42.

46

Perseus Rescues Andromeda

A hanging from the series *The Story of Perseus*

Southern Netherlands, 1515–25
Wool warp; wool and silk wefts
11 ft. × 10 ft. 5 in. (3.35 m × 3.18 m)
17–20 warp yarns per inch; 7–8 per centimeter
Bequest of Adele L. Lehman, in memory of Arthur Lehman, 1965
(65.181.16)

CONDITION

Since there are traces of the original red wool loom heading at both sides of the tapestry, we know that the hanging has lost none of its original width. There are three narrow guards along all four edges of the piece. The guards at the sides have survived intact, but the two outer guards at the top and the outermost of the three at the bottom have been replaced. The right end of the upper border was at some time cut from the top of the side border and then rejoined to it. Nevertheless, and in spite of the fact that the floral band in the upper border is less well woven than it is in the other three sections, the entire upper border appears to be original. There is no indication that the border has ever been cut from the field on any of the four sides.

Most of the silk yarns used to render the highlights throughout the field and border have survived; the rest have deteriorated and been replaced with modern yarns. The most important restorations of this kind occur in the parts of the fabric that represent the right shoulder, sleeve, and breast of Andromeda who stands in the upper left corner of the field, the drapery over the left leg of the queen, in the center foreground, and the hat of the soldier standing in the foreground next to the border at the right. The wool yarns that now appear as dark brown, and many other woolen wefts of different colors that delineate the figures and objects, have also been replaced. However these restorations have not altered the original drawing and modeling significantly. The colors have faded appreciably, but each hue has retained its identity.

DESCRIPTION AND SUBJECT

Perseus stands in the left foreground addressing a king and queen, their courtiers, and military attendants. The young god wears hose, a plain mantle decorated at the edges with a band of leaves, and a velvet tunic over armor that is visible only at his neck, shoulders, and lower arms where the mail gorget, backplate, and lower cannons of the vambrace appear. The tunic is decorated with a repeating pattern unit composed of the letter *p* with a stem that terminates in a pair of knotted and fluttering ribbons. Perseus also wears low shoes and a small, round hat with an upturned brim. A page standing next to him at the left holds his sword, helmet, and gauntlets.

The king, who stands left of center, wears plain hose and a patterned doublet under his long coat, which has wide sleeves and is lined with spotted fur. A sheathed sword hangs from his girdle. An open crown encircles the top of his wide-brimmed round hat. He holds the end of a scepter in his left hand and rests its shaft on his shoulder. With his right hand he gestures—as Perseus also does—toward the upper left corner of the field. The queen, who wears a long mantle lined with leaf-patterned damask over her unpatterned gown, presses the palm of her left hand against the ball of the right one as she bends her left knee and looks up into Perseus' face in an attitude of supplication. Her open crown encircles a high bonnet set at the back of her head.

A large company of male and female courtiers and soldiers surrounds the three main figures in the foreground. A halberdier and a swordsman stand in the middle distance at the far right. Like the king and Perseus, some of these figures gesture toward the upper left corner of the field where, in the middle distance, a young woman dressed in a flowing gown resembling a girded chiton stands tied to a tree stump that grows from a rock. Behind her, in the far distance, Perseus walks toward the right accompanied by Hermes. This god wears hose, a knee-length jacket, and his winged helmet; he carries the serpent-headed caduceus in his right hand. In this scene Perseus is dressed in full armor under his tunic (the greaves and sabatons protecting his lower legs and feet are visible below the hemline). He is wearing wings on his shoulders; his helmet is on his head, and he carries a sword and shield.

Perseus appears a third time in the upper central section of the field, which represents a hilly landscape. He is flying toward a scaly monster whose head and neck rise from a body of water in the middle distance. Perseus raises his sword in his right hand, and with his left hand he holds a shield before the monster's head. The two soldiers standing at the right watch the progress of the battle. Two other figures are visible in the far distance just to the right of Perseus' shield. Beyond them trees, castles, and mountains rise to meet the sky.

The border shows a narrow, dark greenish blue band covered with flowers and flanked by striped guards. The floral ornaments consist of branches or stalks laid end to end. They bear red roses, white daisies, or lavender-and-white pansies.

The episodes here show the story of Perseus rescuing Andromeda from the sea monster. Having killed the Gorgon Medusa and taken her head (with which he turned the inhospitable King Atlas to stone), Perseus made his way to Ethiopia. There he found the people being terrorized by a sea monster sent by Poseidon to punish Queen Cassiopeia for boasting that she was more beautiful than the Nereids. King Cepheus consulted the oracle of the god Amun and learned that to rid his people of the monster he must sacrifice his daughter Andromeda to it to atone for her mother's vain words. When Perseus saw the girl tied to a rock, he fell in love with her and told the distraught parents that he would rescue Andromeda if he could have her in marriage. When they consented, he flew at the monster, slew it, and brought Andromeda home safely.

The designer has represented the critical moments in the story. In the foreground Cassiopeia and Cepheus beg Perseus to rescue their daughter, and he strikes his bargain with them. In the distance at the left he is shown armed with the shield from Athena, the sword from Hermes, the helmet of Hades (which would make him invisible), and wings from the nymphs, and approaching the monster under the protection of Hermes. At the center of the tapestry Perseus attacks the monster from above as Andromeda watches. The rescue itself and Andromeda's return to her parents are not represented.

This story is told in Book IV of Ovid's *Metamorphoses*; but the images shown here and in the other tapestries of the series from which it comes (see Related Tapestries) do not correspond to those that a designer might develop directly from Ovid's account. Among the discrepancies of detail, one might mention these: Ovid says that it was Hermes who gave Perseus a curved sword, whereas in the tapestries it is Athena who gives Perseus not only his shield but also a straight sword; and in Ovid, Perseus is given wings for his feet, not for his shoulders. Delmarcel made a study of later iconographic sources which could have been used by the designer of this and two other sixteenth-century *Story of Perseus* tapestry series. He cited Giovanni Boccaccio's *Genealogia deorum gentilium* (third quarter of the fourteenth century); Christine de Pisan's *L'Epître*

d'Othéa, déesse de Prudence, à Hector (1401); and Raoul Lefèvre's *Recueil des histoires de Troie* (1464). He concluded that the episodes in 46 and three other pieces directly related to it, which emphasize the moral content of the Perseus story, were not based on these accounts but on the so-called *Ovide moralisé*.[1] This early fourteenth-century French poem interpreted Ovid's *Metamorphoses* in ethical terms. About 1340 Pierre Bersuire (or Berçuire, latinized as Petrus Berchorius) composed a prose work in Latin variously called *Metamorphosis Ovidiana moraliter explanata, Liber de Reductione fabularum*, or *Ovidius moralizatus*, that also stressed the same content and furthermore described the main pagan gods in detail. Its introduction inspired a shorter, popular book in Latin, the *Libellus de imaginibus deorum*, which, along with other versions of the introduction, became an important source for late medieval designers and writers who needed to describe and tell the stories of the pagan gods.[2] We do not know which of the many versions of these sources the designer of 46 used.

SOURCE OF THE DESIGN

Göbel (1923, vol. 1, 411) attributed the design of this tapestry and of two related hangings that were formerly in the Raoul Heilbronner collection to Jan van Roome working in association with Philip van Orley. Virch (1965, 98) noted Göbel's attribution and implied that the same might be said for the Metropolitan Museum's tapestry. He also observed that the two Heilbronner pieces are similar to the *Legend of Herkinbald* tapestry in Brussels which is documented as having been designed by Jan van Roome (see fig. 70 in the present catalogue). Calberg (1969, 72) thought that the style of 46 and three others (two formerly in the Heilbronner collection and one in Cracow; see Related Tapestries) she published with it agreed with the full-blown early sixteenth-century style associated with Jan van Roome and the *Herkinbald* tapestry.

The Metropolitan Museum's piece does recall the style of the *Legend of Herkinbald*, as do hundreds of other surviving tapestries of the same class. We see no reason to attribute its design to the hand of Jan van Roome or any other particular artist. The poses, gestures, and facial expressions of all but the few main figures connote general rather than specific content. We can imagine that they were taken from stock patterns that served in any number of different compositions. Some of these figures and groups could have been borrowed from existing prints or paintings. We can cite two examples of what may have been such borrow-

Fig. 167. *Zeus Comes to Danae in a Shower of Gold.* Tapestry, southern Netherlands, here dated 1515–25. Museum Narodowe w Krakowie (National Museum, Cracow).

ings. A pair of male figures in the background of a late fifteenth- or early sixteenth-century Florentine engraving of *Christ and the Samaritan Woman* by Cristofano Robetta could have served (in reverse) as the model for the halberdier and swordsman in the upper right corner of the Metropolitan Museum's tapestry.[3] Delmarcel suggested that the scene of Athena giving arms to Perseus that appears in one of the Heilbronner tapestries (fig. 168) derives from miniature paintings showing Athena (also known as Othea) giving arms to Hector in manuscript editions of Christine de Pisan's *Epître d'Othéa, à Hector.*[4]

The artist who designed a *Story of Perseus* series about 1530–40 (see Related Tapestries) used either these cartoons or a common source for certain scenes. The figures of Danae and the infant Perseus in a boat that appear in the upper left corner of the Heilbronner *Perseus Armed by Athena* appear in the upper right corner of a tapestry from the later series that shows the shower of gold subject and is now in Boston (compare fig. 168 here with Cavallo 1967, pl. 25). The figure of the adult Perseus making his sacrifice and the two principals in the wedding scene appear in both the Heilbronner *Perseus Offers a Sacrifice* and a version of it from the later series that was sold in London in 1962 and again in 1963 (see Calberg 1969, figs. 4 and 5; and note 13 below).

MANUFACTURE AND DATE

When 46 was sold from the Baslini collection in Milan in 1888, it was catalogued as a Flemish piece of the fif-

teenth century. In 1903 and again in 1904, Destrée attributed it to Brussels and dated it at the beginning of the sixteenth century. He gave no reason for assigning the piece to Brussels but expressed the opinion (1903, 36–37) that, except for some details, the costumes dated from the time of Maximilian. Göbel (1923, vol. 1, 137) called one of the two closely related Heilbronner tapestries Brussels work of the first decades of the sixteenth century, and he (1923, vol. 2, fig. 266) assigned a date of 1520 to the other. Later writers, probably following Göbel's opinion regarding these two pieces, attributed 46 to Brussels and dated it in the early sixteenth century. Virch (1965, 98) believed it was woven about 1510–20. Forsyth (1966–67, 87) dated it more generally in the early sixteenth century. Gómez-Moreno (1975, 163) retained Virch's date.

Göbel's opinion concerning the date and place of manufacture of the Heilbronner tapestries was probably based on his belief (1923, vol. 1, 308) that they might be identified with a document mentioning the purchase of eight *Story of Perseus* tapestries by Charles V from the Brussels tapestry merchant Gabriel van der Tombe in 1520.[5] Virch (1965, 98), Calberg (1969, 72–74), and Delmarcel also mentioned this possibility.[6] Certainly, in terms of their date and place of origin, 46 and the closely related piece in Cracow, as well as the two formerly in the Heilbronner collection, could have been among the eight Perseus tapestries mentioned in this record of purchase. As Calberg (1969, 64, 72) observed, these four hangings show details characteristic of tapestries attributed to Brussels, and the style of their compositions is

547

similar to that of the *Legend of Herkinbald* tapestry, a tapestry that we know was designed by the Brussels artist Jan van Roome, produced in Brussels, and completed by 1513. However there may have been other Perseus tapestry cycles available in 1520, and so the record of Charles V's purchase cannot be cited as proof that 46 and the three pieces closely related to it were woven before 1520. Two Perseus tapestries conceived in totally different styles from 46 and from each other, one dating from the late fifteenth century and the other from the end of that century or the early years of the next, have survived. The earlier tapestry, in a private collection in France, shows Perseus astride Pegasus at the head of the Castalian spring, in whose waters three nude nymphs appear.[7] The later tapestry, which shows Perseus rescuing Andromeda, thanking the gods, and marrying Andromeda, is in the Cleveland Museum of Art.[8] Each could have come from a *Story of Perseus* series. The earlier piece, and the series of hangings it may represent, would certainly have looked out of date in 1520, the other less so; but later versions of both could have been produced. Perhaps tapestries from one of those conjectural cycles, or from some other Perseus series of which we have no knowledge, were the ones that Charles V bought in 1520.

Although 46 may have been designed about 1515, it could have been woven as late as 1525, when it would not yet have looked excessively outmoded. As for the place of manufacture, we maintain that while the *Herkinbald* tapestry is known to have been designed and woven by Brussels men, we cannot be sure that similar hangings were not being produced in other parts of the southern Netherlands also.

RELATED TAPESTRIES

Calberg brought together for the first time four tapestries dating from about 1515–25 that must have been woven after a single series of cartoons illustrating the *Story of Perseus*. Not only do the four hangings have the same figure types arranged in the same ways in the same kinds of setting, but also the two pieces showing Perseus in battle dress depict him wearing over his armor a tunic decorated with lowercase letters *p.* The four pieces may be listed as follows:

1. Zeus comes to Danae in a shower of gold: Museum Narodowe w Krakowie (National Museum, Cracow; see fig. 167 here, and Calberg 1969, 61–64, fig. 1). No duplicate hangings are known to have survived.

2. Perseus is armed by Athena and kills Medusa: formerly collection of Raoul Heilbronner, Paris (see fig. 168

here, and Calberg 1969, 64, 68–69, fig. 2). What appears to be the same tapestry was noted some years ago as being in the cathedral at Tarragona, and a tapestry answering a somewhat different description belonged in 1966 to the château de Chaumont.[9]

3. Perseus rescues Andromeda: MMA (see also Calberg 1969, 69–70, fig. 3). No duplicate hanging is known to have survived.

4. Perseus offers a sacrifice of thanksgiving to Zeus, Athena, and Hermes and then marries Andromeda: formerly collection of Raoul Heilbronner, Paris (see Calberg 1969, 70–71, fig. 4). The same or a duplicate hanging was in Tarragona, and a near-duplicate piece (see fig. 169 here) belonged to Sir Lionel Phillips and later to Arthur Curtiss James.[10]

While Calberg (1969, 71) believed that the first tapestry listed for each of the four numbers above probably belonged to one set of hangings, she acknowledged that some of them might have come from other sets. She observed (1969, 71 n. 1) that the field of the Phillips/James *Perseus Offers a Sacrifice* differed slightly from the Heilbronner example of the same subject and that their borders were not the same. However she did not point out that the border of 46 is different from both of the Heilbronner pieces and the Cracow piece, but that it is the same as the border of the Phillips/James tapestry. (The borders of 46 and of the Phillips/James tapestry do not include the lavender iris stalks that accompany the rose branches, daisies, and pansies in the borders of the other three hangings.) This indicates that 46 and the Phillips/James piece do not belong to the set or sets of hangings from which the Cracow and Heilbronner pieces come but to one or two other sets woven after the same cartoons. The fact that their borders match does not prove that they belong to one set of weavings.

We do not know how many compositions there were in the *Story of Perseus* series that 46 represents. However Delmarcel, in his study of sixteenth-century *Story of Perseus* tapestries, offered some valuable suggestions that are supported by the evidence provided by tapestries from other, later cycles. Because he endorsed Calberg in associating the four pieces she published with the eight *Story of Perseus* tapestries bought by Charles V in 1520, and also because three somewhat later documents refer to sets of *Perseus* tapestries in seven pieces, Delmarcel suggested that the cycle to which Calberg's four tapestries belong included three or four more subjects and that, like the four subjects we know, they would have represented important moments in Perseus' life.[11] He specified seven subjects in narrative order and an eighth one out of sequence:

Fig. 168. *Perseus Is Armed by Athena and Kills Medusa.* Tapestry, southern Netherlands, here dated 1515–25. Formerly collection of Raoul Heilbronner.

Fig. 169. *Perseus Offers a Sacrifice of Thanksgiving to Zeus, Athena, and Hermes and then Marries Andromeda.* Tapestry, southern Netherlands, here dated 1515–25. Formerly collections of Sir Lionel Phillips, Bart., and of Arthur Curtiss James.

1. Perseus is born of Danae from the shower of gold.
2. Perseus kills Medusa, and Pegasus rises from her blood.
3. Perseus turns King Atlas to stone.
4. Bellerophon fights the Chimera.
5. Perseus rescues Andromeda.
6. Perseus thanks the gods and marries Andromeda.
7. Perseus unwittingly kills his grandfather Acrisius.
8. Perseus arrives at Joppa, where he rescues Andromeda.

We do not know any examples of Delmarcel's subjects 3, 4, 7, or 8 that were woven after the series of cartoons represented by Calberg's four tapestries, but those subjects or subjects closely related to them appear in later cycles of the *Story of Perseus.* In view of that, and also in view of the fact that certain figures in some of these later pieces may have been taken from the cartoons represented by 46 (see Source of the Design), we are inclined to regard these as the subjects that would have appeared in the *Story of Perseus* cycle that 46 represents.

Calberg and Cavallo published three tapestries from a *Story of Perseus* cycle that dates from about 1530–40 and shows compositions closely related to the ones in the series represented by 46. These three hangings show Delmarcel's subjects 1, 6, and 7. An example of subject number 1, the shower of gold, is preserved in the Museum of Fine Arts, Boston, and there is a reduced and somewhat different version of it in the Zornsamlingarna in Mora, Sweden.[12] A version of number 6, Perseus offering a sacrifice, was put up for sale in London in 1962 and again in 1963.[13] The third hanging in this group, showing subject number 7 that deals with Perseus killing his grandfather Acrisius, was formerly the property of the Lenbach Gallery in Munich and is now in the Burg Linn Museum in Krefeld.[14]

Forti Grazzini called attention to a Brussels tapestry dating from about the middle of the sixteenth century that shows Perseus asking Atlas for hospitality, a scene suggesting Delmarcel's subject number 3. It is in the Palazzo Quirinale in Rome.[15]

Delmarcel and Forti Grazzini published a somewhat later Brussels tapestry, woven about 1560–65, whose subject corresponds to Delmarcel's number 4. The tapestry shows Perseus and his half brother Danaus, having joined forces with Bellerophon in Sicily, fighting the Chimera while Bellerophon battles wild animals on top of a mountain. It is in the Castello Sforzesco in Milan.[16] Delmarcel listed a second tapestry belonging to this same Brussels series whose subject relates to his number 8. It shows Perseus riding out a storm in his vessel

and then arriving at Joppa. It was sold in England in 1932 and its present location is unknown.[17]

Delmarcel apparently discovered later another subject in a third tapestry belonging to the Brussels series of 1560–65. This piece, which shows Perseus and Andromeda leaving her parents, was published by Forti Grazzini in 1984 as having been in the collection of the marquez de Cadaval in Colares, Portugal.[18] This subject may perhaps be considered as a ninth one that might have appeared in the series of cartoons after which 46, the Cracow piece, and the two formerly in the Heilbronner collection were woven. The fact that sets of only seven or eight pieces of the *Story of Perseus* are recorded in the sale of 1520 and three other pertinent sixteenth-century documents (see note 11) does not preclude the possibility that some Perseus sets included nine or more pieces.

HISTORY

Sold, *Collezione Baslini di Milano,* A. Genolini, Milan, November 26 and days following, 1888, no. 699, illus. (in reverse).
Property of Leopold Goldschmidt, Paris, in 1900.
Property of A. S. Drey, Paris.
Property of French and Company, New York.
Acquired by Arthur Lehman from French and Company, 1915.
Bequeathed to the MMA by Adele L. Lehman in memory of Arthur Lehman, 1965.

EXHIBITIONS

Paris, Exposition Universelle de 1900. *L'exposition rétrospective de l'art français des origines à 1800.* Cat. no. 3188 ("Scène de roman")? Lent by Leopold Goldschmidt.
New York, MMA, 1975–76. *Patterns of Collecting: Selected Acquisitions 1965–1975.*

PUBLICATIONS

Destrée, Joseph. "Etude sur les tapisseries exposées à Paris en 1900 au Petit Palais et au Pavillon d'Espagne." *Annales de la Société d'Archéologie de Bruxelles* 17 (1903) pp. 35–38. Described and discussed in detail; illus. p. 36.
Destrée, Joseph. *Maître Philippe auteur de cartons de tapisseries.* Brussels, 1904, p. 25. Mentioned; illus.
Roblot-Delondre, L[ouise]. "Les sujets antiques dans la tapisserie." *Revue Archéologique,* 5th ser., 7 (1918) p. 136. Mentioned as formerly in the Leopold Goldschmidt collection.
Göbel 1923, vol. 1, p. 411. Mentioned as in the Leopold Goldschmidt collection.
Virch, Claus. *The Adele and Arthur Lehman Collection.* MMA, New York, 1965, p. 98. Described and discussed; illus. p. 99.
Forsyth, William H. "Reports of the Departments: Medieval Art and The Cloisters, the Main Building." Annual Report for 1965–1966. In *MMA Bulletin,* n.s. 25 (1966–67) p. 87. Mentioned.
Cavallo, Adolph S. *Tapestries of Europe and of Colonial Peru in the Museum of Fine Arts, Boston.* Boston, 1967, p. 97. Mentioned as formerly in the Goldschmidt collection.
Calberg, Marguerite. "La pluie d'or." *Revue Belge d'Archéologie et*

d'Histoire de l'Art 38 (1969) pp. 64, 69–70, 72. Described in detail and discussed; illus. fig. 3.

C.G.-M. [Carmen Gómez-Moreno]. "Tapestry: The Story of Perseus and Andromeda." In *MMA Notable Acquisitions 1965–1975*. New York, 1975, p. 163. Described and discussed briefly; illus.

NOTES

1. See Guy Delmarcel, "De Legende van Perseus in de vlaamse Tapijtkunst van de 16de eeuw: iconographische Beschouwingen," *XLIII° Congres Sint-Niklaas-Waas 1974: Annalen*, Federatie van Kringen voor Oudheidkunde en Geschiedenis van Belgie vzw, pp. 268–69. Delmarcel also discussed iconographic details in a later *Story of Perseus* cycle (ca. 1560–65) that identify its source as Raoul Lefèvre's *Recueil des histoires de Troie*. See the discussion of the literary source of this later series, with credit to Delmarcel, in Nello Forti Grazzini, *Museo d'Arti Applicate: Arazzi* (Milan, 1984) p. 26.

2. For further information concerning late medieval moralized versions of Ovid's *Metamorphoses*, Delmarcel ("De Legende," p. 269 n. 2) referred readers to Erwin Panofsky, *Renaissance and Renascences in Western Art* (Stockholm, 1960) pp. 78–81 n. 2. For still more information on this subject and its complexities, see Joseph Engels, *Etudes sur l'Ovide moralisé* (Groningen and Batavia, 1945).

3. The author wishes to thank Nadine Orenstein for identifying this possible design source. For the Robetta print, see Mark J. Zucker, *Early Italian Masters*, vol. 25 (Commentary) of *The Illustrated Bartsch* (New York, 1984) pp. 541, 544; illus. p. 543, an example in the Cabinet des Estampes, Bibliothèque Nationale, Paris. The figures in question are the two rightmost in a group of five men standing to the left of a well in the middle distance.

4. Guy Delmarcel, *"The Triumph of the Seven Virtues* and Related Brussels Tapestries of the Early Renaissance," *Acts of the Tapestry Symposium, November 1976*, Fine Arts Museums of San Francisco (San Francisco, 1979) pp. 156–57 and fig. 5.

5. The record of the purchase was first published by Jules Houdoy, *Les tapisseries de haute lisse: Histoire de la fabrication lilloise du XIVᵉ au XVIIIᵉ siècle* (Lille and Paris, 1871) p. 143. It included a total of thirty-one pieces of tapestry, eight showing the *Story of Perseus*; the others showed hunting and birding scenes, shepherds, and woodsmen. The sale is mentioned also in Alphonse Wauters, *Les tapisseries bruxelloises* (Brussels, 1878) p. 74; and in Göbel 1923, vol. 1, p. 308. Marguerite Calberg, "La pluie d'or," *Revue Belge d'Archéologie et d'Histoire de l'Art* 38 (1969) p. 73 n. 3, credits Crick-Kuntziger with the information that this tapestry merchant's name was not van den Tombe, as in Houdoy, or van der Tommen, as in Wauters and Göbel, but van der Tombe.

6. Delmarcel, "De Legende," p. 268.

7. For a discussion and illustrations of this tapestry, see Marthe Crick-Kuntziger, "Un chef-d'oeuvre inconnu du Maître de la 'Dame à la Licorne,'" *Revue Belge d'Archéologie et d'Histoire de l'Art* 23 (1954) pp. 3–20. Comparing it to the *Dame à la licorne* in Paris and the *Penelope* fragment in Boston, Crick-Kuntziger concluded that this hanging could be dated about 1480–90; we believe that it could have been woven even later in the fifteenth century. For a large color illustration of it, see Madeleine Jarry, *World Tapestry: From Its Origins to the Present* (New York, 1969) pp. 118–19.

8. Concerning the Cleveland tapestry, see W.M.M. [William M. Milliken], "'Perseus and Andromeda,' a Gothic Tapestry in the John Huntington Collection," *Bulletin of the Cleveland Museum of Art* 14 (1927) pp. 34–36, illus. pp. 37–40; and also Ella S. Siple, "Art in America: A Late Gothic Tapestry at Cleveland," *Burlington Magazine* 51 (1927) pp. 99–100, not illus.

9. For the tapestry said to be in Tarragona, see a photograph from the Arthur Kingsley Porter collection, now in the Visual Collections in the library at the Fogg Art Museum, Cambridge (mount no. 876/Sp 216/2[d]); it illustrates either the Heilbronner tapestry itself or an exact duplicate of it. The tapestry from the château de Chaumont is described as showing essentially the same episodes but with details that do not correspond to those found in the Heilbronner tapestry. See *Tapisseries françaises et flamandes du XVIᵉ siècle*, exh. cat., Musée d'Arras (Arras, 1966) no. 2, not illus.

10. For the hanging in Tarragona, see a photograph from the Arthur Kingsley Porter collection (as in note 9 here), mount no. 876/Sp 216/(a). For notes on the near-duplicate piece, see *Catalogue of the . . . Collection . . . formed by Sir Lionel Phillips, Bart.*, Christie's, London, April 23 . . . May 8, 1913, no. 497[d], illus.; and *British XVIII Century Portraits . . . Property of the Estate of the Late Arthur Curtiss James*, Parke-Bernet, New York, November 13–15, 1941, no. 393, illus.

11. See Delmarcel's discussion of his list in "De Legende," p. 268, and also p. 269 n. 4, where he refers to three sixteenth-century citations of sets of seven pieces each, the first two known for some years, the third offered by Delmarcel for the first time. The earliest reference is to a set bought by François I from Georges Vezellet (or Vescher, Visscher?) of Antwerp in 1529; the second is to a set listed in the inventory (1539) of James V of Scotland; and the third is to a set mentioned in the inventory (1560) of Beltrán de la Cueva. See Wauters, *Les tapisseries bruxelloises*, p. 114 n. 2; Thomson 1930, p. 274; and *Revista de Archivos, Bibliotecas y Museos* 9 (1883) p. 22.

12. For the tapestry in Boston, see Adolph S. Cavallo, *Tapestries of Europe and of Colonial Peru in the Museum of Fine Arts, Boston* (Boston, 1967) pp. 95–98 and pl. 25. The smaller version in Sweden, which shows essentially the same figures of Zeus and Danae (in reverse), some different figures in the foreground, and less of the action in the background, is discussed briefly in Cavallo, *Tapestries*, p. 97, with references to John Böttiger, *Tapisseries à figures des XVIᵉ et XVIIᵉ siècles, appartenant à des collections privées de la Suède* (Stockholm, 1928) p. 8 and pl. 6, and to an illustration in Göbel 1923, vol. 2, fig. 109.

13. See Calberg, "La pluie d'or," pp. 74, 76–77, and fig. 5. The reference given there is to the second occasion on which the tapestry was offered for sale at Sotheby's, on February 22, 1963, in the catalogue of which this piece, no. 27, is not illustrated. It is described and illustrated in *Catalogue of English Pottery . . . Tapestries . . .*, Sotheby's, London, February 2, 1962, no. 93.

14. Mentioned by Cavallo, *Tapestries*, p. 97, with the source given as the Marillier Subject Index, "Mythology—Perseus and Andromeda." The author thanks Guy Delmarcel for advising him in a letter of the tapestry's present location.

15. See Forti Grazzini, *Museo d'Arti Applicate*, p. 26, and his reference to Elisabeth Dhanens, "Twee Tapijtwerken uit het bezit van Margareta van Parma in het Palazzo del Quirinale te Rome," *Revue Belge d'Archéologie et d'Histoire de l'Art* 20 (1951) pp. 223–36, fig. 3.

16. See Delmarcel, "De Legende," pp. 268–69, and Forti Grazzini, *Museo d'Arti Applicate*, pp. 25–28, pls. 29–33, with credit to Delmarcel for identifying this version of the subject and its source in Lefèvre's *Recueil des histoires de Troie*. In the classical versions, Danaus is not mentioned (Lefèvre took the character from Boccaccio), and it is Bellerophon himself who kills the Chimera.

17. From Delmarcel, "De Legende," p. 269 n. 9, with thanks to Wendy Hefford. The reference comes from the unpublished Marillier Subject Index of Tapestries, Victoria and Albert Museum, London, "Mythology—Heroes, M–Z," with a notation concerning the sale: *Milton Abbey, Dorset. Catalogue of the Entire Contents of the Historic Mansion*, September 19–24, 1932, no. 1872A. See also the discussion and illustration of this piece in Forti Grazzini, *Museo d'Arti Applicate*, p. 26 and Appendix II, fig. 4.

18. See Forti Grazzini, *Museo d'Arti Applicate*, p. 26, where he credits Delmarcel with bringing this tapestry to his attention; illus., Appendix II, fig. 5.

Moses and Aaron before Pharaoh

Two complete and two partial scenes from *The Story of Moses*

Southern Netherlands, 1515–30
Wool warp; wool and silk wefts
9 ft. 1 in. × 16 ft. 5 in. (2.77 m × 5.00 m)
10–12 warp yarns per inch, 4–5 per centimeter
From the Collection of James Stillman, Gift of Dr. Ernest G. Stillman, 1925 (25.177.1 [right half]; 25.177.2 [left half])

CONDITION

At some time the hanging was cut down the center; it came to the Metropolitan Museum in two pieces. The line of the cut, which has since been eliminated by reweaving with new warp and weft yarns, passed directly down the middle of the column that rises in the center of the field. The fact that an outdoor scene showing a shepherd in a meadow continues along the top of the field without interruption behind the column from its left side to its right removes any doubt that the hanging was originally woven in one piece. Columns used in this way to separate one narrative space from its neighbor also appear in hangings from a contemporary and stylistically similar series of the *Story of Daniel and Nebuchadnezzar*.[1]

The hanging retains none of its original edges. It is obvious that a reasonably wide strip was cut off the top since a number of motifs, including the tops of some buildings and the top of the shepherd's head, the tops of the columns, and possibly also shallow arches that may have spanned the spaces between the columns, are all missing.[2]

The hanging has also suffered a number of serious alterations and repairs. Beginning at the left, the half-column has been joined to the rest of the field with new yarns. Its design, color, and texture correspond to those of the piece as a whole, but it is not clear whether the column belonged there originally or was moved to that position from some other tapestry. A seam runs diagonally from the middle of that column to the right eye of the man crouched in the corner; another seam extends from the ends of this man's right fingers directly upward to meet the first seam at a point along the hem of the jacket on the man next to the column. The crouching man's right arm has been completely restored with modern yarns. The figures of both this man and the one sprawling on the floor next to him are surrounded by

seams and restorations. It seems quite certain that these figures were not here originally, that they were taken from another tapestry in the set, and for some unknown reason were patched into this hanging. The fabric in this region has been so much disturbed and reworked that we cannot be certain that the sprawled man's head belongs with his body or that the basin which seems to rest on his left arm (the fingers holding the rim are restorations) belongs with that body. The entire bottom of the left compartment, including the bottom of the half-column and the incomplete armorial shield at its base, the club lying next to it, the entire floor of the room, and the bottom of the central column, including its armorial shield, is modern restoration executed with new warp and weft yarns. There are a number of other places where the fabric has either been patched or simply rejoined, the most important involving the left wrist and hand of the man walking toward the left before Pharaoh's throne and the covered cup he seems to be holding in that hand. A great deal of the fabric in the rest of this compartment has been repaired by reweaving modern weft yarns on the original warp, but the drawing seems to have survived these restorations with relatively little alteration.

The weaving at the bottom of the right compartment, including the fabric representing the base of the half-column at the right and part of an armorial shield shown on it, as well as the entire floor of the room, is also modern. The figure of the leaping dog in the center is surrounded by yarns that have been replaced, and it seems unlikely that it belongs here. The head and upper left shoulder of the man in the foreground at the right have been patched in, as have the torso and head of the second woman behind him and the entire top half of the column next to her, the upper part of which has been restored with a different pattern. The bottom of the patched-in portion of that column (just above the lion-mask) together with the shoulders of the woman next to it have been completely restored with modern yarns. There are a number of long joins in the center of this compartment. One of them runs across the middle of Pharaoh's figure. A second, longer join traces the right edge of the figure of Moses, who stands next to the enthroned Pharaoh at the left; and a third join runs down the center of Moses' body. There are extensive

47

repairs by reweaving modern yarns on the original warp throughout this compartment. The most important passages occur in the upper parts of the bodies of the two men behind (above) Aaron and Moses, in the skirt front and left sleeve of the closer of the two, and in the lower part of Aaron's gown.

The hanging undoubtedly had a border which is now missing. Its pattern may have matched that of a hanging showing Moses leading the Israelites out of Egypt, woven after the same series of cartoons, which belonged to V. and C. Sternberg in London in 1966 (see note 2). Its border had baluster arabesques in the side sections and an arabesque of acanthus leaves in the upper section. The lower section was not present. A different border pattern, showing garlands of leaves, flowers, and grapes on all four sides, appears on another closely related tapestry, sold in Paris in 1936, which shows Moses discovering the Israelites worshiping the golden calf (see note 2). On the other hand the Metropolitan Museum's piece might have shown yet a different border pattern, one using a row of bells along the top of the field and arabesques in the side and bottom border sections, like the borders of a number of stylistically related early sixteenth-century tapestries.[3]

The dyes have faded so much throughout the piece that the colors, now muted and neutralized, read almost exclusively as tones of blue, pink, and brown.

DESCRIPTION AND SUBJECT

The following description refers to the hanging in its present condition. The interpretation of each scene, based on what we surmise may have been the correct and intended disposition of forms, will be considered after the piece has been described.

The field shows episodes set in two interior spaces that are separated by a column in the center of the hanging. Halves of similar columns flank the outer ends of the hanging. This suggests that the cartoons after which 47 was woven showed a series of episodes separated by columns, possibly in the bays of an arcade, a compositional scheme that had been fully developed by this time in the category of choir hangings.[4] The central column in 47 is represented as made of gold or gilt metal with insertions of light-colored stone. It is shaped like a great baluster made up of urns, collars, and cylinders and decorated primarily with acanthus leaves. Lion-masks encircle the column above the center; three links of chain drop from each mouth. The urn-shaped element at the top of the column and the shield of arms at the bottom are totally restored. We cannot say whether this shield (or the other two in the piece) shows the original arms or those of a later owner. The blazon reads as follows: azure a fess or between two trefoils and a crescent argent (or?) in chief and a trefoil argent (or?) in base.

In the center of the left compartment Pharaoh, labeled *fara[o or u?]* above his head, is seated on a throne hung at the back with a patterned velvet or damask cloth of honor. The dais beneath his feet is covered with a patterned pile carpet. He wears a fur-lined velvet or damask robe with a wide collar, a heavy gold necklace, and a low circular hat over a cap. He holds a scepter upright in his left hand, and with his right he gestures toward a man and woman standing at the left. The man, bearded and wearing a turban and a plain velvet robe girdled with a sash, looks at the king but gestures toward the young woman standing at the left. She is dressed in a turban and a fur-lined, unpatterned gown girdled by a ribbon with a beaded and tasseled drop. She holds her hands before her breast in a gesture of supplication or prayer. Three male and two female courtiers and two soldiers stand behind this couple. The space opens out beyond them to show a deep landscape where hills and buildings

rise on the horizon. A man wearing full armor crouches in the lower left corner of the field; he turns his head to the right and grasps a striped serpent in his left hand. Another male figure, wearing a fitted robe, sprawls on the floor behind and to the right of the armored man. His face has dark skin and features that express pain or alarm. A shallow basin containing red stones or embers is below his head, and what appear to be the fingers of his left hand clutch the gadrooned rim of this basin. As noted above (Condition), the fingers are modern restorations, the head may not belong with this body, and the basin may not have been associated with this figure in the original design. A second striped serpent raises its head just above the basin; its body passes behind the sprawled man's right wrist, and its tail is caught under the armored man's left foot. The half-column along the left edge, which may not belong to this field, corresponds in its component elements more or less to the

central column and the half-column at the far right. It shows the same kinds of baluster motifs and the same lion-mask with chain drop, but the upper section is quite different. The base of this column, with acanthus leaves and part of an armorial shield, and the club lying on the floor next to it have been completely restored. The blazon, now practically illegible, may perhaps show the second and fourth quarters of a shield, the second with a field azure strewn with trefoils or, the fourth with a field argent charged with a lion-mask or.

In the right foreground of this compartment a man wearing hose and a short velvet tunic under an unpatterned mantle decorated with a row of stylized leaves or lilies walks toward the left. He has a sword at his left side, and he holds a double cup in his raised left hand toward which he gestures with his right. On his head is a low circular hat with a wide dentated brim set at a rakish angle over a pleated cap. A woman wearing an unpatterned, ermine-lined fitted gown and a hood stands behind this man and gestures as though presenting him to the Pharaoh or the court in general. Two male and two female courtiers and a halberdier stand behind these two figures, between the throne on one side and the central column on the other. In the upper right corner of the compartment the space opens out to show a meadow.

The view into the meadow continues in the upper left corner of the right compartment. There a man dressed as a shepherd in hose, short tunic, and cowl is seated on the grass looking upward and holding his hands in an attitude of prayer. What appear to be letters inscribed on the shepherd's cowl have been heavily restored and are now illegible. Two sheep appear in the middle distance of the meadow and in the far distance rises what seems to be a grove of umbrella-shaped trees and tall rushes but which is in fact a representation of the burning bush (see below). Inside, the room represents Pharaoh's throne room, as in the left compartment. The king, labeled *faraou* across the end of his right sleeve, is seated on the same throne. His costume is the same, but an open crown now tops his hat and the fur lining of his robe is clearly represented as ermine (white with black tails). A halberdier and two male and two female courtiers stand next to the throne at the right while two halberdiers, a shepherd (?), two female courtiers, and one male courtier stand at the left. In the foreground two men stand to the left of the throne. The one closer to it wears a plain long gown and a cowl; the other is dressed like a priest, with a miter on his head and an ermine-lined, dalmatic-like tunic worn over a long gown. A row of capital letters appears in the tunic's wide border; they read N-O-R/A-A (Aaron in reverse). This man looks earnestly at Pharaoh and raises both hands; his attitude makes it clear that he is pleading a cause. The man wearing the cowl holds a long rod upright in his left hand and gestures with his right as he, too, looks directly at the king. A small dog labeled *Adictus* (?) across the back and shoulders leaps up on its hind legs in front of this figure. Facing the two men stands a man wearing an ermine-lined, patterned damask or velvet robe over a patterned gown, with a tasseled cap on his head.

The elements in the lower part of the half-column at the right side of the hanging match those in the central column. In the upper part of the half-column, the lower section has been patched in and the upper section completely reconstructed with modern yarns. Among the acanthus leaves at the bottom of the half-column, where the fabric has been heavily restored, appears a motif that may represent either the dexter half of a small armorial shield or the third quarter of a larger shield. The blazon reads as azure bezanty or, a chief or.

The tapestry shows several incidents in the *Story of Moses* or the *Story of Exodus*. We prefer to use the former title since a number of contemporary references to Moses cycles have survived, but we have none in which *Exodus* is used in the title of a tapestry series. Breck (1922, 58; 1926, 21) wrote of this tapestry that half of it showed Moses and Aaron before Pharaoh and the other half showed "the Miracle of the Rods turned into Serpents." But the representation is more complicated than that. We believe that in its original form the hanging showed, in its left half, the episode of the child Moses being put to the test after breaking Pharaoh's crown and, in its right half, Moses and Aaron pleading with Pharaoh to let the Israelites leave Egypt. However the left-hand compartment has been altered in such a way that it now shows not only the trial scene but also some of the episode of Aaron turning his rod into a serpent and the Egyptian magicians doing the same

(Exodus 7:6–12). As already noted, the crouching and sprawling figures in the lower left corner and the two serpents have been patched in. They were undoubtedly removed from another panel in the series. The main part of this composition, which involves all the other figures and the basin that now appears to be lying in the sprawled figure's hand, concerns the trial of the child Moses, an incident that does not appear in Scripture. It comes from versified editions of the Bible and has survived in a number of different forms. The version we offer here was taken from Herman de Valencienne's twelfth-century *Histoire de la Bible.* There it is said that one day the child Moses took hold of Pharaoh's shining crown and dashed it to the floor. (The tapestry designer has shown Pharaoh here with his hat but without the crown that surmounts it in the scene at the right.) The monarch shouted that the boy, who uncrowned him before his people, should be killed; but a wise man pointed out that the child may have behaved as he did not out of malice but out of childishness. He proposed that two basins be brought in, one containing crystals, the other, burning coals. If the child took an ember, it would indicate that he had not yet developed mature understanding. If he took a crystal, it would show that he knew enough to distinguish between the two. In that case one might assume that he had grasped Pharaoh's crown out of malice and he would be killed. Pharaoh's daughter sadly took the child to the basins. He looked at the crystals but took an ember and put it into his mouth, burning his tongue. At that, Pharaoh realized that the child did not understand what he had done, and he forgave him.[5] Since in Herman's account Pharaoh's daughter holds the child during the test and nudges him away from the crystals but in the tapestry Pharaoh's daughter seems to be the suppliant woman standing at the left, it seems likely that the designer did not use Herman as his source.

This episode became popular in late medieval art through the influence of the *Speculum Humanae Salvationis*, where it appears as a prefiguration of the toppling of idols as the Christ Child rides into Egypt with Mary and Joseph.[6] The *Speculum* also found a number of other parallels between the stories of Moses and those of Christ and the Virgin, which helps explain the popularity of Moses at this time. In chapter 8, when Pharaoh's butler dreams of a vine, the event is likened to the Tiburtine Sibyl's showing Augustus a vision of the Virgin and Child as well as to the birth of Christ and the blooming of Aaron's rod. Chapter 10 compares the ark of the testament, which contained Aaron's flowering rod, to Mary. In chapter 11, Pharaoh's ordering the Israelites' male children to be drowned is compared to Herod's ordering the slaughter of the innocents.[7]

556

The episode of the burning bush (Exodus 3:1–6), which appears in the upper left corner of the right half of the tapestry, introduces the episodes dealing with the manhood of Moses. The bush was also interpreted as a type of the Virgin. In the *Speculum,* Mary, still a virgin after the birth, is likened to the bush which, though covered with flames, was not consumed and remained green. God was in the bush, as He was in Mary's womb.[8] In this scene Moses, having taken Jethro's sheep to the mountain of Horeb in the desert of Midian, first hears the Lord's voice coming to him from the burning bush (Exodus 3:1–3). The next incident, played out in the main part of this composition, deals with the visit that Moses and his brother Aaron made to Pharaoh at the Lord's direction. They ask the king to let the Israelites go into the desert to sacrifice to Him. Pharaoh refuses and instructs his overseers and taskmasters to load more work on the Israelites to keep them from idleness (Exodus 5:1–9). Aaron, dressed as a priest, stands in the foreground at the left; Moses stands between him and Pharaoh. The two men at either side of Pharaoh are clearly objecting to the Israelites' proposal, and the man facing Aaron and Moses seems to be delivering the ruler's negative reply. As noted above (Condition), the dog seems to have been patched into the fabric. Since it has no special significance in this narrative, we assume that it was taken from some other hanging, perhaps from another in this set of tapestries. However the label (*Adictus?*) across its back suggests that it came from a hanging in some allegorical cycle like the story of the *Cerf fragile* (see the very similar hound *peine* in the right foreground of 32b).

SOURCE OF THE DESIGN

Ackerman (1924–25, 268) included this hanging (then still in two pieces) in a list of tapestries she believed were designed by an artist she identified as Anthonne, son of Pierre Ferret of Tournai. We see no reason to attribute the design of 47 to him or any other particular artist. It was certainly the work of that class of anonymous designers who, as Joubert suggested, conceived the closely related tapestry in the Musée de Cluny from the series of the *Story of Daniel and Nebuchadnezzar,* along with a host of stylistically similar pieces.[9]

None of the figures in 47 has been traced to a source. The designers who worked them into groups and full compositions most likely borrowed at least some of them from prints. Some figures represent stock patterns that were also used in completely different contexts. For example, the woman standing to the right of the cupbearer in the trial of the child Moses scene, with her head in profile, her right arm held behind her back, and

her left arm bent up at the elbow, appears again, somewhat differently drawn and dressed, in two pieces from a set of four contemporaneous hunting tapestries in the Musée de Cluny.[10] A male figure striking the same pose appears in the right foreground of one of two *Story of Daniel and Nebuchadnezzar* tapestries in San Simeon.[11] In the left-center foreground of the same tapestry there is a male figure whose head, headdress, and body appear to have been taken from the pattern that was used for the cupbearer in 47.[12] In the other *Daniel and Nebuchadnezzar* tapestry in San Simeon there is a figure of a man standing at the left end of the field which appears to have been based on the pattern that served for the figure of the man interceding for the suppliant lady in the trial scene in 47.[13] Both men use essentially the same gestures, the left hand crossed over the chest and the right hand holding what looks like a pleated piece of paper, and both men wear the same kind of plain velvet robe. However the torso of the man in 47 is twisted sharply to the right, whereas the other man's torso is relaxed.

MANUFACTURE AND DATE

When the hanging (in two pieces) came to the Metropolitan Museum on loan in 1922 and again when it was made a gift, Breck (1922, 58; 1926, 21) attributed it to France; in the earlier publication he observed that although the compositions may be dated in the early sixteenth century, the weaving itself might have been executed later. In the catalogue entry prepared for its exhibition in Jerusalem in 1965, the piece was described as Tournai work of the early sixteenth century. A hanging that was woven after a cartoon in the same series, and that was exhibited by V. and C. Sternberg in London in 1966, was called "late Gothic Tournai" (see note 2).

This piece has been attributed to Tournai because it shows stylistic affinities with some surviving tapestries that are thought to represent tapestry cycles documented as having been sold by Tournai merchants in the first quarter of the sixteenth century.[14] These records do not mention any *Story of Moses* pieces. However we know that in 1514 the Tournai weaver and merchant Clément Sarrasin bequeathed to his brother Jacques one or more cartoons of "Moses," so it seems likely that such pieces were produced in Tournai.[15]

We have other documentary references to *Story of Moses* tapestries dating between the end of the fifteenth century and the middle of the sixteenth, and we also have a number of tapestries that have survived from that period. It is recorded that in 1491 the city of Arras paid Jean Villers, a local tapestry weaver, merchant, or upholsterer, for a tapestry bed and perhaps also other pieces for a chamber, showing the *Story of Moses.*[16] Anne de Bretagne's inventory of 1494 mentions eight pieces of tapestry of *Moses* recently bought from Guillaume Mesnagier of Tours.[17] Some *Moses* tapestries are listed among a number of pieces that Piero de' Medici pawned to Agostini Chigi in Rome in 1496.[18] Among the one hundred thirty tapestries that Cardinal Wolsey bought for Hampton Court in 1522 were four pieces of a *Story of Moses.*[19] According to Thomson there was at Tattershall about 1522 a tapestry "in the which Moses standeth with the tables, and the angel, maketh water issue out of the conducte."[20] In Henry VIII's inventory of 1547 three *Moses* tapestries (two qualified as "olde") were listed at Westminster; five more were at Woodstock; and four at The More showed borders with Cardinal Wolsey's arms, presumably the four that Wolsey had bought in 1522.[21]

The existence of a few other *Moses* tapestries woven after totally different sets of cartoons during the end of the fifteenth century or the first quarter of the sixteenth proves that the cycle to which 47 belongs cannot with any degree of certainty be associated with any of the documentary references cited above and therefore that those references cannot be used to date the Metropolitan Museum's hanging. One such piece, formerly in the cathedral in Zamora and now in the Casa de la Villa (City Hall) in Madrid, shows the rod-into-serpent incident at its left end and in the center and right end the Egyptians drowning in the Red Sea as the Israelites continue on the far shore.[22] It was designed toward the end of the fifteenth century. Another piece, designed about 1500–1510, shows the Egyptians drowning in the Red Sea. It is preserved in the Museum of Fine Arts, Boston.[23] A piece that postdates this by about fifteen years shows Pharaoh's daughter discovering the infant Moses at the riverbank. It is in the parish church of Sankt Maria Lyskirchen, Cologne.[24]

While 47 seems too late in style to have been mentioned before 1514, it could nevertheless represent the cartoon (or series of cartoons) Sarrasin owned or any of the hangings mentioned in the documents of later years. The date of 1514 is a perfectly reasonable one for the fashions in costume represented in the Metropolitan Museum's piece. It seems unlikely that it would have been woven later than about 1530 when such garments would have looked outmoded.

RELATED TAPESTRIES

A tapestry that was woven after the same series of cartoons and another tapestry that was based either on these cartoons or versions of them have survived. The first shows Moses leading the Israelites out of Egypt. In 1966 it was the property of V. and C. Sternberg in London (see note 2). Its height was given as 4.67 meters. The Metropolitan Museum's tapestry is 2.77 meters high, and, even allowing for the loss of the upper and lower borders and part of the top of the field, the difference in height between 47 and the London piece is so great that the two pieces could not have come from the same set. The second closely related tapestry was sold in Paris in 1936; it showed Moses finding the Israelites worshiping the golden calf (see note 2). Despite certain differences in the interpretation of the figures and details of the columns, it is clear that this piece was woven either after a variant version of these cartoons or after the same cartoons interpreted in a different design or weaving shop, perhaps at a different time.

We have no way of determining the number of subjects that might have been shown in a complete set of these tapestries nor the number of pieces it might have contained. The Metropolitan Museum's hanging shows four subjects. They are the trial of the child Moses; Moses seeing the burning bush; Moses and Aaron pleading with Pharaoh; and the episode of the rods turned into serpents. The piece formerly in London represented the Israelites leaving Egypt and the one sold in Paris showed them worshiping the golden calf. That makes a total of six subjects that we are fairly certain were represented in this cycle. Tapestries that have survived from other *Moses* cycles of this period or slightly later show subjects that probably were also represented in this series. The scene of Pharaoh's daughter finding the infant Moses, the subject of the piece in Cologne (see note 24), almost certainly would have been included. One or more incidents in the crossing of the Red Sea, another critical episode which appears, for example, in the earlier tapestry now in the Casa de la Villa in Madrid and the somewhat later one in Boston (see notes 22 and 23), would probably also have been represented. The subject of Moses making water flow from the rock, which was shown in the piece believed to have been at Tattershall about 1522 (see note 20), might have been included, as the rain of manna might also have been. We know that Cardinal Wolsey bought four *Moses* pieces in 1522 and that Anne de Bretagne owned eight pieces of a *Moses* series at the end of the fifteenth century. But there is nothing to indicate how many scenes each of those hangings showed, nor whether one group or the other represented a complete cycle of tapestries.

HISTORY

Given to the MMA by Dr. Ernest G. Stillman, from the collection of James Stillman, 1925.

EXHIBITIONS

New York, MMA, 1922–25.
Intended for exhibition in Jerusalem, Bezalel National Art Museum, Israel Museum, 1965, in *Old Masters and the Bible*, but not exhibited; mentioned and illustrated in the catalogue for that exhibition, no. 30.

PUBLICATIONS

J. B. [Joseph Breck]. "A Loan of Tapestries." *MMA Bulletin* 17 (1922) p. 58. Discussed briefly as two tapestries.
Ackerman, Phyllis. "The Ferrets and the Poissoniers." *Art in America* 13 (1924–25) p. 268. Mentioned as two tapestries.
J. B. [Joseph Breck]. "Accessions and Notes: A Gift of Tapestries." *MMA Bulletin* 21 (1926) p. 21. Discussed briefly as two tapestries.

NOTES

1. A decorative column rather like this one rises from the bottom to the top of the field in the center of the *Daniel and Nebuchadnezzar* tapestry in the Musée de Cluny, and there are similar columns rising somewhat off-center in related pieces now preserved in the château de Langeais and the Museum of Art, Rhode Island School of Design, Providence. See Joubert 1987, no. 19, fig. 177, for the Cluny piece, and for the other two pieces, figs. 179 and 180. See also larger illustrations of the two pieces in France in J. P. Asselberghs, *La tapisserie tournaisienne au XVIᵉ siècle*, exh. cat. (Tournai, 1968) nos. 25 and 26; and of the piece in Rhode Island in Miriam Amy Banks, "A Nebuchadnezzar Tapestry in Providence," *Art in America* 14 (1925–26) p. 149.
2. Compare the distance between the tops of the heads and the top of the field, and also the conformation of the tops of the columns, to the corresponding details in a tapestry showing Moses leading the Israelites out of Egypt that appears to have been woven after the same series of cartoons; it was exhibited in *Four Centuries of Tapestry on Exhibition*, exh. cat., V. and C. Sternberg (London, 1966) no. 2, illus. Also compare the same features in another piece that seems to have been woven after a version of these cartoons and shows the Israelites worshiping the golden calf; see *Tableaux modernes . . . Tapisseries . . .* , Hôtel Drouot, Paris, June 23, 1936, no. 80, illus. The columns at the two ends of this piece support the springings of a shallow arch.
3. See especially the *Story of Daniel and Nebuchadnezzar* hangings at the Musée de Cluny and two related ones in the Hearst Collection, San Simeon, California, as well as tapestries from the cycles of *La condamnation de Banquet* and *L'histoire de Calcou:* Joubert 1987, no. 19, figs. 177, 181–84. The four hangings from the *Story of Hercules* in the MMA (48a–d in the present catalogue) also have such a border, as do a number of other pieces woven in the first quarter of the sixteenth century and associated with Tournai merchants; see Asselberghs, *La tapisserie tournaisienne au XVIᵉ siècle*, p. 8 n. 10 and nos. 5 and 6, illus.
4. For an example of the type showing columns separating the episodes, see the *Lives of Christ and the Virgin* choir hangings of 1511 in the Cathedral Saint-Sauveur in Aix-en-Provence, illus. in *Les tapisseries de la Vie du Christ et de la Vierge d'Aix-en-Provence*, exh. cat., Musée des Tapisseries (Aix-en-Provence, 1977). For hangings that show scenes in the bays of an arcade, see the *Life of the Virgin* choir tapestries of about 1500 in the church of Notre-Dame in Beaune, illus. in Göbel 1928, vol. 2, figs. 324, 325.

5. This account was paraphrased from the French text of a manuscript in the Bibliothèque Nationale, Paris, published in Jean Bonnard, *Les traductions de la Bible en vers français au moyen age* (Paris, 1884; Slatkin reprints, Geneva, 1967) p. 16.
6. Louis Réau, *Iconographie de l'art chrétien* (Paris, 1955–59) vol. 2, pt. 1, p. 182. For the text of the account in an early fifteenth-century manuscript of the *Speculum* illustrated with late fifteenth-century woodcuts, see Avril Henry, *The Mirour of Mans Saluacioun, a Middle English Translation of* Speculum Humanae Salvationis: *A Critical Edition of the Fifteenth-Century Manuscript Illustrated from* Der Spiegel der menschen Behältnis, *Speyer: Drach, c. 1475* (Philadelphia, 1987) ch. 11, ll. 1310–56, illus. with woodcuts, pp. 82, 84.
7. See Henry, *Mirour*, ch. 8, ll. 1070–80; ch. 10, ll. 1244–47; ch. 11, ll. 1357–64; some of these subjects illus. pp. 72, 78.
8. See Henry, *Mirour*, ch. 7, ll. 959–70; the burning bush illus. p. 66.
9. Joubert 1987, p. 185.
10. For her exposition of the similarity of the two figures in the Cluny tapestries, see Joubert 1987, pp. 170–71, illus. figs. 164, 165; also p. 177 and fig. 174.
11. The tapestry in San Simeon is illustrated in Joubert 1987, fig. 181; the figure referred to is the third one from the right in the extreme foreground.
12. See Joubert 1987, fig. 181.
13. See Joubert 1987, fig. 182.
14. Lists of such tapestry cycles and of individual pieces that are believed to have survived from some of them have been discussed by Asselberghs, *La tapisserie tournaisienne au XVIᵉ siècle*, pp. 7–8 and nos. 1, 4–9, 28, all illus., and Joubert 1987, p. 185.
15. See Eugène Soil, *Les tapisseries de Tournai* (Tournai and Lille, 1892) pp. 211, 263. The will itself is not dated but the context in which it was found indicates or suggests the date 1514. Although his transcription (p. 211) of the pertinent clause in the document reads "ung de Moïse qui est de papier," Soil refers (p. 263) to the bequest as "les cartons de l'histoire de Moïse," as though it involved a series of cartoons rather than just a single one.
16. Record of payment cited by E. van Drival, *Les tapisseries d'Arras: Etude artistique et historique* (Arras, 1864) pp. 139–40. The description of the pieces is such that it could refer to the ceiling, cover, and curtains for a bed only or to the bed plus floor and wall coverings for the room in which it stood.
17. Cited by J. P. Asselberghs, *Les tapisseries flamandes de la cathédrale de Zamora*, Ph.D. diss., Université Catholique de Louvain, 1964, p. 207.
18. Asselberghs, *Les tapisseries flamandes de . . . Zamora*, p. 207.
19. Thomson 1930, p. 240.
20. W. G. Thomson, *Tapestry Weaving in England from the Earliest Times to the End of the XVIIIth Century* (London, 1914) p. 41. Thomson was probably referring to Tattershall Castle, Lincolnshire, acquired by Henry VIII as a gift from his mother. If so, this piece may have been among those that were listed in his inventory some years later (see the references in note 21 below).
21. See Thomson 1930, respectively pp. 248, 253, 254.
22. Asselberghs, *Les tapisseries flamandes de . . . Zamora*, pp. 23, 204–7, discusses the tapestry itself and its purchase from the cathedral of Zamora by the city of Madrid. The hanging is illustrated in Eulogio Varela Hervias and D. José Moreno Torres, *Casa de la Villa de Madrid* (Madrid, 1951) pl. XLV.
23. Discussed and illustrated in Adolph S. Cavallo, *Tapestries of Europe and of Colonial Peru in the Museum of Fine Arts, Boston* (Boston, 1967) pp. 87–89; pls. 22–22b.
24. Discussed briefly and illustrated in Hugo Rahtgens, *Die kirchlichen Denkmäler der Stadt Köln*, vol. 2, pt. 1, of Paul Clemen, ed., *Die Kunstdenkmäler der Rheinprovinz*, vol. 7, pt. 1, *Die Kunstdenkmäler der Stadt Köln* (Düsseldorf, 1911) p. 308 and fig. 217.

48a

48
Four Episodes in *The Story of Hercules*

a *The Birth of Hercules and Iphicles*
b *The Wedding of Hercules and Deianeira*
c *Hercules and Iole*
d *The Death of Hercules*

Southern Netherlands, 1515–35
Wool warp; wool and silk wefts
48a: 13 ft. 7 1/2 in. × 10 ft. 8 in. (4.15 m × 3.25 m)
9–12 warp yarns per inch, 4–5 per centimeter
48b: 12 ft. 9 in. × 11 ft. (3.89 m × 3.35 m)
10–12 warp yarns per inch, 4–5 per centimeter
48c: 13 ft. 8 in. × 10 ft. 11 in. (4.17 m × 3.33 m)
Two different warp yarns used: brown, 10–11 per inch, 4 per
centimeter; white, 10–13 per inch, 4–5 per centimeter
48d: 13 ft. 3 in. × 11 ft. 1/2 in. (4.04 m × 3.37 m)
8–11 warp yarns per inch, 3–4 per centimeter
Gift of Mrs. Daniel Guggenheim, in memory of her husband, 1935
(35.79.1–4)

CONDITION

The upper and lower striped outer guards of 48a were replaced with narrow bands of modern weaving. Lengths of the same fabric were inserted along both sides in places where the guard had been lost, but some parts of the original striped guard remain at the sides. The selvage appears in places along the outer edges of the upper and lower floral borders in all four hangings. This suggests that at top and bottom the striped guards were stitched on, not woven as part of the main fabric as the guards at the sides were. With the outer guards, part original and part modern, in place, the hanging has its original dimensions. A second outer guard, made of a different modern fabric and not striped, was applied to all four sides of 48a, increasing the original dimensions by some three inches in both height and width.

Four segments of the floral borders on both sides of 48a, one above center and one below on each side, have been restored with modern warp and weft yarns; these segments show undulating vines or grape clusters instead of the usual bunches of flowers and leaves. There are also major replacements in the field, some patches woven with modern warp and weft yarns, others pieces of weaving taken from closely related tapestries. Among these restorations are the panel with a leaf arabesque pattern hanging directly above the head of the woman with the baby in the upper right quarter of the field; the rectangular panel with a trellis pattern at the foot of the

bed; a smaller rectangle with a leaf pattern just below it, to the right; the front of the skirt worn by the woman holding the infant; a small patch of the floor visible under the body of the greyhound in the lower left corner; and most of the floral unit just to the right of center in the openwork arabesque of plant forms that screens the bottom of the field. However the most important restoration involves the entire figure of the woman in the right foreground who holds a rose branch. Because the warp has been cut and rejoined all around this figure, because she is smaller than the other adult women who stand near her, and because she wears a very different kind of costume, it is clear that the fabric on which she is represented was taken from some other tapestry and inserted here. There are also warp joins along lines that follow the contours of the figure of the baby in the cradle, the linens falling over the side, and the right-hand half of the floral arabesque below. There are long joins along the inner edge of the bed curtain in the right foreground and the inner edge of the upper third of the right inner guard. However those parts of the tapestry seem to belong where they are now. There is a good deal of reweaving with modern wefts on the original warp, especially in the areas of highlight in the garments and some of the contours of the figures, in the roofs of the two buildings, and in the dark ground behind the bells, leaves, and pomegranates that form the border along the top. Much of this restoration involves the use of green wool yarns.

The outer guard of 48b has been replaced with striped modern fabric on all four sides, and a second guard of plain modern weaving has been added outside that. Parts of the bell, leaf, and pomegranate border at the top and of the floral arabesque along the bottom of the field have been replaced with modern fabric. Most of the remaining restoration in these places involves reweaving with modern weft yarns on the original warp. Other passages of this kind appear throughout the field, especially in the contours of the figures and the highlights of their garments. In the dark passages these restorations were executed primarily with brown or green wool yarns.

48b

The striped outer guards of 48c were replaced on all four sides, and a second, plain guard was added. The entire upper right corner of the border, including the two outer bell-and-leaf motifs at the top and the topmost floral bunch at the side, was restored with new warp and weft yarns. Both areas show a slight deviation from the normal pattern rhythm. The same kind of restoration appears in two of the bell-and-leaf motifs in the upper border right of center and in the lower half of the floral arabesque along the bottom of the field. The entire fabric has been heavily repaired by inserting modern weft yarns on the original warp. The shadows and highlights in the garments, the architectural elements, the dark floor tiles, and the dark passages serving as backgrounds for the motifs in the upper border have all been restored in this way.

Double modern outer guards have also been sewn to the four sides of 48d, but there are traces of the original outer guards at the sides. Four small segments of the floral band along the bottom have been replaced with modern fabrics. They appear at each corner and at points left and right of center. The small leafy branch in the field directly above Hercules' head has also been replaced. Some of the highlights in the garments and almost all the dark contours and shadows in the field, as well as the dark ground behind the bell-and-leaf motifs in the upper border, have been repaired by inserting modern wefts on the original warp.

These hangings show a few technical peculiarities that merit special notice. In all four pieces the weavers created a few slits in places where they neither relate to the pattern nor are required by it. A small slit of this sort can be seen in 48b in the train of the bride's dress, just below her right elbow. The warp yarns in 48d were spun of naturally colored brown (rather than white or gray) wool, and in places the weft yarns do not cover them completely. In 48c the warp was made up with yarns of brown or white wool (the brown spun heavier than the white) arranged in bands of random widths.

DESCRIPTION AND SUBJECT

These four hangings represent subjects taken from the story of the ancient mythical hero Hercules. Some of them are difficult to interpret, but we can attempt to identify them by comparing the action represented with the accounts given of certain scenes in the literary sources the designer might have used. Rorimer (1933, 1935) and subsequent writers accepted the titles and interpretations that Hunter developed for these tapestries in two short unpublished essays he wrote apparently about the time Mr. Guggenheim acquired the four

hangings.[1] Hunter did not identify the texts he consulted, but he seems to have used versions of the myth that were based on accounts of Hercules' life written by the Greek writers Apollodorus (second century B.C.) and Diodorus (first century B.C.).

The most comprehensive account of Hercules' life to be compiled during the late Middle Ages, only fifty years or so before these tapestries were designed, appears in the first two books of *Le Recueil des histoires de Troie*, which were written in 1464 by Raoul Lefèvre, chaplain to Philippe le Bon, and based on late classical and thirteenth-century texts (see, in the present catalogue, 13a–c). Crick-Kuntziger, writing about a somewhat earlier fragment of tapestry in Brussels showing scenes from Hercules' childhood, quoted extensively from a philologist's report which traced those scenes to specific passages in the first two books of the *Recueil*.[2] The report suggested furthermore that the designer of the tapestry in Brussels might also have been influenced by the scenario for a mime-drama of the twelve labors of Hercules that was presented in 1468 in Bruges during the wedding celebration of Charles le Téméraire and Margaret of York. In 48a–d the narrative details represented do not tally precisely with the corresponding accounts in Lefèvre's *Recueil*. However the birth, wedding, and death scenes leave no doubt that the person who planned the design either developed his own variations on the *Recueil* or used a text derived from it. Kurth (1942, 242 n. 1 [left col.]) called attention to one such text, *Les proesses et vaillances du preux Hercules*, a prose romance that appears in a fifteenth-century illustrated manuscript now in the Nationalbibliothek in Vienna (Cod. 2586) and as a printed text (Paris, 1500, and later editions).

Since the figures in the Metropolitan Museum's hangings are not labeled and there are no expository texts on banderoles above or below the scenes, we cannot be sure that we have identified all the subjects correctly. Therefore the following interpretations are offered purely as tentative ones.

The first tapestry, 48a, shows groups of figures gathered in two different interior spaces. The main action takes place within a bedroom. Two marble columns with carved capitals, collars, and bases support the left end of the roof. The rear wall of the chamber is made of ashlar masonry and has, in the upper left corner, a small arched window that is partly covered by a latticework screen; there is no front wall depicted. The large bed is hung with plain curtains, a patterned damask or velvet headcloth, and needleworked borders and lambrequins. A carved wooden cabinet stands to the left of it and a ewer and cup rest on top of the cabinet. A woman sits up in bed and addresses a nurse or maid who stands holding an infant. This woman wears a long gown fitted at the torso and waist, a linen shirt cut with a high, round neckline, and a cap and hood. Two more women, similarly dressed, appear to the left; one is kneeling, the other standing. They tend an infant who lies in a cradle at the foot of the bed. A fourth woman in a somewhat different costume—a long, wide bodice over sleeves that bulge out over the upper arm and a skirt lined with fur and parted over a kirtle in the center—stands in the lower right foreground. In the background at the left there is another building, clearly a temple, open at the front to expose its interior space. Two marble columns support the roof at the right. The rear wall, which appears to be curved, is pierced by two ranges of tall, narrow arched windows screened with latticework. A statue of Diana, fully clothed, stands on a circular altar in the center, and a cow is shown leaving the building at the right. Three women sit or kneel on the temple steps. Between the two buildings a low masonry wall, with an orange tree behind it, spans the space in the middle distance. Hills and the turrets of castles appear against the horizon in the far distance.

The main subject of 48a is the birth of Hercules and his half brother Iphicles. Accounts of Hercules' conception and birth differ. The version given here comes from Lefèvre's text (using Latin rather than Greek forms of the characters' names; however we retain Iphicles rather than Lefèvre's Ypecleus).[3] Hercules was conceived by Jupiter who visited his mother, Alcmene, disguised as her husband, Amphytrion; the following night Amphytrion himself fathered Iphicles. We see Alcmene in the bed. The infant Hercules occupies the cradle, and the child held by the nurse is Iphicles. Rorimer (1935, 140) correctly identified the scene at the left as one dealing with the wrath of the ever-jealous Juno and her intervention in the birth. Galantis, Alcmene's governess, went often to pray for her safe delivery in the temple of Diana on the grounds of Amphytrion's castle. Juno, in various disguises, waited in the temple to have news of Alcmene's condition. Learning when Alcmene was about to deliver her child, Juno performed her magic. She sat with her legs crossed, which caused Alcmene to do the same. For three days Juno sat like this, every now and then altering her disguise so that she appeared to be a different person or beast but always in the same posture. The elder female figure sitting apparently cross-legged on the steps of the temple is meant to represent Juno in one of these disguises. Galantis realized that the person or beast always sitting there with legs crossed was evil and was preventing Alcmene from giving birth. To trick the evil power she and another lady

in the household, the two younger women kneeling on the temple steps, at the right, went back to the temple and thanked Diana for the delivery of a fair son to Alcmene. When Juno heard that her magic had failed she transformed herself into a cow, which is shown in the tapestry fleeing from the temple into the fields. Immediately Alcmene was released from the spell and delivered her two sons. The youth seated in the left foreground may represent Ganymede disguised by Jupiter as a porter when he visited Alcmene or even Jupiter himself disguised as the servant he impersonated during that visit. The women attending the infant in the cradle seem to be watching the woman in the right foreground who holds a rose branch in her left hand. However, as noted above (Condition), the entire figure of that woman has been inserted to replace whatever the other women were watching.

The side and bottom segments of the border contain narrow dark blue bands decorated with bunches of fruits, flowers, and leaves in natural colors placed end to end, each bunch tied with a pinkish red ribbon. As noted above (Condition), two segments in each side border of this piece are incorrectly restored. They show undulating floral vines or bunches of grapes. There are striped guards along the inner and outer edges of these bands. At the bottom the inner guard is surmounted by an arabesque of intertwined cresting vines that bear a variety of pomegranates, acanthus leaves, and fanciful blossoms at the summits of the crests. The design of the upper border is totally different. There, segments of vines shaped like letters E laid on their sides run end to end along the top edge. From the center of each E drop pairs of acanthus leaves which flank alternately either a bell suspended on a chain or a fruit that resembles an oval pomegranate. This upper border is rendered as though it were a lambrequin hanging free from the upper outer guard, over the tops of the side borders as well as in front of the space in which the characters act out the story.

The border of 48b is the same, with minor variations in the details of the floral arabesque along the bottom. The scene shows a company of richly dressed ladies and gentlemen gathered in or before an arched and vaulted ashlar masonry building which is identified by a tablet above the capital of the central column that is inscribed, in reverse, TEM[the M inverted?]PLE VENVS. A marble column closes the space at each side. An arch decorated with a frieze of acanthus leaves flanking a central rosette surmounts the opening in the wall behind the figures. Through this opening one sees a patterned velvet or damask curtain that lines the main part of the temple's interior from the height of the columns' capitals downward. Above this curtain one has a glimpse of the temple vaults and of bits of landscape that appear beyond the arched openings in the back wall. A priest wearing a hooded gown stands in the center of the company and is about to join the hands of a young lady at the left and a young man facing her. Over doublet and hose, the man wears a funnel-sleeved coat with a fur collar and inscribed bands at the cuffs and hem. He also wears a low, round hat with an upturned brim and wide, round-toed shoes tied over the insteps. He represents the adult Hercules. Four men dressed more or less like him except for their hats, all different, are gathered behind him. The bride has long wavy hair and wears an unpatterned ermine-lined mantle over a funnel-sleeved fitted gown of patterned velvet or damask, trimmed at the neckline, cuffs, and hemline with jeweled bands. She also wears a necklace and a pendant on a chain, and a crown on her head which identifies her as a lady of royal station. Five women dressed in unpatterned gowns stand behind the bride at the left. The two in the background appear to be matrons; they wear close-fitting hoods and no jewelry. The other three are young ladies, who wear caps or hoods and jewels. The one immediately next to the bride holds up the end of her train.

Hunter (see note 1), Rorimer (1935, 140), and Asselberghs (exh. cat. Tournai 1968, 17) are probably correct in identifying the bride as Deianeira, sister of Meleager, daughter of King Oeneus of Calydon, and Hercules' second wife. Lefèvre's account of this wedding differs in some details from the accounts of others. According to him, King Achelous demanded Deianeira in marriage but King Oeneus demurred and sought Hercules' help in preventing the match.[4] Hercules promptly waged war on Achelous (who in other accounts is described as a river god) and ultimately defeated and killed him. The hero then married Deianeira. However, it is also possible that the designer intended to represent not this wedding but that of Hercules and his first wife, Megara. Lefèvre tells how Hercules, earlier in his career, asked Euristus and Amphytrion to go to King Creon of Thebes and present his suit for the hand of the king's daughter, Megara. Creon gave the match his blessing. Hercules and Megara were married and lived happily together until Lincus accused Megara of having been unfaithful to Hercules with him. Lefèvre then says that Hercules slew both of them, although he notes that, according to the Spanish chronicles, Hercules did not kill Megara but put her into a temple of Diana at Thebes and left her there.[5] However it seems more likely, for reasons that will be given presently, that the wedding represented here is indeed that of Hercules and Deianeira.

The third tapestry, 48c, has essentially the same border pattern as 48a, b, and d. The scene is set within a turreted building with front wall removed to reveal the vaulted space inside. The floor is paved with light and dark tiles in a simple pattern of rectangles, lozenges, and diamonds. The back wall contains three arched openings that give on to a space protected by a high ashlar masonry wall. Beyond the wall and above the building the space opens out into a hilly landscape where turreted castles rise in the middle and far distance in the center and at the right. A marble column stands at each side of the space in the foreground. Some richly dressed ladies and gentlemen are gathered in the interior. The women wear unpatterned fitted gowns with low, square necklines and either funnel-shaped sleeves or tight sleeves cut so as to let parts of the shirt fabric beneath show through. The women all wear hoods and necklaces. Four of the men wear coats over jacket, shirt, and hose; three others wear no coat. Four of them wear low, round hats with upturned brims; a fifth wears a turban-like headdress, a sixth has a hood-like cap, and the seventh is hatless. One couple stands in the foreground at the left and another appears behind them. Two men converse in the middle bay at center back. Another man stands under the arch at the right and seems to be gesturing in refusal to the man kneeling before him. The latter is offering a wrapped object to the former. In front of these two figures a woman seated at the right sings from a sheet of music to the accompaniment of the seated male woodwind player, who reclines against her, and of another seated woman playing a stringed instrument with a bow.

Rorimer (1935, 140), following Hunter (see note 1), identified this scene as showing Hercules wooing Iole. According to one version of the myth, King Eurytus of Oechalia, father of Iole, had promised her in marriage to anyone who defeated him in an archery contest. Hercules won the match, but Eurytus refused to award the prize for fear that Hercules might suffer another attack of madness and kill his children by Iole. In this version of the tale, the king's son Iphitus pleaded in favor of Hercules. According to Hunter and Rorimer, Hercules, standing in the left foreground, is pressing his suit to Iole while Iphitus kneels before his father in the background and urges him to reconsider the marriage. Hunter thought that Iole was shown carrying "a tasseled lace cushion, as a sign of her industrious habits." However the object in question is not a cushion for making bobbin lace, and the girl is not holding it. It is a tasseled purse fixed to the man's girdle.

According to the version of the myth given by Raoul Lefèvre, Iole was the daughter of Prycus, king of Calydonia, not of King Eurytus of Oechalia. Hercules defeated Prycus in battle, killed him, and entered his devastated castle. Inside he found Iole among the king's daughters, fell instantly in love with her, and pleaded with her to return his ardor. She resisted him at first, unwilling to forgive him for killing her father; but at last she succumbed and fell completely in love with him.[6]

The representation in the tapestry does not tally exactly with either of these versions of the myth, although the scene of the young man presenting a wrapped object (a letter?) to an older man in the background could be interpreted as an illustration of Iphitus supporting Hercules' suit before his own father, as Hunter believed. However the elder man is not represented as a king and therefore is probably not meant to represent Eurytus. It is possible that this scene does not concern Iole at all but a moment at or soon after the time that Hercules is sold into the service of Queen Omphale to serve her as a slave for three years to atone for his crime in having murdered Iphitus. The money that Omphale paid for Hercules was to be given to Eurytus, the youth's father, but Eurytus refused to accept it. During those three years Hercules became soft and effeminate and lived in a state of easy indolence. If this is the correct interpretation of the scene, the two men occupying the space in the right background would represent the slave-dealer offering money to Eurytus, who refuses it with the gesture of his right hand. There are arguments against this interpretation also, for as noted above the man refusing the object is not wearing a crown and therefore is probably not intended to represent a king. Further, the story of Omphale was not dealt with by Lefèvre, but he did mention two periods when Hercules would have been found in circumstances like these: first, when Hercules lived in pleasant harmony with Deianeira after their wedding; and, second, when the hero, separated from Deianeira by one of his adventures, lived with Iole in peace and comfort.[7] This scene could represent either one of these periods; but most likely it illustrates the later episode, when word of Hercules' easy and happy life with Iole reached Deianeira. She, outraged, sent to Hercules, by her squire Lichas, a letter objecting to the affair. She charged Lichas to deliver the letter to no one but Hercules himself. If that is the incident represented here, the two men in the right-hand background would represent Lichas attempting to hand the letter to a man who is not Hercules. That man refuses it but looks across the room at Hercules (?), in the right foreground, who returns his glance.

There is no doubt that 48d represents the death of Hercules. Hunter (see note 1) and Rorimer (1933, 1935) referred to the subject as "The Apotheosis of Hercules," which is not strictly correct. According to the myths,

Hercules was not received into the ranks of the immortals until after he had been lifted from the funeral pyre amid claps of thunder. That is not the moment the designer chose to represent in the tapestry. Instead, he shows Hercules, bare-chested and wearing hose and a long shirt, standing on the pyre that he himself had built. Lefèvre tells how the hero, overcome with guilt at having betrayed Deianeira with Iole, went to Mount Oethea to make a sacrifice to Apollo.[8] On the way he encountered Lichas and told him of his plans, which Lichas reported back to Deianeira. She in turn sent him to deliver to Hercules a shirt boiled in a "love" potion given her by Nessus which she believed would restore Hercules' love for her. She did not know that Nessus had given her the potion, in fact a deadly, burning poison, in revenge for the mortal wound Hercules had inflicted upon him for attempting to rape Deianeira.[9] After Hercules put the shirt on, the poison began to burn him, and when he tried to tear it from his body, great pieces of flesh came away with it. In agony, he killed Lichas, gave his bow and arrows to his faithful companion Philoctetes, and then threw his club and himself on the fire he had prepared for his sacrifice to Apollo, preferring to die in its flames rather than by what he thought was the treacherous hand of Deianeira. When she realized what she had unwittingly done, Deianeira took a knife and, protesting that she was innocent of Hercules' death, killed herself. It is she who is shown in the middle distance at the right in the act of committing suicide. Two men near her throw their arms up in horror as they witness this tragedy. A third man, visible at the left between two orange trees, may represent Lichas's companion who, Lefèvre tells us, ran off and hid in a bush when the pain-maddened Hercules threw Lichas against the rocks and killed him. A hilly landscape punctuated with a castle opens out behind these four distant figures. In the foreground Philoctetes, holding the bow and arrow, stands to the right of Hercules and is accompanied by another man. At the left two men stand watching Hercules; one holds a spear upright and the other seems to be drawing his sword. In the foreground at the left a young man is seated at the edge of the burning pyre and leans over to grasp Hercules' right hand. Hunter identified this figure as Lichas, whereas Rorimer (1935, 140) thought he represented Hyllus, son of Hercules and Deianeira. Since the youth seems about to be consumed with Hercules, it is possible that the designer was following some version of the myth in which Hercules punishes Lichas by forcing him to burn with him rather than by dashing him against some rocks. This young man wears a long cloak with a high, standing collar; his low-crowned round hat decorated with a plume rests on

Fig. 170. *Golgotha,* by Lucas van Leyden. Engraving, the Netherlands, dated 1517. MMA, Gift of Felix M. Warburg and his family, 1941 (41.1.29).

the ground next to his left knee. The other men in the scene wear hose and knee-length jackets over doublets except for Philoctetes, who wears breeches and stockings, a short doublet, plate armor on his arms, and a helmet. All the men wear wide, round-toed shoes or boots. The border design is the same as that on 48a–c.

It seems clear that the design of 48a–d was derived in one way or another from Raoul Lefèvre's *Recueil.* Unlike the classical texts, this poem has, in parts, the quality of a romantic love story in which the passions and jealousies of the lovers control their lives and rule their destinies. In the *Recueil,* Hercules' death resulted directly from two passions. The first was Nessus's resolve to avenge the mortal wound Hercules inflicted on him for his attempted rape of Deianeira by giving Deianeira the "love" potion to use on Hercules. The second was Deianeira's jealousy of Hercules' love for Iole. Deianeira was so obsessed with her need to win Hercules back that she used the poison that Nessus had given her without

question and without noticing that two servants died when they used it to prepare the shirt for Hercules (see note 9). Therefore, if, as we believe, 48b represents the wedding of Hercules and Deianeira and 48c shows Hercules in the company of Iole receiving Deianeira's letter of complaint, this group of four hangings tells the story of Hercules and Deianeira specifically, from the moment of his birth to the moment of his death by her agency. If that is correct, this group of four pieces may be complete in itself rather than part of a larger series of hangings telling a broader story of Hercules' life and labors (see Related Tapestries).

SOURCE OF THE DESIGN

Joubert (1987, 185) believed that the character of the drawing and composition in a number of tapestries that are related to the *Story of Hercules* by virtue of the similarity of their borders (see Manufacture and Date) is

569

so mediocre that their sources would not be found in any contemporary paintings. In her opinion these cartoons were produced cheaply by hack artists who were probably working for the great tapestry merchants of Tournai. We have found that five of the accessory figures in 48d were adapted, whether directly or indirectly, from a print by Lucas van Leyden entitled *Golgotha* (fig. 170) or from a source common to both images.[10] The figure of Lichas or Hyllus who sits on the edge of the pyre in the tapestry appears in reverse in the foreground of the *Golgotha* print seated on a rock just to the left of center and wearing the same kind of cloak. The man who stands to the left of Hercules in the tapestry and appears to be drawing his sword may be seen, reversed, in the left foreground of the print. The upper half of his jacket is similar, but from the waist down the costume is quite different. Just behind the swordsman in the tapestry, the same figure is repeated, with a complete change of costume and weapon. The figures of Philoctetes and his companion standing in the right foreground of the tapestry appear in the print, again in reverse, among the figures gathered in the middle distance just left of center. The tapestry designer changed their costumes very little when he moved these figures from the print or the common source to the tapestry.

Although the other figures in 48d and the figures in 48a–c have not yet been traced to their sources, it seems likely that all the accessory figures were taken from prints or tapestry cartoons using figures from prints. Because the costumes in 48d show essentially the same fashions as those in the Lucas print, we may conclude that the other print sources also dated from about 1515–20. The figures in 48a–d that relate specifically to the story of Hercules, like the figures of the hero and the distraught Deianeira in 48d, the key figures in the birth and temple scenes in 48a, the three central figures in 48b, and the critical figures in the left foreground and right background of 48c, must have been designed expressly for this series of cartoons (or a closely related series) or derived from prints dealing with the story of Hercules.

The basic elements in the border pattern, including the tied bunches of flora placed end to end in the central band at the bottom and sides and the lambrequin or valance of bells, pomegranates, and acanthus leaves across the top, were obviously not designed for this set of compositions since they appear in a number of tapestries of approximately the same period that show entirely different subjects (see Manufacture and Date). However the arabesque of vines with flowers and pomegranates across the bottom of the field is not a common feature of this border design. The top of what seems to be a closely related though slightly different arabesque appears along the bottom of two tapestries of a contemporary *Twelve Months of the Year* series attributed to Tournai and now in Dijon.[11]

MANUFACTURE AND DATE

Tapestries illustrating the story of Hercules were being produced at least by the early years of the fifteenth century. A "grant tappiz de Herculez" appears in the 1422–35 inventory of Charles VII of France.[12] The Este inventory of 1457–69 contains entries for "Coltrine quatro de razo cum seda nuove belissime jstoriade de le fadige ov.ro forze de ercules" (four beautiful new tapestry hangings with silk of the labors or strengths of Hercules), and "Uno apparamento de razo nuovo belissimo nominato lo apparamento de Ercules" (a beautiful new set of tapestry bed furnishings called the bed of Hercules).[13] Remnants of sets of Hercules tapestries dating from the last quarter of the fifteenth century and the early years of the sixteenth have survived in a number of collections here and abroad (see below). The inventory taken of Henry VIII's tapestries in the middle of the sixteenth century lists at least forty-one Hercules tapestries in the late king's various residences.[14]

Hunter (1925) attributed 48a–d to Tournai and dated them about 1515 without giving his reasons. Rorimer (1933) dated them in the early sixteenth century and suggested that they were probably among the pieces that the city officials of Tournai commissioned from Clément Sarrasin for presentation to their new English governor in 1513. Later Rorimer (1935, 140–41) qualified this suggestion because the colors and yarn content in 48a–d differ from those specified in the document referring to that commission. He also considered the possibility that these are the four Hercules tapestries mentioned in the inventory taken in 1539 of the stock left by the Tournai merchant Arnould Poissonnier, who died in 1522. He concluded that although that question could not be answered one could at any rate properly attribute the Metropolitan Museum's four pieces to the "school of Tournai" and date them in the first third of the sixteenth century. Asselberghs (exh. cat. Tournai 1968, 17) agreed that in the absence of more precise documents it was impossible to identify 48a–d with the pieces that Sarrasin provided in 1513 or the ones that Poissonnier had finished before his death in 1522.

We believe that Rorimer was correct in dating the tapestries broadly in the first third of the sixteenth century. Several fragments of *Story of Hercules* tapestries dating from the last two decades of the fifteenth century have survived, and all of them are clearly much earlier in style than 48a–d. Three pieces from at least two different sets of hangings woven after one series of cartoons are preserved in Brussels, Paris, and Tournai.[15] Two other pieces woven about 1490–1510 after a different series of cartoons are also in Tournai, and a fragmentary piece duplicating part of one of them is preserved in the Joslyn Art Museum, Omaha.[16] Three other contemporary fragments woven after yet another series of cartoons are to be found in the Rijksmuseum, Amsterdam.[17] These pieces were all designed in the style of the last third of the fifteenth century, with strong surface patterns and no real representation of depth beyond an invitation to read figures in the lower part of the composition as occupying the foreground and the figures in the upper parts as existing in more distant space. On the other hand 48a–d and two other tapestries designed somewhat later (one in the Burrell Collection and one at Hampton Court; see Related Tapestries) show that the artist or artists who created the cartoons worked in a new style that gave a much more convincing illusion of depth and placed less emphasis on the surface pattern. It is the style of tapestry design that appears in archetypal form in 1513 in the *Legend of Herkinbald* in Brussels (see fig. 70). The Metropolitan Museum's pieces and the Burrell Collection and Hampton Court hangings show some garments that were in fashion from about 1510 to about 1520. The fact that the designer of 48d may have taken four figures from a print by Lucas van Leyden dated 1517 (fig. 170) suggests but does not prove that 48a–d were designed no earlier than that year. The tapestry designer repeated the poses of the figures and the basic form of their costumes as they appear in the print, but we cannot be sure that a somewhat earlier source did not exist, one from which both the designer and Lucas borrowed.

The *Life of Hercules* tapestries that the officials of the city of Tournai commissioned from the Tournai merchant Clément Sarrasin on December 17, 1513, were to contain approximately 360 square aunes and to measure 6 aunes (about 13 feet 6 inches) high.[18] Therefore, the unspecified number of hangings would have measured about 60 aunes in aggregate length. The Metropolitan Museum's hangings, without their modern outermost guards, vary in height from 12 feet 6 inches to 13 feet 5 inches, or approximately $5^{1}/_{2}$ to 6 aunes. The average width of the four pieces is 11 feet, or 5 aunes. So, although we do not know how many pieces were involved in the contract of 1513, we can say that twelve hangings having the approximate dimensions of 48a–d would

measure about 6 aunes in height and approximately 60 aunes in aggregate length, or about 360 square aunes in area, the figure named in Clément Sarrasin's contract. Except for the fact that the borders specified in that contract were to be blue scattered with yellow foliage set off by golden-red accents, 48a–d could represent four of those pieces. However the border design could have been changed during the course of production. If the Metropolitan Museum's four hangings did not come from that set of tapestries, they could nevertheless have been woven later after some of the same cartoons. Other documents show that in October 1514, after Sarrasin's death, Estienne de Grimaupont, a *tapissier*, assumed the responsibility for completing the contract and furthermore that he bequeathed the cartoons to his companion or godfather (*compère*).[19]

The four *Story of Hercules* tapestries that Arnould Poissonnier left at his death in 1522 contained 120 square aunes.[20] The Metropolitan Museum's four pieces measure approximately 115 to 120 square aunes. Therefore it is at least possible that 48a–d are those four hangings.

All the evidence we have—the Lucas print, the fashions in clothing, the documents referring to Hercules tapestries produced by Sarrasin, de Grimaupont, and Poissonnier between 1513 and 1522 (and possibly later also by de Grimaupont or his *compère*)—suggests that 48a–d were designed during the second or third decades of the sixteenth century and also woven then or perhaps a bit later.

While the documented series cited here are all connected with tapestry producers who were active in Tournai, we cannot be sure that comparable sets of hangings were not being woven elsewhere in the southern Netherlands at the same time. The border design places 48a–d in a category of hangings that have been associated with Tournai because this border, with its bell, leaf, and pomegranate lambrequin at the top and bands with floral bunches at the sides and bottom, appears in conjunction with field patterns that Asselberghs and others have associated specifically with Tournai. These are the pieces in a number of collections that have been identified with documents dating between 1504 and 1522 and mentioning series of tapestries entitled *Histoire* (or *Condamnation*) *de Banquet, A la manière de Portugal et de Indie, La caravane, L'histoire de gens et de bêtes sauvages à la manière de Calcut, Le voyage de Caluce, L'histoire de Calcou,* and *L'histoire de la Carvene.*[21] All these tapestries were ordered from or supplied by Tournai producers. If we assume—and it is only a likelihood, not a certainty—that this particular kind of border design was used primarily or exclusively by Tournai producers, then it would follow that 48a–d were probably woven in Tournai or through the agency of a Tournai producer. However we cannot be sure that such was the case.

RELATED TAPESTRIES

No other pieces woven after these cartoons are known to have survived. As noted above (Description and Subject), it is possible that 48a–d illustrate specifically the tragic love story of Hercules and Deianeira. If that is so, the set of four pieces may be complete as it is now and may never have included other pieces. We have references in 1504[22] and again in 1539 to groups of four Hercules tapestries, the latter specifically described as "Une serie de 4 pièces," which presumably was complete in four pieces (see note 20).

Two early sixteenth-century *Story of Hercules* tapestries woven after a different series of compositions that are closely related to these in general style are now in the United Kingdom. A *Hercules Storming the Castle of King Prycus* is in the Burrell Collection, Glasgow, and a *Death of Hercules* is preserved at Hampton Court.[23] In the Hampton Court tapestry, Deianeira appears twice in the background, once giving the fatal garment to Lichas and once committing suicide. Lichas appears again, in the left foreground, dashed against the rocks. Behind him stands an altar on which a sacrificial fire burns, and to the right of that is the figure of Hercules, wearing a long tunic rather than a shirt, half-kneeling on his funeral pyre. Philoctetes, represented as a boy, stands in the right foreground next to a tall man in armor who is not identified. The Burrell Collection and Hampton Court pieces have more dramatic impact than the compositions in 48a–d, and the drawing is a bit more sophisticated. The figures are labeled with their names, and there are narrative texts inscribed on banderoles above each scene. At its own left end the Hampton Court piece shows the right end of a scene depicting the death of Liomedes. A carved column separates the two scenes and another appears at the right end of the *Death of Hercules*. The same columns flank the Burrell Collection piece showing Hercules storming Prycus's castle. Therefore it appears that these two hangings were cut from one or more longer tapestries which showed several episodes in the length of their fabrics. The Metropolitan Museum's four hangings share none of these characteristics. Kurth ventured the opinion that the Hampton Court piece could have come from the set of hangings that the officials of the city of Tournai commissioned from Clément Sarrasin in 1513, and also that

that tapestry and the one in Glasgow could have figured among the tapestries listed in Henry VIII's testamentary inventory.[24] We have no grounds for endorsing or refuting these opinions.

HISTORY

In the collection of Daniel Guggenheim, New York.
Given to the MMA by Mrs. Daniel Guggenheim in memory of her husband, 1935.

EXHIBITIONS

New York, MMA, 1932–35. 48a–d lent by Mrs. Daniel Guggenheim.
Tournai, 1968. *La tapisserie tournaisienne au XVIe siècle.* Catalogue by J. P. Asselberghs. Cat. no. 9 [48b], illus.

PUBLICATIONS

Hunter 1925, p. 82. Mentioned, with incorrect observation that there is a duplicate of 48d, with inscription, at Hampton Court.
J. J. R. [James J. Rorimer]. "An Important Loan of Tapestries." *MMA Bulletin* 28 (1933) p. 11. 48a–d mentioned.
Rorimer, James J. "A Gift of Four Tapestries." *MMA Bulletin* 30 (1935) pp. 138–41. 48a–d discussed at length; illus., 48a on cover, 48d p. 139.
Kurth, Betty. "Mediaeval Romances in Renaissance Tapestries." *Journal of the Warburg and Courtauld Institutes* 5 (1942) pp. 242 n. 1 (right col.) and 243. 48a–d mentioned.
Kurz, Otto. "Shakespeare and the Shaven Hercules." *Burlington Magazine* 87 (1945) p. 175. 48a–d mentioned; 48d described and discussed briefly and illus. p. 177.
"Shakespeare and the Shaven Hercules." *Shakespeare Fellowship News-Letter*, March 1946, p. 2. 48d mentioned.
Joubert 1987, p. 185. 48c, d mentioned as though they were the only pieces of this set in the MMA.

NOTES

1. Copies in the files of the MMA Department of Medieval Art; one is entitled simply "The Story of Hercules," the other "Transcript of document presented by George Leland Hunter to Daniel Guggenheim."
2. Comments by F. Desonay, then on the faculty of Romance Philology, University of Liège, quoted in Marthe Crick-Kuntziger, "Les 'compléments' de nos tapisseries gothiques," *Bulletin des Musées Royaux d'Art et d'Histoire*, 3d ser., 3 (1931) pp. 68–74.
3. In the text here the descriptions of subjects as they occur in Lefèvre's *Recueil* are taken from H. Oskar Sommer, ed., *The Recuyell of the Historyes of Troye Written in French by Raoul Lefevre, Translated and Printed by William Caxton (about A.D. 1474),* 2 vols. (London, 1894). The account of the conceptions and births of Hercules and Iphicles is given in vol. 1, pp. 231–39.
4. Sommer, *Recuyell*, vol. 2, pp. 371–85.
5. Sommer, *Recuyell*, vol. 1, p. 312; vol. 2, p. 346.
6. See Sommer, *Recuyell*, vol. 2, pp. 466–75, for Lefèvre's account of Hercules' victory over Prycus and his winning Iole's love.
7. Sommer, *Recuyell*, vol. 2, pp. 385, 475, 484–85.
8. See Sommer, *Recuyell*, vol. 2, pp. 483–99, for Lefèvre's account of the events leading up to Hercules' death and of the death itself.

9. For Lefèvre's version of the story of Nessus's treachery and Deianeira's preparing the fatal shirt, see Sommer, *Recuyell,* vol. 2, pp. 385–87 and 494–95.

10. To Nadine Orenstein go the credit and the author's thanks for having found the five figures in the print.

11. The author thanks Wendy Hefford for bringing this detail in the Dijon tapestries to his attention. See J. P. Asselberghs, *La tapisserie tournaisienne au XVIe siècle,* exh. cat. (Tournai, 1968) nos. 14, 15, illus. Asselberghs (p. 22) had also noted the similarity.

12. Quoted from Göbel 1923, vol. 1, p. 72.

13. Quoted from Nello Forti Grazzini, *L'arazzo ferrarese* (Milan, 1982) pp. 215, 217.

14. See the itemized lists of tapestries in the residences of Henry VIII as given in W. G. Thomson, *Tapestry Weaving in England from the Earliest Times to the End of the XVIIIth Century* (London, 1914) pp. 35–38, 40, 41.

15. All three hangings are fragments of larger tapestries. The piece in the Musées Royaux d'Art et d'Histoire in Brussels shows the birth of Hercules and scenes from his youth; see Marthe Crick-Kuntziger, *Catalogue des tapisseries (XIVe au XVIIIe siècle),* Musées Royaux d'Art et d'Histoire (Brussels, 1956) no. 7, pls. 10, 11; also J. P. Asselberghs, *La tapisserie tournaisienne au XVe siècle,* exh. cat. (Tournai, 1967) no. 3, illus. The piece in the Musée d'Histoire et d'Archéologie in Tournai shows Hercules' adventures on the island of sheep; see Asselberghs, *La tapisserie tournaisienne au XVe siècle,* no. 4, illus.; also Anne Dudant, *Les tapisseries tournaisiennes de la seconde moitié du XVeme siècle au Musée d'Histoire et d'Archéologie de la ville de Tournai* (Mons, 1985) p. 43, illus. pp. 40, 41. The third piece, in the Mobilier National in Paris, shows Hercules attending Hippodamia's wedding, then rescuing her from the centaurs; see Asselberghs, *La tapisserie tournaisienne au XVe siècle,* no. 5, illus.; also Jacques Bacri, "L'histoire d'Hercule: Tapisserie du musée des Gobelins," *Gazette des Beaux-Arts,* 6th ser., 12 (1934) pp. 204–11. Asselberghs (p. 20) believed that the piece in Tournai, though woven after the same cartoons, belonged to a different set of weavings. The cartoons have been dated about 1480 on what the present author believes is unconvincing evidence associating them with Cardinal Charles de Bourbon (see Bacri, "Histoire d'Hercule," pp. 209–11, and Crick-Kuntziger, *Catalogue des tapisseries,* p. 24).

16. For further details on the two pieces in Tournai, which show Laomedon refusing the Argonauts access to Troy and Hercules taking vengeance upon Laomedon, see Asselberghs, *La tapisserie tournaisienne au XVe siècle,* nos. 7 and 8, illus.; also Dudant, *Les tapisseries tournaisiennes,* pp. 39–46, 48, illus. For the fragment in Omaha, which shows the subject of Laomedon refusing the Argonauts, see *Collection of the Late Katherine Deere Butterworth,* sale cat., Parke-Bernet, New York, October 21–23, 1954, no. 342, illus.; also "Tournai Gothic Tapestry from the 'Story of Hercules' series by Jean III le Quien," *Art Quarterly* 18 (1955) p. 219, illus. p. 218.

17. For the three fragments in Amsterdam, which all came from one hanging, see Louise Erkelens, "Drie fragmenten van een Hercules tapijt uit de laatste viftien jaren van de XVe eeuw," *Bulletin van het Rijksmuseum* 2 (1954) pp. 9–14, illus. One piece shows the infant Hercules nursing; the second shows the infant strangling two monsters; and the third shows the adult Hercules being dressed in armor. For the third piece, see also Asselberghs, *La tapisserie tournaisienne au XVe siècle,* no. 6, illus.

18. For the terms of this contract, see Eugène Soil, *Les tapisseries de Tournai* (Tournai and Lille, 1892) pp. 398–99. The Flemish aune, the measure used in the document, was equivalent to 27 inches.

19. Soil, *Les tapisseries de Tournai,* pp. 399, 259. The name of de Grimaupont's *compère* was recorded simply as "Olivier."

20. Soil, *Les tapisseries de Tournai,* pp. 281–82. The reference appears in an inventory of Poissonnier's stock that was drawn up in 1539.

21. The choice and spelling of the words in these references vary according to the source one consults. See Asselberghs, *La tapisserie tournaisienne au XVIe siècle,* pp. 12–16, nos. 3–8, also the borders of nos. 1, 5, 6, 7; also Digby 1980, no. 18, and the border in pl. 29. See also similar borders on other tapestries discussed and illus. in Joubert 1987, pp. 180–85.

22. See Jules Houdoy, *Les tapisseries de haute-lisse: Histoire de la fabrication lilloise du XIVe au XVIIIe siècle* (Lille and Paris, 1871) p. 142. The reference concerns a payment to Adam de Cupère, a merchant weaver or upholsterer at the Antwerp fair, for four pieces of the *Story of Hercules.*

23. See Betty Kurth, "Mediaeval Romances in Renaissance Tapestries," *Journal of the Warburg and Courtauld Institutes* 5 (1942) pp. 241–45, illus. See also Kurth, "Masterpieces of Gothic Tapestry in the Burrell Collection," *Connoisseur* 117 (1946) pp. 7–8, illus. p. 6; and H. C. Marillier, *The Tapestries at Hampton Court Palace* (London, 1962) p. 27, illus. pl. 21.

24. Kurth, "Mediaeval Romances," p. 245.

49a

574

49
Hunting Parks

Four hangings from a set of country-life tapestries

a Hunting for Wild Boar
b Hunting with a Hawk
c Woodcutters Working at a Deer Park
d Hunting for Birds with a Hawk and a Crossbow

Southern Netherlands, 1515–35
Wool warp; wool and silk wefts
49a: 11 ft. × 8 ft. 1 in. (3.35 m × 2.46 m)
10–12 warp yarns per inch, 4–5 per centimeter
Bequest of George Blumenthal, 1941 (41.190.106)
49b: 11 ft. 2^1/$_2$ in. × 7 ft. 11^1/$_2$ in. (3.42 m × 2.43 m)
10–13 warp yarns per inch, 4–5 per centimeter
Bequest of George Blumenthal, 1941 (41.190.107)
49c: 11 ft. 2^1/$_2$ in. × 10 ft. 6^1/$_2$ in. (3.42 m × 3.21 m)
10–13 warp yarns per inch, 4–5 per centimeter
Bequest of George Blumenthal, 1941 (41.190.227)
49d: 11 ft. 1 in. × 12 ft. 7^1/$_2$ in. (3.38 m × 3.85 m)
9–12 warp yarns per inch, 3^1/$_2$–5 per centimeter
Bequest of George Blumenthal, 1941 (41.190.228)

CONDITION

In all four hangings, the upper and lower border sections and the adjoining parts of the side sections have been restored with new warp and weft yarns. Since all or part of the original selvages remain along the upper and lower edges of the fields in 49a, c, and d, we know that those three fields, and apparently also the field of 49b, have lost none of their original height. The side border sections of all four tapestries are integral parts of the fabrics, so we know that the fields have lost none of their original width. Many of the dark brown and black wool wefts in all the pieces have been replaced with modern yarns. A moderate amount of reweaving with modern wool and silk wefts of other colors has been done in all parts of the four hangings, but these restorations have not significantly altered the drawing.

The more important repairs, which have changed the original images to some extent, may be cited as follows. The field of 49b was once cut top to bottom in two places and later rejoined with modern warp and weft yarns. One seam passes directly down the center of the field; the other begins at the left side of the treetop in the upper right corner and goes straight down through the head and chest of the deer below and down the front of the piping figure seated in the lower right corner. Al-most the entire lower half of the right-hand section of this border has been rewoven with modern warp and weft yarns, and the lower left and right corners of the field have been similarly restored.

In 49c the completely restored passages include the face of the woman standing in the lower right corner, bits of the left and right sides of her gown, and the entire clump of large leaves that grows next to her left hand. The fabric was once cut from the bottom of that clump of leaves to the bottom of the field and subsequently rejoined.

Approximately one-fifth of the field of 49d was cut away from the rest and later rejoined to it. The seam follows the inner edge of the tree at the left that the shepherd is clinging to and passes along the outer edge of the left leg of the shepherdess seated in the left foreground. The upper ends of both side sections in the border of 49d show more restoration than do the corresponding passages in the other pieces. There is also a good deal of restoration with new warp and weft yarns in the lower part of the field. These repairs involve the bit of skirt passing over the left knee of the peasant woman in the lower left corner and the bits of earth and water above and below the sheep lying in front of her. Most of the central foreground—including the plant next to the shepherd's right leg, the lower part of his jacket skirt, and the entire passage of land, water, and fowl that extends across the field at the level of his shins from the back of the dog to the trunk of the pomegranate tree at the right—has been completely restored. A narrow strip of sky at the center of the field has also been rewoven.

DESCRIPTION AND SUBJECT

In 49a, b, and d men are shown hunting various kinds of game within circular fenced preserves. In 49c a woodsman is splitting a tree trunk inside the enclosure, and in front of the gate, another hacks at an orange branch with his billhook. The fences are made of pointed wooden pickets, each fastened to two parallel wooden rails that

49b

49c

49d

encircle the entire precinct. Metal and stone posts with ornamental finials, collars, and bases rise from the ground outside the fence and engage it at regular intervals. The two posts at center front support an elaborate ogee arch decorated with acanthus leaves and fleurs-de-lis. In each tapestry, this arch marks the entrance to the precinct or park, and the section of picket fencing beneath it functions as a gate although neither hinges nor latch fittings are visible. An ornamental post decorated slightly differently from the others appears at the center of each gate. This detail distinguishes the gate in these tapestries from those in all other hangings that we know of in the same category (see below).

Except for minor differences of detail, the enclosure, fence, and gate are essentially the same in each of the four tapestries. The ground inside is hilly and covered with grass and a few blossoming plants. It is obviously a relatively undisturbed continuation of the land outside the fence. Orange, pomegranate, and pear trees grow both inside and outside the parks. Their branches have either been pruned high on the trunk or, as Stokstad and Stannard suggested (exh. cat. Lawrence 1983, 134), the lower growth has been eaten away by the deer in winter. A narrow moat or stream surrounds each park, although in many places it is not clearly represented.

What varies significantly from piece to piece is the action taking place in each setting. In 49a, in a small clearing bounded by four fruiting trees at the back of the enclosure, a hunter dressed in hose and a short doublet spears a wild boar in the breast. A valet or kennelman, sounding his horn to announce the kill, stands with his hound at the left; he wears a knee-length, short-sleeved jacket over doublet and hose. Another hunter, similarly dressed, moves in from the right with his greyhound, his sword gripped in his right hand, ready to plunge into the boar for the final kill. Beyond the hunt, unconcerned with it, a woodsman wearing a long jacket over hose and a chaperon on his head hacks branches off a fruit tree with a billhook. A fantastic creature with a camel's head, a leopard's body, and a single hooked, twisted horn rising from its forehead crouches in front of the hunting scene. Next to it stands a small two-humped camel. In the foreground, outside the enclosure, two gentlemen wearing small round hats, knee-length jackets with deeply pleated skirts, and hose flank a kneeling lady dressed in a simple fitted gown and a hood. She holds her hands together in an attitude of prayer or supplication and gazes at the man at the left who sits on his horse watching the activity inside the precinct. The other man, who holds a spear in his right hand, is about to mount his horse. In the background, among the hills rising beyond the enclosure, appear a number of castles.

An irregularly shaped pond, with a duck swimming in it, appears in the center of the park in 49b. Beyond the pond a young falconer dressed in a loose, knee-length jacket over doublet and hose sits astride his rearing horse and waves his left arm as he watches his hawk drop on a bird from above (for a note on the pose of this figure, see Source of the Design). Behind him two does graze peacefully. A third doe lies at its ease in the left foreground, and just beyond it at the left stands a stag. A second stag prances forward at the right side of the park. Beyond the fence, in the upper left of the tapestry, are a kennelman, with horn raised to sound, and his hound; they repeat the figures in the upper left of 49a. Outside the park in the upper right of 49b, a greyhound leaps toward a great fox that is making off with a lamb. The hilly landscape behind these animals shows a single castle. In the foreground, before the enclosure, a couple dressed in simple shepherds' clothes dances at the left while at the right a more fashionably dressed shepherd, or perhaps a huntsman, pipes a tune while his companion tips a bottle to drink. Two sheep and a lamb lie or graze in the center foreground.

In 49c only one human figure, a woodsman, occupies the enclosure. Three does, two stags, and a fawn are also there. The man is working in the midst of a clump of fruit trees. Two great tree trunks lie on the ground near him; he uses a wedge and mallet to split the one he stands on. He wears a long-eared cap on his head and a shirt and doublet over his hose. Another woodsman, similarly dressed, crouches outside the precinct in the center foreground and with his billhook hacks at the severed branch of an orange tree. A fashionably dressed couple approaches from the left and seems to be commenting on his work. The gentleman wears a long, fur-lined coat over his knee-length jacket and hose; his round hat has a raised and slashed brim. The lady wears a long, fitted, fur-lined gown with funnel sleeves and, on her head, a hood with a folded kerchief. Another aristocratic lady stands opposite this pair. Her fur-lined gown is cut like the other lady's, but her hood and jewelry, which includes a pendant cross, two necklaces, and an elaborately worked gold girdle with what may be a pomander at the end of a long cord, are much richer. She holds a globular box or covered cup in her raised right hand. In the background at the left, outside the park, a shepherd discovers one of his sheep lying behind a tree while two more rest beyond the next rise. The hills in the far distance are peppered with castles.

More activity is represented in 49d than in any of the other pieces. The park is larger and it contains more people and animals. Beneath a great orange tree in the center of the enclosure, a young man dressed in a loose tunic over his doublet and hose is swinging a lure to retrieve the hawk flying above the tree. Below this hawk another has just dropped on a heron which struggles to free itself. A hound leaps with excitement as it watches the contest. Another hunter or possibly the falconer's valet, wearing a short, stylishly slashed doublet over his hose, a wide-brimmed hat tied under his chin, and a game bag at his waist, is either vaulting the stream with a pole or spearing a fish. Another hunter, at the right of the park, aims a crossbow at a wide-billed bird perched directly above him in the orange tree. A fawn lies near this hunter. Toward the front of the park a stag lies at the left and a doe stands at the right. Nearby, a ram looks up from grazing and a leopard crouches. On the left side of the park a shepherd stands on the top rail of the fence and hugs the adjacent orange tree for support; he is apparently watching the progress of the sport. His sheep graze outside the park, and two more sheep appear on the right side of the enclosure in the middle distance. Two men, both wearing thigh-length jackets with cowls, and hose and buskins, stand in the immediate foreground outside the enclosure. Asselberghs (exh. cat. Tournai 1970, no. 31) described the man standing and leaning on a stick at the right as a beggar. We believe he is a shepherd. The other man, who is certainly a shepherd, stands in front of the gate holding a *houlette*, or sheep-herding implement, over his left shoulder and his dog's leash in his right hand. The two sheep grazing in front of him are part of the original fabric, but as noted above, the pool, duck, and rocks between them have all been completely restored. Both men look at the shepherdess sitting at the far left. Her skirt is hiked up to her knees to make room in her lap for some blossoms for the chaplet she holds in her right hand. She returns the men's gaze and extends her left arm to gesture as she speaks to them. It is clear that she is making lovers' talk with one or the other of them or flirting with both. The background of the composition represents a hilly landscape dotted with castles. In the near hills outside the park at the left, a falconer stands with his hawk on his left wrist and his hound at his side.

The borders of the four tapestries all show the same pattern. Short garlands of flowering stalks tied together with ribbons are laid end to end on a wide band of dark blue flanked by narrow guards of yellow and reddish orange.

In early publications (Rubinstein-Bloch 1927, Rorimer 1947) the tapestries were referred to with titles that described them simply and directly as "pastoral scene," "wood cutters," or "hunting scene"; but in more recent studies they have excited a certain amount of curiosity

about the interpretation of the subject matter. Because the fenced precinct evokes images of the Garden of Paradise and the *hortus conclusus*; because stags have been used as symbols of purity, of the human soul, and even of Christ Himself (see 24a–e and 32a, b); and because both peasants and nobles inhabit the precincts and the surrounding lands, a number of writers have suggested that the four hangings may have symbolic meaning underlying their immediate subjects.

Calkins observed (exh. cat. Ithaca 1968, no. 114) that 49c, which shows woodcutters working both inside and outside the precinct, belongs to the generic group of hangings of the late fifteenth and early sixteenth centuries which show woodcutters going about their business. He considered the possibility that the woodcutters in 49c refer to the traditional cycle of the labors of the months or of the seasons but tempered that interpretation by noting that it is spring or summer in this tapestry and not winter, the season with which woodcutting is traditionally associated. He also suggested that the piece might carry a deeper meaning, perhaps a reference to the Garden of Paradise or to the Virgin's Immaculate Conception, symbolized by the *hortus conclusus*, and that the stags, "gathered around the tree of life" and representing purity and piety, might confirm that reference. He expressed reservations about this interpretation and asked why the woodcutters were in this hallowed place and who the "Magdalene-like figure on the right with her ointment jar" might be. We agree with Calkins's reservations concerning the symbolic value of these figures and setting and believe that, while some of them may apply in other representations of this kind, they do not apply in 49a–d.

Romanelli (exh. cat. Oklahoma City 1985, nos. 95–97) recalled Calkins's thoughts on this interpretation and concluded that the precinct had no religious connotations. She suggested that it represents instead the classical *locus amoenus*, the "lovely place," set in a garden and filled with pleasant flora and fauna. Romanelli also suggested that the four hangings might be studied further in terms of their relation to the ideal landscape of medieval and Renaissance literature, an interpretation that she believed could explain the fact that the season represented in all four pieces is spring.

Schrader (exh. cat. Lawrence 1969, no. 133) referred to Calkins's suggestions but described 49c as a tapestry showing some of the characteristic rural activities that people of various social stations engaged in. He, like most other writers (including the present one), thought that the meaning of the four subjects was essentially self-evident. Stokstad and Stannard (exh. cat. Lawrence

1983, no. 20) also mentioned Calkins's suggestions, but they concentrated on the idea that 49c shows a deer park isolated from the surrounding wilderness by the woodcutters' labor and that the noble couple in the foreground were probably there to inspect their estate. Vandenbroeck (1987, 66) perceived the subject of 49c in essentially the same terms. Joubert (1987, 177) referred to 49a and b simply as hunting scenes, and Asselberghs (exh. cat. Tournai 1970, nos. 31, 32) referred to 49c and d simply as representations of woodcutters and of shepherds and hunters.

Tapestry designers of the late fifteenth and early sixteenth centuries used the same kind of fenced precinct in so many different contexts it is no wonder that writers have striven to find hidden meanings in 49a–d. Two tapestries that have survived from that period each show a unicorn dipping its horn into a pool of water, and so purifying it for all to drink, in the center of a garden enclosed by a circular wattled fence. There are deer inside the enclosure and beasts outside.[1] In these cases the precinct may have been intended as a reference to either the Garden of Paradise or the *hortus conclusus.*[2]

In another category of precinct tapestries, deer occupy gardens enclosed by wattled fences while other animals roam outside. Most of these pieces show a fountain inside the precinct; a few do not. According to Erkelens, a piece of this type in the Rijksmuseum in Amsterdam contains symbolic Christian meaning: the precinct represents faith, and the deer are the human souls satisfying their thirst at the Fountain of Living Water.[3] However, in considering a similar hanging in Schloss Burg an der Wupper, Roselt noted that the deer are not drinking the water and that thistles have found their way into the garden; that neither the Virgin nor the unicorn is present; and that in short the kind of precinct shown in the tapestry may be seen not only as a reflection of the symbolic garden but also as simply a special kind of setting for allegorical or heraldic subjects or hunting scenes.[4]

Three tapestries representing a type closely related to 49a–d show enclosed precincts where deer roam. In one of them these gentle beasts share the park with savage and fantastic animals like a lion, a griffin, and a cockatrice. A fountain appears in the center of each of the three protected spaces, and humans—shepherds, woodsmen and their families, and in one case a falconer—occupy the space outside. Two of these pieces are now in the Burrell Collection in Glasgow (see fig. 171); the third was last published as belonging in a private collection in Paris.[5] All three pieces show inscribed scrolls floating above the figures. The verses, now largely illegible, are written in what seems to be a French dialect. What words we can make out on the piece in Paris seem to express the idea that an amorous shepherd is giving up "such games," as he feels himself becoming old. In the other two pieces some of the words that can be transcribed indicate that the shepherds in the background are being invited to dance to the music of bagpipes. If we have transcribed correctly what we can read of them, the other verses express a number of ideas that are not clear but may have moralistic or erotic connotations.[6]

A precinct enclosed by a post and rail fence, with a low wattled fence at its center, appears in quite a different context in an early sixteenth-century tapestry now in the Isabella Stewart Gardner Museum in Boston. It shows a crowd of woodsmen standing inside the enclosure listening to a lord and his steward while two fashionably dressed falconing couples lounge outside, one couple watching the meeting, the other concerned only with themselves. Asselberghs suggested that the hanging may represent the Parable of the Workers in the Vineyard (Matthew 20:1–16), while Cavallo limited his interpretation of the subject to some activity that involved the taking in or giving out of money.[7]

None of the subjects in any of these groups of hangings corresponds precisely to the subjects of 49a–d. All the people we see here are directly concerned with hunting, with building or tending the parks, or with carrying on their lives outside the parks. 49a clearly depicts a wild boar hunt, 49b a falconer watching his hawk attack a bird, 49d a falconer retrieving his hawk while an older man aims his crossbow at a luckless bird in a tree, and 49c two woodsmen either performing the final activities in clearing the space in the enclosure or keeping the growth under control. Enclosed hunting parks as well as open forests were to be found on some European estates. Those preserves seem to have been stocked with wild boar as well as deer and other game beasts.[8]

There is no hint of religious symbolism anywhere in 49a–d and—unless the woman standing at the right in 49c represents something other than a third aristocrat out walking—there is no allegory here. It is certainly possible that the cartoons after which these four pieces were woven showed inscribed scrolls like the ones that appear in the three similar pieces in Glasgow and Paris (see note 5 and fig. 171) and that their verses elaborated upon the meaning of the incidents depicted in the foregrounds of 49a–d. Even if that were so and for some reason the verses were not included here, it would still be true that these four precincts are obviously hunting parks. All the parks contain deer except the park in 49a, which seems to be set up for the hunting of wild boar in

Fig. 171. *Deer Park.* Tapestry, southern Netherlands, here dated 1500–1525. The Burrell Collection, Glasgow Museums and Art Galleries.

a space also inhabited by exotic and fabulous beasts—the camel and unicorn-like creature. Other country-life tapestries of the period suggest that exotic creatures like lions and the leopard that appears in 49d may have been kept on great estates.[9]

Two tapestries that were formerly in the collection of Edith Rockefeller McCormick show even more straightforward representations of hunting parks, without the element of picturesque incident that lends a bit of romance to 49a–d. Both parks contain fountains. In one enclosure a boar hunt is in progress. In the other a hunter is shooting ducks with a crossbow; outside, another hunter and his dog attack a bear. The first piece

also shows hounds and hunters outside. A related piece in another collection shows hounds and a kennelman or trainer inside the park, which also contains a fountain, and hunters gathering outside.[10] The fountains need not have any symbolic meaning. They, like the pools and streams inside or around the precincts in 49a–d, provided water for both the domestic and the game animals in the park and on the estate.

SOURCE OF THE DESIGN

We called attention above to the fact that the horn-blowing huntsman with his hound who stands in the

582

upper left corner of 49a appears again, very little changed, in a similar position in 49b. None of the other figures represented in these four hangings repeats itself. However Joubert found that the two horsemen in 49a and the one in 49b are versions of the horsemen in the lower left, lower right, and upper right-central sections of a tapestry in the Musée de Cluny which represents the return of a hawking party.[11] It is curious that the third man, a falconer, carries his hawk on his upraised left hand in the Cluny piece but no longer has it in 49b where, as a result, the gesture has lost its original meaning. These observations make it clear that the designer of 49a–d, like many of his contemporaries, used patterns that he either appropriated from existing cartoons or tapestries or to which he had access, along with other artists, in one or more shops. It is likely that figures of this kind were originally taken from prints and then reworked as needed to suit a particular composition. No such sources for any of the figures or groups in 49a–d have yet been discovered. The fenced enclosure must also have been designed after a stock pattern, but this designer has given it what may have been his own personal touch when he placed the extra post at the center of the gate.

MANUFACTURE AND DATE

Except for Schrader (exh. cat. Lawrence 1969, no. 133), who called 49d Franco-Flemish, almost every other writer attributed 49a–d and all the precinct tapestries related to them to Tournai and dated them in the first quarter of the sixteenth century in general or in some span of years within that quarter-century. Only Rorimer (1947) extended the range of dates to include the first third of the century. Vandenbroeck (1987, 66) qualified with a question mark the attribution of 49c to Tournai. Margerin (1932, 142) included the four hangings in a group of tapestries she attributed to Audenarde because they all show along the top the narrow strip of landscape with buildings that she associated with Audenarde tapestries of the late fifteenth century. We have no evidence that such details were represented only in tapestries woven in Audenarde or any other particular south Netherlandish weaving center.

In 1971 Boccara published the generically related tapestry then in a private collection in Paris (see Description and Subject) as Tournai work of about 1515.[12] When one of the two closely related pieces in the Burrell Collection was exhibited in London in 1975, Wells called it Franco-Flemish and dated it about 1500.[13]

On the basis of pictorial style and the few fashionable details of costume shown in 49a–d—that is, the gentle-

men's shoes and hats, the ladies' gowns and hoods, and the slashed doublet worn by the valet in 49d—it is reasonable to date the design of these four compositions sometime between 1510 and 1520. However since the tapestries were neither exceptionally fashionable nor costly, it is equally reasonable to suggest that they may have been woven after 1520 but no later than 1535, when the finer costumes would have looked out of date.

The attribution to Tournai follows from most writers' acceptance of the traditional assignment to that city of tapestries representing this kind of subject in a rather heavy, awkward style within this kind of border. The prejudice undoubtedly gained momentum from Warburg's article of 1907, in which he associated three surviving tapestries showing woodsmen at work in open forests with tapestries that Philippe le Bon bought from the Tournai merchant Pasquier Grenier in 1461 and 1466 and others that Philippe le Beau bought from Jean Grenier (Pasquier's son and heir to his cartoons) in 1505.[14] While Warburg's point was well taken in relation to the pieces he discussed, it does not apply to the class of hangings under consideration here. Roselt noted Göbel's hypothesis that tapestries of this kind were manufactured in shops at Tournai and then observed that, as Jozef Duverger had written in 1960, such pieces "peuvent tout aussi bien avoir été tissées dans un autre atelier provincial."[15] We agree that tapestries like these could have been woven anywhere in the southern Netherlands.

RELATED TAPESTRIES

We do not know any duplicate tapestries or any pieces that might have formed part of the same series of hangings. Like the two closely related pieces in the Burrell Collection (see fig. 171) and the one last reported as being in a collection in Paris (see note 5), 49b and 49d feature peasants (in the Paris piece there is also a falconer) in the foreground. But the content of the pantomime in 49a–d seems to be simple and direct, without the overtones of allegorical or moralistic content that the action and inscriptions in the other pieces convey. Furthermore none of the other pieces shows a hunt in progress within the park as 49a, b, and d do. Certainly the two groups of tapestries are related in terms of form and style, but we believe they represent two quite distinct cycles.

In her entry for 49b in the exhibition catalogue *Songs of Glory* (1985, 262), Romanelli cited Rubinstein-Bloch (1927) as the source of the observation that 49a–d have been presented as a series only since the nineteenth century; but Romanelli added that the consistency of the border pattern and the details of setting endorse the idea that the four tapestries make a legitimate group. We agree with her and add the observation that the four pieces are very nearly the same height. There were probably more than four compositions in the cycle, but we have no way of determining what the total number might have been. Deer hunting is not portrayed here nor is hunting for otters and swans. Any of these game sports and possibly others, as well as activities connected with the building and maintenance of the hunting parks, might have been represented along with the four episodes shown in 49a–d.

HISTORY

Said to have been in the collection of the comte de Vauguyon, Paris.
In the collection of George and Florence Blumenthal, New York, by 1914.
Bequeathed to the MMA by George Blumenthal, 1941.

EXHIBITIONS

New York, MMA, 1914. 49c and d lent by George and Florence Blumenthal.
Ithaca, New York, Andrew Dickson White Museum of Art, Cornell University, and Utica, Munson-Williams-Proctor Institute, 1968. *A Medieval Treasury: An Exhibition of Medieval Art from the Third to the Sixteenth Century.* Catalogue by Robert G. Calkins. Cat. no. 114 [49c], illus.
Lawrence, University of Kansas Museum of Art, 1969. *The Waning Middle Ages.* Catalogue by J. L. Schrader. Cat. no. 133 [49d], illus. pl. LXXVI.
Tournai, 1970. *Tapisseries héraldiques et de la vie quotidienne.* Catalogue by J. P. Asselberghs. Cat. nos. 31 [49d], 32 [49c], illus.
Mobile, Fine Arts Museum of the South; Midland (Michigan) Center for the Arts; Little Rock, Arkansas Arts Center, 1982. *5000 Years of Art from the Collection of the Metropolitan Museum of Art.* Checklist no. 30B [49c].
Lawrence, Spencer Museum of Art, University of Kansas, 1983. *Gardens of the Middle Ages.* Catalogue by Marilyn Stokstad and Jerry Stannard. Cat. no. 20 [49c], illus.
Oklahoma City, Oklahoma Museum of Art, 1985. *Songs of Glory: Medieval Art from 900–1500.* Cat. nos. 95–97 [49a, b, d], illus.; entries by Susan Romanelli.
New York, Center for African Art, 1988–89. *Africa and the Renaissance: Art in Ivory.* 49a exhibited.

PUBLICATIONS

Rubinstein-Bloch, Stella. *Catalogue of the Collection of George and Florence Blumenthal, New-York.* Vol. 4, *Tapestries and Furniture.* Paris, 1927, pls. VII [49c], VIII [49b], IX [49d], X [49a]. Described in detail, discussed briefly; illus.
Mlle. Margerin. "Les tapisseries de verdure, de leur origine au milieu du XIVᵉ siècle, dans les ateliers d'Arras, de Tournai et d'Audenarde." *Bulletin des Musées de France* 4 (1932) p. 142. 49a–d mentioned.
Rorimer, James J. *Mediaeval Tapestries: A Picture Book.* MMA, New York, 1947. 49d illus. fig. 18.

Boccara, Dario. *Les belles heures de la tapisserie.* Zug, 1971, p. 50. 49a–d mentioned.
Calkins, Robert G. *Programs of Medieval Illumination.* Franklin D. Murphy Lectures 5. Lawrence, Kansas, 1984, p. 144. 49c referred to; illus. p. 145, fig. 101.
Joubert 1987, p. 177. 49a and b mentioned; illus. p. 177, as figs. 172, 173.
Vandenbroeck, Paul. *Over Wilden en Narren, Boeren en Bedelaars. Beeld van de Andere, Vertoog over het Zelf.* Exh. cat., Koninklijk Museum voor Schone Kunsten. Antwerp, 1987, p. 66. 49c discussed briefly; illus. fig. 75.

NOTES

1. See *Gothic Art . . . Assembled by the Count and Countess de Kermaingant,* sale cat., American Art Association, New York, November 27, 1926, no. 179, illus.; and *Les fastes de la tapisserie du XVᵉ au XVIIIᵉ siècle,* exh. cat., Musée Jacquemart-André (Paris, 1984) no. 1, illus. In the second piece the pool surrounds a tall fountain, like a moat, in the center of the precinct.
2. In an early fifteenth-century miniature illustrating a manuscript of Bartholomaeus Anglicus's *Propriétés des Choses,* now in the Fitzwilliam Museum in Cambridge, a unicorn stands prominently next to Eve in the Garden of Paradise, a precinct surrounded by a wattled fence; a spring rises in the center of the enclosure and flows out through the opening at the front. See Margaret B. Freeman, *The Unicorn Tapestries,* MMA (New York, 1976) fig. 28. For images of the unicorn with the Virgin in the *hortus conclusus,* see for example an early fifteenth-century German painting in which the figures appear inside a precinct surrounded by a wattled fence and trees and also a detail of a late fifteenth- or early sixteenth-century tapestry altar hanging that shows the figures in a walled garden, in Freeman, *Unicorn Tapestries,* figs. 52, 51, respectively.
3. See A. M. Louise Erkelens, *Wandtapijten 1: Late gotiek en vroege renaissance,* Facetten der Verzameling, Rijksmuseum, 2d ser., no. 4 (Amsterdam, 1962) no. 16, illus.; or Dario Boccara, *Les belles heures de la tapisserie* (Zug, 1971) p. 54, illus.
4. J. Christof Roselt, "Wildgarten mit Lebensbrunnen: Eine flämische Tapisserie im Bergischen Museum Schloss Burg an der Wupper," in *Miscellanea Jozef Duverger* (Ghent, 1968) vol. 2, pp. 714–15, figs. 1, 2. A number of other tapestries of the same type have survived elsewhere: see for example three pieces in the de Kermaingant sale cat. (see note 1 above), nos. 176–78, and another in Boccara, *Les belles heures,* p. 55, illus.
5. For the first two (now Burrell Collection, reg. nos. 46.132, 46.133), see W. G. Thomson, "The Tapestries at Chilham Castle," *Country Life* 56 (September 27, 1924) pp. liv, lvi, figs. 1 and 2; also *Treasures from the Burrell Collection,* exh. cat. by William Wells, Hayward Gallery (London, 1975) no. 93, illus. The third piece, which had been in the collections of Mme. Lelong, Henri de Souhami, and then a number of others, was published in 1971 as belonging in a private collection in Paris; see Boccara, *Les belles heures,* p. 50, illus.
6. The verses in the piece in Paris were transcribed as follows in sale cat., Sotheby's, London, July 1, 1966, no. 17 (our questions and alternate readings follow in parentheses): *Bergier (Biergier) amourex le cuer ci (et?) joyeulx vay (?) cour de songesse (?)* at the left, and *Je quitte tels jeulx plus jouex (jouer?) n'en veulx j'entr' en viellesse* at the right (Enamored shepherd, the heart . . . I leave such games, I no longer want to play them, I am entering [my] old age). One of the two pieces in Glasgow shows four inscribed scrolls above certain figures; the other shows six. The verses appear to be

584

the same in the scrolls shown in the distance. The key words there are *maulgre tous jalou* (?) *envieulx, dancez . . . dance.* In the middle distance at the left the scroll reads *vant a vant que mil ne muse/faitte voie a la cornemuse;* opposite, the verses are *Aller a gaultier car de ce mestier/nen* (?) *plus* (?) *convenanse* (?). The two scrolls in the foreground of the piece that has them (see fig. 171 in this entry) read (above man handing boy an apple?) *Monami tines che* (?) *pommelet/metelle envous . . .* (?) and (above woman handing a sprig of roses to a little girl) *Mamie tines ce boufflet* (?)/*Donelle a bonami* (?) *mrquet* (?).

7. Discussed and illustrated in Adolph S. Cavallo, *Textiles: Isabella Stewart Gardner Museum* (Boston, 1986) no. 5, pp. 34–37; see also his reference to Jean-Paul Asselberghs, *Les tapisseries flamandes aux Etats-Unis d'Amérique* (Brussels, 1974) p. 12.

8. See George Wingfield Digby assisted by Wendy Hefford, *The Devonshire Hunting Tapestries*, Victoria and Albert Museum (London, 1971) p. 44. For some brief notes concerning later tapestries showing hunts in game parks or forests, see Cavallo, *Textiles*, p. 78.

9. See for example a leopard and also a lion attacking a goat (?) in the foreground of a fifteenth-century *Woodcutters* in the Musée des Arts Décoratifs in Paris; illustrated in Hunter 1925, pl. xxi,h, and also in A. Warburg, "Arbeitende Bauern auf burgundischen Teppichen" (1907), in *A. Warburg, Gesammelte Schriften* (Leipzig and Berlin, 1932) vol. 1, fig. 59. Local animals, including deer, a boar, a bear, oxen, and hares together with exotic creatures like a leopard and a rhinoceros inhabit a forest or game park that also contains a unicorn and a cockatrice—all in a mid-sixteenth-century tapestry that Boccara, *Les belles heures*, p. 81, illustrated and published as being in a private collection in France. The presence of the mythical creatures suggests that the designer was taking liberties in depicting the kind of animal park that did contain certain exotic creatures, if indeed he was representing such a park and not simply a romantic fantasy world.

10. The three hangings are illustrated in Phyllis Ackerman, *The Rockefeller McCormick Tapestries* (New York and London, 1932) pls. 3–6, 10. The third piece was then in a private collection in Barcelona.

11. Joubert 1987, p. 177, illus. pp. 174–75. The tapestry, reg. no. Cl. 22858, has been titled *Retour de la chasse.*

12. Boccara, *Les belles heures*, p. 50.

13. Wells, *Treasures from the Burrell Collection*, no. 93.

14. Warburg, "Arbeitende Bauern," pp. 224–27.

15. Roselt, "Wildgarten," p. 716 and n. 10.

50a

50

Arcades with Riders in Fantastic Thickets

Two fragments of one or more hangings

a   *Rider with Spear and Shield and Rider with Rod*
b   *Rider Hailing and Rider with Club*

Southern Netherlands, 1520–50
Wool warp; wool and silk wefts
50a: 8 ft. 5 in. × 6 ft. 4$^{1}/_{2}$ in. (2.57 m × 1.94 m)
10–13 warp yarns per inch, 4–5 per centimeter
50b: 8 ft. 6 in. × 6 ft. 5 in. (2.59 m × 1.96 m)
11 warp yarns per inch, 4 per centimeter
The Friedsam Collection, Bequest of Michael Friedsam, 1931
(32.100.391, 392)

CONDITION

Both pieces have been cut on all four sides, and bands of modern weaving have been sewn along the edges. The lowest parts of both fields are missing and have been replaced with pieces of weaving either from other parts of the same hangings or from other pieces in the set. In 50a this patching follows a line across the piece on a level with the top of the middle circular ornament on the lower part of the center column. The corresponding line in 50b is more irregular and crosses the piece at a slightly lower level. At some time in the past the left third of 50a was cut almost completely away from the rest of the fabric and then rejoined to it. The seam runs from the top of the arch downward through the figure of the rider and the shoulders of the beast, directly to the bottom of the hanging. It passes through the center of the head and shoulders of another man that appear in the added strip of weaving.

Both pieces have been heavily restored by inserting modern wool or silk weft yarns on the original warp. The repairs appear mostly in the contours of all the forms, but they are also scattered everywhere throughout the fields. These restorations, together with the loss of the bottoms of both fields, have altered the appearance of the pieces significantly. Although we have found no breaks in the fabric along the inner edges of the two outer columns in 50a, the fact that those columns are not positioned to support the outer ends of the arches above them suggests either that the fabric on which the columns are represented was cut, shifted, and then invisibly rejoined or that the weavers altered the cartoon at these places for reasons unknown. The logic of the

architecture should, but does not, correspond to the logic of the spans and supports in 50b and also in a tapestry formerly in Munich (fig. 172) that probably comes from the same set of hangings.

The Metropolitan Museum's fragments could have been taken from different parts of one tapestry or from two or more pieces belonging to the same set of hangings. At the outside edges of 50b the springing of two more arches indicates that the field originally contained at least four bays, so at least half the width of the hanging from which 50b comes is missing. Furthermore, since a number of tapestries with similar field patterns have survived, all with borders, it seems likely that borders with patterns like or related to them once surrounded 50a and 50b. Four of these related pieces have baluster arabesques in the side borders and floral arabesques in the upper and lower borders. One is the piece that was in Munich (fig. 172). Another was owned in 1929 by the same dealer in Munich; a third is in the château at Azay-le-Rideau; and a fourth is in the Art Institute of Chicago.[1] A tapestry with a field very much like those of 50a and 50b, but without the architectural bays or the fantastic blossoms, had a border showing a different pattern, garlands of fruit and flowers tied together at the ends with ribbons. That piece was sold in London in 1934.[2]

The dyes in both 50a and 50b have faded significantly, but the individual hues are still distinct.

DESCRIPTION AND SUBJECT

Each fragment shows an arcade with two bays. In each bay there is a single male figure riding an exotic beast through thickets of shrubs bearing giant acanthus-like leaves and equally oversized, fantastic blossoms. Above the shrubs the view opens out into a distant hilly landscape dotted with buildings silhouetted against the sky. Each of the three columns that support the two arches has a thick central shaft decorated with counter-undulating lines in the upper section and with concentric circles and stripes below. Paired engaged colonnettes wrapped spirally with acanthus leaves flank

50b

the central shafts. The cylindrical capitals are decorated with acanthus leaves (in the center) or acanthus leaves and ribbons (at the sides), and the entablature blocks carrying the ends of the arches have a rosette (center) or row of acanthus leaves (sides). The arches have moldings and dentils and are bordered above and below by acanthus arabesques and rosettes. Garlands of leaves and fruits, capped at the ends with acanthus leaves and tied around the center with a scarf, span the spaces below the arches. The cords issuing from the ends of the garlands are carried in the mouths of masks that decorate the keystones or spandrels of the arches. In 50a an ox-head mask occupies the central spandrel while a mask representing an angel's head surrounded by wings appears at the center of each arch. In 50b the cords are carried in the mouths of an angel mask set in the central spandrel and ox-head masks that occupy each side spandrel. In 50a there are two garlands under each arch, and the columns at the sides have been set so close together that their tops, which disappear behind the outer garlands, cannot support the outer ends of the arches. However, in 50b, as noted above, the relation of arch to column is mechanically viable and the springings of the arches are clearly expressed.

The man in the left bay of 50a wears a low, round hat and a long-sleeved jacket over a skirt girdled at thigh level; he has no hose or foot coverings. He holds a spear in his raised right hand and a circular shield in his left as he rides his fairly correctly represented camel. The man in the right bay wears a simple knee-length tunic that has long sleeves and a wide, falling collar. He, too, has a bare left leg and foot, but there are narrow rings of leaves or feathers around his calf and ankle. His hat is a tall conical structure with a row of narrow panes at its tip. In his left hand he holds the reins of the lion-headed, camel-like beast he is riding, and in his right hand is a twisted rod.

The rider in the left bay of 50b wears a knee-length coat with short sleeves and a deep neck. He is bareheaded, and his right foot and knee are bare except for the leather greaves that cover calf and heel. With his left hand he holds the pommel that rises from the harness encircling the neck of his camel, and he raises his right arm in a salute. The man in the right bay rides a griffin-headed, camel-like beast with stag horns, and he holds the reins in his right hand. A large club, gripped in his left hand, rests on his left shoulder. He wears a simple knee-length, long-sleeved coat and a turban with a tall conical crown.

The subject matter has been interpreted in a number of different ways. Breck (1932, 70) wrote that the tapestries showed "children riding animals amidst foliage."

In 1894, when the hangings were sold in Munich, they were described as showing a representation from the story of the *Minnesänger* with male figures on fantastic animals. On the occasion of their sale in 1918, in Munich, they were said to show fighters riding on fantastic animals. We cannot agree with these interpretations. The riders are not children but grown men. As for representing characters in a courtly love story, as they would be if they came from the *Minnesänger*'s lyrical poems, their bare feet and modest dress belie that notion.

It is also possible to think of the savage-looking men in 50a and b, riding through thickets of unnatural leaves and blossoms on their strange beasts, as European "wild men," those hairy, unkempt, emotionally unstable, and slightly threatening humans who have left the civilized world. As Husband observed, "Sublimated in the wild men were the preeminent phobias of medieval society— chaos, insanity, and ungodliness." In some representations these wild men are shown storming the Castle of Love which, in this context, is no longer a haven of virtue.[3] But the bodies of the men in 50a and b are not covered with hair or leaves like the bodies of wild men; they are smooth-skinned. They are not storming a castle nor are they engaged in combat of any kind. Their environment does share two elements with the environment of the wild men, and it may be this similarity that led the author of the 1894 sale catalogue entry to see in these exotic figures something related to the stories of the love poets. The four riders, like the wild men, move in thickets of giant leaves, and at first glance their steeds seem to resemble the fantastic animals that the wild men associate with. However the beasts in the left bays of both 50a and b are fairly realistic camels. Wild men in this kind of setting appear in a Lower Rhenish ornamental engraving of about 1490–1500 by Israhel van Meckenem.[4] It shows a pair of civilized human lovers seated among vines bearing acanthus leaves and the same sort of fantastic blossoms that appear in 50a and b, and five wild men, one wild woman, a hound-like beast, and three crane-like birds cavort through the leaves. Wild folk also associate with fantastic beasts in an environment of leafy vines in Swiss or Upper Rhenish tapestries of the late fifteenth century, and they engage in domestic, erotic, and aggressive activities on caskets and plates of the period, all in environments of giant swirling leaves where real and fantastic creatures lurk.[5]

It is also tempting to see in 50a a representation of a joust, since the men seem to be pointing lances at each other. Wild men were also occasionally shown jousting. A Lower Rhenish engraving of about 1480 by Israhel van Meckenem shows two wild men, protected by ar-

Fig. 172. *Arcades with Riders in Fantastic Thickets.* Tapestry, southern Netherlands, here dated 1520–50. Formerly the property of L. Bernheimer, Munich; present location unknown. From Göbel 1923, vol. 2, fig. 256.

mor made of curling leaves, using uprooted trees as lances as they joust. A somewhat earlier engraving by the Master E.S. shows a wild man jousting with a wild woman against a background of giant scrolling acanthus leaves; he has a rake for a lance, she has a distaff. A detail in an Alsatian tapestry of about 1400 shows two wild men jousting with forked branches.[6]

True "wild men" riding exotic and fantastic creatures in tapestries of this period are represented in two hangings in Amsterdam and one in Chicago. A comparison of these tapestries with 50a and b should dispel the notion that the four men in the Metropolitan Museum's hangings are wild men. One of the Amsterdam pieces shows a wild boy dressed in a knee-length coat astride a giraffe-like creature while his father's lion-headed beast waits in the foreground. The other shows a wild man dressed in a tunic with open sides and holding a club over his right shoulder as he rides sedately on a lion-headed beast past a wild woman falconer mounted on a fantastic unicorn.[7] The tapestry in Chicago shows two wild men, both dressed in open-sided tunics and riding a fanciful breed of camel, moving toward each other in a landscape in which exotic trees and flowering plants grow in the foreground. The man at the right raises a club, and in a generic way he resembles the man riding in the right-hand bay of 50b; but this man's body is covered with long, thick hair.[8] The piece in Chicago makes it clear that there was some confusion in the iconography, undoubtedly reflecting the late medieval tendency to assign to a single category all people who seemed exotic and uncivilized (*l'homme sauvage*) wherever they lived.[9] In that tapestry the beast carrying the wild man at the right has strapped to his flank a bale that is tied about with line and stamped or painted with what appears to be a merchant's mark. This suggests that the designer was illustrating part of a camel caravan conducted by European "wild men" rather than by Gypsies and East Indians, who would be fairly recognizable, or the unidentifiable, ethnically composite people who appear in a great number of tapestries of the first quarter of the sixteenth century that show scenes of oriental life and commerce.

Many such tapestries are documented as having been produced or sold by tapestry weavers, merchants, and upholsterers in Tournai during this period. When Arnould Poissonnier died in 1522, he left a set of hangings that was referred to in his inventory as "l'histoire de Carrabarra dit des Egiptiens" (The Story of Carrabarra, called the Egyptians), which was then sold in 1539 and may perhaps be identified with four such hangings in the Kasteel-Museum van Gaasbeek, Belgium, and a number of others elsewhere.[10] The people represented in these hangings are not Egyptians but Gypsies who, when they appeared in eastern Europe early in the fifteenth century, claimed to have been sent out of Egypt as expiation for their sins. In the documents referring to the tapestry stocks of Poissonnier and also of Jean and Antoine Grenier, all of Tournai, the following titles appear: "à la manière de Portugal et de Indye" (1504), "la caravane" (1508), "l'histoire de gens et de bestes sauvaiges à la manière de calcut" (1510), "le Voyage de Caluce" (1513), "l'histoire de Calcou" (1522), and "l'histoire de la Carvene" (1522). In 1522 Charles V bought six pieces of *L'histoire indienne à oliffans et jeraffes* from the Brussels producer-merchant Pieter van Aelst.[11]

The rods and clubs that the men in 50a and b carry are not primarily weapons but tools used to make their steeds obey their commands. Men dressed and coiffed like these (but not barefoot) use clubs and rods to keep their camels under control in the middle distance and background of a tapestry dubbed *The Unruly Camels*, now in the Fundaçao Abel de Lacerda in Caramulo, Portugal.[12] One of the men, in the upper left corner of the field, holds a spear rather than a club or rod. In another tapestry of this class, formerly the property of French and Company, oriental men use spears, swords, and bows and arrows to hunt lions and griffins; some of them also have shields, like the man in the left-hand bay of 50a.[13]

We believe that the men in the Metropolitan Museum's two tapestries are Gypsy, East Indian, or other ethnically indefinable caravan hands or hunters like the ones just described, even though their facial features have a more western cast. One of the exotic caravan men, in the left foreground of *The Unruly Camels*, who seems to be offering a monkey to a European trader, is

much smaller than the other man, but his body is not that of a child and he is bald. His legs and feet are bare, and he wears anklets reminiscent of the ones worn by the man in the right-hand bay of 50a. Except for the more oriental cast to his features, he could be one of the four men in 50a or 50b. The designer has lifted these exotic men and their steeds out of their narrative contexts and placed them in the kind of exotic thickets that European "wild men" inhabit. The two themes have been combined in a way that reflects a generalized romantic taste among fashionable Europeans for the wild and exotic during the early years of the sixteenth century, a taste perhaps born of, and fostered by, the growing population of Gypsies and by the reports brought back from Vasco da Gama's visits to Calicut and the Malabar coast and Columbus's voyages in the New World.

SOURCE OF THE DESIGN

The design of the setting belongs in a subgroup of the class of hangings that show giant-leaf thickets teeming with fowl, beasts, and flowers, often but not always enframed by architectural elements. These compositions seem to have been inspired by related tapestry designs, ornamental prints, and the borders of pages in illustrated books (see the discussion of design sources in 52a, b). A tapestry now in the Art Institute of Chicago represents the classical example of this variant pattern.[14] There are two elements that distinguish the giant-leaf thickets in 50a and b from those in the primary class. First, the leaves are exceptionally long, slender, and stiff, and they have prominent veins and deeply dentated edges. Second, the blossoms are like nothing that ever grew in nature. They are extraordinarily large and brilliantly colored, with more hues than appear in any one natural blossom. Their pistils are unnaturally large and resemble pineapples, artichokes, or pomegranates. The petals resemble the leaves of some tropical plant. Less exuberant but equally fantastic blossoms appear in a tapestry cover in the Metropolitan Museum (see 26). They also appear in some of the ornamental German prints that might have inspired the giant-leaf thickets in 50a and b as well as the entire class of sixteenth-century tapestries referred to in recent times as "giant-leaf verdures."[15]

As noted above, the exotic figures and beasts in 50a and b are first cousins of the ones appearing in the host of hangings that deal with scenes of life among the Gypsies, East Indians, or people in the world of caravans. Although many or all of these human and animal figures were probably derived from late fifteenth- or early sixteenth-century prints and drawings purporting to show the flora, fauna, and peoples of the East and perhaps also the New World, the images in the tapestries were undoubtedly designed by Netherlandish artists who specialized in creating exotic scenes like these for tapestry producers.

MANUFACTURE AND DATE

The Metropolitan Museum's fragments were called French and were dated in the seventeenth century when they were sold in 1894. At the next sale, in 1918, they were attributed to Burgundy before 1500. In 1932 Breck published them as work of the first half of the sixteenth century attributed to Tournai. None of these writers explained his reasons for making these attributions. Breck may have been following Göbel, who published a related piece that was in Munich (fig. 172 here) as possibly having been woven in Tournai in the middle of the sixteenth century, and also Ackerman, who published the tapestry that shows a similar thicket, now in the Art Institute of Chicago, as Tournai work of about 1520.[16]

As noted above, we have documents proving that between 1504 and 1522 three tapestry weavers, merchants, and upholsterers in Tournai sold one series of tapestries dealing with Gypsy life and six others illustrating scenes set in exotic lands based on contemporary impressions of India (see notes 10 and 11). Asselberghs and other specialists have associated with those cycles a number of tapestries that have survived from that period. The design of 50a and b places them in the same group. Therefore it seems reasonable to consider the possibility that the Metropolitan Museum's two fragments may have been woven in Tournai or fabricated through the agency of a Tournai producer.

As for the date of weaving, 50a and b depend on tapestries that we believe may be associated with at least some of the documented orientalizing hangings of 1504–22. However the Metropolitan Museum's pieces seem to be derivative ones, so it is unlikely that they were among the first to be designed. Furthermore their design depends also on the class of giant-leaf verdures that seem to have reached the height of fashion about the middle of the century or just before. Therefore it seems correct to suggest that the Metropolitan Museum's two fragments were designed and woven sometime between 1520 and 1550.

RELATED TAPESTRIES

The similar hanging that was owned in Munich (fig. 172) must have been woven after the same series of cartoons. The fact that it has lost approximately the same amount of fabric at the bottom of the field (as well as the lower border) suggests that it may even have come from the same set of hangings. If its arabesque border is original, which seems likely, it shows what the border or borders of 50a and b looked like. We have no way of knowing how many hangings there were in the complete set.

At least one of the closely related pieces that were sold in London in 1934 (see note 2) showed figures that may have been taken from the same designs, but the thickets they occupy are different. While the giant leaves are more or less the same, the flowers are not. Large blossoming plants of relatively naturalistic character take the place of the enormous fantastic blossoms that appear in 50a and b.

HISTORY

Sold, *Die Kunstsammlung des Museums August Riedinger in Augsburg,* Munich, sale conducted by Hugo Helbing, October 22, 1894, and following days, nos. 1198 [50b], 1199 [50a], illus.
Sold, *Antiquitäten . . . Gobelins . . . aus dem Besitz eines süddeutschen Sammlers,* Munich, Galerie Helbing, February 26–27, 1918, no. 315, illus. pls. VIII [50b], IX [50a].
In the collection of Michael Friedsam, New York.
Bequeathed to the MMA by Michael Friedsam, 1931.

EXHIBITIONS

None known.

PUBLICATION

Breck, Joseph. "European Decorative Arts: Tapestries and Textiles." *The Michael Friedsam Collection.* In *MMA Bulletin* 27, no. 11 (November 1932) section 2, p. 70. Described and discussed briefly.

NOTES

1. For illustrations of the three last pieces, see respectively Phyllis Ackerman, *The Rockefeller McCormick Tapestries: Three Early Sixteenth Century Tapestries* (New York, 1932) pl. 15; Paul Vandenbroeck, *Over Wilden en Narren, Boeren en Bedelaars: Beeld van de Andere, Vertoog over het Zelf,* exh. cat., Koninklijk Museum voor Schone Kunsten (Antwerp, 1987) fig. 10; and Ackerman, *Rockefeller McCormick Tapestries,* pls. 1 and 2, or J. P. Asselberghs, *Tapisseries héraldiques et de la vie quotidienne,* exh. cat. (Tournai, 1970) no. 12, illus., with bibliography and references to a similar hanging in the Rijksmuseum, Amsterdam, and a similar fragment in the Museum of Art, Rhode Island School of Design, Providence.
2. See *Catalogue of Porcelain . . . and Tapestry* [various properties], Christie's, London, July 12, 1934, no. 141, illus. Nos. 142 and 143, also listed as whole hangings, and no. 144, two fragments of another, were "en suite" with no. 141.
3. See Timothy Husband, with the assistance of Gloria Gilmore-

House, *The Wild Man: Medieval Myth and Symbolism*, exh. cat., MMA, The Cloisters (New York, 1980) p. 5 and, for a discussion of a Castle of Love besieged by knights and another besieged by wild men, pp. 71–76.

4. Husband with Gilmore-House, *The Wild Man*, fig. 54.

5. See for example a mid-fifteenth-century Swiss tapestry in the Österreichisches Museum für Angewandte Kunst, Vienna; an Upper or Middle Rhineland boxwood coffer of about 1460–70 in the Kunsthistorisches Museum, Vienna; and a print of about 1455 by the Master of the Nuremberg Passion in the Staatliche Graphische Sammlung, Munich, on which the scene carved on the right end panel of the coffer was based; a Portuguese gilt-silver repoussé plate of about 1500 in the MMA; and a Portuguese silver repoussé plate of about 1550 in the Victoria and Albert Museum: all illustrated in Husband with Gilmore-House, *The Wild Man*, figs. 76, 67, 70, 73, 74. For another tapestry of this type, which shows fabulous and real animals wandering in an acanthus thicket where similar but less exuberant flowers bloom and a wild man stands holding a club at one side, see Göbel 1933, fig. 26, a piece then the property of Seidlitz and van Baarn, New York.

6. For illustrations of these two prints, which are respectively in the Art Institute of Chicago and the British Museum, and of the tapestry which is in the Museum der Stadt Regensburg, see Husband with Gilmore-House, *The Wild Man*, figs. 87, 90, 88.

7. Both hangings are preserved in the Rijksmuseum. See Vandenbroeck, *Over Wilden*, figs. 12 and 21; also Ackerman, *Rockefeller McCormick Tapestries*, pls. 13 and 12.

8. See an illustration of this piece when it was exhibited in Chicago in 1926 as the property of Demotte: Phyllis Ackerman, *Catalogue of a Loan Exhibition of Gothic Tapestries*, Arts Club of Chicago (Chicago, 1926) no. 18.

9. For a brief study of this subject as it was treated in late medieval tapestries, see Madeleine Jarry, "L'homme sauvage," *L'Oeil*, no. 183 (March 1970) pp. 14–21.

10. For comments on the "Egyptian" or Gypsy series and pieces that are believed to have survived from it, with bibliography, see J. P. Asselberghs, *La tapisserie tournaisienne au XVIe siècle*, exh. cat. (Tournai, 1968) pp. 7 and 11. One of the pieces in Gaasbeek, a *Return from the Hunt*, is discussed and illustrated as no. 2.

11. Concerning all these cycles with oriental subjects, together with references to surviving pieces believed to represent them, with bibliography, see Asselberghs, *La tapisserie tournaisienne au XVIe siècle*, p. 7 n.8, and pp. 12–13. Some of the extant hangings are discussed and illustrated as nos. 3–8.

12. See Asselberghs, *La tapisserie tournaisienne au XVIe siècle*, no. 7, illus.

13. See Asselberghs, *La tapisserie tournaisienne au XVIe siècle*, no. 6, illus.

14. The Art Institute of Chicago, reg. no. 1934.4; illustrated in Ackerman, *Rockefeller McCormick Tapestries*, pls. 1 and 2; also in Asselberghs, *Tapisseries héraldiques*, no. 12. See note 1 above for references to other pieces showing the same design; also Dario Boccara, *Les belles heures de la tapisserie* (Zug, 1971) pp. 44–45, for illustrations of one of a group of tapestries showing figures of sibyls standing in the same kinds of environments, complete with the acanthus branches and the fantastic blossoms along with large rose blossoms, beasts, and fowl.

15. See an example of such a print, an engraving of about 1490–1500 by Israhel van Meckenem, in Husband with Gilmore-House, *The Wild Man*, fig. 54.

16. Göbel 1923, vol. 2, caption to fig. 256; Ackerman, *Rockefeller McCormick Tapestries*, p. 3.

51

An antependium

Southern Netherlands (probably Sint-Truiden), 1525–50
Wool warp, wool wefts
3 ft. 4 in.×6 ft. 5 in. (1.02 m×1.96 m)
14 warp yarns per inch, 5 $^1/_2$ per centimeter
The Cloisters Collection, 1957 (57.35)

CONDITION

There is some reweaving on the original warp in the region of the arms and hands of the main figures, a few details in the lower parts of their garments, and some negligible details in the figures beneath them. The new weft yarns are mostly brown in color. There are insertions of modern fabric using new warp and weft yarns in the upper part of the left guard, the right-hand four-fifths of the lower guard and bits of the field adjacent to it, and a tall, narrow passage involving the lower third of Saint Catherine's gown and the section of hillock that appears directly beneath it.

Photographs published by Van Ysendyck in 1880 and by Terme in 1910 show the tapestry in its damaged condition, before these repairs were made. In those pictures the restored parts of the left and lower guards and the adjacent bits of the field were simply missing, whereas the restored section beneath Saint Catherine's knees had been filled in with a patch of foreign fabric showing a pattern of lozenges. Curiously, the reproduction published in 1881 by Keuller and Wauters shows the tapestry apparently restored. This indicates either that the repairs were made between 1880 and 1881 and that Terme in 1910 (as well as Smets in 1984) for some reason used an earlier photograph or, more likely, that Keuller and Wauters published an image that made the tapestry appear whole.

Since the two left-hand corners of the guard appear to be intact, we conclude that the hanging has lost none of its original height; and since there is no break in the warp between the ends of the field and the guard bands at both sides, it is clear that the piece has preserved its original width. Except for the lower part of Saint Catherine's gown and the portion of the hillock directly below it, virtually none of the original drawing has been altered. The colors are still bright and fresh. The lines representing the diagonal leading in the windows of

Saint Barbara's tower have been painted on the tapestry fabric; it has not been determined whether the pigment is original.

DESCRIPTION AND SUBJECT

The Virgin stands in the center of the space. She wears a mantle of unpatterned material over an unpatterned, high-waisted gown cut with a high V neckline and a wide, flat collar. There is an open crown on her head; from under it her long, free-flowing hair falls over her shoulders, and down to her waist. A nimbus surrounds her head and a halo composed of sword-shaped shafts of light alternating with undulating tongues of light surrounds her figure. Her feet rest on a deeply curved crescent moon which in turn rests on the body of a dragon. The nude Christ Child sits in the crook of her right arm and holds up the end of a rosary as He leans to the left, toward Saint Catherine of Alexandria. That saint stands on a hillock that rises from the bottom of the field at the left, and her gaze is directed toward the Virgin and Child. She wears a mantle over a high-waisted gown of unpatterned fabric that is cut like the Virgin's dress and has sleeves decorated with small slashings filled with puffs of fabric. She wears a crown like the Virgin's and holds the hilt of a sword in her right hand and a ring in her left hand. A wheel with blades set into its outer rim rests on the ground behind her at the left; on the other side crouches the figure of the emperor Maximinus, at whose order Catherine was to have been executed on the wheel. The wheel broke upon touching her body, however, and the emperor had her beheaded. The sword she holds refers to that martyrdom, and the ring alludes to the legend of her betrothal to Christ. Balancing Saint Catherine's figure, at the right end of the field, is the figure of Saint Barbara, who stands on a hillock in front of a tower. She wears a mantle over a high-waisted gown of unpatterned fabric cut like the other two, and she wears the open crown as well. She holds an open book before her and appears to be reading from it; the end of a palm branch is clasped between the thumb and index finger of her left hand. A small male figure wearing a turban and brandishing a sword in his right hand crouches on the top of the hillock slightly behind the saint's right leg. He represents Barbara's father, at whose hand she was shut up in the tower and ultimately be-headed by the sword he carries.

The figures appear in natural colors against a ground that simulates a silk damask woven in a conventional pomegranate pattern. The design, in dark and light blue, is a diagonal latticework system of ogival compartments containing two major motifs arranged in horizontal rows, each row set one-half unit to the side of the motif above or below it. The larger of the two motifs, which repeats across the lower two-thirds of the field, shows a bouquet of five carnations and a pair of acanthus leaves arranged symmetrically in a vase flanked by pomegranates or pineapples; below each vase appears a crown surrounded by three spotted bands and three fleurs-de-lis. The upper borders of the compartments containing these bouquets are decorated with a motif showing a pair of ivy vines rising in opposite directions from a vase in the center. Directly above these vases appear the centers of the second motif. Each of those ogival units shows a pomegranate surrounded by acanthus leaves, the whole above a crown which in turn surmounts an inverted fleur-de-lis. Along the very top of the field runs a row of inverted fleurs-de-lis which are in fact the lowest part of the larger ogival unit which appears again—mostly out of view—above the row of pomegranate and acanthus motifs. A narrow guard comprising a pair of stripes, a light one running along the inside edge of a slightly wider dark one, completely surrounds the field.

The Virgin represented here is the Virgin of the Apocalypse, of whom it was said in the Apocalypse of Saint John the Apostle (11:19–12:1) in relation to the conquest of the powers of darkness: "And the temple of God was opened in heaven: and the ark of his testament was seen in his temple, and there were lightnings, and voices, and an earthquake, and great hail. And a great sign appeared in heaven: A woman clothed with the sun, and the moon under her feet, and on her head a crown of twelve stars. . . ." The dragon on which the Virgin stands in the tapestry is not the seven-headed monster that appears next in Saint John's account, but nevertheless it represents the Devil in the guise of a dragon, which the Virgin crushes beneath her feet. It seems likely that Mary was chosen to occupy the center of this hanging because it was almost certainly designed and made to be hung in front of the altar dedicated to the Virgin on the north side of the entrance to the choir in the church of the beguinage of Saint Agnes at Sint-Truiden (see Source of the Design, Related Tapestries, and History).

Compositions showing the Virgin of the Apocalypse flanked by saints appear frequently on altar hangings woven during the Middle Ages and later. A German

example, attributed to Alsace, about 1510, and preserved in the Württembergisches Landesmuseum in Stuttgart, shows the Virgin flanked by Saint Margaret at the left and Saint Helena at the right, all against a ground simulating a brocaded voided velvet with a pattern antedating that shown on the Metropolitan Museum's tapestry.[1] Two other German examples, both showing the Virgin accompanied by six saints, may be cited. One of them, in the Historisches Museum in Thun, has been attributed to Switzerland, about 1425–40; the other, in the Kunsthistorisches Museum in Vienna, has been attributed to Swabia and is dated 1502 in the weave.[2] A later example, showing the Virgin flanked by Saint Ulrich at the left and Saint Afra at the right, which has been attributed tentatively to Nuremberg, about 1550, is also in Vienna.[3]

SOURCE OF THE DESIGN

In searching for a design source for this tapestry and its pendant, which is in the Burrell Collection (see Related Tapestries), one must take into account the setting for which the pair is believed to have been woven. There seems to be little doubt that they were made to be hung at the altars flanking the entrance to the choir in the beguinage church at Sint-Truiden, one altar dedicated to the Virgin, the other to Saint Agnes, patroness of the beguinage and its church. Smets (1984, 319–23) offered several arguments supporting this hypothesis. Among them is the fact that the front surface of each of the altars in question measures 1.19 meters in height and 2 meters in width, dimensions that agree reasonably well with those of the two tapestries, each of which is approximately 1.02 by 1.96 meters. Smets also observed that the figures in the tapestries correspond in terms of color and design to the figures painted on the walls of the church when its interior was decorated with murals for the second time, about 1500–1510. In connection with these paintings, Smets noted that the Saint Elizabeth in the Burrell piece wears a costume similar to the one worn by Anne in the scene of the *Presentation of the Virgin in the Temple* painted on the west side of the pillar that rises in front of the Saint Agnes altar in the south aisle of the church. Smets also wondered whether the figures of Saints Catherine and Barbara, who were not included among the saints represented in the second decorating phase, might have been included in the Metropolitan Museum's tapestry to complete the iconographic scheme of those murals. Although the paintings have been restored, it seems likely that the painted figures have always resembled the figures in the two tapestries as much as they do today and furthermore

596

that the cartoons after which the two hangings were woven might have been designed by the mural painters.[4]

The painting style is simple and naive and the forms are strongly outlined. Therefore we are inclined to agree with Buyle, who suggested that the murals were inspired by contemporary woodcuts.[5] In view of the strong family resemblance that relates the figures in these murals to the figures in the tapestries, it follows that the designers of the latter may also have been inspired by woodcuts. Ackerman (exh. cat. Chicago 1926) suggested that because the tapestry compositions remind one of wooden sculptures set in front of a damask wall they might have been designed by an artist who worked for wood-carvers. Since tapestries of this class are often reminiscent of polychrome wood retables, Ackerman's point is well taken and valid in itself. However, in view of the close relationship that has been shown to exist between the murals in the church and the tapestries, her observation now seems irrelevant.

MANUFACTURE AND DATE

On first acquaintance the tapestry recalls pieces woven in Germany. As noted above (Description and Subject; see also notes 1–3), a number of German tapestries showing similar formats have survived from the late Middle Ages, more German examples than Netherlandish ones. However the warp yarns in this piece and its pendant in Glasgow are wool rather than linen, a technical peculiarity that virtually rules out a German origin. However the woodcuts that inspired the figure designs in these two pieces might well have been German. Furthermore, at the time the tapestries were woven, the town of Sint-Truiden, now in Belgium, was in the western reaches of territories that were culturally German.

After considering the available archival material concerning the tapestry industry at Sint-Truiden in the late fifteenth and sixteenth centuries, Smets (1984, 323–25) concluded that the two tapestries may have been woven locally even though they do not correspond to the type of hangings that happen to be mentioned in the early records. Those accounts refer to verdure tapestries and to tapestries showing "feuillages."[6] Göbel (1923, vol. 1, 463) acknowledged that he did not know a single tapestry that could be attributed with any certainty to a manufactory at Sint-Truiden, but he thought it likely that the Metropolitan Museum's tapestry was woven there. Ackerman (exh. cat. Chicago 1926) considered it a local product too, presumably because it belonged in the church of the beguinage there and also because she regarded it as "typically provincial, with the delayed primitiveness and naivete that characterize the work of

the minor centers of weaving." The fact that the two tapestries seem always to have been in the church influenced these three writers and others who studied the hangings before them. Van Ysendyck (1880) attributed 51 to the locality of Sint-Truiden. In the catalogue for the Brussels exhibition of 1880, the pendant was attributed tentatively to Sint-Truiden, and by extension the attribution applied to the Metropolitan Museum's piece as well. When 51 was exhibited in Liège in 1881 no attribution was made in the catalogue entry, but in the same year Keuller and Wauters published it as Sint-Truiden work. When it was shown again in Liège in 1905, Terme referred to 51 as having been woven at Sint-Truiden.

Although the design of this piece and its pendant is naive, the quality of the weaving is professional. In certain German convents there were women who effectively were professional artisans; but we do not know that any women associated with the community at Sint-Truiden were engaging in the same kind of activity. Whether or not this tapestry and its mate in Glasgow were woven in the beguinage of Saint Agnes, it seems clear, because of their close relationship to the interior of its church, that they were woven in the vicinity.

In regard to the date of weaving, the suggestions range from the fourteenth century (Keuller and Wauters 1881) to 1420–40 (Van Ysendyck 1880) to about 1520 (Ackerman, exh. cat. Chicago 1926, and Göbel 1923) to the first third of the sixteenth century (Smets 1984, 321). Smets was the only one of these writers to explain his dating. He believed that the stylish costume worn by Saint Catherine (and also the Magdalen's costume in the Burrell piece) reflects the fashions of about 1515–20. In the present writer's opinion these representations do not contain enough detail to justify a date any more precise than the first third or even first half of the sixteenth century, especially since the costumes were probably derived from a print source of unknown origin and then interpreted in a provincial region. As Smets implied, the weaving itself might have been executed some years later than 1515–20. The pattern in the simulated damask ground seems to have been fashionable throughout the first half of the sixteenth century. A very similar pattern appears in the background of the tapestry portrait of Augustus I of Saxony that was woven by Seger Bombeck in Leipzig in or about 1550.[7] For several reasons—the factor of fashions in clothing and silk patterns, the likelihood that the Metropolitan Museum's tapestry and its pendant were designed to harmonize with the second phase of decoration in the church at Sint-Truiden (about 1500–1510), and the allowance of a time lag because the pieces were produced in a provin-

Fig. 173. *Antependium with Mary Magdalen, Saint Agnes, and Saint Elizabeth.* Tapestry; southern Netherlands, probably woven in Sint-Truiden, here dated 1525-50. The Burrell Collection, Glasgow Museums and Art Galleries.

cial context—it seems correct to date this tapestry in the second quarter of the sixteenth century.

RELATED TAPESTRIES

It has already been noted that this tapestry is one of a pair of altar hangings. The pendant, in the Burrell Collection in Glasgow, shows the same simulated blue damask ground and three female figures arranged in a row, each wearing a mantle over a high-waisted gown and each standing on a hillock from which grow flowering plants (fig. 173).[8] The central figure represents Saint Agnes, patron saint of the beguinage at Sint-Truiden and its church. She holds an open book in her left hand and a palm branch in her right. The lamb, her special attribute, stands on the hillock at her right and places its forehooves against her leg. The Magdalen, more fashionably dressed with an elaborate cap, a veil, a patterned stomacher, peplum, and sleeves decorated with puffed slashings, stands at the left. She holds her attribute, a box of ointment, in both hands. At the right stands the figure of Saint Elizabeth of Hungary, dressed modestly and holding a purse or bag in the crook of her left arm and a loaf of bread, her special attribute alluding to her charity, in her right hand.

HISTORY

In the church of the beguinage of Saint Agnes at Sint-Truiden until at least 1905.
Property of Seidlitz and van Baarn, New York, in 1926.
Said to have been with Frank Partridge, London, in 1936.
Property of Raphael Stora, New York.
Purchased by the MMA, The Cloisters Collection, 1957.

EXHIBITIONS

Brussels, 1880. *Exposition Nationale.* IVe section, Industries d'Art en Belgique antérieures au XIXe siècle, Classe F: Tapisseries, no. 108. Lent by the Eglise principale de Saint-Trond.
Liège, 1881. *Exposition de l'art ancien au Pays de Liège. Catalogue officiel.* 5e section: Mobilier, ivoires, tapisseries, costume, no. 148. Lent by the church of the beguinage of Saint Agnes, Sint-Truiden.
Liège, 1905. *L'exposition universelle de Liège 1905. L'art ancien au Pays de Liège.* Cat. no. 5349-2. Lent by the church of the beguinage of Saint Agnes, Sint-Truiden.
Arts Club of Chicago, 1926. *A Loan Exhibition of Gothic Tapestries.* Catalogue by Phyllis Ackerman. Cat. no. 19a, illus. Lent by Seidlitz and van Baarn.
Bellingham, Washington, Whatcom Museum of History and Art, 1976–77. *5000 Years of Art: An Exhibition from the Collections of The Metropolitan Museum of Art.* Cat. no. 45, illus.
Lincroft, New Jersey, Monmouth Museum, 1978. *Kings, Knights and Knaves.* No exh. cat.

PUBLICATIONS

Van Ysendyck, J. J. *Documents classés de l'art dans les Pays-Bas du Xe au XVIIIe siècle.* Vol. 1, [Antwerp], 1880, litt. A, pl. 6. Discussed briefly; illus. in damaged condition.

Keuller, H.-F., and Alphonse Wauters. *Les tapisseries historiées à l'exposition nationale belge de 1880.* Brussels, 1881, pl. [v]. Discussed briefly; illus. as though restored in a hand-colored black and white photoreproduction.

Terme, G. *L'art ancien au pays de Liège: Mobilier et sculptures. Album publié sous le patronage du comité exécutif de l'Exposition universelle de Liège 1905.* [Liege, 1910], pl. 104, no. 5349-2. Discussed briefly; illus. in damaged condition.

Göbel 1923, vol. 1, p. 463. Described and discussed briefly.

Braun, Joseph. *Der christliche Altar.* Munich, 1924, vol. 2, p. 74. Mentioned.

Smets, L[eon]. "Twee Antependia uit de Begijnhofkerk te Sint-Truiden." *Historische Bijdragen over Sint-Truiden* 4 (1984) pp. 319–25. Described and discussed in detail; illus. fig. 24 on p. 506, in damaged condition.

NOTES

1. Göbel 1933, p. 196, fig. 193b.
2. See, respectively, Kurth 1926, pp. 214–15, 257–58, and pls. 37–39, 236, 237. The first example, in Thun, shows the seven figures standing in the bays of an arcade, with the Virgin of the Apocalypse in the center; to her left are Saints Anthony the Hermit, John the Baptist, and John the Evangelist; to her right stand Saints Maurice, Mary Magdalen, and Catherine of Alexandria. The background pattern is one of flowering vines. The other tapestry, in Vienna, shows the seven figures against a different flowering-vine ground and without the arcade. The Virgin of the Apocalypse stands in the center; to her left are Saints Clara, Bonaventure, and Francis; to her right stand Saints Louis of Toulouse, Anthony, and Bernard.
3. Göbel 1933, p. 239, fig. 218. The tapestry is said to have come from the church of Saint Ulrich in Augsburg, the city where both Saints Ulrich and Afra are guardian patron saints. They stand against a rich ground of tall flowering plants, birds, and beasts. As Göbel noted, the weaving looks like Brussels work.
4. Compare for example the figure of Saint Margaret of Antioch, painted on the east face of one of the pillars in the nave, to the figure of Saint Catherine or Saint Barbara in the Metropolitan Museum's tapestry; see *Het Begijnhof te Sint-Truiden, de Kerk en de Muurschilderingen,* Museum voor Religieuze Kunst, Province Limburg (Sint-Truiden, 1982) illus. p. 7 and diagram on p. 6, no. 14. The painting of Saint Margaret appears also, though less clearly, in an illustration in Marjan Buyle and Leon Smets, "De Begijnhofkerk te Sint-Truiden en haar Muur- en Pijlerschilderingen," *Monumenten en Landschappen* 1 (1982) p. 30.
5. Marjan Buyle, "De Muurschilderingen in de Begijnhofkerk van Sint-Truiden (13de tot 17de eeuw)," in *Archivum Artis Lovaniense* (Louvain, 1981) p. 9. See also Buyle and Smets, "De Begijnhofkerk," p. 34.
6. Concerning the tapestry industry at Sint-Truiden and the tapestries documented as having been woven there, see Jules Guiffrey, *Histoire de la tapisserie depuis le moyen âge jusqu'à nos jours* (Tours, 1886) p. 259; Göbel 1923, vol. 1, pp. 462–63; and especially L[eon] Smets, "Twee Antependia uit de Begijnhofkerk te Sint-Truiden," *Historische Bijdragen over Sint-Truiden* 4 (1984) pp. 323–25.
7. MMA, acc. no. 67.55.97, Bequest of Susan Dwight Bliss, 1966; see Edith Appleton Standen, *European Post-Medieval Tapestries and Related Hangings in The Metropolitan Museum of Art* (New York, 1985) no. 137, illus.
8. The Burrell Collection, Glasgow, reg. no. 46/125. Published together with the Metropolitan Museum's tapestry in Phyllis Ackerman, *Catalogue of a Loan Exhibition of Gothic Tapestries,* Arts Club of Chicago (Chicago, 1926) no. 19b, illus. Said to have been offered for sale (together with the Metropolitan Museum's piece) by Frank Partridge, London, in 1936, it was sold from the collection of Mrs. James Manchester, Lloyd's Neck, Long Island, at Sotheby's, London, May 20, 1955, no. 102, illus. It then passed into the collection of Sir William Burrell. See Smets, "Twee Antependia," pp. 320–21, for a recent discussion, and fig. 23 for an illustration.

52a

52

Thickets with Large Leaves, Flowers, Animals, and Architectural Enframements

Two tapestries woven after different but related sets of cartoons

The Netherlands, about 1540–50
Wool warp; wool wefts with a few silk wefts
52a: 7 ft. 5 $^1/_2$ in. × 6 ft. 8 in. (2.27 m × 2.03 m)
9–10 warp yarns per inch, 3–4 per centimeter
52b: 10 ft. 1 $^1/_2$ in. × 10 ft. 5 in. (3.09 m × 3.18 m)
11 warp yarns per inch, 4–5 per centimeter
Gift of the late James J. Rorimer, made by his widow Katherine S. Rorimer, 1967 (67.47.1, 2)

CONDITION

Tapestry 52a is the upper central section of a hanging whose field (not including the border) was originally about 21 to 22 inches taller and perhaps a bit wider than it is now. It probably had a border that was closely related to but slightly different from the one that survives on 52b (see Description and Subject, and Related Tapestries). All four sides of 52a have been cut and modern guards sewn to the edges. The fabric has been very heavily restored throughout by reweaving, and a great many small holes have been repaired with new warp and new weft yarns. In spite of these restorations, the drawing and pattern appear to have been changed very little. The colors have faded significantly.

Tapestry 52b retains the original extent of its field and almost all of its border. Only a short section at the top of the left border has been replaced with new warp and weft yarns. There are a few small repairs by reweaving along the inner edge of the left border and to the left of the stag's shoulders in the lower central section. Other small repairs using new warp as well as weft yarns have been made in and near the lower left and upper right corners of the field. The colors have faded appreciably.

DESCRIPTION AND SUBJECT

Both tapestries show fields completely filled with giant swirling, curling leaves that have heavy medial veins and deeply cut, ragged edges. These leafy thickets serve as a setting for a profusion of flowering branches and a host of birds and beasts, all shown in their natural colors against the dark green of the leaves. Each tapestry has an elaborate architectural enframement that serves essentially as a proscenium through which one views the thickets. The enframements are similar, but they differ significantly in details. Having lost a good deal of its original height, 52a shows the columns at the sides only from the bottom of the shafts upward; the motif supporting the columns was cut away with the rest of the field. The marble shafts of these columns have fluted bases and gadrooned and foliated collars set halfway between the bases and the capitals, which are Corinthian, the left one having upper parts that were altered through restoration. On the capitals rest the ends of a segmented arch that breaks in the center to accommodate a gadrooned and foliated finial supported by a pair of volutes issuing from behind the two sections of the arch. The face or underside of the arch shows a row of small rectangular windows bordered by paired gadrooned moldings. The upper edge of the arch is deeply cusped. At each end of the arch, above the capitals, a lion sits on a volute and leans forward to grasp the upper edge of the arch as it curves away.

The field of 52a shows two birds perched on giant leaves in the center and a third bird in flight in the upper left corner. A spotted goat-like creature with short, forward-curving horns thrusts its head and shoulders out from behind the leaves in the lower right corner. The upper part of an urn containing a bouquet of flowers and lanceolate leaves occupies the lower left corner of the field. The missing bottom section of the field probably resembled the corresponding section of two tapestries formerly at French and Company (see Related Tapestries and note 30). The upper part of their enframements matches 52a precisely, and it is fair to assume that the lower part, with male busts supporting the columns, shows what the bottom of the enframement in 52a looked like even though there is no trace in 52a of the herms that flank the vase in the other pieces. It is also likely that 52a originally had a narrow border resembling the ones on the French and Company pieces; it is a variant of the border on 52b. Four similar hangings (see Related Tapestries) show leopard-legged satyrs rather than the busts supporting the columns; but since the

52b

rest of the prosceniums in those do not match 52a precisely, it seems likely that 52a had the busts for column supports instead.

In 52b three beasts are arranged across the center of the field. A prancing doe appears among the leaves at the left, a lion with a lamb in its mouth rises just left of center, and a leopard perched on a giant leaf appears at the right. A hound stands in the lower left corner of the field, behind the scrolling balustrade that forms the base of the proscenium. In the inwardly curving center of the balustrade a stag prances at the left and a doe reclines at the right. An urn containing flowers and lanceolate leaves rests atop each of the rectangular podia at the outer ends of the curving center section of the balustrade. At the outer ends of each of the scrolling balustrades a leopard-legged satyr sits and holds the gadrooned base of a column on his head, bracing it with the outward hand and resting the inward hand on the rising curve of the adjacent balustrade. Each column comprises a lower half made of a cylindrical shaft of marble and an upper half consisting of a herm carrying on his head a rectangular block which in turn supports a Corinthian capital. The two capitals hold up an arch made up of two flat outer sections and a curved, segmented inner section. Volutes decorated with masks and cherub heads mark the points where the arch sections meet. This arch, like the one in 52a, has an underside showing small rectangular windows, gadrooned moldings, and a cusped edge. Swags of drapery, held at the ends by satyrs and caught up by ribbon bows, run in countermovement to the arch. Bouquets of flowers, fruits, and vegetables hang down from the ribbons at various points. A narrow border surrounds the entire field. It shows three different quatrefoil motifs alternating with each other and with pairs of small leaves between narrow guards. A blossom or star with eight points occupies each of the four corners.

Although the compositions show beasts and satyrs, they contain no narrative or symbolic subject matter and were intended to be purely decorative.

SOURCE OF THE DESIGN

This kind of thicket with giant leaves, flora, and fauna has never been traced to its ultimate source. There are many avenues to investigate. The large, scrolling, convoluted, decoratively edged leaves recall the elaborate mantlings that flow from helmets in the achievements of arms found in prints, paintings, embroideries, and tapestries of the late fifteenth and early sixteenth centuries (see 16). Furthermore, thickets of scrolling leaves, often enhanced with flowers, birds, beasts, and human

figures, appear in a certain class of German ornamental engravings of the same period.[1] Closely allied to these are the leafy thickets that appear in the backgrounds of a contemporaneous group of Upper Rhenish tapestries.[2] Whatever its source, the motif of a host of giant leaves completely filling the field of a south Netherlandish tapestry had made a firm appearance early in the second quarter of the sixteenth century. The earliest surviving examples are the two armorial hangings woven in 1528 by Henri van Lacke of Enghien for Margaret of Austria that are now in the Iparmüvészeti Múzeum in Budapest.[3] In those tapestries the leaves grow from two intertwined tree trunks; and while they completely cover the field behind five achievements of arms, they seem for that reason to function also as heraldic mantling.

The architectural enframements that surround the thickets in 52a and b relate these pieces to the garden and pergola tapestries that were woven in large numbers primarily during the middle and second half of the sixteenth century. Digby summarized the development of this class of hangings in his discussion of a tapestry in the Victoria and Albert Museum.[4] In this connection both 52a and 52b are related to the *Vertumnus and Pomona* tapestries designed probably by Jan Cornelisz Vermeyen before the middle of the century, and perhaps even more so to the four *Gardens with Figures* hangings in the Isabella Stewart Gardner Museum, Boston, two of which date from the last quarter of the century.[5] The *Vertumnus as a Fisherman* subject shows two arches on the central axis whose lower cusped edges recall the cusped upper edges of the arches in 52a and b. The same is true for the cusped arch that appears in the upper section of the *January* subject in the *Twelve Months of the Year* series woven in Brussels about 1560 and now in the Kunsthistorisches Museum in Vienna.[6] The *Months* tapestries use a decorative vocabulary derived from the great tradition of so-called grotesque ornament that originated in antiquity, was revived in Italy in the decoration of the Borgia apartments and the Loggie at the Vatican in the late fifteenth and early sixteenth centuries, and appeared in France a short time later in the paintings and tapestry designs made for the palace at Fontainebleau and also in the ornamental engravings by Jacques Androuet Du Cerceau and Etienne Delaune. In the Netherlands, Cornelis Bos, Cornelis Floris, and Vredeman de Vries produced ornamental engravings in the grotesque idiom around the middle of the sixteenth century. Some thirty years earlier, tapestry weavers in Brussels were working on the grotesque borders for Raphael's *Acts of the Apostles.* Quantities of south Netherlandish tapestries used this and related orna-

mental systems during the middle and second half of the century, but all of them were more sophisticated, complex, and refined than the system on which the prosceniums in 52a and b are based.[7]

Much as the swags, satyrs, and masks seem to hark back to that tradition of grotesque ornament, they reflect a different, though closely related, kind of decoration—the arabesque ornament that is found, among other places, in certain late fifteenth- and early sixteenth-century manuscript-page borders. The page border illustrated here (fig. 174) represents this tradition. Although the tapestry designers did not use this page as their pattern source, it is clear that they used the kind of source that inspired miniature painters not only

some decades earlier but also well into the sixteenth century.[8] The break in the curved pediment of the niche, the shield in the center, the swags of leaves and fruit, and the fluttering ribbons at the sides all appear in the tapestries and the painting, albeit in somewhat differing form. The cusped edges of the arches in the tapestries recall the scalloped edges of the flutings on the painted pediment. The putti supporting the sculptured torchères at the sides of the painted page reappear, but transformed into busts or satyrs, holding up columns at the sides of the tapestries. The semicircular base of the painted niche and its paired rectangular plinths also derive from the tradition of arabesque ornament that inspired both the designer of the page border and the designer of 52b.

MANUFACTURE AND DATE

When four tapestries that resemble 52b were sold from the Dr. James Simon collection in 1927, they were catalogued as Flemish (Tournai, Enghien, or Grammont) and dated in the second half of the sixteenth century.[9] In 1966, when they were exhibited in Arras (property of French and Company), they were attributed to Enghien with a question mark and dated in the mid-sixteenth century.[10] Crick-Kuntziger suggested Enghien as the place of origin for another, similar tapestry that was then (1934) the property of the Bernheimer firm, but she added that it could just as well have been woven in Grammont or Audenarde.[11] When the same tapestry was exhibited in Strasbourg in 1966, it was catalogued as Flemish, second half of the sixteenth century.[12] A tapestry showing a fifth composition in this series of hangings related to 52b, a piece sold in New York in 1967 and exhibited in Paris in 1984, was catalogued on the latter occasion as Audenarde work and dated around the middle of the sixteenth century.[13]

All of these tapestries, as well as 52a and b, have traditionally been attributed to Grammont, Enghien, or Audenarde because a number of tapestries showing fields filled with giant curling leaves carry in their guards the town marks of these three centers. Another shows the mark of Leiden. One tapestry bearing the Grammont mark is in the Kunsthistorisches Museum in Vienna.[14] Another is preserved in the Museum für Kunst und Gewerbe, Hamburg.[15] Two fragments of a marked Grammont tapestry are in the Metropolitan Museum, and two other marked Grammont pieces are said to be preserved in the Clemens Collection at the Kunstgewerbemuseum in Cologne.[16] An example bearing the mark of Enghien is in the Kunsthistorisches Museum in Vienna.[17] A tapestry with a field showing a related design but with as many flowers as large leaves, and bearing the Enghien mark, is in the Musées Royaux d'Art et d'Histoire in Brussels.[18] A giant-leaf verdure tapestry in the Art Institute of Chicago bears the mark of Audenarde; and two of four pieces in the château d'Ecouen that show Hercules going about his labors against a ground of giant leaves also bear the Audenarde mark.[19] A tapestry with the same general type of thicket field, now in the Lakenhal Museum in Leiden, shows the town mark of Leiden, and another in the Österreichisches Museum für Angewandte Kunst in Vienna bears the town mark of Bruges.[20] The verdure tapestries in the Kunsthistorisches Museum, Vienna, and the Rijksmuseum, Amsterdam, that show the coat of arms of the emperor Charles V in the field and were woven in Brussels in the shop of Willem Pannemaker have often been mentioned in connection with the class of tapestries to which 52a and b belong, but in fact they represent a different though related group of designs.[21] It has been suggested that thicket tapestries of this type were also woven in the Marche district of France, specifically at Aubusson and Felletin.[22] This theory is based on a number of sixteenth- and seventeenth-century inventory references, including one for the château de Saumur in 1615 that lists eight "tapisseries de la Marche avec grands feuillages et bestes sauvages" (tapestries from la Marche with large leafage and wild beasts).[23] However it has happened before that "a la Marche" (woven on a low-warp loom?) has been misread as "de la Marche" (from the Marche), and not having seen the document we are not certain that the same misapprehension has not occurred here. Until more convincing evidence has been found to support an attribution of tapestries of this kind to Aubusson or Felletin, we prefer to regard 52a and b as products of looms operating somewhere in the Netherlands.

These pieces have all been dated in the middle or second half of the sixteenth century. It has been shown above (Source of the Design) that the tradition of these thickets of scrolling leaves traces its origin to the late fifteenth century and that they appear in the art of tapestry at least as early as 1528 in the two armorial hangings in Budapest that show the coats of arms of Margaret of Austria and related people (see note 3). However two related kinds of tapestries appeared even earlier. One example, a small cover in the Musées Royaux d'Art et d'Histoire in Brussels, shows a pair of branches intertwining as they rise from the base of the field and sending out branches bearing acanthus leaves and roses to fill the field completely behind a central unit containing a coat of arms and a motto.[24] The striking but seldom published thistle tapestries, in the Bur-

rell Collection in Glasgow, the Danske Kunstindustri-museum in Copenhagen, and the Palais Jacques-Coeur in Bourges, show rows of giant thistle plants completely covering the ground except for a narrow strip of sky along the top. It has been suggested that they may be identified with a series of thistle tapestries that Pierre, duc de Bourbon, ordered before his death in 1503.[25] Other specialists identify these hangings with some thistle tapestries that Charles V bought in 1518 from Pieter van Aelst of Brussels.[26] Margaret of Austria's armorial hangings were woven just ten years later. The step from those designs to the full-blown giant-leaf thickets was a short one, and it could have been taken in just a few years. At the other end of the scale, tapestries of this type, or pieces that were probably very much like them, were still in fashion about 1575. In September 1572, an auction in Paris of the property of the duc de Roannes included "huict pièces de tapisserie de Flandres, neufves, à feuillages d'eaue, en milieu desquelles y a des lions, liepvres et aultres bestes" (eight pieces of Flemish tapestry, new, with water leaves, in the midst of which are lions, hares, and other animals).[27] In 1576, Spanish soldiers invaded the tapestry marketplace in Antwerp and made off with quantities of fabrics among which were dozens of tapestries described as boscaiges (thickets, variously spelled in the documents) made in Audenarde, Brussels, or Enghien.[28] However much or little these pieces may have resembled the class of tapestries being discussed here, the incident indicates that tapestries showing thickets were being sold at that time.

Since 52a and b show not only the leafy fields but also architectural enframements that seem to derive from the arabesque style of ornament of the late fifteenth and early sixteenth centuries, it seems correct to date them toward the beginning of the fashion for thicket tapestries, about 1540–50, rather than later. Many tapestries of this type that were woven in the third quarter of the sixteenth century have borders showing elements derived from strapwork motifs found in prints made in a new and different grotesque style by artists like Cornelis Bos, Cornelis Floris, and Hieronymus Cock.[29] Therefore it seems likely that 52a and b were woven earlier than they.

RELATED TAPESTRIES

Since their enframements do not match, 52a and b must have been woven after different sets of cartoons. Only two tapestries whose upper enframements exactly match the upper part of the proscenium in 52a are known to have survived. They belonged at one time to

French and Company, but they were sold some years ago and their present locations are unknown.³⁰ As noted above (Description and Subject), there is no trace in 52a of the herms that appear near the bottom of these pieces which have borders different from, but closely related to, the border of 52b. A tapestry with a very similar enframement was sold in Monaco in 1984.³¹ It has the same fluted bases and gadrooned collars on the shafts of the columns; but the columns are supported by leopard-legged satyrs rather than by male busts. The piece differs from 52a also because there are no lions at the springing of the arch and because there is a balustrade along the bottom of the field. Three other tapestries showing the balustrade and satyrs and an enframement much like that in the piece sold in Monaco have been identified. One was sold in Paris in 1962.³² The other two, which show enframements common to both, belonged to Dario Boccara in 1970.³³ These three pieces and the one sold in Monaco show the same border design as 52b which, as noted above (Description and Subject), differs somewhat from that on the two pieces formerly with French and Company that were woven after the same series of cartoons as 52a.

At present we know of nine other whole tapestries and one fragmentary piece that appear to have been woven after other compositions in the series of cartoons that 52b represents. Together, these eleven tapestries show eight variations of essentially the same subject, that is, thickets teeming with flora and fauna viewed through the elaborate proscenium and surrounded by the narrow border that appear in 52b. Four of these tapestries were sold from the collection of Dr. James Simon of Berlin in 1927 (see note 9). They were bought by French and Company and were exhibited by them among other places in Arras in 1966 (see note 10). The next year the four hangings were acquired by the Kunst-gewerbemuseum in Berlin.³⁴ Two of the other five whole tapestries show fields that virtually duplicate that of Simon piece number 315B. Crick-Kuntziger published one of them in 1934. The same piece belonged to Simon Mikaeloff in 1966, when he exhibited it in Strasbourg, and in 1985 it was with Yves Mikaeloff in Paris.³⁵ The other near-duplicate of Simon number 315B was sold at Sotheby Parke Bernet in 1977.³⁶ A fifth variation on the subject, one that does not appear in the Simon group or in any of the other known pieces, appears in a tapestry that was sold at Parke-Bernet in 1967 and then exhibited by the firm of Chevalier in Paris in 1984 (see note 13). A fragmentary piece showing approximately the right half of the same field, truncated at the top, was sold at Christie's in New York in 1990.³⁷ A sixth variation appears in a tapestry that was formerly the property of the firm of Margraf in Berlin, and a seventh variation appears in a piece that was noted in 1901 as belonging to the province of Brabant.³⁸ The Metropolitan Museum's tapestry 52b shows an eighth variation which does not appear in any of the other pieces.

HISTORY

In the collection of Mr. and Mrs. James J. Rorimer, New York.
Given to the MMA by Katherine S. Rorimer in the name of her late husband, James J. Rorimer, 1967.

EXHIBITIONS

None known.

PUBLICATION

Forsyth, Williams H. "Reports of the Departments: Medieval Art and The Cloisters, Main Building." Annual Report for 1966–1967. In *MMA Bulletin*, n.s. 26 (1967–68) p. 83. Mentioned.

NOTES

1. See two ornamental designs of this kind engraved in the last quarter of the fifteenth century by Israhel van Meckenem, one in a rectangular format, the other in a ring: Max Lehrs, *Geschichte und kritischer Katalog des deutschen, niederländischen und französischen Kupferstichs im XV. Jahrhundert* (Vienna, 1908–34; Kraus Reprint, Nendeln, Liechtenstein, 1969) vol. 9, p. 460, no. 619, and p. 401, no. 511.
2. For examples, see Kurth 1926, pls. 83a and b.
3. See Guy Delmarcel, *Tapisseries anciennes d'Enghien* (Mons, 1980) nos. 1 and 2, illus. See also Göbel 1923, vol. 1, pp. 520–21; vol. 2, fig. 475.
4. Digby 1980, p. 56.
5. For the *Vertumnus and Pomona* series, see Ludwig Baldass, *Die Wiener Gobelinssammlung* (Vienna, 1920) pls. 146–54, and Adolph S. Cavallo, *Tapestries of Europe and of Colonial Peru in the Museum of Fine Arts, Boston* (Boston, 1967) pp. 115–18, pl. 32. Both publications contain illustrations of *Vertumnus as a Fisherman*. For the garden tapestries in the Gardner Museum in Boston, see Adolph S. Cavallo, *Textiles: Isabella Stewart Gardner Museum* (Boston, 1986) no. 14, pp. 70–77, illus.
6. See Baldass, *Die Wiener Gobelinssammlung*, pl. 119.
7. There are excellent discussions of grotesque tapestries of this period in two publications by Edith A. Standen: "Some Sixteenth-Century Grotesque Tapestries," *Bulletin des Musées Royaux d'Art et d'Histoire*, 6th ser., 45 (1973) pp. 230–37, and *European Post-Medieval Tapestries and Related Hangings in The Metropolitan Museum of Art* (New York, 1985) pp. 100–109. Both publications contain illustrations and further references.
8. For examples dating in the first third of the sixteenth century, see John Plummer assisted by Gregory Clark, *The Last Flowering: French Painting in Manuscripts, 1420–1530, from American Collections*, exh. cat., Pierpont Morgan Library (New York and London, 1982) esp. nos. 121a and b, 126b, 127, 130a and b, and 131, all illus.
9. *Collection de Dr. James Simon de Berlin*, sale cat., Frederik Muller et Cie., Amsterdam, October 25–26, 1927, nos. 315A–D.

10. *Tapisseries françaises et flamandes du XVIe siècle*, exh. cat., Musée d'Arras (Arras, 1966) nos. 19–22, no. 19 illus. pl. 5 and cover.

11. Marthe Crick-Kuntziger, "Une nouvelle tapisserie: Saint François recevant les stigmates," *Bulletin des Musées Royaux d'Art et d'Histoire*, 3d ser., 6 (1934) p. 128, and n. 2.

12. *Tapisseries du moyen-âge à nos jours*, exh. cat., Ancienne Douane (Strasbourg, 1966) no. 20, illus. pl. 9.

13. *Important Eighteenth Century French & Other Continental Furniture*, sale cat., Parke-Bernet, New York, March 18, 1967, no. 27, illus.; *Les fastes de la tapisserie du XVe au XVIIIe siècle*, exh. cat., Musée Jacquemart-André (Paris, 1984) no. 10, illus., lent by the firm of Chevalier.

14. Baldass, *Die Wiener Gobelinssammlung*, pl. 106.

15. Göbel 1923, vol. 2, fig. 471.

16. Standen, *European Post-Medieval Tapestries*, pp. 177–79.

17. Baldass, *Die Wiener Gobelinssammlung*, pl. 108.

18. Delmarcel, *Tapisseries anciennes d'Enghien*, no. 8, illus.

19. For the tapestry in Chicago, see Jean-Paul Asselberghs, *Les tapisseries flamandes aux Etats-Unis d'Amérique* (Brussels, 1974) p. 27 and fig. 14. For the pieces at Ecouen, see Guy Delmarcel, "Hercules en de Stymfalische Vogels," *Kultureel Jaarboek Oost-Vlaanderen*, n.s. no. 18 (1982) pp. 1–2, 16, illus. figs. 4, 5 (in the offprint).

20. Göbel 1923, vol. 1, p. 562; vol. 2, fig. 510, believed that the initials *WA* on the Leiden piece refer to the weaver Willem Andriesz. de Raet. See also G. T. van Ysselsteyn, *Geschiedenis der Tapijtweverijen in de Noordelijke Nederlanden* (Leiden, 1936) vol. 1, fig. 82. For the Bruges tapestry, see *Bruges et la tapisserie*, exh. cat. by Guy Delmarcel and Erik Duverger, Musée Gruuthuse and Musée Memling (Bruges, 1987) p. 108 and fig. 102.

21. See Digby 1980, pp. 54–55, for a well-considered summary of the various kinds of sixteenth-century verdure tapestries, and Delmarcel, *Tapisseries anciennes d'Enghien*, nos. 3, 7, 8, 9–13, 19, for some examples and illustrations. For the Vienna and Amsterdam tapestries see, respectively, Baldass, *Die Wiener Gobelinssammlung*, pls. 62–64, and A.M.L.E. Mulder-Erkelens, *Wandtapijten 2: Renaissance, Manierisme en Barok*, Facetten der Verzameling, Rijksmuseum, 2d ser., no. 5 (Amsterdam, 1971) pp. 7, 8, fig. 3.

22. See Göbel 1923, vol.1, pp. 177–79; Digby 1980, p. 54, referring to Göbel; and *Les tapisseries d'Aubusson et de Felletin des origines à Lurçat*, exh. cat., Musée d'Arras (Arras, 1963) nos. 6–11, some illus., with bibliography.

23. Quoted in Göbel 1923, vol. 1, p. 178.

24. Marthe Crick-Kuntziger, *Catalogue des tapisseries (XIVe au XVIIIe siècle)*, Musées Royaux d'Art et d'Histoire (Brussels, 1956) no. 11, illus. pl. 15.

25. See Betty Kurth, "En ukendt fransk Gruppe af Verdurer fra Overgangen til det 16. Aarhundrede," *Kunstmuseets Aarsskrift* (Copenhagen) 27 (1940) p. 48, all three pieces illus.

26. Sophie Schneebalg-Perelman, "Un grand tapissier bruxellois: Pierre d'Enghien dit Pierre van Aelst," *De Bloeitijd van de Vlaamse Tapijtkunst* (*Internationaal Colloquium, 23–25 Mei 1961*) (Brussels, 1969) p. 304 and fig. 11.

27. Quoted in Göbel 1923, vol. 1, pp. 178–79.

28. Fernand Donnet, "Les tapisseries de Bruxelles, Enghien et Audenarde pendant la furie espagnole," *Annales de la Société d'Archéologie de Bruxelles* 8 (1894) pp. 449–52.

29. For examples of tapestries with this kind of strapwork in the border, and also in the fields, see Delmarcel, "Hercules en de Stymfalische Vogels," pls. 1–4, and Delmarcel, *Tapisseries anciennes d'Enghien*, no. 9, illus. p. 31. For prints with the strapwork motifs, see Standen, "Some Sixteenth-Century Grotesque Tapestries," pp. 233–37 and pls. 1 and 2.

30. French and Company, former negative/inventory numbers 5398-24303 and 5533-24304, in the J. Paul Getty Photo Archives, Santa Monica, California.

31. *Bel ameublement*, sale cat., Sotheby's Monaco, December 9, 1984, no. 940, illus.

32. *Primitifs italiens et flamands . . . meubles et objets d'art . . .*, sale cat., Palais Galliera, Paris, April 11, 1962, no. 160, illus. pl. LXXIV.

33. See Dario Boccara, *Les belles heures de la tapisserie* (Zug, 1971) nos. 94 and 95, illus.

34. "Jahreschronik 1967," *Jahrbuch Preussischer Kulturbesitz* 5 (1967) p. 149, one piece illus. pl. 28.

35. Crick-Kuntziger, "Une nouvelle tapisserie," p. 127, fig. 4; *Tapisseries du moyen-âge à nos jours*, no. 20, illus. pl. 9; and unpublished note of the present author.

36. *Renaissance and Later Works of Art . . .*, sale cat., Sotheby Parke Bernet, New York, June 24, 1977, no. 57, illus.

37. Formerly at Phillips Academy, Andover, Massachusetts. See *Important French and Continental Furniture, Clocks, Porcelain and Tapestries*, sale cat., Christie's, New York, November 1, 1990, no. 207, illus.

38. Photographs on file in the textile department at the Musées Royaux d'Art et d'Histoire, Brussels, nos. 1550.291 and 1550.135 respectively.

53

53
The Apostles' Creed

European, 1550–1600
Wool warp, wool wefts
11 ft. 11¹/₂ in. × 15 ft. 10 in. (3.64 m × 4.83 m)
8–14 warp yarns per inch, 3–5¹/₂ per centimeter
Gift of The Hearst Foundation, Inc., 1960 (60.182)

CONDITION

The hanging shows cut edges along all four sides. However since there are loom finishes at both ends of the field and the pattern is complete along the top and bottom edges, it is clear that only a bit of the original fabric (the selvages and the very outer edges of the two borders) has been lost. Striped modern tapes have been sewn over the cut edges to serve as an outer guard.

There is no evidence that the tapestry ever had borders at the sides. The borders along the top and bottom seem to belong to the original fabric even though there are two considerations that might indicate the reverse. First, the borders are joined to the field by needle stitches rather than by some form of dovetailing or interlocking during weaving. Second, the very right end of each border contains an incomplete motif woven with new warp and weft yarns. Although this suggests that the borders came from some other hanging and were lengthened to make them fit this field, there is more convincing evidence that they belonged with it originally. As Forsyth (1962–63, 248) pointed out, the motifs in the borders above and below the two columns of figure compositions at the right are slightly different from the motifs bordering the other three columns; and the scenes in the two columns of compartments at the right differ from the others in style (see Description and Subject). The fact that these two parts of the field and border are consistent within themselves although different from each other argues in favor of concluding that the upper and lower borders are part of the original fabric.

There is a fair amount of restoration throughout the field in which both new warp and weft yarns were used. These passages occur particularly along the edges of some of the columns separating the scenes. There are also many repairs where weft yarns have been replaced on the original warp. These appear primarily in the contours of virtually every figure and the highlights and shadows of their garments. The light areas were replaced with silk yarns, the others with wool. Because the re-

storers seem to have respected the original outlines the drawing has been altered very little. The appearance of the hanging has changed only in a minor way in two specific places, one in the Baptism, the other in the Holy Catholic Church scene. In the Baptism a small loincloth to cover Jesus' nudity was woven separately and then applied to the surface of the original fabric. That addition, which appears in every photograph of the hanging that was published up to the present, was removed in 1970. In the scene showing Saint Peter seated before a small basilica, the doorway and the two round windows above it were restored with new warp and weft yarns. It is therefore possible that the contours of these three openings—assuming that there were three of them originally—have been changed.

DESCRIPTION AND SUBJECT

The field is divided into fifteen rectangular compartments of approximately equal size arranged in three horizontal rows, five compartments in each row. Each compartment is delineated at the top by a low arch with a single cusp in the center and, at the sides, by twisted columns with flaring capitals carrying cone-shaped pinnacles. Each stack of three columns rises from a cubical base set into a low masonry wall that runs across the bottom of the field. Along the top of this wall rises a row of what appear to be arrowheads but are surely intended to represent the merlons (the solid parts between the cutout portions) of a battlemented wall seen in perspective, as they appear properly drawn along the top of the similar low wall that runs across the bottom of the two outer bays in the Creed tapestry in the Vatican.[1] The articulation of the columns and cusped arches in the Metropolitan Museum's tapestry was undoubtedly patterned after the kind of articulation that appears in the columns and arches of the Vatican tapestry; but the designer of the Metropolitan Museum's piece did not understand the logic of that system, so that, for example, the conical roofs of a pair of double tabernacles that support the upper range of columns in the central bay, and the gabled roofs of turrets and tabernacles above

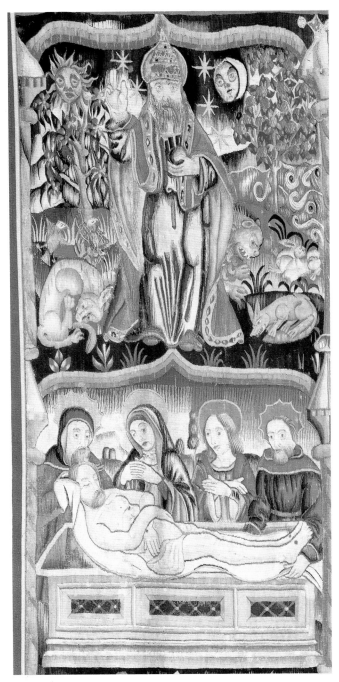

Detail of 53

like the colors in the field—brilliant reds, yellows, greens, and extraordinary ultramarine blues along with pure whites—are startling in their intensity. This is not only the result of the accident of their good state of preservation but also an indication of the designer's and weavers' taste. As most writers have observed when describing the tapestry, it has the naive and provincial air of a piece of folk art. It is the tapestry's extraordinary color scheme that imposes this impression on the observer even more than the character of the drawing of the figures and settings.

The tapestry has another peculiarity that suggests it is not the product of a professional, urban shop. As Forsyth (1962–63, 248–49) noted, the scenes in the two columns of compartments at the right and the adjacent sections of the borders look different from the rest. The dark ultramarine tone is more prominent in these scenes, and they are more crowded with forms and details than the scenes in the left-hand section; the modeling is cruder; and the faces are more stylized. One may add that the columns between these two columns of compartments are more slender than the others and also that the arches are much less regular and in three places are decorated with foliate ornaments or gemstones, a kind of decoration that none of the arches in the left-hand section shows. Furthermore, in most of the scenes in this section small blocks of color of one hue are scattered over ground areas of a different hue—yellow and white on blue; blue on yellow; red, yellow, and white on blue—whereas the device was not much used in the left-hand section, primarily in the Confession scene. Forsyth suggested that the differences are due to the fact that two sets of weavers worked on the tapestry, the right-hand section having been executed after the left-hand section by less skillful artisans, and furthermore that since there is no break in the warp along the line where the style of execution changes, the hanging could not have been woven in two sections that were then joined together. While the compositions of the Nativity, Crucifixion, and Pentecost in the right-hand section show the same kind of formal, symmetrical, and Italianate style of design as most of the compositions in the left-hand section, the other three scenes on this side, in the lower right corner of the field, seem to have come from a different kind of source. Nevertheless, the differences one notes between the left and right parts of the hanging are, as Forsyth suggested, essentially differences of interpretation by two sets of weavers. However there seems to be no certain way of determining which part of the tapestry was woven first.

Each of the fifteen arched compartments contains a scene representing an article of the Apostles' Creed. As

have turned into the curious cone-shaped pinnacles that top the columns in the Museum's piece. The relatively wide upper and lower borders of the Metropolitan Museum's hanging show a repeat of a simple square unit comprising four dentated leaves resembling oak leaves that form a diagonal cross between whose arms issue single blossoms on stems. The colors here—bright green leaves, red and blue blossoms, all on a beige ground—

Forsyth (1962–63, 242) observed, this form of the Creed has been recited since the fourth century A.D. In the Middle Ages it was believed that each of the twelve apostles, inspired by the Holy Ghost, uttered one article of this creed at the Pentecost. After the Council of Nicaea adopted a slightly different and somewhat longer form of the Creed in A.D. 325, that creed, the Nicene Creed, was used in the liturgy of the Mass. However the Apostles' Creed was and is used in other Christian liturgies, and its text, which included the article "He descended into hell" that is missing from the Nicene Creed, was frequently illustrated, often in the form of woodcuts (see Source of the Design). Twelve or more scenes served to illustrate the text. The sheet of German woodcuts made in Augsburg about 1440–60 that Forsyth (1962–63, fig. 2) published in connection with this tapestry shows eighteen scenes. The three articles that are represented there but not in the tapestry are the following ones: "suffered under Pontius Pilate . . . sitteth at the right hand of God the Father almighty . . . the communion of saints. . . ."

The scenes in the tapestry illustrate the articles of the Apostles' Creed in the following order, beginning in the upper left corner of the field and proceeding toward the right to the end of the first row, then beginning at the left end of the second row, and so on to the lower right corner of the field:

1. God the Father standing on the earth, surrounded by animals, trees, flowers, and the sea; above, the sun, moon, and stars in the sky: "I believe in God the Father almighty, maker of Heaven and earth."

2. The Baptism, with the nude Jesus kneeling on the near bank of the river, John standing at the right and sprinkling water on His head, an angel holding what appears to be a chasuble and hovering next to Jesus at the left, and the dove of the Holy Spirit directly above Jesus' head: "And in Jesus Christ his only Son our Lord."

3. The Annunciation, with Mary kneeling on the far side of an altar-like table on which her book and the vase of lilies rest, Gabriel half-kneeling at the right, and the dove of the Holy Spirit above the figures, in the center: "who was conceived by the Holy Ghost."

4. The Nativity, with Mary at the left and Joseph at the right kneeling in adoration before the Christ Child, who lies on the ground between them, two angels hovering above the Child in the center and the ox's head just over the Child, a building in the distance at the left, and the head of the ass in the left foreground: "born of the Virgin Mary."

5. The Crucifixion, with the crucified Christ in the center, Mary standing at the left and John at the right,

and the red roses of sacrificial love (Forsyth 1962–63, 244) in the background: "was crucified."

6. The Entombment, with Joseph of Arimathea at the left and Nicodemus at the right lowering Christ's body on a sheet into a sarcophagus, and Mary and John standing between them on the far side of the tomb: "dead, and buried."

7. The Harrowing of Hell, with Christ wearing the red robe and carrying the cross of the Resurrection standing at the left and gesturing with his left hand toward two nude figures who genuflect as they emerge from the gate of Hell, which is represented as the mouth of a huge dolphin-like head: "He descended into hell."

8. The Resurrection, with Christ, wearing the red robe and carrying the bannered cross, standing in the

Detail of 53

Detail of 53

center foreground before the sarcophagus and flanked by two sleeping and two standing soldiers: "The third day he rose again from the dead."

9. The Ascension, with Mary kneeling in prayer in the left foreground and five of the apostles kneeling behind her while six others kneel at the right; the lower part of Christ's robe and His feet appear in a cloud directly above, in the center of the composition: "He ascended into heaven."

10. The Last Judgment, with Christ seated in heaven surrounded by an oval cloud-like glory bordered with heads of cherubim, a cherub blowing a trumpet in each of the upper corners of the scene, and, beside and below the figure of Christ, two of the living elect and four of the dead, rising from their tombs: "From thence he shall come to judge the quick and the dead." Forsyth (1962–63, 249) suggested that the figure in the lower right corner of this scene, a robed man with his hands crossed on his breast, may represent the donor of the tapestry primarily because he is clothed while the other three reviving figures are nude. However two of the six figures rising from their graves in the general resurrection scene (paragraph 14 below) are robed, whereas the others are nude. Therefore to draw a distinction of this kind between the putative "donor" and the others rising from their tombs in the Last Judgment on the basis of his being robed and they unclothed seems an untenable proposition.

11. The Pentecost, with the Virgin in the center of the kneeling apostles (twelve rather than eleven as in the Ascension) while the dove of the Holy Spirit hovers above them all and sheds rays of light on their heads: "I believe in the Holy Ghost."

12. Saint Peter, wearing the papal tiara and holding a large key in his left hand, genuflects before the facade of a basilica, while half-figures of Christ flanked by John and Paul (?) appear in a cloud above: "the holy catholic Church."

13. Absolution, with a young man kneeling before a tonsured priest who is shown in the act of absolving the youth after hearing the confession an angel encourages the youth to make, as Forsyth (1962–63, 248) suggested, and not Baptism, as Ackerman thought: "the forgiveness of sins."[2]

14. The general resurrection, with an angel blowing a trumpet in each of the upper corners of the scene above a graveyard where six figures, two robed and four nude, rise from their graves: "the resurrection of the body."

15. The Celestial Paradise, with Christ seated in the heavens within a halo of flames and surrounded by cherubs' heads and stars, flanked at the middle of the scene by the kneeling figures of Mary at the left and John

at the right; at the lower center are three figures of saints: "and the life everlasting. Amen."

The form of the composition, with rows of pictures set within an architectural framework, suggests that the tapestry may have been woven to hang as a dossal over a large altar. Painted altarpieces showing related kinds of organization have survived in quantity. A number of tapestry altarpieces with the same kind of system, using pictures set within architectural frameworks, have survived (see, for example, figs. 64 and 66 in the present catalogue), and we also have needlework altar furnishings that show the same kind of pictorial disposition. An example in the Art Institute of Chicago shows a system of columns and arches as the setting for scenes from the life of Christ and figures of apostles. That altarpiece, worked in Spain about 1468, uses fewer, but more elaborately developed, arched bays for its narrative scenes.[3]

SOURCE OF THE DESIGN

Wood (1913–14, 315) recalled that de Ricci thought there were similarities between the Metropolitan Museum's tapestry and the choir hangings both in the church of Notre-Dame in Beaune and the ones in La Chaise-Dieu (see figs. 67, 29, 32 in the present catalogue) and that he noted similarities between the Museum's tapestry and the miniatures in the manuscript of the *Credo de Joinville* in the Bibliothèque Nationale in Paris (nouv. acq. franç. 4509) and some drawings that had been found among the Montfaucon papers in the same collection (MS lat. 11907, fols. 231–32). Wood then suggested a different avenue of research, one that proved more fruitful: that is, the study of the woodcut sheets and books illustrating articles of the Creed, the *Symbolum Apostolicum*, that were made in Germany during the fifteenth century. He pointed out specifically the formal similarity that exists between the general resurrection scene in the tapestry and the corresponding print in Conrad Dinkmut's book of woodcuts illustrating twelve articles of the Creed (Wood 1913–14, pl. v, figs. G and H).[4] Forsyth (1962–63, 244, figs. 18, 19) recalled this comparison and made others based both on Dinkmut's book and on a sheet of woodcuts showing eighteen compositions illustrating the Creed that was printed in Augsburg about 1440–60 (Forsyth 1962–63, fig. 2).[5] However, as Forsyth noted (1962–63, 244), it has not been possible to attribute the design of the fifteen tapestry compositions to one particular source since at the time the tapestry was woven these scenes were part of "a large body of commonplace images—a sort of graphic lingua franca."

Whatever the specific source may have been, it probably was a print or series of prints whose author—wherever he was working—had assimilated for use in most of the subjects shown in the tapestry certain simple, standardized compositions that had been developed in Italy during the late fifteenth and early sixteenth centuries. As for the design of the border, it seems, as Forsyth (1962–63, 248) suggested, to have been inspired by one of the needlework pattern books that circulated throughout Europe during the first half of the sixteenth century. The example Forsyth (1962–63, fig. 21) chose to illustrate in his study of the tapestry came from *Eyn New Künstich Mödelbuech*, published in Cologne in 1544 by Peter Quentel.

MANUFACTURE AND DATE

In 1912, when J. Pierpont Morgan bought the tapestry, it was thought to be German even though it was said to have come from a church near Barcelona.[6] Later that year, when it was exhibited at Jacques Seligmann's gallery in Paris (cat. no. XI, p. 57), de Ricci attributed it to Champagne or Lorraine and dated it in the second half of

Detail of 53

the fifteenth century. A year later he observed that the piece showed a combination of the small pictorial panels of Rhenish tapestries with the large format of French hangings; and, presumably because of this, he (1913, 48) attributed the design of the tapestry to eastern France, specifically to Champagne or Burgundy. Wood (1913–14, 315) did not refute de Ricci's attribution to place but believed that the weaving was the work of less able artisans working perhaps as late as the beginning of the sixteenth century and trying to imitate an earlier style. He, like Hunter (1925, 30), regarded the workmanship as crude and provincial. Noting the similarity that exists between the composition of the general resurrection scene in the tapestry and the one in Dinkmut's woodcut (see Source of the Design), Wood (1913–14, 315) very tentatively suggested that the tapestry might have been woven in Germany, specifically in the Rhineland.

No writer followed Wood in attributing the piece to Germany, even tentatively, until it was published by the Metropolitan Museum (*MMA Bulletin*, 1961–62, 68) as a European work, possibly of German manufacture. It was called French and dated in the middle or second half of the fifteenth century when it was exhibited with the Morgan collection at the Metropolitan Museum in 1914 and again in Brussels in 1935. Only once, when the tapestry was exhibited in Chicago in 1920, was it called Flemish. Crick-Kuntziger, who wrote the catalogue entry for the Brussels exhibition, expressed the opinion that the tapestry, though perhaps of French origin, showed both Rhenish and Italian influences. Forsyth (1962–63, 243, 245, 248) and Ostoia (exh. cat. Los Angeles and Chicago 1970) also observed that there are Italian influences in the tapestry design; but both writers concluded that the piece was woven in Germany. Their arguments rested primarily on their impression that the design and workmanship are direct, naive, and provincial, qualities that they regarded as typical of German weaving of the period.

On the grounds that the design combines Gothic and Renaissance elements, Forsyth (1962–63, 243) dated the piece about 1550, and for the same reason Ostoia (exh. cat. Los Angeles and Chicago 1970) placed it in the second quarter of the sixteenth century or about 1530–40. The undeniable similarities that exist between some of the scenes in the tapestry and German woodcuts of the second half of the fifteenth century figured significantly in both writers' conclusions. As we have noted several times in the present catalogue (see, for example, 8b and 36), the designers or weavers of tapestries that may be attributed with some justification to looms in the southern Netherlands had recourse to German prints among other design sources. The fact that some scenes in 53 resemble those in German woodcuts illustrating the same subjects does not in itself prove that the piece was designed or woven in Germany any more than its small narrative scenes, naive and provincial in both design and execution, necessarily point to Germany as the place of origin. The tapestry could have been woven in any one of a number of provincial weaving shops in other parts of Europe. It could just as well have been woven in Catalonia, as has been suggested informally, as in one of the German-speaking regions of Europe. It seems significant to the present author that neither Kurth nor Göbel, both of whom made intensive studies of medieval German tapestries and both of whom must have known this piece, ever published the tapestry.

In terms of technique the piece depends on the professional traditions of the southern Netherlands. It is provincial work but not the work of amateur or self-trained weavers. Its warp is made of wool yarns, not the linen or other bast fiber yarns that were used in Germany, apparently invariably. Its dimensions are normal for a French or Netherlandish tapestry but extraordinarily large for a German piece of its period. The method of weaving shaded tones, while not so subtle as that ordinarily found in tapestries woven in sophisticated centers, is not typical of the methods that were used in Germany before Netherlandish weavers flourished there. Even the small blocks of color that are scattered about, apparently to enliven large, flat areas of tone, are unlike the checkerboard block-color passages that were woven into many German tapestries to model or lend interest to flat tones. The blocks of color in the Metropolitan Museum's piece probably contain a clue to the place of weaving, but at present we are not in a position to interpret the evidence that this peculiarity offers. We know no other tapestry like this, nothing to compare it with. Until another piece of its kind comes to light, accompanied by a document or other incontrovertible evidence indicating its place of origin, any attempt to attribute the tapestry to a specific locale in Europe is pointless.

As for the date of weaving, it must be placed later than the related German woodcuts of the second half of the fifteenth century and also late enough in the sixteenth century to account for the fact that the Italian High Renaissance compositions of scenes like the Entombment, Resurrection, and Pentecost have become schematic formulas in the world of provincial design. It seems unlikely that the cartoon could have been designed much before 1550, and there is nothing to preclude the possibility that the piece was woven even later in the century.

Wood (1913–14, 248) recognized this hanging as the only one of its kind that is known to have survived. Among the few Creed tapestries that we have from the late Middle Ages, this example is unique in that it treats almost all the articles of the Apostles' Creed in one piece and without inscriptions or figures of prophets and apostles. Therefore it seems more than likely that this hanging was woven as an individual piece and that it never belonged with others in a series of tapestries.

We know from early inventory entries that other Creed tapestries woven in one piece once existed. Wood (1913–14, 248) noted that at the end of the fifteenth century Pope Alexander VI owned "unus magnus pannus cum historia Credo" (a large hanging with the story of the Creed). This brief description does not specify whether the design included figures of prophets or apostles. Other Creed tapestries, both those mentioned in early documents and all the others that are known to have survived, have the figures who, in most cases, hold scrolls inscribed with either prophecies or articles of the Creed. Wood (1913–14, 248) called attention to a piece listed in Philippe le Bon's inventory of 1420 as "ung tapis . . . du Credo fait d'ymages d'Appostres et Prophètes . . . ou quel tapiz est escript es rolleaux que tiennent les diz Apostres tout le Credo et prophesies es roolles que tiennent les diz Prophètes" (a tapestry of the Credo containing figures of apostles and prophets; the whole Credo is written there on the scrolls that the ten apostles hold and prophecies [are written] on the scrolls that the ten prophets hold). Wood also referred as follows to two Creed hangings that Louis, duc d'Orléans, bought from Jacques Dourdin of Paris about 1395: "les deux sont de l'ystoire du Credo à doze prophètes et doze apostres" (the two show the story of the Creed with twelve prophets and twelve apostles). In that case the designer treated the articles of the Creed to be woven in two pieces rather than one. Other Creed tapestries were produced in sets of three, four, and possibly more pieces. Wood mentions three pieces that were listed in Margaret of Austria's inventory of 1523. A hanging in the Museum of Fine Arts, Boston, which shows the first four articles of the Creed and includes representations of four prophets and four apostles with their inscriptions, presumably came from a set of three hangings.[7] A piece in the Vatican, another at Boston College, and a third in the City Hall in Brussels as of 1944 each illustrate three articles of the Creed and therefore probably came from sets of hangings complete in four pieces, assuming that they, like the Museum of Fine Arts, Boston, piece, were based on the scheme of twelve apostles, prophets, and articles of the Creed.[8] Wood, and later Cavallo, mentioned the few other late medieval Creed tapestries that we know have survived.[9]

HISTORY

Said to have come from a church near Barcelona, date unknown.
In the collection of the marqués de Sambola, Gerona.
Property of Jacques Seligmann, Paris, by 1912.
In the collection of J. Pierpont Morgan, May 1912 to 1916.
Property of French and Company, New York.
In the collection of William Randolph Hearst, by 1935.
Given to the MMA by The Hearst Foundation, Inc., 1960.

EXHIBITIONS

Paris, Galerie Jacques Seligmann, 1912. *Description d'une série de tapisseries gothiques appartenant à M. J. Pierpont Morgan, exposées au bénéfice de la Société des Amis du Louvre.* Catalogue by Seymour de Ricci. Cat. no. XI.
New York, MMA, 1914–16. *Loan Exhibition of the J. Pierpont Morgan Collection.* Guidebook, pp. 10–11.
Chicago, Art Institute, 1920. *An Exhibition of Gothic Tapestries of France and Flanders.* Cat. no. 12, illus. Lender's name not recorded.
Brussels, Exposition Universelle et Internationale, 1935. *Cinq Siècles d'Art.* Vol. 2, *Dessins et tapisseries.* Catalogue of tapestries by Marthe Crick-Kuntziger, no. 685, pp. 93–94. Lent by William Randolph Hearst.
Los Angeles County Museum of Art, and Art Institute of Chicago, 1970. *The Middle Ages: Treasures from The Cloisters and The Metropolitan Museum of Art.* Catalogue entry by Vera K. Ostoia, no. 113, illus.

PUBLICATIONS

de Ricci, Seymour. *Catalogue of Twenty Renaissance Tapestries from the J. Pierpont Morgan Collection.* Paris, 1913, no. XIX, pp. 44–48. Described in detail and discussed; illus.
Wood, D. T. B. "'Credo' Tapestries," pls. 1, 2. *Burlington Magazine* 24 (1913–14) pp. 248, 315–16. Described in detail and discussed; illus. pl. V, fig. G.
Hunter 1925, p. 30. Discussed briefly.
Hammer Galleries, Inc. *Art Objects & Furnishings from the William Randolph Hearst Collection: Catalogue Raisonné.* New York, 1941, p. 278, cat. no. 592-9. Mentioned; illus. p. 81.
"Additions to the Collections: Medieval Art and The Cloisters." Annual Report for 1960–1961. In *MMA Bulletin*, n.s. 20 (1961–62) p. 68. Mentioned; illus. complete view, p. 48, detail of Baptism and Harrowing of Hell, p. 49.
Forsyth, William H. "A 'Credo' Tapestry: A Pictorial Interpretation of the Apostles' Creed." *MMA Bulletin*, n.s. 21 (1962–63) pp. 240–51. Described and discussed at length; illus. complete view as fig. 1, details of all fifteen scenes and of lower border as figs. 3–9, 11, 12, 14–17, 19, 20.
Cavallo, Adolph S. *Tapestries of Europe and of Colonial Peru in the Museum of Fine Arts, Boston.* Boston, 1967, p. 87. Mentioned.

NOTES

1. Concerning the Vatican tapestry, see D. T. B. Wood, "'Credo' Tapestries," pt. 1, *Burlington Magazine* 24 (1913–14) pp. 253–54, pl. 1. For further discussion and an illustration in color, see *Ta-*

pisserie de Tournai en Espagne, exh. cat., Halle aux Draps (Tournai, 1985) pp. 110–13.

2. In what appears to be an unpublished description of the tapestry written in connection with the Hearst sale at the Hammer Galleries in 1941 (copy in MMA files), Phyllis Ackerman interpreted this scene as one showing the sacrament of Baptism.

3. Discussed and illustrated in Christa Charlotte Mayer, *Masterpieces of Western Textiles from The Art Institute of Chicago* (Chicago, 1969) p. 127 and pl. 98.

4. *Erklerung der zwölf Artickel des Christenlichen gelaubens,* Cunrad Dinckmut, Ulm, 1485 (see W. L. Schreiber, *Manuel de l'Amateur de la gravure sur bois et sur métal au XVᵉ siècle,* vol. 5 [Leipzig, 1910–11] no. 4106), illustrates sixteen subjects pertaining to the Creed above twelve pairs of prophets and apostles, in twelve prints. The missing subjects concern Christ before Pilate and the communion of saints.

5. An example of the print is in the MMA, Gift of Felix M. Warburg and his family, 1941 (41.1.39), $11^1/16 \times 15^1/16$ inches (see W. L. Schreiber, *Handbuch der Holz- und Metallschnitte des XV. Jahrhunderts,* vol. 4 [Leipzig, 1927] no. 1853). Eight other woodcuts that are believed to have been cut from a sheet of eighteen compositions (different from those in Schreiber no. 1853), representing the articles of the Apostles' or the Nicene Creed (Schreiber no. 1853c) and attributed to Franconia about 1460–70, are in the National Gallery of Art, Washington. See Richard S. Field, *Fifteenth Century Woodcuts and Metalcuts from the National Gallery of Art, Washington, D.C.* (Washington, 1965) nos. 92–99, for a discussion and illustrations of these eight prints and notes on related woodcuts.

6. From unpublished notes developed by James J. Rorimer in 1947, now in the files of the MMA Department of Medieval Art.

7. See Adolph S. Cavallo, *Tapestries of Europe and of Colonial Peru in the Museum of Fine Arts, Boston* (Boston, 1967) pp. 83–87.

8. The three pieces are discussed briefly, with their present locations given, in Cavallo, *Tapestries,* p. 86, and the Vatican and Boston College (referred to as "the Toledo piece") tapestries are discussed at length in Wood, "'Credo' Tapestries," pp. 253–54, 309–10, and illus. on pls. I and III.

9. Wood, "'Credo' Tapestries," pp. 248, 310, 315–16, pls. IV, V. See also Cavallo, *Tapestries,* pp. 86–87, for more current locations.

54

Crucifixion with the Virgin, Saint John the Evangelist, Saint Catherine, and Saint Margaret

Central section of a dossal, choir hanging, or antependium

Tentatively ascribed to the region of the Lake of Constance, 1325–50
Linen warp; wool wefts, with the addition of wool and silk embroidery stitches to render the facial features and a few other details
2 ft. 8 in. × 5 ft. 8 in. (.81 m × 1.73 m)
15 warp yarns per inch, 6 per centimeter
Purchase, Francis L. Leland Fund and Mitchell Samuels Gift, 1916
(16.90)

CONDITION

The fragment has been cut on all four sides. At the bottom the separation was made along a line that passes just below the knees of the standing figures and across Christ's ankles. Since two other pieces of the same hanging, now in Nuremberg (fig. 175), have been diminished along approximately the same line, it seems likely that the loss occurred before this central section was removed from the rest of the hanging (see History).[1] Much of the fabric above the arm of the cross has been lost; the pieces that remain were sewn to a dark foundation fabric. Four grayish stars have been painted on the original dark blue tapestry fabric to the right of Saint Margaret's head. The dark brown wool embroidery yarns that were used to define the facial features have deteriorated and fallen out in many places, but the pale pink silk yarns couched next to them have survived nearly intact. The hues have faded a great deal; however the design in terms of lights and darks has been affected very little. Martin (1981, Appendix) has provided a detailed study of the condition and technical peculiarities of the fragments in New York and Nuremberg as they appeared about 1978.

DESCRIPTION AND SUBJECT

The tortured body of Christ, covered with bleeding wounds from the flagellation, the crowning with thorns, the spear thrust, and the penetration by nails, hangs heavily on a dark green cross in the center of the composition. Around His head is a cruciform halo and above it, fixed to the center of the cross, is a scroll inscribed

INRI. As Martin (1981, 75) noted, the cross is nearly invisible because it was rendered in a tone that almost matches the dark blue background plane. The distracting effect of the six-pointed yellow stars scattered over the ground further obscures the form of the cross. To the left of center stands the Virgin Mary, her head veiled and bowed, her hands clasped together over her breast. She, like the three saints standing with her, faces the crucified Jesus. John the Evangelist stands to the right of the cross. He places the palm of his left hand on his breast and holds a closed book in his right hand, against his shoulder. Saint Catherine of Alexandria stands to the left of the Virgin. She wears a jeweled crown and holds a palm branch in her right hand and a small wheel, the symbol of the instrument of her martyrdom, in her left hand. Saint Margaret of Antioch, also crowned, stands at the right end of the piece, beyond Saint John. She holds a cross in her left hand and a closed book in her right hand. The cross refers to the cross that caused Satan, who had taken the form of a dragon and swallowed the saint, to disgorge her. Milliken (1916, 147) suggested that the tips of flames visible in the lower right corner of the fragment, next to Margaret's knees, represent part of the dragon's fiery breath. However Martin (1981, 75 n. 1) noted that she had found no representations of fire-breathing dragons with Saint Margaret at this period and correctly suggested that the flames may be rising from the torch with which Margaret was tortured. However they could equally well represent the fire in which Saint Margaret was martyred.

The entire image is tapestry woven except for the facial features and the jewels in Saint Catherine's crown. The eyes, eyebrows, noses, and lips were delineated with couched dark brown wool yarns flanked on one side by yarns of pale pink (originally darker pink or red) silk that were couched next to them. Sparsely placed darning stitches made with the pale pink silk yarns form rectangular blocks of color (not circular ones, as Martin [1981, 82] reported) on the cheeks of some of the figures. These would originally have looked much pinker and counted as the blush tone. The polychrome jewels in Saint Margaret's crown were rendered in tapestry weave, but in Catherine's crown they were embroidered with wool

54

yarns in irregular, random, straight stitches. The related fragments in Nuremberg show the same kinds of technical peculiarities with one exception. There, John the Baptist, Peter, and Paul all have lips represented by red wool wefts that were woven into the tapestry web while it was being constructed on the loom. Saint Agnes's crown has jewels woven into the fabric with polychrome wool wefts. In Saint Dorothy's crown the jewels were embroidered into the existing tapestry web with the same kind of straight stitches that were used in Saint Catherine's crown.

The two fragments in Nuremberg were the left and

Fig. 175. Composite hanging incorporating the left- and right-end sections of the tapestry from which 54 was taken. Germanisches Nationalmuseum, Nuremberg.

Fig. 176. Composite photograph showing a reconstruction of most of the original tapestry before it was cut into three sections, with 54 in its proper location between the two end sections now in Nuremberg (see fig. 175).

right quarter sections of the original tapestry before it was cut apart. The two pieces were carefully separated from the center section so as to preserve almost all the details in the pattern flanking the cuts. Thus, when the raw right edge of the left-hand quarter section was brought to the left edge of the right-hand section and joined to it with a strip of new weaving that restored some of the stars and a bit of Saint Dorothy's right arm (details lost when the original tapestry was cut), the hanging looked like a whole tapestry rather than like the composite piece it was (fig. 175). Indeed none of the published illustrations of the hanging shows any sign of a seam or join running down the center. From 1855 when the tapestry was first mentioned as being in the museum in Nuremberg (see History) until 1917 when Meyer-Riefstahl called attention to the fact that it was composed of two fragments, the piece was described as a single fabric, and it was so referred to again by three later authors: that is, by Schmitz about 1919, Migeon in 1929, and Ackerman in 1934 (see Publications). In its present form the Nuremberg piece shows six saints standing against the same starry dark blue sky. The two innermost saints, Agnes at the left and Dorothy of Caesarea at the right, face inward as though addressing one another. In fact they face the line where the two fragments were joined. Agnes stood to the left of Saint Catherine in the original hanging, and Saint Dorothy once stood to the right of Saint Margaret. In other words these four female saints, together with the Virgin and John the Evangelist, all faced inward toward the center of the composition, the figure of the crucified Christ. At the left end of the piece in Nuremberg, John the Baptist turns away from the center—that is, toward the left—to address Saint Clare, whose figure terminates the composition at the left end. At the right end of the Nuremberg piece, Peter turns away from the center to address Paul, whose figure finishes the original composition at the right.

Each of the six saints in the Nuremberg piece, like those in the Metropolitan Museum's fragment, carries one or more attributes. Saint Clare holds a monstrance containing the Host in her left hand. John the Baptist holds a tiny lamb in his left hand and seems to point to it with his right hand. Saint Agnes also holds a lamb, in the crook of her left arm; in her right hand is a palm branch. Dorothy holds a branch of roses in her right hand and a basket of flowers (and apples, according to her legend, fruit from the garden of Paradise brought to her by an angel just before her martyrdom) in her left hand. Peter holds a key in his right hand and gestures with his left hand, as though in conversation. Paul, at the far right end of the composition, holds a sword in his right hand and a closed book in his left hand.

To give an idea of what the complete tapestry looked like before it was cut into pieces, Martin (1981, fig. 4) published a photographic reconstruction of the existing pieces made by joining together photographs printed to the same scale. This graphic reconstruction (fig. 176 here)—the three fragments have never been rejoined in fact—shows a photograph of the Nuremberg piece cut down the middle and mounted at the sides of a photograph of the Metropolitan Museum's fragment. The reconstruction cannot depict the entire tapestry since each of the three existing fragments has lost some fabric along the bottom and the top. Nevertheless the illustration succeeds in showing how most of the composition looked originally. The heads of the six innermost figures flanking the cross describe a downward curve whose lowest point falls at the center. It seems clear that the designer chose this device as a way of concentrating the observer's attention on the figure of the crucified Christ, whose head and arms therefore rise dominantly above the attendant figures. The heads of the four end figures —Clare and John the Baptist at the left and Peter and Paul at the right—appear on a level with Christ's head.

Fig. 177. Antependium showing the Crucifixion with the Virgin and John the Evangelist in the center, flanked by two arcades under which stand Saints Peter, Catherine, and Agnes at the left and Andrew, John the Baptist, and Paul at the right. Appliqué work, Upper Rhineland, second third of the fourteenth century. Bernisches Historisches Museum, Bern.

These figures are not taller than the others; they simply stand higher up in the composition. They probably occupied more elevated ground whose contours we cannot even guess at owing to the absence of the bottoms of all three extant fragments. Martin (1981, 77–78) examined certain similar compositions and found that most of them show the base of the cross fixed in a mound of earth from which the surface of the ground extends to both sides and serves as a baseline on which the attendant figures may stand. In this connection she (1981, 78, fig. 5) compared the reconstructed photograph of the original tapestry to a contemporaneous Upper Rhenish embroidered antependium that is now in Bern (fig. 177 here) to give an approximate indication of how the New York–Nuremberg tapestry might have looked when it had its full height and with the hillock at the foot of the cross.[2] While the two compositions are essentially similar, they differ in that the attendant saints in the embroidered antependium stand within the bays of a pair of triple arcades that flank the central group of Mary, Jesus, and John rather than in the open air. But the loss of fabric at the bottom of the tapestry involves a consideration that is more critical than the question of the missing ground line. The absent strip of weaving might have contained representations of coats of arms and perhaps also representations of one or more donor figures. Since that strip appears to have been lost, any clues it might have contained concerning the place and date of weaving have disappeared with it.

It was Meyer-Riefstahl (1916–17, 151–54) who realized that the Metropolitan Museum's fragment and the two joined-together pieces in Nuremberg came from one and the same hanging. He was not correct, however, in suggesting that the tapestry—whether a choir hanging or a back cloth placed above a row of benches in some

ecclesiastical context—might have been much longer. We agree with Martin (1981, 76–77), who believed that because the two outer pairs of figures form terminating motifs for the left and right ends of the piece, there were never any other figures beyond them. Given the simplicity of the setting, it is equally unlikely that there were any bits of landscape or architecture at the ends. Kurth (1926, 80) agreed that the three fragments were closely related in style, but she was not convinced that they came from one tapestry and suggested that the pieces in Nuremberg might have come from a different hanging in the same set, a piece showing perhaps a figure of the Virgin in the center. However, Göbel (1933, 63) believed that 54 was indeed the central section of the tapestry to which the two pieces in Nuremberg had also belonged. When the Metropolitan Museum's tapestry was conserved and remounted in 1936, the question was settled once and for all. None of the scholars who knew it before that date had seen the extreme left and right ends of the piece because these had been turned under when it was mounted sometime earlier. The later remounting revealed incomplete but unmistakable representations of one red and two white blossoms seemingly floating on the blue ground to the right of Saint Margaret's head. Imagining this edge next to the left edge of the right-hand fragment in Nuremberg (as it appears in fig. 176), one can see quite clearly that the blossoms are in fact three more roses growing on the branch that Saint Dorothy holds in her right hand. Therefore there can be no doubt that these two pieces of the hanging originally belonged next to each other. While there is no comparable evidence for declaring unequivocally that the left-hand fragment in Nuremberg once belonged at the left end of the *Crucifixion* in the Metropolitan Museum, there is no logical reason for doubting it.

Although bits of fabric have probably been lost at both ends of all three pieces of the original hanging, we can nevertheless determine with some degree of accuracy just what its length would have been. Meyer-Riefstahl (1916–17, 154) stated that the combined length of the New York and Nuremberg fragments totaled some 129 inches (3.28 m). Using dimensions recorded by other writers between 1869 and 1978, one can take the maximum figures and come up with a total length of approximately $134^1/8$ inches (3.41 m) or the minimum figures to reach a length of $131^3/8$ inches (3.34 m).[3] Taking into account the fact that bits of the fabric have been lost, we can readily imagine that the whole piece could have been as long as some 135 inches (3.43 m). Martin (1981, 84) noted that some high altars of the period were more than ten feet long, so this hanging, in its original form, might have served as an antependium. The Metropolitan Museum's section now measures 32 inches (.81 m) in height. Judging from the placement of the figures in relation to the bottom edge of the fabric, it is clear that a band of fabric at least as wide as a quarter of the original height—or about 8 inches—is missing there. Some fabric is also missing along the upper edge. Therefore, the hanging must have been somewhat more than 40 inches (1.02 m) tall. While that dimension could easily correspond to the height of a large altar, it could equally well represent the height of a dossal installed either above an altar or a row of choir stalls. Martin (1981, 84) considered the idea that, as was done in early Christian churches, the original tapestry might have been hung around the front and two ends of the altar, with the crucifix and six adjacent figures at the front, Saints Clare and John the Baptist at the left end and Peter and Paul at the right end. Martin rejected this idea for iconographic reasons and suggested instead that the tapestry might have covered just the front of an altar. On the other hand, as noted here, the designer made the figure of the crucified Christ dominate the composition by diminishing the apparent height of the six closest attendant figures. This device would have been most effective when the tapestry was viewed from a distance and installed at a high, rather than low, level. For this reason, it seems more likely that the hanging in its original form was meant to be seen above an altar or a row of choir stalls rather than in front of an altar.

SOURCE OF THE DESIGN

In attributing the tapestry to Constance, Kurth (1926, 80–81, fig. 42) compared it to a wall painting in the upper sacristy of the cathedral church of Constance that shows the Virgin and John the Evangelist flanking the crucified Christ. A dedicatory inscription accompanying the painting bears the date 1348, which establishes its terminus ad quem. Kurth also noted that the tapestry figures of John, the Virgin, and Christ are even more closely related to those shown in a lost fresco painted about 1320–40 in the Dominican monastery (later the Inselhotel) in Constance. The painting, destroyed in 1873, is known only from an old photograph or tracing and a line drawing made after it.[4] Like the New York–Nuremberg tapestry, it showed six saints (but all male) flanking the central group, three at the left and three at the right. The main figures in the center were indeed virtually identical to those in the tapestry, but the representation of John is especially interesting in this connection because from the neck down, his body is shown in the reverse orientation. As a third comparison Kurth cited a roughly contemporaneous stained-glass window of the *Crucifixion* from Constance that is now in the cathedral church of Freiburg im Breisgau. Martin (1981 78, 80, fig. 8) called attention to another representation of the crucified Christ flanked by the Virgin and John that resembles the composition in the center of the tapestry more than any cited thus far. It is a miniature painting of the *Crucifixion* bound in an Upper Rhenish manuscript of the second quarter of the fourteenth century (fig. 178). As Martin (1981, 80 n. 10) also noted, this particular figure of the crucified Christ recurs frequently in representations of the subject from this region and time. For that reason the striking similarity that relates the other two figures in the tapestry's central group to those in the miniature painting is particularly important. It suggests that the tapestry designer or weaver took that part of his composition from some unidentified common source if not from this manuscript or another version of it.

MANUFACTURE AND DATE

According to Martin (1981, 78) and other scholars writing after 1926, it was Kurth (1926, 80) who first identified the New York–Nuremberg tapestry as German and attributed it to Constance, dating it in the mid-fourteenth century. But in fact Müntz had published the Nuremberg hanging as German half a century before Kurth did (see note 1). The year before Kurth published, Hunter (1925, 68–69) referred to the character of the weaving in the Metropolitan Museum's piece as being more German or Swiss than French. He also observed that since both the weave and design in provincial tapestries like this made them look earlier than they were, he would date it in the second half of the fourteenth century rather than in the thirteenth century as his pre-

adozant oñamos. necuñir pñatres. Ceu cclozge ñimes?
acña seraphin. socia crulrane gcelcbiit. Cu qulge cñiae
nozes ñ adinim ulecas cestañt. suphia ecclesie dicentes.
Sos. Sos. Sos. ones os sabaoth. pleñ s. Briors q̃ uenit.

Cigitur clementissime pater per
istm xp̃m filiu tuu dñm ñrñ suppli

Fig. 178. *The Crucifixion*, with the Virgin and John the Evangelist. Miniature painting, Upper Rhineland, about 1330–50. Stiftsbibliothek, Saint Gall (MS cod. 346, fol. 193r).

decessors had done. Before Hunter questioned the idea of a French origin, and Kurth effectively dismissed it, the Metropolitan Museum's tapestry had indeed been called French and dated no later than 1300. Apparently following the new idea that Hunter and Kurth introduced, Göbel (1933, 63–64)—and later Rorimer (1947, 1), Rorimer and Forsyth (1953–54, 135), Heinz (1963, 39–40), Ferrero Viale (1967, col. 915), and Martin (1981, 76)—considered the tapestry to be German work from the area of the Lake of Constance and dated it in the mid-fourteenth century, as Kurth had done. Migeon (1929, 206–7) believed that the tapestry reflected the pictorial styles of the Rhineland and Cologne and placed it in the second quarter of the century.

Meyer-Riefstahl (1916–17, 150–55) had already associated 54 with the hanging in Nuremberg which itself had

been recognized in the literature many years earlier as being of German origin (see note 1), but he treated all three pieces as French works of art of the fourteenth century. Before him Pératé (1911, vol. 1, no. 50), Guiffrey (1911, 10), Vitry (1914, 434), and Milliken (1916, 146) had all attributed the Metropolitan Museum's piece to France and dated it in the thirteenth century. Schmitz (1919, 64, 81–82) did not realize that the three fragments belonged together and published the Metropolitan Museum's example as French, early fourteenth century, and the pieces in Nuremberg as native work of the first third of the same century. Most of these writers regarded the *Crucifixion* as being closely related in terms of style to the *Presentation in the Temple* in Brussels (Martin 1981, fig. 9); and, believing that the latter was a product of Parisian looms, they claimed the Metropolitan Museum's piece too as a Paris tapestry. The stylistic affinity that relates these two weavings to one another and also to the *Apocalypse* series in Angers (which Pératé brought into the discussion) is one of general period style at best, and it bears little weight in any serious discussion of the place of origin and date of the *Crucifixion*. The same may be said of Kurth's (1926, 80, pl. 24) and Göbel's (1933, 64, fig. 43) claims that a fragment of tapestry in the Iklé collection showing the busts of the Virgin and Child is also closely related to the *Crucifixion*. The Iklé piece, with its sophisticated hatchings and highly stylized, elegant faces, is in fact much closer to the Brussels *Presentation* than to the Metropolitan Museum's fragment.

The *Crucifixion* reflects an international style of painting that blossomed toward the end of the thirteenth and beginning of the fourteenth century. During that time Constance was an international cultural center and market. It is not surprising therefore to see French, English, and Flemish influences in works of art produced there in the early fourteenth century.[5] The mural painting in the sacristy in Constance, the one formerly in the Dominican monastery there, the window now in Freiburg im Breisgau (all cited by Kurth and Göbel), and the miniature painting in Saint Gall that Martin published (fig. 178 here) all exemplify the style of the region of Constance around the second quarter of the fourteenth century. However, it is important to acknowledge that the tapestry could have been woven somewhere else after an earlier design conceived in the region of Constance. For that reason, this catalogue entry offers suggestions for the place and date of origin that can be nothing more than tentative.

Martin (1981, 83–84) was the first student of the *Crucifixion* to appreciate and study the possible significance of the presence of Saint Clare of Assisi among the attendant figures shown in the Nuremberg fragments. She suggested that because this founder of the Poor Clares was represented here, the tapestry might have been woven in some house of that Franciscan Second Order or one of the Franciscan Third Order (a lay society), of which there were many in the region of Constance. These establishments were maintained in part by women who practiced handcrafts. Although at present we have no evidence that they were weaving tapestries before the early fifteenth century, it is certainly possible that they were and that the *Crucifixion* was woven in an establishment of the Poor Clares or of the Tertiaries.[6] Furthermore, the presence of Saint Agnes in this company could be interpreted to support Martin's suggestion. Unlikely as it may seem, it is not impossible that the tapestry designer or weaver intended to represent Saint Agnes of Assisi, Clare's sister and cofounder of the Poor Clares, but mistakenly gave her the attribute of the lamb, which is associated with another Saint Agnes, the early Christian martyr of Rome. John the Baptist, who is represented as though conversing with Saint Clare, seems also to be pointing at Saint Agnes and not, as one infers at first, at the lamb he is holding.

RELATED TAPESTRIES

As noted above, the left and right sections of the original tapestry are now in Nuremberg, in the Germanisches Nationalmuseum (see note 1). Kurth's suggestion (1926, 80) that the *Crucifixion* belonged to a series of hangings cannot be dismissed out of hand, but it seems unlikely in view of the devotional rather than narrative character of the subject and the composition.

HISTORY

Separated from the two fragments now in Nuremberg before 1855, when those pieces were first published as being in the Germanisches Nationalmuseum.[7]
In the collection of Georges Hoentschel, Paris, before 1911.
In the collection of J. Pierpont Morgan, by 1912.
Bought by French and Company in 1916.
Purchased from French and Company for the MMA by means of the Francis L. Leland Fund and a gift from Mitchell Samuels, 1916.

EXHIBITIONS

Paris, Galerie Jacques Seligmann, 1912. *Description d'une série de tapisseries gothiques appartenant à M. J. Pierpont Morgan, exposées au bénéfice des Amis du Louvre.* Catalogue by Seymour de Ricci, p. 6. Mentioned.
New York, MMA, 1914–16. *Loan Exhibition of the J. Pierpont Morgan Collection.* Guidebook, p. 27. Briefly described; illus. facing p. 30.
Hartford, Wadsworth Atheneum, 1960. *The Pierpont Morgan Treasures.* Cat. no. 14. Briefly discussed; illus. pl. III (upper image).

PUBLICATIONS

Guiffrey, Jules. *Les tapisseries du XIIᵉ à la fin du XVIᵉ siècle.* Paris, [1911], p. 10. Mentioned; illus. fig. 6.
Pérate, André. *Collections Georges Hoentschel.* Paris, 1911, vol. 1, no. 50. Described in detail; color illus., pl. XLIV.
Vitry, Paul. "Les Collections Pierpont Morgan." *Gazette des Beaux-Arts,* 4th ser., 11 (1914) p. 434. Discussed briefly.
D. F. [Durr Friedley]. "The Morgan Tapestries." *MMA Bulletin* 11 (1916) p. 130. Mentioned.
W. M. M. [William M. Milliken]. "A Late Thirteenth-Century French Tapestry." *MMA Bulletin* 11 (1916) pp. 146–47. Discussed, illus.
Meyer-Riefstahl, R. A. "Three Fragments of the Earliest French Tapestry." *Art in America* 5 (1916–17) pp. 150–55. Discussed at length; illus.
Schmitz, Hermann. *Bildteppiche.* Berlin, [1919], p. 64. Discussed briefly.
Hunter 1925, pp. 68–69. Discussed briefly; illus. pl. IV,f.
Kurth 1926, pp. 80–81, 211. Discussed in detail, with full catalogue entry, bibliography; illus. pl. 23a.
Migeon, Gaston. *Les arts du tissu.* Rev. ed. Paris, 1929, pp. 206–7. Discussed briefly; illus.
Göbel 1933, pp. 63–64. Discussed; illus. fig. 41.
Ackerman, Phyllis. Review of Göbel 1933. *Art Bulletin* 16 (1934) pp. 222. Mentioned.
Rorimer, James J. *Mediaeval Tapestries: A Picture Book.* MMA, New York, 1947, p. [1]. Discussed briefly; illus. p. [2].
Rorimer, James J., and William H. Forsyth. "The Medieval Galleries." *MMA Bulletin,* n.s. 12 (1953–54) p. 135. Discussed briefly; illus.
Heinz, Dora. *Europäische Wandteppiche I.* Brunswick, 1963, pp. 39–40. Discussed briefly; illus. fig. 20.
Ferrero Viale, Mercedes. "Tapestry and Carpets: I. Tapestry." In *Encyclopedia of World Art.* Vol. 13, New York, Toronto, and London, 1967, col. 915. Briefly discussed; illus. pl. 395.
Hibbard, Howard. *The Metropolitan Museum of Art.* New York and Toronto, 1980, p. 168. Discussed briefly; illus. fig. 312 on p. 165.
Martin, Rebecca. "A Fourteenth-Century German Tapestry of the Crucifixion." *Metropolitan Museum Journal* 16 (1981) pp. 75–86. Discussed at length; illus. fig. 1 (full view), fig. 2 (detail of Christ's head and chest), fig. 4 (partial reconstruction of the original tapestry).

NOTES

1. Concerning the two fragments now in Nuremberg, see the following: [A. O. Essenwein], *Katalog der im Germanischen Museum befindlichen Gewebe und Stickereien . . .* (Nuremberg, 1869) p. 14, inv. no. G.101, pl. IX (reproduction of a line drawing; the place where the two fragments are joined is not indicated), called fourteenth century. Eugène Müntz, *Histoire générale de la tapisserie,* pt. 2, *La tapisserie en Italie, en Allemagne, en Angleterre, . . .* (Paris, 1878–84), "Allemagne," p. 5, regarded as German, seemingly fourteenth century. Theodor Hampe, *Katalog der Gewebesammlung des Germanischen Nationalmuseums,* pt. 1, *Gewebe und Wirkereien, Zeugdrucke* (Nuremberg, 1896) p. 111, no. 670 (inv. G.101), pl. VIII (reproduction of a photo, as the rest of the illustrations in this list of references are; none of them shows a seam or join down the middle), called about 1400. Gaston Migeon, *Les arts du tissu* (Paris, 1909) pp. 259, 262, illus., called Nuremberg work, end of the fourteenth century. R. A. Meyer-Riefstahl, "Three Fragments of the Earliest French Tapestry," *Art in America* 5 (1916–17) pp. 150–55, illus. p. 151, called French, fourteenth century. Hermann Schmitz, *Bildteppiche* (Berlin, [1919]) pp. 81, 82, referred to as a single piece, called Nuremberg work, last third of the fourteenth century. Kurth 1926, pp. 80, 211, pl. 23b, called

Constance work, mid-fourteenth century. Göbel 1933, p. 63, fig. 42, called work from the region of the Lake of Constance, about 1350. Dora Heinz, *Europäische Wandteppiche I* (Brunswick, 1963) pp. 39–40, with the same regional attribution and date. Rebecca Martin, "A Fourteenth-Century German Tapestry," *Metropolitan Museum Journal* 16 (1981) pp. 75–86, figs. 3, 4, called probably region of Constance, mid-fourteenth century.

2. For a brief account of the history and condition of the embroidered antependium in Bern, see Michael Stettler and Paul Nizon, *Bildteppiche und Antependien im Historischen Museum Bern* (Bern, 1966) p. 43, illus. Figures from two different sets of embroideries were combined and applied to the dark red velvet ground after 1334–35.

3. The two textile catalogues of the Germanisches National-museum in Nuremberg (1869 and 1896; see note 1 above) gave the dimensions of the composite piece in that collection as .76 by 1.68 meters. Kurth (1926, p. 211) gave the measurements as .75 by 1.64 meters. Martin ("A Fourteenth-Century German Tapestry," caption for fig. 3) gave the approximate dimensions as .737 by 1.651 meters. The dimensions recorded for 54 when the piece was received at the Metropolitan Museum in 1916 were .826 by 2.06 meters. In André Pératé, *Collections Georges Hoentschel* (Paris, 1911) vol. 1, no. 50, the measurements were given as .83 by 1.70 meters. In or about 1978, Martin ("A Fourteenth-Century German Tapestry," caption for fig. 1) recorded the dimensions as approximately .813 by 1.727 meters (32 by 68 in.) and these are accepted in this catalogue entry. As Martin noted (p. 76 n. 4), the ragged condition of the edges of the three fragments makes it nearly impossible to determine their exact dimensions.

4. The line drawing is illustrated as pl. III in Franz Xaver Kraus, ed., *Die Kunstdenkmäler des Grossherzogthums Baden*, vol. 1, *Die Kunstdenkmäler des Kreises Konstanz* (Freiburg im Breisgau,

1887); see also pp. 244–47 there for pertinent text and further bibliography concerning the lost fresco and the visual record of it. According to this source, the drawing was made after a tracing (*Pause*) that Graf Zeppelin had had made of the painting before it was destroyed in 1873, when the monastery church was rebuilt. There is no mention of the "old photograph" of the fresco that both Kurth (1926, p. 81) and Göbel (1933, p. 277 n. 6) referred to. Josef Gramm, *Spätmittelalterliche Wandgemalde im Konstanzer Münster* (Strasbourg, 1905) p. 28, mentions in his discussion of the lost fresco only Graf Zeppelin's *Pause*, or tracing, but no photograph.

5. For a brief but useful view of art in the region of Constance at this period, see *Konstanz: Ein Mittelpunkt der Kunst um 1300*, exh. cat., Rosgarten-Museum (Constance, 1972). As an example of French painting that influenced painting in this region at this time, and specifically the tradition that the tapestry designer called upon, see a Crucifixion page from a Paris missal of about 1270 in the MMA (acc. no. 1981.322), illustrated and discussed by Charles T. Little, "Crucifixion from a Missal," *Notable Acquisitions 1981–1982*, MMA (New York, 1982) pp. 18–19.

6. It is now believed that tapestries produced in convent shops were woven by lay, professional, female weavers. See Anna Rapp Buri and Monica Stucky-Schürer, *Zahm und Wild: Basler und Strassburger Bildteppiche des 15. Jahrhunderts* (Mainz, 1990) pp. 47–51.

7. See *Anzeiger für Kunde der deutschen Vorzeit* [*Anzeiger des Germanischen Nationalmuseums*], 2 (1855) col. 316, a reference kindly cited by Leonie von Wilckens of that museum's staff who also stated that there is no indication that the composite hanging was ever in the church of Saint Lawrence in Nuremberg, where Migeon (*Les arts du tissu*, 1909, p. 259) and Thomson (1930, p. 76, illus. facing p. 76) had published it as being located.

55
A Fantastic Beast

Fragment of a wall hanging

Upper Rhineland, Basel, 1420–35
Linen warp, wool wefts
2 ft. 5³/₄ in. × 2 ft. 10¹/₂ in. (.755 m × .876 m)
15–17 warp yarns per inch, 6–7 per centimeter
The Cloisters Collection, 1990 (1990.211)

CONDITION

The piece has been cut along the four sides, but a bit of one selvage remains along the top edge directly above the leftmost of three tufts of hair at the top of the creature's head. Otherwise, all the edges have been restored with new warp and weft yarns. At the left, the restoration includes all the fabric to the left of a line extending from the middle of the leaf in the upper left corner down through the cuff below and then through the tassel, blossom, and leaves to the bottom edge at a point below the hand holding the leash. The entire right edge of the piece, from the tip of the uppermost leaf to the blossom at the right of the lowest claw on the creature's left rear leg, has been restored. The restorations along the top and bottom edges extend more or less straight across the piece, close to the edges of the field; they do not invade any significant part of the pattern. There are small repairs in the region of the beast's nose, cheek, neck, and two forward claws on the left rear leg as well as in a few spots in the leaves and blossoms of the background plants. Some of the black outlines that delineate the creature, particularly along the tops of the ears and the rump, have been replaced with yarns that are now brownish red.

Small spots of light green and light blue paint are scattered over the front and back surfaces of the fragment. The spots on the front were scraped off at some time, but traces of them are visible. The spots on the reverse have survived intact.

The colors have faded considerably, but a number of bluish green tones in the beast's body are discernible. The blues and greens in the periwinkle vines in the background, the yellow in the creature's talons, and some pinkish tones in the inner sleeve on the arm at the left are still relatively bright.

DESCRIPTION AND SUBJECT

The body of a fantastic beast fills the composition. The creature faces to the left, its weight supported on both hind legs, its forelegs raised (the right higher than the left) in a posture like that of a heraldic lion passant. The beast's head resembles that of a horse, and, while its tongue is like a horse's tongue, its teeth, which are widely spaced and sharply pointed, are those of a carnivore. The base of the left ear has the shape of a horse's ear, but the tips of both ears are elongated and flutter backward like flames. The rest of the body is that of a lion with a thick mane and furry forelegs. At the top of the head the mane, rising in three tufts, resembles a bird's comb. The creature's trunk, rump, and rear left thigh are covered with fish scales. The lower part of the left rear leg and the inner side of the right rear leg are not textured in any way. The feet are lion's feet, but whereas each of the front feet has five toes and claws, each of the rear ones appears to have only three. Tufts of fur resembling plumes flare out from the creature's long, upward twisting tail, its tip fluttering to a point above the animal's shoulders. One end of a leash made of plied cord is tied to a ring in a collar hung with bells, which encircles the beast's neck. The other end has a tassel and is held loosely in the left hand of a figure which is missing except for the lower part of its left arm. The rest of this figure survives at the right end of another fragment of the same wall hanging that is now in the abbey of Muri-Gries, near Bolzano (fig. 180). That fragment together with 55 and a lost fragment that is larger than those two (fig. 179) show the composition of the hanging as a whole, before it was cut into three pieces (see Related Tapestries).

This composition (see figs. 179–81), which also survives in four fragments of a near-duplicate hanging that are now in the Historisches Museum in Basel,[1] shows six elegantly dressed young people, each leading a fantastic beast, standing in a row against a flat backdrop covered with a mass of periwinkle stalks and blossoms in natural colors on a plain ground of dark greenish blue. At the left end, a young woman leads a horned griffin-like creature by a chain connected to its collar. To the right of her is a young man leading a fantastic elephant-feline creature by a plied cord attached to a ring around the beast's trunk. Next comes a young woman leading a beast resembling a basilisk by a chain and, to the right of her, a young man leading a ram-headed beast on a plied cord. The fifth figure from the left end is a young woman who holds the horn of a unicorn-feline creature in both hands. The sixth figure, at the right end of the composi-

625

55

tion, is a young man leading a fantastic beast, the one represented in 55.

Two of the women and three of the men hold a flowering stalk or branch in the hand that is not holding the animal's leash. One gets the impression that the men and women are using the flowers to control the beasts, not only because the people hold the branches and stalks up in front of the animals' heads either as a threat to them or as protection from them, but also because the cords or chains serving as leashes are slack rather than taut and because the young woman with the unicorn-feline creature holds no flowers, presumably since the animal's unicorn component becomes tractable, as a whole unicorn does, in the presence of a maiden.

Rapp and Stucky-Schürer (1990, 68–73, 112–14) published a succinct and pertinent study of the symbolism of plants in the late Middle Ages. They noted (1990, 72, 114) that the periwinkle (*Vinca minor*) against which the beasts and the human figures appear in these tapestry fragments was regarded at that time as an apotropaic talisman, a means of avoiding evil spells, and that it appears in the tapestries for that reason. The authors also offered interpretations for the flowers held by the young people leading the creatures. The young woman at the left end of the composition wears a strawberry crown on her head and carries a nosegay containing a white lily in her right hand. Rapp and Stucky-Schürer (1990, 71, 72) wrote that strawberries were thought to drive away evil demons and that white lilies not only signified purity but were also efficacious weapons used by defenders of the Castle of Love, along with roses, in contemporary love allegories. The man next to this woman, the second man from the left end of the composition, wears a crown of periwinkle and holds an elder branch. Rapp and Stucky-Schürer (1990, 70–72, 73 n. 19) indicated that elder was regarded as a medicinal remedy and as a symbol of true love, among other things, but acknowledged that the symbolism associated with it was extremely complex. The next figure, the young woman standing left of center in the composition, is wearing a crown of pinks and holds a branch bearing both pinks and columbines, the first a symbol of healing power and purity, the other a flower having the ability to arouse erotic desire. The man standing to the right of her holds a cornflower stalk in his left hand, a plant for which Rapp and Stucky-Schürer offered no symbolic interpretation. Next, continuing to the right, comes the young woman holding the unicorn-like creature by its horn, and at the right end of the composition appears the figure leading the beast that appears in 55. This young man, like the second one from the left end, holds an elder branch which, as noted above, was regarded as a symbol of healing and of love, among other things.

As Rapp and Stucky-Schürer (1990, 69–70) acknowledged, the symbolic value of these plants may vary from one context to another, and since several different meanings have been suggested for each plant in the pertinent literature, it is not entirely clear why the designer of this tapestry represented specifically these plants in these contexts. The young people in the composition certainly seem to be controlling their beasts with the aid of the plants, but while two men hold elder branches, the other figures that hold flowers have either cornflower, strawberry, lily, carnation, or columbine. This diversity suggests that each beast succumbs to the power of a particular plant, and this, in turn, suggests that each beast symbolizes a specific quality that is different from the quality symbolized by each of the other creatures. Therefore, it seems that one cannot know what the flowers mean in this context without first knowing what each beast symbolizes.

The theories that have been put forth thus far con-

cerning the nature and significance of the fantastic beasts are not much help: they are as miscellaneous, and sometimes as contradictory, as those concerning the plants. As far as Kurth (1926, 85) was concerned, no one had yet interpreted the creatures correctly. We agree and furthermore believe that her opinion is still valid, despite the suggestions that have been made since her time. Rapp and Stucky-Schürer (1990, 52) noted that as early as 1880 Moritz Heyne interpreted fantastic beasts like these as symbols of the Virtues and Vices and that Lanz accepted that interpretation as late as 1985.[2] In discussing the beast at the right end of the rightmost fragment in Basel, which is the same beast that appears in 55, Lanz referred to it as a symbol of pugnacity. For him, the small creatures in the composition also have allegorical meaning, the opposite meaning to that of the fantastic beasts. For example, Lanz referred to the owl near the unicorn as "diabolical" and the unicorn as "chaste."[3]

Rapp and Stucky-Schürer (1990, 52, 114) believed that the beasts, made up of parts of real animals and thus imbued with the qualities of those animals, are ferocious symbols of what is wild in nature, wildness that must be tamed and mastered. Then, interpreting them in terms of what appears to be a psychoanalytical theory advanced by Christian Müller,[4] these two authors suggested that the creatures symbolize the wilder natures of the young men and ladies who lead the creatures with the help of magic plants and that, in subduing the beasts, the young people are also taming their own wild impulses. Cantzler interpreted fantastic beasts in the same way, also in 1990,[5] and, according to the 1990 sale catalogue entry for 55 and the two pieces sold with it, the fantastic beasts that serve as mounts for wild men in one of those pieces represent vices and the young people leading the beasts are struggling against "their baser instincts." For Bernheimer, the image of men and women leading such beasts had an erotic connotation even when wild men, who were often associated with love themes and rode such beasts, were not represented with the urban figures.[6]

According to some other writers, the fantastic beasts did not have erotic connotations. Heinz believed that the figures and beasts in the four tapestry fragments in Basel symbolize free, unbridled nature as opposed to tightly structured urban society.[7] According to the author of the catalogue entry for a contemporary Basel tapestry in the Österreichisches Museum für Angewandte Kunst in Vienna that was exhibited in Karlsruhe in 1970, the fantastic beasts in that piece symbolize uncorrupted nature and are proper companions for the wild folk who decry the treachery in civi-

Fig. 179. *Three Fashionable Figures and Three Fantastic Beasts.* Fragment of a tapestry, Upper Rhineland, Basel, 1420–35. Formerly collection of Jost Mayer-AmRhyn, Lucerne; present location unknown.

lized man.[8] For Digby, writing somewhat later about a tapestry in the Victoria and Albert Museum related to the one in Vienna, the fantastic beasts are not symbols of "evil passions" but of "uncontaminated Nature."[9] In 1980, Husband made several suggestions concerning the meaning of these fantastic creatures. For him, the wild men in tapestries like the one in the Victoria and Albert Museum found more sympathetic company in these fantastic creatures than in the company of civilized men, and the beasts in idyllic settings, like the one in the Vienna tapestry, represent "uncorrupted nature" whereas in the context of tapestries like the one from which 55 came the beasts are "symbols of hidden vice."[10]

As ingenious as these theories are, only the ones that interpret the creatures as symbols of uncorrupted nature and as sympathetic companions to the wild folk who sometimes appear with them, and also the theories that relate the beasts to love themes, are corroborated by the sense of the inscriptions representing the speech of urban or wild folk in tapestries that show such folk with fantastic beasts. We have found no speeches that indicate the beasts are to be understood as symbols of desire, base instincts, or vice. For example, in the Basel tapestry of about 1430–40 that is in Vienna, four wild men holding scourges stand next to four fantastic beasts.[11] The four inscribed scrolls representing the speech of the men make it clear that they have left the world and joined the beasts because the world is full of evil and lies and they prefer to live out of the world and with these creatures. Another Basel piece, which Rapp and Stucky-Schürer (1990, no. 50) illustrated and dated about 1480, shows a pair of fantastic beasts flanking an elegantly dressed young man and another pair flanking a fashionable young lady. In this hanging, the man claims that he can

defeat any beast with his wiles and the lady answers that she can master wild animals and men with her love. A Basel tapestry fragment that Rapp and Stucky-Schürer (1990, no. 18) illustrated and dated about 1460 shows a fashionably dressed couple standing at either side of a griffin in the main part of the field and most of the figure of another lady at the right. The young man asks the lady at the left to favor him with her love. She answers that the griffin gives her the wit to see that true love no longer exists. It seems to us that nothing in these last two tapestries presents the beasts as symbols of desires which must be tamed. On the contrary, in the example of about 1480 it is the lady's love that can conquer the beast, and in the earlier piece the griffin is a kind of medium that enables the girl to see her companion's bid for love as the insincere thing it is.

Therefore it seems likely that the fantastic beasts may have had different meanings in different contexts, as their companions the wild folk also seem to have done. As stated above, we agree with Kurth (1926, 85), who observed that no one has yet come up with a convincing interpretation of these beasts. We also believe that anyone studying this question in the future might find some suggestions of our own, which for the most part run counter to those that have been made by earlier writers, worth considering. First, we believe it is possible that the guilt lies in the other direction: that is, that the elegant city folk in the Basel fragments and the hanging from which 55 came may be leading what are innocent creatures into their own world of treachery and evil, enticing them with beneficent plants, and perhaps intending to use the beasts as a means of enabling themselves to see through treachery to truth, as the lady in the Basel piece of about 1460 does.

Second, the catalogue entry for the exhibition in

Fig. 180. *Three Fashionable Figures and Two Fantastic Beasts.* Fragment of a tapestry, Upper Rhineland, Basel, 1420–35. Abbey of Muri-Gries, near Bolzano, Italy.

Fig. 181. 55 shown in relation to figs. 179 and 180 to give the approximate appearance of the wall hanging from which the three fragments came.

Karlsruhe of the tapestry in Vienna pointed out that the wild men and fantastic beasts in that tapestry convey not only a sense of misanthropy but also one of playful whimsy, and furthermore that in many late medieval compositions involving wild men it is difficult to tell whether the designer intended to imbue the images with symbolic meaning or whether he was using them simply to convey a satirical comment.[12] Certainly the image of the wild man or woman is outrageously satirical, whatever else it may be; and designers may have wanted to make the beasts they consorted with equally outrageous by making them equally fantastic.

Finally, it seems reasonable to suggest that designers may have chosen to represent these exceptionally decorative animals, with their weird humps and horns, pelts and scales, claws and beaks, primarily to enhance the decorative value of the hangings designed for people who were already familiar with such fantastic creatures through images in bestiaries and through folk traditions and who obviously found them endearing, entertaining, or provocative. All the energy that has gone into studying the beasts has centered on the a priori conviction that they are primarily symbols. What has not yet attracted the attention we believe it deserves is the premise that these fantastic creatures may be, instead, primarily amusing and handsome ornaments which, perhaps, also contain symbolic meanings—meanings that were so much a part of the culture in which they had been developed that no modern iconographic or psychoanalytical explanations can convey them accurately.

SOURCE OF THE DESIGN

As Husband has already noted, fantastic beasts like the ones in the Basel fragments and 55 were probably based on the imaginary animals described in the *Physiologus*, an early Christian collection of allegories, and illustrated in medieval bestiaries where the animals were interpreted primarily in theological terms.[13] The *Physiologus* and the bestiaries dealt both with creatures that exist and with creatures that early writers had imagined or concocted from various unscientific sources or developed from their own interpretations of Scripture.

The designer of the composition that 55 represents almost certainly used one or more such works, illustrated with prints, drawings, or paintings, as the source of the beasts in his composition. The periwinkle vines in the background may have been based on a medieval herbal, and the fashionable human figures from some other preexisting images. No sources that might have served his purpose have been identified.

MANUFACTURE AND DATE

When 55 was sold in 1990, it was attributed to Basel about 1430–40. No explanation was given in the text of the sale catalogue, but it seems likely that the author accepted the attributions that had been published earlier. Burckhardt (1923, 9) regarded the four fragments in Basel and 55 with its two related pieces as Basel work of the second third of the fifteenth century, and he cited fashion in costume as his criterion for the dating. Göbel (1933, 24, caption for fig. 6) attributed these pieces to Basel, partly because he believed Basel weavers had a predilection for fantastic beasts, but he dated these tapestry fragments slightly earlier, in the second quarter of the fifteenth century. Kurth (1926, 85, 212) preferred a date specifically between 1420 and 1440 on the basis of fashion in costume. When 55 was exhibited in Basel in 1936, it was attributed to Basel and dated in the second quarter of the fifteenth century, without any explanation.

Rapp and Stucky-Schürer (1990, 104, 112, 118) set forth in detail their reasons for regarding 55 and the related fragments in Basel and elsewhere as having been woven in Basel between 1410 and 1420 and therefore as the earliest known Basel pieces. They considered the form of the composition, with figures filling the entire height of the field, clearly silhouetted against the ground, as typical of Basel work. Furthermore, they noted that the pleasing faces, with small heart-shaped mouths, could be found in numbers of Upper Rhenish paintings of that period including the *Annunciation* in the Oskar Reinhart Collection in Winterthur; another *Annunciation,* by the Master of the Staufener Altar, in Freiburg im Breisgau; the small *Paradise Garden* in the Städelsches Kunstinstitut in Frankfurt; and the so-called Strawberry Madonna in the Kunstmuseum in Solothurn.[14] As examples of the painting from Basel specifically, they cited (1990, 104–5 and figs. 48, 49) the so-called Offenburg stained-glass window of 1416–18 in Basel and a recently discovered wall painting of about 1424 in Sankt Peterskirche in Basel where there is a figure of Gabriel, whose facial type corresponds precisely to that of the young lady standing at the left end of one of the tapestries in Basel. To support the early date that Rapp and Stucky-Schürer suggested for the tapestry fragments, they noted (1990, 77, 104) that backgrounds with foliate patterns like the periwinkle vines in 55 and the related pieces are found in Basel tapestries in the first half of the fifteenth century and textile-patterned backgrounds in the second half.

If the so-called Toggenburgerbibel of 1411 that Burckhardt (1923, 9) used as one of his criteria in dating the costumes in the Basel tapestry fragments does indeed show representative Upper Rhenish fashions of that year, then the fragments must be assigned a later date. The men's costumes illustrated in the miniatures of Joseph sold by his brothers and Joseph escaping from Potiphar's wife, and two others showing the siege of Jericho, have the pigeon-breasted, swathed, and narrow-hipped silhouette of fashionable French male body garments of the late fourteenth century.[15] Our own study of fashionable German and Upper Rhenish costume in this period suggests that Kurth's dates of 1420 to 1440 are the most convincing but that the terminal date should be placed somewhat earlier, about 1435. Among the comparative pictorial sources she cited are the Wilhelm von Orlens manuscript of 1419, illustrated with pen drawings, in the Württembergische Landesbibliothek, Stuttgart.[16] The men's and women's costumes represented in those drawings show similar fashions and—an important point—the men's hair is

worn short, to or just below the ears. Burckhardt (1923, 9) also compared the costumes in the tapestry fragments to the engraved playing cards in the Württembergische Landesmuseum in Stuttgart which he dated about 1440. However Stange, who discussed and illustrated these cards, which indeed do show figures in similar costumes, dated the cards about 1420 and attributed them to southwest Germany.[17] Stange also illustrated some Upper Rhenish miniature paintings and an Alsatian pen drawing, all dating from about 1420, which show numbers of men wearing garments like those in the Basel tapestry fragments; their curly hair is short and does not fall below the ears.[18] The length of the men's hair is significant, for although costumes with similar silhouettes and elaborately dagged edges, for both men and women, continued to be worn in southwestern Germany almost to 1450, as numbers of prints by the Master of the Playing Cards demonstrate, men at that later date wore their hair loose to the shoulders.[19]

This evidence suggests that 1410 is too early a date for 55 and the pieces related to it and 1450 too late a date. A number of illustrations dated about 1420 show similar garments and men's hair styles, but by about 1440–50 the men's hair had changed noticeably even though the garments had changed less. Therefore, we suggest that the hanging from which 55 comes was designed, and probably woven, no earlier than 1420 and no later than 1435.

RELATED TAPESTRIES

Burckhardt (1923, 7; figs. 7, 8), Kurth (1926, 212, pl. 28/29), and Rapp and Stucky-Schürer (1990, 118–19, fig. 2, left and central sections) discussed and illustrated two other tapestry fragments which, originally joined to each other and to 55, once formed a long and narrow wall hanging that was cut into three pieces sometime after about 1800 (see below). The largest of the three fragments, which showed three human figures and three fantastic creatures (fig. 179 in this entry), constituted the entire left half of the hanging. When that piece was exhibited in Geneva in 1896, it belonged to Jost Meyer-AmRhyn of Lucerne.[20] His collection was dispersed piecemeal until 1923 when the remainder was sold. The present location of the fragment in question is unknown. The next largest fragment of the original hanging (fig. 180 here), which was transferred sometime between 1841 and 1843 from the abbey of Muri in Canton Aargau to the abbey of Muri-Gries near Bolzano, constitutes the entire right half of the tapestry except for 55.[21] This piece shows two complete human figures, two beasts, and most of the last figure at the right end, the man who leads the beast that is now in 55. When 55 was cut off the right end of the piece, this figure lost part of the left side of its head, its left shoulder, and most of its left arm. The lower part of that arm, and the hand, have been partially preserved at the left side of 55. It is not only this correspondence that indicates 55 is part of the wall hanging from which the Meyer-AmRhyn and Muri-Gries fragments came: all three pieces have spots of light green and light blue paint that splattered on the hanging when it was used to cover the floor during an interior decorating project in the abbey of Muri in Canton Aargau.[22] Because spots like these also appeared on some patches of blue and white linen on the backs of some other tapestries that had been used as floor coverings during that project, linen that Rapp and Stucky-Schürer dated to the eighteenth century, but not on the green cotton fabric that was used to line those other pieces after they were transferred to the abbey of Muri-Gries, Rapp and Stucky-Schürer (1990, 11, 118) reasoned that the decorating project had taken place in the eighteenth century and that the hanging from which 55 came was cut up probably about 1800, but certainly before 1841 or 1843 when the fragment now in the abbey of Muri-Gries was acquired there.

As noted above, the hanging was a near-duplicate of one that has survived in four pieces in the Historisches Museum in Basel, pieces that Rapp and Stucky-Schürer (1990, 112–15) have published in detail. The beast in 55 is to be seen again at the right end of one of those fragments, but there are significant differences between these two creatures. The drawing in the Basel fragment is more subtle than it is in 55 where heavy black contours outline every major form and feature. Also, the color range is broader in the Basel piece: there, the beast has a red body, a blue mane, and a red, green, and yellow collar, whereas the entire body of the beast in 55 is bluish green and the collar is yellow and white. The young man leading the beast in Basel wears red hose on one leg and blue on the other, and the shoe on each foot is the same hue as the hose on that leg. The young man in the piece from which 55 was cut (fig. 180) wears red hose on both legs and both of his shoes are beige. The piece in Basel also differs from 55 in terms of weaving technique. In 55 the wide central band in the beast's collar is rendered with a flat neutral tone, whereas in the Basel fragment the central band is shaded and textured with small blocks of green alternating regularly with blocks of yellow. The same technique, using two tones of pink blocks, creates a value midway between the highlights and the shadows on the inner surface of the beast's rear right thigh. The middle tone on the inner surface of the corresponding thigh in 55 was achieved by alternating

the lighter wefts with the darker ones for a few rows of weaving that form a line between the light and dark parts of the leg. The left foreleg of the beast in Basel was modeled by means of hatching, whereas the corresponding foreleg of the creature in 55 is not modeled.

Rapp and Stucky-Schürer (1990, 45, 114) made a careful study of the formal and technical relationship that links the fragments in Basel with the fragments related to 55 and concluded that the two hangings from which the seven fragments came were woven after the same cartoon, and in the same workshop, but by different weavers. In their opinion, the weaver had some freedom in interpreting the cartoon, and that freedom extended to matters of color choice, method of suggesting texture, and shading. Certainly the differences in weaving technique indicate that the weaver who executed the pieces in Basel did not weave the others. However, in regard to the formal differences, we wonder whether the two weavers might have been using two versions of the same cartoon, rather than the very same cartoon, and not necessarily in the same shop. Until we know more about the organization of the tapestry industry in the Upper Rhine at this time, it seems prudent at least to consider the possibility that a tapestry pattern, whether in the form of a preliminary sketch or a cartoon, might have been accessible to more than one weaver or workshop, possibly in more than one version.

HISTORY

As part of a wall hanging, in the Benedictine abbey of Muri, Canton Aargau, Switzerland, from an unknown date. About 1800, or sometime after that but before 1841 or 1843, the hanging was cut into three pieces that were dispersed.

In the collection of Ratsherr Peter Vischer-Sarasin, Schloss Wildenstein, near Bubendorf, Canton Basel, Switzerland, and by descent to Peter Vischer-Milner-Gibson, until 1989.

Sold, *Important European Sculpture and Works of Art*, Christie's, London, July 3, 1990, no. 110[b]. Color illus.

Purchased by the MMA, The Cloisters Collection, 1990.

EXHIBITION

Basel, Musée des Arts Décoratifs (Gewerbemuseum), 1936. *Tapisseries gotiques de la région bâloise provenant du musée historique de Bâle et d'autres collections.* Cat. no. 4. Lent from Schloss Wildenstein.

PUBLICATIONS

Burckhardt, Rudolf F. *Gewirkte Bildteppiche des XV. und XVI. Jahrhunderts im Historischen Museum zu Basel.* Leipzig, 1923, pp. 7–8. Discussed briefly; illus. fig. 9 (before restoration of the edges).

Kurth 1926, pp. 212–13, pl. 28/29c (after restoration of the edges).

Göbel 1933, p. 24. Discussed briefly.

Rapp Buri, Anna, and Monica Stucky-Schürer. *Zahm und Wild: Basler und Strassburger Bildteppiche des 15. Jahrhunderts.* Mainz, 1990, pp. 11, 12, 118–19. Described and discussed; illus. p. 117, fig. 2c (color), and p. 119 lower right (black and white).

NOTES

1. For an authoritative discussion of these pieces, with illustrations in black and white and color, see Anna Rapp Buri and Monica Stucky-Schürer, *Zahm und Wild: Basler und Strassburger Bildteppiche des 15. Jahrhunderts* (Mainz, 1990) pp. 112–15. The authors list additional bibliography on p. 114.

2. For the study by Heyne, see Rapp and Stucky-Schürer, *Zahm und Wild*, p. 413: Moritz Heyne, *Kunst im Hause: Abbildungen von Gegenständen aus der Mittelalterlichen Sammlung zu Basel*, 2 vols. (Basel, 1880–82). See also Hans Lanz, *Die alten Bildteppiche im Historischen Museum Basel* (Basel, 1985) p. 22 (text in German, French, and English).

3. Lanz, *Die alten Bildteppiche*, p. 22.

4. From Rapp and Stucky-Schürer, *Zahm und Wild*, pp. 114 n. 2, 415. Their reference is to Christian Müller, *Studien zur Darstellung und Funktion "wilder Natur" in deutschen Minnedarstellungen des 15. Jahrhunderts*, Diss. Karlsruhe, 1982. Christina Cantzler, *Bildteppiche der Spätgotik am Mittelrhein 1400–1550* (Tübingen, 1990) p. 142, referred to the same work as a Ph.D. dissertation, Tübingen, 1982.

5. Cantzler, *Bildteppiche der Spätgotik*, p. 142.

6. Richard Bernheimer, *Wild Men in the Middle Ages: A Study in Art, Sentiment, and Demonology* (Cambridge, Mass., 1952) p. 161.

7. Dora Heinz, *Mittelalterliche Tapisserien* (Vienna, 1965) pl. 2, text and illustration.

8. *Spätgotik am Oberrhein: Meisterwerke der Plastik und des Kunsthandwerks 1450–1530*, exh. cat., Badisches Landesmuseum (Karlsruhe, 1970), no. 255, illus.

9. Digby 1980, p. 22.

10. Timothy Husband, with the assistance of Gloria Gilmore-House, *The Wild Man: Medieval Myth and Symbolism*, exh. cat., MMA, The Cloisters (New York, 1980) pp. 15, 122–24.

11. *Spätgotik am Oberrhein*, no. 255; Rapp and Stucky-Schürer, *Zahm und Wild*, no. 4.

12. *Spätgotik am Oberrhein*, no. 255.

13. Husband, in *The Wild Man*, p. 122.

14. For illustrations of the two *Annunciations* and the *Paradise Garden*, see I[lse] Futterer, "Zur Malerei des frühen XV. Jahrhunderts im Elsasz," *Jahrbuch der preuszischen Kunstsammlungen* 49 (1928), respectively figs. 8, 9 (the altar from Staufen, captioned as the "Thennenbacher Altar") and 7. For the "Strawberry Madonna," see Irmtraud Himmelheber, *Meisterwerke der oberrheinischen Kunst des Mittelalters* (Honnef am Rhein, 1959) fig. 99.

15. The manuscript (cod. poet 2), entitled *Weltchronik*, now in the Kupferstichkabinett in Berlin, was written for Frederick, count of Toggenburg. The Joseph and Jericho miniatures, along with a few others in the volume, are illustrated in color in Fedja Anzelewsky, *Miniaturen aus der Toggenburg-Chronik aus dem Jahre 1411* (Baden-Baden, 1960) n. pag. For examples of the fashionable silhouette for men in the late fourteenth century, see fig. 73 in the present catalogue, an illustration of a tapestry from the *Story of Jourdain de Blaye* series.

16. See Alwin Schultz, *Deutsches Leben im XIV. und XV. Jahrhundert* (Vienna, 1892) vol. 2, figs. 301–11.

17. Alfred Stange, *Deutsche Malerei der Gotik*, vol. 4, *Südwestdeutschland in der Zeit von 1400 bis 1450* (Munich and Berlin, 1951) pp. 102–3, figs. 140–43.

18. Stange, *Deutsche Malerei der Gotik*, vol. 4, p. 47, figs. 65–67 (the miniatures), and p. 52, fig. 76 (the pen drawing). The miniature paintings are found in MS A.N.III. 17 in the Universitätsbibliothek, Basel; the drawing is in MS cod. pal. germ. 359 in the Universitätsbibliothek, Heidelberg.

19. Using his dating of the fashions represented in these prints as his criterion, Lehrs concluded that the Master of the Playing Cards was active toward the end of the first half of the fifteenth century. See Max Lehrs, *Geschichte und kritischer Katalog des deutschen, niederländischen und französischen Kupferstichs im XV. Jahrhundert* (Vienna, 1908–34; Kraus Reprint, Nendeln, Liechtenstein, 1969) vol. 1, pp. 63–64; plate vol. 1, figs. 7, 12, 18–23. See also Schultz, *Deutsches Leben*, figs. 312–15, for some pen drawings from a Calendarium of 1445 that show men with long hair.

20. We agree with Kurth 1926, p. 86 n. 1, who believed that a tapestry called "le Triomphe des Vertus sur les Vices" that was exhibited by J. Meyer-AmRhyn in Geneva in 1896 was the same piece even though the catalogue entry for it contains only a verbal description of the image and neither an illustration nor notes on the dimensions. See *Catalogue de l'art ancien: Groupe 25*, Exposition Nationale Suisse, Geneva, 1896 (Geneva, 1896) p. 340, no. 3665. According to that catalogue entry, the piece came from the Benedictine abbey of Hermetschwyl, Aargau.

21. We do not know precisely when this fragment, together with some other tapestry weavings, were transferred from the abbey of Muri in Canton Aargau to the abbey of Muri-Gries near Bolzano. According to Rapp and Stucky-Schürer, *Zahm und Wild*, p. 11, the abbey of Muri was dissolved by a decree of the high council of Aargau dated January 20, 1841, and the brothers at the abbey of Gries bei Bozen acquired what church property there was in the abbey of Muri. On p. 118 of the same publication, the date of the dissolution of the abbey of Muri is given as 1843.

22. Rapp and Stucky-Schürer, *Zahm und Wild*, p. 11, explained how the spots of paint came to be on the tapestries. In 1923, Burckhardt, *Gewirkte Bildteppiche*, p. 8, described the spots as drops of colored candle wax, but he also used the spots to argue that 55 was originally part of the fragment now in the abbey of Muri-Gries.

Fragment of a tapestry of unknown subject

Tentatively ascribed to Hesse or Thuringia, 1450–1500
Linen warp, wool wefts
10 in. × 5 ft. 2 in. (.25 m × 1.57 m)
8–9 warp yarns per inch, 3–4 per centimeter
Bequest of Charles F. Iklé, 1963 (64.27.22)

CONDITION

There are narrow bands of plain-weave loom finish at each end of the piece, which prove that the fabric has lost none of its original width. The top edge has been cut, but most of the left third of the bottom edge preserves the original selvage. The rest of the bottom edge shows considerable repair by reweaving that in places imitates the original selvage. Along the top edge there are numerous traces of white and beige yarns, undoubtedly the remains of motifs whose lower contours were cut into when this fragment was separated from the rest of the tapestry. All the pattern elements in the fragment were originally outlined with black yarns. Most of these yarns have deteriorated and fallen out; some have been replaced with needle-worked buff-colored yarns. The same yarns were used to replace missing portions of the white weft yarns that outline the dark brown dog at the far right. It appears that the forelegs of the white hound at the left were never woven. They were added with long-and-short stitches worked with white wool yarn. The weaving throughout the piece is extremely crude.

DESCRIPTION AND SUBJECT

This is a fragment from the bottom of a tapestry. The tops of hillocks and the crowns of plants rise upward from the bottom edge. From these crowns, and from less clearly defined sprouting points, grow small flowering plants that form a miniature forest in which the animals cavort. At the left end of the field a hound chases a doe or perhaps a rabbit—there is no consistent scale in the composition—toward the right, where a parrot-like bird confronts a turkey. At the far right end another hound faces outward, his muzzle touching a border stripe decorated with multicolored diagonal segments. The stripe is repeated at the left end of the field, where it partly obscures the base of a column set on a plinth. All the

flora and fauna are rendered in white and tones of beige, yellow, blue, green, and brown against a ground of blue-green.

Animal scenes like this appear relatively frequently along the bottom of German tapestries. The scenes fall essentially into three groups. One group shows game animals engaged in a chase or simply lounging. Two examples closely related to 56 in terms of both subject and style may be cited here. One, with wild folk tending fabulous animals in the upper three-quarters of the hanging, is in the Schweizerisches Landesmuseum in Zurich. Across the lowest quarter of the field a pattern unit showing a hound chasing a stag is repeated three times; in the central unit there is a second hound (Göbel 1933, fig. 15). The other example, whose main subject is the arrival of Joan of Arc at Chinon, is in the Musée Jeanne d'Arc in Orléans.[1] In the lowest quarter of this piece stags graze while a hound chases a doe.

In the second group of tapestries, creatures totally unconnected with the chase are shown along with the hunt. A *Garden of Love* in the Historisches Museum in Basel is a typical example. Hounds chase deer along the very bottom of the hanging, in and out among the stakes of a wattled fence, while next to them other kinds of creatures, including a butterfly, a rabbit, and a snail, go about their business unconcerned with the hunt.[2] The Metropolitan Museum's fragment, combining as it does a deer or rabbit hunt with incidental creatures like the parrot and the turkey, belongs iconographically with this group.

In the third class of miniature scenes human figures appear along with the animals. A typical example, preserved in the Musées Royaux d'Art et d'Histoire in Brussels, shows tiny animals and a miller, wrestlers, swordsmen, an archer, and other human figures along the bottom of the larger scene, which involves a morality tale enacted by wild folk.[3] There are additional tapestries showing yet other miniature bucolic scenes below large figures engaged in various activities, but since those diminutive incidents are set within rows of hillocks or curling vines rather than in fields or meadows, they differ from the kind of scenes being discussed here.[4]

Miniature rural scenes like these were also used along the bottom of narrative tapestries woven in series, like the *Life of the Virgin* cycle in the cathedral of Halber-

56

stadt.[5] Finally, small animal scenes occasionally appear at the bottom of compositions involving only real and fabulous beasts (Göbel 1933, fig. 65).

In all these examples the degree to which the figures along the bottom are involved formally with the major activity represented above varies considerably. In some cases the lowest quarter or fifth of a tapestry appears to have been designed quite separately and could be removed without compromising the formal or logical integrity of the rest. Kurth illustrates two fragments of a hanging of the *Allegory of Age*, in the convent of Saint Johann bei Zabern, in which the lowest fifth of the field is an animal composition completely unconnected with the main section.[6] In a tapestry of the departure of the twelve apostles the designer demonstrated an even greater tendency to arrange the field in bands—here the field comprises four totally distinct horizontal sections.[7] There is a band of clouds and angels across the top, the main narrative scene occupies the wide central band, and two narrow bands of stylized floral ornament finish the piece at the bottom. Another example, a tapestry showing wild men hunting a unicorn (Göbel 1933, fig. 129b), is designed in such a way that almost the entire left two-thirds of the bottom of the field (where three men and three animals share a space quite apart from that above) could be removed without disturbing the integrity of the main composition. In all of the tapestries discussed here the designer allotted to the miniature scene along the bottom anywhere from a fifth to a quarter of the whole piece. From this we may deduce that the Metropolitan Museum's fragment, which is 10 inches high, was cut from the bottom of a hanging ranging anywhere from about 40 to 50 inches high. While 40

inches represents approximately the standard height of German tapestry altar frontals of this period, the Metropolitan Museum's piece, which preserves its full width of 62 inches, is much narrower than the average antependium. Therefore, it seems likely that this fragment was taken from the bottom of a wall hanging, and not from an altar frontal or dossal.

SOURCE OF THE DESIGN

Since some of the tapestries cited above show animal hunts made up of a single pattern unit that repeats across the width of the piece, it seems clear that, at least for the miniature scenes at the bottom, the weavers were using stock patterns which the designer made up from existing tapestry cartoons or from prints or drawings. For 56 he probably used one source for the dogs and doe or rabbit and then turned to a different model, perhaps a bestiary or patterns based on a bestiary, for the exotic creatures—the parrot and the turkey. The flowers and hillocks probably appeared in the first pattern, as a setting for the doe or rabbit hunt.

MANUFACTURE AND DATE

The drawing and weaving are so coarse that it is difficult to relate this fragment to other German tapestries of similar character. This lack of competence might point on one hand simply to an individual weaver's lack of skill or on the other to a legitimate, positive regional characteristic. Göbel (1933, 71, fig. 46) ascribed this piece to northern Switzerland and dated it about 1460 on stylistic grounds. Kurth assigned the Joan of Arc

tapestry, with deer and rather similar plants along the bottom, to Switzerland, about 1430–40.[8] However, if the peculiarities of weaving and drawing that one sees in 56 are indeed indicative of a regional style, then it may be placed instead in central Germany, either in Hesse or Thuringia. This suggestion is based on attributions made by Kurth and Göbel concerning two other pieces that show the same kind of crude drawing and the same rendering of plants. One of these, now in the Rijksmuseum, Amsterdam, depicts the Holy Family and, in the lower left corner, a tiny figure of a nun, possibly the person who wove the tapestry. Göbel (1933, fig. 101b)

attributed it tentatively to Upper Hesse and dated it about 1485, while Kurth dated it in the last third of the fifteenth century and assigned it to central Germany.[9] The other tapestry is an antependium in the Burrell Collection, Glasgow, showing perhaps even more similar plants and blossoms in the background of a scene of the Coronation of the Virgin flanked at the left by three bishop saints (Eobanus, Adelarius, and Boniface) and at the right by Saints Andrew and Catherine (fig. 182). It too has been dated in the second half of the fifteenth century.[10] Because the three bishop saints are closely associated with Erfurt in Thuringia, it is thought that

Fig. 182. *Coronation of the Virgin, with Five Saints.* Tapestry antependium, Germany, perhaps Erfurt (Thuringia), 1450–1500. The Burrell Collection, Glasgow Museums and Art Galleries.

the tapestry might have been woven there. It has also been suggested that because it was said to have come from Fulda in Hesse, where Saint Boniface founded a monastery and also was buried, the tapestry could have been woven there instead.[11] If Göbel and Kurth are right in locating the origin of these two tapestries in central Germany, which includes both Hesse and Thuringia, and if the community of naive style that links them with the Metropolitan Museum's fragment counts for more than a coincidence, then there is reason to attribute the last to central Germany. In the absence of more convincing arguments than these, it seems prudent now to acknowledge that the tapestry from which 56 was taken certainly was woven in Germany in the second half of the fifteenth century, and probably somewhere other than in the Rhineland, whose tapestries show quite a different community of style.

RELATED TAPESTRIES

No other fragments of this tapestry or of others related to it in a series of hangings or altar furnishings are known to have survived.

HISTORY

In the collection of Fritz Iklé, Saint Gall, Switzerland.
In the collection of Charles F. Iklé, New York.
Bequeathed to the MMA by Charles F. Iklé, 1963.

EXHIBITIONS

None known.

PUBLICATIONS

Göbel 1933, p. 71. Discussed briefly; illus. fig. 46.
Forsyth, William H. "Reports of the Departments: Medieval Art and The Cloisters, the Main Building." Annual Report for 1963–1964. In *MMA Bulletin*, n.s. 23 (1964–65) p. 80. Mentioned.

NOTES

1. Kurth 1926, p. 216, pl. 48, called Swiss, 1430–40.
2. Kurth 1926, pp. 223–24, pls. 75, 76, called Swiss, probably Basel, 1460–80.
3. Kurth 1926, pp. 246–47, pl. 171, called Middle Rhine, 1400–1450.
4. Kurth 1926, p. 213, pls. 30, 31, in Schloss Wildenstein, called Swiss, 1420–40; p. 225, pls. 81, 82, in Basel, Historisches Museum, called Swiss, probably Basel, 1488–1502; p. 244, pl. 162, in Freiburg im Breisgau, Städtische Altertümersammlung, called Upper Rhine, beginning of the fifteenth century.
5. Kurth 1926, pp. 277–78, pls. 333–44, called North German, about 1500.
6. Kurth 1926, p. 234, pls. 122b, c, called Alsace, early sixteenth century, after a prototype of 1400–1433.
7. Kurth 1926, pp. 270–71, pl. 301, then in a private collection, called Frankish, last third of the fifteenth century.
8. Kurth 1926, p. 216, pl. 48.
9. Kurth 1926, p. 256, pl. 230a.
10. Kurth 1926, pp. 161, 256, pl. 229, called Middle German, second half of the fifteenth century; and Göbel 1933, p. 132, fig. 104a, called Upper Hesse or Erfurt (?), second half of the fifteenth century.
11. Göbel 1933, p. 132.

57
Fragment with a Simulated Silk Textile Pattern

Part of a strip of tapestry weaving

Nuremberg or Upper Rhineland (Strasbourg), 1450–1550
Linen warp, wool wefts
23 1/2 in. × 24 1/2 in. (.60 m × .62 m)
13 warp yarns per inch, 5 per centimeter
The Cloisters Collection, 1953 (53.164)

CONDITION

The warp runs vertically in this piece. The fabric has been cut along the top, bottom, and right sides. About one inch of the selvage and some turned-back wefts (without the linen warp yarns that once engaged them there) have survived at the middle of the left side; the rest of that edge has been cut. If, as we believe, the pattern was planned so that when several lengths of the fabric were sewn side by side the half-leaf units along the edges would match up across the seams, then it follows that about one-sixth of the pattern's width is missing at the right side. We can therefore calculate that this fragment may have been about six inches wider than it is at present, or just over 28 inches (.72 m) wide. Although the colors are still bright, the red and yellow areas show the striated effect that usually results when wools from different dye lots have faded.

DESCRIPTION

The fabric shows a late medieval silk velvet or damask pattern based on a leaf-and-stem unit whose outer contour remains constant while its inner conformation changes according to its position in the scheme. The leaves are arranged in diagonal rows so that the spaces around them seem to define a hexagonal mesh or trellis. Each leaf grows from the end of a short, curved stalk that also bears a rosette at the tip of a fine, subsidiary stalk branching off to the right. The centers of the leaves have one of two patterns alternating regularly in the diagonal direction. One center shows a pomegranate silhouetted against an acanthus leaf; from behind the leaf three daisies (or rosettes in profile) grow out to the left and three to the right. In the other center an acanthus leaf is flanked by four rosettes in frontal view, two at the left and two at the right. The pattern is rendered mainly in dark red on a ground of golden yellow. The single rosettes on the subsidiary stems have mauve petals (faded from pinkish lavender, visible on the reverse) and dark golden yellow centers. The two rosettes in the middle leaf along the left edge are beige rather than yellow as they are in the other leaves.

The warp in this fragment runs vertically—that is, parallel to the vertical orientation of the pattern—rather than horizontally. In this respect, as in respect to the pattern, the fabric simulates the silk weaving it was made to substitute for. This piece was perhaps meant to be hung as a narrow curtain, possibly one of a pair at the head of a bed, or in a series of such strips sewn together to make a wide hanging to cover a wall or to hang free as a curtain. A curtain of this kind, made up of lengths of green voided and brocaded silk velvet with a similar pattern, is shown hanging behind the Madonna in a painting published by Stechow as an early work of Stephan Lochner (fig. 183).[1] The fabric could, as well, have been intended as yardage to be cut up (as its silk counterparts often were) for cushion or furniture covers. However the fact that the warp runs vertically tempts one to think that it was meant to be used as part of a hanging since it would have fallen in softer folds than a tapestry with a horizontal warp. It could also have been sewn to more strips and used as a cover for a table or a bier. A tapestry fragment with a similar pattern and a vertical warp, in Nuremberg, shows the Volckamer arms at the lower left edge, so oriented that it can be read properly only if the weaving is lying on a horizontal plane. It was published as a fragment of what might have been a bier cover (see note 5).

SOURCE OF THE DESIGN

There can be no doubt that the pattern was taken or adapted from that of a sumptuous woven silk, probably a velvet or a damask, brocaded with two other colors (the pinkish lavender and the darker golden tone) of silk yarn or perhaps silver and gilt yarns. Great numbers of such silks have survived, some with very similar patterns (fig. 184).[2]

MANUFACTURE AND DATE

Although during the late Middle Ages Netherlandish weavers produced tapestries featuring the patterns of

57

related velvets and damasks (see 51), the linen warp in this fragment indicates that it was woven in a German-speaking region. Also, German tapestries made in this era often had simulated textile patterns as flat backgrounds for single figures or groups of figures.[3] When 57 entered the Metropolitan Museum collection in 1953, it was ascribed to Franconia, an attribution that probably accompanied it when it came from the Figdor and then the Iklé collections. More often than not, tapestries of this kind were traditionally called Franconian. Von Wilckens has offered good reasons to specify Nuremberg as the place of manufacture of some pieces showing woven silk patterns that incorporate formal arrangements of pomegranate motifs.[4] Although the pattern in 57 features leaf units, there are pomegranate motifs in the centers, and so this piece is closely related to the pomegranate-patterned fragment in Nuremberg that has a vertical warp and shows the arms of the Volckamer family of that city, as well as to three other pomegranate-patterned fragments with vertical warps, one in the Burrell Collection in Glasgow (fig. 185), a second in the Musée de l'Oeuvre Notre-Dame, Strasbourg, and a third in the cloister of Saint Jean Saverne in Saverne (near Strasbourg), which Hirschhoff published as the work of nuns in that cloister and which Rapp and Stucky-Schürer published, together with the other two fragments, as Strasbourg work.[5] Therefore, we have good reason to consider both Nuremberg and the Upper Rhineland as the place where 57 might have been woven.

The design formula that links the pattern in this fragment to patterns of a particular group of silks produced in Italy during the first half of the fifteenth century involves the repetition of a single, large leaf or leaf-like motif accompanied by subsidiary related motifs arranged in horizontal or diagonal rows and all heading either toward the left or right or, in some cases, alternately in one direction or the other. The formula, with elaborations that designers eventually abandoned, can be traced back to the first half of the fourteenth century.[6] The velvets and damasks referred to above (Source of the Design) as being most closely related to the pattern in the Metropolitan Museum's piece are believed to have been woven in the first half of the fifteenth century. If we assumed that 57 was woven to be used as a cheaper substitute for sumptuous silks imported from Italy when such velvets and damasks were at the height of fashion there, we would date it between 1400 and 1450. However it seems reasonable to consider a much later date because it undoubtedly took some time for these patterns to become popular outside the centers of fashion. Furthermore, this piece is related technically to the

fragment in the Burrell Collection (fig. 185) whose pattern derives from fine silks of the period 1500–1550.[7] But since we do not know where these tapestry fabrics were woven and used, whether in an urban or a provincial setting, there are no grounds for determining how current the sense of fashion was in the weaving shops or the homes or churches associated with 57 and the Burrell Collection piece. Therefore it seems expedient and necessary to acknowledge for the present that the Metropolitan Museum's fragment might have been woven as early as 1450 and as late as 1550.

Fig. 183. *Virgin Mary Crowned by Angels*, attributed to Stephan Lochner. Panel painting, Germany, perhaps about 1440. The Cleveland Museum of Art.

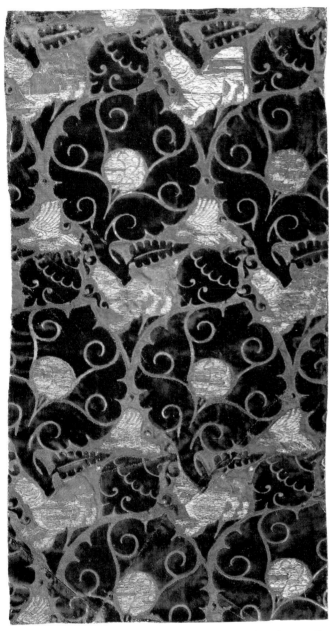

Fig. 184. Cut voided satin velvet. Silk brocaded with metallic yarns; Italy, probably Venice, here dated about 1425–50. MMA, Fletcher Fund, 1946 (46.156.132).

Fig. 185. Strip of tapestry weaving, Germany, attributed to Strasbourg, about 1510–20. The Burrell Collection, Glasgow Museums and Art Galleries.

RELATED TAPESTRIES

No other fragments from the same tapestry strip or set of strips are known to have survived.

HISTORY

In the collection of Dr. Albert Figdor, Vienna, cat. no. 3260.
In the Iklé Collection, Saint Gall, Switzerland.
Purchased by the MMA, The Cloisters Collection, 1953, from Fred Charles Iklé.

EXHIBITIONS

None known.

PUBLICATION

Forsyth, William H. "Reports of the Departments: Medieval Art and The Cloisters, the Main Building." Annual Report for 1963–1964. In *MMA Bulletin*, n.s. 23 (1964–65) p. 80.

NOTES

1. Wolfgang Stechow, "A Youthful Work by Stephan Lochner," *Bulletin of the Cleveland Museum of Art* 55 (1968) pp. 305–14, color illus. on cover.

2. See a few typical examples of silks with related patterns in the following publications: Barbara Markowsky, *Europäische Seidengewebe des 13.–18. Jahrhunderts*, Kunstgewerbemuseum (Cologne, 1976) nos. 26, 28; Renate Jaques and Ernst Flemming, *Encyclopedia of Textiles* (New York, 1958) pl. 63. See also fig. 184 in the present entry. For paintings showing silks with these kinds of patterns, see fig. 183 in the present entry and two other paintings by Stephan Lochner in which curtains made of lengths of patterned silk hang behind standing figures; they are illustrated in Stechow, "A Youthful Work by Stephan Lochner," figs. 10 (an *Angel of the Annunciation* in the cathedral church in Cologne) and 12 (*Madonna with the Violet* in the Diocesan Museum, Cologne). The curtain in fig. 10 shows rows of leaves of two kinds, one moving left, one right. This pattern represents an intermediate stage between the "leaf" silks of this type and the meandering pomegranate-vine velvet patterns that became fashionable in the second half of the fifteenth century; see Adolph S. Cavallo, *Textiles: Isabella Stewart Gardner Museum* (Boston, 1986) no. 124, illus., with accompanying text.

3. Textile patterns that can be found in surviving silks, as well as patterns that look like textiles of which no examples have come down to us, appear in the backgrounds of German tapestries woven in the fourteenth to sixteenth centuries. For a typical example from each period, see the *Wild Men and Moors* of about 1400 in the Museum of Fine Arts, Boston (Adolph S. Cavallo, *Tapestries of Europe and of Colonial Peru in the Museum of Fine Arts, Boston* [Boston, 1967] no. 1); the *Christ Child with Saints* (ca. 1450) in the Bayerisches Nationalmuseum, Munich (Kurth

1926, p. 268, pl. 289b); and the *Augustus I of Saxony*, 1550, MMA (Edith Appleton Standen, *European Post-Medieval and Related Hangings in The Metropolitan Museum of Art* [New York, 1985] no. 137, pp. 753–55); all are illustrated and discussed.

4. See Leonie von Wilckens, in *Gothic and Renaissance Art in Nuremberg 1300–1550*, exh. cat., MMA and Germanisches Nationalmuseum (New York and Nuremberg, 1986) nos. 58, 68, and 69, all illus.

5. The tapestry fragment with the Volckamer arms is preserved in the Germanisches Nationalmuseum in Nuremberg; see Luitpold Herzog in Bayern, *Die Fränkische Bildwirkerei* (Munich, 1925) vol. 1, p. 60, no. 37, vol. 2, fig. 37. For the attribution of the Saverne piece to nuns in that cloister, see C. E. Alexander Hirschhoff, *Die Bildwirkerein von St. Johann bei Zabern: Ein Beitrag zur Kenntnis klösterlichen Kunstschaffens im Elsass* (Frankfurt am Main, 1933) pp. 21, 56, illus. pl. VIII; and for notes on the fragments in Glasgow, Strasbourg, and Saverne, all of which show one pattern, see Anna Rapp Buri and Monica Stucky-Schürer, *Zahm und Wild: Basler und Strassburger Bildteppiche des 15. Jahrhunderts* (Mainz, 1990) p. 410, the Glasgow piece illus. in color.

6. See, for example, a fourteenth-century Italian brocaded satin showing a pattern involving a hawk propelling a dog in a boat from behind which rise a stalk bearing a large lobed leaf tilted toward the left and below that a smaller branch sprouting small leaves and pomegranates tilted toward the right, illustrated in Jaques and Flemming, *Encyclopedia of Textiles*, pl. 53, or Adele Coulin Weibel, *Two Thousand Years of Textiles* (New York, 1952) no. 213.

7. For a silk damask and a tapestry fabric showing virtually identical patterns that also match the pattern in the Burrell, Strasbourg, and Saverne fragments, see Markowsky, *Seidengewebe*, no. 84, dated to 1500–1550 and illustrated, and the tapestry portrait of Augustus I of Saxony, dated to 1550 (see note 3 above).

58
Two Scenes from the Poem
Der Busant (The Buzzard)

Fragment of a wall hanging

Upper Rhineland, Strasbourg, 1480–90
Linen warp; wool, silk, linen, cotton, and metallic wefts
2 ft. 7⁷⁄₈ in. × 4 ft. 4 in. (.81 m × 1.32 m) including the extreme
right end, which has been turned under
18 warp yarns per inch, 7 per centimeter
Gift of The Honorable Murtogh D. Guinness, 1985 (1985.358)

CONDITION

The fabric has been cut along the sides and the bottom. A few bits of the original selvage have survived along the top edge, but most of that edge and the entire bottom edge have been rewoven with modern warp and weft yarns. There are also some insertions of modern weaving in the top of the tree above the unicorn's head and of the foliage just in front of its nose, in the turnover of the banderole at the left, and in the princess's right sleeve, bodice, and skirt. There are a few repairs where modern weft yarns were woven on the original warp. These occur in scattered spots throughout the left-hand three-quarters of the field; they have had little effect on the original drawing. Some of the letters in the inscriptions have been badly restored and they are now illegible. These are the letters between the initial word *ich* in the banderole at the left and the terminal letters *ete* of the word immediately following it. In the banderole at the right the restoration has obscured the two letters preceding *armer*, the second word on that scroll. The colors are still bright throughout the field.

The right-hand end of the field, which consisted mostly of old restoration, was turned under during a recent restoration project. It is not visible in the photograph reproduced here but does appear in the illustration that Kurth published in 1915. The line where the original and modern fabrics meet begins at the top of the field above the left eye of the man standing at the right and continues on a curved path downward through the foliage to the top of the banderole. From there it moves to the right across the crown of the man's head and down the left side of his face, then to the left across his cheek and mouth to the jawline, and then diagonally to the right across his chest to his left armpit. The line then runs down the inside of his left sleeve, across its cuff, along the outer edge of the skirt of his tunic, and then

along the outside of his left leg to the ankle. It then turns to the right and drops straight to the bottom edge of the field at a point just to the right of the plant with the long lanceolate leaves. The fabric between that line and what appears in this illustration as the right end of the piece was entirely rewoven recently. The clouds above the man's head and the plant with lanceolate leaves next to his left calf were introduced into the pattern at that time.

DESCRIPTION AND SUBJECT

In the lower left corner of the field a wild man with fur on his body and a crown on his head appears in the midst of a forest, crawling on all fours. In the middle distance, at the left, a spotted unicorn dashes forward. Above, in the branches of a tree, a bird turns to the left and looks at another, larger bird perched nearby. Only the larger bird's head and the leading edges of its wings are represented in the fabric. One can see that it carries a golden ring in its beak. In the center of the tapestry a young lady wearing a crown and a gown decorated with a damask or voided velvet pattern is seen riding her horse toward the right. Another horse, riderless, trots beside her. An inscribed banderole separates the princess and the horses from the wild man, birds, and unicorn. A second banderole separates her from the space occupied by the man standing at the right. The tiny roe deer in the lower left corner may be a weaver's personal motif, as Rapp and Stucky-Schürer (1990, 363) suggested, or simply one of the miniature creatures that occasionally appear in these tapestries (see 56).

The ring in the larger bird's beak and the princess's girdle and bodice ties are woven with metallic yarns (gilt or silvered membrane wrapped around a linen core yarn) that are now much abraded and darkened. The flowers, the birds' feathers, beaks, and claws, and the gemstones in the crowns are highlighted with silk yarns. The princess's face and hands are rendered with cotton yarns. The yarns used in the border of her gown were spun of linen.

These two scenes represent the climax in the story of *Der Busant* (The Buzzard), a Middle High German poem believed to have originated in Alsace in the early fourteenth century. It was probably based on some earlier

58

source, one from which its French counterpart, *L'Escoufle*, also derives.[1] *Der Busant* deals with the adventures of a young prince of England who goes with his chaplain to Paris, where he attends school. He meets and falls in love with the princess of France, who has been betrothed without her consent to the king of Morocco. The prince and princess make plans to elope on her wedding day. The prince then goes back to England. At the appointed time he returns to France in the guise of a minstrel. He finds the princess and rides off into the woods with her. During a moment of rest, when the princess falls asleep with her head on the young man's lap, he takes a ring from her finger and studies it. Suddenly a buzzard flies down and makes off with the ring. The prince chases the bird, trying to retrieve the ring. He penetrates deeper and deeper into the forest and loses his way. Realizing that he has gone astray from his loved one and cannot find her, he becomes frantic and wild,

abandons his clothing, and begins to live like a beast in the woods, crawling on all fours. Meanwhile the princess wakes and finds her lover gone. Seeking shelter, she is taken in first by a humble miller and later by a kindly duke of the region. After some time passes, the duke's hunters find the wild man and bring him to the castle. The duke, realizing that the man was once civilized, arranges to have him rehabilitated. One day, while hunting with the duke, the prince bites off a buzzard's head and in explanation tells his sad story. The princess hears of this, recognizes her lover, and is reunited with him. The duke sends out messengers to tell the lovers' parents the good news. The prince and princess are finally married amid suitable festivities which include a feast and a tournament.

The Metropolitan Museum's tapestry shows the moment when the prince—having left his beloved behind as he dashed off in pursuit of the buzzard (a moment

Fig. 186. Two scenes from the poem *Der Busant*. Fragment of tapestry weaving that was once joined to the left end of 58 and part of the same wall hanging. Clemens Collection, Museum für Angewandte Kunst, Cologne.

shown in the fragments in Glasgow and Cologne, see fig. 186 and Related Tapestries)—has become a wild man of the forest. He gazes upward and toward the left, as though looking at the taunting bird, which holds the ring in its beak. Since this is the only surviving fragment that shows the prince as a wild man with a unicorn nearby, we cannot say whether the unicorn in this scene has some special significance. The beast may be the wild man's steed, as unicorns often were in these tales, or it may simply be a symbol of the uncorrupted nature of the forest or of the regenerative power of love (if the last, then perhaps as a presentiment of the prince's ultimate rehabilitation). This is also the moment that begins the long period of the lovers' separation. Their plan has been frustrated.

The princess must find shelter and protection now that she is alone in the forest. Luckily she comes upon a gentle miller and asks him (first banderole):

ich . . . ete [unmüete?] frouge [frouwe?] ich biten dich dz [das] du durch got beherbergestz mich

(I, an unhappy lady, beseech you
to give me shelter for God's sake).

The miller answers (second banderole):

*gern . . . [ich?] armer man kein
er [ehre?] ich uch [euch?] erbieten kan*

(Gladly, [though] I, as a poor man,
cannot receive you with the honors [you deserve]).

The transcriptions and translations offered above were suggested by Helmut Nickel in an attempt to make sense of the damaged inscriptions and to produce an acceptable translation into English.[2] None of the earlier transcriptions had made that possible. Kurth (1915, 244) gave the first reading of the inscriptions essentially as they are shown above but without the words presented here within brackets and with *als* (instead of Nickel's *ich*) following *gern* in the miller's speech. She repeated this reading (1926, 240) and was followed in it by Göbel (1933, 285 n. 54) and, with slight variations, by van Ysselsteyn (1969, 171). Von Falke (1930, no. 29) published essentially the same transcription, but he interpreted the *ete* after the first *ich* in the princess's speech as *unstete* and the *kein er* in the miller's speech as *keiner*. Although *unstete* conveys the idea of fickleness and inconstancy, and thus would be irrelevant in this context, it can also mean wandering. Therefore the word in its original form could have been *unstete* or *unmüete* or perhaps some other word that has not yet been suggested. Von Falke's reading of *keiner* is not acceptable in comparison with Nickel's reading of *kein ehre*. Nickel suggested that *frouge* (which cannot be interpreted) may have been a painter's or weaver's mistake for *frouwe*, which in this context makes sense. Rapp and Stucky-Schürer (1990, 364), whose readings are essentially the same as Nickel's, read this word as *frowge*.

SOURCE OF THE DESIGN

As Digby (1980, 25) suggested, the compositions in the long, narrow hanging might have been based on a series of book illustrations. These could have been prints or miniature paintings. No illustrations that might have inspired these compositions have yet been identified.

MANUFACTURE AND DATE

By common consent every writer who published the Metropolitan Museum's piece has attributed it along with most other surviving fragments of *Der Busant* to Alsace, often specifically to Strasbourg, and dated it in the last quarter of the fifteenth century. The attribution to Alsace is based on a number of technical, stylistic, and linguistic considerations and also the evidence of coats of arms that appear in similar pieces. Digby (1980,

644

24) noted that the Alsatian dialect was used in the inscriptions that appear in the various fragments of *Der Busant,* and he referred to a grammatical work dealing with this matter. Some of the fragments, not including the Metropolitan Museum's example, have passages of knotted-pile weaving combined with the tapestry weave, a technique which seems to occur frequently in tapestries attributable to Alsace, specifically to the region of Strasbourg. In discussing the matter of style, writers call attention to regional characteristics in the way plants and landscapes are represented in the various pieces of *Der Busant.* Certainly within the group of surviving late fifteenth-century pieces that have been ascribed to Alsace, these characteristic modes of representation, and also the kinds of figure and facial types that accompany them, do indeed appear consistently. However the arguments for identifying this style with Alsace and this technical peculiarity with Strasbourg depend entirely on the evidence of heraldry. Everything has been deduced by studying the pieces showing the arms of Alsace and Strasbourg families and then isolating the stylistic and technical elements that are common to all of them and calling these elements regional characteristics.

Traditionally a certain group of tapestries has been accepted as typifying late fifteenth-century Alsatian work. These include among other pieces a hunting tapestry in the Kunsthistorisches Museum in Vienna; a piece with lovers on horseback in the Burrell Collection in Glasgow; another showing David and Bathsheba, also in the Burrell Collection; a piece rich with knotted-pile work, showing the story of the *Two Riddles of the Queen of Sheba,* now in the Metropolitan Museum (59); and a tapestry in the Germanisches Nationalmuseum in Nuremberg with scenes from the story of the *Queen of France and the Disloyal Marshal.*[3] All of these tapestries show strikingly similar styles and details; but as Digby (1980, 24) in considering certain pieces in this group has observed, this is not grounds for claiming them all as the work of a single artist. The community of design depends on some other factor, perhaps after all a regional style. As Major demonstrated, two of these pieces show coats of arms belonging to Strasbourg families.[4] The arms represented on the *David and Bathsheba* in the Burrell Collection indicate that the tapestry was woven for Heinrich Ingold, a wealthy Strasbourg merchant (died 1523), and his wife Clara Gerbott (died 1495) probably about 1480. The hunting tapestry in Vienna shows the arms of the Strasbourg families Böcklin and von Mullenheim. Major dated this tapestry about 1490. These two pieces show the stylistic peculiarities that are now associated with Alsace

weaving of the late fifteenth century. The *David and Bathsheba* also has passages of the knotted-pile weaving which occurs in tapestries that are attributed to Strasbourg on grounds of heraldry.

Fragments from at least three separate woven editions of *Der Busant* have survived (see Related Tapestries). Two editions seem to antedate by some years the third weaving, which is represented solely by the long fragment in the Germanisches Nationalmuseum in Nuremberg. The Metropolitan Museum's example belongs to one of the earlier editions, which shows a more delicate style of weaving and earlier fashions in clothing. The difference in fashion is perceptible only when one compares the tournament scene on the tapestry in Nuremberg with the same scene on the fragment in the Louvre. The bulbous headdress worn by the woman at the left in the tournament scene in Nuremberg and also the round-toed shoes of the squires standing on the field represent somewhat later fashions than corresponding details in the Paris piece do.

Considerations of pictorial style and fashion in costume suggest that the Metropolitan Museum's fragment and the edition to which it belongs may properly be dated about the time of the *David and Bathsheba* tapestry in Glasgow and the hunting tapestry in Vienna, which Major dated about 1480 and about 1490, respectively, on the evidence of heraldry. Rapp and Stucky-Schürer (1990, 362) attributed 58 to Strasbourg and dated it about 1480–90.

RELATED TAPESTRIES

All six surviving fragments of tapestries illustrating the story of *Der Busant* were published, together with color plates, by Rapp and Stucky-Schürer (1990, 358–68). In addition to 58, there are pieces in the Victoria and Albert Museum, London; the Museum für Angewandte Kunst, Cologne; the Burrell Collection, Glasgow; the Musée de Cluny (on deposit at the Musée du Louvre), Paris; and the Germanisches Nationalmuseum, Nuremberg. Rapp and Stucky-Schürer demonstrated, both in their exhibition in Basel in 1990 and in their related publication (1990, 362–63), that 58 was at some time cut off the right end of the Cologne piece, and, therefore, that those two fragments belong to a single edition of the weaving. Since the fragment in Glasgow repeats the composition of the piece in Cologne, it is clear that the Glasgow piece comes from a different edition. The long piece in Nuremberg represents a third and later edition. In theory, and pending further technical examinations, it is at least possible that 58 (with the fragment in Cologne) and the Paris piece came from the missing right end of the

London tapestry. If that is not the case, then 58 and its mate in Cologne, and the Paris piece, represent fourth, and possibly fifth, editions of these cartoons.

Among the surviving pieces, the longest one, published and illustrated by Digby (1980, no. 13) as well as by Rapp and Stucky-Schürer (1990, 359–61), is in London. It shows six episodes that occur early in the story. None of the known pieces shows the first episodes, those in which the prince of England goes to Paris with his chaplain and falls in love with the princess of France. In the first scene of the London strip the prince has returned to England. In the second episode he asks for three horses and a fiddle. In the third scene these are brought and he leaves for France. The fourth scene finds him being received at the court of France. Then the king of Morocco arrives to claim his bride in the fifth scene. In the last episode the prince and princess make good their escape.

The story continues with the fragment in the Clemens Collection in the Museum für Angewandte Kunst in Cologne and its near-duplicate in the Burrell Collection in Glasgow,[5] both published by Rapp and Stucky-Schürer (1990, 362–63, 364–65). Here, during a rest in their travels, the princess has fallen asleep with her head in the prince's lap while he holds her ring up and looks at it. In the next scene the prince is running and shaking a stick at the buzzard that took the ring out of his hand and flew away. The tips of the thief's wings are visible at the upper right edge of the piece in Cologne (fig. 186) but not in the Glasgow example. The buzzard's head and shoulders appear at the upper left edge of the next scene in the story, the one shown in the Metropolitan Museum's tapestry. Directly below this is the front part of the unicorn whose rump remains in the representation in Cologne. The prince has turned into a wild man roaming the forest and the princess is seeking shelter with the miller. As Kurth (1926, 240), Göbel (1933, 97), and the author of the Karlsruhe catalogue entry (*Spätgotik am Oberrhein*, 1970, 289) observed, none of the fragments known to have survived shows the episodes that occur between this point and the moment represented in the first of five scenes in the Nuremberg strip where the duke, having found the prince and learned his story, sends messengers to the lovers' parents to tell them the good news. In the second episode the couple are married and in the third they are seated at the wedding feast. In the fourth scene they witness a joust and in the last scene they ride off together on one horse, accompanied by pages. The fragment in the Louvre repeats the last two scenes of the Nuremberg piece with some differences in the details.

Editions of *Der Busant* were produced in the form of long, narrow tapestries in one or more pieces to be hung on the wall of a house above a row of benches (*Rücklaken*). The cumulative length of the London, Cologne, Metropolitan Museum, and Nuremberg fragments, which together show fifteen different scenes from the story, but not every episode in the story, can be calculated from the dimensions given by Rapp and Stucky-Schürer (1990, 359, 362, 367) as approximately $29^{1}/_{2}$ feet (8.98 m). The *Rücklaken* from which 58 came might have been that long or, if it showed all the episodes in the story, even longer.

HISTORY

In the collection of Roman Abt, Lucerne.
In the collection of Dr. Albert Figdor, Vienna. According to Kurth (1926, 240), it was acquired from Bossard, Lucerne.
Sold, *Die Sammlung Dr. Albert Figdor*, Vienna, June 11–13, 1930, pt. 1, vol. 1, no. 29, illus.
In the collection of Walter Edward Guinness, first Baron Moyne.
In the collection of the Honorable Murtogh D. Guinness.
Given to the MMA by the Honorable Murtogh D. Guinness, 1985.

EXHIBITION

Basel, Historisches Museum, 1990. *Zahm und Wild: Basler und Strassburger Bildteppiche des 15. Jahrhunderts.* Checklist no. 64.

PUBLICATIONS

Kurth, Betty. "Mittelhochdeutsche Dichtungen auf Wirkteppichen des XV. Jahrhunderts." *Jahrbuch der Kunsthistorischen Sammlungen des allerhöchsten Kaiserhauses* 32 (1915) pp. 236, 243, 244. Described briefly; illus. figs. 1 (middle row, right end), 6.
Kurth 1926, pp. 132, 240. Discussed in detail; illus. pls. 142, 143, 148.
Drey, Franz. "Deutsche Bildteppiche des Mittelalters," review of Kurth 1926. *Die Kunst für Alle* 44 (1928–29) p. 237. Illus.
von Falke, Otto. *Die Sammlung Dr. Albert Figdor, Wien.* Sale cat., pt. 1, vol. 1. Vienna and Berlin, 1930, no. 29. Described; illus. pl. xv.
Göbel 1933, pp. 97, 285 n. 54. Discussed in detail; illus. fig. 71.
Bernheimer, Richard. *Wild Men in the Middle Ages: A Study in Art, Sentiment, and Demonology.* Cambridge, Mass., 1952. Illus. fig. 8.
Stammler, Wolfgang. "Busant." In Otto Schmidt et al., eds., *Reallexikon zur Deutschen Kunstgeschichte.* Vol. 3, Stuttgart, 1954, col. 238. Mentioned.
Heinz, Dora. *Europäische Wandteppiche I.* Brunswick, 1963, p. 148. Mentioned.
van Ysselsteyn, G. T. *Tapestry: The Most Expensive Industry of the XVth and XVIth Centuries.* The Hague and Brussels, 1969, p. 171, pl. 182. Inscription transcribed and the piece illustrated, but with no mention of its past or present location.
Spätgotik am Oberrhein: Meisterwerke der Plastik und des Kunsthandwerks 1450–1530. Exh. cat., Badisches Landesmuseum. Karlsruhe, 1970, p. 289. Described briefly and as formerly in the Figdor collection, present location unknown.
Digby 1980, p. 25. Mentioned.
Rapp Buri, Anna, and Monica Stucky-Schürer. *Zahm und Wild: Basler und Strassburger Bildteppiche des 15. Jahrhunderts.* Mainz, 1990, pp. 362–69. Described and discussed; color illus. fig. 114b.

NOTES

1. See Digby 1980, p. 25, for a brief discussion of the poem's date and place of origin and a list of publications in which the text may be found. In Digby's opinion, *Der Busant* derived from the thirteenth-century *L'Escoufle,* whereas Göbel 1933, p. 97, believed that both romances were based on some common source.

2. The author wishes to thank Dr. Nickel, who kindly studied the inscription during an informal consultation in August 1987.

3. For the tapestry in Vienna with hunting scenes, see Kurth 1926, pp. 130–31, 238, pls. 138, 139. Also Göbel 1933, pp. 96–97, figs. 68, 69; and Emil Major, *Strassburger Bildteppiche aus gotischer Zeit* (Basel, [1943]) pp. 25–26, figs. 12–15. For the lovers on horseback in the Burrell Collection, where it is called "The Pursuit of Fidelity," see Kurth 1926, pp. 131, 238, pl. 140. Also *Treasures from the Burrell Collection,* exh. cat. by William Wells, Hayward Gallery (London, 1975) no. 70, illus. For the *David and Bathsheba* piece in the same collection, see Kurth 1926, pp. 134–35, 242, pl. 154. Also Göbel 1933, pp. 100–101, fig. 77a. In both of these publications the piece is erroneously located in the museum in Tours, where it was once exhibited but never owned. See also Major, *Strassburger Bildteppiche,* pp. 23–25, fig. 11. For the piece illustrating the story of the *Queen of France and the Disloyal Marshal,* see Kurth 1926, pp. 132–33, 191, 241, pl. 151. Also Göbel 1933, pp. 97–98, fig. 72. For more recent information on these pieces, with illustrations in color, see Anna Rapp Buri and Monica Stucky-Schürer, *Zahm und Wild: Basler und Strassburger Bildteppiche des 15. Jahrhunderts* (Mainz, 1990) respectively pp. 348–49, 350–52, 346–48, 354–58.

4. For discussions of the coats of arms and the dates involved, see Major, *Strassburger Bildteppiche,* respectively pp. 24–25, 26.

5. Concerning the near-duplicate piece in Glasgow, see also *The Burrell Collection: Medieval Tapestries, Sculpture . . . ,* exh. cat., Hatton Gallery, King's College, Newcastle-upon-Tyne, also circulated by The Arts Council of Britain to Sheffield and Swansea (London, 1977) no. 205, illus.

59

59
Two Riddles of the Queen of Sheba

Upper Rhineland, Strasbourg, 1490–1500
Bast fiber warp; wool, silk, and metallic wefts; wool pile yarns
2 ft. 7$^{1}/_{2}$ in. × 3 ft. 4 in. (.80 m × 1.02 m)
15 warp yarns per inch, 6 per centimeter
The Cloisters Collection, 1971 (1971.43)

CONDITION

The presence of a woven heading along the right edge and of a narrow band of plain-weave finish along the left proves that the tapestry has lost none of its original width. The upper and lower edges have been rewoven, but bits of the original selvage have survived in both places. Their presence indicates that the tapestry has lost none of its height. The extent of the reweaving along the top and bottom may be appreciated by comparing the illustration in this entry with a photograph of the piece that was reproduced in the Burlington Fine Arts Club exhibition catalogue of 1906 (see Exhibitions). The earlier photograph shows that the upper and lower edges and the four corners were somewhat worn and broken. These areas have since been restored.[1] There are also small repairs by reweaving in several places along both sides and in a few spots within the field, but none of these has affected the drawing. The colors are still relatively strong, but some of the red tones and the yellows have faded appreciably.

DESCRIPTION AND SUBJECT

The scene is set in a meadow or garden containing large plants including, among others, a thistle, a violet, a columbine, and carnations. Giant lilies of the valley grow atop hills in the far distance at both sides, the plant at the left towering over a tiny castle perched on a precipice. A pomegranate (?) tree rises in the middle distance right of center, and beyond it the view opens to the horizon across a grassy meadow. In the left foreground King Solomon sits on a cushion placed on the seat of his throne. A length of damask or voided velvet covers the back, seat, and floor of the throne, and at the top there is a canopy whose curtains are faced on the outside with voided velvet. The king wears an open crown with jeweled strawberry leaves on the points and holds a cruciform scepter upright against his left shoulder. The Queen of Sheba stands at the right side of the

field and looks across at the king. She wears an ermine-bordered, voided velvet gown with long, tight sleeves. The points of her open crown support lilies. She holds two roses in her right hand. With her left hand she points at two identically dressed children between the king and herself. The child kneeling at the left gathers apples in the skirt of its gown. The other child, standing at the right, holds an apple in its right hand and looks up at the king. A small creature that looks like a bird but is meant to represent a bee flies from the left, just outside the canopy, toward the roses in the queen's hand. The king and queen are engaged in conversation. Their speech is conveyed by the words inscribed on two banderoles that begin their twisting, intertwined courses near the mouth of each speaker. The queen says (in the right-hand scroll):

Bescheyd mich kuing ob blůmen und kind
Glich an art oder unglich sint

(Tell me, King, whether the flowers and children are of the same or different kind).

The king answers:

Die bine ein quote blům nit spart
das knuwen zoigt die wiplich art

(The bee does not pass up a good flower; kneeling shows the female style).

A narrow stripe of multicolored lozenges extends along the full height of the left edge, while at the right the corresponding stripe shows multicolored triangles. In the field, certain details have been specially rendered in order to show the actual textures of the things represented. Thus, the voided velvet outer surface of the canopy curtains, the king's hair, his velvet jerkin, and the pile-surfaced cushion cover, as well as the queen's velvet gown and its ermine borders, have all been rendered with Ghiordes knots tied with woolen yarns whose cut ends convey the texture of velvet pile, hair, and fur as required. Other details have been woven with metallic yarns (strips of gilt or silvered membrane wound on a core of bast fiber yarn): the highlights on the king's crown, his scepter, the finial atop the canopy, and the girdles at the waists of both figures. There are also touches of gilt yarn in the queen's sleeves, suggesting that the fabric of her gown is a gilt-ground voided velvet. The eyes of the figures were woven with white, brown, and blue silk yarns that give them a bit of gloss. Kajitani (1972) has described in detail not only the condition of the tapestry but also the materials and structures that were used to produce it.

The scene illustrates a story in which the Queen of Sheba tests King Solomon's renowned wisdom by asking him two difficult riddles. One riddle concerns the identification of real and artificial flowers; the other concerns the identification of the sexes of two small children. When a bee flies to one of the roses in the queen's hand, Solomon knows it is the real flower; and when one of the children kneels to gather apples in the skirt of its gown, he knows that one is the girl. The story does not occur in the Old Testament (1 Kings 10:1–3), where it is said simply that the Queen of Sheba asked the king a number of difficult questions and that he answered all of them. As Ostoia has shown (1972, 84–88), the story of the riddles does appear in various forms in both Hebrew and Islamic texts. She made an exhaustive study of the origins of these stories and concluded that the most likely source for the riddle of the flowers is an unidentified text referred to in Clément Marot's prologue to the 1527 edition of the *Roman de la Rose.* She noted (1972, 85–87) that a similar version of the riddle of the children's sexes may be found in a manuscript of 1346 entitled *Tractatus de Diversis Historiis Romanorum et Quibusdam Aliis,* a text probably based on some earlier source. (However in that story it is the boy who gathers the apples in the skirt of his gown and the girl who takes the apples in her hands.) Ostoia (1972, 82–91) also considered other pictorial, literary, and theatrical treatments of the riddles. Her examples date from the fifteenth to the seventeenth century.

Despite the relatively small size of the tapestry, it was probably woven to be used as a wall hanging in a domestic interior. Neither end has been cut, so it could not have been extracted from a longer hanging. Rapp and Stucky-Schürer (1990, 372) believed that it could have served as either a wall hanging or a cushion cover.

SOURCE OF THE DESIGN

There is a curious disparity between the style of the two main figures, elegantly drawn and posed, and the rest of the composition. The rather naively rendered sky, hills, and overscaled flowers are the stock-in-trade of tapestry weaving in this place and time. But the figures and throne clearly come from some particular source, some composition designed by a professional artist. Kurth (1926, 133) and Göbel (1933, 100) both noted that the tapestry design was closely related to the work of the Upper Rhenish Master E.S. Ostoia (1972, 76–77, 89–90)

Fig. 187. *The Judgment of Solomon,* by Master E.S. Engraving, Upper Rhineland, about 1467. British Museum, London.

made an extensive search for the source of the tapestry design and succeeded in finding two prints that are closely related to it. She demonstrated that the figure of Solomon on his throne is almost identical to the figure of the king in a *Judgment of Solomon* engraved by the Master E.S. about 1467 (fig. 187 here). The wide-jowled, narrow-chinned head with its curious tilt to the side, the pose of the body, the specific position of the left arm, and the placement of the throne cushion are virtually the same in the tapestry. However in the tapestry the left leg crosses in front of the right, whereas in the print it passes behind. Ostoia (1972, 77, fig. 4) found another print, a woodcut attributed to the Master of the Hausbuch which, although the body faces in the other direction, shows Solomon's legs in precisely the same relationship that they have in the tapestry. In that example the Queen of Sheba is also present. The woodcut appeared in a *Speculum Humanae Salvationis* printed in Speyer about 1478. Ostoia (1972, 76–77) suggested that this composition and the tapestry design might have derived from a common source. She also called attention to other prints and a stained-glass panel in which similar figures of Solomon appear. Finally she discussed and illustrated (1972, 89–90, fig. 14) a late fifteenth-century print by Israhel van Meckenem that was copied after a lost engraving by the Master E.S. It shows the subject of the two riddles (fig. 188 here). While the figures and composition are different from those in the tapestry, it seems likely that the tapestry composition was derived from some print like it. That hypothetical print would have shown not only this figure of Solomon enthroned but also, as the Master E.S./van Meckenem print does, other specific details like the rolled shoulders of the queen's gown and the child holding an apple up to an adult (the child at the right in the tapestry, at the far left in the print).

MANUFACTURE AND DATE

When it was exhibited in London in 1906, the tapestry was called German and dated in the early fifteenth cen-

tury. Migeon (1909, 261) and Pringsheim (1914–15) simply placed it in the fifteenth century. Schmitz (1919) was the first to associate the tapestry with the Upper Rhineland (Basel) and he called it "late gothic." Burckhardt (1923) did not agree that it was made in Basel even though he acknowledged that it was related stylistically to pieces that had been woven there. He was the first to note the similarity between this tapestry and the *David and Bathsheba* that is now in the Burrell Collection in Glasgow; and he suggested furthermore that the two pieces were made in the same shop.[2] Kurth (1926, 133, 242) believed that the style of the Metropolitan Museum's tapestry and the garments represented in it placed the piece firmly in Alsace between 1470 and 1490. Later (1940–41, 234) she referred to it as Upper Rhenish and dated it in the last quarter of the fifteenth century. Göbel (1933, 100) ascribed it to Alsace on the basis of style and dated it about 1480. He also noted the lavish use of pile work which he thought characteristic

Fig. 188. *Two Riddles of the Queen of Sheba,* by Israhel van Meckenem, copied after a print by Master E.S. Engraving, Upper Rhineland, late fifteenth century. Collection Edmond de Rothschild, Musée du Louvre, Paris.

of Strasbourg. Ostoia (1972, 73–76) believed that the Metropolitan Museum's tapestry was woven in the Upper Rhineland, probably in Alsace and possibly in Strasbourg, during the last quarter of the fifteenth century. She based this attribution partly on the use of Alsatian dialect in the inscriptions and partly on stylistic and technical grounds. She (1972, 75) referred to Göbel in discussing the association of knotted-pile work with Strasbourg and noted that there is some pile work in another tapestry in the Metropolitan Museum (61 in this catalogue) that she had attributed tentatively to Basel (1972, 76 n. 5).

In terms of dialect, style, and technique, the *Two Riddles* belongs with the group of tapestries to which the Metropolitan Museum's fragment of *Der Busant* (58) also belongs.[3] All of these tapestries share characteristics that are accepted as being typical of Alsatian work of the late fifteenth century. Three of them show coats of arms representing members of Strasbourg families, and these have been dated in the last quarter of the fifteenth century (see 58 and note 4 in that entry). The pile work in the Metropolitan Museum's *Two Riddles* suggests but does not prove that it was woven in Strasbourg. Rapp and Stucky-Schürer attributed it to that city on considerations of style and dated it about 1490–1500.[4]

RELATED TAPESTRIES

No duplicate tapestry is known to have survived, and we do not know of any that might have belonged with this one in a series of hangings or covers with related subjects. Whether or not such a series ever existed is a matter of conjecture.

Göbel (1933), Kurth (1926 and 1940–41), and Ostoia (1972) collected data and illustrations concerning several other German and Swiss tapestries with the same subject that range in date from 1506 to 1611. In most instances the compositions and inscriptions are similar to those in the Metropolitan Museum's tapestry, but they are not identical.[5]

HISTORY

In the collection of J. Pierpont Morgan from before 1906 to 1916.
With French and Company, New York, briefly in 1916.
In the collection of W. Hinckle Smith, Philadelphia, from 1916 to 1970.
Property of French and Company, 1970–71.
Purchased by the MMA, The Cloisters Collection, 1971.

EXHIBITIONS

London, Burlington Fine Arts Club, 1906. *Exhibition of Early German Art.* Cat. no. 11, pl. LXVIII. Lent by J. Pierpont Morgan.
London, Victoria and Albert Museum, sometime between 1906 and 1912. Lent by J. Pierpont Morgan.

New York, MMA, 1912–16. Lent by J. Pierpont Morgan.
Moscow, Pushkin State Museum of Fine Arts, and Leningrad, The Hermitage, 1990. *Decorative Arts from Late Antiquity to Late Gothic* (from The Metropolitan Museum of Art and The Art Institute of Chicago) (in Russian). Cat. no. 69; illus. in color.
Basel, Historisches Museum, 1990. *Zahm und Wild: Basler und Strassburger Bildteppiche des 15. Jahrhunderts.* Checklist no. 56.

PUBLICATIONS

von der Leyen, Friedrich. "Zu den Rätseln der Konigin von Saba." *Beilage zur Allgemeinen Zeitung* 175 (1907). Described briefly (see below, Ostoia 1972, p. 73 n. 1).
Migeon, Gaston. *Les arts du tissu.* Paris, 1909, p. 263. Described briefly; illus. p. 261.
Hunter 1912, p. 226. Mentioned.
Pringsheim, report recorded in "Berichte: Sitzungen der Kunstwissenschaftlichen Gesellschaft in München 1913–15. Sitzung am 2. Februar 1914." *Münchner Jahrbuch der Bildenden Kunst* 9 (1914–15) p. 246. Discussed briefly.
Schmitz, Hermann. *Bildteppiche.* Berlin, [1919], p. 124. Mentioned.
Burckhardt, Rudolf F. *Gewirkte Bildteppiche des XV. und XVI. Jahrhunderts im Historischen Museum zu Basel.* Leipzig, 1923, pp. 51–52, n. 10. Discussed briefly; illus. fig. 61.
Hunter 1925, pp. 209–10. Described; illus. pl. XIV,a.
Kurth 1926, pp. 133, 135, 242. Discussed in detail; illus. pl. 153.
Saxe, Eleanor B. "A Gothic Pile Fabric." *Metropolitan Museum Studies* 1 (1928–29) pp. 68, 70. Discussed briefly.
Thomson 1930, pp. 130–31. Described.
Göbel 1933, pp. 100, 193. Discussed; illus. fig. 76.
Kurth, Betty. "The Riddles of the Queen of Sheba in Swiss and Alsatian Tapestries." *Connoisseur* 106 (1940–41) pp. 234–35, 266. Discussed; illus. no. 1.
Ostoia, Vera K. "Two Riddles of the Queen of Sheba." *Metropolitan Museum Journal* 6 (1972) pp. 73–96. Complete study of the tapestry, its design sources, iconography, and history; illus. fig. 1.
Kajitani, Nobuko. "Two Riddles of the Queen of Sheba: Technical Notes." *Metropolitan Museum Journal* 6 (1972) pp. 97–103. Appendix to Ostoia article, treating materials, structure, and condition; illus. and with microphotographs and diagrams, figs. 1–9.
J. L. S. [Joseph L. Schrader]. "Tapestry: Two Riddles of the Queen of Sheba." *MMA Notable Acquisitions 1965–1975.* New York, 1975, p. 164. Discussed briefly; illus.
Rapp Buri, Anna, and Monica Stucky-Schürer. *Zahm und Wild: Basler und Strassburger Bildteppiche des 15. Jahrhunderts.* Mainz, 1990, pp. 372–74. Described and discussed in detail; illus. in color p. 373.

NOTES

1. A note in the files of the MMA Department of Medieval Art indicates that "Mr. Samuels" (probably Milton Samuels) said that the tapestry had been repaired before French and Company bought it in 1916. It has been restored further since it has been at the MMA.

2. For discussions and illustrations of the *David and Bathsheba* tapestry in the Burrell Collection, see Kurth 1926, pp. 134–35, 242, pl. 154. See also Emil Major, *Strassburger Bildteppiche aus gotischer Zeit* (Basel, [1943]) pp. 23–25, fig. 11; also *Treasures from the Burrell Collection,* exh. cat. by William Wells, Hayward Gallery (London, 1975) no. 69, not illus. Major (p. 24) deduced from the evidence of the coats of arms displayed on it that the tapestry was woven for the Strasbourg merchant Heinrich Ingold and his wife Clara Gerbott around 1480. See also Anna Rapp Buri and Monica Stucky-Schürer, *Zahm und Wild: Basler und Strassburger*

Bildteppiche des 15. Jahrhunderts (Mainz, 1990) pp. 346–48, illus. in color.

3. See, in this catalogue, 58, note 3, for a list of the tapestries in that group, with references. See also Digby 1980, p. 24, for a note on the Alsatian dialect in the inscriptions of the *Busant* tapestries.

4. The author thanks Anna Rapp Buri and Monica Stucky-Schürer for sharing their opinion with him during a discussion in the Metropolitan Museum in June 1988. See their publication of 59 in *Zahm und Wild*, pp. 372–74.

5. The earliest tapestry in this group is an example that was said to have been dated 1506. It is known only from a description that Carl Becker gave of it in 1878 after he had seen it in the Boasberg Antiquarian Museum in Amsterdam; see Vera K. Ostoia, "Two Riddles of the Queen of Sheba," *Metropolitan Museum Journal* 6 (1972), pp. 80, 82. The second piece, which is the one that Prings-heim reported on in 1914 (see Publications), is dated 1544 (earlier reported as 1541) and is now at the Caramoor Center for Music and the Arts in Katonah, New York; see Ostoia, "Two Riddles," pp. 80–81; it is illustrated in Betty Kurth, "The Riddles of the Queen of Sheba in Swiss and Alsatian Tapestries," *Connoisseur* 106 (1940–41) no. IV. The third example, in the Historisches Museum in Basel, is dated 1561; see Ostoia, "Two Riddles," p. 81 and fig. 8. The fourth piece, dated 1566, was in the parish church of Kirschkau and then with the prince of Reuss in Schleiz; see Ostoia, "Two Riddles," p. 81; illustrated in Kurth, "Riddles," no. III. The fifth example, with a date that Kurth, "Riddles," p. 236 and illus. no. V, believed had been changed through faulty repair from 1611 to 1511, was formerly the property of French and Company; see also Ostoia, "Two Riddles," pp. 81–82, fig. 9. The sixth example is only a fragment of a tapestry that dates from the second quarter of the sixteenth century. It shows the two children handling the apples at the feet of two robed figures and above two armorial shields; see Ostoia, "Two Riddles," p. 82, and Göbel 1933, p. 193 and fig. 182, then the property of Margraf and Company in Berlin. Kurth, "Riddles," pp. 236–37, illus. no. VI, published a sixteenth-century Swiss tapestry that she believed showed the same subject, though misunderstood, with inscriptions that she could not explain.

60

Hanging with a Simulated Silk Textile Pattern

Part of a dossal or wall hanging

Probably Nuremberg, 1475–1525
Linen warp; wool and bast fiber wefts
3 ft. 3⁵/₈ in. × 7 ft. 3⁵/₈ in. (1.01 m × 2.23 m)
14–15 warp yarns per inch, 5–6 per centimeter
The Cloisters Collection, 1949 (49.144)

CONDITION

The fabric has been cut at both ends but retains its original selvages along the top and bottom edges. There are small spots of reweaving scattered throughout the field. The yellow and red wool wefts have faded somewhat. Some of the red yarns have turned from bluish red to brick red and the yellows have turned to a straw tone.

DESCRIPTION

The entire field is covered with a pattern imitating that of a class of silk velvets and damasks, brocaded with gilt yarns, of the second half of the fifteenth century and early sixteenth century. Approximately one and a half vertical repeats of the pattern are represented. The upper two-thirds of the field shows the whole unit, which is made up of rows of larger and smaller ovoid leaves, each leaf having five points, offset to the side one from the other by the width of half a leaf. The leaves are dark red (representing the pile of a voided velvet or one weave face of a damask) against a ground of lighter red (the ground of the velvet or the second weave face of the damask). In the center of each leaf is a symmetrical unit consisting of a pomegranate surrounded by acanthus leaves. The units are larger and more elaborate in the narrow ovoid leaves than in the wide ones. These units, and the three cinquefoils that top each one, are yellow (representing the gilt metal brocading yarns in the velvet or damask). A swag of yellow and red leaves, flowers, and pomegranates separates the bottoms of the narrow leaves from the tops of the wide ones. In this piece swags occur along the top of the field and again about two-thirds of the way down. Narrow guards, each having a white (bast fiber) stripe between two yellow (wool) stripes, border the field at top and bottom.

As indicated below (Related Tapestries), 60 is probably a section from a hanging that showed one or more figures against this ground pattern. Since most of the related pieces that are known to have survived show figures associated with Christian iconography, 60 may once have been part of a dossal that hung above an altar or a row of choir stalls. However one of the related pieces shows a lady with a unicorn, a motif that could have either secular or Christian connotations; therefore it follows that the Metropolitan Museum's piece may have come instead from a hanging meant to be used in a domestic setting. Von Wilckens (exh. cat. New York and Nuremberg 1986, 208–9), who did not treat this piece as a fragment from a larger hanging, believed that it was used in a domestic rather than ecclesiastical context.

SOURCE OF THE DESIGN

The pattern was inspired by a class of gilt-brocaded silk voided velvets and damasks that were woven in Europe during the second half of the fifteenth century and the first quarter of the next. The patterns in surviving silks show many variations on the same theme.[1] A similar pattern appears on a polychrome multiple-harness fabric woven with linen, wool, and metallic yarns that von Wilckens (exh. cat. New York and Nuremberg 1986, 209) attributed to Nuremberg and dated in the early sixteenth century. That hanging is also in the Metropolitan Museum.

MANUFACTURE AND DATE

When von Falke published the hanging in the Figdor sale catalogue (1930, no. 5), he called it Netherlandish and dated it about 1500. In 1949, in a letter to James Rorimer, Charles Iklé wrote that more recent research suggested that 60 was not Dutch but south German and that it may perhaps have been woven in Ulm.[2] Since it has a linen warp and belongs stylistically to a small group of tapestries that was certainly woven in Germany, there can be no question that it, too, was woven there.

60

Tapestries with this kind of silk pattern have traditionally been ascribed to Franconia or to Nuremberg. Göbel published as Franconian a tapestry with figures against the same ground pattern and dated it about 1450.[3] Kurth attributed a fragment showing figures on a similar red, yellow, and white ground to Franconia and dated it about 1450, and another fragment with a more elaborate ground pattern in red and yellow to Eichstätt, not far from Nuremberg, first half of the sixteenth century.[4] Franses (1986, 208) attributed to Franconia, middle of the fifteenth century, a hanging showing the figure of a female martyr saint against the ground pattern that appears in 60 and in the same colors (fig. 189). Von Wilckens (exh. cat. New York and Nuremberg 1986, 208) published the Metropolitan Museum's tapestry as Nuremberg work of the last quarter of the fifteenth century on the strength of its showing a pomegranate pattern which she noted was used occasionally in the background of Nuremberg tapestries of the middle and third quarter of the fifteenth century. A piece with the same field pattern as 60, now in the chapel of Leeds Castle in Maidstone, Kent, is said to have come from a church near Strasbourg.[5]

Therefore, while we have grounds for suggesting that the Metropolitan Museum's hanging may have been woven in Nuremberg, we have no proof that tapestries with patterns like this were being woven only there and not in other parts of Germany as well. The date of manufacture can be estimated roughly from the fact that luxury silks with this kind of pattern were being produced for fashionable markets from about 1450 to 1525. We do not have enough reliable data to determine how early or late each variation of the pattern appeared during that time span. Since textiles with repeat patterns like this were being woven on multiple-harness looms in Germany in the early years of the sixteenth century (see von Wilckens, exh. cat. New York and Nuremberg 1986, 209), it seems reasonable to suggest that 60 would have been designed and woven later than the earliest silks but probably no later than these other German (perhaps Nuremberg) hangings that contain linen, wool, and metallic yarns.

RELATED TAPESTRIES

The similar piece in Leeds Castle hangs as an antependium in the chapel (see note 5). The tapestry showing a female martyr saint standing in front of the same ground (fig. 189) belonged to the firm of S. Franses in London in 1986.[6] Göbel published two other pieces with this ground pattern, one with a lady and unicorn in the center, the other with a figure of Saint Margaret, also in the center.[7] Unfortunately Göbel noted neither the colors used for the textile pattern in those pieces nor their dimensions. Since the Leeds Castle and the Franses pieces show the same pattern as 60 in the same colors, and since the latter is also about the same height as 60, it is possible that these three pieces once belonged to the

Fig. 189. *Female Saint against a Ground of Brocaded Velvet.* Tapestry, here attributed to Germany, perhaps Nuremberg, late fifteenth or early sixteenth century. Collection of S. Franses, Ltd., London.

same hanging or set of hangings. It is also possible that the two pieces published by Göbel belonged with that group: the lady with the unicorn is drawn in the same style as the saint in the Franses tapestry.

HISTORY

According to the Figdor sale catalogue, formerly in the possession of Lorenz Gedon, whose collection was sold by M. Heberle, Munich, June 17–21, 1884. It probably was the piece listed in the Gedon catalogue as no. 881, a wool antependium with yellow motifs on a floral ground, sixteenth century, measuring 1.15 m × 2.10 m, not illus.

Sold, *Die Sammlung Dr. Albert Figdor, Wien*, Vienna, June 11–13, 1930, pt. 1, vol. 1, no. 5, not illus. Catalogued by Otto von Falke.

In the collections of Leopold Iklé and Fred Charles Iklé.

Purchased by the MMA, The Cloisters Collection, from Fred Charles Iklé, 1949.

EXHIBITIONS

Vienna, K. K. Österreichisches Museum für Kunst und Industrie, 1890. Tapestry exhibition, title unknown. Lent by Dr. Albert Figdor.

New York, MMA, and Nuremberg, Germanisches Nationalmuseum, 1986. *Gothic and Renaissance Art in Nuremberg 1300–1550.* Catalogue entry by Leonie von Wilckens, no. 68, illus. in color.

PUBLICATIONS

Riegl, Alois. "Die Gobelins-Ausstellung im Oesterr. Museum." *Mittheilungen des K. K. Oesterreichischen Museums für Kunst und Industrie*, n.s. 5, no. 51 (1890) p. 55. Mentioned.

Franses, Simon. *European Tapestries 1450–1750: A Catalogue of Recent Acquisitions, Spring 1986.* London, 1986, p. 10. Mentioned.

NOTES

1. See, for example, Barbara Markowsky, *Europäische Seidengewebe des 13.–18. Jahrhunderts* (Cologne, 1976) nos. 41, 45, 84, 85, all illus.
2. Letter dated November 12, 1949, in the files of the MMA Department of Medieval Art, not published.
3. Göbel 1933, p. 162, fig. 131.
4. Kurth 1926, p. 268 and pl. 289b, a piece in the Bayerisches Nationalmuseum, Munich, showing the dove of the Holy Spirit, musical angels, Saints Ursula and Agnes, the Christ Child, and the young Saint John the Baptist, called Franconian, mid-fifteenth century; also pp. 193 and 276, and pl. 325a, a fragment in the same museum, showing a small armorial shield against the textile-patterned ground, which Kurth thought had probably been woven in the convent at Eichstätt in the first half of the sixteenth century. See also pieces with related but less similar grounds and Christian figures, like pl. 287, with the Man of Sorrows, and pl. 288, with Saint Anne, the Virgin, and the Christ Child, both pieces in the Germanisches Nationalmuseum, Nuremberg, both called Franconian, probably Nuremberg, mid-fifteenth century.
5. See *Leeds Castle, Maidstone, Kent*, Leeds Castle Foundation (London, 1985) p. 79, view of the chapel in color. The present author is indebted to Simon Franses, who brought this tapestry to his attention.
6. See Simon Franses, *European Tapestries 1450–1750: A Catalogue of Recent Acquisitions, Spring 1986* (London, 1986) pp. 8–10, illus.; detail in color, p. 9.
7. Göbel 1933, p. 162, fig. 131, the unicorn piece, then owned by Julius Böhler, Munich, and p. 162, the Saint Margaret piece, then owned by J. Rosenbaum, Frankfurt am Main, not illus.

61

Scenes from the Life of the Virgin

An antependium

Upper Rhineland, Strasbourg, about 1500
Linen warp; wool, linen, silk, silver, and gilt wefts; wool pile yarns
3 ft. 5 in. × 11 ft. 6 in. (1.04 m × 3.51 m)
15–20 warp yarns per inch, 6–8 per centimeter
Gift of Charles F. Iklé, 1957 (57.126)

CONDITION

The fabric retains its original finish on all four sides. The selvages at the upper and lower edges were covered with narrow yellow tape. As the illustration in the Lipperheide sale catalogue of 1909 shows, the fabric had been damaged by that date. A seam running from top to bottom, following the right edge of the left-hand pictorial panel, showed that the left end of the piece had been cut off and then partially restored: the left-hand panel and the section of vine border above it had been returned, but the panel was placed a bit higher than it had been, presumably to fill the space that the strip of fictive fringe, which was missing, had taken up. Bits of fabric along the right edge of the panel and in the vine border above it were either turned under in the seam or lost. When the tapestry came to the Metropolitan Museum, the piece was still seamed, but the panel and a strip of modern fabric imitating the fringe were in their proper positions.

There are a few small spots of reweaving, especially in the lower right corner, but none of them has altered the drawing. The dyes have faded to some extent but the colors are still strong and rich. The metallic yarns, particularly the silver ones, have lost some color and luster due to oxidation.

DESCRIPTION AND SUBJECT

The tapestry was designed to serve as an altar frontal.[1] Along the top is a simulated superfrontal showing a leafy vine with stylized columbine blossoms of different colors coursing across a ground of solid red. A narrow band of simulated polychrome fringe serves as a border along the bottom of the superfrontal. At the center of this band, two flying angels hold up between them a representation of the veil of Veronica.

The main section of the antependium contains a row of six rectangular compartments, each showing one or more scenes from the life of the Virgin. The left and right ends of this section are finished with narrow stripes covered with polychrome lozenges. The six pictorial compartments show the following subjects from left to right: the Birth of the Virgin, the Annunciation, the Visitation, the Nativity combined with the Annunciation to the Shepherds, the Presentation of the Christ Child in the Temple combined with the Purification of the Virgin, and finally the Coronation of the Virgin. The first, second, and fifth scenes, all set in interior spaces, are viewed through archways. In the Birth scene, Anne is shown sitting up in bed at the left, opening her arms to receive the infant Mary, whom two women standing behind the bed present to her. A rich textile with a damask or voided velvet pattern hangs at the head of the bed, and there are three arched, diamond-paned windows in the back wall of the chamber. A small table with a ewer, a bowl, and a towel stands in the left foreground, and to the right of it a wooden tub of water and another towel on the floor. The same kind of floor covered with rectangular polychrome tiles also appears in the next scene, the Annunciation. The small chamber has a flat planked ceiling with a curtain covering the left part of the rear wall and two rectangular diamond-paned windows in the right part of the wall. The Virgin sits on a bench in the left foreground and faces Gabriel, who kneels at the right. He holds a staff in his right hand and salutes Mary with his left. She has been interrupted while reading a book that lies open on her lap, and she raises her hands in surprise. There is a book box on the floor at her feet and a pot of lilies next to it, between the two figures. Another book lies on the simple bed that extends across the back of the room. A bust of God the Father appears in a curling band of clouds in the upper right corner of the scene, and shafts of light preceded by the dove of the Holy Spirit radiate from it toward the Virgin's head.

In the next compartment to the right the Visitation takes place in a meadow. Mary stands in the foreground at the left opposite Elizabeth, who places her right hand on the Virgin's arm and takes Mary's left hand in her own. There are plants in the foreground, trees, build-

61

ings, and hills in the middle distance, and a line of low shrubs along the horizon. A large dove perches on a rock at the left, and a spotted stag prances in the middle distance at the right. Since the dove has no halo, it could not have been intended as a representation of the Holy Spirit. Ostoia (1965–66, 298) noted that the image of the stag has at times been used as a metaphor for the Virgin or for Christ. She also observed that there may be references here to the Song of Songs, which was included in the Office for the Feast of the Visitation. As she pointed out, some of the names applied in that canticle to the bride were later applied to the Virgin. In this instance the image is that of a dove: "My dove in the clefts of the rock . . ." (Canticle of Canticles 2:14). Also, the bride speaks of her beloved three times in the song as a roe or a young hart, as for example when she says, ". . . he cometh leaping upon the mountains, skipping over the hills. My beloved is like a roe, or a young hart" (Canticle of Canticles 2:8–9; with similar images in 2:17 and 8:14).

In the next scene, the Nativity, which is also set out-of-doors, Joseph and Mary are both shown kneeling in the left foreground. The stable rises behind them. The Christ Child, nude and surrounded by rays of light, lies on the ground between Mary at the left and the end of a wicket fence at the right. The heads of the ox and ass appear above this fence in the middle distance. A shepherd tends his sheep on a distant hill at the right, and an angel appears above him. In the upper right corner of the scene there is a bust of God the Father surrounded by a band of clouds from which emanate rays of light.

The fifth scene is set inside the temple. Three arched, diamond-paned windows appear in the rear wall; the floor is paved with polychrome rectangular tiles. The altar in the middle of the space is covered on the front by a rich damask antependium with a fringed superfrontal and on the top by a diapered cloth. Mary, standing next to the altar at the right, places the nude Christ Child on the altar. Joseph stands behind her. Five coins, each marked with a fleur-de-lis (florins), rest on the altar cloth. All first-born Jewish boys were to be presented in the temple and later serve there as adults; but boys of the tribe of Judah could be redeemed by an offering of five coins. Simeon, wearing over his robe a damask or voided velvet tunic cut rather like a sleeveless dalmatic, stands in the foreground at the left and raises his hands in wonder at the sight of the Child, whom he recognizes as the Redeemer. Jewish law also required that the boy's mother be purified at the time of his presentation. The other figures and objects in the scene refer to that ceremony (the Church celebrated the two events on the same day). The young woman behind the altar in the center of the scene is the maid who came to the temple with Mary and Joseph. She holds a basket containing two turtle doves in her right hand and a lighted candle in her left. As Ostoia (1965–66, 300) indicated, these are both connected with the ceremony of Mary's purification.

In the sixth and last compartment, at the right end of the antependium, Mary kneels in the center foreground before the enthroned figures of God the Father at the left

658

and Christ at the right. Jesus places a crown on His mother's head as the dove of the Holy Spirit appears above. A rich damask or voided velvet fabric covers the back and seat of the throne of majesty. Four angels stand behind the throne; the two outer ones play musical instruments while the two in the center hold their hands in attitudes of prayer. An arch of curling clouds finishes the composition at the top while the lower part is represented as a polychrome tiled floor, essentially the same kind of floor that appears in the interior spaces at the left. Ostoia (1965–66, 301–2) also pointed out the fact that the Coronation scene appears to have been represented here in reverse, with God the Father blessing Mary with His left hand, Christ holding the crown with His left hand, and Christ sitting at the left hand of God the Father rather than the right. However, in a comparable representation on a panel painting illustrated by Ostoia (1965–66, fig. 14), the two deities sit in the same relative positions but use their right hands to make the gestures.

Detail of 61

Detail of 61

659

Detail of 61

Detail of 61

Ostoia (1965–66, 293) noted that the six main subjects represented here were celebrated at the time as feast days of the Virgin, with the Coronation in this case substituting for the Assumption. She also suggested that the choice of subjects could be interpreted as an allusion to the redemption of man and to the Passion. For Rapp and Stucky-Schürer (1990, 378), the six scenes refer among other things to the Passion, which is represented by Veronica's veil. Ostoia, throughout her exhaustive study of this tapestry, also noted and discussed other iconographic details of special interest. In regard to matters of iconography it is important to note, and also curious, that the designer or weaver did not choose to represent some of the other major events in Mary's life, like her presentation in the temple, her marriage, her presence at the Crucifixion and the Deposition, and her assumption. Therefore it seems likely that the tapestry was woven to commemorate a specific set of feast days that the nuns of a particular order or convent favored.

Silver and gilt weft yarns were used to represent objects that would in reality be made of precious metals or of light. Among these are the florins on the altar, the crowns, and details in the nimbuses and certain garments. Bleached linen yarns and colored silks were used to render the eyes and as highlights on a variety of objects. The tassel on the Virgin's cushion in the Annunciation and the pelt of the black sheep in the Annunciation to the Shepherds were executed in knotted (Ghiordes knot) pile work.

SOURCE OF THE DESIGN

Ostoia, after her intensive search for the source of each composition, concluded that the tapestry designs were derived from some series of narrative paintings made to be installed in a retable or from a set of manuscript illustrations or prints or even another series of tapestries. She noted (1965–66, 294) that the composition of the Birth of the Virgin recalls representations in certain

Detail of 61

Detail of 61

Alsatian stained-glass windows reflecting the style of the Master E.S. For the Annunciation, Ostoia (1965–66, 296) connected two compositions with the tapestry either as direct prototypes or as parallel reflections of an unidentified common source. The first is a small panel painting in the Reinhart Collection in Winterthur that has been attributed to the Master of the Frankfurt Paradise Garden, among others, and dated about 1420–40.[2] Fischel (1947, caption fig. 1) attributed the panel to the Master of the Thennenbacher Altar in Freiburg, and Futterer[3] gave it to the master who painted the Coronation of the Virgin in that altar. While there are a few minor differences in the details, the tapestry and the Reinhart panel show the same images but reversed in relation to one another. The left-right orientation of the image in the tapestry agrees with that in a woodcut cited by Ostoia (1965–66, fig. 7) as an alternate possible source. The woodcut is usually attributed to the Master of the Nuremberg Passion and dated in the middle of the fifteenth century.

For the composition of the Visitation scene, Ostoia had no prototype to offer but called attention (1965–66, 298 and fig. 10) to a fragment of early sixteenth-century Upper Rhenish or northern Swiss tapestry that shows two very similar figures. This piece is now in the Burrell Collection, Glasgow (see Related Tapestries). Obviously the two compositions were derived from the same unknown source. Concerning the Presentation in the Temple, Ostoia (1965–66, 300) observed that its form derived in a general way from Italian prototypes. Finally she noted (1965–66, 302) that the style but not the form of the Coronation of the Virgin relates it to the panel with that subject in the Staufen Altar in Freiburg im Breisgau (Fischel, 1947, fig. 6), which has been dated in the first third of the fifteenth century.

At the close of her study, Ostoia propounded an ingenious theory whereby the tapestry designs might have been taken at a very long remove from the compositions in a lost series of six tapestries of the Life of the Virgin that Philippe le Bon bought in 1423 as a gift for Pope

Martin V and whose designs may have influenced wall paintings and woodcuts associated with the cardinal Juan de Torquemada. As Ostoia demonstrated (1965–66, fig. 16), the composition of the woodcut for the Annunciation in Torquemada's *Meditations* (first edition, Rome, 1467) agrees almost precisely with the composition in the Metropolitan Museum's tapestry. However, since the woodcuts for the Nativity and the Presentation in the Temple do not agree with those scenes in the tapestry, it is clear that the prints in the *Meditations* did not serve as the source for the tapestry designer.

There is a detail to add to Ostoia's study. She did not list as a possible source for the Nativity, or as a parallel derivation from some common source, a woodcut with the subject in reverse that has also been attributed to the Master of the Nuremberg Passion. Fischel published it in connection with the tapestry in 1947 (fig. 3), and some twenty years later Koreny (1968, 66–67 n. 2) considered it again. Koreny suggested that this print and the one of the Annunciation, both having the same dimensions, may be the sole survivors of a more extensive series of prints that were probably derived from a series of Upper Rhenish panel paintings. The Nativity scenes have similar figures and settings in print and tapestry, but the correspondence is not virtually exact, as it is in the case of the Annunciation. Nevertheless it is certainly possible that the compositions in the tapestry were derived from Koreny's hypothetical print series, which might also have included, in addition to the other scenes, an Adoration of the Kings, a print that Fischel (1947, fig. 4) published with the Annunciation and the Nativity, all as the work of the Master of the Nuremberg Passion.

MANUFACTURE AND DATE

When it was sold from the collection of Franz-Joseph von Lipperheide in 1909 (see History), the tapestry was dated about 1500 but given no national or regional attribution. Schmitz (1919, 341 n. 21) assigned it to southern Germany but referred to its date simply as "late gothic." It was described in the Iklé sale catalogue in 1923 (see History) as Swabian and dating from the last quarter of the fifteenth century. Kurth (1926, 162) offered elaborate reasons for making the same regional attribution, basing her arguments on the evidence of both style and heraldic motifs. She regarded the figure types, style of composition, and palette as typically Swabian and cited specific paintings of the last quarter of the fifteenth century by Hans Schüchlin, Friedrich Herlin, and Bartholomäus Zeitblom in connection with the tapestry compositions for the Visitation and Nativity. Kurth also believed that the design of the simulated superfrontal—a flowering vine meandering across a red ground—indicated that the Metropolitan Museum's tapestry was manufactured in the same shop that produced two strips of tapestry with a similar pattern; the strips are now in the Germanisches Nationalmuseum, Nuremberg (Kurth 1926, pl. 235). These strips also show two coats of arms, one unidentified, the other identified as the arms of the Swabian family von Knöringen, whose seat was at Augsburg but who also owned lands on the border of Franconia.

We agree with Göbel (1933, 136–37), who found Kurth's arguments concerning style untenable, especially in relation to the specific artists she cited. Göbel also expressed the opinion that the Metropolitan Museum's tapestry seemed to be more like Nuremberg work than Swabian. In discussing the two tapestry strips with vine patterns now in Nuremberg, Göbel noted that since the von Knöringen family held lands on the border of Swabia and Franconia they could have had the strips woven in the general region of Nuremberg. His own attribution for the Metropolitan Museum's tapestry placed it tentatively in Swabia with a date of about 1490. He, like Kurth, believed that the Museum's tapestry and the two ornamental strips were woven in the same shop. We cannot endorse this opinion since the pattern at the top of 61 is only similar to that on the two strips in Nuremberg and not exactly like it as it might have been had it come from the same shop.

It is of some interest that after Ostoia published her study of the tapestry a numismatist in Paris identified the coins represented on the altar in the Presentation scene as belonging to the currency of Strasbourg.[4] In ascribing the tapestry to the Upper Rhine region, Ostoia (1965–66, 287) indicated that she was in fact referring to a region that includes the lower part of old Swabia, the northern part of modern Switzerland, and the southwest corner of modern Germany.

Rorimer and Ostoia believed that the tapestry was woven in the third quarter of the fifteenth century. The other writers dated it in the last quarter, Göbel (1933, fig. 107a) specifying a date about 1490, and the compiler of the von Lipperheide sale catalogue (1909, 108) one about 1500, all presumably on the grounds of style.

After studying the piece at first hand, Rapp and Stucky-Schürer concluded that it could not have been produced before 1500,[5] and they published it (1990, 376) as Strasbourg work of about 1500.

RELATED TAPESTRIES

No other tapestry woven after the same cartoon is known to have survived, nor do we know of any fragments or small pieces that represent any of the individual compositions. Very similar figures of Elizabeth and Mary appear again, with notable changes of costume, in a much wider setting, and with the addition of speech scrolls, in a fragmentary weaving of the Visitation that has been dated about 1505. It is now in the Burrell Collection, Glasgow.[6] The many different details, as well as the breadth of the setting, greater than that in the corresponding section of the Metropolitan Museum's tapestry, indicate that this piece could not have been woven after the same cartoon. At some time in the past it was cut into the shape of a hood for a cope and given a border of metallic galloon and a deep fringe along the sides and bottom. The two tapestry strips in Nuremberg with a pattern similar to that on the simulated superfrontal are not directly related to the Metropolitan Museum's antependium.

HISTORY

Sold, *Kunstbesitz eines bekannten norddeutschen Sammlers* [Franz-Joseph von Lipperheide], pt. 1, *Textilien*, Galerie Helbing, Munich, October 25–30, 1909, no. 2619, pl. 41.
Sold, *Sammlung Leopold Iklé, St. Gallen*, Zunfthaus zur Meise, Zurich, September 18 and following days, 1923, pt. 1, no. 784, pls. 141, 142.
In the collection of Charles F. Iklé until 1957.
Given to the MMA by Charles F. Iklé, 1957.

EXHIBITIONS

None known.

PUBLICATIONS

Schmitz, Hermann. *Bildteppiche*. Berlin, [1919], p. 341 n. 21. Mentioned.
Kurth 1926, pp. 162, 257. Discussed at length; illus. pls. 233, 234.
Göbel 1933, pp. 136–37. Discussed briefly; illus. fig. 107a.
Fischel, Lilli. "Oberrheinische Malerei im Spiegel des frühen Kupferstichs." *Zeitschrift für Kunstwissenschaft* 1 (1947) fig. 5. Illus. detail.
"Additions to the Collections: Medieval Art and The Cloisters." Annual Report for 1959–1960. In *MMA Bulletin*, n.s. 19 (1960–61) p. 61. Described briefly; detail illus. p. 45.
Rorimer, James J., et al. *The Cloisters*. 3d ed., rev. MMA, New York, 1963, pp. ix, 193. Discussed briefly.

Lafontaine-Dosogne, Jacqueline. *Iconographie de l'enfance de la Vierge dans l'empire Byzantin et en Occident*. Brussels, 1964–65, vol. 2, p. 47. Mentioned, with the same attribution that Göbel had made.
Ostoia, Vera K. "A Tapestry Altar Frontal with Scenes from the Life of the Virgin." *MMA Bulletin*, n.s. 24 (1965–66) pp. 287–303. Complete stylistic and iconographic study; illus. figs. 1, 2, 6, 9, 11, 13, 15, full view and details of each of the six pictorial compositions.
von Gynz-Rekowski, Georg. "Der Marienteppich im Dommuseum zu Halberstadt." *Niederdeutsche Beiträge zur Kunstgeschichte* 7 (1968) p. 168. Mentioned with reference to the angels in the Coronation of the Virgin.
Koreny, Fritz. "Über die Anfänge der Reproduktionsgraphik Nördlich der Alpen." Ph.D. diss., University of Vienna, 1968, pp. 66–67 and nn. 1, 2. Discussed briefly; illus. figs. 3, 3a, full view and detail of the Annunciation.
Wells, William. *Treasures from the Burrell Collection*. Exh. cat., Hayward Gallery. London, 1975, no. 75. Mentioned; illus.
Rapp Buri, Anna, and Monica Stucky-Schürer. *Zahm und Wild: Basler und Strassburger Bildteppiche des 15. Jahrhunderts*. Mainz, 1990, pp. 376–78. Described and discussed in detail; color illus. pp. 376–77.

NOTES

1. Anna Rapp Buri and Monica Stucky-Schürer, *Zahm und Wild: Basler und Strassburger Bildteppiche des 15. Jahrhunderts* (Mainz, 1990) pp. 376, 378, questioned whether this piece is an antependium. They believed that it had served as a wall hanging and noted that the border along the top seemed to be a later addition. However, since the lower edge of the composite border—really a fictive superfrontal—is connected to the row of pictorial panels with double-interlocked wefts, it is clear that the border is part of the original weaving.
2. Walter Hugelshofer made this attribution in his "Eine Verkündigung vom Meisters des Frankfurter Paradiesgärtleins," *Pantheon* 1 (1928) p. 66, color illus. facing p. 58.
3. I[lse] Futterer, "Zur Malerei des frühen XV. Jahrhunderts im Elsasz," *Jahrbuch der preuszischen Kunstsammlungen* 49 (1928) p. 197 and fig. 9. The Thennenbacher Altar, which Lilli Fischel, "Oberrheinische Malerei im Spiegel des frühen Kupferstichs," *Zeitschrift für Kunstwissenschaft* 1 (1947) caption for fig. 6, called the "Altar aus Staufen," is preserved in the Augustinermuseum, Freiburg.
4. From correspondence conducted between Bonnie Young, The Cloisters, and M. Dhenin, Cabinet des Médailles, Bibliothèque Nationale, Paris, in 1978. Letter in the files at The Cloisters.
5. The author thanks Doctors Monica Stucky-Schürer and Anna Rapp, who were making an intensive study of Upper Rhenish tapestries of this period, for sharing their opinion with him during a discussion held at the Metropolitan Museum in June 1988.
6. See Göbel 1933, fig. 40; see also *Treasures from the Burrell Collection*, exh. cat. by William Wells, Hayward Gallery (London, 1975) no. 75, text and illus.; see also Rapp and Stucky-Schürer, *Zahm und Wild*, p. 409, color illus.

62

Three Scenes from the Life of the Virgin

A wall hanging, dossal, or antependium

Tentatively ascribed to the Upper Rhineland, region of northern Switzerland, 1538–50
Linen warp; wool, linen, and metallic wefts
3 ft. 3/4 in. × 7 ft. 3 3/8 in. (.93 m × 2.22 m)
15–18 warp yarns per inch, 6–7 per centimeter
Gift of Richard C. Hunt, in memory of his grandfather, Richard M. Hunt, 1948 (48.161.4)

CONDITION

All four sides have been cut, and narrow blue tapes have been sewn along the edges. The dark brown wefts used as contours in the design have deteriorated and fallen out in many places, leaving the brownish linen warp yarns exposed to view. In some places these bare warp yarns have been stitched close together in an attempt to close the gaps that had opened in the fabric. The dark brown ground in the lower part of the hanging is restoration. There are a few small repairs by reweaving, especially along the top and left edges. All of the numerals in the date have been partly rewoven, but the repair does not seem to have changed the conformation of the figures. The colors have faded appreciably throughout.

DESCRIPTION AND SUBJECT

The hanging shows three episodes in the life of the Virgin. Each scene is framed by one of three arches in an arcade that stretches entirely across the field parallel to the picture plane. Only two of the four columns carrying the three arches are visible; the two outer ones disappear behind the strips of polychrome lozenges (right) or triangles (left) that border the field at the sides. The columns have capitals and bases trimmed with plain circular moldings; the shafts are decorated from the bottom upward to mid-height with relief carvings that resemble tall, thin acanthus leaves.

The subjects represented in the arched openings are, left to right, the Adoration of the Magi, the Annunciation, and the Marriage of Mary and Joseph. The sequence of episodes and each image itself have been presented to the viewer in reverse. Gabriel's greeting (inscribed on the scroll twisted around his staff), AVE

MARIA GRACIA, is in reverse, as is the date 1538 inscribed on the wall above the column right of center. Gabriel salutes Mary with his left hand, and in the marriage scene the couple join their left, rather than right, hands. After examining both faces of the weaving carefully and finding that what is now the back was never intended to be used as the front, we are sure that the reversals are not due simply to someone's having turned the tapestry back to front at some time in the past in order to have the brighter colors on the front, as was done with 26. It is clear that the pattern for 62 was woven in reverse, perhaps by mistake and most likely by an illiterate weaver.

In the Adoration of the Magi, Mary sits at the right in the foreground and holds the Child on her knees. He leans forward and runs His hands over the gold coins in a coffer held by the Magus kneeling at the left, looking not at the Magi but over His left shoulder at His mother. The dark-skinned Magus holding a horn full of incense stands at the far left side of the scene while the third king, who holds a ciborium containing myrrh, stands in the center behind the main figures and converses with the dark king. The upper part of the figure of Joseph appears above and behind Mary's head at the right. He is standing in the entrance of the stable which rises in the background, a small ashlar masonry building covered with a gabled roof of timber and straw. The ox and ass peer out from their places inside the stable; somehow their chins overlap the Virgin's halo, which glows a distance in front of them. In the upper left corner of the scene the vista opens out into the distance, with mountains at the left and a star shining high in the sky toward the right. All the figures are dressed in civilian costumes of the period. The Virgin wears a high-waisted gown with a low square neckline and straight long sleeves, a high-collared linen shirt, and a long veil. Each of the Magi has a hat with a narrow round brim and a low round crown encircled by an open golden crown.

The little building that serves as the setting for the Annunciation seems to be part of the same ashlar structure that serves as the stable in the Adoration. There is one rectangular window in the back wall and another in the side wall which is set at an acute angle at the right.

62

The floor is represented as a meadow with flowers growing along the front edge. The Virgin kneels before a prie-dieu in the left foreground of the scene. An open book rests on a cloth that has been thrown over the slanted reading surface, and a pot containing three lilies stands on the ground next to the forward edge of the prie-dieu. Gabriel, both wings raised, rushes into the room from the right. Behind him the view opens out into a distant landscape. He greets the Virgin with his upraised left hand and addresses her, the words on a scroll wrapped around his staff (in reverse, as noted), AVE MARIA GRACIA.

The marriage scene at the right takes place in an outdoor setting with flowers growing on the ground, trees and mountains in the distance, and three heavenly bodies or round clouds riding in the sky above. Mary stands at the left, Joseph at the right. Their left hands are clasped, and the angel covers them with his own right hand and raises his left hand in benediction. A narrow curtain decorated with a damask or voided velvet pattern and trimmed along the bottom with fringe stretches across the scene just behind the three figures. Mary wears her veil, shirt, and gown. Joseph wears a simple coat and a hooded cloak over it.

Undyed linen weft yarns were used to represent the Virgin's linen shirt, the angels' collars, the book and part of the cloth on the prie-dieu, Gabriel's scroll, and various highlights. Metallic yarns made of linen core yarns wrapped with strips of membrane coated with silver and/or gold leaf (the yarns are so much deteriorated that

one cannot now distinguish one metal from the other) were used to represent Mary's halos in the center and left scenes, the kings' crowns, and the angels' tiaras. A different metallic yarn, linen core yarn wrapped with narrow, flat gold-colored wire, was used to represent Mary's halo in the marriage scene.

Among surviving Germanic tapestries of the period, this piece is not unique in showing the chronological sequence of events in reverse. Göbel published two pieces of a somewhat later wall hanging with scenes from the life of Christ. One piece shows, from left to right, the Circumcision, the Adoration of the Shepherds, the Visitation, and the Annunciation. The other, apparently once attached to the first, shows, left to right, the Young Christ among the Doctors, the Flight into Egypt, the Presentation in the Temple, and the Adoration of the Magi.[1] However in those examples the characters seem to be right-handed, and while Gabriel gestures to Mary with his left hand in the Annunciation scene, the greeting inscribed on his scroll is not reversed.

Although 62 seems somewhat narrow for an antependium, it could have been made for a small altar in a convent chapel. It could also have served as a dossal above an altar or as a wall hanging (*Rücklaken*).

SOURCE OF THE DESIGN

No source has been identified. It seems likely that the three compositions were borrowed from prints.

665

Manufacture and Date

The attribution to the Upper Rhineland region of northern Switzerland is offered only as a tentative suggestion. The drawing and execution are so crude that it is pointless to attempt to relate this piece to others that were produced by more experienced hands. Nevertheless, the figure and facial types relate positively in a general way to those found in the Metropolitan Museum's tapestries showing Esther before Ahasuerus or the Madonna with eight saints (63 and 64), both of which were probably woven in that part of the Upper Rhineland. The date 1538 woven into this tapestry seems correct for the style of the composition and the fashion of Mary's gown. Therefore it seems reasonable to accept this date as representing the year in which the cartoon was painted. The weaving could have been executed some years later, certainly as late as 1550.[2]

Related Tapestries

No other tapestries that may have formed a set of hangings or altar decorations with this piece are known to have survived. Kurth published a small wall hanging or altar frontal (.88 m × 1.81 m) that shows three scenes from the life of the Virgin depicted in narrow, vertical rectangular compartments.[3] Left to right the scenes are as follows: the Annunciation, the Visitation, and the Nativity. Beyond the similarity of subject matter and general arrangement of the composition, that piece, which was woven in Nuremberg, bears no relation to 62.

History

Exhibition

Lincroft, New Jersey, Monmouth Museum, 1978–79. *The Glory of Angels.*

Publication

"Reports of the Departments: Medieval Art and The Cloisters, Gifts Received." Annual Report for 1948. In *MMA Bulletin*, n.s. 8 (1949–50) p. 22. Mentioned.

Notes

1. Göbel 1933, p. 187 and fig. 168. Göbel attributed the piece to northern Switzerland and dated it in the second half of the sixteenth century. It is preserved in the Historisches Museum in Basel.
2. Anna Rapp Buri and Monica Stucky-Schürer indicated to the author, in a conversation held at the Metropolitan Museum in 1988, that they believed the style of this piece points to a date well after 1538.
3. Kurth 1926, pp. 185, 270; pl. 299. The tapestry, which Kurth dated between 1461 and 1501, is preserved in the Sebalduskirche in Nuremberg.

63
Esther Pleading before Ahasuerus

A wall hanging

Tentatively ascribed to the Upper Rhineland, region of northern
Switzerland, 1540–60
Linen warp; wool, linen, and metallic wefts
3 ft. 7³/₄ in. × 7 ft. 1 in. (1.11 m × 2.16 m)
11–14 warp yarns per inch, 4–6 per centimeter
The Cloisters Collection, 1953 (53.35.4)

CONDITION

The original height and width of the fabric have survived intact. The tapestry still has its selvages along the top and bottom edges as well as its original warp finishes along the right and left sides. There are a few small spots of reweaving along the top edge and in several parts of Ahasuerus's robe. In other places, especially in the inscription bearing Ahasuerus's name, several places in his costume, and also in Haman's hat and right cuff, the original black weft yarns have deteriorated and fallen out and the bare warp is exposed. Parts of Esther's headdress, necklace, girdle, and the widest sleeve band have been rewoven with modern metal-wrapped yarn as have also parts of Ahasuerus's crown and girdle and of Haman's hat. The other gilt yarns, and the silver yarns, are original (see Description and Subject). The dyes, especially the reds, have faded a good deal on the face of the fabric. The bright green wefts used to weave the background plane have faded selectively according to the different dye lots that were used. As a result the background is now streaked with various tones of green that favor yellow in some places, blue in others.

DESCRIPTION AND SUBJECT

Six figures are ranged along the front of what appears to be a shallow meadow in which grow lilies of the valley and other flowering plants. The rest of the background appears as a striated green plane that is mostly covered by an arabesque of leafy vines bearing pomegranates and a variety of stylized blossoms. This kind of setting for figures arranged in parallel lines along the front of the composition is a traditional device that in tapestries from this region can be traced back at least to the second quarter of the fifteenth century.[1]

Esther, cousin and foster daughter of the Jew Mordecai, and now queen to King Ahasuerus of Persia, kneels in the center at the king's feet. Ahasuerus is seated on a tall throne covered with velvet or damask. Their names, HESTER and ASWERVS, appear inscribed on scrolls that float above their heads. Haman, also named on a scroll above his head, stands to the right of the throne and addresses a man in the lower right corner of the field. Two ladies stand behind Esther in the lower left third of the field. Diagonally striped narrow borders appear along the left and right edges of the field.

The scene derives from the Book of Esther in the Old Testament. Queen Esther has just learned that at the urging of his favorite minister, Haman, King Ahasuerus has sent out orders that all Jews in his kingdom are to be killed and their property taken. Esther goes to the king, kneels before him, and begs him to rescind the decree (Esther 8:3). Ahasuerus grants her petition, withdraws his decree against the Jews, and has Haman hanged. The two women at the left are the handmaidens who accompanied Esther on her mission to the throne room. At the right of the scene, an earlier moment in the story is represented, when Haman instructs a courier to distribute the king's decree against the Jews to the governors in all the king's provinces.

The words of Esther's petition and of the king's reply are inscribed on meandering banderoles that hover above the characters' heads. At each end the scrolls wind around adjacent stalks of the background vines. The queen says:

O künig lass mich gnad uṁ dich erwerben
d[a]z min folck nit also müsse sterben

(Oh, King, let me have your mercy
so that my people need not die).

And Ahasuerus answers:

Hester was din hertz begert
das soltu von mir gewert

(Esther, whatever your heart desires
you shall have from me).

The women's faces and the white parts of their costumes were woven with white linen weft yarns. The men's faces were rendered with pink and beige wool

63

yarns. Metallic yarns (narrow, flat wires of silver or gilt metal, wrapped on core yarns of white or yellow silk respectively) were used to represent objects made of precious metals, like the crowns, the point of Ahasuerus's scepter, the jewelry, girdles, and other costume details on some of the figures. Although the tapestry's dimensions would suit it for use as a frontal for a rather tall and narrow altar, both the dimensions and the subject matter suggest that it was probably made instead as a wall hanging for a domestic interior.

SOURCE OF THE DESIGN

The figures were probably derived from one or more prints in a book or illustrated Bible and then combined with a standard setting by the cartoon painter.

MANUFACTURE AND DATE

In Leopold Iklé's private (unpublished) catalogue of his tapestry collection, this piece was listed as south German, late fifteenth century. Göbel (1933, caption, fig. 154) attributed it to the Upper Rhineland and dated it at the end of the sixteenth century. Rorimer dated it in the middle of the century and noted that it represented "a type popular in South Germany and Switzerland." None

of these writers gave reasons for his attributions. The figure and facial types are like those in tapestries that have traditionally been attributed to the region encompassing the Upper Rhineland, the lower part of old Swabia, and the northern part of modern Switzerland; but at present we have no scientific proof that tapestries designed in this style were manufactured only in that district. It has been suggested that because the inscriptions were written in the dialect of the region, the tapestry ought to be regarded as Upper Rhenish work.[2]

As for placing the tapestry in time, the evidence of fashion in costume argues for a date no later than the second third of the sixteenth century. Since the garments represented in this piece are particularly splendid, it may be fair to assume that the tapestry would not have been woven very long after these forms had gone out of fashion. The basic style of the women's garments corresponds reasonably well to two small tapestries illustrated by Göbel (1933, figs. 149, 151a) as examples of work produced in Basel; they are dated in the weave 1548 and 1549 respectively. Comparing these pieces to another Upper Rhenish tapestry, dated 1566, one finds that the changes in the form of the female costumes, while less drastic than the changes in the men's clothes, are nevertheless perceptible.[3] In these examples and also in a tapestry-woven group portrait of the Echter von

668

Mespelbrunn family woven in the Middle Rhine region about 1564, the bodices of the women's gowns are longer and more tapered and the skirts have a fullness at the back.[4] This is quite unlike the short-waisted, round-skirted gowns of the earlier period, specifically the gowns represented in 63. In a wall hanging woven in Hesse in 1540 that shows examples of the artfulness of women, the costumes worn by Esther and Ahasuerus in a scene at the left end are very similar in both form and detail to their costumes in 63.[5] A scene of Herod's feast that appears at the right end of a north Swiss or Alsatian tapestry dated 1548 includes the figure of a serving girl in a costume that almost duplicates the one worn by the second handmaiden from the left in 63.[6] There can be little doubt that the costumes of both the men and the women in 63 place it firmly in the period about 1540–60.

RELATED TAPESTRIES

No hangings related to 63 in terms of style and subject matter are known to have survived. The subject of Esther pleading for the lives and rights of her people was an immensely popular one throughout the history of tapestry weaving. A few examples woven in the German-speaking territories during the sixteenth century have survived.[7]

HISTORY

In the collection of Leopold Iklé, Saint Gall, Switzerland; listed as no. 4326 in the unpublished catalogue of the collection.

In the collection of Fritz Iklé, Saint Gall.
In the collection of the Iklé family, Switzerland.
Purchased by the MMA, The Cloisters Collection, 1953.

EXHIBITIONS

New York, MMA, The Cloisters, 1953. Exhibition of new acquisitions.
New York, MMA (Uris Center), 1986. *A Picture of Medieval Life.*
Carlisle, Pennsylvania, The Trout Art Gallery, Emil R. Weiss Center for the Arts, 1987. *Medieval and Renaissance Art.*
Carlisle, Pennsylvania, The Trout Art Gallery, Emil R. Weiss Center for the Arts, 1987–91.

PUBLICATIONS

Göbel 1933, pp. 183–84, fig. 154. Discussed briefly; illus.
Rorimer, James J. "Acquisitions for The Cloisters." *MMA Bulletin,* n.s. 11 (1952–53) p. 282. Illus.; briefly discussed in caption.

NOTES

1. See Göbel 1933, figs. 6, 7a, 7b.
2. Noted in the files of the MMA Department of Medieval Art as a suggestion made in 1960 by E. Steingraber, Bayerisches Nationalmuseum, Munich.
3. See Göbel 1933, fig. 152b.
4. See Göbel 1934, fig. 5.
5. See Göbel 1934, fig. 6.
6. See Göbel 1933, fig. 171.
7. See Kurth 1926, pp. 242–43, pl. 156, a tapestry with the coats of arms of two Alsatian families, woven about 1500, in the Altertümersammlung in Stuttgart. See also Göbel 1933, fig. 152b, an example dated 1566, then the property of French and Company, New York, and fig. 153, an example dated 1590, in the Musée de Cluny, Paris; Göbel attributed both of these tapestries to the Upper Rhineland.

64
Madonna with Eight Saints

An antependium

Tentatively ascribed to the Upper Rhineland, region of northern
Switzerland, 1550–1600
Linen warp; wool, silk, and metallic wefts; silk embroidery yarns
3 ft. × 7 ft. 4 in. (.91 m × 2.24 m)
16–18 warp yarns per inch, 6–7 per centimeter
Gift of Mrs. Leo S. Bing, 1951 (51.50)

CONDITION

Since the original loom finish is present at both ends of
the piece, we know that the tapestry has lost none of its
original width. Both selvages are missing; but since the
names ranged along the top of the field are still present,
it is clear that very little of the fabric is missing along
that edge. The pattern finishes well within the bounds
of the bottom edge, so it seems likely that none of the
design has been lost there. This edge has been restored
with a strip of modern weaving that runs entirely across
the field and the bottoms of both ornamental borders at
the sides. This restoration is approximately 2 1/2 inches
(6.4 cm) high at the left end; it tapers downward as it
moves to the right, and at that end of the piece it is about
1 1/2 inches (3.8 cm) high. Identical strips of modern
tapestry weaving have been sewn along the top and

bottom edges of the piece. They are approximately one-
half inch (1 cm) wide, and in design they imitate the
polychrome striped pattern of the guard bands at both
ends of the field. There are small spots of reweaving
throughout the piece. The colors are bright. Selective
fading of the different dye lots used for the red wefts in
the background and the green wefts in the meadow has
caused the spaces behind and in front of the figures to
appear striated.

DESCRIPTION AND SUBJECT

The field shows a shallow grassy and flowering meadow
in the foreground. A squirrel and a rabbit sit on the
ground left of center, and a bird preens its feathers between some plants just right of center. Behind this, parallel to the edge of the meadow, a row of eight richly
dressed figures sits on a rocky ledge. The space behind
the figures is represented as a flat plane of brick red, with
an arabesque of leafy green vines bearing real and fanciful blossoms, berries, and pomegranates. Four birds are
perched on the vine at different points along its course,
and a fifth one flies in front of it near the upper left
corner. A narrow border decorated with polychrome

64

lozenges set on the diagonal finishes each end of the field. Flanking both borders are narrow guard bands decorated with polychrome stripes.

The main figure in the center represents the Virgin Mary. She is seated on a tasseled cushion and holds the nude Christ Child on her right hip and a scepter in her left hand. She wears a gold-ground voided velvet or gold-brocaded damask gown cut with a low round neck and a long fitted bodice. She also wears a closed crown and a necklace with a pendant cross. The figure seated next to her, toward the right, represents Saint Nicholas, bishop of Myra. He wears a damask or velvet cope over his chasuble and alb and, on his head, a miter with lappets. The book of the Gospels rests on his lap and in his right hand he holds a crosier. Next to him sits Saint Catherine of Alexandria. She wears a damask or velvet gown cut with a low round neckline, a long bodice, and sleeves slashed at the elbow to allow the pleated linen shirt beneath to show through. She also wears a double gold necklace with a small pendant. The sword she holds by the pommel in both hands, the wheel at her feet, and the crown on her head are symbols of her martyrdom. Next to her sits Saint Agatha, who turns to her own left to address Saint Margaret. Over her gown Agatha wears a damask or velvet robe with pendant sleeves. She holds a lighted candle in her left hand and seems to be warming her right hand over its flame. This attribute refers to her having been tortured by fire. She also wears the martyr's crown. Saint Margaret of Antioch, seated at the extreme right end of the ledge, wears a plain gown cut like the Virgin's and a gold chain around her neck. She holds a processional cross in her left hand and in the other hand the leash of a dragon that crouches like a tame dog at her feet. Along with these symbols of her martyrdom she wears the martyr's crown.

At the far left end of the row of figures sits Saint Agnes, who turns slightly to the right, like the three saints next to her, to face toward the Virgin. She wears a damask or velvet gown cut with a low round neckline, a long bodice, and slashed sleeves. She holds her attributes —a book and a lamb—in her lap, and she wears the martyr's crown. Next to her sits Saint Anne, mother of the Virgin, who wears a plain gown cut with a low square neck, a short wide bodice, and sleeves that fall loose over the upper arm and tight from elbow to wrist. She wears an elaborate headdress that resembles the martyrs' coronets but is not a crown. Her only attribute is the stalk of lilies that she holds in her left hand, a reference to Christ's having been conceived and born free of original sin. Saint Barbara, who sits next to Anne, turns to speak to her. She wears a gown of velvet or damask cut with a low round neckline, a long bodice,

and funnel-shaped linen sleeves. She holds in her hands, two of her attributes—a chalice (as patroness of the dying, though the Host is not visible here) and a palm branch (as a martyr)—and she wears the martyr's crown. Saint Mary Magdalen is seated between Barbara and the Virgin. The Magdalen wears a damask or velvet gown, cut like Saint Agatha's, as well as two chain necklaces and a bonnet. She holds the jar of ointment in her left hand and an open book on her lap.

Each figure is labeled with his or her name directly above, along the top of the field. The names are written alternately in blue and red (and in two instances in both colors), as follows (left to right): *S Agnes, S Anna, S barbara, S Maria Magdalēa, S Maria, S Nicolaus, S Katherina, S Agata,* and *S Margareta.* Each figure also has a nimbus. The inner halo is colored alternately blue or pink except for the first at the left, which is golden brown. In each instance the outer ring is woven with gilt yarn, and the cross within the Child's nimbus is also gold. Gilt yarns were used to render the pattern on the Virgin's gown, her jewelry, and scepter. Gilt and silver yarns appear in the other jewelry, the lappets of Saint Nicholas's miter, Saint Barbara's chalice, and in some details of costume. The tapestry is noteworthy for the lavish use of these metallic yarns, which are composed of narrow, flat silver or gilt wires wrapped around white or yellow core yarns. All the facial features were rendered with needlework stitches after the weaving was completed.

SOURCE OF THE DESIGN

The arrangement of the figures is sophisticated in form and it has narrative content. The composition is certainly not the result of haphazard borrowing from several sources. It was designed by a professional artist, one who might nevertheless have based some or all of his figures on existing sources, either prints or paintings. The plants and animals in the setting are the stock-in-trade of Germanic tapestry weaving at this time (see a similar setting in 63) and must have been available to many cartoon painters and weavers.

MANUFACTURE AND DATE

Braun (1924), who first published 64, dated it simply in the sixteenth century, as Rorimer (1952–53), who called it German, also did some years later. Neither writer attempted to assign the piece a place of origin within Germany. The tapestry shows all the qualities of form and detail that have traditionally been associated with pieces believed to have been woven in the north Swiss region of the Upper Rhineland (see Manufacture and Date for 63). There is no evidence except fashion in clothing to help date the tapestry. Its richness in terms of color and material suggests that the gowns of the female saints (except for Saint Anne's) represent the height of fashion even though the patterns of the damasks or velvets of which they are made correspond to patterns that were in favor during the second half of the fifteenth century and the early years of the sixteenth. It is the cut of the gowns, with their low, round necklines and long, fitted bodices, that places them firmly in the second half of the sixteenth century.[1] On the other hand Saint Anne's gown, with its square neckline and short, wide bodice, represents an earlier moment of fashion, a style of the second quarter of the century (see the Virgin's gowns in 62). Contemporary eyes would therefore have perceived this figure as an old-fashioned one. The designer undoubtedly used this device deliberately to emphasize the fact that Anne was older than the other women represented here.

RELATED TAPESTRIES

No other tapestries that relate to 64 in terms of style, subject matter, or history are known to have survived.

HISTORY

In the Collegium Germanicum in Rome in 1924 (see Braun under Publications).
In the collection of Mrs. Leo S. Bing, New York.
Given to the MMA by Mrs. Leo S. Bing, 1951.

EXHIBITION

Columbia (South Carolina) Museum of Art, 1967. *Landscape in Art: Origin and Development*. Cat. no. 10, illus.

PUBLICATIONS

Braun, Joseph. *Der christliche Altar.* Munich, 1924, vol. 2, p. 73. Described briefly; illus. pl. 130.
Rorimer, James J. "Reports of the Departments: Medieval Art and The Cloisters." Annual Report for 1951. In *MMA Bulletin*, n.s. 11 (1952–53) pp. 29, 30. Mentioned; illus.

NOTE

1. See the discussion of fashion in costume under 63. For the longer, fitted bodice of the second half of the sixteenth century, see Göbel 1933, figs. 152b and 156; also Göbel 1934, fig. 5. For the earlier bodice, see Göbel 1933, figs. 149, 151a; and Göbel 1934, fig. 6.

Concordance of Accession and Catalogue Numbers

07.57.1	7a	37.80.5	20e	45.128.23	25e
07.57.2	7b	37.80.6	20f	45.128.24	25f
07.57.3	7c	38.28	29b	46.58.1	3a
07.57.4	7d	38.29	29a	46.58.2	9
07.57.5	7e	38.51.1	20g	46.175	1
09.137.1	8a	38.51.2	20h	47.101.1	2c
09.137.2	8b	39.74	13c	47.101.2	2d
09.137.3	8c	41.100.195	37	47.101.3	2e
09.172	10	41.100.196	34	47.101.4	2f
14.40.707	18	41.100.214	27c	47.101.5	2g
14.40.709	22	41.100.215	17	47.152	2h
15.121.1	21	41.100.231	8d	48.161.4	62
15.121.2	41a	41.167.1	33b	49.7.118	45
15.121.3	41b	41.167.2	33a	49.123	2i
16.90	54	41.190.89	42a	49.144	60
17.189	15	41.190.92	42b	50.145.4	32a
22.60.34	44	41.190.94	43	50.145.5	32b
25.177.1,2	47	41.190.106	49a	51.50	64
25.177.3	28	41.190.107	49b	52.34	14
32.100.391	50a	41.190.227	49c	52.69	13a
32.100.392	50b	41.190.228	49d	53.35.4	63
32.130a,b	2a, b	41.190.229	12	53.80	27a
35.67	26	42.152.6	19	53.81	27b
35.79.1	48a	42.202	40	53.164	57
35.79.2	48b	43.70.1	4	55.39	13b
35.79.3	48c	43.70.2	3b	56.47	30
35.79.4	48d	45.76	5	57.35	51
37.80.1	20a	45.128.19	25a	57.126	61
37.80.2	20b	45.128.20	25b	59.85	6
37.80.3	20c	45.128.21	25c	60.127.1	16
37.80.4	20d	45.128.22	25d	60.182	53

64.27.22	56	65.181.19	24b	67.155.8	35
64.277	38	65.181.20	24c	1971.43	59
65.181.14	39	65.181.21	24d	1971.135	11
65.181.15	23	65.181.22	24e	1974.228.2	36
65.181.16	46	67.47.1	52a	1985.358	58
65.181.17	31	67.47.2	52b	1990.211	55
65.181.18	24a				

Photograph Credits

Photography of all Museum holdings is by the Photograph Studio, The Metropolitan Museum of Art. Other photographs were supplied by the owners of works of art listed in the captions, except as noted:

© ACL Brussels (Institut Royal du Patrimoine Artistique), figs. 46, 57, 70, 71, 102, 103, 113, 115, 129, 141, 147; Administration Générale du Mobilier National et des Manufactures Nationales des Gobelins, figs. 64, 155; A.F.S. B.A.S. Firenze, fig. 45; Alinari/Art Resource, NY, fig. 61; Ampliaciones y Reproducciones Mas, figs. 44, 106, 128, 135, 139; © ARS, NY/Arch. Phot., figs. 69, 95; © ARS, NY/SPADEM, Paris, fig. 161; © 1988, The Art Institute of Chicago, fig. 121; © 1990, The Art Institute of Chicago, fig. 156; Bildarchiv Foto Marburg, figs. 80, 84; Bildarchiv Preussischer Kulturbesitz, fig. 41; photo by Peter Blaikie, courtesy of the Center for Tapestry Arts, fig. 8; reproduced by courtesy of the Trustees of the British Museum, fig. 187; Cliché Inventaire Général F. Lasa–P. Giraud, fig. 55; photos by Julien Coffinet, courtesy of Mme. Coffinet, figs. 4, 10; © CNHMS/ARS, NY/SPADEM, figs. 29, 32, 49, 63, 67, 72, 76; photos by Yves Debraine, courtesy of M. Debraine, figs. 6, 7, 12, 21; © 1987, The Detroit Institute of Arts, fig. 154; Documentation de la Réunion des Musées Nationaux, Paris, figs. 30, 35, 39, 50, 65, 66, 68, 74, 79, 94, 105, 130, 131, 140, 157, 162, 163, 164, 188; Master Weavers in the Dovecot Studios of the Edinburgh Tapestry Co., Ltd., photo courtesy of the Edinburgh Tapestry Co., Ltd., fig. 22; Getty Center for the History of Art and the Humanities, Photo Archives, fig. 122; Giraudon/Art Resource, NY, fig. 26; photo © Graffilm SA, Geneva, fig. 9; © Historisches Museum, Basel, photo by M. Babey, fig. 179; photos by Herbert Laesslé, courtesy of Mme. Julien Coffinet, figs. 5, 11; Lichtbildwerkstätte Alpenland, figs. 42, 145, 146; Ingeborg Limmer Fotomeisterin, fig. 85; photo by John Mills, fig. 112; reproduced by courtesy of the Trustees, The National Gallery, London, fig. 58; National Trust Photographic Library, fig. 75; Royal Collection, St. James's Palace © 1991 Her Majesty Queen Elizabeth II, fig. 142; reproduced by kind permission of His Grace the 10th Duke of Rutland, fig. 114; SBAS Firenze, fig. 25; The Watson Library, MMA, figs. 86, 107, 168, 169, 172.

Index

Bruce, Mrs. Mellon, 15, 501
Bruegel, Peter, the Elder, 445n26
Brummer, Joseph, 94, 111, 121
Brunavillani of Treviso arms, 528
bulrushes, 423
Burckhardt, Rudolf F., 629, 630, 651
Burgkmair, Hans, 141
Burgundy
  duchess of. *See* Marie de Bourgogne
  dukes of, 65, 69
    Priam as ancestor of, 233
    See also Charles le Téméraire; Jean sans Peur; Philippe II le Hardi; Philippe III le Bon; Philippe VI
Buri, Anna Rapp. *See* Rapp Buri, Anna
Burning Bush, 264, 555, 557, 558
Busant, Der. See Buzzard, The
Busts of Achilles, Agamemnon, and Hector in Conference, 229, 231, 239
Buyle, Marjan, 597
Buys, Cornelius, 344
Buzzard, The (*Der Busant*, a poem), two scenes from, 15, 642–47, *643, 644*, 652

C

Cadaval, marquez de, 550
Caesar, Julius, 406, 410. *See: Julius Caesar; Story of Caesar*
Calabria, duke of, 205, 206
Calatrava, Order of, 334, 340, 341n19
Calberg, Marguerite, 546–50
Calkins, Robert G., 580, 581, 584
Callmann, Ellen, 293–95
camels, *574, 579*, 589–91
Cameron, Kenneth M., 263, 265
Campin, Robert, 140, 164, 266, 267, 268
Candee, Helen Churchill, 180, 184, 185
Cantzler, Christina, 73, 627
Capars, Jean, 65
Capella, Martianus, 73
carbon 14 test, 218, 222n12
Cardon, Ch. L., 442
Carew, Sir John, 275
carnations, 627, 649
  symbolism of, 527
Cartari, Vincenzo, 469
Carter, John, 243–46
cartoons
  dates of, and dates of tapestry, 45, 61, 185
  definition of, 18
  in Germany, 75
  merchants holding stocks of, 66, 67

in *Nine Worthies*, 115–16
preparation of, by cartoon painter, 37, 42–44, *43*
as substitutes for tapestries in churches, 31
in weaving process, *19*, 24–25
Cassiopeia, Queen, 546
Castelains, Jean, 65
Castle of Love, 589, 627
Catalonia, 144
Catherine of Alexandria, Saint, *594, 595, 596*, 617–19, *618–20*, 635, *635*, 670, 671
Caurrée, Ysabeau, 64
Cavallo, Adolfo S., 90, 160, *163*, 428, 431, 433, 436–40, 442, 479, 483–86, 509, 547, 550, 581, 615
Caxton, William, 234
Cenami, Giovanna, *48*
centaur. *See* Sagittary
Cepheus, King, 546
Cetto, Anna Maria, 164, 167
Chabrières-Arlès, M., 121
Chalcas, 245
Chamans, Michel de, 67, 71
chambers, definition of, 27
chaperon (hood), *126–27, 128, 149*, 150, 179, *191, 194,* 287
Chappey, Edouard, 418, 420
Charlemagne (emperor), 98, 105, 111, 114, 117, 120, 382, 386, 391, 402–6, 411, 412n17, 464, 465, 467
Charlemagne tapestry (Halberstadt), 73–74
Charles le Téméraire (duke of Burgundy), 29–31, 36, 66–68, 142, 242, 243, 247, 248, 438, 565
Charles V (Holy Roman Emperor), 70, 247, 505, 547–48, 591, 605
Charles V (king of France), 27, 113, 117, 118, 182
Charles VI (king of France), 29, 64, 113, 116–18, 120, 121, 153, 182
Charles VII (king of France), 27–29, *29*, 143–44, 182, 183, 185, 241, 570
Charles VIII (king of France), 36, 67, 205, 206, 208n9, 227, 242, 243, 384–87, 400, 408–9
Châtelet, Albert, 165, 167, 243
Chavagnac d'Amandine of Auvergne family, 320
chess-playing, 508–9
Chevalier, Etienne, 184
Chevrot, Jean, 157, 166–69
Chigi, Agostino, 558
Childhood of Hercules. See: Episodes in the Childhood of Hercules

Chillón Sampedro, Bartolomé, 243
Chimera, the, 550
China, tapestry in, 61
choir hangings, 71, 333, 347
  The Adoration of the Magi (Sens Cathedral), 328–33, *329*
  The Annunciation (1460–80), 15, 210–23, *210–13*
  Crucifixion with the Virgin, Saint John the Evangelist, Saint Catherine, and Saint Margaret, 617–24, *618, 619*
  in La Chaise-Dieu church, *30*, 31, 33, 34
  Lives of Christ and the Virgin, 52, *53*, 289, 540, 559n4
  possible examples of, 347–57, *348, 349, 351, 352, 354*
  in Tournai cathedral, 45, 47, 58
  See also antependiums; dossals
Chope, R. Pearse, 274
Christ
  Glorification of Christ, 70, 387, 396
  infant, 62, *138, 139–40*, 255, *257, 286, 287*, 387, *391, 416, 427, 432, 433, 438, 594, 595*, 611, *658, 660, 664, 665*, 670, 671
    Christ Child with Saints, 641n3
    The Holy Family with Saint Anne, 339, 342–46, *343*
    Rest on the Flight into Egypt, 344
    See also: Adoration of the Magi, The; Baptism of Christ; Infant Christ Pressing the Wine of the Eucharist; Nativity
  life of. *See: Fall and Redemption of Man, The;* Incarnation; *Lives of Christ and the Virgin*
  passion of. *See: Christ Carrying the Cross;* Crucifixion; Passion
  resurrection of. *See* Resurrection
  Second Coming of, 392, 396–99
  stag as symbol for, 355, 580
  in *The Story of the Redemption of Man*, 424, 426, 431–36, 438
  as unicorn, 313, 315–17
Christ and the Adulteress, 282
Christ Appearing to His Mother (painting), 538
Christ Ascends to Heaven and

Man Is Reconciled to God (two tapestries), *435*, 443
Christ before Pilate, 540
Christ Carrying the Cross, 70, 540, 541, 542n18
Christ Child. *See* Christ—infant; Nativity
Christian Worthies, 402, 410
  Christian Worthies, 102–3, 103–7, 111, 114–17, 121
Christine de Pisan, 152, 546, 547
Christ Is Born as Man's Redeemer, 333n4, 421, 422, 426–28, 430–31, 431–32, 442
Christ Makes His Last Judgment and the Vices Are Vanquished (two tapestries), 435, 436, 443
Christ of the Mystic Winepress, 336, 337, 338
Christ Rises and Rescues Man from Hell (two tapestries), 434, 436, 442–43
Christ tapestry (Halberstadt), 73
Christ the Judge on the Throne of Majesty and Other Subjects, 15, 70, 377–412, 378–83, 390, 392–98, 400, 401, 403–5, 417, 418, 521n3
Christ the Savior as a Child (two tapestries), 432, 442
Christ Washing the Disciples' Feet, 541
Cicero, 467
Ciervo, Joaquín, 168
Cimbri women, 194
cinquefoil rosettes, 220
ciphers, in *The Hunt of the Unicorn*, 313, 318–22
Circumcision, the, 331, 433, 665
Clare of Assisi, Saint, 619, 621–23
Clark, Susan Vanderpoel, 15, 487
Claude (queen of France), 315, 324
Claude de France (daughter of Louis XII), 474, 475
Clement VI (pope), 88, 90, 91
Clement VII (antipope), 118
Cleopatra, 391
Cles, Bernard, 541
Cleve, Joos van, 338, 344, 345
Clopas, Mary, 278
clothing. *See* costume
Coat of Arms and Emblems of Philippe le Bon, 68, 69, 73
Cock, Hieronymus, 605
Coe, William R., 206, 209n18
Coëtivy Master, 241, 322
Coeur, Jacques, 182, 189n6
Coffinet, Julien, 18, 87, 91, 118, 119, 131, 134, 143, 144, 193, 226, 268, 324

Manfredi, Astore II, 68
Manises majolica, 144–45
Mankind, "frail stag" as metaphor for, 349–50, 353–54, 461
Margaret, Saint, 655
Margaret of Antioch, Saint, 596, 599n4, 517, 617, 618–19, 620, 670, 671
Margaret of Austria, 68, 165, 276, 290n8, 366, 386, 408–9, 603, 605, 615
Margaret of York, 234, 438, 565
Margerin, Mlle., 131, 583
Marguerite de Barbezieux, 314, 320
Marguerite of Flanders, 321
Mariacher, Giovanni, 91
Marie de Bourgogne (Mary of Burgundy), 68, 223n18, 271n17, 386
Marillier, H. C., 94, 111, 121, 165, 171, 214, 218, 243, 324, 375, 439, 442
Marmion, Simon, 61
Marot, Clément, 650
Marriage at Cana (painting), 505n1
Marriage at Cana, 331
Marriage of Mercury and Philology, The, 73, 74
Martin V (pope), 66, 145, 661–62
Martin, Rebecca, 617, 619–23
Mary Magdalen, 436, 580, 670, 671
  Antependium with Mary Magdalen, Saint Agnes, and Saint Elizabeth, 597, 598, 598
  The Lamentation, 278, 279–80, 282
  The Resurrected Christ Appearing to Mary Magdalen in the Garden, 15, 446, 447–51
  The Resurrection, 536, 537
Mary Queen of Heaven (painting), 288, 289
Mass of Saint Gregory, 69, 70, 282, 283, 409, 436
Massys, Quentin, 266, 282, 288, 344, 407
Master b g, 373, 376n3
Master E.S., 508, 590, 650–51, 650, 651, 661
Master h w, 373, 376n3
Master of Saint Severin, 438
Master of the Combat of the Virtues and Vices, 407
Master of the Ehningen Altar, 538, 539
Master of the Frankfurt Paradise Garden, 661
Master of the Hausbuch, 650
Master of the Love Gardens, 181, 184, 508
Master of the Nuremberg Passion, 593n5, 661, 662

Master of the Playing Cards, 184, 630, 632n19
Master of the Saint Lucy Legend, 288, 289
Master of the Staufener Altar, 630
Master of the Thennenbacher Altar, 661
Master of the View of Saint Gudule, 69, 437, 437
Matrimony, in *Seven Sacraments* tapestry, 157, 158, 163, 164
Matteo dei Pasti, 472
Matthias Corvinus (king of Hungary), 242, 293
Matton, Auguste, 242
Maximilian I (Holy Roman Emperor), 68, 70, 386, 408, 439
Maximinus (Roman emperor), 595
Mayer, Christa Charlotte, 490, 493
Mayer AmRhyn, Jost, 628, 630, 631, 632n20
Mazarin tapestry (*Triumph of Christ*), 379, 384, 386, 391–401, 406–10, 412n11
Medici, Cosimo de', 472
Medici, Giovanni de', 37, 61, 68
Medici, Piero de', 61, 558
medieval, definition of, 11
Medusa, 546, 549, 550
Megara, 567
Mège, Charles, 228, 497
Meiss, Millard, 114, 115, 119, 143
Melchior, 330–31
Melchizedek, 157, 160, 170–71
Meleager, 567
Mélian, Paul, 66
Mellon, Andrew W., 501
Memling, Hans, 41–42, 42, 227, 271n17, 319, 407
Mendoza, Pedro González de, 293
Menelaus, 229, 231, 235, 238, 239, 245
Menon, 239, 244
Mercury, 244
Merle-Smith, Mrs. Van Santvoord, 14, 510
Mesnagier, Guillaume, 558
Messenger before Pilate. See: Imperial Messenger before Pilate
metallic oxides, 25
metallic yarns. *See* silver, silvergilt, and metallic yarns
Methuselah, 465, 466, 469
Meunier, Gaston, 509, 510
Meyer-Riefstahl, R. A., 619–22
Michael, Archangel, 62, 73, 76
  Michael and His Angels Defeating Satan and His Angels, 46

Micheas, 428
Michel, Jehan, 202, 208n3
Midoux, Etienne, 242
Migeon, Gaston, 180, 181, 185, 227, 324, 329, 332, 619, 622, 651
Mikaeloff, Simon, 606
Mikaeloff, Yves, 606
millefleurs tapestries, 33, 71–73, 474, 503
  A Mon Seul Désir, 72, 72, 323
  anticipations of, 152, 183
  Arma Christi, 250–53, 251
  The Armorial Bearings and Badges of John, Lord Dynham, 15, 272, 273–77, 505
  Birds, Beasts, and Rosebushes on a Millefleurs Ground, 503, 504
  Concert (Le concert), 491, 493, 509
  dating of, 53
  falconing scenes on, 35, 488, 490, 492, 495, 496, 498, 499–501
  Five Youths Playing Blindman's Buff, 452, 453–57, 454–55
  Flowering Plants and Rosebushes, 502, 503–5
  La vie seigneuriale, 491, 493, 508
  red-ground, 498, 499–501
  Royal Arms of England, 273, 275
  shepherd scenes on, 480, 481, 484–86, 485
  stag hunts on, 360–61, 364–65, 368–70, 371–72, 458, 459–62, 460
  wreaths on, 294
Millet, Jacques, 233
Milliken, William M., 617, 622
Minerva, 246, 356
Miolard (*tapissier*), 71
miracle and mystery plays, 34, 202, 233, 444nn4, 5, 9, 11
Miracle of Saint Julien, 35
Miraculous Statue Is Brought to Brussels, The, 54
Mirimonde, A. P. de, 509
Moab, king of, 402
Molinet, Jean, 152
Monarch and a Lady Exchanging a Covered Cup or Box, A (Metropolitan Museum), 517–20, 519
Monarch and a Lady Exchanging a Cup or Box, A (Glasgow), 520, 520
monkeys, 181, 188n2
Monod, François, 288, 339
Montaigne, Pasquier de, 71
Montefeltro, Federico da, 67
months. *See: Twelve Months of the Year*

morality plays. *See* miracle and mystery plays
mordants, 25
Mordecai, 389, 391, 399, 400, 667
Morelowski, Marjan, 164, 166–68
Morgan, J. Pierpont, 13, 171, 187, 445n30, 613, 615, 623, 652
morris dancers, 375, 375
Moses, 157, 160, 257–58, 263–65, 415, 417, 426, 431, 448
  Moses and Aaron before Pharaoh, 13, 552–59, 553–55
  other tapestries of, 558
Mounted Knight with the Arms of Jean de Daillon, 58, 59, 73, 505, 505n5
Mullenheim family, 645
Müller, Christian, 627
Munsey, Frank A., 121
Müntz, Eugène, 57, 240, 472, 478nn4, 11, 621
mystery plays. *See* miracle and mystery plays

N

Naamah, 406
Namaan Being Cleansed in the Jordan, 157, 159, 160, 161, 168, 169
Naomi, 194, 195
Narcissus, 509
Nathan, 157, 160
Nativity, 255–56, 257, 263, 266, 412n22, 427, 433, 437, 666
  in *The Apostles' Creed*, 611
  Nativity (Budapest), 541
  Nativity (Patrimonio Nacional, Madrid), 436
  Nativity (Trent), 541
  in *Scenes from the Life of the Virgin*, 658, 660
  See also Christ—infant; Virgin Mary
nature, fantastic beasts as symbols for, 627–28
Nature (Natura), 431–33, 436
Nature Sets Her Hound Youth after the Stag, 347, 348, 350
Nebuchadnezzar (king of Assyria), 192, 195
Nero Sends Vespasian and Titus to Wage War on Jerusalem, 203, 206
Nessus, 568, 569
Nestor, 469
Netherlandish tapestries, 32, 34–38, 41, 43, 45–53, 46, 48–53, 56, 64–72
  general development of, 11
  marks required for, 71
  new ideas about space in, 540
Neuf Preuses. See female Worthies
Neuf Preux. See: Nine Worthies

Porcher, Jean, 240
Porter, Arthur Kingsley, 257,
    258, 266–68, 441nn9, 10
Portinari, Tommaso, 37, 68, 227
Pottequin, Jehanne, 66
Pourtalès, Count and Countess
    Hubert de, 121
Pratt, George D., 14, 295, 477
Pratt, Mr. and Mrs. Frederic B.,
    14, 125, 132, 134, 136
Pratt, Mr. and Mrs. Harold Irv-
    ing, 137, 145
Pratt, Harriet Barnes, 14, 137, 145
*Preparing to Undo the Stag in
    the Field*, 359, 363, 367,
    368, 371
Presentation
    Presentation in the Temple, 622
    *Presentation of the Child in
        the Temple*, 436
    in *Scenes from the Life of the
        Virgin*, 658, 661, 662
Prestre, Jehan le, 116
Preuses. See female Worthies
Preux. See: Nine Worthies,
    Worthies
Priam, 232, 233, 239, 240,
    245–47
primroses, 423
    symbolism of, 281
Prince des Malices, 220
Pringsheim (author), 651
Prodigal Son, 402, 428, 430,
    523, 524n2
    *Departure of the Prodigal
        Son*, 530–32, 531
    Parable of the Prodigal Son, 514
    *Story of the Prodigal Son
        (Louisville)*, 437, 438
    *Story of the Prodigal Son
        (Walters Art Gallery)*,
        395, 407, 408, 437
    *Two Episodes from the Para-
        ble of the Prodigal Son*,
        281, 512, 513–16
Prudentius, Aurelius Clemens,
    420n6, 428
Prycus, King, 567–68, 572
Pseudo-Bonaventure, 139, 432,
    444n11
Pseudo-Jacquemart, 123–24n22
puer parvulus formatus, 140
Pyrrhus, 246
Pythagoras's bivium, 113

Q

*Queen of France and the Dis-
    loyal Marshal*, 645
Queen of Sheba, 387, 410, 519,
    523
    *Queen of Sheba Presenting
        Gifts to Solomon*, 380, 388
    *See also: Two Riddles of the
        Queen of Sheba*
Quentel, Peter, 613

R

rabbits, 134, 135, 292, 293–95,
    295, 298, 300–301, 479,
    480, 633, 670, 670
Ramírez de Fuenreal (or, de Vi-
    llaescusa), Don Diego, 269
Ramsden, Sir John, 515
Raphael, 11, 70, 603
Rapp Buri, Anna, 73, 75, 626–
    28, 630, 631, 644–46,
    650, 652, 660, 662
Rave, Jean de, 68
reading stands, 142
Réau, Louis, 416, 448
*Redemption of Man. See: Story
    of the Redemption of
    Man, The*
Redmond, Roland L., 151
Reinach, Salomon, 187
Renaissance, definition of, 11
Resurrection, 263
    in *The Apostles' Creed*, 611–
        12, 613
    *Christ Rises and Rescues
        Man from Hell* (two tap-
        estries), 434, 436, 442–43
    painting of, 538, 539
    pre-11th-century depiction
        of, 536
    *Resurrected Christ Appearing
        to Mary Magdalen in the
        Garden*, 15, 446, 447–51
    The Resurrection (Louvre), 144
    The Resurrection (Metropolitan
        Museum), 14, 534, 535–43
    The Resurrection (Trent), 70,
        439, 541
    The Resurrection (Victoria and
        Albert Museum), 537,
        537, 538, 540, 542nn1, 2
Rewarding the Hounds, 359,
    363, 369, 371
Reynaud, Nicole, 205–7, 240–44,
    247, 321–23, 355, 356
rhinoceros, 584n9
Ricci, Seymour de, 234, 438,
    613–14
Richard, M., 440–42
Richard (painter), 246
Richard II (king of England), 28
Richard III (king of England), 274
Riedinger, August, 592
Ripa, Cesare, 466, 469
Roannes, duc de, 605
Robb, David, 140
Robert de Monchaux, 204
Robertet, Florimond, 353
Robertet, Jehan, 467, 472,
    478nn12, 13
Roberts, Mary Fanton, 539
Robetta, Cristofano, 547
Robinson, Edward, 167
Rockefeller, John D., Jr., 14, 325
Rodière, R., 318, 320, 321
Rodríguez de Fonseca, Juan,
    428, 438, 441–43

Roen, Peter, 215
Rogers, Meyric R., 165, 181,
    184, 186, 201, 205, 264,
    266, 268, 313, 318, 332,
    345, 416, 418, 454, 481,
    490, 493, 531, 539, 557, 589
Rogier van der Weyden. *See*
    Weyden, Rogier van der
Rohan, Charles de, 73
Rohan, Pierre de, 505n4
Rohan master, 143–44, 143
Rolin, Nicolas, 321
Rolland, Paul, 166, 167, 169–71
Romanelli, Susan, 580, 583, 584
*Romans Enter Jerusalem and
    Find the Inhabitants
    Starving*, 202
Rorimer, James J., 13–15, 94–97,
    112–19, 121, 134, 136,
    141, 142, 144, 153, 157,
    162, 165, 166, 168, 169,
    171, 180, 201, 226, 227,
    240, 247, 251–52, 268,
    282, 311, 314–19, 322,
    324, 332, 375, 377–78,
    382–87, 389, 396, 400,
    403, 406–8, 474, 481, 496,
    499, 510, 565–67, 570, 583,
    606, 622, 662, 668, 671
Rorimer, Katherine S., 15, 606
Rose Garden tapestry. *See: Fig-
    ures in a Rose Garden*
Roselt, J. Christof, 581, 583
Rosenthal, Erwin, 181, 184
roses, 84, 85, 86, 417, 428, 498,
    499, 513, 546, 649–50
    *Birds, Beasts, and Rose-
        bushes on a Millefleurs
        Ground*, 503, 504
    *Flowering Plants and Rose-
        bushes*, 502, 503–5
    *Honor Making a Chaplet of
        Roses*, 15, 148–55, 149
    symbolism of, 281, 344, 448,
        538, 611, 627
rosettes, 220, 637, 638
Rothschild, Edmond de, 164–65
Rousseau, Theodore, Jr., 433
Royal Arms of England, 273, 275
Royalty of Christ, 385, 396
Roybet, F. G., 244, 248
Rubinstein-Bloch, Stella, 180–
    82, 184–86, 226, 227,
    282, 379, 402–6, 408,
    479, 481, 496, 518, 520,
    523, 524, 580, 583
Rücklaken, 646, 665
Ruíz, Raimondo, 248
Ruth, 194, 195
Ryerson, Martin A., 528

S

Sagittary, 229, 230, 231, 235–37,
    235, 238, 244
*Saint Anatoile's Body Trans-

    ported in State to the
    Church of Saint Sym-
    phorien at Salins*, 53
Saint Hillaire, Jean de, 67
Saint Jerome in His Study
    (painting), 337, 451n12
*Saint Luke Drawing the Virgin
    and Child*, 32, 33, 39–41
Saint-Notaire, Jacques de, 30
*Saint Peter Released from
    Prison*, 217, 220
*Saint Piat Begins His Preaching
    in Tournai*, 47
Salet, Francis, 60, 63–64, 116,
    247, 311–13, 315–17, 319,
    320, 467, 472–75, 481,
    491, 493
Salome, Mary, 278, 279–80
Saluzzo, Tommaso di, 111, 112
Sambola, marqués de, 615
Samson, 68, 472
Samuel, 402
Samuels, Michael, 13, 623
Sánchez Cantón, Francisco Ja-
    vier, 167, 269, 270
Sanderus (historian of Tournai),
    166
Sarrazin, Clément, 70, 570, 572
Satan (the Tempter), 423, 433–34
    *Michael and His Angels De-
        feating Satan and His
        Angels*, 46
    overcome by the Virgin Mary,
        193
    in *The Story of the Redemp-
        tion of Man*, 430, 433, 436
satyrs, 601, 603, 604, 606
Scedius, 235
Scellier, Philippe le, 61
*Scenes from a Courtly Ro-
    mance*, 130
*Scenes from the Life of the Vir-
    gin* (1490–1510), 13, 285–
    91, 286
*Scenes from the Life of the Vir-
    gin* (about 1500), 657–63,
    658–61
Scheicher, Elisabeth, 466, 472–
    75, 477
Scherer, Margaret R., 234, 237
Schickler, Baron Arthur, 121, 411
Schmitz, Hermann, 164, 165,
    181, 185, 205, 240, 287,
    619, 622, 662
Schneebalg-Perelman, Sophie,
    134, 324, 481
Schottmüller, Frida, 375
Schouvaloff, Count, 246
Schrader, J. L., 244–46, 248, 580,
    583
Schüchlin, Hans, 662
Schumann, Paul, 241–42
Schutz, Fernand, 440, 481
seasons of the year, 226–27
Segorbe, dukes of, 251–52
Seidlitz and van Baarn, 598
Seligman, Germain, 180, 187